# ECHOES FROM THE CAVE

## Philosophical Conversations since Plato

EDITED BY LISA GANNETT

**OXFORD**

UNIVERSITY PRESS

# OXFORD
## UNIVERSITY PRESS

Oxford University Press is a department of the University of Oxford.
It furthers the University's objective of excellence in research, scholarship,
and education by publishing worldwide. Oxford is a registered trade mark of
Oxford University Press in the UK and in certain other countries.

Published in Canada by
Oxford University Press
8 Sampson Mews, Suite 204,
Don Mills, Ontario M3C 0H5 Canada
www.oupcanada.com

First Edition published in 2014

**Library and Archives Canada Cataloguing in Publication**

Echoes from the cave : philosophical conversations since
Plato / edited by Lisa Gannett.

Includes bibliographical references, filmography, and index.
ISBN 978-0-19-543369-2

1. Philosophy—Introductions.  I. Gannett, Lisa, 1961-

BD21.E25 2013          190          C2013-900645-1

Cover image: Terry Wilson/iStockphoto

This book is printed on permanent acid-free paper ∞

Printed and bound in the United States of America

1  2  3  4 — 17  16  15  14

# Contents

# Part III ▸ The Good   301

## Introduction   301

## Moral Foundations   314

## Challenges to Moral Foundations   346

## Gender and Morality   377

## Film Notes   411

# Part IV ▸ The Just   415

## Introduction   415

## Civil Disobedience   428

## Democratic Government   453

# Preface

*E*choes from the Cave: Philosophical Conversations since Plato is an anthology for use in introductory philosophy courses that take a problem-oriented approach to the subject. Thoughtfully edited readings from historical and contemporary sources welcome students to participate in conversations of Western philosophy that have been ongoing since Plato's time. The anthology is divided into five sections that cover the main areas of philosophy: metaphysics ("The Real"), epistemology ("The True"), morality ("The Good"), politics ("The Just"), and aesthetics ("The Beautiful"). Each section begins with a selection from Plato. The philosophical problems included in each section are designed to appeal to the interests of a broad range of students while providing a solid foundation for further study in philosophy. An effort has been made to include Canadian philosophers and problems such as multiculturalism that resonate for Canadian audiences. The historical legacy of philosophy as a discipline shaped predominantly by socio-economically privileged European men is interrogated in several readings by feminist, post-colonial, and anti-racist authors.

Each section of the anthology opens with a short introduction. Students are given an explanation of the theme for the section: what it is for a philosophical problem to count as a problem in metaphysics, epistemology, morality, politics, or aesthetics. A synopsis of the Platonic dialogue for the section is provided, and an effort is made to relate the philosophical problems of the section to issues raised by Plato over two millennia ago. The authors' various solutions to the problems are compared, providing an overview that allows students and instructors to appreciate how the readings fit together as a whole. Discussion questions and suggestions for further reading round out the introductions. The anthology's readings have been carefully edited in order to facilitate comprehension and confine readings to a length suitable for a single class: text has been eliminated (including all but the most important authors' endnotes), sections with headings have been introduced, and language has been modernized. Square brackets are indicative of editorial changes, including ellipses in square brackets that are placed where text has been excised in the midst of a section. An introductory headnote containing background information on the author and work precedes each reading. Words that may be unfamiliar to students are indicated with bold type, and definitions for these are found in the glossary. Study questions provided at the end of each selection focus on key concepts and arguments and will be helpful for students and instructors alike in preparing for classes and tests.

I am grateful for the help I received in writing the headnotes. Student assistants wrote some of the headnotes, as the accompanying initials indicate: Jonah Flanagan (JF), Terissa Rafuse (TR), and Georgia Schurman (GS). The headnote for Martin Luther King's

"Letter from Birmingham Jail" was written by my nine-year-old nephew, Tynan Gannett (TG). Headnotes rely on information from the Stanford Encyclopedia of Philosophy (http://plato.stanford.edu) and the Internet Encyclopedia of Philosophy (www.iep.utm.edu), both of which are excellent, peer-reviewed resources for instructors and students to consult. The glossary relies on information from these and additional sources: Tufts University's Perseus Digital Library (www.perseus.tufts.edu/hopper), the British Broadcasting Corporation's history site (www.bbc.co.uk/history), Public Broadcasting Service website resources (www.pbs.org), the Metropolitan Museum of Art's Heilbrunn Timeline of Art History (www.metmuseum.org/toah), and artist A–Z lookups at the National Gallery, London (www.nationalgallery.org.uk/artists) and National Gallery of Canada (www.gallery.ca/en/see/collections/artist_index.php).

"Film Notes" at the end of each section recommend films that are relevant to one or more of the philosophical problems for the section. A brief description of each film is provided to allow instructors to decide which films are worth screening for possible inclusion on the syllabus and to encourage students to explore philosophical themes introduced in class on their own. An effort has been made to include a range of films: Hollywood classics and blockbusters, and Canadian and international fare. In addition, the National Film Board makes documentaries available for viewing on its website (www.nfb.ca). Instructors will find that including films on their syllabus helps to introduce students to philosophical ideas and stimulate discussion and debate in class. Examples from assigned or well-known films can be used to illustrate philosophical ideas by including screen shots or short clips in lectures. The Wachowski brothers' *The Matrix* is a perennial favourite for illustrating themes from Descartes' *Meditations*, such as skepticism about the existence of the external world and the nature of the relationship between mind and body. Locke's account of personal identity can be explored by forgoing the usual thought experiments involving brain transplants and opting for the more realistic portrayal of a woman with Alzheimer's disease in Sarah Polley's *Away from Her*. Another advantage of including film on the syllabus is that it encourages discussion and debate by creating a shared experience. This is especially helpful for a polarizing and sensitive issue such as abortion: complex character development in Mike Leigh's *Vera Drake*, a film set in England in the 1950s, when abortion was illegal, serves to promote moral reflection and respect. Films can also project students forward in time, allowing them to fathom existentialist crises about the meaning of life provoked by middle age, as in Sam Mendes' *American Beauty*, or impending death, as in Akira Kurosawa's *Ikiru*.

Acknowledgements are heartfelt and many. Janet Sisson generously contributed a previously unpublished translation of Plato's *Meno* and allowed me to edit it for length; she also provided helpful advice about Plato's dialogues more generally. At Oxford University Press Canada, acquisitions editor Ryan Chynces came onboard with the project when I first broached the idea with him, and his enthusiasm buoyed and carried me throughout the planning stages. I am indebted to the OUP Canada editors who oversaw production, especially for their remarkable patience: Peter Chambers, Stephen Kotowych, Lisa Peterson, and Eric Sinkins. Tara Tovell did a wonderful job as copy editor. I would also like to thank my philosophy colleagues at Saint Mary's University and elsewhere, who generously shared their ideas about what to include in an introductory anthology, especially the anonymous referees for OUP Canada who weighed in at one or more stages of an extensive review process with thoughtful and judicious recommendations. I am grateful to the Student Employment Experience Program (SEEP) at Saint Mary's University for the funding that made it possible to hire undergraduate students as editorial assistants. Cameron Fenton, Jonah Flanagan, Andrew Inkpen, Stephanie Pronk, Terissa Rafuse, Georgia Schurman, Jessica Smith, and Kathleen Van Ekris carried out a wide range of tasks: reformatting and correcting texts, recommending problems and readings for inclusion, making editing suggestions for readings, identifying words for the glossary, writing headnotes, screening films, and more. They were always a pleasure to work with as they tackled these tasks—no matter how mundane, tedious, or challenging—with diligence and good cheer. My five years of experience in teaching Philosophy 1201, "Introduction to Philosophy," at Saint Mary's University has left an indelible mark on *Echoes from the Cave*. It is impossible to recognize by name all those students who contributed to the project by bringing their curiosity, questions, and ideas to class, but the assistance of at least some bears mention: my thanks to Amaris Desmond and Kelley Sheppard for their film ideas; Renée Doucet, Judy Stewart, and Garth Williams for their feedback on readings; Rachel MacDonald for her vigilance in catching typos; Terissa Rafuse for her generosity in volunteering extra hours; and Georgia Schurman for her passion for the project from its inceptions.

# PART I

# The Real

## ▶ Introduction

Philosophical study of "the real," of what exists and the nature of being, is called metaphysics. The word "metaphysics" is derived from the original Greek *meta ta phusika*, which means beyond or after the physics: a treatise of Aristotle's was given this title centuries after his death, likely to indicate that it was to be studied after his *Physics*. Traditionally, those philosophers called metaphysicians have been interested in such problems as whether universals exist, the nature of space and time, what causation is, if there is a god, etc. Metaphysics includes presuppositions of scientific theories (e.g., that every event has a cause) and, for empirically inclined philosophers, any aspect of reality that lies beyond detection by the senses. The question of whether universals exist asks if properties, relations, kinds, etc. exist apart from particulars that exhibit properties, enter relations, are classified into kinds, etc.—for example, whether redness exists apart from individual things that are red, such as your shoes, my sweater, etc. Plato answers affirmatively, as we shall see. The other readings in the section cover three additional topics in metaphysics: personal identity, freedom and determinism, and natural and social kinds.

### Plato's "Cave Allegory"

Part 1, "The Real," begins with Plato's famous allegory of the cave in *The Republic*, from which the title of the anthology, *Echoes from the Cave: Philosophical Conversations since Plato*, comes. Plato holds that fundamental reality consists of an abstract (non-spatiotemporal) realm of objects called "the forms," a view that seems counter-intuitive to many of us today, though perhaps not mathematicians and students of mathematics. Sensible things—the book whose weight you feel in your hands, the cellphone whose blaring alarm woke you far too early this morning, the sun whose rays are streaming through your classroom window—are real only in a derivative sense. The book in your hands is an imperfect copy: what makes it a book, and makes similar such things in your university library and classmates' hands also books, is that these particulars manifest the universal property "being a book"—a property exhibited perfectly in the Platonic form Book. Whereas your cellphone will all too soon end up in a toxic pile of broken, discarded electronics, the Platonic form Cellphone is changeless and eternal. While there are many solar systems, there is only one Platonic form Sun.

## Personal Identity

Plato's theory of the forms can be understood as responding to metaphysical questions concerning individuation: What makes something the kind of thing it is and not some other kind of thing? What makes something the same and not a different thing across time and place?

In the late seventeenth century, John Locke posed such questions of material bodies, plants, animals, humans, and persons. In "Of Identity and Diversity," Locke argues that these different sorts of things require different criteria of identity. He considers consciousness to be the criterion for what constitutes a person and the same person over time, and holds that consciousness is distinct from whatever substance, material or immaterial, in which it might inhere. According to Locke, conscious beings do not simply perceive but perceive that they perceive, and this allows them to distinguish their own selves from others. A person remains the same person for as long as her or his consciousness extends to past thoughts and actions. This implies that individuals who suffer memory loss are no longer the persons they once were.

In "The Lost Mariner," neurologist Oliver Sacks presents the case study of Jimmie G., a patient with Korsakov's syndrome, a condition in which it becomes impossible to form memories because of damage to the brain's mammillary bodies, often due to alcoholism. Initially, Sacks considers Jimmie G. to be an apt illustration of eighteenth-century philosopher David Hume's "bundle theory" of personal identity. For Hume, the self was "nothing but a bundle or collection of different perceptions, which succeed each other with an inconceivable rapidity, and are in a perpetual flux and movement."[1] Subsequently, however, Sacks concludes that there is more to a person than memory—that Jimmie G.'s absorption in activities like religious mass, gardening, and music reveal something "soul-like" in him.

Although Jimmie G. provides Sacks with an actual case, theories of personal identity often appeal to imaginary cases devised by thought experiments. Locke asks us to imagine that consciousness accompanies a little finger after it is severed from the body. In "Personal Identity," Derek Parfit draws explicitly on Locke's example to present a thought experiment in which a man divides in half to produce two bodies, each housing a fully conscious half brain. Parfit inserts a wedge between survival and identity to argue that while the person who underwent fission *survives as* both individuals, it is *not* the case that he *is* both individuals. Parfit's contention that "psychological continuity" may underlie a person's survival without that person being the same person thus departs from Locke's account of personal identity.

Marya Schechtman challenges the reliance of Parfit and other philosophers on the principle of psychological continuity in "The Same and the Same." She does so by distinguishing between the numerical sameness and qualitative sameness of the psychological subject. Psychological continuity theorists rely on qualitative sameness (possessing the same qualities), but this fails to make sense of the practical importance that Locke attaches to personal identity, which demands numerical sameness (being one and the same). Schechtman's alternative view "places the limits of the person at the limits of the self-conception." Projection of one's self backwards and forwards in time provides a narrative context within which present experience is interpreted.

Locke, Sacks, Parfit, and Schechtman all adopt psychological approaches to personal identity. However, we are not merely conscious beings; our conscious experiences are always also embodied experiences, which are shaped by the sorts of bodies we have and the ways in which these bodies interact with our surroundings. We are not only physical beings but social beings: our social relationships and cultural upbringings contribute to making us who we are.

In Simone de Beauvoir's famous words in *The Second Sex*, "One is not born but becomes a woman." Beauvoir distinguishes between sex and gender: "every female human being is not necessarily a woman"; this requires "femininity." Beauvoir argues that neither **conceptualism** nor **nominalism** provides an adequate account of femininity: there is no corresponding concept (mental entity), nor is it a mere name (linguistic entity). Rather, gender identity is constructed socially, though not symmetrically: man is constructed as the human norm, woman a deviation from that norm; man is accorded positive value as "the One," woman negative value as "the Other"; man is dominant, woman subordinate. Only in the freedom exercised by pursuing "an authentic existence" is full personhood achieved.

Thomas King exemplifies the narrative approach to personal identity suggested by Schechtman: "The truth about stories," he writes, "is that that's all we are." King reminds us that we choose what stories we tell about ourselves and others, and are responsible for those choices. Dominant groups (e.g., whites) construct stories about the groups they subordinate (e.g., Aboriginals) often in ways that are contrary to fact, inattentive to actual people's lives, and rooted in stereotypes. These "fixed ideas" are not Platonic forms: they are cultural inventions, imaginings, by which the authenticity of people belonging to the subordinate group comes to be measured by people belonging to the dominant group (as the title "You're Not the Indian I Had in Mind" suggests).

## Freedom and Determinism

In the cave analogy, Plato tells us that the soul's active principle of rationality is responsible for its "yearning" for "that sojourn above" whereby the forms are grasped and knowledge attained. To ascend from the sensible realm of particulars to the abstract realm of universals, the rational soul must escape the material confines of the body. Mind–body dualism is also assumed by the Christian doctrine of free will, a subject of debate for Enlightenment philosophers Baron d'Holbach, David Hume, and Immanuel Kant.

Like others of his time, Holbach was impressed by the culmination of the mechanical world view of the scientific revolution in Newtonian physics. Holbach was a materialist and an atheist: he believed that all phenomena can be explained in terms of matter in motion—that there is no immaterial soul wherein a capacity for free will might reside. In "Of the System of Man's Free Agency," he argues that the motives and desires that bring about our actions are themselves mechanically caused, whether internally (e.g., by our temperament) or externally (e.g., by objects that create desires). Holbach tells us that we are unable to "swerve" from the "line" nature "commands" us to follow, that we are determined, not free.

The freedom–determinism debate is not limited to metaphysics but carries implications for moral and legal responsibility. Is it legitimate to reward or punish people for what they did not freely choose and could not have avoided doing? Holbach says no. But what if determinism is false? Quantum physics raises the possibility that the universe is indeterministic, that some events are uncaused. But is it any more legitimate to reward or punish people for what they did not freely choose but did randomly? Compatibilists such as Hume, Kant, and Moritz Schlick insist that it is a mistake to consider freedom and determinism to be incompatible theses.

Hume's famous skeptical account of causation underlies his treatment of what in *A Treatise of Human Nature* he calls the "long disputed question concerning *liberty and necessity*." Hume questions what knowledge we have of physical necessity and concludes that we have sense experience only of the "constant union" of causes and effects and that habit is responsible for the mind's further inference that effects follow necessarily from their causes. For Hume, the idea that "like causes produce like effects" is true no less for our internal motives and consequent actions than for the interactions of external bodies. But, unlike Holbach, Hume does not find this troubling for religion and morality since reward and punishment themselves depend on causal reasoning: we hold people responsible for their actions only when these flow from their characters.

Kant is a compatibilist of a quite different sort; in fact, it is a matter of philosophical debate whether he is a compatibilist at all. In Kant's "Antinomy of Pure Reason," the third antinomy proves the truth of contradictory claims: the thesis that there is a causality of freedom and a causality of laws of nature and the antithesis that there is no causality of freedom but only a causality of laws of nature. Kant's antinomies are designed to show that such conflicts arise when reason illegitimately applies concepts of the understanding beyond the bounds of experience. Kant tells us that we are able to reconcile freedom and determinism once we realize that the sensible world of appearances is not the "absolute reality" of things in themselves. An action is freely chosen when reason determines the will independently of the sensible world of appearances in which it is carried out.

Schlick belonged to the twentieth-century school of logical positivism, which was strongly influenced by Hume. Indeed, in "When Is a Man Responsible?" Schlick begins by characterizing the problem of freedom of the will as a "pseudo-problem" that is due to confusion about meanings of words and was already solved by Hume. Schlick locates that confusion in the conflation of meanings of "law" in natural science and practical affairs. The solution is suggested by Hume's assertion that the "liberty of spontaneity" as "that which is opposed to violence" is the only liberty worth keeping. In natural science, the laws of psychology merely describe how we behave and do not compel that behaviour. In practical affairs, our actions are free when they are caused by our own desires and not compelled (e.g., at gunpoint or due to mental illness).

In "Alternate Possibilities and Moral Responsibility," Harry Frankfurt intervenes in the freedom–determinism debate to point out that all parties—whether compatibilists or incompatibilists, whether hard determinists, soft determinists, or libertarians—subscribe to the principle of alternate possibilities: the principle that "a person is morally responsible for what he has done only if he could have done otherwise." Frankfurt argues that this principle is false.

Scientific research into genetic causes of behaviour raises questions about freedom and responsibility. In "Crime, Genes, and Responsibility," Marcia Baron reminds us that a so-called violence gene would incline or predispose an individual to act violently, but not necessitate that action. Although the action might be harder to avoid, it would not be impossible to avoid. Baron questions whether scientific discovery of such genes would constitute a great advance, as many assume. She concludes that it would be more beneficial to focus on environmental conditions that predispose to crime, many of which are likely triggers for genetic predispositions anyways.

## Natural and Social Kinds

Baron raises a question relevant to metaphysical debates about natural and social kinds. She points out that when genes and criminal behaviour are discussed, it is often unclear to what behaviours such genetic markers would mark a genetic predisposition: anger, premeditated violence, aggressiveness, non-violent crimes such as tax evasion or shoplifting? Presumably, scientists want categories of classification that capture differences that matter, whether in nature or society. Plato's cave allegory suggests that only through knowledge of the forms are we able to discern these truths. A different metaphor of Plato's, found in the *Phaedrus*, that of "cutting nature at its joints," more frequently enters debates about natural kinds.

For nominalists like John Locke, particulars are all that exist and all that we experience. There are no Platonic Forms, and nature has no joints. In "Of Words," Locke argues that we arrive at general ideas through abstraction: we begin with ideas we have of various things and retain only what is common. It is to these abstract ideas, which Locke calls "nominal essences," "species," or "sorts" of things, that we attach general names. Thus, the word "gold" refers to the abstract idea "gold," which is a product of the understanding; however, the similarities shared by the particulars sorted together as gold things are a product of nature. "Real essences" are the unknown and unknowable internal constitutions of particular things that are responsible for their sensible properties and therefore the similarities by which they are sorted.

In "Meaning and Reference," Hilary Putnam challenges Locke's intensional theory of meaning, whereby the meaning of a word is the concept attached to it. Putnam defends a position called "semantic externalism," which holds that the meaning of a word is fixed by the thing to which it refers, i.e., its extension. Putnam's famous Twin Earth thought experiment is designed to convince us that meanings cannot be "in the head": two individuals, one on Earth and the other on Twin Earth, may have identical ideas about water (that it is transparent, odourless, etc.) even though, unbeknownst to both, the chemical composition of "water" on Earth is $H_2O$ and on Twin Earth is XYZ. Putnam submits that the word "water" has different meanings in each place.

In "Natural Kinds and Biological Taxa," John Dupré notes that Locke's skepticism concerning our ability to know real essences was "premature" given subsequent progress in physics and chemistry: for Putnam, writing in the twentieth century, the extensions of many ordinary language terms (e.g., "water") turn out to be natural kinds whose essential microstructural properties (e.g., $H_2O$) are discoverable by scientists. However, Dupré points out that Putnam's theory encounters problems in biology. Species lack essential properties. An ordinary language term such as "lily" does not correspond to a recognized biological taxon: the species we call lilies belong to different genera within the lily family. Scientific taxonomy likewise places onions and garlics in the lily family, but their culinary importance distinguishes them in ordinary language.

As Ian Hacking notes in "Madness: Biological or Constructed?" arguments in the "science wars" of the 1990s were often cast in terms of one side saying, "X is real" and the other side saying, "No, X is constructed." Hacking is interested in psychopathologies such as mental retardation, schizophrenia, and childhood autism. Whereas realists argue that these conditions are caused by underlying genetic, neurological, or biochemical problems, social constructionists emphasize how changing attitudes in society have led to different classifications at different times. Hacking introduces a "less tired set of opposites," "interactive" and "indifferent" kinds, which, aided by Putnam's theory of reference, show how a condition such as childhood autism can be both socially constructed and real.

Whereas Hacking attempts to reconcile (biological) realist and social constructionist camps, the final two readings are situated squarely within social constructionism.

Sally Haslanger asks: "Gender and Race: (What) Are They? (What) Do We Want Them To Be?" Haslanger's approach to these questions is "descriptive" (about whether the gender and racial terms we use adequately track natural and/or social kinds) and "analytic" (about what it is we want concepts of gender and race to do for us). Haslanger treats gender and race as social classes that reflect the hierarchical positioning of individuals within a complex of oppressive social relations, with bodily differences used as physical markers of dominant or subordinate status. Given the role of gender and race in oppression, Haslanger wonders whether we should "refuse to be gendered man or woman, refuse to be raced."

Michel Foucault's *The Order of Things* tells us that classifying things on the basis of similarities and differences is not simply an empirical task, as Locke believed. Bringing about order depends on language, perception, values, and practices, all of which are embedded in particular cultures—this is evident in Haslanger's account of gender and race. But more fundamental yet, according to Foucault, is the historically and culturally contingent epistemological field or *episteme* that is "anterior to words, perceptions, and gestures" and makes order possible. Foucault argues that the human sciences emerged only with the Modern age: not until the beginning of the nineteenth century did "man" belong to the "order of things."

## ▶ Note

1. *A Treatise of Human Nature*, vol. 1 (London: J. M. Dent & Sons and New York: E.P. Dutton, 1911), 239.

## ▶ Discussion Questions

1. Consider a photo taken when you were a baby or a small child. What makes you the same person as you were then? Consider your classmates, all closer to you in age and likely more similar to you (in beliefs, interests, etc.) than the baby or small child you once were. What makes you a different person than your classmates?
2. How important is sex, gender, race, or ethnicity to who you are as a person? How important is sex, gender, race, or ethnicity to who you take others to be as persons?
3. Consider some of your actions today: whether you got out of bed when the alarm rang or hit the snooze button; whether you ate breakfast and what you ate; whether you walked, cycled, bussed, or drove to school; whether you did your assigned reading before coming to class. Did you freely choose these actions? Could you have done otherwise?
4. Are we justified in holding individuals morally and/or legally responsible for actions they performed due to factors beyond their control (their genes, childhoods, etc.)?
5. Do the ways in which scientists classify things reflect the way the world is? Do the ways in which scientists classify things reflect their own ideas and interests?

## ▶ Further Reading

Bird, Alexander. "Natural Kinds." *Philosophy of Science*. Montreal and Kingston: McGill-Queens University Press, 1998. 95–120.

Dupré, John. *Humans and Other Animals*. Oxford: Clarendon Press, 2002.

Honderich, Ted. *How Free Are You?: The Determinism Problem*, 2nd ed. New York: Oxford University Press, 2002.

Kane, Robert. *A Contemporary Introduction to Free Will*. New York: Oxford University Press, 2005.

Shrage, Laurie J., ed. *"You've Changed": Sex Reassignment and Personal Identity*. Oxford: Oxford University Press, 2009.

Wilkes, Kathleen V. *Personal Identity without Thought Experiments*. New York: Oxford University Press, 1994.

# Plato

Plato (429–347 BCE) is so important to philosophy's inceptions and subsequent development as a discipline that the philosopher and mathematician Alfred North Whitehead once wrote, "The safest general characterization of the European philosophical tradition is that it consists of a series of footnotes to Plato."[1] This excerpt from *Republic*, Bk. 7, the famous allegory of the cave, introduces readers to Plato's theory of the forms and his views on education and the philosopher's proper role in society.

## Cave Allegory

From *The Republic*

Characters: **Socrates**, **Glaucon**

1. "Next," said I [Socrates], "compare our nature in respect of education and its lack to such an experience as this. Picture men dwelling in a sort of subterranean cavern with a long entrance open to the light on its entire width. Conceive them as having their legs and necks fettered from childhood, so that they remain in the same spot, able to look forward only, and prevented by the fetters from turning their heads. Picture further the light from a fire burning higher up and at a distance behind them, and between the fire and the prisoners and above them a road along which a low wall has been built, as the exhibitors of puppet-shows have partitions before the men themselves, above which they show the puppets." "All that I see," he [Glaucon] said. "See also, then, men carrying past the wall implements of all kinds that rise above the wall, and human images and shapes of animals as well, wrought in stone and wood and every material, some of these bearers presumably speaking and others silent." "A strange image you speak of," he said, "and strange prisoners." "Like to us," I said; "for, to begin with, tell me do you think that these men would have seen anything of themselves or of one another except the shadows cast from the fire on the wall of the cave that fronted them?" "How could they," he said, "if they were compelled to hold their heads unmoved through life?" "And again, would not the same be true of the objects carried past them?" "Surely." "If then they were able to talk to one another, do you not think that they would suppose that in naming the things that they saw they were naming the passing objects?" "Necessarily." "And if their prison had an echo from the wall opposite them, when one of the passersby uttered a sound, do you think that they would suppose anything else than the passing shadow to be the speaker?" "By Zeus, I do not," said he. "Then in every way such prisoners would deem reality to be nothing else than the shadows of the artificial objects." "Quite inevitably," he said. "Consider, then, what would be the manner of the release and healing from these bonds and this folly if in the course of nature something of this sort should happen to them: When one was freed from his fetters and compelled to stand up suddenly and turn his head around and walk and to lift up his eyes to the light, and in doing all this felt pain and, because of the dazzle and glitter of the light, was unable to discern the objects whose shadows he formerly saw, what do you suppose would be his answer if someone told him that what he had seen before was all a cheat and an illusion, but that now, being nearer to reality and turned toward more real things, he saw more truly? And if also one should point out to him each of the passing objects and constrain him by questions to say what it is, do you not think that he would be at a loss and that he would regard what he formerly saw as more real than the things now pointed out to him?" "Far more real," he said.

2. "And if he were compelled to look at the light itself, would not that pain his eyes, and would he not turn away and flee to those things which he is able to discern and regard them as in very deed more clear and exact than the objects pointed out?" "It is so," he said. "And if," said I, "someone should drag him thence by force up the ascent which is rough and steep, and not let him go before he had drawn him out into the light of the sun, do you not think that he would find it painful to be so haled along, and would chafe at it, and when he came out into the light, that his eyes would be filled with its beams so that he would not be able to see even one of the things that we call real?" "Why, no, not immediately," he said. "Then there would be need of habituation, I take it, to enable him to see the things higher up. And at first he would most easily discern the shadows and, after that, the likenesses or reflections in water of men and other things, and later, the things themselves, and from these he would go on to contemplate the appearances in the heavens and heaven itself, more easily by night, looking at the light of the stars and the moon, than by day the sun and the sun's light." "Of course." "And so, finally, I suppose, he would be able to look upon the sun itself and see its true nature, not by reflections in water or phantasms of it in an alien setting, but in and by itself in its own place." "Necessarily," he said. "And at this point he would infer and conclude that this it is that provides the seasons and the courses of the year and presides over all things in the visible region, and is in some sort the cause of all these things that they had seen." "Obviously," he said, "that would be the next step." "Well then, if he recalled to mind his first habitation and what passed for wisdom there, and his fellow-bondsmen, do you not think that he would count himself happy in the change and pity them?" "He would indeed." "And if there had been honours and commendations among them which they bestowed on one another and prizes for the man who is quickest to make out the shadows as they pass and best able to remember their customary precedences, sequences and co-existences, and so most successful in guessing at what was to come, do you think he would be very keen about such

rewards, and that he would envy and emulate those who were honoured by these prisoners and lorded it among them, or that he would feel with **Homer** (*Odyss.* 11.489) and 'greatly prefer while living on earth to be serf of another, a landless man', and endure anything rather than opine with them and live that life?" "Yes," he said, "I think that he would choose to endure anything rather than such a life." "And consider this also," said I, "if such a one should go down again and take his old place would he not get his eyes full of darkness, thus suddenly coming out of the sunlight?" "He would indeed." "Now if he should be required to contend with these perpetual prisoners in 'evaluating' these shadows while his vision was still dim and before his eyes were accustomed to the dark—and this time required for habituation would not be very short—would he not provoke laughter, and would it not be said of him that he had returned from his journey aloft with his eyes ruined and that it was not worthwhile even to attempt the ascent? And if it were possible to lay hands on and to kill the man who tried to release them and lead them up, would they not kill him[2]?" "They certainly would," he said.

3. "This image then, dear Glaucon, we must apply as a whole to all that has been said, likening the region revealed through sight to the habitation of the prison, and the light of the fire in it to the power of the sun. And if you assume that the ascent and the contemplation of the things above is the soul's ascension to the intelligible region, you will not miss my surmise, since that is what you desire to hear. But God knows whether it is true. But, at any rate, my dream as it appears to me is that in the region of the known the last thing to be seen and hardly seen is the idea of good, and that when seen it must needs point us to the conclusion that this is indeed the cause for all things of all that is right and beautiful, giving birth in the visible world to light, and the author of light and itself in the intelligible world being the authentic source of truth and reason, and that anyone who is to act wisely in private or public must have caught sight of this." "I concur," he said, "so far as I am able." "Come then," I said, "and join me in this further thought, and do not be surprised

that those who have attained to this height are not willing to occupy themselves with the affairs of men, but their souls ever feel the upward urge and the yearning for that sojourn above. For this, I take it, is likely if in this point too the likeness of our image holds." "Yes, it is likely." "And again, do you think it at all strange," said I, "if a man returning from divine contemplations to the petty miseries of men cuts a sorry figure and appears most ridiculous, if, while still blinking through the gloom, and before he has become sufficiently accustomed to the environing darkness, he is compelled in courtrooms or elsewhere to contend about the shadows of justice or the images that cast the shadows and to wrangle in debate about the notions of these things in the minds of those who have never seen justice itself?" "It would be by no men strange," he said. "But a sensible man," I said, "would remember that there are two distinct disturbances of the eyes arising from two causes, according as the shift is from light to darkness or from darkness to light, and, believing that the same thing happens to the soul too, whenever he saw a soul perturbed and unable to discern something, he would not laugh unthinkingly, but would observe whether coming from a brighter life its vision was obscured by the unfamiliar darkness, or whether the passage from the deeper dark of ignorance into a more luminous world and the greater brightness had dazzled its vision. And so he would deem the one happy in its experience and way of life and pity the other, and if it pleased him to laugh at it, his laughter would be less laughable than that at the expense of the soul that had come down from the light above." "That is a very fair statement," he said.

4. "Then, if this is true, our view of these matters must be this, that education is not in reality what some people proclaim it to be in their professions. What they aver is that they can put true knowledge into a soul that does not possess it, as if they were inserting vision into blind eyes." "They do indeed," he said. "But our present argument indicates," said I, "that the true analogy for this indwelling power in the soul and the instrument whereby each of us apprehends is that of an eye that could not be converted to the light from the darkness except by turning the whole body. Even so this organ of knowledge must be turned around from the world of becoming together with the entire soul, like the scene-shifting periact[3] in the theatre, until the soul is able to endure the contemplation of essence and the brightest region of being. And this, we say, is the good, do we not?" "Yes." "Of this very thing, then," I said, "there might be an art, an art of the speediest and most effective shifting or conversion of the soul, not an art of producing vision in it, but on the assumption that it possesses vision but does not rightly direct it and does not look where it should, an art of bringing this about." "Yes, that seems likely," he said. "Then the other so-called virtues of the soul do seem akin to those of the body. For it is true that where they do not pre-exist, they are afterwards created by habit and practice. But the excellence of thought, it seems, is certainly of a more divine quality, a thing that never loses its potency, but, according to the direction of its conversion, becomes useful and beneficent, or, again, useless and harmful. Have you never observed in those who are popularly spoken of as bad, but smart men, how keen is the vision of the little soul, how quick it is to discern the things that interest it, a proof that it is not a poor vision which it has, but one forcibly enlisted in the service of evil, so that the sharper its sight the more mischief it accomplishes?" "I certainly have," he said. "Observe then," said I, "that this part of such a soul, if it had been hammered from childhood, and had thus been struck free of the leaden weights, so to speak, of our birth and becoming, which attaching themselves to it by food and similar pleasures and gluttonies turn downwards the vision of the soul— If, I say, freed from these, it had suffered a conversion towards the things that are real and true, that same faculty of the same men would have been most keen in its vision of the higher things, just as it is for the things toward which it is now turned." "It is likely," he said. "Well, then," said I, "is not this also likely and a necessary consequence of what has been said, that neither could men who are uneducated and inexperienced in truth ever adequately preside over a state, nor could those who had been permitted to

linger on to the end in the pursuit of culture—the one because they have no single aim and purpose in life to which all their actions, public and private, must be directed, and the others, because they will not voluntarily engage in action, believing that while still living they have been transported to the Islands of the Blest." "True," he said. "It is the duty of us, the founders, then," said I, "to compel the best natures to attain the knowledge which we pronounced the greatest, and to win to the vision of the good, to scale that ascent, and when they have reached the heights and taken an adequate view, we must not allow what is now permitted." "What is that?" "That they should linger there," I said, "and refuse to go down again among those bondsmen and share their labours and honours, whether they are of less or of greater worth." "Do you mean to say that we must do them this wrong, and compel them to live an inferior life when the better is in their power?"

5. "You have again forgotten, my friend," said I, "that the law is not concerned with the special happiness of any class in the state, but is trying to produce this condition in the city as a whole, harmonizing and adapting the citizens to one another by persuasion and compulsion, and requiring them to impart to one another any benefit which they are severally able to bestow upon the community, and that it itself creates such men in the state, not that it may allow each to take what course pleases him, but with a view to using them for the binding together of the commonwealth." "True," he said, "I did forget it." "Observe, then, Glaucon," said I, "that we shall not be wronging, either, the philosophers who arise among us, but that we can justify our action when we constrain them to take charge of the other citizens and be their guardians. For we will say to them that it is natural that men of similar quality who spring up in other cities should not share in the labours there. For they grow up spontaneously from no volition of the government in the several states, and it is justice that the self-grown, indebted to none for its breeding, should not be zealous either to pay to anyone the price of its nurture. But you we have engendered for yourselves and the rest of the city to be, as it were, king-bees and leaders in the hive. You

have received a better and more complete education than the others, and you are more capable of sharing both ways of life. Down you must go then, each in his turn, to the habitation of the others and accustom yourselves to the observation of the obscure things there. For once habituated you will discern them infinitely better than the dwellers there, and you will know what each of the 'idols' is and whereof it is a semblance, because you have seen the reality of the beautiful, the just, and the good. So our city will be governed by us and you with waking minds, and not, as most cities now which are inhabited and ruled darkly as in a dream by men who fight one another for shadows and wrangle for office as if that were a great good, when the truth is that the city in which those who are to rule are least eager to hold office must needs be best administered and most free from dissension, and the state that gets the contrary type of ruler will be the opposite of this." "By all means," he said. "Will our alumni, then, disobey us when we tell them this, and will they refuse to share in the labours of state each in his turn while permitted to dwell the most of the time with one another in that purer world[4]?" "Impossible," he said: "for we shall be imposing just commands on men who are just. Yet they will assuredly approach office as an unavoidable necessity, and in the opposite temper from that of the present rulers in our cities." "For the fact is, dear friend," said I, "if you can discover a better way of life than office-holding for your future rulers, a well-governed city becomes a possibility. For only in such a state will those rule who are really rich, not in gold, but in the wealth that makes happiness—a good and wise life. But if, being beggars and starvelings from lack of goods of their own, they turn to affairs of state thinking that it is thence that they should grasp their own good, then it is impossible. For when office and rule become the prizes of contention, such a civil and internecine strife destroys the office-seekers themselves and the city as well." "Most true," he said. "Can you name any other type or ideal of life that looks with scorn on political office except the life of true philosophers?" I asked. "No, by Zeus," he said. "But what we require," I said, "is that those who take office should not be lovers of rule.

Otherwise there will be a contest with rival lovers." "Surely." "What others, then, will you compel to undertake the guardianship of the city than those who have most intelligence of the principles that are the means of good government and who possess distinctions of another kind and a life that is preferable to the political life?" "No others," he said.

## Notes

1. Alfred North Whitehead, *Process and Reality: An Essay in Cosmology* (New York: Humanities Press, 1929), 63.—LG
2. Tr.: An obvious allusion to the fate of Socrates.
3. Tr.: Probably a reference to the triangular prisms on each side of the stage. They revolved on an axis and had different scenes painted on their three faces.
4. Tr.: The world of ideas, the upper world as opposed to that of the cave.

## Study Questions

1. Draw a picture that illustrates Plato's cave allegory. Explain how the goings-on of the cave serve as an allegory for Plato's theory of the forms.
2. How do the concrete and particular objects of our sense-experience relate to the abstract and universal objects that inhabit Plato's realm of the forms?
3. What does Plato's cave allegory suggest about how students should be educated? Once educated, what is the proper role of the philosopher in society, according to Plato?

# ⌣ PERSONAL IDENTITY ⌣

## John Locke

John Locke (1632–1704) was an English philosopher and physician. He is especially known for his 1689 *An Essay Concerning Human Understanding*. In the first two books of the *Essay*, Locke defends empiricism and the theory of the mind as a *tabula rasa*, or blank slate: knowledge is not innate but arises from the mind's capacities to act on ideas gained entirely through the senses. In this chapter on personal identity, added to the second edition of the *Essay*, Locke rejects Descartes' equation of the person with the immaterial soul.—TR

## Of Identity and Diversity

From *An Essay Concerning Human Understanding*

4. [. . .] **Principium Individuationis.** The *principium individuationis* [. . .], it is plain, is existence itself [. . .]: e.g., let us suppose an atom [. . .] existing in a determined time and place; it is evident that considered in any instant of its existence, it is in that instant the same with itself. For, being at that instant what it is and nothing else, it is the same, and so must continue as long as its existence is continued; for so long it will be the same, and no other. In like manner, if two or more atoms be joined together into the same mass, every one of those atoms will be the same by the foregoing rule: and whilst they exist united together, the mass, consisting of the same atoms, must be the same mass, or the same body, let the parts be ever so differently jumbled. But if one of these atoms be taken away, or one new one added, it is no longer the same mass or the same body. In the state of living creatures, their identity depends not on a mass of the same particles, but on something else. For in them the variation of great parcels of matter alters not the identity: an oak growing from a plant to a great tree, and then lopped, is still the same oak; and a colt grown up to a horse, sometimes fat, sometimes lean, is all the while the same horse: though, in both these cases, there may be a manifest change of the parts, so that truly they are not either of them the same masses of matter, though they be truly one of them the same oak, and the other the same horse. The reason whereof is that, in these two cases—a *mass of matter* and a *living body*, identity is not applied to the same thing.

5. **Identity of Vegetables.** We must therefore consider wherein an oak differs from a mass of matter, and that seems to me to be in this, that the one is only the cohesion of particles of matter anyhow united, the other such a disposition of them as constitutes the parts of an oak, and such an organization of those parts as is fit to receive and distribute nourishment, so as to continue and frame the wood, bark, and leaves, etc., of an oak, in which consists the vegetable life. That being then one plant which has such an organization of parts in one coherent body, partaking of one common life, it continues to be the same plant as long as it partakes of the same life, though that life be communicated to new particles of matter vitally united to the living plant, in a like continued organization conformable to that sort of plants. For this organization, being at any one instant in any one collection of matter, is in that particular concrete distinguished from all other, and *is* that individual life, which existing constantly from that moment both forwards and backwards, in the same continuity of insensibly succeeding parts united to the living body of the plant, it has that identity which makes the same plant, and all the parts of it parts of the same plant, during all the time that they exist united in that continued organization which is fit to convey that common life to all the parts so united.

6. **Identity of Animals.** The case is not so much different in *brutes* but that anyone may hence see what makes an animal and continues it the same. Something we have like this in machines, and may serve to illustrate it. For example, what is a watch? It is plain it is nothing but a fit organization or construction of parts to a certain end, which, when a sufficient force is added to it, it is capable to attain. If we would suppose this machine one continued body, all whose organized parts were repaired, increased, or diminished by a constant addition or separation of insensible parts, with one common life, we should have something very much like the body of an animal—with this difference: that in an animal, the fitness of the organization and the motion wherein life consists begin together, the motion coming from within; but in machines, the force coming sensibly from without is often away when the organ is in order, and well fitted to receive it.

7. **The Identity of Man.** This also shows wherein the identity of the same *man* consists: viz., in nothing but a participation of the same continued life, by constantly fleeting particles of matter, in succession vitally united to the same organized body. He that shall place the identity of man in anything else but, like that of other animals, in one fitly organized body taken in any one instant, and from thence continued under one organization of life in several successively fleeting particles of matter united to it, will find it hard to make an embryo, one of years, mad and sober the *same* man by any supposition that will not make it possible for **Seth**, **Ishmael**, **Socrates**, **Pilate**, St Austin [**St Augustine**], and **Caesar Borgia** to be the same man. For if the identity of *soul alone* makes the same *man*, and there be nothing in the nature of matter why the same individual spirit may not be united to different bodies, it will be possible that those men, living in distant ages and of different tempers, may have been the same man: which way of speaking must be from a very strange use of the word man, applied to an idea out of which body and shape are excluded. And that way of speaking would agree yet worse with the notions of those philosophers who allow of transmigration, and are of opinion that the souls of men may, for their miscarriages, be detruded into the bodies of beasts, as fit habitations, with organs suited to the satisfaction of their brutal inclinations. But yet I think nobody, could he be sure that the *soul* of **Heliogabalus** were in one of his hogs, would yet say that hog were a *man* or *Heliogabalus*.

8. **Idea of Identity Suited to the Idea It Is Applied To.** It is not therefore unity of substance that comprehends all sorts of identity, or will determine it in every case; but to conceive and judge of it aright, we must consider what idea the word it is applied to stands for: it being one thing to be the same *substance*, another the same *man*, and a third the same *person*, if *person*, *man*, and *substance* are three names standing for three different ideas;—for such as is the idea belonging to that name, such must be the identity; which, if it had been a little more carefully attended to, would possibly have prevented a great deal of that confusion which often occurs about this matter, with no small seeming difficulties, especially concerning *personal* identity, which therefore we shall in the next place a little consider. [. . .]

11. **Personal Identity.** This being premised, to find wherein personal identity consists, we must consider what *person* stands for;—which, I think, is a thinking intelligent being, that has reason and reflection, and can consider itself as itself, the same thinking thing, in different times and places; which it does only by that consciousness which is inseparable from thinking, and, as it seems to me, essential to it: it being impossible for anyone to perceive without *perceiving* that he does perceive. When we see, hear, smell, taste, feel, meditate, or will anything, we know that we do so. Thus it is always as to our present sensations and perceptions: and by this everyone is to himself that which he calls *self*:—it not being considered, in this case, whether the same self be continued in the same or diverse substances. For, since consciousness always accompanies thinking, and it is that which makes everyone to be what he calls self, and thereby distinguishes himself from all other thinking things, in this alone consists personal identity, i.e., the sameness of a rational being: and as far as this consciousness can be extended backwards to any past action or thought, so far reaches

the identity of that person; it is the same self now it was then; and it is by the same self with this present one that now reflects on it that that action was done.

12. **Consciousness Makes Personal Identity.** But it is further inquired, whether it be the same identical substance. This few would think they had reason to doubt of, if these perceptions, with their consciousness, always remained present in the mind, whereby the same thinking thing would be always consciously present, and, as would be thought, evidently the same to itself. But that which seems to make the difficulty is this, that this consciousness being interrupted always by forgetfulness, there being no moment of our lives wherein we have the whole train of all our past actions before our eyes in one view, but even the best memories losing the sight of one part whilst they are viewing another; and we sometimes, and that the greatest part of our lives, not reflecting on our past selves, being intent on our present thoughts, and in sound sleep having no thoughts at all, or at least none with that consciousness which remarks our waking thoughts,—I say, in all these cases, our consciousness being interrupted, and we losing the sight of our past selves, doubts are raised whether we are the same thinking thing, i.e., the same *substance* or no. Which, however reasonable or unreasonable, concerns not *personal* identity at all, the question being what makes the same person, and not whether it be the same identical substance which always thinks in the same person, which, in this case, matters not at all: different substances, by the same consciousness (where they do partake in it) being united into one person, as well as different bodies by the same life are united into one animal, whose identity is preserved in that change of substances by the unity of one continued life. For, it being the same consciousness that makes a man be himself to himself, personal identity depends on that only, whether it be annexed solely to one individual substance, or can be continued in a succession of several substances. For as far as any intelligent being *can* repeat the idea of any past action with the same consciousness it had of it at first, and with the same consciousness it has of any present action, so far it is the same personal self. For it is by the consciousness it has of its present thoughts and actions that it is *self to itself* now, and so will be the same self as far as the same consciousness can extend to actions past or to come, and would be, by distance of time or change of substance, no more two persons than a man be two men by wearing other clothes today than he did yesterday, with a long or a short sleep between: the same consciousness uniting those distant actions into the same person, whatever substances contributed to their production.

13. **Personal Identity in Change of Substance.** That this is so, we have some kind of evidence in our very bodies: all whose particles, whilst vitally united to this same thinking conscious self, so that *we feel* when they are touched, and are affected by, and conscious of good or harm that happens to them, are a part of ourselves—i.e., of our thinking conscious self. Thus, the limbs of his body are to everyone a part of himself; he sympathizes and is concerned for them. Cut off a hand, and thereby separate it from that consciousness he had of its heat, cold, and other affections, and it is then no longer a part of that which is himself, anymore than the remotest part of matter. Thus, we see the *substance* whereof personal self consisted at one time may be varied at another, without the change of personal identity, there being no question about the same person, though the limbs which but now were a part of it be cut off.

14. **Personality in Change of Substance.** But the question is, whether if the same substance which thinks be changed, it can be the same person, or, remaining the same, it can be different persons?

And to this I answer: First, this can be no question at all to those who place thought in a purely material animal constitution, void of an immaterial substance. For, whether their supposition be true or no, it is plain they conceive personal identity preserved in something else than identity of substance, as animal identity is preserved in identity of life, and not of substance.

15. **Whether in Change of Thinking Substances There Can Be One Person.** But next, as to the first part of the question, whether, if the same thinking substance (supposing immaterial substances only to think) be changed, it can be the same person?

I answer, that cannot be resolved but by those who know what kind of substances they are that do think, and whether the consciousness of past actions can be transferred from one thinking substance to another. I grant were the same consciousness the same individual action it could not: but it being a present representation of a past action, why it may not be possible that that may be represented to the mind to have been which really never was will remain to be shown. [. . .] Why one intellectual substance may not have represented to it, as done by itself, what *it* never did, and was perhaps done by some other agent—why, I say, such a representation may not possibly be without reality of matter of fact as well as several representations in dreams are, which yet whilst dreaming we take for true—will be difficult to conclude from the nature of things. And that it never is so will by us, till we have clearer views of the nature of thinking substances, be best resolved into the goodness of God, who, as far as the happiness or misery of any of his sensible creatures is concerned in it, will not, by a fatal error of theirs, transfer from one to another that consciousness which draws reward or punishment with it. [. . .] But yet, [. . .] it must be allowed that if the same consciousness [. . .] can be transferred from one thinking substance to another, it will be possible that two thinking substances may make but one person. For the same consciousness being preserved, whether in the same or different substances, the personal identity is preserved.

16. **Whether, the Same Immaterial Substance Remaining, There Can Be Two Persons.** As to the second part of the question, whether the same immaterial substance remaining there may be two distinct persons, which question seems to me to be built on this,—whether the same immaterial being, being conscious of the action of its past duration, may be wholly stripped of all the consciousness of its past existence, and lose it beyond the power of ever retrieving it again: and so, as it were beginning a new account from a new period, have a consciousness that *cannot* reach beyond this new state. All those who hold pre-existence are evidently of this mind, since they allow the soul to have no remaining consciousness of what it did in that pre-existent state, either wholly separate from body or informing any other body; and if they should not, it is plain experience would be against them. [. . .] Let anyone reflect upon himself and conclude that he has in himself an immaterial spirit, which is that which thinks in him and in the constant change of his body keeps him the same, and is that which he calls *himself*: let him also suppose it to be the same soul that was in **Nestor or Thersites at the siege of Troy** (for souls being, as far as we know anything of them, in their nature indifferent to any parcel of matter, the supposition has no apparent absurdity in it), which it may have been as well as it is now the soul of any other man: but he now having no consciousness of any of the actions either of Nestor or Thersites, does or can he conceive himself the same person with either of them? Can he be concerned in either of their actions? Attribute them to himself, or think them his own, more than the actions of any other men that ever existed? So that this consciousness, not reaching to any of the actions of either of those men, he is no more one *self* with either of them than if the soul or immaterial spirit that now informs him had been created and began to exist when it began to inform his present body, though it were never so true that the same *spirit* that informed Nestor's or Thersites' body were numerically the same that now informs his. For this would no more make him the same person with Nestor than if some of the particles of matter that were once a part of Nestor were now a part of this man—the same immaterial substance, without the same consciousness, no more making the same person by being united to any body than the same particle of matter, without consciousness, united to any body makes the same person. But let him once find himself conscious of any of the actions of Nestor, he then finds himself the same person with Nestor.

17. **The Body, as well as the Soul, Goes to the Making of a Man.** And thus may we be able, without any difficulty, to conceive the same person at the resurrection, though in a body not exactly in make or parts the same which he had here,—the same consciousness going along with the soul that inhabits it. But yet the soul alone in the change of

bodies would scarce, to anyone but to him that makes the soul the man, be enough to make the same man. For should the soul of a prince, carrying with it the consciousness of the prince's past life, enter and inform the body of a cobbler, as soon as deserted by his own soul, everyone sees he would be the same *person* with the prince, accountable only for the prince's actions: but who would say it was the same *man*? The body too goes to the making the man, and would, I guess, to everybody determine the man in this case, wherein the soul, with all its princely thoughts about it, would not make another man: but he would be the same cobbler to everyone besides himself. I know that in the ordinary way of speaking, the same person and the same man stand for one and the same thing. And indeed everyone will always have a liberty to speak as he pleases, and to apply what articulate sounds to what ideas he thinks fit, and change them as often as he pleases. But yet, when we will inquire what makes the same *spirit*, *man*, or *person*, we must fix the ideas of spirit, man, or person in our minds; and having resolved with ourselves what we mean by them, it will not be hard to determine, in either of them, or the like, when it is the same, and when not.

18. **Consciousness Alone Unites Actions into the Same Person.** But though the same immaterial substance or soul does not alone, wherever it be, and in whatsoever state, make the same *man*; yet it is plain, consciousness, as far as ever it can be extended—should it be to ages past—unites existences and actions very remote in time into the same *person*, as well as it does the existences and actions of the immediately preceding moment: so that whatever has the consciousness of present and past actions is the same person to whom they both belong. Had I the same consciousness that I saw the ark and Noah's flood, as that I saw an overflowing of the Thames last winter, or as that I write now, I could no more doubt that I who write this now, that saw the Thames overflowed last winter, and that viewed the flood at the general deluge was the same *self*—place that self in what *substance* you please—than that I who write this am the same *myself* now whilst I write (whether I consist of all the same substance,

material or immaterial, or no) that I was yesterday. For as to this point of being the same self, it matters not whether this present self be made up of the same or other substances—I being as much concerned, and as justly accountable for any action that was done a thousand years since, appropriated to me now by this self-consciousness, as I am for what I did the last moment.

19. **Self Depends on Consciousness, Not on Substance.** *Self* is that conscious thinking thing—whatever substance made up of (whether spiritual or material, simple or compounded, it matters not)—which is sensible or conscious of pleasure and pain, capable of happiness or misery, and so is concerned for itself, as far as that consciousness extends. Thus everyone finds that, whilst comprehended under that consciousness, the little finger is as much a part of himself as what is most so. Upon separation of this little finger, should this consciousness go along with the little finger and leave the rest of the body, it is evident the little finger would be the person, the same person; and self then would have nothing to do with the rest of the body. As in this case it is the consciousness that goes along with the substance when one part is separate from another which makes the same person and constitutes this inseparable self, so it is in reference to substances remote in time. That with which the consciousness of this present thinking thing *can* join itself makes the same person, and is one self with it and with nothing else, and so attributes to itself, and owns all the actions of that thing, as its own, as far as that consciousness reaches, and no further—as everyone who reflects will perceive.

20. **Persons, Not Substances, the Objects of Reward and Punishment.** In this personal identity is founded all the right and justice of reward and punishment, happiness and misery being that for which everyone is concerned for *himself*, and not mattering what becomes of any *substance* not joined to, or affected with that consciousness. For, as it is evident in the instance I gave but now, if the consciousness went along with the little finger when it was cut off, that would be the same self which was concerned for the whole body yesterday, as making part of itself, whose actions then it cannot but admit

as its own now. Though, if the same body should still live, and immediately from the separation of the little finger have its own peculiar consciousness, whereof the little finger knew nothing, it would not at all be concerned for it, as a part of itself, or could own any of its actions, or have any of them imputed to him.

21. **Which Shows Wherein Personal Identity Consists.** This may show us wherein personal identity consists: not in the identity of substance, but, as I have said, in the identity of consciousness, wherein if Socrates and the present mayor of Queenborough agree, they are the same person: if the same Socrates waking and sleeping do not partake of the same consciousness, Socrates waking and sleeping is not the same person. And to punish Socrates waking for what sleeping Socrates thought, and waking Socrates was never conscious of, would be no more of right than to punish one twin for what his brother-twin did, whereof he knew nothing, because their outsides were so like that they could not be distinguished, for such twins have been seen.

22. **Absolute Oblivion Separates What Is Thus Forgotten from the Person, But Not from the Man.** But yet possibly it will still be objected,—Suppose I wholly lose the memory of some parts of my life, beyond a possibility of retrieving them, so that perhaps I shall never be conscious of them again; yet am I not the same person that did those actions, had those thoughts that I once was conscious of, though I have now forgot them? To which I answer, that we must here take notice what the word *I* is applied to; which, in this case, is the *man* only. And the same man being presumed to be the same person, I is easily here supposed to stand also for the same person. But if it be possible for the same man to have distinct incommunicable consciousness at different times, it is past doubt the same man would at different times make different persons; which, we see, is the sense of mankind in the solemnest declaration of their opinions, human laws not punishing the mad man for the sober man's actions, nor the sober man for what the mad man did,—thereby making them two persons: which is somewhat explained by our way of speaking in English when we say such an one is "not himself," or is "beside himself"; in which phrases it is insinuated, as if those who now, or at least first used them, thought that self was changed; the selfsame person was no longer in that man. [. . .]

## Study Questions

1. Describe Locke's criteria for being the same material substance, the same plant or animal, and the same person.
2. What are Locke's criteria for being *a human* and for being *a person*? In Locke's view, are all humans persons? In Locke's view, are all persons humans?
3. Outline the arguments Locke offers to justify the independence of consciousness from any substance, material or immaterial, in which it might inhere.
4. Is Locke correct to claim that the law does not punish "the mad man for the sober man's actions, nor the sober man for what the mad man did"?

# Oliver Sacks

Oliver Sacks is an Oxford-educated neurologist whose books tell real-life stories of patients with neurological disorders. By substituting clinical tales for case studies, Sacks wants readers to see the person behind the disorder. But what is a person? This chapter from *The Man Who Mistook His Wife for a Hat* questions the role of memory in personal identity.—TR

## The Lost Mariner

From *The Man Who Mistook His Wife for a Hat*

*You have to begin to lose your memory, if only in bits and pieces, to realise that memory is what makes our lives. Life without memory is no life at all. . . . Our memory is our coherence, our reason, our feeling, even our action. Without it, we are nothing . . . (I can only wait for the final amnesia, the one that can erase an entire life, as it did my mother's . . .)*

—Luis Buñuel

This moving and frightening segment in Buñuel's recently translated memoirs raises fundamental questions—clinical, practical, existential, philosophical: what sort of a life (if any), what sort of a world, what sort of a self, can be preserved in a man who has lost the greater part of his memory and, with this, his past, and his moorings in time?

It immediately made me think of a patient of mine in whom these questions are precisely exemplified: charming, intelligent, memoryless Jimmie G., who was admitted to our Home for the Aged near New York City early in 1975, with a cryptic transfer note saying, "Helpless, demented, confused and disoriented."

Jimmie was a fine-looking man, with a curly bush of grey hair, a healthy and handsome forty-nine-year-old. He was cheerful, friendly, and warm.

"Hiya, Doc!" he said. "Nice morning! Do I take this chair here?" He was a genial soul, very ready to talk and to answer any questions I asked him. He told me his name and birth date, and the name of the little town in Connecticut where he was born. He described it in affectionate detail, even drew me a map. He spoke of the houses where his family had lived—he remembered their phone numbers still. He spoke of school and school days, the friends he'd had, and his special fondness for mathematics and science. He talked with enthusiasm of his days in the navy—he was seventeen, had just graduated from high school when he was drafted in 1943. With his good engineering mind he was a "natural" for radio and electronics, and after a crash course in Texas found himself assistant radio operator on a submarine. He remembered the names of various submarines on which he had served, their missions, where they were stationed, the names of his shipmates. He remembered Morse code, and was still fluent in Morse tapping and touch-typing.

A full and interesting early life, remembered vividly, in detail, with affection. But there, for some reason, his reminiscences stopped. He recalled, and almost relived, his war days and service, the end of the war, and his thoughts for the future. He had come to love the navy, thought he might stay in it. But with the **GI Bill**, and support, he felt he might do best to go to college. His older brother was in accountancy school and engaged to a girl, a "real beauty," from Oregon.

With recalling, reliving, Jimmie was full of animation; he did not seem to be speaking of the past but of the present, and I was very struck by the change of tense in his recollections as he passed from his school days to his days in the navy. He had been using the past tense, but now used the present—and (it seemed to me) not just the formal or fictitious present tense of recall, but the actual present tense of immediate experience.

A sudden, improbable suspicion seized me.

"What year is this, Mr G.?" I asked, concealing my perplexity under a casual manner.

"Forty-five, man. What do you mean?" He went on, "We've won the war, **FDR**'s dead, **Truman**'s at the helm. There are great times ahead."

"And you, Jimmie, how old would you be?"

Oddly, uncertainly, he hesitated a moment, as if engaged in calculation.

"Why, I guess I'm 19, Doc. I'll be 20 next birthday."

Looking at the grey-haired man before me, I had an impulse for which I have never forgiven myself—it was, or would have been, the height of cruelty had there been any possibility of Jimmie's remembering it.

"Here," I said, and thrust a mirror toward him. "Look in the mirror and tell me what you see. Is that a 19-year-old looking out from the mirror?"

He suddenly turned ashen and gripped the sides of the chair. "Jesus Christ," he whispered. "Christ, what's going on? What's happened to me? Is this a nightmare? Am I crazy? Is this a joke?"—and he became frantic, panicked.

"It's okay, Jimmie," I said soothingly. "It's just a mistake. Nothing to worry about. Hey!" I took him to the window. "Isn't this a lovely spring day. See the kids there playing baseball?" He regained his colour and started to smile, and I stole away, taking the hateful mirror with me.

Two minutes later I re-entered the room. Jimmie was still standing by the window, gazing with pleasure at the kids playing baseball below. He wheeled around as I opened the door, and his face assumed a cheery expression.

"Hiya, Doc!" he said. "Nice morning! You want to talk to me—do I take this chair here?" There was no sign of recognition on his frank, open face.

"Haven't we met before, Mr G.?" I asked casually.

"No, I can't say we have. Quite a beard you got there. I wouldn't forget *you*, Doc!"

"Why do you call me "Doc"?"

"Well, you are a doc, ain't you?"

"Yes, but if you haven't met me, how do you know what I am?"

"You *talk* like a doc. I can *see* you're a doc."

"Well, you're right, I am. I'm the neurologist here."

"Neurologist? Hey, there's something wrong with my nerves? And 'here'—where's 'here'? What is this place anyhow?"

"I was just going to ask you—where do you think you are?"

"I see these beds, and these patients everywhere. Looks like a sort of hospital to me. But hell, what would I be doing in a hospital— and with all these old people, years older than me. I feel good, I'm strong as a bull. Maybe I *work* here. . . . Do I work? What's my job? . . . No, you're shaking your head, I see in your eyes I don't work here. If I don't work here, I've been *put* here. Am I a patient, am I sick and don't know it, Doc? It's crazy, it's scary. . . . Is it some sort of joke?"

"You don't know what the matter is? You really don't know? You remember telling me about your childhood, growing up in Connecticut, working as a radio operator on submarines? And how your brother is engaged to a girl from Oregon?"

"Hey, you're right. But I didn't tell you that, I never met you before in my life. You must have read all about me in my chart."

"Okay," I said. "I'll tell you a story. A man went to his doctor complaining of memory lapses. The doctor asked him some routine questions, and then said, "These lapses. What about them?" "What lapses?" the patient replied."

"So that's my problem," Jimmie laughed. "I kinda thought it was. I do find myself forgetting things, once in a while—things that have just happened. The past is clear, though."

"Will you allow me to examine you, to run over some tests?"

"Sure," he said genially. "Whatever you want."

On intelligence testing he showed excellent ability. He was quick-witted, observant, and logical, and had no difficulty solving complex problems and puzzles—no difficulty, that is, if they could be done quickly. If much time was required, he forgot what he was doing. He was quick and good at tic-tac-toe and checkers, and cunning and aggressive—he easily beat me. But he got lost at chess—the moves were too slow.

Homing in on his memory, I found an extreme and extraordinary loss of recent memory—so that whatever was said or shown to him was apt to be forgotten in a few seconds' time. Thus I laid out my watch, my tie, and my glasses on the desk, covered them, and asked him to remember these. Then, after a minute's chat, I asked him what I had put under the cover. He remembered none of them— or indeed that I had even asked him to remember. I repeated the test, this time getting him to write down the names of the three objects; again he forgot, and when I showed him the paper with his writing on it he was astounded, and said he had no recollection of writing anything down, though he acknowledged that it was his own writing, and then got a faint "echo" of the fact that he had written them down.

He sometimes retained faint memories, some dim echo or sense of familiarity. Thus five minutes after I had played tic-tac-toe with him, he recollected that "some doctor" had played this with him "a while back"—whether the "while back" was minutes or months ago he had no idea. He then paused and said, "It could have been you?" When I said it *was* me, he seemed amused. This faint amusement and indifference were very characteristic, as were the involved cogitations to which he was driven by being so disoriented and lost in time. When I asked Jimmie the time of the year, he would immediately look around for some clue—I was careful to remove the calendar from my desk—and would work out the time of year, roughly, by looking through the window.

It was not, apparently, that he failed to register in memory, but that the memory traces were fugitive in the extreme, and were apt to be effaced within a minute, often less, especially if there were distracting or competing stimuli, while his intellectual and perceptual powers were preserved, and highly superior.

Jimmie's scientific knowledge was that of a bright high school graduate with a penchant for mathematics and science. He was superb at arithmetical (and also algebraic) calculations, but only if they could be done with lightning speed. If there were many steps, too much time, involved, he would forget where he was, and even the question. He knew the elements, compared them, and drew the periodic table—but omitted the transuranic elements.

"Is that complete?" I asked when he'd finished.

"It's complete and up-to-date, sir, as far as I know."

"You wouldn't know any elements beyond uranium?"

"You kidding? There's 92 elements, and uranium's the last."

I paused and flipped through a *National Geographic* on the table. "Tell me the planets," I said, "and something about them." Unhesitatingly, confidently, he gave me the planets—their names, their discovery, their distance from the sun, their estimated mass, character, and gravity.

"What is this?" I asked, showing him a photo in the magazine I was holding.

"It's the moon," he replied.

"No, it's not," I answered. "It's a picture of the earth taken from the moon."

"Doc, you're kidding! Someone would've had to get a camera up there!"

"Naturally."

"Hell! You're joking—how the hell would you do that?"

Unless he was a consummate actor, a fraud simulating an astonishment he did not feel, this was an utterly convincing demonstration that he was still in the past. His words, his feelings, his innocent wonder, his struggle to make sense of what he saw, were precisely those of an intelligent young man in the forties faced with the future, with what had not yet happened, and what was scarcely imaginable. "This more than anything else," I wrote in my notes, "persuades me that his cut-off around 1945 is genuine. . . . What I showed him, and told him, produced the authentic amazement which it would have done in an intelligent young man of the pre-Sputnik era."

I found another photo in the magazine and pushed it over to him.

"That's an aircraft carrier," he said. "Real ultramodern design. I never saw one quite like that."

"What's it called?" I asked.

He glanced down, looked baffled, and said, "The *Nimitz*!"

"Something the matter?"

"The hell there is!" he replied hotly. "I know 'em all by name, and I *don't know a Nimitz*. . . . Of course there's an Admiral Nimitz, but I never heard they named a carrier after him."

Angrily he threw the magazine down.

He was becoming fatigued, and somewhat irritable and anxious, under the continuing pressure of anomaly and contradiction, and their fearful implications, to which he could not be entirely oblivious. I had already, unthinkingly, pushed him into panic, and felt it was time to end our session. We wandered over to the window again, and looked down at the sunlit baseball diamond; as he looked his face relaxed, he forgot the *Nimitz*, the satellite photo, the other horrors and hints, and became absorbed in the game below. Then, as a savoury smell drifted up from the dining room, he smacked his lips, said "Lunch!," smiled, and took his leave.

And I myself was wrung with emotion—it was heartbreaking, it was absurd, it was deeply perplexing, to think of his life lost in limbo, dissolving.

"He is, as it were," I wrote in my notes, "isolated in a single moment of being, with a moat or lacuna of forgetting all round him. . . . He is man without a past (or future), stuck in a constantly changing, meaningless moment." And then, more prosaically, "The remainder of the neurological examination is entirely normal. Impression: probably Korsakov's syndrome, due to alcoholic degeneration of the mammillary bodies." My note was a strange mixture of facts and observations, carefully noted and itemized, with irrepressible meditations on what such problems might "mean," in regard to who and what and where this poor man was—whether, indeed, one could speak of an "existence," given so absolute a privation of memory or continuity.

I kept wondering, in this and later notes—unscientifically—about "a lost soul," and how one might establish some continuity, some roots, for he was a man without roots, or rooted only in the remote past.

"Only connect"—but how could he connect, and how could we help him to connect? What was life without connection? "I may venture to affirm,"

Hume wrote, "that we are nothing but a bundle or collection of different sensations, which succeed each other with an inconceivable rapidity, and are in a perpetual flux and movement." In some sense, he had been reduced to a "Humean" being—I could not help thinking how fascinated Hume would have been at seeing in Jimmie his own philosophical "chimaera" incarnate, a gruesome reduction of a man to mere disconnected, incoherent flux and change.

Perhaps I could find advice or help in the medical literature—a literature which, for some reason, was largely Russian, from Korsakov's original thesis about such cases of memory loss, which are still called "Korsakov's syndrome," to Luria's *Neuropsychology of Memory* (which appeared in translation only a year after I first saw Jimmie). Korsakov wrote in 1887: "Memory of recent events is disturbed almost exclusively; recent impressions apparently disappear soonest, whereas impressions of long ago are recalled properly, so that the patient's ingenuity, his sharpness of wit, and his resourcefulness remain largely unaffected."

To Korsakov's brilliant but spare observations, almost a century of further research has been added—the richest and deepest, by far, being Luria's. And in Luria's account science became poetry, and the pathos of radical lostness was evoked. "Gross disturbances of the organization of impressions of events and their sequence in time can always be observed in such patients," he wrote. "In consequence, they lose their integral experience of time and begin to live in a world of isolated impressions." Further, as Luria noted, the eradication of impressions (and their disorder) might spread backward in time—"in the most serious cases—even to relatively distant events."

Most of Luria's patients, as described in this book, had massive and serious cerebral tumours, which had the same effects as Korsakov's syndrome, but later spread and were often fatal. Luria included no cases of "simple" Korsakov's syndrome, based on the self-limiting destruction that Korsakov described—neuron destruction, produced by alcohol, in the tiny but crucial mammillary bodies, the rest of the brain being preserved. And so there was no long-term follow-up of Luria's cases.

I had at first been deeply puzzled, and dubious, even suspicious, about the apparently sharp cut-off in 1945, a point, a date, which was also symbolically so sharp. I wrote in a subsequent note:

> There is a great blank. We do not know what happened then—or subsequently. . . . We must fill in these "missing" years—from his brother, or the navy, or hospitals he has been to. . . . Could it be that he sustained some massive trauma at this time, some massive cerebral or emotional trauma in combat, in the war, and that this may have affected him ever since? . . . was the war his "high point," the last time he was really alive, and existence since one long anti-climax?

We did various tests on him (EEG, brain scans), and found no evidence of massive brain damage, although atrophy of the tiny mammillary bodies would not show up on such tests. We received reports from the navy indicating that he had remained in the navy until 1965, and that he was perfectly competent at that time.

Then we turned up a short nasty report from Bellevue Hospital, dated 1971, saying that he was "totally disoriented . . . with an advanced organic brain-syndrome, due to alcohol" (cirrhosis had also developed by this time). From Bellevue he was sent to a wretched dump in the Village, a so-called "nursing home" whence he was rescued—lousy, starving—by our Home in 1975.

We located his brother, whom Jimmie always spoke of as being in accountancy school and engaged to a girl from Oregon. In fact he had married the girl from Oregon, had become a father and grandfather, and been a practising accountant for 30 years.

Where we had hoped for an abundance of information and feeling from his brother, we received a courteous but somewhat meagre letter. It was obvious from reading this—especially reading between the lines—that the brothers had scarcely seen each other since 1943, and gone separate ways, partly through the vicissitudes of location and profession, and partly through deep (though not estranging) differences of temperament. Jimmie, it seemed, had never "settled down," was "happy-go-lucky," and "always a drinker." The navy, his brother felt, provided a structure, a life, and the real problems started when he left it, in 1965. Without his habitual structure and anchor Jimmie had ceased to work, "gone to pieces," and started to drink heavily. There had been some memory impairment, of the Korsakov type, in the middle and especially the late sixties, but not so severe that Jimmie couldn't "cope" in his nonchalant fashion. But his drinking grew heavier in 1970.

Around Christmas of that year, his brother understood, he had suddenly "blown his top" and become deliriously excited and confused, and it was at this point he had been taken into Bellevue. During the next month, the excitement and delirium died down, but he was left with deep and bizarre memory lapses, or "deficits," to use the medical jargon. His brother had visited him at this time—they had not met for 20 years—and, to his horror, Jimmie not only failed to recognize him, but said, "Stop joking! You're old enough to be my father. My brother's a young man, just going through accountancy school."

When I received this information, I was more perplexed still: why did Jimmie not remember his later years in the navy, why did he not recall and organize his memories until 1970? I had not heard then that such patients might have a retrograde amnesia [. . .]. "I wonder, increasingly," I wrote at this time, "whether there is not an element of hysterical or fugal amnesia—whether he is not in flight from something too awful to recall," and I suggested he be seen by our psychiatrist. Her report was searching and detailed—the examination had included a sodium amytal test, calculated to "release" any memories which might be repressed. She also attempted to hypnotize Jimmie, in the hope of eliciting memories repressed by hysteria—this tends to work well in cases of hysterical amnesia. But it failed because Jimmie could not be hypnotized, not because of any "resistance," but because of his extreme amnesia, which caused him to lose track of what the hypnotist was saying. [. . .]

"I have no feeling or evidence," the psychiatrist wrote, "of any hysterical or "put-on" deficit. He lacks both the means and the motive to make a facade. His memory deficits are organic and permanent and incorrigible, though it is puzzling they should go back so long." Since, she felt, he was "unconcerned . . . manifested no special anxiety . . . constituted no management problem," there was nothing she could offer, or any therapeutic "entrance" or "lever" she could see.

At this point, persuaded that this was, indeed, "pure" Korsakov's, uncomplicated by other factors, emotional or organic, I wrote to Luria and asked his opinion. He spoke in his reply of his patient Bel (see Luria 250–2), whose amnesia had retroactively eradicated ten years. He said he saw no reason why such a retrograde amnesia should not thrust backward decades, or almost a whole lifetime. "I can only wait for the final amnesia," Buñuel writes, "the one that can erase an entire life." But Jimmie's amnesia, for whatever reason, had erased memory and time back to 1945—roughly—and then stopped. Occasionally, he would recall something much later, but the recall was fragmentary and dislocated in time. Once, seeing the word "satellite" in a newspaper headline, he said offhandedly that he'd been involved in a project of satellite tracking while on the ship *Chesapeake Bay*, a memory fragment coming from the early or mid-sixties. But, for all practical purposes, his cut-off point was during the mid- (or late) forties, and anything subsequently retrieved was fragmentary, unconnected. This was the case in 1975, and it is still the case now, nine years later.

What could we do? What should we do? "There are no prescriptions," Luria wrote, "in a case like this. Do whatever your ingenuity and your heart suggest. There is little or no hope of any recovery in his memory. But a man does not consist of memory alone. He has feeling, will, sensibilities, moral being—matters of which neuropsychology cannot speak. And it is here, beyond the realm of an impersonal psychology, that you may find ways to touch him, and change him. And the circumstances of your work especially allow this, for you work in a Home, which is like a little world, quite different from the clinics and institutions where I work. Neuropsychologically, there is little or nothing you can do; but in the realm of the Individual, there may be much you can do."

Luria mentioned his patient Kur as manifesting a rare self-awareness, in which hopelessness was mixed with an odd equanimity. "I have no memory of the present," Kur would say. "I do not know what I have just done or from where I have just come. . . . I can recall my past very well, but I have no memory of my present." When asked whether he had ever seen the person testing him, he said, "I cannot say yes or no, I can neither affirm nor deny that I have seen you." This was sometimes the case with Jimmie; and, like Kur, who stayed many months in the same hospital, Jimmie began to form a sense of familiarity; he slowly learned his way around the home—the whereabouts of the dining room, his own room, the elevators, the stairs, and in some sense recognized some of the staff, although he confused them, and perhaps had to do so, with people from the past. He soon became fond of the nursing sister in the Home; he recognized her voice, her footfalls, immediately, but would always say that she had been a fellow pupil at his high school, and was greatly surprised when I addressed her as "Sister."

"Gee!" he exclaimed, "the damnedest things happen. I'd never have guessed you'd become a religious, Sister!"

Since he's been at our Home—that is, since early 1975—Jimmie has never been able to identify anyone in it consistently. The only person he truly recognizes is his brother, whenever he visits from Oregon. These meetings are deeply emotional and moving to observe—the only truly emotional meetings Jimmie has. He loves his brother, he recognizes him, but he cannot understand why he looks so old: "Guess some people age fast," he says. Actually his brother looks much younger than his age, and has the sort of face and build that change little with the years. These are true meetings, Jimmie's only connection of past and present, yet they do nothing to provide any sense of history or continuity. If anything they emphasize—at least to his brother, and to others who see them together—that Jimmie still lives, is fossilized, in the past.

All of us, at first, had high hopes of helping Jimmie—he was so personable, so likable, so quick and intelligent, it was difficult to believe that he might be beyond help. But none of us had ever encountered, even imagined, such a power of amnesia, the possibility of a pit into which everything, every experience, every event, would fathomlessly drop, a bottomless memory-hole that would engulf the whole world.

I suggested, when I first saw him, that he should keep a diary, and be encouraged to keep notes every day of his experiences, his feelings, thoughts, memories, reflections. These attempts were foiled, at first, by his continually losing the diary: it had to be attached to him—somehow. But this too failed to work: he dutifully kept a brief daily notebook but could not recognize his earlier entries in it. He does recognize his own writing, and style, and is always astounded to find that he wrote something the day before.

Astounded—and indifferent—for he was a man who, in effect, had no "day before." His entries remained unconnected and unconnecting and had no power to provide any sense of time or continuity. Moreover, they were trivial—"Eggs for breakfast," "Watched ballgame on TV"—and never touched the depths. But were there depths in this unmemoried man, depths of an abiding feeling and thinking, or had he been reduced to a sort of Humean drivel, a mere succession of unrelated impressions and events?

Jimmie both was and wasn't aware of this deep, tragic loss in himself, loss *of* himself. (If a man has lost a leg or an eye, he knows he has lost a leg or an eye; but if he has lost a self—himself—he cannot know it, because he is longer there to know it.) Therefore I could not question him intellectually about such matters.

He had originally professed bewilderment at finding himself amid patients, when, as he said, he himself didn't feel ill. But what, we wondered, did he feel? He was strongly built and fit, he had a sort of animal strength and energy, but also a strange inertia, passivity, and (as everyone remarked) "unconcern"; he gave all of us an overwhelming sense of

"something missing," although this, if he realized it, was itself accepted with an odd "unconcern." One day I asked him not about his memory, or past, but about the simplest and most elemental feelings of all:

"How do you feel?"

"How do I feel," he repeated, and scratched his head. "I cannot say I feel ill. But I cannot say I feel well. I cannot say I feel anything at all."

"Are you miserable?" I continued.

"Can't say I am."

"Do you enjoy life?"

"I can't say I do . . ."

I hesitated, fearing that I was going too far, that I might be stripping a man down to some hidden, unacknowledgeable, unbearable despair.

"You don't enjoy life," I repeated, hesitating somewhat. "How then *do* you feel about life?"

"I can't say that I feel anything at all."

"You feel alive though?"

"Feel alive? Not really. I haven't felt alive for a very long time."

His face wore a look of infinite sadness and resignation.

Later, having noted his aptitude for, and pleasure in, quick games and puzzles, and their power to "hold" him, at least while they lasted, and to allow, for a while, a sense of companionship and competition—he had not complained of loneliness, but he looked so alone; he never expressed sadness, but he looked so sad—I suggested he be brought into our recreation programs at the Home. This worked better—better than the diary. He would become keenly and briefly involved in games, but soon they ceased to offer any challenge: he solved all the puzzles, and could solve them easily; and he was far better and sharper than anyone else at games. And as he found this out, he grew fretful and restless again, and wandered the corridors, uneasy and bored and with a sense of indignity—games and puzzles were for children, a diversion. Clearly, passionately, he wanted something to do: he wanted to do, to be, to feel—and could not; he wanted sense, he wanted purpose—in **Freud**'s words, "Work and Love."

Could he do "ordinary" work? He had "gone to pieces," his brother said, when he ceased to work in 1965.

He had two striking skills—Morse code and touch-typing. We could not use Morse, unless we invented a use; but good typing we could use, if he could recover his old skills—and this would be real work, not just a game. Jimmie soon did recover his old skill and came to type very quickly—he could not do it slowly—and found in this some of the challenge and satisfaction of a job. But still this was superficial tapping and typing; it was trivial, it did not reach to the depths. And what he typed, he typed mechanically—he could not hold the thought—the short sentences following one another in a meaningless order.

One tended to speak of him, instinctively, as a spiritual casualty—a "lost soul": was it possible that he had really been "de-souled" by a disease? "Do you think he *has* a soul?" I once asked the Sisters. They were outraged by my question, but could see why I asked it. "Watch Jimmie in chapel," they said, "and judge for yourself."

I did, and I was moved, profoundly moved and impressed, because I saw here an intensity and steadiness of attention and concentration that I had never seen before in him or conceived him capable of. I watched him kneel and take the Sacrament on his tongue, and could not doubt the fullness and totality of Communion, the perfect alignment of his spirit with the spirit of the Mass. Fully, intensely, quietly, in the quietude of absolute concentration and attention, he entered and partook of the Holy Communion. He was wholly held, absorbed, by a feeling. There was no forgetting, no Korsakov's then, nor did it seem possible or imaginable that there should be; for he was no longer at the mercy of a faulty and fallible mechanism—that of meaningless sequences and memory traces—but was absorbed in an act, an act of his whole being, which carried feeling and meaning in an organic continuity and unity, a continuity and unity so seamless it could not permit any break.

Clearly Jimmie found himself, found continuity and reality, in the absoluteness of spiritual attention and act. The Sisters were right—he did find his soul here. And so was Luria, whose words now came back to me: "A man does not consist of memory alone. He

has feeling, will, sensibility, moral being. . . . It is here . . . you may touch him, and see a profound change." Memory, mental activity, mind alone, could not hold him; but moral attention and action could hold him completely.

But perhaps "moral" was too narrow a word—for the aesthetic and dramatic were equally involved. Seeing Jim in the chapel opened my eyes to other realms where the soul is called on, and held, and stilled, in attention and communion. The same depth of absorption and attention was to be seen in relation to music and art: he had no difficulty, I noticed, "following" music or simple dramas, for every moment in music and art refers to, contains, other moments. He liked gardening, and had taken over some of the work in our garden. At first he greeted the garden each day as new, but for some reason this had become more familiar to him than the inside of the Home. He almost never got lost or disoriented in the garden now; he patterned it, I think, on loved and remembered gardens from his youth in Connecticut.

Jimmie, who was so lost in extensional "spatial" time, was perfectly organized in **Bergson**ian "intentional" time; what was fugitive, unsustainable, as formal structure, was perfectly stable, perfectly held, as art or will. Moreover, there was something that endured and survived. If Jimmie was briefly "held" by a task or puzzle or game or calculation, held in the purely mental challenge of these, he would fall apart as soon as they were done, into the abyss of his nothingness, his amnesia. But if he was held in emotional and spiritual attention—in the contemplation of nature or art, in listening to music, in taking part in the Mass in chapel—the attention, its "mood," its quietude, would persist for a while, and there would be in him a pensiveness and peace we rarely, if ever, saw during the rest of his life at the Home.

I have known Jimmie now for nine years—and neuropsychologically, he has not changed in the least. He still has the severest, most devastating Korsakov's, cannot remember isolated items for more than a few seconds, and has a dense amnesia going back to 1945. But humanly, spiritually, he is at times a different man altogether—no longer fluttering, restless, bored, and lost, but deeply attentive to the beauty and soul of the world, rich in all the **Kierkegaard**ian categories—[the] aesthetic, the moral, the religious, the dramatic. I had wondered, when I first met him, if he was not condemned to a sort of "Humean" froth, a meaningless fluttering on the surface of life, and whether there was any way of transcending the incoherence of his Humean disease. Empirical science told me there was not—but empirical science, empiricism, takes no account of the soul, no account of what constitutes and determines personal being. Perhaps there is a philosophical as well as a clinical lesson here: that in Korsakov's, or dementia, or other such catastrophes, however great the organic damage and Humean dissolution, there remains the undiminished possibility of reintegration by art, by communion, by touching the human spirit: and this can be preserved in what seems at first a hopeless state of neurological devastation. [. . .]

## Work Cited

Luria, A.R. *The Neuropsychology of Memory.* Washington: V.H. Winston, 1976.

## Study Questions

1. Apply Locke's criteria for being the same material substance, the same human, and the same person to the example of Sacks's patient Jimmie G.
2. Why does Sacks (at least initially) remark, "I could not help thinking how fascinated Hume would have been at seeing in Jimmie his own philosophical 'chimaera' incarnate"?
3. Explain why, as he works further with Jimmie G., Sacks becomes skeptical that any empirically based account of personal identity manages adequately to capture what it is to be a person.
4. What theory of personal identity does Sacks himself ultimately formulate?

# Derek Parfit

Derek Parfit is interested in problems of personal identity, rationality, and ethics. He is a senior research fellow at All Souls College, Oxford, and visiting professor of philosophy at New York University, Harvard University, and Rutgers University. In this well-known essay, Parfit recommends that we give up talk about personal identity.—TR

## Personal Identity

### 1. Fission Thought Experiment

We can start by considering the much-discussed case (implicit in John **Locke**'s *An Essay Concerning Human Understanding*, Ch. 27 s. [20]) of the man who, like an amoeba, divides.

Wiggins has recently dramatized this case (50). He first referred to the operation imagined by Shoemaker (22). We suppose that my brain is transplanted into someone else's (brainless) body, and that the resulting person has my character and apparent memories of my life. Most of us would agree, after thought, that the resulting person is me. I shall here assume such agreement.

Wiggins then imagined his own operation. My brain is divided, and each half is housed in a new body. Both resulting people have my character and apparent memories of my life.

What happens to me? There seem only three possibilities: (1) I do not survive; (2) I survive as one of the two people; (3) I survive as both.

The trouble with (1) is this. We agreed that I could survive if my brain were successfully transplanted. And people have in fact survived with half their brains destroyed. It seems to follow that I could survive if half my brain were successfully transplanted and the other half were destroyed. But if this is so, how could I *not* survive if the other half were also successfully transplanted? How could a double success be a failure?

We can move to the second description. Perhaps one success is the maximum score. Perhaps I shall be one of the resulting people.

The trouble here is that in Wiggins' case each half of my brain is exactly similar, and so, to start with, is each resulting person. So how can I survive as only one of the two people? What can make me one of them rather than the other?

It seems clear that both of these descriptions—that I do not survive, and that I survive as one of the people—are highly implausible. Those who have accepted them must have assumed that they were the only possible descriptions.

What about our third description: that I survive as both people?

It might be said, "If 'survive' implies identity, this description makes no sense—you cannot be two people. If it does not, the description is irrelevant to a problem about identity."

I shall later deny the second of these remarks. But there are ways of denying the first. We might say, "What we have called 'the two resulting people' are not two people. They are one person. I do survive Wiggins' operation. Its effect is to give me two bodies and a divided mind."

It would shorten my argument if this were absurd. But I do not think it is. It is worth showing why.

We can, I suggest, imagine a divided mind. We can imagine a man having two simultaneous experiences, in having each of which he is unaware of having the other.

We may not even need to imagine this. Certain actual cases, to which Wiggins referred, seem to be best described in these terms. These involve the cutting of the bridge between the hemispheres of the brain. The aim was to cure epilepsy. But the result appears to be, in the surgeon's words, the creation of "two separate spheres of consciousness" (Sperry 299), each of which controls one half of the patient's body. What is experienced in each is, presumably, experienced by the patient.

There are certain complications in these actual cases. So let us imagine a simpler case.

Suppose that the bridge between my hemispheres is brought under my voluntary control. This would enable me to disconnect my hemispheres as easily as if I were blinking. By doing this I would divide my mind. And we can suppose that when my mind is divided I can, in each half, bring about reunion.

This ability would have obvious uses. To give an example: I am near the end of a math exam, and see two ways of tackling the last problem. I decide to divide my mind, to work, with each half, at one of two calculations, and then to reunite my mind and write a fair copy of the best result.

What shall I experience?

When I disconnect my hemispheres, my consciousness divides into two streams. But this division is not something that I experience. Each of my two streams of consciousness seems to have been straightforwardly continuous with my one stream of consciousness up to the moment of division. The only changes in each stream are the disappearance of half my visual field and the loss of sensation in, and control over, half my body.

Consider my experiences in what we can call my "right-handed" stream. I remember that I assigned my right hand to the longer calculation. This I now begin. In working at this calculation I can see, from the movements of my left hand, that I am also working at the other. But I am not aware of working at the other. So I might, in my right-handed stream, wonder how, in my left-handed stream, I am getting on.

My work is now over. I am about to reunite my mind. What should I, in each stream, expect? Simply that I shall suddenly seem to remember just having thought out two calculations, in thinking out each of which I was not aware of thinking out the other. This, I submit, we can imagine. And if my mind was divided, these memories are correct.

In describing this episode, I assumed that there were two series of thoughts, and that they were both mine. If my two hands visibly wrote out two calculations, and if I claimed to remember two corresponding series of thoughts, this is surely what we should want to say.

If it is, then a person's mental history need not be like a canal, with only one channel. It could be like a river, with islands, and with separate streams.

To apply this to Wiggins' operation: we mentioned the view that it gives me two bodies and a divided mind. We cannot now call this absurd. But it is, I think, unsatisfactory.

There were two features of the case of the exam that made us want to say that only one person was involved. The mind was soon reunited, and there was only one body. If a mind was permanently divided and its halves developed in different ways, the point of speaking of one person would start to disappear. Wiggins' case, where there are also two bodies, seems to be over the borderline. After I have had his operation, the two "products" each have all the attributes of a person. They could live at opposite ends of the earth. (If they later met, they might even fail to recognize each other.) It would become intolerable to deny that they were different people.

Suppose we admit that they are different people. Could we still claim that I survived as both, using "survive" to imply identity?

We could. For we might suggest that two people could compose a third. We might say, "I do survive Wiggins' operation as two people. They can be different people, and yet be me, in just the way in which the **Pope's three crowns** are one crown."

This is a possible way of giving sense to the claim that I survive as two different people, using "survive" to imply identity. But it keeps the language of identity only by changing the concept of a person. And there are obvious objections to this change.[1]

The alternative, for which I shall argue, is to give up the language of identity. We can suggest that I survive as two different people without implying that I am these people.

When I first mentioned this alternative, I mentioned this objection: "If your new way of talking does not imply identity, it cannot solve our problem. For that is about identity. The problem is that all the possible answers to the question about identity are highly implausible."

We can now answer this objection.

We can start by reminding ourselves that this is an objection only if we have one or both of the [following] beliefs [. . .].

The first [is] the belief that to any question about personal identity, in any describable case, there must be a true answer. For those with this belief, Wiggins' case is doubly perplexing. If all the possible answers are implausible, it is hard to decide which of them is true, and hard even to keep the belief that one of them must be true. If we give up this belief, as I think we should, these problems disappear. We shall then regard the case as like many others in which, for quite unpuzzling reasons, there is no answer to a question about identity. (Consider "Was England the same nation after 1066?")[2]

Wiggins' case makes the first belief implausible. It also makes it trivial. For it undermines the second belief. This [is] the belief that important questions turn upon the question about identity. (It is worth pointing out that those who have only this second belief do not think that there must be an answer to this question, but rather that we must decide upon an answer.)

Against this second belief my claim is this. Certain questions do presuppose a question about personal identity. And because these questions are important, Wiggins' case does present a problem. But we cannot solve this problem by answering the question about identity. We can solve this problem only by taking these important questions and prizing them apart from the question about identity. After we have done this, the question about identity (though we might for the sake of neatness decide it) has no further interest.

Because there are several questions which presuppose identity, this claim will take some time to fill out.

We can first return to the question of survival. This is a special case, for survival does not so much presuppose the retaining of identity as seem equivalent to it. It is thus the general relation which we need to prize apart from identity. We can then consider particular relations, such as those involved in memory and intention.

"Will I survive?" seems, I said, equivalent to "Will there be some person alive who is the same person as me?"

If we treat these questions as equivalent, then the least unsatisfactory description of Wiggins' case is, I think, that I survive with two bodies and a divided mind.

Several writers have chosen to say that I am neither of the resulting people. Given our equivalence, this implies that I do not survive, and hence, presumably, that even if Wiggins' operation is not literally death, I ought, since I will not survive it, to regard it *as* death. But this seemed absurd.

It is worth repeating why. An emotion or attitude can be criticized for resting on a false belief, or for being inconsistent. A man who regarded Wiggins' operation as death must, I suggest, be open to one of these criticisms.

He might believe that his relation to each of the resulting people fails to contain some element which is contained in survival. But how can this be true? We agreed that he *would* survive if he stood in this very same relation to only *one* of the resulting people. So it cannot be the nature of this relation which makes it fail, in Wiggins' case, to be survival. It can only be its duplication.

Suppose that our man accepts this, but still regards division as death. His reaction would now seem wildly inconsistent. He would be like a man who, when told of a drug that could double his years of life, regarded the taking of this drug as death. The only difference in the case of division is that the extra years are to run concurrently. This is an interesting difference. But it cannot mean that there are *no* years to run.

I have argued this for those who think that there must, in Wiggins' case, be a true answer to the question about identity. For them, we might add, "Perhaps the original person does lose his identity. But there may be other ways to do this

than to die. One other way might be to multiply. To regard these as the same is to confuse nought with two."

For those who think that the question of identity is up for decision, it would be clearly absurd to regard Wiggins' operation as death. These people would have to think, "We could have chosen to say that I should be one of the resulting people. If we had, I should not have regarded it as death. But since we have chosen to say that I am neither person, I *do*." This is hard even to understand.

My first conclusion, then, is this. The relation of the original person to each of the resulting people contains all that interests us—all that matters—in any ordinary case of survival. This is why we need a sense in which one person can survive as two.

One of my aims in the rest of this paper will be to suggest such a sense. But we can first make some general remarks.

## 2. Psychological Continuity and Identity

Identity is a one–one relation. Wiggins' case serves to show that what matters in survival need not be one–one.

Wiggins' case is of course unlikely to occur. The relations which matter are, in fact, one–one. It is because they are that we can imply the holding of these relations by using the language of identity.

This use of language is convenient. But it can lead us astray. We may assume that what matters *is* identity and, hence, has the properties of identity.

In the case of the property of being one–one, this mistake is not serious. For what matters is in fact one–one. But in the case of another property, the mistake *is* serious. Identity is all-or-nothing. Most of the relations which matter in survival are, in fact, relations of degree. If we ignore this, we shall be led into quite ill-grounded attitudes and beliefs.

The claim that I have just made—that most of what matters are relations of degree—I have yet to support. Wiggins' case shows only that these relations need not be one–one. The merit of the case is not that it shows this in particular, but that it makes the first break between what matters and identity. The belief that identity *is* what matters is hard to overcome. This is shown in most discussions of the problem cases which actually occur: cases, say, of amnesia or of brain damage. Once Wiggins' case has made one breach in this belief, the rest should be easier to remove.

To turn to a recent debate: most of the relations which matter can be provisionally referred to under the heading "psychological continuity" (which includes causal continuity). My claim is thus that we use the language of personal identity in order to imply such continuity. This is close to the view that psychological continuity provides a criterion of identity.

Williams has attacked this view with the following argument. Identity is a one–one relation. So any criterion of identity must appeal to a relation which is logically one–one. Psychological continuity is not logically one–one. So it cannot provide a criterion.

Some writers have replied that it is enough if the relation appealed to is always in fact one–one.

I suggest a slightly different reply. Psychological continuity is a ground for speaking of identity when it is one–one.

If psychological continuity took a one–many or branching form, we should need, I have argued, to abandon the language of identity. So this possibility would not count against this view.

We can make a stronger claim. This possibility would count in its favour.

The view might be defended as follows. Judgments of personal identity have great importance. What gives them their importance is the fact that they imply psychological continuity. This is why, whenever there is such continuity, we ought, if we can, to imply it by making a judgment of identity.

If psychological continuity took a branching form, no coherent set of judgments of identity could correspond to, and thus be used to imply, the branching form of this relation. But what we ought to do, in such a case, is take the importance which would attach to a judgment of identity and attach this importance directly to each limb of the branching relation. So this case helps to show that judgments

of personal identity do derive their importance from the fact that they imply psychological continuity. It helps to show that when we can, usefully, speak of identity, this relation is our ground. [. . .]

The criterion might be sketched as follows. "X and Y are the same person if they are psychologically continuous and there is no person who is contemporary with either and psychologically continuous with the other." We should need to explain what we mean by "psychologically continuous" and say how much continuity the criterion requires. We should then, I think, have described a sufficient condition for speaking of identity.[3]

We need to say something more. If we admit that psychological continuity might not be one–one, we need to say what we ought to do if it were not one–one. Otherwise our account would be open to the objections that it is incomplete and arbitrary.

I have suggested that if psychological continuity took a branching form, we ought to speak in a new way, regarding what we describe as having the same significance as identity. This answers these objections.

We can now return to our discussion. We have three remaining aims. One is to suggest a sense of "survive" which does not imply identity. Another is to show that most of what matters in survival are relations of degree. A third is to show that none of these relations needs to be described in a way that presupposes identity.

We can take these aims in the reverse order.

## 3. Survival Relations and Identity

The most important particular relation is that involved in memory. This is because it is so easy to believe that its description must refer to identity. This belief about memory is an important cause of the view that personal identity has a special nature. But it has been well discussed by Shoemaker and by Wiggins. So we can be brief.

It may be a logical truth that we can only remember our own experiences. But we can frame a new concept for which this is not a logical truth. Let us call this "*q*-memory."

To sketch a definition I am *q*-remembering an experience if (1) I have a belief about a past experience which seems in itself like a memory belief, (2) someone did have such an experience, and (3) my belief is dependent upon this experience in the same way (whatever that is) in which a memory of an experience is dependent upon it.

According to (1) *q*-memories seem like memories. So I *q*-remember *having* experiences.

This may seem to make *q*-memory presuppose identity. One might say, "My apparent memory of *having* an experience is an apparent memory of *my* having an experience. So how could I *q*-remember my having other people's experiences?"

This objection rests on a mistake. When I seem to remember an experience, I do indeed seem to remember *having* it. But it cannot be a part of what I seem to remember about this experience that I, the person who now seems to remember it, am the person who had this experience.[4] That I am is something that I automatically assume. (My apparent memories sometimes come to me simply as the belief that *I* had a certain experience.) But it is something that I am justified in assuming only because I do not in fact have *q*-memories of other people's experiences.

Suppose that I did start to have such *q*-memories. If I did, I should cease to assume that my apparent memories must be about my own experiences. I should come to assess an apparent memory by asking two questions: (1) Does it tell me about a past experience? (2) If so, whose?

Moreover (and this is a crucial point) my apparent memories would now come to me *as q*-memories. Consider those of my apparent memories which do come to me simply as beliefs about my past: for example, "I did that." If I knew that I could *q*-remember other people's experiences, these beliefs would come to me in a more guarded form: for example, "Someone—probably I—did that." I might have to work out who it was.

I have suggested that the concept of *q*-memory is coherent. Wiggins' case provides an illustration. The resulting people, in his case, both have apparent memories of living the life of the original person.

If they agree that they are not this person, they will have to regard these as only *q*-memories. And when they are asked a question like "Have you heard this music before?" they might have to answer "I am sure that I *q*-remember hearing it. But I am not sure whether I remember hearing it. I am not sure whether it was I who heard it, or the original person."

We can next point out that on our definition every memory is also a *q*-memory. Memories are, simply, *q*-memories of one's own experiences. Since this is so, we could afford now to drop the concept of memory and use in its place the wider concept *q*-memory. If we did, we should describe the relation between an experience and what we now call a "memory" of this experience in a way which does not presuppose that they are had by the same person.

This way of describing this relation has certain merits. It vindicates the "memory criterion" of personal identity against the charge of circularity. And it might, I think, help with the problem of other minds.

But we must move on. We can next take the relation between an intention and a later action. It may be a logical truth that we can intend to perform only our own actions. But intentions can be redescribed as *q*-intentions. And one person could *q*-intend to perform another person's actions.

Wiggins' case again provides the illustration. We are supposing that neither of the resulting people is the original person. If so, we shall have to agree that the original person can, before the operation, *q*-intend to perform their actions. He might, for example, *q*-intend, as one of them, to continue his present career, and, as the other, to try something new. (I say "*q*-intend *as* one of them" because the phrase "*q*-intend *that* one of them" would not convey the directness of the relation which is involved. If I intend that someone else should do something, I cannot get him to do it simply by forming this intention. But if I am the original person, and he is one of the resulting people, I can.)

The phrase "*q*-intend *as* one of them" reminds us that we need a sense in which one person can survive as two. But we can first point out that the concepts of *q*-memory and *q*-intention give us our model for the others that we need: thus, a man who can *q*-remember could *q*-recognize, and be a *q*-witness of, what he has never seen; and a man who can *q*-intend could have *q*-ambitions, make *q*-promises, and be *q*-responsible for.

To put this claim in general terms: many different relations are included within, or are a consequence of, psychological continuity. We describe these relations in ways which presuppose the continued existence of one person. But we could describe them in new ways which do not.

This suggests a bolder claim. It might be possible to think of experiences in a wholly "impersonal" way. I shall not develop this claim here. What I shall try to describe is a way of thinking of our own identity through time which is more flexible, and less misleading, than the way in which we now think.

This way of thinking will allow for a sense in which one person can survive as two. A more important feature is that it treats survival as a matter of degree.

## 4. Degrees of Survival

We must first show the need for this second feature. I shall use two imaginary examples.

The first is the converse of Wiggins' case: fusion. Just as division serves to show that what matters in survival need not be one–one, so fusion serves to show that it can be a question of degree.

Physically, fusion is easy to describe. Two people come together. While they are unconscious, their two bodies grow into one. One person then wakes up.

The psychology of fusion is more complex. One detail we have already dealt with in the case of the exam. When my mind was reunited, I remembered just having thought out two calculations. The one person who results from a fusion can, similarly, *q*-remember living the lives of the two original people. None of their *q*-memories need be lost.

But some things must be lost. For any two people who fuse together will have different characteristics, different desires, and different intentions. How can these be combined?

We might suggest the following. Some of these will be compatible. These can coexist in the one resulting person. Some will be incompatible. These, if of equal strength, can cancel out, and if of different strengths, the stronger can be made weaker. And all these effects might be predictable.

To give examples—first, of compatibility: I like **Palladio** and intend to visit Venice. I am about to fuse with a person who likes **Giotto** and intends to visit Padua. I can know that the one person we shall become will have both tastes and both intentions. Second, of incompatibility: I hate red hair, and always vote Labour. The other person loves red hair, and always votes Conservative. I can know that the one person we shall become will be indifferent to red hair, and a floating voter.

If we were about to undergo a fusion of this kind, would we regard it as death?

Some of us might. This is less absurd than regarding division as death. For after my division the two resulting people will be in every way like me, while after my fusion the one resulting person will not be wholly similar. This makes it easier to say, when faced with fusion, "I shall not survive," thus continuing to regard survival as a matter of all-or-nothing.

This reaction is less absurd. But here are two analogies which tell against it.

First, fusion would involve the changing of some of our characteristics and some of our desires. But only the very self-satisfied would think of this as death. Many people welcome treatments with these effects.

Second, someone who is about to fuse can have, beforehand, just as much "intentional control" over the actions of the resulting individual as someone who is about to marry can have, beforehand, over the actions of the resulting couple. And the choice of a partner for fusion can be just as well considered as the choice of a marriage partner. The two original people can make sure (perhaps by "trial fusion") that they do have compatible characters, desires, and intentions.

I have suggested that fusion, while not clearly survival, is not clearly failure to survive, and hence that what matters in survival can have degrees.

To reinforce this claim we can now turn to a second example. This is provided by certain imaginary beings. These beings are just like ourselves except that they reproduce by a process of natural division.

We can illustrate the histories of these imagined beings with the aid of a diagram [see below]. The lines on the diagram represent the spatiotemporal paths which would be traced out by the bodies of these beings. We can call each single line (like the double line) a "branch"; and we can call the whole structure a "tree." And let us suppose that each "branch" corresponds to what is thought of as the life of one individual. These individuals are referred to as "A," "B + 1," and so forth.

Now, each single division is an instance of Wiggins' case. So A's relation to both B + 1 and B + 2 is just as good as survival. But what of A's relation to B + 30?

I said earlier that what matters in survival could be provisionally referred to as "psychological continuity." I must now distinguish this relation from another, which I shall call "psychological connectedness."

Let us say that the relation between a $q$-memory and the experience $q$-remembered is a "direct" relation. Another "direct" relation is that which holds between a $q$-intention and the $q$-intended action. A third is that which holds between different expressions of some lasting $q$-characteristic.

"Psychological connectedness," as I define it, requires the holding of these direct psychological relations. "Connectedness" is not transitive, since these relations are not transitive. Thus, if $X$ $q$-remembers most of $Y$'s life, and $Y$ $q$-remembers most of $Z$'s life, it does not follow that $X$ q-remembers most of $Z$'s life. And if $X$ carries out the $q$-intentions of $Y$, and $Y$ carries out the $q$-intentions of $Z$, it does not follow that $X$ carries out the $q$-intentions of $Z$.

"Psychological continuity," in contrast, only requires overlapping chains of direct psychological relations. So "continuity" is transitive.

To return to our diagram. $A$ is psychologically continuous with $B + 30$. There are between the two continuous chains of overlapping relations. Thus, $A$ has $q$-intentional control over $B + 2$, $B + 2$ has $q$-intentional control over $B + 6$, and so on up to $B + 30$. Or $B + 30$ can $q$-remember the life of $B + 14$, $B + 14$ can $q$-remember the life of $B + 6$, and so on back to A.[5]

$A$, however, need not be psychologically connected to $B + 30$. Connectedness requires direct relations. And if these beings are like us, $A$ cannot stand in such relations to every individual in his indefinitely long "tree." Q-memories will weaken with the passage of time, and then fade away. Q-ambitions, once fulfilled, will be replaced by others. Q-characteristics will gradually change. In general, $A$ stands in fewer and fewer direct psychological relations to an individual in his "tree" the more remote that individual is. And if the individual is (like $B + 30$) sufficiently remote, there may be between the two no direct psychological relations.

Now that we have distinguished the general relations of psychological continuity and psychological connectedness, I suggest that connectedness is a more important element in survival. As a claim about our own survival, this would need more arguments than I have space to give. But it seems clearly true for my imagined beings. $A$ is as close psychologically to $B + 1$ as I today am to myself

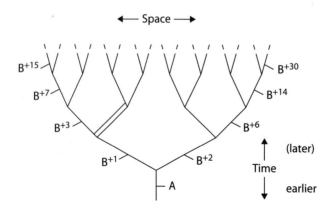

tomorrow. *A* is as distant from *B* + 30 as I am from my great-great-grandson.

Even if connectedness is not more important than continuity, the fact that one of these is a relation of degree is enough to show that what matters in survival can have degrees. And in any case the two relations are quite different. So our imagined beings would need a way of thinking in which this difference is recognized.

## 5. Survival without Identity

What I propose is this.

First, *A* can think of any individual, anywhere in his "tree," as "a descendant self." This phrase implies psychological continuity. Similarly, any later individual can think of any earlier individual on the single path which connects him to *A* as "an ancestral self."

Since psychological continuity is transitive, "being an ancestral self of" and "being a descendant self of" are also transitive.

To imply psychological connectedness I suggest the phrases "one of my future selves" and "one of my past selves."

These are the phrases with which we can describe Wiggins' case. For having past and future selves is, what we needed, a way of continuing to exist which does not imply identity through time. The original person does, in this sense, survive Wiggins' operation: the two resulting people are his later selves. And they can each refer to him as "my past self." (They can share a past self without being the same self as each other.)

Since psychological connectedness is not transitive, and is a matter of degree, the relations "being a past self of" and "being a future self of" should themselves be treated as relations of degree. We allow for this series of descriptions: "my most recent self," "one of my earlier selves," "one of my distant selves," "hardly one of *my* past selves (I can only *q*-remember a few of his experiences)," and, finally, "not in any way one of *my* past selves—just an ancestral self." [. . .]

## Notes

1. Suppose the resulting people fight a duel. Are there three people fighting, one on each side, and one on both? And suppose one of the bullets kills. Are there two acts, one murder and one suicide? How many people are left alive? One? Two? (We could hardly say, "One and a half.")

2. 1066 is the date of the Norman invasion of England: after English king Harold's defeat and death in the Battle of Hastings, William of Normandy claimed the nation's crown.—LG

3. But not a necessary condition, for in the absence of psychological continuity bodily identity might be sufficient.

4. This is what so many writers have overlooked. Cf. **Thomas Reid**: "My memory testifies not only that this was done, but that it was done by me who now remember it" (203).

5. The chain of continuity must run in one direction of time. *B* + 2 is not, in the sense I intend, psychologically continuous with *B* + 1.

## Works Cited

Reid, T. "Of Identity." *Essays on the Intellectual Powers of Man*. Ed. A.D. Woozley. London: Macmillan, 1941. 200–6.

Shoemaker, S. *Self-Knowledge and Self-Identity*. Ithaca: Cornell University Press, 1963.

Sperry, R.W. "Brain Bisection and Mechanisms of Consciousness." *Brain and Conscious Experience*. Ed. J.C. Eccles. New York: Springer-Verlag, 1966. 298–313.

Wiggins, D. *Identity and Spatio-Temporal Continuity*. Oxford: Blackwell, 1967.

Williams, B.A.O. "Bodily Continuity and Personal Identity." *Analysis* 21, 2 (1960): 43–8.

## Study Questions

1. What three possible responses to the fission thought experiment does Parfit identify?
2. Parfit's ultimate response to the fission thought experiment is that it is possible to *survive* as two people without *being* two people. What role do "*q*-memory" and "*q*-intention" play in this argument?
3. How does Parfit's fusion thought experiment contribute to his argument that survival, unlike identity, is a matter of degree?
4. How does Parfit distinguish between "psychological continuity" and "psychological connectedness," and why does he consider the latter more important than the former when it comes to a person's survival?

---

## Marya Schechtman

Marya Schechtman specializes in personal identity, practical reasoning, and philosophy of mind. She received her PhD from Harvard University in 1988 and is currently a professor of philosophy at the University of Illinois at Chicago. Schechtman's essay draws on Locke's insight about the practical importance of personal identity.—TR

## The Same and the Same: Two Views of Psychological Continuity

### 1. Introduction

There are two competing sets of intuitions concerning the nature of personal identity. On the one hand, it seems that the continuation of the same person over time consists in the continued existence of the same human body, and on the other that it consists in the continued existence of the same psychological subject. The former view is supported by the observation that persons are, in fact, usually reidentified through the reidentification of human bodies; the latter on the sense, uncovered by **Locke**, that a substance-based identity criterion cannot make sense of the tremendous practical importance that attaches to judgments of personal identity.

The latter view has been represented in the current literature by psychological continuity theories of personal identity that take Locke's original insight and develop it into a fully defined identity criterion. These views have, like all views, been subject to a number of objections. Among them is the charge that they cannot make sense of the tremendous practical importance facts about personal identity bear. This objection is taken quite seriously but, surprisingly, in no place in the literature is it pointed out that it charges the psychological continuity theory with deficiency in respect to its raison d'être. [. . .]

The thesis of this paper is that [. . .] contemporary psychological continuity theories do not genuinely represent the Lockean insight. The intuitions that Locke uncovers and that contemporary theorists use to support their views are that something akin to numerical sameness of psychological subject over time is required to explain the importance of identity. Psychological continuity theorists, however, define identity in terms of a relation akin to qualitative sameness of psychological life and so are in no better position to make sense of the importance of identity than those who hold a substance-based criterion.

This is important because it is taken for granted in the literature that psychological continuity theories adequately express the Lockean insight, so that, if they fail, the insight fails. Realizing that these theories do not capture the intuitions supporting a psychological account of identity provides an alternative. The discussion which follows will first argue that standard objections show psychological continuity theories to fail in their goal of developing the Lockean insight, and then sketch a promising alternative approach to its development.

## 2. Psychological Continuity Theories

The case for the psychological continuity theory is made by appealing to the fact that persons' identification with themselves as psychological subjects is more primitive and powerful than their identification with their physical selves. The idea is that in utterances like "I want to survive" or "I love John," "I" and "John" do not refer primarily to a body or even an immaterial soul but to a subject, and that this subject must continue if the person is to continue to exist.

The intuitions at play here are powerful, and they run very deep. They are expressed in the fact that for most people irretrievable loss of consciousness is a very real form of death. There is an important sense in which "surviving" an accident in a deep coma from which one never emerges is not surviving at all—not in the sense that matters. These intuitions are also expressed in the standard descriptions, religious and otherwise, of what is involved in surviving the death of the body. Whether or not one believes in the possibility of such survival, it is at least generally accepted that, if psychological life persisted beyond the body, it would constitute a form of survival. So there is general agreement that the continuation of conscious psychological life without the body is sufficient for survival.

These are the intuitions on which those who offer psychological accounts of identity base their views. Starting with Locke and continuing in the work of contemporary theorists, arguments for a psychologically based account of identity have been made almost exclusively through the use of hypothetical cases that serve as thought experiments. In these, one is asked to imagine situations in which

the psychological subject is separated in thought from the body (or soul) to which it is attached. The assumption is that in these cases it will be clear that the *person* goes where the psychological subject goes, and not where the body or soul goes. Locke, for instance, describes a case in which the consciousness of a prince enters and informs the body of a cobbler and says that, although the cobbler is the same *human being* he always was, "every one sees he would be the same Person with the Prince, accountable only for the Prince's Actions" (340). Similarly he suggests imagining someone with the same soul or body as Nestor or Thersites at the siege of Troy but without their consciousness and asks "can he conceive himself the same Person with either of them? Can he be concerned in either of their Actions?" (339).

Contemporary puzzle cases are more high-tech than Locke's—and more varied—but they follow essentially the same strategy. Shoemaker, for instance, proposes a case in which the brain of one person, with all of his consciousness, is transplanted into the body of another. Parfit describes teletransportation, a means of interplanetary travel in which all of the states of one's brain and body are recorded, the original body destroyed, and an exact duplicate built. [. . .] Others describe fission, in which one person splits into two; fusion, in which two fuse into one; and a variety of similar cases. These cases and cases like them are absolutely standard and provide the basic support for psychological accounts of personal identity. It is assumed that those who imagine these cases will judge that the person continues in all and only those in which the psychological subject continues.

A close look at these cases reveals that they rely heavily on facts about the practical importance of personal identity. In Locke's case of the prince and cobbler, for instance, the immediate question under consideration is who is to be held *accountable* for the prince's actions after the switch. In the case of the person having Nestor's soul, the issue is whether he can be *concerned* in Nestor's actions. Similar considerations are called into play in the contemporary puzzle cases. The person imagining such cases is supposed to decide whom he would rather see tortured and whom rewarded; whether he would be relieved or comforted to know of the existence of the resultant person; or whether that person's existence would leave him anxious about his own survival. He is asked to consider in which cases he feels concerned for the well-being of the future person as he is usually concerned for his own future well-being, in which cases he feels that gains to the future person could compensate him for sacrifices he makes now, and so on.

It is emphasis on these aspects of personhood that fuels the sense that the only view that could adequately capture what is required for a person's continued existence is that sameness of person consists in sameness of psychological subject: if David's psychological life could somehow be placed into Peter's body and Peter's in David's, then surely David should care in a self-interested way about what happens to the erstwhile Peter-body after the transfer; it is this body which is fairly punished for what David did before the transfer, and so on. This seems right because it seems true that questions of self-interest and responsibility arise only with consciousness. This is the Lockean insight and the support for contemporary psychological continuity theories.

The insight is, as it stands, somewhat vague. Contemporary theorists take up the task of turning it into a more fully articulated identity criterion, which turns out to be a difficult undertaking. While it may seem compelling to say that personal identity is constituted by sameness of psychological subject, it is not obvious what it means to say that a subject persists through time. A subject is not to be construed as an object. A subject is not a brain, not a body, not even an immaterial soul; and it is only insofar as it is none of these things that a psychologically based view of personal identity has the appeal it does. This means, however, that a psychological subject cannot persist through time in the same way substances do; and so it is not clear what is asserted by the claim that psychological continuation makes a person at time $t_2$ the same person as a person at time $t_1$.

This difficulty can be made clearer by considering an exchange between Locke and his contemporaries. **Butler**, for instance, asserts that consciousness is "successive" and, therefore, "cannot be the same in any two moments, nor consequently the personality constituted by it" (102). **Reid** argues that "Consciousness, and every kind of thought are transient and momentary, and have no continued existence. . . ." (116). Locke himself acknowledges that "the same Consciousness" is not the same "individual Action" but "a present representation of a past Action" (337). Consciousness is, at least according to these theorists, a momentary phenomenon and does not remain numerically the same over time. The Lockean view holds that continuation of the consciousness *itself* (or, in the terms that have been used so far, the psychological subject itself), not of the body or soul in which that consciousness resides, is necessary for identity. Given this view of consciousness, it is not clear what it means to say that the same consciousness has continued to exist.

One possibility is offered by Reid, who observes that the *contents* of consciousness at different times can be *qualitatively* like or unlike one another, and in this sense it is possible for the consciousness of one person to be the same as that of someone else, or for a single person's consciousness to be the same at different times. He concludes that it must be this sort of sameness Locke has in mind when he offers his view of personal identity. He says,

> When Mr. Locke, therefore, speaks of "the same consciousness being continued through a succession of different substances"; when he speaks of "repeating a past action with the same consciousness we had of it at the first," and of "the same consciousness extending to actions past and to come"; these expressions are to me unintelligible, unless he means not the same individual consciousness, but a consciousness that is similar, or of the same kind. (116)

With this understanding, the view that personal identity is constituted by sameness of consciousness becomes the view that a person at time $t_2$ is the same person as a person at time $t_1$ if the person at $t_2$ has contents of consciousness qualitatively like those of the person at $t_1$.

The basic sentiment of this reading of sameness of consciousness has been adopted by psychological continuity theorists. They do not hold the crude view described in the above paragraph, but take it as a starting point. They point out that it is not occurrent psychological states alone that are part of one's psychological make-up, but underlying traits and dispositions as well. Furthermore, the kind of similarity necessary for continuity, they say, is not a static psychological sameness but a smoothly flowing psychological life in which what change occurs is gradual, natural, and directed. [. . .]

This view is not, on the surface, an intuitively unappealing understanding of what is involved in personal identity over time. Certainly part of what concerns people in thinking about their own survival is that their personalities not change too much or too rapidly. Persons identify themselves with their values, goals, and character traits and feel that the stability of these is somehow crucial to remaining the same person. It is not, however, a faithful rendering of the nature of psychological continuity that the original puzzle cases show to be crucial to an account of personal identity. This can best be seen by looking at the way in which the original arguments for the psychological continuity theory turn into an argument against it.

## 3. Difficulties for Psychological Continuity Theories

Once psychologically based views of identity are offered, they are almost immediately charged with an inability to make sense of the practical importance of personal identity. This objection is raised against Locke by Butler, who, having concluded that consciousness cannot literally persist through time, observes that if Locke's view is correct,

> . . . it is a fallacy upon ourselves, to charge our present selves with any thing we did, or to imagine our present selves interested in any thing which befell us yesterday, or that our present self will be interested in what will befall us to-morrow; since our present self is not, in reality, the same with the self of yesterday, but another like self or person coming in its room, and mistaken for it; to which another self will succeed tomorrow. (102)

This objection, labelled "The Extreme Claim" by Parfit (307), is very much alive in the contemporary discussion. [. . .]

The basic contours of the argument for the extreme claim are easy to understand. It is based on the well-founded assumption that there are certain attitudes and practices appropriate only in cases where one and the same psychological subject continues throughout time and that *similarity* of subject is not enough. There is, for instance, a special kind of concern based on anticipation that one can feel for only oneself. A person may be very sorry that someone she cares about will be in pain tomorrow, but she should not expect to *feel* that person's pain. The degree of similarity that person has to her may affect how *much* she cares—she may feel worse about the suffering of a kindred spirit than of someone alien—but she can no more correctly *anticipate* the suffering of one than the other.

Similarly, only benefits to *oneself* can compensate one for present sacrifices. Making Susan work after school so that she can go to college is one thing; making her twin sister work after school so that Susan can go to college is quite another. This is why people receive paycheques for *their* hours and not anyone else's. Again, similarity seems irrelevant here. It does not matter if the person who gets Susan's paycheque is more *like* her than someone else; she is compensated only if *she* gets to enjoy spending the money. The same case can be made about moral responsibility. It is deemed fair only to punish someone for her own actions, not for the actions of anyone else, no matter how similar to her that other person may be.

The claim is that psychological continuity theories collapse the distinction between person A *being* person B and person A merely being *like* person B. True, they do not give a simple qualitative similarity view of identity, but they do give a view on which there is no deeper connection between a person now and himself in the future than there is between a person now and others who are very like him psychologically. The psychological subject who is here now to plan the evil crime or put in the extra hours is not, on this view, really around to languish in prison or enjoy the vacation bought with the overtime pay. This is a direct consequence of the view that consciousness cannot literally persist and that continuity of consciousness consists in no more than certain external relations of similarity between moments of consciousness that are really distinct.

The view that each moment of consciousness is distinct from all the others entails the fact that persisting persons can be psychological subjects in only a secondary or derivative sense. A *person* can experience a pleasure or pain, or intend an action, only if that pleasure or pain is experienced, or that intention formed, by one of the interrelated moments of consciousness that make up that person. The moments of consciousness will thus be the primary subjects of action and experience, with the persisting person being their subject only by including one or more moments of consciousness. On this view, for the same person who committed the crime to be punished for it, or for the same person who worked overtime to enjoy the vacation, is only for the momentary consciousness that suffers the punishment or soaks up the sun to be related by overlapping chains of similarity and like relations to the momentary consciousness that planned the crime or worked the extra hours. Similarity, however, is *not* a strong enough relation to underlie responsibility or compensation. [. . .]

A psychological continuity theorist might answer this charge as follows. Thought experiments demonstrate that the persistence of substance cannot provide a basis for the importance of identity, and it is natural to conclude that identity must be constituted by the continued existence of the psychological subject. A look at the nature of consciousness, however, reveals that all that psychological continuation can be is a modified relation of qualitative similarity; and so the continuation of subject cannot provide a basis for that importance either. It thus follows that

no basis for this importance *can* be provided and that the attribution of such importance to identity is ungrounded. This is essentially Parfit's view.

This response is consistent but does not constitute a definitive response to the extreme claim. Denying the importance of identity requires the denial of one of the most fundamental beliefs about persons, and these arguments do not seem strong enough to warrant such a radical move. The sole reason offered for this move is the assumption that the psychological continuity theory presents the only possible definition of the continuation of a psychological subject. This is not, however, correct. It is not necessary to give up on the importance of identity so quickly, because there is an alternative understanding of sameness of consciousness that can capture the Lockean insight.

## 4. An Alternative View

The Lockean insight is, after all, Locke's, and his work contains crucial hints about what an alternative definition of sameness of consciousness might look like. The view that follows is not being offered as a reading of Locke, but rather as a strand that can be extracted from his text and that helps the present discussion by providing the beginnings of an alternative way of defining sameness of consciousness.

Locke's discussion of sameness of consciousness begins with observations concerning the way in which presently existing material substance becomes part of one's body. He says that the particles of one's body,

. . . whilst vitally united to this same thinking conscious self, so that we feel when they are touch'd, and are affected by, and conscious of good or harm that happens to them, are a part of our *selves*: i.e., of our thinking conscious *self*. Thus, the Limbs of his Body are to every one a part of *himself*: He sympathizes and is concerned for them. Cut off an hand, and thereby separate it from that consciousness, we had of its Heat, Cold, and other Affections; and it is then no longer a part of that which is *himself* any more than the remotest part of Matter. (336–7)

The same principle, he says, holds true for immaterial substance. Insofar as mental states are states of an immaterial soul, a soul becomes that of a particular person when she is conscious of those mental states; that is, when she experiences them, and they cause her pain or pleasure.

The idea here is simple. A fundamental part of what it is to be a conscious being is to be a creature who can be, from a first-person, phenomenological perspective, better or worse off. Some states of consciousness are pleasurable, some are painful; and it is a fundamental feature of our experience that some subjective states are intrinsically preferable to others. The notion of well-being and the possibility of valuing some states over others emerge as dimensions of experience for the first time with consciousness, and are intimately linked to it. To be conscious is always to be in a better or worse state of mind, more or less comfortable and happy; and everything experienced consciously affects the subject somewhere on the continuum of pleasure and pain.

Locke's next move is to claim that present consciousness includes in itself temporally distant actions and experiences in precisely the same way it does present ones. He says that a present self "extends it *self* beyond present Existence to what is past, only by consciousness, whereby it becomes concerned and accountable, owns and imputes to it *self* past Actions, *just upon the same ground, and for the same reason,* that it does the present" (346; my emphasis). In the present, persons' own actions [. . .] affect their well-being or cause them pleasure and pain. If past and future actions become those of a particular person in precisely the same way, they must do so by affecting her well-being and causing her pleasure and pain. To understand this view, then, it is necessary to understand how past and future actions and experiences can presently cause a person pleasure or pain.

This is not difficult to see, it is obvious that temporally distant actions and experiences do affect a person's present well-being in any number of ways. When someone is, at present, tortured by guilt or warmed by happy memories, when he measures his current successes by comparison with past ones, or when his anticipation of a pleasant evening out cheers him through the drudgery of the boring tasks he must complete during the day, past and future experiences are having a direct impact on his current well-being, and hence, by the Lockean criterion, are part of his present consciousness as are his cold hands or warm feet. This is not to say that actions and experiences that have not yet taken place can somehow reach back through time and cause pleasure or pain, nor even that actions and experiences that have taken place can reach forward and do so. It points only to the obvious psychological fact that adult humans project themselves backwards and forwards in time. A person not only remembers her past successes, she also views her present self as the same person who had those successes; and this alters the way her present successes are experienced. Similarly, she not only knows that there will be revelry tonight, but also thinks that she will be there and that the associated pleasures will be hers; and this makes her feel better now.

This phenomenon is not most accurately described by saying that a person is affected in the present by memories of the past or anticipations of the future, because this description implies that the effect comes from some particular state (a memory or anticipation), perhaps added to another state (self-ascription). This presents the wrong picture. The projection of oneself into the past and future, and the attendant affect, are not local psychological events but a way of organizing consciousness. There is a background presupposition that one has had a past and will have a future, and that their character is relevant to one's well-being. This presupposition is expressed in, but not equivalent to, particular memories and anticipations.

The sense of oneself as temporally extended is a *background presupposition* of psychological life in that it provides a context in terms of which immediate stimuli are interpreted. This can be seen in a number of ways. First, there are the *kinds* of states and events that typically make up a person's psychological life. Many of these are intrinsically forward or backward looking and depend conceptually on the assumption that the subject is temporally persistent. This is especially evident in some of the more complex elements of human psychology. Shame, remorse, nostalgia, and regret are all states that logically presuppose that the subject has a past; anxiety and anticipation assume that the subject will have a future. Even an experience as basic as pain can be said to be forward-looking. It is common to define pain at least partially in terms of a desire for its cessation, and pleasure in terms of a desire for its continuance. These desires are not separate states but part of the very phenomenology of pleasure and pain.

The assumption that one will continue to exist affects not only the kinds of states one has, but also the character of particular experiences. It is rare for a person to experience anything in total isolation. Instead, present circumstances are automatically interpreted in terms of the supposition that they take place within the context of an ongoing life, and their character will differ depending on the role they play in that life. This effect, too, can be seen at the level of both the most basic and the most sophisticated features of human psychological life.

It is a commonplace, for instance, that pain suffered with the knowledge that it is for a good cause, or that it will soon cease, is a great deal more bearable than pain of unknown origin that one expects may go on indefinitely. Similarly, a graduate student struggling along with virtually no money may be able to view her poverty as a romantic rite of passage, or at least as a survivable stage leading to greater financial security. Such poverty has a much different character than a lack of resources with no foreseeable end, even if the day to day details are exactly the same. The expectations in the former instance will cause those details to be experienced quite differently than in the latter. [. . .]

The view described here is thus the view that persons are essentially creatures who perceive themselves as subjects, persisting through time, and that they extend their consciousness over time through their self-conceptions. As Locke expresses it, a person is ". . . a thinking intelligent Being, that has reason and reflection, and can consider it self as it self, the same thinking thing, in different times and places . . ." (335). And that "where-ever a Man finds, what he calls *himself,* there I think, another may say is the same *Person*" (346). "Self-conception" is, however, a rather vague term, and it is

important to be clear that on this view not just *any* self-conception will truly extend consciousness. To extend oneself over time in the way that is definitive of personhood, one must have a self-conception essentially like that of an ordinary adult human being.

## 5. Self-Constitution and the Lockean Insight

It remains to be shown that the view described above captures the intuitions supporting a psychological account of identity better than the qualitative sameness view does. Observe first that the original impetus behind the psychological criterion is the idea that persons have a distinctive sort of psychological life and that it is this they are most interested in preserving. Observe further that the features that make the psychological lives of persons unique are precisely those linked to their unique kind of self-conception. The sense of oneself as a continuing subject makes possible the whole range of psychological activities involving self-regarding emotions and self-interpretation and it is these that are peculiar to persons, distinguishing them from other sentient creatures. With a sense of oneself as a persisting subject, one no longer simply reacts to the stimuli immediately presented but interprets and conditions those stimuli by reference to the past and future. It therefore stands to reason that having this sort of self-conception is essential to the identity that is important to us.

It is important to be clear that forming a self-conception does not merely involve adding a few new psychological states to one's repertoire. The view of sameness of consciousness presented here does not just replace the qualitative similarity view with a view for which consciousness is equally disjointed, but for which the consciousness-slice at $t_2$ must now, in addition to being similar to the consciousness-slice at $t_1$, also contain something like the thought "these actions (at $t_1$) are mine" or a feeling of guilt about an action at $t_1$. Such a view would gain very little over the qualitative similarity view in terms of explaining or supporting the special concern we have for our futures because it would still provide no real unity of consciousness over time.

Because a self-conception is a general organizing feature of psychological life and not an occurrent state, the formation of a self-conception of the sort described above will actually alter the nature of consciousness by genuinely extending it. This is a difficult claim to defend directly, but a reminder of the best supported views of human development will help make it plausible. As infants develop into adulthood, gaining a self-conception and the capacities of persons, there are major changes in the nature of their experience. Infants are certainly sentient, but their consciousness is thought to be quite different from that of adults. Here is a real example of the disjointed, unprocessed moments of experience that exist when there is no unity of consciousness. Infants are not fully self-conscious, nor are they capable of many of the sorts of experiences adults have. They do not yet have the cognitive capacity to connect different moments and features of experience into more complex wholes. As a child grows, is socialized, and develops cognitively, the nature of experience changes, the child gradually awakens to its own existence, and with this awakening comes a different *sort* of consciousness than was present before. The child changes from an unreflective creature acting on instinct to a self-conscious agent capable of acting from reasons—a change in capacity that implies a phenomenological change.

This explains part of what is so horrifying about the contemplation of senility. The loss of the ability to process our experience as we ordinarily do represents a return to a state of consciousness more like that of infancy than that of adult life. A senile person is unable to remember who and what she is, what she has done, what roles she has played in the lives of others, or they in hers. These deficits make it impossible to form a coherent self-conception. The senile person cannot manage to get the story straight on who she is, and so lives in confusion. She is, furthermore, robbed of the capacities necessary for engaging in the activities and practices definitive of persons. It is important to realize that in such cases there are believed to be pronounced phenomenological differences accompanying the outward changes of senility; this is what makes it most horrific to

contemplate. As one imagines sinking deeper and deeper into senility, one imagines sinking deeper and deeper into a twilight state of semi-consciousness, a consciousness qualitatively unlike ordinary adult consciousness.

Infancy and senility provide two examples of disunified consciousness. There are undoubtedly many others.[1] In those cases which *are* seen as cases of disunified consciousness, it is assumed that the subjective quality of experience is different from that of ordinary adults. This indicates, however, that the formation of a self-conception, and the appropriation of temporally distant actions and experiences, does more than provide a formal connection between separate time-slices, it alters the nature of consciousness and subjectivity.

The unity of consciousness over time that has developed in this way is deep enough to support the fundamental features of personhood that psychological continuity theories are meant to support. This claim can be made more compelling by considering once again unity of consciousness at a time and its relation to unity of consciousness over time. No one denies that there is a real unity among psychological states co-conscious at a time; that the various elements that are part of a person's conscious experience at a given moment bear a deep connection to one another that they do not bear to the contents of anyone else's consciousness. The intuitions supporting a psychological account of personal identity require that this relation be extended over time to past and future psychological states, and the self-constitution view suggested here involves just such an extension. Consider what it is for different psychological components to be part of the same consciousness at a time. It is not possible to offer a complete analysis of this relation here, but part of what is involved is the fact that the various beliefs, desires, images, and so on that are part of the same consciousness at a given time interact in such a way that each provides a context in which to interpret the others. The difference between one person thinking a six-word sentence and six people each thinking one word of that sentence is, at least in part, that in the former case each of the words provides an interpretive context that constrains the understanding of the others so that what is experienced is not the same as six separate words side by side, but a single six-word unit. The meanings of the other five words are, in a sense, already present in the consciousness of each word when one is conscious of such a sentence.

Consider now that on the self-constitution view described here it is precisely this relation that makes psychological features at different times part of the same consciousness. To extend consciousness over time is to weave temporally distant actions or experiences into the network of one's conception of oneself. This requires that the effects of certain past experiences and the anticipation of certain future ones affect and condition one's present experience. Appropriating past and future experiences, however, consists precisely in taking them as the interpretive context for present experience. It cannot be stressed

enough that this view is not committed to the unrealistic claim that each time a person has an experience she consciously considers the past and future and decides how to understand the present on that basis, any more than in understanding a six-word sentence one need always consciously attend to the interactions of the words. The view suggests only that when a person feels his present disappointment more profoundly because it comes at the end of a long string of disappointments, or when a shadow is cast over a person's eating and drinking pleasure by her guilt at not keeping her resolutions and her awareness that she will regret it in the morning, the past and future are providing the context within which the present is experienced and condition the nature of that experience. This, then, is a sketch of the view alternative to the qualitative similarity view offered by psychological continuity theorists. It places the limits of the person at the limits of the self-conception. [. . .]

## Note

1. For a nice example of this, look at the description of "Jimmy," the Korsakov's victim described by Oliver Sacks in *The Man Who Mistook His Wife for a Hat*.

## Works Cited

Butler, J. "Of Personal Identity." *Personal Identity*. Ed. J. Perry. Berkeley and Los Angeles: University of California Press, 1975. 99–105.

Locke, J. *An Essay Concerning Human Understanding*. Ed. P.H. Nidditch. Oxford: Clarendon Press, 1979.

Parfit, D. *Reasons and Persons*. Oxford: Oxford University Press, 1984.

Reid, T. "Of Mr. Locke's Account of Our Personal Identity." *Personal Identity*. Ed. J. Perry. Berkeley and Los Angeles: University of California Press, 1975. 113–8.

Shoemaker, S. "Personal Identity: A Materialist's Account." *Personal Identity*. Ed. S. Shoemaker and R. Swinburne. Oxford: Basil Blackwood Ltd., 1984. 67–132.

## Study Questions

1. How do *qualitative sameness* and *numerical sameness* differ? Provide an example.
2. Schechtman considers the reliance of psychological continuity theories of personal identity on qualitative sameness to be intuitively appealing but also problematic. Explain why.
3. Why does Schechtman believe that her theory of personal identity, by placing "the limits of the person at the limits of the self-conception," better captures the insights of Locke's account than do psychological continuity theories?
4. Why might Schechtman's theory of personal identity be considered a *narrative* theory?

# Simone de Beauvoir

Simone de Beauvoir (1908–86) was a Sorbonne-educated existentialist author of novels, plays, and memoirs, as well as philosophical essays on metaphysics, ethics, and politics. Her novel *The Mandarins* won the Prix Goncourt, France's most prestigious literary award. Beauvoir's famous line in *The Second Sex*, "One is not born, but rather becomes, a woman," inaugurated "second wave" feminism's sex–gender distinction and raised hope that if gendered social roles are socially constructed and not biologically determined, they could be otherwise.—TR

## Introduction to *The Second Sex*

For a long time I have hesitated to write a book on woman. The subject is irritating, especially to women; and it is not new. Enough ink has been spilled in quarrelling over feminism, and perhaps we should say no more about it. It is still talked about, however, for the voluminous nonsense uttered during the last century seems to have done little to illuminate the problem. After all, is there a problem? And if so, what is it? Are there women, really? Most assuredly the theory of the eternal feminine still has its adherents who will whisper in your ear: "Even in Russia women still are *women*"; and other erudite persons—sometimes the very same—say with a sigh: "Woman is losing her way, woman is lost." One wonders if women still exist, if they will always exist, whether or not it is desirable that they should, what place they occupy in this world, what their place should be. "What has become of women?" was asked recently in an ephemeral magazine.

But first we must ask: what is a woman? "*Tota mulier in utero*," says one, "woman is a womb." But in speaking of certain women, connoisseurs declare that they are not women, although they are equipped with a uterus like the rest. All agree in recognizing the fact that females exist in the human species; today as always they make up about one half of humanity. And yet we are told that femininity is in danger; we are exhorted to be women, remain women, become women. It would appear, then, that every female human being is not necessarily a woman; to be so considered she must share in that mysterious and threatened reality known as femininity. Is this attribute something secreted by the ovaries? Or is it a Platonic essence, a product of the philosophic imagination? Is a rustling petticoat enough to bring it down to earth? Although some women try zealously to incarnate this essence, it is hardly patentable. It is frequently described in vague and dazzling terms that seem to have been borrowed from the vocabulary of the seers, and indeed in the times of **St Thomas** [**Aquinas**] it was considered an essence as certainly defined as the somniferous virtue of the poppy.

But **conceptualism** has lost ground. The biological and social sciences no longer admit the existence of unchangeably fixed entities that determine given characteristics, such as those ascribed to woman, the Jew, or the Negro. Science regards any characteristic as a reaction dependent in part upon a *situation*. If today femininity no longer exists, then it never existed. But does the word *woman*, then, have no specific content? This is stoutly affirmed by those who hold to the philosophy of the enlightenment, of rationalism, of nominalism; women, to them, are merely the human beings arbitrarily designated by the word *woman*. Many American women particularly are prepared to think that there is no longer any place for woman as such; if a backward individual still takes herself for a woman, her friends advise her to be psychoanalyzed and thus get rid of this obsession. In regard to a work, *Modern Woman: The Lost Sex*, which in other respects has its irritating features, **Dorothy Parker** has written: "I cannot be just to books which treat of woman as woman. . . .

My idea is that all of us, men as well as women, should be regarded as human beings." But **nominalism** is a rather inadequate doctrine, and the antifeminists have had no trouble in showing that women simply *are not* men. Surely woman is, like man, a human being; but such a declaration is abstract. The fact is that every concrete human being is always a singular, separate individual. To decline to accept such notions as the eternal feminine, the black soul, the Jewish character, is not to deny that Jews, Negroes, women exist today—this denial does not represent a liberation for those concerned, but rather a flight from reality. [. . .] In truth, to go for a walk with one's eyes open is enough to demonstrate that humanity is divided into two classes of individuals whose clothes, faces, bodies, smiles, gaits, interests, and occupations are manifestly different. Perhaps these differences are superficial, perhaps they are destined to disappear. What is certain is that they do most obviously exist.

If her functioning as a female is not enough to define woman, if we decline also to explain her through "the eternal feminine," and if nevertheless we admit, provisionally, that women do exist, then we must face the question: what is a woman?

To state the question is, to me, to suggest, at once, a preliminary answer. The fact that I ask it is in itself significant. A man would never set out to write a book on the peculiar situation of the human male. But if I wish to define myself, I must first of all say: "I am a woman"; on this truth must be based all further discussion. A man never begins by presenting himself as an individual of a certain sex; it goes without saying that he is a man. The terms *masculine* and *feminine* are used symmetrically only as a matter of form, as on legal papers. In actuality the relation of the two sexes is not quite like that of two electrical poles, for man represents both the positive and the neutral, as is indicated by the common use of *man* to designate human beings in general; whereas woman represents only the negative, defined by limiting criteria, without reciprocity. In the midst of an abstract discussion it is vexing to hear a man say: "You think thus and so because you are a woman"; but I know that my only defence is to reply: "I think thus and so

because it is true," thereby removing my subjective self from the argument. It would be out of the question to reply: "And you think the contrary because you are a man," for it is understood that the fact of being a man is no peculiarity. A man is in the right in being a man; it is the woman who is in the wrong. It amounts to this: just as for the ancients there was an absolute vertical with reference to which the oblique was defined, so there is an absolute human type, the masculine. Woman has ovaries, a uterus: these peculiarities imprison her in her subjectivity, circumscribe her within the limits of her own nature. It is often said that she thinks with her glands. Man superbly ignores the fact that his anatomy also includes glands, such as the testicles, and that they secrete hormones. He thinks of his body as a direct and normal connection with the world, which he believes he apprehends objectively, whereas he regards the body of woman as a hindrance, a prison, weighed down by everything peculiar to it. "The female is a female by virtue of a certain *lack* of qualities," said **Aristotle**; "we should regard the female nature as afflicted with a natural defectiveness." And St Thomas for his part pronounced woman to be an "imperfect man," an "incidental" being. This is symbolized in Genesis where Eve is depicted as made from what **Bossuet** called "a supernumerary bone" of Adam.

Thus humanity is male and man defines woman not in herself but as relative to him; she is not regarded as an autonomous being. [. . .] And she is simply what man decrees; thus she is called "the sex," by which is meant that she appears essentially to the male as a sexual being. For him she is sex—absolute sex, no less. She is defined and differentiated with reference to man and not he with reference to her; she is the incidental, the inessential as opposed to the essential. He is the Subject, he is the Absolute—she is the Other. [. . .]

No group ever sets itself up as the One without at once setting up the Other over against itself. If three travellers chance to occupy the same compartment, that is enough to make vaguely hostile "others" out of all the rest of the passengers on the train. In small-town eyes all persons not belonging to the village are "strangers" and suspect; to the native of a country all who inhabit other countries are "foreigners"; Jews are "different" for the anti-Semite, Negroes are "inferior" for American racists, aborigines are "natives" for colonists, proletarians are the "lower class" for the privileged. [. . .]

Following **Hegel**, we find in consciousness itself a fundamental hostility towards every other consciousness; the subject can be posed only in being opposed—he sets himself up as the essential, as opposed to the other, the inessential, the object.

But the other consciousness, the other ego, sets up a reciprocal claim. The native travelling abroad is shocked to find himself in turn regarded as a "stranger" by the natives of neighbouring countries. As a matter of fact, wars, festivals, trading, treaties, and contests among tribes, nations, and classes tend to deprive the concept *Other* of its absolute sense and to make manifest its relativity; willy-nilly, individuals and groups are forced to realize the reciprocity of their relations. How is it, then, that this reciprocity has not been recognized between the sexes, that one of the contrasting terms is set up as the sole essential, denying any relativity in regard to its correlative and defining the latter as pure otherness? Why is it that women do not dispute male sovereignty? No subject will readily volunteer to become the object, the inessential; it is not the Other who, in defining himself as the Other, establishes the One. The Other is posed as such by the One in defining himself as the One. But if the Other is not to regain the status of being the One, he must be submissive enough to accept this alien point of view. Whence comes this submission in the case of woman?

There are, to be sure, other cases in which a certain category has been able to dominate another completely for a time. Very often this privilege depends upon inequality of numbers—the majority imposes its rule upon the minority or persecutes it. But women are not a minority, like the American Negroes or the Jews; there are as many women as men on earth. Again, the two groups concerned have often been originally independent; they may have been formerly unaware of each other's existence, or perhaps they recognized each other's autonomy.

But a historical event has resulted in the subjugation of the weaker by the stronger. The scattering of the Jews, the introduction of slavery into America, the conquests of imperialism are examples in point. In these cases the oppressed retained at least the memory of former days; they possessed in common a past, a tradition, sometimes a religion or a culture.

The parallel drawn by **Bebel** between women and the proletariat is valid in that neither ever formed a minority or a separate collective unit of mankind. And instead of a single historical event it is in both cases a historical development that explains their status as a class and accounts for the membership of *particular individuals* in that class. But proletarians have not always existed, whereas there have always been women. They are women in virtue of their anatomy and physiology. Throughout history they have always been subordinated to men, and hence their dependency is not the result of a historical event or a social change—it was not something that *occurred*. The reason why otherness in this case seems to be an absolute is in part that it lacks the contingent or incidental nature of historical facts. A condition brought about at a certain time can be abolished at some other time, as the **Negroes of Haiti** and others have proved: but it might seem that a natural condition is beyond the possibility of change. In truth, however, the nature of things is no more immutably given, once for all, than is historical reality. If woman seems to be the inessential which never becomes the essential, it is because she herself fails to bring about this change. Proletarians say "We"; Negroes also. Regarding themselves as subjects, they transform the bourgeois, the whites, into "others." But women do not say "We," except at some congress of feminists or similar formal demonstration; men say "women," and women use the same word in referring to themselves. They do not authentically assume a subjective attitude. The proletarians have accomplished the revolution in Russia, the Negroes in Haiti, the Indo-Chinese are battling for it in Indo-China; but the women's effort has never been anything more than a symbolic agitation. They have gained only what men have been willing to grant; they have taken nothing, they have only received.

The reason for this is that women lack concrete means for organizing themselves into a unit which can stand face to face with the correlative unit. They have no past, no history, no religion of their own; and they have no such solidarity of work and interest as that of the proletariat. They are not even promiscuously herded together in the way that creates community feeling among the American Negroes, the ghetto Jews, the workers of Saint-Denis, or the factory hands of Renault. They live dispersed among the males, attached through residence, housework, economic condition, and social standing to certain men—fathers or husbands—more firmly than they are to other women. If they belong to the bourgeoisie, they feel solidarity with men of that class, not with proletarian women; if they are white, their allegiance is to white men, not to Negro women. The proletariat can propose to massacre the ruling class, and a sufficiently fanatical Jew or Negro might dream of getting sole possession of the atomic bomb and making humanity wholly Jewish or black; but woman cannot even dream of exterminating the males. The bond that unites her to her oppressors is not comparable to any other. The division of the sexes is a biological fact, not an event in human history. Male and female stand opposed within a primordial *Mitsein*, and woman has not broken it. The couple is a fundamental unity with its two halves riveted together, and the cleavage of society along the line of sex is impossible. Here is to be found the basic trait of woman: she is the Other in a totality of which the two components are necessary to one another.

One could suppose that this reciprocity might have facilitated the liberation of woman. When Hercules sat at the feet of Omphale and helped with her spinning, his desire for her held him captive; but why did she fail to gain a lasting power? To revenge herself on Jason, Medea killed their children; and this grim legend would seem to suggest that she might have obtained a formidable influence over him through his love for his offspring. In *Lysistrata* **Aristophanes** gaily depicts a band of women who joined forces to gain social ends through the sexual needs of their men; but this is only a play.

In the legend of the Sabine women, the latter soon abandoned their plan of remaining sterile to punish their ravishers. In truth woman has not been socially emancipated through man's need—sexual desire and the desire for offspring—which makes the male dependent for satisfaction upon the female.

Master and slave, also, are united by a reciprocal need, in this case economic, which does not liberate the slave. In the relation of master to slave the master does not make a point of the need that he has for the other; he has in his grasp the power of satisfying this need through his own action; whereas the slave, in his dependent condition, his hope and fear, is quite conscious of the need he has for his master. Even if the need is at bottom equally urgent for both, it always works in favour of the oppressor and against the oppressed. That is why the liberation of the working class, for example, has been slow.

Now, woman has always been man's dependant, if not his slave; the two sexes have never shared the world in equality. And even today woman is heavily handicapped, though her situation is beginning to change. Almost nowhere is her legal status the same as man's, and frequently it is much to her disadvantage. Even when her rights are legally recognized in the abstract, long-standing custom prevents their full expression in the mores. In the economic sphere men and women can almost be said to make up two castes; other things being equal, the former hold the better jobs, get higher wages, and have more opportunity for success than their new competitors. In industry and politics men have a great many more positions and they monopolize the most important posts. In addition to all this, they enjoy a traditional prestige that the education of children tends in every way to support, for the present enshrines the past—and in the past all history has been made by men. At the present time, when women are beginning to take part in the affairs of the world, it is still a world that belongs to men—they have no doubt of it at all and women have scarcely any. To decline to be the Other, to refuse to be a party to the deal—this would be for women to renounce all the advantages conferred upon them by their alliance with the superior caste. Man-the-sovereign will provide woman-the-liege with material protection and will undertake the moral justification of her existence; thus she can evade at once both economic risk and the metaphysical risk of a liberty in which ends and aims must be contrived without assistance. Indeed, along with the ethical urge of each individual to affirm his subjective existence, there is also the temptation to forgo liberty and become a thing. This is an inauspicious road, for he who takes it—passive, lost, ruined—becomes henceforth the creature of another's will, frustrated in his transcendence and deprived of every value. But it is an easy road; on it one avoids the strain involved in undertaking an authentic existence. When man makes of woman the *Other*, he may, then, expect to manifest deep-seated tendencies towards complicity. Thus, woman may fail to lay claim to the status of subject because she lacks definite resources, because she feels the necessary bond that ties her to man regardless of reciprocity, and because she is often very well pleased with her role as the *Other*.

But it will be asked at once: how did all this begin? It is easy to see that the duality of the sexes, like any duality, gives rise to conflict. And doubtless the winner will assume the status of absolute. But why should man have won from the start? It seems possible that women could have won the victory; or that the outcome of the conflict might never have been decided. How is it that this world has always belonged to the men and that things have begun to change only recently? Is this change a good thing? Will it bring about an equal sharing of the world between men and women?

These questions are not new, and they have often been answered. But the very fact that woman *is the Other* tends to cast suspicion upon all the justifications that men have ever been able to provide for it. These have all too evidently been dictated by men's interest. A little-known feminist of the seventeenth century, Poulain de la Barre, put it this way: "All that has been written about women by men should be suspect, for the men are at once judge and party to the lawsuit." [. . .]

Legislators, priests, philosophers, writers, and scientists have striven to show that the subordinate position of woman is willed in heaven and advantageous on earth. The religions invented by men reflect this wish for domination. In the legends of Eve and Pandora men have taken up arms against women. They have made use of philosophy and theology, as the quotations from Aristotle and St Thomas have shown. Since ancient times satirists and moralists have delighted in showing up the weaknesses of women. [. . .] This hostility may at times be well founded, often it is gratuitous; but in truth it more or less successfully conceals a desire for self-justification. As **Montaigne** says, "It is easier to accuse one sex than to excuse the other." Sometimes what is going on is clear enough. For instance, the Roman law limiting the rights of woman cited "the imbecility, the instability of the sex" just when the weakening of family ties seemed to threaten the interests of male heirs. And in the effort to keep the married woman under guardianship, appeal was made in the sixteenth century to the authority of **St Augustine**, who declared that "woman is a creature neither decisive nor constant," at a time when the single woman was thought capable of managing her property. [. . .]

In proving woman's inferiority, the anti-feminists [. . .] draw not only upon religion, philosophy, and theology, [. . .] but also upon science—biology, experimental psychology, etc. At most they were willing to grant "equality in difference" to the *other* sex. That profitable formula is most significant; it is precisely like the "equal but separate" formula of the **Jim Crow laws** aimed at the North American Negroes. As is well known, this so-called equalitarian segregation has resulted only in the most extreme discrimination. The similarity just noted is in no way due to chance, for whether it is a race, a caste, a class, or a sex that is reduced to a position of inferiority, the methods of justification are the same. "The eternal feminine" corresponds to "the black soul" and to "the Jewish character." True, the Jewish problem is on the whole very different from the other two—to the anti-Semite the Jew is not so much an inferior as he is an enemy for whom there is to be granted no place on earth, for whom annihilation is the fate desired. But there are deep similarities between the situation of woman and that of the Negro. Both are being emancipated today from a like paternalism, and the former master class wishes to "keep them in their place"—that is, the place chosen for them. In both cases the former masters lavish more or less sincere eulogies, either on the virtues of "the good Negro" with his dormant, childish, merry soul—the submissive Negro—or on the merits of the woman who is "truly feminine"—that is, frivolous, infantile, irresponsible—the submissive woman. In both cases the dominant class bases its argument on a state of affairs that it has itself created. As **George Bernard Shaw** puts it, in substance, "The American white relegates the black to the rank of shoeshine boy; and he concludes from this that the black is good for nothing but shining shoes." This vicious circle is met with in all analogous circumstances; when an individual (or a group of individuals) is kept in a situation of inferiority, the fact is that he *is* inferior. But the significance of the verb *to be* must be rightly understood here; it is in bad faith to give it a static value when it really has the dynamic Hegelian sense of "to have become." Yes, women on the whole *are* today inferior to men; that is, their situation affords them fewer possibilities. The question is: should that state of affairs continue?

Many men hope that it will continue; not all have given up the battle. The conservative bourgeoisie still see in the emancipation of women a menace to their morality and their interests. Some men dread feminine competition. Recently a male student wrote in the *Hebdo-Latin*: "Every woman student who goes into medicine or law robs us of a job." He never questioned his rights in this world. [. . .]

But men profit in many more subtle ways from the otherness, the alterity of woman. Here is a miraculous balm for those afflicted with an inferiority complex, and indeed no one is more arrogant towards women, more aggressive or scornful, than the man who is anxious about his virility. Those who are not fear-ridden in the presence of their fellow men are much more disposed to recognize a fellow creature in woman; but even to these the myth of Woman, the Other, is precious for many reasons. They cannot be blamed for not cheerfully relinquishing all the benefits they derive from the myth, for they realize what they would lose in relinquishing woman as they fancy her to be, while they fail to realize what they have to gain from the woman of tomorrow. Refusal to pose oneself as the Subject, unique and absolute, requires great self-denial. [. . .]

We should consider the arguments of the feminists with no less suspicion, however, for very often their controversial aim deprives them of all real value. If the "woman question" seems trivial, it is because masculine arrogance has made of it a "quarrel"; and when quarrelling one no longer reasons well. People have tirelessly sought to prove that woman is superior, inferior, or equal to man. Some say that, having been created after Adam, she is evidently a secondary being; others say on the contrary that Adam was only a rough draft and that God succeeded in producing the human being in perfection when He created Eve. Woman's brain is smaller; yes, but it is relatively larger. Christ was made a man; yes, but perhaps for his greater humility. Each argument at once suggests its opposite, and both are often fallacious. If we are to gain understanding, we must get out of these ruts; we must discard the vague notions of superiority, inferiority, equality which have hitherto corrupted every discussion of the subject and start afresh.

Very well, but just how shall we pose the question? And, to begin with, who are we to propound it at all? Man is at once judge and party to the case; but so is woman. What we need is an angel—neither man nor woman—but where shall we find one? Still, the angel would be poorly qualified to speak, for an angel is ignorant of all the basic facts involved in the problem. With a hermaphrodite we should be no better off, for here the situation is most peculiar; the hermaphrodite is not really the combination of a whole man and a whole woman, but consists of parts of each and thus is neither. [. . .]

But it is doubtless impossible to approach any human problem with a mind free from bias. The way in which questions are put, the points of view assumed, presuppose a relativity of interest; all characteristics imply values, and every objective description, so called, implies an ethical background. Rather than attempt to conceal principles more or less definitely implied, it is better to state them openly, at the beginning. This will make it unnecessary to specify on every page in just what sense one uses such words as *superior, inferior, better, worse, progress, reaction*, and the like. If we survey some of the works on woman, we note that one of the points of view most frequently adopted is that of the public good, the general interest; and one always means by this the benefit of society as one wishes it to be maintained or established. For our part, we hold that the only public good is that which assures the private good of the citizens; we shall pass judgment on institutions according to their effectiveness in giving concrete opportunities to individuals. But we do not confuse the idea of private interest with that of happiness, although that is another common point of view. Are not women of the harem more happy than women voters? Is not the housekeeper happier than the workingwoman? It is not too clear just what the word *happy* really means and still less what true values it may mask. There is no possibility of measuring the happiness of others, and it is always easy to describe as happy the situation in which one wishes to place them.

In particular those who are condemned to stagnation are often pronounced happy on the pretext that happiness consists in being at rest. This notion we reject, for our perspective is that of existentialist ethics. Every subject plays his part as such specifically through exploits or projects that serve as a mode of transcendence; he achieves liberty only through a continual reaching out towards other liberties. There is no justification for present existence other than its expansion into an indefinitely open future. Every time

transcendence falls back into immanence, stagnation, there is a degradation of existence into the "*en-sois*"—the brutish life of subjection to given conditions—and of liberty into constraint and contingence. This downfall represents a moral fault if the subject consents to it; if it is inflicted upon him, it spells frustration and oppression. In both cases it is an absolute evil. Every individual concerned to justify his existence feels that his existence involves an undefined need to transcend himself, to engage in freely chosen projects.

Now, what peculiarly signalizes the situation of woman is that she—a free and autonomous being like all human creatures—nevertheless finds herself living in a world where men compel her to assume the status of the Other. They propose to stabilize her as object and to doom her to immanence since her transcendence is to be overshadowed and forever transcended by another ego (*conscience*) which is essential and sovereign. The drama of woman lies in this conflict between the fundamental aspirations of every subject (ego)—who always regards the self as the essential—and the compulsions of a situation in which she is the inessential. How can a human being in woman's situation attain fulfilment? What roads are open to her? Which are blocked? How can independence be recovered in a state of dependency? What circumstances limit woman's liberty and how can they be overcome? These are the fundamental questions on which I would fain throw some light. This means that I am interested in the fortunes of the individual as defined not in terms of happiness but in terms of liberty. [. . .]

## Study Questions

1. Provide an example of a group of people that constitutes itself as "the One" by at the same time constituting another group of people as "the Other." Explain what Beauvoir means when she says that this opposition of the One and the Other is generally both "relative" and "reciprocal," except when it comes to men and women.
2. Why might Beauvoir's *The Second Sex* be said to provide an account of identity that is relational and social, rather than individualistic? Why might Beauvoir instead be said to reinforce an

individualistic approach to identity?
3. What is the significance of Beauvoir's now-famous words "One is not born, but rather becomes, a woman"? On what basis might we say the same thing about men, and on what basis, if we take Beauvoir seriously, might we resist saying the same thing about men? Can a similar analysis be applied to race?
4. What role does "authenticity" play in Beauvoir's account?

# Thomas King

Thomas King writes novels, short stories, and screenplays. You may have heard him on CBC Radio One's *The Dead Dog Café Comedy Hour* or come across a murder mystery penned under his pseudonym, Hartley GoodWeather. Born in California to a Greek mother and Cherokee father, King received his PhD in American studies/English at the University of Utah in 1986 and is currently a professor of English and theatre studies at the University of Guelph. This reading comes from the CBC Massey lecture delivered by King in 2003.—TR

## You're Not the Indian I Had in Mind

There is a story I know. It's about the earth and how it floats in space on the back of a turtle. I've heard this story many times, and each time someone tells the story, it changes. Sometimes the change is simply in the voice of the storyteller. Sometimes the change is in the details. Sometimes in the order of events. Other times it's the dialogue or the response of the audience. But in all the tellings of all the tellers, the world never leaves the turtle's back. And the turtle never swims away.

One time, it was in Lethbridge I think, a young boy in the audience asked about the turtle and the earth. If the earth was on the back of the turtle, what was below the turtle? Another turtle, the storyteller told him. And below that turtle? Another turtle. And below that? Another turtle.

The boy began to laugh, enjoying the game, I imagine. So how many turtles are there? he wanted to know. The storyteller shrugged. No one knows for sure, she told him, but it's turtles all the way down.

The truth about stories is that that's all we are. "You can't understand the world without telling a story," the Anishinabe writer Gerald Vizenor tells us. "There isn't any centre to the world but a story" (Coltelli 156).

In 1994, I came up with the bright idea of travelling around North America and taking black-and-white portraits of Native artists. For a book. A millennium project. I figured I'd spend a couple of months each year on the road travelling to cities and towns and reserves in Canada and the United States, and when 2000 rolled around, I'd be with a terrific coffee-table book to welcome the next thousand years.

I should tell you that I had not come up with this idea on my own. As a matter of fact, Edward Sheriff Curtis had already done it. Photographed Indians, that is. Indeed, Curtis is probably the most famous of the Indian photographers. He started his project of photographing the Indians of North America around 1900, and for the next 30 years he roamed the continent, producing some 40,000 negatives, of which more than 2,200 were published.

Curtis was fascinated by the idea of the North American Indian, obsessed with it. And he was determined to capture that idea, that image, before it vanished. This was a common concern among many intellectuals and artists and social scientists at the turn of the nineteenth century, who believed that, while Europeans in the New World were poised on the brink of a new adventure, the Indian was poised on the brink of extinction.

In literature in the United States, this particular span of time is known as the American Romantic Period, and the Indian was tailor-made for it. With its emphasis on feeling, its interest in nature, its fascination with exoticism, mysticism, and eroticism, and its preoccupation with the glorification of the past, American Romanticism found in the Indian a symbol in which all these concerns could be united. Prior to the nineteenth century, the prevalent image of the Indian had been that of an inferior being. The Romantics imagined their Indian as dying. But in that dying, in that passing away, in that disappearing from the stage of human progress, there was also a sense of nobility.

One of the favourite narrative strategies was to create a single, heroic Indian (male, of course)—James Fenimore Cooper's Chingachgook, John Augustus Stone's Metamora, Henry Wadsworth Longfellow's Hiawatha—who was the last of his race. Indeed, during this period, death and nobility were sympathetic ideas that complemented one another, and writers during the first half of the nineteenth century used them in close association, creating a literary shroud in which to wrap the Indian. And bury him.

Edgar Allan Poe believed that the most poetic topic in the world was the death of a beautiful woman. From the literature produced during the nineteenth century, second place would have to go to the death of the Indian.

Not that Indians were dying. To be sure, while many of the tribes who lived along the east coast of North America, in the interior of Lower Canada, and in the Connecticut, Ohio, and St Lawrence river valleys had been injured and disoriented by the years of almost continuous warfare, by European diseases, and by the destructive push of settlers for cheap land, the vast majority of the tribes were a comfortable distance away from the grave.

This was the Indian of fact.

In 1830, when the American president, Andrew Jackson, fulfilling an election promise to his western and southern supporters, pushed the Removal Act through Congress, he did so in order to get rid of thousands of Indians—particularly the Cherokees, Choctaws, Chickasaws, Creeks, and Seminoles—who were not dying and not particularly interested in going anywhere.

These were not the Indians Curtis went west to find.

Curtis was looking for the literary Indian, the dying Indian, the imaginative construct. And to make sure that he would find what he wanted to find, he took along boxes of "Indian" paraphernalia—wigs, blankets, painted backdrops, clothing—in case he ran into Indians who did not look as the Indian was supposed to look.

I collect postcards. Old ones, new ones. Postcards that depict Indians or Indian subjects. I have one from the 1920s that shows an Indian lacrosse team in Oklahoma. Another is a hand-coloured rendering of the Sherman Indian School in California. A third is a cartoon of an Indian man fishing in the background while, in the foreground, a tourist takes a picture of the man's wife and their seven kids with the rather puerile caption "And what does the chief do when he's not fishing?"

One of my favourites is a photograph of a group of Indians, in full headdresses, golfing at the Banff Springs Hotel golf course in 1903. The photograph was taken by Byron Harmon and shows Jim Brewster and Norman Luxton, two Banff locals, caddying for what looks to be five Indians who are identified only as "two Stoney Indian Chiefs." I like this particular postcard because there is an element of play in the image of Indians in beaded outfits and full headdresses leaning on their golf clubs while their horses graze in the background, and because I can't tell if the person on the tee with bobbed hair, wearing what looks to be a dress and swinging the club, is an Indian or a white, a man or a woman.

But the vast majority of my postcards offer no such mysteries. They are simply pictures and paintings of Indians in feathers and leathers, sitting in or around teepees or chasing buffalo on pinto ponies.

Some of these postcards are old, but many of them are brand new, right off the rack. Two are contemporary pieces from the Postcard Factory in Markham, Ontario. The first shows an older Indian man in a full beaded and fringed leather outfit with an eagle feather war bonnet and a lance, sitting on a horse, set against a backdrop of trees and mountains. The second is a group of five Indians, one older man in a full headdress sitting on a horse and four younger men on foot: two with bone breastplates, one with a leather vest, and one bare chested. The interesting thing about these two postcards is that the solitary man on his horse is identified only as a "Cree Indian," while the group of five is designated as "Native Indians," much like the golfers, as if none of them had names or identities other than the cliché. Though to give them identities, to reveal them to be actual people, would be, I suppose, a violation of the physical laws governing matter and antimatter, that the Indian and Indians cannot exist in the same imagination.

Which must be why the white caddies on the Banff postcard have names.

And the Indians do not.

It is my postcard Indian that Curtis was after. And in spite of the fact that Curtis met a great variety of Native people who would have given the lie to the construction, in spite of the fact that he fought vigorously for Native rights and published articles and books that railed against the government's treatment of Indians, this was the Indian that Curtis believed in.

I probably sound a little cranky. I don't mean to. I know Curtis paid Indians to shave away any facial hair. I know he talked them into wearing wigs. I know that he would provide one tribe of Indians with clothing from another tribe because the clothing looked more "Indian."

So his photographs would look authentic.

And while there is a part of me that would have preferred that Curtis had photographed his Indians as he found them, the men with crewcuts and moustaches, the women in cotton print dresses, I am grateful that we have his images at all, for the faces of the mothers and fathers, aunts and uncles, sisters and brothers who look at you from the depths of these photographs are not romantic illusions, they are real people.

Native culture, as with any culture, is a vibrant, changing thing, and when Curtis happened upon it, it was changing from what it had been to what it would become next. But the idea of "the Indian" was already fixed in time and space. Even before Curtis built his first camera, that image had been set. His task as he visited tribe after tribe was to sort through what he saw in order to find what he needed.

But to accuse Curtis of romantic myopia is to be petty and to ignore the immensity of the project and the personal and economic ordeal that he undertook. He spent his life photographing and writing about Indians. He died harnessed to that endeavour, and, when I look at his photographs, I can imagine this solitary man moving across the prairies, through the forests, along the coast, dragging behind him an enormous camera and tripod and the cultural expectations of an emerging nation, and I am humbled.

So when I set out in the fall of 1995 on what I had pompously decided to call the Medicine River Photographic Expedition, I was stuffed full of high expectations. My brother Christopher, who is a fine woodworker and three years younger than I, wanted to come along. He told me that the expedition sounded like fun and the prospect of meeting other Native artists was appealing.

My mother, fearful that her only children might get lost in the heart of the heart of the country, cooked and packed us six roast chickens, twenty dozen chocolate chip cookies, an entire tree of bananas, a vineyard of grapes, an orchard of apples and oranges, four loaves of bread, a case of drinking water, candy (in case we ran out of cookies, I guess), and four pounds of butter. Along with a complete set of maps of the provinces and states, three flashlights of varying sizes, a highway hazard warning light, a car-battery charging system with an electrical tire inflater, several pamphlets on how to survive in the wilderness, and a compass.

After we had packed and said our goodbyes, she walked alongside the car all the way to the street and had us roll down the window so she could tell us to drive carefully.

As we slipped onto the interstate, the Volvo stuffed with camera gear and the better part of a grocery store, and began following my bright idea down to the American Southwest, I can remember thinking that Curtis couldn't have been any better outfitted.

In Roseville, California, where I grew up, race was little more than a series of cultural tributaries that flowed through the town, coming together in confluences, swinging away into eddies. There were at least three main streams, Mexicans, the Mediterranean folk—Italians and Greeks—and the general mix of Anglo-Saxons that a Japanese friend of mine, years later, would refer to as the Crazy Caucasoids. But in Roseville in the late 1950s and early 1960s, there were no Asian families that I can remember, and the picture I have of my 1961 graduating class does not contain a single black face.

If there was a racial divide in the town, it was the line between the Mexicans and everyone else. Some of the Mexican families had been in the area long before California fell to the Americans in 1848 as a spoil of war. The rest had come north later to work the fields and had settled in Roseville and the other small towns—Elk Grove, Lodi, Stockton, Turlock, Merced, Fresno—that ran through the heart of the Sacramento and San Joaquin valleys.

I went to school with Hernandezes and Gomezes. But I didn't socialize with them, didn't even know where they lived. My brother and I kept pretty much to our own neighbourhood, a five- or six-block area on the northwestern edge of town bounded by auction yards and an ocean of open fields.

Racism is a funny thing, you know. Dead quiet on occasion. Often dangerous. But sometimes it has a peculiar sense of humour. The guys I ran with looked at Mexicans with a certain disdain. I'd like to say that I didn't, but that wasn't true. No humour here. Except that while I was looking at Mexicans, other people, as it turned out, were looking at me.

In my last year of high school, I mustered enough courage to ask Karen Butler to go to the prom with me. That's not her real name, of course. I've changed it so I don't run the risk of embarrassing her for something that wasn't her fault.

I should probably begin by saying that at 18, I was not the prettiest of creatures. Tall and skinny, with no more coordination than a three-legged stepladder, I also had drawn the pimple card to brighten my adolescence.

Pimples. The word has an almost dainty sound to it. Like "dimples." But my pimples were not annoying little flares that appeared here and there but rather large, erupting pustules that hurled magma and spewed lava. They crowded against the sides of my nose, burrowed around my lips, and spread out across my chin and forehead like a cluster of volcanic islands.

Roseville was a railroad town. Until the hospital and the shopping centre were built on the southeast side, most everyone lived north of the tracks. Karen was from the south side, one of the new subdivisions, what cultural theorists in the late twentieth century would call "havens of homogeneity."

Karen's mother was a schoolteacher. Her father was a doctor. My mother ran a small beauty shop out of a converted garage. Karen's family was upper middle class. We weren't. Still, there was a levelling of sorts, for Karen had a heart defect. It didn't affect her so far as I could tell, but I figured that being well off with a heart defect was pretty much the same as being poor with pimples. So I asked her if she wanted to go to the prom with me, and she said yes.

Then about a week before the big evening, Karen called me to say that she couldn't go to the dance after all. I'm sorry, she told me. It's my father. He doesn't want me dating Mexicans.

It took my brother and me four days to drive to New Mexico. We could have made the trip in three days, but we kept getting sidetracked by interesting stops. My favourite was a McDonald's on the Will Rogers Turnpike near Claremore, Oklahoma. I generally avoid places like McDonald's but this one had a tiny Will Rogers museum on the first floor of the restaurant, as well a statue of Rogers himself in the parking lot standing next to a flagpole, twirling a rope.

Tourists pulling off the turnpike and seeing the statue for the first time would probably think Rogers was some kind of famous cowboy. In fact, he was a famous Indian, a sort of Indian/cowboy, a Cherokee to be exact.

But most importantly, he was what the political and literary theorist Antonio Gramsci called an "organic" intellectual, an individual who articulates the understandings of a community or a nation. During the 1930s Rogers was probably the most famous man in North America. He performed in circuses and Wild West shows. He starred in the Ziegfeld Follies, and from 1933 to 1935 he was the top male motion-picture box-office attraction. Over 40 million people read his newspaper columns on everything from gun control to Congress, and even more listened to his weekly radio show. He did just about everything with the exception of running for office. "I ain't going to try that," he said. "I've got some pride left."

Rogers was born near Claremore, Oklahoma, and his family was prominent in the Cherokee Nation. But he didn't look Indian. Not in that constructed way. Certainly not in the way Curtis wanted Indians to look. And tourists pulling into the parking lot and seeing the statue for the first time would never know that this was an Indian as famous as Sitting Bull or Crazy Horse or Geronimo.

Christopher must have read my mind. The Indians we're going to photograph, he said, walking over to the statue. What if they all look like Rogers? I know he's Indian, said my brother, and you know he's Indian, but how is anyone else going to be able to tell?

Curtis wasn't the only photographer in the early twentieth century who was taking pictures of Indians. So was Richard Throssel. Unless you're a photography buff, you won't know the name and will therefore have no way of knowing that Throssel was not only a contemporary of Curtis's, but that he was also Native. Cree to be exact. Adopted by the Crow. Throssel even met Curtis, when Curtis came to the Crow reservation.

Throssel took many of the same sort of romantic photographs as Curtis, photographs such as "The Sentinel," which shows an Indian in a feathered headdress, holding a lance, and sitting on a horse, all in silhouette, set against a dramatic sky, or "The Feathered Horsemen," which records a party of Indians on horses coming through a stand of teepees, the men wearing feathered headdresses and carrying bows and arrows and lances.

But he also took other photographs, photographs that moved away from romance toward environmental and social comment, photographs that did not imagine the Indian as dying or particularly noble, photographs that suggested that Indians were contemporary as well as historical figures. His photograph of Bull Over the Hill's home titled "The Old and the New," which shows a log house with a tipi in the background, and his 1910 photograph "Interior of the Best Indian Kitchen on the Crow Reservation," which shows an Indian family dressed in "traditional" clothing sitting at an elegantly set table in their very contemporary house having tea, suggest that Native people could negotiate the past and the present with relative ease. His untitled camp scene that juxtaposes traditional teepees with contemporary buggies and a family of pigs, rather than with unshod ponies and the prerequisite herd of buffalo, suggests, at least to my contemporary sensibilities, that Throssel had a penchant for satiric play.

But I'm probably imagining the humour. Throssel was, after all, a serious photographer trying to capture a moment, perhaps not realizing that tripping the shutter captures nothing, that everything on the ground glass changes before the light hits the film plane. What the camera allows you to do is to invent, to create. That's really what photographs are. Not records of moments, but rather imaginative acts.

Still, neither Curtis nor Throssel had to deal with the Rogers conundrum. Or perhaps neither chose to. Throssel's Indians, even the ones set against contemporary backdrops, were, like Curtis's Indians, all visually Indian. And when we look at his photographs, we see what we expect to see.

The Choctaw-Cherokee-Irish writer Louis Owens, in his memoir *I Hear the Train: Reflections, Inventions, Refractions,* deals with the issue of photographs and expectations. Looking through a collection of old photographs of his mixed-blood family, Owens can find no "Indians." "This family from whom I am descended," he says, "wears no recognizably Indian cultural artifacts; nor are they surrounded by any such signifiers. (Though there is possibility in the blanket nailed across the cabin door: what if my great-grandfather had perversely wrapped the blanket around himself for this picture?) . . . To find the Indian in the photographic cupboard, I must narratively construct him out of his missing presence, for my great-grandfather was Indian but not *an Indian*" (91–2).

Of course, all this—my expedition, Throssel's images, Owens's family portraits—are reminders of how hard it is to break free from the parochial and paradoxical considerations of identity and authenticity. Owens, in a particularly wry moment, notes that "few looking at [these] photos of mixedbloods would be likely to say, "But they don't look like

Irishmen," but everyone seems obligated to offer an opinion regarding the degree of Indianness represented" (103).

In Curtis's magnum opus, *Portraits from North American Indian Life,* we don't see a collection of photographs of Indian people. We see race. Never mind that race is a construction and an illusion. Never mind that it does not exist in either biology or theology, though both have, from time to time, been enlisted in the cause of racism. Never mind that we can't hear it or smell it or taste it or feel it. The important thing is that we believe we can see it.

In fact, we hope we can see it. For one of the conundrums of the late twentieth century that we've hauled into the twenty-first is that many of our mothers and fathers, who were pursued by missionaries, educators, and government officials (armed with residential schools, European history, legislation such as the Indian Act, the Termination Act, and the Relocation Program of the 1950s), who were forcibly encouraged to give up their identities, now have children who are *determined* to be *seen* as Indians. Louis Owens isn't the only Native person who has sorted through old photographs and looked in cold mirrors for that visual confirmation.

When I was going to university, there was an almost irresistible pull to become what Gerald Vizenor calls a "cultural ritualist," a kind of "pretend" Indian, an Indian who has to dress up like an Indian and act like an Indian in order to be recognized as an Indian. And in the 1970s, being recognized as an Indian was critical. And here tribal affiliation was not a major consideration. We didn't dress up as nineteenth-century Cherokees or as the Apache, Choctaw, Lakota, Tlingit, Ojibway, Blackfoot, or Haida had dressed. We dressed up as the "Indian" dressed. We dressed up in a manner to substantiate the cultural lie that had trapped us, and we did so with a passion. I have my own box of photographs. Pictures of me in my "Indian" outfits, pictures of me being "Indian," pictures of me in groups of other "Indians."

Not wanting to be mistaken for a Mexican or a white, I grew my hair long, bought a fringed leather pouch to hang off my belt, threw a four-strand bone choker around my neck, made a headband out of an old neckerchief, and strapped on a beaded belt buckle that I had bought at a trading post on a reservation in Wyoming. Trinkets of the trade.

I did resist feathers but that was my only concession to cultural sanity.

Not that university was my first experience with the narrow parameters of race. In 1964, I fell into a job as a junior executive at the Bank of America in San Francisco. Junior executive sounds grand, but as I discovered after the first few days, this was what the bank called men who worked as tellers, as opposed to the women who worked as tellers and who were just called tellers. These terms, though I didn't understand it at the time, were innate promises that men had possibilities of advancement, while women did not.

In any case, it was a boring job, and by the end of the first month I was looking for another career. I didn't find it, but I did meet a woman who worked for a steamship company. Each week, on Friday, she would come in and deposit the company's earnings. I was bored. She was bored. So we talked. The steamship company she worked for was called Columbus Lines, an irony that was not lost on me, and, occasionally, she told me, they would take on "passengers" who could earn their one-way passage to Australia by working aboard the ship.

As it happened, I knew quite a bit about Australia. Just before I moved to San Francisco, I had worked at South Shore Lake Tahoe, a gambling, fun-in-the-sun mecca in the Sierra Nevada Mountains, where I had dated a woman from Australia. Her name was Sharon or Sherry and she told me all about the country, its beaches, the outback, the sharks. To hear her tell it, the place was bristling with adventure, and, three weeks into our relationship, I applied for an immigration visa. At eight weeks our relationship was over. At the twelve-week mark, just as I was packing to go to San Francisco, my visa arrived. I put it in the box with the books and forgot about it.

Amazing the way things come around.

The next week I asked the woman from the steamship company what the chances were of my getting a one-way job on one of the company's ships, and she told me she thought they were good. I must admit I could hardly contain my excitement.

Tom King, on a tramp steamer. Tom King, sailing off on a great adventure. Tom King, explorer of known worlds.

So I was disappointed when she came back the next week to tell me that the list of people who wanted to work their way to Australia was quite long and that nothing would come open for at least a year. However, there was a ship sailing for New Zealand in a week, and there was one spot left on the crew. If I wanted it, she said, it was mine.

And so I went. Packed everything I owned into two cheap metal trunks and hauled them to the docks. By the end of the week, I was at sea.

The ship was a German vessel out of Hamburg, the SS *Cap Colorado*. The captain was German. The crew was German. The cook was German. I wasn't German. As a matter of fact, none of the crew was sure what I was. When I told them I was Cherokee, or to keep matters simple, a North American Indian, they were intrigued.

And suspicious.

The cook, who could speak passable English, told me that he had read all of Karl May's novels and had a fair idea of what Indians were supposed to look like and that I wasn't what he had imagined.

"You're not the Indian I had in mind," he told me.

Here was a small dilemma. Of all the crew members on that ship, the one person I didn't want to offend was the cook. I knew that Indians came in all shapes and sizes and colours, but I hadn't read Karl May, had no idea who he was. The cook had read May but had never actually seen an Indian. So we compromised. I confessed that I was a mixed-blood, and he allowed that this was possible, since May had described full-blood Apaches and not mixed-blood Cherokees.

I discovered some years later that May had never seen an Indian, either, but on board that ship it was probably just as well that I did not know this.

I spent almost a year in New Zealand. I worked as a deer culler, a beer bottle sorter, a freezer packer, and a photographer. I liked the country and might well have stayed had it not been for a phone call I got early one morning. It was a British-sounding man who introduced himself as an official with the immigration department.

If I'm not mistaken, he said, clipping the edges off each consonant, you entered the country eleven months ago on a 30-day tourist visa and are therefore in violation of New Zealand immigration laws.

I agreed that he was probably correct.

When might we expect you to leave? he wanted to know.

As I said, I liked the place, had no plans to leave. So I asked him if there was any chance of applying for an immigration visa.

It turned out my immigration man had only newly arrived from England the month before to take up his duties and wasn't sure if this was possible. But he would check into it, he told me. In the meantime, would I give him some of my particulars.

It was the usual stuff. Name. Colour of hair. Colour of eyes. Height. Weight. Race.

Black, brown, six feet six inches, 230 pounds. Indian.

Dear me, he said. I don't believe we take applications from Indians.

I have to admit I was stunned. Why not? I wanted to know.

Policy, said the immigration man.

Do you get many? I asked.

Oh, yes, he said. Thousands.

I hadn't heard of any mass exodus of Native peoples from Canada or the States. These Indians, I asked him, where are they from? Alberta? Saskatchewan? Arizona? South Dakota? Oklahoma?

Dear me, no, said my British voice. They're from, you know, New Delhi, Bombay. . .

When Karen told me her father wouldn't let me take her to the prom because he didn't want her dating Mexicans, I told her I wasn't Mexican. I was Indian.

When the immigration officer told me I couldn't apply for a visa because I was Indian, I told him I wasn't East Indian, I was North American Indian.

As if that was going to settle anything.

Without missing a beat, and at the same time injecting a note of enthusiasm into his otherwise precise voice, the immigration man said, What? Do you mean like cowboys and Indians?

The next week, I was on a ship for Australia. As it turned out, that immigration visa I had was still good. As for Karen, well, I went to the prom that year. But I went alone.

The first three or four months I was in Australia, I travelled around, working my way up the east coast and into the interior. At Rockhampton, I made pocket money helping a man and his son dismantle a small house. At Tennent Creek, I worked at a mine shovelling ore into sacks. In Adelaide, I cleaned trucks. But in all my travels, I never met an indigenous Australian. In New Zealand, I had met a great many Maoris, and while there had been friction between Maoris and Europeans, the two groups seemed to have organized themselves around an uneasy peace between equals. In Australia, there was no such peace. Just a damp, sweltering campaign of discrimination that you could feel on your skin and smell in your hair.

The Aboriginal people, I was told, were failing. They were dying off at such a rate that they wouldn't last another decade. It was sad to see them passing away, but their problem, according to the men who gathered in the bars after work, was that they did not have the same mental capacities as whites. There was no point in educating them because they had no interest in improving their lot and were perfectly happy living in poverty and squalor.

The curious thing about these stories was I had heard them all before, knew them, in fact, by heart.

Eventually I wound up in Sydney and lied my way into a job as a journalist with a third-rate magazine called *Everybody's*—a disingenuous name if ever there was one. I got the job, in part, because I was an American and an Indian—the exotic combination being too much for folks to resist—and I was sent out on jobs that required the firm hand of a reporter of exotic background. I filed stories about teenagers having a good time drinking themselves into a stupor and jumping off cliffs into the ocean, about escorting a chimpanzee around the city and showing her the sights, about spending an exhilarating afternoon with the self-proclaimed king of tic-tac-toe, discussing strategies and secret moves.

Almost certainly, the high point of my journalistic career was dragging one of those plastic blow-up dollies around on a date that included dinner and a movie. You'll probably think poorly of me, but I didn't really mind doing these idiotic assignments. Actually, many of them were fun. Best of all, I had a professional job. Race, which had periodically been something of a burden, was suddenly something of an advantage.

There was a photographer who worked for the magazine. Let's say that, after all these years, I've forgotten his name. So, we'll call him Lee. Lee was a decent enough guy, but on Friday afternoons when we got paid and adjourned to the local pub to drink and review the week, he would turn into a boor. The kind of boor who, after half a dozen beers and a few whisky chasers, liked to expound on what was wrong with the country. Government was at the top of his list, followed closely by Australia's "Abo" problem—"Abo" being Australia's derogatory term for the Aboriginal people. And because there were no Aboriginal people in the immediate vicinity, Lee spent many of these smoky evenings sharpening his soggy wit on me.

Lee didn't know any more about Indians than had the cook on the tramp steamer or Karl May or the immigration man, but he reckoned that North Americans had taken care of the problem in a reasonably expedient fashion. I'm embarrassed to repeat his exact words but the gist of it was that North Americans had shot Native men and bred Native women until they were white.

In a perverse way, I've always liked people like Lee. They are, by and large, easy to deal with. Their racism is honest and straightforward. You don't have to go looking for it in a phrase or a gesture. And you don't have to wonder if you're being too sensitive. Best of all, they remind me how the past continues to inform the present.

One Monday, Lee stopped by my desk with a present for me. It was a cartoon that he had gotten one of the guys in the art department to work up. It showed a stereotypical Indian in feathers and leathers with a bull's eye on his crotch and flies buzzing around him. "Office of Chief Screaching [sic] Eagle Goldstein," the caption read. "Payola and bribes acceptable in the form of checks or money orders. No silver please." Just above the Indian was "Happy Barmizvah Keemosaby" and just below was "only living Cherokee Jew."

Lee stood at my desk, waiting for me to smile. I told him it was funny as hell, and he said, yeah, everyone he had showed it to thought it was a scream. I had the cartoon mounted on a board and stuck it on my desk.

I still have it. Just in case I forget.

So it was unanimous. Everyone knew who Indians were. Everyone knew what we looked like. Even Indians. But standing in that parking lot in Oklahoma with my brother, looking at the statue of Will Rogers, I realized, for perhaps the first time, that I didn't know. Or more accurately, I didn't know how I wanted to represent Indians. My brother was right. Will Rogers did not look like an Indian. Worse, as I cast my mind across the list of Native artists I had come west to photograph, many of them friends, I realized that a good number of them didn't look Indian, either.

Yet how can something that has never existed—the Indian—have form and power while something that is alive and kicking—Indians—are invisible?

Edward Sheriff Curtis.

James Fenimore Cooper, George Catlin, Paul Kane, Charles Bird King, Karl May, the Atlanta Braves, the Washington Redskins, the Chicago Blackhawks, Pontiac (the car, not the Indian), Land O'Lakes butter, Calumet baking soda, Crazy Horse Malt Liquor, *A Man Called Horse,* Iron Eyes Cody, *Dances with Wolves, The Searchers*, the Indian Motorcycle Company, American Spirit tobacco, Native American Barbie, Chippewa Springs Golf Course, John Augustus Stone, the Cleveland Indians, Disney's Pocahontas, Geronimo shoes, the Calgary Stampede, Cherokee brand underwear, the Improved Order of Red Men, Ralph Hubbard and his Boy Scout troop, Mutual of Omaha, Buffalo Bill's Wild West Show, the Boston Tea Party, Frank Hamilton Cushing, William Wadsworth Longfellow, the Bank of Montreal, Chief's Trucking, Grey Owl, *The Sioux Spaceman*, Red Man chewing tobacco, Grateful Dead concerts, Dreamcatcher perfume.

In the end, there is no reason for the Indian to be real. The Indian simply has to exist in our imaginations.

But for those of us who are Indians, this disjunction between reality and imagination is akin to life and death. For to be seen as "real," for people to "imagine" us as Indians, we must be "authentic."

In the past, authenticity was simply in the eye of the beholder. Indians who looked Indian were authentic. Authenticity only became a problem for Native people in the twentieth century. While it is true that mixed-blood and full-blood rivalries predate this period, the question of who was an Indian and who was not was easier to settle. What made it easy was that most Indians lived on reserves of one sort or another (out of sight of Europeans) and had strong ties to a particular community, and the majority of those people who "looked Indian" and those who did not at least had a culture and a language in common.

This is no longer as true as it once was, for many Native people now live in cities, with only tenuous ties to a reserve or a nation. Many no longer speak their Native language, a gift of colonialism, and the question of identity has become as much a personal matter as it is a matter of blood. N. Scott Momaday has suggested that being Native is an idea that an individual has of themselves. Momaday, who is Kiowa, is not suggesting that anyone who wants to can imagine themselves to be Indian. He is simply acknowledging that language and narrow definitions of culture are not the only ways identity can be constructed. Yet, in the absence of visual confirmation, these "touchstones"—race, culture, language, blood—still form a kind of authenticity test, a racial-reality game that contemporary Native people are forced to play. And here are some of the questions.

Were you born on a reserve? Small, rural towns with high Native populations will do. Cities will not.

Do you speak your Native language? Not a few phrases here and there. Fluency is the key. No fluency, no Indian.

Do you participate in your tribe's ceremonies? Being a singer or a dancer is a plus, but not absolutely required.

Are you a full-blood?

Are you a status Indian?

Are you enrolled?

You may suspect me of hyperbole, but many of these were questions that I was asked by a selection committee when I applied for a Ford Foundation Grant for American Indians in order to complete my PhD. I've told this story a number of times at various events, and each time I've told it, one or two non-Natives have come up to me afterwards and apologized for the stereotypical attitudes of a few misguided whites. But the truth of the matter is that the selection committee was composed entirely of Native people. And the joke, if there is one, is that most of the committee couldn't pass this test, either, for these questions were not designed to measure academic potential or to ensure diversity, they were designed to exclude. For the real value of authenticity is in the rarity of a thing.

Of course, outside grant selection committees and possibly guards at the new and improved US border crossings, not many people ask these questions. They don't have to. They're content simply looking at you. If you don't look Indian, you aren't. If you don't look white, you're not.

As I pulled out of the McDonald's parking lot, I began thinking about my dilemma in earnest. Edward Sheriff Curtis had been successful in raising money and getting his photographs in print because he was fulfilling a national fantasy, and because he documented the only antiquity that North America would ever have. Indians might not have been Greeks or Romans or Egyptians, but Indians were all the continent had to offer to a society that relished the past. I could not photograph that particular antiquity, not because it had vanished, but because it had changed.

When I came up with my bright idea for a photographic expedition, I sat down with a number of granting agencies to see if there was any chance of getting some financial support for the project. Several of them thought the idea had merit, but they weren't sure why I wanted to do it.

Which Indians did I have in mind, they wanted to know. How would I find these Indians? How would taking photographs of Native artists benefit Native people?

Had **J.P. Morgan** asked that question of Edward Curtis, Curtis probably would have told him that such photographs were necessary because the Indian was dying, and if he hesitated, the Noble Red Man would be gone and that part of America's antiquity would be lost forever. Curtis might have even thrown up John Audubon and Audubon's great endeavour to paint the birds of North America, many of whom were on the verge of extinction and might well have been helped on their way, since, in order to paint the birds, Audubon first had to kill them.

So they wouldn't move and spoil the sitting.

How will taking photographs of Native artists benefit Native people?

It wasn't a question I would have ever asked. It was a question—and I understood this part clearly—that came out of a Western Judeo-Christian sense of responsibility and that contained the unexamined implication that the lives of Native people needed improvement. I knew, without a doubt, that the pictures I was taking would not change the lives of the people I photographed any more than the arrivals and departures of, say, anthropologists on Native reserves had done anything to improve the lives of the people they came to study.

I teach at a university, so I know all about the enthusiasm for creating social change through intellectual and artistic activity, especially within what we ironically call the "humanities." And while we have had our fair share of literary critics who have believed in the potentials of literature—Sir Philip Sidney, Matthew Arnold, F.R. and Queenie Leavis—it goes without saying, I think, that, apart from recent feminist and Marxist critics who seek to engage literature in the enterprise of social and political transformation, the study of literature, especially in the wake of New Criticism, has not had a sustained political component.

So I was, in many ways, delighted to see post-colonial studies arrive on campus, not only because it expanded the canon by insisting that we read, consider, and teach the literatures of colonized peoples, but because it promised to give Native people a place at the table. I know that post-colonial studies is not a panacea for much of anything. I know that it never promised explicitly to make the colonized world a better place for colonized peoples. It did, however, carry with it the implicit expectation that, through exposure to new literatures and cultures and challenges to hegemonic assumptions and power structures, lives would be made better.

At least the lives of the theorists.

But perhaps that was it. Perhaps I was travelling around the country taking portraits of Native artists because the project promised to make my life better, to make me feel valuable, to make me feel important.

How will photographing Native artists benefit Native people? You see this basic kind of question in various guises on the "human study" portion of grant applications, and you hear it debated on talk shows and in churches. Politicians use it as a ploy because they know that political memory is not even short term. Advertisers transform the question into a glimmering promise that if you buy their products—deodorants, frozen pizzas, magic beans—your life will improve. It is the great Western come-on. The North American Con. The Caucasoid Sting.

Actually, I'm no better. If you've been paying attention, you will have noticed that I've defined identity politics in a rather narrow and self-serving fashion.

Appearance.

I want to look Indian so that you will see me as Indian because I want to be Indian, even though being Indian and looking Indian is more a disadvantage than it is a luxury.

Just not for me.

Middle-class Indians, such as myself, can, after all, afford the burden of looking Indian. There's little danger that *we'll* be stuffed into the trunk of a police cruiser and dropped off on the outskirts of Saskatoon.[1] Not much chance that *we'll* come before the courts and be incarcerated for a longer period of time than our non-Indian brethren. Hardly any risk that *our* children will be taken from us because we are unable to cope with the potentials of poverty.

That sort of thing happens to those other Indians. My relatives. My friends.

Just not me.

To date, I've photographed about 500 Native artists. In that time some of the people, such as the Navajo artist Carl Gorman, have died. Before I finish, more will pass away, and new ones will take their place. I may never finish the project, may never see the book I had imagined when my brother and I headed off that first time almost ten years ago. But it doesn't matter. The photographs themselves are no longer the issue. Neither are the questions of identity. What's important are the stories I've heard along the way. And the stories I've told. Stories we make up to try to set the world straight.

Take Will Rogers's story, for instance. It's yours. Do with it what you will. Make it the topic of a discussion group at a scholarly conference. Put it on the Web. Forget it. But don't say in the years to come that you would have lived your life differently if only you had heard this story.

You've heard it now.

## Note

1. In November 1990, 17-year-old Neil Stonechild, last seen in the back of a Saskatoon Police cruiser, was found dead of hypothermia in a field on the outskirts of the city. Several other Aboriginal men died in similar circumstances before a Saskatchewan government inquiry into Stonechild's death was held more than a decade later.—LG

## Works Cited

Coltelli, L. *Winged Words: American Indian Writers Speak*. Lincoln: University of Nebraska Press, 1990.

Owens, L. *I Hear the Train: Reflections, Inventions, Refractions*. Norman: University of Oklahoma Press, 2001.

## Study Questions

1. King presents a narrative account of personal identity: he writes, "The truth about stories is that that's all we are." Explain what he means by this.
2. King asks: "Yet how can something that has never existed—the Indian—have form and power while something that is alive and kicking—Indians—are invisible?" Explain the significance of this question.
3. What role does "authenticity" play in King's account?
4. About the "honest and straightforward" racism of people like his magazine photographer colleague "Lee," King writes: "Best of all, they remind me how the past continues to inform the present." Do you think that racist attitudes alleging the biologically based inferiority of some groups compared to others persist today?

## ⌐ FREEDOM AND DETERMINISM ⌐

---

## Baron d'Holbach

---

French Enlightenment philosopher Paul-Henri Thiry, Baron d'Holbach (1723–89) lived in Paris, famously hosting dinner parties attended by leading intellectuals of his day, such as philosophers David Hume and Jean-Jacques Rousseau. *The System of Nature*, which was published under the pseudonym M. Mirabaud in 1770, was condemned by the Paris parliament and publicly burned because Holbach's materialist metaphysics denied the existence of god, the soul, and free will.—TR

# Of the System of Man's Free Agency

From *The System of Nature*

## 1. Materialism

Those who have pretended that the *soul* is distinguished from the body, is immaterial, draws its ideas from its own peculiar source, acts by its own energies, without the aid of any exterior object, have, by a consequence of their own system, enfranchised it from those physical laws according to which all beings of which we have a knowledge are obliged to act. They have believed that the soul is mistress of its own conduct, is able to regulate its own peculiar operations, has the faculty to determine its will by its own natural energy; in a word, they have pretended that man is a *free agent*.

It has been already sufficiently proved that the soul is nothing more than the body considered relatively to some of its functions more concealed than others: it has been shown that this soul, even when it shall be supposed immaterial, is continually modified conjointly with the body, is submitted to all its motion, and that without this it would remain inert and dead: that, consequently, it is subjected to the influence of those material and physical causes which give impulse to the body; of which the mode of existence, whether habitual or transitory, depends upon the material elements by which it is surrounded, that form its texture, constitute its temperament, enter into it by means of the aliments, and penetrate it by their subtility. The faculties which are called *intellectual*, and those qualities which are styled *moral*, have been explained in a manner purely physical and natural. In the last place it has been demonstrated that all the ideas, all the systems, all the affections, all the opinions, whether true or false, which man forms to himself, are to be attributed to his physical and material senses. Thus man is a being purely physical; in whatever manner he is considered, he is connected to universal nature, and submitted to the necessary and immutable laws that she imposes on all the beings she contains, according to their peculiar essences or conformable to the respective properties with which, without consulting them, she endows each particular species. Man's life is a line that nature commands him to describe upon the surface of the earth, without his ever being able to swerve from it, even for an instant. He is born without his own consent; his organization does in nowise depend upon himself; his ideas come to him involuntarily; his habits are in the power of those who cause him to contract them; he is unceasingly modified by causes, whether visible or concealed, over which he has no control, which necessarily regulate his mode of existence, give the hue to his way of thinking, and determine his manner of acting. He is good or bad, happy or miserable, wise or foolish, reasonable or irrational, without his will being for anything in these various states. Nevertheless, despite the shackles by which he is bound, it is pretended he is a free agent, or that independent of the causes by which he is moved, he determines his own will and regulates his own condition.

However slender the foundation of this opinion, of which everything ought to point out to him the error, it is current at this day and passes for an incontestable truth with a great number of people, otherwise extremely enlightened; it is the basis for religion, which, supposing relations between man and the unknown being she has placed above nature, has been incapable of imagining how man could either merit reward or deserve punishment from this being, if he was not a free agent. Society has been believed interested in this system because an idea has gone abroad that if all the actions of man were to be contemplated as necessary, the right of punishing those who injure their associates would no longer exist. At length human vanity accommodated itself to a hypothesis which, unquestionably, appears to distinguish man from all other physical beings, by assigning to him the special privilege of a total independence of all other causes, but of which a very little reflection would have shown him the impossibility.

## 2. Will as a Modification of the Brain

The will, as we have elsewhere said, is a modification of the brain, by which it is disposed to action, or prepared to give play to the organs. This will is necessarily determined by the qualities, good or bad, agreeable or painful, of the object or the motive that acts upon his senses, or of which the idea remains with him, and is resuscitated by his memory. In consequence, he acts necessarily, his action is the result of the impulse he receives either from the motive, from the object, or from the idea which has modified his brain, or disposed his will. When he does not act according to this impulse, it is because there comes some new cause, some new motive, some new idea, which modifies his brain in a different manner, gives him a new impulse, determines his will in another way, by which the action of the former impulse is suspended: thus, the sight of an agreeable object, or its idea, determines his will to set him in action to procure it; but if a new object or a new idea more

powerfully attracts him, it gives a new direction to his will, annihilates the effect of the former, and prevents the action by which it was to be procured. This is the mode in which reflection, experience, reason, necessarily arrests or suspends the action of man's will: without this he would of necessity have followed the anterior impulse which carried him towards a then desirable object. In all this he always acts according to necessary laws, from which he has no means of emancipating himself.

If when tormented with violent thirst, he figures to himself in idea, or really perceives a fountain, whose limpid streams might cool his feverish want, is he sufficient master of himself to desire or not to desire the object competent to satisfy so lively a want? It will no doubt be conceded that it is impossible he should not be desirous to satisfy it; but it will be said—if at this moment it is announced to him that the water he so ardently desires is poisoned, he will, notwithstanding his vehement thirst, abstain from drinking it: and it has, therefore, been falsely concluded that he is a free agent. The fact, however, is that the motive in either case is exactly the same: his own conservation. The same necessity that determined him to drink before he knew the water was deleterious, upon this new discovery equally determines him not to drink; the desire of conserving himself either annihilates or suspends the former impulse; the second motive becomes stronger than the preceding, that is, the fear of death, or the desire of preserving himself, necessarily prevails over the painful sensation caused by his eagerness to drink: but, it will be said, if the thirst is very parching, an inconsiderate man without regarding the danger will risk swallowing the water. Nothing is gained by this remark: in this case, the anterior impulse only regains the ascendency; he is persuaded that life may possibly be longer preserved, or that he shall derive a greater good by drinking the poisoned water than by enduring the torment, which, to his mind, threatens instant dissolution: thus, the first becomes the strongest and necessarily urges him on to action. Nevertheless, in either case, whether he partakes of the water, or whether he does not, the two actions will be equally necessary; they will be the effect of that motive which finds itself most powerful, which consequently acts in the most coercive manner upon his will.

This example will serve to explain the whole phenomenon of the human will. This will, or rather the brain, finds itself in the same situation as a bowl, which, although it has received an impulse that drives it forward in a straight line, is deranged in its course whenever a force superior to the first obliges it to change its direction. The man who drinks the poisoned water appears a madman; but the actions of fools are as necessary as those of the most prudent individuals.

### 3. Choice Does Not Prove Freedom

Choice by no means proves the free agency of man: he only deliberates when he does not yet know which to choose of the many objects that move him, he is then in an embarrassment, which does not terminate until his will is decided by the greater advantage he believes he shall find in the object he chooses, or the action he undertakes. From whence it may be seen that choice is necessary, because he would not determine for an object, or for an action, if he did not believe that he should find in it some direct advantage. That man should have free agency it were needful that he should be able to will or choose without motive, or that he could prevent motives coercing his will. Action always being the effect of his will once determined, and as his will cannot be determined but by a motive which is not in his own power, it follows that he is never the master of the determination of his own peculiar will; that consequently he never acts as a free agent. It has been believed that man was a free agent because he had a will with the power of choosing; but attention has not been paid to the fact that even his will is moved by causes independent of himself; is owing to that which is inherent in his own organization, or which belongs to the nature of the beings acting on him. Is he the master of willing not to withdraw his hand from the fire when he fears it will be burnt? Or has he the power to take away from fire the property which makes him fear it? Is he the master of not choosing a dish of meat,

which he knows to be agreeable, or analogous to his palate; of not preferring it to that which he knows to be disagreeable or dangerous? It is always according to his sensations, to his own peculiar experience, or to his suppositions, that he judges of things, either well or ill; but whatever may be his judgment, it depends necessarily on his mode of feeling, whether habitual or accidental, and the qualities he finds in the causes that move him, which exist in spite of himself. [. . .]

Despite these proofs of the want of free agency in man, so clear to unprejudiced minds, it will, perhaps, be insisted upon with no small feeling of triumph that if it be proposed to anyone to move or not to move his hand, an action in the number of those called *indifferent*, he evidently appears to be the master of choosing; from which it is concluded that evidence has been offered of his free agency. The reply is, this example is perfectly simple; man in performing some action which he is resolved on doing does not by any means prove his free agency: the very desire of displaying this quality, excited by the dispute, becomes a necessary motive, which decides his will either for the one or the other of these actions: what deludes him in this instance, or that which persuades him he is a free agent at this moment, is that he does not discern the true motive which sets him in action, namely, the desire of convincing his opponent: if in the heat of the dispute he insists and asks, "Am I not the master of throwing myself out of the window?" I shall answer him, no; that whilst he preserves his reason there is no probability that the desire of proving his free agency will become a motive sufficiently powerful to make him sacrifice his life to the attempt; if, notwithstanding this, to prove he is a free agent, he should actually precipitate himself from the window, it would not be a sufficient warranty to conclude he acted freely, but rather that it was the violence of his temperament which spurred him on to this folly. Madness is a state that depends upon the heat of the blood, not upon the will. A fanatic or a hero braves death as necessarily as a more phlegmatic man or a coward flies from it.[1]

## 4. Freedom Is Not Absence of Constraint

It is said that free agency is the absence of those obstacles competent to oppose themselves to the actions of man, or to the exercise of his faculties: it is pretended that he is a free agent whenever, making use of these faculties, he produces the effect he has proposed to himself. In reply to this reasoning, it is sufficient to consider that it in nowise depends upon himself to place or remove the obstacles that either determine or resist him; the motive that causes his action is no more in his own power than the obstacle that impedes him, whether this obstacle or motive be within his own machine or exterior of his person: he is not master of the thought presented to his mind, which determines his will; this thought is excited by some cause independent of himself.

To be undeceived on the system of his free agency, man has simply to recur to the motive by which his will is determined; he will always find this motive is out of his own control. It is said that in consequence of an idea to which the mind gives birth, man acts freely if he encounters no obstacle. But the question is, what gives birth to this idea in his brain? Was he the master either to prevent it from presenting itself, or from renewing itself in his brain? Does not this idea depend either upon objects that strike him exteriorly despite himself, or upon causes that without his knowledge act within himself and modify his brain? Can he prevent his eyes, cast without design upon any object whatever, from giving him an idea of this object, and from moving his brain? He is not more master of the obstacles; they are the necessary effects of either interior or exterior causes, which always act according to their given properties. A man insults a coward, this necessarily irritates him against his insulter, but his will cannot vanquish the obstacle that cowardice places to the object of his desire because his natural conformation, which does not depend upon himself, prevents his having courage. [. . .]

The partisans of the system of free agency appear ever to have confounded constraint with necessity. Man believes he acts as a free agent every time he does not see anything that places obstacles to his actions; he does not perceive that the motive which causes him to will is always necessary and independent of himself. A prisoner loaded with chains is compelled to remain in prison; but he is not a free agent in the desire to emancipate himself; his chains prevent him from acting, but they do not prevent him from willing; he would save himself if they would loose his fetters; but he would not save himself as a free agent; fear or the idea of punishment would be sufficient motives for his action.

Man may, therefore, cease to be restrained, without, for that reason, becoming a free agent: in whatever manner he acts, he will act necessarily, according to motives by which he shall be determined. He may be compared to a heavy body that finds itself arrested in its descent by any obstacle whatever: take away this obstacle, it will gravitate or continue to fall; but who shall say this dense body is free to fall or not? Is not its descent the necessary effect of its own specific gravity? The virtuous Socrates submitted to the laws of his country, although they were unjust; and though the doors of his jail were left open to him, he would not save himself; but in this he did not act as a free agent: the invisible chains of opinion, the secret love of decorum, the inward respect for the laws, even when they were iniquitous, the fear of tarnishing his glory, kept him in his prison; they were motives sufficiently powerful with this enthusiast for virtue to induce him to wait death with tranquillity; it was not in his power to save himself because he could find no potential motive to bring him to depart, even for an instant, from those principles to which his mind was accustomed.

## 5. Multiplicity of Causes Mistaken for Freedom

When it is said that man is not a free agent, it is not pretended to compare him to a body moved by a simple impulsive cause: he contains within himself causes inherent to his existence; he is moved by an interior organ, which has its own peculiar laws, and is itself necessarily determined in consequence of ideas formed from perceptions resulting from sensations which it receives from exterior objects. As the mechanism of these sensations, of these perceptions, and the manner they engrave ideas on the brain of man are not known to him; because he is unable to unravel all these motions; because he cannot perceive the chain of operations in his soul, or the motive principle that acts within him, he supposes himself a free agent; which, literally translated, signifies that he moves himself by himself; that he determines himself without cause: when he rather ought to say that he is ignorant how or for why he acts in the manner he does. It is true the soul enjoys an activity peculiar to itself: but it is equally certain that this activity would never be displayed, if some motive or some cause did not put it in a condition to exercise itself: at least it will not be pretended that the soul is able either to love or to hate without being moved, without knowing the objects, without having some idea of their qualities. Gunpowder has unquestionably a particular activity, but this activity will never display itself, unless fire be applied to it; this, however, immediately sets it in motion.

It is the great complication of motion in man, it is the variety of his action, it is the multiplicity of causes that move him, whether simultaneously or in continual succession, that persuades him he is a free agent: if all his motions were simple, if the causes that move him did not confound themselves with each other, if they were distinct, if his machine were less complicated, he would perceive that all his actions were necessary because he would be enabled to recur instantly to the cause that made him act. [. . .]

It is, then, for want of recurring to the causes that move him; for want of being able to analyze, from not being competent to decompose the complicated motion of his machine, that man believes himself a free agent: it is only upon his own ignorance that he founds the profound yet deceitful notion he has of his free agency; that he builds those opinions which he brings forward as a striking proof of his pretended freedom of action. If, for a short time, each man was willing to examine his own peculiar actions, search out their true motives to discover their concatenation, he would remain convinced that the sentiment he has of his natural free agency is a chimera that must speedily be destroyed by experience.

## 6. Morals

However this may be, man either sees or believes he sees much more distinctly the necessary relation of effects with their causes in natural philosophy than in the human heart: at least he sees in the former that sensible causes constantly produce sensible effects, ever the same, when the circumstances are alike. After this he hesitates not to look upon physical effects as necessary; whilst he refuses to acknowledge necessity in the acts of the human will: these he has, without any just foundation, attributed to a motive-power that acts independently by its own peculiar energy, which is capable of modifying itself without the concurrence of exterior causes, and which is distinguished from all material or physical beings. Agriculture is founded upon the assurance, afforded by experience, that the earth, cultivated and sown in a certain manner, when it has otherwise the requisite qualities, will furnish grain, fruit, and flowers, either necessary for subsistence or pleasing to the senses. If things were considered without prejudice, it would be perceived that in morals, education is nothing more than *the agriculture of the mind*; that, like the earth, by reason of its natural disposition, of the culture bestowed upon it, of the seeds with which it is sown, of the seasons, more or less favourable that conduct it to maturity, we may be assured that the soul will produce either virtue or vice—*moral fruit*, that will be either salubrious for man or baneful to society. *Morals* is the science of the relations that subsist between the minds, the wills, and the actions of men, in the same manner that geometry is the science of the relations that are found between bodies. Morals would be a chimera and would have no certain principles, if it was not founded upon the knowledge of the motives which must necessarily have an influence upon the human will, and which must necessarily determine the actions of human beings.

If, in the moral as well as in the physical world, a cause, of which the action is not interrupted, be necessarily followed by a given effect, it flows consecutively that a reasonable education, grafted upon truth, and founded upon wise laws; that honest principles instilled during youth; virtuous examples continually held forth; esteem attached solely to merit and good actions; contempt and shame and chastisements regularly visiting vice and falsehood and crime, are causes that would necessarily act on the will of man, and would determine the greater number of his species to exhibit virtue. But if, on the contrary, religion, politics, example, public opinion, all labour to countenance wickedness and to train man viciously; if, instead of fanning his virtues, they stifle good principles; if, instead of directing his studies to his advantage, they render his education either useless or unprofitable; if this education itself, instead of grounding him in virtue, only inoculates him with vice; if, instead of inculcating reason, it imbues him with prejudice; if, instead of making him enamoured of truth, it furnishes him with false notions and with dangerous opinions; if, instead of fostering mildness and forbearance, it kindles in his breast only those passions which are incommodious to himself and hurtful to others; it must be of necessity that the will of the greater number shall determine them to evil. [. . .]

In spite of the gratuitous ideas which man has formed to himself on his pretended free agency; in defiance of the illusions of this supposed intimate sense, which, notwithstanding his experience, persuades him that he is master of his will; all his institutions are really founded upon necessity: on this, as on a variety of other occasions, practice throws aside speculation. Indeed, if it was not believed that certain motives embraced the power requisite to determine the will of man, to arrest the progress of his passions; to direct them towards an end, to modify him, of what use would be the faculty of speech? What benefit could arise from education, from legislation, from morals, even from religion itself? What does education achieve, save give the first impulse to the human will; make man contract habits; oblige him to persist in them; furnish him with motives, whether true or false, to act after a given manner? When the father either menaces his son with punishment, or promises him a

reward, is he not convinced these things will act upon his will? What does legislation attempt except it be to present to the citizens of a state those motives which are supposed necessary to determine them to perform some actions that are considered worthy; to abstain from committing others that are looked upon as unworthy? What is the object of morals, if it be not to show man that his interest exacts he should suppress the momentary ebullition of his passions, with a view to promote a more certain happiness, a more lasting well being, than can possibly result from the gratification of his transitory desires? Does not the religion of all countries suppose the human race, together with the entire of nature, submitted to the irresistible will of a necessary being who regulates their condition after the eternal laws of immutable wisdom?

## 7. Necessity

From all that has been advanced in this chapter, it results that in no one moment of his existence man is a free agent. He is not the architect of his own conformation, which he holds from nature; he has no control over his own ideas, or over the modification of his brain; these are due to causes that, in spite of him, and without his own knowledge, unceasingly act upon him; he is not the master of not loving or coveting that which he finds amiable or desirable; he is not capable of refusing to deliberate when he is uncertain of the effects certain objects will produce upon him; he cannot avoid choosing that which he believes will be most advantageous to him; in the moment when his will is determined by his choice, he is not competent to act otherwise than he does. In what instance, then, is he the master of his own actions? In what moment is he a free agent?

That which a man is about to do, is always a consequence of that which he has been—of that which he is—of that which he has done up to the moment of the action: his total and actual existence, considered under all its possible circumstances, contains the sum of all the motives to the action he is about to commit; this is a principle, the truth of which no thinking being will be able to refuse accrediting: his life is a series of necessary moments; his conduct, whether good or bad, virtuous or vicious, useful or prejudicial, either to himself or to others, is a concatenation of action, as necessary as all the moments of his existence. *To live*, is to exist in a necessary mode during the points of that duration which succeed each other necessarily: *to will*, is to acquiesce or not in remaining such as he is: *to be free*, is to yield to the necessary motives he carries within himself.

If he understood the play of his organs, if he was able to recall to himself all the impulsions they have received, all the modifications they have undergone, all the effects they have produced, he would perceive that all his actions are submitted to that *fatality*, which regulates his own particular system, as it does the entire system of the universe: no one effect in him, any more than in nature, produces itself by *chance*; this, as has been before proved, is a word void of sense. All that passes in him; all that is done by him; as well as all that happens in nature, or that is attributed to her, is derived from necessary causes, which act according to necessary laws, and which produce necessary effects from whence necessarily flow others.

*Fatality*, is the eternal, the immutable, the necessary order, established in nature; or the indispensable connection of causes that act, with the effects they operate. Conforming to this order, heavy bodies fall; light bodies rise; that which is analogous in matter reciprocally attracts; that which is heterogeneous mutually repels; man congregates himself in society, modifies each his fellow; becomes either virtuous or wicked; either contributes to his mutual happiness, or reciprocates his misery; either loves his neighbour, or hates his companion necessarily,

according to the manner in which the one acts upon the other. From whence it may be seen that the same necessity which regulates the physical, also regulates the moral world, in which everything is in consequence submitted to fatality. Man, in running over, frequently without his own knowledge, often in spite of himself, the route which nature has marked out for him, resembles a swimmer who is obliged to follow the current that carries him along: he believes himself a free agent because he sometimes consents, sometimes does not consent, to glide with the stream, which, notwithstanding, always hurries him forward; he believes himself the master of his condition because he is obliged to use his arms under the fear of sinking.

The false ideas he has formed to himself upon free agency, are in general thus founded: there are certain events which he judges *necessary*; either because he sees that they are effects constantly and invariably linked to certain causes, which nothing seems to prevent; or because he believes he has discovered the chain of causes and effects that is put in play to produce those events: whilst he contemplates as *contingent* other events of whose causes he is ignorant, and with whose mode of acting he is unacquainted: but in nature, where everything is connected by one common bond, there exists no effect without a cause. In the moral as well as in the physical world, everything that happens is a necessary consequence of causes, either visible or concealed, which are of necessity obliged to act after their peculiar essences. *In man, free agency is nothing more than necessity contained within himself.* [. . .]

## Note

1. There is, in point of fact, no difference between the man that is cast out of the window by another, and the man who throws himself out of it, except that the impulse in the first instance comes immediately from without, whilst that which determines the fall in the second case, springs from within his own peculiar machine, having its more remote cause also exterior.

## Study Questions

1. Explain the significance of Holbach's materialism for his treatment of the problem of freedom and determinism.

2. Let's say I try to prove to you that humans have free agency by choosing to move or not move my hand at will. What would Holbach's response be?

3. The position we know today as compatibilism defines freedom as the absence of constraint. Do you find Holbach's argument against compatibilism convincing?

4. Describe Holbach's views on chance and the status of statistical laws and probabilistic explanations in science.

# David Hume

Scottish Enlightenment philosopher and historian David Hume (1711–76) was 11 years old when he began his education at Edinburgh University and 28 when *A Treatise of Human Nature* was published. Hume's reputation as an atheist and skeptic, however, blocked him from holding any academic posts. This excerpt from the *Treatise* defends a compatibilist position on freedom and determinism that draws on Hume's skeptical account of causation, an account so philosophically challenging that Kant said it "interrupted" his "dogmatic slumber" and diverted him in a direction that ultimately led to his critical philosophy.—JF

## Of Liberty and Necessity

From *A Treatise of Human Nature*

### Section 1

We come now to explain the *direct* passions, or the impressions which arise immediately from good or evil, from pain or pleasure. Of this kind are, *desire and aversion*, *grief and joy*, *hope and fear*.

Of all the immediate effects of pain and pleasure, there is none more remarkable than the *will*; and though, properly speaking, it be not comprehended among the passions, yet, as the full understanding of its nature and properties is necessary to the explanation of them, we shall here make it the subject of our inquiry. I desire it may be observed that by the *will*, I mean nothing but *the internal impression we feel, and are conscious of, when we knowingly give rise to any new motion of our body, or new perception of our mind.* This impression, [. . .] it is impossible to define and needless to describe any further, for which reason we shall cut off all those definitions and distinctions with which philosophers are wont

to perplex rather than clear up this question, and entering at first upon the subject shall examine that long-disputed question concerning *liberty and necessity*, which occurs so naturally in treating of the will.

It is universally acknowledged that the operations of external bodies are necessary and that in the communication of their motion, in their attraction, and mutual cohesion, there are not the least traces of indifference or liberty. Every object is determined by an absolute fate to a certain degree and direction of its motion, and can no more depart from that precise line in which it moves than it can convert itself into an angel, or spirit, or any superior substance. The actions, therefore, of matter are to be regarded as instances of necessary actions, and whatever is, in this respect, on the same footing with matter must be acknowledged to be necessary. That we may know whether this be the case with the actions of the mind, we shall begin with examining matter and considering on what the idea of a necessity in its operations is founded and why we conclude one body or action to be the infallible cause of another.

It has been observed already that in no single instance the ultimate connection of any objects is discoverable either by our senses or reason and that we can never penetrate so far into the essence and construction of bodies as to perceive the principle on which their mutual influence depends. It is their constant union alone with which we are acquainted, and it is from the constant union the necessity arises. If objects had not a uniform and regular conjunction with each other, we should never arrive at any idea of cause and effect, and even after all, the necessity which enters into that idea is nothing but a determination of the mind to pass from one object to its usual attendant and infer the existence of one from that of the other. Here then are two particulars which we are to consider as essential to necessity, viz., the constant *union* and the *inference* of the mind, and wherever we discover these, we must acknowledge a necessity. As the actions of matter have no necessity but what is derived from these circumstances, and it is not by any insight into the essence of bodies we discover their connection, the absence of this insight, while the union and inference remain, will never, in any case, remove the necessity. It is the observation of the union which produces the inference, for which reason it might be thought sufficient if we prove a constant union in the actions of the mind in order to establish the inference along with the necessity of these actions. But that I may bestow a greater force on my reasoning, I shall examine these particulars apart, and shall first prove from experience that our actions have a constant union with our motives, tempers, and circumstances before I consider the inferences we draw from it.

To this end a very slight and general view of the common course of human affairs will be sufficient. There is no light in which we can take them that does not confirm this principle. Whether we consider mankind according to the difference of sexes, ages, governments, conditions, or methods of education, the same uniformity and regular operation of natural principles are discernible. Like causes still produce like effects, in the same manner as in the mutual action of the elements and powers of nature.

There are different trees which regularly produce fruit whose relish is different from each other, and this regularity will be admitted as an instance of necessity and causes in external bodies. But are the products of Guienne and of Champagne more regularly different than the sentiments, actions, and passions of the two sexes, of which the one are distinguished by their force and maturity, the other by their delicacy and softness?

Are the changes of our body from infancy to old age more regular and certain than those of our mind and conduct? And would a man be more ridiculous who would expect that an infant of four years old will raise a weight of three hundred pounds than one who, from a person of the same age, would look for a philosophical reasoning, or a prudent and well concerted action?

We must certainly allow that the cohesion of the parts of matter arises from natural and necessary principles, whatever difficulty we may find in explaining them, and for a like reason we must allow that human society is founded on like principles. Our reason in the latter case is better than even that in the former because we not only observe that men *always* seek society, but can also explain the principles on which this universal propensity is founded. For is it more certain that two flat pieces of marble will unite together than two young savages of different sexes will copulate? Do the children arise from this copulation more uniformly than does the parents' care for their safety and preservation? And after they have arrived at years of discretion by the care of their parents, are the inconveniencies attending their separation more certain than their foresight of these inconveniencies and their care of avoiding them by a close union and confederacy?

The skin, pores, muscles, and nerves of a day-labourer are different from those of a man of quality: so are his sentiments, actions, and manners. The different stations of life influence the whole fabric, external and internal, and these different stations arise necessarily, because uniformly, from the necessary and uniform principles of human nature. Men cannot live without society and cannot be associated without government. Government makes a distinction of property and establishes the different ranks of men. This produces industry, traffic, manufactures, lawsuits, war, leagues, alliances, voyages, travels, cities, fleets, ports, and all those other actions and objects which cause such a diversity, and at the same time maintain such an uniformity in human life.

Should a traveller returning from a far country tell us that he had seen a climate in the fiftieth degree of northern latitude where all the fruits ripen and come to perfection in the winter and decay in the summer, after the same manner as in England they are produced and decay in the contrary seasons, he would find few so credulous as to believe him. I am apt to think a traveller would meet with as little credit who should inform us of people exactly of the same character with those in Plato's republic on the one hand, or those in **Hobbes'** *Leviathan* on the other. There is a general course of nature in human actions, as well as in the operations of the sun and the climate. There are also characters peculiar to different nations and particular persons, as well as common to mankind. The knowledge of these characters is founded on the observation of a uniformity in the actions that flow from them, and this uniformity forms the very essence of necessity.

I can imagine only one way of eluding this argument, which is by denying that uniformity of human actions on which it is founded. As long as actions have a constant union and connection with the situation and temper of the agent, however we may in words refuse to acknowledge the necessity, we really allow the thing. Now, some may perhaps find a pretext to deny this regular union and connection. For what is more capricious than human actions? What more inconstant than the desires of man? And what creature departs more widely, not only from right reason, but from his own character and disposition? An hour, a moment is sufficient to make him change from one extreme to another, and overturn what cost the greatest pain and labour to establish. Necessity is regular and certain.

Human conduct is irregular and uncertain. The one therefore proceeds not from the other.

To this I reply that in judging of the actions of men, we must proceed upon the same maxims as when we reason concerning external objects. When any phenomena are constantly and invariably conjoined together, they acquire such a connection in the imagination that it passes from one to the other without any doubt or hesitation. But below this there are many inferior degrees of evidence and probability, nor does one single contrariety of experiment entirely destroy all our reasoning. The mind balances the contrary experiments, and deducting the inferior from the superior, proceeds with that degree of assurance or evidence which remains. Even when these contrary experiments are entirely equal, we remove not the notion of causes and necessity, but, supposing that the usual contrariety proceeds from the operation of contrary and concealed causes, we conclude that the chance or indifference lies only in our judgment on account of our imperfect knowledge, not in the things themselves, which are in every case equally necessary, though, to appearance, not equally constant or certain. No union can be more constant and certain than that of some actions with some motives and characters, and if, in other cases, the union is uncertain, it is no more than what happens in the operations of body; nor can we conclude anything from the one irregularity which will not follow equally from the other.

It is commonly allowed that madmen have no liberty. But, were we to judge by their actions, these have less regularity and constancy than the actions of wise men, and consequently are farther removed from necessity. Our way of thinking in this particular is, therefore, absolutely inconsistent, but is a natural consequence of these confused ideas and undefined terms which we so commonly make use of in our reasonings, especially on the present subject.

We must now show that as the *union* between motives and actions has the same constancy as that in any natural operations, so its influence on the understanding is also the same in *determining* us to infer the existence of one from that of another. If this shall appear, there is no known circumstance that enters into the connection and production of the actions of matter that is not to be found in all the operations of the mind, and consequently we cannot, without a manifest absurdity, attribute necessity to the one and refuse it to the other.

There is no philosopher whose judgment is so riveted to this fantastical system of liberty as not to acknowledge the force of *moral evidence*, and both in speculation and practice proceed upon it, as upon a reasonable foundation. Now, moral evidence is nothing but a conclusion concerning the actions of men, derived from the consideration of their motives, temper, and situation. [. . .] [This] kind of reasoning runs through politics, war, commerce, economy, and indeed mixes itself so entirely in human life that it is impossible to act or subsist a moment without having recourse to it. A prince who imposes a tax upon his subjects expects their compliance. A general who conducts an army makes account of a certain degree of courage. A merchant looks for fidelity and skill in his factor or supercargo. A man who gives orders for his dinner doubts not of the obedience of his servants. In short, as nothing more nearly interests us than our own actions and those of others, the greatest part of our reasonings is employed in judgments concerning them. Now I assert that whoever reasons after this manner does *ipso facto* [by that very fact] believe the actions of the will to arise from necessity, and that he knows not what he means when he denies it.

All those objects, of which we call the one *cause* and the other *effect*, considered in themselves, are as distinct and separate from each other as any two things in nature; nor can we ever, by the most accurate survey of them, infer the existence of the one from that of the other. It is only from experience and the observation of their constant union that we are able to form this inference, and even after all, the inference is nothing but the effects of custom on the imagination. We must not here be content with saying that the idea of cause and effect arises from objects constantly united but must affirm that

it is the very same with the idea of these objects, and that the *necessary connection* is not discovered by a conclusion of the understanding but is merely a perception of the mind. Wherever, therefore, we observe the same union, and wherever the union operates in the same manner upon the belief and opinion, we have the idea of cause and necessity, though perhaps we may avoid those expressions. Motion in one body, in all past instances that have fallen under our observation, is followed upon impulse by motion in another. It is impossible for the mind to penetrate further. From this constant union it *forms* the idea of cause and effect, and by its influence *feels* the necessity. As there is the same constancy and the same influence in what we call moral evidence, I ask no more. What remains can only be a dispute of words.

And indeed, when we consider how aptly *natural* and *moral* evidence cement together and form only one chain of argument between them, we shall make no scruple to allow that they are of the same nature and derived from the same principles. A prisoner who has neither money nor interest discovers the impossibility of his escape as well from the obstinacy of the jailer as from the walls and bars with which he is surrounded, and in all attempts for his freedom, chooses rather to work upon the stone and iron of the one than upon the inflexible nature of the other. The same prisoner, when conducted to the scaffold, foresees his death as certainly from the constancy and fidelity of his guards as from the operation of the axe or wheel. His mind runs along a certain train of ideas: the refusal of the soldiers to consent to his escape; the action of the executioner; the separation of the head and body, bleeding, convulsive motions, and death. Here is a connected chain of natural causes and voluntary actions, but the mind feels no difference between them in passing from one link to another, nor is less certain of the future event than if it were connected with the present impressions of the memory and senses by a train of causes cemented together by what we are pleased to call a *physical necessity*. The same experienced union has the same effect on the mind, whether the united objects be motives, volitions, and actions, or figure and motion. We may change the names of things, but their nature and their operation on the understanding never change.

I dare be positive no one will ever endeavour to refute these reasonings otherwise than by altering my definitions and assigning a different meaning to the terms of *cause, and effect, and necessity, and liberty, and chance*. According to my definitions, necessity makes an essential part of causation, and consequently liberty, by removing necessity, removes also causes, and is the very same thing with chance. As chance is commonly thought to imply a contradiction and is at least directly contrary to experience, there are always the same arguments against liberty or free-will. If anyone alters the definitions, I cannot pretend to argue with him till I know the meaning he assigns to these terms.

## Section 2

I believe we may assign the three following reasons for the prevalence of the doctrine of liberty, however absurd it may be in one sense, and unintelligible in any other. First, after we have performed any action, though we confess we were influenced by particular views and motives, it is difficult for us to persuade ourselves [that] we were governed by necessity and that it was utterly impossible for us to have acted otherwise, the idea of necessity seeming to imply something of force, and violence, and constraint, of which we are not sensible. Few are capable of distinguishing between the liberty of *spontaneity*, as it is called in the schools, and the liberty of *indifference*, between that which is opposed to violence and that which means a negation of necessity and causes. The first is even the most common sense of the word, and as it is only that species of liberty which it concerns us to preserve, our thoughts have been principally turned towards it and have almost universally confounded it with the other.

Secondly, there is a *false sensation or experience* even of the liberty of indifference, which is regarded as an argument for its real existence. The necessity

of any action, whether of matter or of the mind, is not properly a quality in the agent but in any thinking or intelligent being who may consider the action, and consists in the determination of his thought to infer its existence from some preceding objects: as liberty or chance, on the other hand, is nothing but the want of that determination and a certain looseness which we feel in passing or not passing from the idea of one to that of the other. Now, we may observe that though in reflecting on human actions, we seldom feel such a looseness or indifference, yet it very commonly happens that in performing the actions themselves, we are sensible of something like it: and as all related or resembling objects are readily taken for each other, this has been employed as a demonstrative, or even an intuitive proof of human liberty. We feel that our actions are subject to our will on most occasions and imagine we feel that the will itself is subject to nothing because when, by a denial of it, we are provoked to try, we feel that it moves easily every way and produces an image of itself even on that side on which it did not settle. This image or faint motion, we persuade ourselves, could have been completed into the thing itself because, should that be denied, we find, upon a second trial, that it can. But these efforts are all in vain; whatever capricious and irregular actions we may perform, as the desire of showing our liberty is the sole motive of our actions, we can never free ourselves from the bonds of necessity. We may imagine we feel a liberty within ourselves, but a spectator can commonly infer our actions from our motives and character, and even where he cannot, he concludes in general that he might, were he perfectly acquainted with every circumstance of our situation and temper, and the most secret springs of our complexion and disposition. Now this is the very essence of necessity, according to the foregoing doctrine.

A third reason why the doctrine of liberty has generally been better received in the world than its antagonist proceeds from *religion*, which has been very unnecessarily interested in this question. There is no method of reasoning more common, and yet none more blameable, than in philosophical debates to endeavour to refute any hypothesis by a pretext of its dangerous consequences to religion and morality. When any opinion leads us into absurdities, it is certainly false; but it is not certain an opinion is false because it is of dangerous consequence. Such topics, therefore, ought entirely to be forborne, as serving nothing to the discovery of truth but only to make the person of an antagonist odious. This I observe in general, without pretending to draw any advantage from it. I submit myself frankly to an examination of this kind, and dare venture to affirm that the doctrine of necessity, according to my explication of it, is not only innocent but even advantageous to religion and morality.

I define necessity two ways, conformable to the two definitions of *cause*, of which it makes an essential part. I place it either in the constant union and conjunction of like objects or in the inference of the mind from the one to the other. Now, necessity, in both these senses, has universally, though tacitly, in the schools, in the pulpit, and in common life been allowed to belong to the will of man, and no one has ever pretended to deny that we can draw inferences concerning human actions, and that those inferences are founded on the experienced union of like actions with like motives and circumstances. The only particular in which anyone can differ from me is either that perhaps he will refuse to call this necessity [. . .] or that he will maintain there is something else in the operations of matter. Now, whether it be so or not is of no consequence to religion, whatever it may be to natural philosophy. I may be mistaken in asserting that we have no idea of any other connection in the actions of body, and shall be glad to be further instructed on that head: but sure I am, I ascribe nothing to the actions of the mind but what must readily be allowed of. Let no one, therefore, put an invidious construction on my words by saying simply that I assert the necessity of human actions and place them on the same footing with the operations of senseless matter. I do not ascribe to the will that unintelligible necessity which is supposed to lie in matter. But I ascribe to matter that

intelligible quality, call it necessity or not, which the most rigorous orthodoxy does or must allow to belong to the will. I change, therefore, nothing in the received systems with regard to the will, but only with regard to material objects.

Nay, I shall go further and assert that this kind of necessity is so essential to religion and morality that without it there must ensue an absolute subversion of both, and that every other supposition is entirely destructive to all laws, both *divine* and *human*. It is indeed certain that as all human laws are founded on rewards and punishments, it is supposed as a fundamental principle that these motives have an influence on the mind, and both produce the good and prevent the evil actions. We may give to this influence what name we please; but as it is usually conjoined with the action, common sense requires it should be esteemed a cause, and be looked upon as an instance of that necessity which I would establish.

This reasoning is equally solid when applied to *divine* laws, so far as the Deity is considered as a legislator, and is supposed to inflict punishment and bestow rewards with a design to produce obedience. But I also maintain that even where he acts not in his magisterial capacity but is regarded as the avenger of crimes merely on account of their odiousness and deformity, not only it is impossible without the necessary connection of cause and effect in human actions that punishments could be inflicted compatible with justice and moral equity, but also that it could ever enter into the thoughts of any reasonable being to inflict them. The constant and universal object of hatred or anger is a person or creature endowed with thought and consciousness, and when any criminal or injurious actions excite that passion, it is only by their relation to the person or connection with him. But according to the doctrine of liberty or chance, this connection is reduced to nothing, nor are men more accountable for those actions which are designed and premeditated than for such as are the most casual and accidental. Actions are, by their very nature, temporary and perishing, and where they proceed not from some cause in the characters and dispositions of the person who performed them, they infix not themselves upon him and can neither redound to his honour, if good, nor infamy, if evil. The action itself may be blameable; it may be contrary to all the rules of morality and religion: but the person is not responsible for it, and as it proceeded from nothing in him that is durable or constant and leaves nothing of that nature behind it, it is impossible he can, upon its account, become the object of punishment or vengeance. According to the hypothesis of liberty, therefore, a man is as pure and untainted after having committed the most horrid crimes as at the first moment of his birth, nor is his character any way concerned in his actions since they are not derived from it, and the wickedness of the one can never be used as a proof of the depravity of the other. It is only upon the principles of necessity that a person acquires any merit or demerit from his actions, however the common opinion may incline to the contrary.

But so inconsistent are men with themselves that though they often assert that necessity utterly destroys all merit and demerit either towards mankind or superior powers, yet they continue still to reason upon these very principles of necessity in all their judgments concerning this matter. Men are not blamed for such evil actions as they perform ignorantly and casually, whatever may be their consequences. Why but because the causes of these actions are only momentary and terminate in them alone. Men are less blamed for such evil actions as they perform hastily and unpremeditatedly than for such as proceed from thought and deliberation. For what reason but because a hasty temper, though a constant cause in the mind, operates only by intervals and infects not the whole character. Again, repentance wipes off every crime, especially if attended with an evident reformation of life and manners. How is this to be accounted for but by asserting that actions render a person criminal merely as they are proofs of criminal passions or principles in the mind, and when, by any alteration of these principles, they cease to be just proofs, they likewise cease to be criminal. But according to the doctrine of *liberty* or *chance*, they never were just proofs, and consequently never were criminal.

Here, then, I turn to my adversary and desire him to free his own system from these odious consequences before he charges them upon others. Or, if he rather chooses that this question should be decided by fair arguments before philosophers than by declamations before the people, let him return to what I have advanced to prove that liberty and chance are synonymous and concerning the nature of moral evidence and the regularity of human actions. Upon a review of these reasonings, I cannot doubt of an entire victory, and therefore, having proved that all actions of the will have particular causes, I proceed to explain what these causes are and how they operate. [. . .]

## Study Questions

1. In what two ways does Hume explain the necessity that is "universally acknowledged" to characterize "the operations of external bodies"?

2. Hume argues that necessity characterizes "human affairs" no less than it does "operations of external bodies": making reference to examples, explain the two ways in which this is so. Why does Hume consider necessity to be conducive, not opposed, to morality and religion?

3. Right now, as you sit in your seat, you have a sense that you can freely choose whether to stand or remain seated. It does not seem unreasonable for us to take this as evidence that determinism is false. What are Hume's two objections?

4. Describe Hume's views on chance and the status of statistical laws and probabilistic explanations in science.

# Immanuel Kant

Immanuel Kant (1724–1804) was educated at the University of Königsberg. After gradua-
tion, he tutored privately for six years before returning to the university to teach for the rest
of his career. Kant is especially known for his three Critiques: *Critique of Pure Reason* (1781,
1787), *Critique of Practical Reason* (1788), and *Critique of the Power of Judgment* (1790). The
first Critique, excerpted here, cautions against seeking knowledge by employing reason
beyond the limits of experience.—TR

# The Antinomy of Pure Reason

From *Critique of Pure Reason*

## 1. Antithetic of Pure Reason [Sec. 2]

If thetic be the name for any body of dogmatic
doctrines, antithetic may be taken as meaning, not
dogmatic assertions of the opposite, but the conflict
of the doctrines of seemingly dogmatic knowledge
(*thesis cum antithesi*) in which no one assertion can
establish superiority over another. The antithetic
does not, therefore, deal with one-sided assertions.
It treats only of the conflict of the doctrines of reason with one another and the causes of this conflict.
The transcendental antithetic is an enquiry into the
antinomy of pure reason, its causes and outcome.
If in employing the principles of understanding we
do not merely apply our reason to objects of experience, but venture to extend these principles beyond
the limits of experience, there arise *pseudo-rational*
doctrines which can neither hope for confirmation
in experience nor fear refutation by it. Each of them
is not only in itself free from contradiction, but
finds conditions of its necessity in the very nature
of reason—only that, unfortunately, the assertion of
the opposite has, on its side, grounds that are just as
valid and necessary.

## 1.1. Third Conflict of the Transcendental Ideas

### Thesis

Causality in accordance with laws of nature is not
the only causality from which the appearances of the
world can one and all be derived. To explain these
appearances it is necessary to assume that there is
also another causality, that of freedom.

### Proof

Let us assume that there is no other causality than
that in accordance with laws of nature. This being
so, everything which *takes place* presupposes a preceding state upon which it inevitably follows according to a rule. But the preceding state must itself be
something which has taken place (having come to
be in a time in which it previously was not); for if it
had always existed, its consequence also would have
always existed, and would not have only just arisen.
The causality of the cause through which something
takes place is itself, therefore, something that has *taken
place*, which again presupposes, in accordance with
the law of nature, a preceding state and its causality,
and this in similar manner a still earlier state, and so
on. If, therefore, everything takes place solely in accordance with laws of nature, there will always be only a
relative and never a first beginning, and consequently
no completeness of the series on the side of the causes
that arise the one from the other. But the law of nature
is just this, that nothing takes place without a cause
*sufficiently* determined a priori. The proposition that
no causality is possible save in accordance with laws
of nature, when taken in unlimited universality, is
therefore self-contradictory; and this cannot, therefore, be regarded as the sole kind of causality.

We must, then, assume a causality through which something takes place, the cause of which is not itself determined, in accordance with necessary laws, by another cause antecedent to it, that is to say, an *absolute spontaneity* of the cause, whereby a series of appearances, which proceeds in accordance with laws of nature, begins *of itself*. This is transcendental freedom, without which, even in the ordinary course of nature, the series of appearances on the side of the causes can never be complete.

## Antithesis

There is no freedom; everything in the world takes place solely in accordance with laws of nature.

## Proof

Assume that there is freedom in the transcendental sense, as a special kind of causality in accordance with which the events in the world can have come about, namely, a power of absolutely beginning a state, and therefore also of absolutely beginning a series of consequences of that state; it then follows that not only will a series have its absolute beginning in this spontaneity, but that the very determination of this spontaneity to originate the series, that is to say, the causality itself, will have an absolute beginning; there will be no antecedent through which this act, in taking place, is determined in accordance with fixed laws. But every beginning of action presupposes a state of the not yet acting cause; and a *dynamical* beginning of the action, if it is also a first beginning, presupposes a state which has no *causal* connection with the preceding state of the cause, that is to say, in nowise follows from it. Transcendental freedom thus stands opposed to the law of causality; and the kind of connection which it assumes as holding between the successive states of the active causes renders all unity of experience impossible. It is not to be met with in any experience, and is therefore an empty thought-entity.

In nature alone, therefore, not in freedom, must we seek for the connection and order of cosmical events. Freedom (independence) from the laws of nature is no doubt a liberation from compulsion, but also from the guidance of all rules. For it is not permissible to say that the *laws* of freedom enter into the causality exhibited in the course of nature, and so take the place of natural laws. If freedom were determined in accordance with laws, it would not be freedom; it would simply be nature under another name. Nature and transcendental freedom differ as do conformity to law and lawlessness. Nature does indeed impose upon the understanding the exacting task of always seeking the origin of events ever higher in the series of causes, their causality being always conditioned. But in compensation it holds out the promise of thoroughgoing unity of experience in accordance with laws. The illusion of freedom, on the other hand, offers a point of rest to the enquiring understanding in the chain of causes, conducting it to an unconditioned causality which begins to act of itself. This causality is, however, blind, and abrogates those rules through which alone a completely coherent experience is possible.

## 1.2. Observation on the Third Antinomy

### On the Thesis

The transcendental idea of freedom does not by any means constitute the whole content of the psychological concept of that name, which is mainly empirical. The transcendental idea stands only for the absolute spontaneity of an action, as the proper ground of its imputability. This, however, is, for philosophy, the real stumbling-block; for there are insurmountable difficulties in the way of admitting any such type of unconditioned causality. What has always so greatly embarrassed speculative reason in dealing with the question of the freedom of the will is its strictly transcendental aspect. The problem, properly viewed, is solely this: whether we must admit a power of *spontaneously* beginning a series of successive things or states. How such a power is possible is not a question which requires to be answered in this case, any more than in regard to causality in accordance with the laws of nature. For, as we have found, we have to remain satisfied with the a priori knowledge that this latter type of causality must be presupposed; we are not in the least able to comprehend how it can be possible that through one existence the existence of another is determined, and for this reason must be guided by experience alone. The necessity of a first beginning, due to freedom, of a series of appearances we have demonstrated only insofar as it is required to make an origin of the world conceivable; for all the later following states can be taken as resulting according to purely natural laws. But since the power of spontaneously beginning a series in time is thereby proved (though not understood), it is now also permissible for us to admit within the course of the world different series as capable in their causality of beginning of themselves, and so to attribute to their substances a power of acting from freedom. And we must not allow ourselves to be prevented from drawing this conclusion by a misapprehension, namely that, as a series occurring in the world can have only a relatively first beginning, being always preceded in the world by some other state of things, no absolute first beginning of a series is possible during the course of the world. For the absolutely first beginning of which we are here speaking is not a beginning in time, but in causality. If, for instance, I at this moment arise from my chair, in complete freedom, without being necessarily determined thereto by the influence of natural causes, a new series, with all its natural consequences *in infinitum*, has its absolute beginning in this event, although as regards time this event is only the continuation of a preceding series. For this resolution and act of mine do not form part of the succession of purely natural effects, and are not a mere continuation of them. In respect of its happening, natural causes exercise over it no determining influence whatsoever. It does indeed follow upon them, but without arising out of them; and accordingly, in respect of causality though not of time, must be entitled an absolutely first beginning of a series of appearances.

This requirement of reason, that we appeal in the series of natural causes to a first beginning, due to freedom, is amply confirmed when we observe that all the philosophers of antiquity, with the sole exception of the **Epicurean** School, felt themselves obliged, when explaining cosmical movements, to assume a *prime mover*, that is, a freely acting cause, which first and of itself began this series of states. They made no attempt to render a first beginning conceivable through nature's own resources.

### On the Antithesis

The defender of an omnipotent nature (transcendental *physiocracy*), in maintaining his position against the pseudo-rational arguments offered in support of the counter-doctrine of freedom, would argue as follows. *If you do not, as regards time, admit anything as being mathematically first in the world, there is no necessity, as regards causality, for seeking something that is dynamically first.* What authority have you for inventing an absolutely first state of the world, and therefore an absolute beginning of the ever-flowing series of appearances, and so of procuring a resting place for your imagination by setting bounds to limitless nature? Since the substances in the world have always existed—at least the unity of experience renders necessary such a supposition—there is no difficulty in assuming that change of their states, that is, a series of their alterations, has likewise always existed, and therefore that a first beginning, whether mathematical or dynamical, is not to be looked for. The possibility of such an infinite derivation, without a first member to which all the rest is merely a sequel, cannot indeed, in respect of its possibility, be rendered comprehensible. But if for this reason you refuse to recognize this enigma in nature, you will find yourself compelled to reject many fundamental **synthetic** properties and forces, which as little admit of comprehension. The possibility even of alteration itself would have to be denied. For were you not assured by experience that alteration actually occurs, you would never be able to excogitate a priori the possibility of such a ceaseless sequence of being and not being.

Even if a transcendental power of freedom be allowed, as supplying a beginning of happenings in the world, this power would in any case have to be outside the world (though any such assumption that over and above the sum of all possible intuitions there exists an object which cannot be given in any possible perception is still a very bold one). But to ascribe to substances in the world itself such a power can never be permissible; for, should this be done, that connection of appearances determining one another with necessity according to universal laws, which we entitle nature, and with it the criterion of empirical truth, whereby experience is distinguished from dreaming, would almost entirely disappear. Side by side with such a lawless faculty of freedom, nature as an ordered system is hardly thinkable; the influences of the former would so unceasingly alter the laws of the latter that the appearances which in their natural course are regular and uniform would be reduced to disorder and incoherence.

## 2. The Empirical Employment of the Regulative Principle of Reason, in Respect of All Cosmological Ideas [Sec. 9]

### 2.1. Solution of the Cosmological Idea of Totality in the Derivation of Cosmical Events from their Causes

When we are dealing with what happens there are only two kinds of causality conceivable by us; the causality is either according to *nature* or arises from *freedom*. The former is the connection in the sensible world of one state with a preceding state on which it follows according to a rule. Since the causality of appearances rests on conditions of time, and the preceding state, if it had always existed, could not have produced an effect which first comes into being in time, it follows that the causality of the cause of that which happens or comes into being must itself also have *come into being*, and that in accordance with the principle of the understanding it must in its turn itself require a cause.

By freedom, on the other hand, in its cosmological meaning, I understand the power of beginning a state *spontaneously*. Such causality will not, therefore, itself stand under another cause determining it in time, as required by the law of nature. Freedom, in this sense, is a pure transcendental idea, which, in the first place, contains nothing borrowed from experience, and which, secondly, refers to an object that

cannot be determined or given in any experience. That everything which happens has a cause is a universal law, conditioning the very possibility of all experience. Hence the causality of the cause, which *itself happens* or comes to be, must itself in turn have a cause; and thus the entire field of experience, however far it may extend, is transformed into a sum-total of the merely natural. But since in this way no absolute totality of conditions determining causal relation can be obtained, reason creates for itself the idea of a spontaneity which can begin to act of itself, without requiring to be determined to action by an antecedent cause in accordance with the law of causality.

It should especially be noted that the practical concept of freedom is based on this *transcendental* idea, and that in the latter lies the real source of the difficulty by which the question of the possibility of freedom has always been beset. Freedom in the practical sense is the will's independence of coercion through sensuous impulses. For a will is sensuous, insofar as it is *pathologically affected*, i.e., by sensuous motives; it is *animal* (*arbitrium brutum*), if it can be pathologically *necessitated*. The human will is certainly an *arbitrium sensitivum*, not, however, *brutum* but *liberum*. For sensibility does not necessitate its action. There is in man a power of self-determination, independently of any coercion through sensuous impulses.

Obviously, if all causality in the sensible world were mere nature, every event would be determined by another in time, in accordance with necessary laws. Appearances, in determining the will, would have in the actions of the will their natural effects, and would render the actions necessary. The denial of transcendental freedom must, therefore, involve the elimination of all practical freedom. For practical freedom presupposes that although something has not happened, it *ought* to have happened, and that its cause, as found in the field of appearance, is not, therefore, so determining that it excludes a causality of our will—a causality which, independently of those natural causes, and even contrary to their force and influence, can produce something that is determined in the time-order in accordance with empirical laws, and which can therefore begin a series of events *entirely of itself*. [. . .]

The difficulty which then meets us, in dealing with the question regarding nature and freedom, is whether freedom is possible at all, and if it be possible, whether it can exist along with the universality of the natural law of causality. Is it a truly disjunctive proposition to say that every effect in the world must arise *either* from nature *or* from freedom; or must we not rather say that in one and the same event, in different relations, both can be found? That all events in the sensible world stand in thoroughgoing connection in accordance with unchangeable laws of nature is an established principle of the Transcendental Analytic, and allows of no exception. The question, therefore, can only be whether freedom is completely excluded by this inviolable rule, or whether an effect, notwithstanding its being thus determined in accordance with nature, may not at the same time be grounded in freedom. The common but fallacious presupposition of the *absolute reality* of appearances here manifests its injurious influence, to the confounding of reason. For if appearances are things in themselves, freedom cannot be upheld. Nature will then be the complete and sufficient determining cause of every event. The condition of the event will be such as can be found only in the series of appearances; both it and its effect will be necessary in accordance with the law of nature. If, on the other hand, appearances are not taken for more than they actually are; if they are viewed not as things in themselves, but merely as representations, connected according to empirical laws, they must themselves have grounds which are not appearances. The effects of such an intelligible cause appear, and accordingly can be determined through other appearances, but its causality is not so determined. While the effects are to be found in the series of empirical conditions, the intelligible cause, together with its causality, is outside the series. Thus the effect may be regarded as free in respect of its intelligible cause, and at the same time in respect of appearances as resulting from them according to the necessity of nature.

This distinction, when stated in this quite general and abstract manner, is bound to appear extremely subtle and obscure, but will become clear in the course of its application. My purpose has only been to point out that since the thoroughgoing connection of all appearances, in a context of nature, is an inexorable law, the inevitable consequence of obstinately insisting upon the reality of appearances is to destroy all freedom. Those who thus follow the common view have never been able to reconcile nature and freedom.

## 2.2. Explanation of the Cosmological Idea of Freedom in its connection with Universal Natural Necessity

Let us apply this to experience. Man is one of the appearances of the sensible world, and insofar one of the natural causes the causality of which must stand under empirical laws. Like all other things in nature, he must have an empirical character. This character we come to know through the powers and faculties which he reveals in his actions. In lifeless, or merely animal, nature we find no ground for thinking that any faculty is conditioned otherwise than in a merely sensible manner. Man, however, who knows all the rest of nature solely through the senses, knows himself also through pure apperception; and this, indeed, in acts and inner determinations which he cannot regard as impressions of the senses. He is thus to himself, on the one hand phenomenon, and on the other hand, in respect of certain faculties the action of which cannot be ascribed to the receptivity of sensibility, a purely intelligible object. We entitle these faculties understanding and reason. The latter, in particular, we distinguish in a quite peculiar and especial way from all empirically conditioned powers. For it views its objects exclusively in the light of ideas, and in accordance with them determines the understanding, which then proceeds to make an empirical use of its own similarly pure concepts.

That our reason has causality, or that we at least represent it to ourselves as having causality, is evident from the *imperatives* which in all matters of conduct we impose as rules upon our active powers. "*Ought*" expresses a kind of necessity and of connection with grounds which is found nowhere else in the whole of nature. The understanding can know in nature only what is, what has been, or what will be. We cannot say that anything in nature *ought to be* other than what in all these time-relations it actually is. When we have the course of nature alone in view, "*ought*" has no meaning whatsoever. It is just as absurd to ask what ought to happen in the natural world as to ask what properties a circle ought to have. All that we are justified in asking is: what happens in nature? what are the properties of the circle?

This "*ought*" expresses a possible action the ground of which cannot be anything but a mere concept; whereas in the case of a merely natural action the ground must always be an appearance. The action to which the "*ought*" applies must indeed be possible under natural conditions. These conditions, however, do not play any part in determining the will itself, but only in determining the effect and its consequences in the field of appearance. No matter how many natural grounds or how many sensuous impulses may impel me to *will*, they can never give rise to the "*ought*," but only to a willing which, while very far from being necessary, is always conditioned; and the "*ought*" pronounced by reason confronts such willing with a limit and an end—nay more, forbids or authorizes it. Whether what is willed be an object of mere sensibility (the pleasant) or of pure reason (the good), reason will not give way to any ground which is empirically given. Reason does not here follow the order of things as they present themselves in appearance, but frames for itself with perfect spontaneity an order of its own according to ideas, to which it adapts the empirical conditions, and according to which it declares actions to be necessary, even although they have never taken place, and perhaps never will take place. And at the same time reason also presupposes that it can have causality in regard to all these actions, since otherwise no empirical effects could be expected from its ideas. [. . .]

In order to illustrate this regulative principle of reason by an example of its empirical employment—not, however, to confirm it, for it is useless to endeavour to prove transcendental propositions by examples—let us take a voluntary action, for example, a malicious lie by which a certain confusion has been caused in society. First of all, we endeavour to discover the motives to which it has been due, and then, secondly, in the light of these, we proceed to determine how far the action and its consequences can be imputed to the offender. As regards the first question, we trace the empirical character of the action to its sources, finding these in defective education, bad company, in part also in the viciousness of a natural disposition insensitive to shame, in levity and thoughtlessness, not neglecting to take into account also the occasional causes that may have intervened. We proceed in this enquiry just as we should in ascertaining for a given natural effect the series of its determining causes. But although we believe that the action is thus determined, we nonetheless blame the agent, not indeed on account of his unhappy disposition, nor on account of the circumstances that have influenced him, nor even on account of his previous way of life; for we presuppose that we can leave out of consideration what this way of life may have been, that we can regard the past series of conditions as not having occurred and the act as being completely unconditioned by any preceding state, just as if the agent in and by himself began in this action an entirely new series of consequences. Our blame is based on a law of reason whereby we regard reason as a cause that irrespective of all the above-mentioned empirical conditions could have determined, and ought to have determined, the agent to act otherwise. This causality of reason we do not regard as only a cooperating agency, but as complete in itself, even when the sensuous impulses do not favour but are directly opposed to it; the action is ascribed to the agent's intelligible character; in the moment when he utters the lie, the guilt is entirely his. Reason, irrespective of all empirical conditions of the act, is completely free, and the lie is entirely due to its default. [. . .]

## Study Questions

1. Kant proves the thesis of freedom and antithesis of determinism by beginning with the opposite premise and generating a contradiction (what is called "proof by contradiction"). Outline Kant's two proofs.

2. Kant reconciles freedom and determinism by appealing to two realms and two faculties: the phenomenal realm of "appearances" and noumenal realm of "things in themselves," and the faculty of understanding and faculty of reason. Describe his solution.

3. Right now, as you sit in your seat, you have a sense that you can freely choose whether to stand or remain seated. It does not seem unreasonable for us to take this as evidence that humans have free agency and determinism is false. How would Kant respond?

4. Using his example of someone who tells a "malicious lie," explain why Kant considers the person to be morally responsible even though the act was determined by causes both internal and external.

---

# Moritz Schlick

---

Moritz Schlick (1882–1936) completed his PhD in physics in 1904 and habilitation in logic in 1910. Appointed chair in philosophy of the inductive sciences at University of Vienna in 1922, Schlick founded the Vienna Circle, a group of scientists and philosophers who advocated a scientific—logical, empirical, and anti-metaphysical—approach to philosophy known as "logical positivism." Schlick's life was cut short when he was murdered by a mentally ill former student while on his way to class. Hume's influence on logical positivists such as Schlick is evident in this reading.

## When Is a Man Responsible?

From *Problems of Ethics*

### 1. The Pseudo-Problem of Freedom of the Will

With hesitation and reluctance I prepare to add this chapter to the discussion of ethical problems. For in it I must speak of a matter which, even at present, is thought to be a fundamental ethical question, but which got into ethics and has become a much discussed problem only because of a misunderstanding. This is the so-called problem of the freedom of the will. Moreover, this pseudo-problem has long since been settled by the efforts of certain sensible persons; and, above all, the state of affairs just described has been often disclosed—with exceptional clarity by Hume. Hence it is really one of the greatest scandals of philosophy that again and again so much paper and printer's ink is devoted to this matter, to say nothing of the expenditure of thought, which could have been applied to more important problems (assuming that it would have sufficed for these). Thus I should truly be ashamed to write a chapter on "freedom." In the chapter heading, the word "responsible" indicates what concerns ethics, and designates the point at which misunderstanding arises. Therefore the concept of responsibility constitutes our theme, and if in the process of its clarification I also must speak of the concept of freedom, I shall, of course, say only what others have already said better, consoling myself with the thought that in this way alone can anything be done to put an end at last to that scandal.

The main task of ethics [. . .] is to explain moral behaviour. To explain means to refer back to laws: every science, including psychology, is possible only insofar as there are such laws to which the events can be referred. Since the assumption that *all* events are subject to universal laws is called the principle of causality, one can also say, "Every science presupposes the principle of causality." Therefore every explanation of human behaviour must also assume the validity of causal laws, in this case the existence of psychological laws. [. . .] All of our experience strengthens us in the belief that this presupposition is realized, at least to the extent required for all purposes of practical life in intercourse with nature and human beings, and also for the most precise demands of technique. Whether, indeed, the principle of causality holds universally, whether, that is, *determinism* is true, we do not know; no one knows. But we do know that it is impossible to settle the dispute between determinism and indeterminism by mere reflection and speculation, by the consideration of so many reasons for and so many reasons against (which collectively and individually are but pseudo-reasons). Such an attempt becomes especially ridiculous when one considers with what enormous expenditure of experimental and logical skill contemporary physics carefully approaches the question of whether causality can be maintained for the most minute intra-atomic events.

But the dispute concerning "freedom of the will" generally proceeds in such fashion that its advocates attempt to refute, and its opponents to prove, the validity of the causal principle, both using hackneyed arguments, and neither in the least abashed by the magnitude of the undertaking. [. . .] Others distinguish two realms, in one of which determinism holds, but not in the other. This line of thought (which was unfortunately taken by **Kant**) is, however, quite the most worthless (though **Schopenhauer** considered it to be Kant's most profound idea).

Fortunately, it is not necessary to lay claim to a final solution of the causal problem in order to say what is necessary in ethics concerning responsibility; there is required only an analysis of the concept, the careful determination of the meaning which is in fact joined to the words "responsibility" and "freedom" as these are actually used. If men

had made clear to themselves the sense of those propositions, which we use in everyday life, that pseudo-argument which lies at the root of the pseudo-problem, and which recurs thousands of times within and outside of philosophical books, would never have arisen.

The argument runs as follows: "If determinism is true, if, that is, all events obey immutable laws, then my will too is always determined, by my innate character and my motives. Hence my decisions are necessary, not free. But if so, then I am not responsible for my acts, for I would be accountable for them only if I could do something about the way my decisions went; but I can do nothing about it, since they proceed with necessity from my character and the motives. And I have made neither, and have no power over them: the motives come from without, and my character is the necessary product of the innate tendencies and the external influences which have been effective during my lifetime. Thus determinism and moral responsibility are incompatible. Moral responsibility presupposes freedom, that is, exemption from causality."

This process of reasoning rests upon a whole series of confusions, just as the links of a chain hang together. We must show these confusions to be such, and thus destroy them.

## 2. Two Meanings of the Word "Law"

It all begins with an erroneous interpretation of the meaning of "law." In practice this is understood as a rule by which the state prescribes certain behaviour to its citizens. These rules often contradict the natural desires of the citizens (for if they did not do so, there would be no reason for making them), and are in fact not followed by many of them; while others obey, but under *compulsion*. The state does in fact compel its citizens by imposing certain sanctions (punishments) which serve to bring their desires into harmony with the prescribed laws.

In natural science, on the other hand, the word "law" means something quite different. The natural law is not a *pre*scription as to how something should behave, but a formula, a *de*scription of how something does in fact behave. The two forms of "laws" have only this in common: both tend to be expressed in *formulae*. Otherwise they have absolutely nothing to do with one another, and it is very blameworthy that the same word has been used for two such different things, but even more so that philosophers have allowed themselves to be led into serious errors by this usage. Since natural laws are only descriptions of what happens, there can be in regard to them no talk of "compulsion." The laws of celestial mechanics do not prescribe to the planets how they have to move, as though the planets would actually like to move quite otherwise, and are only forced by these burdensome laws of **Kepler** to move in orderly paths; no, these laws do not in any way "compel" the planets, but express only what in fact planets actually do.

If we apply this to volition, we are enlightened at once, even before the other confusions are discovered. When we say that a man's will "obeys psychological laws," these are not civic laws, which compel him to make certain decisions, or dictate desires to him, which he would in fact prefer not to have. They are laws of nature, merely expressing which desires he *actually has* under given conditions; they describe the nature of the will in the same manner as the astronomical laws describe the nature of planets. "Compulsion" occurs where man is prevented from realizing his natural desires. How could the rule according to which these natural desires arise itself be considered as "compulsion"?

## 3. Compulsion and Necessity

But this is the second confusion to which the first leads almost inevitably: after conceiving the laws of nature, anthropomorphically, as order imposed *nolens volens* upon the events, one adds to them the concept of "necessity." This word, derived from "need," also comes to us from practice, and is used there in the sense of inescapable compulsion. To apply the word with this meaning to natural laws is of course senseless, for the presupposition of an opposing desire is lacking; and it is then confused with something altogether different, which is actually an attribute of natural laws. That is, universality. It is of the essence

of natural laws to be universally valid, for only when we have found a rule which holds of events without exception do we *call* the rule a law of nature. Thus when we say "a natural law holds necessarily" this has but one legitimate meaning: "It holds in *all* cases where it is applicable." It is again very deplorable that the word "necessary" has been applied to natural laws (or, what amounts to the same thing, with reference to causality), for it is quite superfluous, since the expression "universally valid" is available. Universal validity is something altogether different from "compulsion"; these concepts belong to spheres so remote from each other that once insight into the error has been gained one can no longer conceive the possibility of a confusion.

The confusion of two concepts always carries with it the confusion of their contradictory opposites. The opposite of the universal validity of a formula, of the existence of a law, is the nonexistence of a law, indeterminism, acausality; while the opposite of compulsion is what in practice everyone calls "freedom." Here emerges the nonsense, trailing through centuries, that freedom means "exemption from the causal principle," or "not subject to the laws of nature." Hence it is believed necessary to vindicate indeterminism in order to save human freedom.

## 4. Freedom and Indeterminism

This is quite mistaken. Ethics has, so to speak, no moral interest in the purely theoretical question of "determinism or indeterminism?," but only a theoretical interest, namely: insofar as it seeks the laws of conduct, and can find them only to the extent that causality holds. But the question of whether man is morally free (that is, has that freedom which, as we shall show, is the presupposition of moral responsibility) is altogether different from the problem of determinism. Hume was especially clear on this point. He indicated the inadmissible confusion of the concepts of "indeterminism" and "freedom"; but he retained, inappropriately, the word "freedom" for both, calling the one freedom of "the will," the other, genuine kind, "freedom of conduct." He showed that morality is interested only in the latter, and that such freedom, in general, is unquestionably to be attributed to mankind. And this is quite correct. Freedom means the opposite of compulsion; a man is *free* if he does not act under *compulsion*, and he is compelled or unfree when he is hindered from without in the realization of his natural desires. Hence he is unfree when he is locked up, or chained, or when someone forces him at the point of a gun to do what otherwise he would not do. This is quite clear, and everyone will admit that the everyday or legal notion of the lack of freedom is thus correctly interpreted, and that a man will be considered quite free and responsible if no such external compulsion is exerted upon him. There are certain cases which lie between these clearly described ones, as, say, when someone acts under the influence of alcohol or a narcotic. In such cases we consider the man to be more or less unfree, and hold him less accountable, because we rightly view the influence of the drug as "external," even though it is found within the body; it prevents him from making decisions in the manner peculiar to his nature. If he takes the narcotic of his own will, we make him completely responsible for *this* act and transfer a part of the responsibility to the consequences, making, as it were, an average or mean condemnation of the whole. In the case also of a person who is mentally ill, we do not consider him free with respect to those acts in which the disease expresses itself because we view the illness as a disturbing factor which hinders the normal functioning of his natural tendencies. We make not him but his disease responsible.

## 5. The Nature of Responsibility

But what does this really signify? What do we mean by this concept of responsibility which goes along with that of "freedom," and which plays such an important role in morality? It is easy to attain complete clarity in this matter; we need only carefully determine the manner in which the concept is used. What is the case in practice when we impute "responsibility" to a person? What is our aim in doing this? The judge has to discover who is responsible for a given act in order

that he may *punish* him. We are inclined to be less concerned with the inquiry as to who deserves *reward* for an act, and we have no special officials for this; but of course the principle would be the same. But let us stick to punishment in order to make the idea clear. What is punishment, actually? The view still often expressed, that it is a natural *retaliation* for past wrong, ought no longer to be defended in cultivated society; for the opinion that an increase in sorrow can be "made good again" by further sorrow is altogether barbarous. Certainly the origin of punishment may lie in an impulse of retaliation or vengeance; but what is such an impulse except the instinctive desire to destroy the *cause* of the deed to be avenged, by the destruction of or injury to the malefactor? Punishment is concerned only with the institution of causes, of *motives* of conduct, and this alone is its meaning. Punishment is an educative measure, and as such is a means to the formation of motives, which are in part to prevent the wrongdoer from repeating the act (reformation) and in part to prevent others from committing a similar act (intimidation). Analogously, in the case of reward we are concerned with an incentive.

Hence the question regarding responsibility is the question: Who, in a given case, is to be punished? Who is to be considered the true wrongdoer? This problem is not identical with that regarding the original instigator of the act; for the great-grandparents of the man, from whom he inherited his character, might in the end be the cause, or the statesmen who are responsible for his social milieu, and so forth. But the "doer" is the one *upon whom the motive must have acted* in order, with certainty, to have prevented the act (or called it forth, as the case may be).

Consideration of remote causes is of no help here, for in the first place their actual contribution cannot be determined, and in the second place they are generally out of reach. Rather, we must find the person in whom the decisive junction of causes lies. The question of who is responsible is the question concerning the *correct point of application of the motive*. And the important thing is that in this its meaning is completely exhausted; behind it there lurks no mysterious connection between transgression and requital, which is merely *indicated* by the described state of affairs. It is a matter only of knowing who is to be punished or rewarded, in order that punishment and reward function as such—be able to achieve their goal.

Thus, all the facts connected with the concepts of responsibility and imputation are at once made intelligible. We do not charge an insane person with responsibility, for the very reason that he offers no unified point for the application of a motive. It would be pointless to try to affect him by means of promises or threats, when his confused soul fails to respond to such influence because its normal mechanism is out of order. We do not try to give him motives, but try to heal him (metaphorically, we make his sickness responsible, and try to remove its causes). When a man is forced by threats to commit certain acts, we do not blame him but the one who held the pistol at his breast. The reason is clear: the act would have been prevented had we been able to restrain the person who threatened him; and this person is the one whom we must influence in order to prevent similar acts in the future.

## 6. The Consciousness of Responsibility

But much more important than the question of when a man is said to be responsible is that of when he *himself* feels responsible. Our whole treatment would be untenable if it gave no explanation of this. It is, then, a welcome confirmation of the view here developed that the subjective feeling of responsibility coincides with the objective judgment. It is a fact of experience that, in general, the person blamed or condemned is conscious of the fact that he was "rightly" taken to account—of course, under the supposition that no error has been made, that the assumed state of affairs actually occurred. What is this consciousness of having been the true doer of the act, the actual instigator? Evidently not merely that it was he who took the steps required for its performance; but there must be added the awareness that he did it "independently," "of his own initiative," or however it be expressed. This feeling is simply the consciousness of *freedom,* which is merely the

knowledge of having acted of one's *own* desires. And "one's own desires" are those which have their origin in the regularity of one's character in the given situation, and are not imposed by an external power, as explained above. The absence of the external power expresses itself in the well-known feeling (usually considered characteristic of the consciousness of freedom) *that one could also have acted otherwise.* How this indubitable experience ever came to be an argument in favour of indeterminism is incomprehensible to me. It is of course obvious that I should have acted differently had I *willed* something else; but the feeling never says that I could also have willed something else, even though this is true, if, that is, other motives had been present. And it says even less that under *exactly the same* inner and outer conditions I could also have willed something else. How could such a feeling inform me of anything regarding the purely theoretical question of whether the principle of causality holds or not? Of course, after what has been said on the subject, I do not undertake to demonstrate the principle, but I do deny that from any such fact of consciousness the least follows regarding the principle's validity. This feeling is not the consciousness of the absence of a cause, but of something altogether different, namely, of *freedom,* which consists in the fact that I can act as I desire.

Thus the feeling of responsibility assumes that I acted freely, that my own desires impelled me; and if because of this feeling I willingly suffer blame for my behaviour or reproach myself, and thereby admit that I might have acted otherwise, this means that other behaviour was compatible with the laws of volition—of course, granted other motives. And I myself desire the existence of such motives and bear the pain (regret and sorrow) caused me by my behaviour so that its repetition will be prevented. To blame oneself means just to apply motives of improvement to oneself, which is usually the task of the educator. But if, for example, one does something under the influence of torture, feelings of guilt and regret are absent, for one knows that according to the laws of volition no other behaviour was possible—no matter what ideas, because of their feeling tones, might have functioned as motives. The important thing, always, is that the feeling of responsibility means the realization that one's self, one's own psychic processes constitute the point at which motives must be applied in order to govern the acts of one's body.

## 7. Causality as the Presupposition of Responsibility

We can speak of motives only in a causal context; thus it becomes clear how very much the concept of responsibility rests upon that of causation, that is, upon the regularity of volitional decisions. In fact if we should conceive of a decision as utterly without any cause (this would in all strictness be the indeterministic presupposition) then the act would be entirely a matter of *chance*, for chance is identical with the absence of a cause; there is no other opposite of causality. Could we under such conditions make the agent responsible? Certainly not. Imagine a man, always calm, peaceful and blameless, who suddenly falls upon and begins to beat a stranger. He is held and questioned regarding the motive of his action, to which he answers, in his opinion truthfully, as we assume: "There was no motive for my behaviour. Try as I may I can discover no reason. My volition was without any cause—I desired to do so, and there is simply nothing else to be said about it." We should shake our heads and call him insane, because we have to believe that there was a cause, and lacking any other we must assume some mental disturbance as the only cause remaining; but certainly no one would hold him to be responsible. If decisions were causeless there would be no sense in trying to influence men; and we see at once that this is the reason why we could not bring such a man to account, but would always have only a shrug of the shoulders in answer to his behaviour. One can easily determine that in practice we make an agent the more responsible the more motives we can find for his conduct. If a man guilty of an atrocity was an enemy of his victim, if previously he had shown violent tendencies, if some special circumstance angered him, then we impose severe punishment

upon him; while the fewer the reasons to be found for an offence the less do we condemn the agent, but make "unlucky chance," a momentary aberration, or something of the sort, responsible. We do not find the causes of misconduct in his character, and therefore we do not try to influence it for the better: this and only this is the significance of the fact that we do not put the responsibility upon him. And he too feels this to be so, and says, "I cannot understand how such a thing could have happened to me."

In general we know very well how to discover the causes of conduct in the characters of our fellow men, and how to use this knowledge in the prediction of their future behaviour, often with as much certainty as that with which we know that a lion and a rabbit will behave quite differently in the same situation. From all this it is evident that in practice no one thinks of questioning the principle of causality, that, thus, the attitude of the practical man offers no excuse to the metaphysician for confusing freedom from compulsion with the absence of a cause. If one makes clear to himself that a causeless happening is identical with a chance happening, and that, consequently, an indetermined will would destroy all responsibility, then every desire will cease which might be father to an indeterministic thought. No one can prove determinism, but it is certain that we assume its validity in all of our practical life, and that in particular we can apply the concept of responsibility to human conduct only insofar as the causal principle holds of volitional processes.

For a final clarification I bring together again a list of those concepts which tend, in the traditional treatment of the "problem of freedom," to be confused. In the place of the concepts on the left are put, mistakenly, those of the right, and those in the vertical order form a chain, so that sometimes the previous confusion is the cause of that which follows:

| | |
|---|---|
| Natural Law. | Law of State. |
| Determinism (Causality). | Compulsion. |
| (Universal Validity). | (Necessity). |
| Indeterminism (Chance). | Freedom. |
| (No Cause). | (No Compulsion). |

## Study Questions

1. On what grounds does a soft determinist like Schlick reject the belief shared by hard determinists and libertarians that freedom and determinism are incompatible?

2. In analyzing the concept of responsibility, Schlick concludes that when we ask who is responsible for an action we are really asking who should be punished or rewarded for that action. By making reference to an example of an action for which someone might conceivably be punished or rewarded, explain how Schlick goes about determining responsibility.

3. Right now, as you sit in your seat, you have a sense that you can freely choose whether to stand or remain seated. It does not seem unreasonable for us to take this as evidence that humans have free agency and determinism is false. What is Schlick's response regarding the significance of our subjective experience for the question of freedom and determinism?

4. Describe Schlick's views on chance and the status of statistical laws and probabilistic explanations in science.

# Harry G. Frankfurt

Harry G. Frankfurt received his PhD from Johns Hopkins University in 1954. Now emeritus professor of philosophy at Princeton University, Frankfurt's contributions to metaphysics and moral philosophy include writings on such questions as personal identity, responsibility, and love. In 2005, Frankfurt's book *On Bullshit* reached number one on the *New York Times* best-seller list, earning him an appearance on *The Daily Show with Jon Stewart*. In this influential essay, Frankfurt challenges an underlying assumption shared by all parties to the freedom–determinism debate.—TR

## Alternate Possibilities and Moral Responsibility

### 1. Introduction

A dominant role in nearly all recent inquiries into the free-will problem has been played by a principle which I shall call "the principle of alternate possibilities." This principle states that a person is morally responsible for what he has done only if he could have done otherwise. Its exact meaning is a subject of controversy, particularly concerning whether someone who accepts it is thereby committed to believing that moral responsibility and determinism are incompatible. Practically no one, however, seems inclined to deny or even to question that the principle of alternate possibilities (construed in some way or other) is true. It has generally seemed so overwhelmingly plausible that some philosophers have even characterized it as an a priori truth. People whose accounts of free will or of moral responsibility are radically at odds evidently find in it a firm and convenient common ground upon which they can profitably take their opposing stands.

But the principle of alternate possibilities is false. A person may well be morally responsible for what he has done even though he could not have done otherwise. The principle's plausibility is an illusion, which can be made to vanish by bringing the relevant moral phenomena into sharper focus.

### 2. Framing Counterexamples to the Principle of Alternate Possibilities

In seeking illustrations of the principle of alternate possibilities, it is most natural to think of situations in which the same circumstances both bring it about that a person does something and make it impossible for him to avoid doing it. These include, for example, situations in which a person is coerced into doing something, or in which he is impelled to act by a hypnotic suggestion, or in which some inner compulsion drives him to do what he does. In situations of these kinds there are circumstances that make it impossible for the person to do otherwise, and these very circumstances also serve to bring it about that he does whatever it is that he does.

However, there may be circumstances that constitute sufficient conditions for a certain action to be performed by someone and that therefore make it impossible for the person to do otherwise, but that do not actually impel the person to act or in any way produce his action. A person may do something in circumstances that leave him no alternative to doing it, without these circumstances actually moving him or leading him to do it—without them playing any role, indeed, in bringing it about that he does what he does.

An examination of situations characterized by circumstances of this sort casts doubt, I believe, on the relevance to questions of moral responsibility of the fact that a person who has done something could not have done otherwise. I propose to develop some examples of this kind in the context of a discussion of coercion and to suggest that our moral intuitions concerning these examples tend to disconfirm the principle of alternate possibilities. Then I will discuss the principle in more general terms, explain what I think is wrong with it, and describe briefly and without argument how it might appropriately be revised.

## 3. Doctrine that Coercion Excuses Not a Version of the Principle of Alternate Possibilities

It is generally agreed that a person who has been coerced to do something did not do it freely and is not morally responsible for having done it. Now the doctrine that coercion and moral responsibility are mutually exclusive may appear to be no more than a somewhat particularized version of the principle of alternate possibilities. It is natural enough to say of a person who has been coerced to do something that he could not have done otherwise. And it may easily seem that being coerced deprives a person of freedom and of moral responsibility simply because it is a special case of being unable to do otherwise. The principle of alternate possibilities may in this way derive some credibility from its association with the very plausible proposition that moral responsibility is excluded by coercion.

It is not right, however, that it should do so. The fact that a person was coerced to act as he did may entail both that he could not have done otherwise and that he bears no moral responsibility for his action. But his lack of moral responsibility is not entailed by his having been unable to do otherwise. The doctrine that coercion excludes moral responsibility is not correctly understood, in other words, as a particularized version of the principle of alternate possibilities.

Let us suppose that someone is threatened convincingly with a penalty he finds unacceptable and that he then does what is required of him by the issuer of the threat. We can imagine details that would make it reasonable for us to think that the person was coerced to perform the action in question, that he could not have done otherwise, and that he bears no moral responsibility for having done what he did. But just what is it about situations of this kind that warrants the judgment that the threatened person is not morally responsible for his act?

This question may be approached by considering situations of the following kind. Jones decides for reasons of his own to do something, then someone threatens him with a very harsh penalty (so harsh that any reasonable person would submit to the threat) unless he does precisely that, and Jones does it. Will we hold Jones morally responsible for what he has done? I think this will depend on the roles we think were played, in leading him to act, by his original decision and by the threat.

One possibility is that Jones$_1$ is not a reasonable man: he is, rather, a man who does what he has once decided to do no matter what happens next and no matter what the cost. In that case, the threat actually exerted no effective force upon him. He acted without any regard to it, very much as if he were not aware that it had been made. If this is indeed the way it was, the situation did not involve coercion at all. The threat did not lead Jones$_1$ to do what he did. Nor was it in fact sufficient to have prevented him from doing otherwise: if his earlier decision had been to do something else, the threat would not have deterred him in the slightest. It seems evident that in these circumstances the fact that Jones$_1$ was threatened in no way reduces the moral responsibility he would otherwise bear for his act. This example, however, is not a counterexample either to the doctrine that coercion excuses or to the principle of alternate possibilities. For we have supposed that Jones$_1$ is a man upon whom the threat had no coercive effect and, hence, that it did not actually deprive him of alternatives to doing what he did.

Another possibility is that Jones$_2$ was stampeded by the threat. Given that threat, he would have performed that action regardless of what decision he had already made. The threat upset him so profoundly, moreover, that he completely forgot his own earlier decision and did what was demanded of him entirely because he was terrified of the penalty with which he was threatened. In this case, it is not relevant to his having performed the action that he had already decided on his own to perform it. When the chips were down he thought of nothing but the threat, and fear alone led him to act. The fact that at an earlier time Jones$_2$ had decided for his own reasons to act in just that way may be relevant to an evaluation of his character; he may bear full moral responsibility for having made *that* decision. But he can hardly be said to be morally responsible for his action. For he performed the action simply as a result of the coercion to which he was subjected. His earlier decision played no role in bringing it about that he did what he did, and it would therefore be gratuitous to assign it a role in the moral evaluation of his action.

Now consider a third possibility. Jones$_3$ was neither stampeded by the threat nor indifferent to it. The threat impressed him, as it would impress any reasonable man, and he would have submitted to it wholeheartedly if he had not already made a decision that coincided with the one demanded of him. In fact, however, he performed the action in question on the basis of the decision he had made

before the threat was issued. When he acted, he was not actually motivated by the threat but solely by the considerations that had originally commended the action to him. It was not the threat that led him to act, though it would have done so if he had not already provided himself with a sufficient motive for performing the action in question.

No doubt it will be very difficult for anyone to know, in a case like this one, exactly what happened. Did Jones$_3$ perform the action because of the threat, or were his reasons for acting simply those which had already persuaded him to do so? Or did he act on the basis of two motives, each of which was sufficient for his action? It is not impossible, however, that the situation should be clearer than situations of this kind usually are. And suppose it is apparent to us that Jones$_3$ acted on the basis of his own decision and not because of the threat. Then I think we would be justified in regarding his moral responsibility for what he did as unaffected by the threat even though, since he would in any case have submitted to the threat, he could not have avoided doing what he did. It would be entirely reasonable for us to make the same judgment concerning his moral responsibility that we would have made if we had not known of the threat. For the threat did not in fact influence his performance of the action. He did what he did just as if the threat had not been made at all.

## 4. More on Jones$_3$

The case of Jones$_3$ may appear at first glance to combine coercion and moral responsibility, and thus to provide a counterexample to the doctrine that coercion excuses. It is not really so certain that it does so, however, because it is unclear whether the example constitutes a genuine instance of coercion. Can we say of Jones$_3$ that he was coerced to do something, when he had already decided on his own to do it and when he did it entirely on the basis of that decision? Or would it be more correct to say that Jones$_3$ was not coerced to do what he did, even though he himself recognized that there was an irresistible force at work in virtue of which he had to do it? My own linguistic intuitions lead me toward the second alternative, but they are somewhat equivocal. Perhaps we can say either of these things, or perhaps we must add a qualifying explanation to whichever of them we say.

This murkiness, however, does not interfere with our drawing an important moral from an examination of the example. Suppose we decide to say that Jones$_3$ was *not* coerced. Our basis for saying this will clearly be that it is incorrect to regard a man as being coerced to do something unless he does it *because of* the coercive force exerted against him. The fact that an irresistible threat is made will not, then, entail that the person who receives it is coerced to do what he does. It will also be necessary that the threat is what actually accounts for his doing it. On the other hand, suppose we decide to say that Jones$_3$ *was* coerced. Then we will be bound to admit that being coerced does not exclude being morally responsible. And we will also surely be led to the view that coercion affects the judgment of a person's moral responsibility only when the person acts as he does because he is coerced to do so—i.e., when the fact that he is coerced is what accounts for his action.

Whichever we decide to say, then, we will recognize that the doctrine that coercion excludes moral responsibility is not a particularized version of the principle of alternate possibilities. Situations in which a person who does something cannot do otherwise because he is subject to coercive power are either not instances of coercion at all, or they are situations in which the person may still be morally responsible for what he does if it is not because of the coercion that he does it. When we excuse a person who has been coerced, we do not excuse him because he was unable to do otherwise. Even though a person is subject to a coercive force that precludes his performing any action but one, he may nonetheless bear full moral responsibility for performing that action.

## 5. Black and Jones$_4$ as Counter-example to the Principle of Alternate Possibilities

To the extent that the principle of alternate possibilities derives its plausibility from association with the doctrine that coercion excludes moral responsibility, a clear understanding of the latter diminishes the appeal of the former. Indeed

the case of Jones$_3$ may appear to do more than illuminate the relationship between the two doctrines. It may well seem to provide a decisive counter-example to the principle of alternate possibilities and thus to show that this principle is false. For the irresistibility of the threat to which Jones$_3$ is subjected might well be taken to mean that he cannot but perform the action he performs. And yet the threat, since Jones$_3$ performs the action without regard to it, does not reduce his moral responsibility for what he does.

The following objection will doubtless be raised against the suggestion that the case of Jones$_3$ is a counter-example to the principle of alternate possibilities. There is perhaps a sense in which Jones$_3$ cannot do otherwise than perform the action he performs, since he is a reasonable man and the threat he encounters is sufficient to move any reasonable man. But it is not this sense that is germane to the principle of alternate possibilities. His knowledge that he stands to suffer an intolerably harsh penalty does not mean that Jones$_3$, strictly speaking, *cannot* perform any action but the one he does perform. After all it is still open to him, and this is crucial, to defy the threat if he wishes to do so and to accept the penalty his action would bring down upon him. In the sense in which the principle of alternate possibilities employs the concept of "could have done otherwise," Jones$_3$'s inability to resist the threat does not mean that he cannot do otherwise than perform the action he performs. Hence the case of Jones$_3$ does not constitute an instance contrary to the principle.

I do not propose to consider in what sense the concept of "could have done otherwise" figures in the principle of alternate possibilities, nor will I attempt to measure the force of the objection I have just described. For I believe that whatever force this objection may be thought to have can be deflected by altering the example in the following way. Suppose someone—Black, let us say—wants Jones$_4$ to perform a certain action. Black is prepared to go to considerable lengths to get his way, but he prefers to avoid showing his hand unnecessarily. So he waits until Jones$_4$ is about to make up his mind what to do, and he does nothing unless it is clear to him (Black is an excellent judge of such things) that

Jones$_4$ is going to decide to do something *other* than what he wants him to do. If it does become clear that Jones$_4$ is going to decide to do something else, Black takes effective steps to ensure that Jones$_4$ decides to do, and that he does do, what he wants him to do. Whatever Jones$_4$' initial preferences and inclinations, then, Black will have his way.

What steps will Black take, if he believes he must take steps, in order to ensure that Jones$_4$ decides and acts as he wishes? Anyone with a theory concerning what "could have done otherwise" means may answer this question for himself by describing whatever measures he would regard as sufficient to guarantee that, in the relevant sense, Jones$_4$ cannot do otherwise. Let Black pronounce a terrible threat, and in this way both force Jones$_4$ to perform the desired action and prevent him from performing a forbidden one. Let Black give Jones$_4$ a potion, or put him under hypnosis, and in some such way as these generate in Jones$_4$ an irresistible inner compulsion to perform the act Black wants performed and to avoid others. Or let Black manipulate the minute processes of Jones$_4$' brain and nervous system in some more direct way, so that causal forces running in and out of his synapses and along the poor man's nerves determine that he chooses to act and that he does act in the one way and not in any other. Given any conditions under which it will be maintained that Jones$_4$ cannot do otherwise, in other words, let Black bring it about that those conditions prevail. The structure of the example is flexible enough, I think, to find a way around any charge of irrelevance by accommodating the doctrine on which the charge is based.[1]

Now suppose that Black never has to show his hand because Jones$_4$, for reasons of his own, decides to perform and does perform the very action Black wants him to perform. In that case, it seems clear, Jones$_4$ will bear precisely the same moral responsibility for what he does as he would have borne if Black had not been ready to take steps to ensure that he do it. It would be quite unreasonable to excuse Jones$_4$ for his action, or to withhold the praise to which it would normally entitle him, on the basis of the fact that he could not have done otherwise. This fact played no role at all in leading him to act as he did.

He would have acted the same even if it had not been a fact. Indeed, everything happened just as it would have happened without Black's presence in the situation and without his readiness to intrude into it.

In this example there are sufficient conditions for Jones$_4$' performing the action in question. What action he performs is not up to him. Of course it is in a way up to him whether he acts on his own or as a result of Black's intervention. That depends upon what action he himself is inclined to perform. But whether he finally acts on his own or as a result of Black's intervention, he performs the same action. He has no alternative but to do what Black wants him to do. If he does it on his own, however, his moral responsibility for doing it is not affected by the fact that Black was lurking in the background with sinister intent, since this intent never comes into play.

## 6. Replacing, Not Revising, the Principle of Alternate Possibilities

The fact that a person could not have avoided doing something is a sufficient condition of his having done it. But, as some of my examples show, this fact may play no role whatever in the explanation of why he did it. It may not figure at all among the circumstances that actually brought it about that he did what he did, so that his action is to be accounted for on another basis entirely. Even though the person was unable to do otherwise, that is to say, it may not be the case that he acted as he did *because* he could not have done otherwise. Now if someone had no alternative to performing a certain action but did not perform it because he was unable to do otherwise, then he would have performed exactly the same action even if he *could* have done otherwise. The circumstances that made it impossible for him to do otherwise could have been subtracted from the situation without affecting what happened or why it happened in any way. Whatever it was that actually led the person to do what he did, or that made him do it, would have led him to do it or made him do it even if it had been possible for him to do something else instead.

Thus it would have made no difference, so far as concerns his action or how he came to perform it, if the circumstances that made it impossible for him to avoid performing it had not prevailed. The fact that he could not have done otherwise clearly provides no basis for supposing that he *might* have done otherwise if he had been able to do so. When a fact is in this way irrelevant to the problem of accounting for a person's action it seems quite gratuitous to assign it any weight in the assessment of his moral responsibility. Why should the fact be considered in reaching a moral judgment concerning the person when it does not help in any way to understand either what made him act as he did or what, in other circumstances, he might have done?

This, then, is why the principle of alternate possibilities is mistaken. It asserts that a person bears no moral responsibility—that is, he is to be excused—for having performed an action if there were circumstances that made it impossible for him to avoid performing it. But there may be circumstances that make it impossible for a person to avoid performing some action without those circumstances in any way bringing it about that he performs that action. It would surely be no good for the person to refer to circumstances of this sort in an effort to absolve himself of moral responsibility for performing the action in question. For those circumstances, by hypothesis, actually had nothing to do with his having done what he did. He would have done precisely the same thing, and he would have been led or made in precisely the same way to do it, even if they had not prevailed.

We often do, to be sure, excuse people for what they have done when they tell us (and we believe them) that they could not have done otherwise. But this is because we assume that what they tell us serves to explain why they did what they did. We take it for granted that they are not being disingenuous, as a person would be who cited as an excuse the fact that he could not have avoided doing what he did but who knew full well that it was not at all because of this that he did it.

What I have said may suggest that the principle of alternate possibilities should be revised so as to assert that a person is not morally responsible for what he has done if he did it because he could not have done otherwise. It may be noted that this revision of the

principle does not seriously affect the arguments of those who have relied on the original principle in their efforts to maintain that moral responsibility and determinism are incompatible. For if it was causally determined that a person perform a certain action, then it will be true that the person performed it because of those causal determinants. And if the fact that it was causally determined that a person perform a certain action means that the person could not have done otherwise, as philosophers who argue for the incompatibility thesis characteristically suppose, then the fact that it was causally determined that a person perform a certain action will mean that the person performed it because he could not have done otherwise. The revised principle of alternate possibilities will entail, on this assumption concerning the meaning of "could have done otherwise," that a person is not morally responsible for what he has done if it was causally determined that he do it. I do not believe, however, that this revision of the principle is acceptable.

Suppose a person tells us that he did what he did because he was unable to do otherwise; or suppose he makes the similar statement that he did what he did because he had to do it. We do often accept statements like these (if we believe them) as valid excuses, and such statements may well seem at first glance to invoke the revised principle of alternate possibilities. But I think that when we accept such statements as valid excuses it is because we assume that we are being told more than the statements strictly and literally convey. We understand the person who offers the excuse to mean that he did what he did *only because* he was unable to do otherwise, or *only because* he had to do it. And we understand him to mean, more particularly, that when he did what he did it was not because that was what he really wanted to do. The principle of alternate possibilities should thus be replaced, in my opinion, by the following principle: a person is not morally responsible for what he has done if he did it only because he could not have done otherwise. This principle does not appear to conflict with the view that moral responsibility is compatible with determinism.

The following may all be true: there were circumstances that made it impossible for a person to avoid doing something; these circumstances actually played a role in bringing it about that he did it, so that it is correct to say that he did it because he could not have done otherwise; the person really wanted to do what he did; he did it because it was what he really wanted to do, so that it is not correct to say that he did what he did only because he could not have done otherwise. Under these conditions, the person may well be morally responsible for what he has done. On the other hand, he will not be morally responsible for what he has done if he did it only because he could not have done otherwise, even if what he did was something he really wanted to do.

## Note

1. The example is also flexible enough to allow for the elimination of Black altogether. Anyone who thinks that the effectiveness of the example is undermined by its reliance on a human manipulator, who imposes his will on Jones$_4$, can substitute for Black a machine programmed to do what Black does. If this is still not good enough, forget both Black and the machine and suppose that their role is played by natural forces involving no will or design at all.

## Study Questions

1. What is the "principle of alternate possibilities"?
2. Is Frankfurt correct in saying that parties to the freedom and determinism debate—hard determinists, soft determinists, and libertarians alike—despite their differences, assume the truth of the principle of alternate possibilities?
3. Describe how each of the various characters named Jones—Jones$_1$, Jones$_2$, Jones$_3$, and Jones$_4$—makes a distinct contribution to Frankfurt's argument in defence of his thesis that the principle of alternate possibilities is false.
4. Pretend that there is a "violence gene" that does not just predispose someone to commit a crime but provides a sufficient cause. According to Frankfurt, does having such a gene mitigate a person's responsibility for a crime?

## Marcia Baron

Marcia Baron specializes in moral philosophy, moral psychology, and philosophy of criminal law. She received her PhD at the University of North Carolina in 1982, and is currently Rudy Professor of Philosophy at Indiana University, Bloomington, and a professor of philosophy at the University of St Andrews. This essay was written for a 1995 University of Maryland conference that generated controversy for its discussion of genetic research and criminal behaviour—TR

## Crime, Genes, and Responsibility

### 1. Introduction

As ethicists and metaphysicians we have been asked by the conference organizers to discuss freedom, responsibility, and desert in connection with the possibility that a genetic marker will be discovered for "criminality" or aggressiveness. Some have thought that if there were a marker, then individuals with the marker could not be held responsible for whatever criminal or aggressive behaviour they might engage in. Would we, they worry, be morally justified in punishing a murderer or a rapist if this person's genes predisposed him toward violent behaviour?

Before answering this question, we should note a problem in its formulation. I have used as if they were interchangeable all of the following: "criminality," "aggressiveness," and "violent behaviour." Of course, they are not interchangeable terms, but the problem is that we don't know what a genetic marker, if found, would mark. Toward what would a person with the marker be predisposed? Anger? Or calculated, premeditated violence? Some sort of generic criminality (whatever that might be)? Or a sort of generic aggressiveness—a tendency to try to get one's way by force rather than by asking or negotiating? Or something more specific: a tendency to beat "loved" ones when they seem to be getting too independent? Or something specific and criminal but non-violent: tax evasion or embezzlement or shoplifting?

The fact that we don't know what a marker, if discovered, would mark, generally goes unnoticed, and I think it is of considerable importance. Not knowing what a marker would mark, we put some face on it. But we do so without realizing it. And the face we put on it then affects our view of the meaning and importance of research into a link between genes and crime. When someone speaks of crime without giving any indication of what sort of crime is meant, most of us don't think of embezzling or writing bad checks. We picture violent crime of one sort or another. And indeed it seems that what we think we are looking for is a tendency toward violence of one sort or another. [. . .] We need, therefore, to bear in mind that we do not know what a marker, if discovered, would mark. I take it that the most serious concern is that there might be a marker for violent behaviour, and I focus primarily, though not exclusively, on that possibility.

## 2. Genes, Like Environments, Incline But Do Not Necessitate

So, to ask the question again: would we be morally justified in punishing a murderer or a rapist if this person's genes predisposed him toward violent behaviour?

The answer is, I think, fairly straightforward. Suppose there were a genetic factor in crime and a test that disclosed whether the individual had the marker. The individual who tested positive would simply be genetically *predisposed* toward such behaviour. He or she would, as philosophers sometimes say, be *inclined but not necessitated* to act violently. The person's position would be the same as that of people whose environment—including, especially, their past environment and, in particular, their childhoods—significantly increased the chance that they would become violent offenders.[1] Both the person with the genetic marker and the person whose environmental factors significantly increase the chance that he or she will become a criminal are likely to have a harder time than they otherwise would (and than other people have) leading a life in which they do not act violently. Neither is "caused" to commit violent crimes; it is simply harder for them than it is for others not to commit violent crimes. If we do not regard the individual whose upbringing significantly increased the chance that he would become a violent offender as therefore not responsible for his crimes, I see no basis for thinking that someone with a genetic marker for criminality should not be held responsible for crimes that he committed.

Why might there be a temptation not to hold someone responsible for a crime if we knew that she was genetically predisposed to commit crimes of this sort? The reason, I think, is that we would judge her to be less free to refrain from committing such crimes than the rest of us are. But if she is less free, so is the person who is "environmentally predisposed" to commit such crimes (and, for that matter, so is the person whose non-genetic medical condition predisposed her to commit such crimes). So again, I don't see that the possibility that a genetic marker for criminality will be discovered and readily tested for raises new problems concerning freedom and responsibility.

The same point holds regarding desert: the fact that the person is genetically predisposed to commit violent crimes should be a mitigating factor just to the extent that the fact that environmental factors dispose the person to do so is a mitigating factor. And so my tentative conclusion to the question of responsibility, desert, and freedom is this: the possibility of genetic markers for aggressiveness or criminality or violent criminality does not pose any new problems regarding responsibility, etc. that are not already posed by environmental (and other familiar) factors.

## 3. Or Is There Something Special about Genetic Factors?

Now, a complication. I have said that a genetic predisposition to act in certain ways—or to suffer certain behavioural problems—would only incline the person to such behaviour, rather than necessitate it. There are different ways of being inclined, however, and some ways may provide reasons for considering the person so minimally free to refrain from the objectionable behaviour that to hold her fully responsible for her conduct is not justifiable. If someone has a condition that drastically reduces her willpower, so that no matter how firmly she believes that arson is wrong, and no matter how fervently she wishes never to set fires, and no matter how many precautions she takes—keeping no matches or lighters in her house, for instance—and despite seeking counselling or taking special classes for pyromaniacs, she nonetheless commits arson, this condition surely calls for our sympathy and may be grounds for not holding her fully responsible for her actions. It certainly should be a mitigating factor, a reason to give her a more lenient sentence, if in fact we do hold her responsible and do convict her.

Now, if certain genetic influences were to affect us much more dramatically than any other influences, predisposing us to violent, criminal behaviour more, or in a significantly different way than other influences do, this would of course be noteworthy. I don't see that the research points in this direction, however; and in any case, the point remains that the fact that the influence is *genetic* is itself of no importance. Moreover, the primary reason for thinking that in a

case such as the one I describe the agent deserves a lighter sentence than usual (and arguably should not be held responsible at all) is that she tried so hard not to commit arson (not that it was so hard for her to refrain from doing so).

Consider the following three examples. Imagine someone—let's call him A—who feels a strong sexual attraction to children. He abhors this desire in himself, tries to extinguish it, tries to avoid situations in which the temptation will be strong and where the opportunity to satisfy the desire will be present. Despite his efforts, he sexually molests children. Now imagine B. What was just said of A is true of B, as well. But unlike A, B has a genetic abnormality which has been correlated with impulsivity. In the case of B we have a bit more of an explanation of why it is that B fails to refrain from molesting children. But I don't see that we have any more reason not to hold B responsible for his acts of child molesting than not to hold A responsible, or any more reason for leniency in sentencing B than for leniency in sentencing A (if we do hold them responsible and do convict them). Finally consider C, who like B has a genetic abnormality that is correlated with impulsivity and, like both B and A, has sexually molested children. But in the case of C, we understand the mechanism at work and see that the underlying problem is that, as Greenspan puts it, C has inadequate resources for behavioural control. There is "an absence of 'enabling' causes of normal control such as adequate supply of serotonin and other electrotransmitters" (244). (I assume for simplicity that no treatment for the defect was available at the time the defendant committed the offences.) There may be some temptation to think that C deserves greater leniency, perhaps, but I think that is only because we are more certain that C is really doing his best and just cannot control his untoward impulses. If we fully accept that A and B are doing all they can, is there any reason to hold them more responsible than C? I don't think so.

My more general point is that, with one exception, it does not matter what the source of the problem is (the problem being that it is unusually difficult for the person to do what he firmly believes he should do, and fervently wants to do). Whether it is genetic or not does not matter. The one exception is that if the source of the problem is something that he did, we *may* (reasonably) feel less sympathetic toward A than toward B or C. We *may*; it will depend on what he did and why.

## 4. Are Environmental Factors More Superficial?

Still, some might feel that, although they are not sure why, a gene linked to criminality would render the person *less free* to refrain from committing crimes of the sort to which he is disposed than would environmental factors. Is there reason to believe that a genetic factor limits one's freedom more than environmental factors? Are there (and the answer to this question might possibly be different) reasons for treating a genetic predisposition toward committing (certain) crimes as a more fully mitigating factor than an environmental predisposition? I very much doubt it (in each case); but I can think of reasons why some might think otherwise. Genes sound like the sorts of things that determine us completely. If a trait has a genetic basis, we may erroneously assume that, in some interestingly robust sense, we have to be that way. [. . .] My guess is that many think that any trait with a genetic basis is rather like having blue eyes; it is something determined by one's genes, and one cannot do anything about it. (Of course one can wear tinted contact lenses that alter the way one's eyes *look*. But still one's eyes are blue.) By contrast, we've all been taught that no matter how impoverished one's background, any American can, if he or she only tries hard enough, become wealthy, famous, and maybe even a US president. Thus, environmental factors are seen by many to be more superficial, more surmountable, than genetic factors.

Obviously, one's political leanings will influence how one thinks about these matters. Those who accept the idea that any American can become wealthy, no matter how dire the poverty into which she was born and how grave the injustices that her parents and grandparents suffered, will see environmental factors to "incline" one less than will those who reject it. But this disagreement does not run very deep. For the point remains that genetic predispositions only predispose; they don't necessitate. Thus, while acknowledging our political differences, we can all agree that with respect to conduct (as opposed to eye colour) environmental factors and genetic factors alike incline but do not necessitate.

## 5. A Question of Evidence

There is, however, a somewhat stronger reason why jurors might be more sympathetic to an unfree-to-do-otherwise argument in the case of someone who is genetically predisposed to commit crimes than they are to the same argument used in the case of someone whose childhood environment was marked by violence, sexual abuse, lack of love, dire poverty, hunger, terrible schools, and so on. We have *medical proof* in the first case that the person is genetically predisposed to commit crimes—that is, assuming a scenario in which a marker had been found and where medical tests would show decisively whether the individual had the marker. But there's no "proof," a lawyer might convince jurors, that the murderer with the terrible childhood was *really* predisposed to commit murders. There's something irrefutable in the first case, and not in the second. To put it differently: "Anyone," it might be claimed (with some exaggeration), "can be said to have had so lousy a childhood that it marked him for life; but not everyone can be said to have the genetic marker. There's a test for the genetic marker, and no one will say under oath that the person has been tested and found to have the marker unless it's true."

The difference seems to be one of evidence—of how convincing the claim is—rather than that environmental factors limit one's freedom less than a genetic marker for criminality does. If this is right, there is no reason to think that those with the genetic marker are less responsible for their crimes than those who lack the marker but were disposed by environmental factors over which they had no control—the socio-economic and familial conditions into which they were born—to commit crimes that they indeed did commit. There is, in the scenario we are imagining, merely more room for doubt about whether the individual who has committed a crime was "environmentally disposed" than there is about whether such a person was genetically disposed. Even this is not altogether clear, however. For the fact that we do not know what the marker marks bears on the issue. If it marks a tendency to unaggravated property offences, do we say that the marker made someone less able to refrain from the crime of armed robbery that she committed? It may be difficult to judge how much the marker disposes her to. If this is the case, the medical testimony may in fact leave as much room for doubt as the social worker's or the psychologist's testimony that her early childhood marked her for life, leaving her less able than most of us to refrain from committing crimes.

## 6. Would Discovering a Genetic Marker for Criminality Be an Advance?

I have argued that there is no good reason to believe that genetic predispositions to criminality undermine responsibility more than environmental predispositions do [. . .]. Nonetheless, many people may believe that they do, and some of these people may be jurors. In that sense a discovery of a genetic predisposition to crime may raise issues regarding responsibility, freedom, and desert. It will be seen to raise new issues because genes are believed by many to determine us more fully than they do. The supposition that there is something very special—and wonderful—about a genetic explanation is prominent in the popular literature on genes and crime. It is also prominent in works on related topics, such as *The Bell Curve* (Herrnstein and Murray), a book that received a great deal of attention a few years ago.

Readers of *The Bell Curve*—and readers (or "auditors") of the many enthusiastic summaries of that work in magazines, newspapers and on radio and television—are left with the impression that a genetic

basis for *x* means that *x* cannot be altered by improved education, a more supportive environment, or the like.

Recognizing that a genetic marker for some sort of criminal tendency may raise social issues that it would not raise were it not for (induced?) ignorance, we do well to broaden our topic and ask how things would be different if we discovered and had a test for a genetic marker. In particular, what would be gained?

It is common to assume that the discovery would be a great advance. The following view, expressed by a former Maryland state delegate, is not unusual (though more cautious in its optimism than is typical): "(Most) experts in the field doubt there are 'criminal genes' or that genetic markers could be found that would identify potential wrongdoers at an early age. But, on the other hand, amazing genetic breakthroughs occur routinely. These advances can improve the quality of life for all of us" (Mooney). How so? The assumption that such a scientific advance would "improve the quality of life for all of us" needs to be examined.

Our thinking on this topic is no doubt affected by the way we think of other genetic markers. Perhaps we assume that finding a marker for criminality would improve our quality of life because of our views concerning the value of finding some other marker (of a sort that it is easier to imagine finding, or that has already been found).

Consider the benefits and the costs of finding a genetic marker for a disease, for example, colon cancer. The negative effects are not negligible. Insurance companies may review applicants" (and members') family histories, require those with a worrisome family history to be tested for the marker, and, if they test positive, reject their applications (or terminate their insurance). There is, moreover, the possibility that prospective (or actual) employers will gain access to such information and avoid hiring (or perhaps fire) those who have the marker for colon cancer. As markers for more and more diseases are discovered, they might be factored into a ranking system and used by insurance companies and some employers to avoid "costly" clients or employees. Other drawbacks (at least from the standpoint of the person found to have the genetic marker) are anxiety and a sense of doom. Moreover, parents' knowledge that their young children have the marker could have a damaging effect on the child. Education might alleviate the last two problems, and legislation forbidding insurance companies and employers from obtaining this information would offset the former problems. Still, none of these problems can be discounted.

On the other hand, there could be significant benefits to having a marker (and a reliable and reasonably inexpensive test for it). Those who learn that they do have the marker can have frequent diagnostic tests to facilitate early detection and thus reduce the likelihood that they'll die from colon cancer. (With or without a marker, we could, of course, all have these tests, but the cost is high and the tests are unpleasant.) And the news that they have the marker should motivate those in need of motivation to redouble their efforts to improve their diets so as to reduce the likelihood that they will get the disease (since, after all, having the marker does not mean that one is certain to get the disease) or at least postpone the onset of the disease until old age. These are the sorts of measures that many people are prone to avoid but which perhaps they would pursue if they found out that they are genetically prone to the disease. (Admittedly this is optimistic; the notion that genes determine our fates is hard to shake, and many who learn they have the marker may simply resign themselves to what they assume will inevitably be an early death.) Those who learn that they do not have the marker will enjoy the relief afforded by that news (without assuming, of course, that they are guaranteed not to get colon cancer). In addition, they can reasonably opt for less frequent diagnostic tests than their family history of cancer would otherwise have indicated.

Would the discovery of a genetic link to crime and a test to determine who has the marker benefit people in some similar ways? Not likely. It might benefit people—possibly even the people in whom the marker was found—but not in any way analogous to the way in which a marker for cancer or some other sometimes curable diseases would be beneficial. The dissimilarities are striking. The benefit of a marker for a sometimes curable, sometimes fatal disease, a disease whose early detection greatly increases one's chances of survival, is evident—and it is primarily a benefit for the person with the marker. It is hard to see how someone would benefit from knowing that he or she had a genetic marker for criminality or violence.

Now there is one scenario in which a test for a marker for criminality would be highly beneficial, probably even for the affected person, and it parallels the way in which a test for a gene linked to cancer is beneficial. As noted earlier, a genetic predisposition to crime would only make a person more likely to commit crimes; it would not ensure that he or she would commit crimes. But suppose that we knew that in certain conditions the person genetically disposed to commit crimes is far more likely to commit them than he or she would be in other conditions. And suppose that these conditions were not simply the same as the conditions in which everyone is far more likely to commit crimes. After all, we have a pretty good idea of the conditions that render it more likely that a person will commit crimes: the person is addicted to an illegal and expensive drug and is not wealthy (and, we might add, the waiting lists for drug treatment centres are very long); and so on. Suppose, rather, that the environmental conditions that triggered those genetically predisposed to commit crimes were something like this: the person had recently consumed four ounces or more of a sports drink or had recently consumed two ounces or more of blue cheese. Imagine that people who were genetically predisposed to criminality needed only to avoid drinking or eating these substances— and, if they did, their predisposition would, in effect, be nullified. They would then be no more likely to commit violent crimes than people without the genetic predisposition.

If this were the situation, the existence and availability of a test for the marker would be a real benefit to those who test positive for it. For there would be something to do about it, and the something would not be costly (unlike, say, being kept permanently on drugs that have serious side effects). There would be a benefit to others, as well: there would be less violence in the world, if a substantial number (even if it were a substantial minority) of those with the marker abstained (at least most of the time) from the sports drink or blue cheese or whatever. Even here the existence and use of a test for the marker is not without its costs to the individual. Would it be possible for parents to be instructed in proper diet for their child, and convinced of the importance of adhering rigidly to the diet, if they were not told that the child had this genetic abnormality? Would it be ethical not to inform the parents of the abnormality? Yet if the parents are told, the likelihood that the child will be raised with the expectation, or at least fear, that he or she will grow up to be a criminal is worrisomely high. Confidence that all the usual disturbing behaviours young children exhibit (biting other children, kicking their parents, screaming "I'm going to kill you") mean nothing would be hard to maintain. ("I knew this diet wouldn't work; he's clearly a sociopath.") In addition, there is the risk of social stigma, a further cost to the individual with the marker.

What I have described is, of course, an unduly rosy picture of how, on balance, the person with the genetic marker would be affected by the existence and implementation of a test for it. In the more likely scenario, the predisposition would not be nullified by a simple dietary measure. The conditions that triggered the feared behaviour would most probably be environmental, and very likely (I would venture to guess) the same sorts of conditions that trigger violent behaviour in people without the genetic predisposition. These conditions include others—parents, in particular—not having confidence in the child. The very knowledge that the child has the marker is likely to increase the risk that the child will exhibit the behaviour associated with it. It is, in short, extremely difficult to see how the person with the genetic marker is better off if we have a test for the marker; and in this respect a genetic marker for violence (or aggression or criminality) stands in striking contrast to markers for various cancers.

Are there benefits to others in having (and implementing, say, on all newborns) a test for the marker? Unless there is some reasonably simple way to prevent the problem from ever surfacing—dietary measures or, better yet, administration of a harmless drug at infancy—it is unlikely. Of course, if we were willing to engage in obviously unacceptable strategies for dealing with it, such as forcible isolation of those with the marker from the rest of the population, knowing who has the marker would be useful.

In general, there seems to be little benefit, all told, if the aim is to implement large-scale testing to find out who has the marker. The risks seem clearly to outweigh the benefits. This is not to say, however, that genetic research concerning criminality does not yield benefits that outweigh its risks; on that point I am agnostic. The risks, however, are great, and one would like to see a concerted effort to address the risks by correcting common misconceptions—for example, the belief that a genetic predisposition to X means that one is virtually guaranteed to do X, and the related assumptions that environmental conditions such as schooling would have no bearing on whether one ever engages in the undesirable conduct to which one is genetically predisposed.

Genetic research may well be of value in a number of ways. For instance, studies of identical twins reared apart might yield information on environmental protective factors that help to explain why one twin commits crimes whereas the other genetically identical twin does not (Raine 50). If it could be known that the twins had the genetic marker for criminality (or whatever the marker marks), that would make studies of twins reared apart all the more useful. We could compare pairs with the marker with those without it, and if there were enough pairs in which one committed crimes and the other did not, we could see if the environmentally protective factors differed between those who have and those who lack the marker. (Notice, though, that this research is tricky: if the parents knew or suspected that their children had the genetic marker, worries about their children would, in addition to—and by way of—harming the children and their relationships with them, throw off the study.)

A discovery of a marker might be helpful within that research. Tracking those with a marker, as well as a control group, to look for environmentally protective factors that explain why some with the marker commit crimes and others do not might even lead to a discovery of what can be done to avoid "triggering" the predisposition to violence or criminality. But, in general, having a test for a marker does not seem likely to improve either the lives of those found to have the marker or the welfare of society as a whole. It seems most likely that the conditions that trigger the feared behaviour in the genetically predisposed person are not of a sort that are very easily corrected (e.g., by diet). It is only a hunch, but my hunch is that the conditions that trigger the undesirable behaviour in the genetically predisposed person would turn out to be no different from those that trigger it in everyone else. This is one reason why research to find a genetic marker should not be a very high priority.

Would it not be more to the point to focus on altering the social conditions that trigger such behaviour? Why so much interest in figuring out ways to detect which people are the "problems"—which people are flawed by an internal defect? If we deemed it morally appropriate to isolate the "problem people"—to send them away to an internment camp, perhaps, or require them to undergo medical treatment designed to tame them—there would be some point to the search for a marker. Or again, if we thought it a good social policy to screen fetuses routinely for the marker and urge pregnant women whose fetuses tested positive to have abortions, then again, there would be a real point to the test. But unless we favour such policies, and unless the triggering conditions turn out to be something like consumption of more than four ounces of a sports drink, altering (some of) the environmental conditions that make the commission of crimes more likely (no matter what one's genes are) seems more to the point.

## Note

1. I say "especially" and "in particular" because of their lack of control over their childhood environments. Arguably they bear, in at least some cases, some responsibility for their current environments; it would be hard to make such an argument with respect to their childhood environments.

## Works Cited

Greenspan, P.S. "Genes, Electrotransmitters, and Free Will." *Genetics and Criminal Behavior*. Ed. David Wasserman and Robert Wachbroit. Cambridge: Cambridge University Press, 2001. 243–58.

Herrnstein, R.J., and C. Murray. *The Bell Curve: Intelligence and Class Structure in American Life*. New York: Free Press, 1994.

Mooney, T.J. "Viewpoint." *Prince George's Journal* (November 3, 1992): A4.

Raine, A. *The Psychopathology of Crime*. San Diego: Academic Press, 1993.

## Study Questions

1. On a 2001 episode of *Law & Order: SVU*, the defence attorney blames a "violence gene" for the rape committed by his client. Why does Baron argue that genetic factors are no different than environmental factors in assessing criminal responsibility?

2. What explanation does Baron offer for why so many people mistakenly believe that freedom is limited more by genetic than environmental factors?

3. Baron points out that the availability of medical evidence might make jurors more sympathetic to an accused who was genetically predisposed to commit a crime than an accused who was environmentally predisposed to commit a crime. Why does she argue that they are mistaken?

4. According to Baron, what costs and benefits are likely to result from discovering a genetic marker for a disease like colon cancer? Why is Baron skeptical that similar benefits would arise from discovering a genetic marker for criminality?

## ◜ NATURAL AND SOCIAL KINDS ◝

### John Locke

John Locke (1632–1704) was an English philosopher educated at Christ Church College, Oxford. While at Oxford, Locke joined a circle of experimental philosophers led by John Wilkins and Robert Boyle, from which the Royal Society of London emerged. *An Essay Concerning Human Understanding*, Book 3, applies Locke's empiricism to Boyle's corpuscularianism: since the corpuscles (or atoms) of which physical substances are composed are too minute to be perceived by our senses, knowledge of "real essences" is deemed impossible.—TR

## Of Words

From *An Essay Concerning Human Understanding*

### Of General Terms [Ch. 3]

1. **The Greatest Part of Words Are General Terms.** All things that exist being particulars, it may perhaps be thought reasonable that words, which ought to be conformed to things, should be so too—I mean in their signification: but yet we find quite the contrary. The far greatest part of words that make all languages are general terms: which has not been the effect of neglect or chance, but of reason and necessity.

2. **That Every Particular Thing Should Have a Name for Itself Is Impossible.** First, it is impossible that every particular thing should have a distinct peculiar name. For, the signification and use of words depending on that connection which the mind makes between its ideas and the sounds it uses as signs of them, it is necessary, in the application of names to things, that the mind should have distinct ideas of the things, and retain also the particular name that belongs to everyone, with its peculiar appropriation to that idea. But it is beyond the power of human capacity to frame and retain distinct ideas of all the particular things we meet with: every bird and beast men saw, every tree and plant that affected the senses, could not find a place in the most capacious understanding. If it be looked on as an instance of a prodigious memory that some generals have been able to call every soldier in their army by his proper name, we may easily find a reason why men

have never attempted to give names to each sheep in their flock or crow that flies over their heads, much less to call every leaf of plants or grain of sand that came in their way by a peculiar name.

3. **And Would Be Useless, If It Were Possible.** Secondly, if it were possible, it would yet be useless, because it would not serve to the chief end of language. Men would in vain heap up names of particular things that would not serve them to communicate their thoughts. Men learn names, and use them in talk with others, only that they may be understood: which is then only done when, by use or consent, the sound I make by the organs of speech excites in another man's mind who hears it the idea I apply it to in mine when I speak it. This cannot be done by names applied to particular things; whereof I alone having the ideas in my mind, the names of them could not be significant or intelligible to another, who was not acquainted with all those very particular things which had fallen under my notice.

4. **A Distinct Name for Every Particular Thing Not Fitted for Enlargement of Knowledge.** Thirdly, but yet, granting this also feasible (which I think is not), yet a distinct name for every particular thing would not be of any great use for the improvement of knowledge: which, though founded in particular things, enlarges itself by general views to which things reduced into sorts, under general names, are properly subservient. These, with the names belonging to

them, come within some compass, and do not multiply every moment, beyond what either the mind can contain, or use requires. And therefore, in these, men have for the most part stopped: but yet not so as to hinder themselves from distinguishing particular things by appropriated names where convenience demands it. And therefore in their own species, which they have most to do with, and wherein they have often occasion to mention particular persons, they make use of proper names; and there distinct individuals have distinct denominations. [. . .]

6. **How General Words Are Made.** The next thing to be considered is: how general words come to be made. For, since all things that exist are only particulars, how come we by general terms; or where find we those general natures they are supposed to stand for? Words become general by being made the signs of general ideas: and ideas become general by separating from them the circumstances of time and place, and any other ideas that may determine them to this or that particular existence. By this way of abstraction they are made capable of representing more individuals than one; each of which having in it a conformity to that abstract idea is (as we call it) of that sort.

7. **Shown by the Way We Enlarge Our Complex Ideas from Infancy.** But, to deduce this a little more distinctly, it will not perhaps be amiss to trace our notions and names from their beginning, and observe by what degrees we proceed, and by what steps we enlarge our ideas from our first infancy. There is nothing more evident than that the ideas of the persons children converse with (to instance in them alone) are, like the persons themselves, only particular. The ideas of the nurse and the mother are well framed in their minds and, like pictures of them there, represent only those individuals. The names they first gave to them are confined to these individuals; and the names of *nurse* and *mamma*, the child uses, determine themselves to those persons. Afterwards, when time and a larger acquaintance have made them observe that there are a great many other things in the world that in some common agreements of shape and several other qualities resemble their father and mother and those persons they have been used to, they frame an idea, which they find those many particulars do partake

in, and to that they give, with others, the name *man*, for example. And thus they come to have a general name, and a general idea. Wherein they make nothing new but only leave out of the complex idea they had of Peter and James, Mary and Jane, that which is peculiar to each, and retain only what is common to them all.

8. **And Further Enlarge Our Complex Ideas, by Still Leaving Out Properties Contained in Them.** By the same way that they come by the general name and idea of *man*, they easily advance to more general names and notions. For, observing that several things that differ from their idea of man, and cannot therefore be comprehended under that name, have yet certain qualities wherein they agree with man, by retaining only those qualities and uniting them into one idea, they have again another and more general idea, to which having given a name they make a term of a more comprehensive extension: which new idea is made, not by any new addition, but only as before by leaving out the shape and some other properties signified by the name man, and retaining only a body, with life, sense, and spontaneous motion, comprehended under the name animal. [. . .]

12. **Abstract Ideas Are the Essences of Genera and Species.** The next thing therefore to be considered is: what kind of signification it is that general words have. For, as it is evident that they do not signify barely one particular thing—for then they would not be general terms but proper names, so, on the other side, it is as evident they do not signify a plurality; for *man* and *men* would then signify the same; and the distinction of numbers (as the grammarians call them) would be superfluous and useless. That then which general words signify is a *sort* of things; and each of them does that by being a sign of an abstract idea in the mind; to which idea, as things existing are found to agree, so they come to be ranked under that name, or, which is all one, be of that sort. Whereby it is evident that the *essences* of the sorts, or, if the Latin word pleases better, *species* of things, are nothing else but these abstract ideas. [. . .] From whence it is easy to observe that the essences of the sorts of things, and, consequently,

the sorting of things, is the workmanship of the understanding that abstracts and makes those general ideas.

13. **They Are the Workmanship of the Understanding, but Have Their Foundation in the Similitude of Things.** I would not here be thought to forget, much less to deny, that Nature, in the production of things, makes several of them alike: there is nothing more obvious, especially in the races of animals, and all things propagated by seed. But yet I think we may say, *the sorting of them under names is the workmanship of the understanding, taking occasion from the similitude it observes amongst them to make abstract general ideas*, and set them up in the mind, with names annexed to them, as patterns or forms (for, in that sense, the word *form* has a very proper signification) to which as particular things existing are found to agree, so they come to be of that species, have that denomination, or are put into that *classis*. For when we say this is a man, that a horse; this justice, that cruelty; this a watch, that a jack; what do we else but rank things under different specific names, as agreeing to those abstract ideas, of which we have made those names the signs? And what are the essences of those species set out and marked by names but those abstract ideas in the mind, which are, as it were, the bonds between particular things that exist and the names they are to be ranked under? And when general names have any connection with particular beings, these abstract ideas are the medium that unites them: so that the essences of species, as distinguished and denominated by us, neither are nor can be anything but those precise abstract ideas we have in our minds. And therefore the supposed real essences of substances, if different from our abstract ideas, cannot be the essences of the species *we* rank things into. For two species may be one, as rationally as two different essences be the essence of one species: and I demand, what are the alterations that may or may not be made in a *horse* or *lead* without making either of them to be of another species? In determining the species of things by *our* abstract ideas, this is easy to resolve: but if anyone will regulate himself herein by supposed *real* essences, he will, I suppose, be at a loss: and he will never be able to know when anything precisely ceases to be of the species of a *horse* or *lead*. [. . .]

15. **Several Significations of the Word Essence: Real Essences and Nominal Essences.** But since the essences of things are thought by some (and not without reason) to be wholly unknown, it may not be amiss to consider the several significations of the word *essence*.

First, essence may be taken for the very being of anything, whereby it is what it is. And thus the real internal, but generally (in substances) unknown constitution of things, whereon their discoverable qualities depend, may be called their essence. This is the proper original signification of the word, as is evident from the formation of it—*essentia*, in its primary notation, signifying properly, being. And in this sense it is still used, when we speak of the essence of *particular* things, without giving them any name.

Secondly, the learning and disputes of the schools having been much busied about *genus* and *species*, the word *essence* has almost lost its primary signification: and, instead of the real constitution of things, has been almost wholly applied to the artificial constitution of *genus* and *species*. It is true, there is ordinarily supposed a real constitution of the sorts of things; and it is past doubt, there must be some real constitution on which any collection of simple ideas coexisting must depend. But, it being evident that things are ranked under names into sorts or species only as they agree to certain abstract ideas to which we have annexed those names, the essence of each *genus*, or sort, comes to be nothing but that abstract idea which the general, or sortal (if I may have leave so to call it from sort, as I do general from genus) name stands for. And this we shall find to be that which the word essence imports in its most familiar use.

These two sorts of essences, I suppose, may not unfitly be termed, the one the *real*, the other *nominal* essence. [. . .]

## Of the Names of Substances [Ch. 6]

1. **The Common Names of Substances Stand for Sorts.** The common names of substances, as well as

other general terms, stand for *sorts*: which is nothing else but the being made signs of such complex ideas wherein several particular substances do or might agree, by virtue of which they are capable of being comprehended in one common conception, and signified by one name. I say do or might agree: for though there be but one sun existing in the world, yet the idea of it being abstracted, so that more substances (if there were several) might each agree in it, it is as much a sort as if there were as many suns as there are stars. They want not their reasons who think there are, and that each fixed star would answer the idea the name sun stands for, to one who was placed in a due distance: which, by the way, may show us how much the sorts, or, if you please, *genera* and *species* of things (for those Latin terms signify to me no more than the English word sort) depend on such collections of ideas as men have made, and not on the real nature of things; since it is not impossible but that, in propriety of speech, that might be a sun to one which is a star to another.

2. **The Essence of Each Sort of Substance Is Our Abstract Idea to Which the Name Is Annexed.** The measure and boundary of each sort or species, whereby it is constituted that particular sort and distinguished from others, is that we call its *essence*, which is nothing but that abstract idea to which the name is annexed so that everything contained in that idea is essential to that sort. This, though it be all the essence of natural substances that *we* know, or by which we distinguish them into sorts, yet I call it by a peculiar name, the *nominal essence*, to distinguish it from the real constitution of substances upon which depends this nominal essence and all the properties of that sort, which, therefore, as has been said, may be called the *real essence*: e.g., the nominal essence of gold is that complex idea the word gold stands for, let it be, for instance, a body yellow, of a certain weight, malleable, fusible, and fixed. But the real essence is the constitution of the insensible parts of that body on which those qualities and all the other properties of gold depend. How far these two are different, though they are both called essence, is obvious at first sight to discover.

3. **The Nominal and Real Essence Different.** For, though perhaps voluntary motion, with sense

and reason, joined to a body of a certain shape, be the complex idea to which I and others annex the name *man*, and so be the nominal essence of the species so called: yet nobody will say that complex idea is the real essence and source of all those operations which are to be found in any individual of that sort. The foundation of all those qualities which are the ingredients of our complex idea is something quite different: and had we such a knowledge of that constitution of man (from which his faculties of moving, sensation, and reasoning, and other powers flow, and on which his so regular shape depends, as it is possible angels have, and it is certain his Maker has), we should have a quite other idea of his essence than what now is contained in our definition of that species, be it what it will: and our idea of any individual man would be as far different from what it is now, as is his who knows all the springs and wheels and other contrivances within of the **famous clock at Strasburg**, from that which a gazing countryman has of it, who barely sees the motion of the hand, and hears the clock strike, and observes only some of the outward appearances.

4. **Nothing Essential to Individuals.** That *essence*, in the ordinary use of the word, relates to sorts, and that it is considered in particular beings no further than as they are ranked into sorts, appears from hence: that, take but away the abstract ideas by which we sort individuals, and rank them under common names, and then the thought of anything essential to any of them instantly vanishes: we have no notion of the one without the other, which plainly shows their relation. It is necessary for me to be as I am; God and nature has made me so: but there is nothing I have that is essential to me. An accident or disease may very much alter my colour or shape; a fever or fall may take away my reason or memory, or both; and an apoplexy leave neither sense, nor understanding, no, nor life. Other creatures of my shape may be made with more and better, or fewer and worse faculties than I have; and others may have reason and sense in a shape and body very different from mine. None of these are essential to the one or the other, or to any individual whatever, till the mind refers it to some sort or species of things; and then presently, according

to the abstract idea of that sort, something is found essential. Let anyone examine his own thoughts, and he will find that as soon as he supposes or speaks of essential, the consideration of some species, or the complex idea signified by some general name, comes into his mind; and it is in reference to that that this or that quality is said to be essential. So that if it be asked, whether it be essential to me or any other particular corporeal being to have reason? I say, no—no more than it is essential to this white thing I write on to have words in it. But if that particular being be to be counted of the sort *man*, and to have the name *man* given it, then reason is essential to it, supposing reason to be a part of the complex idea the name man stands for: as it is essential to this thing I write on to contain words, if I will give it the name *treatise*, and rank it under that species. So that essential and not essential relate only to our abstract ideas and the names annexed to them, which amounts to no more than this: that whatever particular thing has not in it those qualities which are contained in the abstract idea which any general term stands for cannot be ranked under that species, nor be called by that name, since that abstract idea is the very essence of that species. [. . .]

6. **Even the Real Essences of Individual Substances Imply Potential Sorts.** It is true, I have often mentioned a *real essence*, distinct in substances from those abstract ideas of them, which I call their nominal essence. By this real essence, I mean that real constitution of anything, which is the foundation of all those properties that are combined in, and are constantly found to coexist with the nominal essence; that particular constitution which everything has within itself, without any relation to anything without it. But essence, even in this sense, *relates to a sort, and supposes a species*. For, being that real constitution on which the properties depend, it necessarily supposes a sort of things, properties belonging only to species and not to individuals: e.g., supposing the nominal essence of gold to be a body of such a peculiar colour and weight, with malleability and fusibility, the real essence is that constitution of the parts of matter on which these qualities and their union depend, and is also the foundation of its solubility in *aqua regia* and other properties accompanying

that complex idea. Here are essences and properties, but all upon supposition of a sort or general abstract idea, which is considered as immutable; but there is no individual parcel of matter to which any of these qualities are so annexed as to be essential to it or inseparable from it. That which is essential belongs to it as a condition whereby it is of this or that sort: but take away the consideration of its being ranked under the name of some abstract idea, and then there is nothing necessary to it, nothing inseparable from it. Indeed, as to the real essences of substances, we only suppose their being, without precisely knowing what they are; but that which annexes them still to the species is the nominal essence, of which they are the supposed foundation and cause.

7. **The Nominal Essence Bounds the Species for Us.** The next thing to be considered is, by which of those essences it is that substances are determined into sorts or species; and that, it is evident, is by the nominal essence. For it is that alone that the name, which is the mark of the sort, signifies. It is impossible, therefore, that anything should determine the sorts of things, which *we* rank under general names, but that idea which that name is designed as a mark for—which is that, as has been shown, which we call nominal essence. Why do we say this is a horse, and that a mule; this is an animal, that an herb? How comes any particular thing to be of this or that sort, but because it has that nominal essence—or, which is all one, agrees to that abstract idea that name is annexed to? And I desire anyone but to reflect on his own thoughts, when he hears or speaks any of those or other names of substances, to know what sort of essences they stand for.

8. **The Nature of Species as Formed by Us.** And that the species of things to us are nothing but the ranking them under distinct names, according to the complex ideas in *us*, and not according to precise, distinct, real essences in *them*, is plain from hence: that we find many of the individuals that are ranked into one sort, called by one common name, and so received as being of one species, have yet qualities, depending on their real constitutions, as far different one from another as from others from which they are accounted to differ specifically. This, as it is easy to be observed by all who have to do with natural bodies, so chemists especially are often, by sad

experience, convinced of it, when they, sometimes in vain, seek for the same qualities in one parcel of sulphur, antimony, or vitriol, which they have found in others. For, though they are bodies of the same species, having the same nominal essence, under the same name, yet do they often, upon severe ways of examination, betray qualities so different one from another, as to frustrate the expectation and labour of very wary chemists. But if things were distinguished into species, according to their real essences, it would be as impossible to find different properties in any two individual substances of the same species, as it is to find different properties in two circles, or two equilateral triangles.

9. **Not the Real Essence, or Texture of Parts, Which We Know Not.** Nor indeed can we rank and sort things, and consequently (which is the end of sorting) denominate them, by their real essences because we know them not. Our faculties carry us no further towards the knowledge and distinction of substances than a collection of *those sensible ideas which we observe in them*, which, however made with the greatest diligence and exactness we are capable of, yet is more remote from the true internal constitution from which those qualities flow than, as I said, a countryman's idea is from the inward contrivance of that famous clock at Strasburg, whereof he only sees the outward figure and motions. There is not so contemptible a plant or animal that does not confound the most enlarged understanding. Though the familiar use of things about us take off our wonder, yet it cures not our ignorance. When we come to examine the stones we tread on, or the iron we daily handle, we presently find we know not their make,

and can give no reason of the different qualities we find in them. It is evident the internal constitution, whereon their properties depend, is unknown to us: for to go no further than the grossest and most obvious we can imagine amongst them, What is that texture of parts, that real essence, that makes lead and antimony fusible, wood and stones not? What makes lead and iron malleable, antimony and stones not? And yet how infinitely these come short of the fine contrivances and inconceivable real essences of plants or animals, everyone knows. The workmanship of the all-wise and powerful God in the great fabric of the universe, and every part thereof, further exceeds the capacity and comprehension of the most inquisitive and intelligent man than the best contrivance of the most ingenious man doth the conceptions of the most ignorant of rational creatures. Therefore we in vain pretend to range things into sorts, and dispose them into certain classes under names, by their real essences, that are so far from our discovery or comprehension. A blind man may as soon sort things by their colours, and he that has lost his smell as well distinguish a lily and a rose by their odours, as by those internal constitutions which he knows not.

10. **Not the Substantial Form, Which We Know Less.** Those, therefore, who have been taught that the several species of substances had their distinct internal *substantial forms*, and that it was those *forms* which made the distinction of substances into their true species and genera, were led yet further out of the way by having their minds set upon fruitless inquiries after "substantial forms," wholly unintelligible, and whereof we have scarce so much as any obscure or confused conception in general. [. . .]

## Study Questions

1. Give an example of a general term and an example of a particular term. What three reasons does Locke provide for why, in our language, we have so many more general terms than particular terms?

2. When Locke writes "All things that exist being particulars," what metaphysical position is he defending? If all that exists is particulars, how

do we come up with general ideas and general terms, according to Locke? Provide an example.

3. Explain Locke's distinction between real and nominal essences. Provide an example.

4. What is the significance of Locke's references to the "famous clock at Strasburg" in his discussion of real and nominal essences?

# Hilary Putnam

Hilary Putnam, a well-known American philosopher, received his PhD at the University of California, Los Angeles, in 1951 and spent most of his career at Harvard University, retiring in 2000. He has done comprehensive work in many areas, including philosophy of language and science. In this article, Putnam defends semantic externalism: the position that meanings of words are fixed by physical facts and linguistic practices, not internal mental states.—GS

## Meaning and Reference

### 1. Introduction

Unclear as it is, the traditional doctrine that the notion "meaning" possesses the extension/intension ambiguity has certain typical consequences. The doctrine that the meaning of a term is a concept carried the implication that meanings are mental entities. **Frege**, however, rebelled against this "psychologism." Feeling that meanings are *public* property—that the *same* meaning can be "grasped" by more than one person and by persons at different times—he identified concepts (and hence "intensions" or meanings) with abstract entities rather than mental entities. However, "grasping" these abstract entities was still an individual psychological act. None of these philosophers doubted that understanding a word (knowing its intension) was just a matter of being in a certain psychological state (somewhat in the way in which knowing how to factor numbers in one's head is just a matter of being in a certain very complex psychological state).

Secondly, the timeworn example of the two terms 'creature with a kidney' and 'creature with a heart' does show that two terms can have the same extension and yet differ in intension. But it was taken to be obvious that the reverse is impossible: two terms cannot differ in extension and have the same intension. Interestingly, no argument for this impossibility was ever offered. Probably it reflects the tradition of the ancient and medieval philosophers, who assumed that the concept corresponding to a term was just a conjunction of predicates, and hence that the concept corresponding to a term must *always*

provide a necessary and sufficient condition for falling into the extension of the term. For philosophers like **Carnap**, who accepted the **verifiability theory of meaning**, the concept corresponding to a term provided (in the ideal case, where the term had "complete meaning") a *criterion* for belonging to the extension (not just in the sense of "necessary and sufficient condition," but in the strong sense of *way of recognizing* whether a given thing falls into the extension or not). So theory of meaning came to rest on two unchallenged assumptions:

1. That knowing the meaning of a term is just a matter of being in a certain psychological state (in the sense of "psychological state," in which states of memory and belief are "psychological states"; no one thought that knowing the meaning of a word was a continuous state of consciousness, of course).
2. That the meaning of a term determines its extension (in the sense that sameness of intension entails sameness of extension).

I shall argue that these two assumptions are not jointly satisfied by *any* notion, let alone any notion of meaning. The traditional concept of meaning is a concept which rests on a false theory.

### 2. Are Meanings in the Head?

For the purpose of the following science-fiction examples, we shall suppose that somewhere there is a planet we shall call Twin Earth. Twin Earth is very much like Earth: in fact, people on Twin Earth even speak *English*. In fact, apart from the differences we shall specify in our science-fiction examples, the reader may suppose that Twin Earth is *exactly* like Earth. He may even suppose that he has a *Doppelganger*—an identical copy—on Twin Earth, if he wishes, although my stories will not depend on this.

Although some of the people on Twin Earth (say, those who call themselves "Americans" and those who call themselves "Canadians" and those who call themselves "Englishmen," etc.) speak English, there are, not surprisingly, a few tiny differences between the dialects of English spoken on Twin Earth and standard English.

One of the peculiarities of Twin Earth is that the liquid called "water" is not $H_2O$ but a different liquid whose chemical formula is very long and complicated. I shall abbreviate this chemical formula simply as XYZ. I shall suppose that XYZ is indistinguishable from water at normal temperatures and pressures. Also, I shall suppose that the oceans and lakes and seas of Twin Earth contain XYZ and not water, that it rains XYZ on Twin Earth and not water, etc.

If a space ship from Earth ever visits Twin Earth, then the supposition at first will be that 'water' has the same meaning on Earth and on Twin Earth. This supposition will be corrected when it is discovered that "water" on Twin Earth is XYZ, and the Earthian space ship will report somewhat as follows.

"On Twin Earth the word 'water' means XYZ."

Symmetrically, if a space ship from Twin Earth ever visits Earth, then the supposition at first will be that the word 'water' has the same meaning on Twin Earth and on Earth. This supposition will be corrected when it is discovered that "water" on Earth is $H_2O$, and the Twin Earthian space ship will report:

"On Earth the word 'water' means $H_2O$."

Note that there is no problem about the extension of the term 'water': the word simply has two different meanings (as we say); in the sense in which it is used on Twin Earth, the sense of water$_{TE}$, what *we* call "water" simply isn't water, while in the sense in which it is used on Earth, the sense of water$_E$, what the Twin Earthians call "water" simple isn't

water. The extension of 'water' in the sense of water$_E$ is the set of all wholes consisting of $H_2O$ molecules, or something like that; the extension of water in the sense of water$_{TE}$ is the set of all wholes consisting of XYZ molecules, or something like that.

Now let us roll the time back to about 1750.[1] The typical Earthian speaker of English did not know that water consisted of hydrogen and oxygen, and the typical Twin-Earthian speaker of English did not know that "water" consisted of XYZ. Let Oscar$_1$ be such a typical Earthian English speaker, and let Oscar$_2$ be his counterpart on Twin Earth. You may suppose that there is no belief that Oscar$_1$ had about water that Oscar$_2$ did not have about "water." If you like, you may even suppose that Oscar$_1$ and Oscar$_2$ were exact duplicates in appearance, feelings, thoughts, interior monologue, etc. Yet the extension of the term 'water' was just as much $H_2O$ on Earth in 1750 as in 1950; and the extension of the term 'water' was just as much XYZ on Twin Earth in 1750 as in 1950. Oscar$_1$ and Oscar$_2$ understood the term 'water' differently in 1750 *although they were in the same psychological state,* and although, given the state of science at the time, it would have taken their scientific communities about fifty years to discover that they understood the term 'water' differently. Thus the extension of the term 'water' (and, in fact, its "meaning" in the intuitive pre-analytical usage of that term) is *not* a function of the psychological state of the speaker by itself.[2]

But, it might be objected, why should we accept it that the term 'water' had the same extension in 1750 and in 1950 (on both Earths)? Suppose I point to a glass of water and say "this liquid is called water." My "ostensive definition" of water has the following empirical presupposition: that the body of liquid I am pointing to bears a certain sameness relation (say, *x is the same liquid as y,* or *x is the same$_L$ as y*) to most of the stuff I and other speakers in my linguistic community have on other occasions called "water." If this presupposition is false because, say, I am— unknown to me—pointing to a glass of gin and not a glass of water, then I do not intend my ostensive definition to be accepted. Thus the ostensive definition conveys what might be called a "defeasible" necessary and sufficient condition: the necessary and sufficient condition for being water is bearing the relation $same_L$ to the stuff in the glass; but this is the necessary and sufficient condition only if the empirical presupposition is satisfied. If it is not satisfied, then one of a series of, so to speak, "fallback" conditions becomes activated.

The key point is that the relation $same_L$ is a *theoretical* relation: whether something is or is not the same liquid as *this* may take an indeterminate amount of scientific investigation to determine. Thus, the fact that an English speaker in 1750 might have called XYZ "water," whereas he or his successors would not have called XYZ water in 1800 or 1850 does not mean that the "meaning" of 'water' changed for the average speaker in the interval. In 1750 or in 1850 or in 1950 one might have pointed to, say, the liquid in Lake Michigan as an example of "water." What changed was that in 1750 we would have mistakenly thought that XYZ bore the relation $same_L$ to the liquid in Lake Michigan, whereas in 1800 or 1850 we would have known that it did not.

Let us now modify our science-fiction story. I shall suppose that molybdenum pots and pans *can't* be distinguished from aluminum pots and pans save by an expert. (This could be true for all I know, and, *a fortiori*, it could be true for all I know by virtue of "knowing the meaning" of the words *aluminum* and *molybdenum*.) We will now suppose that molybdenum is as common on Twin Earth as aluminum is on Earth, and that aluminum is as rare on Twin Earth as molybdenum is on Earth. In particular, we shall assume that "aluminum" pots and pans are made of molybdenum on Twin Earth. Finally, we shall assume that the words 'aluminum' and 'molybdenum' are *switched* on Twin Earth: 'aluminum' is the name of *molybdenum*, and 'molybdenum' is the name of *aluminum*. If a space ship from Earth visited Twin Earth, the visitors from Earth probably would not suspect that the "aluminum" pots and pans on Twin Earth were not made of aluminum, especially when the Twin Earthians *said* they were. But there is one important difference between the two cases. An Earthian metallurgist could tell very easily that "aluminum" was molybdenum, and a Twin Earthian metallurgist could tell equally easily that aluminum was "molybdenum." (The shudder quotes in the preceding sentence indicate Twin Earthian usages.) Whereas in 1750 no one on either Earth or Twin Earth could have distinguished water from "water," the confusion of aluminum with "aluminum" involves only a part of the linguistic communities involved.

This example makes the same point as the preceding example. If $Oscar_1$ and $Oscar_2$ are standard speakers of Earthian English and Twin Earthian English, respectively, and neither is chemically or metallurgically sophisticated, then there may be no difference at all in their psychological states when they use the word 'aluminum'; nevertheless, we have to say that 'aluminum' has the extension *aluminum* in the idiolect of $Oscar_1$ and the extension *molybdenum* in the idiolect of $Oscar_2$. (Also we have to say that $Oscar_1$ and $Oscar_2$ mean different things by 'aluminum'; that 'aluminum' has a different meaning on Earth than it does on Twin Earth, etc.) Again we see that the psychological state of the speaker does *not* determine the extension (*or* the "meaning," speaking preanalytically) of the word.

Before discussing this example further, let me introduce a *non*-science-fiction example. Suppose you are like me and cannot tell an elm from a beech tree. We still say that the extension of 'elm' in my idiolect is the same as the extension of 'elm' in anyone else's, viz., the set of all elm trees, and that the set of all beech trees is the extension of 'beech' in *both* of our idiolects. Thus 'elm' in my idiolect has a different extension from 'beech' in your idiolect (as it should). Is it really credible that this difference in extension is brought about by some difference in our *concepts*? My *concept* of an elm tree is exactly the same as my concept of a beech tree (I blush to confess). If someone heroically attempts to maintain that the difference between the extension of 'elm' and the extension of 'beech' in *my* idiolect is explained by a difference in my psychological state, then we can always refute him by constructing a "Twin Earth" example—just let the words 'elm' and 'beech' be switched on Twin Earth (the way 'aluminum' and 'molybdenum' were in the previous example).

Moreover, suppose I have a *Doppelganger* on Twin Earth who is molecule for molecule "identical" with me. If you are a dualist, then also suppose my Doppelganger thinks the same verbalized thoughts I do, has the same sense data, the same dispositions, etc. It is absurd to think *his* psychological state is one bit different from mine: yet he "means" *beech* when he says "elm," and I "mean" *elm* when I say "elm." Cut the pie any way you like, "meanings" just ain't in the *head*!

## 3. A Sociolinguistic Hypothesis

The last two examples depend upon a fact about language that seems, surprisingly, never to have been pointed out: that there is *division of linguistic labour*. We could hardly use such words as 'elm' and 'aluminum' if no one possessed a way of recognizing elm trees and aluminum metal; but not everyone to whom the distinction is important has to be able to make the distinction. Let us shift the example; consider *gold*. Gold is important for many reasons: it is a precious metal; it is a monetary metal; it has symbolic value (it is important to most people that the "gold" wedding ring they wear *really* consist of gold and not just *look* gold); etc. Consider our community as a "factory": in this "factory" some people have the "job" of *wearing gold wedding rings*; other people have the "job" of *selling gold wedding rings*; still other people have the job of *telling whether or not something is really gold*. It is not at all necessary or efficient that every one who wears a gold ring (or a gold cufflink, etc.), or discusses the "gold standard," etc., engage in buying and selling gold. Nor is it necessary or efficient that everyone who buys and sells gold be able to tell whether or not something is really gold in a society where this form of dishonesty is uncommon (selling fake gold) and in which one can easily consult an expert in case of doubt. And it is *certainly* not necessary or efficient that everyone who has occasion to buy or wear gold be able to tell with any reliability whether or not something is really gold.

The foregoing facts are just examples of mundane division of labour (in a wide sense). But they engender a division of linguistic labour: everyone to whom gold is important for any reason has to *acquire* the word 'gold'; but he does not have to acquire the *method of recognizing* whether something is or is not gold. He can rely on a special subclass of speakers. The features that are generally thought to be present in connection with a general name—necessary and sufficient conditions for membership in the extension, ways of recognizing whether something is in the extension, etc.—are all present in the linguistic community *considered as a collective body*; but that collective body divides the "labour" of knowing and employing these various parts of the "meaning" of 'gold'.

This division of linguistic labour rests upon and presupposes the division of *non*linguistic labour, of course. If only the people who know how to tell whether some metal is really gold or not have any reason to have the word 'gold' in their vocabulary, then the word 'gold' will be as the word 'water' was in 1750 with respect to that subclass of speakers, and the other speakers just won't acquire it at all. And some words do not exhibit any division of linguistic labour: 'chair', for example. But with the increase of division of labour in the society and the rise of science, more and more words begin to exhibit this kind of division of labour. 'Water', for example, did not exhibit it at all before the rise of chemistry. Today it is obviously necessary for every speaker to be able to recognize water (reliably under normal conditions), and probably most adult speakers even know the necessary and sufficient condition "water is $H_2O$," but only a few adult speakers could distinguish water from liquids that superficially resembled water. In case of doubt, other speakers would rely on the judgment of these "expert" speakers. Thus the way of recognizing possessed by these "expert" speakers is also, through them, possessed by the collective linguistic body, even though it is not possessed by each individual member of the body, and in this way the most *recherché* fact about water may become part of the *social* meaning of the word although unknown to almost all speakers who acquire the word.

It seems to me that this phenomenon of division of linguistic labour is one that it will be very important for sociolinguistics to investigate. In connection with it, I should like to propose the following hypothesis:

HYPOTHESIS OF THE UNIVERSALITY OF THE DIVISION OF LINGUISTIC LABOUR: Every linguistic community exemplifies the sort of division of linguistic labour just described; that is, it possesses at least some terms whose associated "criteria" are known only to a subset of the speakers who acquire the terms, and whose use by the other speakers depends upon a structured cooperation between them and the speakers in the relevant subsets.

It is easy to see how this phenomenon accounts for some of the examples given above of the failure of the assumptions (1 and 2). When a term is subject to the division of linguistic labour, the "average" speaker who acquires it does not acquire anything that fixes its extension. In particular, his individual psychological state *certainly* does not fix its extension; it is only the sociolinguistic state of the collective linguistic body to which the speaker belongs that fixes the extension.

We may summarize this discussion by pointing out that there are two sorts of tools in the world: there are tools like a hammer or a screwdriver which can be used by one person; and there are tools like a steamship which require the cooperative activity of a number of persons to use. Words have been thought of too much on the model of the first sort of tool.

## 4. Indexicality and Rigidity

The first of our science-fiction examples—'water' on Earth and on Twin Earth in 1750—does not involve division of linguistic labour, or at least does not involve it in the same way the examples of 'aluminum' and 'elm' do. There were not (in our story, anyway) any "experts" on water on Earth in 1750, nor any experts on "water" on Twin Earth. The example *does* involve things which are of fundamental importance to the theory of reference and also to the theory of necessary truth, which we shall now discuss.

Let $W_1$ and $W_2$ be two possible worlds in which I exist and in which this glass exists and in which

I am giving a meaning explanation by pointing to this glass and saying "This is water." Let us suppose that in $W_1$ the glass is full of $H_2O$ and in $W_2$ the glass is full of XYZ. We shall also suppose that $W1$ is the *actual* world, and that XYZ is the stuff typically called "water" in the world $W_2$ (so that the relation between English speakers in $W_1$ and English speakers in $W_2$ is exactly the same as the relation between English speakers on Earth and English speakers on Twin Earth). Then there are two theories one might have concerning the meaning of 'water':

1. One might hold that 'water' was *world-relative* but *constant* in meaning (i.e., the word has a constant relative meaning). On this theory, 'water' means the same in $W_1$ and $W_2$; it's just that water is $H_2O$ in $W_1$, and water is XYZ in $W_2$.
2. One might hold that water is $H_2O$ in all worlds (the stuff called "water" in $W_2$ isn't water), but 'water' doesn't have the same meaning in $W_1$ and $W_2$.

If what was said before about the Twin Earth case was correct, then (2) is clearly the correct theory. When I say "*this* (liquid) is water," the "this" is, so to speak, a *de re* "this"—i.e., the force of my explanation is that "water" is whatever bears a certain equivalence relation (the relation we called "*same*$_L$" above) to the piece of liquid referred to as "this" *in the actual world*. [. . .]

Kripke calls a designator "rigid" (in a given sentence) if (in that sentence) it refers to the same individual in every possible world in which the designator designates. If we extend this notion of rigidity to substance names, then we may express Kripke's theory and mine by saying that the term 'water' is *rigid*.

The rigidity of the term 'water' follows from the fact that when I give the "ostensive definition": "*this* (liquid) is water," I intend (2) and not (1).

We may also say, following Kripke, that when I give the ostensive definition "*this* (liquid) is water," the demonstrative 'this' is *rigid*. [. . .]

Words like 'now', 'this', 'here' have long been recognized to be *indexical*, or *token-reflexive*—i.e., to have an extension which varies from context to context or token to token. For these words, no one has ever suggested the traditional theory that "intension determines extension." To take our Twin Earth example: if I have a *Doppelganger* on Twin Earth, then when I think "I have a headache," *he* thinks "I have a headache." But the extension of the particular token of 'I' in his verbalized thought is himself (or his unit class, to be precise), while the extension of the token of 'I' in *my* verbalized thought is *me* (or my unit class, to be precise). So the same word, 'I', has two different extensions in two different idiolects; but it does not follow that the concept I have of myself is in any way different from the concept my Doppelganger has of himself.

Now then, we have maintained that indexicality extends beyond the *obviously* indexical words and morphemes (e.g., the tenses of verbs). Our theory can be summarized as saying that words like 'water' have an unnoticed indexical component: "water" is stuff that bears a certain similarity relation to the water *around here*. Water at another time or in another place or even in another possible world has to bear the relation *same*$_L$ to *our* "water" *in order to be water*. Thus the theory that (1) words have "intensions," which are something like concepts associated with the words by speakers; and (2) intension determines extension—cannot be true of natural-kind words like 'water' for the same reason it cannot be true of obviously indexical words like 'I'.

The theory that natural-kind words like 'water' are indexical leaves it open, however, whether to say that 'water' in the Twin Earth dialect of English has the same *meaning* as 'water' in the Earth dialect and a different extension—which is what we normally say about 'I' in different idiolects—thereby giving up the doctrine that "meaning (intension) determines extension," or to say, as we have chosen to do, that difference in extension is *ipso facto* a difference in meaning for natural-kind words, thereby giving up the doctrine that meanings are concepts, or, indeed, mental entities of *any* kind.[3]

It should be clear, however, that Kripke's doctrine that natural-kind words are rigid designators and our doctrine that they are indexical are but two ways of making the same point.

We have now seen that the extension of a term is not fixed by a concept that the individual speaker has in his head, and this is true both because extension is, in general, determined *socially*—there is division of linguistic labour as much as of "real" labour—and because extension is, in part, determined *indexically*. The extension of our terms depends upon the actual nature of the particular things that serve as paradigms, and this actual nature is not, in general, fully known to the speaker. Traditional semantic theory leaves out two contributions to the determination of reference—the contribution of society and the contribution of the real world; a better semantic theory must encompass both.

## Notes

1. In the early 1780s, it was discovered that water is not a simple substance but composed of two gases, which the French chemist Antoine Lavoisier (1743–94) named oxygen and hydrogen.—LG
2. See note 3 [. . .] and the corresponding text.
3. Our reasons for rejecting the first option—to say that 'water' has the same meaning on Earth and on Twin Earth, while giving up the doctrine that meaning determines reference—are presented in "The Meaning of 'Meaning'." They may be illustrated thus: Suppose 'water' has the same meaning on Earth and on Twin Earth. Now, let the word 'water' become phonemically different on Twin Earth—say, it becomes 'quaxel'. Presumably, this is not a change in meaning per se, on any view. So 'water' and 'quaxel' have the same meaning (although they refer to different liquids). But this is highly counterintuitive. Why not say, then, that 'elm' in my idiolect has the same meaning as 'beech' in your idiolect, although they refer to different trees?

## Study Questions

1. What is the difference between "intension" and "extension" when it comes to meaning?
2. Describe Putnam's famous Twin Earth example. Explain how the Twin Earth example challenges the traditional theory of meaning and supports Putnam's theory of meaning.
3. With the help of an example, outline Putnam's theory of the division of linguistic labour.
4. What role does indexicality as a property of natural-kind terms play in Putnam's defence of his theory of meaning of such terms?

---

# John Dupré

---

John Dupré received his PhD at Cambridge in 1981, and taught at Stanford University and Birkbeck College, University of London, before becoming director of Egenis, the Economic and Social Research Council Centre for Genomics in Society at the University of Exeter. Dupré has published on a wide range of topics in philosophy of science, including reductionism, human nature, genomics, Darwin, and, the focus of this essay, natural kinds.—GS

## Natural Kinds and Biological Taxa

### 1. Introduction

The main topic of this paper is the theory of natural kinds that has been developed by Putnam and Kripke. One area to which this analysis has seemed particularly appropriate is that of general terms naming biological organisms. My strategy will be to compare the requirements of this analysis with some actual biological facts and theories. It will appear that these diverge to an extent which, I will claim, is fatal to the theory. Toward the end of the paper I will also make some more constructive remarks about the nature of biological classification.

In the first section of the paper I will outline the theory in question, particularly as it has been developed by Putnam, and touch on some related historical and contemporary issues. In the second section I will assume the interpretation of biological taxonomy most favourable to Putnam's theory, and show that even this is often not as Putnam needs it to be. In the third section I will move to a more defensible account of biological taxonomy that renders the theory increasingly untenable. In the fourth section I will make some more constructive remarks about the relations between different ways of classifying organisms,

and in the fifth and final section I will discuss the nature of species. The account I will offer, I believe, lends support to the contentions of earlier sections.

### 2. Putnam's Theory of Natural Kind Terms

A good point of entry to the present issue is provided by **Locke**'s theory of real and nominal essences. The distinction between real and nominal essence is, roughly, that between what accounts for the properties characteristic of a particular kind ("the being of anything whereby it is what it is" [Locke 26]), and the means whereby we distinguish things as belonging to that kind ("the abstract idea which the general, or sortal . . . name stands for" [ibid]). For something like a triangle, which Locke took to be a wholly conceptual object, the real and nominal essences coincide. Since the properties of a triangle flow only from the way it is defined, contemplation of the latter could provide insight into the former. But one point of the distinction was to emphasize the futility of the scholastic, contemplative view of science. Contemplation of forms, nominal essences if anything, would be a source of knowledge of real substances only if nominal essences were also real essences. But they are not, so it is not. In the case of material things Locke, like his successors, thought that the real essence was some feature of the microscopic structure; i.e., that the microscopic structure was the real source of the phenomenal properties of a thing, and that microstructural similarities accounted for the homogeneity of macroscopic kinds. Of the practical value of this notion, on the other hand, Locke was skeptical. Regretting, famously, our lack of microscopic eyes, he doubted whether knowledge of real essences was possible, and also whether real essences, if they were discovered, would coincide with the nominal kinds we had previously distinguished. Thus he held that sorts of things were demarcated by nominal essences only (63). Subsequent scientific history has convinced some philosophers that Locke's skepticism was premature. Chemistry and physics have, since Locke's time, revealed a good deal about the microstructure of things, and antecedently distinguished classes of things have proved to share important structural properties.

The contemporary theory I want to discuss may now be crudely stated in Lockean terms as follows: (1) real essences demarcate natural kinds; (2) such natural kinds provide the extension of many terms in ordinary language. The theory does not attempt to conflate real and nominal essence. As we will see, Putnam has a theory of meaning that incorporates, and sharply distinguishes, both real and nominal essence. But it is the real essence that is supposed to determine the extension of the term. It is with the feasibility of this role that I will be mainly concerned.

Henceforward, I will use the term "natural kind" to refer to a class of objects defined by common possession of some theoretically important property (generally, but not necessarily, microstructural). The traditional view, to which Locke may be counted a subscriber, is that terms of ordinary language refer to kinds whose extension is determined by a nominal essence, and hence not to natural kinds;[1] and that science, on the other hand, attempts to discover those kinds that are demarcated by real essences. It is compatible with this view that in some cases real

and nominal kinds will coincide. But this would be largely fortuitous. This position does not require that ordinary language is entirely independent of science, for several reasons. First, the explanation of our recognition of a kind might, in some cases, trace back to a theoretical feature that defined a natural kind. Second, terms that originate in scientific theory may become incorporated in ordinary language; we should certainly not suppose that these are separated by a sharp or impassable boundary. And third, it is widely accepted that even the most straightforwardly observational terms are to some extent "theory-laden," though the exact extent of this is much debated. At any rate, the general picture is of science as a largely autonomous activity, in spite of subtle and pervasive interactions with the main body of language. It is one of the great attractions of Putnam's essentialism that it promises to provide much stronger links between science and ordinary language, since many terms of the latter are shown to refer to kinds demarcated by the former.

Putnam's theory resolves the meaning of a natural kind term into four components, referred to as a syntactic marker, a semantic marker, a stereotype, and an extension. To illustrate, the term "elephant" might have as syntactic marker "noun," as semantic marker "animal," as stereotype "large grey animal with flapping ears, a long nose, etc.," and an extension determined by the microstructural (or other theoretical) truth about elephants. It is with the last two of these, which are approximately equivalent to nominal and real essences, (the stereotype being the nominal essence, stripped of its reference-fixing function) that I will be concerned.

The distinction between the stereotype and the extension is reflected in a distinction between mere competence in the use of a term, and (full) knowledge of the meaning of the term. The former requires only the first three components of meaning. In fact, the stereotype is explained as the set of features that must be known by any competent speaker of the language, regardless of whether it provides a good guide to the actual extension of the term. All this ignorant talk is facilitated by what Putnam describes as "the division of linguistic labour." If, for any reason, it is important that items be assigned to the correct classes, it is necessary that there be experts familiar with the really essential properties of the kinds in question, and who are therefore able to perform this function. We generally take it on authority, for instance, whether something is made of gold. We may note, however, that we can never be sure even that the experts fully know the meaning of the term. For there is no guarantee that they have yet got right the real essence of the kind in question.

The central question raised by Putnam's analysis is how the nominal, or stereotypic, kinds of ordinary language are to be correlated with the natural kinds discovered by science. That is to say, granted that there are these real, empirically discoverable, natural kinds, how do we know which to assign to a particular term. Putnam answers this question by appealing to a previously unnoticed indexical component of meaning. This consists in the reference, in using a natural kind term, to whatever natural kind paradigmatic instances of the extension of the term "in our world" belong. Such a paradigm may be identified either ostensively, or operationally through the stereotype. Having identified the paradigmatic exemplar, the kind is then defined as consisting of all those individuals that bear an appropriate "sameness relation" to this individual. This sameness relation is Putnam's exact equivalent of Locke's real essence. My fundamental objection to the theory as a theory of biological kinds is that no such sameness relations suitable for Putnam's theory can be found in it.

## 3. Problems for Putnam's Theory Even Assuming Taxonomic Realism

Putnam's theory requires that there be kinds discriminated by science appropriate for providing the extensions of certain kinds of terms in ordinary language. A very encouraging source of examples for this thesis is available in biology, and it is these examples that I want to consider. The part of biology that is concerned with the classification of biological organisms is taxonomy. Within taxonomy, an organism is classified by assigning it to a hierarchical series of taxa, the narrowest of which is the species.[2] Thus a complete taxonomic theory could be displayed as a tree, the smallest branches of which would represent species. Rules would be required for assigning individual organisms to species, and an individual that belonged to a particular species would also belong to all higher taxa in a direct line from that species to the trunk of the tree. (In practice, an organism is classified by assigning it to successively narrower taxa. But as will emerge, this does not reflect the theoretical relations of successive taxonomic levels.) Let us assume what might be called "taxonomic realism." This is the view that there is one unambiguously correct taxonomic theory. At each taxonomic level there will be clear-cut and universally applicable criteria that generate an exhaustive partition of individuals into taxa. Each individual will then have the essential properties of all the taxa to which it belongs. We may even assume that the appropriate number of taxonomic levels to recognize is somehow implicit in the nature of the organisms. The claim that there are natural kinds in biology demarcated by real essences (and a *fortiori* Putnamian privileged sameness relations) would thus be entirely sustained. My first aim will be to show that even under these circumstances Putnam's theory faces serious difficulties of application.

The central difficulty I have in mind is that it is far from universally the case that the preanalytic extension of a term of ordinary language corresponds to *any* recognized biological taxon. (Of course, I am not assuming that present biological theory includes the best possible taxonomy. But there can be no reason to anticipate a general trend towards coincidence with ordinary language distinctions.) In a sense this claim is not easy to substantiate, because the general terms in question are in fact extremely vague, and their application indeterminate. However, I think this indeterminacy can be seen to corroborate my thesis.

The richest source of illustrations for this difficulty is the vegetable kingdom, where specific differences tend to be much less clear than among animals, and considerable developmental plasticity is the rule. Any observant person who has explored the deserts of the Southwest United States will have little difficulty distinguishing a prickly pear from a cholla. Yet taxonomically both these kinds of cacti belong to the same genus, *Opuntia*. Several species of this genus are certainly (to the ordinary man in the desert) prickly pears, and several are certainly chollas. Taxonomy does not recognize any important relation between *Opuntia polyacantha* and *Opuntia fragilis* (two species of prickly pear) that either does not share with *Opuntia bigelovia* (a species of cholla). Ordinary language does make such a distinction, and on the basis of perfectly intelligible and readily perceptible criteria. Thus the property of being a prickly pear is just not recognized in biology.

Or consider the lilies. Species which are commonly referred to as lilies occur in numerous genera of the lily family (Liliaceae). To take a few examples from the flora of the Western United States again, the Lonely Lily belongs to the genus *Eremocrinum*, the Avalanche Lily to the genus *Erythronium*, the Adobe Lily to the genus *Fritillaria*, and the Desert Lily to the genus *Hesperocallis*. The White and Yellow Globe Lilies and the Sego Lily belong to the genus *Calochortus*; but this genus is shared with various species of Mariposa Tulips and the Elegant Cat's Ears (or Star Tulip). I would not want to undertake the task of describing the taxonomic extension of the English term "lily." However, it is fairly clearly well short of including the entire family. To include the onions and garlics (genus *Allium*, and, incidentally, another good example of the point of the previous paragraph) would surely amount to a debasement of the English term. [. . .]

A rather desperate attempt might be made to save the theory from such examples, by going for the best available taxon and accepting some revisionary consequences for ordinary language. Thus one might claim that the extension of "lily" was the whole family Liliaceae [. . .]. We would just have to accept the fact that onions had turned out to be lilies [. . .]. In defence of such claims, it could be pointed out that ordinary language has indeed come to accept such scientifically motivated changes as

the rejection of the view that whales are fish in favour of the belief that they are mammals. But actually this example is by no means as clear-cut as is sometimes assumed. In the first place, "mammal" is more a term of biological theory than of prescientific usage. One cannot recognize mammals at a glance, but must learn quite sophisticated criteria of mammalhood. "Fish," by contrast, is certainly a prescientific category. What is more doubtful is whether it is genuinely a postscientific category, for it is another term that lacks a tidy taxonomic correlate. I assume that the three chordate classes Chrondichthyes, Osteichthyes, and Agnatha would all equally be referred to as fish (unless sharks and lampreys are just as good nonfish as whales). But unless there is some deep scientific reason for lumping these classes together but excluding the class Mammalia, the claim that whales are not fish might be a debatable one. Perhaps "fish" just means aquatic vertebrate, so that whales are both fish and mammals, and this well-worn example is just wrong. [. . .]

The second difficulty for the application of Putnam's theory that occurs even against a background assumption of taxonomic realism, concerns the hierarchical structure of taxonomy. Putnam's theory, it will be recalled, determines the extension of a natural kind term by means of a theoretical "sameness relation" to a suitable exemplar. Suppose we want to discover the extension of the English word "beetle." A suitable exemplar will no doubt have to satisfy the condition that it be readily recognizable as a beetle by a linguistically competent layman; but probably this would not eliminate a very large proportion of the approximately 290,000 recognized species. Any particular exemplar will belong to one particular species. Given taxonomic realism, there will then be some sameness relation that it displays to other members of that species, some relation that applies within its particular genus, and so on up, not just to the relation that holds between all members of the order Coleoptera, which is approximately coextensional with the term "beetle," but beyond, as far as the relation that holds between it and all animals but no plants. One may well wonder how the appropriate sameness relation is supposed to be selected from these numerous alternatives.

## 4. Taxonomic Realism Fails above Species Level

I have not meant to deny that very many general terms for living organisms do have a reasonably clear taxonomic correlate. But to investigate the extent of this correlation, it is first necessary to say something about the word "ordinary." For almost all species of birds and large vertebrates, for many flowering plants, and for some species of fish and insects, there is something (or sometimes a list of things) referred to as a common name. It is not obvious whether these should be thought of as part of ordinary language, or as part of a technical vocabulary. Certainly if competence in English does not require enough biological know-how to distinguish a beech from an elm, then surely it cannot require an awareness even of the existence of the solitary Pussytoes, the Flammulated Owl, or the Chinese Matrimony Vine. If such charming terms are assigned with their Latin equivalents to scientific taxonomy, and we restrict our attention to terms with which the layman can reasonably be expected to be familiar, then one thing we will find is that where there is a recognizable corresponding taxon, it is generally of higher level than the species.

For the case of large mammals, where human interest (and empathy) is at its highest, most familiar terms do refer to quite small groups of species; and common specific names are often widely known (as Blue Whale, Indian Elephant, or White-Tailed Deer). Most well-known names of trees refer quite neatly to genera, as, e.g., oak, beech, elm, willow, etc. (The various cedars, by contrast, are not closely related. It is reasonable to suppose that the term "cedar" has more to do with a kind of timber than with a biological kind.) With birds the situation is highly varied. Ducks, wrens, and woodpeckers form families. Gulls and terns form subfamilies. Kingbirds and cuckoos correspond to genera, while owls and pigeons make up whole orders. The

American Robin, finally, is a true species, though it is interesting that in Britain "robin" refers to a quite different species, and in Australia, I am told, it refers to a genus of flycatchers. For insects, where the number of species is much greater, and the degree of human interest generally lower, the mapping is predictably coarser. Such things as hump-backed flies, pleasing fungus beetles, brush-footed butterflies, and darkling beetles make up whole families (the last-named, for instance, having some 1,400 known North American species). More familiar things, like beetles and bugs, refer to whole orders. (Must the competent speaker of (American) English know that a beetle is not a bug? Or is the word "bug" ambiguous?)

The significance of the preceding point is that whereas there is an interesting case to be made for the reality of the species, there seems to be almost no case for taxonomic realism at any higher level of classification. Among biologists, "lumpers" and "splitters" do indeed dispute such questions as how many genera are to be distinguished within a family. Such disputes may be based on estimates of morphological or physiological similarity within groups of species, or on considerations of practical utility for field classification; they do not appear to involve deep theoretical interests, or to embody the assumption that such questions admit of true or false answers. (There is a possible claim that such distinctions reflect phylogenetic matters of fact, but I will postpone consideration of this suggestion.)

It will be recalled that Putnam's theory requires that there be some sameness relation between any two members of a natural kind. This might be called a "privileged sameness relation" since it is not supposed to be just any relation that happens to demarcate the kind, but rather some discoverable relation that constitutes the real nature of that kind. But biological theory offers no reason to expect that any such privileged relations exist, since higher taxa are assumed to be arbitrarily distinguished and do not reflect the existence of real kinds. This claim will be reinforced in the final section of this paper, where I will argue that even for the case of species no privileged sameness relations exist. Since this is a rather more controversial question, however, I should emphasize that I do not think the argument against Putnam depends in any way on this question. For as I have indicated, a species is seldom a candidate for the extension of an ordinary language term.

## 5. Promiscuous Realism

In this section I will make some more constructive suggestions about the relationship between the classifications of organisms in ordinary language (OLC) and in scientific taxonomy (TC). The natural way to contrast these classificatory schemes, it seems to me, is in terms of the different functions that they serve.

The functions of OLC, unsurprisingly enough, are overwhelmingly anthropocentric. A group of organisms may be distinguished in ordinary language for any of various reasons: because it is economically or sociologically important (Colorado beetles, silkworms, or Tsetse flies); because its members are intellectually intriguing (trap-door spiders or porpoises); furry and empathetic (hamsters and Koala bears); or just very noticeable (tigers and giant redwoods). This list could no doubt be extended almost indefinitely, which merely reflects the immense variety of human interests. From this standpoint many apparent anomalies between OLC terms and TC terms are readily explicable. An example I mentioned earlier is illustrative here. It would be a severe culinary misfortune if no distinction were drawn between garlic and onions. But we have seen that this is not a distinction reflected in TC. Presumably there is no reason why taxonomy should pay special attention to the gastronomic properties of its subject matter.

A slightly more elaborate example is the following. The taxonomic classes birds and mammals are both part of ordinary language (though the latter less clearly). By contrast, the much larger class of angiosperms (flowering plants) receives no such recognition. There is a very familiar term of ordinary language, "tree," the extension of which undoubtedly includes oak trees and pine trees (though perhaps not their seedlings). The extension of the TC term "angiosperm," on the other hand, includes daisies, cacti, and oak trees, but excludes pine trees. It is no surprise that such a grouping finds few uses outside biology; for most purposes it is much more relevant whether something is a tree or not than whether its seeds develop in an ovary. This seems sufficient to explain why there is no taxonomic equivalent of "tree" and no ordinary language equivalent of "angiosperm."

Where organisms are of little interest to non-specialists, they are typically coarsely discriminated in OLC. Thus it is that despite the vastly greater number of arthropod than vertebrate species, OLC distinguishes many more kinds of the latter. The factors I mentioned before may all apply here. Vertebrates are more likely to be useful (nutritious), interesting (empathetic), furry (useful), noticeable (big), etc. Thus arthropod classifications in OLC typically cover enormous numbers of species. In fact, the useful distinctions tend to be more on the model of "small red beetle" and "large black beetle," than of specific identification. Still with this functionalist viewpoint in mind, we can also see that there may be other, specialized vocabularies that do not coincide with either TC or OLC. The vocabularies of the timber merchant, the furrier, or even the herbalist may involve subtle distinctions between types of organisms; there is no obligation that these distinctions coincide with those of the taxonomist. (Recall, for instance, my earlier suggestion about the term "cedar.")

TC, hopefully, avoids this anthropocentric viewpoint. The number of species names is here intended to reflect the number of species that exist. Nonetheless, even here there is an anthropomorphic aspect. For an adequate taxonomy must not only meet theoretical constraints, but should also be practicably usable. The strongest theoretical constraints apply at the level of the species, for the obvious reason that this is the level with the greatest theoretical significance. Thus it has recently been recognized that a large number of groups that had been taken for species were in fact groups of very similar but distinct species (so-called "sibling species"). There is no requirement that taxonomy must be easy.

A taxonomic system is not merely a list of species, but must also include a selection of features by which they are to be recognized. Such features may be called "diagnostic." If it were possible to discover some privileged sameness relation for species, then clearly this relation should be used as diagnostic for the species. In the final part of this paper I will consider and reject some candidates for such a relation. For now I will assume that the existence of a species consists in the general co-occurrence of a large number of characteristics. If this is right, then the selection of diagnostic features must be greatly underdetermined, and hence, in a sense, arbitrary. Of course, there will be certain desiderata for such a choice, such as minimal developmental plasticity, or just ease of determination. In practice, a suitable feature or set of features is generally taken as providing a conclusive identification. But this should not be taken as showing that the features selected are privileged. And indeed, a slight acquaintance with field biology suggests that even the best selected diagnostic features will occasionally fall foul of atypical specimens or obscure hybrids. [. . .]

The position I would like to advocate might be described as promiscuous realism.[3] The realism derives from the fact that there are many sameness relations that serve to distinguish classes of organisms in ways that are relevant to various concerns; the promiscuity derives from the fact that none of these relations is privileged. The class of trees, for example, is just as real as the class of angiosperms; it is just that we have different reasons for distinguishing them. It is true that in the case of species there is a largely, though not wholly, determinate range of classes that we are aiming to identify. The existence of species, I suggest, may be seen as consisting in the following fact. If it were possible to map individual organisms on a multidimensional quality space, we would find numerous clusters or bumps. In some parts of biology these clusters will be almost entirely discrete. In other areas there will be a continuum of individuals between the peaks. It can then be seen as the business of taxonomy to identify these peaks. This picture also makes it easy to see why the deliverances of taxonomy need not provide the distinctions that are relevant for more specialized interests. As is demonstrated by

the existence of sibling species, the properties that covary in a species and distinguish it from other similar species may be very subtle (at least subtle enough to have escaped biologists for a long time). When the classificatory problem is approached from a more restricted point of view, that is, with an interest only in a certain range of properties, many peaks will disappear, while others may be emphasized. As an example of the former, analysis of the vocalizations of frogs have revealed numerous sibling species. But this hardly need be a matter of concern to the gourmet unless there are also variations in the texture or flavour of frogs' legs. Again, the gourmet puts more emphasis on the distinction between garlic and onions than is implicit in taxonomy. Even within biology different interests call for the emphasis of different distinctions. Thus the primary unit of significance in ecology is not the species but the population.

## 6. No Species Essences

I will now review and criticize three strategies that might be attempted for identifying privileged sameness relations between the members of a species. These strategies are based, respectively, on intrinsic properties of the individuals, on reproductive isolation of a group of individuals, and on evolutionary descent of a group of individuals. They will be considered in that order.

A traditional assumption that dates back at least to **Aristotle** is that organisms could be unambiguously sorted into discrete kinds on the basis of overt morphological characteristics. Since the theory of evolution undermined the belief in the fixity of species, this assumption has become increasingly untenable. It is now widely agreed that gross morphological properties are not sufficient for the unambiguous and exhaustive partition of individuals into species. Crudely, this is because there is considerable intraspecific variation with respect to any such property, and the range of variation of a property within a species will often overlap the range of variation of the same property within other species.

At the same time it is still sometimes thought that a more covert, probably microstructural, property could be discovered that would be adequate for the unambiguous assignment of individuals to species. More specifically, it may be thought that some description of the genetic material could capture a genuinely essential, or at least privileged, property (e.g., Putnam 141). It is assumed that the morphological and physiological properties are causally conditioned by interaction between the organism's genetic endowment and its environment. Thus it is imaginable that all members of a species do share the same genetic blueprint, or one with certain essential features, but that intraspecific differences are attributable to differences in environmental factors. But it is equally possible that there should be as much or more genetic variability as morphological variability. That is, intraspecific genetic variability may overlap interspecific variation as much as, or more than, morphological variability does. In fact, there are good reasons for supposing this to be the case. [. . .]

Much importance is attached in theoretical biology to the notion of reproductive isolation. It is suggested that a species can be defined as a group of interbreeding individuals, reproductively isolated from all other individuals; this is often referred to as the "biological" species concept, and may be considered a second candidate for providing a privileged relation between members of a species. Set against the desirability of genetic variation, there is a need for a species to maintain the integrity of a well-adapted gene pool. This requires insulation against the introgression of alien genes. Furthermore, it is generally supposed that the process of speciation is not completed until effective mechanisms have been established to prevent such introgression. Thus there is a certain sense in which reproductive isolation is an essential property of the species: the species would not have come into existence if it had not, to a sufficient degree, acquired this property. The important point here is that this is a property of the species, or gene pool, but only secondarily of the individuals that make up the species. [. . .]

Adequate reproductive isolation of a species does not require complete isolation of all its members.

Hybridization occurs throughout the natural world, though more particularly among plants, fishes, and amphibians. (A recently publicized case of successful mating between two monkeys of different species has brought this fact to more general attention.) This need not lead to significant gene introgression. In some cases hybrid individuals are sterile. In more complex cases there may be a band of hybridization where the geographic ranges of two species meet. (A readily noticeable example occurs with primroses and cowslips.) In such cases the continued existence of the two species is made possible by the competitive superiority of each within its preferred range. Since this superiority will normally apply also over hybrids, the alien genes will not penetrate much beyond the area of overlap. Thus the suggestion that this criterion for species provides a privileged relation between its constituent individuals fails on two counts. First, there will be individuals that would not be assigned to any species on this criterion; and second, there will be reproductive links connecting individuals that certainly belong to different species. The latter point is reinforced by the fact that the ability to produce viable offspring is not transitive. There exist chains of species, any two adjacent members of which can produce viable offspring, but the terminal members of which are not able to interbreed. Finally, as has often been observed, this criterion is completely useless for asexual species, since it would imply that every asexual organism constituted an entire species.

The third, and final, proposal I will consider is one based directly on evolutionary history. The underlying idea is that it should be possible, in theory, to construct a family tree for all life on Earth. It is then hoped that the classificatory taxonomic tree could converge on this phylogenetic tree. Hence any taxon will correspond to a historically real evolutionary process. This proposal has the considerable advantage that it appears to be equally applicable to the species and to higher taxa. Since it is certainly hoped that taxonomy and phylogeny should at least be mutually illuminating, this suggestion is in some sympathy with biological theory. [. . .]

To assess the present hypothesis it is first necessary to explain how a taxonomic tree could also be interpreted as an evolutionary tree. This requires that something be said about speciation. Qua taxonomy, each taxon also includes all the lower taxa "descended" from it. Thus the American Robin belongs simultaneously to the species *migratorius*, the genus *Turdus*, the family Turdidae, etc. The present suggestion interprets this as also embodying an evolutionary hypothesis. A species is composed of a number of populations that may be more or less differentiated from one another, both genetically and morphologically. When a population acquires some characteristic that isolates it genetically from the rest of the species, it is said to have achieved the status of a species. Thus the relevant evolutionary hypothesis would assert that at one time "turdidae" would have referred merely to a population of a larger species. Subsequently, this population would have achieved full species status, and still later divided into further species which now constitute the various genera in the family Turdidae. The particular genus *Turdus*, in turn, must have divided into further species, of which one is *migratorius*.

It remains to be seen whether this phylogenetic interpretation of the taxonomic tree can do anything to supply the taxon with a real essence, or privileged internal relation. Against the suggestion that evolutionary history could be essential to members of a taxon, one might deploy a Putnam-Kripke type argument. If, say, a chicken began to lay perfectly ordinary walnuts which were planted and grew into walnut trees, I would not wish to refer to this result as the production of a grove of chickens. If accepted, this intuition shows that the right ancestry is not a sufficient condition for taxon membership. My intuition, moreover, is that the trees in question might prove to be genuine walnut trees, which is to deny that ancestry is even a necessary condition. However, having expressed

suspicion of this style of argument, I do not want to rest any weight on this example of it. A more general argument is the following. Any sorting procedure that is based on ancestry presupposes that at some time in the past the ancestral organisms could have been subjected to some kind of sorting. One can imagine drawing up a phylogenetic tree and naming some branch of it; but the objective reality of the branch can be no greater than the objective reality of the grouping of organisms that constitutes the beginning of the branch. But I have claimed that, given all the organisms existing at a single time, there are no privileged properties or relations by means of which these can be sorted unambiguously and exhaustively into objectively significant classes. In short, the phylogenetic criterion must be parasitic on some other, synchronic, principle of taxonomy. It cannot generate privileged properties on its own.

As I have tried to stress, I do not mean to claim that species are unreal; only that they lack essential properties, and that their members cannot be distinguished by some privileged sameness relation. In fact, the existence of discrete species is one of the most striking and least disputable of biological data. If one examines the trees or birds in a particular area, it is apparent that these fall into a number of classes that differ from one another in numerous respects. But the essentialist conclusion that one might be tempted to draw from this fact is dissipated first by more careful study, which reveals that these distinguishing characteristics are by no means constant within the classes, and second by extending the scope of the investigation in both space and time, whereupon the limitations both of intraspecific similarity and interspecific difference will become increasingly apparent. [. . .]

## Notes

1. I use the term "nominal essence" here very broadly to include definitions, criteria, clusters of symptoms, etc. I do not mean to imply that every kind requires an essential property.

2. Taxonomic levels above the species include genus, family, order, class, phylum, and kingdom.—LG

3. I am grateful to John Perry for suggesting this term.

## Works Cited

Locke, J. *An Essay Concerning Human Understanding.* Vol. 2. Ed. Alexander Campbell Fraser. Oxford: Clarendon Press, 1894.

Putnam, H. "Is Semantics Possible?" *Mind, Language, and Reality, Vol. 2 of Philosophical Papers.* Cambridge: Cambridge University Press, 1975.

## Study Questions

1. Describe Putnam's four-component theory of the meaning of natural kind terms. How does this theory (a) incorporate Locke's distinction between nominal and real essences, and (b) provide a framework for understanding Putnam's account of the division of linguistic labour?

2. What does Dupré mean by "taxonomic realism"? Even if we assume taxonomic realism, what two problems does Dupré tell us confront Putnam's theory that the natural kinds investigated by scientists provide an extension for many of our ordinary language terms?

3. What does Dupré mean by "promiscuous realism," and what does this position imply about the relationship between ordinary and scientific language?

4. Biologists tend to believe that species, unlike higher taxonomic classes, are real. What three species definitions does Dupré compare, and on what grounds does he argue that each fails to provide Putnam with the privileged sameness relations his theory of natural kinds requires?

---

# Ian Hacking

---

Philosopher of science Ian Hacking received his BA in mathematics and physics from the University of British Columbia in 1956 and a PhD in moral sciences from Cambridge University in 1962. Hacking is an emeritus professor at the University of Toronto, a Companion of the Order of Canada, and holds a permanent chair at the Collège de France. In *The Social Construction of What?* Hacking intervenes in the "science wars" of the 1990s by making sense of talk about social construction.—GS

## Madness: Biological or Constructed?

From *The Social Construction of What?*

### 1. Introduction

[. . .] It is easy to be skeptical about many of the entries in contemporary diagnostic manuals. How about Intermittent Explosive Disorder? Certainly, some people fly off the handle all too easily, but do they suffer from a mental illness, IED? Or is this just some construct concocted by psychiatrists? We suspect that IED has to do with medicalizing disagreeable patterns of behaviour. It is easily argued that IED is not a diagnosis but a disciplinary devise. If someone said that Intermittent Explosive Disorder is a social construct, I might wince at the overuse of social-construct talk, but would understand roughly what was meant.

Other mental illnesses are what I call transient. I do not mean that they last only for a time in the life of an individual. I mean that they show up only at some times and some places, for reasons which we can only suppose are connected with the culture of those times and places. The classic example is hysteria in late-nineteenth-century France. There is multiple personality in recent America. There is anorexia—of which young women can die—which is quite local in its history; at present it is more virulent in Argentina than anywhere else. It is all too tempting to call these social constructs.

Here I will not discuss transient mental illnesses, which I examine, in a very different way, in my book *Mad Travelers*, nor will I discuss the disciplinary diagnoses such as Intermittent Explosive Disorder. Instead, I will examine illnesses such as schizophrenia and conditions such as mental retardation. These, it will be said, contrast strongly with anorexia, in that they have been with the human race in most places and times. There are no mental retardation epidemics in Argentina, even if the various words used to describe the condition, such as "feeble minded," were used only at a specific time and place and very strongly reflect social attitudes and institutional practices. The name "schizophrenia" was invented only in 1908. So what? These are "real" illnesses and conditions. And yet, and yet, there is a minority that will say that these disorders—and not just our ideas about them—are social constructs. Very often arguments are expressly put as: *X* is real—No, *X* is constructed.

It is not only the "constructed" that confuses us here, but also the "real." Hilary Putnam hit the nail on the head, when he wrote about a "common philosophical error of supposing that "reality" must refer to a single super thing, instead of looking at the ways in which we endlessly renegotiate—and are *forced* to renegotiate—our notion of reality as our language and our life develops" ("Sense" 452). One of the reasons that we become confused in debates about whether an illness is real or not is that we fail to attend carefully to the grammar of the word itself. But in the special context of mental illness we have, for the past two centuries, been constantly renegotiating our notion of reality.

"Social construct" and "real" do seem terribly at odds with each other. Part of the tension between the "real" and the "constructed" results from interaction between the two, between, say, child abuse, which is real enough, and the idea of child abuse, which is "constructed." But that is not all. We can also confuse more complex types of interactions, which make people think of antique dualisms between mind and body. These come out most clearly when we turn to the very habitus of mind and body, psychopathology. Most present-day research scientists take schizophrenia to be at the bottom a biochemical and neurological or genetic disorder (perhaps all three). A minority of critics think that in important ways the disease has been socially constructed. I do not want to take sides, but to create a space in which both ideas can be developed without too much immediate confrontation—and without much social construction talk either.

What difficult terrain we enter! One of the reasons that I dislike talk of social construction is that it is like a miasma, a curling mist within which hover will-o'-the-wisps luring us to destruction. Yet such talk will no more go away than will our penchant for talking about reality. There are deep-seated needs for both ideas. Nothing I could say would discourage anyone from talking about reality or social construction. Hilary Putnam, just quoted, said something very useful, but it is not going to change the way that even those who read him talk about reality. So instead I shall suggest some other ways to think about questions posed by the ideas of social construction—and reality. There are many difficult questions to address, so it is good to start with something relatively easy to follow.

## 2. Children

The distinction between objects and ideas [. . .] conceals a very difficult issue. The trouble is that ideas often *interact* with states, conditions, behaviour, actions, and individuals. Recall Philippe Ariès's well-known *Centuries of Childhood*. In the wake of that book, childhood has been called a social construct. Some people mean that the idea of childhood (and all that implies) has been constructed. Others mean that a certain state of person, or even a period in the life of a human being, an actual span of time, has been constructed. Some thinkers may even mean that children, as they exist today, are constructed. States, conditions, stages of development, and children themselves are worldly objects, not ideas.

Thus it may be contended that children now—take two small individuals named Sam and Charlie-boy—are different from children at some other time, because the idea of childhood—the matrix of childhood—is different now. It may be argued that the state in which Sam and Charlie find themselves now is different from what it was for their ancestors, or even their mothers, Jane and Rachel, when they were very young. Conversely, the idea of childhood may have changed from what it was long ago, if children now are different from children then.

To use a less grand example than the whole of childhood, there has been a historical succession of ideas: fidgety, hyperactive, attention deficit, and Attention Deficit Hyperactivity Disorder. Perhaps the children to which these terms have been applied over the course of this century are themselves different. Perhaps children diagnosed with ADHD are different from children once called fidgety—in part because of the theories held about them, and the remedies that have been put in place around their bad habits. Conversely, it may be that the resulting changes in the children have contributed to the evolution of ideas about problem children. That is an example of interaction.

I want to focus not on the children but on the classification, those *kinds* of children, fidgety, hyperactive, attention-deficient. They are *interactive kinds*. I do not mean that hyperactive children, the individuals, are "interactive." Obviously hyperactive children, like any other children, interact with innumerable people and things in innumerable ways. "Interactive" is a new concept that applies not to people but to classifications, to kinds, to the kinds that can influence what is classified. And because kinds can interact with what is classified, the classification itself may be modified or replaced.

I do not necessarily mean that hyperactive children, as individuals, on their own, become aware of how they are classified, and thus react to the classification. Of course they may, but the interaction occurs in the larger matrix of institutions and

practices surrounding this classification. There was a time when children described as hyperactive were placed in "stim-free" classrooms: classrooms in which stimuli were minimized, so that the children would have no occasion for excess activity. Desks were far apart. The walls had no decoration. The windows were curtained. The teacher wore a plain black dress with no ornaments. The walls were designed for minimum noise reflection. The classification *hyperactive* did not interact with the children simply because the individual children heard the word and changed accordingly. It interacted with those who were so described in institutions and practices that were predicated upon classifying children as hyperactive.

## 3. Interactive Kinds

There is a big difference between quarks and children. Children are conscious, self-conscious, very aware of their social environment, less articulate than many adults, perhaps, but, in a word, aware. People, including children, are agents, they act, as the philosophers say, under descriptions. The courses of action they choose, and indeed their ways of being, are by no means independent of the available descriptions under which they may act. Likewise, we experience ourselves in the world as being persons of various kinds. [. . .] It is said that "the experiences of being female or of having a disability are socially constructed" (Asch and Fine 5–6). That means, in part, that we are affected by the ways in which being female or having a disability are conceived, described, ordained by ourselves and the network of milieus in which we live.

Here I am concerned with kinds of people, their behaviour, and their experiences involving action, awareness, agency, and self-awareness. The awareness may be personal, but more commonly is an awareness shared and developed within a group of people, embedded in practices and institutions to which they are assigned in virtue of the way in which they are classified.

We are especially concerned with classifications that, when known by people or by those around them, and put to work in institutions, change the ways in which individuals experience themselves—and may even lead people to evolve their feelings and behaviour in part because they are so classified. Such kinds (of people and their behaviour) are interactive kinds. This ugly phrase has the merit of recalling actors, agency and action. The *inter* may suggest the way in which the classification and the individual classified may interact, the way in which the actors may become self-aware as being of a kind, if only because of being treated or institutionalized as of that kind, and so experiencing themselves in that way.

## 4. Indifferent Kinds

The word "kind" was first used as a free-standing noun in the philosophy of the sciences by **William Whewell** and **John Stuart Mill**, some 160 years ago. Here I use it to draw attention to the principle of classification, the kind itself, which interacts with those classified. And vice-versa, of course, it is people who interact with the classification.

There can be strong interactions. What was known about people of a kind may become false because people of that kind have changed in virtue of how they have been classified, what they believe about themselves, or because of how they have been treated as so classified. There is a looping effect.

I have not defined "interactive kind," but only pointed. Kinds that are the subject of intense scientific scrutiny are of special interest. There is a constant drive in the social and psychological sciences to emulate the natural sciences, and to produce true natural kinds of people. This is evidently true for basic research on pathologies such as schizophrenia and autism, but it is also, at present, equally true for some but only some investigators who study homosexuality (the search for the homosexual gene) or violent crime (is that an innate and heritable propensity?). There is a picture of an object to be searched out, the right kind, the kind that is true to nature, a fixed target if only we can get there. But perhaps it is a moving target, just because of the looping effect of human kinds? That is, new knowledge about "the

criminal" or "the homosexual" becomes known to the people classified, changes the way these individuals behave, and loops back to force changes in the classifications and knowledge about them.

The notion of an interactive kind is fuzzy but not useless. Plenty of classifications differ fundamentally from any of the human kinds just mentioned. **Quarks** are not aware. A few of them may be affected by what people do to them in accelerators. Our knowledge about quarks affects quarks, but not because they become aware of what we know, and act accordingly. What name shall we give to classifications like that? Too much philosophy has been built into the epithet "natural kind." All I want is a contrast to interactive kinds. *Indifferent* will do. The classification "quark" is indifferent in the sense that calling a quark a quark makes no difference to the quark.

Indifferent does not imply passive. The classification *plutonium* is indifferent, but plutonium is singularly nonpassive. It kills. It exists only because human beings have created it. (That is not quite true: it was once thought that transuranic evolution had never, in nature, got to plutonium; in fact natural plutonium has been identified). Plutonium has a quite extraordinary relationship with people. They made it, and it kills them. But plutonium does not interact with the idea of plutonium, in virtue of being aware that it is called plutonium, or experiencing existence in plutonium institutions like reactors, bombs, and storage tanks. So I call it indifferent.

**Microbes**, not individually but as a class, may well interact with the way in which we intervene in the life of microbes. We try to kill bad microbes with penicillin derivatives. We cultivate good ones such as the acidophilus and bifidus we grow to make yogurt. In evolutionary terms, it is very good for these benevolent organisms that we like yogurt, and cultivate them. But some of the malevolent ones do pretty well too. Disease microbes that we try to kill may as a class, a species, respond to our murderous onslaught. They mutate. There is some evidence for what is called directed mutation. Under environmental stress, such as lack of edible food (lactates) that can be ingested by the microbes in a culture, the microbes mutate in a nonrandom, species-beneficial way so that they can feed. Maybe that is how disease microbes so quickly become resistant to our poisons. [. . .]

Do not microbes adapt themselves to us, quickly evolving strains that resist our antibacterial medications? Is there not a looping effect between the microbe and our knowledge? My simple-minded reply is that microbes do not do all these things because, either individually or collectively, they are aware of what we are doing to them. The classification *microbe* is indifferent, not interactive, although we are certainly not indifferent to microbes, and they do interact with us. But not because they know what they are doing.

## 5. Natural Kinds

When philosophers talk about natural kinds, they take the indifference—in my technical sense—of natural kinds for granted. That is to be expected. At the end of this chapter I shall make heavy use of the natural-kind philosophy and semantics that we owe to Hilary Putnam and Saul Kripke. Their innovative ideas were, in one respect, very conservative. They are part of a tradition that reaches back into the industrial revolution, when William Whewell and John Stuart Mill put the idea of natural kinds into philosophical circulation. At that time, more than ever before in human history, the distinctions between humans and nature, minds and matter, took a distinctive turn. The earth became covered by active machines, made by and tended by people, but running more or less on their own, thoroughly active and somewhat autonomous. In the seventeenth century, mechanical watches and an automatic clock on the spire at Strasbourg had moved philosophers to flights of fancy. But those devices *did* nothing. They were semantic; they were signifiers; they told us the time. In the early nineteenth century, the steam engine at the pit head, the steam locomotive, the spinning jenny accomplished unimaginable feats.

Nature, despite the way that Romantics were fascinated by the sublime and the wild, continued to be thought of as passive, at least in the laboratory. Nature was acted on by us, and now by our creatures, the machines. Hence the concept of the natural kind

came into currency, as something indifferent. The things classified by the natural-kind terms favoured in philosophical writing are not aware of how they are classified, and do not interact with their classifications. The canonical examples have been: water, sulphur, horse, tiger, lemon, multiple sclerosis, heat and the colour yellow. What an indifferent bunch! None is aware that it is SO classified. Of course people and horses interact. Black Beauty and Flicka were (fictional) horses that attended to the humans who loved them, who in turn attended to the horses they loved. In denying that *horse* is an interactive kind, I am not denying that people and horses interact. I am saying that horses are no different for being classified as horses. Indeed it will make a difference, in law and to a Shetland pony, whether ponies are classified as horses: but not because the ponies know the law.

## 6. Psychopathologies

What happens if something is both an interactive kind and an indifferent kind? Psychopathology furnishes obvious candidates. I do not want to insist on any one psychopathology, but will mention a range of cases. Each of them is to some extent a dreadful mystery, a veritable pit of human ignorance: mental retardation, childhood autism, schizophrenia. It is true that childhood autism was diagnosed only in 1943, and that schizophrenia was named only in 1908, but there is a widespread conviction that these disorders are here to stay, and were with us long before they were named.

There are competing theses about these three examples. One type of thesis tends, speaking very loosely, to the constructionist camp. The other type tends, once again speaking loosely, to the biological camp. In the constructionist camp, these disorders are interactive kinds of illness. In the biological camp, they are thought of as indifferent kinds. Here is a very sharp instance of the fundamental tension between the "real" and the "constructed." I am attempting to address the felt tension with a less tired set of opposites.

We need to make room, especially in the case of our most serious psychopathologies, for both the constructionist and the biologist. That is not to say that I favour one or the other, only that I want spaces in which each can work, without interfering too much with the positive parts of the other's research programs. I shall begin by stating the constructionist attitude to three severe mental disorders.

## 6.1. The Feeble Mind

On the construction side we have, for example, *Inventing the Feeble Mind* (Trent), a book that shows how the seemingly inevitable classification, "retarded child," overlaps with and has evolved from a host of earlier labels: ill-balanced, idiots, imbeciles, morons, feebleminded, mental deficients, moral imbeciles, subnormals, retardates. Each of these classifications has had its moment of glory. The populations singled out overlap markedly. Each label was thought of as a classification or subclassification that improved on previous ones. Each classification has been associated with a regimen of treatment, schooling, exclusion, or inclusion. Each has surely affected the experience both of those so classified and of their families, their schoolmates, their teachers. At various times in our history each classification has been an interactive kind. At the time that each classification was in use, it seemed somewhat inevitable, a perfectly natural way to classify children with various sorts of deficit. Yet when we see the parade of ungainly labels, we quickly realize that these classifications are highly contingent. Each reflects the medical and social attitude of a particular epoch. They could have been otherwise. [. . .]

The idea of mental retardation (and all those other names just listed) [is unmasked as] being part of an ideology whose extra-theoretical function (Mannheim) was to control difficult children, divert them away from schools or school buses into institutions or regimens of treatment. And the retarded have fought back. Every public school in California is required to integrate a certain number of "special education" children into every classroom. This is a splendid example of ideas operating within an extended matrix. One very helpful accident for special education programs was the fact that President John F. Kennedy had a retarded sister, so he set in

motion, long ago, federal programs that have ended up as special education in California.

California's programs provide a wonderful illustration of how interactive kinds work. First, the classification has become embedded in a complex matrix of institutions and practices wherein a certain number of children, designated in a certain way, must be assigned to every class, although they are also removed from the class for more individualized tuition. The regular teachers complain bitterly that the result is class disruption; the specially educated know how they are classified; they develop not only individual but collective new patterns of behaviour. One can make a strong prediction that not only will the procedures be modified, but also the ways in which these children are classified will be modified because of the new kinds of behaviour that have emerged.

These looping patterns also show up in the past. Those changes in terminology referring to retarded children were not the result of a better classification of individuals as pure beings-in-themselves, but reclassification of individuals in the light of how those individuals had altered, in the light of a previous classification and because of the theories, practices, and institutions associated with that classification. One regular refrain in the history of mental retardation is the claim that now we are getting to understand things—as if it were the same thing being understood all along.

## 6.2. Schizophrenia

Or take schizophrenia. Here we have for example *Schizophrenia: A Scientific Delusion?* by Mary Boyle who, in her preface, avows that she is a social constructionist. Her subject is seemingly less amenable to such treatment than that of mental retardation. Instead of a string of sad and inapt labels for the people classified, moral imbeciles and all the rest, we have only a few neologisms made from Latin or Greek, *schizophrenia* and its precursor *dementia praecox*, and then classifications that no one today has ever heard of, such as *hebephrenia*. Once Eugen Bleuler had given us the name in the first decade of the twentieth century, it stuck.

As Boyle herself says, she concentrates not on schizophrenics but on those who diagnose schizophrenia. She recounts the history of this "kind" of patient. She notes stark mutations in the concept of schizophrenia. She claims that clinicians are often benignly unaware of them. She argues that the introduction, definition, and characterization of this theoretical notion fails to satisfy criteria of adequacy [. . .]. She argues that psychiatrists, patients, families, welfare agencies, all "need" the idea of schizophrenia. Her conclusion, stated baldly, is that schizophrenia is a construct. Attempts to identify its etiology by neurochemistry are doomed. Schizophrenia is not a kind of disease. The motley of impaired individuals that at different times, and in different ways, have been handily lumped together as schizophrenics are not of a kind. [. . .]

One of the reasons for the changing symptom profile of schizophrenia is, I suspect, that it is a moving target. There are certain rather widespread phenomena that often lead to the diagnosis of schizophrenia—auditory hallucinations, for example. But even the ways in which people diagnosed as schizophrenic describe these delusive hearings have changed, and the content of the hallucinations has changed. Moreover, the role of hallucinations in the diagnosis of schizophrenia is itself mobile. The founding fathers, Emil Kraepelin and Eugen Bleuler, emphasized above all flat affect, and held that many mental illnesses are accompanied by hallucinations. Just before World War II, Kurt Schneider, intending to operationalize the concept, produced a list of some 12 First Rank Symptoms with auditory hallucinations top of the list. When First Rank Symptoms ruled the diagnostic yard, a lot more people became schizophrenic than would ever have made it in the wards of the Burghölzli hospital during Bleuler's reign.

I conjecture a remarkable looping effect here. Bleuler allowed fairly free expression of auditory hallucinations. They were not important; there were other aspects of one's life to come to grips with. He took hallucinations in stride and paid little heed to them. Hallucinations became ordinary, not to be worried about, neither to be the voice of God to be proud of, nor something to hide from the doctor. Hallucinations became so freely available, unproblematic, that schizophrenics said they had them. So Schneider made them almost a sine qua non of schizophrenia, and yes, they were, at that time. But then as schizophrenia passed from being a disorder that was somewhat in fashion to a diagnosis not wanted any more, flat affect came back, and hallucinations, in the most recent diagnostic manuals, are no longer key. The schizophrenic, as a kind of person, is a moving target, and the classification is an interactive kind.

## 6.3. Childhood Autism

My third example, childhood autism, bridges my first two. The name "autism" was invented by Bleuler to describe a characteristic family of symptoms in the group of schizophrenias. Adult patients lost the usual sense of social relationships, they became withdrawn, gave inappropriate responses, a phenomenon deeply disturbing to family and friends. Then the word "autism" was applied to some children previously regarded as feeble-minded, or even deaf-and-dumb. This was the result of Leo Kanner's many years of study of a quite small number of children. He published it in 1943. At that time the prevailing view, influenced by the (brief!) dominance of psychoanalysis in American psychiatry, was that the autistic child had a "refrigerator mother," one who could not express emotion to the child. This doctrine has by and large passed. Similar if subtler notions do persist in some schools of psychoanalysis, for example, that of Jacques Lacan, in which childhood autism is still connected with problematic relations between mother and child at a critical stage of maturation.

Cognitive science now rules some roosts. Since autistic children have many linguistic and other deficits, theories of cognition may be invoked. A recent fashion has been to argue that the autistic child lacks a "theory of mind." A single ingenious experiment originally suggested by philosophers has spawned an experimental industry.[1] That is often the case in psychology, where new experimental ideas are as rare and as hard to invent as deep mathematical proofs or truly new magic tricks. But as with retardation and schizophrenia, there continues to be a substantial iconoclastic literature urging that autism is not something people just have, and that autism is no single disorder. Thus we read sentences like this: "Mental retardation is not something you have, like blue eyes or a bad heart" (AAMR 9). "Autism is the 'way people are' rather than 'a thing people have'"(Donellan and Leary 46).

Autism may seem problematic for my idea of an interactive kind. Autistic children by definition have severe problems of communication. So how can the classification interact with the children? Part of the answer is that they are in their own ways aware, conscious, reflective, and, in the experience of those who work with autistic children, very good at manipulating other people, despite their problems of lack of affect and rapport. But the example brings out that by interaction I do not mean only the self-conscious reaction of a single individual to how she is classified. I mean the consequences of being so classified for the whole class of individuals and other people with whom they are intimately connected. The autistic family, as we might call it—a family with an autistic child—was severely influenced, and some would say damaged, by the doctrine of the refrigerator mother. The subsequent changes in the family contributed to a rethinking of what childhood autism is—not because one found out more about it, but because the behaviour itself changed. Most of the behaviours described by Kanner seem not to exist any more.

## 6.4. Indifferent versus Interactive

There is, then, not only a strong pull towards a constructionist attitude to many mental disorders, but also a great interest in what the classifications do to the individuals classified. One of the defects of social-construction talk is that it suggests a one-way street: society (or some fragment of it) constructs the disorder (and that is a bad thing, because the disorder does not really exist as described, or would

not really exist unless so described). By introducing the idea of an interactive kind, I want to make plain that we have a two-way street, or rather a labyrinth of interlocking alleys.

There is obviously another side to this story. There is a deep-seated conviction that retarded children, schizophrenics, and autistic people suffer from one or more fundamental neurological or biochemical problems which will, in the future, be identified. It is not claimed that every person now diagnosed will have the same problem. In the case of schizophrenia, some researchers conjecture that there are at least two distinct disorders, one of which declares itself in late adolescence and is genetic, and another of which may not be inherited. No one maintains that mental retardation is a single disorder, but many believe that specific types of retardation have clear biological causes, to the extent that we can say these disorders simply are biological in nature.

Autism is instructive. There was a debate long ago between the anti-psychiatrist, Thomas Szasz, and Robert Spitzer, who as editor of the Diagnostic and Statistical Manuals has directed American psychiatric nosology since 1974. Szasz argued that MDs should treat only what they know to be diseases. Psychiatrists treat troubled people, but cannot identify any genuine medical conditions, so they should leave the treatment to healers, shamans, priests, counsellors. Psychiatry is not a branch of medicine. Spitzer replied: what about childhood autism? We know it *must* be neurological in nature, but we have no idea what the neurology is, so we treat it symptomatically, as psychologists. Is it wrong for us as doctors to try to help autistic children just because we do not yet know the neurology?[2] He took this to be a knockdown argument.

We need not argue that nearly all children diagnosed with autism today have exactly one and the same biological disorder. We need only hold possible that there are a few (possibly just one) basic fundamental biological disorders that produce the symptoms currently classified as autistic. Imagine, however, that there is just one such pathology, call it *P*, and that in reasonable time, we discover what $P$ is. A great discovery is reported: "Autism is $P$." Optimists will say that we won't have to wait long. As this book goes to press in July 1998, the International Molecular Genetic Study of Autism Consortium has just announced the first major linkage of autism to a region on a certain chromosome.

There is a question as to what kind of entity $P$ will prove to be. Imagine that in the future it is established that a certain set of genetic markers indicates an inherited biological mechanism producing a certain neurological deficit accompanied by biochemical imbalance. Is the pathology genetic, neurological, or biochemical? It is of no moment, to the present discussion, what sort of thing $P$ is. Different hypotheses going the rounds involve a range of genetic, neurological, and biochemical conjectures. [. . .]

By hypothesis the pathology $P$ will be an indifferent kind. The neuro-geno-biochemical state $P$ is not aware of what we find out. It is not affected simply by the fact that we have found out about it, although of course our new knowledge may, with luck, enable us to intervene and either prevent or ameliorate the pathology. In more traditional jargon, $P$ would be a natural kind.

## 7. A Dilemma

Suppose that childhood autism is at bottom a biological pathology $P$, namely what has traditionally been called a "natural" kind and what I here call an indifferent kind. What then happens to the claim that childhood autism is an interactive kind? That is, a kind in which the humans classified may indeed change through looping effects, because of the ways in which the people classified react to being so classified? How can it be an interactive kind and also an indifferent kind?

This is one way in which to address an issue that troubles many cautious people, the idea that something can apparently be both socially constructed and yet "real." [. . .] Here we want to say both that childhood autism *is* (is identical to) a certain biological

pathology $P$, and so is a "natural" kind or an indifferent kind. At the same time, we want to say that childhood autism is an interactive kind, interacting with autistic children, evolving and changing as the children change.

The pathology $P$ causes havoc in the behaviour, life, and emotions of conscious, judging, moral, aware, somewhat autonomous human beings, namely autistic children. But pathology $P$ is, by hypothesis, not what it is in virtue of anything conscious, self-aware. The greater the role of fundamental genetics, of molecular identification in the pathology $P$, the more people say that human genome is the place to look, then the more obvious it will seem that we are in the realm of indifferent, "natural" kinds.

## 7.1. Semantic Resolution

At this juncture, philosophers may like to think of childhood autism and the postulated pathology $P$ in terms of the theories of reference advocated by Hilary Putnam ("Meaning of 'Meaning'") and Saul Kripke. The term "autism" is what they would call a natural-kind-term, analogous to the multiple sclerosis that Putnam long used as an example (even before working out his theory on the meaning of "meaning.") If there is in fact exactly one definite biological pathology $P$ underlying a broad class of autistic children, then the reference of the name "childhood autism" is $P$. Under this hypothesis, the name "childhood autism" is, in Kripke's terms, a rigid designator of a natural kind, namely the pathology $P$. In my terms, the pathology $P$ is an indifferent kind, and "childhood autism" is the name of that kind.

Our difficulty then seems merely verbal. Yes, if there is precisely one neuropathology $P$ underlying what we now call autism, then, in Kripke-Putnam semantics, the kind-term "childhood autism" rigidly designates that pathology. Shall we say that when Kanner coined the name "childhood autism," it referred to pathology $P$? Some would give him what Putnam calls the "benefit of the dubbed"—yes, he referred to P, even though he (like ourselves) had not the remotest idea what childhood autism really is, namely P.

Putnam's theory of meaning presents meaning as a vector, or ordered tuple. This vector is in most ways like a dictionary entry: part of speech, category, down through stereotype, but ending in an item no dictionary, or anything else, can ever present: the extension of the term being defined. That is, the class of things falling under the term, the class of things to which the term applies. In our example, the final entry in the meaning of "meaning" vector for "autism" is the pathology P, or perhaps all instances of the pathology P.

We can perfectly well keep Putnam's machinery, but suppose that in the Putnam-style meaning of "autism" (and of a great many other words) we put an enriched stereotype of childhood autism, the current idea of childhood autism, accompanied by definite examples and descriptions of prototypical autistic children. So-called definitions of mental disorders commonly proceed by giving clinical examples prototypes. We need not now concern ourselves with details. In the vector for the meaning of "childhood autism" we should include both the current idea of autism—prototypes, theories, hypotheses, therapies, attitudes, the lot—and the reference, if there is one, namely the pathology P.

Now for the bottom line. Someone writes a paper titled "The Social Construction of Childhood Autism." The author could perfectly well maintain (a) there is probably a definite unknown neuropathology P that is the cause of prototypical and most other examples of what we now call childhood autism; (b) the idea of childhood autism is a social construct that interacts not only with therapists and psychiatrists in their treatments, but also interacts with autistic children themselves, who find the current mode of being autistic a way for themselves to be.

In this case we have several values for the X in the social construction of X = childhood autism: (a) the idea of childhood autism, and what that involves; (b) autistic children, actual human beings, whose way of being is in part constructed. But not (c) the neuropathology P, which, ex-hypothesi, we are treating as an indifferent kind, and which Putnam would call a natural kind. A follower of Kripke might call P the essence of autism. For us, the interest would be not in the semantics but the dynamics. How would the discovery of P affect how autistic children and their families conceive of themselves; how would it affect their behaviour? What would be the looping affect on the stereotype of autistic children? Which children, formerly classified as autistic, would now be excluded, and what would that do to them? [. . .]

My position here is rather curious. I have already made amply plain that I do not, myself, favour the language of social construction. I am discussing it in connection with psychopathologies because many deeply committed critics of psychiatric establishments find social-construction talk helpful. It enables them to begin with a critique of practices about which they are deeply sceptical. I respect their concerns, and have, I hope, represented them fairly, if cautiously. On the other hand, I also respect the biological program of research into the most troubling of psychiatric disorders. That creates a dilemma.

I have suggested a semantic way for a philosopher to make peace with the dilemma. Some would say that it is more than that—it is a tidy resolution of the dilemma. But not only am I ambivalent, or worse, about social construction; I am also ambivalent about the use of rigid designation in connection with disease and disorder. [. . .]

Semantical theories like those of Kripke and Putnam are [. . .] tools [. . .] not literally correct descriptions of natural language. They are artificial ways of construing natural languages for this or that purpose. [. . .] In the present case, putting a theory of reference alongside social construction shows how to diminish a felt dilemma. If this approach helps, then it does a real service, for it enables us to move on to more significant issues, to what I call the dynamics, rather than the semantics, of classification. [. . .]

## Notes

1. Jack and Jill are shown a box with plastic dinosaurs in it. Jack is sent out of the room. The dinosaurs are replaced by candies. Jack is asked to come back into the room, but before he enters Jill is asked, "What will Jack think is in the box?"
   If Jill says dinosaurs, she has a theory of mind, but if she says candies, she does not.
2. I take the anecdote from a talk by Spitzer to the annual convention of the American Psychological Association, Toronto, 10 August 1996.

## Works Cited

AAMR. *Handbook of the American Association for the Mentally Retarded.* X (1992): 9.

Asch, A., and M. Fine. "Introduction: Beyond Pedestals." *Women with Disabilities: Essays in Psychology, Culture, and Politics.* Ed. A. Asch and M. Fine. Philadelphia: Temple University Press, 1988.

Boyle, M. *Schizophrenia: A Scientific Delusion?* London: Routledge, 1990.

Donellan, A.M., and M.A. Leary. *Movement Differences and Diversity in Autism/Mental Retardation: Appreciating and Accommodating People with Communication and Behavior Challenges.* Madison, WI: DRI Press, 1995.

Hacking, I. *Mad Travelers: Reflections on the Reality of Transient Mental Illnesses.* Charlottesville: University Press of Virginia, 1998.

IMGAC (International Molecular Genetic Study of Autism Consortium). "A Full Genome Screen for Linkage to a Region on Chromosome 7q." *Human Molecular Genetics* 7 (1998): 571–8.

Kripke, S. *Naming and Necessity.* Cambridge, MA: Harvard University Press, 1980.

Mannheim, K. "The Problem of a Sociology of Knowledge." *Essays on the Sociology of Knowledge.* London: Routledge & Kegan Paul, 1952. 134–90.

Putnam, H. "The Meaning of 'Meaning.'" *Mind, Language and Reality, Vol. 2 of Philosophical Papers.* Cambridge: Cambridge University Press, 1975.

Putnam, H. "Sense, Nonsense and the Senses: An Inquiry into the Powers of the Human Mind. *The Journal of Philosophy* 91 (1994): 445–517.

Trent, J.W. *Inventing the Feeble Mind: A History of Mental Retardation in the United States.* Berkeley: University of California Press, 1994.

## Study Questions

1. According to Hacking, how do "intermittent explosive disorder" (IED) and hysteria illustrate two different ways in which psychopathologies are often said to be socially constructed?
2. For Hacking, how does childhood provide an example of (a) the social construction of an idea, and (b) the social construction of an object in the world?
3. Explain Hacking's distinction between interactive and indifferent kinds.
4. What use does Hacking make of Putnam's approach to the semantics of natural kind terms to try to resolve the dilemma faced when it appears possible that a condition like childhood autism is both an indifferent and interactive kind?

# Sally Haslanger

Sally Haslanger acquired her PhD from University of California, Berkeley, in 1985. She is a professor of philosophy and linguistics and director of women's and gender studies at the Massachusetts Institute of Technology. This article's critical analysis of the categories of "gender" and "race" combines Haslanger's philosophical interests in metaphysics and feminist theory.—GS

# Gender and Race: (What) Are They? (What) Do We Want Them To Be?

## 1. Introduction

It is always awkward when someone asks me informally what I'm working on and I answer that I'm trying to figure out what gender is. For outside a rather narrow segment of the academic world, the term "gender" has come to function as the polite way to talk about the sexes. And one thing people feel pretty confident about is their knowledge of the difference between males and females. Males are those human beings with a range of familiar primary and secondary sex characteristics, most important being the penis; females are those with a different set, most important being the vagina or, perhaps, the uterus. Enough said. Against this background, it isn't clear what could be the point of an inquiry, especially a philosophical inquiry, into "what gender is."

But within that rather narrow segment of the academic world concerned with gender issues, not only is there no simple equation of sex and gender, but the seemingly straightforward anatomical distinction between the sexes has been challenged as well. What began as an effort to note that men and women differ socially as well as anatomically has prompted an explosion of different uses of the term "gender." Within these debates, not only is it unclear what gender is and how we should go about understanding it, but whether it is anything at all.

The situation is similar, if not worse, with respect to race. The self-evidence of racial distinctions in everyday American life is at striking odds with the uncertainty about the category of race in law and the academy. Work in the biological sciences has informed us that our practices of racial categorization don't map neatly onto any useful biological classification; but that doesn't settle much, if anything. For what should we make of our tendency to classify individuals according to race, apparently on the basis of physical appearance? And what are we to make of the social and economic consequences of such classifications? Is race real or is it not?

## 2. The Question(s)

[Concerning] the questions, "What is race?" or "What is gender?" we can distinguish [. . .] three projects with importantly different priorities: *conceptual*, *descriptive*, and *analytical*.

A *conceptual* inquiry into race or gender would seek an articulation of our *concepts* of race or gender. To answer the conceptual question, one way to proceed would be to use the method of reflective equilibrium. (Although within the context of analytic philosophy this might be seen as a call for a conceptual *analysis* of the term(s), I want to reserve the term "analytical" for a different sort of project, described below.)

In contrast to the conceptual project, a *descriptive* project is not concerned with exploring the nuances of our concepts (or anyone else's for that matter); it focuses instead on their extension. Here, the task is to develop potentially more accurate concepts through careful consideration of the phenomena, usually relying on empirical or quasi-empirical methods. Paradigm descriptive projects occur in studying natural phenomena. [. . .] However, a descriptive approach need not be confined to a search for *natural* or *physical* kinds; inquiry into what it is to be, e.g., a human right, a citizen, a democracy, might begin by considering the full range of what has counted as such to determine whether there is an underlying (possibly social) kind that explains the temptation to group the cases together. Just as natural science can enrich our "folk" conceptualization of natural phenomena, social sciences (as well as the arts and humanities) can enrich our "folk" conceptualization of social phenomena. So, a descriptive inquiry into race and gender need not presuppose that race and gender are biological kinds; instead it might ask whether our uses of race and gender vocabularies are tracking social kinds, and if so which ones.

The third sort of project takes an *analytical* approach to the question, "What is gender?" or "What is race?" On this approach the task is not to explicate our ordinary concepts; nor is it to investigate the kind that we may or may not be tracking with our everyday conceptual apparatus; instead we begin by considering more fully the pragmatics of our talk employing the terms in question. What is the point of having these concepts? What cognitive or practical task do they (or should they) enable us to accomplish? Are they effective tools to accomplish our (legitimate) purposes; if not, what concepts would serve these purposes better? In the limit case of an analytical approach the concept in question is introduced by stipulating the meaning of a new term, and its content is determined entirely by the role it plays in the theory. But if we allow that our everyday vocabularies serve both cognitive and practical purposes, purposes that might also be served by our theorizing, then a theory offering an improved understanding of our (legitimate) purposes and/or improved conceptual resources for the tasks at hand might reasonably represent itself as providing a (possibly revisionary) account of the everyday concepts.

So, on an analytical approach, the questions "What is gender?" or "What is race?" require us to consider what work we want these concepts to do for us; why do we need them at all? The responsibility is ours to define them for our purposes. In doing so we will want to be responsive to some aspects of ordinary usage (and to aspects of both the connotation and extension of the terms). However, neither ordinary usage nor empirical investigation is overriding, for there is a stipulative element to the project: *this* is the phenomenon we need to be thinking about. Let the term in question refer to it. On this approach, the world by itself can't tell us what gender is, or what race is; it is up to us to decide what in the world, if anything, they are.

This essay pursues an analytical approach to defining race and gender. [. . .]

The goal of the project is to consider what work the concepts of gender and race might do for us in a critical—specifically feminist and antiracist—social theory, and to suggest concepts that can accomplish at least important elements of that work. So to start: why might feminist antiracists want or need the concepts of gender and race? What work can they do for us?

At the most general level, the task is to develop accounts of gender and race that will be effective tools in the fight against injustice.

## 3. What Is Gender?

Even a quick survey of the literature reveals that a range of things have counted as "gender" within feminist theorizing. The guiding idea is sometimes expressed with the slogan: "gender is the social meaning of sex." But like any slogan, this one allows for different interpretations. Some theorists use the term "gender" to refer to the subjective experience of sexed embodiment, or a broad psychological orientation to the world ("gender identity"); others to a set of attributes or ideals that function as norms for males and females ("masculinity" and "femininity"); others to a system of sexual symbolism; and still others to the traditional social roles of men and women. My strategy is to offer a focal analysis that defines gender, in the primary sense, as a social class. A focal analysis undertakes to explain a variety of connected phenomena in terms of their relations to one that is theorized as the central or core phenomenon. As I see it, the core phenomenon to be addressed is the pattern of social relations that constitute the social classes of men as dominant and women as subordinate. [. . .] I see my emphasis as falling within, though not following uncritically, the tradition of materialist feminism. [. . .]

The main strategy of materialist feminist accounts of gender has been to define gender in terms of women's subordinate position in systems of male dominance. Although there are materialist feminist roots in Marxism, contemporary versions resist the thought that all social phenomena can be explained in or reduced to economic terms; and although materialist feminists emphasize the role of language and culture in women's oppression, there is a wariness of extreme forms of linguistic constructivism and a commitment to staying grounded in the material realities of women's lives. In effect, there is a concerted effort to show how gender oppression is jointly sustained by both cultural and material forces.

Critiques of universalizing feminisms have taught us to be attentive to the variety of forms gender takes and the concrete social positions females occupy. However it is compatible with these commitments to treat the category of gender as a genus that is realized in different ways in different contexts; doing so enables us to recognize significant patterns in the ways that gender is instituted and embodied. Working at the most general level, then, the materialist strategy offers us three basic principles to guide us in understanding gender:

(i)   Gender categories are defined in terms of how one is socially positioned, where this is a function of, e.g., how one is viewed, how one is treated, and how one's life is structured socially, legally, and economically; gender is not defined in terms of an individual's intrinsic physical or psychological features.

(This allows that there may be other categories—such as sex—that are defined in terms of intrinsic physical features. Note, however, that once we focus our attention on gender as social position, we must allow that one can be a woman without ever (in the ordinary sense) "acting like a woman," "feeling like a woman," or even having a female body.)

(ii)   Gender categories are defined hierarchically within a broader complex of oppressive relations; one group (viz., women) is socially positioned as subordinate to the other (viz., men), typically within the context of other forms of economic and social oppression.

(iii)   Sexual difference functions as the physical marker to distinguish the two groups, and is used in the justification of viewing and treating the members of each group differently.

(Tentatively) we can capture these main points in the following analyses:

- S *is a woman* iff$_{df}$ [if and only if, by definition] S is systematically subordinated along some dimension (economic, political, legal, social, etc.), and S is "marked" as a target for this treatment by observed or imagined bodily features presumed to be evidence of a female's biological role in reproduction.

- S *is a man* iff$_{df}$ S is systematically privileged along some dimension (economic, political, legal, social, etc.), and S is "marked" as a target for this treatment by observed or imagined bodily features presumed to be evidence of a male's biological role in reproduction.

It is a virtue, I believe, of these accounts, that depending on context, one's sex may have a very different meaning and it may position one in very different kinds of hierarchies. The variation will clearly occur from culture to culture (and subculture to subculture); so e.g., to be a Chinese woman of the 1790s, a Brazilian woman of the 1890s, or an American woman of the 1990s may involve very different social relations, and very different kinds of oppression. Yet on the analysis suggested, these groups count as women insofar as their subordinate positions are marked and justified by reference to (female) sex. Similarly, this account allows that the substantive import of gender varies even from individual to individual within a culture depending on how the meaning of sex interacts with other socially salient characteristics (e.g., race, class, sexuality, etc.). For example, a privileged white woman and a black woman of the underclass will both be women insofar as their social positions are affected by the social meanings of being female; and yet the social implications of being female vary for each because sexism is intertwined with race and class oppression.

## 4. What Is Oppression?

There are points in the proposed analysis that require clarification, however. What does it mean to say that someone is "systematically subordinated" or "privileged," and further, that the subordination occurs "on the basis of" certain features? The background idea is that women are *oppressed*, and that they are oppressed *as women*. But we still need to ask: What does it mean to say that women are oppressed, and what does the qualification "as women" add?

Marilyn Frye's account of oppression with Iris Young's elaborations provides a valuable starting point. [. . .] Oppression in the intended sense is a structural phenomenon that positions certain groups as disadvantaged and others as advantaged or privileged in relation to them. Oppression consists of, "an enclosing structure of forces and barriers which tends to the immobilization and reduction of a group or category of people" (Frye 11). Importantly, such structures, at least as we know them, are not designed and policed by those in power, rather, ". . . oppression refers to the vast and deep injustices some groups suffer as a consequence of often unconscious assumptions and reactions of well-meaning people in ordinary interactions, media and cultural stereotypes, and structural features of bureaucratic hierarchies and market mechanisms—in short, the normal processes of everyday life" (Young 41).

Developing this concept of oppression, Young specifies five forms it can take: exploitation, marginalization, powerlessness, cultural imperialism, and (systematic) violence. The key point for us is that oppression comes in different forms, and even if one is privileged along some dimension (e.g., in income or respect), one might be oppressed in others. In fact, one might be systematically subordinated along some social axis, and yet still be tremendously privileged in one's *overall* social position.

It is clear that women are oppressed in the sense that women are members of groups that suffer exploitation, marginalization, etc. But how should we understand the claim that women are oppressed *as women*. Frye explains this as follows:

> One is marked for application of oppressive pressures by one's membership in some group or category. . . . In the case at hand, it is the category, *woman*. . . . If a woman has little or no economic or political power, or achieves little of what she wants to achieve, a major causal factor in this is that she is a woman. For any woman of any race or economic class, being a woman is significantly attached to whatever disadvantages and deprivations she suffers, be they great or small. . . . [In contrast,] being male is something [a man] has going *for* him, even if race or class or age or disability is going against him. (15–6)

But given the diffusion of power in a model of structural oppression how are we to make sense of one's being "marked" and the "application" of pressures? In the context of oppression, certain properties of individuals are socially meaningful. This is to say that the properties play a role in a broadly accepted (though usually not fully explicit) representation of the world that functions to justify and motivate particular forms of social intercourse. The significant properties in question—in the cases at hand, assumed or actual properties of the body—mark you "for application of oppressive pressures" insofar as the attribution of these properties is interpreted as adequate, in light of this background representation, to explain and/or justify your position in a structure of oppressive social relations. In the case of women, the idea is that societies are guided by representations that link being female with other facts that have implications for how one should be viewed and treated; insofar as we structure our social life to accommodate the cultural meanings of the female (and male) body, females occupy an oppressed social position.

Although I agree with Frye that in sexist societies social institutions are structured in ways that on the whole disadvantage females and advantage males, we must keep in mind that societies are not monolithic and that sexism is not the only source of oppression. For example, in the contemporary US, there are contexts in which being black *and male* marks one as a target for certain forms of systematic violence (e.g., by the police). In those contexts, contrary to Frye's suggestion, *being male* is not something that a man "has going *for* him"; though there are other contexts (also in the contemporary US) in which black males benefit from being male. In examples of this sort, the systematic violence against males *as males* is emasculating (and may be intended as such); but there are important differences between an emasculated man and a woman. On the sort of view we're considering, a woman is someone whose subordinated status is marked by reference to (assumed) *female* anatomy; someone marked for subordination by reference to (assumed) *male* anatomy does not qualify as a woman, but also, *in the particular context*, is not socially positioned as a man.

## 5. What Is Race?

One advantage of this account of gender is the parallel it offers for race. To begin, let me review a couple of points that I take to be matters of established fact: First, there are no racial genes responsible for the complex morphologies and cultural patterns we associate with different races. Second, in different contexts racial distinctions are drawn on the basis of different characteristics, e.g., the Brazilian and US classification schemes for who counts as "black" differ. For these reasons and others, it appears that race, like gender, could be fruitfully understood as a position within a broad social network.

Although suggestive, this idea is not easy to develop. It is one thing to acknowledge that race is *socially* real, even if a biological fiction; but it is another thing to capture in general terms "the social meaning of colour." There seem to be too many different forms race takes. Note, however, that we encountered a similar problem with gender: is there any prospect for a unified analysis of "the social meaning of sex"? The materialist feminist approach offered a helpful strategy: don't look for an analysis that assumes that the meaning is always and everywhere the same; rather, consider how members of the group are *socially positioned*, and what *physical markers* serve as a supposed basis for such treatment.

How might we extend this strategy to race? Transposing the slogan, we might say that race is the social meaning of the geographically marked body, familiar markers being skin colour, hair type, eye shape, physique. To develop this, I propose the following account [. . .]:[1]

> A group is *racialized* iff$_{df}$ its members are socially positioned as subordinate or privileged along some dimension (economic, political, legal, social, etc.), and the group is "marked" as a target for this treatment by observed or imagined bodily features presumed to be evidence of ancestral links to a certain geographical region.

[. . .] In other words, races are those groups demarcated by the geographical associations accompanying perceived body type, when those associations take on evaluative significance concerning how members of the group should be viewed and treated. As in the case of gender, the ideology need not use physical morphology or geography as the entire basis for "appropriate" treatment; these features may instead simply be "markers" of other characteristics that the ideology uses to justify the treatment in question.

Given this definition, we can say that S is of the white (black, Asian . . .) race iff [if and only if] whites (blacks, Asians . . .) are a racialized group, and S is a member. [. . .] [W]hether a group is racialized, and so how and whether an individual is raced, is not an absolute fact, but will depend on context. For example, blacks, whites, Asians, Native Americans, are currently racialized in the US insofar as these are all groups defined in terms of physical features associated with places of origin, and insofar as membership in the group functions socially as a basis for evaluation. However, some groups are not currently racialized in the US, but have been so in the past and possibly could be again (and in other contexts are), e.g., the Italians, the Germans, the Irish.

It is useful to note a possible contrast between race and ethnicity. I don't have a theory of ethnicity to offer; these are some preliminary comparisons. One's ethnicity concerns one's ancestral links to a certain geographical region (perhaps together with participation in the cultural practices of that region); often ethnicity is associated with characteristic physical features. For our purposes, however, it might be useful to employ the notion of "ethnicity" for those groups that are like races as I've defined them except that they do not experience systematic subordination or privilege in the context in question.[2] Ethnic groups can be (and are) racialized, however, and when they are, one's membership in the group positions one in a social hierarchy; but (on the view I'm sketching) the occurrence of this hierarchical positioning means that the group has gone beyond simply being an ethnic group and functions in that context as a race. In short, we can distinguish between grouping individuals on the basis of their (assumed) origins, and grouping them *hierarchically* on the basis of their (assumed) origins, and the contrast between race and ethnicity might be a useful way to capture this distinction.

## 6. Negotiating Terms

Let me now turn to summarize some of the advantages of the proposed definitions. At this point we could bracket the terminological issues and just consider whether the groups in question are ones that are important to consider given the goals of our inquiry. I hope it is clear from what I've already said how the analyses can help us identify and critique broad patterns of racial and sexual oppression, and how they accommodate the intersectionality of social categories. But a further and, I think, more interesting question is whether it is useful to think of these groups *in these terms*: Does it serve both the goal of understanding racial and sexual oppression, and of achieving sexual and racial equality to think of ourselves as *men* or *women*, or *raced* in the ways proposed?

By appropriating the everyday terminology of race and gender, the analyses I've offered invite us to acknowledge the force of oppressive systems in framing our personal and political identities. Each of us has some investment in our race and gender: I am a White woman. On my accounts, this claim locates me within social systems that in some respects privilege and in others subordinate me. Because gender and racial inequality are not simply a matter of public policy but implicate each of us at the heart of our self-understandings, the terminological shift calls us to reconsider who we think we are.

This point highlights why the issue of terminological appropriation is especially sensitive when the terms designate categories of social identity. Writing in response to a *NY Times* editorial supporting the terminological shift from "black" to "African-American," Trey Ellis responded: "When somebody tries to tell me what to call myself in all its uses just because they come to some decision at a cocktail party to which I wasn't even invited, my mama raised me to tell them to kiss my black ass. In many cases, *African-American* just won't do." The issue is not just what words we should use, and who gets to say what words to use, but who we take ourselves to be, and so, in some sense, who we are. Terms for social groups can function as descriptive terms: it may be accurate to say that someone is a woman when she satisfies certain conditions. However, terms for social groups serve other rhetorical purposes. Typically the act of classifying someone as a member of a social group invokes a set of "appropriate" (contextually specific) norms and expectations. It positions her in a social framework and makes available certain kinds of evaluation; in short, it carries prescriptive force. Accepting or identifying with the classification typically involves an endorsement of some norms and expectations, however, not always the socially sanctioned ones. [. . .]

Although "identifying" someone as a member of a social group invokes a set of "appropriate" norms, what these norms are is not fixed. What it means to be a woman, or to be white, or to be Latino, in this sense, is unstable and always open to contest. The instability across time is necessary to maintain the basic structure of gender and race relations through other social changes: as social roles change—prompted by the economy, immigration, political movements, natural disasters, war, etc.—the contents of normative race and gender identities adjust. The flexibility across contexts accommodates the complexity of social life: what norms are assumed to apply depends on the dominant social structure, the ideological context, and other dimensions of one's identity (such as class, age, ability, sexuality). But this instability and flexibility is exactly what opens the door for groups to redefine themselves in new ways. One strategy is for the group to adopt new names ("African-American," "womyn"); another is to appropriate old names with a normative twist ("queer"); but in some cases the contest is over the meanings of the standard terms ("Ain't I a woman?"). [. . .]

Given the normative force and political potential of identifying someone (or self-identifying) in racial or gendered terms, how do we evaluate a terminological appropriation of the kind I'm proposing? For example, isn't there something disingenuous about appropriating race and gender terminology *because* it is used to frame how we think of ourselves and each other, in order to use them for new concepts that are *not* part of our self-understandings?

This latter question is especially pressing because the appropriation under consideration intentionally invokes what many find to be positive self-understandings—being Latina, being a white man—and offers analyses of them which emphasize the broader context of injustice. Thus there is an invitation not only to revise one's understanding of these categories (given their instability, this happens often enough), but to revise one's relationship to their prescriptive force. By offering these analyses

of our ordinary terms, I call upon us to reject what seemed to be positive social identities. I'm suggesting that we should work to undermine those forces that make being a man, a woman, or a member of a racialized group possible; we should refuse to be gendered man or woman, refuse to be raced. This goes beyond denying essentialist claims about one's embodiment and involves an active political commitment to live one's life differently (Stoltenberg). In one sense this appropriation is "just semantics": I'm asking us to use an old term in a new way. But it is also politics: I'm asking us to understand ourselves and those around us as deeply moulded by injustice and to draw the appropriate prescriptive inference. This, I hope, will contribute to empowering critical social agents. However, whether the terminological shift I'm suggesting is politically useful will depend on the contexts in which it is employed and the individuals employing it. The point is not to legislate what terms to use in all contexts, but to offer resources that should be used judiciously.

## 7. Lingering Concerns, Promising Alternatives

There is, nonetheless, a broader concern one might have about the strategy I've employed: Why build hierarchy into the definitions? Why not define gender and race as those social positions motivated and justified by cultural responses to the body, without requiring that the social positions are hierarchical? Wouldn't that provide what we need without implying (implausibly) that women are, by definition, subordinate, men, by definition, privileged, and races, by definition, hierarchically positioned?

If we were to remove hierarchy from the definitions, then there would be two other benefits: first, by providing a place in our model for cultural representations of the body *besides* those that contribute to maintaining subordination and privilege, we could better acknowledge that there are positive aspects to having a gender and a race. And second, the accounts would provide a framework for envisioning the sorts of constructive changes needed to create a more just world. The suggestion that we must eliminate race and gender may be a powerful rallying call to those who identify with radical causes, but it is not at all clear that societies can or should avoid giving meanings to the body, or organizing themselves to take sexual and reproductive differences into account. [. . .]

Consider gender. I am sympathetic to radical rethinkings of sex and gender. In particular, I believe that we should refuse to use anatomy as a primary basis for classifying individuals and that any distinctions between kinds of sexual and reproductive bodies are importantly political and open to contest. Some authors have argued that we should acknowledge the continuum of anatomical differences and recognize at least five sexes (Fausto-Sterling). And if sexual distinctions become more complex, we would also need to rethink sexuality, given that sexual desire would not fit neatly within existing homosexual/heterosexual paradigms.

However, one can encourage the proliferation of sexual and reproductive options without maintaining that we can or should eliminate *all* social implications of anatomical sex and reproduction. Given that as a species there are substantial differences in what human bodies contribute to reproduction, and what sorts of bodies bear the main physical burdens of reproduction, and given further that reproduction cannot really help but be a socially significant fact (it does, after all, produce children), it can seem difficult to imagine a functioning society, more specifically, a functioning *feminist* society, that doesn't acknowledge in some way the difference between those kinds of bodies that are likely able to bear children, and those that aren't. [. . .]

I will not debate here the degree to which a just society must be attentive to sexual and reproductive differences. Whether we, as feminists, ought to recommend the construction of (new) non-hierarchical genders or work to abolish gender entirely is a normative issue I leave for another occasion. Nonetheless, at the very least it would help to have terminology to debate these issues. I propose that we use the definitions of *man* and *woman* offered above: it is clear that these dominant nodes of our current gender structures are hierarchical. But borrowing strategies employed before, we can define gender in

generic terms under which the previous definitions of man and women fall, thus allowing the possibility of non-hierarchical genders and breaking the binary opposition between man and woman.

A group G is *a gender* relative to context C iff$_{df}$ members of G are (all and only) those:

(i)   who are regularly observed or imagined to have certain bodily features presumed in C to be evidence of their reproductive capacities;

(ii)   whose having (or being imagined to have) these features marks them within the context of the ideology in C as motivating and justifying some aspect(s) of their social position; and

(iii)   whose satisfying (i) and (ii) plays (or would play) a role in C in their social position's having one or another of these designated aspects.

I offer this analysis as a way of capturing the standard slogan: gender is the social meaning of sex. Note, however, that in imagining "alternative" genders we should be careful not to take for granted that the relevant biological divisions will correspond to what *we* consider "sex." (Alternative groupings could include: "pregnant persons," "lactating persons," "menstruating persons," "infertile persons," [. . .]). Neither should we assume that membership in a gender will constitute one's personal or psychological identity to any significant degree. Recall that on the accounts of gender and race I am proposing, both are to be understood first and foremost as social groups defined within a structure of social relations; whatever links there might be to identities and norms are highly contingent and would depend on the details of the picture. For example, we might imagine that "after the revolution" gender is a component of one's overall social position because, for example, there are legal protections or medical entitlements granted to individuals classified as having a certain sort of "sexed" body; but this need not have broad implications for psychological identity or everyday social interactions, for the "sex" of bodies might not even be publicly marked.

Turning briefly to race, the parallel issue arises: Do we need a concept of non-hierarchical "races" in order to frame and debate different visions of a "racially" just society? It would seem that we have the terminological resources available without a further definition: let races be, as previously defined, those hierarchically organized groups that are defined (roughly) by physical features and (assumed) geographical origins, and call those that aren't hierarchically organized (in the context in question) "ethnicities." Admittedly, ethnicity as we know it does have implications for social status and power, so my proposal is to employ the term for a somewhat idealized conception.

As in the case of gender, the question arises whether it ought to be part of an anti-racist project to recommend the preservation of existing ethnic groups or the formation of "new" ethnicities. And more generally, we need to ask whether a feminist anti-racism should treat genders and ethno-racial groups in the same way over the long term. Should we seek, e.g., to eliminate all genders and ethnoracial groupings; to preserve and proliferate them; to eliminate gender but not ethnicity (or vice versa)? These questions deserve careful attention but I cannot address them here.

## 8. Conclusion

On the accounts I've offered, there are striking parallels between race and gender. Both gender and race are real, and both are social categories. Neither gender nor race is chosen, but the forms they take can be resisted or mutated. Both race and gender (as we know it) are hierarchical, but the systems that sustain the hierarchy are contingent. And although the ideologies of race and gender and the hierarchical structures they sustain are substantively very different, they are intertwined.

There are many different types of human bodies; it is not the case that there is a unique "right" way of classifying them, though certain classifications will be more useful for some purposes than others. How we classify bodies can and does matter politically, for our laws, social institutions, and personal identities are profoundly linked to understandings of the body and its possibilities. This is compatible with the idea that what possibilities a human body has is not wholly a function of our understandings of it. Our bodies often outdo us, and undo us, in spite of the meanings we give them.

Within the framework I've sketched, there is room for theoretical categories such as *man*, *woman*, and *race* (and particular racial groups), that take hierarchy to be a constitutive element, and those such as *gender* and *ethnicity* that do not. As I have suggested before, I am willing to grant that there are other ways to define race or gender, man or woman, that are useful to answer different questions, motivated by different concerns and priorities. I'm sure we need several concepts to do all the work needed in understanding the complex systems of racial and gender subordination.

In short, (speaking of my analyses) I'm less committed to saying that *this* is what gender is and what race is, than to saying that *these* are important categories that a feminist antiracist theory needs. [. . .] To return to the point made much earlier in characterizing analytic projects: it is our responsibility to define gender and race for our theoretical purposes. The world itself can't tell us what gender is. The same is true for race. [. . .] Of course, in defining our terms, we must keep clearly in mind our political aims both in analyzing the past and present, and in envisioning alternative futures. But rather than worrying, "what is gender, really?" or "what is race, really?" I think we should begin by asking (both in the theoretical and political sense) what, if anything, we want them to be.

## Notes

1. On this I am deeply indebted to Stevens, Ch. 4, and Omi and Winant, esp. pp. 53–61.
2. We may want to allow there to be kinds of social stratification among ethnic groups that fall short of the kind of systematic subordination constitutive of race. My account remains vague on this point.

## Works Cited

Ellis, T. *Village Voice,* 13 June 1989.

Fausto-Sterling, A. "The Five Sexes: Why Male and Female Are Not Enough." *The Sciences* 33, 2 (1993): 20–4.

Frye, M. *The Politics of Reality*. Freedom, CA: Crossing Press, 1983.

Omi, M., and H. Winant. *Racial Formation in the United States*. New York: Routledge, 1994.

Stevens, J. *Reproducing the State*. Princeton: Princeton University Press, 1999.

Young, I. *Justice and the Politics of Difference*. Princeton: Princeton University Press, 1990.

## Study Questions

1. Haslanger outlines three different approaches that philosophers might take in response to the questions "What is gender?" and "What is race?" Compare these approaches using an example other than gender or race.
2. On Haslanger's material feminist approach, it is within a matrix of social relations that we become an individual of a particular gender and race. Explain how this happens by attending to the specifics of Haslanger's account and using your own gender and race as an example.
3. What norms and expectations does society prescribe for individuals of the same gender and race as you? Can you identify any ways in which these norms and expectations incorporate the oppressive relations Haslanger argues are basic to classification by gender and race?
4. Haslanger suggests that "we should work to undermine those forces that make being a man, a woman, or a member of a racialized group possible; we should refuse to be gendered man or woman, refuse to be raced." Do you agree or disagree?

---

# Michel Foucault

---

Michel Foucault (1926–84) was a famous French thinker who became a professor of the history of systems of thought at the renowned Collège de France in 1969, and held this position until his death. Foucault is known for analyzing how power and knowledge operate through institutions such as the prison and clinic. In *The Order of Things*, Foucault argues that "man" is the "recent invention" of a system of thought (*episteme*) that emerged only at the beginning of the nineteenth century.—GS

## Preface to *The Order of Things*

This book first arose out of a passage in **Borges**,[1] out of the laughter that shattered, as I read the passage, all the familiar landmarks of my thought—*our* thought, the thought that bears the stamp of our age and our geography—breaking up all the ordered surfaces and all the planes with which we are accustomed to tame the wild profusion of existing things, and continuing long afterwards to disturb and threaten with collapse our age-old distinction between the Same and the Other. This passage quotes a "certain Chinese encyclopaedia" in which it is written that "animals are divided into: (a) belonging to the Emperor, (b) embalmed, (c) tame, (d) sucking pigs, (e) sirens, (f) fabulous, (g) stray dogs, (h) included in the present classification, (i) frenzied, (j) innumerable, (k) drawn with a very fine camelhair brush, (l) *et cetera*, (m) having just broken the water pitcher, (n) that from a long way off look like flies." In the wonderment of this taxonomy, the thing we apprehend in one great leap, the thing that, by means of the fable, is demonstrated as the exotic charm of another system of thought, is the limitation of our own, the stark impossibility of thinking *that*.

But what is it impossible to think, and what kind of impossibility are we faced with here? Each of these strange categories can be assigned a precise meaning and a demonstrable content; some of them do certainly involve fantastic entities—fabulous animals or sirens—but, precisely because it puts them into categories of their own, the Chinese encyclopedia localizes their powers of contagion; it distinguishes carefully between the very real animals (those that are frenzied or have just broken the water pitcher) and those that reside solely in the realm of imagination. The possibility of dangerous mixtures has been exorcized, heraldry and fable have been relegated to their own exalted peaks: no inconceivable amphibious maidens, no clawed wings, no disgusting, squamous epidermis, none of those polymorphous and demoniacal faces, no creatures breathing fire. The quality of monstrosity here does not affect any real body, nor does it produce modifications of any kind in the bestiary of the imagination; it does not lurk in the depths of any strange power. It would not even be present at all in this classification had it not insinuated itself into the empty space, the interstitial blanks *separating* all these entities from one another. It is not the "fabulous" animals that are impossible, since they are designated as such, but the narrowness of the distance separating them from (and juxtaposing them to) the stray dogs, or the animals that from a long way off look like flies. What transgresses the boundaries of all imagination, of all possible thought, is simply that alphabetical series (a, b, c, d) which links each of those categories to all the others.

Moreover, it is not simply the oddity of unusual juxtapositions that we are faced with here. We are all familiar with the disconcerting effect of the proximity of extremes, or, quite simply, with the sudden vicinity of things that have no relation to each other; the mere act of enumeration that heaps them all together

has a power of enchantment all its own: "I am no longer hungry," Eusthenes said. "Until the morrow, safe from my saliva all the following shall be: Aspics, Acalephs, Acanthocephalates, Amoebocytes, Ammonites, Axolotls, Amblystomas, Aphislions, Anacondas, Ascarids, Amphisbaenas, Angleworms, Amphipods, Anaerobes, Annelids, Anthozoans. . . ." But all these worms and snakes, all these creatures redolent of decay and slime are slithering, like the syllables which designate them, in Eusthenes' saliva: that is where they all have their *common locus*, like the umbrella and the sewing-machine on the operating table;[2] startling though their propinquity may be, it is nevertheless warranted by that *and*, by that *in*, by that *on* whose solidity provides proof of the possibility of juxtaposition. It was certainly improbable that arachnids, ammonites, and annelids should one day mingle on Eusthenes' tongue, but, after all, that welcoming and voracious mouth certainly provided them with a feasible lodging, a roof under which to coexist.

The monstrous quality that runs through Borges's enumeration consists, on the contrary, in the fact that the common ground on which such meetings are possible has itself been destroyed. What is impossible is not the propinquity of the things listed, but the very site on which their propinquity would be possible. The animals "(i) frenzied, (j) innumerable, (k) drawn with a very fine camel-hair brush"—where could they ever meet, except in the immaterial sound of the voice pronouncing their enumeration, or on the page transcribing it? Where else could they be juxtaposed except in the non-place of language? Yet, though language can spread them before us, it can do so only in an unthinkable space. The central category of animals "included in the present classification," with its explicit reference to paradoxes we are familiar with, is indication enough that we shall never succeed in defining a stable relation of contained to container between each of these categories and that which includes them all: if all the animals divided up here can be placed without exception in one of the divisions of this list, then aren't all the other divisions to be found in that one division too? And then again, in what space would that single, inclusive division have *its* existence? Absurdity destroys the *and* of the enumeration by making impossible the *in* where the things enumerated would be divided up. Borges adds no figure to the atlas of the impossible; nowhere does he strike the spark of poetic confrontation; he simply dispenses with the least obvious, but most compelling, of necessities; he does away with the *site*, the mute ground upon which it is possible for entities to be juxtaposed. A vanishing trick that is masked or, rather, laughably indicated by our alphabetical order, which is to be taken as the clue (the only visible one) to the enumerations of a Chinese encyclopedia. . . . What has been removed, in short, is the famous "operating table"; and rendering to **Roussel** a small part of what is still his due, I use that word "table" in two superimposed senses: the nickel-plated, rubbery table swathed in white, glittering beneath a glass sun devouring all shadow—the table where, for an instant, perhaps forever, the umbrella encounters the sewing-machine; and also a table, a *tabula*, that enables thought to operate upon the entities of our world, to put them in order, to divide them into classes, to group them according to names that designate their similarities and their differences— the table upon which, since the beginning of time, language has intersected space.

That passage from Borges kept me laughing a long time, though not without a certain uneasiness that I found hard to shake off. Perhaps because there arose in its wake the suspicion that there is a worse kind of disorder than that of the *incongruous*, the linking together of things that are inappropriate; I mean the disorder in which fragments of a large number of possible orders glitter separately in the dimension, without law or geometry, of the *heteroclite*; and that word should be taken in its most literal, etymological sense: in such a state, things are "laid," "placed," "arranged" in sites so very different from one another that it is impossible to find a place of residence for them, to define a *common locus* beneath them all. *Utopias* afford consolation: although they have no real locality there is nevertheless a fantastic, untroubled region in which they are able to unfold; they open up cities with vast avenues, superbly planted gardens, countries where life is easy, even though the road to them is chimerical. *Heterotopias* are disturbing, probably because they secretly undermine language, because they make it impossible to name this *and* that, because they shatter or tangle common names, because they destroy "syntax" in advance, and not only the syntax with which we construct sentences but also that less apparent syntax which causes words and things (next to and also opposite one another) to "hold together." This is why utopias permit fables and discourse: they run with the very grain of language and are part of the fundamental dimension of the *fabula*; heterotopias (such as those to be found so often in Borges) desiccate speech, stop words in their tracks, contest the very possibility of grammar at its source; they dissolve our myths and sterilize the lyricism of our sentences.

It appears that certain aphasiacs, when shown various differently coloured skeins of wool on a table top, are consistently unable to arrange them into any coherent pattern; as though that simple rectangle were unable to serve in their case as a homogeneous and neutral space in which things could be placed so as to display at the same time the continuous order of their identities or differences as well as the semantic field of their denomination. Within this simple space in which things are normally arranged and given names, the aphasiac will create a multiplicity of tiny, fragmented regions in which nameless resemblances agglutinate things into unconnected islets; in one corner, they will place the lightest-coloured skeins, in another the red ones, somewhere else those that are softest in texture, in yet another place the longest, or those that have a tinge of purple or those that have been wound up into a ball. But no sooner have they been adumbrated than all these groupings dissolve again, for the field of identity that sustains them, however limited it may be, is still too wide not to be unstable; and so the sick mind continues to infinity, creating groups then dispersing them again, heaping up diverse similarities, destroying those that seem clearest, splitting up things that are identical, superimposing different criteria, frenziedly beginning all over again, becoming more and more disturbed, and teetering finally on the brink of anxiety.

The uneasiness that makes us laugh when we read Borges is certainly related to the profound distress of those whose language has been destroyed: loss of what is "common" to place and name. Atopia, aphasia. Yet our text from Borges proceeds in another direction; the mythical homeland Borges assigns to that distortion of classification that prevents us from applying it, to that picture that lacks all spatial coherence, is a precise region whose name alone constitutes for the West a vast reservoir of utopias. In our dreamworld, is not China precisely this privileged *site* of *space?* In our traditional imagery, the Chinese culture is the most meticulous, the most rigidly ordered, the one most deaf to temporal events, most attached to the pure delineation of space; we think of it as a civilization of dikes and dams beneath the eternal face of the sky; we see it, spread and frozen, over the entire surface of a continent surrounded by walls. Even its writing does not reproduce the fugitive flight of the voice in horizontal lines; it erects the motionless and still-recognizable images of things themselves in vertical columns. So much so that the Chinese encyclopedia quoted by Borges, and the taxonomy it proposes, lead to a kind of thought without space, to words and categories that lack all life and place, but are rooted in a ceremonial space, overburdened with complex figures, with tangled paths, strange places, secret passages, and unexpected communications. There would appear to be, then, at the other extremity of the earth we inhabit, a culture entirely devoted to the ordering of space, but one that does not distribute the multiplicity of existing things into any of the categories that make it possible for us to name, speak, and think.

When we establish a considered classification, when we say that a cat and a dog resemble each other less than two greyhounds do, even if both are tame or embalmed, even if both are frenzied, even if both have just broken the water pitcher, what is the ground on which we are able to establish the validity of this classification with complete certainty? On what "table," according to what grid of identities, similitudes, analogies, have we become accustomed to sort out so many different and similar things? What is this coherence—which, as is immediately apparent, is neither determined by an a priori and necessary concatenation, nor imposed on us by immediately perceptible contents? For it is not a question of linking consequences, but of grouping and isolating, of analyzing, of matching and pigeon-holing concrete contents; there is nothing more tentative, nothing more empirical (superficially, at least) than the process of establishing an order among things; nothing that demands a sharper eye or a surer, better-articulated language; nothing that more insistently requires that one allow oneself to be carried along by the proliferation of qualities and forms. And yet an eye not consciously prepared might well group together certain similar figures and distinguish between others on the basis of such and such a difference: in fact, there is no similitude and no distinction, even for the wholly untrained perception, that is not the result of a precise operation and of the application of a preliminary criterion. A "system of elements"—a definition of the segments by which the resemblances and differences can be shown, the types of variation by which those segments can be affected, and, lastly, the threshold above which there is a difference and below which there is a similitude—is indispensable for the establishment of even the simplest form of order. Order is, at one and the same time, that which is given in things as their inner law, the hidden network that determines the way they confront one another, and also that which has no existence except in the grid created by a glance, an examination, a language; and it is only in the blank spaces of this grid that order manifests itself in depth as though already there, waiting in silence for the moment of its expression.

The fundamental codes of a culture—those governing its language, its schemas of perception, its exchanges, its techniques, its values, the hierarchy of its practices—establish for every man, from the very first, the empirical orders with which he will be dealing and within which he will be at home. At the other extremity of thought, there are the scientific theories or the philosophical interpretations which explain why order exists in general, what universal law it obeys, what principle can account for it, and why this particular order has been established and not some other. But between these two regions, so distant from one another, lies a domain which, even though its role is mainly an intermediary one, is nonetheless fundamental: it is more confused, more obscure, and probably less easy to analyze. It is here that a culture, imperceptibly deviating from the empirical orders prescribed for it by its primary codes, instituting an initial separation from them, causes them to lose their original transparency, relinquishes its immediate and invisible powers, frees itself sufficiently to discover that these orders are perhaps not the only possible ones or the best ones; this culture then finds itself faced with the stark fact that there exists, below the level of its spontaneous orders, things that are in themselves capable of being ordered, that belong to a certain unspoken order; the fact, in short, that order *exists*. As though emancipating itself to some extent from its linguistic, perceptual, and practical grids, the culture superimposed on them another kind of grid which neutralized them, which by this superimposition both revealed and excluded them at the same time, so that the culture, by this very process, came face to face with order in its primary state. It is on the basis of this newly perceived order that the codes of language, perception, and practice are criticized and rendered partially invalid. It is on the basis of this order, taken as a firm foundation, that general theories as to the ordering of things, and the interpretation that such an ordering involves, will be constructed. Thus, between the already "encoded" eye and reflexive knowledge there is a middle region which liberates order itself: it is here that it appears, according to the culture and the age in question, continuous and graduated or discontinuous and piecemeal, linked to space or constituted anew at each instant by the driving force of time, related to a series of variables or defined by separate systems of coherences, composed of resemblances which are either successive or corresponding, organized around increasing differences, etc. This middle region, then, insofar as it makes manifest the modes of being of order, can be posited as the most fundamental of all: anterior to words, perceptions, and gestures, which are then taken to be more or less exact, more or less happy, expressions of it (which is why this experience of order in its pure primary state always plays a

critical role); more solid, more archaic, less dubious, always more "true" than the theories that attempt to give those expressions explicit form, exhaustive application, or philosophical foundation. Thus, in every culture, between the use of what one might call the ordering codes and reflections upon order itself, there is the pure experience of order and of its modes of being.

The present study is an attempt to analyze that experience. I am concerned to show its developments, since the sixteenth century, in the mainstream of a culture such as ours: in what way, as one traces—against the current, as it were—language as it has been spoken, natural creatures as they have been perceived and grouped together, and exchanges as they have been practised; in what way, then, our culture has made manifest the existence of order, and how, to the modalities of that order, the exchanges owed their laws, the living beings their constants, the words their sequence and their representative value; what modalities of order have been recognized, linked with space and time, in order to create the positive basis of knowledge as we find it employed in grammar and philology, in natural history and biology, in the study of wealth and political economy. Quite obviously, such an analysis does not belong to the history of ideas or of science: it is rather an inquiry whose aim is to rediscover on what basis knowledge and theory became possible; within what space of order knowledge was constituted; on the basis of what historical a priori, and in the element of what positivity, ideas could appear, sciences be established, experience be reflected in philosophies, rationalities be formed, only, perhaps, to dissolve and vanish soon afterwards. I am not concerned, therefore, to describe the progress of knowledge towards an objectivity in which today's science can finally be recognized; what I am attempting to bring to light is the epistemological field, the *episteme* which knowledge, envisaged apart from all criteria having reference to its rational value or to its objective forms, grounds its positivity and thereby manifests a history which is not that of its growing perfection, but rather that of its conditions of possibility; in this account, what should appear are those configurations within the *space* of knowledge which have given rise to the diverse forms of empirical science. Such an enterprise is not so much a history, in the traditional meaning of that word, as an "archaeology."

Now, this archaeological inquiry has revealed two great discontinuities in the *episteme* of Western culture: the first inaugurates the Classical age (roughly halfway through the seventeenth century) and the second, at the beginning of the nineteenth century, marks the beginning of the modern age. The order on the basis of which we think today does not have the same mode of being as that of the Classical thinkers. Despite the impression we may have of an almost uninterrupted development of the European *ratio* from the **Renaissance** to our own day, despite our possible belief that the classifications of **Linnaeus**, modified to a greater or lesser degree, can still lay claim to some sort of validity, that **Condillac**'s theory of value can be recognized to some extent in nineteenth-century marginalism, that **Keynes** was well aware of the affinities between his own analyses and those of **Cantillon**, that the language of *general grammar* (as exemplified in the **authors of Port-Royal** or in Bauzée [**Beauzée**]) is not so very far removed from our own—all this quasi-continuity on the level of ideas and themes is doubtless only a surface appearance; on the archaeological level, we see that the system of positivities was transformed in a wholesale fashion at the end of the eighteenth and beginning of the nineteenth century. Not that reason made any progress: it was simply that the mode of being of things, and of the order that divided them up before presenting them to the understanding, was profoundly altered. If the natural history of **Tournefort**, Linnaeus, and **Buffon** can be related to anything at all other than itself, it is not to biology, to **Cuvier**'s comparative anatomy, or to **Darwin**'s theory of evolution, but to Bauzée's general grammar, to the analysis of money and wealth as found in the works of **Law**, or **Véron de Fortbonnais**, or **Turgot**. Perhaps knowledge succeeds in engendering knowledge, ideas in transforming themselves and actively modifying one another (but how?—historians have not yet enlightened us on this point); one thing, in any case, is certain: archaeology, addressing itself to the general space of knowledge, to its configurations, and to the mode of being of the things that appear in it, defines systems of simultaneity, as well as the series of mutations necessary and sufficient to circumscribe the threshold of a new positivity.

In this way, analysis has been able to show the coherence that existed, throughout the classical age, between the theory of representation and the theories of language, of the natural orders, and of wealth and value. It is this configuration that, from the nineteenth century onward, changes entirely; the theory of representation disappears as the universal foundation of all possible orders; language as the spontaneous *tabula*, the primary grid of things, as an indispensable link between representation and things, is eclipsed in its turn; a profound historicity penetrates into the heart of things, isolates and defines them in their own coherence, imposes upon them the forms of order implied by the continuity of time; the analysis of exchange and money gives way to the study of production, that of the organism takes precedence over the search for taxonomic characteristics, and, above all, language loses its privileged position and becomes, in its turn, a historical form coherent with the density of its own past. But as things become increasingly reflexive, seeking the principle of their intelligibility only in their own development, and abandoning the space of representation, man enters in his turn, and for the first time, the field of Western knowledge. Strangely enough, man—the study of whom is supposed by the naive to be the oldest investigation since **Socrates**—is probably no more than a kind of rift in the order of things, or, in any case, a configuration whose outlines are determined by the new position he has so recently taken up in the field of knowledge. Whence all the chimeras of the new humanisms, all the facile solutions of an "anthropology" understood as a universal reflection on man, half-empirical, half-philosophical. It is comforting, however, and a source of profound relief to think that man is only a recent invention, a figure not yet two centuries old, a new wrinkle in our knowledge, and that he will disappear again as soon as that knowledge has discovered a new form.

It is evident that the present study is, in a sense, an echo of my undertaking to write a history of madness in the Classical age; it has the same articulations in time, taking the end of the Renaissance as its starting point, then encountering, at the beginning of the nineteenth century, just as my history of madness did, the threshold of a modernity that we have not yet left behind. But whereas in the history of madness I was investigating the way in which a culture can determine in a massive, general form the difference that limits it, I am concerned here with observing how a culture experiences the propinquity of things, how it establishes the *tabula* of their relationships and the order by which they must be considered. I am concerned, in short, with a history of resemblance: on what conditions was Classical thought able to reflect relations of similarity or equivalence between things, relations that would provide a foundation and a justification for their words, their classifications, their systems of exchange? What historical a priori provided the starting-point from which it was possible to define the great checkerboard of distinct identities established against the confused, undefined, faceless, and, as it were, indifferent background of differences? The history of madness would be the history of the Other—of that which, for a given culture, is at once interior and foreign, therefore to be excluded (so as to exorcize the interior danger) but by being shut away

(in order to reduce its otherness); whereas the history of the order imposed on things would be the history of the Same—of that which, for a given culture, is both dispersed and related, therefore to be distinguished by kinds and to be collected together into identities.

And if one considers that disease is at one and the same time disorder—the existence of a perilous otherness within the human body, at the very heart of life—and a natural phenomenon with its own constants, resemblances, and types, one can see what scope there would be for an archaeology of the medical point of view. From the limit-experience of the Other to the constituent forms of medical knowledge, and from the latter to the order of things and the conceptions of the Same, what is available to archaeological analysis is the whole of Classical knowledge, or rather the threshold that separates us from Classical thought and constitutes our modernity. It was upon this threshold that the strange figure of knowledge called man first appeared and revealed a space proper to the human sciences. In attempting to uncover the deepest strata of Western culture, I am restoring to our silent and apparently immobile soil its rifts, its instability, its flaws; and it is the same ground that is once more stirring under our feet.

## Notes

1. The passage Foucault cites is from Borges' essay "John Wilkins' Analytical Language."
2. The Uruguayan-French poet Isidore Ducasse (1846–70), pseudonym Comte de Lautréamont, penned the line "as beautiful as the chance encounter between a sewing machine and an umbrella on an operating table," an image that inspired Surrealists.

## Study Questions

1. What contrast does Foucault draw between Ducasse's umbrella and sewing machine on the operating table and Borges' Chinese encyclopedia, and how does this illustrate his thesis?
2. Provide an example of how a classification of things on the basis of similarities and differences can be seen to depend, as Foucault contends, on a "preliminary criterion" of ordering.
3. Why might Foucault have chosen to call his project an "archaeological inquiry"?
4. We suppose that we have long taken Socrates' advice "know thyself" to heart, but Foucault tells us that the human sciences have existed only since the beginning of the nineteenth century. Why is this?

# Film Notes

### Personal Identity

*Away from Her* (Canada 2006, Sarah Polley, 109 min): Based on Alice Munro's short story "The Bear Came Over the Mountain." About a woman with Alzheimer's disease and her husband's grief as he faces losing her.

*Being John Malkovich* (USA 1999, Spike Jonze, 112 min): A financially strapped puppeteer discovers a portal into the brain of actor John Malkovich.

*C.R.A.Z.Y.* (Canada 2005, Jean-Marc Vallée, 129 min; French with subtitles): In 1970s working-class Montreal, a teenager struggles to express his homosexuality.

*Double Happiness* (Canada 1994, Mina Shum, 92 min): Sandra Oh plays an aspiring 22-year-old Vancouver actress forced to balance her wishes against the expectations of her traditional Chinese family.

*Eternal Sunshine of the Spotless Mind* (USA 2004, Michel Gondry, 108 min): Difficulty moving on from a bad breakup? A romantic comedy about an experimental procedure that selectively erases memories from the brain.

*The Man without a Past* (Finland/France/Germany 2002, Aki Kaurismäki, 97 min; Finnish with subtitles): A man who is mugged and almost dies leaves the hospital with no memories of his past and no idea who he is.

*Moon* (UK 2008, Duncan Jones, 97 min): Nearing the end of a three-year contract, an astronaut who extracts the moon's helium for use as energy on Earth finds that all is not as it appears.

*Orlando* (UK/Italy/France/Netherlands 1992, Sally Potter, 93 min): Orlando is an attractive youth, a favourite of the aging Queen Elizabeth I who bequeaths him an estate on condition that he not grow old. Partway across the ensuing centuries, Orlando becomes a woman.

*Smoke Signals* (USA 1998, Chris Eyre, 88 min): Two young men take a road trip from Idaho's Coeur d'Alene reservation to Phoenix to pick up the ashes of one's estranged father.

### Freedom and Determinism

*A Clockwork Orange* (UK 1971, Stanley Kubrick, 137 min): Set in what was then the near future of the late 1970s/early 1980s. A sadistic juvenile delinquent undergoes behavioural modification in order to be released from jail.

*Babel* (USA 2006, Alejandro González Iñárritu, 142 min): What appear to be separate lives unfolding in different parts of the globe—Morocco, the United States, Mexico, and Japan—are actually causally linked.

*Gattaca* (USA 1997, Andrew Niccol, 112 min): About a society not far into the future. Naturally born "In-Valid" Vincent dreams of becoming an astronaut, but the job is restricted to genetically engineered "Valids."

*M* (Germany 1931, Fritz Lang, 105 min; German with subtitles): Berlin's underworld takes over from the police to catch a child murderer. "M" claims he is not responsible because he cannot control his impulses.

*The Matrix Reloaded* (USA 2003, Andy and Larry Wachowski, 138 min): Morpheus, Neo, and Trinity travel to Zion, humanity's only remaining outpost. But Neo's role as messiah and human freedom itself come into question.

*Minority Report* (USA 2002, Steven Spielberg, 144 min): Set in Washington, DC, in 2054. A detective in the "Precrime" unit becomes a fugitive when the "precogs" predict he will commit murder.

*Run, Lola, Run* (Germany 1998, Tom Tykwer, 81 min; German with subtitles): Lola receives a panicked phone call from her petty criminal boyfriend Manni who needs 100,000 deutschmarks in 20 minutes. Three different versions of ensuing events unfold.

*The Shawshank Redemption* (USA 1994, Frank Darabont, 142 min): About a prison friendship between two men and the ability to exercise freedom and hold onto hope while inside prison walls.

## Personal Identity/Freedom and Determinism

*Dark City* (USA 1998, Alex Proyas, 101 min): A city of the future under the control of villainous Strangers from another solar system. The hero awakes bloodied in a bathtub, amnesiac, and accused of serial murder.

*Memento* (USA 2000, Christopher Nolan, 116 min): A man's short-term memory is destroyed in the same violent crime that killed his wife. As he pursues her killer, notes, photos, and even tattoos must substitute for memories.

## Natural and Social Kinds

*A Beautiful Mind* (USA 2001, Ron Howard, 134 min): About mathematician John Forbes Nash, Jr., who won a Nobel Prize for his contributions to game theory despite struggles with schizophrenia.

*The Fly* (USA 1958, Kurt Neumann, 94 min; USA and Canada 1986, David Cronenberg, 96 min): A scientist experimenting with a "matter transmitter" in the 1958 version and a "telepod" in the 1986 version manages to exchange his matter with a fly's.

*Freaks* (USA 1932, Tod Browning, 66 min): About members of a circus community and the code of ethics that binds and protects them.

*Rain Man* (USA 1988, Barry Levinson, 128 min): A self-absorbed man who discovers that an autistic older brother he never knew he had has inherited their father's estate comes to accommodate their differences during a cross-country road trip.

## Personal Identity/Natural and Social Kinds

*Boys Don't Cry* (USA 1999, Kimberly Peirce, 116 min): Based on the life of transgendered Brandon Teena, who met a violent death soon after moving to Falls City, Nebraska.

*Club Native* (Canada 2008, Tracey Deer, 78 min): NFB documentary about four women from Kahnawake whose identities as Mohawk are threatened by community rules against marrying and having children with whites.

*Ma Vie en Rose* (Belgium/France/UK 1997, Alain Berliner, 90 min; French with subtitles): Seven-year-old Ludovic is convinced he is a girl. His parents do their best, but Ludovic's plan to marry his father's boss's son when he gets older does not help matters.

*Prom Night in Mississippi* (USA/Canada 2008, Paul Saltzman, 90 min): Charleston's high school was finally desegregated in the 1970s, but separate black and white proms were held until actor Morgan Freeman's offer to pay for an integrated prom was accepted in 2008.

*Skin* (South Africa/UK 2008, Anthony Fabian, 107 min): About the life of Sandra Laing, born with dark skin to white parents in apartheid-era South Africa.

*Spider* (Canada/UK 2002, David Cronenberg, 98 min): A schizophrenic man released from an asylum to a halfway house has fragmented and distorted memories of a traumatic childhood.

*XXY* (Argentina/France/Spain 2007, Lucía Puenzo, 86 min; Spanish with subtitles): To her parents' consternation, Alex, who is 15 years old, intersex, and raised as a girl, explores a growing interest in sex and decides to stop hormonal treatments.

# PART II

# The True

## ▶ Introduction

Philosophical study of "the true," of what we can know and the nature of knowledge, is called epistemology. The word "epistemology" is derived from the Greek *episteme*, which translates as "knowledge," and *logos*, which translates as "theory." It is worthwhile to distinguish epistemology from metaphysics. Metaphysicians make knowledge claims about what exists and the nature of reality: whether there is a god, what space and time are, if minds are material or immaterial, whether freedom or determinism is true. Epistemologists are interested in the bases for making such knowledge claims: whether to rely on reason or the senses, how to define truth, what counts as evidence for a belief, if knowledge is even possible.

### Plato's *Meno*

Plato believed that the sensible things we are disposed to take as constituents of reality are merely derivative. Ultimate reality consists of an abstract realm of objects called "the forms." Knowledge of the forms (e.g., "excellence" or "virtue" in *Meno*) is gained through reason, not the senses. In *Meno*, Plato both describes and justifies his rationalist epistemology. As Socrates guides Meno's slave boy in proving the geometrical theorem that the diagonal of any square is equal in length to the side of a square twice as large, we are introduced to the dialectical, or Socratic, method. Socrates is not teaching the boy, and the boy is not learning: instead, the boy is remembering (or recollecting) what his immortal, and repeatedly reincarnated, soul once knew. Thus, Plato provides an account of innate, a priori knowledge.

### Knowledge of the External World

René Descartes shares the rationalist epistemology of Plato's *Meno*: Euclidean geometry, with its deduction of theorems from self-evident truths or axioms, is his model for scientific knowledge. In *Meditations on First Philosophy*, Descartes pioneers the use of "methodic doubt." He canvasses his existing beliefs and discards any that are not certain with the goal of establishing new, secure "foundations" that will support a "stable" and "lasting" science. Because our senses sometimes deceive us, Descartes discards his beliefs about the reality of objects and even his own body. Descartes ultimately reaches one foundational belief: his existence as a thinking thing, i.e., the reality of his own mind. Thus, a representational gap opens between the mind of the knowing subject and the world external to that mind that consists (ostensibly) of material things, the body, and other minds.

The empiricism of George Berkeley and David Hume opposes the rationalism of Plato and Descartes. For Berkeley and Hume, sense experience provides the foundations of knowledge.

In Berkeley's *Three Dialogues*, Philonous challenges the primary–secondary quality distinction in order to convince his opponent Hylas (*hyle* is Greek for "matter") of the truth of immaterialism: Berkeley's belief that only mind exists. Philosophers of the early modern period considered "primary qualities" to be mind-independent and "secondary qualities" to be mind-dependent: as Hylas says, "extension, figure, solidity, gravity, motion, and rest . . . exist really in bodies" whereas "Colours, sounds, tastes . . . have certainly no existence without the mind." Whether or not we accept Berkeley's immaterialist metaphysics, if he convinces us that primary qualities are no less mind-dependent than secondary qualities, subjective idealism as an epistemological position follows. For subjective idealists, the representational gap is unbridgeable: as knowers, we have access only to our own ideas, not to a world external to these.

Descartes' scepticism is wholly methodic: by the end of the *Meditations*, he assures us not only that the external world exists but that we have trustworthy knowledge of it. In response to Hylas's worries that skepticism will lead to atheism, Philonous/ Berkeley insists that he is not a skeptic: sensible things do not depend on his or any other finite mind but exist in God's infinite mind. While Hume considered Descartes and Berkeley to be among his greatest philosophical influences, his skepticism, unlike theirs, is thoroughgoing. Hume's skepticism is based on his empiricism. In *An Enquiry Concerning Human Understanding*, Hume contends that metaphysical claims about the existence of immaterial souls or material bodies are illegitimate because they do not contain ideas that are copied from sense impressions. Hume also stresses the limits of empirical knowledge. Although the idea of cause and effect is derived from the constant conjunction of particular objects in experience, Hume contends that reasoning inductively that similar causes will bring about similar effects is justified neither by reason nor experience. Custom alone is responsible.

Hume's skeptical accounts of causation and induction challenged his contemporaries and continue to vex philosophers today. In *Prolegomena to Any Future Metaphysics*, Immanuel Kant famously writes of being awoken from his "dogmatic slumber" by Hume's discovery that causation has no a priori basis in reason but arises from the "subjective necessity of habit." Kant argues that the mind structures experience and makes knowledge possible. The faculty of sensibility contributes the forms of space and time, and the faculty of understanding contributes concepts like causation. We have knowledge not of things as they are in themselves, the "noumena," but things as they appear to us, the "phenomena." Thus, Kant's "critical idealism" mediates between rationalism and empiricism to close the representational gap opened by Descartes.

Nelson Goodman's "Words, Works, Worlds" draws on Berkeley's subjective idealism and Kant's critical idealism. For Berkeley, it is impossible to have knowledge of a world external to the mind; for Goodman, it is impossible to have knowledge of a world external to language: "We can have words without a world but no world without words." However, Goodman, like Kant, discounts "the pure given" that empiricists like Berkeley and Hume find in immediate sense experience: there is no "perception without conception." Despite sharing Kant's constructionalism, Goodman's approach is relativist and pragmatist: "worldmaking" incorporates particular "frames of reference," and so, we have "worlds that are but versions," the "rightness" of which depends on purposes underlying their construction.

In "Realism and Anti-Realism; Metaphysics and Empiricism," Anjan Chakravartty challenges the legacy of empiricists such as Berkeley and Hume in philosophy of science. Chakravartty defines scientific realism as, roughly, "the view that scientific theories correctly describe the nature of a mind-independent world." This epistemological stance carries with it, of course, the metaphysical assumption that there *is* a mind-independent world—exactly what Berkeley's idealism denies. But there are additional anti-realist challenges. Empiricists since Hume have been skeptical about the existence of unobservables—objects of science inaccessible to our unaided senses such as electrons and genes—and therefore about the truth of those scientific theories that refer to them. However, Chakravartty argues that empiricism does not necessarily present a challenge to realism.

## ▶ Knowledge of the Mind

Descartes' *Meditations* defends metaphysical dualism: that the universe comprises two distinct substances, immaterial mind and material body. This section's readings are concerned not so much with the metaphysical question about whether the mind is material or immaterial but with the epistemological question about how best to understand mental processes.

In Plato's *Meno*, Meno poses a paradox to Socrates concerning inquiry: we do not seek what we already know, and yet, we cannot seek what we do not know. The paradox provides a basis for exploring Maurice Merleau-Ponty's criticisms of empiricism and rationalism in *Phenomenology of Perception*: empiricism ignores that we cannot look for what we do not know we are looking for and rationalism ignores that we would not look for what we know we are looking for.[1] The chapter "The Experience of the Body and Classical Psychology" rejects classical psychology's incorporation of Cartesian mind–body and subject–object dualisms in its representation of the body as part of objective reality. Merleau-Ponty's approach is phenomenological: the body thinks and perceives and makes experience possible, and as "that by which there are objects" cannot itself be an object.

In *Philosophical Investigations,* Ludwig Wittgenstein departs from the philosophical approach of Plato's Meno, whereby knowledge of the forms, e.g., excellence, is sought through essential definitions that provide necessary and sufficient conditions.

"Language games" embedded in "forms of life" instead determine meaning. Knowledge of the rules governing a word's meaning is achieved not by grasping the abstract concept it represents but by understanding how it is used in a variety of contexts, and thus, "family resemblances" replace necessary and sufficient conditions. Wittgenstein's famous "private language argument" emphasizes the incoherence of the idea that a person could invent a language that refers to her or his private sensations: without shared standards, it makes no sense to speak of a language at all.

Descartes' use of methodic doubt in the *Meditations* promotes solipsism: the position that only the reality of one's own mind can be known with certainty—not material things, the body, or, indeed, other minds. By forgoing Cartesian rationalism for intersubjective accounts of knowledge, both Merleau-Ponty and Wittgenstein manage to escape solipsism. The problem of solipsism has long intrigued philosophers, however; philosopher-poet Troy Jollimore pokes gentle fun at such thinking in his poem "The Solipsist."

Wittgenstein's "private language argument" has been interpreted, although controversially, as providing support for a behaviourist philosophy of mind. Behaviourists hold that when we attribute a mental state to someone, we are actually referring to a behavioural disposition: to experience pain is simply to be disposed to wince or cry in certain situations. In "Sensations and Brain Processes," J.J.C. Smart finds behaviourism "congenial" because it is consistent with physicalism: unlike the Cartesian dualist, the behaviourist makes no commitment to sensations or states of consciousness over and above the arrangement of physical particles that make us up. Smart, however, defends physicalism outright. He argues that sensations and other mental states are simply brain processes, not behavioural dispositions or modifications of an immaterial substance. The mind is therefore best studied using the mechanical approach of physics.

Like the behaviourism attributed to Wittgenstein, but unlike Smart's physicalism, the functionalism Hilary Putnam defends in "The Nature of Mental States" is consistent with, but does not require, the denial of mind–body dualism. For functionalists, to be in the same mental state (e.g., pain) is to be in the same functional state that connects sensory input (e.g., pinprick) to behavioural output (e.g., withdrawal). Putnam argues that his hypothesis that pain is a functional state of the whole organism is better supported empirically than competing brain-process and behavioural-disposition hypotheses, especially when cross-species comparisons are made. Functionalism is popular with artificial intelligence enthusiasts: Putnam introduces the idea of a "probabilistic automaton," which is similar to a Turing machine (see http://plato.stanford.edu/entries/turing-machine) but probabilistic rather than deterministic in connecting sensory inputs to behavioural outputs.

In "What Is It Like to be a Bat?" Thomas Nagel argues that consciousness is something over and above behavioural dispositions, brain processes, or functional states. For organisms that have consciousness, "there is something it is like to *be* that organism." According to Nagel, we lack knowledge of this phenomenological fact about bats, for example, because, without sonar, it is impossible for us to adopt the point of view of a bat. For Nagel, there is an irreducibly "subjective character of experience" that is tied to a species-specific point of view. In contrast, the physicalist reduction of lightning to electrical discharge is possible for human and Martian scientists alike because objectivity is achieved by successfully detaching from the species-specific point of view (i.e., discarding the bright yellow flash of phenomenological experience).

## Methods of Scientific Inquiry

Francis Bacon's *Novum Organum* shares with Descartes' *Meditations* the goal of securing new foundations for natural philosophy. Both philosophers contributed to those developments of the sixteenth and seventeenth centuries that became known as the scientific revolution, but they promote different methods of scientific inquiry. Descartes favours the rationalism of Plato's *Meno*, which takes Euclidean geometry as the model for natural philosophy. Bacon prefers empiricism, holding that "true induction" begins with particulars of sense experience and proceeds in a "gradual and unbroken ascent" from "middle axioms" (empirical rules) to "the most general axioms" (laws of nature). This method, Bacon argues, promotes scientific objectivity by keeping his famous four "idols"—of the cave, tribe, marketplace, and theatre—at bay.

In "A Survey of Some Fundamental Problems," Karl Popper defends deductive logic as the method of the empirical sciences, and by doing so, claims to have solved Hume's famous problem of induction. Popper argues that the invention of theories does not involve inductive logic but an "irrational element." He also argues that theories can be justified without relying on inductive logic. If the prediction deduced from the theory is falsified, deductive logic falsifies the theory. If the prediction is verified, the theory is said to be "corroborated." Corroboration makes no commitment to the theory's truth or probable truth but merely reports that the theory has survived an attempt to falsify it. By replacing verifiability with falsifiability as the criterion that demarcates empirical science from metaphysics, Popper also claims to have solved "Kant's problem."

Whereas ancient philosophers such as Plato and Aristotle conceived of nature as an organism, early modern philosophers such as Bacon and Descartes conceived of it as a machine. The goal was to provide mechanical explanations, appealing to matter in motion alone, for all natural phenomena. The contemplative ideal of the Greeks was replaced by an interventionist ideal, and experimentation and technological innovation became central to scientific discovery.

Kathleen Okruhlik's title "Birth of a New Physics or Death of Nature?" refers to the contested legacy of the scientific revolution. The period is often characterized as the triumph of genius over superstition. However, environmentalists point to harmful ecological consequences arising from the reductionistic treatment of nature as a machine, and feminists point to harmful consequences to women arising from construing nature as female and knowers as male. Okruhlik analyzes these claims by returning to ontological, epistemological, and methodological notions of objectivity associated with the seventeenth-century distinction between primary and secondary qualities. She concludes that reductionism and mechanism are not inherently harmful to women and that feminists should reconstruct objectivity and rationality as methodological norms.

Despite the reductionism and mechanism of the scientific revolution, teleological explanations appealing to final causes (a thing's purpose or end, *telos* in Greek) persisted, especially in biology. Final causation was understood sometimes in theological terms as God's own design and at other times in Kantian terms as an a priori "regulative idea." Only with Darwin's *Origin of Species* in 1859, with natural selection providing an explanation for the adaptedness of organisms, is the demise of teleology at the hands of mechanism considered to have been accomplished. However, in "Teleology and the Relationship Between Biology and the Physical Sciences in the Nineteenth Century," John Beatty argues that Darwin's contemporaries disagreed on his attitude toward teleology: they alternately praised and criticized him, both for promoting and undermining teleology.

Scientists are charged with seeking evidence in support of hypotheses and, as Popper emphasizes, being prepared to relinquish those hypotheses if contradictory evidence obtains. In "Public Knowledge, Public Trust," Lorraine Code argues that this course expected of "normal science" did not unfold in the well-publicized case of Nancy Olivieri, the Toronto haematologist responsible for clinical trials testing the drug deferiprone in patients with thalassemia before turning "whistleblower." Code suggests that the importance of trust in science has been ignored because of assumptions that science occupies an autonomous realm, free of social influences. Code urges a democratization of scientific practice that shares epistemic responsibility with a participatory public.

## ▶ Note

1. M.C. Dillon, *Merleau-Ponty's Ontology*, 2nd ed. Evanston, IL: Northwestern University Press, 1998.

## ▶ Discussion Questions

1. Is this really a book that you have in your hands? How do you know that you are not dreaming that you have a book in your hands? How do you know that you are not "a brain in a vat" being manipulated by an "evil scientist" to think that you have hands holding a book?
2. Can we gain knowledge of the world independently of sense experience?
3. Can consciousness and other aspects of the mind be fully understood by science?
4. Descartes' famous words "I think, therefore I am" are supposed to assure us that we exist as thinking things. Can we be certain that other minds exist? Do non-human as well as human animals have minds? Is it possible for computers to have minds?
5. What is meant by "the scientific method"? Is there indeed a method shared by all the various branches of science?

## ▶ Further Reading

Kim, Jaegwon. *Philosophy of Mind*, 2nd ed. Boulder, CO: Westview Press, 2006.

Kuhn, Thomas S. *The Structure of Scientific Revolutions*, 2nd ed. Chicago: University of Chicago Press, 1970.

Longino, Helen E. *Science as Social Knowledge: Values and Objectivity in Scientific Inquiry*. Princeton, NJ: Princeton University Press, 1990.

Russell, Bertrand. *The Problems of Philosophy*. Oxford: Oxford University Press, 1959.

Searle, John. *Minds, Brains and Science*. Cambridge, MA: Harvard University Press, 1986.

# Plato

Plato (429–347 BCE) was a citizen of the ancient Greek city-state of Athens. Plato's works are not treatises but take the form of dialogues, in which Socrates is usually the main character. Plato's family knew Socrates, and Plato probably began discussions with Socrates at an early age. Plato is thought to have travelled widely after Socrates' death in 399 BCE, returning to Athens around 387 BCE to found a school (a *Mouseion*, dedicated to the Muses) in the grove of the hero Academe. In *Meno*, Plato investigates the question of what excellence (or virtue) is and introduces a theory of knowledge as remembering (or recollection).—JS

## From *Meno*[1]

Characters: Meno, Socrates, Meno's slave

### 1. What Is Excellence?

MENO. Can you tell me, Socrates, is excellence teachable? Or is it not teachable, but acquired by practice? Or is it neither acquired by practice nor learned, but something which comes to men by nature or in some other way?

SOCRATES. Meno, the Thessalians used to be famous and much admired among the Greeks for their horsemanship and their wealth; nowadays, I think, they have a reputation for wisdom as well, especially the citizens of **Larissa**, where your companion Aristippus comes from. For this change in you, Gorgias is responsible because when he arrived at your city, he made lovers of his wisdom out of the highest of the Aleuadai, among them your own lover Aristippus, and the other Thessalians too. What is more, he made you adopt the habit of answering confidently and with great style whatever anyone asked you, as befits those who have knowledge, since he is himself ready to answer any Greek who wishes to ask him anything whatever, and never lacks an answer. But here at Athens, my dear Meno, the opposite has happened. It's as if the supply of wisdom had dried up, and perhaps it has left these parts to be with you. At any rate, if you propose to put that question to people here, there isn't a single person who won't laugh and say "Stranger, I must seem to you to be a lucky man—at least if you think that I know whether excellence is teachable or how

it comes. But I'm so far from knowing whether excellence is teachable or not, that I don't even know what excellence itself is at all." So that's my position too, Meno: I'm just as poor as my fellow-citizens in this respect, and blame myself for not knowing about excellence at all. But where I don't know what something is, how could I know what sort of a thing it is? Or do you think that it is possible for someone, who doesn't know at all who Meno is, to know whether he is beautiful or rich or nobly-born, or the opposite of these? Do you really think that's possible?

M. I don't. But do *you*, Socrates, really not even know what excellence is? Are we to take home this news about you?

S. Not only that, but you can add that I've never yet met anyone else who did, as far as I can tell.

M. What! Didn't you meet Gorgias when he was here?

S. I did.

M. Then you didn't think that he knew?

S. I don't have a very good memory, Meno, so I can't say now what I thought then. But perhaps he does know, and you too know what he said: so do remind me of how he spoke. Or, if you like, tell me yourself. I suppose that you think as he does.

M. I do.

S. Then let's forget about him, since anyway he isn't here: but, for heaven's sake, Meno, what do *you* say excellence is? Do tell me and don't refuse to give me the chance of discovering that I am fortunate to be caught out in a falsehood, if it proves that you and Gorgias do know, when I said that I'd never yet met anyone who knew.

M. It's not difficult to explain, Socrates. First of all, let's take a man's excellence, that's easy. A man's excellence is this: to be capable in handling the affairs of the city, and, while so doing, to help his friends and harm his enemies, taking care not to suffer anything of the sort himself. Now take a woman's excellence, that's not difficult to describe: she must manage the household well, watch over all household affairs and be obedient to her husband. Different again is the excellence of a child, male or female, so too that of an older man, whether free or slave. And there are a great many other different excellences, so that one is at no loss to say about excellence what it is: corresponding to each action and time of life, and to every function, there is, for each of us, the appropriate excellence and likewise, I'd say, Socrates, the appropriate defect.

S. I seem to have had very good luck, Meno: I was looking for a single excellence and I discover a swarm of them all around you. But, Meno, to pursue this image of swarms, suppose I asked you about the essential nature of bees, what it is, and you said that there were many different kinds of bees, how would you answer me if I asked "Do you hold that they are of many kinds and different from one another in respect of being bees? Isn't it rather that they don't differ at all in this respect, but only in others, as in beauty or size or the like?" Tell me, what answer would you give to that question?

M. What I'd say is that one is no different from another insofar as they are bees.

S. Suppose I said next: "Then tell me this, Meno: what do you say this is, in respect of which they are no different but all the same? You'd have a reply for me, I think?

M. I would.

S. Then do the same for the excellences: even if they are of many different kinds, at any rate they have this one common character, because of which they are all excellences, and which it's as well to keep your eye on if you're giving an answer to the question: "What is excellence?" Or don't you understand what I mean?

M. I think I do: but I don't yet grasp the question as well as I'd like to.

S. In your opinion, Meno, is it only in the case of excellence that there's a different one for a man and for a woman and so on? Or do you think that the same holds for health and size and strength? Do you think that there is one kind of health for a man and another for a woman? Or is it the same character everywhere, provided that it's health, whether it's in a man or in anything else whatever?

M. Health seems to me to be the same whether in man or woman.

S. Surely this applies to size and strength as well? If a woman is strong, will she be strong because of the same kind of thing, the same strength? What I mean by "the same" here is this: strength is no different in respect of being strength whether it is in a man or in a woman. Or do you think that there is a difference?

M. I don't.

S. Will excellence be any different in respect of being excellence whether it is in a child or an elder, in a woman or in a man?

M. I'm inclined to think, Socrates, that this case is not the same as those other ones.

S. Well, didn't you say that a man's excellence was to run a city well, while a woman's was to run a house well?

M. I did.

S. Is it possible to run a city or a house or anything else well, if one doesn't run it sensibly and justly?

M. No.

S. And surely, if they run anything justly and sensibly, they will run it with justice and good sense?

M. Necessarily.

S. So both a man and a woman will need the same things, justice and good sense, if they are going to be good?

M. So it appears.

S. What about a child or an elder? Could they ever possibly be good if they lacked good sense or were unjust?

M. Indeed not.

S. But if they were sensible and just, they could be?

M. Yes.

S. So everyone is good in the same way; for it is by acquiring the same things that they become good.

M. It seems so.

S. Now surely, they wouldn't all be good in the same way, unless it was the same excellence they possessed.

M. Indeed not.

S. Then since they all possess the same excellence, try to tell me or to remember what Gorgias, and you too, say it is.

M. What else can it be but to be capable of ruling people? If, that is, you are looking for one thing that applies to every case.

S. Indeed I am. But will a child possess this same excellence, Meno, and will a slave be capable of ruling his master? Do you think such a ruler would be a slave any longer?

M. No, I don't think that at all, Socrates.

S. No, it's not likely, my friend: and consider this next point. You say "to be capable of ruling." Shouldn't we add "justly and not unjustly"?

M. I agree because justice, Socrates, is excellence.

S. Excellence, Meno, or *an* excellence?

M. What do you mean?

S. Like any other case. As, for example, I'd say of roundness that it is *a* shape, not simply that it is shape. I'd say this because there are other shapes as well.

M. You'd be right to say that, and I'd say that justice is not alone; there are other excellences as well.

S. What are they? Do tell me. Just as I would tell you of other shapes, if you asked me to, so you tell me of other excellences.

M. I think that courage is an excellence and so are good sense and wisdom and nobility of style, and lots of others.

S. The same thing has happened to us again, Meno: when we were looking for one excellence, we've found lots, though in a different way from just now. But we can't discover that single one which runs through all of them.

M. I can't yet, Socrates, grasp the one excellence that you seek, applying to every case, as in the other examples.

S. That's quite understandable: but I will try, if I can, to get us closer to it. I'm sure you understand that this is a general point: if anyone had asked you as I did just now, "What is shape, Meno?" then if you had told him it was roundness and if he had said to you as I did "Is roundness shape or *a* shape?" you'd have said, I think, that it was *a* shape.

M. Of course.

S. Presumably because there are other shapes as well?

M. Yes.

S. And if he'd then asked you what those were, you'd have said?

M. I would.

S. And if he'd asked you about colour in the same way, what it is, and if when you'd said that it was white, he had followed up your reply by asking "Is white colour or *a* colour?" You'd have said it was a colour because there happen to be others?

M. I would.

S. And if he asked you to cite other colours, you'd have mentioned others, which are colours no less than white is?

M. Yes.

S. So if he pursued the argument, as I did, and said "We always come across several, but I don't want that. Since you speak of those many things by one name, and you say that there is not one of them which is not shape, although they are also opposites of one another, what is this thing, which embraces the round no less than the straight, which you call shape, and say that the curved is no more shape than the straight is?" Isn't that what you say?

M. I do.

S. Well, when you say that, do you hold that the round is no more round than straight, or the straight no more straight than round?

M. Of course not, Socrates.

S. But you do hold that the round is no more shape than the straight is, and vice versa.

M. That's true.

S. What, then, is it, that thing whose name is "shape"? Try to explain. If you'd replied to the man asking you these questions about shape or colour by saying "But I don't understand what you want, sir, I don't know what you mean," he would probably have been surprised and said "Don't you understand that I am looking for what is the same in all these cases?" Wouldn't you even have anything to say along these lines, if someone asked you "What is it that applies to the round and the straight and to everything else that you call shapes, which is the same in all of them?" Try to say, to give yourself some practice for the answer about excellence.

M. No, Socrates, you answer.

S. You want me to humour you?

M. Yes.

S. Will you give me your answer about excellence, if I do?

M. I will.

S. Then I must try hard: it will be worth it.

M. It certainly will.

S. Well then, let's try to tell you what shape is. See if you accept it as this: let us take shape to be the only one of the things that are which always accompanies colour. Will that satisfy you or are you looking for some other kind of answer? I'd be delighted if you would give me an answer like that about excellence.

M. But that's a naïve answer, Socrates.

S. How so?

M. On your account, shape is what always accompanies colour. Well, suppose that someone said he didn't know what colour was, but was just as much at a loss here as about shape. What answer would you think you had given him?

S. A true one: and if my questioner was one of those clever, contentious and argumentative people, I'd tell him: "I've had my say: if it isn't right, it's your job to take up the argument and refute it." But if friends like you and me want to have a discussion, they must make their replies more considerate and more properly dialectical. To answer more dialectically is perhaps not only to give true answers, but also to reply in terms that the questioner agrees that he knows. I'll try to reply to you like that. Tell me: is there something you call an end? I mean something that is a limit or an extremity—I say that all these are one and the same: perhaps **Prodicus** would distinguish them for us, but I assume that you would say that anything which has been limited has also been ended—that's all I mean, nothing complicated.

M. I do say that, and I think I understand what you mean.

S. Well, is there something that you call a plane and something else you call a solid, for example those mentioned in geometry?

M. I do.

S. Then you should already understand from those what I mean by shape. Because I say of every shape that it is that in which a solid ends—which I could put shortly as "shape is the limit of a solid."

M. And what do you say colour is, Socrates.

S. You're quite shameless, Meno: you keep demanding answers from an old man, when you won't use your memory and explain what Gorgias says excellence is.

M. But I will answer you, when you've explained this, Socrates.

S. Anyone could tell, Meno, even if he were blindfolded, that you are beautiful and still have lovers from the way you talk.

M. Why?

S. Because in your conversation, you do nothing but lay down the law, as spoilt boys do, who are tyrants as long as they're attractive. Besides you've realized that I can't resist anything beautiful: so I'll satisfy you and give you an answer.

M. Yes, do satisfy me.

S. Do you want me to give you an answer in Gorgias' style, which you would find easiest to follow?

M. Of course I'd like that.

S. You both hold that things that are have effluences, as **Empedocles'** theory states?

M. Yes indeed.

S. And that they have passages into which and through which these effluences travel?

M. Yes.

S. And that some of the effluences fit certain of the passages, but others are too small or too large?

M. That's so.

S. Is there something you call sight?

M. There is.

S. Given this, then, "See what it is I mean" as **Pindar** says. Because colour is an effluence shapes have, which is commensurate with sight and perceived by it.

M. I think you've given an excellent answer there, Socrates.

S. Probably because it's the kind you're used to hearing. And no doubt you see that you could go on from this to say what sound is, and smell and lots of other things of that kind.

M. Yes, indeed.

S. It sounds a grand answer, Meno, so you prefer it to the answer about shape.

M. I do.

S. But I've convinced myself that it isn't the best one—the other one is. And I suspect that you would think so, if you didn't, as you said yesterday, have to go away before the mysteries, but could stay here and be initiated.

M. Oh but I would stay, Socrates, if you kept on talking to me like that.

S. You can be sure that I shan't be lacking in enthusiasm for talking like that, for my sake as well as yours: but I'm afraid that I won't be able to say much more in that vein. Come on now, you have a try, and do as you promised, explain excellence to me as a whole, saying what it is, and stop making a multitude out of one, as jokers say when people break things; leave it whole and tell me what excellence is when intact. You've had some examples from me. [. . .]

## 2. Learning as Remembering

MENO. Socrates, I was told even before I met you that you're always puzzled yourself and that you make other people puzzled too. And now, I'd say, you are using spells and drugs and positively bewitching me, so that I'm just a mass of perplexity. And, to be frivolous for a moment, you seem to me to be exactly like one of those flat sea-going electric rays; both in your appearance and in other ways. Because it numbs anyone who approaches and touches it, and that's just what you seem to have done to me now. My mind and my lips have really gone numb and I don't know what reply to give you. Yet thousands of times I've made long speeches about excellence to large audiences, and did it very well, or so I fancied: but now there isn't a single thing that I can say. It seems to me that you would be well advised not to leave Athens or go to live elsewhere: if you behaved like this as a stranger in some foreign city, you'd probably be arrested as a sorcerer.

SOCRATES. You wretch, Meno, you nearly fooled me.

M. How so, Socrates?

S. I know why you used a simile about me.

M. Why, do you think?

S. So that I would return the compliment. I've discovered that all those who are beautiful enjoy having comparisons made about them—because they gain by it: for likenesses of beautiful things are themselves beautiful—but I'm not going to give you one in exchange for yours. I am like the electric ray, if it numbs others by being numb itself: but if it doesn't then I'm not. It's not that I am well off myself when I puzzle others, but rather I'm so puzzled that I make others puzzled too. And now, as regards excellence, I don't know what it is, and though you perhaps used to know before you came into contact with me, still, now it's just as if you didn't. However, I am ready to join you in investigating and trying to look for what it is.

M. And how will you look for this, Socrates, when you don't know at all what it is? For, which of the things that you don't know are you going to take this to be when you go looking for it? Or if you should happen to come across it, how will you know that this is what you didn't know?

S. I understand what you mean, Meno. Do you see that you are introducing that eristic [controversial] argument that a man cannot try to find out either what he knows or what he doesn't know? He wouldn't seek what he knows—for as he knows it, he has no need to make the inquiry—nor for what he doesn't know—for then he doesn't even know what he is to look for.

M. Don't you think that argument is a sound one, Socrates?

S. I do not.

M. Can you say why?

S. I can: because I have heard from men and women who are wise in matters of religion. . .

M. What account did they give?

S. One that was true, I thought, and beautiful.

M. What was this account and who were the people who told it to you?

S. They are holy men and women who are interested in being able to give an account of the activities in which they engage: Pindar talks of it too, and so do other divinely-inspired poets. What they say is this—just see if they seem to you to be speaking the truth. Because they say that man's soul is immortal, and at one time comes to an end—which they call dying—but at another is born, and is never totally annihilated. Because of this, one must live out one's life in as righteous a manner as one can. [. . .] Thus, since the soul is immortal and has come to be many times, and has seen both what is on earth and what is in Hades, all things, in fact, there is nothing which it has not learned: so it is not surprising that it is able to remember what it formerly knew, both about excellence and other things. Since all nature is related, and the soul is in a state of having learned everything, once someone has remembered one thing—this is what people *call* learning—nothing prevents him from finding out everything, provided he is stouthearted and does not tire of his inquiry: for all seeking and learning is remembering. So we mustn't accept that eristic argument, because it would make us lazy, and is one that pleases weak men. The other makes people hardworking and eager inquirers: I trust in its truth and am willing to join you in trying to find out what excellence is.

M. Yes, Socrates. But what do you mean when you say that we don't learn, but that what we call learning is remembering? Can you teach me how this is so?

S. Didn't I call you a wretch just now, Meno, and here you are, when I say that there is no teaching, only remembering, asking me if I can teach you, so that I shall immediately be caught in an obvious contradiction.

M. No, no, Socrates, I didn't have that in mind, I was using the word out of habit. But if you have any way of showing me that things are as you say, please do show me.

S. Well, it's not easy, but for your sake, I'm willing to make the effort. Call over for me one of this crowd of servants you have here, any you like, so that I can use him to give you a demonstration.

M. Of course. [TO BOY] Come here.

S. He is a Greek and Greek-speaking?

M. Certainly, born in our house.

S. Pay attention then, and see whether he seems to you to be remembering or learning from me.

M. I'll do that.

S. Tell me, boy, do you recognize a square as a figure like this? [SOCRATES DRAWS A SQUARE]

BOY. I do.

S. So is a square a figure having all these lines equal, four of them? [INDICATING THE SIDES]

B. Yes.

S. Isn't it one having also these lines going through the middle equal? [IT IS LEFT TO THE READER TO DECIDE WHICH LINES THESE ARE]

B. Yes.

S. Such a figure could be larger or smaller?

B. Yes.

S. So if this side were two feet long, and this side two feet, how many feet would the whole be? Think of it like this: if it was two feet on this side, but only one foot on this one, the figure would be two feet by one, wouldn't it?

B. Yes.

S. But since it is two feet on this side, can it come to anything but twice two?

B. It comes to that.

S. So it comes to twice two feet?

B. Yes.

S. How many feet are twice two? Work it out and tell me.

B. Four, Socrates.

S. There could be, couldn't there, another figure twice the size of this one, and of the same kind, having all these lines equal like this one?

B. Yes.

S. How many feet will it be?

B. Eight.

S. Well now, try and tell me how long each of its lines will be. This one has a line of two feet: What is the line of the double square?

B. Obviously, Socrates, it is double.

S. Do you see, Meno, that I'm not teaching him anything, but always asking questions? He now thinks that he knows what kind of line it is from which the eight-foot figure will come to be; don't you agree?

M. I do.

S. So does he know?

M. By no means.

S. He thinks it is from the double line?

M. Yes.

S. Just watch him remembering in order, as one should remember. [SOCRATES TURNS BACK TO THE BOY] Tell me: you say the double figure comes to be from the double line? What I mean is not a figure that is long in one direction and short in another, but one that is to be equal in every direction like this one, but an eight-foot one, double its size. Do you still think that it will come to be from the double line?

B. I do.

S. Won't a line double that one come to be if we add another similar line to it?

B. Of course.

S. It is from this line, you say, that the eight-foot figure will be constructed, if there were four similar lines?

B. Yes.

S. Let's draw in the four equal lines. This will be what you say the eight-foot figure is, won't it?

B. Of course.

S. Surely there are in this figure these four figures, each of which is equal to the original four-foot square?

B. Yes.

S. So how big is it? Isn't it four times the size?

B. It must be.

S. So is what is four times the size double?

B. Certainly not.

S. But how many times as big?

B. Four times.

S. Then from the double line, boy, it's not a double figure that is generated, but one four times as big?

B. That's true.

S. Because four by four is sixteen, isn't it?

B. Yes.

S. What line gives the eight-foot one? Doesn't this line give a figure four times the size?

B. I agree.

S. And from the one half its length, the four-foot figure?

B. Yes.

S. Well; isn't the eight-foot figure double this one and half that?

B. Yes.

S. Won't it be generated from a line greater than one of this length, but less than one of that?

B. I think so.

S. Good. Do answer what you think. Tell me, wasn't this line two feet long, and this one four?

B. Yes.

S. So the line for the eight-foot figure must be longer than this two-foot one, but shorter than the four-foot one.

B. It must.

S. Now try and tell me how long you think it is.

B. Three feet.

S. If it's to be three feet, shall we increase this line by half and will that be three feet? Because this length is two feet and this is one: and from here again, this is two feet and this is one: and here is the figure which you mention.

B. Yes.

S. Surely if it's three feet this way and three that, the whole figure will come to be three by three feet?

B. It looks like it.

S. How many is three by three feet?

B. Nine.

S. How many is the double figure to be?

B. Eight.

S. So the eight-foot figure doesn't come to be from the three-foot line either?

B. Obviously not.

S. Then from what line? Try to tell us exactly: or if you don't want to put a number to it, then indicate its length.

B. My goodness, Socrates, I just don't know.

S. Do you see, Meno, where he has now got to in his journey of remembering? To begin with he didn't know what the line of the eight-foot figure is, just as now he still doesn't know, but of course then he thought he knew it and answered confidently, like one who knows, and he didn't suppose he was at a loss. Now, though, he does suppose he's at a loss and he still doesn't know—but he doesn't think he knows either.

M. That's true.

S. Surely he's now better off as regards the thing which he didn't know?

M. I'd agree with that.

S. So by making him puzzled and numbing him like an electric ray, have we really done him any harm?

M. I don't think so.

S. In fact we've done him a service, as far as finding out how things are is concerned: because now he will be glad to investigate, since he doesn't know, but previously he would have thought he could easily often have made fine speeches before large audiences about the double figure, saying that it must have a line double the length.

M. Presumably.

S. So do you think that he would then have tried to investigate or to learn what he didn't know but thought he knew, before he came to suppose he didn't know, fell into perplexity, and started wanting the knowledge?

M. I don't think so, Socrates.

S. So being numbed has helped him?

M. I think so.

S. Now see what, starting from this puzzlement, he'll discover, investigating with my help, when I do nothing but ask questions and don't do any teaching: watch out in case you catch me teaching or explaining to him, and not just asking for his opinions. [TURNING BACK TO THE BOY, SOCRATES BEGINS TO DRAW A NEW FIGURE.] Tell me, isn't this our four-foot figure? Do you understand?

B. I do.

S. We could add another one equal to it here?

B. Yes.

S. And a third equal to each of these?

B. Yes.

S. Then we could complete this space in the corner?

B. Certainly.

S. So these will be four equal figures?

B. Yes.

S. Well: how many times the size of this original figure is this whole one?

B. Four times.

S. But what we needed was one double the size, if you remember.

B. Of course.

S. Isn't this line from corner to corner one which cuts each of these figures in half?

B. Yes.

S. Don't these four lines turn out to be equal lines, enclosing this figure here?

B. They do.

S. Think then; what size is this figure?

B. I don't understand.

S. Doesn't each line cut off the inner half of each of these four figures?

B. Yes.

S. How many halves are there in this figure?

B. Four.

S. How many in this one?

B. Two.

S. What multiple is four of two?

B. Double.

S. So how many feet does this figure come to?

B. Eight feet.

S. From which line?

B. From this one.

S. From the one stretching from angle to angle of the four-foot figure?

B. Yes.

S. **Sophists** call this the "diagonal": so if its name is the diagonal, it would be from the diagonal, in your opinion, Meno's boy, that the double square would come to be.

B. Of course, Socrates.

S. What do you think, Meno? Has he expressed any opinion not his own when he answered?

M. No, all his own.

S. And yet he didn't know, as we said a little while ago.

M. That's true.

S. Still, these opinions were somehow in him, weren't they?

M. Yes.

S. So in one who doesn't know whatever it is he doesn't know, there are true opinions about those things which he doesn't know.

M. So it appears.

S. And just for now these opinions have been freshly aroused in him as if in a dream: but if anyone asks him these same things on many occasions and in many ways, you know very well that he will end up knowing about these things as accurately as anybody.

M. It seems so.

S. Surely he will know not from someone teaching him but from questioning, himself taking up the knowledge from himself?

M. Yes.

S. For oneself to take up knowledge that's in oneself—isn't that to remember?

M. Of course. [. . .]

## Note

1. Trans. Janet D. Sisson (2008). Sisson has an MA in Literae Humaniores and a BPhil in Philosophy from the University of Oxford and a PhD from the University of Calgary. A specialist in ancient philosophy, Sisson was a tenured lecturer at the University of Glasgow until 1987. She has also taught at the Universities of Leicester, Oxford, Kansas, Alberta, Calgary, and most recently at Mount Royal University, Calgary.—LG

## Study Questions

1. Meno repeatedly goes wrong in searching for a definition of "excellence." Explain how Socrates uses his examples of bees and shapes to set Meno straight.
2. What definitions of "shape" and "colour" does Socrates propose in order to help Meno arrive at a definition of "excellence"? What might explain Socrates' preference for his definition of "shape" over his definition of "colour"?
3. What is the pedagogical significance of accepting, with Socrates, that what we call learning is actually remembering?
4. Why does Socrates reject the "eristic argument" that seems so convincing to Meno?

# ∽ KNOWLEDGE OF THE EXTERNAL WORLD ∽

## René Descartes

René Descartes (1596–1650), who is considered to be the first modern philosopher, also made important contributions to mathematics and physics. Descartes was born in La Haye, France, and received a Jesuit education before attending the University of Poitiers, where he graduated in law. In *Meditations on First Philosophy*, Descartes methodically casts doubt on his most deeply held beliefs in order to provide new, secure foundations for scientific knowledge.—JF

## From *Meditations on First Philosophy*

### Meditation I: Of the Things on Which We May Doubt

Several years have now elapsed since I first became aware that I had accepted, even from my youth, many false opinions for true and that, consequently, what I afterward based on such principles was highly doubtful; and from that time I was convinced of the necessity of undertaking once in my life to rid myself of all the opinions I had adopted, and of commencing anew the work of building from the foundation, if I desired to establish a firm and abiding superstructure in the sciences. But as this enterprise appeared to me to be one of great magnitude, I waited until I had attained an age so mature as to leave me no hope that at any stage of life more advanced I should be better able to execute my design. On this account, I have delayed so long that I should henceforth consider I was doing wrong were I still to consume in deliberation any of the time that now remains for action. Today, then, since I have opportunely freed my mind from all cares and am happily disturbed by no passions, and since I am in the secure possession of leisure in a peaceable retirement, I will at length apply myself earnestly and freely to the general overthrow of all my former opinions. But, to this end, it will not be necessary for me to show that the whole of these are false—a point, perhaps, which I shall never reach; but as even now my reason convinces me that I ought not the less carefully to withhold belief from what is not entirely certain and indubitable than from what is manifestly false, it will be sufficient to justify the rejection of the whole if I shall find in each some ground for doubt. Nor for this purpose will it be necessary even to deal with each belief individually, which would be truly an endless labour; but, as the removal from below of the foundation necessarily involves the downfall of the whole edifice, I will at once approach the criticism of the principles on which all my former beliefs rested.

All that I have, up to this moment, accepted as possessed of the highest truth and certainty, I received either from or through the senses. I observed, however, that these sometimes misled us; and it is the part of prudence not to place absolute confidence in that by which we have even once been deceived.

But it may be said, perhaps, that although the senses occasionally mislead us respecting minute objects, and such as are so far removed from us as to be beyond the reach of close observation, there are yet many other of their informations (presentations), of the truth of which it is manifestly impossible to doubt: as for example, that I am in this place, seated by the fire, clothed in a winter dressing gown, that I hold in my hands this piece of paper, with other intimations of the same nature. But how could I deny that I possess these hands and this body, and withal escape being classed with persons in a state of insanity, whose brains are so disordered and clouded by dark bilious vapours as to cause them pertinaciously to assert that they are monarchs when they are in the greatest poverty; or clothed in gold and purple when destitute of any covering; or that their head is made of clay, their body of glass, or that they are gourds? I should certainly be not less insane than they, were I to regulate my procedure according to examples so extravagant.

Though this be true, I must nevertheless here consider that I am a man, and that, consequently, I am in the habit of sleeping, and representing to myself in dreams those same things, or even sometimes others less probable, which the insane think are presented to them in their waking moments. How often have I dreamt that I was in these familiar circumstances, that I was dressed and occupied this place by the fire, when I was lying undressed in bed? At the present moment, however, I certainly look upon this paper with eyes wide awake; the head which I now move is not asleep; I extend this hand consciously and with express purpose, and I perceive it; the occurrences in sleep are not so distinct as all this. But I cannot forget that, at other times, I have been deceived in sleep by similar illusions; and, attentively considering those cases, I perceive so clearly that there exist no certain marks by which the state of waking can ever be distinguished from sleep, that I feel greatly astonished; and in amazement I almost persuade myself that I am now dreaming.

Let us suppose, then, that we are dreaming, and that all these particulars—namely, the opening of the eyes, the motion of the head, the forth-putting of the hands—are merely illusions, and even that we really possess neither an entire body nor hands such as we see. Nevertheless it must be admitted at least that the objects which appear to us in sleep are, as it were, painted representations, which could not have been formed unless in the likeness of realities, and, therefore, that those general objects, at all events, namely, eyes, a head, hands, and an entire body, are not simply imaginary, but really existent. For, in truth, painters themselves, even when they study to represent sirens and satyrs by forms the most fantastic and extraordinary, cannot bestow upon them natures absolutely new, but can only make a certain medley of the members of different animals; or if they chance to imagine something so novel that nothing at all similar has ever been seen before, and such as is, therefore, purely fictitious and absolutely

false, it is at least certain that the colours of which this is composed are real.

And on the same principle, although these general objects, viz., a body, eyes, a head, hands, and the like, be imaginary, we are nevertheless absolutely necessitated to admit the reality at least of some other objects still more simple and universal than these, of which, just as of certain real colours, all those images of things, whether true and real, or false and fantastic, that are found in our consciousness (*cogitatio*) are formed.

To this class of objects seem to belong corporeal nature in general and its extension: the figure of extended things, their quantity or magnitude, and their number, as also the place in, and the time during, which they exist, and other things of the same sort. We will not, therefore, perhaps reason illegitimately if we conclude from this that Physics, Astronomy, Medicine, and all the other sciences that have for their end the consideration of composite objects are indeed of a doubtful character, but that Arithmetic, Geometry, and the other sciences of the same class, which regard merely the simplest and most general objects, and scarcely inquire whether or not these are really existent, contain somewhat that is certain and indubitable: for whether I am awake or dreaming, it remains true that two and three make five, and that a square has but four sides; nor does it seem possible that truths so apparent can ever fall under a suspicion of falsity or incertitude.

Nevertheless, the belief that there is a God who is all powerful, and who created me, such as I am, has, for a long time, obtained steady possession of my mind. How, then, do I know that he has not arranged that there should be neither earth, nor sky, nor any extended thing, nor figure, nor magnitude, nor place, providing at the same time, however, for the rise in me of the perceptions of all these objects, and the persuasion that these do not exist otherwise than as I perceive them? And further, as I sometimes think that others are in error respecting matters of which they believe themselves to possess a perfect knowledge, how do I know that I am not also deceived each time I add together two and three, or number the sides of a square, or form some judgment still more simple, if more simple indeed can be imagined? But perhaps Deity has not been willing that I should be thus deceived, for he is said to be supremely good. If, however, it were repugnant to the goodness of Deity to have created me subject to constant deception, it would seem likewise to be contrary to his goodness to allow me to be occasionally deceived; and yet it is clear that this is permitted. Some, indeed, might perhaps be found who would be disposed rather to deny the existence of a Being so powerful than to believe that there is nothing certain. But let us for the present refrain from opposing this opinion, and grant that all which is here said of a Deity is fabulous: nevertheless, in whatever way it be supposed that I reached the state in which I exist, whether by fate, or chance, or by an endless series of antecedents and consequents, or by any other means, it is clear (since to be deceived and to err is a certain defect) that the probability of my being so imperfect as to be the constant victim of deception will be increased exactly in proportion as the power possessed by the cause to which they assign my origin is lessened. To these reasonings I have assuredly nothing to reply, but am constrained at last to avow that there is nothing of all that I formerly believed to be true of which it is impossible to doubt, and that not through thoughtlessness or levity, but from cogent and maturely considered reasons; so that henceforward, if I desire to discover anything certain, I ought not the less carefully to refrain from assenting to those same opinions than to what might be shown to be manifestly false.

But it is not sufficient to have made these observations; care must be taken likewise to keep them in remembrance. For those old and customary opinions perpetually recur—long and familiar usage giving them the right of occupying my mind, even almost against my will, and subduing my belief; nor will I lose the habit of deferring to them and confiding in them so long as I shall consider them to be what in truth they are, viz., opinions to some extent doubtful, as I have already shown, but still highly probable, and such as it is much more reasonable to believe than deny. It is for this reason

I am persuaded that I shall not be doing wrong, if, taking an opposite judgment of deliberate design, I become my own deceiver, by supposing, for a time, that all those opinions are entirely false and imaginary, until at length, having thus balanced my old by my new prejudices, my judgment shall no longer be turned aside by perverted usage from the path that may conduct to the perception of truth. For I am assured that, meanwhile, there will arise neither peril nor error from this course, and that I cannot for the present yield too much to distrust, since the end I now seek is not action but knowledge.

I will suppose, then, not that Deity, who is sovereignly good and the fountain of truth, but that some malignant demon, who is at once exceedingly potent and deceitful, has employed all his artifice to deceive me; I will suppose that the sky, the air, the earth, colours, figures, sounds, and all external things are nothing better than the illusions of dreams, by means of which this being has laid snares for my credulity; I will consider myself as without hands, eyes, flesh, blood, or any of the senses, and as falsely believing that I am possessed of these; I will continue resolutely fixed in this belief, and if indeed by this means it be not in my power to arrive at the knowledge of truth, I shall at least do what is in my power, viz., suspend my judgment, and guard with settled purpose against giving my assent to what is false and being imposed upon by this deceiver, whatever be his power and artifice.

But this undertaking is arduous, and a certain indolence insensibly leads me back to my ordinary course of life; and just as the captive, who, perchance, was enjoying in his dreams an imaginary liberty when he begins to suspect that it is but a vision, dreads awakening and conspires with the agreeable illusions that the deception may be prolonged, so I, of my own accord, fall back into the train of my former beliefs and fear to arouse myself from my slumber, lest the time of laborious wakefulness that would succeed this quiet rest, in place of bringing any light of day, should prove inadequate to dispel the darkness that will arise from the difficulties that have now been raised.

## Meditation II: Of the Nature of the Human Mind; and That It Is More Easily Known Than the Body

The Meditation of yesterday has filled my mind with so many doubts that it is no longer in my power to forget them. Nor do I see, meanwhile, any principle on which they can be resolved; and, just as if I had fallen all of a sudden into very deep water, I am so greatly disconcerted as to be unable either to plant my feet firmly on the bottom or sustain myself by swimming on the surface. I will, nevertheless, make an effort, and try anew the same path on which I had entered yesterday, that is, proceed by casting aside all that admits of the slightest doubt, not less than if I had discovered it to be absolutely false; and I will continue always in this track until I shall find something that is certain, or at least, if I can do nothing more, until I shall know with certainty that there is nothing certain. **Archimedes**, that he might transport the entire globe from the place it occupied to another, demanded only a point that was firm and immovable; so, also, I shall be entitled to entertain the highest expectations, if I am fortunate enough to discover only one thing that is certain and indubitable.

I suppose, accordingly, that all the things which I see are false (fictitious); I believe that none of those objects which my fallacious memory represents ever existed; I suppose that I possess no senses; I believe that body, figure, extension, motion, and place are merely fictions of my mind. What is there, then, that can be esteemed true? Perhaps this only, that there is absolutely nothing certain.

But how do I know that there is not something different altogether from the objects I have now enumerated, of which it is impossible to entertain the slightest doubt? Is there not a God, or some being, by whatever name I may designate him, who causes these thoughts to arise in my mind? But why suppose such a being, for it may be I myself am capable of producing them? Am I, then, at least not something? But I before denied that I possessed senses or a body; I hesitate, however, for what follows from that? Am I so dependent on the body and the senses that without these I cannot exist? But I had the persuasion that there was absolutely nothing in the world, that there was no sky and no earth, neither minds nor bodies; was I not, therefore, at the same time, persuaded that I did not exist? Far from it; I assuredly existed, since I was persuaded. But there is I know not what being, who is possessed at once of the highest power and the deepest cunning, who is constantly employing all his ingenuity in deceiving me. Doubtless, then, I exist, since I am deceived; and, let him deceive me as he may, he can never bring it about that I am nothing, so long as I shall be conscious that I am something. So that it must, in fine, be maintained, all things being maturely and carefully considered, that this proposition (*pronunciatum*) I am, I exist, is necessarily true each time it is expressed by me, or conceived in my mind.

But I do not yet know with sufficient clearness what I am, though assured that I am; and hence, in the next place, I must take care, lest perchance I inconsiderately substitute some other object in room of what is properly myself, and thus wander from truth, even in that knowledge (cognition) which I hold to be of all others the most certain and evident. For this reason, I will now consider anew what I formerly believed myself to be, before I entered on the present train of thought; and of my previous opinion I will retrench all that can in the least be invalidated by the grounds of doubt I have adduced, in order that there may at length remain nothing but what is certain and indubitable. What then did I formerly think I was? Undoubtedly I judged that I was a man. But what is a man? Shall I say a rational animal? Assuredly not; for it would be necessary forthwith to inquire into what is meant by animal, and what by rational, and thus, from a single question, I should insensibly glide into others, and these more difficult than the first; nor do I now possess enough of leisure to warrant me in wasting my time amid subtleties of this sort. I prefer here to attend to the thoughts that sprung up of themselves in my mind, and were inspired by my own nature alone, when I applied myself to the consideration of what I was. In the first place, then, I thought that I possessed a countenance, hands, arms, and all the fabric of members that appears in a corpse, and which I called by the name of body. It further occurred to me that I was nourished, that I walked, perceived, and thought, and all those actions I referred to the soul; but what the soul itself was I either did not stay to consider, or, if I did, I imagined that it was something extremely rare and subtle, like wind, or flame, or ether, spread through my grosser parts. As regarded the body, I did not even doubt of its nature, but thought I distinctly knew it, and if I had wished to describe it according to the notions I then entertained, I should have explained myself in this manner: By body I understand all that can be terminated by a certain figure; that can be comprised in a certain place, and so fill a certain space as therefrom to exclude every other body; that can be perceived either by touch, sight, hearing, taste, or smell; that can be moved in different ways, not indeed of itself, but by something foreign to it by which it is touched and from which it receives the impression; for the power of self-motion, as likewise that of perceiving and thinking, I held as by no means pertaining to the nature of body; on the contrary, I was somewhat astonished to find such faculties existing in some bodies.

But as to myself, what can I now say that I am, since I suppose there exists an extremely powerful, and, if I may so speak, malignant being, whose whole endeavours are directed toward deceiving me? Can I affirm that I possess any one of all those attributes of which I have lately spoken as belonging to the nature of body? After attentively considering them in my own mind, I find none of them that can properly be said to belong to myself. To recount them were idle and tedious. Let us pass, then, to the attributes of the soul. The first mentioned were the powers of nutrition and walking; but, if it be true that I have no body, it is true likewise that I am capable neither of walking nor of being nourished. Perception is another attribute of the soul; but perception too is impossible without the body; besides, I have frequently, during sleep, believed that I perceived objects which I afterward observed I did not in reality perceive. Thinking is another attribute of the soul; and here I discover what properly

belongs to myself. This alone is inseparable from me. I am—I exist: this is certain; but how often? As often as I think; for perhaps it would even happen, if I should wholly cease to think, that I should at the same time altogether cease to be. I now admit nothing that is not necessarily true. I am therefore, precisely speaking, only a thinking thing, that is, a mind (*mens sive animus*), understanding, or reason, terms whose signification was before unknown to me. I am, however, a real thing, and really existent; but what thing? The answer was, a thinking thing. The question now arises, am I aught besides? I will stimulate my imagination with a view to discover whether I am not still something more than a thinking being. Now it is plain I am not the assemblage of members called the human body; I am not a thin and penetrating air diffused through all these members, or wind, or flame, or vapour, or breath, or any of all the things I can imagine; for I supposed that all these were not, and, without changing the supposition, I find that I still feel assured of my existence.

But it is true, perhaps, that those very things which I suppose to be nonexistent because they are unknown to me are not in truth different from myself whom I know. This is a point I cannot determine, and do not now enter into any dispute regarding it. I can only judge of things that are known to me: I am conscious that I exist, and I who know that I exist inquire into what I am. It is, however, perfectly certain that the knowledge of my existence, thus precisely taken, is not dependent on things, the existence of which is as yet unknown to me: and consequently it is not dependent on any of the things I can feign in imagination. Moreover, the phrase itself, I frame an image (*effingo*), reminds me of my error; for I should in truth frame one if I were to imagine myself to be anything, since to imagine is nothing more than to contemplate the figure or image of a corporeal thing; but I already know that I exist, and that it is possible at the same time that all those images, and in general all that relates to the nature of body, are merely dreams or chimeras. From this I discover that it is not more reasonable to say, I will excite my imagination that I may know more distinctly what I am, than to express myself as follows: I am now awake, and perceive something real; but because my perception is not sufficiently clear, I will of express purpose go to sleep that my dreams may represent to me the object of my perception with more truth and clearness. And, therefore, I know that nothing of all that I can embrace in imagination belongs to the knowledge which I have of myself, and that there is need to recall with the utmost care the mind from this mode of thinking, that it may be able to know its own nature with perfect distinctness.

But what, then, am I? A thinking thing, it has been said. But what is a thinking thing? It is a thing that doubts, understands conceives, affirms, denies, wills, refuses; that imagines also, and perceives. Assuredly it is not little, if all these properties belong to my nature. But why should they not belong to it? Am I not that very being who now doubts of almost everything; who, for all that, understands and conceives certain things; who affirms one alone as true, and denies the others; who desires to know more of them, and does not wish to be deceived; who imagines many things, sometimes even despite his will; and is likewise percipient of many, as if through the medium of the senses. Is there nothing of all this as true as that I am, even although I should be always dreaming, and although he who gave me being employed all his ingenuity to deceive me? Is there also any one of these attributes that can be properly distinguished from my thought, or that can be said to be separate from myself? For it is of itself so evident that it is I who doubt, I who understand, and I who desire, that it is here unnecessary to add anything by way of rendering it more clear. And I am as certainly the same being who imagines; for although it may be (as I before supposed) that nothing I imagine is true, still the power of imagination does not cease really to exist in me and to form part of my thought. In fine, I am the same being who perceives, that is, who apprehends certain objects as by the organs of sense, since, in truth, I see light, hear a noise, and feel heat. But it will be said that these presentations are false, and that I am dreaming. Let it be so. At all events it is certain that I seem to see light, hear a noise, and feel heat; this cannot be false, and this is what in me is properly called perceiving (*sentire*), which is nothing else than thinking. From this I begin to know what I am with somewhat greater clearness and distinctness than heretofore.

But, nevertheless, it still seems to me, and I cannot help believing, that corporeal things, whose images are formed by thought which fall under the senses, and are examined by the same, are known with much greater distinctness than that I know not what part of myself which is not imaginable; although, in truth, it may seem strange to say that I know and comprehend with greater distinctness things whose existence appears to me doubtful, that are unknown, and do not belong to me, than others of whose reality I am persuaded, that are known to me, and appertain to my proper nature; in a word, than myself. But I see clearly what is the state of the case. My mind is apt to wander, and will not yet submit to be restrained within the limits of truth. Let us therefore leave the mind to itself once more, and, according to it every kind of liberty permit it to consider the objects that appear to it from without, in order that, having afterward withdrawn it from these gently and opportunely and fixed it on the consideration of its being and the properties it finds in itself, it may then be the more easily controlled.

Let us now accordingly consider the objects that are commonly thought to be the most easily, and likewise the most distinctly known, viz., the bodies we touch and see—not, indeed, bodies in general, for these general notions are usually somewhat more confused, but one body in particular. Take, for example, this piece of wax: it is quite fresh, having been but recently taken from the beehive; it has not yet lost the sweetness of the honey it contained; it still retains somewhat of the odour of the flowers from which it was gathered; its colour, figure, size are apparent (to the sight); it is hard, cold, easily handled; and sounds when struck upon with the finger. In fine, all that contributes to make a body as distinctly known as possible is found in the one before us. But, while I am speaking, let it be placed near the fire—what remained of the taste exhales, the smell evaporates, the colour changes, its figure is destroyed, its size increases, it becomes liquid, it grows hot, it can hardly be handled, and, although struck upon, it emits no sound. Does the same wax still remain after this change? It must be admitted that it does remain; no one doubts it, or judges otherwise. What, then, was it I knew with so much distinctness in the piece of wax? Assuredly, it could be nothing of all that I observed by means of the senses, since all the things that fell under taste, smell, sight, touch, and hearing are changed, and yet the same wax remains. It was perhaps what I now think, viz., that this wax was neither the sweetness of honey, the pleasant odour of flowers, the whiteness, the figure, nor the sound, but only a body that a little before appeared to me conspicuous under these forms, and which is now perceived under others. But, to speak precisely, what is it that I imagine when I think of it in this way? Let it be attentively considered, and, retrenching all that does not belong to the wax, let us see what remains. There certainly remains nothing, except something extended, flexible, and movable. But what is meant by flexible and movable? Is it not that I imagine that the piece of wax, being round, is capable of becoming square, or of passing from a square into a triangular figure? Assuredly such is not the case, because I conceive that it admits of an infinity of similar changes; and I am, moreover, unable to compass this infinity by imagination, and consequently this conception which I have of the wax is not the product of the faculty of imagination. But what now is this extension? Is it not also unknown? For it becomes greater when the wax is melted, greater when it is boiled, and greater still when the heat increases; and I should not conceive clearly and according to truth the wax as it is, if I did not suppose that the piece we are considering admitted even of a wider variety of extension than I ever imagined. I must, therefore, admit that I cannot even comprehend by imagination what the piece of wax is, and that it is the mind alone (*mens*, Lat., *entendement*, F.) which perceives it. I speak of one piece in particular; for as to wax in general, this is still more evident. But what is the piece of wax that can be perceived only by the understanding or mind? It is certainly the same which I see, touch,

imagine; and, in fine, it is the same which, from the beginning, I believed it to be. But (and this it is of moment to observe) the perception of it is neither an act of sight, of touch, nor of imagination, and never was either of these, though it might formerly seem so, but is simply an intuition (*inspectio*) of the mind, which may be imperfect and confused, as it formerly was, or very clear and distinct, as it is at present, according as the attention is more or less directed to the elements which it contains, and of which it is composed.

But, meanwhile, I feel greatly astonished when I observe the weakness of my mind, and its proneness to error. For although, without at all giving expression to what I think, I consider all this in my own mind, words yet occasionally impede my progress, and I am almost led into error by the terms of ordinary language. We say, for example, that we see the same wax when it is before us, and not that we judge it to be the same from its retaining the same colour and figure: whence I should forthwith be disposed to conclude that the wax is known by the act of sight, and not by the intuition of the mind alone, were it not for the analogous instance of human beings passing on in the street below, as observed from a window. In this case I do not fail to say that I see the men themselves, just as I say that I see the wax; and yet what do I see from the window beyond hats and cloaks that might cover artificial machines, whose motions might be determined by springs? But I judge that there are human beings from these appearances, and thus I comprehend, by the faculty of judgment alone which is in the mind, what I believed I saw with my eyes.

The man who makes it his aim to rise to knowledge superior to the common ought to be ashamed to seek occasions of doubting from the vulgar forms of speech: instead, therefore, of doing this, I shall proceed with the matter in hand, and inquire whether I had a clearer and more perfect perception of the piece of wax when I first saw it, and when I thought I knew it by means of the external sense itself, or, at all events, by the common sense (*sensus communis*), as it is called, that is, by the imaginative faculty; or whether I rather apprehend it more clearly at present, after having examined with greater care, both what it is, and in what way it can be known. It would certainly be ridiculous to entertain any doubt on this point. For what, in that first perception, was there distinct? What did I perceive which any animal might not have perceived? But when I distinguish the wax from its exterior forms, and when, as if I had stripped it of its vestments, I consider it quite naked, it is certain, although some error may still be found in my judgment, that I cannot, nevertheless, thus apprehend it without possessing a human mind.

But, finally, what shall I say of the mind itself, that is, of myself? For as yet I do not admit that I am anything but mind. What, then! I who seem to possess so distinct an apprehension of the piece of wax, do I not know myself, both with greater truth and certitude, and also much more distinctly and clearly? For if I judge that the wax exists because I see it, it assuredly follows, much more evidently, that I myself am or exist, for the same reason: for it is possible that what I see may not in truth be wax, and that I do not even possess eyes with which to see anything; but it cannot be that when I see, or, which comes to the same thing, when I think I see, I myself who think am nothing. So likewise, if I judge that the wax exists because I touch it, it will still also follow that I am; and if I determine that my imagination, or any other cause, whatever it be, persuades me of the existence of the wax, I will still draw the same conclusion. And what is here remarked of the piece of wax is applicable to all the other things that are external to me. And further, if the notion or perception of wax appeared to me more precise and distinct, after not only sight and touch but many other causes besides rendered it manifest to my apprehension, with how much greater distinctness must I now know myself, since all the reasons that contribute to the knowledge of the nature of wax, or of any body whatever, manifest still better the nature of my mind? And there are, besides, so many other things in the mind itself that contribute to the illustration of its nature that those dependent on the body, to which I have here referred, scarcely merit to be taken into account.

But, in conclusion, I find I have insensibly reverted to the point I desired; for, since it is now manifest to me that bodies themselves are not properly perceived by the senses nor by the faculty of imagination, but by the intellect alone; and since they are not perceived because they are seen and touched, but only because they are understood or rightly comprehended by thought, I readily discover that there is nothing more easily or clearly apprehended than my own mind. But because it is difficult to rid one's self so promptly of an opinion to which one has been long accustomed, it will be desirable to tarry for some time at this stage, that, by long continued meditation, I may more deeply impress upon my memory this new knowledge.

## Study Questions

1. Detail Descartes' employment of methodological scepticism in the *Meditations*: be sure to consider each of the devices he uses and the specific role it plays for him.

2. What is the subject matter of the sciences of arithmetic and geometry?

3. In the second Meditation, Descartes determines the certainty of these two propositions: (i) "I am, I exist"; and (ii) "I am . . . in the strict sense only a thing that thinks, that is, I am a mind, or intelligence, or intellect, or reason." How do these two propositions differ in their philosophical significance?

4. According to Descartes, what is the essence of material things? On what bases does Descartes argue that we arrive at this knowledge through reason, not through our senses or imagination?

# George Berkeley

George Berkeley (1685–1753) was born near Kilkenny, Ireland, and completed his education at Trinity College, Dublin. Berkeley's best-known works, including *Three Dialogues*, arose in critical response to the writings of Descartes, Locke, and other modern philosophers while he was a fellow at Trinity College between 1707 and 1724. An ordained Anglican priest, Berkeley was appointed dean of Derry in 1724 and bishop of Cloyne in 1734. Between 1728 and 1731, Berkeley lived in Rhode Island, waiting in vain for a promised parliamentary grant in support of his planned seminary in Bermuda.—JF

## From *Three Dialogues between Hylas and Philonous, in Opposition to Skeptics and Atheists*

### The First Dialogue

PHILONOUS. Good morrow, Hylas: I did not expect to find you abroad so early.

HYLAS. It is indeed something unusual: but my thoughts were so taken up with a subject I was discoursing of last night that finding I could not sleep, I resolved to rise and take a turn in the garden.

P. It happened well, to let you see what innocent and agreeable pleasures you lose every morning. Can there be a pleasanter time of the day, or a more delightful season of the year? That purple sky, those wild but sweet notes of birds, the fragrant bloom upon the trees and flowers, the gentle influence of the rising sun, these and a thousand nameless beauties of nature inspire the soul with secret transports; its faculties too, being at this time fresh and lively, are fit for these meditations, which the solitude of a garden and tranquillity of the morning naturally dispose us to. But I am afraid I interrupt your thoughts; for you seemed very intent on something.

H. It is true, I was, and shall be obliged to you if you will permit me to go on in the same vein; not that I would by any means deprive myself of your company, for my thoughts always flow more easily in conversation with a friend than when I am alone: but my request is, that you would suffer me to impart my reflections to you.

P. With all my heart, it is what I should have requested myself, if you had not prevented me.

H. I was considering the odd fate of those men who have in all ages, through an affectation of being distinguished from the vulgar, or some unaccountable turn of thought, pretended either to believe nothing at all, or believe the most extravagant things in the world. This however might be borne, if their paradoxes and skepticism did not draw after them some consequences of general disadvantage to mankind. But the mischief lieth here: that when men of less leisure see them who are supposed to have spent their whole time in the pursuits of knowledge professing an entire ignorance of all things, or advancing such notions as are repugnant to plain and commonly received principles, they will be tempted to entertain suspicions concerning the most important truths, which they had hitherto held sacred and unquestionable.

P. I entirely agree with you, as to the ill tendency of the affected doubts of some philosophers, and fantastical conceits of others. I am even so far gone of late in this way of thinking that I have quitted several of the sublime notions I had got in their schools for vulgar opinions. And I give it you on my word, since this revolt from metaphysical notions to the plain dictates of nature and common sense, I find my understanding strangely enlightened, so that I can now easily comprehend a great many things which before were all mystery and riddle.

H. I am glad to find there was nothing in the accounts I heard of you.

P. Pray, what were those?

H. You were represented in last night's conversation as one who maintained the most extravagant opinion that ever entered into the mind of man, to wit, that there is no such thing as *material substance* in the world.

P. That there is no such thing as what philosophers call *material substance*, I am seriously persuaded: but if I were made to see anything absurd or skeptical in this, I should then have the same reason to renounce this that I imagine I have now to reject the contrary opinion.

H. What! Can anything be more fantastical, more repugnant to common sense, or a more manifest piece of skepticism than to believe there is no such thing as *matter*?

P. Softly, good Hylas. What if it should prove that you, who hold there is, are by virtue of that opinion a greater skeptic, and maintain more paradoxes and repugnancies to common sense, than I who believe no such thing?

H. You may as soon persuade me, the part is greater than the whole as that, in order to avoid absurdity and skepticism, I should ever be obliged to give up my opinion in this point.

P. Well then, are you content to admit that opinion for true, which upon examination shall appear most agreeable to common sense and remote from skepticism?

H. With all my heart. Since you are for raising disputes about the plainest things in nature, I am content for once to hear what you have to say.

P. Pray, Hylas, what do you mean by a *skeptic*?

H. I mean what all men mean, one that doubts of everything.

P. He then who entertains no doubts concerning some particular point, with regard to that point cannot be thought a *skeptic*.

H. I agree with you.

P. Whether doth doubting consist in embracing the affirmative or negative side of a question?

H. In neither; for whoever understands English cannot but know that *doubting* signifies a suspense between both.

P. He then that denieth any point can no more be said to doubt of it than he who affirmeth it with the same degree of assurance.

H. True.

P. And consequently, for such his denial is no more to be esteemed a *skeptic* than the other.

H. I acknowledge it.

P. How cometh it to pass then, Hylas, that you pronounce me a *skeptic* because I deny what you affirm, to wit, the existence of matter? Since, for aught you can tell, I am as peremptory in my denial, as you in your affirmation.

H. Hold, Philonous, I have been a little out in my definition; but every false step a man makes in discourse is not to be insisted on. I said, indeed, that a *skeptic* was one who doubted of everything; but I should have added, or who denies the reality and truth of things.

P. What things? Do you mean the principles and theorems of sciences? But these you know are universal intellectual notions, and consequently independent of matter; the denial therefore of this doth not imply the denying them.

H. I grant it. But are there no other things? What think you of distrusting the senses, of denying the real existence of sensible things, or pretending to know nothing of them? Is not this sufficient to denominate a man a *skeptic*?

P. Shall we therefore examine which of us it is that denies the reality of sensible things, or professes the greatest ignorance of them, since, if I take you rightly, he is to be esteemed the greatest *skeptic*?

H. That is what I desire.

P. What mean you by sensible things?

H. Those things which are perceived by the senses. Can you imagine that I mean anything else?

P. Pardon me, Hylas, if I am desirous clearly to apprehend your notions, since this may much shorten our inquiry. Suffer me then to ask you this further question. Are those things only perceived by the senses which are perceived immediately? Or may those things properly be said to be *sensible* which are perceived mediately, or not without the intervention of others?

H. I do not sufficiently understand you.

P. In reading a book, what I immediately perceive are the letters, but mediately, or by means of these, are suggested to my mind the notions of God, virtue, truth, etc. Now that the letters are truly sensible things, or perceived by sense, there is no doubt: but I would know whether you take the things suggested by them to be so too.

H. No, certainly, it were absurd to think *God* or *virtue* sensible things, though they may be signified and suggested to the mind by sensible marks, with which they have an arbitrary connection.

P. It seems, then, that by *sensible things* you mean those only which can be perceived immediately by sense.

H. Right.

P. Doth it not follow from this that though I see one part of the sky red, and another blue, and that my reason doth thence evidently conclude there must be some cause of that diversity of colours, yet that cause cannot be said to be a sensible thing, or perceived by the sense of seeing?

H. It doth.

P. In like manner, though I hear variety of sounds, yet I cannot be said to hear the causes of those sounds.

H. You cannot.

P. And when by my touch I perceive a thing to be hot and heavy, I cannot say with any truth or propriety that I feel the cause of its heat or weight?

H. To prevent any more questions of this kind, I tell you once for all that by *sensible things* I mean those only which are perceived by sense, and that in truth the senses perceive nothing which they do not perceive immediately: for they make no inferences. The deducing therefore of causes or occasions from effects and appearances, which alone are perceived by sense, entirely relates to reason.

P. This point then is agreed between us, that *sensible things are those only which are immediately perceived by sense*. You will further inform me, whether we immediately perceive by sight anything beside light, and colours, and figures: or by hearing anything but sounds: by the palate, anything beside tastes: by the smell, besides odours: or by the touch, more than tangible qualities.

H. We do not.

P. It seems, therefore, that if you take away all sensible qualities, there remains nothing sensible.

H. I grant it.

P. Sensible things therefore are nothing else but so many sensible qualities, or combinations of sensible qualities.

H. Nothing else.

P. Heat then is a sensible thing.

H. Certainly.

P. Doth the reality of sensible things consist in being perceived? Or is it something distinct from their being perceived, and that bears no relation to the mind?

H. To *exist* is one thing, and to be *perceived* is another.

P. I speak with regard to sensible things only; and of these I ask, whether by their real existence you mean a subsistence exterior to the mind, and distinct from their being perceived?

H. I mean a real absolute being, distinct from, and without any relation to their being perceived.

P. Heat, therefore, if it be allowed a real being, must exist without the mind.

H. It must. [. . .]

P. Can any doctrine be true that necessarily leads a man into an absurdity?

H. Without doubt it cannot.

P. Is it not an absurdity to think that the same thing should be at the same time both cold and warm?

H. It is.

P. Suppose now one of your hands hot and the other cold, and that they are both at once put into the same vessel of water in an intermediate state; will not the water seem cold to one hand and warm to the other?

H. It will.

P. Ought we not therefore by your principles to conclude, it is really both cold and warm at the same time, that is, according to your own concession, to believe an absurdity?

H. I confess it seems so.

P. Consequently, the principles themselves are false, since you have granted that no true principle leads to an absurdity.

H. But after all, can anything be more absurd than to say, *there is no heat in the fire*?

P. To make the point still clearer; tell me, whether in two cases exactly alike, we ought not to make the same judgment?

H. We ought.

P. When a pin pricks your finger, doth it not rend and divide the fibres of your flesh?

H. It doth.

P. And when a coal burns your finger, doth it any more?

H. It doth not.

P. Since therefore you neither judge the sensation itself occasioned by the pin nor anything like it to be in the pin, you should not, conformably to what you have now granted, judge the sensation occasioned by the fire or anything like it to be in the fire.

H. Well, since it must be so, I am content to yield this point, and acknowledge that heat and cold are only sensations existing in our minds: but there still remain qualities enough to secure the reality of external things.

P. But what will you say, Hylas, if it shall appear that the case is the same with regard to all other sensible qualities, and that they can no more be supposed to exist without the mind than heat and cold?

H. Then indeed you will have done something to the purpose; but that is what I despair of seeing proved.

P. Let us examine them in order. What think you of tastes, do they exist without the mind, or no?

H. Can any man in his senses doubt whether sugar is sweet, or wormwood bitter?

P. Inform me, Hylas. Is a sweet taste a particular kind of pleasure or pleasant sensation, or is it not?

H. It is.

P. And is not bitterness some kind of uneasiness or pain?

H. I grant it.

P. If therefore sugar and wormwood are unthinking corporeal substances existing without the mind, how can sweetness and bitterness, that is, pleasure and pain, agree to them?

H. Hold, Philonous; I now see what it was deluded me all this time. You asked whether heat and cold, sweetness and bitterness, were not particular sorts of pleasure and pain; to which I answered simply, that they were. Whereas I should have thus distinguished: those qualities, as perceived by us, are pleasures or pains, but not as existing in the external objects. We must not therefore conclude absolutely that there is no heat in the fire, or sweetness in the sugar, but only that heat or sweetness, as perceived by us, are not in the fire or sugar. What say you to this?

P. I say it is nothing to the purpose. Our discourse proceeded altogether concerning sensible things, which you defined to be the things we *immediately perceive by our senses*. Whatever other qualities therefore you speak of, as distinct from these, I know nothing of them, neither do they at all belong to the point in dispute. You may indeed pretend to have discovered certain qualities which you do not perceive, and assert those insensible qualities exist in fire and sugar. But what use can be made of this to your present purpose, I am at a loss to conceive. Tell me then once more, do you acknowledge that heat and cold, sweetness and bitterness (meaning those qualities which are perceived by the senses), do not exist without the mind?

H. I see it is to no purpose to hold out, so I give up the cause as to those mentioned qualities. Though I profess it sounds oddly to say that sugar is not sweet.

P. But for your further satisfaction, take this along with you: that which at other times seems sweet shall to a distempered palate appear bitter. And nothing can be plainer than that diverse persons perceive different tastes in the same food, since that which one man delights in, another abhors. And how could this be, if the taste was something really inherent in the food?

H. I acknowledge I know not how.

P. In the next place, odours are to be considered. And with regard to these, I would fain know, whether what hath been said of tastes doth not exactly agree to them? Are they not so many pleasing or displeasing sensations?

H. They are.

P. Can you then conceive it possible that they should exist in an unperceiving thing?

H. I cannot.

P. Or can you imagine that filth and ordure affect those brute animals that feed on them out of choice with the same smells which we perceive in them?

H. By no means.

P. May we not therefore conclude of smells, as of the other forementioned qualities, that they cannot exist in any but a perceiving substance or mind?

H. I think so.

P. Then as to sounds, what must we think of them: are they accidents really inherent in external bodies, or not?

H. That they inhere not in the sonorous bodies is plain from hence: because a bell struck in the exhausted receiver of an air-pump sends forth no sound. The air therefore must be thought the subject of sound.

P. What reason is there for that, Hylas?

H. Because when any motion is raised in the air, we perceive a sound greater or lesser, according to the air's motion; but without some motion in the air, we never hear any sound at all.

P. And granting that we never hear a sound but when some motion is produced in the air, yet I do not see how you can infer from thence that the sound itself is in the air.

H. It is this very motion in the external air that produces in the mind the sensation of *sound*. For striking on the drum of the ear, it causeth a vibration, which by the auditory nerves being communicated to the brain, the soul is thereupon affected with the sensation called *sound*.

P. What! Is sound then a sensation?

H. I tell you, as perceived by us, it is a particular sensation in the mind.

P. And can any sensation exist without the mind?

H. No, certainly.

P. How then can sound, being a sensation, exist in the air, if by the *air* you mean a senseless substance existing without the mind.

H. You must distinguish, Philonous, between sound, as it is perceived by us, and as it is in itself; or, (which is the same thing) between the sound we immediately perceive, and that which exists without us. The former indeed is a particular kind of sensation, but the latter is merely a vibrative or undulatory motion in the air.

P. I thought I had already obviated that distinction by the answer I gave when you were applying it in a like case before. But to say no more of that: are you sure then that sound is really nothing but motion?

H. I am.

P. Whatever therefore agrees to real sound may with truth be attributed to motion.

H. It may.

P. It is then good sense to speak of *motion*, as of a thing that is *loud*, *sweet*, *acute*, or *grave*.

H. I see you are resolved not to understand me. Is it not evident, those accidents or modes belong only to sensible sound, or *sound* in the common acceptation of the word, but not to *sound* in the real and philosophic sense, which, as I just now told you, is nothing but a certain motion of the air?

P. It seems then there are two sorts of sound, the one vulgar, or that which is heard, the other philosophical and real.

H. Even so.

P. And the latter consists in motion.

H. I told you so before.

P. Tell me, Hylas, to which of the senses, think you, the idea of motion belongs: to the hearing?

H. No, certainly, but to the sight and touch.

P. It should follow, then, that according to you, real sounds may possibly be *seen* or *felt*, but never *heard*.

H. Look you, Philonous, you may if you please make a jest of my opinion, but that will not alter the truth of things. I own, indeed, the inferences you draw me into sound something oddly: but common language, you know, is framed by, and for, the use of the vulgar: we must not therefore wonder if expressions adapted to exact philosophic notions seem uncouth and out of the way.

P. Is it come to that? I assure you, I imagine myself to have gained no small point since you make so light of departing from common phrases and opinions, it being a main part of our inquiry to examine whose notions are widest of the common road, and most repugnant to the general sense of the world. But can you think it no more than a philosophical paradox to say that *real sounds are never heard*, and that the idea of them is obtained by some other sense. And is there nothing in this contrary to nature and the truth of things?

H. To deal ingenuously, I do not like it. And after the concessions already made, I had as well grant that sounds too have no real being without the mind.

P. And I hope you will make no difficulty to acknowledge the same of colours.

H. Pardon me; the case of colours is very different. Can anything be plainer than that we see them on the objects? [. . .]

P. What! Are then the beautiful red and purple we see on yonder clouds really in them? Or do you imagine they have in themselves any other form than that of a dark mist or vapour?

H. I must own, Philonous, those colours are not really in the clouds as they seem to be at this distance. They are only apparent colours.

P. *Apparent* call you them? How shall we distinguish these apparent colours from real?

H. Very easily. Those are to be thought apparent which, appearing only at a distance, vanish upon a nearer approach.

P. And those I suppose are to be thought real, which are discovered by the most near and exact survey.

H. Right.

P. Is the nearest and exactest survey made by the help of a microscope, or by the naked eye?

H. By a microscope, doubtless.

P. But a microscope often discovers colours in an object different from those perceived by the unassisted sight. And in case we had microscopes magnifying to any assigned degree, it is certain that no object whatsoever viewed through them would appear in the same colour which it exhibits to the naked eye.

H. And what will you conclude from all this? You cannot argue that there are really and naturally no colours on objects because by artificial managements they may be altered, or made to vanish.

P. I think it may evidently be concluded from your own concessions that all the colours we see with our naked eyes are only apparent as those on the clouds since they vanish upon a more close and accurate inspection which is afforded us by a microscope. Then as to what you say by way of prevention, I ask you, whether the real and natural state of an object is better discovered by a very sharp and piercing sight, or by one which is less sharp.

H. By the former without doubt.

P. Is it not plain from *dioptrics* that microscopes make the sight more penetrating, and represent objects as they would appear to the eye in case it were naturally endowed with a most exquisite sharpness?

H. It is.

P. Consequently the microscopical representation is to be thought that which best sets forth the real nature of the thing, or what it is in itself. The colours therefore by it perceived are more genuine and real than those perceived otherwise. [. . .]

H. I frankly own, Philonous, that it is in vain to stand out any longer. Colours, sounds, tastes, in a word, all those termed *secondary qualities*, have certainly no existence without the mind. But by this acknowledgment I must not be supposed to derogate anything from the reality of matter or external objects, seeing it is no more than several philosophers maintain, who nevertheless are the furthest imaginable from denying matter. For the clearer understanding of this, you must know sensible qualities are by philosophers divided into *primary* and *secondary*. The former are extension, figure, solidity, gravity, motion, and rest. And these they hold exist really in bodies. The latter are those above enumerated, or briefly, all sensible qualities beside the primary, which they assert are only so many sensations or ideas existing nowhere but in the mind. But all this, I doubt not, you are already apprised of. For my part, I have been a long time sensible there was such an opinion current among philosophers, but was never thoroughly convinced of its truth till now.

P. You are still then of opinion that extension and figures are inherent in external unthinking substances.

H. I am.

P. But what if the same arguments which are brought against secondary qualities will hold proof against these also?

H. Why then I shall be obliged to think, they too exist only in the mind.

P. Is it your opinion, the very figure and extension which you perceive by sense exist in the outward object or material substance?

H. It is.

P. Have all other animals as good grounds to think the same of the figure and extension which they see and feel?

H. Without doubt, if they have any thought at all.

P. Answer me, Hylas. Think you the senses were bestowed upon all animals for their preservation and well-being in life? Or were they given to men alone for this end?

H. I make no question but they have the same use in all other animals.

P. If so, is it not necessary they should be enabled by them to perceive their own limbs, and those bodies which are capable of harming them?

H. Certainly.

P. A mite therefore must be supposed to see his own foot, and things equal or even less than it, as bodies of some considerable dimension; though at the same time they appear to you scarce discernible, or at best as so many visible points.

H. I cannot deny it.

P. And to creatures less than the mite they will seem yet larger.

H. They will.

P. Insomuch that what you can hardly discern will to another extremely minute animal appear as some huge mountain.

H. All this I grant.

P. Can one and the same thing be at the same time in itself of different dimensions?

H. That were absurd to imagine.

P. But from what you have laid down it follows that both the extension by you perceived and that perceived by the mite itself, as likewise all those perceived by lesser animals, are each of them the true extension of the mite's foot, that is to say, by your own principles you are led into an absurdity.

H. There seems to be some difficulty in the point.

P. Again, have you not acknowledged that no real inherent property of any object can be changed without some change in the thing itself?

H. I have.

P. But as we approach to or recede from an object, the visible extension varies, being at one distance ten or a hundred times greater than at another. Doth it not therefore follow from hence likewise that it is not really inherent in the object?

H. I own I am at a loss what to think.

P. Your judgment will soon be determined, if you will venture to think as freely concerning this quality as you have done concerning the rest. Was it not admitted as a good argument that neither heat nor cold was in the water because it seemed warm to one hand and cold to the other?

H. It was.

P. Is it not the very same reasoning to conclude, there is no extension or figure in an object because to one eye it shall seem little, smooth, and round, when at the same time it appears to the other, great, uneven, and angular?

H. The very same. But does this latter fact ever happen?

P. You may at any time make the experiment by looking with one eye bare, and with the other through a microscope.

H. I know not how to maintain it, and yet I am loath to give up *extension*; I see so many odd consequences following upon such a concession.

P. Odd, say you? After the concessions already made, I hope you will stick at nothing for its oddness. But on the other hand should it not seem very odd, if the general reasoning which includes all other sensible qualities did not also include extension? If it be allowed that no idea nor anything like an idea can exist in an unperceiving substance, then surely it follows that no figure or mode of extension, which we can either perceive or imagine, or have any idea of, can be really inherent in matter—not to mention the peculiar difficulty there must be in conceiving a material substance, prior to and distinct from extension, to be the *substratum* of extension. Be the sensible quality what it will—figure, or sound, or colour, it seems alike impossible it should subsist in that which doth not perceive it.

H. I give up the point for the present, reserving still a right to retract my opinion, in case I shall hereafter discover any false step in my progress to it.

P. That is a right you cannot be denied. Figures and extension being dispatched, we proceed next to *motion*. Can a real motion in any external body be at the same time both very swift and very slow?

H. It cannot.

P. Is not the motion of a body swift in a reciprocal proportion to the time it takes up in describing any given space? Thus a body that describes a mile in an hour moves three times faster than it would in case it described only a mile in three hours.

H. I agree with you.

P. And is not time measured by the succession of ideas in our minds?

H. It is.

P. And is it not possible ideas should succeed one another twice as fast in your mind as they do in mine, or in that of some spirit of another kind?

H. I own it.

P. Consequently the same body may to another seem to perform its motion over any space in half the time that it doth to you. And the same reasoning will hold as to any other proportion: that is to say, according to your principles (since the motions perceived are both really in the object) it is possible one and the same body shall be really moved the same way at once, both very swift and very slow. How is this consistent either with common sense, or with what you just now granted?

H. I have nothing to say to it.

P. Then as for *solidity*: either you do not mean any sensible quality by that word, and so it is beside our inquiry: or if you do, it must be either hardness or resistance. But both the one and the other are plainly relative to our senses: it being evident that what seems hard to one animal may appear soft to another, who hath greater force and firmness of limbs. Nor is it less plain that the resistance I feel is not in the body.

H. I own the very sensation of resistance, which is all you immediately perceive, is not in the *body*, but the cause of that sensation is.

P. But the causes of our sensations are not things immediately perceived, and therefore not sensible. This point I thought had been already determined.

H. I own it was; but you will pardon me if I seem a little embarrassed: I know not how to quit my old notions.

P. To help you out, do but consider that if extension be once acknowledged to have no existence without the mind, the same must necessarily be granted of motion, solidity, and gravity, since they all evidently suppose extension. It is therefore superfluous to inquire particularly concerning each of them. In denying extension, you have denied them all to have any real existence.

## The Second Dialogue

HYLAS. I beg your pardon, Philonous, for not meeting you sooner. All this morning my head was so filled with our late conversation that I had not leisure to think of the time of the day, or indeed of anything else.

PHILONOUS. I am glad you were so intent upon it, in hopes if there were any mistakes in your concessions, or fallacies in my reasonings from them, you will now discover them to me.

H. I assure you, I have done nothing ever since I saw you but search after mistakes and fallacies, and with that view have minutely examined the whole series of yesterday's discourse: but all in vain, for the notions it led me into, upon review, appear still more clear and evident; and the more I consider them, the more irresistibly do they force my assent. [. . .]

P. Well then, are you at length satisfied that no sensible things have a real existence, and that you are in truth an arrant *skeptic*?

H. It is too plain to be denied. [. . .] My comfort is, you are as much a *skeptic* as I am.

P. There, Hylas, I must beg leave to differ from you.

H. What! Have you all along agreed to the premises, and do you now deny the conclusion, and leave me to maintain those paradoxes by myself which you led me into? This surely is not fair.

P. I deny that I agreed with you in those notions that led to skepticism. You indeed said, the reality of sensible things consisted in an *absolute existence* out of the minds of spirits, or distinct from their being perceived. And pursuant to this notion of reality, you are obliged to deny sensible things any real existence: that is, according to your own definition, you profess yourself a *skeptic*. But I neither said nor thought the reality of sensible things was to be defined after that manner. To me it is evident, for the reasons you allow of, that sensible things cannot exist otherwise than in a mind or spirit. Whence I conclude, not that they have no real existence, but that seeing they depend not on my thought, and have all existence distinct from being perceived by me, *there must be some other mind wherein they exist.* As sure therefore as the sensible world really exists, so sure is there an infinite, omnipresent Spirit who contains and supports it.

H. What! This is no more than I and all Christians hold; nay, and all others too who believe there is a God, and that he knows and comprehends all things.

P. Ay, but here lies the difference. Men commonly believe that all things are known or perceived by God because they believe the being of a God, whereas I, on the other side, immediately and necessarily conclude the being of a God because all sensible things must be perceived by him.

H. But so long as we all believe the same thing, what matter is it how we come by that belief?

P. But neither do we agree in the same opinion. For philosophers, though they acknowledge all corporeal beings to be perceived by God, yet they attribute to them an absolute subsistence distinct from their being perceived by any mind whatever, which I do not. [. . .]

## Study Questions

1. Explain the distinction between primary and secondary qualities. Describe one of Philonous's arguments against the mind-independent existence of sensible things that is directed toward a secondary quality. Describe one of Philonous's arguments against the mind-independent existence of sensible things that is directed toward a primary quality.
2. What positions do Berkeley's two characters, Philonous and Hylas, take regarding the claim "*Esse est percipi*" ("To be is to be perceived")?
3. Why is Berkeley considered to be an idealist—specifically, a "subjective idealist"?
4. We have all heard that crazy-sounding question: If a tree falls in the forest and no one is around to hear, does it make a sound? Making reference to the distinction between primary and secondary qualities, explain why this question actually has philosophical depth. What is your response? Justify your response by addressing a likely objection.

---

# David Hume

---

David Hume (1711–76) is considered today to be history's greatest English-language philosopher, but during his lifetime, his reputation as an atheist and skeptic blocked him from holding any academic posts. Employment as Librarian to the Edinburgh Faculty of Advocates during the 1750s offered Hume the opportunity to write his six-volume *History of England*, which became a best-seller and provided him with financial independence. While serving in a diplomatic capacity in Paris during the 1760s, Hume associated with *philosophes* such as Diderot, d'Holbach, and Rousseau. Hume's *Enquiry* recasts arguments from the *Treatise of Human Understanding* in order to reach a wider audience.

## From *An Enquiry Concerning Human Understanding*

### Of the Origin of Ideas [Section 2]

Everyone will readily allow that there is a considerable difference between the perceptions of the mind when a man feels the pain of excessive heat or the pleasure of moderate warmth, and when he afterwards recalls to his memory this sensation or anticipates it by his imagination. These faculties may mimic or copy the perceptions of the senses, but they never can entirely reach the force and vivacity of the original sentiment. The utmost we say of them, even when they operate with greatest vigour, is that they represent their object in so lively a manner that we could *almost* say we feel or see it. But, except the mind be disordered by disease or madness, they never can arrive at such a pitch of vivacity as to render these perceptions altogether undistinguishable. All the colours of poetry, however splendid, can never paint natural objects in such a manner as to make the description be taken for a real landscape. The most lively thought is still inferior to the dullest sensation.

We may observe a like distinction to run through all the other perceptions of the mind. A man in a fit of anger is actuated in a very different manner from one who only thinks of that emotion. If you tell me that any person is in love, I easily understand your meaning and form a just conception of his situation, but never can mistake that conception for the real disorders and agitations of the passion. When we reflect on our past sentiments and affections, our thought is a faithful mirror and copies its objects truly, but the colours which it employs are faint and dull, in comparison of those in which our original perceptions were clothed. It requires no nice discernment or metaphysical head to mark the distinction between them.

Here therefore we may divide all the perceptions of the mind into two classes or species, which are distinguished by their different degrees of force and vivacity. The less forcible and lively are commonly denominated *Thoughts* or *Ideas*. The other species want a name in our language and in most others—I suppose because it was not requisite for any but philosophical purposes to rank them under a general term or appellation. Let us, therefore, use a little freedom and call them *Impressions*, employing that word in a sense somewhat different from the usual. By the term *impression*, then, I mean all our more lively perceptions, when we hear, or see, or feel, or love, or hate, or desire, or will. And impressions are distinguished from ideas, which are the less lively perceptions, of which we are conscious when we reflect on any of those sensations or movements above mentioned.

Nothing, at first view, may seem more unbounded than the thought of man, which not only escapes all human power and authority but is not even restrained within the limits of nature and reality. To form monsters and join incongruous shapes and appearances costs the imagination no more trouble than to conceive the most natural and familiar objects. And while the body is confined to one planet, along which it creeps with pain and difficulty, the thought can in an instant transport us into the most distant regions of the universe, or even beyond the universe into the unbounded chaos, where nature is supposed to lie in total confusion. What never was seen or heard of may yet be conceived; nor is anything beyond the power of thought, except what implies an absolute contradiction.

But though our thought seems to possess this unbounded liberty, we shall find upon a nearer examination that it is really confined within very narrow limits, and that all this creative power of the mind amounts to no more than the faculty of compounding, transposing, augmenting, or diminishing the materials afforded us by the senses and experience. When we think of a golden mountain, we only join two consistent ideas, *gold* and *mountain*, with which we were formerly acquainted. A virtuous horse we can conceive because from our own feeling, we can conceive virtue, and this we may unite to the figure and shape of a horse, which is an animal familiar to us. In short, all the materials of thinking are derived either from our outward or inward sentiment: the mixture and composition of these belongs alone to the mind and will. Or, to express myself in philosophical language, all our ideas or more feeble perceptions are copies of our impressions or more lively ones.

To prove this, the two following arguments will, I hope, be sufficient. First, when we analyze our thoughts or ideas, however compounded or sublime, we always find that they resolve themselves into such simple ideas as were copied from a precedent feeling or sentiment. Even those ideas, which at first view seem the most wide of this origin, are found, upon a nearer scrutiny, to be derived from it. The idea of

God, as meaning an infinitely intelligent, wise, and good Being, arises from reflecting on the operations of our own mind, and augmenting, without limit, those qualities of goodness and wisdom. We may prosecute this enquiry to what length we please, where we shall always find that every idea which we examine is copied from a similar impression. Those who would assert that this position is not universally true nor without exception have only one easy method of refuting it: by producing that idea, which, in their opinion, is not derived from this source. It will then be incumbent on us, if we would maintain our doctrine, to produce the impression, or lively perception, which corresponds to it.

Secondly. If it happens, from a defect of the organ, that a man is not susceptible of any species of sensation, we always find that he is as little susceptible of the correspondent ideas. A blind man can form no notion of colours, a deaf man of sounds. Restore either of them that sense in which he is deficient, by opening this new inlet for his sensations, you also open an inlet for the ideas, and he finds no difficulty in conceiving these objects. The case is the same if the object proper for exciting any sensation has never been applied to the organ. A Laplander or Negro has no notion of the relish of wine. And though there are few or no instances of a like deficiency in the mind where a person has never felt or is wholly incapable of a sentiment or passion that belongs to his species, yet we find the same observation to take place in a lesser degree. A man of mild manners can form no idea of inveterate revenge or cruelty, nor can a self-ish heart easily conceive the heights of friendship and generosity.

There is, however, one contradictory phenomenon, which may prove that it is not absolutely impossible for ideas to arise independent of their correspondent impressions. I believe it will readily be allowed that the several distinct ideas of colour which enter by the eye or those of sound which are conveyed by the ear are really different from each other, though, at the same time, resembling. Now, if this be true of different colours, it must be no less so of the different shades of the same colour—that each shade produces a distinct idea, independent of the rest. For if this should be denied, it is possible by the continual gradation of shades to run a colour insensibly into what is most remote from it; and if you will not allow any of the means to be different, you cannot without absurdity deny the extremes to be the same. Suppose, therefore, a person to have enjoyed his sight for thirty years, and to have become perfectly acquainted with colours of all kinds except one particular shade of blue, for instance, which it never has been his fortune to meet with. Let all the different shades of that colour except that single one be placed before him, descending gradually from the deepest to the lightest; it is plain that he will perceive a blank where that shade is wanting and will be sensible that there is a greater distance in that place between the contiguous colours than in any other. Now I ask, whether it be possible for him, from his own imagination, to supply this deficiency and raise up to himself the idea of that particular shade, though it had never been conveyed to him by his senses? I believe there are few but will be of opinion that he can. This may serve as a proof that the simple ideas are not always, in every instance, derived from the correspondent impressions; though this instance is so singular that it is scarcely worth our observing, and does not merit that for it alone we should alter our general maxim.

Here, therefore, is a proposition, which not only seems in itself simple and intelligible, but, if a proper use were made of it, might render every dispute equally intelligible and banish all that jargon which has so long taken possession of metaphysical reasonings and drawn disgrace upon them. All ideas, especially abstract ones, are naturally faint and obscure; the mind has but a slender hold of them; they are apt to be confounded with other resembling ideas; and when we have often employed any term, though without a distinct meaning, we are apt to imagine it has a determinate idea annexed to it. On the contrary, all impressions, that is, all sensations, either outward or inward, are strong and vivid; the limits between them are more exactly determined; nor is it easy to fall into any error or mistake with regard to them. When we entertain, therefore, any suspicion that a philosophical term is employed without any meaning or idea (as is but too frequent), we need but enquire, *from what impression is that supposed idea derived?* And if it be impossible to assign any, this will serve to confirm our suspicion. By bringing ideas into so clear a light, we may reasonably hope to remove all dispute which may arise concerning their nature and reality.

## Skeptical Doubts Concerning the Operations of the Understanding [Section 4]

### Part I. On Cause and Effect

All the objects of human reason or enquiry may naturally be divided into two kinds, to wit, *Relations of Ideas* and *Matters of Fact*. Of the first kind are the sciences of Geometry, Algebra, and Arithmetic; and in short, every affirmation which is either intuitively or demonstratively certain. *That the square of the hypotenuse is equal to the square of the two sides* is a proposition which expresses a relation between these figures. *That three times five is equal to the half of thirty* expresses a relation between these numbers. Propositions of this kind are discoverable by the mere operation of thought, without dependence on what is anywhere existent in the universe. Though there never were a circle or triangle in nature, the truths demonstrated by Euclid would forever retain their certainty and evidence.

Matters of fact, which are the second objects of human reason, are not ascertained in the same manner; nor is our evidence of their truth, however great, of a like nature with the foregoing. The contrary of every matter of fact is still possible because it can never imply a contradiction, and is conceived by the mind with the same facility and distinctness as if ever so conformable to reality. *That the sun will not rise tomorrow* is no less intelligible a proposition, and implies no more contradiction than the affirmation, *that it will rise*. We should in vain, therefore, attempt to demonstrate its falsehood. Were it demonstratively false, it would imply a contradiction, and could never be distinctly conceived by the mind.

It may, therefore, be a subject worthy of curiosity to enquire what is the nature of that evidence which assures us of any real existence and matter of fact beyond the present testimony of our senses, or the records of our memory.

All reasonings concerning matter of fact seem to be founded on the relation of *Cause and Effect*. By means of that relation alone we can go beyond the evidence of our memory and senses. If you were to ask a man why he believes any matter of fact which is absent—for instance, that his friend is in the country or in France, he would give you a reason, and this reason would be some other fact—as a letter received from him, or the knowledge of his former resolutions and promises. A man finding a watch or any other machine in a desert island would conclude that there had once been men in that island. [. . .] If we anatomize all the other reasonings of this nature, we shall find that they are founded on the relation of cause and effect, and that this relation is either near or remote, direct or collateral. Heat and light are collateral effects of fire, and the one effect may justly be inferred from the other.

If we would satisfy ourselves, therefore, concerning the nature of that evidence which assures us of matters of fact, we must enquire how we arrive at the knowledge of cause and effect.

I shall venture to affirm, as a general proposition which admits of no exception, that the knowledge of this relation is not in any instance attained by reasonings a priori, but arises entirely from experience when we find that any particular objects are constantly conjoined with each other. Let an object be presented to a man of ever so strong natural reason and abilities, and if that object be entirely new to him, he will not be able, by the most accurate examination of its sensible qualities, to discover any of its causes or effects. Adam, though his rational faculties be supposed at the very first entirely perfect, could not have inferred from the fluidity and transparency of water that it would suffocate him, or from the light and warmth of fire that it would consume him.

This proposition, *that causes and effects are discoverable, not by reason but by experience*, will readily be admitted with regard to such objects as we remember to have once been altogether unknown to us, since we must be conscious of the utter inability which we then lay under of foretelling what would arise from them. Present two smooth pieces of marble to a man who has no tincture of natural philosophy, and he will never discover that they will adhere together in such a manner as to require great force to separate them in a direct line, while they make so small a resistance to a lateral pressure. Such events as bear little analogy to the common course of nature are also readily confessed to be known only by experience; nor does any man imagine that the explosion of gunpowder or the attraction of a loadstone could ever be discovered by arguments a priori. In like manner, when an effect is supposed to depend upon an intricate machinery or secret structure of parts, we make no difficulty in attributing all our knowledge of it to experience. Who will assert that he can give the ultimate reason why milk or bread is proper nourishment for a man, but not for a lion or a tiger?

But the same truth may not appear, at first sight, to have the same evidence with regard to events which have become familiar to us from our first appearance in the world, which bear a close analogy to the whole course of nature, and which are supposed to depend on the simple qualities of objects without any secret structure of parts. We are apt to imagine that we could discover these effects by the mere operation of our reason, without experience. We fancy that were we brought suddenly into this world, we could at first have inferred that one billiard ball would communicate motion to another upon impulse, and that we needed not to have waited for the event in order to pronounce with certainty concerning it. Such is the influence of custom that where it is strongest, it not only covers our natural ignorance but even conceals itself and seems not to take place, merely because it is found in the highest degree.

But to convince us that all the laws of nature, and all the operations of bodies without exception, are known only by experience, the following reflections may, perhaps, suffice. Were any object presented to us, and were we required to pronounce concerning the effect which will result from it without consulting past observation, after what manner, I beseech you, must the mind proceed in this operation? It must invent or imagine some event which it ascribes to the object as its effect, and it is plain that this invention must be entirely arbitrary. The mind can never possibly find the effect in the supposed cause by the most accurate scrutiny and examination. For the effect is totally different from the cause and consequently can never be discovered in it. Motion in the second billiard ball is a quite distinct event from motion in the first; nor is there anything in the one to suggest the smallest hint of the other. A stone or piece of metal raised into the air and left without any support immediately falls, but to consider the matter a priori, is there anything we discover in this situation which can beget the idea of a downward, rather than an upward or any other motion in the stone or metal?

And as the first imagination or invention of a particular effect in all natural operations is arbitrary where we consult not experience, so must we also esteem the supposed tie or connection between the cause and effect which binds them together and renders it impossible that any other effect could result from the operation of that cause. When I see, for instance, a billiard ball moving in a straight line towards another, even suppose motion in the second ball should by accident be suggested to me as the result of their contact or impulse, may I not conceive that a hundred different events might as well follow from that cause? May not both these balls remain at absolute rest? May not the first ball return in a straight line, or leap off from the second in any line or direction? All these suppositions are consistent and conceivable. Why then should we give the preference to one, which is no more consistent or conceivable than the rest? All our reasonings a priori will never be able to show us any foundation for this preference.

In a word, then, every effect is a distinct event from its cause. It could not, therefore, be discovered in the cause, and the first invention or conception of it, a priori, must be entirely arbitrary. And even after it is suggested, the conjunction of it with the cause must appear equally arbitrary, since there are always many other effects, which, to reason, must seem fully as consistent and natural. In vain, therefore, should we pretend to determine any single event, or infer any cause or effect, without the assistance of observation and experience.

## Part II. On Induction

But we have not yet attained any tolerable satisfaction with regard to the question first proposed. Each solution still gives rise to a new question as difficult as the foregoing, and leads us on to further enquiries. When it is asked, *What is the nature of all our reasonings concerning matter of fact?* the proper answer seems to be that they are founded on the relation of cause and effect. When again it is asked, *What is the foundation of all our reasonings and conclusions concerning that relation?* it may be replied in one word, Experience. But if we still carry on our sifting humour and ask, *What is the foundation of all conclusions from experience?* this implies a new question, which may be of more difficult solution and explication. [. . .]

I shall content myself in this section with an easy task, and shall pretend only to give a negative answer to the question here proposed. I say, then, that even after we have experience of the operations of cause and effect, our conclusions from that experience are *not* founded on reasoning or any process of the understanding. This answer we must endeavour both to explain and to defend.

It must certainly be allowed that nature has kept us at a great distance from all her secrets, and has afforded us only the knowledge of a few superficial qualities of objects, while she conceals from us those powers and principles on which the influence of those objects entirely depends. Our senses inform us of the colour, weight, and consistency of bread, but neither sense nor reason can ever inform us of those qualities which fit it for the nourishment and support of a human body. [. . .] But notwithstanding this ignorance of natural powers and principles, we always

presume when we see like sensible qualities that they have like secret powers, and expect that effects similar to those which we have experienced will follow from them. If a body of like colour and consistency with that bread which we have formerly eaten be presented to us, we make no scruple of repeating the experiment, and foresee, with certainty, like nourishment and support. Now this is a process of the mind or thought of which I would willingly know the foundation. It is allowed on all hands that there is no known connection between the sensible qualities and the secret powers, and consequently, that the mind is not led to form such a conclusion concerning their constant and regular conjunction by anything which it knows of their nature. As to past *Experience*, it can be allowed to give *direct* and *certain* information of those precise objects only, and that precise period of time, which fell under its cognizance: but why this experience should be extended to future times, and to other objects which for aught we know may be only in appearance similar, this is the main question on which I would insist. The bread which I formerly ate nourished me, that is, a body of such sensible qualities was at that time endued with such secret powers: but does it follow that other bread must also nourish me at another time, and that like sensible qualities must always be attended with like secret powers? The consequence seems nowise necessary. At least, it must be acknowledged that there is here a [. . .] process of thought and an inference which wants to be explained. These two propositions are far from being the same: *I have found that such an object has always been attended with such an effect*, and *I foresee that other objects which are in appearance similar will be attended with similar effects*. I shall allow, if you please, that the one proposition may justly be inferred from the other: I know, in fact, that it always is inferred. But if you insist that the inference is made by a chain of reasoning, I desire you to produce that reasoning. The connection between these propositions is not intuitive. There is required a medium which may enable the mind to draw such an inference, if indeed it be drawn by reasoning and argument. What that medium is, I must confess, passes my comprehension; and it is incumbent on those to produce it, who assert that it really exists and is the origin of all our conclusions concerning matter of fact.

This negative argument must certainly, in process of time, become altogether convincing, if many penetrating and able philosophers shall turn their enquiries this way and no one be ever able to discover any connecting proposition or intermediate step which supports the understanding in this conclusion. But as the question is yet new, every reader may not trust so far to his own penetration as to conclude, because an argument escapes his enquiry, that therefore it does not really exist. For this reason it may be requisite to venture upon a more difficult task, and enumerating all the branches of human knowledge, endeavour to show that none of them can afford such an argument.

All reasonings may be divided into two kinds, namely, demonstrative reasoning, or that concerning relations of ideas, and moral reasoning, or that concerning matter of fact and existence. That there are no demonstrative arguments in the case seems evident since it implies no contradiction that the course of nature may change, and that an object, seemingly like those which we have experienced, may be attended with different or contrary effects. May I not clearly and distinctly conceive that a body falling from the clouds which in all other respects resembles snow has yet the taste of salt or feeling of fire? Is there any more intelligible proposition than to affirm that all the trees will flourish in December and January and decay in May and June? Now whatever is intelligible, and can be distinctly conceived, implies no contradiction, and can never be proved false by any demonstrative argument or abstract reasoning a priori.

If we be, therefore, engaged by arguments to put trust in past experience and make it the standard of our future judgment, these arguments must be probable only, or such as regard matter of fact and real existence, according to the division above mentioned. But that there is no argument of this kind must appear if our explication of that species of reasoning be admitted as solid and satisfactory. We have said that all arguments concerning existence are founded on the relation of cause and effect, that our knowledge of that relation is derived entirely from experience, and that all our experimental

conclusions proceed upon the supposition that the future will be conformable to the past. To endeavour, therefore, the proof of this last supposition by probable arguments, or arguments regarding existence, must be evidently going in a circle, and taking that for granted which is the very point in question.

In reality, all arguments from experience are founded on the similarity which we discover among natural objects, and by which we are induced to expect effects similar to those which we have found to follow from such objects. And though none but a fool or madman will ever pretend to dispute the authority of experience or to reject that great guide of human life, it may surely be allowed a philosopher to have so much curiosity at least as to examine the principle of human nature which gives this mighty authority to experience and makes us draw advantage from that similarity which nature has placed among different objects. From causes which appear *similar* we expect similar effects. This is the sum of all our experimental conclusions. Now it seems evident that if this conclusion were formed by reason, it would be as perfect at first, and upon one instance, as after ever so long a course of experience. But the case is far otherwise. Nothing is so like as eggs, yet no one, on account of this appearing similarity, expects the same taste and relish in all of them. It is only after a long course of uniform experiments in any kind that we attain a firm reliance and security with regard to a particular event. Now, where is that process of reasoning, which from one instance draws a conclusion so different from that which it infers from a hundred instances that are nowise different from that single one?

Should it be said that from a number of uniform experiments, we *infer* a connection between the sensible qualities and the secret powers, this, I must confess, seems the same difficulty, couched in different terms. The question still recurs, on what process of argument this *inference* is founded? Where is the medium, the interposing ideas, which join propositions so very wide of each other? It is confessed that the colour, consistence, and other sensible qualities of bread appear not, of themselves, to have any connection with the secret powers of nourishment and support. For otherwise we could infer these secret powers from the first appearance of these sensible qualities without the aid of experience, contrary to the sentiment of all philosophers, and contrary to plain matter of fact. Here, then, is our natural state of ignorance with regard to the powers and influence of all objects. How is this remedied by experience? It only shows us a number of uniform effects resulting from certain objects, and teaches us that those particular objects, at that particular time, were endowed with such powers and forces. When a new object endowed with similar sensible qualities is produced, we expect similar powers and forces, and look for a like effect. From a body of like colour and consistence with bread we expect like nourishment and support. But this surely is a step or progress of the mind, which wants to be explained. When a man says, *I have found, in all past instances, such sensible qualities conjoined with such secret powers*, and when he says, *Similar sensible qualities will always be conjoined with similar secret powers*, he is not guilty of a **tautology**, nor are these propositions in any respect the same. You say that the one proposition is an inference from the other. But you must confess that the inference is not intuitive; neither is it demonstrative. Of what nature is it, then? To say it is experimental is begging the question. For all inferences from experience suppose as their foundation that the future will resemble the past, and that similar powers will be conjoined with similar sensible qualities. If there be any suspicion that the course of nature may change, and that the past may be no rule for the future, all experience becomes useless, and can give rise to no inference or conclusion. It is impossible, therefore, that any arguments from experience can prove this resemblance of the past to the future, since all these arguments are founded on the supposition of that resemblance. Let the course of things be allowed hitherto ever so regular; that alone, without some new argument or inference, proves not that, for the future, it will continue so. In vain do you pretend to have learned the nature of bodies from your past experience. Their secret nature, and consequently all their effects and influence, may change, without any change in their sensible qualities. This happens sometimes, and with regard to some objects: Why may it not happen always, and with regard to all objects? What logic, what process of argument secures you against this supposition? My practice, you say,

refutes my doubts. But you mistake the purport of my question. As an agent, I am quite satisfied in the point; but as a philosopher, who has some share of curiosity, I will not say scepticism, I want to learn the foundation of this inference. No reading, no enquiry has yet been able to remove my difficulty, or give me satisfaction in a matter of such importance. Can I do better than propose the difficulty to the public, even though, perhaps, I have small hopes of obtaining a solution? We shall at least, by this means, be sensible of our ignorance, if we do not augment our knowledge.

## Skeptical Solution of These Doubts [Section 5]

Though we should conclude, for instance, as in the foregoing section, that in all reasonings from experience, there is a step taken by the mind which is not supported by any argument or process of the understanding, there is no danger that these reasonings, on which almost all knowledge depends, will ever be affected by such a discovery. If the mind be not engaged by argument to make this step, it must be induced by some other principle of equal weight and authority, and that principle will preserve its influence as long as human nature remains the same. What that principle is may well be worth the pains of enquiry.

Suppose a person, though endowed with the strongest faculties of reason and reflection, be brought suddenly into this world. He would, indeed, immediately observe a continual succession of objects and one event following another, but he would not be able to discover anything farther. He would not, at first, by any reasoning, be able to reach the idea of cause and effect since the particular powers by which all natural operations are performed never appear to the senses. Nor is it reasonable to conclude, merely because one event, in one instance, precedes another, that therefore the one is the cause, the other the effect. Their conjunction may be arbitrary and casual. There may be no reason to infer the existence of one from the appearance of the other. And in a word, such a person, without more experience, could never employ his conjecture or reasoning concerning any matter of fact, or be assured of anything beyond what was immediately present to his memory and senses.

Suppose, again, that he has acquired more experience, and has lived so long in the world as to have observed familiar objects or events to be constantly conjoined together; what is the consequence of this experience? He immediately infers the existence of one object from the appearance of the other. Yet he has not, by all his experience, acquired any idea or knowledge of the secret power by which the one object produces the other; nor is it by any process of reasoning he is engaged to draw this inference. But still he finds himself determined to draw it: And though he should be convinced that his understanding has no part in the operation, he would nevertheless continue in the same course of thinking. There is some other principle which determines him to form such a conclusion.

This principle is Custom or Habit. For wherever the repetition of any particular act or operation produces a propensity to renew the same act or operation, without being impelled by any reasoning or process of the understanding, we always say that this propensity is the effect of *Custom*. By employing that word, we pretend not to have given the ultimate reason of such a propensity. We only point out a principle of human nature, which is universally acknowledged, and which is well known by its effects. Perhaps we can push our enquiries no farther, or pretend to give the cause of this cause, but must rest contented with it as the ultimate principle which we can assign of all our conclusions from experience. It is sufficient satisfaction that we can go so far, without repining at the narrowness of our faculties because they will carry us no farther. And it is certain we here advance a very intelligible proposition at least, if not a true one, when we assert that, after the constant conjunction of two objects—heat and flame, for instance, weight and solidity—we are determined by custom alone to expect the one from the appearance of the other. This hypothesis seems even the only one which explains the difficulty, why we draw from a thousand instances an inference which we are not able to draw from one instance that is in no respect different from them. Reason is incapable of any such variation. The conclusions which it draws from considering one circle are the same which it would form upon surveying all the circles in the universe. But no man having seen only one body move after being impelled by another could infer that every other body will move after a like impulse. All inferences from experience, therefore, are effects of custom, not of reasoning.

Custom, then, is the great guide of human life. It is that principle alone which renders our experience useful to us, and makes us expect for the future a similar train of events with those which have appeared in the past. Without the influence of custom, we should be entirely ignorant of every matter of fact beyond what is immediately present to the memory and senses. We should never know how to adjust means to ends, or to employ our natural powers in the production of any effect. There would be an end at once of all action, as well as of the chief part of speculation. [. . .]

## Study Questions

1. What is Hume's copy thesis, and how does it illustrate his empiricism? Explain how the "missing shade of blue" counter-example challenges Hume's copy thesis. Do you find Hume's response to this challenge convincing?

2. How do "relations of ideas" and "matters of fact" differ? Provide an example of each.

3. What proposition does Hume suggest we use to banish metaphysical "jargon" from philosophy? What does this entail for our notion of "laws of nature"?

4. Why does Hume claim that reason cannot provide any basis for certainty in induction? Why does Hume claim that experience cannot provide any basis for even probabilistic assurance in induction? What principle does underlie induction?

# Immanuel Kant

Immanuel Kant (1724–1804), like other philosophers of the Enlightenment, held that reason allows us to think for ourselves rather than relying on political and religious authorities. In the *Critique of Pure Reason*, Kant sought to show, however, that Newtonian science is consistent with traditional moral and religious beliefs. After disappointing reviews, Kant wrote the *Prolegomena* as an effort to clarify the main points of the *Critique*.

# From *Prolegomena to Any Future Metaphysics*

## Introduction

Since the Essays of **Locke** and **Leibniz**, or rather since the origin of metaphysics so far as we know its history, nothing has ever happened which was more decisive to its fate than the attack made upon it by **David Hume**. He threw no light on this species of knowledge, but he certainly struck a spark from which light might have been obtained, had it caught some inflammable substance and had its smouldering fire been carefully nursed and developed.

Hume started from a single but important concept in Metaphysics, viz., that of Cause and Effect (including its derivatives force and action, etc.). He challenges reason, which pretends to have given birth to this idea from herself, to answer him by what right she thinks anything to be so constituted, that if that thing be posited, something else also must necessarily be posited; for this is the meaning of the concept of cause. He demonstrated irrefutably that it was perfectly impossible for reason to think a priori and by means of concepts a combination involving necessity. We cannot at all see why, in consequence of the existence of one thing, another must necessarily exist, or how the concept of such a combination can arise a priori. Hence he inferred that reason was altogether deluded with reference to this concept, which she erroneously considered as one of her children, whereas in reality it was nothing but a bastard of imagination, impregnated by experience, which subsumed certain representations under the Law of Association, and mistook the subjective necessity of habit for an objective necessity arising from insight. Hence he inferred that reason had no power to think such combinations, even generally, because her concepts would then be purely fictitious, and all her pretended a priori cognitions nothing but common experiences marked with a false stamp. In plain language there is not, and cannot be, any such thing as metaphysics at all. [. . .]

The question was not whether the concept of cause was right, useful, and even indispensable for our knowledge of nature, for this Hume had never doubted, but whether that concept could be thought by reason a priori, and consequently whether it possessed an inner truth, independent of all experience, implying a wider application than merely to the objects of experience. This was Hume's problem. It was a question concerning the *origin*, not concerning the *indispensable need* of the concept. Were the former decided, the conditions of the use and the sphere of its valid application would have been determined as a matter of course. [. . .]

I openly confess, the suggestion of David Hume was the very thing which many years ago first interrupted my dogmatic slumber and gave my investigations in the field of speculative philosophy quite a new direction. I was far from following him in the conclusions at which he arrived by regarding not the whole of his problem but a part, which by itself can give us no information. If we start from a well-founded but undeveloped thought which another has bequeathed to us, we may well hope by continued reflection to advance farther than the acute man to whom we owe the first spark of light. [. . .]

## First Part of the Transcendental Problem: How Is Pure Mathematics Possible?

6. Here is a great and established branch of knowledge, encompassing even now a wonderfully large domain and promising an unlimited extension in the future. Yet it carries with it thoroughly apodeictical certainty, i.e., absolute necessity, which therefore rests upon no empirical grounds. Consequently it is a pure product of reason, and moreover is thoroughly **synthetical**. Here the question arises:

"How then is it possible for human reason to produce a cognition of this nature entirely a priori?" [. . .]

9. [. . .] in one way only can my intuition (*Anschauung*) anticipate the actuality of the object, and be a cognition a priori, viz.: if my intuition contains nothing but the form of sensibility, antedating in my subjectivity all the actual impressions through which I am affected by objects.

For that objects of sense can only be intuited according to this form of sensibility I can know a priori. Hence it follows: that propositions which concern this form of sensuous intuition only are possible and valid for objects of the senses; as also, conversely, that intuitions which are possible a priori can never concern any other things than objects of our senses.

10. Accordingly, it is only the form of sensuous intuition by which we can intuit things a priori, but by which we can know objects only as they *appear* to us (to our senses), not as they are in themselves; and this assumption is absolutely necessary if synthetical propositions a priori be granted as possible, or if, in case they actually occur, their possibility is to be comprehended and determined beforehand.

Now, the intuitions which pure mathematics lays at the foundation of all its cognitions and judgments which appear at once apodeictic and necessary are Space and Time. For mathematics must first have all its concepts in intuition, and pure mathematics in pure intuition, that is, it must construct them. If it proceeded in any other way, it would be impossible to make any headway, for mathematics proceeds, not

analytically by dissection of concepts but synthetically, and if pure intuition be wanting, there is nothing in which the matter for synthetical judgments a priori can be given. Geometry is based upon the pure intuition of space. Arithmetic accomplishes its concept of number by the successive addition of units in time; and pure mechanics especially cannot attain its concepts of motion without employing the representation of time. Both representations, however, are only intuitions; for if we omit from the empirical intuitions of bodies and their alterations (motion) everything empirical, or belonging to sensation, space and time still remain, which are therefore pure intuitions that lie a priori at the basis of the empirical. Hence they can never be omitted, but at the same time, by their being pure intuitions a priori, they prove that they are mere forms of our sensibility, which must precede all empirical intuition, or perception of actual objects, and conformably to which objects can be known a priori, but only as they appear to us.

11. The problem of the present section is therefore solved. Pure mathematics, as synthetical cognition a priori, is only possible by referring to no other objects than those of the senses. At the basis of their empirical intuition lies a pure intuition (of space and of time) which is a priori. This is possible because the latter intuition is nothing but the mere form of sensibility, which precedes the actual appearance of the objects, in that it, in fact, makes them possible. [. . .]

## Appearances vs. Things-in-Themselves [Remark II]

Whatever is given us as object must be given us in intuition. All our intuition however takes place by means of the senses only; the understanding intuits nothing, but only reflects. And as we have just shown that the senses never and in no manner enable us to know things in themselves, but only their appearances, which are mere representations of the sensibility, we conclude that "all bodies, together with the space in which they are, must be considered nothing but mere representations in us, and exist nowhere but in our thoughts." You will say: Is not this manifest idealism?

Idealism consists in the assertion that there are none but thinking beings, all other things, which we think are perceived in intuition, being nothing but representations in the thinking beings, to which no object external to them corresponds in fact. Whereas I say, that things as objects of our senses existing outside us are given, but we know nothing of what they may be in themselves, knowing only their appearances, i.e., the representations which they cause in us by affecting our senses. Consequently I grant by all means that there are bodies without us, that is, things which, though quite unknown to us as to what they are in themselves, we yet know by the representations which their influence on our sensibility procures us, and which we call bodies, a term signifying merely the appearance of the thing which is unknown to us, but not therefore less actual. Can this be termed idealism? It is the very contrary.

Long before Locke's time, but assuredly since him, it has been generally assumed and granted without detriment to the actual existence of external things that many of their predicates may be said to belong not to the things in themselves but to their appearances, and to have no proper existence outside our representation. Heat, colour, and taste, for instance, are of this kind. Now, if I go farther, and for weighty reasons rank as mere appearances the remaining qualities of bodies also, which are called primary, such as extension, place, and in general space, with all that which belongs to it (impenetrability or materiality, space, etc.)—no one in the least can adduce the reason of its being inadmissible. As little as the man who admits colours not to be properties of the object in itself, but only as modifications of the sense of sight, should on that account be called an idealist, so little can my system be named idealistic, merely because I find that more, nay,

*All the properties which constitute the intuition of a body belong merely to its appearance.*

The existence of the thing that appears is thereby not destroyed, as in genuine idealism, but it is only shown that we cannot possibly know it by the senses as it is in itself.

I should be glad to know what my assertions must be in order to avoid all idealism. Undoubtedly, I should say that the representation of space is not only perfectly conformable to the relation which our sensibility has to objects—that I have said—but that it is quite similar to the object,—an assertion in which I can find as little meaning as if I said that the sensation of red has a similarity to the property of vermilion, which in me excites this sensation.

## Critical Idealism [Remark III]

Hence we may at once dismiss an easily foreseen but futile objection, "that by admitting the ideality of space and of time the whole sensible world would be turned into mere sham." At first all philosophical insight into the nature of sensuous cognition was spoiled by making the sensibility merely a confused mode of representation, according to which we still know things as they are, but without being able to reduce everything in this our representation to a clear consciousness; whereas proof is offered by us that sensibility consists, not in this logical distinction of clearness and obscurity, but in the genetical one of the origin of cognition itself. For sensuous perception represents things not at all as they are, but only the mode in which they affect our senses, and consequently by sensuous perception appearances only and not things themselves are given to the understanding for reflection. After this necessary corrective, an objection rises from an unpardonable and almost intentional misconception, as if my doctrine turned all the things of the world of sense into mere illusion.

When an appearance is given us, we are still quite free as to how we should judge the matter. The appearance depends upon the senses, but the judgment upon the understanding, and the only question is, whether in the determination of the object there is truth or not. But the difference between truth and dreaming is not ascertained by the nature of the representations which are referred to objects (for they are the same in both cases), but by their connection according to those rules which determine the coherence of the representations in the concept of an object, and by ascertaining whether they can subsist together in experience or not. And it is not the fault of the appearances if our cognition takes illusion for truth, i.e., if the intuition by which an object is given us is considered a concept of the thing or of its existence also, which the understanding can only think. The senses represent to us the paths of the planets as now progressive, now retrogressive, and herein is neither falsehood nor truth, because as long as we hold this path to be nothing but appearance, we do not judge of the objective nature of their motion. But as a false judgment may easily arise when the understanding is not on its guard against this subjective mode of representation being considered objective, we say they appear to move backward; it is not the senses however which must be charged with the illusion but the understanding, whose province alone it is to give an objective judgment on appearances.

Thus, even if we did not at all reflect on the origin of our representations, whenever we connect our intuitions of sense (whatever they may contain) in space and in time according to the rules of the coherence of all cognition in experience, illusion or truth will arise according as we are negligent or careful. It is merely a question of the use of sensuous representations in the understanding, and not of their origin. In the same way, if I consider all the representations of the senses, together with their form, space and time, to be nothing but appearances, and space and time to be a mere form of the sensibility, which is not to be met with in objects out of it, and if I make use of these representations in reference to possible experience only, there is nothing in my regarding them as appearances that can lead astray or cause illusion. [. . .]

But if I venture to go beyond all possible experience with my notions of space and time, which I cannot refrain from doing if I proclaim them qualities inherent in things in themselves (for what should prevent me from letting them hold good of the same things, even though my senses might be different and unsuited to them?), then a grave error may arise due to illusion, for thus I would proclaim to be universally valid what is merely a subjective condition of the intuition of things and sure only for all objects of sense, viz., for all possible experience; I would refer this condition to things in themselves, and do not limit it to the conditions of experience. [. . .]

Inasmuch, therefore, as I leave to things as we obtain them by the senses their actuality and only limit our sensuous intuition of these things to this, that they represent in no respect, not even in the pure intuitions of space and of time, anything more than mere appearance of those things but never their constitution in themselves, this is not a sweeping illusion invented for nature by me. My protestation too against all charges of idealism is so valid and clear as even to seem superfluous, were there not incompetent judges, who, while they would have an old name for every deviation from their perverse though common opinion and never judge of the spirit of philosophic nomenclature but cling to the letter only, are ready to put their own conceits in the place of well-defined notions, and thereby deform and distort them. I have myself given this my theory the name of transcendental idealism, but that cannot authorize anyone to confound it either with the empirical idealism of **Descartes**, (indeed, his was only an insoluble problem owing to which he thought everyone at liberty to deny the existence of the corporeal world because it could never be proved satisfactorily), or with the mystical and visionary idealism of **Berkeley**, against which and other similar phantasms our Critique contains the proper antidote. My idealism concerns not the existence of things (the doubting of which, however, constitutes idealism in the ordinary sense), since it never came into my head to doubt it, but it concerns the sensuous representation of things, to which space and time especially belong. Of these viz., space and time, consequently of all appearances in general,

I have only shown, that they are neither things (but mere modes of representation), nor determinations belonging to things in themselves. But the word "transcendental," which with me means a reference of our cognition, i.e., not to things but only to the cognitive faculty, was meant to obviate this misconception. Yet rather than give further occasion to it by this word, I now retract it, and desire this idealism of mine to be called critical. But if it be really an objectionable idealism to convert actual things (not appearances) into mere representations, by what name shall we call him who conversely changes mere representations to things? It may, I think, be called "dreaming idealism," in contradistinction to the former, which may be called "visionary," both of which are to be refuted by my transcendental, or, better, critical idealism.

## Second Part of the Transcendental Problem: How Is the Science of Nature Possible?

[. . .] 17. [. . .]Accordingly we shall here be concerned with experience only, and the universal conditions of its possibility which are given a priori. Thence we shall determine nature as the whole object of all possible experience. I think it will be understood that I here do not mean the rules of the observation of a nature that is already given, for these already presuppose experience. I do not mean how (through experience) we can study the laws of nature, for these would not then be laws a priori and would yield us no pure science of nature; but I mean to ask how the conditions a priori of the possibility of experience are at the same time the sources from which all the universal laws of nature must be derived.

18. In the first place we must state that while all judgments of experience (*Erfahrungsurtheile*) are empirical (i.e., have their ground in immediate sense-perception), vice versa, all empirical judgments (*empirische Urtheile*) are not judgments of experience, but, besides the empirical, and in general besides what is given to the sensuous intuition, particular concepts must yet be superadded—concepts

which have their origin quite a priori in the pure understanding, and under which every perception must be first of all subsumed and then by their means changed into experience.

Empirical judgments, so far as they have objective validity, are *judgments of experience*; but those which are only subjectively valid, I name mere *judgments of perception*. The latter require no pure concept of the understanding, but only the logical connection of perception in a thinking subject. But the former always require, besides the representation of the sensuous intuition, particular *concepts originally begotten in the understanding*, which produce the objective validity of the judgment of experience. [. . .]

19. [. . .] To illustrate the matter: When we say, "the room is warm, sugar sweet, and wormwood bitter,"[1]—we have only subjectively valid judgments. I do not at all expect that I or any other person shall always find it as I now do; each of these sentences only expresses a relation of two sensations to the same subject, to myself, and that only in my present state of perception; consequently they are not valid of the object. Such are judgments of perception. Judgments of experience are of quite a different nature. What experience teaches me under certain circumstances, it must always teach me and everybody; and its validity is not limited to the subject nor to its state at a particular time. Hence I pronounce all such judgments as being objectively valid. For instance, when I say the air is elastic, this judgment is as yet a judgment of perception only—I do nothing but refer two of my sensations to one another. But, if I would have it called a judgment of experience, I require this connection to stand under a condition, which makes it universally valid. I desire therefore that I and everybody else should always connect necessarily the same perceptions under the same circumstances.

20. We must consequently analyze experience in order to see what is contained in this product of the senses and of the understanding, and how the judgment of experience itself is possible. The foundation is the intuition of which I become conscious, i.e., perception (*perceptio*), which pertains merely to the

senses. But in the next place, there are acts of judging (which belong only to the understanding). But this judging may be twofold—first, I may merely compare perceptions and connect them in a particular state of my consciousness; or, secondly, I may connect them in consciousness generally. The former judgment is merely a judgment of perception, and of subjective validity only: it is merely a connection of perceptions in my mental state, without reference to the object. Hence it is not, as is commonly imagined, enough for experience to compare perceptions and to connect them in consciousness through judgment; there arises no universality and necessity, for which alone judgments can become objectively valid and be called experience.

Quite another judgment therefore is required before perception can become experience. The given intuition must be subsumed under a concept, which determines the form of judging in general relatively to the intuition, connects its empirical consciousness in consciousness generally, and thereby procures universal validity for empirical judgments. A concept of this nature is a pure a priori concept of the Understanding, which does nothing but determine for an intuition the general way in which it can be used for judgments. Let the concept be that of cause, then it determines the intuition which is subsumed under it, e.g., that of air, relative to judgments in general, viz., the concept of air serves with regard to its expansion in the relation of antecedent to consequent in a hypothetical judgment. The concept of cause accordingly is a pure concept of the understanding, which is totally disparate from all possible perception, and only serves to determine the representation subsumed under it, relatively to judgments in general, and so to make a universally valid judgment possible.

Before, therefore, a judgment of perception can become a judgment of experience, it is requisite that the perception should be subsumed under some such a concept of the understanding; for instance, air ranks under the concept of causes, which determines our judgment about it in regard to its expansion as hypothetical.[2] Thereby the expansion of the air is represented not as merely belonging to

the perception of the air in my present state or in several states of mine, or in the state of perception of others, but as belonging to it necessarily. The judgment, "the air is elastic," becomes universally valid, and a judgment of experience, only by certain judgments preceding it, which subsume the intuition of air under the concept of cause and effect: and they thereby determine the perceptions not merely as regards one another in me, but relatively to the form of judging in general, which is here hypothetical, and in this way they render the empirical judgment universally valid.

If all our synthetical judgments are analyzed so far as they are objectively valid, it will be found that they never consist of mere intuitions connected only (as is commonly believed) by comparison into a judgment; but that they would be impossible were not a pure concept of the understanding superadded to the concepts abstracted from intuition, under which concept these latter are subsumed, and in this manner only combined into an objectively valid judgment. [. . .]

27. Now we are prepared to remove Hume's doubt. He justly maintains that we cannot comprehend by reason the possibility of Causality, that is, of the reference of the existence of one thing to the existence of another, which is necessitated by the former. [. . .] But I am very far from holding [this concept] to be derived merely from experience, and the necessity represented in [it], to be imaginary and a mere illusion produced in us by long habit. [. . .]

29. When making an experiment with Hume's problematical concept (his *crux metaphysicorum*), the concept of cause, we have, in the first place, given a priori, by means of logic, the form of a conditional judgment in general, i.e., we have one given cognition as antecedent and another as consequence. But it is possible that in perception we may meet with a rule of relation which runs thus: that a certain phenomenon is constantly followed by another (though not conversely), and this is a case for me to use the hypothetical judgment, and, for instance, to say, if the sun shines long enough upon a body, it grows warm. Here there is indeed as yet no necessity of connection, or concept of cause. But I proceed

and say, that if this proposition, which is merely a subjective connection of perceptions, is to be a judgment of experience, it must be considered as necessary and universally valid. Such a proposition would be, "the sun is by its light the cause of heat." The empirical rule is now considered as a law, and as valid not merely of appearances but valid of them for the purposes of a possible experience which requires universal and therefore necessarily valid rules. I therefore easily comprehend the concept of cause as a concept necessarily belonging to the mere form of experience, and its possibility as a synthetical union of perceptions in consciousness generally; but I do not at all comprehend the possibility of a thing generally as a cause because the concept of cause denotes a condition not at all belonging to things, but to experience. It is nothing in fact but an objectively valid cognition of appearances and of their succession, so far as the antecedent can be conjoined with the consequent according to the rule of hypothetical judgments.

30. Hence if the pure concepts of the understanding do not refer to objects of experience but to things in themselves (*noumena*), they have no signification whatever. They serve, as it were, only to decipher appearances, that we may be able to read them as experience. The principles which arise from their reference to the sensible world only serve our understanding for empirical use. Beyond this they are arbitrary combinations, without objective reality, and we can neither cognize their possibility a priori nor verify their reference to objects, let alone make it intelligible by any example; because examples can only be borrowed from some possible experience, consequently the objects of these concepts can be found nowhere but in a possible experience.

This complete (though to its originator unexpected) solution of Hume's problem rescues for the pure concepts of the understanding their a priori origin, and for the universal laws of nature their validity as laws of the understanding, yet in such a way as to limit their use to experience because their possibility depends solely on the reference of the understanding to experience, but with a completely reversed mode of connection which never occurred to Hume, not by deriving them from experience, but by deriving experience from them.

This is therefore the result of all our foregoing inquiries: "All synthetical principles a priori are nothing more than principles of possible experience, and can never be referred to things in themselves, but to appearances as objects of experience. And hence pure mathematics as well as a pure science of nature can never be referred to anything more than mere appearances, and can only represent either that which makes experience generally possible, or else that which, as it is derived from these principles, must always be capable of being represented in some possible experience." [. . .]

32. Since the oldest days of philosophy inquirers into pure reason have conceived, besides the things of sense, or appearances (phenomena), which make up the sensible world, certain creations of the understanding (*Verstandeswesen*), called noumena, which should constitute an intelligible world. And as appearance and illusion were by those men identified (a thing which we may well excuse in an undeveloped epoch), actuality was only conceded to the creations of thought.

And we indeed, rightly considering objects of sense as mere appearances, confess thereby that they are based upon a thing in itself, though we know not this thing in its internal constitution but only know its appearances, viz., the way in which our senses are affected by this unknown something. The understanding therefore, by assuming appearances, grants the existence of things in themselves also, and so far we may say, that the representation of such things as form the basis of phenomena, consequently of mere creations of the understanding, is not only admissible but unavoidable.

Our critical deduction by no means excludes things of that sort (noumena), but rather limits the principles of the Aesthetic (the science of the sensibility) to this, that they shall not extend to all things, as everything would then be turned into mere appearance, but that they shall only hold good of objects of possible experience. Hereby then objects of the understanding are granted, but with the inculcation of this rule which admits of no exception: "that we neither know nor can know anything at all definite of these pure objects of the understanding because our pure concepts of the understanding as well as our pure intuitions extend to nothing but objects of possible experience, consequently to mere things of sense, and as soon as we leave this sphere these concepts retain no meaning whatever." [. . .]

## Notes

1. I freely grant that these examples do not represent such judgments of perception as ever could become judgments of experience, even though a concept of the understanding were superadded, because they refer merely to feeling, which everybody knows to be merely subjective, and which of course can never be attributed to the object, and consequently never become objective. [. . .] An example of the judgments of perception, which become judgments of experience by superadded concepts of the understanding, will be given in the next note.

2. As an easier example, we may take the following: "When the sun shines on the stone, it grows warm." This judgment, however often I and others may have perceived it, is a mere judgment of perception, and contains no necessity; perceptions are only usually conjoined in this manner. But if I say, "The sun warms the stone," I add to the perception a concept of the understanding, viz., that of cause, which connects with the concept of sunshine that of heat as a necessary consequence, and the synthetical judgment becomes of necessity universally valid, viz., objective, and is converted from a perception into experience.

## Study Questions

1. Explain why, for Kant, truths of arithmetic (e.g., 2 + 3 = 5) and geometry (e.g., "The internal angles of a triangle add up to 180 degrees") are a priori, not a posteriori; synthetic, not analytic; and necessary, not contingent.

2. What is Kant's response to Descartes' dream hypothesis and the brand of idealism that results from taking it seriously?

3. Why does Kant consider his "transcendental" or "critical idealism" to provide "the proper antidote" for Berkeley's "mystical and visionary idealism"?

4. What about Hume's philosophy so impressed and challenged Kant that he was awoken from a "dogmatic slumber" and encouraged to set off in a "new direction" in his own work? What solution does Kant offer to the challenge posed by Hume?

# Nelson Goodman

Nelson Goodman (1906–98) received BS and PhD degrees from Harvard University and was appointed professor there in 1968 after positions at Tufts University, the University of Pennsylvania, and Brandeis University. Goodman's specialities include epistemology, metaphysics, logic, and aesthetics. The interest Goodman displays in art was more than theoretical: he was a collector and gallery director, and was married to painter Katharine Sturgis. In *Ways of Worldmaking*, Goodman argues that the external world we claim to know is one that we, ourselves, have constructed.

## Words, Works, Worlds

From *Ways of Worldmaking*

### 1. Questions

Countless worlds made from nothing by use of symbols—so might a satirist summarize some major themes in the work of **Ernst Cassirer**. These themes—the multiplicity of worlds, the speciousness of "the given," the creative power of the understanding, the variety and formative function of symbols— are also integral to my own thinking. Sometimes, though, I forget how eloquently they have been set forth by Cassirer (e.g., in *Language and Myth*), partly perhaps because his emphasis on myth, his concern with the comparative study of cultures, and his talk of the human spirit have been mistakenly associated with current trends toward mystical obscurantism, anti-intellectual intuitionism, or anti-scientific humanism. Actually these attitudes are as alien to Cassirer as to my own skeptical, analytic, constructionalist orientation.

My aim in what follows is less to defend certain theses that Cassirer and I share than to take a hard look at some crucial questions they raise. In just what sense are there many worlds? What distinguishes genuine from spurious worlds? What are worlds made of? How are they made? What role do symbols play in the making? And how is worldmaking related to knowing? These questions must be faced even if full and final answers are far off.

### 2. Versions and Visions

As intimated by **William James'** equivocal title *A Pluralistic Universe*, the issue between monism and pluralism tends to evaporate under analysis. If there is but one world, it embraces a multiplicity of contrasting aspects; if there are many worlds, the collection of them all is one. The one world may be taken as many, or the many worlds taken as one; whether one or many depends on the way of taking.

Why, then, does Cassirer stress the multiplicity of worlds? In what important and often neglected sense are there many worlds? Let it be clear that the question here is not of the possible worlds that many of my contemporaries, especially those near Disneyland, are busy making and manipulating. We are not speaking in terms of multiple possible alternatives to a single actual world but of multiple actual worlds. How to interpret such terms as "real," "unreal," "fictive," and "possible" is a subsequent question.

Consider, to begin with, the statements "The sun always moves" and "The sun never moves" which, though equally true, are at odds with each other. Shall we say, then, that they describe different worlds, and indeed that there are as many different worlds as there are such mutually exclusive truths? Rather, we are inclined to regard the two strings of words not as complete statements with truth-values of their own but as elliptical for some such statements as "Under frame of reference *A*, the sun always moves" and "Under frame of reference *B*, the sun never moves"— statements that may both be true of the same world.

Frames of reference, though, seem to belong less to what is described than to systems of description: and each of the two statements relates what is described to such a system. If I ask about the world, you can offer to tell me how it is under one or more frames of reference; but if I insist that you tell me how it is apart from all frames, what can you say? We are confined to ways of describing whatever is described. Our universe, so to speak, consists of these ways rather than of a world or of worlds.

The alternative descriptions of motion, all of them in much the same terms and routinely transformable into one another, provide only a minor and rather pallid example of diversity in accounts of the world. Much more striking is the vast variety of versions and visions in the several sciences, in the works of different painters and writers, and in our perceptions as informed by these, by circumstances, and by our own insights, interests, and past experiences. Even with all illusory or wrong or dubious versions dropped, the rest exhibit new dimensions of disparity. Here we have no neat set of frames of reference, no ready rules for transforming physics, biology, and psychology into one another, and no way at all of transforming any of these into **Van Gogh**'s vision, or Van Gogh's into **Canaletto**'s. Such of these versions as are depictions rather than descriptions have no truth-value in the literal sense, and cannot be combined by conjunction. The difference between juxtaposing and conjoining two statements has no evident analogue for two pictures or for a picture and a statement. The dramatically contrasting versions of the world can of course be relativized: each is right under a given system—for a given science, a given artist, or a given perceiver and situation. Here again we turn from describing or depicting "the world" to talking of descriptions and depictions, but now without even the consolation of intertranslatability among or any evident organization of the several systems in question.

Yet doesn't a right version differ from a wrong one just in applying to the world, so that rightness itself depends upon and implies a world? We might better say that "the world" depends upon rightness. We cannot test a version by comparing it with a world undescribed, undepicted, unperceived, but only by other means that I shall discuss later. While we may speak of determining what versions are right as "learning about the world," "the world" supposedly being that which all right versions describe, all we learn about the world is contained in right versions of it; and while the underlying world, bereft of these, need not be denied to those who love it, it is perhaps on the whole a world well lost. For some purposes, we may want to define a relation that will so sort versions into clusters that each cluster constitutes a world, and the members of the cluster are versions of that world; but for many purposes, right world-descriptions and world-depictions and world-perceptions, the ways-the-world-is, or just versions, can be treated as our worlds.

Since the fact that there are many different world-versions is hardly debatable, and the question how many if any worlds-in-themselves there are is virtually empty, in what non-trivial sense are there, as Cassirer and like-minded pluralists insist, many worlds? Just this, I think: that many different world-versions are of independent interest and importance, without any requirement or presumption of reducibility to a single base. The pluralist, far from being anti-scientific, accepts the sciences at full value. His typical adversary is the monopolistic materialist or physicalist who maintains that one system, physics, is preeminent and all-inclusive, such that every other version must eventually be reduced to it or rejected as false or meaningless. If all right versions could somehow be reduced to one and only one, that one might with some semblance of plausibility be regarded as the only truth about the only world. But the evidence for such reducibility is negligible, and even the claim is nebulous since physics itself is fragmentary and unstable and the kind and consequences of reduction envisaged are vague. (How do you go about reducing **Constable**'s or **James Joyce**'s world-view to physics?) I am the last person likely to underrate construction and reduction. A reduction from one system to another can make a genuine contribution to understanding the interrelationships among world-versions; but reduction in any reasonably strict sense is rare, almost always partial, and seldom if ever unique. To demand full and sole reducibility to physics or any other one version is to forego nearly all other versions. The pluralists" acceptance of versions other than physics implies no relaxation of rigour but a recognition that standards different from yet no less exacting than those applied in science are appropriate for appraising what is conveyed in perceptual or pictorial or literary versions.

So long as contrasting right versions not all reducible to one are countenanced, unity is to be sought not in an ambivalent or neutral *something* beneath these versions but in an overall organization embracing them. Cassirer undertakes the search through a cross-cultural study of the development of myth, religion, language, art, and science. My approach is rather through an analytic study of types and functions of symbols and symbol systems. In neither case should a unique result be anticipated; universes of worlds as well as worlds themselves may be built in many ways.

## 3. How Firm a Foundation?

The non-**Kant**ian theme of multiplicity of worlds is closely akin to the Kantian theme of the vacuity of the notion of pure content. The one denies us a unique world, the other the common stuff of which worlds are made. Together these theses defy our intuitive demand for something stolid underneath, and threaten to leave us uncontrolled, spinning out our own inconsequent fantasies.

The overwhelming case against perception without conception, the pure given, absolute immediacy, the innocent eye, substance as substratum, has been so fully and frequently set forth—by **Berkeley**, Kant, Cassirer, [. . .] and many others—as to need no restatement here. Talk of unstructured content or an unconceptualized given or a substratum without properties is self-defeating; for the talk imposes structure, conceptualizes, ascribes properties. Although conception without perception is merely *empty*, perception without conception is *blind* (totally inoperative). Predicates, pictures, other labels, schemata, survive want of application, but content vanishes without form. We can have words without a world but no world without words or other symbols.

The many stuffs—matter, energy, waves, phenomena—that worlds are made of are made along with the worlds. But made from what?

Not from nothing, after all, but *from other worlds*. Worldmaking as we know it always starts from worlds already on hand; the making is a remaking. Anthropology and developmental psychology may study social and individual histories of such world-building, but the search for a universal or necessary beginning is best left to theology. My interest here is rather with the processes involved in building a world out of others.

With false hope of a firm foundation gone, with the world displaced by worlds that are but versions, with substance dissolved into function, and with the given acknowledged as taken, we face the questions how worlds are made, tested, and known.

## 4. Ways of Worldmaking

Without presuming to instruct the gods or other worldmakers, or attempting any comprehensive or systematic survey, I want to illustrate and comment on some of the processes that go into worldmaking. Actually, I am concerned more with certain relationships among worlds than with how or whether particular worlds are made from others.

### (a) Composition and Decomposition

Much but by no means all worldmaking consists of taking apart and putting together, often conjointly: on the one hand, of dividing wholes into parts and partitioning kinds into subspecies, analyzing complexes into component features, drawing distinctions; on the other hand, of composing wholes and kinds out of parts and members and subclasses, combining features into complexes, and making connections. Such composition or decomposition is normally effected or assisted or consolidated by the application of labels: names, predicates, gestures, pictures, etc. Thus, for example, temporally diverse events are brought together under a proper name or identified as making up "an object" or "a person"; or snow is sundered into several materials under terms of the Eskimo vocabulary. [. . .]

Identification rests upon organization into entities and kinds. The response to the question "Same or not the same?" must always be "Same what?" Different soandsos may be the same such-and-such: what we point to or indicate, verbally or otherwise, may be different events but the same object, different towns but the same state, different members but the same club or different clubs but the same members, different innings but the same ball game. "The ball-in-play" of a single game may be comprised of temporal segments of a dozen or more baseballs. The psychologist asking the child to judge constancy when one vessel is emptied into another must be careful to consider *what* constancy is in question—constancy of volume or depth or shape or kind of material, etc. Identity or constancy in a world is identity with respect to what is within that world as organized.

Motley entities cutting across each other in complicated patterns may belong to the same world. We do not make a new world every time we take things apart or put them together in another way; but worlds may *differ* in that not everything belonging to one belongs to the other. The world of the Eskimo who has not grasped the comprehensive concept of snow differs not only from the world of the Samoan but also from the world of the New Englander who has not grasped the Eskimo's distinctions. In other cases, worlds differ in response to theoretical rather than practical needs. A world with points as elements cannot be the **Whitehead**ian world having points as certain classes of nesting volumes or having points as certain pairs of intersecting lines or as certain triples of intersecting planes. That the points of our everyday world can be equally well defined in any of these ways does not mean that a point can be identified in any one world with a nest of volumes and a pair of lines and a triple of planes; for all these are different from each other. Again the world of a system taking minimal concrete phenomena as atomic cannot admit qualities as atomic parts of these concretra.

Repetition as well as identification is relative to organization. A world may be unmanageably heterogeneous or unbearably monotonous according to how events are sorted into kinds. Whether or not today's experiment repeats yesterday's, however much the two events may differ, depends upon whether they test a common hypothesis; as Sir George Thomson puts it: "There will always be something different. . . . What it comes to when you say you repeat an experiment is that you repeat all the features of an experiment which a theory determines are relevant. In other words you repeat the experiment as an example of the theory" (85). Likewise, two musical performances that differ drastically are nevertheless performances of the same work if they conform to the same score. The notational system distinguishes constitutive from contingent features, thus picking out the performance-kinds that count as works. And things "go on in the same way" or not according to what is regarded as the same way; "now I can go on," in **Wittgenstein**'s sense, when I have found a familiar pattern, or a tolerable variation of one, that fits and goes beyond the cases given. Induction requires taking some classes to the exclusion of others as relevant kinds. Only so, for example, do our observations of emeralds exhibit any regularity and confirm that all emeralds are green rather than that all are grue (i.e., examined before a given date and green, or not so examined and blue—Goodman 72–80). The uniformity of nature we marvel at or the unreliability we protest belongs to a world of our own making.

In these latter cases, worlds differ in the relevant kinds they comprise. I say "relevant" rather than "natural" for two reasons: first, "natural" is an inapt term to cover not only biological species but such artificial kinds as musical works, psychological experiments, and types of machinery; and second, "natural" suggests some absolute categorical or psychological priority, while the kinds in question are rather habitual or traditional or devised for a new purpose.

## (b) Weighting

While we may say that in the cases discussed some relevant kinds of one world are missing from another, we might perhaps better say that the two worlds contain just the same classes sorted differently into relevant and irrelevant kinds. Some relevant kinds of the one world, rather than being absent from the other, are present as irrelevant kinds; some differences among worlds are not so much in entities comprised as in emphasis or accent, and these differences are no less consequential. Just as to stress all syllables is to stress none, so to take all classes as relevant kinds is to take none as such. In one world there may be many kinds serving different purposes; but conflicting purposes may make for irreconcilable accents and contrasting worlds, as may conflicting conceptions of what kinds serve a given purpose. Grue cannot be a relevant kind for induction in the same world as green, for that would preclude some of the decisions, right or wrong, that constitute inductive inference.

Some of the most striking contrasts of emphasis appear in the arts. Many of the differences among portrayals by **Daumier**, **Ingres**, **Michelangelo**, and **Rouault** are differences in aspects accentuated. What counts as emphasis, of course, is departure from the relative prominence accorded the several features in the current world of our everyday seeing. With changing interests and new insights, the visual weighting of features of bulk or line or stance or light alters, and yesterday's level world seems strangely perverted—yesterday's realistic calendar landscape becomes a repulsive caricature.

These differences in emphasis, too, amount to a difference in relevant kinds recognized. Several portrayals of the same subject may thus place it according to different categorical schemata. Like a green emerald and a grue one, even if the same emerald, a **Piero della Francesca** *Christ* and a **Rembrandt** one belong to worlds organized into different kinds. [. . .]

Emphasis or weighting is not always binary as is a sorting into relevant and irrelevant kinds or into important and unimportant features. Ratings of relevance, importance, utility, value often yield hierarchies rather than dichotomies. Such weightings are also instances of a particular type of ordering.

## (c) Ordering

Worlds not differing in entities or emphasis may differ in ordering; for example, the worlds of different constructional systems differ in order of derivation. As nothing is at rest or is in motion apart from a frame of reference, so nothing is primitive or is derivationally prior to anything apart from a constructional system. However, derivation unlike motion is of little immediate practical interest; and thus in our everyday world, although we almost always adopt a frame of reference at least temporarily, we seldom adopt a derivational basis. Earlier I said that the difference between a world having points as pairs of lines and a world having lines as composed of points is that the latter but not the former admits as entities nonlinear elements comprised within lines. But alternatively we may say that these worlds differ in their derivational ordering of lines and points of the not-derivationally-ordered world of daily discourse.

Orderings of a different sort pervade perception and practical cognition. The standard ordering of brightness in colour follows the linear increase in physical intensity of light, but the standard ordering of hues curls the straight line of increasing wavelength into a circle. Order includes periodicity as well as proximity; and the standard ordering of tones is by pitch and octave. Orderings alter with circumstances and objectives. Much as the nature of shapes changes under different geometries, so do perceived patterns change under different orderings; the patterns perceived under a 12-tone scale are quite different from those perceived under the traditional 8-tone scale, and rhythms depend upon the marking off into measures. [. . .]

All measurement, furthermore, is based upon order. Indeed, only through suitable arrangements and groupings can we handle vast quantities of material perceptually or cognitively. Gombrich discusses the decimal periodization of historical time into decades, centuries, and millennia. Daily time is marked off into 24 hours, and each of these into 60 minutes of 60 seconds each. Whatever else may be said of these modes of organization, they are not "found in the world" but *built into a world*. Ordering, as well as composition and decomposition and weighting of wholes and kinds, participates in worldmaking.

## (d) Deletion and Supplementation

Also, the making of one world out of another usually involves some extensive weeding out and filling—actual excision of some old and supply of some new material. Our capacity for overlooking is virtually unlimited, and what we do take in usually consists of significant fragments and clues that need massive supplementation. Artists often make skillful use of this: a lithograph by **Giacometti** fully presents a walking man by sketches of nothing but the head, hands, and feet in just the right postures and positions against an expanse of blank paper; and a drawing by Katharine Sturgis conveys a hockey player in action by a single charged line.

That we find what we are prepared to find (what we look for or what forcefully affronts our expectations), and that we are likely to be blind to what neither helps nor hinders our pursuits, are commonplaces of everyday life and amply attested in the psychological laboratory. In the painful experience of proofreading and the more pleasurable one of watching a skilled magician, we incurably miss something that is there and see something that is not there. Memory edits more ruthlessly; a person with equal command of two languages may remember a learned list of items while forgetting in which language they were listed (Kolers 78–86). And even within what we do perceive and remember, we dismiss as illusory or negligible what cannot be fitted into the architecture of the world we are building.

The scientist is no less drastic, rejecting or purifying most of the entities and events of the world of ordinary things while generating quantities of filling for curves suggested by sparse data, and erecting elaborate structures on the basis of meagre observations. Thus does he strive to build a world conforming to his chosen concepts and obeying his universal laws.

Replacement of a so-called analog by a so-called digital system through the articulation of separate steps involves deletion; for example, to use a digital thermometer with readings in tenths of a degree is to recognize no temperature as lying between 90 and 90.1 degrees. Similar deletion occurs under standard musical notation, which recognizes no pitch between *c* and *c#* and no duration between a sixty-fourth and a one hundred-and-twenty-eighth note. On the other hand, supplementation occurs when, say, an analog replaces a digital instrument for registering attendance, or reporting money raised, or when a violinist performs from a score.

### (e) Deformation

Finally, some changes are reshapings or deformations that may according to point of view be considered either corrections or distortions. The physicist smooths out the simplest rough curve that fits all his data. Vision stretches a line ending with arrowheads pointing *in* while shrinking a physically equal line ending with arrowheads pointing *out,* and tends to expand the size of a smaller more valuable coin in relation to that of a larger less valuable one. Caricaturists often go beyond overemphasis to actual distortion. **Picasso** starting from **Velásquez**'s *Las Meninas*, and **Brahms** starting from a theme of **Haydn**'s, work magical variations that amount to revelations.

These then are ways that worlds are made. I do not say *the* ways. My classification is not offered as comprehensive or clearcut or mandatory. Not only do the processes illustrated often occur in combination but the examples chosen sometimes fit equally well under more than one heading; for example, some changes may be considered alternatively as reweightings or reorderings or reshapings or as all of these, and some deletions are also matters of differences in composition. All I have tried to do is to suggest something of the variety of processes in constant use. While a tighter systematization could surely be developed, none can be ultimate; for as remarked earlier, there is no more a unique world of worlds than there is a unique world.

## 5. Trouble with Truth

With all this freedom to divide and combine, emphasize, order, delete, fill in and fill out, and even distort, what are the objectives and the constraints? What are the criteria for success in making a world?

Insofar as a version is verbal and consists of statements, truth may be relevant. But truth cannot be defined or tested by agreement with "the world"; for not only do truths differ for different worlds but the nature of agreement between a version and a world apart from it is notoriously nebulous. Rather [. . .] a version is taken to be true when it offends no unyielding beliefs and none of its own precepts. Among beliefs unyielding at a given time may be long-lived reflections of laws of logic, short-lived reflections of recent observations, and other convictions and prejudices ingrained with varying degrees of firmness. Among precepts, for example, may be choices among alternative frames of reference, weightings, and derivational bases. But the line between beliefs and precepts is neither sharp nor stable. Beliefs are framed in concepts informed by precepts; and if a **Boyle** ditches his data for a smooth curve just missing them all, we may say either that observational volume and pressure are different properties from theoretical volume and pressure or that the truths about volume and pressure differ in the two worlds of observation and theory. Even the staunchest belief may in time admit alternatives; "The earth is at rest" passed from dogma to dependence upon precept.

Truth, far from being a solemn and severe master, is a docile and obedient servant. The scientist who supposes that he is single-mindedly dedicated to the search for truth deceives himself. He is unconcerned with the trivial truths he could grind out endlessly; and he looks to the multifaceted and irregular results of observations for little more than suggestions of overall structures and significant generalizations. He seeks system, simplicity, scope; and when satisfied on these scores he tailors truth to fit. He as much decrees as discovers the laws he sets forth, as much designs as discerns the patterns he delineates.

Truth, moreover, pertains solely to what is said, and literal truth solely to what is said literally. [. . .] In a scientific treatise, literal truth counts most; but in a poem or novel, metaphorical or allegorical truth may matter more, for even a literally false statement may be metaphorically true and may mark or make new associations and discriminations, change emphases, effect exclusions and additions. And statements whether literally or metaphorically true or false may show what they do not say, may work as trenchant literal or metaphorical examples of unmentioned features and feelings. In Vachel Lindsay's *The Congo*, for example, the pulsating pattern of drumbeats is insistently exhibited rather than described.

Finally, for nonverbal versions and even for verbal versions without statements, truth is irrelevant. We risk confusion when we speak of pictures or predicates as "true of" what they depict or apply to; they have no truth-value and may represent or denote some things and not others, while a statement does have truth-value and is true of everything

if of anything. A nonrepresentational picture such as a **Mondrian** says nothing, denotes nothing, pictures nothing, and is neither true nor false, but shows much. Nevertheless, showing or exemplifying, like denoting, is a referential function; and much the same considerations count for pictures as for the concepts or predicates of a theory: their relevance and their revelations, their force and their fit—in sum their *rightness*. Rather than speak of pictures as true or false we might better speak of theories as right or wrong; for the truth of the laws of a theory is but one special feature and is often, as we have seen, overridden in importance by the cogency and compactness and comprehensiveness, the informativeness and organizing power of the whole system.

"The truth, the whole truth, and nothing but the truth" would thus be a perverse and paralyzing policy for any worldmaker. The whole truth would be too much; it is too vast, variable, and clogged with trivia. The truth alone would be too little, for some right versions are not true—being either false or neither true nor false—and even for true versions rightness may matter more.

## 6. Relative Reality

Shouldn't we now return to sanity from all this mad proliferation of worlds? Shouldn't we stop speaking of right versions as if each were, or had, its own world, and recognize all as versions of one and the same neutral and underlying world. The world thus regained, as remarked earlier, is a world without kinds or order or motion or rest or pattern—a world not worth fighting for or against.

We might, though, take the real world to be that of some one of the right versions (or groups of them bound together by some principle of reducibility or translatability) and regard all others as versions of that same world differing from the standard version in accountable ways. The physicist takes his world as the real one, attributing the deletions, additions, irregularities, emphases of other versions to the imperfections of perception, to the urgencies of practice, or to poetic license. The phenomenalist regards the perceptual world as fundamental, and the excisions, abstractions, simplifications, and distortions of other versions as resulting from scientific or practical or artistic concerns. For the man-in-the-street, most versions from science, art, and perception depart in some ways from the familiar serviceable world he has jerry-built from fragments of scientific and artistic tradition and from his own struggle for survival. This world, indeed, is the one most often taken as real; for reality in a world, like realism in a picture, is largely a matter of habit.

Ironically, then, our passion for *one* world is satisfied, at different times and for different purposes, in *many* different ways. Not only motion, derivation, weighting, order, but even reality is relative. That right versions and actual worlds are many does not obliterate the distinction between right and wrong versions, does not recognize merely possible worlds answering to wrong versions, and does not imply that all right alternatives are equally good for every or indeed for any purpose. Not even a fly is likely to take one of its wing-tips as a fixed point; we do not welcome molecules or concreta as elements of our everyday world, or combine tomatoes and triangles and typewriters and tyrants and tornadoes into a single kind; the physicist will count none of these among his fundamental particles; the painter who sees the way the man-in-the-street does will have more popular than artistic success. And the same philosopher who here metaphilosophically contemplates a vast variety of worlds finds that only versions meeting the demands of a dogged and deflationary nominalism suit his purposes in constructing philosophical systems.

Moreover, while readiness to recognize alternative worlds may be liberating, and suggestive of new avenues of exploration, a willingness to welcome all worlds builds none. Mere acknowledgement of the many available frames of reference provides us with no map of the motions of heavenly bodies; acceptance of the eligibility of alternative bases produces no scientific theory or philosophical system; awareness of varied ways of seeing paints no pictures. A broad mind is no substitute for hard work.

## 7. Notes on Knowing

What I have been saying bears on the nature of knowledge. On these terms, knowing cannot be exclusively or even primarily a matter of determining what is true. Discovery often amounts as when I place a piece in a jigsaw puzzle, not to arrival at a proposition for declaration or defence, but to finding a fit. Much of knowing aims at something other than true, or any, belief. An increase in acuity of insight or in range of comprehension, rather than a change in belief, occurs when we find in a pictured forest a face we already knew was there, or learn to distinguish stylistic differences among works already classified by artist or composer or writer, or study a picture or a concerto or a treatise until we see or hear or grasp features and structures we could not discern before. Such growth in knowledge is not by formation or fixation of belief (Peirce) but by the advancement of understanding.

Furthermore, if worlds are as much made as found, so also knowing is as much remaking as reporting. All the processes of worldmaking I have discussed enter into knowing. Perceiving motion, we have seen, often consists in producing it. Discovering laws involves drafting them. Recognizing patterns is very much a matter of inventing and imposing them. Comprehension and creation go on together. [. . .]

## Works Cited

Cassirer, E. *Language and Myth*. Trans. S. Langer. New York: Harper, 1946.

Gombrich, E.H. "Zeit, Zahl, und Zeichen." Delivered at the Cassirer celebration in Hamburg, 1974.

Goodman, N. *Fact, Fiction, and Forecast*, 3rd edn. Indianapolis: Bobbs-Merrill, 1973.

Kolers, P. "Bilinguals and Information Processing." *Scientific American* 218 (1968): 78–86.

Peirce, C.S. "The Fixation of Belief." *Collected Papers of Charles Sanders Peirce*. Vol. 5. Pp. 223–47. Cambridge, MA: Harvard University Press, 1934.

Thomson, G. "Some Thoughts on Scientific Method." *Boston Studies in the Philosophy of Science*. Vol. 2. New York: Humanities Press, 1965.

Wittgenstein, L. *Philosophical Investigations*. Trans. G.E.M. Anscombe. Oxford: Blackwell, 1953.

## Study Questions

1. Goodman is considered to be an idealist. Is his idealism more like Berkeley's or Kant's?
2. Why does Goodman use the terminology of "relevant" rather than "natural" kinds?
3. Making reference to specific "ways of worldmaking" in science, painting and literature, or perception, explain what Goodman means when he describes himself as having a "constructionalist orientation."
4. Knowledge is generally considered to involve the accumulation of beliefs that are true—i.e., beliefs that accurately represent the world as it really is, "undescribed, undepicted, unperceived." If we accept with Goodman that such a world is "perhaps on the whole a world well lost," where does this leave truth and the possibility of knowledge?

## Anjan Chakravartty

Anjan Chakravartty is a professor of philosophy at the University of Notre Dame, having moved there from the University of Toronto's Institute for the History and Philosophy of Science and Technology. Chakravartty earned his PhD and MPhil in history and philosophy of science at the University of Cambridge and an MA in philosophy and BSc in biophysics at the University of Toronto. *A Metaphysics for Scientific Realism* won the Canadian Philosophical Association Book Prize in 2009.

# Realism and Anti-realism; Metaphysics and Empiricism

From *A Metaphysics for Scientific Realism: Knowing the Unobservable*

## 1. The Trouble with Common Sense

Hanging in my office is a framed photograph of an armillary sphere, which resides in the Whipple Museum of the History of Science in Cambridge, England. An armillary sphere is a celestial globe. It is made up of a spherical model of the planet Earth (the sort we all played with as children), but the model is surrounded by an intricate skeleton of graduated rings, representing the most important celestial circles. Armillary spheres were devised in ancient Greece and developed as instruments for teaching and astronomical calculation. During the same period, heavenly bodies were widely conceived as fixed to the surfaces of concentrically arranged crystalline spheres, which rotate around the Earth at their centre.

This particular armillary sphere has, I expect, many fascinating historical stories to tell, but there is a specific reason I framed the picture. Once upon a time, astronomers speculated about the causes and mechanisms of the motions of the planets and stars, and their ontology of crystalline spheres was a central feature of astronomical theory for hundreds of years. But crystalline spheres are not the sorts of things one can observe, at least not with the naked eye from the surface of the Earth. Even if it had turned out that they exist, it is doubtful one would have been able to devise an instrument to detect them before the days of satellites and space shuttles. Much of the energy of the sciences is consumed in the attempt to work out and describe things that are inaccessible to the unaided senses, whether in practice or in principle. My armillary sphere, with its glorious and complicated mess of interwoven circles, is a reminder of past testaments to that obsession.

In describing the notion of a crystalline sphere, I have already made some distinctions. There are things that one can, under favourable circumstances, perceive with one's unaided senses. Let us call them "observables," though this is to privilege vision over the other senses for the sake of terminological convenience. Unobservables, then, are things one cannot perceive with one's unaided senses, and this category divides into two subcategories. Some unobservables are nonetheless detectable through the use of instruments with which one hopes to "extend" one's senses, and others are simply undetectable. These distinctions are important, because major controversies about how to interpret the claims of the sciences revolve around them. In this chapter, I will briefly outline the most important positions engaged in these controversies, and consider how the tension between speculative metaphysics and empiricism has kept them alive.

There are occasional disputes about what counts as science—concerning how best to exclude astrology but include astronomy, about what to say to creationists unhappy with the teaching of evolutionary biology in schools, etc. I leave these disputes to one side here, and begin simply with what are commonly regarded as sciences today. It is widely held that the sciences are not merely knowledge-producing endeavours, but *the* means of knowledge production *par excellence*. Scientific inquiry is our best hope for gaining knowledge of the world, the things that compose it, its structure, its laws, and so on. And the more one investigates, the better it gets. Scientific knowledge is progressive; it renders the natural world with increasing accuracy.

*Scientific realism*, to a rough, first approximation, is the view that scientific theories correctly describe the nature of a mind-independent world. Outside of philosophy, realism is usually regarded as common sense, but philosophers enjoy subjecting commonplace views to thorough scrutiny, and this one certainly requires it. The main consideration in favour of realism is ancient, but more recently referred to as the "miracle argument" (or "no-miracles argument") after the memorable slogan coined by Hilary Putnam that realism "is the only philosophy that doesn't make the success of science a miracle" (73). Scientific theories are amazingly successful in that they allow us to predict, manipulate, and participate in worldly phenomena, and the most straightforward explanation of this is that they correctly describe the nature of the

world, or something close by. In the absence of this explanation the success afforded by the sciences might well seem miraculous, and, given the choice, one should always choose common sense over miracles.

Some have questioned the need for an explanation of the success of science at all. Bas van Fraassen (23–5, 34–40), for example, suggests that successful scientific theories are analogous to well-adapted organisms. There is no need to explain the success of organisms, he says. Only well-adapted organisms survive, just as only well-adapted theories survive, where "well-adapted" in the latter case means adequate to the tasks to which one puts theories. These tasks are generally thought to include predictions and retrodictions (predictions concerning past phenomena), and perhaps most impressively novel predictions (ones about classes of things or phenomena one has yet to observe). A well-adapted theory is one whose predictions, retrodictions, and novel predictions, if any, are borne out in the course of observation and experimentation. But saying that successful theories are ones that are well-adapted may be tantamount to the **tautology** that successful theories are successful, which is not saying much. Whatever the merits of the Darwinian analogy for theories generally, one might still wonder why any *given* theory (organism) survives for the time it does, and this may require a more specific consideration of the properties of the theory (organism) in virtue of which it is well adapted. [. . .]

The attempt to satisfy the desire for an explanation of scientific success has produced the bulk of the literature on scientific realism. As arguments go, the miracle argument is surprisingly poor, all things considered, and consequently alternatives to realism have flourished. The poverty of the miracle argument and consequent flourishing of rivals to realism stem from difficulties presented by three general issues, which I will mention only briefly:

1. the use of abductive inference, or inference to the best explanation (IBE)
2. the underdetermination of theory choice by data or evidence (UTD)
3. discontinuities in scientific theories over time, yielding a pessimistic induction (PI)

Abduction is a form of inference famous from the writings of **Charles Sanders Peirce**, inspiring what is now generally called "inference to the best explanation" (some use the term synonymously with "abduction" while others, more strictly, distinguish it from Peirce's version). IBE offers the following advice to inference makers: infer the hypothesis that, if true, would provide the best explanation for whatever it is you hope to explain. Note that the miracle argument itself is an abductive argument. Why are scientific theories so successful at making predictions and accounting for empirical data? One answer is that they are true, and this seems, to the realist at any rate, the best explanation. One might even think it the only conceivable explanation, but as we shall see, in light of UTD and PI, this is highly contestable. First, however, let us turn from the particular case of the miracle argument to the merits of IBE as a form of inference in general. There is little doubt that this sort of inferential practice is fundamental to everyday and scientific reasoning. The decision to adopt one theory as opposed to its rivals, for example, is generally a complex process involving many factors, but IBE will most certainly figure at some stage.

Antirealists are quick to point out that in order for an instance of IBE to yield the truth, two conditions must be met. Firstly, one must rank the rival hypotheses under consideration correctly with respect to the likelihood that they are true. Secondly, the truth must be among the hypotheses one is considering. But can one ensure that these conditions are met? Regarding the first, it is difficult to say what features a truth-likely explanation should have. Beyond the minimum criterion of some impressive measure of agreement with outcomes of observation and experiment, possible indicators of good explanations have been widely discussed. Some hold that theories characterized by features such as simplicity, elegance, and unity (with other theories or domains of inquiry) are preferable. Quite apart from the matter of describing what these virtues are, however, and knowing how to compare and prioritize them, it is not immediately obvious that such virtues have anything to do with truth. There is no a priori reason, one might argue, to reject the possibility that

natural phenomena are rather complex, inelegant, and disjoint. And regarding the second condition for successful IBE, in most cases it is difficult to see how one could know in advance that the true hypothesis is among those considered. (A case in which one does have this knowledge is where rival hypotheses are contradictions.)

In practice it is often difficult to produce even one theory that explains the empirical data, let alone rivals. This, however, does not diminish the seriousness of the problem. In fact, it turns out that it may be irrelevant whether one ever has a choice to make between rival theories in practice. For some maintain that rival theories are always possible, whether or not one has thought of them, and this is sufficient to raise concerns about IBE. Confidence in the possibility of rivals stems from the underdetermination thesis, or UTD. Its canonical formulation due to **Pierre Duhem**, later expressed in rather different terms by **W.V.O. Quine** (hence also called the "Duhem-Quine thesis"), goes this way. Theoretical hypotheses rarely if ever yield predictions by themselves. Rather, they must be conjoined with auxiliary hypotheses—background theories, related theories, theories about the measurement of relevant parameters, etc.—in order to yield predictions. If observation and experimentation produce data that are not as one predicts, one has a choice to make concerning which of the prediction-yielding hypotheses is culpable. One can always preserve a favoured hypothesis at the expense of something else. Since there are different ways of choosing how to account for recalcitrant data, different overall theories or conjunctions of hypotheses may be used to account for the empirical evidence. Thus, in general, there is always more than one overall theory consistent with the data.

In more contemporary discussions, UTD is usually explicated differently. Given a theory, $T_1$, it is always possible to generate an empirically equivalent but different theory, $T_2$. $T_2$ is a theory that makes precisely the same claims regarding observable phenomena as $T_1$, but differs in other respects. $T_2$, might, for example, exclude all of the unobservable entities and processes of $T_1$, or replace some or all of these with others, or simply alter them, but in such a way as to produce exactly the same observable predictions. Given that this sort of manoeuvring is always possible, how does one decide between rival theories so constructed? Here again the realist must find a way to infer to a particular theory at the expense of its rivals, with the various difficulties this engenders.

In addition to challenges concerning IBE and UTD, at least one anti-realist argument aspires to the status of an empirical refutation of realism. PI, or as it is often called, the "pessimistic meta-induction," can be summarized as follows. Consider the history of scientific theories in any particular domain. From the perspective of the present, most past theories are considered false, strictly speaking. There is evidence of severe discontinuity over time, regarding both the entities and processes described. This evidence makes up a catalogue of instability in the things to which theories refer. By induction based on these past cases, it is likely that present-day theories are also false and will be recognized as such in the future. Realists are generally keen to respond that not even they believe that theories are true *simpliciter*. Scientific theorizing is a complex business, replete with things like approximation, abstraction, and idealization. What is important is that successive theories get better with respect to the truth, coming closer to it over time. It is the progress sciences make in describing nature with increasing accuracy that fuels realism. Good theories, they say, are normally "approximately true," and more so as the sciences progress. Giving a precise account of what "approximate truth" means, however, is no easy task.

So much for common sense. The promise of scientific realism is very much open to debate, and in light of IBE, UTD, and PI, this debate has spawned many positions. Let us take a look at the main players, so as to gain a better understanding of the context of realism.

## 2. A Conceptual Taxonomy

Earlier I described realism as the view that scientific theories correctly describe the nature of a mind-independent world. This is shorthand for the various and more nuanced commitments realists tend to make. For example, many add that they are not realists about all theories, just ones that are genuinely successful. The clarification is supplied to dissolve the potential worry that realists must embrace theories that seem artificially successful—those that do not make novel predictions and simply incorporate past empirical data on an *ad hoc* basis, for instance. Realists often say that their position extends only to theories that are sufficiently "mature." Maturity is an admittedly vague notion, meant to convey the idea that a theory has withstood serious testing in application to its domain over some significant period of time, and some correlate the maturity of disciplines more generally with the extent to which their theories make successful, novel predictions. Finally, as I have already mentioned, it is also standard to qualify that which theories are supposed to deliver: it is said that theoretical descriptions may not be true, *per se*, but that they are nearly or approximately true, or at least more so than earlier descriptions.

With these caveats in mind it may be instructive to situate scientific realism in a broader context, as a species of the genus of positions historically described as realisms. Traditionally, "realism" simply denotes a belief in the reality of something—an existence that does not depend on minds, human or otherwise. Consider an increasingly ambitious sequence of items about which one might be a realist. One could begin with the objects of one's perceptions (goldfish, fishbowls), move on to objects beyond one's sensory abilities to detect (genes, electrons), and further still, beyond the realm of the concrete to the realm of the abstract, to non-spatiotemporal things such as numbers, sets, universals, and propositions. The sort of realist one is, if at all, can be gauged from the sorts of things one takes to qualify for mind-independent existence. Though I have just described these commitments as forming a sequence, it should be understood that realism at any given stage does not necessarily entail realism about anything prior to that stage. Some Platonists, for example, appear to hold that ultimately, the only real objects are abstract ones, the Forms, or that the Forms are in some sense "more real" than observables. Scientific realism, in committing to something approaching the truth of scientific theories, makes a commitment to their subject matter: entities and processes involving their interactions, at the level of both the observable and the unobservable. Anything more detailed is a matter for negotiation, and realists have many opposing views beyond this shared, minimal commitment. [. . .]

I said that "realism" traditionally denotes a belief in the reality of something, but in the context of scientific realism the term has broader connotations. The most perspicuous way of understanding these aspects is in terms of three lines of inquiry: ontological, semantic, and epistemological. Ontologically, scientific realism is committed to the existence of a mind-independent world or reality. A realist semantics implies that theoretical claims about this reality have truth values, and should be construed literally, whether true or false. I will consider an example of what it might mean to construe claims in a non-literal way momentarily. Finally, the epistemological commitment is to the idea that these theoretical claims give us knowledge of the world. That is, predictively successful (mature, non-*ad hoc*) theories, taken literally as describing the nature of a mind-independent reality are (approximately) true. The things our best scientific theories tell us about entities and processes are

decent descriptions of the way the world really is. Henceforth I will use the term "realism" to refer to this scientific variety only. We are now ready to locate it and various other positions in a conceptual space.

If by "anti-realism" one means any view opposed to realism, many different positions will fit the bill. Exploiting the differences in commitments along our three lines of inquiry, one may construct a taxonomy of views discussed in connection with these debates. Table 1 lists the most prominent of these, and for each notes how it stands on the existence of a mind-independent world, on whether theoretical statements should be taken literally, and on whether such claims yield knowledge of their putative subject matter. This is a blunt instrument; an impressive array of viewpoints is not adequately reflected in this simple classificatory scheme, and the reflections present are imprecise. There are many ways, for example, in which to be a sceptic. But the core views sketched in Table 1 offer some basic categories for locating families of related commitments.

Traditionally and especially in the early twentieth century, around the time of the birth of modern analytic philosophy, realist positions were contrasted with idealism, according to which there is no world external to and thus independent of the mental. The classic statement of this position is credited to Bishop George Berkeley, for whom reality is constituted by thoughts and ultimately sustained by

## Table 1  Scientific realism and anti-realisms

| | The ontological question: mind-independent reality? | The semantic question: theories literally construed? | The epistemological question: knowledge? |
|---|---|---|---|
| Realism | yes | yes | yes |
| Constructive empiricism | yes | yes | observables: yes unobservables: no |
| Skepticism | yes | yes | no |
| Logical positivism/empiricism | yes/no/? | observables: yes unobservables: no | yes |
| Traditional instrumentalism | yes | observables: yes unobservables: no | observables: yes unobservables: no |
| Idealism | no | no | yes |

the mind of God. Idealism need not invoke a deity, though. A phenomenalist, for instance, might be an idealist without appealing to the divine. Given an idealist ontology, it is no surprise that scientific claims cannot be construed literally, since they are not about what they seem to describe at face value, but this of course does not preclude knowledge of a mind-*dependent* reality. As Table 1 shows, idealism is the only position considered here to take an unambiguous antirealist stand with respect to ontology.

Instrumentalism is a view shared by a number of positions, all of which have the following contention in common: theories are merely instruments for predicting observable phenomena or systematizing observation reports. Traditional instrumentalism is an even stronger view according to which, furthermore, claims involving unobservable entities and processes have no meaning at all. Such "theoretical claims," as they are called ("claims about unobservables" is better, I think, since theories describe observables too), do not have truth values. They are not even capable of being true or false; rather, they are mere tools for prediction. In common usage, however, some now employ the term in a weaker sense, to describe views that grant truth values to claims involving unobservables while maintaining that one is not in a position, for whatever reason, to determine what these truth values are. In this latter, weaker sense, constructive empiricism is sometimes described as a form of instrumentalism. And though I have represented instrumentalists in Table 1 as subscribing to realism in ontology, some would include those who do not.

Logical positivism, famously associated with the philosophers and scientists of the **Vienna Circle**, and its later incarnation, logical empiricism, are similar to traditional instrumentalism in having a strict policy regarding the unobservable. But where traditional instrumentalism holds that claims about unobservables are meaningless, logical empiricism assigns meaning to some of these claims by interpreting them non-literally. Rather than taking these claims at face value as describing the things they

appear to describe, claims about unobservables are meaningful for logical empiricists if and only if their unobservable terms are linked in an appropriate way to observable terms. The unobservable vocabulary is then treated as nothing more than a shorthand for the observation reports to which they are tied. "Electron," for example, might be shorthand in some contexts for "white streak in a cloud chamber," given the path of water droplets one actually sees in a cloud chamber experiment, along what is theoretically described as the trajectory of an electron. It is by means of such "correspondence rules" or "bridge principles" that talk of the unobservable realm is interpreted. Given a translation manual of this sort, theories construed non-literally are thought to yield knowledge of the world. The label "logical positivism/empiricism" covers vast ground, however, and views regarding the ontological status of the world described by science are far from univocal here. **Rudolf Carnap**, for instance, held that while theories furnish frameworks for systematizing knowledge, ontological questions "external" to such frameworks are meaningless, or have no cognitive content.

While traditional instrumentalism banishes meaningful talk about unobservables altogether and logical empiricism interprets it non-literally, constructive empiricism, the view advocated by van Fraassen, adopts a realist semantics. The anti-realism of this latter position is thus wholly manifested in its epistemology. For the constructive empiricist the observable–unobservable distinction is extremely important, but only in the realm of knowledge, and this feature marks the position as an interesting halfway house between realism and various kinds of skepticism. By skepticism here, I intend any position that agrees with the realist concerning ontology and semantics, but offers epistemic considerations to suggest that one does not have knowledge of the world, or at least that one is not in a position to know that one does. Constructive empiricism goes along with the skeptic part way, denying that one can have knowledge of the unobservable, but also with the realist part way, accepting that one can have knowledge of the observable. (More strictly, constructive empiricism is the view that the aim of science is true claims about observables, not truth more generally, but this is usually interpreted in the way I have suggested.) By adopting a realist semantics, constructive empiricism avoids the semantic difficulties that were in large part responsible for the demise of logical empiricism in the latter half of the twentieth century, and has taken its place as the main rival to realism today.

Table 1 does not exhaust the list of "isms" opposed to realism. It does, however, provide a fairly comprehensive list of the reasons and motivations one might have for being an anti-realist. For example, the discipline known as the sociology of scientific knowledge is predominantly anti-realist. This is not a logical consequence, however, of the desire to study science from a sociological perspective. Sociologists who are anti-realists are usually so inclined because of commitments they share with one or more of the antirealist positions outlined in Table 1. Though I will not consider this approach to thinking about the sciences in any detail here, it is important to appreciate its influence. Sociological and related methodologies, which attempt to explicate scientific practice and its social, political, and economic relations, both internal and external, represent the major alternative approach to the study of the sciences today, contrasting with the more straightforwardly philosophical approach of realism and constructive empiricism.

## 3. Metaphysics, Empiricism, and Scientific Knowledge

Armed with a basic summary of realism and its principal rivals, let us turn to the central focus of this work. Earlier I said that much of the controversy surrounding these positions concerns the question of how one should understand scientific claims, in light of the distinctions between the observable and unobservable on one hand, and between the two categories of the unobservable, the detectable and undetectable, on the other. By examining these distinctions one may begin to shed some light on the roles that metaphysics and empiricism play in the interpretation of scientific claims, and the dialectic between them. The first distinction, between observables and unobservables, concerns things that one can under favourable circumstances perceive with one's unaided senses, and things one cannot. Note that this use of "observable" and "unobservable" is different from what is often the case in the sciences themselves. In scientific practice the label "observable" is usually applied permissively to anything with which one can forge some sort of causal contact, as one does when one uses instruments (such as microscopes) for detection. In the present discussion, however, observables are strictly things one can perceive with the unmediated senses. As Table 1 attests, almost everyone thinks one can have knowledge of the observable. This is not to say, however, that interpreting claims about observables is necessarily straightforward. It may be, for example, that the categories of objects and processes one employs to express one's knowledge of the observable are interestingly shaped by the theories one adopts. Indeed, that this is the case for both observables and unobservables is a central tenet of the influential views of **Thomas Kuhn**, the sociological approaches that followed him, and even some of the logical empiricists who preceded him, who held that "conceptual schemes" shape one's knowledge of the world. [. . .]

It is the status of the unobservable that has proved most controversial. Logical positivism was, in effect, the founding movement of modern philosophy of science, and the radical empiricism of the positivists has had a lasting impact. It will be useful [. . .] to clarify my second distinction, between unobservables that are detectable and those that are not. Let me reserve the word "detectable" for unobservables one can detect using instruments but not otherwise, and "undetectable" for those one cannot detect at all (see Figure 1). The mitochondrion, for example, is a cellular organelle in which substances are oxidized to produce energy. Though unobservable, one can detect mitochondria using microscopy. A celebrated historical example of a more indirect case of detection is the neutrino, a subatomic particle originally posited by Wolfgang Pauli and theorized about by Enrico Fermi in the 1930s. The neutrino was hypothesized to allow for the conservation of mass-energy and angular momentum in certain subatomic interactions, such as the $\beta$-decay of radium-210, and detections of such interactions might thus be viewed as indirect detections of neutrinos. It was not until 1956 that Frederick Reines and Clyde Cowan successfully performed an experiment in which neutrinos were detected more directly. Now consider unobservables whose putative existence cannot be the subject of empirical investigation, whether in practice or in principle. Examples include Newton's conceptions of position and velocity with respect to absolute space, and causally inefficacious entities such as mathematical objects. Even if they exist, such things are undetectable.

Historically, the most pressing challenges to realism have come from those adopting some form of empiricism. This is not to say, however, that all empiricists are anti-realists! It may be helpful here to note that empiricism is traditionally associated with two strands of thought which often come together, interwoven. One strand is the idea that sensory experience is the *source* of all knowledge

of the world, and this by itself does not preclude an empiricist from being a realist. A realist might accept this first strand while further believing that one can infer the existence of certain unobservables on the basis of the evidence of one's senses. The second strand of empiricism is the idea that all knowledge of the world is *about* experience, and it is this tenet that conflicts with realism, since realists believe claims about things that transcend experience in addition to claims about observables. So an empiricist of the first strand alone may be a realist, but not one of the first and second strands combined. The most adamant critiques of realism stem from those who are committed to the second strand of empiricism, and to violate this commitment is to engage in what its advocates view as a fruitless and misconceived philosophical activity: speculative metaphysics.

What is this metaphysics, then, of which so many empiricists disapprove? To say that there is a conflict between metaphysics and empiricism *simpliciter* is too strong, since many empiricists do metaphysics as it is understood most broadly, as the study of the first or basic principles of philosophy,

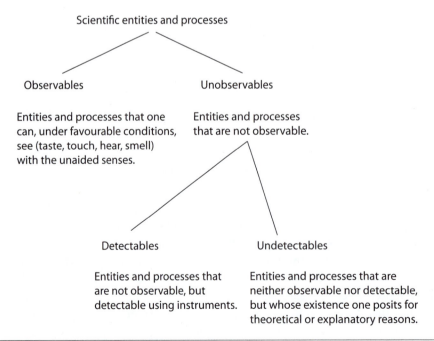

**Figure 1     Observables and unobservables**

being *qua* being, and the natures of things that exist. The metaphysics that empiricists disavow concerns the unobservable, and thus any position that endorses speculation of this sort, leading to substantive beliefs about detectables or undetectables, is unacceptable to them. This includes not only speculations about things like universals and causal necessity, which are familiar topics within metaphysics, but also speculations about mitochondria and neutrinos, which are familiar topics within the sciences. But empiricists are generally happy to do metaphysics so long as it does not involve believing speculations about the unobservable. Thus Hume gives an account of causation, not in terms of undetectable necessary connections, but solely in terms of observable events that follow one another. And thus nominalists speak of properties, not as abstract entities like universals, but as sets of observable things to which the predicates associated with these properties apply. The unobservable is likewise an anathema to many empiricist accounts of science. The scientific realist, in maintaining that one can have knowledge of scientific unobservables, engages in the very sort of metaphysical speculation these empiricists reject. [. . .]

The metaphysics of the sciences concerns the observable and unobservable parts of the world described by scientific theories, both explicitly and implicitly. The epistemology of the sciences concerns the specific methods used to generate scientific claims, the justification or confirmation of these claims, whether they constitute knowledge, and if so, what sort. The influence of logical positivism during the birth of the philosophy of science as a separate discipline in the late nineteenth century, and throughout most of the twentieth century, led to a vestigial neglect of metaphysical questions in connection with realism. Those investigating problems such as the nature of causation, laws of nature, and conceptions of natural kinds have done so largely in isolation from debates between realists and antirealists. Metaphysical issues have been the purview of the philosophy of particular sciences: space and time, evolutionary biology, quantum mechanics, and so on. The neglect of metaphysics in the context of realism, however, is a mistake. For there is a sense in which the metaphysics of science is a precursor to its epistemology. One cannot fully appreciate what it might mean to be a realist until one has a clear picture of what one is being invited to be a realist about. [. . .]

## Works Cited

Carnap, R. "Empiricism, Semantics and Ontology." *Revue Internationale de Philosophie* 4 (1950): 20–40.

Kuhn, T.S. *The Structure of Scientific Revolutions*. Chicago: University of Chicago Press, 1970/1962.

Putnam, H. *Mathematics, Matter and Method*. Cambridge: Cambridge University Press, 1975.

van Fraassen, B.C. *The Scientific Image*. Oxford: Oxford University Press, 1980.

## Study Questions

1. Chakravartty notes that although scientific realism seems like common sense, it is a matter of philosophical debate. Outline the debate between Putnam and van Fraassen over whether the success of science justifies scientific realism.

2. What challenges do inference to the best explanation, under-determination of theory choice by data, and pessimistic induction pose for scientific realism?

3. Describe the ontological, semantic, and epistemological commitments of scientific realism. Explain how each of these commitments is challenged by some variety of anti-realism.

4. How does Chakravartty distinguish between "observables" and "unobservables"? Making reference to this distinction, assess the empiricist challenge to metaphysics.

# ↜ KNOWLEDGE OF THE MIND ↜

## Maurice Merleau-Ponty

French phenomenologist and existentialist Maurice Merleau-Ponty (1908–61) earned degrees at École Normale Supérieure in Paris. He taught at the *lycée* level and then at University of Lyon and the Sorbonne before becoming, in 1952, the youngest-ever chair of philosophy at Collège de France. In *Phenomenology of Perception*, Merleau-Ponty criticizes both empiricist and rationalist approaches to the philosophy of mind for neglecting the embodiment of experience.

## The Experience of the Body and Classical Psychology

From *Phenomenology of Perception*

### 1. Classical Psychology and the Body's Permanence from the Point of View of the Self

In its descriptions of the body from the point of view of the self, classical psychology was already wont to attribute to it "characteristics" incompatible with the status of an object. In the first place it was stated that my body is distinguishable from the table or the lamp in that I can turn away from the latter whereas my body is constantly perceived. It is therefore an object which does not leave me. But in that case is it still an object? If the object is an invariable structure, it is not one *in spite of* the changes of perspective, but *in* that change or *through* it. It is not the case that ever-renewed perspectives simply provide it with opportunities of displaying its permanence, and with contingent ways of presenting itself to us. It is an object, which means that it is standing in front of us, only because it is observable: situated, that is to say, directly under our hand or gaze, indivisibly over-thrown and re-integrated with every movement they make. Otherwise it would be true like an idea and not present like a thing. It is particularly true that an object is an object only insofar as it can be moved away from me, and ultimately disappear from my field of vision. Its presence is such that it entails a possible absence. Now the permanence of my own body is entirely different in kind: it is not at the extremity of some indefinite exploration; it defies exploration and is always presented to me from the same angle. Its permanence is not a permanence in the world, but a permanence on my part. To say that it is always near me, always there for me, is to say that it is never really in front of me, that I cannot array it before my eyes, that it remains marginal to all my perceptions, that it is *with* me. It is true that external objects too never turn one of their sides to me without hiding the rest, but I can at least freely choose the side which they are to present to me. They could not appear otherwise than in perspective, but the particular perspective which I acquire at each moment is the outcome of no more than physical necessity, that is to say, of a necessity which I can use and which is not a prison for me: from my window only the tower of the church is visible, but this limitation simultaneously holds out the promise that from elsewhere the whole church could be seen. It is true, moreover, that if I am a prisoner the church will be restricted, for me, to a truncated steeple. If I did not take off my clothes I could never see the inside of them, and it will in fact be seen that my clothes may become appendages of my body. But this fact does not prove that the presence of my body is to be compared to the *de facto* permanence of certain objects, or the organ compared to a tool which is always available. It shows that conversely those actions in which I habitually engage incorporate their instruments into themselves and make them play a part in the original structure of my own body. As for the latter, it is my basic habit, the one which conditions all the others, and by means of which they are mutually comprehensible. Its permanence near to me, its unvarying perspective are not a *de facto* necessity, since such necessity presupposes them: in order that my window may impose upon me a point of view of the church, it is necessary in the first place that my body should impose upon me one of the world; and the first necessity can be merely physical only in virtue of the fact that the second is metaphysical; in short, I am accessible to factual situations only if my nature is such that there are factual situations for me. In other words, I observe external objects with my body, I handle them, examine them, walk round them, but my body itself is a thing which I do not observe: in order to be able to do so, I should need the use of a second body which itself would be unobservable. When I say that my body is always perceived by me, these words are not to be taken in a purely statistical sense, for there must be, in the way my own body presents itself, something which makes its absence or its variation inconceivable. What can it be? My head is presented to my sight only to the extent of my nose end and the boundaries of my eye-sockets. I can see my eyes in three mirrors, but they are the eyes of someone observing, and I have the utmost difficulty in catching my living glance when a mirror in the street unexpectedly reflects my image back at me. My body in the mirror never stops following my intentions like their shadow, and if observation consists in varying the point of view while keeping the object fixed, then it escapes observation and is given to me as a simulacrum of my tactile body since it imitates the body's actions instead of responding to them by a free unfolding of perspectives. My visual body is certainly an object as far as its parts far removed from my head are concerned, but as we come nearer to the eyes, it becomes divorced from objects, and reserves among them a quasi-space to which they have no access, and when I try to fill this void by recourse to the image in the mirror, it refers me back to an original of the body which is not out there among things, but in my own province, on this side of all things

seen. It is no different, in spite of what may appear to be the case, with my tactile body, for if I can, with my left hand, feel my right hand as it touches an object, the right hand as an object is not the right hand as it touches: the first is a system of bones, muscles and flesh brought down at a point of space, the second shoots through space like a rocket to reveal the external object in its place. Insofar as it sees or touches the world, my body can therefore be neither seen nor touched. What prevents its ever being an object [. . .] is that it is that by which there are objects. It is neither tangible nor visible insofar as it is that which sees and touches. The body therefore is not one more among external objects, with the peculiarity of always being there. If it is permanent, the permanence is absolute and is the ground for the relative permanence of disappearing objects, real objects. The presence and absence of external objects are only variations within a field of primordial presence, a perceptual domain over which my body exercises power. Not only is the permanence of my body not a particular case of the permanence of external objects in the world, but the second cannot be understood except through the first: not only is the perspective of my body not a particular case of that of objects, but furthermore the presentation of objects in perspective cannot be understood except through the resistance of my body to all variation of perspective. If objects may never show me more than one of their facets, this is because I am myself in a certain place from which I see them and which I cannot see. If nevertheless I believe in the existence of their hidden sides and equally in a world which embraces them all and co-exists with them, I do so insofar as my body, always present for me, and yet involved with them in so many objective relationships, sustains their co-existence with it and communicates to them all the pulse of its duration. Thus the permanence of one's own body, if only classical psychology had analyzed it, might have led it to the body no longer conceived as an object of the world, but as our means of communication with it, to the world no longer conceived as a collection of determinate objects, but as the horizon latent in all our experience and itself ever-present and anterior to every determining thought.

## 2. Classical Psychology and the Body's "Double Sensations," Affectivity, and "Kinesthetic Sensations" from the Point of View of the Self

The other "characteristics" whereby one's own body was defined were no less interesting, and for the same reasons. My body, it was said, is recognized by its power to give me "double sensations": when I touch my right hand with my left, my right hand, as an object, has the strange property of being able to feel too. We have just seen that the two hands are never simultaneously in the relationship of touched and touching to each other. When I press my two hands together, it is not a matter of two sensations felt together as one perceives two objects placed side by side, but of an ambiguous set-up in which both hands can alternate the roles of "touching" and being "touched." What was meant by talking about "double sensations" is that, in passing from one role to the other, I can identify the hand touched as the same one which will in a moment be touching. In other words, in this bundle of bones and muscles which my right hand presents to my left, I can anticipate for an instant the integument or incarnation of that other right hand, alive and mobile, which I thrust towards things in order to explore them. The body catches itself from the outside engaged in a cognitive process; it tries to touch itself while being touched, and initiates "a kind of reflection" (Husserl 81) which is sufficient to distinguish it from objects, of which I can indeed say that they "touch" my body, but only when it is inert, and therefore without ever catching it unawares in its exploratory function.

It was also said that the body is an affective object, whereas external things are from my point of view merely represented. This amounted to stating a third time the problem of the status of my own body. For if I say that my foot hurts, I do not simply mean that it is a cause of pain in the same way as the nail which is cutting into it, differing only in being nearer to me; I do not mean that it is the last of the objects in the external world, after which a more intimate kind of pain should begin, an unlocalized awareness of pain in itself, related to the foot only by some causal connection and within the closed system of experience.

I mean that the pain reveals itself as localized, that it is constitutive of a "pain-infested space." "My foot hurts" means not: "I think that my foot is the cause of this pain," but: "the pain comes from my foot" or again "my foot has a pain." This is shown clearly by the "primitive voluminousness of pain" formerly spoken of by psychologists. It was therefore recognized that my body does not present itself as the objects of external impressions do, and that perhaps even these latter objects do no more than stand out against the affective background which in the first place throws onsciousness outside itself.

Finally when the psychologists tried to confine "kinesthetic sensations" to one's own body, arguing that these sensations present the body's movements to us globally, while attributing the movements of external objects to a mediating perception and to a comparison between successive positions, it could have been objected that movement, expressing a relationship, cannot be felt, but demands a mental operation. This objection, however, would merely have been an indictment of their language. What they were expressing, badly it is true, by "kinesthetic sensation," was the originality of the movements which I perform with my body: they directly anticipate the final situation, for my intention initiates a movement through space merely to attain the objective initially given at the starting point; there is as it were a germ of movement which only secondarily develops into an objective movement. I move external objects with the aid of my body, which takes hold of them in one place and shifts them to another. But my body itself I move directly, I do not find it at one point of objective space and transfer it to another, I have no need to look for it, it is already with me—I do not need to lead it towards the movement's completion, it is in contact with it from the start and propels itself towards that end. The relationships between my decision and my body are, in movement, magic ones.

## 3. The Body as a Subject-Object

If the description of my own body given by classical psychology already offered all that is necessary to distinguish it from objects, how does it come about that psychologists have not made this distinction or that they have in any case seen no philosophical consequence flowing from it? The reason is that, taking a step natural to them, they chose the position of impersonal thought to which science has been committed as long as it believed in the possibility of separating, in observation, on the one hand what belongs to the situation of the observer and on the other the properties of the absolute object. For the living subject his own body might well be different from all external objects; the fact remains that for the unsituated thought of the psychologist the experience of the living subject became itself an object and, far from requiring a fresh definition of being, took its place in universal being. It was the life of the "psyche" which stood in opposition to the real, but which was treated as a second reality, as an object of scientific investigation to be brought under a set of laws. It was postulated that our experience, already besieged by physics and biology, was destined to be completely absorbed into objective knowledge, with the consummation of the system of the sciences. Thenceforth the experience of the body degenerated into a "representation" of the body; it was not a phenomenon but a fact of the psyche. In the matter of living appearance, my visual body includes a large gap at the level of the head, but biology was there ready to fill that gap, to explain it through the structure of the eyes, to instruct me in what the body really is, showing that I have a retina and a brain like other men and like the corpses which I dissect, and that, in short, the surgeon's instrument could infallibly bring to light in this indeterminate zone of my head the exact replica of plates illustrating the human anatomy. I apprehend my body as a subject-object, as capable of "seeing" and "suffering," but these confused representations were so many psychological oddities, samples of a magical variety of thought the laws of which are studied by psychology and sociology and which has its place assigned to it by them, in the system of the real world, as an object of scientific investigation. This imperfect picture of my body, its marginal presentation, and its equivocal status as touching and touched, could not therefore be *structural* characteristics of the body itself; they did not affect the idea of it; they became "distinctive characteristics" of those *contents*

of consciousness which make up our representation of the body: these contents are consistent, affective, and strangely duplicated in "double sensations," but apart from this the representation of the body is a representation like any other and correspondingly the body is an object like any other. Psychologists did not realize that in treating the experience of the body in this way they were simply, in accordance with the scientific approach, shelving a problem which ultimately could not be burked. The inadequacy of my perception was taken as a *de facto* inadequacy resulting from the organization of my sensory apparatus; the presence of my body was taken as a *de facto presence* springing from its constant action on my receptive nervous system; finally the union of soul and body, which was presupposed by these two explanations, was understood, in **Cartesian fashion**, as a *de facto union* whose *de jure* possibility need not be established, because the fact, as the starting point of knowledge, was eliminated from the final result. Now the psychologist could imitate the scientist and, for a moment at least, see his body as others saw it, and conversely see the bodies of others as mechanical things with no inner life. The contribution made from the experiences of others had the effect of dimming the structure of his own, and conversely, having lost contact with himself he became blind to the behaviour of others. He thus saw everything from the point of view of universal thought which abolished equally his experience of others and his experience of himself. But as a psychologist he was engaged in a task which by nature pulled him back into himself, and he could not allow himself to remain unaware to this extent. For whereas neither the physicist nor the chemist are the objects of their own investigation, the psychologist *was himself,* in the nature of the case, the fact which exercised him. This representation of the body, this magical experience, which he approached in a detached frame of mind, was himself; he lived it while he thought about it. It is true that, as has been shown (Guillaume), it was not enough for him to be a psyche in order to know this, for this knowledge, like other knowledge, is acquired only through our relations with other people. It does not emerge from any recourse to an ideal of introspective psychology, and between himself and others no less than between himself and himself, the psychologist was able and obliged to rediscover a pre-objective relationship. But as a psyche speaking of the psyche, he *was* all that he was *talking* about. This history of the psyche which he was elaborating in adopting the objective attitude was one whose outcome he already possessed within himself, or rather he was, in his existence, its contracted outcome and latent memory. The union of soul and body had not been brought about once and for all in a remote realm; it came into being afresh at every moment beneath the psychologist's thinking, not as a repetitive event which each time takes the psyche by surprise, but as a necessity that the psychologist knew to be in the depths of his being as he became aware of it as a piece of knowledge. The birth of perception from "sense-data" to "world" had to be renewed with each act of perception, otherwise the sense-data would have lost the meaning they owed to this development. Hence the "psyche" was not an object like others: it had done everything that one was about to say of it before it could be said; the psychologist's being knew more about itself than he did; nothing that had happened or was happening according to science was completely alien to it. Applied to the psyche, the notion of fact, therefore, underwent a transformation. The de facto psyche, with its "peculiarities," was no longer an event in objective time and in the external world, but an event with which we were in internal contact, of which we were ourselves the ceaseless accomplishment or upsurge, and which continually gathered within itself its past, its body, and its world. Before being an objective fact, the union of soul and body had to be, then, a possibility of consciousness itself and the question arose as to what the perceiving subject is and whether he must be able to experience a body as his own. There was no longer a fact passively submitted to, but one assumed. To be a consciousness or rather *to be an experience* is to hold inner communication with the world, the body, and other people, to be with them instead of being beside them. To concern oneself with psychology is necessarily to encounter, beneath objective thought which moves among ready-made things, a first opening upon things without which there would be no objective knowledge. The psychologist could not fail to rediscover himself as experience, which means as an immediate presence to the past, to the world, to the body, and to others at the very moment when he was trying to see himself as an object among objects. [. . .]

## Works Cited

Guillaume, P. "L'Objectivité en Psychologie." *Journal de psychologie 29* (1932): 682–743.

Husserl, E. *Méditations cartésiennes: introduction à la phénoménologie.* Trans. G. Pfeiffer and E. Levinas. Paris: Armand Colin, 1931.

## Study Questions

1. What does Merleau-Ponty mean by "classical psychology"? How do classical psychologists approach the problem of pain, according to Merleau-Ponty?
2. Merleau-Ponty writes, "my own body . . . is not a permanence in the world, but a permanence on my part." Explain what he means by this, and how the "permanence" of one's own body relates to the "permanence" of other things.
3. Describe the "double sensations" and "kinesthetic sensations" identified by classical psychology. How do these sensations distinguish one's own body from other things?
4. According to Merleau-Ponty, what philosophical consequence is implied by classical psychology's descriptions of the body from the point of view of the self, and why have classical psychologists failed to appreciate this?

# Ludwig Wittgenstein

Born into a wealthy industrial family in Vienna, Austria, Ludwig Wittgenstein (1889–1951) became interested in the foundations of mathematics while studying aeronautical engineering at Manchester University and transferred to Cambridge University to study philosophy with Bertrand Russell. Wittgenstein's career is divided into two stages. The "early Wittgenstein" of *Tractatus Logico-Philosophicus* conceived meaning as logical form and philosophy as clarification and criticism. The "later Wittgenstein" of *Philosophical Investigations* conceived meaning as use and philosophy as therapy.

## From *Philosophical Investigations*

[. . .] 256. Now, what about the language which describes my inner experiences and which only I myself can understand? *How* do I use words to stand for my sensations?—As we ordinarily do? Then are my words for sensations tied up with my natural expressions of sensation? In that case my language is not a "private" one. Someone else might understand it as well as I.—But suppose I didn't have any natural expression for the sensation, but only had the sensation? And now I simply *associate* names with sensations and use these names in descriptions.—

257. "What would it be like if human beings showed no outward signs of pain (did not groan, grimace, etc.)? Then it would be impossible to teach a child the use of the word 'tooth-ache.'"— Well, let's assume the child is a genius and itself invents a name for the sensation!—But then, of course, he couldn't make himself understood when he used the word.—So does he understand the name, without being able to explain its meaning to anyone?—But what does it mean to say that he has "named his pain"?—How has he done this naming of pain?! And whatever he did, what was its purpose?—When one says "He gave a name to his sensation" one forgets that a great deal of stage-setting in the language is presupposed if the mere act of naming is to make sense. And when we speak of someone's having given a name to pain, what is presupposed is the existence of the grammar of the word "pain"; it shows the post where the new word is stationed.

258. Let us imagine the following case. I want to keep a diary about the recurrence of a certain sensation. To this end I associate it with the sign "S" and write this sign in a calendar for every day on which I have the sensation.—I will remark first of all that a definition of the sign cannot be formulated.—But still I can give myself a kind of ostensive definition.—How? Can I point to the sensation? Not in the ordinary sense. But I speak, or write the sign down, and at the same time I concentrate my attention on the sensation—and so, as it were, point to it inwardly.—But what is this ceremony for? For that is all it seems to be! A definition surely serves to establish the meaning of a sign.—Well, that is done precisely by the concentrating of my attention; for in this way I impress on myself the connection between the sign and the sensation.—But "I impress it on myself" can only mean: this process brings it about that I remember the connection *right* in the future. But in the present case I have no criterion of correctness. One would like to say: whatever is going to seem right to me is right. And that only means that here we can't talk about 'right.'

259. Are the rules of the private language *impressions* of rules?—The balance on which impressions are weighed is not the *impression* of a balance.

260. "Well, I *believe* that this is the sensation S again."—Perhaps you *believe* that you believe it!

Then did the man who made the entry in the calendar make a note of *nothing whatever*?—Don't consider it a matter of course that a person is making a note of something when he makes a mark—say in a calendar. For a note has a function, and this "S" so far has none.

(One can talk to oneself.—If a person speaks when no one else is present, does that mean he is speaking to himself?)

261. What reason have we for calling "S" the sign for a *sensation*? For "sensation" is a word of our common language, not of one intelligible to me alone. So the use of this word stands in need of a justification which everybody understands.—And it would not help either to say that it need not be a *sensation*; that when he writes "S," he has *something*—and that is all that can be said. "Has" and "something" also belong to our common language.—So in the end when one is doing philosophy one gets to the point where one would like just to emit an inarticulate sound.—But such a sound is an expression only as it occurs in a particular language-game, which should now be described.

262. It might be said: if you have given yourself a private definition of a word, then you must inwardly *undertake* to use the word in such-and-such a way. And how do you undertake that? Is it to be assumed that you invent the technique of using the word; or that you found it ready-made?

263. "But I can (inwardly) undertake to call THIS 'pain' in the future."—"But is it certain that you have undertaken it? Are you sure that it was enough for this purpose to concentrate your attention on your feeling?"—A queer question.—

264. "Once you know *what* the word stands for, you understand it, you know its whole use."

265. Let us imagine a table (something like a dictionary) that exists only in our imagination. A dictionary can be used to justify the translation of a word X by a word Y. But are we also to call it a justification if such a table is to be looked up only in the imagination?—"Well, yes; then it is a subjective justification."—But justification consists in appealing to something independent.—"But surely I can appeal from one memory to another. For example, I don't know if I have remembered the time of departure of a train right and to check it I call to mind how a page of the time-table looked. Isn't it the same here?"—No; for this process has got

to produce a memory which is actually *correct*. If the mental image of the time-table could not itself be *tested* for correctness, how could it confirm the correctness of the first memory? (As if someone were to buy several copies of the morning paper to assure himself that what it said was true.)

Looking up a table in the imagination is no more looking up a table than the image of the result of an imagined experiment is the result of an experiment.

266. I can look at the clock to see what time it is: but I can also look at the dial of a clock in order to *guess* what time it is; or for the same purpose move the hand of a clock till its position strikes me as right. So the look of a clock may serve to determine the time in more than one way. (Looking at the clock in imagination.)

267. Suppose I wanted to justify the choice of dimensions for a bridge which I imagine to be building, by making loading tests on the material of the bridge in my imagination. This would, of course, be to imagine what is called justifying the choice of dimensions for a bridge. But should we also call it justifying an imagined choice of dimensions?

268. Why can't my right hand give my left hand money?—My right hand can put it into my left hand. My right hand can write a deed of gift and my left hand a receipt.—But the further practical consequences would not be those of a gift. When the left hand has taken the money from the right, etc., we shall ask: "Well, and what of it?" And the same could be asked if a person had given himself a private definition of a word; I mean, if he has said the word to himself and at the same time has directed his attention to a sensation.

269. Let us remember that there are certain criteria in a man's behaviour for the fact that he does not understand a word: that it means nothing to him, that he can do nothing with it. And criteria for his "thinking he understands," attaching some meaning to the word, but not the right one. And, lastly, criteria for his understanding the word right. In the second case one might speak of a subjective understanding. And sounds which no one else understands but which I "*appear to understand*" might be called a "private language".

270. Let us now imagine a use for the entry of the sign "S" in my diary. I discover that whenever I have a particular sensation a manometer shows that my blood-pressure rises. So I shall be able to say that my blood-pressure is rising without using any apparatus. This is a useful result. And now it seems quite indifferent whether I have recognized the sensation *right* or not. Let us suppose I regularly identify it wrong, it does not matter in the least. And that alone shows that the hypothesis that I make a mistake is mere show. (We as it were turned a knob which looked as if it could be used to turn on some part of the machine; but it was a mere ornament, not connected with the mechanism at all.)

And what is our reason for calling "S" the name of a sensation here? Perhaps the kind of way this sign is employed in this language-game.—And why a "particular sensation," that is, the same one every time? Well, aren't we supposing that we write "S" every time?

271. "Imagine a person whose memory could not retain *what* the word 'pain' meant—so that he constantly called different things by that name—but nevertheless used the word in a way fitting in with the usual symptoms and presuppositions of pain"—in short he uses it as we all do. Here I should like to say: a wheel that can be turned though nothing else moves with it, is not part of the mechanism.

272. The essential thing about private experience is really not that each person possesses his own exemplar, but that nobody knows whether other people also have *this* or something else. The assumption would thus be possible—though unverifiable—that one section of mankind had one sensation of red and another section another.

273. What am I to say about the word "red"?—that it means something "confronting us all" and that everyone should really have another word, besides this one, to mean his *own* sensation of red? Or is it like this: the word "red" means something known to everyone; and in addition, for each person, it means something known only to him? (Or perhaps rather: it *refers* to something known only to him.)

274. Of course, saying that the word "red" "refers to" instead of "means" something private does not help us in the least to grasp its function; but it is the more psychologically apt expression for a particular experience in doing philosophy. It is as if when I uttered the word I cast a sidelong glance at the private sensation, as it were in order to say to myself: I know all right what I mean by it.

275. Look at the blue of the sky and say to yourself "How blue the sky is!"—When you do it spontaneously—without philosophical intentions—the idea never crosses your mind that this impression of colour belongs only to *you*. And you have no hesitation in exclaiming that to someone else. And if you point at anything as you say the words you point at the sky. I am saying: you have not the feeling of pointing-into-yourself, which often accompanies 'naming the sensation' when one is thinking about 'private language.' Nor do you think that really you ought not to point to the colour with your hand, but with your attention. (Consider what it means "to point to something with the attention.")

276. But don't we at least *mean* something quite definite when we look at a colour and name our colour-impression? It is as if we detached the colour-*impression* from the object, like a membrane. (This ought to arouse our suspicions.)

277. But how is even possible for us to be tempted to think that we use a word to *mean* at one time the colour known to everyone—and at another the 'visual impression' which *I* am getting *now*? How can there be so much as a temptation here?—I don't turn the same kind of attention on the colour in the two cases. When I mean the colour impression that (as I should like to say) belongs to me alone I immerse myself in the colour—rather like when I 'cannot get my fill of a colour.' Hence it is easier to produce this experience when one is looking at a bright colour, or at an impressive colour-scheme.

278. "I know how the colour green looks to *me*"—surely that makes sense!—Certainly: what use of the proposition are you thinking of?

279. Imagine someone saying: "But I know how tall I am!" and laying his hand on top of his head to prove it.

280. Someone paints a picture in order to show how he imagines a theatre scene. And now I say: "This picture has a double function: it informs others, as pictures or words inform—but for the one who gives the information it is a representation

(or piece of information?) of another kind: for him it is the picture of his image, as it can't be for anyone else. To him his private impression of the picture means what he has imagined, in a sense in which the picture cannot mean this to others."—And what right have I to speak in this second case of a representation or piece of information—if these words were rightly used in the *first* case?

281. "But doesn't what you say come to this: that there is no pain, for example, without *pain-behaviour*?"—It comes to this: only of a living human being and what resembles (behaves like) a living human being can one say: it has sensations; it sees; is blind; hears; is deaf; is conscious or unconscious.

282. "But in a fairy tale the pot too can see and hear!" (Certainly; but it *can* also talk.)

"But the fairy tale only invents what is not the case: it does not talk *nonsense*."—It is not as simple as that. Is it false or nonsensical to say that a pot talks? Have we a clear picture of the circumstances in which we should say of a pot that it talked? (Even a nonsense-poem is not nonsense in the same way as the babbling of a child.)

We do indeed say of an inanimate thing that it is in pain: when playing with dolls for example. But this use of the concept of pain is a secondary one. Imagine a case in which people ascribed pain *only* to inanimate things; pitied *only* dolls! (When children play at trains their game is connected with their knowledge of trains. It would nevertheless be possible for the children of a tribe unacquainted with trains to learn this game from others, and to play it without knowing that it was copied from anything. One might say that the game did not make the same *sense* to them as to us.)

283. What gives us *so much as the idea* that living beings, things, can feel?

Is it that my education has led me to it by drawing my attention to feelings in myself, and now I transfer the idea to objects outside myself? That I recognize that there is something there (in me) which I can call "pain" without getting into conflict with the way other people use this word?—I do not transfer my idea to stones, plants, etc.

Couldn't I imagine having frightful pains and turning to stone while they lasted? Well, how do I know, if I shut my eyes, whether I have not turned into a stone? And if that has happened, in what sense will *the stone* have the pains? In what sense will they be ascribable to the stone? And why need the pain have a bearer at all here?!

And can one say of the stone that it has a soul and *that* is what has the pain? What has a soul, or pain, to do with a stone?

Only of what behaves like a human being can one say that it *has* pains.

For one has to say it of a body, or, if you like of a soul which some body *has*. And how can a body *have* a soul?

284. Look at a stone and imagine it having sensations.—One says to oneself: How could one so much as get the idea of ascribing a *sensation* to a *thing*? One might as well ascribe it to a number!—And now look at a wriggling fly and at once these difficulties vanish and pain seems able to get a foothold here, where before everything was, so to speak, too smooth for it.

And so, too, a corpse seems to us quite inaccessible to pain.—Our attitude to what is alive and to what is dead, is not the same. All our reactions are different.—If anyone says: "That cannot simply come from the fact that a living thing moves about in such-and-such a way and a dead one not," then I want to intimate to him that this is a case of the transition "from quantity to quality."

285. Think of the recognition of *facial expressions*. Or of the description of facial expressions—which does not consist in giving the measurements of the face! Think, too, how one can imitate a man's face without seeing one's own in a mirror.

286. But isn't it absurd to say of a *body* that it has pain?—And why does one feel an absurdity in that? In what sense is it true that my hand does not feel pain, but I in my hand?

What sort of issue is: Is it the *body* that feels pain?—How is it to be decided? What makes it plausible to say that it is *not* the body?—Well, something like this: if someone has a pain in his hand, then the hand does not say so (unless it writes it) and one does not comfort the hand, but the sufferer: one looks into his face.

287. How am I filled with pity for this *for this man*? How does it come out what the object of my

pity is? (Pity, one may say, is a form of conviction that someone else is in pain.)

**288.** I turn to stone and my pain goes on.—Suppose I were in error and it was no longer *pain*?—But I can't be in error here; it means nothing to doubt whether I am in pain!—That means: if anyone said "I do not know if what I have got is a pain or something else," we should think something like, he does not know what the English word "pain" means; and we should explain it to him.—How? Perhaps by means of gestures, or by pricking him with a pin and saying: "See, that's what pain is!" This explanation, like any other, he might understand right, wrong, or not at all. And he will show which he does by his use of the word, in this as in other cases.

If he now said, for example: "Oh, I know what "pain" means; what I don't know is whether *this*, that I have now, is pain"—we should merely shake our heads and be forced to regard his words as a queer reaction which we have no idea what to do with. (It would be rather as if we heard someone say seriously: "I distinctly remember that some time before I was born I believed. . . .")

That expression of doubt has no place in the language-game; but if we cut out human behaviour, which is the expression of sensation, it looks as if I might *legitimately* begin to doubt afresh. My temptation to say that one might take a sensation for something other than what it is arises from this: if I assume the abrogation of the normal language-game with the expression of a sensation, I need a criterion of identity for the sensation; and then the possibility of error also exists.

**289.** "When I say 'I am in pain' I am at any rate justified *before myself*."—What does that mean? Does it mean: "If someone else could know what I am calling "pain," he would admit that I was using the word correctly"?

To use a word without a justification does not mean to use it without right.

**290.** What I do is not, of course, to identify my sensation by criteria: but to repeat an expression. But this is not the *end* of the language-game: it is the beginning.

But isn't the beginning the sensation—which I describe?—Perhaps this word "describe" tricks us here. I say "I describe my state of mind" and "I describe my room." You need to call to mind the differences between the language-games.

**291.** What we call "*descriptions*" are instruments for particular uses. Think of a machine-drawing, a cross-section, an elevation with measurements, which an engineer has before him. Thinking of a description as a word-picture of the facts has something misleading about it: one tends to think only of such pictures as hang on our walls: which seem simply to portray how a thing looks, what it is like. (These pictures are as it were idle.)

**292.** Don't always think that you read off what you say from the facts; that you portray these in words according to rules. For even so you would have to apply the rule in the particular case without guidance.

**293.** If I say of myself that it is only from my own case that I know what the word "pain" means—must I not say the same of other people too? And how can I generalize the *one* case so irresponsibly?

Now someone tells me that *he* knows what pain is only from his own case!—Suppose everyone had a box with something in it: we call it a "beetle." No one can look into anyone else's box, and everyone says he knows what a beetle is only by looking at *his* beetle.—Here it would be quite possible for everyone to have something different in his box. One might even imagine such a thing constantly changing.—But suppose the word "beetle" had a use in these people's language?—If so it would not be used as the name of a thing. The thing in the box has no place in the language-game at all; not even as a *something*: for the box might even be empty.—No, one can "divide through" by the thing in the box; it cancels out, whatever it is.

That is to say: if we construe the grammar of the expression of sensation on the model of "object and designation" the object drops out of consideration as irrelevant.

**294.** If you say he sees a private picture before him, which he is describing, you have still made an assumption about what he has before him. And that means that you can describe it or do describe it more closely. If you admit that you haven't any notion what kind of thing it might be that he has before him—then what leads you into saying, in spite of that, that he has something before him? Isn't it as if I were to say of someone: "He *has* something. But I don't know whether it is money, or debts, or an empty till."

295. "I know . . . only from my *own* case"—what kind of proposition is this meant to be at all? An experiential one? No.—A grammatical one?

Suppose everyone does say about himself that he knows what pain is only from his own pain.—Not that people really say that, or are even prepared to say it. But *if* everybody said it—it might be a kind of exclamation. And even if it gives no information, still it is a picture, and why should we not want to call up such a picture? Imagine an allegorical painting take the place of those words.

When we look into ourselves as we do philosophy, we often get to see just such a picture. A full-blown pictorial representation of our grammar. Not facts; but as it were illustrated turns of speech.

296. "Yes, but there is *something* there all the same accompanying my cry of pain. And it is on account of that that I utter it. And this something is what is important—and frightful."—Only whom are we informing of this? And on what occasion?

297. Of course, if water boils in a pot, steam comes out of the pot and also pictured steam comes out of the pictured pot. But what if one insisted on saying that there must also be something boiling in the picture of the pot?

298. The very fact that we should so much like to say: "*This* is the important thing"—while we point privately to the sensation—is enough to show how much we are inclined to say something which gives no information.

299. Being unable—when we surrender ourselves to philosophical thought—to help saying such-and-such; being irresistibly inclined to say it—does not mean being forced into an *assumption*, or having an immediate perception or knowledge of a state of affairs.

300. It is—we should like to say—not merely the picture of the behaviour that plays a part in the language-game with the words "he is in pain," but also the picture of the pain. Or, not merely the paradigm of the behaviour, but also that of the pain.—It is a misunderstanding to say "The picture of pain enters into the language-game with the word 'pain.'" The image of pain is not a picture and *this* image is not replaceable in the language-game by anything that we should call a picture.—The image of pain certainly enters into the language game in a sense; only not as a picture.

301. An image is not a picture, but a picture can correspond to it.

302. If one has to imagine someone else's pain on the model of one's own, this is none too easy a thing to do: for I have to imagine pain which I *do not feel* on the model of the pain which I *do feel*. That is, what I have to do is not simply to make a transition in imagination from one place of pain to another. As, from pain in the hand to pain in the arm. For I am not to imagine that I feel pain in some region of his body. (Which would also be possible.)

Pain-behaviour can point to a painful place—but the subject of pain is the person who gives it expression.

303. "I can only *believe* that someone else is in pain, but I *know* it if I am."—Yes: one can make the decision to say "I believe he is in pain" instead of "He is in pain." But that is all.—What looks like an explanation here, or like a statement about a mental process, is in truth an exchange of one expression for another which, while we are doing philosophy, seems the more appropriate one.

Just try—in a real case—to doubt someone else's fear or pain.

304. "But you will surely admit that there is a difference between pain-behaviour accompanied by pain and pain-behaviour without any pain?"—Admit it? What greater difference could there be?—"And yet you again and again reach the conclusion that the sensation itself is a *nothing*."—Not at all. It is not a *something*, but not a *nothing* either! The conclusion was only that a nothing would serve just as well as a something about which nothing could be said. We have only rejected the grammar which tries to force itself on us here.

The paradox disappears only if we make a radical break with the idea that language always functions in one way, always serves the same purpose: to convey thoughts—which may be about houses, pains, good and evil, or anything else you please. [ . . .]

## Study Questions

1. In the *Meditations*, **Descartes** assumes that he can talk sensibly about his inner experiences (e.g., his sensations) while at the same time maintaining a thoroughgoing skepticism about the existence of the external world. How does Wittgenstein's example of keeping a diary about the recurrence of a certain sensation cast doubt on this?

2. What is Wittgenstein's response to the argument that words like "red" and "blue" have a shared linguistic *meaning* but *refer* to private sensations that could differ among individuals?

3. Describe Wittgenstein's example of the beetle in the box. What support does this example lend to his doctrine of meaning as use?

4. Do you find support in Wittgenstein's writings for a behaviourist approach to the philosophy of mind, whereby talk of mental states can be replaced by talk of behavioural dispositions?

# Troy Jollimore

Born in Liverpool, Nova Scotia, Troy Jollimore earned his BA at the University of King's College and Dalhousie University and his PhD at Princeton University, and is an associate professor at California State University, Chico. Besides being a philosopher, Jollimore is a poet. His first book of poetry, *Tom Thomson in Purgatory*, won the National Book Critics Circle Award in 2006.—GS

## The Solipsist

Don't be misled:
that sea-song you hear
when the shell's at your ear?
It's all in your head.

That primordial tide—
the slurp and salt-slosh
of the brain's briny wash—
is on the inside.

Truth be told, the whole place,
everything that the eye
can take in, to the sky
and beyond into space,

lives inside of your skull.
When you set your sad head
down on Procrustes' bed,
you lay down the whole

universe. You recline
on the pillow: the cosmos

grows dim. The soft ghost
in the squishy machine,

which the world is, retires.
Someday it will expire.
Then all will go silent
and dark. For the moment,

however, the black-
ness is just temporary.
The planet you carry
will shortly swing back

from the far nether regions.
And life will continue—
but only *within* you.
Which raises a question

that comes up again and again,
as to why
God would make ear and eye
to face *outward*, not in?

## Study Questions

1. What is solipsism?

2. What ideas about solipsism are expressed in Jollimore's poem?

# J.J.C. Smart

J.J.C. Smart graduated from Oxford with a BPhil in 1948. He spent 22 years as chair of philosophy at the University of Adelaide and is currently an emeritus professor at Monash University. Smart's interests are in metaphysics, philosophy of science, and philosophy of mind. In this article, Smart defends physicalism: since things are no more than their physical parts, when we talk about the mind, we are really talking about the brain.—GS

## Sensations and Brain Processes

### 1. Wittgenstein and Behaviourism as a Response to Dualism

Suppose that I report that I have at this moment a roundish, blurry-edged after-image which is yellowish towards its edge and is orange towards its centre. What is it that I am reporting? One answer to this question might be that I am not reporting anything, that when I say that it looks to me as though there is a roundish yellowy orange patch of light on the wall I am expressing some sort of temptation, the *temptation* to say that there is a roundish yellow orange patch on the wall (though I may know that there is not such a patch on the wall). This is perhaps **Wittgenstein**'s view in the *Philosophical Investigations*. Similarly, when I "report" a pain, I am not really reporting anything (or, if you like, I am reporting in a queer sense of "reporting"), but am doing a sophisticated sort of wince. (See paragraph 244: "The verbal expression of pain replaces crying and does not describe it." Nor does it describe anything else?) I prefer most of the time to discuss an after-image rather than a pain, because the word "pain" brings in something which is irrelevant to my purpose: the notion of "distress." I think that "he is in pain" entails "he is in distress," that is, that he is in a certain agitation-condition. Similarly, to say "I am in pain" may be to do more than "replace pain behaviour": it may be partly to report something, though this something is quite non-mysterious, being an agitation-condition, and so susceptible of behaviouristic analysis. The suggestion I wish if possible to avoid is a different one, namely that "I am in pain" is a genuine report, and that what it reports is an irreducibly psychical something. And similarly the suggestion I wish to resist is also that to say "I have a yellowish orange after-image" is to report something irreducibly psychical.

Why do I wish to resist this suggestion? Mainly because of **Occam's razor**. It seems to me that science is increasingly giving us a viewpoint whereby organisms are able to be seen as physico-chemical mechanisms: it seems that even the behaviour of man himself will one day be explicable in mechanistic terms. There does seem to be, so far as science is concerned, nothing in the world but increasingly complex arrangements of physical constituents. All except for one place: in consciousness. That is, for a full description of what is going on in a man you would have to mention not only the physical processes in his tissue, glands, nervous system, and so forth, but also his states of consciousness: his visual, auditory, and tactual sensations, his aches and pains. That these should be *correlated* with brain processes does not help, for to say that they are *correlated* is to say that they are something "over and above." You cannot correlate something with itself. You correlate footprints with burglars, but not Bill Sikes the burglar with Bill Sikes the burglar. So sensations, states of consciousness, do seem to be the one sort of thing left outside the physicalist picture, and for various reasons I just cannot believe that this can be so. That everything should be explicable in terms of physics (together of course with descriptions of the ways in which the parts are put together—roughly, biology is to physics as radio-engineering is to electro-magnetism) except the occurrence of sensations seems to me to be frankly unbelievable. Such sensations would be "nomological danglers," to use **Feigl**'s expression (428). It is not often realized how odd would be the laws whereby these nomological danglers would dangle. It is sometimes asked, "Why can't there be psycho-physical laws which are of a novel sort, just as the laws of electricity and magnetism were novelties from the standpoint of **Newton**ian mechanics?" Certainly we are pretty sure in the future to come across new ultimate laws of a novel type, but I expect them to relate simple constituents: for example, whatever ultimate particles are then in vogue. I cannot believe that ultimate laws of nature could relate simple constituents to configurations consisting of perhaps billions of neurons (and goodness knows how many billion billions of ultimate particles) all put together for all the world as though their main purpose in life was to be a negative feedback mechanism of a complicated sort. Such ultimate laws would be like nothing so far known in science. They have a queer "smell" to them. I am just unable to believe in the nomological danglers themselves, or in the laws whereby they would dangle. If any philosophical arguments seemed to compel us to believe in such things, I would suspect a catch in the argument. In any case it is the object of this paper to show that there are no philosophical arguments which compel us to be dualists.

The above is largely a confession of faith, but it explains why I find Wittgenstein's position (as I construe it) so congenial. For on this view there are, in a sense, no sensations. A man is a vast arrangement of physical particles, but there are not, over and above this, sensations or states of consciousness. There are just behavioural facts about this vast mechanism, such as that it expresses a temptation (behaviour disposition) to say "there is a yellowish-red patch on the wall" or that it goes through a sophisticated sort of wince, that is, says "I am in pain." Admittedly Wittgenstein says that though the sensation "is not a something," it is nevertheless "not a nothing either" (paragraph 304) but this need only mean that the word "ache" has a use. An ache is a thing, but only in the

innocuous sense in which the plain man, in the first paragraph of **Frege**'s *Foundations of Arithmetic*, answers the question "what is the number one?" by "a thing." It should be noted that when I assert that to say "I have a yellowish-orange after-image" is to express a temptation to assert the physical-object statement "there is a yellowish-orange patch on the wall," I mean that saying "I have a yellowish-orange after-image" is (partly) the exercise of the disposition which is the temptation. It is not to *report* that I have the temptation, any more than is "I love you" normally a report that I love someone. Saying "I love you" is just part of the behaviour which is the exercise of the disposition of loving someone.

## 2. Physicalism

Though, for the reasons given above, I am very receptive to the above "expressive" account of sensation statements, I do not feel that it will quite do the trick. Maybe this is because I have not thought it out sufficiently, but it does seem to me as though, when a person says "I have an after-image," he *is* making a genuine report, and that when he says "I have a pain," he *is* doing more than "replace pain-behaviour," and that "this more" is not just to say that he is in distress. I am not so sure, however, that to admit this is to admit that there are non-physical correlates of brain processes. Why should not sensations just be brain processes of a certain sort? There are, of course, well-known (as well as lesser-known) philosophical objections to the view that reports of sensations are reports of brain-processes, but I shall try to argue that these arguments are by no means as cogent as is commonly thought to be the case.

Let me first try to state more accurately the thesis that sensations are brain processes. It is not the thesis that, for example, "after-image" or "ache" means the same as "brain process of sort *X*" (where "*X*" is replaced by a description of a certain sort of brain process). It is that, in so far as "after-image" or "ache" is a report of a process, it is a report of a process that *happens to be* a brain process. It follows that the thesis does not claim that sensation statements can be *translated* into statements about brain processes. Nor does it claim that the logic of a sensation statement is the same as that of a brain-process statement. All it claims is that insofar as a sensation statement is a report of something, that something is in fact a brain process. Sensations are nothing over and above brain processes. Nations are nothing "over and above" citizens, but this does not prevent the logic of nation statements being very different from the logic of citizen statements, nor does it ensure the translatability of nation statements into citizen statements. [. . .]

*Remarks on identity.* When I say that a sensation is a brain process or that lightning is an electric discharge, I am using "is" in the sense of strict identity. (Just as in the—in this case necessary—proposition "7 is identical with the smallest prime number greater than 5.") When I say that a sensation is a brain process or that lightning is an electric discharge I do not mean just that the sensation is somehow spatially or temporally continuous with the brain process or that the lightning is just spatially or temporally continuous with the discharge. When on the other hand I say that the successful general is the same person as the small boy who stole the apples I mean only that the successful general I see before me is a time slice of the same four-dimensional object of which the small boy stealing apples is an earlier time slice. However, the four-dimensional object which has the general-I-see-before-me for its late time slice is identical in the strict sense with the four-dimensional object which has the small-boy-stealing-apples for an early time slice. I distinguish these two senses of "is identical with" because I wish to make it clear that the brain-process doctrine asserts identity in the *strict* sense.

## 3. Replies to Possible Objections

I shall now discuss various possible objections to the view that the processes reported in sensation statements are in fact processes in the brain. Most of us have met some of these objections in our first year as philosophy students. All the more reason to take a good look at them. Others of the objections will be more recondite and subtle.

*Objection 1.* Any illiterate peasant can talk perfectly well about his after-images, or how things look or feel to him, or about his aches and pains, and yet he may know nothing whatever about neurophysiology. A man may, like **Aristotle**, believe that the brain is an organ for cooling the body without any impairment of his ability to make true statements about his sensations. Hence the things we are talking about when we describe our sensations cannot be processes in the brain.

*Reply.* You might as well say that a nation of slug-abeds, who never saw the morning star or knew of its existence, or who had never thought of the expression "the Morning Star," but who used the expression "the Evening Star" perfectly well, could not use this expression to refer to the same entity as we refer to (and describe as) "the Morning Star."

You may object that the Morning Star is in a sense not the very same thing as the Evening Star, but only something spatiotemporally continuous with it. That is, you may say that the Morning Star is not the Evening Star in the strict sense of "identity" that I distinguished earlier. I can perhaps forestall this objection by considering the slug-abeds to be New Zealanders and the early risers to be Englishmen. Then the thing the New Zealanders describe as "the [Evening] Star" could be the very same thing (in the strict sense) as the Englishmen describe as "the [Morning] Star." And yet they could be ignorant of this fact.

There is, however, a more plausible example. Consider lightning. Modern physical science tells us that lightning is a certain kind of electrical discharge due to ionization of clouds of water-vapour in the atmosphere. This, it is now believed, is what the true nature of lightning is. Note that there are not two things: a flash of lightning and an electrical discharge. There is one thing, a flash of lightning, which is described scientifically as an electrical discharge to the earth from a cloud of ionized water-molecules. The case is not at all like that of explaining a footprint by reference to a burglar. We say that what lightning really is, what its true nature as revealed by science is, is an electric discharge. (It is not the true nature of a footprint to be a burglar.)

To forestall irrelevant objections, I should like to make it clear that by "lightning" I mean the publicly observable physical object, lightning, not a visual sense-datum of lightning. I say that the publicly observable physical object lightning is in fact the electric discharge, not just a correlate of it. The sense-datum, or at least the having of the sense-datum, the "look" of lightning, may well in my view be a correlate of the electric discharge. For in my view it is a brain state *caused* by the lightning. But we should no more confuse sensations of lightning with lightning than we confuse sensations of a table with the table.

In short, the reply to Objection 1 is that there can be contingent statements of the form "A is identical with B," and a person may well know that something is an A without knowing that it is a B. An illiterate peasant might well be able to talk about his sensations without knowing about his brain processes, just as he can talk about lightning though he knows nothing of electricity.

*Objection 2.* It is only a contingent fact (if it is a fact) that when we have a certain kind of sensation there is a certain kind of process in our brain. Indeed it is possible, though perhaps in the highest degree unlikely, that our present physiological theories will be as out of date as the ancient theory connecting mental processes with goings-on in the heart. It follows that when we report a sensation we are not reporting a brain-process.

*Reply.* The objection certainly proves that when we say "I have an after-image" we cannot *mean* something of the form "I have such and such a brain-process." But this does not show that what we report (having an after-image) is not *in fact* a brain process. "I see lightning" does not *mean* "I see an electric discharge." Indeed, it is logically possible (though highly unlikely) that the electrical discharge account of lightning might one day be given up. Again, "I see the Evening Star" does not *mean* the same as "I see the Morning Star," and yet "the Evening Star and the Morning Star are one and the same thing" is a contingent proposition. Possibly Objection 2 derives some of its apparent strength from a "Fido"—Fido theory of meaning. If the meaning of an expression were what the expression named, then of course it *would* follow from the fact that "sensation" and "brain-process" have different meanings that they cannot name one and the same thing.

*Objection 3.* Even if Objections 1 and 2 do not prove that sensations are something over and above brain-processes, they do prove that the qualities of sensations are something over and above the qualities of brain-processes. That is, it may be possible to get out of asserting the existence of irreducibly psychic processes, but not out of asserting the existence of irreducibly psychic *properties*. For suppose we identify the Morning Star with the Evening Star. Then there must be some properties which logically imply that of being the Morning Star, and quite distinct properties which entail that of being the Evening Star. Again, there must be some properties (for example, that of being a yellow flash) which are logically distinct from those in the physicalist story.

Indeed, it might be thought that the objection succeeds at one jump. For consider the property of "being a yellow flash." It might seem that this property lies inevitably outside the physicalist framework within which I am trying to work (either by "yellow" being an objective emergent property of physical objects, or else by being a power to produce yellow sense-data, where "yellow," in this second instantiation of the word, refers to a purely phenomenal or introspectible quality). I must therefore digress for a moment and indicate how I deal with secondary qualities. I shall concentrate on colour.

First of all, let me introduce the concept of a normal percipient. One person is more a normal percipient than another if he can make colour discriminations that the other cannot. For example, if A can pick a lettuce leaf out of a heap of cabbage leaves, whereas B cannot though he can pick a lettuce leaf out of a heap of beetroot leaves, then A is more normal than B. (I am assuming that A and B are not given time to distinguish the leaves by their slight difference in shape, and so forth.) From the concept of "more normal than" it is easy to see how we can introduce the concept of "normal." Of course, Eskimos may make the finest discriminations at the blue end of the spectrum, Hottentots at the red end. In this case the concept of a normal percipient is a slightly idealized one, rather like that of "the mean sun" in astronomical chronology. There is no need to go into such subtleties now. I say that "This is red" means something roughly like "A normal percipient would not easily pick this out of a clump of geranium petals though he would pick it out of a clump of lettuce leaves." Of course it does not exactly mean this: a person might know the meaning of "red" without knowing anything about geraniums, or even about normal percipients. But the point is that a person can be *trained* to say "This is red" of objects which would not easily be picked out of geranium petals by a normal percipient, and so on. (Note that even a colour-blind person can reasonably assert that something is red, though of course he needs to use another human being, not just himself, as his "colour meter.") This account of secondary qualities explains their unimportance in physics. For obviously the discriminations and lack of discriminations made by a very complex neurophysiological mechanism are hardly likely to correspond to simple and non-arbitrary distinctions in nature.

I therefore elucidate colours as powers, in **Locke's** sense,[1] to evoke certain sorts of discriminatory responses in human beings. They are also, of course, powers to cause sensations in human beings (an account still nearer Locke's). But these sensations, I am arguing, are identifiable with brain processes.

Now how do I get over the objection that a sensation can be identified with a brain process only if it has some phenomenal property, not possessed by brain processes, whereby one-half of the identification may be, so to speak, pinned down?

My suggestion is as follows. When a person says, "I see a yellowish-orange after-image," he is saying something like this: "*There is something going on which is like what is going on when* I have my eyes open, am awake, and there is an orange illuminated in good light in front of me, that is, when I really see an orange." (And there is no reason why a person should not say the same thing when he is having a veridical sense-datum, so long as we construe "like" in the last sentence in such a sense that something can be like itself.) Notice that the italicized words, namely "there is something going on which is like what is going on when," are all quasi-logical or topic-neutral words. This explains why the ancient Greek peasant's reports about his sensations can be neutral between dualistic metaphysics or my materialistic metaphysics. It explains how sensations can be brain-processes and yet how those who report them need know nothing about brain-processes. For he reports them only very abstractly as "something going on which is like what is going on when . . ." Similarly, a person may say "someone is in the room," thus reporting truly that the doctor is in the room, even though he has never heard of doctors. (There are not two people in the room: "someone" *and* the doctor.) [. . .]

This, then, is how I would reply to Objection 3. The strength of my reply depends on the possibility of our being able to report that one thing is like another without being able to state the respect in which it is like. I am not sure whether this is so or not, and that is why I regard Objection 3 as the strongest with which I have to deal. [. . .]

*Objection 5.* It would make sense to say of a molecular movement in the brain that it is swift or slow, straight or circular, but it makes no sense to say this of the experience of seeing something yellow.

*Reply.* So far we have not given sense to talk of experiences as swift or slow, straight or circular. But I am not claiming that "experience" and "brain-process" mean the same or even that they have the same logic. "Somebody" and "the doctor" do not have the same logic, but this does not lead us to suppose that talking about somebody telephoning is talking about someone over and above, say, the doctor. The ordinary man when he reports an experience is reporting that something is going on, but he leaves it open as to what sort of thing is going on, whether in a material solid medium, or perhaps in some sort of gaseous medium, or even perhaps in some sort of non-spatial medium (if this makes sense). All that I am saying is that "experience" and "brain-process" may in fact refer to the same thing, and if so we may easily adopt a convention (which is not a change in our present rules for the use of experience words but an addition to them) whereby it would make sense to talk of an experience in terms appropriate to physical processes.

*Objection 6.* Sensations are private, brain processes are *public*. If I sincerely say, "I see a yellowish-orange after-image" and I am not making a verbal mistake, then I cannot be wrong. But I can be wrong about a brain-process. The scientist looking into my brain might be having an illusion. Moreover, it makes sense to say that two or more people are observing the same brain-process but not that two or more people are reporting the same inner experience.

*Reply.* This shows that the language of introspective reports has a different logic from the language of material processes. It is obvious that until the brain-process theory is much improved and widely accepted there will be no *criteria* for saying "Smith has an experience of such-and-such a sort" *except* Smith's introspective reports. So we have adopted a rule of language that (normally) what Smith says goes. [. . .]

*Objection 8.* The "beetle in the box" objection (see Wittgenstein, *Philosophical Investigations,* paragraph 293). How could descriptions of experiences, if these are genuine reports, get a foothold in language? For any rule of language must have public criteria for its correct application.

*Reply.* The change from describing how things are to describing how we feel is just a change from uninhibitedly saying "this is so" to saying "this looks so." That is, when the naïve person might be tempted to say, "There is a patch of light on the wall which moves whenever I move my eyes" or "A pin is being stuck into me," we have learned how to resist this temptation and say "It *looks as though* there is a patch of light on the wallpaper" or "It *feels as though* someone were sticking a pin into me." The introspective account tells us about the individual's state of consciousness in the same way

as does "I see a patch of light" or "I feel a pin being stuck into me": it differs from the corresponding perception statement insofar as (a) in the perception statement the individual "goes beyond the evidence of his senses" in describing his environment and (b) in the introspective report he withholds descriptive epithets he is inclined to ascribe to the environment, perhaps because he suspects that they may not be appropriate to the actual state of affairs. Psychologically speaking, the change from talking about the environment to talking about one's state of consciousness is simply a matter of inhibiting descriptive reactions not justified by appearances alone, and of disinhibiting descriptive reactions which are normally inhibited because the individual has learned that they are unlikely to provide a reliable guide to the state of the environment in the prevailing circumstances. To say that something looks green to me is to say that my experience is like the experience I get when I see something that really is green. In my reply to Objection 3, I pointed out the extreme openness or generality of statements which report experiences. This explains why there is no language of private qualities. (Just as "someone," unlike "the doctor," is a colourless word.)[2]

If it is asked what is the difference between those brain processes which, in my view, are experiences and those brain processes which are not, I can only reply that this is at present unknown.

## 4. Empirical Thesis?

I have now considered a number of objections to the brain-process thesis. I wish now to conclude by some remarks on the logical status of the thesis itself. **U.T. Place** seems to hold that it is a straight-out scientific hypothesis. If so, he is partly right and partly wrong. If the issue is between (say) a brain-process thesis and a heart thesis, or a liver thesis, or a kidney thesis, then the issue is a purely empirical one, and the verdict is overwhelmingly in favour of the brain. The right sorts of things don't go on in the heart, liver, or kidney, nor do these organs possess the right sort of complexity of structure. On the other hand, if the issue is between a brain-or-heart-or-liver-or-kidney thesis (that is, some form of materialism) on the one hand and epiphenomenalism on the other hand, then the issue is not an empirical one. For there is no conceivable experiment which could decide between materialism and epiphenomenalism. This latter issue is not like the average straight-out empirical issue in science, but like the issue between the nineteenth-century English naturalist Philip Gosse and the orthodox geologists and paleontologists of his day. According to Gosse, the earth was created about 4000 BCE, exactly as described in *Genesis*, with twisted rock strata, "evidence" of erosion, and so forth, and all sorts of fossils, all in their appropriate strata, just as if the usual evolutionist story had been true. Clearly this theory is in a sense irrefutable: no evidence can possibly tell against it. Let us ignore the theological setting in which Philip Gosse's hypothesis had been placed, thus ruling out objections of a theological kind, such as "what a queer God who would go to such elaborate lengths to deceive us." Let us suppose that it is held that the universe just *began* in 4004 BCE with the initial conditions just everywhere as they were in 4004 BCE, and in particular that our own planet began with sediment in the rivers, eroded cliffs, fossils in the rocks, and so on. No scientist would ever entertain this as a serious hypothesis, consistent though it is with all possible evidence. The hypothesis offends against the principles of parsimony and simplicity. There would be far too many brute and inexplicable facts. Why are pterodactyl bones just as they are? No explanation in terms of the evolution of pterodactyls from earlier forms of life would any longer be possible. We would have millions of facts about the world as it was in 4004 BCE that just have to be *accepted*.

The issue between the brain-process theory and epiphenomenalism seems to be of the above sort. (Assuming that a behaviouristic reduction of introspective reports is not possible.) If it be agreed that there are no cogent philosophical arguments which force us into accepting dualism, and if the brain process theory and dualism are equally consistent with the facts, then the principles of parsimony and simplicity seem to me to decide overwhelmingly in favour of the brain-process theory. As I pointed out earlier, dualism involves a large number of irreducible psychophysical laws (whereby the "nomological danglers" dangle) of a queer sort, that just have to be taken on trust, and are just as difficult to swallow as the irreducible facts about the paleontology of the earth with which we are faced on Philip Gosse's theory.

## Notes

1. On the English philosopher and physician John Locke's (1632–1704) causal theory of perception, external objects have powers that act on the sense organs to produce ideas.—LG
2. The "beetle in the box" objection is, if it is sound, an objection to any view, and in particular the Cartesian one, that introspective reports are genuine reports. So it is no objection to a weaker thesis that I would be concerned to uphold, namely, that if introspective reports of "experiences" are genuinely reports, then the things they are reports of are in fact brain processes.

## Works Cited

Feigl, H. "The "Mental" and the "Physical"." *Minnesota Studies in the Philosophy of Science* 2 (1958): 370–497.

Place, U.T. "Is Consciousness a Brain Process?" *British Journal of Psychology* 47 (1956): 44–50.

## Study Questions

1. What does Smart mean by "physicalism"? Why does he tell us that we should accept physicalism even though it is not an empirical (i.e., scientific) hypothesis?
2. Smart considers his physicalist thesis that sensations are brain processes to be an assertion of strict identity analogous to the claim "The Morning Star is the Evening Star." Use this example to outline Smart's responses to the first three objections.
3. Explain why Wittgenstein's famous "beetle in a box" example presents an objection to the view that introspective reports (e.g., "I have a pain") are genuine reports. Why does Smart believe that unlike the dualist, his thesis that introspective reports are genuine reports escapes Wittgenstein's objection?
4. Smart admits that his physicalist thesis that sensations are brain processes is not an empirical (i.e., scientific) hypothesis since no experiment could decide in its favour. Nevertheless, using evolutionism vs. creationism as an analogy, he tells us that we should accept physicalism. Why?

# Hilary Putnam

Hilary Putnam, a well-known American philosopher, received his PhD at the University of California, Los Angeles, in 1951 and spent most of his career at Harvard University, retiring in 2000. He has done comprehensive work in many areas of philosophy, including language, science, and mind. In this article, Putnam defends a functionalist approach that identifies mental states with machine states.—GS

# The Nature of Mental States

## 1. Introduction

The typical concerns of the Philosopher of Mind might be represented by three questions: (1) How do we know that other people have pains? (2) Are pains brain states? (3) What is the analysis of the concept *pain*? I do not wish to discuss questions (1) and (3) in this chapter. I shall say something about question (2).

## 2. Identity Questions

"Is pain a brain state?" (Or, "Is the property of having a pain at time *t* a brain state?") It is impossible to discuss this question sensibly without saying something about the peculiar rules which have grown up in the course of the development of "analytical philosophy"—rules which, far from leading to an end to all conceptual confusions, themselves represent considerable conceptual confusion. These rules—which are, of course, implicit rather than explicit in the practice of most analytical philosophers—are (1) that a statement of the form "being A is being B" (e.g., "being in pain is being in a certain brain state") can be *correct* only if it follows, in some sense, from the meaning of the terms A and B; and (2) that a statement of the form "being A is being B" can be philosophically *informative* only if it is in some sense reductive (e.g., "being in pain is having a certain unpleasant sensation" is not philosophically informative; "being in pain is having a certain behaviour disposition" is, if true, philosophically informative). These rules are excellent rules if we still believe that the program of reductive analysis (in the style of the 1930s) can be carried out; if we don't, then they turn analytical philosophy into a mug's game, at least so far as "is" questions are concerned.

In this paper I shall use the term "property" as a blanket term for such things as being in pain, being in a particular brain state, having a particular behaviour disposition, and also for magnitudes such as temperature, etc.—i.e., for things which can naturally be represented by one-or-more-place predicates or functors. I shall use the term "concept" for things which can be identified with synonymy-classes of expressions. Thus the concept *temperature* can be identified (I maintain) with the synonymy-class of the word "temperature." (This is like saying that the number 2 can be identified with the class of all pairs. This is quite a different statement from the peculiar statement that 2 *is* the class of all pairs. I do not maintain that concepts *are* synonymy-classes, whatever that might mean, but that they can be identified with synonymy-classes, for the purpose of formalization of the relevant discourse.)

The question "What is the concept *temperature*?" is a very "funny" one. One might take it to mean "What is temperature? Please take my question as a conceptual one." In that case an answer might be (pretend for a moment "heat" and "temperature" are synonyms) "temperature is heat," or even "the concept of temperature is the same concept as the concept of heat." Or one might take it to mean "What are *concepts*, really? For example, what is 'the concept of temperature'?" In that case heaven knows what an "answer" would be. (Perhaps it would be the statement that concepts *can be identified with* synonymy-classes.)

Of course, the question "What is the property temperature?" is also "funny." And one way of interpreting it is to take it as a question about the concept of temperature. But this is not the way a physicist would take it.

The effect of saying that the property $P_1$ can be identical with the property $P_2$ only if the terms $P_1$, $P_2$ are in some suitable sense "synonyms" is, to all intents and purposes, to collapse the two notions of "property" and "concept" into a single notion. The view that concepts (intensions) are the same as properties has been explicitly advocated by **Carnap** (e.g., in *Meaning and Necessity*). This seems an unfortunate view, since

"temperature is mean molecular kinetic energy" appears to be a perfectly good example of a true statement of identity of properties, whereas "the concept of temperature is the same concept as a concept of mean molecular kinetic energy" is simply false.

Many philosophers believe that the statement "pain is a brain state" violates some rules or norms of English. But the arguments offered are hardly convincing. For example, if the fact that I can know that I am in pain without knowing that I am in brain state $S$ shows that pain cannot be brain state $S$, then, by exactly the same argument, the fact that I can know that the stove is hot without knowing that the mean molecular kinetic energy is high (or even that molecules exist) shows that it is *false* that temperature is mean molecular kinetic energy, physics to the contrary. In fact, all that immediately follows from the fact that I can know that I am in pain without knowing that I am in brain state $S$ is that the concept of pain is not the same concept as the concept of being in brain state $S$. But either pain, or the state of being in pain, or some pain, or some pain state, might still be brain state $S$. After all, the concept of temperature is not the same concept as the concept of mean molecular kinetic energy. But temperature is mean molecular kinetic energy.

Some philosophers maintain that both "pain is a brain state" and "pain states are brain states" are unintelligible. The answer is to explain to these philosophers, as well as we can, given the vagueness of all scientific methodology, what sorts of considerations lead one to make an empirical reduction (i.e., to say such things as "water is $H_2O$," "light is electro-magnetic radiation," "temperature is mean molecular kinetic energy"). If, without giving reasons, he still maintains in the face of such examples that one cannot imagine parallel circumstances for the use of "pains are brain states" (or, perhaps, "pain states are brain states") one has grounds to regard him as perverse.

Some philosophers maintain that "$P_1$ is $P_2$" is something that can be true, when the "is" involved is the "is" of empirical reduction, only when the properties $P_1$ and $P_2$ are (a) associated with a spatio-temporal region; and (b) the region is one and the same in both cases. Thus "temperature is mean molecular kinetic energy" is an admissible empirical reduction, since the temperature and the molecular energy are associated with the same space–time region, but "having a pain in my arm is being in a brain state" is not, since the spatial regions involved are different.

This argument does not appear very strong. Surely no one is going to be deterred from saying that mirror images are light reflected from an object and then from the surface of a mirror by the fact that an image can be "located" three feet *behind* the mirror! (Moreover, one can always find *some* common property of the reductions one is willing to allow— e.g. temperature is mean molecular kinetic energy— which is not a property of some one identification one wishes to disallow. This is not very impressive unless one has an argument to show that the very purposes of such identification depend upon the common property in question.)

Again, other philosophers have contended that all the predictions that can be derived from the conjunction of neurophysiological laws with such statements as "pain states are such-and-such brain states" can equally well be derived from the conjunction of the same neurophysiological laws with "being in pain is correlated with such-and-such brain states," and hence (*sic*!) there can be no methodological grounds for saying that pains (or pain states) *are* brain states, as opposed to saying that they are *correlated* (invariantly) with brain states. This argument, too, would show that light is only correlated with electromagnetic radiation. The mistake is in ignoring the fact that, although the theories in question may indeed lead to the same predictions, they open and exclude different *questions*. "Light is invariantly correlated with electromagnetic radiation" would leave open the questions "What is the light, then, if it isn't the same as the electromagnetic radiation?" and "What makes the light accompany the electromagnetic radiation?"— questions which are excluded by saying that the light *is* the electromagnetic radiation. Similarly, the purpose of saying that pains are brain states is precisely to exclude from empirical meaningfulness the questions "What is the pain, then, if it isn't the same as the brain state?" and "What makes the pain accompany the brain state?" If there are grounds to suggest that these questions represent, so to speak, the wrong way to look at the matter, then those grounds are grounds for a theoretical identification of pains with brain states.

If all arguments to the contrary are unconvincing, shall we then conclude that it is meaningful (and perhaps true) to say either that pains are brain states or that pain states are brain states?

1. It is perfectly meaningful (violates no "rule of English," involves no "extension of usage") to say "pains are brain states."
2. It is not meaningful (involves a "changing of meaning" or "an extension of usage," etc.) to say "pains are brain states."

My own position is not expressed by either (1) or (2). It seems to me that the notions "change of meaning" and "extension of usage" are simply so ill defined that one cannot in fact say *either* (1) or (2). I see no reason to believe that either the linguist, or the man-on-the-street, or the philosopher possesses today a notion of "change of meaning" applicable to such cases as the one we have been discussing. The *job* for which the notion of change of meaning was developed in the history of the language was just a *much* cruder job than this one.

But, if we don't assert either (1) or (2)—in other words, if we regard the "change of meaning" issue as a pseudo-issue in this case—then how are we to discuss the question with which we started? "Is pain a brain state?"

The answer is to allow statements of the form "pain is *A*," where "pain" and "*A*" are in no sense synonyms, and to see whether any such statement can be found which might be acceptable on empirical and methodological grounds. This is what we shall now proceed to do.

## 3. Is Pain a Brain State?

We shall discuss "Is pain a brain state?" then. And we have agreed to waive the "change of meaning" issue.

Since I am discussing not what the concept of pain comes to, but what pain is, in a sense of "is" which requires empirical theory-construction (or, at least, empirical speculation), I shall not apologize for advancing an empirical hypothesis. Indeed, my strategy will be to argue that pain is *not* a brain state, not on a priori grounds, but on the grounds that another hypothesis is more plausible. The detailed development and verification of my hypothesis would be just as Utopian a task as the detailed development and verification of the brain-state hypothesis. But the putting-forward, not of detailed and scientifically "finished" hypotheses, but of schemata for hypotheses, has long been a function of philosophy. I shall, in short, argue that pain is not a brain state, in the sense of a physical-chemical state of the brain (or even the whole nervous system), but another *kind* of state entirely. I propose the hypothesis that pain, or the state of being in pain, is a functional state of a whole organism.

To explain this it is necessary to introduce some technical notions. In previous papers I have explained the notion of a **Turing Machine** and discussed the use of this notion as a model for an organism. The notion of a Probabilistic Automaton is defined similarly to a Turing Machine, except that the transitions between "states" are allowed to be with various probabilities rather than being "deterministic." (Of course, a Turing Machine is simply a special kind of Probabilistic Automaton, one with transition probabilities 0, 1.) I shall assume the notion of a Probabilistic Automaton has been generalized to allow for "sensory inputs" and "motor outputs"—that is, the Machine Table specifies, for every possible combination of a "state" and a complete set of "sensory inputs," an "instruction" which determines the probability of the next "state," and also the probabilities of the "motor outputs." (This replaces the idea of the Machine as printing on a tape.) I shall also assume that the physical realization of the sense organs responsible for the various inputs, and of the motor organs, is specified, but that the "states" and the "inputs" themselves are, as usual, specified only "implicitly"—i.e., by the set of transition probabilities given by the Machine Table.

Since an empirically given system can simultaneously be a "physical realization" of many different Probabilistic Automata, I introduce the notion of a *Description* of a system. A Description of $S$, where $S$ is a system, is any true statement to the effect that $S$ possesses distinct states $S_1, S_2 \ldots Sn$ which are related to one another and to the motor outputs and sensory inputs by the transition probabilities given in such-and-such a Machine Table. The Machine Table mentioned in the Description will then be called the Functional Organization of $S$ relative to that Description, and the $Si$ such that $S$ is in state $Si$ at a given time will be called the Total State of $S$ (at the time) relative to that Description. It should be noted that knowing the Total State of a system relative to a Description involves knowing a good deal about how the system is likely to "behave," given various combinations of sensory inputs, but does *not* involve knowing the physical realization of the $Si$ as, e.g., physical-chemical states of the brain. The $Si$, to repeat, are specified only *implicitly* by the Description—i.e., specified *only* by the set of transition probabilities given in the Machine Table.

The hypothesis that "being in pain is a functional state of the organism" may now be spelled out more exactly as follows:

1. All organisms capable of feeling pain are Probabilistic Automata.
2. Every organism capable of feeling pain possesses at least one Description of a certain kind (i.e., being capable of feeling pain *is* possessing an appropriate kind of Functional Organization).
3. No organism capable of feeling pain possesses a decomposition into parts which separately possess Descriptions of the kind referred to in (2).
4. For every Description of the kind referred to in (2), there exists a subset of the sensory inputs such that an organism with that Description is in pain when and only when some of its sensory inputs are in that subset.

This hypothesis is admittedly vague, though surely no vaguer than the brain-state hypothesis in its present form. For example, one would like to know more about the kind of Functional Organization that an organism must have to be capable of feeling pain, and more about the marks that distinguish the subset of the sensory inputs referred to in (4). With respect to the first question, one can probably say that the Functional Organization must include something that resembles a "preference function," or at least a preference partial ordering, and something that resembles an "inductive logic" (i.e., the Machine must be able to "learn from experience"). [. . .] In addition, it seems natural to require that the Machine possess "pain sensors," i.e., sensory organs which normally signal damage to the Machine's body, or dangerous temperatures, pressures, etc., which transmit a special subset of the inputs, the subset referred to in (4). Finally, and with respect to the second question, we would want to require at least that the inputs in the distinguished subset have a high disvalue on the Machine's preference function or ordering [. . .]. The purpose of condition (3) is to rule out such "organisms" (if they can count as such) as swarms of bees as single pain-feelers. The condition (1) is, obviously, redundant, and is only introduced for expository reasons. (It is, in fact, empty, since everything is a Probabilistic Automaton under *some* Description.)

I contend, in passing, that this hypothesis, in spite of its admitted vagueness, is far *less* vague than the "physical-chemical state" hypothesis is today, and far more susceptible to investigation of both a mathematical and an empirical kind. Indeed, to investigate this hypothesis is just to attempt to produce "mechanical" models of organisms—and isn't this, in a sense, just what psychology is about? The difficult step, of course, will be to pass from models to *specific* organisms to a *normal form* for the psychological description of organisms—for this is what is required to make (2) and (4) precise. But this too seems to be an inevitable part of the program of psychology.

I shall now compare the hypothesis just advanced with (a) the hypothesis that pain is a brain state, and (b) the hypothesis that pain is a behaviour disposition.

## 4. Functional State versus Brain State

It may, perhaps, be asked if I am not somewhat unfair in taking the brain-state theorist to be talking about *physical-chemical* states of the brain. But (a) these are the only sorts of states ever mentioned by brain-state theorists. (b) The brain-state theorist usually mentions (with a certain pride, slightly reminiscent of the Village Atheist) the incompatibility of his hypothesis with all forms of dualism and mentalism. This is natural if physical-chemical states of the brain are what is at issue. However, functional states of whole systems are something quite different. In particular, the functional-state hypothesis is not incompatible with dualism! Although it goes without saying that the hypothesis is "mechanistic" in its inspiration, it is a slightly remarkable fact that a system consisting of a body and a "soul," if such things there be, can perfectly well be a Probabilistic Automaton. (c) One argument advanced by Smart is that the brain-state theory assumes only "physical" properties, and Smart finds "non-physical" properties unintelligible. The Total States and the "inputs" defined above are, of course, neither mental nor physical *per se*, and I cannot imagine a functionalist advancing this argument. (d) If the brain-state theorist does mean (or at least allow) states other than physical-chemical states, then his hypothesis is completely empty, at least until he specifies *what* sort of "states" he *does* mean.

Taking the brain-state hypothesis in this way, then, what reasons are there to prefer the functional-state hypothesis over the brain-state hypothesis? Consider what the brain-state theorist has to do to make good his claims. He has to specify a physical-chemical state such that *any* organism (not just a mammal) is in pain if and only if (a) it possesses a brain of a suitable physical-chemical structure; and (b) its brain is in that physical-chemical state. This means that the physical-chemical state in question must be a possible state of a mammalian brain, a reptilian brain, a mollusc's brain (octopuses are mollusca, and certainly feel pain), etc. At the same time, it must *not* be a possible (physically possible) state of the brain of any physically possible creature that cannot feel pain. Even if such a state can be found, it must be nomologically certain that it will also be a state of the brain of any extraterrestrial life that may be found that will be capable of feeling pain before we can even entertain the supposition that it may *be* pain.

It is not altogether impossible that such a state will be found. Even though octopus and mammal are examples of parallel (rather than sequential) evolution, for example, virtually identical structures (physically speaking) have evolved in the eye of the octopus and in the eye of the mammal, notwithstanding the fact that this organ has evolved from different kinds of cells in the two cases. Thus it is at least possible that parallel evolution, all over the universe, might *always* lead to *one and the same* physical "correlate" of pain. But this is certainly an ambitious hypothesis.

Finally, the hypothesis becomes still more ambitious when we realize that the brain-state theorist is not just saying that *pain* is a brain state; he is, of course, concerned to maintain that *every* psychological state is a brain state. Thus if we can find even one psychological predicate which can clearly be applied to both a mammal and an octopus (say "hungry"), but whose physical-chemical "correlate" is different in the two cases, the brain-state theory has collapsed. It seems to me overwhelmingly probable that we can do this. Granted, in such a case the brain-state theorist can save himself by *ad hoc* assumptions (e.g., defining the disjunction of two states to be a single "physical-chemical state"), but this does not have to be taken seriously.

Turning now to the considerations *for* the functional-state theory, let us begin with the fact that we identify organisms as in pain, or hungry, or angry, or in heat, etc., on the basis of their *behaviour*. But it is a truism that similarities in the behaviour of two systems are at least a reason to suspect similarities in the functional organization of the two systems, and a much *weaker* reason to suspect similarities in the actual physical details. Moreover, we expect the various psychological states—at least the basic ones, such as hunger, thirst, aggression, etc.—to have more or less similar "transition probabilities" (within wide and ill defined limits, to be sure) with each other and with behaviour in the case of different species, because this is an artifact of the way in which we identify these states. Thus, we would not count an animal as *thirsty* if its "unsatiated" behaviour did not seem to be directed toward drinking and was not

followed by "satiation for liquid." Thus any animal that we count as capable of these various states will at least *seem* to have a certain rough kind of functional organization. And, as already remarked, if the program of finding psychological laws that are not species-specific—i.e., of finding a normal form for psychological theories of different species—ever succeeds, then it will bring in its wake a delineation of the kind of functional organization that is necessary and sufficient for a given psychological state, as well as a precise definition of the notion "psychological state." In contrast, the brain-state theorist has to hope for the eventual development of neurophysiological laws that are species-independent, which seems much less reasonable than the hope that psychological laws (of a sufficiently general kind) may be species-independent, or, still weaker, that a species-independent *form* can be found in which psychological laws can be written.

## 5. Functional State versus Behaviour-Disposition

The theory that being in pain is neither a brain state nor a functional state but a behaviour disposition has one apparent advantage: it appears to agree with the way in which we verify that organisms are in pain. We do not in practice know anything about the brain state of an animal when we say that it is in pain; and we possess little if any knowledge of its functional organization, except in a crude intuitive way. In fact, however, this "advantage" is no advantage at all: for, although statements about how we verify that *x* is *A* may have a good deal to do with what the concept of being *A* comes to, they have precious little to do with what the property *A is*. To argue on the ground just mentioned that pain is neither a brain state nor a functional state is like arguing that heat is not mean molecular kinetic energy from the fact that ordinary people do not (they think) ascertain the mean molecular kinetic energy of something when they verify that it is hot or cold. It is not necessary that they should; what is necessary is that the marks that they take as indications of heat should in fact be explained by the mean molecular kinetic energy.

And, similarly, it is necessary to our hypothesis that the marks that are taken as behavioural indications of pain should be explained by the fact that the organism is in a functional state of the appropriate kind, but not that speakers should *know* that this is so.

The difficulties with "behaviour disposition" accounts are so well known that I shall do little more than recall them here. The difficulty—it appears to be more than a "difficulty," in fact—of specifying the required behaviour disposition except as "the disposition of $X$ to behave as if $X$ were in *pain*," is the chief one, of course. In contrast, we *can* specify the functional state with which we propose to identify pain, at least roughly, without using the notion of pain. Namely, the functional state we have in mind is the state of receiving sensory inputs which play a certain role in the Functional Organization of the organism. This role is characterized, at least partially, by the fact that the sense organs responsible for the inputs in question are organs whose function is to detect damage to the body, or dangerous extremes of temperature, pressure, etc., and by the fact that the "inputs" themselves, whatever their physical realization, represent a condition that the organism assigns a high disvalue to. [. . .] This does *not* mean that the Machine will always *avoid* being in the condition in question ("pain"); it only means that the condition will be avoided unless not avoiding it is necessary to the attainment of some more highly valued goal. Since the behaviour of the Machine (in this case, an organism) will depend not merely on the sensory inputs, but also on the Total State (i.e., on other values, beliefs, etc.), it seems hopeless to make any general statement about how an organism in such a condition *must* behave; but this does not mean that we must abandon hope of characterizing the condition. Indeed, we have just characterized it.

Not only does the behaviour-disposition theory seem hopelessly vague; if the "behaviour" referred to is peripheral behaviour, and the relevant stimuli are peripheral stimuli (e.g., we do not say anything about what the organism will do if its brain is operated upon), then the theory seems clearly false. For example, two animals with all motor nerves cut will have the same actual and potential "behaviour" (namely, none to speak of); but if one has cut pain fibres and the other has uncut pain fibres, then one will feel pain and the other won't. Again, if one person has cut pain fibres, and another suppresses all pain responses deliberately due to some strong compulsion, then the actual and potential peripheral behaviour may be the same, but one will feel pain and the other won't. (Some philosophers maintain that this last case is conceptually impossible, but the only evidence for this appears to be that *they* can't, or don't want to, conceive of it.) If, instead of pain, we take some sensation the "bodily expression" of which is easier to suppress—say, a slight coolness in one's left little finger—the case becomes even clearer.

Finally, even if there *were* some behaviour disposition invariantly correlated with pain (species-independently!), and specifiable without using the term "pain," it would still be more plausible to identify being in pain with some state whose presence *explains* this behaviour disposition—the brain state or functional state—than with the behaviour disposition itself. Such considerations of plausibility may be somewhat subjective; but if other things *were* equal (of course, they aren't) why shouldn't we allow considerations of plausibility to play the deciding role?

## 6. Methodological Considerations

So far we have considered only what might be called the "empirical" reasons for saying that being in pain is a functional state, rather than a brain state or a behaviour disposition; namely, that it seems more likely that the functional state we described is invariantly "correlated" with pain, species-independently, than that there is either a physical-chemical state of the brain (must an organism have a *brain* to feel pain? perhaps some ganglia will do) or a behaviour disposition so correlated. If this is correct, then it follows that the identification we proposed is at least a candidate for consideration. What of methodological considerations?

The methodological considerations are roughly similar in all cases of reduction, so no surprises need be expected here. First, identification of psychological states with functional states means that the laws of psychology can be derived from statements of the form "such-and-such organisms have such-and-such Descriptions" together with the identification statements ("being in pain is such-and-such a functional state," etc.). Secondly, the presence of the functional state (i.e., of inputs which play the role we have described in the Functional Organization of the organism) is not merely "correlated with" but actually explains the pain behaviour on the part of the organism. Thirdly, the identification serves to exclude questions which (if a naturalistic view is correct) represent an altogether wrong way of looking at the matter, e.g., "What *is* pain if it isn't either the brain state or the functional state?" and "What causes the pain to be always accompanied by this sort of functional state?" In short, the identification is to be tentatively accepted as a theory which leads to both fruitful predictions and to fruitful *questions*, and which serves to discourage fruitless and empirically senseless questions, where by "empirically senseless" I mean "senseless" not merely from the standpoint of verification, but from the standpoint of what there in fact *is*.

## Study Questions

1. Explain the importance of Putnam's distinction between concepts and properties for the empirical approach he adopts in addressing the question "Is pain a brain state?"
2. What use does Putnam make use of the idea of a "Probabilistic Automaton" in defending his hypothesis that being in pain is not a brain state but a functional state of the whole organism? Why does Putnam consider the functional-state hypothesis, unlike the brain-state hypothesis, to be compatible with Cartesian dualism?
3. What empirical reasons does Putnam provide to try to convince us that his functional-state hypothesis does better than the brain-state hypothesis when it comes to the mental states of such divergent creatures as mammals, molluscs, and Martians?
4. Putnam criticizes the behaviour-disposition theory of mind on the grounds that it is not just vague and implausible but false. Why does he consider it false?

---

# Thomas Nagel

---

Born in Belgrade, Serbia, Thomas Nagel earned his BPhil at Oxford and PhD at Harvard. He has been a professor of law and philosophy at New York University since 1980. Philosophy of mind is one of Nagel's specialties. In this famous article, Nagel argues that subjective experience of consciousness cannot be explained in a reductionist framework.—GS

## What Is It Like to Be a Bat?

### 1. Introduction

Consciousness is what makes the mind–body problem really intractable. Perhaps that is why current discussions of the problem give it little attention or get it obviously wrong. The recent wave of reductionist euphoria has produced several analyses of mental phenomena and mental concepts designed to explain the possibility of some variety of materialism, psychophysical identification, or reduction [e.g., Smart 1963]. But the problems dealt with are those common to this type of reduction and other types, and what makes the mind–body problem unique, and unlike the water-$H_2O$ problem or the Turing machine-IBM machine problem or the lightning-electrical discharge problem or the gene-DNA problem or the oak tree-hydrocarbon problem, is ignored.

Every reductionist has his favourite analogy from modern science. It is most unlikely that any of these unrelated examples of successful reduction will shed light on the relation of mind to brain. But philosophers share the general human weakness for explanations of what is incomprehensible in terms suited for what is familiar and well understood, though entirely different. This has led to the acceptance of implausible accounts of the mental largely because they would permit familiar kinds of reduction. I shall try to explain why the usual examples do not help us to understand the relation between mind and body—why, indeed, we have at present no conception of what an explanation of the physical nature of a mental phenomenon would be. Without consciousness the mind–body problem would be much less interesting. With consciousness it seems hopeless. The most important and characteristic feature of conscious mental phenomena is very poorly understood. Most reductionist theories do not even try to explain it. And careful examination will show that no currently available concept of reduction is applicable to it. Perhaps a new theoretical form can be devised for the purpose, but such a solution, if it exists, lies in the distant intellectual future.

## 2. Consciousness

Conscious experience is a widespread phenomenon. It occurs at many levels of animal life, though we cannot be sure of its presence in the simpler organisms, and it is very difficult to say in general what provides evidence of it. (Some extremists have been prepared to deny it even of mammals other than man.) No doubt it occurs in countless forms totally unimaginable to us, on other planets in other solar systems throughout the universe. But no matter how the form may vary, the fact that an organism has conscious experience *at all* means, basically, that there is something it is like to *be* that organism. There may be further implications about the form of the experience; there may even (though I doubt it) be

implications about the behaviour of the organism. But fundamentally an organism has conscious mental states if and only if there is something that it is like to *be* that organism—something it is like *for* the organism.

We may call this the subjective character of experience. It is not captured by any of the familiar, recently devised reductive analyses of the mental, for all of them are logically compatible with its absence. It is not analyzable in terms of any explanatory system of functional states, or intentional states, since these could be ascribed to robots or automata that behaved like people though they experienced nothing. It is not analyzable in terms of the causal role of experiences in relation to typical human behaviour—for similar reasons. I do not deny that conscious mental states and events cause behaviour, nor that they may be given functional characterizations. I deny only that this kind of thing exhausts their analysis. Any reductionist program has to be based on an analysis of what is to be reduced. If the analysis leaves something out, the problem will be falsely posed. It is useless to base the defence of materialism on any analysis of mental phenomena that fails to deal explicitly with their subjective character. For there is no reason to suppose that a reduction which seems plausible when no attempt is made to account for consciousness can be extended to include consciousness. Without some idea, therefore, of what the subjective character of experience is, we cannot know what is required of a physicalist theory.

While an account of the physical basis of mind must explain many things, this appears to be the most difficult. It is impossible to exclude the phenomenological features of experience from a reduction in the same way that one excludes the phenomenal features of an ordinary substance from a physical or chemical reduction of it—namely, by explaining them as effects on the minds of human observer. If physicalism is to be defended, the phenomenological features must themselves be given a physical account. But when we examine their subjective character it seems that such a result is impossible. The reason is that every subjective phenomenon is essentially connected with a single point of view, and it seems inevitable that an objective, physical theory will abandon that point of view.

Let me first try to state the issue somewhat more fully than by referring to the relation between the subjective and the objective, or between the *pour-soi* and the *en-soi*. This is far from easy. Facts about what it is like to be an *X* are very peculiar, so peculiar that some may be inclined to doubt their reality, or the significance of claims about them. To illustrate the connection between subjectivity and a point of view, and to make evident the importance of subjective features, it will help to explore the matter in relation to an example that brings out clearly the divergence between the two types of conception, subjective and objective.

## 3. Inner Lives of Bats

I assume we all believe that bats have experience. After all, they are mammals, and there is no more doubt that they have experience than that mice or pigeons or whales have experience. I have chosen bats instead of wasps or flounders because if one travels too far down the phylogenetic tree, people gradually shed their faith that there is experience there at all. Bats, although more closely related to us than those other species, nevertheless present a range of activity and a sensory apparatus so different from ours that the problem I want to pose is exceptionally vivid (though it certainly could be raised with other species). Even without the benefit of philosophical reflection, anyone who has spent some time in an enclosed space with an excited bat knows what it is to encounter a fundamentally *alien* form of life.

I have said that the essence of the belief that bats have experience is that there is something that it is like to be a bat. Now we know that most bats (the *microchiroptera*, to be precise) perceive the external world primarily by sonar, or echolocation, detecting the reflections, from objects within range, of their own rapid, subtly modulated, high-frequency shrieks. Their brains are designed to correlate the outgoing impulses with the subsequent echoes, and the information thus acquired enables bats to make precise discriminations of distance, size, shape, motion, and texture comparable to those we make

by vision. But bat sonar, though clearly a form of perception, is not similar in its operation to any sense that we possess, and there is no reason to suppose that it is subjectively like anything we can experience or imagine. This appears to create difficulties for the notion of what it is like to be a bat. We must consider whether any method will permit us to extrapolate to the inner life of the bat from our own [human] case, and if not, what alternative methods there may be for understanding the notion.

Our own experience provides the basic material for our imagination, whose range is therefore limited. It will not help to try to imagine that one has webbing on one's arms, which enables one to fly around at dusk and dawn catching insects in one's mouth; that one has very poor vision, and perceives the surrounding world by a system of reflected high-frequency sound signals; and that one spends the day hanging upside down by one's feet in an attic. Insofar as I can imagine this (which is not very far), it tells me only what it would be like for *me* to behave as a bat behaves. But that is not the question. I want to know what it is like for a *bat* to be a bat. Yet if I try to imagine this, I am restricted to the resources of my own mind, and those resources are inadequate to the task. I cannot perform it either by imagining additions to my present experience, or by imagining segments gradually subtracted from it, or by imagining some combination of additions, subtractions, and modifications.

To the extent that I could look and behave like a wasp or a bat without changing my fundamental structure, my experiences would not be anything like the experiences of those animals. On the other hand, it is doubtful that any meaning can be attached to the supposition that I should possess the internal neurophysiological constitution of a bat. Even if I could by gradual degrees be transformed into a bat, nothing in my present constitution enables me to imagine what the experiences of such a future stage of myself thus metamorphosed would be like. The best evidence would come from the experiences of bats, if we only knew what they were like.

So if extrapolation from our own case is involved in the idea of what it is like to be a bat, the extrapolation must be incompletable. We cannot form more than a schematic conception of what it *is* like. For example, we may ascribe general *types* of experience on the basis of the animal's structure and behaviour. Thus we describe bat sonar as a form of three-dimensional forward perception; we believe that bats feel some versions of pain, fear, hunger, and lust, and that they have other, more familiar types of perception besides sonar. But we believe that these experiences also have in each case a specific subjective character, which it is beyond our ability to conceive. And if there is conscious life elsewhere in the universe, it is likely that some of it will not be describable even in the most general experiential terms available to us. (The problem is not confined to exotic cases, however, for it exists between one person and another. The subjective character of the experience of a person deaf and blind from birth is not accessible to me, for example, nor presumably is mine to him. This does not prevent us each from believing that the other's experience has such a subjective character.)

## 4. Phenomenological Facts

If anyone is inclined to deny that we can believe in the existence of facts like this whose exact nature we cannot possibly conceive, he should reflect that in contemplating the bats we are in much the same position that intelligent bats or Martians would occupy if they tried to form a conception of what it was like to be us. The structure of their own minds might make it impossible for them to succeed, but we know they would be wrong to conclude that there is not anything precise that it is like to be us: that only certain general types of mental state could be ascribed to us (perhaps perception and appetite would be concepts common to us both; perhaps not). We know they would be wrong to draw such a sceptical conclusion because we know what it is like to be us. And we know that while it includes an enormous amount of variation and complexity, and while we do not possess the vocabulary to describe it adequately, its subjective character is highly specific, and in some respects describable in terms that can be understood only by creatures like us. The fact that we cannot expect

ever to accommodate in our language a detailed description of Martian or bat phenomenology should not lead us to dismiss as meaningless the claim that bats and Martians have experiences fully comparable in richness of detail to our own. It would be fine if someone were to develop concepts and a theory that enabled us to think about those things; but such an understanding may be permanently denied to us by the limits of our nature. And to deny the reality or logical significance of what we can never describe or understand is the crudest form of cognitive dissonance.

This brings us to the edge of a topic that requires much more discussion than I can give it here: namely, the relation between facts on the one hand and conceptual schemes or systems of representation on the other. My realism about the subjective domain in all its forms implies a belief in the existence of facts beyond the reach of human concepts. Certainly it is possible for a human being to believe that there are facts which humans never *will* possess the requisite concepts to represent or comprehend. Indeed, it would be foolish to doubt this, given the finiteness of humanity's expectations. After all, there would have been **transfinite numbers** even if everyone had been wiped out by the **Black Death** before **Cantor** discovered them. But one might also believe that there are facts which *could* not ever be represented or comprehended by human beings, even if the species lasted forever—simply because our structure does not permit us to operate with concepts of the requisite type. This impossibility might even be observed by other beings, but it is not clear that the existence of such beings, or the possibility of their existence, is a precondition of the significance of the hypothesis that there are humanly inaccessible facts. (After all, the nature of beings with access to humanly inaccessible facts is presumably itself a humanly inaccessible fact.) Reflection on what it is like to be a bat seems to lead us, therefore, to the conclusion that there are facts that do not consist in the truth of propositions expressible in a human language. We can be compelled to recognize the existence of such facts without being able to state or comprehend them.

I shall not pursue this subject, however. Its bearing on the topic before us (namely, the mind–body problem) is that it enables us to make a general observation about the subjective character of experience. Whatever may be the status of facts about what it is like to be a human being, or a bat, or a Martian, these appear to be facts that embody a particular point of view.

I am not adverting here to the alleged privacy of experience to its possessor. The point of view in question is not one accessible only to a single individual. Rather it is a *type*. It is often possible to take up a point of view other than one's own, so the comprehension of such facts is not limited to one's own case. There is a sense in which phenomenological facts are perfectly objective: one person can know or say of another what the quality of the other's experience is. They are subjective, however, in the sense that even this objective ascription of experience is possible only for someone sufficiently similar to the object of ascription to be able to adopt his point of view—to understand the ascription in the first person as well as in the third, so to speak. The more different from oneself the other experiencer is, the less success one can expect with this enterprise. In our own case we occupy the relevant point of view, but we will have as much difficulty understanding our own experience properly if we approach it from another point of view as we would if we tried to understand the experience of another species without taking up *its* point of view.

## 5. Mind–Body Problem

This bears directly on the mind–body problem. For if the facts of experience—facts about what it is like *for* the experiencing organism—are accessible only from one point of view, then it is a mystery how the true character of experiences could be revealed in the physical operation of that organism. The latter is a domain of objective facts *par excellence*—the kind that can be observed and understood from many points of view and by individuals with differing perceptual systems. There are no comparable imaginative obstacles to the acquisition of knowledge about bat neurophysiology by human scientists, and

intelligent bats or Martians might learn more about the human brain than we ever will.

This is not by itself an argument against reduction. A Martian scientist with no understanding of visual perception could understand the rainbow, or lightning, or clouds as physical phenomena, though he would never be able to understand the human concepts of rainbow, lightning, or cloud, or the place these things occupy in our phenomenal world. The objective nature of the things picked out by these concepts could be apprehended by him because, although the concepts themselves are connected with a particular point of view and a particular visual phenomenology, the things apprehended from that point of view are not: they are observable from the point of view but external to it; hence they can be comprehended from other points of view also, either by the same organisms or by others. Lightning has an objective character that is not exhausted by its visual appearance, and this can be investigated by a Martian without vision. To be precise, it has a *more* objective character than is revealed in its visual appearance. [. . .]

In the case of experience, on the other hand, the connection with a particular point of view seems much closer. It is difficult to understand what could be meant by the *objective* character of an experience, apart from the particular point of view from which its subject apprehends it. After all, what would be left of what it was like to be a bat if one removed the viewpoint of the bat? But if experience does not have, in addition to its subjective character, an objective nature that can be apprehended from many different points of view, then how can it be supposed that a Martian investigating my brain might be observing physical processes which were my mental processes (as he might observe physical processes which were bolts of lightning), only from a different point of view? How, for that matter, could a human physiologist observe them from another point of view?

We appear to be faced with a general difficulty about psycho-physical reduction. In other areas the process of reduction is a move in the direction of greater objectivity, toward a more accurate view of the real nature of things. This is accomplished by reducing our dependence on individual or species-specific points of view toward the object of investigation. We describe it not in terms of the impressions it makes on our senses, but in terms of its more general effects and of properties detectable by means other than the human senses. The less it depends on a specifically human viewpoint, the more objective is our description. It is possible to follow this path because although the concepts and ideas we employ in thinking about the external world are initially applied from a point of view that involves our perceptual apparatus, they are used by us to refer to things beyond themselves—toward which we *have* the phenomenal point of view. Therefore we can abandon it in favour of another, and still be thinking about the same things.

Experience itself, however, does not seem to fit the pattern. The idea of moving from appearance to reality seems to make no sense here. What is the analogue in this case to pursuing a more objective understanding of the same phenomena by abandoning the initial subjective viewpoint toward them in favour of another that is more objective but concerns the same thing? Certainly it *appears* unlikely that we will get closer to the real nature of human experience by leaving behind the particularity of our human point of view and striving for a description in terms accessible to beings that could not imagine what it was like to be us. If the subjective character of experience is fully comprehensible only from one point of view, then any shift to greater objectivity—that is, less attachment to a specific viewpoint—does not take us nearer to the real nature of the phenomenon: it takes us farther away from it.

In a sense, the seeds of this objection to the reducibility of experience are already detectable in successful cases of reduction; for in discovering sound to be, in reality, a wave phenomenon in air or other media, we leave behind one viewpoint to take up another, and the auditory, human or animal viewpoint that we leave behind remains unreduced. Members of radically different species may both understand the same physical events in objective terms, and this does not require that they understand the phenomenal forms in which those events appear to the senses of members of the other species. Thus it is a condition of their referring to a common reality that their more particular viewpoints are not part of the common reality that they both apprehend. The reduction can succeed only if the species-specific viewpoint is omitted from what is to be reduced.

But while we are right to leave this point of view aside in seeking a fuller understanding of the external world, we cannot ignore it permanently, since it is the essence of the internal world, and not merely a point of view on it. Most of the neobehaviourism of recent philosophical psychology results from the effort to substitute an objective concept of mind for the real thing, in order to have nothing left over which cannot be reduced. If we acknowledge that a physical theory of mind must account for the subjective character of experience, we must admit that no presently available conception gives us a clue how this could be done. The problem is unique. If mental processes are indeed physical processes, then there is something it is like, intrinsically, to undergo certain physical processes. What it is for such a thing to be the case remains a mystery.

## 6. Physicalism

What moral should be drawn from these reflections, and what should be done next? It would be a mistake to conclude that physicalism must be false. Nothing is proved by the inadequacy of physicalist hypotheses that assume a faulty objective analysis of mind. It would be truer to say that physicalism is a position we cannot understand because we do not at present have any conception of how it might be true. Perhaps it will be thought unreasonable to require such a conception as a condition of understanding. After all, it might be said, the meaning of physicalism is clear enough: mental states are states of the body; mental events are physical events. We do not know *which* physical states and events they are, but that should not prevent us from understanding the hypothesis. What could be clearer than the words "is" and "are"?

But I believe it is precisely this apparent clarity of the word "is" that is deceptive. Usually, when we are told that X is Y we know *how* it is supposed to be true, but that depends on a conceptual or theoretical background and is not conveyed by the "is" alone. We know how both "X" and "Y" refer, and the kinds of things to which they refer, and we have a rough idea how the two referential paths might converge on a single thing, be it an object, a person, a process, an event, or whatever. But when the two terms of the identification are very disparate it may not be so clear how it could be true. We may not have even a rough idea of how the two referential paths could converge, or what kind of things they might converge on, and a theoretical framework may have to be supplied to enable us to understand this. Without the framework, an air of mysticism surrounds the identification.

This explains the magical flavour of popular presentations of fundamental scientific discoveries, given out as propositions to which one must subscribe without really understanding them. For example, people are now told at an early age that all matter is really energy. But despite the fact that they know what "is" means, most of them never form a conception of what makes this claim true, because they lack the theoretical background.

At the present time the status of physicalism is similar to that which the hypothesis that matter is energy would have had if uttered by a pre-Socratic philosopher. We do not have the beginnings of a conception of how it might be true. In order to understand the hypothesis that a mental event is a physical event, we require more than an understanding of the word "is." The idea of how a mental and a physical term might refer to the same thing is lacking, and the usual analogies with theoretical identification in other fields fail to supply it. They fail because if we construe the reference of mental terms to physical events on the usual model, we either get a reappearance of separate subjective events as the effects through which mental reference to physical events is secured, or else we get a false account of how mental terms refer (for example, a causal behaviourist one).

Strangely enough, we may have evidence for the truth of something we cannot really understand. Suppose a caterpillar is locked in a sterile safe by someone unfamiliar with insect metamorphosis, and weeks later the safe is reopened, revealing a butterfly. If the person knows that the safe has been shut the whole time, he has reason to believe that the butterfly is or was once the caterpillar, without having any idea in what sense this might be so. (One possibility is that the caterpillar contained a tiny winged parasite that devoured it and grew into the butterfly.)

It is conceivable that we are in such a position with regard to physicalism. Donald Davidson has argued that if mental events have physical causes and effects, they must have physical descriptions. He holds that we have reason to believe this even though we do not—and in fact *could* not—have a general psychophysical theory. His argument applies to intentional mental events, but I think we also have some reason to believe that sensations are physical processes, without being in a position to understand how. Davidson's position is that certain physical events have irreducibly mental properties, and perhaps some view describable in this way is correct. But nothing of which we can now form a conception corresponds to it; nor have we any idea what a theory would be like that enabled us to conceive of it.

Very little work has been done on the basic question (from which mention of the brain can be entirely omitted) whether any sense can be made of experiences' having an objective character at all. Does it make sense, in other words, to ask what my experiences are *really* like, as opposed to how they appear to me? We cannot genuinely understand the hypothesis that their nature is captured in a physical description unless we understand the more fundamental idea that they *have* an objective nature (or that objective processes can have a subjective nature).[1]

## 7. Conclusion

I should like to close with a speculative proposal. It may be possible to approach the gap between subjective and objective from another direction. Setting aside temporarily the relation between the mind and the brain, we can pursue a more objective understanding of the mental in its own right. At present we are completely unequipped to think about the subjective character of experience without relying on the imagination—without taking up the point of view of the experiential subject. This should be regarded as a challenge to form new concepts and devise a new method—an objective phenomenology not dependent on empathy or the imagination. Though presumably it would not capture everything, its goal would be to describe, at least in part, the subjective character of experiences in a form comprehensible to beings incapable of having those experiences.

We would have to develop such a phenomenology to describe the sonar experiences of bats; but it would also be possible to begin with humans. One might try, for example, to develop concepts that could be used to explain to a person blind from birth what it was like to see. One would reach a blank wall eventually, but it should be possible to devise a method of expressing in objective terms much more than we can at present, and with much greater precision. The loose intermodal analogies—for example, "Red is like the sound of a trumpet"—which crop up in discussions of this subject are of little use. That should be clear to anyone who has both heard a trumpet and seen red. But structural features of perception might be more accessible to objective description, even though something would be left out. And concepts alternative to those we learn in the first person may enable us to arrive at a kind of understanding even of our own experience which is denied us by the very ease of description and lack of distance that subjective concepts afford.

Apart from its own interest, a phenomenology that is in this sense objective may permit questions about the physical basis of experience to assume a more intelligible form. Aspects of subjective experience that admitted this kind of objective description might be better candidates for objective explanations of a more familiar sort. But whether or not this guess is correct, it seems unlikely that any physical theory of mind can be contemplated until more thought has been given to the general problem of subjective and objective. Otherwise we cannot even pose the mind–body problem without sidestepping it.

## Note

1. This question also lies at the heart of the problem of other minds, whose close connection with the mind–body problem is often overlooked. If one understood how subjective experience could have an objective nature, one would understand the existence of subjects other than oneself.

## Works Cited

Davidson, D. "Mental Events." *Experience and Theory*. Eds. L. Foster and J.W. Swanson. Amherst: University of Massachusetts Press, 1970. 207–27.

Smart, J.J.C. *Philosophy and Scientific Realism*. London: Routledge and Kegan Paul, 1963.

## Study Questions

1. Outline Nagel's criticisms of the philosophical theories of the mind encountered elsewhere in previous readings: physical reductionism (Smart), functionalism (Putnam), and behaviourism (Wittgenstein).
2. Explain what Nagel means by his construal of consciousness as "the subjective character of experience." Why does Nagel wonder what it is like to be a bat, instead of, say, a wasp or a gorilla?
3. How does Nagel define "subjectivity" and "objectivity"? Given these definitions, explain why Nagel considers a phenomenon like lightning to be physically reducible (to an electrical discharge) but not a phenomenon like consciousness (to a brain state).
4. Interestingly, Nagel does not conclude that physicalism is false. What "speculative proposal" does Nagel offer as a possible means of arriving at a physical theory of mind?

# ～ METHODS OF SCIENTIFIC INQUIRY ～

## Francis Bacon

Francis Bacon (1561–1626) was a lawyer, politician, and natural philosopher. His political offices included member of Parliament, solicitor general, attorney general, Privy Council member, lord keeper of the Great Seal, and lord chancellor. Bacon's works in natural philosophy challenged the scholastic tradition: these aphorisms come from the first book of Bacon's *Novum Organum Scientiarum*, a reference to the *Organon*, Aristotle's collected works on logic. Ironically, the empirical scientific method Bacon promoted proved his downfall: he died of pneumonia after experiments with ice.—TR

## Aphorisms Concerning the Interpretation of Nature and the Kingdom of Man

From *Novum Organum Scientiarum*

### New Foundations for Science

1. Man, being the servant and interpreter of Nature, can do and understand so much and so much only as he has observed in fact or in thought of the course of nature: beyond this he neither knows anything nor can do anything. [. . .]

3. Human knowledge and human power meet in one; for where the cause is not known the effect cannot be produced. Nature to be commanded must be obeyed; and that which in contemplation is as the cause is in operation as the rule. [. . .]

5. The study of nature with a view to works is engaged in by the mechanic, the mathematician, the physician, the alchemist, and the magician; but by all (as things now are) with slight endeavour and scanty success. [. . .]

8. The works already known are due to chance and experiment rather than to sciences; for the sciences we now possess are merely systems for the nice ordering and setting forth of things already invented, not methods of invention or directions for new works. [. . .]

11. As the sciences which we now have do not help us in finding out new works, so neither does the logic which we now have help us in finding out new sciences. [. . .]

14. The syllogism consists of propositions, propositions consist of words, words are symbols of notions. Therefore if the notions themselves (which is the root of the matter) are confused and over-hastily abstracted from the facts, there can be no firmness in the superstructure. Our only hope therefore lies in a true induction. [. . .]

19. There are and can be only two ways of searching into and discovering truth. The one flies from the senses and particulars to the most general axioms, and from these principles, the truth of which it takes for settled and immoveable, proceeds to judgment and to the discovery of middle axioms. And this way is now in fashion. The other derives axioms from the senses and particulars, rising by a gradual and unbroken ascent, so that it arrives at the most general axioms last of all. This is the true way, but as yet untried. [. . .]

26. The conclusions of human reason as ordinarily applied in matter of nature, I call for the sake of distinction *Anticipations of Nature* (as a thing rash or premature). That reason which is elicited from facts by a just and methodical process, I call *Interpretation of Nature*. [. . .]

30. Though all the wits of all the ages should meet together and combine and transmit their labours, yet will no great progress ever be made in science by means of anticipations; because radical errors in the first concoction of the mind are not to be cured by the excellence of functions and remedies subsequent.

31. It is idle to expect any great advancement in science from the superinducing and engrafting of new things upon old. We must begin anew from the very foundations, unless we would revolve forever in a circle with mean and contemptible progress. [. . .]

## Four Idols

38. The idols and false notions which are now in possession of the human understanding, and have taken deep root therein, not only so beset men's minds that truth can hardly find entrance, but even after entrance obtained, they will again in the very instauration of the sciences meet and trouble us, unless men being forewarned of the danger fortify themselves as far as may be against their assaults.

39. There are four classes of Idols which beset men's minds. To these for distinction's sake I have assigned names, calling the first class *Idols of the Tribe*; the second, *Idols of the Cave*; the third, *Idols of the Marketplace*; the fourth, *Idols of the Theatre*.

40. The formation of ideas and axioms by true induction is no doubt the proper remedy to be applied for the keeping off and clearing away of idols. To point them out, however, is of great use; for the doctrine of Idols is to the Interpretation of Nature what the doctrine of the refutation of Sophisms is to common Logic.

41. The Idols of the Tribe have their foundation in human nature itself, and in the tribe or race of men. For it is a false assertion that the sense of man is the measure of things. On the contrary, all perceptions as well of the sense as of the mind are according to the measure of the individual and not according to the measure of the universe. And the human understanding is like a false mirror, which, receiving rays irregularly, distorts and discolours the nature of things by mingling its own nature with it.

42. The Idols of the Cave are the idols of the individual man. For everyone (besides the errors common to human nature in general) has a cave or den of his own, which refracts and discolours the light of nature, owing either to his own proper and peculiar nature; or to his education and conversation with others; or to the reading of books, and the authority of those whom he esteems and admires; or to the differences of impressions, accordingly as they take place in a mind preoccupied and predisposed or in a mind indifferent and settled; or the like. So that the spirit of man (according as it is meted out to different individuals) is in fact a thing variable and full of perturbation, and governed as it were by chance.

43. There are also Idols formed by the intercourse and association of men with each other, which I call Idols of the Marketplace, on account of the commerce and consort of men there. For it is by discourse that men associate; and words are imposed according to the apprehension of the vulgar. And therefore the ill and unfit choice of words wonderfully obstructs the understanding. Nor do the definitions or explanations wherewith in some things learned men are wont to guard and defend themselves by any means set the matter right. But words plainly force and overrule the understanding, and throw all into confusion, and lead men away into numberless empty controversies and idle fancies.

44. Lastly, there are Idols which have immigrated into men's minds from the various dogmas of philosophies, and also from wrong laws of demonstration. These I call Idols of the Theatre because in my judgment all the received systems are but so many stage-plays, representing worlds of their own creation after an unreal and scenic fashion. Nor is it only of the systems now in vogue, or only of the ancient sects and philosophies, that I speak; for many more plays of the same kind may yet be composed and in like artificial manner set forth, seeing that errors the most widely different have nevertheless causes for the most part alike. Neither again do I mean this only of entire systems, but also of many principles and axioms in science, which by tradition, credulity, and negligence have come to be received.

But of these several kinds of Idols I must speak more largely and exactly, that the understanding may be duly cautioned.

45. The human understanding is of its own nature prone to suppose the existence of more order and regularity in the world than it finds. And though there be many things in nature which are singular

and unmatched, yet it devises for them parallels and conjugates and relatives which do not exist. Hence the fiction that all celestial bodies move in perfect circles, spirals and dragons being (except in name) utterly rejected. Hence too the element of Fire with its orb is brought in, to make up the square with the other three which the sense perceives. Hence also the ratio of density of the so-called elements is arbitrarily fixed at ten to one. And so on of other dreams. And these fancies affect not dogmas only, but simple notions also.

46. The human understanding when it has once adopted an opinion (either as being the received opinion or as being agreeable to itself) draws all things else to support and agree with it. And though there be a greater number and weight of instances to be found on the other side, yet these it either neglects and despises or else by some distinction sets aside and rejects, in order that by this great and pernicious predetermination the authority of its former conclusions may remain inviolate. [. . .] Besides, [. . .] it is the peculiar and perpetual error of the human intellect to be more moved and excited by affirmatives than by negatives, whereas it ought properly to hold itself indifferently disposed towards both alike. Indeed in the establishment of any true axiom, the negative instance is the more forcible of the two.

47. The human understanding is moved by those things most which strike and enter the mind simultaneously and suddenly, and so fill the imagination; and then it feigns and supposes all other things to be somehow, though it cannot see how, similar to those few things by which it is surrounded.

48. The human understanding is unquiet; it cannot stop or rest, and still presses onward, but in vain. Therefore it is that we cannot conceive of any end or limit to the world; but always as of necessity it occurs to us that there is something beyond. [. . .] But this inability interferes more mischievously in the discovery of causes: for although the most general principles in nature ought to be held merely positive, as they are discovered, and cannot with truth be referred to a cause, nevertheless the human understanding being unable to rest still seeks something prior in the order of nature. And then it is that in struggling towards that which is further off it falls back upon that which

is more nigh at hand—namely, on final causes: which have relation clearly to the nature of man rather than to the nature of the universe, and from this source have strangely defiled philosophy.

49. The human understanding is no dry light but receives an infusion from the will and affections, whence proceed sciences which may be called "sciences as one would." For what a man had rather were true he more readily believes. Therefore he rejects difficult things from impatience of research; sober things, because they narrow hope; the deeper things of nature, from superstition; the light of experience, from arrogance and pride, lest his mind should seem to be occupied with things mean and transitory; things not commonly believed, out of deference to the opinion of the vulgar. Numberless in short are the ways, and sometimes imperceptible, in which the affections colour and infect the understanding.

50. But by far the greatest hindrance and aberration of the human understanding proceeds from the dullness, incompetency, and deceptions of the senses, in that things which strike the sense outweigh things which do not immediately strike it, though they be more important. Hence it is that speculation commonly ceases where sight ceases, insomuch that of things invisible there is little or no observation. Hence all the working of the spirits enclosed in tangible bodies lies hid and unobserved of men. So also all the more subtle changes of form in the parts of coarser substances (which they commonly call alteration, though it is in truth local motion through exceedingly small spaces) is in like manner unobserved. And yet unless these two things just mentioned be searched out and brought to light, nothing great can be achieved in nature, as far as the production of works is concerned.

51. The human understanding is of its own nature prone to abstractions and gives a substance and reality to things which are fleeting. But to resolve nature into abstractions is less to our purpose than to dissect her into parts, as did the school of **Democritus**, which went further into nature than the rest. Matter rather than forms should be the object of our attention, its configurations and changes of configuration, and simple action, and law of action or motion; for forms are figments of the human mind.

52. Such then are the idols which I call *Idols of the Tribe* [. . .].

53. The *Idols of the Cave* take their rise in the peculiar constitution, mental or bodily, of each individual; and also in education, habit, and accident. Of this kind there is a great number and variety, but I will instance those the pointing out of which contains the most important caution and which have most effect in disturbing the clearness of the understanding.

54. Men become attached to certain particular sciences and speculations, either because they fancy themselves the authors and inventors thereof, or because they have bestowed the greatest pains upon them and become most habituated to them. But men of this kind, if they betake themselves to philosophy and contemplations of a general character, distort and colour them in obedience to their former fancies—a thing especially to be noticed in **Aristotle**, who made his natural philosophy a mere bond-servant to his logic, thereby rendering it contentious and well nigh useless.

55. There is one principal and as it were radical distinction between different minds in respect of philosophy and the sciences, which is this: that some minds are stronger and apter to mark the differences of things, others to mark their resemblances. The steady and acute mind can fix its contemplations and dwell and fasten on the subtlest distinctions; the lofty and discursive mind recognizes and puts together the finest and most general resemblances. Both kinds however easily err in excess, by catching the one at gradations the other at shadows.

56. There are found some minds given to an extreme admiration of antiquity, others to an extreme love and appetite for novelty, but few so duly tempered that they can hold the mean, neither carping at what has been well laid down by the ancients nor despising what is well introduced by the moderns. This however turns to the great injury of the sciences and philosophy since these affectations of antiquity and novelty are the humours of partisans rather than judgments and truth is to be sought for not in the felicity of any age, which is an unstable thing, but in the light of nature and experience, which is eternal.

57. Contemplations of nature and of bodies in their simple form break up and distract the understanding, while contemplations of nature and bodies in their composition and configuration overpower and dissolve the understanding: a distinction well seen in the school of **Leucippus** and Democritus as compared with the other philosophies. For that school is so busied with the particles that it hardly attends to the structure; while the others are so lost in admiration of the structure that they do not penetrate to the simplicity of nature. These kinds of contemplation should therefore be alternated and taken by turns—that so the understanding may be rendered at once penetrating and comprehensive. [. . .]

59. But the *Idols of the Marketplace* are the most troublesome of all: idols which have crept into the understanding through the alliances of words and names. For men believe that their reason governs words, but it is also true that words react on the understanding, and this it is that has rendered philosophy and the sciences sophistical and inactive. Now words, being commonly framed and applied according to the capacity of the vulgar, follow those lines of division which are most obvious to the vulgar understanding. And whenever an understanding of greater acuteness or a more diligent observation would alter those lines to suit the true divisions of nature, words stand in the way and resist the change. Whence it comes to pass that the high and formal discussions of learned men end oftentimes in disputes about words and names, with which (according to the use and wisdom of the mathematicians) it would be more prudent to begin, and so by means of definitions reduce them to order. Yet even definitions cannot cure this evil in dealing with natural and material things since the definitions themselves consist of words, and those words beget others: so that it is necessary to recur to individual instances.

60. The idols imposed by words on the understanding are of two kinds. They are either names of things which do not exist (for as there are things left unnamed through lack of observation, so likewise are there names which result from fantastic suppositions and to which nothing in reality corresponds), or they are names of things which exist, but yet confused and ill-defined, and hastily and irregularly derived from realities. Of the former kind are Fortune, the Prime Mover, Planetary Orbits, Element

of Fire, and like fictions which owe their origin to false and idle theories. And this class of idols is more easily expelled because to get rid of them it is only necessary that all theories should be steadily rejected and dismissed as obsolete.

But the other class, which springs out of a faulty and unskilful abstraction, is intricate and deeply rooted. Let us take for example such a word as *humid*, and see how far the several things which the word is used to signify agree with each other; and we shall find the word *humid* to be nothing else than a mark loosely and confusedly applied to denote a variety of actions which will not bear to be reduced to any constant meaning. For it both signifies that which easily spreads itself round any other body; and that which in itself is indeterminate and cannot solidify; and that which readily yields in every direction; and that which easily divides and scatters itself; and that which easily unites and collects itself; and that which readily flows and is put in motion; and that which readily clings to another body and wets it; and that which is easily reduced to a liquid, or being solid easily melts. Accordingly when you come to apply the word, if you take it in one sense, flame is humid; if in another, air is not humid; if in another, fine dust is humid; if in another, glass is humid. So that it is easy to see that the notion is taken by abstraction only from water and common and ordinary liquids, without any due verification. [. . .]

62. *Idols of the Theatre*, or of Systems, are many, and there can be and perhaps will be yet many more. [. . .] For as on the phenomena of the heavens many hypotheses may be constructed, so likewise (and more also) many various dogmas may be set up and established on the phenomena of philosophy. And in the plays of this philosophical theatre you may observe the same thing which is found in the theatre of the poets, that stories invented for the stage are more compact and elegant, and more as one would wish them to be, than true stories out of history.

In general, however, there is taken for the material of philosophy either a great deal out of a few things or a very little out of many things, so that on both sides philosophy is based on too narrow a foundation of experiment and natural history, and decides on the authority of too few cases. For the Rational School of philosophers snatches from experience a variety of common instances, neither duly ascertained nor diligently examined and weighed, and leaves all the rest to meditation and agitation of wit.

There is also another class of philosophers who having bestowed much diligent and careful labour on a few experiments have thence made bold to educe and construct systems, wresting all other facts in a strange fashion to conformity therewith.

And there is yet a third class, consisting of those who out of faith and veneration mix their philosophy with theology and traditions, among whom the vanity of some has gone so far aside as to seek the origin of sciences among spirits and genii. So that this parent stock of errors—this false philosophy—is of three kinds: the Sophistical, the Empirical, and the Superstitious.

63. The most conspicuous example of the first class was Aristotle, who corrupted natural philosophy by his logic: fashioning the world out of categories; assigning to the human soul, the noblest of substances, a genus from words of the second intention; doing the business of density and rarity (which is to make bodies of greater or less dimensions, that is, occupy greater or less spaces) by the frigid distinction of act and power; asserting that single bodies have each a single and proper motion, and that if they participate in any other, then this results from an external cause; and imposing countless other arbitrary restrictions on the nature of things. [. . .] Nor let any weight be given to the fact that in his books on animals and his problems, and other of his treatises, there is frequent dealing with experiments. For he had come to his conclusion before; he did not consult experience, as he should have done, in order to the framing of his decisions and axioms; but having first determined the question according to his will, he then resorts to experience, and bending her into conformity with his placets leads her about like a captive in a procession—so that even on this count he is more guilty than his modern followers, the schoolmen, who have abandoned experience altogether.

64. But the Empirical school of philosophy gives birth to dogmas more deformed and monstrous

than the Sophistical or Rational school. For it has its foundations not in the light of common notions (which though it be a faint and superficial light is yet in a manner universal and has reference to many things) but in the narrowness and darkness of a few experiments. To those therefore who are daily busied with these experiments, and have infected their imagination with them, such a philosophy seems probable and all but certain; to all men else incredible and vain. Of this there is a notable instance in the alchemists and their dogmas, though it is hardly to be found elsewhere in these times, except perhaps in the philosophy of **Gilbert**. Nevertheless, with regard to philosophies of this kind, there is one caution not to be omitted; for I foresee that if ever men are roused by my admonitions to betake themselves seriously to experiment and bid farewell to sophistical doctrines, then indeed through the premature hurry of the understanding to leap or fly to universals and principles of things, great danger may be apprehended from philosophies of this kind.

65. But the corruption of philosophy by superstition and an admixture of theology is far more widely spread and does the greatest harm, whether to entire systems or to their parts. For the human understanding is obnoxious to the influence of the imagination no less than to the influence of common notions. For the contentious and sophistical kind of philosophy ensnares the understanding; but this kind, being fanciful and tumid and half poetical, misleads it more by flattery. [. . .]

Of this kind we have among the Greeks a striking example in **Pythagoras**, though he united with it a coarser and more cumbrous superstition; another in Plato and his school, more dangerous and subtle. It shows itself likewise in parts of other philosophies, in the introduction of abstract forms and final causes and first causes, with the omission in most cases of causes intermediate and the like. Upon this point the greatest caution should be used. For nothing is so mischievous as the apotheosis of error, and it is a very plague of the understanding for vanity to become the object of veneration. Yet in this vanity some of the moderns have with extreme levity indulged so far as to attempt to found a system of natural philosophy

on the first chapter of Genesis, on the book of Job, and other parts of the sacred writings; [. . .] from this unwholesome mixture of things human and divine there arises not only a fantastic philosophy but also an heretical religion. [. . .]

## Benefits of Science

129. It remains for me to say a few words touching the excellency of the end in view. [. . .]

In the first place then, the introduction of famous discoveries appears to hold by far the first place among human actions; and this was the judgment of the former ages. For to the authors of inventions they awarded divine honours; while to those who did good service in the state (such as founders of cities and empires, legislators, saviours of their country from long endured evils, quellers of tyrannies, and the like) they decreed no higher honours than heroic. And certainly if a man rightly compare the two, he will find that this judgment of antiquity was just. For the benefits of discoveries may extend to the whole race of man, civil benefits only to particular places; the latter last not beyond a few ages, the former through all time. Moreover the reformation of a state in civil matters is seldom brought in without violence and confusion; but discoveries carry blessings with them, and confer benefits without causing harm or sorrow to any. [. . .]

Again, let a man only consider what a difference there is between the life of men in the most civilized province of Europe, and in the wildest and most barbarous districts of New India; he will feel it be great enough to justify the saying that "man is a god to man," not only in regard of aid and benefit, but also by a comparison of condition. And this difference comes not from soil, not from climate, not from race, but from the arts.

Again, it is well to observe the force and virtue and consequences of discoveries; and these are to be seen nowhere more conspicuously than in those three which were unknown to the ancients, and of which the origin, though recent, is obscure and inglorious: namely, printing, gunpowder, and the magnet. For these three have changed the whole face and state of things throughout the world—the first in literature, the second in warfare, the third in navigation; whence have followed innumerable changes, insomuch that no empire, no sect, no star seems to have exerted greater power and influence in human affairs than these mechanical discoveries.

Further, it will not be amiss to distinguish the three kinds and as it were grades of ambition in mankind. The first is of those who desire to extend their own power in their native country; which kind is vulgar and degenerate. The second is of those who labour to extend the power of their country and its dominion among men. This certainly has more dignity, though not less covetousness. But if a man endeavour to establish and extend the power and dominion of the human race itself over the universe, his ambition (if ambition it can be called) is without doubt both a more wholesome thing and a more noble than the other two. Now the empire of man over things depends wholly on the arts and sciences. For we cannot command nature except by obeying her. [. . .]

Lastly, if the debasement of arts and sciences to purposes of wickedness, luxury, and the like be made a ground of objection, let no one be moved thereby. For the same may be said of all earthly goods—of wit, courage, strength, beauty, wealth, light itself, and the rest. Only let the human race recover that right over nature which belongs to it by divine bequest, and let power be given it, the exercise thereof will be governed by sound reason and true religion.

## Study Questions

1. What does Bacon mean by "true induction" as the method that will provide new foundations for science?
2. What are Bacon's four Idols? Provide a specific example of each.
3. Explain how Bacon's inductive method might serve, in his words, as "the proper remedy to be applied for the keeping off and clearing away of idols"?
4. What reasons does Bacon give for why we should value the contributions of inventors over statesmen? Do these reasons hold for the examples of technologies Bacon gives: printing, gunpowder, and the magnet?

---

# Karl R. Popper

---

*The Logic of Scientific Discovery* established Karl Popper (1902–94) as an early critic of logical positivism, despite his PhD from the University of Vienna and close ties to the Vienna Circle. Forced like other Jewish intellectuals to leave Austria by the rise of Nazism, Popper held positions at the University of Canterbury, the London School of Economics, and the University of London. Apart from his work on the philosophy of science, he is known for his social and political writings opposing totalitarianism.—TR

## A Survey of Some Fundamental Problems

From *The Logic of Scientific Discovery*

### 1. Introduction

A scientist, whether theorist or experimenter, puts forward statements, or systems of statements, and tests them step by step. In the field of the empirical sciences, more particularly, he constructs hypotheses, or systems of theories, and tests them against experience by observation and experiment.

I suggest that it is the task of the logic of scientific discovery, or the logic of knowledge, to give a logical analysis of this procedure; that is, to analyze the method of the empirical sciences.

But what are these "methods of the empirical sciences"? And what do we call "empirical science"?

## 2. The Problem of Induction

According to a widely accepted view [. . .] the empirical sciences can be characterized by the fact that they use "*inductive methods*," as they are called. According to this view, the logic of scientific discovery would be identical with inductive logic, i.e., with the logical analysis of these inductive methods.

It is usual to call an inference "inductive" if it passes from *singular statements* (sometimes also called "particular" statements), such as accounts of the results of observations or experiments, to *universal statements*, such as hypotheses or theories.

Now it is far from obvious, from a logical point of view, that we are justified in inferring universal statements from singular ones, no matter how numerous; for any conclusion drawn in this way may always turn out to be false: no matter how many instances of white swans we may have observed, this does not justify the conclusion that *all* swans are white.

The question whether inductive inferences are justified, or under what conditions, is known as *the problem of induction*.

The problem of induction may also be formulated as the question of how to establish the truth of universal statements which are based on experience, such as the hypotheses and theoretical systems of the empirical sciences. For many people believe that the truth of these universal statements is "*known by experience*"; yet it is clear that an account of an experience—of an observation or the result of an experiment—can in the first place be only a singular statement and not a universal one. Accordingly, people who say of a universal statement that we know its truth from experience usually mean that the truth of this universal statement can somehow be reduced to the truth of singular ones, and that these singular ones are known by experience to be true; which amounts to saying that the universal statement is based on inductive inference. Thus to ask whether there are natural laws known to be true appears to be only another way of asking whether inductive inferences are logically justified.

Yet if we want to find a way of justifying inductive inferences, we must first of all try to establish a *principle of induction*. A principle of induction would be a statement with the help of which we could put inductive inferences into a logically acceptable form. In the eyes of the upholders of inductive logic, a principle of induction is of supreme importance for scientific method: "this principle," says **Reichenbach**, "determines the truth of scientific theories. To eliminate it from science would mean nothing less than to deprive science of the power to decide the truth or falsity of its theories. Without it, clearly, science would no longer have the right to distinguish its theories from the fanciful and arbitrary creations of the poet's mind" (186).

Now this principle of induction cannot be a purely logical truth like a **tautology** or an **analytic** statement. Indeed, if there were such a thing as a purely logical principle of induction, there would be no problem of induction; for in this case, all inductive inferences would have to be regarded as purely logical or tautological transformations, just like inferences in deductive logic. Thus the principle of induction must be a **synthetic** statement; that is, a statement whose negation is not self-contradictory but logically possible. So the question arises why such a principle should be accepted at all, and how we can justify its acceptance on rational grounds.

Some who believe in inductive logic are anxious to point out, with Reichenbach, that "the principle of induction is unreservedly accepted by the whole of science and that no man can seriously doubt this principle in everyday life either" (67). Yet even supposing this were the case—for after all, "the whole of science" might err—I should still contend that a principle of induction is superfluous, and that it must lead to logical inconsistencies.

That inconsistencies may easily arise in connection with the principle of induction should have been clear from the work of **Hume**; also, that they can be avoided, if at all, only with difficulty. For the principle of induction must be a universal statement in its turn. Thus if we try to regard its truth as known from experience, then the very same problems which occasioned its introduction will arise all over again. To justify it, we should have to employ inductive inferences; and to justify these we should have to assume an inductive principle of a higher order; and so on. Thus the attempt to base the principle of induction on experience breaks down, since it must lead to an infinite regress.

**Kant** tried to force his way out of this difficulty by taking the principle of induction (which he formulated as the "principle of universal causation") to be "a priori valid." But I do not think that his ingenious attempt to provide an a priori justification for synthetic statements was successful.

My own view is that the various difficulties of inductive logic here sketched are insurmountable. So also, I fear, are those inherent in the doctrine, so widely current today, that inductive inference, although not "strictly valid," *can attain some degree of "reliability" or of "probability."* According to this doctrine, inductive inferences are "probable inferences." "We have described," says Reichenbach, "the principle of induction as the means whereby science decides upon truth. To be more exact, we should say that it serves to decide upon probability. For it is not given to science to reach either truth or falsity . . . but scientific statements can only attain continuous degrees of probability whose unattainable upper and lower limits are truth and falsity" (186). [. . .]

[But] if a certain degree of probability is to be assigned to statements based on inductive inference, then this will have to be justified by invoking a new principle of induction, appropriately modified. And this new principle in its turn will have to be justified, and so on. Nothing is gained, moreover, if the principle of induction, in its turn, is taken not as "true" but only as "probable." In short, like every other form of inductive logic, the logic of probable inference, or "probability logic," leads either to an infinite regress, or to the doctrine of apriorism.

The theory to be developed in the following pages stands directly opposed to all attempts to operate with the ideas of inductive logic. It might be described as the theory of *the deductive method of testing*, or as the view that a hypothesis can only be empirically *tested*—and only *after* it has been advanced.

Before I can elaborate this view (which might be called "deductivism," in contrast to "inductivism") I must first make clear the distinction between the *psychology of knowledge* which deals with empirical facts, and the *logic of knowledge* which is concerned only with logical relations. For the belief in inductive logic is largely due to a confusion of psychological problems with epistemological ones. It may be worth noticing, by the way, that this confusion spells trouble not only for the logic of knowledge but for its psychology as well.

## 3. Elimination of Psychologism

I said above that the work of the scientist consists in putting forward and testing theories.

The initial stage, the act of conceiving or inventing a theory, seems to me neither to call for logical analysis nor to be susceptible of it. The question how it happens that a new idea occurs to a man—whether it is a musical theme, a dramatic conflict, or a scientific theory—may be of great interest to empirical psychology; but it is irrelevant to the logical analysis of scientific knowledge. This latter is concerned not with *questions of fact* (Kant's *quid facti?*), but only with questions of *justification or validity* (Kant's *quid juris?*). Its questions are of the following kind. Can a statement be justified? And if so, how? Is it testable? Is it logically dependent on certain other statements? Or does it perhaps contradict them? In order that a statement may be logically examined in this way, it must already have been presented to us. Someone must have formulated it, and submitted it to logical examination.

Accordingly I shall distinguish sharply between the process of conceiving a new idea, and the methods and results of examining it logically. As to the task of the logic of knowledge—in contradistinction to the psychology of knowledge—I shall proceed on the assumption that it consists solely in investigating the methods employed in those systematic tests to which every new idea must be subjected if it is to be seriously entertained.

Some might object that it would be more to the purpose to regard it as the business of epistemology to produce what has been called a "*rational reconstruction*" of the steps that have led the scientist to a discovery—to the finding of some new truth. But the question is: what, precisely, do we want to reconstruct? If it is the processes involved in the stimulation and release of an inspiration which are to be reconstructed, then I should refuse to take it as the task of the logic of knowledge. Such processes are the concern of empirical psychology but hardly of logic. It is another matter if we want to reconstruct rationally the *subsequent tests* whereby the inspiration may be discovered to be a discovery, or become known to be knowledge. Insofar as the scientist critically judges, alters, or rejects his own inspiration we may, if we like, regard the methodological analysis undertaken here as a kind of "rational reconstruction" of the corresponding thought-processes. But this reconstruction would not describe these processes as they actually happen: it can give only a logical skeleton of the procedure of testing. Still, this is perhaps all that is meant by those who speak of a "rational reconstruction" of the ways in which we gain knowledge. [. . .]

My view of the matter, for what it is worth, is that there is no such thing as a logical method of having new ideas, or a logical reconstruction of this process. My view may be expressed by saying that every discovery contains "an irrational element," or "a creative intuition," in **Bergson**'s sense. In a similar way **Einstein** speaks of "the search for those highly universal . . . laws from which a picture of the world can be obtained by pure deduction. There is no logical path," he says, "leading to these . . . laws. They can only be reached by intuition, based upon something like an intellectual love ("*Einfühlung*") of the objects of experience" (125).

## 4. Deductive Testing of Theories

According to the view that will be put forward here, the method of critically testing theories, and selecting them according to the results of tests, always proceeds on the following lines. From a new idea, put up tentatively, and not yet justified in any way—an anticipation, a hypothesis, a theoretical system, or what you will—conclusions are drawn by means of logical deduction. These conclusions are then compared with one another and with other relevant statements, so as to find what logical relations (such as equivalence, derivability, compatibility, or incompatibility) exist between them.

We may if we like distinguish four different lines along which the testing of a theory could be carried out. First there is the logical comparison of the conclusions among themselves, by which the internal consistency of the system is tested. Secondly, there is the investigation of the logical form of the theory, with the object of determining whether it has the character of an empirical or scientific theory, or whether it is, for example, tautological. Thirdly, there is the comparison with other theories, chiefly with the aim of determining whether the theory would constitute a scientific advance should it survive our various tests. And finally, there is the testing of the theory by way of empirical applications of the conclusions which can be derived from it.

The purpose of this last kind of test is to find out how far the new consequences of the theory—whatever may be new in what it asserts—stand up to the demands of practice, whether raised by purely scientific experiments, or by practical technological applications. Here too the procedure of testing turns out to be deductive. With the help of other statements, previously accepted, certain singular statements—which we may call "predictions"—are deduced from the theory; especially predictions that are easily testable or applicable. From among these statements, those are selected which are not derivable from the current theory, and more especially those which the current theory contradicts. Next we seek a decision as regards these (and other) derived statements by comparing them with the results of practical applications and experiments. If this decision is positive, that is, if the singular conclusions turn out to be acceptable, or *verified*, then the theory has, for the time being, passed its test: we have found no reason to discard it. But if the decision is negative, or in other words, if the conclusions have been *falsified*, then their falsification also falsifies the theory from which they were logically deduced.

It should be noticed that a positive decision can only temporarily support the theory, for subsequent negative decisions may always overthrow it. So long as a theory withstands detailed and severe tests and is not superseded by another theory in the course of scientific progress, we may say that it has "proved its mettle" or that it is "*corroborated.*"

Nothing resembling inductive logic appears in the procedure here outlined. I never assume that we can argue from the truth of singular statements to the truth of theories. I never assume that by force of "verified" conclusions, theories can be established as "true," or even as merely "probable."

## 5. The Problem of Demarcation

Of the many objections which are likely to be raised against the view here advanced, the most serious is perhaps the following. In rejecting the method of induction, it may be said, I deprive empirical science of what appears to be its most important characteristic; and this means that I remove the barriers which separate science from metaphysical speculation. My reply to this objection is that my main reason for rejecting inductive logic is precisely that *it does not provide a suitable distinguishing mark* of the empirical, non-metaphysical, character of a theoretical system; or in other words, that *it does not provide a suitable "criterion of demarcation."*

The problem of finding a criterion which would enable us to distinguish between the empirical sciences on the one hand, and mathematics and logic as well as "metaphysical" systems on the other, I call the *problem of demarcation.*

This problem was known to Hume who attempted to solve it. With Kant it became the central problem of the theory of knowledge. If, following Kant, we call the problem of induction "Hume's problem," we might call the problem of demarcation "Kant's problem."

Of these two problems—the source of nearly all the other problems of the theory of knowledge—the problem of demarcation is, I think, the more fundamental. Indeed, the main reason why epistemologists with empiricist leanings tend to pin their faith to the "method of induction" seems to be their belief that this method alone can provide a suitable criterion of demarcation. This applies especially to those empiricists who follow the flag of "positivism."

The older positivists wished to admit, as scientific or legitimate, only those *concepts* (or notions or ideas) which were, as they put it, "derived from experience"; those concepts, that is, which they believed to be logically reducible to elements of sense-experience, such as sensations (or sense-data), impressions, perceptions, visual or auditory memories, and so forth. Modern positivists are apt to see more clearly that science is not a system of concepts but rather a system of *statements*. Accordingly, they wish to admit, as scientific or legitimate, only those statements which are reducible to elementary (or "atomic") statements of experience—to "judgments of perception" or "atomic propositions" or "protocol-sentences" or what not. It is clear that the implied criterion of demarcation is identical with the demand for an inductive logic.

Since I reject inductive logic I must also reject all these attempts to solve the problem of demarcation. With this rejection, the problem of demarcation gains in importance for the present inquiry. Finding an acceptable criterion of demarcation must be a crucial task for any epistemology which does not accept inductive logic.

Positivists usually interpret the problem of demarcation in a *naturalistic* way; they interpret it as if it were a problem of natural science. Instead of taking it as their task to propose a suitable convention, they believe they have to discover a difference, existing in the nature of things, as it were, between empirical science on the one hand and metaphysics on the other. They are constantly trying to prove that metaphysics by its very nature is nothing but nonsensical twaddle—"sophistry and illusion," as Hume says, which we should "commit to the flames."

If by the words "nonsensical" or "meaning-less" we wish to express no more, by definition, than "not belonging to empirical science," then the characterization of metaphysics as meaningless non-sense would be trivial; for metaphysics has usually been defined as non-empirical. But of course, the positivists believe they can say much more about metaphysics than that some of its statements are non-empirical. The words "meaningless" or "nonsensical" convey, and are meant to convey, a derogatory evalu-ation; and there is no doubt that what the positivists really want to achieve is not so much a successful demarcation as the final overthrow (Carnap 219) and the annihilation of metaphysics. However this may be, we find that each time the positivists tried to say more clearly what "meaningful" meant, the attempt led to the same result—to a definition of "meaning-ful sentence" (in contradistinction to "meaningless pseudo-sentence") which simply reiterated the crite-rion of demarcation of their *inductive logic*.

This "shows itself" very clearly in the case of **Wittgenstein**, according to whom every meaningful proposition must be *logically reducible* to elementary (or atomic) propositions, which he characterizes as descriptions or "pictures of reality" (a characterization, by the way, which is to cover all meaningful propo-sitions). We may see from this that Wittgenstein's criterion of meaningfulness coincides with the induc-tivists" criterion of demarcation, provided we replace their words "scientific" or "legitimate" by "meaning-ful." And it is precisely over the problem of induction that this attempt to solve the problem of demarcation comes to grief: positivists, in their anxiety to anni-hilate metaphysics, annihilate natural science along with it. For scientific laws, too, cannot be logically reduced to elementary statements of experience. If consistently applied, Wittgenstein's criterion of meaningfulness rejects as meaningless those natural laws the search for which, as Einstein says, is "the supreme task of the physicist": they can never be accepted as genuine or legitimate statements. This view, which tries to unmask the problem of induction as an empty pseudo-problem, has been expressed by **Schlick** in the following words: "The problem of induction consists in asking for a logical justification

of *universal statements* about reality. . . . We recognize, with Hume, that there is no such logical justification: there can be none, simply because *they are not genuine statements*" (156; the italics are mine).

This shows how the inductivist criterion of demarcation fails to draw a dividing line between scientific and metaphysical systems, and why it must accord them equal status; for the verdict of the positivist dogma of meaning is that both are systems of meaningless pseudo-statements. Thus instead of eradicating metaphysics from the empirical sciences, positivism leads to the invasion of metaphysics into the scientific realm.

In contrast to these anti-metaphysical strata-gems—anti-metaphysical in intention, that is—my business, as I see it, is not to bring about the over-throw of metaphysics. It is, rather, to formulate a suitable characterization of empirical science, or to define the concepts "empirical science" and "meta-physics" in such a way that we shall be able to say of a given system of statements whether or not its closer study is the concern of empirical science.

My criterion of demarcation will accordingly have to be regarded as a *proposal for an agreement or convention*. As to the suitability of any such convention opinions may differ; and a reason-able discussion of these questions is only possible between parties having some purpose in common. The choice of that purpose must, of course, be ulti-mately a matter of decision, going beyond rational argument.

Thus anyone who envisages a system of abso-lutely certain, irrevocably true statements as the end and purpose of science will certainly reject the pro-posals I shall make here. [. . .]

The aims of science which I have in mind are different. I do not try to justify them, however, by representing them as the true or the essential aims of science. This would only distort the issue, and it would mean a relapse into positivist dogmatism. There is only *one* way, as far as I can see, of argu-ing rationally in support of my proposals. This is to analyze their logical consequences: to point out their fertility—their power to elucidate the problems of the theory of knowledge.

Thus I freely admit that in arriving at my proposals I have been guided, in the last analysis, by value judgments and predilections. But I hope that my proposals may be acceptable to those who value not only logical rigour but also freedom from dogmatism; who seek practical applicability, but are even more attracted by the adventure of science, and by discoveries which again and again confront us with new and unexpected questions, challenging us to try out new and hitherto undreamed-of answers.

The fact that value judgments influence my proposals does not mean that I am making the mistake of which I have accused the positivists—that of trying to kill metaphysics by calling it names. I do not even go so far as to assert that metaphysics has no value for empirical science. For it cannot be denied that along with metaphysical ideas which have obstructed the advance of science there have been others—such as speculative atomism—which have aided it. And looking at the matter from the psychological angle, I am inclined to think that scientific discovery is impossible without faith in ideas which are of a purely speculative kind, and sometimes even quite hazy; a faith which is completely unwarranted from the point of view of science, and which, to that extent, is "metaphysical."

## 6. Falsifiability as a Criterion of Demarcation

The criterion of demarcation inherent in inductive logic—that is, the positivistic dogma of meaning—is equivalent to the requirement that all the statements of empirical science (or all "meaningful" statements) must be capable of being finally decided, with respect to their truth *and* falsity; we shall say that they must be "*conclusively decidable.*" This means that their form must be such that *to verify them and to falsify them* must both be logically possible. Thus Schlick says: "a genuine statement must be capable of *conclusive verification*" (150); and **Waismann** says still more clearly: "If there is no possible way to *determine whether a statement is true* then that statement has no meaning whatsoever.

For the meaning of a statement is the method of its verification" (229).

Now in my view there is no such thing as induction. Thus inference to theories, from singular statements which are "verified by experience" (whatever that may mean), is logically inadmissible. Theories are, therefore, *never* empirically verifiable. If we wish to avoid the positivist's mistake of eliminating, by our criterion of demarcation, the theoretical systems of natural science, then we must choose a criterion which allows us to admit to the domain of empirical science even statements which cannot be verified.

But I shall certainly admit a system as empirical or scientific only if it is capable of being *tested* by experience. These considerations suggest that not the *verifiability* but the *falsifiability* of a system is to be taken as a criterion of demarcation. In other words: I shall not require of a scientific system that it shall be capable of being singled out, once and for all, in a positive sense; but I shall require that its logical form shall be such that it can be singled out, by means of empirical tests, in a negative sense: *it must be possible for an empirical scientific system to be refuted by experience.*

(Thus the statement, "It will rain or not rain here tomorrow" will not be regarded as empirical, simply because it cannot be refuted; whereas the statement, "It will rain here tomorrow" will be regarded as empirical.)

Various objections might be raised against the criterion of demarcation here proposed. In the first place, it may well seem somewhat wrong-headed to suggest that science, which is supposed to give us positive information, should be characterized as satisfying a negative requirement such as refutability. However, [. . .] this objection has little weight, since the amount of positive information about the world which is conveyed by a scientific statement is the greater the more likely it is to clash, because of its logical character, with possible singular statements. (Not for nothing do we call the laws of nature "laws": the more they prohibit the more they say.)

Again, the attempt might be made to turn against me my own criticism of the inductivist criterion of demarcation; for it might seem that objections can be raised against falsifiability as a criterion of demarcation similar to those which I myself raised against verifiability.

This attack would not disturb me. My proposal is based upon an *asymmetry* between verifiability and falsifiability; an asymmetry which results from the logical form of universal statements. For these are never derivable from singular statements, but can be contradicted by singular statements. Consequently it is possible by means of purely deductive inferences (with the help of the *modus tollens* of classical logic) to argue from the truth of singular statements to the falsity of universal statements. Such an argument to the falsity of universal statements is the only strictly deductive kind of inference that proceeds, as it were, in the "inductive direction"—that is, from singular to universal statements.

A third objection may seem more serious. It might be said that even if the asymmetry is admitted, it is still impossible, for various reasons, that any theoretical system should ever be conclusively falsified. For it is always possible to find some way of evading falsification, for example by introducing *ad hoc* an auxiliary hypothesis, or by changing *ad hoc* a definition. It is even possible without logical inconsistency to adopt the position of simply refusing to acknowledge any falsifying experience whatsoever. Admittedly, scientists do not usually proceed in this way, but logically such procedure is possible; and this fact, it might be claimed, makes the logical value of my proposed criterion of demarcation dubious, to say the least.

I must admit the justice of this criticism; but I need not therefore withdraw my proposal to adopt falsifiability as a criterion of demarcation. For I am going to propose that the *empirical method* shall be characterized as a method that excludes precisely those ways of evading falsification which, as my imaginary critic rightly insists, are logically admissible. According to my proposal, what characterizes the empirical method is its manner of exposing to falsification, in every conceivable way, the system to be tested. Its aim is not to save the lives of untenable systems but, on the contrary, to select the one which is by comparison the fittest, by exposing them all to the fiercest struggle for survival.

The proposed criterion of demarcation also leads us to a solution of Hume's problem of induction—of the problem of the validity of natural laws. The root of this problem is the apparent contradiction between what may be called "the fundamental thesis of empiricism"—the thesis that experience alone can decide upon the truth or falsity of scientific statements—and Hume's realization of the inadmissibility of inductive arguments. This contradiction arises only if it is assumed that all empirical scientific statements must be "conclusively decidable," i.e., that their verification and their falsification must both in principle be possible. If we renounce this requirement and admit as empirical also statements which are decidable in one sense only—unilaterally decidable and, more especially, falsifiable—and which may be tested by systematic attempts to falsify them, the contradiction disappears: the method of falsification presupposes no inductive inference, but only the tautological transformations of deductive logic whose validity is not in dispute. [. . .]

## Works Cited

Carnap, R. "Überwindung der Metaphysik durch logische Analyse der Sprache." *Erkenntnis* 2 (1931): 219–41.

Einstein, A. *The World as I See It*. Trans. A. Harris. London: John Lane, 1935.

Kant, I. *Critique of Pure Reason*. Trans. N. Kemp Smith. London: Macmillan, 1933.

Reichenbach, H. "Kausalität und Wahrscheinlichkeit." *Erkenntnis* 1 (1930/31): 158–88.

Schlick, M. "Die Kausalität in der gegenwartigan Physik." *Naturwissenschaften* 19 (1931): 145–62.

Waismann, F. "Logische Analyse des Wahrscheinlichkeitsbegriffs." *Erkenntnis* 1 (1930/31): 228–48.

Wittgenstein, L. *Tractatus Logico-Philosophicus*. London: Kegan Paul, Trench, Trubner, 1933.

## Study Questions

1. What is inductive reasoning? Provide an example.

2. What is the "problem of induction," and why does it pose as much of a problem for arriving at probable theories as it does for arriving at true theories?

3. Describe the distinction Popper draws between the "psychology of knowledge" and the "logic of knowledge." How does Popper make use of this distinction in his avowed solution of the "problem of induction," known as "Hume's problem"?

4. Popper argues that the "problem of demarcation" should be known as "Kant's problem" just as the "problem of induction" is known as "Hume's problem." What is the "problem of demarcation"? What is Popper's solution?

---

## Kathleen Okruhlik

---

Kathleen Okruhlik received her PhD in history and philosophy of science at the University of Pittsburgh. Okruhlik is currently an associate professor at the University of Western Ontario, where she has served as founding director of women's studies and feminist research, chair of philosophy, and dean of the faculty of arts and humanities. Okruhlik's research interests include laws of nature, feminist critiques of science, and science and values. This essay provides a feminist assessment of the legacy of the scientific revolution.—TR

## Birth of a New Physics or Death of Nature?

### 1. Introduction

The title of this essay is derived from the names of two books that describe those events of the sixteenth and seventeenth centuries known collectively as the scientific revolution. The first, *The Birth of a New Physics*, by I.B. Cohen, represents a point of view that is familiar, at least in its broad outlines, to all of us. The period in question is portrayed as a time of unparalleled genius, a time when the human intellect triumphed against the forces of superstition and liberated itself from the chains of ignorance through heroic exercise of the imagination. Cohen encapsulates this point of view in the book's final sentence, where he asks, "Who, after studying **Newton**'s magnificent contribution to thought, could deny that pure science exemplifies the creative accomplishment of the human spirit at its pinnacle?" (184).

Some feminist theorists writing about the events of the scientific revolution have been rather less enthralled. Carolyn Merchant's 1980 book, *The Death of Nature: Women, Ecology, and the Scientific Revolution*, is an important example. She describes the period in question as profoundly gynophobic and argues that the mechanistic worldview developed at that time has led to ecological disaster and to a socioeconomic order that subordinates women. The damage done to the environment and the injury to women are linked through the identification of nature as feminine and of woman as natural. A dualism of nature and culture is said by Merchant to be a key factor in Western civilization's advance at the expense of nature. She argues that, since the seventeenth century, European culture has increasingly set itself above and apart from all that is symbolized by nature, with disastrous results for the environment and for women.

Merchant pursues this theme by tracing the demise of the Aristotelian and neo-Platonic world views and their replacement during the seventeenth century by mechanism. The world that was lost at that time was organic in its conception: for sixteenth-century Europeans, the root metaphor binding together the self, society, and the cosmos was that of an *organism*. This metaphor was a flexible one that could function simultaneously at several levels. So, for example, nature in a generalized sense was seen as female; but also the earth or geocosm was universally viewed as a nurturing mother—a living human body with breath, blood, sweat, and elimination systems. The mother earth was able to give birth to stones and metals within her womb through marriage to the sun (24–5).

The important thing here is not the metaphorical description per se but the normative structure associated with it. Merchant argues that the view of Earth as a nurturing mother brought with it moral constraints against exploitation—as, for example, in mining, which was often identified as a sort of rape of Mother Earth. She cites **Agricola**'s 1556 work, *De Re Metallica.*

> The Earth does not conceal and remove from our eyes those things which are useful and necessary to mankind, but, on the contrary, like a beneficent and kindly mother she yields in large abundance from her bounty and brings into light of day the herbs, vegetables, grains, and fruits, and trees. The minerals, on the other hand, she buries far beneath in the depth of the ground, therefore they should not be sought. (34)

Merchant traces the changes in the metaphorical representation of nature as woman as these develop in the sixteenth and seventeenth centuries. Nature ceases to be represented so much as a loving, nurturing mother and re-emerges as a lewd and lusty whore who must be exploited and dominated by the new science and technology. Some of the more notorious and most often cited metaphors are those employed by **Francis Bacon**, as in the following example from *De Dignitate et Augmentis Scientiarum.*

> For you have but to follow and as it were hound nature in her wanderings, and you will be able when you like to lead and drive her afterward to the same place again. . . . Neither ought a man to make scruple of entering and

penetrating into these holes and corners, when the inquisition of truth is his whole object. (4: 296)

[. . .] Merchant argues that passages like this reveal that the new philosophy implicitly embodies the view of a male knower who manipulates, dominates, and exploits the object of his knowledge.

Although Evelyn Fox Keller reaches somewhat different conclusions from Merchant regarding the role of gender metaphors during the scientific revolution, she too argues that attention to these is crucial to a proper understanding of modern science. In particular, she maintains that the scientific revolution provided crucial support for the polarization of gender required by industrial capitalism. Concepts of rationality, objectivity, and the will to dominate nature supported *both* the new science and the institutionalization of a new definition of manhood.

> The scientific mind is set apart from what is known, that is, from nature, and its autonomy is guaranteed . . . by setting apart its modes of knowing from those in which that dichotomy is threatened. In this process, the characterization of both the scientific mind and its modes of access to knowledge as masculine is indeed significant. Masculine here connotes, as it so often does, autonomy, separation, and distance . . . a radical rejection of any commingling of subject and object. (79)

In a similar vein, Susan Bordo argues that Cartesian rationalism and objectivism are best understood not simply as the articulation of a new epistemological ideal, but as a defensive intellectual "flight from the feminine," resulting from anxiety over separation from the organic female universe. "The result," she says, "was a "super-masculinized" model of knowledge in which detachment, clarity, and transcendence of the body are all key requirements" (8).

The suggestion that sometimes emerges from this line of thought is that our concepts of rationality and objectivity are so deeply masculinist in their seventeenth-century origins that any truly feminist account of science must be premised upon their rejection. The dangers of this response, however, are very great. We surely do not wish to accept the patriarchal identification of women with nature, thereby supporting the inference that if the mechanical philosophy was bad for nature then it must have been bad for women too. Nor do we want to accede too hastily to the attribution of certain (subjective, personal, empathetic, intuitive, interactive, relational, or holistic) "ways of knowing" to women when these attributions, too, are the products of a deeply sexist culture. Finally and most importantly, we want to be able to argue that feminist theories are *better* than their androcentric or sexist rivals, in the sense of being more rational and more objective; but this hope is lost to us if we surrender, as masculinist, the very concepts of rationality and objectivity.

Therefore, I should like to look a little more closely at our seventeenth-century heritage with an eye to disentangling the various threads of that inheritance. In particular, I shall focus on the distinction between primary and secondary qualities as the site at which several of those threads intersect and an important site for the development of our notion of objectivity. My hope is to show that we can jettison the physical ontology that underlay that distinction as well as certain metaphysical and epistemological positions associated with it while retaining a fairly robust notion of objectivity. I shall then go on to examine the scope and limits of that notion, arguing that we shall do better to account for the persistence of sexist science by attending to the epistemic limits acknowledged by irreducibly comparative models of theory choice instead of focusing on the simple exclusion of certain psychological and epistemological attitudes alleged to be characteristic of women.

## 2. Primary/Secondary Qualities Distinction

The first step [. . .] is to set the stage for the primary/secondary qualities distinction.

When the Aristotelian and neo-Platonic world views gave way to the mechanistic world view, it was not simply the case that the dominant scientific metaphor switched from that of a living body to that of a great clockwork. Instead, several distinct intellectual trends came together and formed a new constellation of ideas. In addition to the mechanization of the world view, there are two developments to bear in mind here. The first is the notion of human beings (men?) as more than just passive observers of nature, but as interveners and manipulators. We have already seen Francis Bacon advocating experiment over mere observation [. . .]. Although this contrasts sharply with the Aristotelian view, which promoted passive observation of the living organism, there are strong continuities here with the **neo-Platonic or Hermetic view** of the magus as one who could manipulate and operate upon nature. Conjoined with the new view of the universe as a machine, this interventionist view makes the scientist a sort of mechanic who comes to understand the great clockwork of the universe by taking it apart and breaking it down to its smallest machine parts. Organisms are perhaps best understood in terms of overall function, but machines are best understood in terms of their component parts.

In addition to the machine metaphor and the emphasis on the interventionist role of the scientist, we must consider (perhaps most important of all) the role of mathematization in the making of the scientific revolution. In some ways, the whole point of banishing the organic view of nature was to make matter amenable to mathematical treatment. Organisms are self-moving and indeterminate. Therefore, so long as nature was seen as permeated by living forces, so long as there was an *anima mundi* (or world soul), mathematical treatment of moving bodies could not succeed. The death of nature was brought about (nature was killed) in order to make possible the mathematical treatment of physical phenomena. It is true that the ontology that replaced the living ontology of **Aristotle** was likened to a giant machine clockwork at the macrolevel, but this clockwork also had a corpuscular microstructure that guaranteed the smooth, regular, determinate functioning of the universal clockwork.

It was believed that the smallest elements of bodies possessed a number of non-relational, purely intrinsic, and fundamental properties that were amenable to mathematical treatment. These properties were called *primary* properties; and they included extension, mass, impenetrability, and mobility. These primary properties (and perhaps a few others) were thought to account for the real structure of the external world. Other properties, those not possessed by single corpuscles in isolation, were called *secondary* properties, and they included colours, tastes, sounds, and smells. The ultimate inventory of the universe's furniture would not require reference to any but primary properties. Reference to secondary properties could be reduced to a description in terms of primary properties, and this reduction had explanatory primacy.

This was one way of drawing the primary/secondary distinction; but it is probably not the one familiar to most readers today. While the distinction sketched here is tied very closely to a particular physical ontology, the familiar distinction is generally couched in somewhat more epistemological terms. So, for example, one is asked to consider what happens if one hand is immersed in cold water and another in hot before placing both in a sink of tepid water. The tepid water will feel warm to the hand previously immersed in cold water and cool to the one previously immersed in hot water. The same water feels different to the two hands; and so it is concluded that the properties of being warm or cool are not properties of the object (i.e., the water) but of the perceiving subject. Those properties or qualities that are located in the independently existing external object are called primary; those that are in the perceiving subject are called secondary.

These two ways of drawing the primary/secondary distinction were made to yield the same lists of properties, but it is important to remember that their conceptual foundations are distinct. The drive to separate appearance from reality already had a long and varied history by the seventeenth century. What was new at the time of the scientific revolution was the identification of the real with the mathematizable properties of corpuscles. Representational realism was the epistemology that developed to go along with this corpuscular ontology. According to

representational realism, there is an external world that exists entirely independently of us and to which we have epistemic access through ideas. In particular, our ideas of primary properties reflect real features of this independently existing world, whereas our ideas of secondary properties do not.

## 3. Three Senses of Objectivity

From these metaphysical and epistemological commitments, certain methodological desiderata flow.

If science is to develop an accurate picture of reality, within this account, then it must rely upon methods that privilege primary properties and systematically screen out the secondary; only those ideas that directly mirror elements of external reality have a place in science. This means that not only sensory qualities must be systematically eliminated, but also any trace of emotion, value, or personal interest; for, in addition to being colourless, tasteless, odourless, and so on, external reality is devoid of emotion and value-neutral. Insofar as the methods of scientific inquiry could successfully screen out subjective elements of all kinds, they guaranteed theoretical objectivity. Originally, this meant that they ensured that the theory had an objective referent; but gradually, another sense of theoretical objectivity evolved alongside this one. An objective theory was not just one with an objective referent, but one that had been arrived at using the methods of science. These methods were meant to exclude bias, partiality, arbitrariness, and idiosyncrasy as a means of guaranteeing reference to an independently existing object; but later the two considerations (ontological and methodological) became separable. So a theory could be objective either in the sense that it successfully referred to what is metaphysically real or in the sense that it was arrived at through the employment of objective methods.

We could even go so far as to distinguish three senses in which the ascription of a property might be said to be objective: (1) the property in question is primary rather than secondary; (2) the ascription succeeds in picking out a referent in the external world; and (3) methods of inquiry designed to yield impartial and nonarbitrary claims led to the ascription.

The first sense of objectivity is tied to a particular physical ontology, that of seventeenth-century mechanism. The second is tied to metaphysical realism, the doctrine that there is one true description of the world, which exists independently of us and our epistemic activities. The third is committed to no particular physical or metaphysical ontology. My claim is that feminist critics should have no qualms about discarding the first two senses of objectivity (which have outlived their usefulness anyway), but that the third (methodological) sense is indispensable to feminist theory and practice. Let me now try to unpack these claims.

The particular physical ontology posited by seventeenth-century mechanism is the one deplored by Carolyn Merchant as marking the death of nature and the beginning of ecological disaster. The chief source of difficulty would seem to lie in the type of part–whole relationship prescribed by corpuscularianism whereby ultimate reality is said to lie in the smallest parts of matter. This gives rise to a quite literal, physical sense of reduction. Generally, when we say that one theory *reduces* to another, we mean simply that the objects and properties of the first can be fully explained in terms of the second; but, in the mechanical philosophy, this sort of reduction goes in tandem with a sort of decomposition, a *physical* reduction to smallest parts, the properties of which are (in the ideal case) mathematizable and purely intrinsic. This particular bit of ontology has been outgrown by modern science, although the general view that some sort of physicalism is an aim of science remains. Advocating a role for holism in the ecological sciences (and, thereby, rejecting a specific brand of reductionism) does not, therefore, entail the rejection of scientific objectivity in all its senses.

A related question that remains to be confronted is whether reductionism in this broader sense (understood as a commitment to physicalism) is intrinsically dangerous to feminist theorizing. As a matter of fact, the rhetoric of debates in biology, in the social sciences, and, most notoriously, in sociobiology sometimes seems to suggest that this must be

the case. When feminists argue for the importance of history and current culture in accounting for the subordinate status of women (or the subordinate status of some racial groups), they are often accused of substituting a political for a scientific agenda. Philip Kitcher has expressed the problem nicely: "To deny that biology is the key to understanding human behaviour and human society is allegedly to take refuge in a non-physical "mind" or "will" or to appeal to a fictitious entity "culture" with peculiar and ill-defined characteristics" (201). In other words, introducing historical and cultural considerations into the understanding of human behaviour is portrayed as analogous to reintroducing vital forces or the *anima mundi* [world soul]—the very undoing of the achievements of the scientific revolution.

But this is nonsense. To say that human behaviour must be understood largely in terms of history and present culture is not to say that we must introduce a new, non-physical entity called "Culture" that has to be added to our inventory of forces. It does not require us to abandon physicalism at all but only to insist that group characteristics cannot be treated as the mere summation of the characteristics of individuals. It is true that we have left behind a particular view of the part-whole relationship that was embedded in the mechanical philosophy; but that is true generally. We have not abandoned, I want to argue, the search for a unified and objective account of human experience. We have simply pointed out that such an account cannot be achieved unless we abandon a particularly crude form of reductionism, already discredited in other areas.

Giving up the physical ontology of the seventeenth century does not, however, force us to abandon metaphysical realism. We could remain committed to the view that there is an external reality, the structure and representation of which are independent of all human epistemic activity, while admitting that our earlier attempt to characterize that reality failed. In this case, the second (metaphysical realist) sense of objectivity would still be relevant. We might, on the other hand, maintain that **Kant** discredited the notion that it is possible to make meaningful reference to reality as it exists independent of rational activity. Nothing we can say about any object describes the object as it is "in itself," independently of its effect on us; all knowledge depends upon a contribution from the knowing subject. And so the clean distinction between purely objective and purely subjective properties is no longer tenable.

The important point, however, is that in giving up "the subject–object split," Kant did not surrender the notion of objectivity; he certainly believed that we have objective knowledge. The truth of our objective knowledge claims, however, did not depend, for Kant, upon a definition of "truth" as correspondence to some noumenal reality. Instead, "truth" itself was defined in terms of the *methodological* requirement to seek systematic unity in nature (Okruhlik). Thus, the objectivity that Kant embraced fits nicely under the third of the three senses in the preceding discussion.

## 4. Scope and Limits of Methodological Objectivity

Contemporary philosophers of science who are sympathetic to Kant's rejection of metaphysical realism do not usually follow him in trying to establish an ahistorical and universal framework for objective knowledge claims, but they do seek a methodological basis for objectivity. Generally, they find it in the rigorous application of the prevailing canons of scientific theory acceptance, maintaining that the search for objective accounts of human experience can continue so long as it is recognized that the objectivity being sought is modest, in the sense that it is only objectivity-for-human-beings.

Feminist critics, however, may scoff at this claim and argue that even the ideal of objectivity-for-human-beings is a masculine illusion, which has contributed to the subordination of women as well as the poor and a variety of racial groups. Even this allegedly modest conception of objectivity is far too pretentious because it has allowed scientists to deny their own biases and to ignore the centrality of lived experience.

This last phrase, "the centrality of lived experience," is bound to cause trouble for those who pride themselves on being hard-headed and analytic. But it can be understood in two ways: as referring to the lived experience of the human subject who is being studied by the social scientist, for example (i.e., the lived experience of the known, the object of the knowledge), or to the lived experience of the knower, the subject of the knowledge. It is the first sense that Elizabeth Fee has in mind in the following passage.

> The relationship of scientific authority to the population, or expert to non-expert, is one of an immense and protected distance. It parallels the privileged relationship of the producer of knowledge, the subject, to the object of knowledge: the knowing mind is active, the object of knowledge entirely passive. This relationship of domination has been immensely productive in allowing the manipulation and transformation of natural processes to serve particular human ends; when transferred to the social sciences, it also serves as a justification for the attempted manipulation of human beings as the passive objects of social engineering. Women, who have already been defined as natural objects in relation to man, and who have been viewed traditionally as passive, have special reason to question the political power relation expressed in this epistemological distancing. (386)

Here the problem is that methods appropriate for an impartial and complete understanding of inanimate objects are not appropriate for an impartial and complete understanding of conscious objects. To treat centres of consciousness as if they were objects is to fail to be objective in the methodologically defined sense, to ignore the lived experience of research subjects is to fail epistemically as well as morally. Objectivity, in this case, demands that we take subjectivity into account. The problem here stems not so much from the seventeenth-century distinction between subject and object as from later problems introduced by the rise of positivism and the growth of the social sciences in the nineteenth and twentieth centuries.

Let me turn my attention, therefore, to the second question: whether the lived experience of the knower, the epistemological agent, influences the content of science. The traditional story is that the scientific method, rigorously applied, allows the content of science to transcend biases of time, place, gender, race, politics, and so on. [. . .] This notion must be modified in the light of feminist and other critiques [. . .].

Traditionally, philosophy of science has been quite willing to grant that social and psychological factors (including, perhaps, gender) play a role in science; but that role has been a strictly delimited one, contained entirely within the so-called context of discovery or, alternatively, within those episodes called "bad science" in which the canons of rationality were clearly violated in favour of other interests.

In the context of discovery or theory generation, says the traditional story, anything goes: the source of one's hypotheses is epistemically irrelevant; all that matters is the context of justification. If you arrived at your hypothesis by reading tea leaves, it does not matter so long as the hypothesis is confirmed or corroborated in the context of justification. You test the hypothesis in the tribunal of nature and, if it holds up, then you are justified in holding on to it—whatever its origins. The idea here is that the canons of scientific theory choice supply a sort of filter that removes social, psychological, and political contaminants as a hypothesis passes from one context to the next. This view made a certain amount of sense in the first half of the twentieth century, when models of theory evaluation held that hypotheses were compared directly to nature or to theory-neutral observation reports.

But this view, which shears the context of discovery or theory generation of all epistemic significance, makes no sense at all given current models of scientific rationality that view theory choice as irreducibly comparative. That is, we now recognize that one does not actually compare the test hypothesis to nature directly in the hope of getting a yes or no (true or false) answer; nor does one compare it to all possible rival hypotheses. We can only compare a hypothesis to its extant rivals—that is, to other hypotheses that have actually been articulated to account for phenomena in the same domain and developed to the point of being testable.[1] So the picture underlying current debates regarding theory choice looks something like Figure 1.

Each of the nodes is meant to represent a decision point at which the scientist must choose among alternative rivals. Methodological objectivists argue that as long as the proper machinery of theory assessment is brought to bear at each of the nodes, the rationality of science is preserved. How the nodes were generated in the first place is irrelevant, as long as the right decisions are made at each juncture. There may be interesting sociological stories to tell about the generation of the various alternative

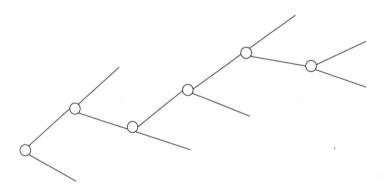

**Figure 1** **Diagram representing comparative models of rational theory choice. Each of the nodes represents a point at which a decision must be made among rival theories.**

hypotheses, but sociological influences are effectively screened from affecting the content of science by the decision procedure operating at the nodes. This procedure will tell us which theory is preferable to its extant rivals on purely objective grounds.

My point, however, is that this procedure, even if it operates perfectly, will not insulate the content of science from sociological influences once we grant that these influences do affect theory generation. If our choice among rivals is irreducibly comparative, as it is in this model, then scientific methodology cannot guarantee (even in the most optimistic scenario) that the preferred theory is true—only that it is epistemically superior to the other actually available contenders. But if all these contenders have been affected by sociological factors, nothing in the appraisal machinery will completely "purify" the successful theory.

Suppose, for the sake of example, that Figure 1 represents the history of theories about female behaviour. These theories may, in many respects, be quite different from one another; but if they have all been generated by males operating in a deeply sexist culture, all will be contaminated by sexism. Non-sexist rivals will never even be generated. Hence, the theory that is selected by the canons of scientific appraisal will simply be the best of the sexist rivals; the very *content* of science will be sexist, no matter how rigorously we apply objective standards of assessment in the context of justification. It is the conjunction of the old-fashioned view of the relationship between discovery and justification with newfangled models of irreducibly comparative theory evaluation that is untenable.

So, if my account is right, it does not necessarily follow that the presence of androcentrism and sexism in science makes rational theory choice impossible, but it does follow that the scientific method, by itself as currently understood, cannot be counted upon to eliminate sexist or androcentric bias from science. In light of this, we can either content ourselves with much more modest claims for rationality, understood in this narrow sense (i.e., scientific method in the context of justification), or we can enlarge our concept of rationality by reclaiming the epistemic

significance of the social and political factors that inform the context of theory generation by trying to take into account the ways in which the situation of knowers may influence the range of hypotheses from among which we make our rational choices. Bacon's theory of scientific rationality, whatever its failings, was consonant with his social and political theories: just as he believed that the monarch could represent the political interests of all members of the kingdom, so he assumed that a privileged male elite could represent the needs and interests of all humanity in the advancement of science. Our theories of scientific rationality, however, reflect no progress in social or political thought since Bacon.

## 5. Conclusion

Bearing this in mind, let me make a few final remarks about whether the seventeenth century marked the birth of a new physics or the death of nature. Clearly it did both; but neither description will allow us to deal adequately with the relationship of feminist theory to our seventeenth-century heritage. The traditional, very optimistic account of the origins of science does little to help us understand how so much sexist theory has been able to hide behind the mantle of science. Merchant's very important account, too, fails to satisfy completely although it raises many provocative questions. Some of my dissatisfaction stems from a failure to understand how tightly Merchant wants to link her analyses of nature and women. Her thesis about nature, that the view of nature as a machine to be exploited legitimated the destruction of the natural environment, is supported by a clear and sustained argument. One can see very well how ecological concerns might have been better served had nature continued to be viewed metaphorically as an organism rather than a machine.

The situation, however, is not so clear with respect to women. We do not want to say that whatever is bad for nature is bad for women because that is to buy into the very identification of women and nature that feminist theory *ought* to be resisting. This is not meant to denigrate in any way the importance of metaphor in the shaping of thought; it just seems that the ontology of the mechanical worldview and the new methodology of science should have opened a window of opportunity for women. At least the *literal* ontology of the mechanistic worldview was sexless and genderless (as well as colourless, odourless, etc.); and at least the *rhetoric* of the new methodology was egalitarian in opposition to the older rhetorics of privileged access. What happened to women as a result of the scientific revolution, then, cannot be understood simply in terms of changing ontologies or transformations of dominant metaphors.

We must consider, also, what happened to the relationship between women and *reason* as a result of developments in the seventeenth century. Reason became increasingly identified with the employment of the scientific method to the exclusion of a variety of earlier faculties including, for example, practical reasoning. Although, in principle, the methods of science were to have been as accessible to women as to men, in practice they were not. Women were not allowed the education, the leisure, or the laboratory space necessary to participate fully in this new form of rationality, which, as Genevieve Lloyd points out, became a sort of cultural attainment rather than a natural faculty (39). The incredible success of the new science further concentrated power in the hands of a small class of men, not because it was intrinsically more sexist or more androcentric than the earlier science, but because it was more successful. That the virtual exclusion of women from the making of modern science has been harmful to women goes, I should think, without saying; that it has also been harmful to science and to our conceptions of rationality and objectivity is one of the things I hope to have demonstrated.

## Note

1. It is important to stress that the argument developed here does not presuppose or entail that value-ladenness depends on the acceptance of comparative models of theory testing. A theory that was never compared to or tested against other theories would be no less value-laden on that account. Indeed such a theory would be generally more vulnerable to error insofar as its implicit values and assumptions could not be recognized, tested, and replaced with better alternatives.

## Works Cited

Bacon, F. *De Dignitate et Augmentis Scientarum. The Works of Francis Bacon*. Ed. James Spedding, Robert Leslie Ellis, and Douglas Devon Heath. 14 vols. London: Longmans Green, [1623]1870.

Bordo, S. *The Flight to Objectivity: Essays on Cartesianism and Culture*. Albany, NY: SUNY Press, 1987.

Cohen, I.B. *The Birth of New Physics*. 2nd ed. New York: Norton, 1985.

Fee, E. "Is Feminism a Threat to Scientific Objectivity?" *International Journal of Women's Studies* 4 (1981): 387–93.

Keller, E.F. *Reflections on Gender and Science*. New Haven: Yale University Press, 1985.

Kitcher, P. *Vaulting Ambition: Sociobiology and the Quest for Human Nature*. Cambridge, MA: MIT Press, 1985.

Lloyd, G. *The Man of Reason: "Male" and "Female" in Western Philosophy*. Minneapolis: University of Minnesota Press, 1984.

Merchant, C. *The Death of Nature: Women, Ecology, and the Scientific Revolution*. San Francisco: Harper and Row, 1980.

Okruhlik, K. "Kant on Realism and Methodology." *Kant's Philosophy of Physical Science*. Ed. R.E. Butts. Dordrecht, Netherlands: Reidel, 1986. 307–32.

## Study Questions

1. Does Okruhlik agree or disagree with Merchant's argument in *The Death of Nature* that the scientific revolution's replacement of the metaphor of world as organism with world as machine promoted both ecological destruction and the subordination of women?

2. Describe the ontological, epistemological, and methodological aspects of the seventeenth-century distinction between primary and secondary qualities.

3. What are the three senses of "objectivity" identified by Okruhlik? According to Okruhlik, which of these senses should feminists discard and which should they retain?

4. Describe how the distinction between the context of discovery and context of justification is drawn. On what basis does Okruhlik argue that the discovery–justification distinction cannot protect the content of scientific knowledge from the intrusion of social biases?

---

# John Beatty

---

John Beatty has an undergraduate degree in biology and chemistry and received his PhD in the history and philosophy of science at Indiana University in 1979. Beatty is a professor of philosophy at the University of British Columbia; he taught previously at Harvard University, Arizona State University, and the University of Minnesota. Beatty's research focuses on methodology, theoretical foundations, and socio-political dimensions of genetics and evolutionary biology. This essay examines the opposition between mechanistic and teleological thinking from the scientific revolution to Darwin.—TR

## Teleology and the Relationship between Biology and the Physical Sciences in the Nineteenth Century

### 1. Introduction

In his 1869 address, "The Aim and Progress of Physical Science," **Helmholtz** recounted a series of discoveries from **Galileo** to **Newton**, and finally to **Darwin**, all of which contributed to the "ultimate aim of physical science" (231), which was "to reduce all phenomena to mechanics." Darwin's role in this series of developments, as Helmholtz imagined it, had consisted in perhaps the ultimate extension of mechanistic thinking. For Darwin had succeeded in providing a mechanical alternative to teleological reasoning about the living world (237ff).

The most striking thing about the living world, Helmholtz admitted, was the adaptation of organisms to their environments. Teleologists had urged that this sort of appropriateness could not be explained solely in terms of mechanical causes that are blind to their consequences. Organisms must have the characteristics they do at least in part because of the adaptive utility of those characteristics. But, according to Helmholtz, Darwinism made clear precisely "how adaptation in the structure of organisms can result from the blind rule of a law of nature" (238).

Helmholtz's mechanistic aspirations, and Darwin's, if we adopt the fairly common understanding of Darwin's achievement exemplified by Helmholtz, were a good deal more radical than those of many of the scientists that we associate with the rise of the mechanical worldview. Mechanists of the likes of Newton and **Boyle** never dreamed that nature could be understood wholly in mechanical terms. Complete understanding of nature would require knowing also the purposes that God had in mind when he employed this rather than that particular mechanism in the construction of the world. As Newton reasoned in the "General Scholium" that concluded the *Principia*, "mere mechanical causes" could not account for such things as the fact that the stars are so distant from one another. Rather, one would also have to take into account God's ends in designing the universe in this way. The good thing about having the stars so far apart, and especially so distant from our own solar system, is that they do not thereby collapse upon one another through their mutual gravitational forces. Rather more infamous is Newton's insistence that a mere mechanical explanation could not account for the origin of a solar system so orderly as our own. Only in terms of God's aesthetic ends could one account for the neatly nested concentric, and nearly uniplanar orbits of the planets and their moons, and for the common direction of their axial rotations and revolutions around the sun.

But the inorganic world did not really present anything like the opportunity for teleological reasoning offered by the organic. Even Boyle, a staunch defender of the place of teleology within the mechanical world view, had concerns about the usefulness of teleological reasoning in the physical sciences. In his "Disquisition about the Final Causes of Natural Things," he admitted that, "for my part, I am apt to think, there is more of admirable contrivance in a man's muscles than in (what we know of) the coelestial orbs; and that the eye of a fly is (at least as far as appears to us) a more curious piece of workmanship than the body of the sun" (403). And while he admitted that a purely mechanical account of the formation of different stones and metals might suffice, he would not allow the same for plants and animals (403–4).

**Kant**, who was in so many other respects concerned to make sense of Newton, departed from him in this regard: not by denying the need for teleological reasoning in science, but by restricting it to the biological sciences. Kant distinguished between the nonliving realm of nature that we can hope to understand completely in terms of "mechanical principles," and the living world that we cannot; our understanding of the living world requires in addition the notions of purpose and design. It is absurd, he maintained in the *Critique of Judgment*, to expect that "another Newton will arise in the future who will make even the production of a blade of grass understandable by us according to natural laws which no design has ordered . . . we must absolutely deny this insight to men" (54).

To be sure, Kant acknowledged, the formation of organisms and their parts is to be understood to some extent in terms of mechanical processes—"accretion" and the like—but the fact that the parts of organisms should take shapes so appropriate for their possessors, and that they should be placed so appropriately, "must always be estimated teleologically" (23–6).

Kant, in his style, considered purpose and design not so much a part of nature as of our cognitive apparatus; the notions of purpose and design were, for him, a priori "regulative ideas" that "guide [our] reflection upon nature" and make possible a unified conception of the otherwise very diverse living world (26). Kant believed that we could hardly reflect upon purpose and design without invoking an intelligent Being whose purposes and designs are at issue. However, he also considered this additional inference to be "extravagant" as far as science itself is concerned and unnecessary as far [as] the possibility of achieving a unified conception of the living world (31–4). But what is most important here is just Kant's attitude toward the need for teleological, not strictly mechanical, thinking in biology, if not in the physical sciences.

Kant's attitude is nicely exemplified in his *Theory of the Heavens*, where he proposed a purely mechanical alternative to Newton's teleological account of the origin of the solar system (although he did not explicitly single out Newton for criticism on this occasion). However, Kant felt the need to preface the presentation of his nebular hypothesis with the acknowledgement that he foresaw no similar mechanical explanation of "even a single herb or caterpillar" (29).

The nebular hypothesis of **Laplace** received considerably more attention than Kant's, in part because of the (now well known) moral that Laplace drew from his achievement, namely, that "If we trace the history of the progress of the human mind, and of its errors, we shall observe final causes perpetually receding, according as the boundaries of our knowledge are extended" (333) (Laplace did explicitly criticize Newton in this regard [331]). And thus it was to be expected (according to Laplace) that the origins of the various forms of life would also be explained one day in purely mechanical terms (332–3). But it remained for such an account to be provided— much less generally accepted. [. . .]

So from the point of view of some of the most influential early mechanical philosophers, and many of their intellectual descendants, teleological reasoning had a place in science, though much more so, and according to some exclusively so, in the biological sciences. The pursuit of purposes actually served to distinguish quite neatly the practice of biology from that of astronomy, physics, and chemistry.

To the extent that Darwin succeeded in replacing teleological with mechanistic explanations in biology, then, he did away with one of the last (legitimate) remnants of teleological reasoning in the sciences, and also did away with a traditional way of distinguishing the biological from the physical sciences. In the process, he (would have) effected a radical change in, not just an extension of, the mechanical worldview of Boyle, and especially Newton.

But the question whether Darwin actually succeeded in replacing the teleological approach is a very difficult one, and I do not just mean in retrospect and from a purely philosophical point of view. My main concern here is with evaluations of Darwin by his contemporaries. After briefly introducing a few of the many varieties of teleological reasoning in nineteenth-century biology, and the nature of Darwin's alternative, I will then take up some of the very disparate perceptions that Darwin's supporters and critics had of his attitude toward teleology. Darwin was praised for abandoning teleology and criticized for pretending that it could be abandoned, but he was also criticized for being a teleologist and even praised for accommodating that approach.

## 2. Darwin and Teleology in the Nineteenth Century

In nineteenth-century biology (more generally, but at least in this context), teleology and mechanism were rarely characterized independently of one another, and rarely independently of the notion of chance as absence of purpose, or coincidence, or accident. As the German biologist Ernst Haeckel distinguished between the teleological and purely mechanical approaches,

> One group of philosophers affirms, in accordance with its teleological conception, that the whole cosmos is an orderly system, in which every phenomenon has its aim and purpose; there is no such thing as chance. The other group, holding a mechanical theory, expresses itself thus: The development of the universe is a monistic process, in which we discover no aim or purpose whatever; what we call design in the organic world is a special result of biological agencies; neither in the evolution of the heavenly bodies nor in that of the crust of our earth do we find any trace of a controlling purpose—all is the result of chance. (273–4)

Examples of nineteenth-century teleologists so characterized are numerous. Consider for instance the German embryologist Karl Ernst von Baer. Von Baer could not fathom how the wonderfully adaptive characteristics of developing organisms could be the result of chance—mere coincidences, accidents. As an example, he pointed out how chicks still in the egg develop two hard spikes on the tips of their beaks at just the time when their backbones are well enough developed for them to move and stretch their necks (198–9). By these movements, and with these two spikes, they break their eggs and emerge. Is the coincident timing of these phenomena just an *accident*? Surely the breaking of the egg and the emergence of the chick is the *purpose* of the appearance of the spikes. Sarcastically, von Baer formulated the alternative, mechanistic perspective of the phenomenon: instead of saying that the chick developed the spikes for the purpose of breaking the egg, the mechanist would say, "Because the hard spikes are there, it is possible for the egg to be broken from within" (199). But then why, von Baer pressed, do the spikes fall off just after the chick emerges, when they serve no further purpose?

There were many versions of teleological reasoning in nineteenth-century biology, of which I will discuss just a few. One involved the invocation of purposeful vital forces—von Baer was a proponent of this approach. He invoked vitalistic, organizational "types" to explain what physics and chemistry alone could not explain about the development and functioning of organisms, namely, the appropriate integration of the various physical and chemical processes that occurred. Type-guided development was not strictly mechanical: the principles of physics and chemistry were controlled, if not violated, in the process. The materials and principles of physics and chemistry were, in this sense, means to an end—that end being the manifestation of the type. There had to be some way of guiding physical and chemical processes to an appropriately adaptive result. For, just as a productive laboratory needs a chemist, and not just chemicals and chemical principles, so too adaptively organized organisms must have some way of integrating their own various chemical processes (188). [. . .]

The version of teleology that predominated in the land of Darwin was the sort that identified purposes in the organic world with the purposes God had in mind when he fashioned living beings. The Reverend William Paley defended this approach forcefully at the very beginning of the nineteenth century in his immensely popular book, *Natural Theology*. His line of reasoning is still familiar.

On what grounds do we infer that a telescope, or any other obvious object of contrivance was indeed so contrived? Surely we infer a maker for such an object on the ground that its parts are so constructed and arranged as to suit their purposes relative to the overall purpose of the object. If a telescope can be so understood, then why not an eye? Like a telescope, the eye has a lens for the refraction of light rays to an area where the image is registered. And like a telescope, whose lens positions can be manipulated to focus on objects near and far, the lens of the eye also changes shape to focus on objects at different distances. Better even than a telescope, the eye has an automatic protective cover, and an automatic cleaning system, as well as a mechanism for directing it to objects of interest. The eye is clearly an object of contrivance, its purposefulness clearly a reflection of the purposes of its Designer (19–52).

To understand nature in terms of no more than the interplay of mechanical forces, without acknowledging the purposes of its Architect, would be to construe the wonderful adaptations of nature as mere coincidences—the results of chance alone. But, as Paley reasoned,

> What does chance ever do for us? In the human body, for instance, chance, i.e., the operation of causes without design, may produce a wen, a wart, a mole, a pimple, but never an eye. Amongst inanimate substances, a clod, a pebble, a liquid drip, might be; but never was a watch, a telescope, an organized body of any kind, answering a valuable purpose by a complicated mechanism, the effect of chance. In no assignable instance hath such a thing existed without intention somewhere. (46)

The nine Bridgewater Treatises published in 1839 represent the epitome of this particular theological, teleological, anti-chance view of nature.

Von Baer blamed this sort of theological teleology for much of the "teleophobia" of his time (73). The theological brand of teleology had proven not only misleading, but positively silly, as was illustrated by the tale of the schoolmaster who explained the location of the world's major rivers by arguing that God had put them there to supply water to the world's major cities (61–2).

Among those more positively influenced by theological teleology was the young Charles Darwin. Having pursued that line of reasoning for some time, he was then considered by many to have demolished it, the greatest blow coming with the publication in 1859 of his *On the Origin of Species*. [. . .]

On Darwin's account of the unity and diversity of life, chance in the sense of absence of purpose, or chance in the sense of coincidence or accident, played a large role. Darwin usually invoked chance or accident specifically with reference to how new variations arise from time to time among the members of a species. Suppose, for instance, as Darwin did, that among the wolves of a certain area some speedier wolves happened "by chance" to be born—suppose, that is, that the original occurrence of these speedier wolves was independent of the fact that speed is beneficial for these wolves. Such speedier wolves would likely outreproduce and outsurvive the others. Assuming not only that they left more offspring but also that their offspring inherited their greater speediness, then a greater proportion of the next generation of wolves in this area would be speedier. And the proportion would continue to increase over time. Note that speediness would not increase among wolves if their circumstances did not make speed important to survival and reproduction, as, Darwin suggested, in the case of a certain form of North American wolf whose chief prey consists of sheep. Thus, wolves might diverge evolutionarily to the extent that their circumstances differ (*Origin* 90–1). Extrapolating, Darwin proposed to explain how all forms of organisms come to have characteristics suited to their particular circumstances.

The important point for now concerns the particular role of chance in all of this. To say that advantageous variations arise by chance is to say that their occurrence is not occasioned by the fact that they promote the survival and reproduction of

their possessors, though, of course, the persistence and increase in frequency of those characteristics does depend on their effects in their possessors. As Darwin more eloquently explained the role of chance variation,

> [Evolution by natural selection] absolutely depends on what we in our ignorance call spontaneous or accidental variability. Let an architect be compelled to build an edifice with uncut stones, fallen from a precipice. The shape of each fragment may be called accidental. Yet the shape of each has been determined . . . by events and circumstances, all of which depend on natural laws; but there is no relation between these laws and the purpose for which each fragment is used by the builder. In the same manner the variations of each creature are determined by fixed and immutable laws; but these bear no relation to the living structure which is slowly built up through the power of selection (*Variation* 236).

So, in other words, it is a matter of chance that there should have fallen from the precipice a stone suitable for a particular use in a building. But of course it is not merely a matter of chance that we find the stone put to that use. Similarly, again, it is a matter of chance that a variation suitable to the survival or reproductive needs of members of a particular species should arise within that species, but it is not merely a matter of chance that variation should continue to increase in frequency within the species.

## 3. Reception of the *Origin* by Darwin's Contemporaries

This seemingly (misleadingly) simple concept nevertheless lent itself to widely different interpretations by Darwin's contemporaries, especially with regard to the question of whether it accommodated, or was a substitute for, teleological reasoning. As I mentioned earlier, Darwin was both praised and criticized for abandoning teleology, but he was also praised and criticized for not doing so (see Figure 1). I will consider, briefly, examples of each of the four possible positions; suffice it to say that there are more examples of each position. [. . .]

Among those convinced that Darwinism accommodated teleology was the American botanist Asa Gray. A longtime confidant of Darwin, Gray took issue with reviewers of the *Origin* who claimed that Darwin had repudiated teleological thinking; instead, Gray argued, "Darwin's particular hypothesis, if we understand it, would leave the doctrines of final causes, utility, and special design, just where they were before" (119).

> As to all this, nothing is easier than to bring out in the conclusion what you introduce in the premises. If you import atheism into your conception of variation and natural selection, you can readily exhibit it in the result. If you do not put it in, perhaps there need be none come out. (126)

This much Darwin would have been happy to acknowledge. What he objected to was the nature of the role that Gray had assigned to God in relation to evolution by natural selection, namely, the role of directing the occurrence of beneficial variations upon which selection could act.

> [W]e should advise Mr. Darwin to assume, in the philosophy of his hypothesis, that variation has been let along certain beneficial lines. Streams flowing over a sloping plane by gravitation (here the concept of natural selection) may have worn their actual channels as they flowed; yet their particular courses may have been assigned; and where we see them forming definite and useful lines of irrigation, after a manner unaccountable on the laws of gravitation and dynamics, we should believe that the distribution was designed. (121–2)

But, as Darwin rejoined, to reason thus was to miss the whole point about variation being a matter of chance. And this was essential to his notion of evolution by natural selection. Natural selection is rather "superfluous" if God just directs variation along beneficial lines (*Variation* 427–8).

Darwin did not have to point out the essentially accidental aspects of evolution by natural selection to those like von Baer, who criticized him for having completely ignored teleology and abandoning the organic world to chance. For all its emphasis on chance variation, Darwin's account of evolution was patently absurd to von Baer.

That evolution by the natural selection of chance variations would ever lead to well adapted forms of life seemed to von Baer no more likely than that the residents of the isle of Laputa would ever succeed in developing knowledge in the manner reported by Gulliver [in Jonathan Swift's 1726–7 novel, *Gulliver's Travels*]. At the Academy of Lagado, in Laputa, a very mechanical approach to the acquisition of knowledge was supposedly being tried. The members of the Academy had inscribed words in all their grammatical forms on the sides of wooden dice.

|  | For Promoting Teleology | For Undermining Teleology |
|---|---|---|
| Praised by | Gray | Huxley<br>Helmholtz<br>duBois-Reymond |
| Criticized by | Kölliker | Von Baer |

**Figure 1  Darwin praised and criticized**

They had then connected the dice in such a way that the dice could be spun independently, and such that strings of words could be read off. After each spin of the dice, the strings of words were reviewed and those that formed sensible phrases were recorded. The dice were then spun again, with the hope that additional phrases would appear that could be conjoined with the former, and thus knowledge would be obtained. "The elimination of those that did not go together was . . . completely mechanical, and was completed much more rapidly than occurs in the 'struggle for existence'" (419). Unfortunately, no one had taken Gulliver's account seriously, or they might have been in a better mind-set to appreciate Darwin's theory.

> For a long time the author of these reports was taken to be joking, because it is self-evident that nothing useful and significant could ever result from chance events. On the contrary, order must emerge as a complete whole at the outset, even though there might well be room for considerable improvement. Now we must acknowledge this philosopher as a deep thinker since he foresaw the present triumphs of science! (419)

Just as it was incomprehensible to von Baer that knowledge could be generated in any other way than by choosing one's words carefully, so too it was incomprehensible to him that adaptation could be generated by chance.

Of course, the Laputans did not rely entirely on chance, and neither does evolution by natural selection. It was not just a matter of chance that sensible truths (vs. senseless phrases) would fill the pages of the books of the Academy of Lagado. The Laputans employed a selection mechanism in addition to their spins of the dice. Nor was it just a matter of chance that evolution by natural selection would produce adapted life forms. Unlike his countryman von Baer, the anatomist Albert von Kölliker saw considerable evidence of teleological thought in Darwin's work, and he brought Darwin to task for that reason:

> Darwin is, in the fullest sense of the word, a Teleologist. He says quite distinctly . . . that every particular in the structure of an animal has been created for its benefit, and he regards the whole series of animal forms only from this point of view.
>
> The teleological general conception adopted by Darwin is a mistaken one.
>
> Varieties arise irrespective of the notion of purpose, or of utility, according to general laws of Nature, and may be either useful, or hurtful, or indifferent.
>
> The assumption that an organism exists only on account of some definite end in view, and represents something more than the incorporation of a general idea, or law, implies a one-sided conception of the universe. Assuredly, every organism has, and every organism fulfills, its end, but its purpose is not the condition of its existence. (175, 178)

In order to appreciate the nature of Kölliker's objections to Darwinism as outlined above, it is necessary to expand somewhat upon the alternative explanatory approaches available to biologists in the early to mid-nineteenth century. One important alternative, which we have yet to discuss, was the so-called "unity-of-plan" approach. From this perspective, the characteristics of members of a species were best accounted for not so much in terms of the adaptive significance of those characteristics, but rather, first and foremost, in terms of resemblances between members of that and other species. Explaining the presence of a particular bone among members of a particular species—say, a species of bird—involved demonstrating first that this bone and the bone of another species of bird, perhaps also the bone of a fish, and perhaps also the bone of a mammal, are all, despite some differences, instances of the "same" bone, all "homologues." Thus, a common plan, repeated throughout nature, and underlying its variety, is revealed. As the French comparative anatomist Etienne Geoffroy St. Hilaire, one of the earliest systematic proponents of this view of nature claimed,

It is known that nature works constantly with the same materials. She is ingenious to vary only the forms. As if, in fact, she were restricted to the [same] primitive ideas, one sees her tend always to cause the same elements to reappear in the same number, in the same circumstances, and with the same connections. (in Appel 89)

If, as Geoffroy and others reasoned, organic form were so well tailored to the adaptive needs of organisms—if, for instance, fish were so well adapted to life under water and reptiles to life on land—then there would be no reason to expect such extensive similarities between them. As the English anatomist Richard Owen reasoned, there is no more reason to expect similarities in the organic world on the basis of Divine contrivance alone than appears among the products of human contrivance. Think how much more similar in terms of skeletal anatomy are birds, fishes, and land mammals than hot-air balloons, boats, and locomotives (9–10).

Proponents of the unity-of-plan approach argued that the teleological approach placed too much emphasis on utility in nature. Unity-of-plan thinkers did not altogether deny that many characteristics of organisms are useful for the survival and reproduction of their possessors. But many characteristics are not. A favourite example was male nipples. The teleological approach also made little sense of the fact that organisms inhabiting very different environments (for example the temperate zones and the arctic), and hence supposedly adapted to very different environments, are often very much alike (as, for instance, in the case of the wolves of the temperate and arctic regions). Similarly, organisms in very similar environments can be very different. Thus, unity-of-plan thinkers advocated understanding the diversity of nature primarily as variations on a common theme, and only secondarily as adaptive variations. [. . .]

It is with respect to the virtues of unity-of-plan reasoning that Kölliker perceived Darwin as just a

teleologist, and faulted him for it. Darwin's emphasis on the respects in which natural selection resulted in useful combinations of traits made him too much of a utilitarian from Kölliker's more unity-of-plan point of view. [. . .]

Actually, Darwin imagined himself to have found in evolution by natural selection the perfect compromise to the teleological and unity-of-plan approaches. In his scheme, common ancestor species substituted for the archetypes or themes upon which a variety of different descendant species were generated. The variety of descendant species was generated by natural selection adapting each to the particular circumstances it encountered. But this was not satisfactory to Kölliker, who complained that Darwin had not accounted for unity of type in terms of any law of nature guaranteeing that effect [. . .] but rather "merely" as a matter of ancestry (175).

The rebukes of Kölliker by "Darwin's Bulldog," **T.H. Huxley**, [. . .] did not emphasize the distinction between the teleological and unity-of-plan approaches, nor Darwin's self-professed reconciliation. [. . .] Rather alarmed by Kölliker's appraisal of Darwin, Huxley retorted, "It is singular how differently one and the same book will impress different minds. That which struck the present writer most forcibly in his first perusal of the 'Origin of Species' was the conviction that Teleology, as commonly understood, had received its deathblow at Mr. Darwin's hands" (82).

To be a teleologist, as Huxley understood the enterprise, involved believing that organisms of different species take the different forms they do in response to a constructive agent that shapes them so that they *will* be suited, and *perfectly* suited, to the circumstances in which they find themselves. Darwinism, he argued, was quite at odds with this point of view. The suitability of a characteristic in a particular set of circumstances is relevant to the *persistence* and *increase* of that characteristic over the course of generations, but not to the *original occurrence* of that characteristic. An advantageous characteristic does not come into being on account of the adaptive advantages it offers in some set of circumstances. Moreover, the characteristics that do persist will be those that offer *better* survival and reproductive advantages to their possessors, not necessarily the *best possible*. In his own words,

> Cats catch mice, small birds and the like, very well. Teleology tells us that they do so because they were expressly constructed for so doing—that they are perfect mousing apparatuses. . . . Darwinism affirms, on the contrary, that there was no express construction concerned in the matter; but that among the multitudinous variations of the Feline stock, many of which died out from want of power to resist opposing influences, some, the cats, were better fitted to catch mice than others, whence they throve and persisted, in proportion to the advantage over their fellows thus offered to them.
>
> Far from imagining that cats exist *in order* to catch mice well, Darwinism supposes that cats exist because they catch mice well—mousing being not the end, but the condition of their existence. (85)

Huxley was a reductionist; his assessment of Darwin's role in purging biology of teleology fit in well with his view that biology was just a branch of physics and chemistry. Similarly, the German reductionists Helmholtz and Emil du Bois-Reymond saw in Darwin's work the replacement of one of the last remnants of teleological thinking in science, and at the same time a significant extension of the boundaries of physical science. Helmholtz's interpretation of Darwin served as an introduction to my essay. I will add here only that it is indeed telling that an extended discussion of Darwin's accomplishments should have such a central place in Helmholtz's essay, "The Aim and Structure of Physical Science."

The notion that Darwin paved the way for the incorporation of biology into the physical sciences was also expressed forcefully by du Bois-Reymond, in his well-known essay, "Seven World Problems." There were, as he explained there, seven questions yet to receive answers in terms of the physical sciences: the origin of matter and force, the origin of motion, the origin of life, the teleological character of life, conscious sensation, language and intelligent thought, and free will. As for the "apparently" teleological character of life, he remarked, "organic laws of formation cannot work adaptively unless matter was created with adaptive purpose in the beginning; and they are inconsistent with the mechanical view of nature." He continued, "The difficulty is, however, not absolutely transcendent, for Mr. Darwin has pointed out in his doctrine of natural selection a possible way of overcoming it, and of explaining the inner suitableness of organic creation to its purposes and its adaptation to inorganic conditions through a concatenation of circumstances operating by a kind of mechanism in connection with natural necessity" (438).

Helmholtz and du Bois-Reymond had considerably more faith in Darwinism than the majority of biologists of their time. As Peter Bowler and others have recently emphasized, Darwin's theory was anything but an overnight sensation, and was in fact just one of many rival theories of evolution in the late nineteenth and early twentieth centuries. But du Bois-Reymond for one, whose reductionist interpretation of Darwinism made Darwin an ally, found the theory of evolution by natural selection appealing enough to cling to, and the image of clinging is not my own: "We might always, . . . while we hold to this theory, have the feeling of the otherwise helpless sinking man, who is cleaving to a plank that just bears him up even with the surface of the water. In the choice between the plank and destruction, the advantage is decidedly on the side of the plank" (438).

Did Darwin replace teleological thinking, or accommodate it? And in which direction did scientific progress lie? At least among Darwin's contemporaries, these were much disputed questions. So it was by no means immediately clear whether and/or how Darwin had affected the practice of biology vis-à-vis the physical sciences. [. . .]

## Works Cited

Appel, T. *The Cuvier-Geoffroy Debate: French Biology in the Decades before Darwin*. Oxford: Oxford University Press, 1987.

Bowler, P.J. *The Eclipse of Darwinism: Anti-Darwinian Evolution Theories in the Decades Around 1900*. Baltimore: Johns Hopkins University Press, 1983.

Boyle, R. "Disquisitions about the Final Causes of Natural Things" [17XX]. *The Works of the Honorable Robert Boyle*, new ed. London: Rivington, 1722. Vol. 5. 394–444.

Darwin, C. *On the Origin of Species by Means of Natural Selection*. London: Murray, 1859. Facsimile edited and with an introduction by E. Mayr. Cambridge: Harvard University Press, 1964.

Darwin, C. *Variation of Animals and Plants Under Domestication*. Vol. 2. London: Murray, 1968.

du Bois-Reymond, E. "The Seven World Problems." *The Popular Science Monthly* 5 (1882): 433–47.

Gray, A. "Natural Selection not Inconsistent with Natural Theology" [1860]. *Darwiniana* [1876]. Ed. A.H. Dupree. Cambridge: Harvard University Press, 1963.

Haeckel, E. *The Riddle of the Universe* [1899]. Tr. J. McCabe. New York: Harper and Brothers, 1900.

Helmholtz, H. von. "The Aim and Progress of Physical Science" [1869]. *Selected Writings of Hermann von Helmholtz*. Ed. R. Kahl. Middletown, CT: Wesleyan University Press, 1971. 223–45.

Huxley, T.H. "Criticisms on the Origin of Species" [1864]. *Darwinians* [1893]. New York: Appleton, 1898. 80–106.

Kant, I. *Critique of Judgment* [1790]. Tr. J.C. Meredith. Oxford: Oxford University Press, 1928.

Kant, I. *Universal Natural History and Theory of the Heavens* [1755]. Tr. W. Hastie. Kant's Cosmogony. New York: Johnson Reprint Corporation, 1970.

Kölliker, A. von. "Ueber die Darwin'sche Schöpfungstheorie." *Zeitschrift für Wissenschaftliche Zoologie* 14 (1864): 174–86.

Laplace, P.S. *The System of the World* [5th ed., 1824]. Tr. H.H. Harte. Dublin: University of Dublin Press, 1830.

Newton, I. *Mathematical Principles of Natural Philosophy*, 3rd ed. [1726], Vol. 2. Tr. A. Motte [1729]. Ed. F. Cajori. Berkeley: University of California Press, 1934. 543–4.

Owen, R. *On the Nature of Limbs*. London: Voorst, 1849.

Paley, W. *Natural Theology, or Evidences of the Existence and Attributes of the Deity, Collected from the Appearances of Nature*. London: Fauldner, 1802.

von Baer, K.E. *Reden gehalten in wissenschaftllichen Versammlungen und kleinere Aufsätze vermischten Inhalts*. St. Petersburg: Schmitzdorff, 1876.

von Baer, K.E. "The Controversy over Darwinism" [1873]. Tr. D.L. Hull. *Darwin and his Critics*. Ed. D.L. Hull. Cambridge: Harvard University Press, 1973. 416–25.

## Study Questions

1. Compare Helmholtz's and Kant's positions on reductionism and the relationship between physics and biology.

2. The scientific revolution's mechanical worldview is supposed to have eliminated the need to appeal to final causes. And yet, Newton, the greatest of all scientists of that era, appealed to final causes. Which nineteenth-century teleologist did Newton's appeal to final causes resemble more: von Baer or Paley?

3. Describe the early to mid-nineteenth-century debate between proponents of the teleological and unity-of-plan approaches. Why did Darwin believe he had resolved this debate?

4. It seems that Darwin and his theory of natural selection couldn't win: he was praised and criticized for promoting teleology and praised and criticized for undermining teleology. Who among his supporters and critics got Darwin's views right? Who among his supporters and critics got Darwin's views wrong?

# Lorraine Code

Lorraine Code is an emeritus professor at York University and a fellow of the Royal Society of Canada since 2005. She received a BA from Queen's University and an MA and a PhD from the University of Guelph. Code's research focuses on feminist epistemology and the politics of knowledge. Code's influential 1991 book *What Can She Know?* is excerpted in a number of first-year anthologies; this reading is from her more recent *Ecological Thinking.*—TR

## Public Knowledge, Public Trust: Toward Democratic Epistemic Practices

From *Ecological Thinking: The Politics of Epistemic Location*

### 1. Introduction

Captioned "Whistle Blower," the cover photograph of the 16 November 1998 issue of *Maclean's: Canada's Weekly Newsmagazine* features Dr Nancy Olivieri, a hematologist at the University of Toronto and Toronto's Hospital for Sick Children (Figure 1). It names her principled breaking of a confidentiality agreement with a pharmaceutical company whose product she had been testing as the catalyst for "a debate over money and morality . . . raging through the medical world." The Olivieri case, which I read through diverse lenses in this chapter, exposes tangled issues peculiar to late-twentieth- and early-twenty-first-century politics of knowledge, which indeed require—and invite—multiple points of address and analysis. [Among] these issues figure [. . .] the preservation of public trust and the creation of responsible epistemic citizenship—concerns notably absent from putatively universal, a priori theories of knowledge and action. They show how knowledge claims advanced and substantiated even by the most authoritative of knowers—an eminent doctor and research scientist—are vulnerable to undermining by features of her social-political-ecological location. With respect to money, they generate questions about patronage in knowledge production and circulation, about open and closed research practices and communities, where openness can influence the availability or otherwise of funding and other infrastructural support. With respect to morality, they require re-examining relations of trust among producers of knowledge and re-evaluating trustworthy approaches

within epistemic communities, to "consumers" of the knowledge produced. In public deliberations prompted by the Olivieri case, both issues have tended to be addressed as matters of academic freedom in institutions of knowledge production and the societies that house and support them, and thence as

**Figure 1**    *Maclean's,* **16 November 1998. Photograph by Peter Bregg/Rogers Media.**

requiring reconstructed science policies/knowledge policies and practices, capable of promoting habitable, democratic epistemic community. I will suggest, however, that academic freedom is just one of several matters of concern the case exposes.

## 2. The Olivieri Affair

The broad outlines of the Olivieri affair are as follows. In the *New England Journal of Medicine* (*NEJM*) in 1994, Dr Nancy Olivieri, (then) of the Division of Haematology/Oncology at Toronto's Hospital for Sick Children (HSC) and professor of medicine at the University of Toronto, published a team-authored article, "Survival in Medically Treated Patients with Homozygous B-Thalassemia," reporting on "transfusion and iron-chelation therapy" (administered in a drug called deferiprone-L1) for the treatment of patients (mainly children) with thalassemia major, a genetically transmitted condition of the blood, prevalent around the Mediterranean, in the Middle East and Southeast Asia, and in Canada among children of Chinese, Greek, and Italian parents. Characterized by abnormalities in red blood cell production, thalassemia major (also called Mediterranean anemia) results in oxygen depletion in the body and, if untreated, can cause death within a few years. Growth failure, bone deformities, enlarged liver and spleen, which begin to appear within the first year of life, are some of its indications. Before deferiprone was available, patients had required monthly blood transfusions, administered by connecting them for as much as 12 hours a day to a drug infusion pump, a treatment whose effects include a dangerous iron build-up. Because the procedure for clearing the iron is so onerous, many patients opted out of treatment in their teenaged years, and many died in their twenties. Thus 1993 press reports herald deferiprone as a "revolutionary new treatment," promising "an entire new way to treat these diseases" (= thalassemia and sickle-cell anemia) (Priest), citing testimony from parents relieved at the prospect of taking their children off the intravenous pump, and children pleased with their newfound freedom.

Nonetheless, just a year after the first article appeared, Olivieri published concerns about deferiprone's long-term effects, in response to emerging evidence that, for some patients, it, too, could produce iron overload serious enough to cause heart, liver, and endocrine damage. In a 1995 letter to the *New England Journal of Medicine* she cautions: "When new therapies are introduced, it is important to confirm promising initial findings . . . so that false hope and expectation on the part of patients with chronic disease can be avoided." And in 1998, a second team-authored article (Olivieri et al. 420-1) concludes:

> Deferiprone is not an effective means of iron-chelation therapy in patients with thalassemia major and may be associated with worsening of hepatic fibrosis, even in patients whose hepatic iron concentrations have stabilized or decreased. After a mean of 4.6 years of deferiprone therapy, body iron burden was at concentrations associated with a greatly increased risk of cardiac disease and early death . . . in 7 of 18 patients (39%).

For western scientists, philosophers of science, and an informed public alike, these events fit easily into received images of "normal science," following a standard trajectory from positive initial findings through cautionary warnings to (partial) refutation of a hypothesis in light of new evidence, with modifications of (putative) knowledge and treatment and/or withdrawal of the drug as its outcome. Yet in this instance the trajectory was blocked: what could and *should* have been a set of uncontroversial epistemic and ethical decisions devolved into a contest of wills and interests, generating the "debate over money and morality" announced in *Maclean's* cover story.

Deferiprone research had been generously financed by Apotex Inc, "one of Canada's most high-powered pharmaceutical firms" (Papp); in 1993 and again in 1995, Olivieri had signed confidentiality agreements prohibiting disclosure of information about the drug's trials without written permission from the company; and Apotex was negotiating a large donation to the University of Toronto. Thus, making new evidence public, exposing the fallibility/corrigibility of the initial findings, cautioning parents and patients, withdrawing the drug from circulation, were not as straightforward as allegedly value-neutral empiricist epistemologies contend, according to which error suspected or exposed forces a re-evaluation of knowledge claims, if it does not simply negate them. When, despite a warning from the Research Ethics Board (REB) at HSC, Olivieri insisted on modifying consent forms to warn patients of the dangers, Apotex threatened legal action, and both the hospital and the university refused to support her decision. Nonetheless, Olivieri publicly "defied the confidentiality clause and the company's threats to sue, arranged for her own legal counsel, informed her patients and the [hospital's] REB, informed the federal government's Health Protection Branch, reported her research at a medical conference" (Valpy, "Salvage Group" A9) and published the 1998 *NEJM* article. In consequence, she was dismissed from her position as head of the hospital's hemoglobinopathy program. Although subsequent collegial and public pressure forced a review of the case, and a settlement brokered by the Canadian Association of University Teachers (CAUT), with two of the world's other leading experts in blood disease testifying to Olivieri's scientific integrity and worldwide eminence, was instrumental in bringing about her early-1999 reinstatement, the story does not end there. Even a putative ending that Olivieri reports in October 2001 scarcely counts as a "resolution." Nor is there any clear indication of justice having been done either for Olivieri and her supporters or in addressing the wider issues of "money and morality," academic freedom, corporate sponsorship, and public trust that permeate the case and its aftermath, with ongoing ripples spreading through western medical and scientific institutions.

## 3. The Scientific Imaginary

The claim that science—and thus medical science and technology—figures in the present-day western epistemic imaginary as the most objective, certain, and sophisticated knowledge humankind has achieved requires no argument to support it. Nor does the claim that expert scientific practitioners occupy positions of acknowledged epistemic authority, commonly stretching well beyond the boundaries of their specific domains of professional expertise. Merely prefacing a newspaper or television report with the words *science has proved* generates a public presumption in favour of taking the report seriously, accords it a credibility that frequently exceeds its evidential warrant, works to mask such agendas and vested interests as might underlie its presentation to the public eye. This same epistemic imaginary, with its adherence to an autonomy-of-knowledge credo, promotes a belief that scientific knowledge production takes place, appropriately, in enclosed, segregated laboratory settings—locations allegedly removed from the structures of power and privilege constitutive of all human institutions, practices, and societies—and in science itself as one such institution. Although self-critical work by scientists, and by philosophers and others in critical science studies, reveals this imaginary to be neither seamless nor impervious to critique, its tenacity in the public eye has not diminished to keep pace with these interventions. It sustains an imaginary of science (often cursorily essentialized) as self-contained and politically neutral—an imaginary within which members of an informed public judge and debate reported scientific "facts" and advance their own, derivative, claims to know. [. . .]

The operative public image of laboratory science in this imaginary—however incongruous it may be with "the facts"—is of an esoteric, authoritative inquiry, practised by privileged, mainly white men in "enclosed communities" (Hunter 104), sealed off from open public discourse by a language in which even the well-educated, literate, and privileged members of a non-scientific public cannot readily find their place. It effectively masks the human—thus fallible—provenance of scientific discoveries behind impersonal, passive locutions such as "it has been shown" or claims such as "the data show" or "science has proved," which erase the specificities, and thence the responsibilities, of human agency. The esoteric aura this discourse engenders creates a protected insularity for laboratory life, separating quests for knowledge itself from the social-political-ethical effects of its circulation and enactment, often dismissively labelled its "uses" that, in this rhetorical frame, are extraneous to science and epistemology proper. It underwrites a mystique of official secrecy in which a confidentiality agreement such as Nancy Olivieri signed would pass merely as a matter of course. Such rhetorical tropes may partially account for the efforts of Olivieri's detractors to contain her story by labelling it "a scientific controversy," situating it within procedures and rules that pose as self-justifying and thus impersonally apolitical (Olivieri observes: "Having created this fiction, they were able to express the desirability of "not taking sides"" ["Money and Truth" 53, 59]). The strategy echoes what Evelyn Fox Keller calls an "unspoken agreement that privilege[s] questions of truth over questions of consequences . . . [and] demarcat[es] the internal dynamics of science from its social and political influences" (84)—a strategy adept [. . .] at protecting a laboratory "club culture" (Hunter 30) from the public accountability regularly demanded of more secular forms of knowing. That such external factors would be operative in knowledge production is neither a surprise nor a sin; but in shielding them from view, an institution of knowledge production defies expectations of the transparency integral to public trust, thereby compromising its responsibly authoritative status.

The metaphor of the *hortus conclusus* in medieval painting—the walled garden, complete in itself, isolated from the outside world and protected from unwanted (unwonted?) intruders by the stone wall surrounding it—conveys the flavour of how the laboratory figures in this imaginary. Michèle Le Dœuff, to whom [. . .] I am indebted in my thinking about epistemic and social imaginaries, invokes a related image in her conception of philosophy's islanded consciousness (8), elaborated from **Kant's** reference to the "territory of pure understanding" as "an island, enclosed by nature itself within unalterable limits" (257). Kant's first *Critique* endeavours to "prevent the understanding, which has at last applied itself to its proper, empirical employment, from wandering off elsewhere," leaving its rightful, island domain, Le Dœuff (10, 11) contends. These rhetorical images prefigure the "enclosed communities" of present-day laboratory science, where whistle-blowers are bound to be vilified, pilloried, excommunicated

from the ranks of those whose domain they threaten to unsettle. Residues of a chemistry-set imagery of the laboratory and of a tabula rasa theory of mind, yielding a picture of white-coated (thus pure white, politically innocent) practitioners engaged in solitary, value-, and theory-neutral quests for truth, still tacitly shape secular visions of scientific inquiry. They sustain an imaginary of scientific methodology and discovery as autonomous, internally justifying, and hence immune to the ethico-political critiques enunciated by feminists and other Others.

The Olivieri case challenges these aspects of scientific self-presentation head on. It exposes some of the strategies that institutional authorities employ to shore up cherished beliefs in scientific purity and isolation, as laboratory science has no choice but to emerge into public discourse to address matters of confidentiality in conflict with principles of informed consent. Moreover, as I will elaborate with regard to its implication with "the gender question," the case shows something of why medical science's social-ecological location as a *specifically populated* institution of knowledge production cannot be ignored.

## 4. The Gender Question?

Clearly, the mere fact of a high-profile *female* doctor as the main protagonist—and in some reports the victim—is not sufficient to cast the events in the Olivieri affair, unequivocally, as effects of gender politics. Despite, or more likely because of, their often having been instrumental in forcing public inquiry into conflict of interest and other unethical practices in medicine, science more generally, and other public practices, whistle-blowers of any gender, race, class, religion, ethnicity put themselves seriously at risk. Yet since so much coverage of this case focuses on Olivieri herself, rather than on the knowledge and/or its misuses under investigation, it stands as a persuasive example of how even the most authoritative practitioners" allegations of research misconduct are vulnerable to critique that enlists aspects of their social-ecological location. Thus in my view, examining how Olivieri's female presence figures in and shapes public understandings of what happened in this exposure of the research laboratory and its inhabitants to scrutiny adds a vital dimension to projects of determining why the events unfolded as they did, accompanied as they were by a media chorus in which gender functioned as a recurrent, if secondary, *Leitmotiv* [theme about a character]. In a society where hierarchies of gendered power and privilege remain firmly in place even after almost three decades of feminist research in epistemology, this case raises crucial issues about the politics of representation, especially when the press as a source of public knowledge is so active a participant in the unfolding, positioning, and judging of what happened.

To a feminist eye, some early media reports point—if obliquely—to gendered assumptions at the core of the attacks directed at Olivieri: First, in the months leading up to her dismissal, the HSC publicly debunked—mocked—Olivieri's claims that the administration was threatening to dismiss her; second, a CBC television documentary characterized by one of her strong supporters as full of "grave factual errors and innuendo," claimed that Olivieri was "not only an incompetent scientist but carries responsibility for the suffering and death of thousands of patients worldwide" (Shafer). Third, a Toronto newspaper carried the heading "Firm axes outspoken scientist's research: Woman went public with concerns about drug's safety" (Papp). Fourth, a caller to *Maclean's* magazine from inside the hospital "accused her of stealing money from her research grant, treating her patients unethically, and sleeping with some of the scientists who looked favourably on her research findings," while another, with links to Apotex, "stubbornly referred to the trained medical specialist as "Miss Oliveria" (O'Hara 66). And fifth, the pediatrician-in-chief at the HSC maintained that patient care would be unaffected by Olivieri's removal from the research program: she would "actually have more time to care for her patients" (Foss and Taylor, "Sick Kids"). Regardless of how the case is ultimately evaluated, these remarks expose a gendered subtext beneath the dominant readings. Discrediting a woman's take on events is a familiar ploy; just as, in the politics of discourse, "outspoken" is rarely a gender-neutral term; nor is labelling

her a "woman" who went public—not a doctor or scientist—a gender-neutral action. Attributing a woman's professional success to her having slept her way to the top is a common strategy in the politics of gender, as is casually "forgetting" her name and professional title; and announcing that her time would be better spent with her patients trivializes Olivieri's scientific stature, relegating her to a caring position where she will, assuredly, "be better off." In gendered divisions of labels and labour, these are familiar scripts for designating a woman's place in a man-made world and cautioning her should she fail to know that place.

Even these items are not enough to establish a pivotal role for gender in the politics of knowledge and ethics of inquiry operative here, for explicitly gendered comments are sufficiently rare in the early press coverage that sceptics can easily discount them as mere slips of the pen. But there are exceptions, so telling as to make the larger silences resoundingly audible: A reference to "the dysfunctional patriarchy in which she works—The Hospital for Sick Children" describes it as "a place where senior scientists are scolded like schoolgirls and their concerns ignored" (Valpy, "Science Friction" 28); a feminist columnist quotes a male colleague and supporter of Olivieri at the University of Toronto saying: "If she were a six foot two male football player, her concerns for her patients' well-being would not have been treated this way" (Landsberg). And the HSC's CEO Michael Strofolino refers to her as "this poor little innocent researcher" (O'Hara 66), a comment unlikely to be made of a man.

Striking as they are, these examples combine neither to support a focus on gender nor to single it out as an explanatory-causal factor, for male scientists face comparable sanctions from pharmaceutical sponsors and/or universities devoted to protecting their financial assets. To cite just three well-known examples, Dr Arpad Pusztai of the University of Aberdeen found his contract terminated after he spoke out about the risks of genetically modified foods (see, e.g., Flynn and Gillard); Dr David Healy's offer of an appointment as clinical director of the University of Toronto's Centre for Addiction and Mental Health was revoked when he published concerns about increased suicide risks among patients taking antidepressants (Horton 7); and Olivieri compares her experiences with threats directed at Dr David Kern, formerly of Brown University, in response to concerns he expressed about interstitial lung disease in workers at the industrial plant Microfibers ("Money and Truth" 58). Nor are gender issues explicitly named in reports of the professional harassment directed at Dr Ann Clark of the Plant Agriculture Department at the University of Guelph, following her opposition to the development and use of genetically modified seeds (although reading her situation through a feminist lens could yield quite a different interpretation) (see Clark). Yet (partial) media silence notwithstanding, there is every reason to evaluate gender as an analytic category in analyzing this case, given a scientific-research climate where a sexualized politics of knowledge sustains hierarchies of credibility, epistemic authority and trust in ways detrimental to open, democratic epistemic negotiation. [. . .]

## 5. Toward Democratic Epistemic Practices?

[. . .] Questions posed by how corporate interests are served in pharmaceutical and other private research funding are about epistemic responsibility preserved, threatened, enhanced, compromised, even destroyed in reliance on commercial sponsorship at all levels, from the traditional contexts of discovery and justification, to circulation and practical deployment. They call urgently for democratic debate and collective rethinking of the very idea of trustworthy epistemic, scientific, and communicative practices. Yet in the twentieth and early twenty-first centuries, [. . .] trust has not ranked unequivocally as an epistemic virtue or value. Nor, for epistemologists and philosophers of science who carry positivism's legacy forward, is its low epistemic status surprising. Autonomous, impartial knowledge seems to risk being destabilized beyond tenability when trust figures among necessary and sufficient conditions for knowledge in general. Hence, Steven Shapin persuasively maintains, epistemologists have defined "legitimate knowledge" by "its rejection of trust": indeed, "trust and authority

stand against the very idea of *science*" (16) as the putatively most reliable form of human knowledge. He exposes a curious paradox: "Knowledge is supposed to be the product of a sovereign individual confronting the world; reliance upon the views of others produces error. The very *distrust* which social theorists have identified as the most potent way of dissolving social order is said to be the most potent means of constructing our knowledge" (17; emphasis added). *Knowledge production*, on this account, is strangely anomalous among human practices: it is paradigmatically asocial, kept apart and isolated from the networks of social interdependence constitutive of viable human lives. [. . .] Shapin contends, by contrast, that concerns with trust and trustworthiness were manifested, in early modern England, in the co-operation of "gentlemanly society" with the new "practice of empirical science" ("gentlewomen" were not judged equivalently trustworthy, nor were non-white, non-affluent, non-heterosexual, non-Christian men). He sees the combination of a scientific method founded on individual epistemic self-reliance with an ethic for which the reliability of its gentleman practitioners could be taken on trust as providing a "local resolution of a pervasive problem about the grounds and adequacy of knowledge" (42). It took a sharp separation of the contexts of discovery and justification, instituted by the positivism of the Vienna Circle, to banish trust once more from the epistemic terrain. [. . .]

In post-1969 naturalistic and social epistemology and at points where they intersect, a space opens for reintroducing responsibility and trust into epistemic discourse. [. . .]

Recall John Hardwig's now-classic illustration of epistemic interdependence in laboratory science, announced on the title page of a report of a physics experiment where ninety-nine "authors" are listed. He observes: "No one person could have done the experiment . . . and many of the authors of an article like this will not even know how a given number in the article was arrived at" ("Epistemic Dependence" 347). Analogously, with the division of intellectual labour in the Olivieri affair, it would be impossible for every author listed for the 1998 *NEJM* article to repeat the experiment for her/himself. They have to *take on trust* a commitment of their coauthors to responsible epistemic practice, in order to contribute knowledgeably to the enterprise; and the case shows how fragile such trust can be. If knowing "is a privileged state at all," Hardwig comments, "it is a privileged *social* state" ("Role of Trust" 697; emphasis added). Hence, I am affirming the *epistemological* significance of the structures—the situations, places, societies—that position some people as knowers and others not; I am presenting the Olivieri affair as exemplary for developing an analysis at once politically fraught and illustrative of the complexity of establishing the public epistemic status and trustworthiness of knowers, and of scientific truths, in the real world of empirical science, vested interest, power, and patronage.

Locating my discussion in a space where trust and epistemic responsibility are addressed and debated more publicly than in scholarly/professional journals, I have enlisted newspaper reports and media imagery as sources, reading them as a midlevel locus/site of the making-public of knowledge, as a place in mass societies where a deliberative democratic public forum is often conducted. They are commonly partisan, thus neither perfectly, objectively reliable; but neither are they always irresponsibly sensationalist, ideological. Public knowledge—albeit frequently contestable, merely putative knowledge—commonly derives from such sources and their analogues, where trust accumulates or diminishes, at least in part, according to judgments about the credibility of the testimonial claims of one or several report(s), and thus even of a particular reporter. [. . .]

In the Olivieri affair, responsibilities devolve across the epistemic and moral planes, as lines of confidentiality and trust become tangled in this head-on collision of "truths" and financial interest. Apotex's public responsibilities are both epistemic and moral: *epistemic* in the requirement to take new evidence seriously into account, following precepts assumed by a tacit "normative realism"; *moral* in the requirement to evaluate the impact for ordinary and professional human lives and for knowledge (hence not just for financial gain) of failing to do so. When such failures of responsibility are exposed, the fabric of epistemic reliance is torn. It is always more

difficult to repair a fractured trust than to establish it initially.

In the individualistic language of *Epistemic Responsibility*, I advocate honesty and humility: "Honesty not to pretend to know what one does not know (and *knows* one does not) or to ignore its relevance; humility not to yield to temptations to suppress facts damning to one's theory" (137). These injunctions translate, with modifications and refinements, into the socially-ecologically framed discourse of the present discussion. An informed public placing its trust in public knowledge tends, in western affluent societies, to expect such intellectual virtues to count, ex officio—so to speak—among the credentials of practising scientists and other knowledge makers and for their patrons and sponsors, thus offsetting risks of epistemic imperialism and the oppressive effects of such putative knowings beyond the confines of the laboratory or other institution. Hence epistemic responsibility requirements are peculiarly stringent when it is mooted that the profit motive might take "precedence over scientific rigour" or "the researchers themselves [may] lose their objectivity" (Foss and Taylor, "Volatile Mix"), in consequence of these conflicts.

Apparently, Nancy Olivieri did not "lose her objectivity." Her cautionary 1995 letter to the editor of the *New England Journal of Medicine*, with its language of confirming findings, ensuring against false hope and expectation, tells in favour of maintaining public trust in her scientific responsibility, and many of the media assessments tend in this direction. [. . .] Olivieri's responsibilities are analogous to those of Apotex, but they differ in her relationship to a wider scientific and secular public wondering how far to trust *her* knowledge as she reports on it publicly. They differ also in relation to the patients from whom she must, in good faith, ask informed consent, confident in her capacity to provide knowledge sufficiently sound and complete to inform that consent.

This discussion redirects the question "whose knowledge are we talking about?"[1] toward larger matters of *democratic* epistemic-scientific practice: democratic in the sense of facilitating informed public participation in deliberating science and knowledge policies, fostering open debate, building bridges between accredited expertise and people reliant upon it across a range of specialized and everyday practices. It focuses on cultivating public sensitivity to the specificity of diverse social circumstances and positionings, in diverse habitats, and with acknowledged differences in habitus and ethos. My interest is in developing strategies and policies to address the ecological implications and effects of socializing and naturalizing epistemology in these ways, thus to locate inquiry in a community that bears—or shares—the burdens of epistemic responsibility. I think it is from similar interests that Ursula Franklin deplores the loss of moral literacy in an age of increasing technological literacy, and the rarity of public discussion about "the merits or problems of adopting a particular technology." Advocating public inquiry, open debate, she contends that "what the real world of technology needs more than anything else are citizens with a sense of humility" (69, 91), echoing Rachel Carson's plea for intellectual-moral humility in scientific inquiry and scientifically informed practice. Such democratic, participatory inquiry would engage critically and subversively with social arrangements that position citizens unequally in relation to sources of public knowledge, posing obstacles to democratic participation, and with patterns of informed consent and confidentiality as they inflect these larger issues.

It would be naive to imagine the mere act of locating epistemic practices within a social, communal frame as a straightforward solution, capable of redistributing burdens of justification or proof, enabling ready agreement and smooth epistemic negotiations. Situating knowledge socially and ecologically could not produce instant consensus within a community—nor is even the highest degree of consensus truth- or justice-guaranteeing. It could, as readily, close down interrogation and dissent: Apotex's silencing efforts are one pertinent example. [. . .] Practices like those Donna Haraway advocates in *Modest Witness* suggest a productive model for democratic deliberation. [. . .] She writes of a Danish practice of "establishing panels of ordinary citizens, selected from pools of people who indicate an interest, but not

professional expertise or a commercial or other organized stake, in an area of technology. . . . [They] hear testimony, cross-examine experts, read briefings, deliberate among themselves, and issue reports to a national press conference" (95–7). The debates generated in the Canadian press by the Olivieri case bear some informal resemblance to this process, as, more formally, does Doctors for Research Integrity, "an independent, non-profit group that seeks to promote research integrity and academic freedom," established by Olivieri and her colleagues after the Olivieri vs. Apotex affair (see their website www.doctorsintegrity.org/media/allmedia.htm). In societies where scientific-technological discourse remains largely inaccessible to a public comprised of people who have to make wise decisions about how, when, and why to confer or withhold trust, such debate could advance projects to establish properly deliberative democracy, whose citizens—when they can—have to assume some responsibility for interrogating the taken-for-granted status of institutions of knowledge production. [. . .]

Enacting such responsibilities cannot be represented as a universal requirement, given the uneven social distribution of practical and structural access to sources of knowledge making and the contested relationship to patronage that twenty-first-century research scientists have often to maintain. But the present-day variation on the gentlemanly scientific culture Shapin details, which is as exclusive and exclusionary in its membership and esotericism as Shapin's society of gentlemen, has to be opened to social-political critique. In such cultures trust and credibility tend to attach less to putative truths than to their makers and promulgators; ordinary lay access to scientific facts is rarely unmediated, and practices of mediation, as with Apotex, are kept closed to scrutiny. When public knowledge can be crudely controlled by mechanisms such as Apotex's confidentiality clause, [. . .] principled, informed critique has a vitally important part to play.

The issues are not simple. Patronage, which literally makes so much research and thus knowledge possible has long been in place, if not in the forms it takes in this era of multinational corporations and multimillion dollar funding. Shapin's gentlemen, like western laboratory scientists now, comprise a distinct, predominately male segment of civil society, privileged by class, race, and gender, even when such specificities go unmarked in the imagined naturalness of the social order and the presumed autonomy of scientific inquiry. When patronage makes truth subservient to profit or ideology, the very possibility of evaluating knowledge and public trust collides head on with a power that simultaneously thwarts inquiry and, in a complex doubling back upon itself, immobilizes investigations of the very conditions of inquiry it is bent on examining.

The task, then, for philosophers and other citizens is to work through questions about collective responsibility and opportunities for critical intervention, in relation both to publicly and to privately funded institutions of knowledge production. Despite the notoriety of its conduct, Apotex is not solely answerable for the Olivieri affair: it is a symptom, not the disease. The social practices and institutions that make its funding style possible demand ongoing social-political intervention, committed to democratic, ecologically attuned epistemic-scientific process whose purposes include honouring the responsibilities capable of contributing to viable, habitable community. [. . .]

## Note

1. Code notes in an earlier part of the chapter that "it is feminists who have moved the question "whose knowledge are we talking about?" to centre stage in epistemology" (264).—LG

## Works Cited

Clark, E.A. "Academia in the Service of Industry: The Ag Biotech Model." *The Corporate Campus: Commercialization and the Dangers to Canada's Colleges and Universities.* Ed. J.L. Turk. Toronto: Canadian Association of University Teachers, 2000. 69–86.

Code, L. *Epistemic Responsibility.* Hanover, NH: University Press of New England, 1987.

Flynn, L., and M.S. Gillard. "GM Food Scandal Puts Labour on Spot." *Guardian Weekly,* 21 February 1999.

Foss, K., and P. Taylor. "Volatile Mix Meant Trouble at Sick Kids." *Toronto Globe and Mail,* 22 August 1998, A1, A4.

Foss, K., and P. Taylor. "Sick Kids Demotes Controversial MD." *Toronto Globe and Mail,* 8 January 1999, A12.

Franklin, U. *The Real World of Technology.* Toronto: Anansi, 1992.

Haraway, D.J. *Modest_Witness@Second_Millennium. Female_Man©_Meets_OncoMouseTM: Feminism and Technoscience.* New York: Routledge, 1997.

Hardwig, J. "Epistemic Dependence." *Journal of Philosophy* 82, 5 (1985): 335–49.

Hardwig, J. "The Role of Trust in Knowledge." *Journal of Philosophy* 88, 12 (1991): 693–708.

Horton, R. "The Dawn of McScience." *New York Review of Books* 51, 4 (March 2004): 7–9.

Hunter, L. *Critiques of Knowing: Situated Textualities in Science, Computing, and the Arts.* London: Routledge, 1999.

Kant, I. *Critique of Pure Reason.* Trans. N.K. Smith. London: Macmillan, 1970.

Keller, E.F. *Secrets of Life, Secrets of Death: Essays on Language, Gender, and Science.* New York: Routledge, 1992.

Landsberg, M. "U of T Should Back Demoted Doctor." *Toronto Sunday Star,* 17 January 1999, A2.

Le Dœuff, M. *The Philosophical Imaginary.* Trans. C. Gordon. Stanford: Stanford University Press, 1989.

O'Hara, Jane. "Whistle-Blower." *Maclean's,* 16 November 1998, 65–69.

Olivieri, N. "When Money and Truth Collide." *The Corporate Campus: Commercialization and the Dangers to Canada's Colleges and Universities.* Ed. J. L. Turk. Toronto: Canadian Association of University Teachers, 2000. 53–62.

Olivieri, N. Letter to the editor. *New England Journal of Medicine* 333, 9 (1995): 1287–88.

Olivieri, N. "Scientific Inquiry: The Fight's Just Starting." *The Globe and Mail*, 31 October 2001, A17.

Olivieri, N., G.M. Brittenham, C.E. McLaren, D.M. Templeton, R.G. Cameron, R.A. McClelland, A.D. Burt, and K.A. Fleming. "Long-Term Safety and Effectiveness of Iron-Chelation Therapy with Deferiprone for Thalassemia Major." *New England Journal of Medicine* 339, 7 (1998): 417–23.

Papp, L. "Firm Axes Outspoken Scientist's Research: Woman Went Public with Concerns about Drug's Safety." *Toronto Star*, 26 January 1997, A2.

Priest, L. "Sick Kids Doctor Finds Anemia Drug." *Toronto Star*, 14 January 1993, A3.

Shafer, A. "Science Wars: Olivieri under Media Folly." *Toronto Star*, 10 April 2000.

Shapin, S. *A Social History of Truth: Civility and Science in Seventeenth-Century England.* Chicago: University of Chicago Press, 1994.

Valpy, M. "Science Friction." *Elm Street* 3, 3 (1998): 28.

Valpy, M. "Salvage Group Tackles Sick Kids" Image Disaster." *Toronto Globe and Mail*, 2 November 1998, A1, A9.

## Study Questions

1. Why was the drug deferiprone considered to be a promising therapy for patients with thalassemia? As clinical trials proceeded, what concerns led Olivieri to modify patient consent forms, thus, according to Apotex, violating the confidentiality agreement she had signed?

2. What does Code mean by the "scientific imaginary," and how does the metaphor of the walled garden serve to convey this meaning?

3. In what ways do media reports suggest that gender stereotypes were implicated in the Olivieri affair? Why does Code nevertheless avoid singling out gender as the explanation of what transpired?

4. Code characterizes Apotex as "a symptom, not the disease" in the Olivieri affair. What does Code diagnose as the "disease," and what remedy does she suggest?

# Film Notes

## Knowledge of the External World

*Abre los ojos* (Spain 1997, Alejandro Amenábar, 117 min; Spanish with subtitles). Dreams and reality become entangled after a handsome playboy is disfigured in a car crash caused by a jealous ex-lover. Remade as *Vanilla Sky* (USA 2001, Cameron Crowe, 135 min).

*eXistenZ* (Canada/UK 1999, David Cronenberg, 97 min): The virtual reality game "eXistenZ" downloads directly into players through a "bioport" inserted at the base of the spine.

*Spider* (Canada/UK 2002, David Cronenberg, 98 min): A schizophrenic man released from an asylum to a halfway house has fragmented and distorted memories of a traumatic childhood.

*The Truman Show* (USA 1998, Peter Weir, 103 min): Truman Burbank has unknowingly lived almost his entire life on the set of a television show followed by millions of viewers.

*Waking Life* (USA 2001, Richard Linklater, 99 min): About a man dreaming, awakening into yet another dream, and engaging in philosophical conversations throughout.

*The Wild Hunt* (Canada 2009, Alexandre Franchi, 96 min): Afraid he is losing his girlfriend to a fantasy world, Erik is drawn into a Live Action Role Playing battle between Vikings and Celts.

## Knowledge of the Mind

*2001: A Space Odyssey* (UK/USA 1968, Stanley Kubrick, 141 min): About the place of intelligence in the universe: apes discovering tools, humans interacting with their space shuttle's onboard computer, and alien-built monoliths that make this progress possible.

*A. I. Artificial Intelligence* (USA 2001, Steven Spielberg, 146 min): David is a lovable humanoid robot, abandoned by the couple who brought him home, who embarks on a quest to become a real boy and win back his mother's love.

*Being John Malkovich* (USA 1999, Spike Jonze, 112 min): A financially strapped puppeteer discovers a portal into the brain of actor John Malkovich.

*Bicentennial Man* (USA/Germany 1999, Chris Columbus, 132 min): Andrew, a robo-butler, receives upgrades that make him more humanlike as he is passed through four generations of a family.

*Blade Runner* (USA/Hong Kong 1982, Ridley Scott, 117 min): In circa-2020 Los Angeles, Harrison Ford plays a "blade runner," a cop who has the job of tracking down and killing genetically engineered human "replicants."

*I, Robot* (USA/Germany 2004, Alex Proyas, 115 min): In circa-2035 Chicago, a police detective with a deep distrust of robots despite Asimov's Three Laws of Robotics investigates the apparent suicide of a robot designer.

*Invasion of the Body Snatchers* (USA 1956, Don Siegel, 80 min): A small-town doctor discovers that people are being replaced by replicas grown from plant-like pods. Remade as *Invasion of the Body Snatchers* (USA 1978, Philip Kaufman, 115 min) set in San Francisco and *Body Snatchers* (USA 1993, Abel Ferrara, 87 min) set on an Alabama army base.

## Knowledge of the External World/Knowledge of the Mind

*The Matrix* (USA/Australia 1999, Andy and Larry Wachowski, 136 min): Neo is a software designer/computer hacker turned possible messiah for a rebel force working to free human minds programmed to live a virtual reality.

## Methods of Scientific Inquiry

*The Constant Gardener* (UK/Germany 2005, Fernando Meirelles, 128 min; some subtitles): The activist wife of a British diplomat posted in Africa is murdered after discovering collusion between governments and pharmaceutical companies conducting research on AIDS patients.

*Galileo* (UK/USA 1975, Joseph Losey, 145 min): Based on Bertolt Brecht's play, the film covers Galileo's scientific achievements, personal foibles, and troubles with the Inquisition, including his miscalculations of support within the Church.

*Gorillas in the Mist* (USA 1988, Michael Apted, 129 min): About Dian Fossey's life studying and protecting the mountain gorillas of central Africa, her love affair with a *National Geographic* photographer, the enemies she made, and her 1985 murder.

*The Insider* (USA 1999, Michael Mann, 157 min): The producer of CBS's *60 Minutes* convinces a former tobacco scientist to reveal secrets about the industry but must battle his litigation-wary network to run the program.

*Madame Curie* (USA 1943, Mervyn LeRoy, 124 min): A somewhat sentimental portrayal of the life of physicist Marie Sklodowska Curie and the laboratory research that led to the discovery of radium in collaboration with her husband, Pierre.

*Mr. Death: The Rise and Fall of Fred A. Leuchter, Jr.* (UK/USA 1999, Errol Morris, 91 min): Leuchter is the son of a prison warden who put his engineer training into designing better death row machines and later joined the Holocaust denial circuit.

*Rashomon* (Japan 1950, Akira Kurosawa, 88 min; Japanese with subtitles): A local bandit is suspected in the murder of a samurai and the rape of his wife, but eyewitness accounts conflict.

*Rear Window* (USA 1954, Alfred Hitchcock, 112 min): A photographer confined to a wheelchair spies on his neighbours through his apartment window and comes to believe that a murder has been committed.

*Twelve Angry Men* (USA 1957, Sidney Lumet, 96 min): A man presses his fellow jurors, who are ready to convict a Latino teenager accused of killing his father, to consider whether they have proof beyond a reasonable doubt. Remade as *12* (Russia 2007, Nikita Mikhalkov, 159 min; Russian and Chechen with subtitles), with a Chechen teenager accused of killing his Russian stepfather.

## Knowledge of the External World/Methods of Scientific Inquiry

*MindWalk* (USA 1990, Bernt Capra, 112 min): On the medieval island of Mont Saint Michel, a politician, poet, and physicist converse about systems theory and scientific responsibility.

## Knowledge of the Mind/Methods of Scientific Inquiry

*Planet of the Apes* (USA 1968, Franklin J. Schaffner, 112 min): A space traveller from Earth, who crashes on a planet where apes rank higher than humans, must prove his intelligence.

# PART III

# The Good

## ▶ Introduction

For Plato, "the good" is the most important of the forms. In *The Republic* (508e, 509b), the role of the good in the intelligible realm is compared to that of the sun in the sensible realm. Metaphysically, the "the objects of knowledge" derive their "very existence and essence" and "their truth" from the good, just as living things do from the sun. Epistemologically, the good gives "the power of knowing to the knower" and "their being known" to "the objects of knowledge" by aiding the soul's use of reason, just as sunlight aids the eyes' vision. The readings of this section, however, are concerned with knowledge of the good insofar as this guides us in leading good lives and acting rightly: the subject matter of ethics and morality.

### Plato's *Euthyphro*

*Euthyphro* begins with a chance meeting between Socrates and Euthyphro, a professional priest, at the court of the king-archon. We find out the charges against Socrates that result in his trial (see Plato's *Apology*) and execution (see Plato's *Crito*): not believing in the city's gods, introducing new gods, and corrupting the young. Euthyphro is laying charges against his own father, convinced that he is acting rightly and it is not "unholy for a son to prosecute his father for murder." Socrates questions Euthyphro about what holiness and unholiness, piety and impiety, are (an especially significant question because impiety is the charge brought against Socrates), but Euthyphro repeatedly fails "to tell the essential aspect, by which all holy acts are holy."

The central philosophical question of *Euthyphro* concerns the dilemma Socrates poses to Euthyphro: "Is that which is holy loved by the gods because it is holy, or is it holy because it is loved by the gods?" Divine command theory sides with the second choice: what is holy, pious, or good is holy, pious, or good because it is loved by the gods. In the monotheistic tradition, morality and religion coincide. If we do what God commands—follow scripture, obey the rabbi, priest, or imam—we will lead good lives and act rightly. The secular philosophical tradition inaugurated by Socrates and Plato favours the first choice: what is holy, pious, or good is holy, pious, or good on the basis of some rational standard that is independent of the gods, but which they—and we, no less—can employ. Morality and religion need not coincide. But what is this rational standard? How does philosophical inquiry lead us to knowledge of what is good? What it is to be a good person, lead a good life, adopt a good intent, perform a good act? What *is* goodness?

## Moral Foundations

The readings in this section cover various attempts to answer the problem Socrates leaves us with in *Euthyphro*.

Aristotle, Plato's student, defends a virtue theory of morality in *The Nichomachean Ethics*. Through practice, a virtuous person has developed the disposition to exercise moderation in feelings and actions. Such virtue fulfills "man's nature" as "a political animal," and for Aristotle, as for Plato, it is by performing our function well that we live well and attain happiness (*eudaimonia*). But this life "is happy only in a secondary degree." The "best" and "happiest" life is the contemplative life. Exercise of the rational principle of the soul distinguishes "man" (i.e., male, non-slave humans) from other animals and is the "supreme Good."

For Immanuel Kant, in *Fundamental Principles of the Foundations of Ethics*, what is good in itself is "a good will," and a person's will is good when the intent behind an action conforms to duty. An intent conforms to duty when it yields to the demands of rationality. What rationality demands is that principles underlying actions be universalizable (i.e., able to be willed without contradiction for everyone in similar circumstances to follow), the ends of other rational beings ("persons") be respected, and rules that bind us be those to which we willingly assent. These are the three forms of the "categorical imperative."

In contrast, the utilitarianism of John Stuart Mill is consequentialist: what matters are an action's consequences, not the intent behind it. Pleasure is the only thing that is good in itself—this is the "life of enjoyment" Aristotle considered "vulgar," "utterly slavish," and "only a life for cattle." For Mill, in *Utilitarianism*, right actions are those that maximize pleasure and minimize pain. Mill seeks the greatest amount of happiness for the greatest number, arguing that everyone affected by an action matters equally. This principle of utility, in contrast to Kant's categorical imperative, is a posteriori not a priori, empirical not rational.

In "On the Cognitive Content of Morality," Jürgen Habermas emphasizes the importance of distinguishing between the "ethical point of view," which is Aristotelian, concerns the "good," and involves "value-orientations," and the "moral point of view," which is Kantian, concerns the "right," and involves "obligations." Habermas is especially concerned that in "pluralistic, modern societies," without a common conception of "the good," justice risks becoming just another value. Habermas's solution is his theory of "discourse ethics." On this "proceduralist" approach, a rule is valid if it can be freely accepted by all concerned through participation in "rational discourse."

## Challenges to Moral Foundations

The readings in this section pose a variety of challenges to moral foundations.

In *Twilight of the Idols*, Friedrich Nietzsche advocates a naturalistic morality that celebrates the passions and promotes actions that satisfy physiological instincts—not, as Kant demands, their sublimation to reason. Nietzsche rejects Aristotle's belief that virtue causes happiness, arguing instead that virtue is the consequence of living happily, by which Nietzsche means living according to instinct. Nietzsche dismisses the impartiality of Mill's utility principle: instead, he insists, we should be egoists who seek our own advantage.

Like Habermas, A.J. Ayer belongs to the "linguistic turn" in twentieth-century philosophy, in which sentences replace ideas as targets of analysis. According to Ayer and other logical positivists, only the logical and empirical claims of science are meaningful. In "Critique of Ethics," Ayer argues that claims about what we "should" or "ought" to do, what is "good" and "bad" or "right" and "wrong," are meaningless. Such sentences express feelings but say nothing—a position called "emotivism." Not only are the normative theories of Aristotle, Kant, and Mill deemed illegitimate, so is the entire branch of philosophy to which they belong.

In contrast to Ayer, Sartre is skeptical about science, especially when it comes to claims about human nature. Sartre argues in *Existentialism and Humanism* that "Man is nothing else but that which he makes of himself." Contra Aristotle, there is no purpose determined by nature that must be fulfilled to lead a good life; contra Kant, there is no universal principle of rationality whose commands must be obeyed to act rightly; contra Mill, pleasure and happiness are not inherently good. Nor does a transcendent realm of abstract Platonic forms prescribe our values. Sartre tells us that we bring values into existence through the choices we make.

In "Cultural Relativism and Cultural Values," anthropologist Melville Herskovits argues that there are no "fixed values" or "absolute moral standards": those defended by Aristotle, Kant, or Mill, he would say, "however objectively arrived at, are nonetheless the product of a given time or place." Herskovits defends "cultural relativism": morality is a "universal" that exists in all cultures, but it takes different forms, and we are urged to respect those differences. Unlike Nietzsche's egoism, Ayer's emotivism, and Sartre's existentialism, Herskovits' challenge to moral foundations does not hold that morality is subjective for individuals. Values are relative to time and place, but they exist and are valid for those whose values they are.

## Gender and Morality

Aristotle, Kant, Mill, Habermas, Nietzsche, Ayer, Sartre: all philosophers, all male. Does the predominance of males in the Western philosophical canon make a difference to the theories we have inherited?

Martha Nussbaum's topic in "Judging Other Cultures" is the traditional practice of female genital mutilation (FGM), still carried out as a rite of passage in many African cultures. Nussbaum confronts the cultural relativism she finds among not only anthropologists like Herskovits but her undergraduate students with the serious health effects and coercion associated with FGM. Nussbaum argues that FGM is a violation of women's human rights and Westerners should support activists living in countries where FGM continues to be practised in their efforts to stop it.

Carol Gilligan is a psychologist, not a philosopher. "Moral Orientation and Moral Development" concerns gender differences in moral reasoning that Gilligan has discovered through empirical research: a care perspective is more likely to be adopted by girls and women, and a justice perspective is more likely to be adopted by boys and men. Kant's categorical imperative, Mill's principle of utility, and the proceduralism of Habermas's discourse ethics are examples of the justice perspective's rule-based approach to morality. Gilligan argues that the care perspective offers "a different voice" in the assessment of moral problems.

Certainly, as Susan Sherwin points out in "Ethics, "Feminine" Ethics, and Feminist Ethics," philosophers like Aristotle and Kant theorize in ways that denigrate women's abilities and sanction their subordination. Aristotle's virtues for women include obedience and silence; Kant holds that women are unfit for public life because their sentiments cannot take a backseat to reason. Gender bias may enter in more subtle ways. Like Gilligan, Sherwin notes that the impartiality emphasized by both deontologists and utilitarians fails to accommodate the reality of women's moral lives—that women tend to be charged with the responsibility of caring for children, the sick and elderly, and male partners and colleagues. However, drawing a distinction between "feminine" and "feminist" ethics, Sherwin cautions that valorizing the care perspective *as* a woman's perspective risks perpetuating the subordination of women by men that has been associated with caring relationships.

Catherine Wilson notes that unlike "the old philosophers" Aristotle and Kant, contemporary moral philosophers tend to ignore sex and gender altogether. Sociobiologists and evolutionary psychologists, in contrast, are likely to explain women's subordination much as Aristotle and Kant do: in terms of "nature's plan." In "Moral Equality and 'Natural' Subordination," Wilson investigates such claims and concludes that any small effects favourable to men due to biology have been leveraged by discriminatory social institutions over the years into much larger ones.

## ▶ Work Cited

Plato, *The Republic*, vol. 2, trans. Paul Shorey (Cambridge, MA: Harvard University Press and London: William Heinemann, 1935).

## ▶ Discussion Questions

1. What is an action you consider to be clearly right? What is an action you consider to be clearly wrong? What makes the right action right and the wrong action wrong?
2. Who is someone you consider to be living an unquestionably good life? Who is someone you consider to be living an unquestionably bad life? What makes the good life good and the bad life bad?

3. Identify some specific examples of ways in which cultural practices vary across place and time. Is it legitimate to make value judgments about another culture's practices?

4. Girls and boys still tend to be brought up differently: dressed in pink or blue, handed dolls or trucks, encouraged to plié in tutus or climb trees. Why do we do this, and should we? What impact do gender norms have on how we behave and how we assess the behaviour of others?

## ▶ Further Reading

de Waal, Frans. *Primates and Philosophers: How Morality Evolved*. Ed. Stephen Macedo and Josiah Ober. Princeton and Oxford: Princeton University Press, 2006.

Gilligan, Carol. *In a Different Voice: Psychological Theory and Women's Development*. Cambridge, MA: Harvard University Press, 1982.

MacIntyre, Alasdair. *After Virtue: A Study in Moral Theory*. South Bend, IN: University of Notre Dame Press, 1981.

Singer, Peter. *Practical Ethics*, 3rd ed. Cambridge: Cambridge University Press, 2011.

## Plato

> *Euthyphro* is considered to be one of Plato's (429–347 BCE) early dialogues, also known as the "Socratic" dialogues because in these we encounter the historical Socrates, a philosopher whom Aristotle described as focused on questions about how to lead a good life, preoccupied with seeking, though without success, definitions of ethical concepts—here, of "holiness" or "piety."

## *Euthyphro* (or *On Holiness,* a Tentative Dialogue)

Characters: Euthyphro, **Socrates**

EUTHYPHRO. What strange thing has happened, Socrates, that you have left your accustomed haunts in the **Lyceum** and are now haunting the portico where the **king archon** sits? For it cannot be that you have an action before the king, as I have.

SOCRATES. Our Athenians, Euthyphro, do not call it an action, but an indictment.

E. What? Somebody has, it seems, brought an indictment against you; for I don't accuse you of having brought one against anyone else.

S. Certainly not.

E. But someone else against you?

S. Quite so.

E. Who is he?

S. I don't know the man very well myself, Euthyphro, for he seems to be a young and unknown person. His name, however, is Meletus, I believe. And he is of the **deme** of Pitthus, if you remember any Pitthian Meletus, with long hair and only a little beard, but with a hooked nose.

E. I don't remember him, Socrates. But what sort of an indictment has he brought against you?

S. What sort? No mean one, it seems to me; for the fact that, young as he is, he has apprehended so important a matter reflects no small credit upon him. For he says he knows how the youth are corrupted and who those are who corrupt them. He must be a wise man; who, seeing my lack of wisdom and that I am corrupting his fellows, comes to the State, as a boy runs to his mother, to accuse me. And he seems to me to be the only one of the public men who begins in the right way; for the right way is to take care of the young men first, to make them as good as possible, just as a good husbandman will naturally take care of the young plants first and afterwards of the rest. And so Meletus, perhaps, is first clearing away us who corrupt the young plants, as he says; then after this, when he has turned his attention to the older men, he will bring countless most precious blessings upon the State—at least, that is the natural outcome of the beginning he has made.

E. I hope it may be so, Socrates; but I fear the opposite may result. For it seems to me that he begins by injuring the State at its very heart when he undertakes to harm you. Now tell me, what does he say you do that corrupts the young?

S. Absurd things, my friend, at first hearing. For he says I am a maker of gods; and because I make new gods and do not believe in the old ones, he indicted me for the sake of these old ones, as he says.

E. I understand, Socrates; it is because you say the divine monitor keeps coming to you. So he has brought the indictment against you for making innovations in religion, and he is going into court to slander you, knowing that slanders on such subjects are readily accepted by the people. Why, they even laugh at me and say I am crazy when I say anything in the assembly about divine things and foretell the future to them. And yet there is not one of the things I have foretold that is not true; but they are jealous of all such men as you and I are. However, we must not be disturbed, but must come to close quarters with them.

S. My dear Euthyphro, their ridicule is perhaps of no consequence. For the Athenians, I fancy, are not much concerned if they think a man is clever, provided he does not impart his clever notions to others; but when they think he makes others to be like himself, they are angry with him, either through jealousy, as you say, or for some other reason.

E. I don't much desire to test their sentiments toward me in this matter.

S. No, for perhaps they think that you are reserved and unwilling to impart your wisdom. But I fear that because of my love of men they think that I not only pour myself out copiously to anyone and everyone without payment, but that I would even pay something myself, if anyone would listen to me. Now if, as I was saying just now, they were to laugh at me, as you say they do at you, it would not be at all unpleasant to pass the time in the court with jests and laughter; but if they are in earnest, then only soothsayers like you can tell how this will end.

E. Well, Socrates, perhaps it won't amount to much, and you will bring your case to a satisfactory ending, as I think I shall mine.

S. What is your case, Euthyphro? Are you defending or prosecuting?

E. Prosecuting.

S. Whom?

E. Such a man that they think I am insane because I am prosecuting him.

S. Why? Are you prosecuting one who has wings to fly away with?

E. No flying for him at his ripe old age.

S. Who is he?

E. My father.

S. Your father, my dear man?

E. Certainly.

S. But what is the charge, and what is the suit about?

E. Murder, Socrates.

S. Heracles! Surely, Euthyphro, most people do not know where the right lies; for I fancy it is not everyone who can rightly do what you are doing, but only one who is already very far advanced in wisdom.

E. Very far, indeed, Socrates, by Zeus.

S. Is the one who was killed by your father a relative? But of course he was; for you would not bring a charge of murder against him on a stranger's account.

E. It is ridiculous, Socrates, that you think it matters whether the man who was killed was a stranger or a relative, and do not see that the only thing to consider is whether the action of the slayer was justified or not, and that if it was justified one ought to let him alone, and if not, one ought to proceed against him, even if he share one's hearth and eat at one's table. For the pollution is the same if you associate knowingly with such a man and do not purify yourself and him by proceeding against him. In this case, the man who was killed was a hired workman of mine, and when we were farming at Naxos, he was working there on our land. Now he got drunk, got angry with one of our house slaves, and butchered him. So my father bound him hand and foot, threw him into a ditch, and sent a man here to Athens to ask the religious adviser what he ought to do. In the meantime he paid no attention to the man as he lay there bound, and neglected him, thinking that he was a murderer and it did not matter if he were to die. And that is just what happened to him. For he died of hunger and cold and his bonds before the messenger came back from the adviser. Now my father and the rest of my relatives are angry with me, because for the sake of this murderer I am prosecuting my father for murder. For they say he did not kill him, and if he had killed him never so much, yet since the dead man was a murderer, I ought not to trouble myself about such a fellow because it is unholy for a son to prosecute his father for murder. Which shows how little they know what the divine law is in regard to holiness and unholiness.

S. But, in the name of Zeus, Euthyphro, do you think your knowledge about divine laws and holiness and unholiness is so exact that, when the facts are as you say, you are not afraid of doing something unholy yourself in prosecuting your father for murder?

E. I should be of no use, Socrates, and Euthyphro would be in no way different from other men, if I did not have exact knowledge about all such things.

S. Then the best thing for me, my admirable Euthyphro, is to become your pupil and, before the suit with Meletus comes on, to challenge him and say that I always thought it very important before to know about divine matters and that now, since he says I am doing wrong by acting carelessly and making innovations in matters of religion, I have become your pupil. And "Meletus," I should say, "if you acknowledge that Euthyphro is wise in such matters, then believe that I also hold correct opinions, and do not bring me to trial; and if you do not acknowledge that, then bring a suit against him, my teacher, rather than against me, and charge him with corrupting the old, namely, his father and me, which he does by teaching me and by correcting and punishing his father." And if he does not do as I ask and does not release me from the indictment or bring it against you in my stead, I could say in the court the same things I said in my challenge to him, could I not?

E. By Zeus, Socrates, if he should undertake to indict me, I fancy I should find his weak spot, and it would be much more a question about him in court than about me.

S. And I, my dear friend, perceiving this, wish to become your pupil; for I know that neither this fellow Meletus, nor anyone else, seems to notice you at all, but he has seen through me so sharply and so easily that he has indicted me for impiety. Now in the name of Zeus, tell me what you just now asserted that you knew so well. What do you say is the nature of piety and impiety, both in relation to murder and to other things? Is not holiness always the same with itself in every action, and, on the other hand, is not unholiness the opposite of all holiness, always the same with itself, and whatever is to be unholy possessing some one characteristic quality?

E. Certainly, Socrates.

S. Tell me then, what do you say holiness is, and what unholiness?

E. Well then, I say that holiness is doing what I am doing now, prosecuting the wrongdoer who commits murder or steals from the temples or does any such thing, whether he be your father, or your mother or anyone else, and not prosecuting him is unholy. And, Socrates, see what a sure proof I offer you—a proof I have already given to others—that this is established and right and that we ought not to let him who acts impiously go unpunished, no matter who he may be. Men believe that Zeus is the best and most just of the gods, and they acknowledge that he put his father in bonds because he wickedly devoured his children, and he in turn had mutilated his father for similar reasons; but they are incensed against me because I proceed against my father when he has done wrong, and so they are inconsistent in what they say about the gods and about me.

S. Is not this, Euthyphro, the reason why I am being prosecuted, because when people tell such stories about the gods I find it hard to accept them? And therefore, probably, people will say I am wrong. Now if you, who know so much about such things, accept these tales, I suppose I too must give way. For what am I to say, who confess frankly that I know nothing about them? But tell me, in the name of Zeus, the god of friendship, do you really believe these things happened?

E. Yes, and still more wonderful things than these, Socrates, which most people do not know.

S. And so you believe that there was really war between the gods, and fearful enmities and battles and other things of the sort, such as are told of by the poets and represented in varied designs by the great artists in our sacred places and especially on the robe which is carried up to the Acropolis at the great **Panathenaea**, for this is covered with such representations? Shall we agree that these things are true, Euthyphro?

E. Not only these things, Socrates; but, as I said just now, I will, if you like, tell you many other things about the gods, which I am sure will amaze you when you hear them.

S. I dare say. But you can tell me those things at your leisure some other time. At present try to tell more clearly what I asked you just now. For, my friend, you did not give me sufficient information before, when I asked what holiness was, but you told me that this was holy which you are now doing, prosecuting your father for murder.

E. Well, what I said was true, Socrates.

S. Perhaps. But, Euthyphro, you say that many other things are holy, do you not?

E. Why, so they are.

S. Now call to mind that this is not what I asked you, to tell me one or two of the many holy acts, but to tell the essential aspect, by which all holy acts are holy; for you said that all unholy acts were unholy and all holy ones holy by one aspect. Or don't you remember?

E. I remember.

S. Tell me then what this aspect is, that I may keep my eye fixed upon it and employ it as a model and, if anything you or anyone else does agrees with it, may say that the act is holy, and if not, that it is unholy.

E. If you wish me to explain in that way, I will do so.

S. I do wish it.

E. Well then, what is dear to the gods is holy, and what is not dear to them is unholy.

S. Excellent, Euthyphro, now you have answered as I asked you to answer. However, whether it is true, I am not yet sure; but you will, of course, show that what you say is true.

E. Certainly.

S. Come then, let us examine our words. The thing and the person that are dear to the gods are holy, and the thing and the person that are hateful to the gods are unholy; and the two are not the same, but the holy and the unholy are the exact opposites of each other. Is not this what we have said?

E. Yes, just this.

S. And it seems to be correct?

E. I think so, Socrates.

S. Well then, have we said this also, that the gods, Euthyphro, quarrel and disagree with each other, and that there is enmity between them?

E. Yes, we have said that.

S. But what things is the disagreement about, which causes enmity and anger? Let us look at it in this way. If you and I were to disagree about number, for instance, which of two numbers were the greater, would the disagreement about these matters make us enemies and make us angry with each other, or should we not quickly settle it by resorting to arithmetic?

E. Of course we should.

S. Then, too, if we were to disagree about the relative size of things, we should quickly put an end to the disagreement by measuring?

E. Yes.

S. And we should, I suppose, come to terms about relative weights by weighing?

E. Of course.

S. But about what would a disagreement be, which we could not settle and which would cause us to be enemies and be angry with each other? Perhaps you cannot give an answer offhand; but let me suggest it. Is it not about right and wrong, and noble and disgraceful, and good and bad? Are not these the questions about which you and I and other people become enemies, when we do become enemies, because we differ about them and cannot reach any satisfactory agreement?

E. Yes, Socrates, these are the questions about which we should become enemies.

S. And how about the gods, Euthyphro? If they disagree, would they not disagree about these questions?

E. Necessarily.

S. Then, my noble Euthyphro, according to what you say, some of the gods too think some things are right or wrong, and noble or disgraceful, and good or bad, and others disagree; for they would not quarrel with each other if they did not disagree about these matters. Is that the case?

E. You are right.

S. Then the gods in each group love the things which they consider good and right and hate the opposites of these things?

E. Certainly.

S. But you say that the same things are considered right by some of them and wrong by others; and it is because they disagree about these things that they quarrel and wage war with each other. Is not this what you said?

E. It is.

S. Then, as it seems, the same things are hated and loved by the gods, and the same things would be dear and hateful to the gods.

E. So it seems.

S. And then the same things would be both holy and unholy, Euthyphro, according to this statement.

E. I suppose so.

S. Then you did not answer my question, my friend. For I did not ask you what is at once holy and unholy; but, judging from your reply, what is dear to the gods is also hateful to the gods. And so, Euthyphro, it would not be surprising if, in punishing your father as you are doing, you were performing an act that is pleasing to Zeus, but hateful to Cronus and Uranus, and pleasing to Hephaestus, but hateful to Hera, and so forth in respect to the other gods, if any disagree with any other about it.

E. But I think, Socrates, that none of the gods disagrees with any other about this, or holds that he who kills anyone wrongfully ought not to pay the penalty.

S. Well, Euthyphro, to return to men, did you ever hear anybody arguing that he who had killed anyone wrongfully, or had done anything else whatever wrongfully, ought not to pay the penalty?

E. Why, they are always arguing these points, especially in the law courts. For they do very many wrong things, and then there is nothing they will not do or say, in defending themselves, to avoid the penalty.

S. Yes, but do they acknowledge, Euthyphro, that they have done wrong and, although they acknowledge it, nevertheless say that they ought not to pay the penalty?

E. Oh, no, they don't do that.

S. Then there is something they do not do and say. For they do not, I fancy, dare to say and argue that if they have really done wrong, they ought not to pay the penalty; but, I think, they say they have not done wrong; do they not?

E. You are right.

S. Then they do not argue this point, that the wrongdoer must not pay the penalty; but perhaps they argue about this, who is a wrongdoer, and what he did, and when.

E. That is true.

S. Then is not the same thing true of the gods, if they quarrel about right and wrong, as you say, and some say others have done wrong, and some say they have not? For surely, my friend, no one, either of gods or men, has the face to say that he who does wrong ought not to pay the penalty.

E. Yes, you are right about this, Socrates, in the main.

S. But I think, Euthyphro, those who dispute, both men and gods, if the gods do dispute, dispute about each separate act. When they differ with one another about any act, some say it was right and others that it was wrong. Is it not so?

E. Certainly.

S. Come now, my dear Euthyphro, inform me, that I may be made wiser, what proof you have that all the gods think that the man lost his life wrongfully, who, when he was a servant, committed murder, was bound by the master of the man he killed, and died as a result of his bonds before the master who had bound him found out from the advisers what he ought to do with him, and that it is right on account of such a man for a son to proceed against his father and accuse him of murder. Come, try to show me clearly about this, that [9b] the gods surely believe that this conduct is right; and if you show it to my satisfaction, I will glorify your wisdom as long as I live.

E. But perhaps this is no small task, Socrates; though I could show you quite clearly.

S. I understand; it is because you think I am slower to understand than the judges, since it is plain that you will show them that such acts are wrong and that all the gods hate them.

E. Quite clearly, Socrates—that is, if they listen to me.

S. They will listen, if they find that you are a good speaker. But this occurred to me while you were talking, and I said to myself: "If Euthyphro should prove to me no matter how clearly that all the gods think such a death is wrongful, what have I learned from Euthyphro about the question, what is holiness and what is unholiness?" For this act would, as it seems, be hateful to the gods; but we saw just now that holiness and its opposite are not defined in this way; for we saw that what is hateful to the gods is also dear to them; and so I let you off any discussion of this point, Euthyphro. If you like, all the gods may think it wrong and may hate it. But shall we now emend our definition and say that whatever all the gods hate is unholy and whatever they all love is holy, and what some love and others hate is neither or both? Do you wish this now to be our definition of holiness and unholiness?

E. What is to hinder, Socrates?

S. Nothing, so far as I am concerned, Euthyphro, but consider your own position, whether by adopting this definition you will most easily teach me what you promised.

E. Well, I should say that what all the gods love is holy and, on the other hand, what they all hate is unholy.

S. Then shall we examine this again, Euthyphro, to see if it is correct, or shall we let it go and accept our own statement, and those of others, agreeing that it is so if anyone merely says that it is? Or ought we to inquire into the correctness of the statement?

E. We ought to inquire. However, I think this is now correct.

S. We shall soon know more about this, my friend. Just consider this question: Is that which is holy loved by the gods because it is holy, or is it holy because it is loved by the gods?

E. I don't know what you mean, Socrates.

S. Then I will try to speak more clearly. We speak of being carried and of carrying, of being led and of leading, of being seen and of seeing; and you understand—do you not?—that in all such expressions the two parts differ one from the other in meaning, and how they differ.

E. I think I understand.

S. Then, too, we conceive of a thing being loved and of a thing loving, and the two are different?

E. Of course.

S. Now tell me, is a thing which is carried a carried thing because one carries it, or for some other reason?

E. No, for that reason.

S. And a thing which is led is led because one leads it, and a thing which is seen is so because one sees it?

E. Certainly.

S. Then one does not see it because it is a seen thing, but, on the contrary, it is a seen thing because one sees it; and one does not lead it because it is a led thing, but it is a led thing because one leads it; and one does not carry it because it is a carried thing, but it is a carried thing because one carries it. Is it clear, Euthyphro, what I am trying to say? I am trying to say this, that if anything becomes or undergoes, it does not become because it is in a state of becoming, but it is in a state of becoming because it becomes, and it does not undergo because it is a thing which undergoes, but because it undergoes it is a thing which undergoes; or do you not agree to this?

E. I agree.

S. Is not that which is beloved a thing which is either becoming or undergoing something?

E. Certainly.

S. And is this case like the former ones: those who love it do not love it because it is a beloved thing, but it is a beloved thing because they love it?

E. Obviously.

S. Now what do you say about that which is holy, Euthyphro? It is loved by all the gods, is it not, according to what you said?

E. Yes.

S. For this reason, because it is holy, or for some other reason?

E. No, for this reason.

S. It is loved because it is holy, not holy because it is loved?

E. I think so.

S. But that which is dear to the gods is dear to them and beloved by them because they love it.

E. Of course.

S. Then that which is dear to the gods and that which is holy are not identical, but differ one from the other.

E. How so, Socrates?

S. Because we are agreed that the holy is loved because it is holy and that it is not holy because it is loved; are we not?

E. Yes.

S. But we are agreed that what is dear to the gods is dear to them because they love it, that is, by reason of this love, not that they love it because it is dear.

E. Very true.

S. But if that which is dear to the gods and that which is holy were identical, my dear Euthyphro, then if the holy were loved because it is holy, that which is dear to the gods would be loved because it is dear, and if that which is dear to the gods is dear because it is loved, then that which is holy would be holy because it is loved; but now you see that the opposite is the case, showing that the two are different from each other. For the one becomes lovable from the fact that it is loved, whereas the other is loved because it is in itself lovable. And, Euthyphro, it seems that when you were asked what holiness is you were unwilling to make plain its essence, but you mentioned something that has happened to this holiness, namely, that it is loved by the gods. But you did not tell as yet what it really is. So, if you please, do not hide it from me, but begin over again and tell me what holiness is, no matter whether it is loved by the gods or anything else happens to it; for we shall not quarrel about that. But tell me frankly, What is holiness, and what is unholiness?

E. But, Socrates, I do not know how to say what I mean. For whatever statement we advance, somehow or other it moves about and won't stay where we put it.

S. Your statements, Euthyphro, are like works of my ancestor Daedalus,[1] and if I were the one who made or advanced them, you might laugh at me and say that on account of my relationship to him my works in words run away and won't stay where they are put. But now—well, the statements are yours, so some other jest is demanded; for they stay fixed, as you yourself see.

E. I think the jest does very well as it is; for I am not the one who makes these statements move about and not stay in the same place, but you are the Daedalus; for they would have stayed, so far as I am concerned.

S. Apparently then, my friend, I am a more clever artist than Daedalus, inasmuch as he made only his own works move, whereas I, as it seems, give motion to the works of others as well as to my own. And the most exquisite thing about my art is that I am clever against my will; for I would rather have my words stay fixed and stable than possess the wisdom of Daedalus and the wealth of Tantalus besides. But enough of this. Since you seem to be indolent, I will aid you myself, so that you may instruct me about holiness. And do not give it up beforehand. Just see whether you do not think that everything that is holy is right.

E. I do.

S. But is everything that is right also holy? Or is all which is holy right, and not all which is right holy, but part of it holy and part something else?

E. I can't follow you, Socrates.

S. And yet you are as much younger than I as you are wiser; but, as I said, you are indolent on account of your wealth of wisdom. But exert yourself, my friend; for it is not hard to understand what I mean. What I mean is the opposite of what the poet said, who wrote: "Zeus the creator, him who made all things, thou wilt not name; for where fear is, there also is reverence." Now I disagree with the poet. Shall I tell you how?

E. By all means.

S. It does not seem to me true that where fear is, there also is reverence; for many who fear diseases and poverty and other such things seem to me to fear, but not to reverence at all these things which they fear. Don't you think so, too?

E. Certainly.

S. But I think that where reverence is, there also is fear; for does not everyone who has a feeling of reverence and shame about any act also dread and fear the reputation for wickedness?

E. Yes, he does fear.

S. Then it is not correct to say "where fear is, there also is reverence." On the contrary, where reverence is, there also is fear; but reverence is not everywhere where fear is, since, as I think, fear is more comprehensive than reverence; for reverence is a part of fear, just as the odd is a part of number, so that it is not true that where number is, there also is the odd, but that where the odd is, there also is number. Perhaps you follow me now?

E. Perfectly.

S. It was something of this sort that I meant before, when I asked whether where the right is, there also is holiness, or where holiness is, there also is the right; but holiness is not everywhere where the right is, for holiness is a part of the right. Do we agree to this, or do you dissent?

E. No, I agree; for I think the statement is correct.

S. Now observe the next point. If holiness is a part of the right, we must, apparently, find out what part of the right holiness is. Now if you asked me about one of the things I just mentioned, as, for example, what part of number the even was, and what kind of a number it was, I should say, "that which is not indivisible by two, but divisible by two"; or don't you agree?

E. I agree.

S. Now try in your turn to teach me what part of the right holiness is, that I may tell Meletus not to wrong me anymore or bring suits against me for impiety, since I have now been duly instructed by you about what is, and what is not, pious and holy. [. . .]

## Note

1. Tr.: Socrates was the son of a sculptor and was himself educated to be a sculptor. This is doubtless the reason for his reference to Daedalus as an ancestor. Daedalus was a half mythical personage whose statues were said to have been so lifelike that they moved their eyes and walked about.

## Study Questions

1. Do you think that Euthyphro's father acted wrongly in the death of his servant? If so, do you think that Euthyphro is acting rightly or wrongly in bringing charges against his father?
2. Outline the several ways in which Euthyphro fails in his attempts to define what is holy and unholy, pious and impious?
3. How does Socrates suggest concepts be properly defined?
4. What is your response to Socrates' question, "Is that which is holy [good] loved by the gods because it is holy [good], or is it holy [good] because it is loved by the gods?"?

# ~ MORAL FOUNDATIONS ~

## Aristotle

Aristotle (384–322 BCE) was born in the northern Greek city of Stagira; his father was physician to King Amyntas III of Macedonia. At age 17, Aristotle went to Athens to study at Plato's Academy. Aristotle left Athens after Plato's death and studied natural history in Mysea and Lesbos before becoming tutor to King Philip II of Macedonia's son Alexander—later Alexander the Great—in Pella. After Alexander became king, Aristotle returned to Athens and opened his own school at the Lyceum. *The Nicomachean Ethics* discusses what is the best kind of life for a human being to live.

# From *The Nicomachean Ethics*

## Book 1

[. . .]

2. If [. . .] among the ends at which our actions aim there be one which we wish for its own sake, while we wish the others only for the sake of this, and if we do not choose everything for the sake of something else (which would obviously result in a process ad infinitum, so that all desire would be futile and vain), it is clear that this one ultimate End must be the Good, and indeed the Supreme Good. Will not then a knowledge of this Supreme Good be also of great practical importance for the conduct of life? Will it not better enable us to attain what is fitting, like archers having a target to aim at? If this be so, we ought to make an attempt to determine [. . .] what exactly this Supreme Good is, and of which of the theoretical or practical sciences it is the object. [. . .]

4. [. . .] [I]nasmuch as all studies and undertakings are directed to the attainment of some good, let us discuss what it is that we pronounce to be the aim of Politics, that is, what is the highest of all the goods that action can achieve. As far as the name goes, we may almost say that the great majority of mankind are agreed about this; for both the multitude and persons of refinement speak of it as Happiness,[1] and conceive "the good life" or "doing well" to be the same thing as "being happy." But what constitutes happiness is a matter of dispute; and the popular account of it is not the same as that given by the philosophers. Ordinary people identify it with some obvious and visible good, such as pleasure or wealth or honour—some say one thing and some another, indeed very often the same man says different things at different times: when he falls sick he thinks health is happiness, when he is poor, wealth. At other times, feeling conscious of their own ignorance, men admire those who propound something grand and above their heads; and it has been held by some thinkers, viz., Plato and the Academy, that beside the many good things we have mentioned, there exists another Good, that is good in itself, and stands to all those goods as the cause of their being good.

Now perhaps it would be a somewhat fruitless task to review all the different opinions that are held. It will suffice to examine those that are most widely prevalent, or that seem to have some argument in their favour. [. . .]

5. [. . .] To judge from men's lives, the more or less reasoned conceptions of the Good or Happiness that seem to prevail among them are the following. On the one hand the generality of men and the most vulgar identify the Good with pleasure, and accordingly are content with the Life of Enjoyment—for there are three specially prominent Lives, the one just mentioned, the Life of Politics, and thirdly, the Life of Contemplation. The generality of mankind then show themselves to be utterly slavish,

by preferring what is only a life for cattle; but they get a hearing for their view as reasonable because many persons of high position share the feelings of Sardanapallus.[2]

Men of refinement, on the other hand, and men of action think that the Good is honour—for this may be said to be the end of the Life of Politics. But honour after all seems too superficial to be the Good for which we are seeking; since it appears to depend on those who confer it more than on him upon whom it is conferred, whereas we instinctively feel that the Good must be something proper to its possessor and not easy to be taken away from him. Moreover men's motive in pursuing honour seems to be to assure themselves of their own merit; at least they seek to be honoured by men of judgment and by people who know them, that is, they desire to be honoured on the ground of virtue. It is clear therefore that in the opinion [. . .] of men of action, virtue is a greater good than honour; and one might perhaps accordingly suppose that virtue rather than honour is the end of the Political Life. But even virtue proves on examination to be too incomplete to be the End; since it appears possible to possess it while you are asleep, or without putting it into practice throughout the whole of your life; and also for the virtuous man to suffer the greatest misery and misfortune—though no one would pronounce a man living a life of misery to be happy, unless for the sake of maintaining a paradox. [. . .]

The third type of life is the Life of Contemplation, which we shall consider in the sequel.

6. [. . .] Now there do appear to be several ends at which our actions aim; but as we choose some of them—for instance wealth, or flutes, and instruments generally—as a means to something else, it is clear that not all of them are final ends; whereas the Supreme Good seems to be something final. Consequently if there be some one thing which alone is a final end, this thing—or if there be several final ends, the one among them which is the most final—will be the Good which we are seeking. In speaking of degrees of finality, we mean that a thing pursued as an end in itself is more final than one pursued as a means to something else, and that a

thing never chosen as a means to anything else is more final than things chosen both as ends in themselves and as means to that thing; and accordingly a thing chosen always as an end and never as a means we call absolutely final. Now happiness above all else appears to be absolutely final in this sense, since we always choose it for its own sake and never as a means to something else; whereas honour, pleasure, intelligence, and excellence in its various forms, we choose indeed for their own sakes (since we should be glad to have each of them although no extraneous advantage resulted from it), but we also choose them for the sake of happiness, in the belief that they will be a means to our securing it. But no one chooses happiness for the sake of honour, pleasure, etc., nor as a means to anything whatever other than itself. [. . .]

To say however that the Supreme Good is happiness will probably appear a truism; we still require a more explicit account of what constitutes happiness. Perhaps then we may arrive at this by ascertaining what is man's function. For the goodness or efficiency of a flute-player or sculptor or craftsman of any sort, and in general of anybody who has some function or business to perform, is thought to reside in that function; and similarly it may be held that the good of man resides in the function of man, if he has a function.

Are we then to suppose that, while the carpenter and the shoemaker have definite functions or businesses belonging to them, man as such has none, and is not designed by nature to fulfill any function? Must we not rather assume that, just as the eye, the hand, the foot and each of the various members of the body manifestly has a certain function of its own, so a human being also has a certain function over and above all the functions of his particular members? What then precisely can this function be? The mere act of living appears to be shared even by plants, whereas we are looking for the function peculiar to man; we must therefore set aside the vital activity of nutrition and growth. Next in the scale will come some form of sentient life; but this too appears to be shared by horses, oxen, and animals generally. There remains therefore what may be called the practical[3] life of the rational part of man. [. . .] Rational life again has two meanings; let us assume that we are here concerned with the active exercise[4] of the rational faculty, since this seems to be the more proper sense of the term. If then the function of man is the active exercise of the soul's faculties in conformity with rational principle, or at all events not in dissociation from rational principle, and if we acknowledge the function of an individual and of a good individual of the same class (for instance, a harpist and a good harpist, and so generally with all classes) to be generically the same, the qualification of the latter's superiority in excellence being added to the function in his case (I mean that if the function of a harpist is to play the harp, that of a good harpist is to play the harp well): if this is so, and if we declare that the function of man is a certain form of life, and define that form of life as the exercise of the soul's faculties and activities in association with rational principle, and say that the function of a good man is to perform these activities well and rightly, and if a function is well performed when it is performed in accordance with its own proper excellence—from these premises it follows that the Good of man is the active exercise of his soul's faculties in conformity with excellence or virtue, or if there be several human excellences or virtues, in conformity with the best and most perfect among them. Moreover this activity must occupy a complete lifetime; for one swallow does not make spring, nor does one fine day; and similarly one day or a brief period of happiness does not make a man supremely blessed and happy.

## Book 2

1. [. . .] [M]oral or ethical virtue is the product of habit (*ethos*), and has indeed derived its name (*ethos* for "character"), with a slight variation of form, from that word. And therefore it is clear that none of the moral virtues is engendered in us by nature, for no natural property can be altered by habit. For instance, it is the nature of a stone to move downwards, and it cannot be trained to move upwards, even though you should try to train it to do so by throwing it up into the air ten thousand times; nor can fire be trained to move downwards, nor can anything else that naturally behaves in one way be trained into a habit of behaving in another way. The virtues therefore are engendered in us neither by nature nor yet in violation of nature; nature gives us the capacity to receive them, and this capacity is brought to maturity by habit.

Moreover, the faculties given us by nature are bestowed on us first in a potential form; we exhibit their actual exercise afterwards. This is clearly so with our senses: we did not acquire the faculty of sight or hearing by repeatedly seeing or repeatedly listening, but the other way about—because we had the senses we began to use them, we did not get them by using them. The virtues on the other hand we acquire by first having actually practised them, just as we do the arts. We learn an art or craft by doing the things that we shall have to do when we have learnt it: for instance, men become builders by building houses, harpists by playing on the harp. Similarly we become just by doing just acts, temperate by doing temperate acts, brave by doing brave acts. [. . .] Again, the actions from or through which any virtue is produced are the same as those through which it also is destroyed—just as is the case with skill in the arts, for both the good harpists and the bad ones are produced by harping, and similarly with builders and all the other craftsmen: as you will become a good builder from building well, so you will become a bad one from building badly. Were this not so, there would be no need for teachers of the arts, but everybody would be born a good or bad craftsman as the case might be. The same then is true of the virtues. It is by taking part in transactions with our fellow-men that some of us become just and others unjust; by acting in dangerous situations and forming a habit of fear or of confidence we become courageous or cowardly. And the same holds good of our dispositions with regard to the appetites, and anger; some men become temperate and gentle, others profligate and irascible, by actually comporting themselves in one way or the other in relation to those passions. In a word, our moral dispositions are formed as a result of the corresponding activities. Hence it is incumbent on us to control the character of our activities, since on the quality of these depends the quality of our dispositions. It is therefore not of small moment whether we are trained from childhood in one set of habits or another; on the contrary it is of very great, or rather of supreme, importance. [. . .]

4. A difficulty may however be raised as to what we mean by saying that in order to become just men must do just actions, and in order to become temperate they must do temperate actions. For if they do just and temperate actions, they are just and temperate already, just as, if they spell correctly or play in tune, they are scholars or musicians.

But perhaps this is not the case even with the arts. It is possible to spell a word correctly by chance, or because someone else prompts you; hence you will be a scholar only if you spell correctly in the scholar's way, that is, in virtue of the scholarly knowledge which you yourself possess.

Moreover the case of the arts is not really analogous to that of the virtues. Works of art have their merit in themselves, so that it is enough if they are produced having a certain quality of their own; but acts done in conformity with the virtues are not done justly or temperately if they themselves are of a certain sort, but only if the agent also is in a certain state of mind when he does them: first he must act with knowledge; secondly he must deliberately choose the act, and choose it for its own sake; and thirdly the act must spring from a fixed and permanent disposition of character. For the possession of an art, none of these conditions is included, except the mere qualification of knowledge; but for the possession of the virtues, knowledge is of little or no avail, whereas the other conditions, so far from being of little moment, are all-important, inasmuch as virtue results from the repeated performance of just and temperate actions. Thus although actions are entitled just and temperate when they are such acts as just and temperate men would do, the agent is just and temperate not when he does these acts merely, but when he does them in the way in which just and temperate men do them. It is correct therefore to say that a man

becomes just by doing just actions and temperate by doing temperate actions; and no one can have the remotest chance of becoming good without doing them. But the mass of mankind, instead of doing virtuous acts, have recourse to discussing virtue, and fancy that they are pursuing philosophy and that this will make them good men. In so doing they act like invalids who listen carefully to what the doctor says, but entirely neglect to carry out his prescriptions. That sort of philosophy will no more lead to a healthy state of soul than will the mode of treatment produce health of body.

5. We have next to consider the formal definition of virtue.

A state of the soul is either (l) an emotion, (2) a capacity, or (3) a disposition; virtue therefore must be one of these three things. By the emotions, I mean desire, anger, fear, confidence, envy, joy, friendship, hatred, longing, jealousy, pity; and generally those states of consciousness which are accompanied by pleasure or pain. The capacities are the faculties in virtue of which we can be said to be liable to the emotions, for example, capable of feeling anger or fear or pity. The dispositions are the formed states of character in virtue of which we are well or ill disposed in respect of the emotions; for instance, we have a bad disposition in regard to anger if we are disposed to get angry too violently or not violently enough, a good disposition if we habitually feel a moderate amount of anger; and similarly in respect of the other emotions.

Now the virtues and vices are not emotions because we are not pronounced good or bad according to our emotions, but we are according to our virtues and vices; nor are we either praised or blamed for our emotions—a man is not praised for being frightened or angry, nor is he blamed for being angry merely, but for being angry in a certain way—but we are praised or blamed for our virtues and vices. Again, we are not angry or afraid from choice, but the virtues are certain modes of choice, or at all events involve choice. Moreover, we are said to be "moved" by the emotions, whereas in respect of the virtues and vices we are not said to be "moved" but to be "disposed" in a certain way.

And the same considerations also prove that the virtues and vices are not capacities; since we are not pronounced good or bad, praised or blamed, merely by reason of our capacity for emotion. Again, we possess certain capacities by nature, but we are not born good or bad by nature: of this however we spoke before.

If then the virtues are neither emotions nor capacities, it remains that they are dispositions.

Thus we have stated what virtue is generically.

6. But it is not enough merely to define virtue generically as a disposition; we must also say what species of disposition it is. It must then be premised that all excellence has a twofold effect on the thing to which it belongs: it not only renders the thing itself good, but it also causes it to perform its function well. For example, the effect of excellence in the eye is that the eye is good *and* functions well; since having good eyes means having good sight. Similarly excellence in a horse makes it a good horse, and also good at galloping, at carrying its rider, and at facing the enemy. If therefore this is true of all things, excellence or virtue in a man will be the disposition which renders him a good man and also which will cause him to perform his function well. We have already indicated what this means; but it will throw more light on the subject if we consider what constitutes the specific nature of virtue.

Now of everything that is continuous and divisible, it is possible to take the larger part, or the smaller part, or an equal part, and these parts may be larger, smaller, and equal either with respect to the thing itself or relatively to us; the equal part being a mean between excess and deficiency. By the mean of the thing I denote a point equally distant from either extreme, which is one and the same for everybody; by the mean relative to us, that amount which is neither too much nor too little, and this is not one and the same for everybody. For example, let 10 be many and 2 few; then one takes the mean with respect to the thing if one takes 6; since $6 - 2 = 10 - 6$, and this is the mean according to arithmetical proportion. But we cannot arrive by this method at the mean relative to us. Suppose that 10 lb. of food is a large ration for anybody and 2 lb. a small

one: it does not follow that a trainer will prescribe 6 lb., for perhaps even this will be a large ration, or a small one, for the particular athlete who is to receive it; it is a small ration for a Milo [a famous wrestler], but a large one for a man just beginning to go in for athletics. And similarly with the amount of running or wrestling exercise to be taken. In the same way then an expert in any art avoids excess and deficiency, and seeks and adopts the mean—the mean, that is, not of the thing but relative to us. If therefore the way in which every art or science performs its work well is by looking to the mean and applying that as a standard to its productions (hence the common remark about a perfect work of art, that you could not take from it nor add to it—meaning that excess and deficiency destroy perfection, while adherence to the mean preserves it)—if then, as we say, good craftsmen look to the mean as they work, and if virtue, like nature, is more accurate and better than any form of art, it will follow that virtue has the quality of hitting the mean. [. . .] For example, one can be frightened or bold, feel desire or anger or pity, and experience pleasure and pain in general, either too much or too little, and in both cases wrongly; whereas to feel these feelings at the right time, on the right occasion, towards the right people, for the right purpose and in the right manner, is to feel the best amount of them, which is the mean amount—and the best amount is of course the mark of virtue. And similarly there can be excess, deficiency, and the due mean in actions. Now feelings and actions are the objects with which virtue is concerned; and in feelings and actions excess and deficiency are errors, while the mean amount is praised, and constitutes success; and to be praised and to be successful are both marks of virtue. [. . .]

Virtue then is a settled disposition of the mind determining the choice of actions and emotions, consisting essentially in the observance of the mean relative to us, this being determined by principle, that is, as the prudent man would determine it.

And it is a mean state between two vices, one of excess and one of defect. Furthermore, it is a mean state in that whereas the vices either fall short of or exceed what is right in feelings and in actions, virtue ascertains and adopts the mean. Hence while in respect of its substance and the definition that states what it really is in essence virtue is the observance of the mean, in point of excellence and rightness it is an extreme. [. . .]

9. Enough has now been said to show that moral virtue is a mean, and in what sense this is so, namely that it is a mean between two vices, one of excess and the other of defect; and that it is such a mean because it aims at hitting the middle point in feelings and in actions. This is why it is a hard task to be good, for it is hard to find the middle point in anything: for instance, not everybody can find the centre of a circle, but only someone who knows geometry. So also anybody can become angry—that is easy, and so it is to give and spend money; but to be angry with or give money to the right person, and to the right amount, and at the right time, and for the right purpose, and in the right way—this is not within everybody's power and is not easy; so that to do these things properly is rare, praiseworthy, and noble.

Hence the first rule in aiming at the mean is to avoid that extreme which is the more opposed to the mean, as Calypso advises (*Od.* xii, 219)[5]—

Steer the ship clear of yonder spray and surge.

For of the two extremes one is a more serious error than the other. Hence, inasmuch as to hit the mean extremely well is difficult, the second best way to sail,[6] as the saying goes, is to take the least of the evils; and the best way to do this will be the way we enjoin.

The second rule is to notice what are the errors to which we are ourselves most prone (as different men are inclined by nature to different faults)—and we shall discover what these are by observing the pleasure or pain that we experience—; then we must drag ourselves away in the opposite direction, for by steering wide of our besetting error we shall make a middle course. This is the method adopted by carpenters to straighten warped timber.

Thirdly, we must in everything be most of all on our guard against what is pleasant and against pleasure; for when pleasure is on her trial we are not impartial judges. The right course is therefore to feel towards pleasure as the elders of the people felt towards Helen (*Iliad* iii, 156–160), and to apply their words to her on every occasion; for if we roundly bid her be gone, we shall be less likely to err.

These then, to sum up the matter, are the precautions that will best enable us to hit the mean. [. . .]

## Book 10

[. . .]

7. But if happiness consists in activity in accordance with virtue, it is reasonable that it should be activity in accordance with the highest virtue; and this will be the virtue of the best part of us. Whether then this be the intellect, or whatever else it be that is thought to rule and lead us by nature, and to have cognizance of what is noble and divine, either as being itself also actually divine, or as being relatively the divinest part of us, it is the activity of this part of us in accordance with the virtue proper to it that will constitute perfect happiness; and [. . .] this activity is the activity of contemplation.

And that happiness consists in contemplation may be accepted as agreeing both with the results already reached and with the truth. For contemplation is at once the highest form of activity (since the intellect is the highest thing in us, and the objects with which the intellect deals are the highest things that can be known). [. . .] Also the activity of contemplation may be held to be the only activity that is loved for its own sake: it produces no result beyond the actual act of contemplation, whereas from practical pursuits we look to secure some advantage, greater or smaller, beyond the action itself. [. . .]

Such a life as this however will be higher than the human level: not in virtue of his humanity will a man achieve it, but in virtue of something within him that is divine; and by as much as this something is superior to his composite nature, by so much is its activity superior to the exercise of the other forms of virtue. If then the intellect is something divine in comparison with man, so is the life of the intellect divine in comparison with human life. Nor ought we to obey those who enjoin that a man should have man's thoughts and a mortal the thoughts of mortality, but we ought so far as possible to achieve immortality, and do all that man may to live in accordance with the highest thing in him; for though this be small in bulk, in power and value it far surpasses all the rest.

It may even be held that this is the true self of each, inasmuch as it is the dominant and better part; and therefore it would be a strange thing if a man should choose to live not his own life but the life of some other than himself.

Moreover what was said before will apply here also: that which is best and most pleasant for each creature is that which is proper to the nature of each; accordingly the life of the intellect is the best and the pleasantest life for man, inasmuch as the intellect more than anything else is man; therefore this life will be the happiest.

8. The life of moral virtue, on the other hand, is happy only in a secondary degree. For the moral activities are purely human: Justice, I mean, Courage and the other virtues we display in our intercourse with our fellows, when we observe what is due to each in contracts and services and in our various actions, and in our emotions also; and all of these things seem to be purely human affairs. And some moral actions are thought to be the outcome of the physical constitution, and moral virtue is thought to have a close affinity in many respects with the passions. Moreover, Prudence is intimately connected with Moral Virtue, and this with Prudence, inasmuch as the first principles which Prudence employs are determined by the Moral Virtues, and the right standard for the Moral Virtues is determined by Prudence. But these being also connected with the passions are related to our composite nature; now the virtues of our composite nature are purely human; so therefore also is the life that manifests these virtues, and the happiness that belongs to it. Whereas the happiness that belongs to the intellect is separate [. . .].[7] And such happiness would appear to need but little external equipment, or less than the happiness based on moral virtue. Both, it may be granted, require the mere necessaries of life, and that in an equal degree (though the politician does as a matter of fact take more trouble about bodily requirements and so forth than the philosopher); for in this respect there may be little difference between them. But for the purpose of their special activities their requirements will differ widely. The liberal man will need wealth in order to do liberal actions, and so indeed will the just man in order to discharge his obligations (since mere intentions are invisible, and even the unjust pretend to wish to act justly); and the brave man will need strength if he is to perform any action displaying his virtue; and the temperate man opportunity for indulgence: otherwise how can he, or the possessor of any other virtue, show that he is virtuous? [. . .] But the student, so far as the pursuit of his activity is concerned, needs no external apparatus: on the contrary, worldly goods may almost be said to be a hindrance to contemplation; though it is true that, being a man and living in the society of others, he chooses to engage in virtuous action, and so will need external goods to carry on his life as a human being. [. . .]

## Notes

1. Tr.: This translation of *eudaimonia* can hardly be avoided, but it would perhaps be more accurately rendered by "Well-being" or "Prosperity"; and it will be found that the writer does not interpret it as a state of feeling but as a kind of activity.

2. Tr.: Sardanapallus was a mythical Assyrian king; two versions of his epitaph are recorded by Athenaeus, one containing the words "Eat, drink, play, since all else is not worth that snap of the fingers"; the other ends "I have what I ate; and the delightful deeds of wantonness and love which I did and suffered; whereas all my wealth is vanished."

3. Tr.: "Practice" for Aristotle denotes purposeful conduct, of which only rational beings are capable.

4. Tr.: In contrast with the mere state of possessing the faculty.
5. Tr.: Really the words are said by Odysseus, conveying to his steersman Circe's advice, to avoid the whirlpool of Charybdis which will engulf them all, and steer nearer to the monster Scylla who will devour only some of them.
6. Tr.: A proverb, meaning to take to the oars when the wind fails.
7. Tr.: In *De anima* III.5, Aristotle distinguishes the active from the passive intellect, and pronounces the former to be "separate or separable (from matter, or the body), unmixed and impassible."

## Works Cited

Homer. *The Odyssey*. Trans. Samuel Butler. London: Longmans, Green, and Co., 1900.

Homer. *The Iliad*. Trans. A.T. Murray. Cambridge, MA: Harvard University Press and London: William Heinemann, 1924.

## Study Questions

1. Provide an example of an action you do for its own sake and an example of an action you do for the sake of other ends.
2. According to Aristotle, what are three prevailing conceptions of the "good life," what "good" is specific to each, and which of these is truly a happy life?
3. What three kinds of "states of the soul" does Aristotle identify, and which of these is virtue?
4. Aristotle tells us that "the mark of virtue" is to feel or act "at the right time, on the right occasion, toward the right people, for the right purpose and in the right manner." Can you give an example that illustrates what he means?

# Immanuel Kant

Immanuel Kant (1724–1804) rejected the moral sentimentalism of his Scottish empiricist contemporaries (e.g., Hume): for Kant, actions motivated by feelings have no moral worth. Kant held that the highest principle of practical philosophy is the moral law, which depends only on the nature of reason. By means of our (human) capacity for reason, we discover what the moral law requires of us. Also called *Groundwork of the Metaphysic of Morals*, this is Kant's foundational work on morality.

# From *Fundamental Principles of the Metaphysic of Ethics*

## First Section. Transition from the Common Rational Knowledge of Morality to the Philosophical

Nothing can possibly be conceived in the world, or even out of it, which can be called good without qualification except a Good Will. Intelligence, wit, judgment, and the other *talents* of the mind, however they may be named, or courage, resolution, perseverance, as qualities of temperament, are undoubtedly good and desirable in many respects; but these gifts of nature may also become extremely bad and mischievous if the will which is to make use of them, and which, therefore, constitutes what is called *character*, is not good. It is the same with the *gifts of fortune*. Power, riches, honour, even health and the general well-being and contentment with one's condition which is called *happiness*, inspire pride and often presumption if there is not a good will to correct the influence of these on the mind, and with this also to rectify the whole principle of acting and adapt it to its end. The sight of a being who is not adorned with a single feature of a pure and good will enjoying unbroken prosperity can never give pleasure to an impartial rational spectator. Thus a good will appears to constitute the indispensable condition even of being worthy of happiness.

There are even some qualities which are of service to this good will itself and may facilitate its action, yet which have no intrinsic unconditional value but always presuppose a good will, and this qualifies the esteem that we justly have for them and does not permit us to regard them as absolutely good. Moderation in the affections and passions, self-control, and calm deliberation are not only good in many respects but even seem to constitute part of the intrinsic worth of the person; but they are far from deserving to be called good without qualification, although they have been so unconditionally praised by the ancients. For without the principles of a good will, they may become extremely bad, and the coolness of a villain not only makes him far more dangerous but also directly makes him more abominable in our eyes than he would have been without it.

A good will is good not because of what it performs or effects, not by its aptness for the attainment of some proposed end, but simply by virtue of the volition—that is, it is good in itself, and considered by itself is to be esteemed much higher than all that can be brought about by it in favour of any inclination, nay, even of the sum-total of all inclinations. Even if it should happen that owing to special disfavour of fortune or the niggardly provision of a step-motherly nature, this will should wholly lack power to accomplish its purpose, if with its greatest efforts it should yet achieve nothing and

there should remain only the good will (not, to be sure, a mere wish, but the summoning of all means in our power), then, like a jewel, it would still shine by its own light, as a thing which has its whole value in itself. [. . .]

We have then to develop the notion of a will which deserves to be highly esteemed for itself and is good without a view to anything further, a notion which exists already in the sound natural understanding requiring rather to be cleared up than to be taught, and which in estimating the value of our actions always takes the first place and constitutes the condition of all the rest. In order to do this we will take the notion of duty, which includes that of a good will, although implying certain subjective restrictions and hindrances. These, however, far from concealing it or rendering it unrecognizable, rather bring it out by contrast and make it shine forth so much the brighter. [. . .]

[I]t is a duty to maintain one's life; and, in addition, everyone has also a direct inclination to do so. But on this account the often anxious care which most men take for it has no intrinsic worth, and their maxim has no moral import. They preserve their life *as duty requires*, no doubt, but not *because duty requires*. On the other hand, if adversity and hopeless sorrow have completely taken away the relish for life, if the unfortunate one, strong in mind, indignant at his fate rather than desponding or dejected, wishes for death, and yet preserves his life without loving it—not from inclination or fear but from duty—then his maxim has a moral worth.

To be beneficent when we can is a duty; and besides this, there are many minds so sympathetically constituted that, without any other motive of vanity or self-interest, they find a pleasure in spreading joy around them and can take delight in the satisfaction of others so far as it is their own work. But I maintain that in such a case an action of this kind, however proper, however amiable it may be, has nevertheless no true moral worth, [. . .] deserv[ing] praise and encouragement but not esteem. For the maxim lacks the moral import, namely, that such actions be done *from duty*, not from inclination. Put the case that the mind of that philanthropist were clouded by sorrow of his own, extinguishing all sympathy with the lot of others, and that while he still has the power to benefit others in distress, he is not touched by their trouble because he is absorbed with his own; and now suppose that he tears himself out of this dead insensibility and performs the action without any inclination to it but simply from duty, then first has his action its genuine moral worth. Further still, if nature has put little sympathy in the heart of this or that man; if he, supposed to be an upright man, is by temperament cold and indifferent to the sufferings of others, perhaps because in respect of his own he is provided with the special gift of patience and fortitude, and supposes, or even requires, that others should have the same—and such a man would certainly not be the meanest product of nature; but if nature had not specially framed him for a philanthropist, would he not still find in himself a source from whence to give himself a far higher worth than that of a good-natured temperament could be? Unquestionably. It is just in this that the moral worth of the character is brought out which is incomparably the highest of all, namely, that he is beneficent not from inclination but from duty. [. . .]

The second[1] proposition is: That an action done from duty derives its moral worth *not from the purpose* which is to be attained by it but from the maxim by which it is determined, and therefore does not depend on the realization of the object of the action but merely on the *principle of volition* by which the action has taken place without regard to any object of desire. It is clear from what precedes that the purposes which we may have in view in our actions, or their effects regarded as ends and springs of the will, cannot give to actions any unconditional or moral worth. In what, then, can their worth lie if it is not to consist in the will and in reference to its expected effect? It cannot lie anywhere but in the *principle of the will* without regard to the ends which can be attained by the action. For the will stands between its a priori principle, which is formal, and its a posteriori spring, which is material, as between two roads, and as it must be determined by something, it follows that it must be determined by the formal principle of volition when an action is done from duty, in which case every material principle has been withdrawn from it.

The third proposition, which is a consequence of the two preceding, I would express thus: *Duty is the necessity of acting from respect for the law.* I may have *inclination* for an object as the effect of my proposed action but I cannot have *respect* for it, just for this reason, that it is an effect and not an energy of will. Similarly, I cannot have respect for inclination, whether my own or another's; I can at most, if my own, approve it; if another's, sometimes even love it, i.e., look on it as favourable to my own interest. It is only what is connected with my will as a principle, by no means as an effect—what does not subserve my inclination but overpowers it, or at least in case of choice excludes it from its calculation—in other words, simply the law of itself, which can be an object of respect and hence a command. Now an action done from duty must wholly exclude the influence of inclination and, with it, every object of the will, so that nothing remains which can determine the will except objectively the *law* and subjectively *pure respect* for this practical law, and consequently the maxim that I should follow this law even to the thwarting of all my inclinations.

Thus the moral worth of an action does not lie in the effect expected from it, nor in any principle of action which requires to borrow its motive from this expected effect. For all these effects—agreeableness of one's condition and even the promotion of the happiness of others—could have been also brought about by other causes, so that for this there would have been no need of the will of a rational being, whereas it is in this alone that the supreme and unconditional good can be found. The preeminent good which we call moral can therefore consist in nothing else than *the conception of law* in itself, *which certainly is only possible in a rational being* insofar as this conception, and not the expected effect, determines the will. This is a good which is already present in the person who acts accordingly, and we have not to wait for it to appear first in the result. [. . .]

## Second Section. Transition from Popular Moral Philosophy to the Metaphysic of Morals

[. . .]

The conception of an objective principle, insofar as it is obligatory for a will, is called a command (of reason), and the formula of the command is called an Imperative. [. . .]

Now all *imperatives* command either *hypothetically* or *categorically*. The former represent the practical necessity of a possible action as means to something else that is willed (or at least which one might possibly will). The categorical imperative would be that which represented an action as necessary of itself without reference to another end, i.e., as objectively necessary. [. . .]

We will first inquire whether the mere conception of a categorical imperative may not perhaps supply us also with the formula of it, containing the proposition which alone can be a categorical imperative. [. . .]

When I conceive a hypothetical imperative, in general I do not know beforehand what it will contain until I am given the condition. But when I conceive a categorical imperative, I know at once what it contains. For as the imperative contains besides the law only the necessity that the maxims shall conform to this law, while the law contains no conditions restricting it, there remains nothing but the general statement that the maxim of the action should conform to a universal law, and it is this conformity alone that the imperative properly represents as necessary.

There is therefore but one categorical imperative, namely this: *Act only on that maxim whereby thou canst at the same time will that it should become a universal law.*

Now if all imperatives of duty can be deduced from this one imperative as from their principle, then, although it should remain undecided whether what is called duty is not merely a vain notion, yet at least we shall be able to show what we understand by it and what this notion means.

Since the universality of the law according to which effects are produced constitutes what is properly called *nature* in the most general sense (as to form), that is, the existence of things so far as it is determined by general laws, that imperative of duty may be expressed thus: *Act as if the maxim of thy action were to become by thy will a Universal Law of Nature.*

We will now enumerate a few duties, adopting the usual division of them into duties to ourselves and to others, and into perfect and imperfect duties.[2]

1. A man reduced to despair by a series of misfortunes feels wearied of life, but is still so far in possession of his reason that he can ask himself whether it would not be contrary to his duty to himself to take his own life. Now he inquires whether the maxim of his action could become a universal law of nature. His maxim is: From self-love I adopt it as a principle to shorten my life when its longer duration is likely to bring more evil than satisfaction. It is asked then simply whether this principle founded on self-love can become a universal law of nature. Now we see at once that a system of nature of which it should be a law to destroy life by means of the very feeling whose special nature it is to impel to the improvement of life would contradict itself, and therefore could not exist as a system of nature; hence that maxim cannot possibly exist as a universal law of nature, and consequently would be wholly inconsistent with the supreme principle of all duty.

2. Another finds himself forced by necessity to borrow money. He knows that he will not be able to repay it, but sees also that nothing will be lent to him unless he promises stoutly to repay it in a definite time. He desires to make this promise, but he has still so much conscience as to ask himself: Is it not unlawful and inconsistent with duty to get out of a difficulty in this way? Suppose, however, that he resolves to do so, then the maxim of his action would be expressed thus: When I think myself in want of money, I will borrow money and promise to repay it, although I know that I never can do so. Now this principle

of self-love or of one's own advantage may perhaps be consistent with my whole future welfare; but the question now is, is it right? I change then the suggestion of self-love into a universal law, and state the question thus: How would it be if my maxim were a universal law? Then I see at once that it could never hold as a universal law of nature but would necessarily contradict itself. For supposing it to be a universal law that everyone when he thinks himself in a difficulty should be able to promise whatever he pleases with the purpose of not keeping his promise, the promise itself would become impossible, as well as the end that one might have in view in it, since no one would consider that anything was promised to him but would ridicule all such statements as vain pretences.

3. A third finds in himself a talent which with the help of some culture might make him a useful man in many respects. But he finds himself in comfortable circumstances, and prefers to indulge in pleasure rather than to take pains in enlarging and improving his happy natural capacities. He asks, however, whether his maxim of neglect of his natural gifts, besides agreeing with his inclination to indulgence, agrees also with what is called duty. He sees then that a system of nature could indeed subsist with such a universal law, although men (like the South Sea islanders) should let their talents rust and resolve to devote their lives merely to idleness, amusement, and propagation of their species—in a word, to enjoyment; but he cannot possibly *will* that this should be a universal law of nature, or be implanted in us as such by a natural instinct. For, as a rational being, he necessarily wills that his faculties be developed, since they serve him, and have been given him, for all sorts of possible purposes.

4. A fourth, who is in prosperity, while he sees that others have to contend with great wretchedness and that he could help them, thinks: What concern is it of mine? Let everyone be as happy as heaven pleases, or as he can make himself; I will take nothing from him nor even envy him, only I do not wish to contribute anything to his welfare or to his assistance in distress! Now no doubt if

such a mode of thinking were a universal law, the human race might very well subsist, and doubtless even better than in a state in which everyone talks of sympathy and good-will, or even takes care occasionally to put it into practice, but, on the other side, also cheats when he can, betrays the rights of men, or otherwise violates them. But although it is possible that a universal law of nature might exist in accordance with that maxim, it is impossible to *will* that such a principle should have the universal validity of a law of nature. For a will which resolved this would contradict itself inasmuch as many cases might occur in which one would have need of the love and sympathy of others, and in which, by such a law of nature sprung from his own will, he would deprive himself of all hope of the aid he desires.

These are a few of the many actual duties, or at least what we regard as such, which obviously fall into two classes on the one principle that we have laid down. We must be *able to will* that a maxim of our action should be a universal law. This is the canon of the moral appreciation of the action generally. Some actions are of such a character that their maxim cannot without contradiction be even *conceived* as a universal law of nature, far from it being possible that we should *will* that it *should* be so. In others this intrinsic impossibility is not found, but still it is impossible to *will* that their maxim should be raised to the universality of a law of nature, since such a will would contradict itself. It is easily seen that the former violate strict or rigorous (inflexible) duty, the latter only laxer (meritorious) duty. Thus it has been completely shown by these examples how all duties depend as regards the nature of the obligation (not the object of the action) on the same principle. [. . .]

The question then is this: Is it a necessary law *for all rational beings* that they should always judge of their actions by maxims of which they can themselves will that they should serve as universal laws? If it is so, then it must be connected (altogether a priori) with the very conception of the will of a rational being generally. But in order to discover this connection we must, however reluctantly, take a step into metaphysic, although into a domain of it which is distinct from speculative philosophy, namely, the metaphysic of morals. [. . .]

The will is conceived as a faculty of determining oneself to action *in accordance with the conception of certain laws*. And such a faculty can be found only in rational beings. Now that which serves the will as the objective ground of its self-determination is the *end*, and if this is assigned by reason alone, it must hold for all rational beings. On the other hand, that which merely contains the ground of possibility of the action of which the effect is the end, this is called the *means*. The subjective ground of the desire is the *spring*; the objective ground of the volition is the motive: hence the distinction between subjective ends which rest on springs and objective ends which depend on motives valid for every rational being. Practical principles are *formal* when they abstract from all subjective ends; they are *material* when they assume these, and therefore particular springs of action. The ends which a rational being proposes to himself at pleasure as *effects* of his actions (material ends) are all only relative, for it is only their relation to the particular desires of the subject that gives them their worth, which therefore cannot furnish principles universal and necessary for all rational beings and for every volition, that is to say, practical laws. Hence all these relative ends can give rise only to hypothetical imperatives.

Supposing, however, that there were something *whose existence* has *in itself* an absolute worth, something which, being *an end in itself*, could be a source of definite laws, then in this and this alone would lie the source of a possible categorical imperative, i.e., a practical law.

Now I say: man and generally any rational being *exists* as an end in himself, *not merely as a means* to be arbitrarily used by this or that will, but in all his actions, whether they concern himself or other rational beings, must be always regarded at the same time as an end. All objects of the inclinations have only a conditional worth, for if the inclinations and the wants founded on them did not exist, then their object would be without value. But the inclinations themselves, being sources of

want, are so far from having an absolute worth for which they should be desired that, on the contrary, it must be the universal wish of every rational being to be wholly free from them. Thus the worth of any object which is *to be acquired* by our action is always conditional. Beings whose existence depends not on our will but on nature's have nevertheless, if they are irrational beings, only a relative value as means, and are therefore called *things*; rational beings, on the contrary, are called *persons* because their very nature points them out as ends in themselves, that is, as something which must not be used merely as means, and so far therefore restricts freedom of action (and is an object of respect). These, therefore, are not merely subjective ends, whose existence has a worth *for us* as an effect of our action, but *objective ends*, that is, things whose existence is an end in itself: an end, moreover, for which no other can be substituted which they should subserve *merely* as means, for otherwise nothing whatever would possess *absolute worth*; but if all worth were conditioned and therefore contingent, then there would be no supreme practical principle of reason whatever.

If then there is a supreme practical principle or, in respect of the human will, a categorical imperative, it must be one which, being drawn from the conception of that which is necessarily an end for everyone because it is *an end in itself*, constitutes an *objective* principle of will, and can therefore serve as a universal practical law. The foundation of this principle is: *rational nature exists as an end in itself*. Man necessarily conceives his own existence as being so: so far then this is a *subjective* principle of human actions. But every other rational being regards its existence similarly, just on the same rational principle that holds for me: so that it is at the same time an *objective* principle from which, as a supreme practical law, all laws of the will must be capable of being deduced. Accordingly the practical imperative will be as follows: *So act as to treat humanity, whether in thine own person or in that of any other, in every case as an end withal, never as means only.* We will now inquire whether this can be practically carried out.

To abide by the previous examples:

*Firstly*, under the head of necessary duty to oneself: he who contemplates suicide should ask himself whether his action can be consistent with the idea of humanity *as an end in itself*. If he destroys himself in order to escape from painful circumstances, he uses a person merely as *a mean* to maintain a tolerable condition up to the end of life. But a man is not a thing, that is to say, something which can be used merely as means, but must in all his actions be always considered as an end in himself. I cannot, therefore, dispose in any way of a man in my own person so as to mutilate him, to damage or kill him. [. . .]

*Secondly*, as regards necessary duties, or those of strict obligation, towards others: he who is thinking of making a lying promise to others will see at once that he would be using another man *merely as a mean*, without the latter containing at the same time the end in himself. For he whom I propose by such a promise to use for my own purposes cannot possibly assent to my mode of acting towards him, and therefore cannot himself contain the end of this action. This violation of the principle of humanity in other men is more obvious if we take in examples of attacks on the freedom and property of others. For then it is clear that he who transgresses the rights of men intends to use the person of others merely as means, without considering that as rational beings they ought always to be esteemed also as ends, that is, as beings who must be capable of containing in themselves the end of the very same action.

*Thirdly*, as regards contingent (meritorious) duties to oneself: it is not enough that the action does not violate humanity in our own person as an end in itself, it must also *harmonize with* it. Now there are in humanity capacities of greater perfection which belong to the end that nature has in view in regard to humanity in ourselves as the subject: to neglect these might perhaps be consistent with the *maintenance* of humanity as an end in itself, but not with the *advancement* of this end.

*Fourthly*, as regards meritorious duties towards others: the natural end which all men have is their own happiness. Now humanity might indeed subsist although no one should contribute anything to the happiness of others, provided he did not intentionally withdraw anything from it; but after all, this would only harmonize negatively, not positively, with *humanity as an end in itself* if everyone does not also endeavour, as far as in him lies, to forward the ends of others. For the ends of any subject which is an end in himself ought as far as possible to be *my* ends also, if that conception is to have its *full* effect with me.

This principle that humanity and generally every rational nature is *an end in itself* (which is the supreme limiting condition of every man's freedom of action) is not borrowed from experience: *firstly*, because it is universal, applying as it does to all rational beings whatever, and experience is not capable of determining anything about them; *secondly*, because it does not present humanity as an end to men (subjectively), that is as an object which men do of themselves actually adopt as an end, but as an objective end, which must as a law constitute the supreme limiting condition of all our subjective ends, let them be what we will; it must therefore spring from pure reason. In fact the objective principle of all practical legislation lies (according to the first principle) in *the rule* and its form of universality which makes it capable of being a law (say, e.g., a law of nature); but the *subjective* principle is in the *end*; now by the second principle, the subject of all ends is each rational being, inasmuch as it is an end in itself. Hence follows the third practical principle of the will, which is the ultimate condition of its harmony with the universal practical reason, viz., the idea of *the will of every rational being as a universally legislative will*.

On this principle all maxims are rejected which are inconsistent with the will being itself universal legislator. Thus the will is not subject simply to the law, but so subject that it must be regarded *as itself giving the law*, and on this ground only, subject to the law (of which it can regard itself as the author). [. . .]

I will therefore call this the principle of *Autonomy* of the will, in contrast with every other which I accordingly reckon as *Heteronomy*.

The conception of every rational being as one which must consider itself as giving in all the maxims of its will universal laws, so as to judge itself and its actions from this point of view—this conception leads to another which depends on it and is very fruitful, namely, that of *a kingdom of ends*.

By a *kingdom* I understand the union of different rational beings in a system by common laws. Now since it is by laws that ends are determined as regards their universal validity, hence, if we abstract from the personal differences of rational beings, and likewise from all the content of their private ends, we shall be able to conceive all ends combined in a systematic whole (including both rational beings as ends in themselves, and also the special ends which each may propose to himself), that is to say, we can conceive a kingdom of ends, which on the preceding principles is possible.

For all rational beings come under the *law* that each of them must treat itself and all others *never merely as a means*, but in every case *at the same time as ends in themselves*. Hence results a systematic union of rational beings by common objective laws, i.e., a kingdom which may be called a kingdom of ends, since what these laws have in view is just the relation of these beings to one another as ends and means. It is certainly only an ideal. [. . .]

## Notes

1. Tr: The first proposition was that to have moral worth an action must be done from duty.

2. I understand by a perfect duty one that admits no exception in favour of inclination.

## Study Questions

1. For Kant, what makes an action a good action, and what is good in itself?
2. Although Kant specifies that there is "but one categorical imperative," he characterizes it in three different ways in order to help us apply it in practice. Describe the three forms of the categorical imperative, and show how each applies by making reference to an example.
3. Kant's theory is a "deontological" theory, a term derived from Greek *deon*, which means "duty." Describe Kant's classification of duties into perfect vs. imperfect duties and duties to oneself vs. others, providing an example for each of the four classes.
4. On Kant's account, is a child a person? A fetus? A comatose patient? Someone senile? What moral implications result?

# John Stuart Mill

John Stuart Mill (1806–73), considered the most influential English-speaking philosopher of the nineteenth century, was born in London, the son of Scottish political theorist **James Mill** (1773–1836), who, with his friend Jeremy Bentham (1748–1832), founder of utilitarianism, home-schooled his son with the goal of cultivating the perfect utilitarian mind. Mill came to believe that this education had stunted his emotional growth, contributing to the severe depression he suffered at age 20. In *Utilitarianism*, Mill goes beyond Bentham's hedonistic calculus to count quality as well as quantity of pleasure as morally relevant.

## What Utilitarianism Is

From *Utilitarianism*

### 1. Utility, or the Greatest Happiness Principle

The creed which accepts as the foundation of morals, Utility, or the Greatest Happiness Principle, holds that actions are right in proportion as they tend to promote happiness, wrong as they tend to produce the reverse of happiness. By happiness is intended pleasure and the absence of pain; by unhappiness, pain and the privation of pleasure. To give a clear view of the moral standard set up by the theory, much more requires to be said: in particular, what things it includes in the ideas of pain and pleasure, and to what extent this is left an open question. But these supplementary explanations do not affect the theory of life on which this theory of morality is grounded—namely, that pleasure and freedom from pain are the only things desirable as ends; and that all desirable things (which are as numerous in the utilitarian as in any other scheme) are desirable either for the pleasure inherent in themselves, or as means to the promotion of pleasure and the prevention of pain.

Now, such a theory of life excites in many minds, and among them in some of the most estimable in feeling and purpose, inveterate dislike. To suppose that life has (as they express it) no higher end than pleasure, no better and nobler object of desire and pursuit, they designate as utterly mean and grovelling—as a doctrine worthy only of swine, to whom the followers of **Epicurus** were, at a very early period, contemptuously likened; and modern holders of the doctrine are occasionally made the subject of equally polite comparisons by its German, French, and English assailants.

When thus attacked, the Epicureans have always answered that it is not they but their accusers who represent human nature in a degrading light, since the accusation supposes human beings to be capable of no pleasures except those of which swine are capable. If this supposition were true, the charge could not be gainsaid but would then be no longer an imputation, for if the sources of pleasure were precisely the same to human beings and to swine, the rule of life which is good enough for the one would be good enough for the other. The comparison of the Epicurean life to that of beasts is felt as degrading precisely because a beast's pleasures do not satisfy a human being's conceptions of happiness. Human beings have faculties more elevated than the animal appetites and, when once made conscious of them, do not regard anything as happiness which does not include their gratification. I do not, indeed, consider the Epicureans to have been by any means faultless in drawing out their scheme of consequences from the utilitarian principle. To do this in any sufficient manner, many **Stoic**, as well as Christian, elements require to be included. But there is no known Epicurean theory of life which does not assign to the pleasures of the intellect, of the feelings and imagination, and of the moral sentiments a much higher value as pleasures than to those of mere sensation. It must be admitted, however, that utilitarian writers in general have placed the superiority of mental over bodily pleasures chiefly in the greater permanency, safety, uncostliness, etc., of the former—that is, in their circumstantial advantages rather than in their intrinsic nature. And on all these points utilitarians have fully proved their case; but they might have taken the other, and, as it may be called, higher, ground with entire consistency. It is quite compatible with the principle of utility to recognize the fact that some *kinds* of pleasure are more desirable and more valuable than others. It would be absurd that while, in estimating all other things, quality is considered as well as quantity, the estimation of pleasures should be supposed to depend on quantity alone.

## 2. Higher and Lower Pleasures

If I am asked what I mean by difference of quality in pleasures, or what makes one pleasure more valuable than another, merely as a pleasure, except its being greater in amount, there is but one possible answer. Of two pleasures, if there be one to which all or almost all who have experience of both give a decided preference, irrespective of any feeling of moral obligation to prefer it, that is the more desirable pleasure. If one of the two is, by those who are competently acquainted with both, placed so far above the other that they prefer it, even though knowing it to be attended with a greater amount of discontent, and would not resign it for any quantity of the other pleasure which their nature is capable of, we are justified in ascribing to the preferred enjoyment a superiority in quality, so far outweighing quantity as to render it, in comparison, of small account.

Now it is an unquestionable fact that those who are equally acquainted with, and equally capable of appreciating and enjoying, both do give a most marked preference to the manner of existence which employs their higher faculties. Few human creatures would consent to be changed into any of the lower animals for a promise of the fullest allowance of a beast's pleasures; no intelligent human being would consent to be a fool, no instructed person would be an ignoramus, no person of feeling and conscience would be selfish and base, even though they should be persuaded that the fool, the dunce, or the rascal is better satisfied with his lot than they are with theirs. They would not resign what they possess more than he for the most complete satisfaction of all the desires which they have in common with him. If they ever fancy they would, it is only in cases of unhappiness so extreme that to escape from it they would exchange their lot for almost any other, however undesirable in their own eyes. A being of higher faculties requires more to make him happy, is capable probably of more acute suffering, and certainly accessible to it at more points, than one of an inferior type; but in spite of these liabilities, he can never really wish to sink into what he feels to be a lower grade of existence. [. . .] Whoever supposes that this preference takes place at a sacrifice of happiness—that the superior being, in anything like equal circumstances, is not happier than the inferior—confounds the two very different ideas, of happiness and content. It is indisputable that the being whose capacities of enjoyment are low has the greatest chance of having them fully satisfied; and a highly endowed being will always feel that any happiness which he can look for, as the world is constituted, is imperfect. But he can learn to bear its imperfections, if they are at all bearable; and they will not make him envy the being who is indeed unconscious of the imperfections, but only because he feels not at all the good which those imperfections qualify. It is better to be a human being dissatisfied than a pig satisfied; better to be Socrates dissatisfied than a fool satisfied. And if the fool, or the pig, are of a different opinion, it is because they only know their own side of the question. The other party to the comparison knows both sides.

It may be objected that many who are capable of the higher pleasures, occasionally, under the influence of temptation, postpone them to the lower. But this is quite compatible with a full appreciation of the intrinsic superiority of the higher. Men often, from infirmity of character, make their election for the nearer good, though they know it to be the less valuable—and this no less when the choice is between two bodily pleasures than when it is between bodily and mental. They pursue sensual indulgences to the injury of health, though perfectly aware that health is the greater good. It may be further objected that many who begin with youthful enthusiasm for everything noble, as they advance in years, sink into indolence and selfishness. But I do not believe that those who undergo this very common change voluntarily choose the lower description of pleasures in preference to the higher. I believe that before they devote themselves exclusively to the one, they have already become incapable of the other. Capacity for the nobler feelings is in most natures a very tender plant, easily killed not only by hostile influences but by mere want of sustenance; and in the majority of young persons it speedily dies away if the occupations to which their position in life has devoted them, and the society into which it has thrown them, are not favourable to keeping that higher capacity in exercise. [. . .]

From this verdict of the only competent judges, I apprehend there can be no appeal. On a question which is the best worth having of two pleasures, or which of two modes of existence is the most grateful to the feelings, apart from its moral attributes and from its consequences, the judgment of those who are qualified by knowledge of both, or, if they differ, that of the majority among them, must be admitted as final. And there needs be the less hesitation to accept this judgment respecting the quality of pleasures, since there is no other tribunal to be referred to even on the question of quantity. What means are there of determining which is the acutest of two pains, or the intensest of two pleasurable sensations, except the general suffrage of those who are familiar with both? Neither pains nor pleasures are homogeneous, and pain is always heterogeneous with pleasure. What is there to decide whether a particular pleasure is worth purchasing at the cost of a particular pain, except the feelings and judgment of the experienced? When, therefore, those feelings and judgment declare the pleasures derived from

the higher faculties to be preferable *in kind*, apart from the question of intensity, to those of which the animal nature disjoined from the higher faculties is susceptible, they are entitled on this subject to the same regard.

I have dwelt on this point as being a necessary part of a perfectly just conception of Utility or Happiness, considered as the directive rule of human conduct. But it is by no means an indispensable condition to the acceptance of the utilitarian standard; for that standard is not the agent's own greatest happiness but the greatest amount of happiness altogether; and if it may possibly be doubted whether a noble character is always the happier for its nobleness, there can be no doubt that it makes other people happier, and that the world in general is immensely a gainer by it. Utilitarianism, therefore, could only attain its end by the general cultivation of nobleness of character, even if each individual were only benefited by the nobleness of others, and his own, so far as happiness is concerned, were a sheer deduction from the benefit. But the bare enunciation of such an absurdity as this last renders refutation superfluous.

## 3. Utility as the Standard of Morality

According to the Greatest Happiness Principle, as above explained, the ultimate end, with reference to and for the sake of which all other things are desirable (whether we are considering our own good or that of other people), is an existence exempt as far as possible from pain and as rich as possible in enjoyments, both in point of quantity and quality—the test of quality and the rule for measuring it against quantity being the preference felt by those who in their opportunities of experience, to which must be added their habits of self-consciousness and self-observation, are best furnished with the means of comparison. This being, according to the utilitarian opinion, the end of human action is necessarily also the standard of morality, which may accordingly be defined, the rules and precepts for human conduct. [. . .]

Unquestionably it is possible to do without happiness; it is done involuntarily by nineteen-twentieths of mankind, even in those parts of our present world which are least deep in barbarism; and it often has to be done voluntarily by the hero or the martyr for the sake of something which he prizes more than his individual happiness. But this something, what is it, unless the happiness of others, or some of the requisites of happiness? It is noble to be capable of resigning entirely one's own portion of happiness, or chances of it: but, after all, this self-sacrifice must be for some end; it is not its own end; and if we are told that its end is not happiness but virtue, which is better than happiness, I ask, would the sacrifice be made if the hero or martyr did not believe that it would earn for others immunity from similar sacrifices? Would it be made if he thought that his renunciation of happiness for himself would produce no fruit for any of his fellow creatures but to make their lot like his and place them also in the condition of persons who have renounced happiness? All honour to those who can abnegate for themselves the personal enjoyment of life when by such renunciation they contribute worthily to increase the amount of happiness in the world; but he who does it, or professes to do it, for any other purpose is no more deserving of admiration than the ascetic mounted on his pillar. He may be an inspiriting proof of what men *can* do, but assuredly not an example of what they *should*. [. . .]

I must again repeat what the assailants of utilitarianism seldom have the justice to acknowledge, that the happiness which forms the utilitarian standard of what is right in conduct is not the agent's own happiness but that of all concerned. As between his own happiness and that of others, utilitarianism requires him to be as strictly impartial as a disinterested and benevolent spectator. In the golden rule of Jesus of Nazareth, we read the complete spirit of the ethics of utility. To do as you would be done by, and to love your neighbour as yourself, constitute the ideal perfection of utilitarian morality. As the means of making the nearest approach to this ideal, utility would enjoin: first, that laws and social arrangements should place the happiness, or (as speaking practically it may be called) the interest, of every individual as nearly as possible in harmony with the interest of the whole; and secondly, that education and opinion, which have so vast a power over human character, should so use that power as to establish in the mind of every individual an indissoluble association between his own happiness and the good of the whole—especially between his own happiness and the practice of such modes of conduct, negative and positive, as regard for the universal happiness prescribes, so that not only he may be unable to conceive the possibility of happiness to himself consistently with conduct opposed to the general good but also that a direct impulse to promote the general good may be in every individual one of the habitual motives of action, and the sentiments connected therewith may fill a large and prominent place in every human being's sentient existence. If the impugners of the utilitarian morality represented it to their own minds in this its true character, I know not what recommendation possessed by any other morality they could possibly affirm to be wanting to it: what more beautiful or more exalted developments of human nature any other ethical system can be supposed to foster, or what springs of action not accessible to the utilitarian such systems rely on for giving effect to their mandates.

## 4. Responses to Objections

The objectors to utilitarianism cannot always be charged with representing it in a discreditable light. On the contrary, those among them who entertain anything like a just idea of its disinterested character sometimes find fault with its standard as being too high for humanity. They say it is exacting too much to require that people shall always act from the inducement of promoting the general interests of society. But this is to mistake the very meaning of a standard of morals and confound the rule of action with the motive of it. It is the business of ethics to tell us what are our duties, or by what test we may know them; but no system of ethics requires that the sole motive of all we do shall be a feeling of duty; on the contrary, ninety-nine-hundredths of all our actions are done from other motives, and rightly so done, if the rule of duty does not condemn them. It is the more unjust to utilitarianism that this particular misapprehension should be made a ground of objection to it, inasmuch as utilitarian moralists have gone beyond almost all others in affirming that the motive has nothing to do with the morality of the action, though much with the worth of the agent. He who saves a fellow creature from drowning does what is morally right, whether his motive be duty or the hope of being paid for his trouble; he who betrays the friend that trusts him is guilty of a crime, even if his object be to serve another friend to whom he is under greater obligations. But to speak only of actions done from the motive of duty and in direct obedience to principle: it is a misapprehension of the utilitarian mode of thought to conceive it as implying that people should fix their minds upon so wide a generality as the world, or society at large. The great majority of good actions are intended not for the benefit of the world but for that of individuals, of which the good of the world is made up; and the thoughts of the most virtuous man need not on these occasions travel beyond the particular persons concerned, except so far as is necessary to assure himself that in benefiting them he is not violating the rights, that is, the legitimate and authorized expectations, of anyone else. The multiplication of happiness is, according to the utilitarian ethics, the object of virtue: the occasions on which any person (except one in a thousand) has it in his power to do this on an extended scale, in other words to be a public benefactor, are but exceptional; and on these occasions alone is he called on to consider public utility; in every other case, private utility, the interest or happiness of some few persons, is all he has to attend to. Those alone the influence of whose actions extends to society in general need concern themselves habitually about so large an object. [. . .]

The same considerations dispose of another reproach against the doctrine of utility, founded on a still grosser misconception of the purpose of a standard of morality and of the very meaning of the words right and wrong. It is often affirmed that utilitarianism renders men cold and unsympathizing; that it chills their moral feelings towards individuals; that it makes them regard only the dry and hard consideration of the consequences of actions, not taking into their moral estimate the qualities from which those actions emanate. If the assertion means that they do not allow their judgment respecting the rightness or wrongness of an action to be influenced by their opinion of the qualities of the person who does it, this is a complaint not against utilitarianism but against having any standard of morality at all; for certainly no known ethical standard decides an action to be good or bad because it is done by a good or a bad man, still less because done by an amiable, a brave, or a benevolent man, or the contrary. These considerations are relevant not to the estimation of actions but of persons, and there is nothing in the utilitarian theory inconsistent with the fact that there are other things which interest us in persons besides the rightness and wrongness of their actions. The Stoics, indeed, with the paradoxical misuse of language which was part of their system, and by which they strove to raise themselves above all concern about anything but virtue, were fond of saying that he who has that has everything; that he, and only he, is rich, is beautiful, is a king. But no claim of this description is made for the virtuous man by the utilitarian doctrine. Utilitarians are quite aware that there are other desirable possessions and qualities besides virtue, and are perfectly willing to allow to all of them their full worth. They are also aware that a right action does not necessarily indicate a virtuous character, and that actions which are blameable often proceed from qualities entitled to praise. When this is apparent in any particular case, it modifies their estimation, not certainly of the act but of the agent. I grant that they are, notwithstanding, of opinion that in the long run the best proof of a good character is good actions, and resolutely refuse to consider any mental disposition as good of which the predominant tendency is to produce bad conduct. This makes them unpopular with many people; but it is an unpopularity which they must share with everyone who regards the distinction between right and wrong in a serious light; and the reproach is not one which a conscientious utilitarian need be anxious to repel. [. . .]

It may not be superfluous to notice a few more of the common misapprehensions of utilitarian ethics, even those which are so obvious and gross that it might appear impossible for any person of candour and intelligence to fall into them—since persons, even of considerable mental endowments, often give themselves so little trouble to understand the bearings of any opinion against which they entertain a prejudice, and men are in general so little conscious of this voluntary ignorance as a defect that the vulgarest misunderstandings of ethical doctrines are continually met with in the deliberate writings of persons of the greatest pretensions both to high principle and to philosophy. We not uncommonly hear the doctrine of utility inveighed against as a *godless* doctrine. If it be necessary to say anything at all against so mere an assumption, we may say that the question depends upon what idea we have formed of the moral character of the Deity. If it be a true belief that God desires, above all things, the happiness of his creatures, and that this was his purpose in their creation, utility is not only not a godless doctrine but more profoundly religious than any other. If it be meant that utilitarianism does not recognize the revealed will of God as the supreme law of morals, I answer that a utilitarian who believes in the perfect goodness and wisdom of God necessarily believes that whatever God has thought fit to reveal on the subject of morals must fulfil the requirements of utility in a supreme degree. But others besides utilitarians have been of opinion that the Christian revelation was intended, and is fitted, to inform the hearts and minds of mankind with a spirit which should enable them to find for themselves what is right and incline them to do it when found, rather than to tell them, except in a very general way, what it is; and that we need a doctrine of ethics, carefully followed out, to *interpret* to us the will of God. Whether this opinion is correct or not, it is superfluous here to discuss since whatever aid religion, either natural or revealed, can afford to ethical investigation is as open to the utilitarian moralist as to any other. He can use it as the testimony of God to the usefulness or hurtfulness of any given course of action by as good a right as others can use it for the indication of a transcendental law having no connection with usefulness or with happiness.

Again, Utility is often summarily stigmatized as an immoral doctrine by giving it the name of Expediency, and taking advantage of the popular use of that term to contrast it with Principle. But the Expedient, in the sense in which it is opposed to the Right, generally means that which is expedient for the particular interest of the agent himself, as when a minister sacrifices the interest of his country to keep himself in place. When it means anything better than this, it means that which is expedient for some immediate object, some temporary purpose, but which violates a rule whose observance is expedient in a much higher degree. The Expedient, in this sense, instead of being the same thing with the useful, is a branch of the hurtful. Thus, it would often be expedient, for the purpose of getting over some momentary embarrassment, or attaining some object immediately useful to ourselves or others, to tell a lie. But inasmuch as the cultivation in ourselves of a sensitive feeling on the subject of veracity is one of the most useful, and the enfeeblement of that feeling one of the most hurtful, things to which our conduct can be instrumental; and inasmuch as any, even unintentional, deviation from truth does that much towards weakening the trustworthiness of human assertion, which is not only the principal support of all present social well-being but the insufficiency of which does more than any one thing that can be named to keep back civilization, virtue, everything on which human happiness on the largest scale depends, we feel that the violation for a present advantage of a rule of such transcendent expediency is not expedient and that he who for the sake of a convenience to himself or to some other individual does what depends on him to deprive mankind of the good and inflict upon them the evil involved in the greater or less reliance which they can place in each other's word acts the part of one of their worst enemies. Yet, that even this rule, sacred as it is, admits of possible exceptions is acknowledged by all moralists: the chief of which is when the withholding of some fact (as of information from a malefactor, or of bad news from a person dangerously ill) would save an individual (especially an individual other than oneself) from great and unmerited evil, and when the withholding can only be effected by denial. But in order that the exception may not extend itself beyond the need, and may have the least possible effect in weakening reliance on veracity, it ought to be recognized, and, if possible, its limits defined; and if the principle of utility is good for anything, it must be good for weighing these conflicting utilities against one another, and marking out the region within which one or the other preponderates.

Again, defenders of utility often find themselves called upon to reply to such objections as this—that there is not time, previous to action, for calculating and weighing the effects of any line of conduct on the general happiness. This is exactly as if anyone were to say that it is impossible to guide our conduct by Christianity because there is not time, on every occasion on which anything has to be done, to read through the Old and New Testaments. The answer to the objection is that there has been ample time, namely, the whole past duration of the human species. During all that time, mankind have been learning by experience the tendencies of actions—on which experience all the prudence, as well as all the morality of life, are dependent. People talk as if the commencement of this course of experience had hitherto been put off, and as if at the moment when some man feels tempted to meddle with the property or life of another, he had to begin considering for the first time whether murder and theft are injurious to human happiness. Even then I do not think that he would find the question very puzzling; but, at all events, the matter is now done to his hand. It is truly a whimsical supposition that if mankind were agreed in considering utility to be the test of morality, they would remain without any agreement as to what *is* useful, and would take no measures for having their notions on the subject taught to the young and enforced by law and opinion. There is no difficulty in proving any ethical standard whatever to work ill if we suppose universal idiocy to be conjoined with it; but on any hypothesis short of that, mankind must by this time have acquired positive beliefs as

to the effects of some actions on their happiness; and the beliefs which have thus come down are the rules of morality for the multitude, and for the philosopher until he has succeeded in finding better. That philosophers might easily do this, even now, on many subjects; that the received code of ethics is by no means of divine right; and that mankind have still much to learn as to the effects of actions on the general happiness, I admit, or rather, earnestly maintain. The corollaries from the principle of utility, like the precepts of every practical art, admit of indefinite improvement, and in a progressive state of the human mind, their improvement is perpetually going on. But to consider the rules of morality as improvable is one thing; to pass over the intermediate generalizations entirely, and endeavour to test each individual action directly by the first principle, is another. It is a strange notion that the acknowledgment of a first principle is inconsistent with the admission of secondary ones. To inform a traveller respecting the place of his ultimate destination is not to forbid the use of landmarks and direction-posts on the way. The proposition that happiness is the end and aim of morality does not mean that no road ought to be laid down to that goal, or that persons going thither should not be advised to take one direction rather than another. [. . .]

The remainder of the stock arguments against utilitarianism mostly consist in laying to its charge the common infirmities of human nature and the general difficulties which embarrass conscientious persons in shaping their course through life. We are told that a utilitarian will be apt to make his own particular case an exception to moral rules, and, when under temptation, will see a utility in the breach of a rule greater than he will see in its observance. But is utility the only creed which is able to furnish us with excuses for evil doing and means of cheating our own conscience? They are afforded in abundance by all doctrines which recognize as a fact in morals the existence of conflicting considerations—which all doctrines do that have been believed by sane persons. It is not the fault of any creed but of the complicated nature of human affairs that rules of conduct cannot be so framed as to require no exceptions, and that hardly any kind of action can safely be laid down as either always obligatory or always condemnable. There is no ethical creed which does not temper the rigidity of its laws by giving a certain latitude, under the moral responsibility of the agent, for accommodation to peculiarities of circumstances; and under every creed, at the opening thus made, self-deception and dishonest casuistry get in. There exists no moral system under which there do not arise unequivocal cases of conflicting obligation. These are the real difficulties, the knotty points both in the theory of ethics and in the conscientious guidance of personal conduct. They are overcome practically, with greater or with less success, according to the intellect and virtue of the individual; but it can hardly be pretended that anyone will be the less qualified for dealing with them from possessing an ultimate standard to which conflicting rights and duties can be referred. If utility is the ultimate source of moral obligations, utility may be invoked to decide between them when their demands are incompatible. Though the application of the standard may be difficult, it is better than none at all. [. . .]

## Study Questions

1. For Mill, what makes an action a good action, and what is good in itself?
2. How are Bentham's and Mill's different approaches to utilitarianism illustrated by their respective words: "Pushpin is as good as poetry" (Bentham) and "It is better to be a human being dissatisfied than a pig satisfied; better to be Socrates dissatisfied than a fool satisfied" (Mill)? Do you find Mill's justification of his position convincing?
3. Why does Mill consider the principle of utility to provide an impartial and disinterested standard of morality? How does he answer the objection that such a standard is "too high for humanity"?
4. It is often feared that without God, there is no morality: in Dostoyevsky's words, "everything is permitted." How does Mill respond to the criticism that utilitarianism is a "godless doctrine"?

---

# Jürgen Habermas

---

German philosopher and sociologist Jürgen Habermas's contributions to social-political theory, epistemology, language, aesthetics, and religion successfully bridge the continental and Anglo-American philosophical traditions. Habermas spent his career at the University of Heidelberg, Max Planck Institute in Starnberg, and Institute for Social Research in Frankfurt. A true public intellectual, he has continued to write and lecture since retiring in 1993. In this article, Habermas distinguishes between the ethical point of view of Aristotle the and moral point of view of Kant, and introduces his own theory of discourse ethics.

## On the Cognitive Content of Morality

### Introduction

Moral statements or utterances, assuming they can be justified, have a cognitive content. Thus in order to clarify the possible cognitive content of morality we must examine what it means "to justify something morally." Here we must distinguish between the moral–*theoretical* question of whether moral utterances indeed express knowledge and, if they do, how they can be justified, and the phenomenological question of what cognitive meaning those who participate in moral conflicts themselves associate with their utterances. I will use the term "moral justification" at first in a descriptive manner to refer to the rudimentary practice of justification which has its proper place in the everyday interactions of the lifeworld.

In this context we make statements through which we demand certain conduct of others (that is, hold them to an obligation), commit ourselves to a course of action (incur an obligation), reproach ourselves or others, acknowledge mistakes, make excuses, offer to make amends, and so forth. On this first level, moral utterances serve to coordinate the actions of different actors in a binding or obligatory fashion. "Obligation" presupposes the intersubjective recognition of moral norms or customary practices which prescribe *in a convincing fashion* for a community what actors are obliged to do and what they can expect from one another. "In a convincing manner" means that the members of a moral community appeal to these norms whenever the coordination of action breaks down at the first level and present them as presumably convincing "reasons" for claims and critical positions. Moral utterances are made against a background of potential reasons which can be actualized in moral disputes.

Moral rules are self-reflexive; their action-coordinating power proves itself on two interrelated levels of interaction. They direct social action immediately by binding the will of actors and orienting it in a particular direction; at the same time they govern the critical positions actors adopt when conflicts arise. The morality of a community not only lays down how its members should act; it also provides grounds for the consensual resolution of relevant practical conflicts. To the moral language game belong disagreements which can be resolved in a convincing manner from the perspective of participants on the basis of potential justifications that are equally accessible to all. Sociologically speaking, moral obligations recommend themselves by their internal relation to the gentle rational force of reasons as an alternative to forms of conflict-resolution which are not oriented to reaching understanding.

If morality did not possess a credible cognitive content for members of the community, it would have no advantage over other, more costly forms of action coordination (such as the use of direct force or the exercise of influence through the threat of sanctions or the promise of rewards).

When we examine moral disagreements, we must include affective reactions in the class of moral utterances. The key concept of obligation already refers not only to the content of moral injunctions but also to the peculiar character of the validity (*Sollgeltung*) which is also reflected in the feeling of being obligated. The critical and self-critical stances we adopt towards transgressions find expression in affective attitudes: from the third person perspective, in abhorrence, indignation, and contempt; from the perspective of those affected, in feelings of violation or resentment towards second persons; and from the first person perspective, in shame and guilt (Strawson). To these correspond the positive emotional reactions of admiration, loyalty, gratitude, etc. Because they express implicit judgments, these attitudinal feelings stand in a relation of correspondence to evaluations. We judge actions and intentions to be "good" or "bad," whereas our terms for virtues refer to personal qualities of agents. The claim that moral judgments admit of justification also betrays itself in these moral feelings and evaluations, for they differ from other feelings and evaluations in being tied to obligations that function as reasons. We do not regard these utterances as expressions of mere sentiments and preferences.

From the fact that moral norms are "valid" for the members of a community it does not follow, of course, that they have cognitive content viewed in themselves. A sociological observer might be able to describe a moral language game as a social fact, and even explain why members are "convinced" of their moral rules, without being able to render their reasons and interpretations plausible to himself. But a philosopher cannot remain content with this. He will pursue the phenomenology of the relevant moral disagreements further in order to comprehend what members of the community do when they justify something morally. Of course, "comprehend" here means something different from simply "understanding" utterances. The reflection on the everyday practice of justification in which we ourselves participate as laypersons permits reconstructive translations which should foster critical understanding. In this methodological attitude the philosopher extends the participant perspective *from within* beyond the circle of *immediate* participants.

The results of such efforts can be gauged by examining modern programs in moral philosophy. [. . .]

*Strong non-cognitivism* exposes the presumed cognitive content of moral language in general as an illusion. It attempts to show that behind the utterances which appear to participants as moral judgments and stances that admit of justification, there lurk merely subjective feelings, attitudes, and decisions. Utilitarianism, which traces the "binding" force of evaluative orientations and obligations back to preferences, arrives at similar revisionist descriptions. But in contrast with emotivism (e.g., that of **Stevenson**) and decisionism (e.g., that of **Popper** or the early **Hare**), utilitarianism replaces the unreflective moral self-understanding of participants by a utility calculation undertaken from an observer's point of view.

*Weak non-cognitivism* offers explanations that do justice to the self-understanding of morally *acting* subjects, whether in terms of moral feelings (as in the tradition of Scottish moral philosophy) or in terms of the orientation to accepted norms (as in **Hobbesian contractualism**). However, the self-understanding of morally *judging* subjects succumbs to revision. On this account, their supposedly objectively grounded positions and judgments in fact express merely rational "motives," be they preferences or feelings which must be justified in the same purposive-rational manner.

*Weak cognitivism* leaves the self-understanding of the practice of moral justification intact to the extent that it ascribes a certain epistemic status to "strong" evaluations. Reflection on what is "good" for me (or for us) all things considered or on what is "advisable" for my (or for our) consciously pursued life-plan yields to a rational assessment of

evaluative orientations (in the wake of **Aristotle** or **Wittgenstein**). What in each instance is valuable or authentic forces itself upon us in a certain sense and differs from mere preferences in its binding character, that is, in the fact that it points beyond the subjectivity of needs and preferences. Only the intuitive understanding of justice is still subject to revision. From the perspective of each individual's conception of the good, justice, which is tailored to interpersonal relations, appears as just one value among others (however pronounced), not as a context-independent standard of impartial judgment.

*Strong cognitivism* seeks in addition to give an account of the categorical validity claim of moral obligations. It attempts to reconstruct the complete range of the presumed cognitive content of the moral language game. The **Kant**ian tradition is not only concerned with clarifying a practice of moral justification which unfolds *within* the horizon of unquestioningly recognized norms but with the justification of a moral point of view from which such norms can themselves be judged in an impartial fashion. Here moral theory grounds the possibility of moral justification by reconstructing the point of view which members of post-traditional societies themselves intuitively adopt when they must have recourse to rational grounds because basic moral norms have become problematic.

I will proceed directly to the discussion of the latter two positions which draw, respectively, on Aristotle and Kant (sections 2 and 3); this will prepare the way for my [. . .] theoretical justification [of the moral point of view] (section 5).

## Section 2. Weak Cognitivism: Aristotelian Tradition

Weak non-cognitivism assumes that the faculty of choice (*Willkür*) can only be affected by practical reason in a single way, namely, by reflection on how I can best satisfy my wishes and realize corresponding goals. If, by contrast, practical reason is no longer identified with instrumental reason, the constellation of reason and will changes, and with it the concept of subjective freedom. Freedom is no longer exhausted by the capacity to bind the will through the rational choice of maxims of prudence but finds expression in the will's capacity to bind itself through insight. "Insight" signifies that a decision can be justified on the basis of "epistemic" reasons. Since epistemic reasons generally support the truth of assertoric statements, the use of the expression "epistemic" in practical contexts is in need of explication. "Pragmatic" reasons I call rational motives that reflect the contingent preferences and goals of particular persons. Only the agent himself, who knows his own preferences and goals, has the final epistemic authority to judge these data. Practical reflection can lead to "insights," however, when it extends beyond the subjective world to which the actor has privileged access to the contents of an intersubjectively shared social world. Reflection on shared experiences, practices, and forms of life brings to awareness things we do not already "know" through the epistemic authority of the first person.

Of course, to bring something implicitly known to consciousness is not the same as the acquisition of factual knowledge (Williams). Scientific knowledge in particular is counterintuitive, whereas reflexively achieved "insight" only makes explicit the pre-theoretical knowledge which communicatively socialized individuals have already acquired in the lifeworld. This applies to ethical knowledge, the most general elements of which have become sedimented in evaluative vocabulary and in the rules for the use of normative sentences. Because we intuitively know what is attractive and repulsive, right or wrong, and in general what is relevant, here the moment of insight can be distinguished from a corresponding disposition or preference. It consists of an intersubjectively shared know-how which has gained acceptance in the lifeworld and has "proved" itself in practice. As the shared possession of a cultural form of life, it enjoys "objectivity" in virtue of its social diffusion and acceptance. Hence the practical reflection which *critically* appropriates this intuitive knowledge calls for a *socially expanded* perspective, extending beyond the first person singular perspective of

somebody acting on her preferences. Here I want to distinguish from the outset between value-orientations (*Wertorientierungen*) and obligations (*Verpflichtungen*). We judge value-orientations, and in general the evaluative self-understanding of persons or groups, from the *ethical* point of view, duties, norms, and categorical imperatives from the *moral* point of view.

Ethical questions arise from the first person plural perspective as questions concerning a shared ethos: how we understand ourselves as members of our community, how we should orient our lives, what is best for us in the long run and all things considered. Similar questions arise from the first person singular perspective: who I am and who I would like to be, how I should lead my life. Such existential concerns differ from considerations of prudence not only in the dimensions of the temporal and substantive generalization of the question: what *in the long run and all things considered* is best for me. In these questions the first person perspective no longer signifies an egocentric restriction to my preferences; it points rather to the totality of an individual life history which is always already embedded in intersubjectively shared traditions and forms of life. The attractiveness of values in whose light I understand myself and my life cannot be clarified within the limits of the world of subjective experiences to which I have privileged access. In the case of ethical questions in general, my preferences are no longer simply given but are themselves a matter for discussion (Taylor); they can undergo reasoned change together with my or our self-understanding in reflection on what has intrinsic value *for me or for us* within the horizon of our shared social world.

From the ethical point of view we clarify clinical questions of the successful and happy, or better, not misspent, life, which arise in the context of a particular collective form of life or of an individual life history. Practical reflection takes the form of a process of hermeneutic self-clarification. It articulates strong evaluations in light of which I orient my self-understanding. In this context the critique of self-deceptions and of symptoms of a compulsive or alienated mode of life takes its yardstick from the idea of a consciously guided and coherent course of life, where the authenticity of a life-project can be understood as a higher-level validity claim on an analogy with the claim to truthfulness of expressive speech acts. [. . .]

However, the limits of the ethical point of view become manifest once questions of justice come into play: for from this perspective justice counts in the final analysis as just one value among others. It discloses that moral obligations are more important for one person than they are for another and are of greater significance in one context than in another. Certainly, one can allow for the semantic difference between the binding character of values and moral obligations also from the ethical point of view by according questions of justice a certain priority over questions of the good life: "Ethical life itself is important, but it can see that things other than itself are important. . . . There is one kind of ethical consideration that directly connects importance and deliberative priority, and this is obligation" (Williams 184f). But as long as duties are viewed *solely* from the ethical point of view, an *absolute* priority of the right over the good, which alone would be commensurate with the categorical validity of moral duties, cannot be upheld: "These kinds of obligations very often command the highest deliberative priority. . . . However, we can also see how they need not always command the highest priority, even in ethically well disposed agents" (Williams 187). As long as justice is treated as an integral part of a particular conception of the good, there is no ground for the requirement that, in cases of conflict, duties can only be "trumped" by duties and rights by rights (as Dworkin puts it).

An ethically neutral conception of justice is impossible unless the right is accorded priority over the good. This has unfortunate consequences for equal treatment in societies characterized by a pluralism of worldviews. For the equal treatment of different individuals and groups each with their own individual or collective identity could only be granted by standards that fit into a shared conception of the good equally recognized by all.

The same condition would hold *mutatis mutandis* [necessary changes having been made] for the just regulation of international relations between states, for cosmopolitan relations between world citizens, and for global relations between cultures. The improbability of this requirement of a shared conception of the good shows why neo-Aristotelian approaches have difficulties in accounting for the universalistic content of a morality of equal respect and solidaristic responsibility for everyone. For the projection of a globally shared collective good, on which the solidarity of all human beings—including future generations—could be founded, calls for two problematic operations. The abstraction from all local contexts would destroy the concept of the good itself and the anticipation of the happiness of future generations would entail an intolerable paternalism.

In order to do justice to the *presumptive* impartiality of moral judgments and to the categorical validity *claim* of binding norms, we must uncouple the horizontal perspective in which interpersonal relations are regulated from the vertical perspective of my or our own life-project and treat moral questions separately. The abstract question of what is equally in the interest of all *goes beyond* the context-bound ethical question of what is best "for me" or "for us." Nevertheless, the intuition that issues of justice evolve from an idealizing extension of the ethical problematic retains a genuine heuristic value.

If we interpret justice as what is equally good for all, the "good" which has been extended to the "right" forms a bridge between justice and solidarity. For universal justice also requires that one person should take responsibility for another, and even that each person should stand in and answer for a stranger who has formed his identity in completely different circumstances and who understands himself in terms of alien traditions. The remnant of the good at the core of the right reminds us that moral consciousness does indeed depend on a particular self-understanding of moral persons who recognize that they *belong* to the moral community. All individuals who have been socialized into any communicative form of life belong to this community. Socialized individuals are particularly vulnerable in their integrity and are consequently in special need of protection because they can only stabilize their identities in relations of reciprocal recognition. They therefore need to be able to appeal to an authority beyond their own community—**G.H. Mead** speaks of the "ever wider community." Every concrete community depends on the moral community as its "better self," so to speak. As members of this community, individuals expect from one another an equal treatment that assumes that each person treats everyone else as "one of us." From this perspective, solidarity is only the reverse side of justice.

This connection inspired Kant to elucidate the point of view from which questions of justice can be impartially judged in terms of the **Rousseau**ean model of self-legislation: "Consequently every rational being must act as if by his maxims he were at all times a legislative member of the universal realm of ends" (55). Kant speaks of a "realm of ends" because each of its members regards himself and all other members never merely as means but always also as "ends in themselves." As a legislator, nobody is subordinated to an alien will; but at the same time every person is subject like everyone else to the laws that he gives himself. By replacing the figure of the contract derived from civil law with that of republican legislation derived from public law, in the case of morality Kant can *combine* in one and the same person the two roles which are separated in law, that of the citizen who participates in legislation and that of the private legal person who is subject to the law. For the morally free person it must be possible to understand herself simultaneously as the author of moral commands to which she is subject as addressee. This is possible in turn only if she does not exercise the legislative competence in which she "participates" in an arbitrary manner (as on a positivistic conception of the law), but in accordance with the constitution of a commonwealth whose citizens govern themselves. And there only laws can hold sway which could have been adopted "by each for all and by all for each."

## Section 3. Strong Cognitivism: Kantian Tradition

A law is valid in the moral sense when it could be accepted by everybody from the perspective of each individual. Because only "general" laws fulfil the condition that they regulate matters in the equal interest of all, practical reason is brought to bear under the aspect of the generalizability of the interests expressed in the law. Thus a person takes the moral point of view when he deliberates with himself *in the manner of* a democratic legislator whether the practice that would result from the general observance of a hypothetically proposed norm could be accepted by all those possibly affected as potential co-legislators. In the role of co-legislator, each person participates in a *co-operative* undertaking and thereby adopts an intersubjectively extended perspective from which it can be determined whether a controversial norm can count as generalizable from the point of view of each participant. Pragmatic and ethical reasons, which retain their internal connection to the interests and self-understanding of individual persons, also play a role in these deliberations; but these actor-relative reasons no longer *count* as the motives and value-orientations of individual persons but as epistemic contributions to a discourse in which norms are examined with the aim of reaching a communicative agreement. Because this legislative practice can only be undertaken in common, a monological, egocentric exercise of the generalization test in the manner of the Golden Rule will not suffice (Habermas, *Justification* 7f).

Moral reasons bind the faculty of choice in a way different from pragmatic and ethical reasons. [. . .]

The normativity which is rooted in the will's capacity to bind itself *as such* does not as yet have a moral meaning. When an agent adopts technical rules of skill or pragmatic rules of prudence, he lets his faculty of choice be guided by practical reason but the operative reasons have determining force only in relation to contingent preferences and goals. That holds even for ethical reasons, though in a different way. The authenticity of value-commitments points beyond the subject-centred horizon of instrumental rationality. But strong evaluations achieve objective force for determining the will only in connection with contingent, though intersubjectively shared, experiences, practices, and forms of life. In both cases the corresponding imperatives claim only conditional validity: they hold on the condition of subjectively given interests or intersubjectively shared traditions.

Moral obligations achieve unconditional or categorical validity on the assumption that they proceed from laws which emancipate the will, if only it commits itself to them, from all contingent determinations, and in a sense assimilate it to practical reason itself. For the contingent goals, preferences, and value-orientations which otherwise determine the will from without can then be subjected to critical evaluation in light of norms which are justified from the moral point of view. The heteronomous will can also be motivated by reasons to adopt maxims; but its commitment remains bound to pre-existing interests and context-dependent value-orientations through pragmatic and ethical reasons. Only when the former are examined as to their compatibility with the interests and values of all others from the moral point of view, has the will freed itself from heteronomy.

The abstract opposition between autonomy and heteronomy narrows the theoretical focus on the individual subject. In addition, transcendental background assumptions ascribe the free will to an intelligible Ego situated in the realm of ends. Thus Kant once again attributes the self-legislation, which in its original meaning is a co-operative undertaking in which the individual merely "participates" (52), to the sole competence of the individual. It is no accident that the categorical imperative is addressed to a second person singular and gives the impression that each individual could undertake the required testing of norms for himself *in foro interno* [by his own conscience]. But in fact the reflexive application of the universalization test calls for a form of deliberation in which each is compelled to adopt the perspective of all others in order to examine whether a norm could be willed by all *from the perspective of each.* This is the situation of a *rational discourse* oriented to reaching understanding in which all concerned take

part. Even the mere idea of a discursively produced understanding imposes a greater burden of argument on the individually judging subject than a monologically applied universalization test.

Kant may have been so inclined to foreshorten an intersubjective concept of autonomy in an individualistic manner because he failed to distinguish ethical questions sufficiently from pragmatic questions. Anyone who seriously entertains questions of ethical self-understanding runs up against the unique cultural meaning of the historically changing images of self and world of individuals and groups which stands in need of interpretation. Kant, who still thinks in an unhistorical way, overlooks this layer of traditions in which identities are formed. He tacitly assumes that in making moral judgments each individual can project himself sufficiently into the situation of everyone else *in virtue of his own imagination.* But when the participants can no longer rely on a transcendental pre-understanding—rooted in more or less homogeneous conditions of life and interests, one might add—the moral point of view can only be realized under conditions of communication which ensure that each individual tests the acceptability of a norm, implemented in a general practice, also from the perspective of his own understanding of himself and of the world. In this way the categorical imperative receives a discourse-theoretical interpretation. Its place is taken by the discourse principle "D" which states that: "only those norms can claim validity that could meet with the agreement of all concerned in their capacity as participants in a practical discourse" (Habermas, "Discourse Ethics" 66).

This proceduralist interpretation of the moral point of view seeks to preserve the cognitive content of morality even under conditions of the modern pluralism of world views.

## Section 5. Theoretical Justification of the Moral Point of View

Discourse ethics defends a morality of equal respect and solidaristic responsibility for everyone. But it does this in the first instance only by way of the rational reconstruction of the contents of a moral tradition whose religious foundations have been undermined. It thus remains to provide a theoretical justification of the moral point of view itself. Let me start from the following genealogical scenario.

The discourse principle tries to resolve a predicament in which the members of *any* moral community find themselves when, in making the transition to a modern, pluralistic society, they face the dilemma that, while they still argue about moral judgments and beliefs with reasons, an encompassing value-consensus on basic moral norms has been shattered. They are entangled in action conflicts in need of regulation, and they still regard them as moral and hence as rationally resolvable conflicts, although their shared ethos has disintegrated. As the participants do not wish to resolve these conflicts through violence or even compromise, but through communication, their initial impulse is, let us assume, to engage in deliberation and work out a shared ethical self-understanding. But under the differentiated social conditions of pluralistic societies they will soon realize that their strong evaluations lead to competing conceptions of the good.

If the participants remain steadfast in their resolve to engage in deliberation and not abandon the moral regulation of their coexistence for a negotiated *modus Vivendi* [accommodation of differences], they find that, in the absence of a substantive agreement on particular norms, they must rely on the "neutral" circumstance that each of them participates in *some* communicative form of life—a form of life which is structured by linguistically mediated understanding. Since such communicative processes and forms of life have certain structural aspects in common, they might further ask whether these features contain normative contents that could form a basis for shared orientations. Theories in the tradition of **Hegel**, **Humboldt**, and G.H. Mead which view morality as grounded in relations of symmetrical recognition have taken this route. But the particularism of given forms of life does not per se yield to a transition to symmetrical and inclusive relations of recognition, and thus to the viewpoint of an egalitarian universalism.

Hence, the participants find themselves constrained to fall back on those common features they already *currently* share as a result of having undertaken the co-operative endeavour of practical reasoning. The actual situation of performing a deliberative practice certainly offers only a poor, because formal, supply of commonalities; but the neutral content of this common store may also afford an opportunity in view of the predicament posed by the pluralism of worldviews. The prospect of an equivalent for the traditional substance of a received value consensus exists when the form of communication in which the joint deliberation takes place itself offers an aspect under which a justification of moral norms would be possible in virtue of its impartiality. The missing "transcendent good" can only be compensated for in an "immanent" fashion by some intrinsic feature of the practice of deliberation. From here, I believe, three steps lead to a theoretical justification of the moral point of view.

(a) If the practice of deliberation itself is regarded as the sole possible resource for a standpoint of impartial justification of moral questions, then the appeal to moral contents must be replaced by the self-referential appeal to the form of this practice. "D" gives expression to just this understanding of the situation: only those norms can claim validity that could meet with the acceptance of all concerned in practical discourses. Of course, the "acceptance" achieved under conditions of rational discourse has the force of an agreement (*Einverständnis*) motivated by epistemic reasons; it cannot be understood as a contract (*Vereinbarung*) which is rationally motivated from the egocentric perspective of each individual. Admittedly, the principle of discourse leaves open the type of argumentation, and hence the route, by which a discursive agreement can be reached. "D" does not by itself state that a justification of moral norms is possible without recourse to a substantive background agreement.

(b) The hypothetically posited principle "D" specifies the condition which valid norms would fulfil if they *could* be justified. For the moment let us assume that only the concept of a moral norm is clear. The participants also share an intuitive understanding of how one engages in argumentation. Though they are only familiar with the justification of assertoric sentences and do not yet know whether moral validity claims can be decided in a similar way, they can conceive (without prejudging the issue) what it *would* mean to justify a norm. What is still required for the operationalization of "D" is a rule of argumentation that specifies how moral norms can be justified.

While the principle of universalization "U" is inspired by "D," initially it is nothing more than a hypothesis arrived at in an abductive fashion. It states that:

> a norm is valid when the foreseeable consequences and side-effects of its general observance for the interests and value-orientations of *each individual* could be freely accepted *jointly* by *all* concerned.

Three points are in need of clarification here. With "interests and value-orientations" the pragmatic and ethical reasons of the individual participants are taken into account. These inputs are intended to prevent the marginalization of the world views of particular individuals or groups and, in general, to promote a hermeneutic sensitivity to a sufficiently broad spectrum of contributions. Furthermore, generalized reciprocal perspective-taking ("of each," "jointly by all") requires not only empathy but also interpretive intervention in the self-understanding of participants who must remain open to revisions in their descriptions of themselves and of others (and the language in which these are formulated). Finally, the goal of "free joint acceptance" specifies the respect in which the reasons introduced lose the actor-relative meaning of practical motives and assume an epistemic meaning under the aspect of symmetrical consideration.

(c) The participants themselves will perhaps be content with this (or a similar) rule of argumentation as long as it proves its usefulness and does not lead to counterintuitive results. It must first be *shown* that a practice of justification conducted in this manner succeeds in selecting norms which are capable of gaining general agreement—e.g., those that enshrine human

rights. But from the perspective of the moral theorist a final step in justification remains to be made. We may assume that the practice of deliberation and justification which we call "argumentation" is found in all cultures and societies (if not in institutionalized form, then at least as an informal practice) and that there is no functionally equivalent alternative to this mode of problem-solving. In view of the universal diffusion and non-substitutability of the practice of argumentation, it may be difficult to dispute the neutrality of the principle of discourse. But ethnocentric assumptions, and hence a specific conception of the good which is not shared by other cultures, may have insinuated themselves into the abduction of "U." The suspicion that the understanding of morality operationalized in "U" reflects eurocentric prejudices could be dispelled if this explication of the moral point of view could be made plausible in an "immanent" fashion, that is, on the basis of the general understanding of what it means to engage in the practice of argumentation. Hence the discourse-ethical idea of justification suggests that the basic principle "U" can be derived from the implicit content of universal presuppositions of argumentation in conjunction with the conception of normative justification in general, as it is expressed in "D."

It is easy to understand in an intuitive way how this idea can be realized [. . .] . Here I will content myself with some hints for an explanation of that intuition. Let me start from the observation that we engage in argumentation with the intention of convincing one another of the rightness of the validity claims that proponents raise for their statements and are ready to defend against opponents. The practice of argumentation sets in train a *co-operative* competition for the better argument, where the orientation to the goal of a communicatively reached agreement unites the participants from the outset. The assumption that the competition can lead to "rationally acceptable," hence "convincing," results rests on specific features of the process of argumentation itself, the four most important of which are: (a) that nobody who could make a relevant contribution may be excluded; (b) that all participants are afforded an equal opportunity to make contributions; (c) that the participants must mean what they say: only truthful utterances are admissible; and (d) that communication must be freed from external and internal compulsion so that the "yes"/"no" stances that participants adopt on criticizable validity claims are motivated solely by the rational force of the better reasons. On the assumption that (a)–(d) express unavoidable pragmatic presuppositions of rational discourse, we may back the adoption of "U" by the following considerations. If everyone who engages in argumentation must make at least these pragmatic presuppositions, then in virtue of (a) the public character of practical discourses and the inclusion of all concerned and (b) the equal communicative rights of all participants, only reasons which take account of the interests and evaluative orientations of all equally can have an impact on the outcome of practical discourses; and because of the absence of (c) deception and (d) compulsion, only reasons can be decisive in the acceptance of a controversial norm. Finally, this "free" acceptance can only occur "jointly" on the assumption that the orientation to communicative agreement is reciprocally imputed to all participants. [. . .]

## Works Cited

Habermas, J. "Discourse Ethics: Notes on a Program of Philosophical Justification." *Moral Consciousness and Communicative Action*. Trans. C. Lenhardt and S. Weber Nicholsen. Cambridge: Polity Press, 1990. 43–115.

Habermas, J. *Justification and Application*. Trans. C. Cronin. Cambridge: Polity Press, 1993.

Kant, I. *Foundations of the Metaphysics of Morals*. Trans. L.W. Beck. New York: Macmillan, 1990.

Strawson, P.F. *Freedom and Resentment*. Methuen: London, 1974.

Taylor, C. *The Sources of the Self*. Cambridge, MA: Harvard University Press, 1989.

Williams, B. *Ethics* and *the Limits of Philosophy*. Cambridge, MA: Harvard University Press, 1985.

## Study Questions

1. Habermas identifies four different approaches to moral philosophy. How do "cognitivist" and "non-cognitivist" approaches differ? How do "strong" and "weak" cognitivism differ? How do "strong" and "weak" non-cognitivism differ?

2. Habermas distinguishes between two points of view: the ethical point of view concerned with the "good" and the moral point of view concerned with the "right." Explain the basis of Habermas's distinction and why he considers the ethical point of view as Aristotelian and the moral point of view as Kantian.

3. Habermas's "discourse ethics" is indebted to, and a repudiation of, Kantian concepts like "kingdom of ends" and "categorical imperative." Explain why.

4. Habermas's discourse theory of morality is supposed to supply a deliberative procedure that can adjudicate competing claims of justice in "modern, pluralistic societies." Choose a relevant example (e.g., Canadian Charter case, international human rights), and explain how the procedure works.

# ∽ CHALLENGES TO MORAL FOUNDATIONS ∽

## Friedrich Nietzsche

Friedrich Nietzsche (1844–1900) studied philology at the Universities of Bonn and Leipzig and was a professor in philology at the University of Basel from 1869 until 1879, when illness forced him to leave. Nietzsche's main philosophical works were written during the nomadic 10 years that followed. *Twilight of the Idols*, completed in 1888, was one of his last books; after a mental breakdown the next year, he was an invalid for the rest of his life. Nietzsche's works celebrated creative energy, animal instinct, and will-to-power, and criticized reason, slave morality, and Christianity.

## Morality as Anti-Nature

From *Twilight of the Idols, or How to Philosophize with a Hammer*

1. There is a time with all passions when they are merely fatalities, when they drag their victim down with the weight of their folly—and a later, very much later time when they are wedded with the spirit, when they are "spiritualized." Formerly one made war on passion itself on account of the folly inherent in it: one conspired for its extermination—all the old moral monsters are unanimous that "*il faut tuer les passions.*" The most famous formula for doing this is contained in the New Testament, in the Sermon on the Mount, where, by the way, things are not at all regarded from a *lofty* standpoint. There, for example, it is said, with reference to sexuality, "if thy eye offend thee, pluck it out": fortunately no Christian follows this prescription. To *exterminate* the passions and desires merely in order to do away with their folly and its unpleasant consequences—this itself seems to us today merely an acute form of folly. We no longer admire dentists who *pull out* the teeth to stop them hurting. [. . .]

2. The same expedient—castration, extirpation—is instinctively selected in a struggle against a desire by those who are too weak-willed, too degenerate to impose moderation upon it: by those natures which need La Trappe,[1] to speak metaphorically (and not metaphorically—), some sort of definitive declaration of hostility, a *chasm* between themselves and a passion.

It is only the degenerate who cannot do without radical expedients; weakness of will, more precisely the inability *not* to react to a stimulus, is itself merely another form of degeneration. [. . .] That hostility, that hatred reaches its height, moreover, only when such natures are no longer sufficiently sound even for the radical cure, for the renunciation of their "devil." Survey the entire history of priests and philosophers, and that of artists as well: the most virulent utterances against the senses have *not* come from the impotent, *nor* from ascetics, but from those who found it impossible to be ascetics, by those who stood in need of being ascetics . . . [. . .]

3. The spiritualization of sensuality is called *love*: it is a great triumph over Christianity. A further triumph is our spiritualization of *enmity*. It consists in profoundly grasping the value of having enemies: in brief, in acting and thinking in the reverse of the way in which one formerly acted and thought. The church has at all times desired the destruction of its enemies: we, we immoralists and anti-Christians, see that it is to our advantage that the Church exist. [. . .]

We adopt the same attitude towards the "enemy within": there too we have grasped its *value*. One is *fruitful* only at the cost of being rich in contradictions; one remains *young* only on condition the soul does not relax does not long for peace.

Nothing has grown more alien to us than that desideratum of former times "peace of soul," the *Christian* desideratum; nothing arouses less envy in us than the moral cow and the fat contentment of the good conscience. [. . .]

In many cases, to be sure, "peace of soul" is merely a misunderstanding—something *else* that simply does not know how to give itself a more honest name. Here, briefly and without prejudice, are a few of them. "Peace of soul" can, for example, be the gentle radiation of a rich animality into the moral (or religious) domain. Or the beginning of weariness, the first of the shadows which evening, every sort of evening, casts. Or a sign that the air is damp, that south winds are on the way. Or unconscious gratitude for a good digestion (sometimes called "philanthropy"). Or the quiescence of the convalescent for whom all things have a new taste and who waits.

Or the condition which succeeds a vigorous gratification of our ruling passion, the pleasant feeling of a rare satiety. Or the decrepitude of our will, our desires, our vices. Or laziness persuaded by vanity to deck itself out as morality. Or the appearance of a certainty, even a dreadful certainty, after the protracted tension and torture of uncertainty. Or the expression of ripeness and mastery in the midst of action, creation, endeavour, volition, a quiet breathing, "freedom of will" *attained*.

*Twilight of the Idols:* who knows? perhaps that too is only a kind of "peace of soul.". . .

4. —I formulate a principle. All naturalism in morality, that is all *healthy* morality, is dominated by an instinct of life—some commandment of life is fulfilled through a certain canon of "shall" and "shall not," some hindrance and hostile element on life's road is thereby removed. *Anti-natural* morality, that is virtually every morality that has hitherto been taught, reverenced and preached, turns on the contrary precisely *against* the instincts of life—it is a now secret, now loud and impudent *condemnation* of these instincts. By saying "God sees into the heart" it denies the deepest and the highest desires of life and takes God for the *enemy of life*.

The saint in whom God takes pleasure is the ideal castrate.

Life is at an end where the "kingdom of God" *begins . . .*

5. If one has grasped the blasphemous of such a rebellion against life as has, in Christian morality, become virtually sacrosanct, one has fortunately therewith grasped something else as well: the uselessness, illusoriness, absurdity, *falsity* of such a rebellion. For a condemnation of life by the living is after all no more than the symptom of a certain kind of life: the question whether the condemnation is just or unjust has not been raised at all. One would have to be situated *outside* life, and on the other hand to know it as thoroughly as any, as many, as all who have experienced it, to be permitted to touch on the problem of the *value* of life at all: sufficient reason for understanding that this problem is for us an inaccessible problem. When we speak of values we do so under the inspiration and from the perspective of life: life itself evaluates through us *when* we establish values.

From this it follows that even that *anti-nature of a morality* which conceives God as the contrary concept to and condemnation of life is only a value judgment on the part of life—of *what* life? of *what* kind of life?—But I have already given the answer: of declining, debilitated, weary, condemned life. Morality as it has been understood hitherto—as it was ultimately formulated by **Schopenhauer** as "denial of the will to life"—is the *instinct of decadence* itself, which makes out of itself an imperative: it says: "Perish!"—it is the judgment of the judged . . .

6. Let us consider finally what naivety it is to say "man *ought* to be thus and thus!" Reality shows us an enchanting wealth of types, the luxuriance of a prodigal play and change of forms: and does some pitiful journeyman moralist say at the sight of it: "No! Man ought to be *different*"?

He even knows *how* man ought to be, this bigoted wretch; he paints himself on the wall and says "*ecce homo*"! (Behold the man!)

But even when the moralist merely turns to the individual and says to him: "*You* ought to be thus and thus" he does not cease to make himself ridiculous. The individual is, in his future and in his past, a piece of fate, one law more, one necessity more for everything that is and everything that will be. To say to him "change yourself" means to demand that everything should change, even in the past.

And there have indeed been consistent moralists who wanted man to be different, namely virtuous, who wanted him in their own likeness, namely that of a bigot: to that end, they *denied* the world! No mean madness! No modest presumption!

Insofar as morality *condemns* as morality and *not* with regard to the aims and objects of life, it is a specific error with which one should show no sympathy, an *idiosyncrasy of the degenerate* which has caused an unspeakable amount of harm!

We others, we immoralists, have on the contrary opened wide our hearts to every kind of understanding, comprehension, *approval.* We do not readily deny, we seek our honour in *affirming.* We have come more and more to appreciate that economy which needs and knows how to use all that which the holy lunacy of the priest, the *diseased* reason of the priest rejects; that economy in the law of life which derives advantage even from the repellent species of the bigot, the priest, the virtuous man— *what* advantage?—But we ourselves, we immoralists, are the answer to that . . .

## The Four Great Errors

1. *The error of confusing cause and consequence.* There is no more dangerous error than that of *mistaking the consequence for the cause*: I call it reason's intrinsic form of corruption. Nonetheless, this error is among the most ancient and most recent habits of mankind: it is even sanctified among us, it bears the names "religion" and "morality." *Every* proposition formulated by religion and morality contains it; priests and moral legislators are the authors of this corruption of reason. [. . .]

2. The most general formula at the base of every religion and morality is: "Do this and this, refrain from this and this—and you will be happy! Otherwise. . . ." Every morality, every religion *is* this imperative—I call it the great original sin of reason, *immortal unreason.* In my mouth this formula is converted into its reverse—*first* example of my

"revaluation of all values": a well-constituted human being, a "happy one," *must* perform certain actions and instinctively shrinks from other actions, he transports the order of which he is the physiological representative into his relations with other human beings and with things. In a formula: his virtue is the *consequence* of his happiness. [. . .]

The Church and morality say: "A race, a people perishes through vice and luxury." My *restored* reason says: when a people is perishing, degenerating physiologically, vice and luxury (that is to say the necessity for stronger and stronger and more and more frequent stimulants, such as every exhausted nature is acquainted with) *follow* therefrom. A young man grows prematurely pale and faded. His friends say: this and that illness is to blame. I say: *that* he became ill, *that* he failed to resist the illness, was already the consequence of an impoverished life, a hereditary exhaustion. [. . .] Every error, of whatever kind, is a consequence of degeneration of instinct, disgregation of will: one has thereby virtually defined the *bad.* Everything *good* is instinct—and consequently easy, necessary, free. Effort is an objection, the *god* is typically distinguished from the hero (in my language: *light* feet are the first attribute of divinity).

3. *The error of a false causality.*—We have always believed we know what a cause is; but whence did we derive our knowledge, more precisely our belief we possessed this knowledge? From the realm of the celebrated "inner facts," none of which has up till now been shown to be factual. We believed ourselves to be causal agents in the act of willing; we at least thought we were there *catching causality in the act.* It was likewise never doubted that all the *antecedentia* of an action, its causes, were to be sought in the consciousness and could be discovered there if one sought them—as "motives": for otherwise one would not have been *free* to perform it, *responsible* for it. Finally, who would have disputed that a thought is caused? that the ego causes the thought?

Of these three "inner facts" through which causality seemed to be guaranteed the first and most convincing was that of *will as cause*; the conception of a consciousness ("mind") as cause and later still that of the ego (the "subject") as cause are merely after-products after causality had, on the basis of will, been firmly established as a given fact, as *empiricism*.

Meanwhile we have thought better. Today we do not believe a word of it. The "inner world" is full of phantoms and false lights: the will is one of them. The will no longer moves anything, consequently no longer explains anything—it merely accompanies events, it can also be absent. The so-called "motive": another error. Merely a surface phenomenon of consciousness, an accompaniment to an act, which conceals rather than exposes the *antecedentia* of the act. And as for the ego! It has become a fable, a fiction, a play on words: it has totally ceased to think, to feel and to will!

What follows from this? There are no spiritual causes at all! The whole of the alleged empiricism which affirmed them has gone to the devil! *That is what follows!*—And we had made a nice misuse of that "empiricism," we had *created* the world on the basis of it as a world of causes, as a world of will, as a world of spirit. [. . .] Man projected his three "inner facts," that in which he believed more firmly than in anything else, will, spirit, ego, outside himself—he derived the concept "being" only from the concept "ego," he posited "things" as possessing being according to his own image, according to his concept of the ego as cause. No wonder he later always discovered in things only *that which he had put into them!* [. . .]

And even our atom, *messieurs* mechanists and physicists, how much error, how much rudimentary psychology, still remains in your atom!—To say nothing of the "thing in itself," that *horrendum pudendum* (ugly shameful part) of the metaphysicians! The error of spirit as cause mistaken for reality! And made the measure of reality! And called *God!*—

4. *The error of imaginary causes.* [. . .] Most of our general feelings—every sort of restraint, pressure, tension, explosion in the play and counter-play of our organs, likewise and especially the condition of the *nervus sympathicus*—excite our cause-creating drive: we want to have a *reason* for feeling *as we do*—for feeling well or for feeling ill. It never suffices us simply to establish the mere fact *that* we feel as we

do: we acknowledge this fact—become *conscious* of it—only *when* we have furnished it with a motivation of some kind.—The memory, which in such a case becomes active without our being aware of it, calls up earlier states of a similar kind and the causal interpretations which have grown out of them—*not* their causality. To be sure, the belief that these ideas, the accompanying occurrences in the consciousness, were causes is also brought up by the memory. Thus there arises a *habituation* to a certain causal interpretation which in truth obstructs and even prohibits an *investigation* of the cause. [. . .]

6. *The entire realm of morality and religion falls under this concept of imaginary causes.*—"Explanation" of *unpleasant* general feelings. They arise from beings hostile to us (evil spirits: most celebrated case—hysterics misunderstood as witches). They arise from actions we cannot approve of (the feeling of "sin," of "culpability" foisted upon a physiological discomfort—one always finds reasons for being discontented with oneself). They arise as punishments, as payment for something we should not have done, should not have *been* [. . .] . They arise as the consequences of rash actions which have turned out badly (—the emotions, the senses assigned as "cause," as "to blame"; physiological states of distress construed, with the aid of *other* states of distress, as "deserved").— Explanation" of *pleasant* general feelings. They arise from trust in God. They arise from the consciousness of good actions (the so-called "good conscience," a physiological condition sometimes so like a sound digestion as to be mistaken for it). They arise from the successful outcome of undertakings (—naïve fallacy: the successful outcome of an undertaking certainly does not produce any pleasant general feelings in a hypochondriac or a **Pascal**). They arise from faith, hope and charity—the Christian virtues.—In reality all these supposed explanations are *consequential* states and as it were translations of pleasurable and unpleasurable feelings into a false dialect: one is in a state in which one can experience hope *because* the physiological basic feeling is once more strong and ample; one trusts in God *because* the feeling of plenitude and strength makes one calm.—Morality and religion

fall entirely under the *psychology of error*: in every single case cause is mistaken for effect; or the effect of what is *believed* true is mistaken for the truth; or a state of consciousness is mistaken for the causation of this state.

7. *The error of free will.*—We no longer have any sympathy today with the concept of "free will": we know only too well what it is—the most infamous of all the arts of the theologian for making mankind "accountable" in his sense of the word, that is to say for *making mankind dependent on him.*

I give here only the psychology of making men accountable.—Everywhere accountability is sought, it is usually the instinct for *punishing and judging* which seeks it. One has deprived becoming of its innocence if being in this or that state is traced back to will, to intentions, to accountable acts: the doctrine of will has been invented essentially for the purposes of punishment, that is of *finding guilty.* The whole of the old-style psychology, the psychology of will, has as its precondition the desire of its authors, the priests at the head of the ancient communities, to create for themselves a *right* to ordain punishments— or their desire to create for God a right to do so.

Men were thought of as "free" so that they could become *guilty*: consequently, every action *had* to be thought of as willed, the origin of every action as lying in the consciousness. [. . .]

Today, when we have started to move in the *reverse* direction, when we immoralists especially are trying with all our might to remove the concept of guilt and the concept of punishment from the world and to purge psychology, history, nature, the social institutions and sanctions of them, there is in our eyes no more radical opposition that that of the theologians, who continue to infect the innocence of becoming with "punishment" and "guilt" by means of the concept of the "moral world-order." Christianity is a hangman's metaphysics. . . .

8. What alone can *our* teaching be?—That no one *gives* a human being his qualities: not God, not society, not his parents or ancestors, not *he himself* (—the nonsensical idea here last rejected was propounded, as "intelligible freedom," by Kant, and perhaps also by Plato before him). *No one* is accountable for existing at all, or for being constituted as he is, or for living in the circumstances and surroundings in which he lives. The fatality of his nature cannot be disentangled from the fatality of all that which has been and will be. He is *not* the result of a special design, a will, a purpose; he is *not* the subject of an attempt to attain to an "ideal of man" or an "ideal of happiness" or an "ideal of morality"—it is absurd to want to *hand over* his nature to some purpose or other. *We* invented the concept "purpose": in reality purpose is *lacking.*

One is necessary, one is a piece of fate, one belongs to the whole, one *is* in the whole—there exists nothing which could judge, measure, compare, condemn the whole.

*But nothing exists apart from the whole!*—That no one is any longer made accountable, that the kind of being manifested cannot be traced back to a *causa prima* (first cause), that the world is a unity neither as sensorium nor as "spirit," *this alone is the great liberation*—thus alone is the *innocence* of becoming restored.

This concept "God" has hitherto been the greatest *objection* to existence.

We deny God; in denying God, we deny accountability: only by doing *that* do we redeem the world.— [. . .]

## Expeditions of an Untimely Man

[. . .]

29. *From a doctorate exam.*—"What is the task of all higher education?"—To turn a man into a machine.— "By what means?"—He has to learn how to feel bored.—"How is that achieved?— Through the concept of duty.—"Who is his model?"—The philologist: he teaches how to *grind.*—"Who is the perfect man?"—The civil servant.—"Which philosophy provides the best formula for the civil servant?"—Kant's: the civil servant as thing in itself set as judge over the civil servant as appearance.— [. . .]

33. *The natural value of egoism.*—The value of egoism depends on the physiological value of him who possesses it: it can be very valuable, it can

be worthless and contemptible. Every individual may be regarded as representing the ascending or descending line of life. When one has decided which, one has thereby established a canon for the value of his egoism. If he represents the ascending line his value is in fact extraordinary—and for the sake of the life-collective, which with him takes a step *forward*, the care expended on his preservation, on the creation of optimum conditions for him, may even be extreme. For the individual, the "single man," as people and philosophers have hitherto understood him, is an error: he does not constitute a separate entity, an atom, a "link in the chain," something merely inherited from the past—he constitutes the entire *single* line "man" up to and including himself.

If he represents the descending development, decay, chronic degeneration, sickening (—sickness is, broadly speaking, already a phenomenon consequent upon decay, *not* the cause of it), then he can be accorded little value, and elementary fairness demands that he *take away* as little as possible from the well-constituted. He is no better than a parasite on them. [. . .]

35. *A criticism of decadence morality.*—An "altruistic" morality, a morality under which egoism *languishes*—is under all circumstances a bad sign. This applies to individuals, it applies especially to peoples. The best are lacking when egoism begins to be lacking. To choose what is harmful to *oneself*, to be *attracted* by "disinterested" motives, almost constitutes the formula for *decadence*. "Not to seek *one's own* advantage"—that is merely a moral figleaf for a quite different, namely physiological fact: "I no longer know how to *find* my advantage."

Disgregation of the instincts!—Man is finished when he becomes altruistic.—Instead of saying simply "I am no longer worth anything," the moral lie in the mouth of the *decadent* says: "Nothing is worth anything—*life* is not worth anything."

Such a judgment represents, after all, a grave danger, it is contagious—on the utterly morbid soil of society it soon grows up luxuriously, now in the form of religion (Christianity), now in that of philosophy (Schopenhauerism). In some circumstances the vapours of such a poison-tree jungle sprung up out of putrefaction can poison *life* for years ahead, for thousands of years ahead. [. . .]

37. *Whether we have grown more moral.*—As was only to be expected, the whole *ferocity* of the moral stupidity which, as is well known, is considered morality as such in Germany, has launched itself against my concept "beyond good and evil": I could tell some pretty stories about it. Above all, I was invited to reflect on the "undeniable superiority" of our age in moral judgment, our real *advance* in this respect: compared with *us*, a **Cesare Borgia** was certainly not to be set up as a "higher man," as a kind of *superman*, in the way I set him up.

A Swiss editor [. . .] went so far—not without expressing his admiration of the courage for so hazardous an enterprise—as to "understand" that the meaning of my work lay in a proposal to abolish all decent feeling. [. . .] By way of reply I permit myself to raise the question *whether we have really grown more moral*. That all the world believes so is already an objection to it.

We modern men, very delicate, very vulnerable and paying and receiving consideration in a hundred ways, imagine in fact that this sensitive humanity which we represent, this *achieved* unanimity in forbearance, in readiness to help, in mutual trust, is a positive advance, that with this we have gone far beyond the men of the Renaissance. But every age thinks in this way, *has* to think in this way. What is certain is that we would not dare to place ourselves in Renaissance conditions, or even imagine ourselves in them: our nerves would not endure that reality, not to speak of our muscles. This incapacity, however, demonstrates, not an advance, but only a different, a more belated constitution, a weaker, more delicate, more vulnerable one, out of which is necessarily engendered a morality *which is full of consideration*. If we think away our delicacy and belatedness, our physiological aging, then our morality of "humanization" too loses its value at once—no morality has any value in itself—: we would despise it. On the other hand, let us be in no doubt that we modern men, with our thick padding of humanity which dislikes to give the slightest offence, would provide the contemporaries of Cesare Borgia with a side-splitting comedy. We are, in fact, involuntarily funny beyond all measure, we with our modern "virtues."

The decay of our hostile and mistrust-arousing instincts—and that is what constitutes our advance—represents only one of the effects attending our general decay of *vitality*: it costs a hundred times more effort, more foresight, to preserve so dependent, so late an existence as we are. Here everyone helps everyone else, here everyone is to a certain degree an invalid and everyone a nurse. This is then called "virtue"—: among men who knew a different kind of life, a fuller, more prodigal, more overflowing life, it would be called something else: "cowardice," perhaps, "pitiableness," "old women's morality."

Our softening of customs—this is my thesis, my *innovation* if you like—is a consequence of decline; stern and frightful customs can, conversely, be a consequence of a superabundance of life. For in the latter case much may be risked, much demanded and much squandered. What was formerly a spice of life would be *poison* to us.

We are likewise too old, too belated, to be capable of indifference—also a form of strength: our morality of pity, against which I was the first to warn, that which one might call *l'impressionisme morale*, is one more expression of the physiological over-excitability pertaining to everything *decadent*. That movement which with Schopenhauer's *morality of pity* attempted to present itself as scientific—a very unsuccessful attempt!—is the actual *decadence* movement in morality; as such it is profoundly related to Christian morality. Strong ages, *noble* cultures, see in pity, in "love of one's neighbour," in a lack of self and

self-reliance, something contemptible.—Ages are to be assessed according to their *positive forces*—and by this assessment the age of the Renaissance, so prodigal and so fateful, appears as the last *great* age, and we, we moderns with our anxious care for ourselves and love of our neighbour, with our virtues of work, of unpretentiousness, of fair play, of scientificality—acquisitive, economical, machine-minded—appear as a *weak* age.

Our virtues are conditioned, are *demanded* by our weakness.

"Equality," a certain actual rendering similar of which the theory of "equal rights" is only the expression, belongs essentially to decline: the chasm between man and man, class and class, the multiplicity of types, the will to be oneself, to stand out—that which I call *pathos of distance*—characterizes every *strong* age. The tension, the range between the extremes is today growing less and less—the extremes themselves are finally obliterated to the point of similarity. [. . .]

**42.** *Where faith is needed.*—Nothing is rarer among moralists and saints than integrity; perhaps they say the opposite, perhaps they even *believe* it. For when faith is more useful, effective, convincing than *conscious* hypocrisy, hypocrisy instinctively and forthwith becomes *innocent*: first principle for the understanding of great saints. In the case of philosophers too, a different kind of saint, their entire trade demands that they concede only certain truths: namely those through which their trade receives *public* sanction—in Kantian terms, truths of *practical* reason. They know what they *have* to prove, they are practical in that—they recognize one another by their agreement over "truths."—"Thou shalt not lie"—in plain words: *take care*, philosopher, not to tell the truth. . . . [. . .]

## Note

1. Tr.: The abbey at Soligny from which the Trappist order—characterized by the severity of its discipline—takes its name.

## Study Questions

1. Why does Nietzsche say that Christian morality and all other moralities are "anti-nature"? What does Nietzsche, as a self-proclaimed "immoralist and anti-Christian," want instead?

2. In discussing the value of life, Nietzsche takes a "perspectivalist" approach. What is perspectivalism, and how does it challenge moral foundations?

3. What are Nietzsche's "four great errors," and how does each challenge morality?

4. What criticisms does Nietzsche make of morality's ideals of altruism, progress, and equality?

---

# A.J. Ayer

A.J. (Alfred Jules) Ayer (1910–1989) belongs to the British empiricist tradition of Locke, Hume, and Russell. After graduating from Christ Church, Oxford, Ayer studied with Moritz Schlick in Vienna, lectured at Christ Church, and after his wartime service, spent his career as a professor at University College London and then Oxford. Ayer's 1936 book, *Language, Truth and Logic*, brought the logical positivism of the Vienna Circle to an English-speaking audience. In this excerpt, Ayer defends emotivism: the position that as mere expressions of emotion, ethical "claims" are meaningless.

## Critique of Ethics

From *Language, Truth and Logic*

### 1. Introduction

There is still one objection to be met before we can claim to have justified our view that all **synthetic** propositions are empirical hypotheses. This objection is based on the common supposition that our speculative knowledge is of two distinct kinds—that which relates to questions of empirical fact, and that which relates to questions of value. It will be said that "statements of value" are genuine synthetic propositions, but that they cannot with any show of justice be represented as hypotheses, which are used to predict the course of our sensations; and, accordingly, that the existence of ethics [. . .] as [a] branch of speculative knowledge presents an insuperable objection to our radical empiricist thesis.

In face of this objection, it is our business to give an account of "judgments of value" which is both satisfactory in itself and consistent with our general empiricist principles. We shall set ourselves to show

that insofar as statements of value are significant, they are ordinary "scientific" statements; and that insofar as they are not scientific, they are not in the literal sense significant, but are simply expressions of emotion which can be neither true nor false. [. . .]

The ordinary system of ethics, as elaborated in the works of ethical philosophers, is very far from being a homogeneous whole. Not only is it apt to contain pieces of metaphysics, and analyses of non-ethical concepts: its actual ethical contents are themselves of very different kinds. We may divide them, indeed, into four main classes. There are, first of all, propositions which express definitions of ethical terms, or judgments about the legitimacy or possibility of certain definitions. Secondly, there are propositions describing the phenomena of moral experience, and their causes. Thirdly, there are exhortations to moral virtue. And, lastly, there are actual ethical judgments. It is unfortunately the case that the distinction between these four classes, plain as it is, is commonly ignored by ethical philosophers; with the result that it is often very difficult to tell from their works what it is that they are seeking to discover or prove.

In fact, it is easy to see that only the first of our four classes, namely that which comprises the propositions relating to the definitions of ethical terms, can be said to constitute ethical philosophy. The propositions which describe the phenomena of moral experience, and their causes, must be assigned to the science of psychology, or sociology. The exhortations to moral virtue are not propositions at all, but ejaculations or commands which are designed to provoke the reader to action of a certain sort. Accordingly, they do not belong to any branch of philosophy or science. As for the expressions of ethical judgments, we have not yet determined how they should be classified. But inasmuch as they are certainly neither definitions nor comments upon definitions, nor quotations, we may say decisively that they do not belong to ethical philosophy. A strictly philosophical treatise on ethics should therefore make no ethical pronouncements. But it should, by giving an analysis of ethical terms, show what is the category to which all such pronouncements belong. And this is what we are now about to do.

## 2. Subjectivism, Utilitarianism, and Absolutism

A question which is often discussed by ethical philosophers is whether it is possible to find definitions which would reduce all ethical terms to one or two fundamental terms. But this question, though it undeniably belongs to ethical philosophy, is not relevant to our present inquiry. We are not now concerned to discover which term, within the sphere of ethical terms, is to be taken as fundamental; whether, for example, "good" can be defined in terms of "right" or "right" in terms of "good," or both in terms of "value." What we are interested in is the possibility of reducing the whole sphere of ethical terms to non-ethical terms. We are inquiring whether statements of ethical value can be translated into statements of empirical fact.

That they can be so translated is the contention of those ethical philosophers who are commonly called subjectivists, and of those who are known as utilitarians. For the utilitarian defines the rightness of actions, and the goodness of ends, in terms of the pleasure, or happiness, or satisfaction, to which they give rise; the subjectivist, in terms of the feelings of approval which a certain person, or group of people, has towards them. Each of these types of definition makes moral judgments into a subclass of psychological or sociological judgments; and for this reason they are very attractive to us. For, if either was correct, it would follow that ethical assertions were not generically different from the factual assertions which are ordinarily contrasted with them; and the account which we have already given of empirical hypotheses would apply to them also.

Nevertheless we shall not adopt either a subjectivist or a utilitarian analysis of ethical terms. We reject the subjectivist view that to call an action right, or a thing good, is to say that it is generally approved of, because it is not self-contradictory to assert that some actions which are generally approved of are not right, or that some things which are generally approved of are not good. And we reject the alternative subjectivist view that a man who asserts that a certain action is right, or that a certain thing is good, is saying that he himself approves of it, on the ground that a man who confessed that he sometimes approved of what was bad or wrong would not be contradicting himself. And a similar argument is fatal to utilitarianism. We cannot agree that to call an action right is to say that of all the actions possible in the circumstances it would cause, or be likely to cause, the greatest happiness, or the greatest balance of pleasure over pain, or the greatest balance of satisfied over unsatisfied desire, because we find that it is not self-contradictory to say that it is sometimes wrong to perform the action which would actually or probably cause the greatest happiness, or the greatest balance of pleasure over pain, or of satisfied over unsatisfied desire. And since it is not self-contradictory to say that some pleasant things are not good, or that some bad things are desired, it cannot be the case that the sentence "x is good" is equivalent to "x is pleasant," or to "x is desired." And to every other variant of utilitarianism with which I am acquainted the same objection can be made. And therefore we should, I think, conclude that the validity of ethical judgments is not determined by the felicific tendencies of actions, any more than by the nature of people's feelings; but that it must be regarded as "absolute" or "intrinsic," and not empirically calculable.

If we say this, we are not, of course, denying that it is possible to invent a language in which all ethical symbols are definable in non-ethical terms, or even that it is desirable to invent such a language and adopt it in place of our own; what we are denying is that the suggested reduction of ethical to non-ethical statements is consistent with the conventions of our actual language. That is, we reject utilitarianism and subjectivism, not as proposals to replace our existing ethical notions by new ones, but as analyses of our existing ethical notions. Our contention is simply that, in our language, sentences which contain normative ethical symbols are not equivalent to sentences which express psychological propositions, or indeed empirical propositions of any kind.

It is advisable here to make it plain that it is only normative ethical symbols, and not descriptive ethical symbols, that are held by us to be indefinable in factual terms. There is a danger of confusing these two types of symbols, because they are commonly constituted by signs of the same sensible form. Thus a complex sign of the form "$x$ is wrong" may constitute a sentence which expresses a moral judgment concerning a certain type of conduct, or it may constitute a sentence which states that a certain type of conduct is repugnant to the moral sense of a particular society. In the latter case, the symbol "wrong" is a descriptive ethical symbol, and the sentence in which it occurs expresses an ordinary sociological proposition; in the former case, the symbol "wrong" is a normative ethical symbol, and the sentence in which it occurs does not, we maintain, express an empirical proposition at all. It is only with normative ethics that we are at present concerned; so that whenever ethical symbols are used in the course of this argument without qualification, they are always to be interpreted as symbols of the normative type.

In admitting that normative ethical concepts are irreducible to empirical concepts, we seem to be leaving the way clear for the "absolutist" view of ethics—that is, the view that statements of value are not controlled by observation, as ordinary empirical propositions are, but only by a mysterious "intellectual intuition." A feature of this theory, which is seldom recognized by its advocates, is that it makes statements of value unverifiable. For it is notorious that what seems intuitively certain to one person may seem doubtful, or even false, to another. So that unless it is possible to provide some criterion by which one may decide between conflicting intuitions, a mere appeal to intuition is worthless as a test of a proposition's validity. But in the case of moral judgments, no such criterion can be given. Some moralists claim to settle the matter by saying that they "know" that their own moral judgments are correct. But such an assertion is of purely psychological interest, and has not the slightest tendency to prove the validity of any moral judgment. For dissentient moralists may equally well "know" that their ethical views are correct. And, as far as subjective certainty goes, there will be nothing to choose between them. When such differences of opinion arise in connection with an ordinary empirical proposition, one may attempt to resolve them by referring to, or actually carrying out, some relevant empirical test. But with regard to ethical statements, there is, on the "absolutist" or "intuitionist" theory, no relevant empirical test. We are therefore justified in saying that on this theory ethical statements are held to be unverifiable. They are, of course, also held to be genuine synthetic propositions.

Considering the use which we have made of the principle that a synthetic proposition is significant only if it is empirically verifiable, it is clear that the acceptance of an "absolutist" theory of ethics would undermine the whole of our main argument. And as we have already rejected the "naturalistic" theories which are commonly supposed to provide the only alternative to "absolutism" in ethics, we seem to have reached a difficult position. We shall meet the difficulty by showing that the correct treatment of ethical statements is afforded by a third theory, which is wholly compatible with our radical empiricism.

## 3. Emotivism

We begin by admitting that the fundamental ethical concepts are unanalyzable, inasmuch as there is no criterion by which one can test the validity of the judgments in which they occur. So far we are in agreement with the absolutists. But, unlike the absolutists, we are able to give an explanation of this fact about ethical concepts. We say that the reason why they are unanalyzable is that they are mere pseudo-concepts. The presence of an ethical symbol in a proposition adds nothing to its factual content. Thus if I say to someone, "You acted wrongly in stealing that money," I am not stating anything more than if I had simply said, "You stole that money." In adding that this action is wrong I am not making any further statement about it. I am simply evincing my moral disapproval of it. It is as if I had said, "You stole that money," in a peculiar tone of horror, or written it with the addition of some special exclamation marks. The tone, or the exclamation marks, adds nothing to the literal meaning of the sentence. It merely serves to show that the expression of it is attended by certain feelings in the speaker.

If now I generalize my previous statement and say, "stealing money is wrong," I produce a sentence which has no factual meaning—that is, expresses no proposition which can be either true or false. It is as if I had written "stealing money!!"—where the shape and thickness of the exclamation marks show, by a suitable convention, that a special sort of moral disapproval is the feeling which is being expressed. It is clear that there is nothing said here which can be true or false. Another man may disagree with me about the wrongness of stealing, in the sense that he may not have the same feelings about stealing as I have, and he may quarrel with me on account of my moral sentiments. But he cannot, strictly speaking, contradict me. For in saying that a certain type of action is right or wrong, I am not making any factual statement, not even a statement about my own state of mind. I am merely expressing certain moral sentiments. And the man who is ostensibly contradicting me is merely expressing his moral sentiments. So that there is plainly no sense in asking which of us is in the right. For neither of us is asserting a genuine proposition.

What we have just been saying about the symbol "wrong" applies to all normative ethical symbols. Sometimes they occur in sentences which record ordinary empirical facts besides expressing ethical feeling about those facts: sometimes they occur in sentences which simply express ethical feeling about a certain type of action, or situation, without making any statement of fact. But in every case in which one would commonly be said to be making an ethical judgment, the function of the relevant ethical word is purely "emotive." It is used to express feeling about certain objects, but not to make any assertion about them.

It is worth mentioning that ethical terms do not serve only to express feeling. They are calculated also to arouse feeling, and so to stimulate action. Indeed some of them are used in such a way as to give the sentences in which they occur the effect of commands. Thus the sentence "It is your duty to tell the truth" may be regarded both as the expression of a certain sort of ethical feeling about truthfulness and as the expression of the command "Tell the truth." The sentence "You ought to tell the truth" also involves the command "Tell the truth," but here the tone of the command is less emphatic. In the sentence "It is good to tell the truth" the command has become little more than a suggestion. And thus the "meaning" of the word "good," in its ethical usage, is differentiated from that of the word "duty" or the word "ought." In fact we may define the meaning of the various ethical words in terms both of the different feelings they are ordinarily taken to express, and also the different responses which they are calculated to provoke.

We can now see why it is impossible to find a criterion for determining the validity of ethical judgments. It is not because they have an "absolute" validity which is mysteriously independent of ordinary sense-experience, but because they have no objective validity whatsoever. If a sentence makes no statement at all, there is obviously no sense in asking whether what it says is true or false. And we have seen that sentences which simply express moral judgments do not say anything. They are pure expressions of feeling and as such do not come under the category of truth and falsehood. They are unverifiable for the same reason as a cry of pain or a word of command is unverifiable—because they do not express genuine propositions.

Thus, although our theory of ethics might fairly be said to be radically subjectivist, it differs in a very important respect from the orthodox subjectivist theory. For the orthodox subjectivist does not deny, as we do, that the sentences of a moralizer express genuine propositions. All he denies is that they express propositions of a unique non-empirical character. His own view is that they express propositions about the speaker's feelings. If this were so, ethical judgments clearly would be capable of being true or false. They would be true if the speaker had the relevant feelings, and false if he had not. And this is a matter which is, in principle, empirically verifiable. Furthermore they could be significantly contradicted. For if I say, "Tolerance is a virtue," and someone answers, "You don't approve of it," he would, on the ordinary subjectivist theory, be contradicting me. On our theory, he would not be contradicting me, because, in saying that tolerance was a virtue, I should not be making any statement about my own feelings or about anything else. I should simply be evincing my feelings, which is not at all the same thing as saying that I have them.

The distinction between the expression of feeling and the assertion of feeling is complicated by the fact that the assertion that one has a certain feeling often accompanies the expression of that feeling, and is then, indeed, a factor in the expression of that feeling. Thus I may simultaneously express boredom and say that I am bored, and in that case my utterance of the words, "I am bored," is one of the circumstances which make it true to say that I am expressing or evincing boredom. But I can express boredom without actually saying that I am bored. I can express it by my tone and gestures, while making a statement about something wholly unconnected with it, or by an ejaculation, or without uttering any words at all. So that even if the assertion that one has a certain feeling always involves the expression of that feeling, the expression of a feeling assuredly does not always involve the assertion that one has it. And this is the important point to grasp in considering the distinction between our theory and the ordinary subjectivist theory. For whereas the subjectivist holds that ethical statements actually assert the existence of certain feelings, we hold that ethical statements are expressions and excitants of feeling which do not necessarily involve any assertions.

## 4. Objection

We have already remarked that the main objection to the ordinary subjectivist theory is that the validity of ethical judgments is not determined by the nature of their author's feelings. And this is an objection which our theory escapes. For it does not imply that the existence of any feelings is a necessary and sufficient condition of the validity of an ethical judgment. It implies, on the contrary, that ethical judgments have no validity.

There is, however, a celebrated argument against subjectivist theories which our theory does not escape. It has been pointed out by Moore that if ethical statements were simply statements about the speaker's feelings, it would be impossible to argue about questions of value. To take a typical example: if a man said that thrift was a virtue, and another replied that it was a vice, they would not, on this theory, be disputing with one another. One would be saying that he approved of thrift, and the other that he didn't; and there is no reason why both these statements should not be true. Now Moore held it to be obvious that we do dispute about questions of value, and accordingly concluded that the particular form of subjectivism which he was discussing was false.

It is plain that the conclusion that it is impossible to dispute about questions of value follows from our theory also. For as we hold that such sentences as "Thrift is a virtue" and "Thrift is a vice" do not express propositions at all, we clearly cannot hold that they express incompatible propositions.

We must therefore admit that if Moore's argument really refutes the ordinary subjectivist theory, it also refutes ours. But, in fact, we deny that it does refute even the ordinary subjectivist theory. For we hold that one really never does dispute about questions of value.

This may seem, at first sight, to be a very paradoxical assertion. For we certainly do engage in disputes which are ordinarily regarded as disputes about questions of value. But, in all such cases, we find, if we consider the matter closely, that the dispute is not really about a question of value, but about a question of fact. When someone disagrees with us about the moral value of a certain action or type of action, we do admittedly resort to argument in order to win him over to our way of thinking. But we do not attempt to show by our arguments that he has the "wrong" ethical feeling towards a situation whose nature he has correctly apprehended. What we attempt to show is that he is mistaken about the facts of the case. We argue that he has misconceived the agent's motive: or that he has misjudged the effects of the action, or its probable effects in view of the agent's knowledge; or that he has failed to take into account the special circumstances in which the agent was placed. Or else we employ more general arguments about the effects which actions of a certain type tend to produce, or the qualities which are usually manifested in their performance. We do this in the hope that we have only to get our opponent to agree with us about the nature of the empirical facts for him to adopt the same moral attitude towards them as we do. And as the people with whom we argue have generally received the same moral education as ourselves, and live in the same social order, our expectation is usually justified. But if our opponent happens to have undergone a different process of moral "conditioning" from ourselves, so that, even when he acknowledges all the facts, he still disagrees with us about the moral value of the actions under discussion, then we abandon the attempt to convince him by argument. We say that it is impossible to argue with him because he has a distorted or undeveloped moral sense; which signifies

merely that he employs a different set of values from our own. We feel that our own system of values is superior, and therefore speak in such derogatory terms of his. But we cannot bring forward any arguments to show that our system is superior. For our judgment that it is so is itself a judgment of value, and accordingly outside the scope of argument. It is because argument fails us when we come to deal with pure questions of value, as distinct from questions of fact, that we finally resort to mere abuse.

In short, we find that argument is possible on moral questions only if some system of values is presupposed. If our opponent concurs with us in expressing moral disapproval of all actions of a given type $t$, then we may get him to condemn a particular action A, by bringing forward arguments to show that A is of type $t$. For the question whether A does or does not belong to that type is a plain question of fact. Given that a man has certain moral principles, we argue that he must, in order to be consistent, react morally to certain things in a certain way. What we do not and cannot argue about is the validity of these moral principles. We merely praise or condemn them in the light of our own feelings.

If anyone doubts the accuracy of this account of moral disputes, let him try to construct even an imaginary argument on a question of value which does not reduce itself to an argument about a question of logic or about an empirical matter of fact. I am confident that he will not succeed in producing a single example. And if that is the case, he must allow that its involving the impossibility of purely ethical arguments is not, as Moore thought, a ground of objection to our theory, but rather a point in favour of it.

## 5. Conclusion

Having upheld our theory against the only criticism which appeared to threaten it, we may now use it to define the nature of all ethical inquiries. We find that ethical philosophy consists simply in saying that ethical concepts are pseudo-concepts and therefore unanalyzable. The further task of describing the different feelings that the different ethical terms are used to express, and the different reactions that they customarily provoke, is a task for the psychologist. There cannot be such a thing as ethical science, if by ethical science one means the elaboration of a "true" system of morals. For we have seen that, as ethical judgments are mere expressions of feeling, there can be no way of determining the validity of any ethical system, and, indeed, no sense in asking whether any such system is true. All that one may legitimately inquire in this connection is, What are the moral habits of a given person or group of people, and what causes them to have precisely those habits and feelings? And this inquiry falls wholly within the scope of the existing social sciences.

It appears, then, that ethics, as a branch of knowledge, is nothing more than a department of psychology and sociology. And in case anyone thinks that we are overlooking the existence of casuistry, we may remark that casuistry is not a science, but is a purely analytical investigation of the structure of a given moral system. In other words, it is an exercise in formal logic.

When one comes to pursue the psychological inquiries which constitute ethical science, one is immediately enabled to account for the Kantian and hedonistic theories of morals. For one finds that one of the chief causes of moral behaviour is fear, both conscious and unconscious, of a god's displeasure, and fear of the enmity of society. And this, indeed, is the reason why moral precepts present themselves to some people as "categorical" commands. And one finds, also, that the moral code of a society is partly determined by the beliefs of that society concerning the conditions of its own happiness—or, in other words, that a society tends to encourage or discourage a given type of conduct by the use of moral sanctions according as it appears to promote or detract from the contentment of the society as a whole. And this is the reason why altruism is recommended in most moral codes and egotism condemned. It is from the observation of this connection between morality and happiness that hedonistic or eudæmonistic theories of morals ultimately spring, just as the moral theory of Kant is based on the fact, previously explained, that moral precepts have for some people the force of inexorable commands. As each of these theories ignores the fact which lies at the root of the other, both may be criticized as being one-sided; but this is not the main objection to either of them. Their essential defect is that they treat propositions which refer to the causes and attributes of our ethical feelings as if they were definitions of ethical concepts. And thus they fail to recognize that ethical concepts are pseudo-concepts and consequently indefinable. [. . .]

It should now be clear that the only information which we can legitimately derive from the study of our [. . .] moral experiences is information about our own mental and physical make-up. We take note of these experiences as providing data for our psychological and sociological generalizations. And this is the only way in which they serve to increase our knowledge. It follows that any attempt to make our use of ethical [. . .] concepts the basis of a metaphysical theory concerning the existence of a world of values, as distinct from the world of facts, involves a false analysis of these concepts. Our own analysis has shown that the phenomena of moral experience cannot fairly be used to support any rationalist or metaphysical doctrine whatsoever. In particular, they cannot, as Kant hoped, be used to establish the existence of a transcendent god. [. . .]

## Work Cited

Moore, G.E. "The Nature of Moral Philosophy." *Philosophical Studies*. London: Routledge and Kegan Paul, 1922.

## Study Questions

1. How do utilitarians attempt to reduce ethical statements to empirical statements? Why does Ayer argue that this attempt fails?

2. Ayer defends "emotivism," which he describes as "radically subjectivist." How does he distinguish this position from "orthodox" subjectivism?

3. Given the failure of "naturalistic" approaches to ethics (subjectivism, utilitarianism) to reduce ethical statements to empirical statements, one might conclude that ethical "absolutism" is the correct position. Why does Ayer argue that this would be a mistake?

4. Why does Ayer contend that ethical concepts are "pseudo-concepts"? What are the implications for moral disputes? What are the implications for ethics as a branch of philosophical inquiry?

---

# Jean-Paul Sartre

---

Jean-Paul Sartre (1905–80) was a Parisian philosopher, novelist, playwright, literary critic, and political activist. Sartre graduated from École Normale Supérieure in 1929; taught philosophy at the lycée level through the 1930s; spent the war as a French soldier, then German prisoner, then Resistance member and philosophy professor; and, at the war's end, became a full-time writer. "Existentialism and Humanism" was given as a public lecture in Paris in 1945.

## From "Existentialism and Humanism"

### 1. What Is Existentialism?

[. . .] I have entitled this brief exposition "Existentialism and Humanism." Many may be surprised at the mention of humanism in this connection, but we shall try to see in what sense we understand it. In any case, we can begin by saying that existentialism, in our sense of the word, is a doctrine that does render human life possible; a doctrine, also, which affirms that every truth and every action imply both an environment and a human subjectivity. [. . .] At bottom, what is alarming in the doctrine that I am about to try to explain to you is—is it not?—that it confronts man with a possibility of choice. To verify this, let us review the whole question upon the strictly philosophic level. What, then, is this that we call existentialism?

Most of those who are making use of this word would be highly confused if required to explain its meaning. For since it has become fashionable, people cheerfully declare that this musician or that painter is "existentialist." A columnist in *Clartés* signs himself "The Existentialist," and, indeed, the word is now so loosely applied to so many things that it no longer means anything at all. It would appear that, for the lack of any novel doctrine such as that of surrealism, all those who are eager to join in the latest scandal or movement now seize upon this philosophy in which, however, they can find nothing to their purpose. For in truth this is of all teachings the least scandalous and the most austere: it is intended strictly for technicians and philosophers. All the same, it can easily be defined.

The question is only complicated because there are two kinds of existentialists. There are, on the one hand, the Christians, amongst whom I shall name **Jaspers** and **Gabriel Marcel**, both professed Catholics; and on the other the existential atheists, amongst whom we must place **Heidegger** as well as the **French existentialists** and myself. What they have in common is simply the fact that they believe that *existence* comes before *essence*—or, if you will, that we must begin from the subjective. What exactly do we mean by that?

If one considers an article of manufacture as, for example, a book or a paper-knife—one sees that it has been made by an artisan who had a conception of it; and he has paid attention, equally, to the conception of a paper-knife and to the pre-existent technique of production which is a part of that conception and is, at bottom, a formula. Thus the paper-knife is at the same time an article producible in a certain manner and one which, on the other hand, serves a definite purpose, for one cannot suppose that a man would produce a paper-knife without knowing what it was for. Let us say, then, of the paper-knife that its essence—that is to say the sum of the formulae and the qualities which made its production and its definition possible—precedes its existence. The presence of such-and-such a paper-knife or book is thus determined before my eyes. Here, then, we are viewing the world from a technical standpoint, and we can say that production precedes existence.

When we think of God as the creator, we are thinking of him, most of the time, as a supernal artisan. Whatever doctrine we may be considering, whether it be a doctrine like that of **Descartes**, or of **Leibniz** himself, we always imply that the will follows, more or less, from the understanding or at least accompanies it, so that when God creates he knows precisely what he is creating. Thus, the conception of man in the mind of God is comparable to that of the paper-knife in the mind of the artisan: God makes man according to a procedure and a conception, exactly as the artisan manufactures a paper-knife, following a definition and a formula. Thus each individual man is the realization of a certain conception which dwells in the divine understanding. In the philosophic atheism of the eighteenth century, the notion of God is suppressed, but not, for all that, the idea that essence is prior to existence; something of that idea we still find everywhere, in **Diderot**, in **Voltaire**, and even in **Kant**. Man possesses a human nature; that "human nature," which is the conception of human being, is found in every man; which means that each man is a particular example of a universal conception, the conception of Man. In Kant,

this universality goes so far that the wild man of the woods, man in the state of nature, and the bourgeois are all contained in the same definition and have the same fundamental qualities. Here again, the essence of man precedes that historic existence which we confront in experience.

Atheistic existentialism, of which I am a representative, declares with greater consistency that if God does not exist there is at least one being whose existence comes before its essence, a being which exists before it can be defined by any conception of it. That being is man or, as Heidegger has it, the human reality. What do we mean by saying that existence precedes essence? We mean that man first of all exists, encounters himself, surges up in the world—and defines himself afterwards. If man as the existentialist sees him is not definable, it is because to begin with he is nothing. He will not be anything until later, and then he will be what he makes of himself. Thus, there is no human nature, because there is no God to have a conception of it. Man simply is. Not that he is simply what he conceives himself to be, but he is what he wills, and as he conceives himself after already existing—as he wills to be after that leap towards existence. Man is nothing else but that which he makes of himself. That is the first principle of existentialism. And this is what people call its "subjectivity," using the word as a reproach against us. But what do we mean to say by this, but that man is of a greater dignity than a stone or a table? For we mean to say that man primarily exists—that man is, before all else, something which propels itself towards a future and is aware that it is doing so. Man is, indeed, a project which possesses a subjective life, instead of being a kind of moss, or a fungus, or a cauliflower. [. . .] If, however, it is true that existence is prior to essence, man is responsible for what he is. Thus, the first effect of existentialism is that it puts every man in possession of himself as he is, and places the entire responsibility for his existence squarely upon his own shoulders. And, when we say that man is responsible for himself, we do not mean that he is responsible only for his own individuality, but that he is responsible for all men. The word "subjectivism" is to be understood in two senses, and our adversaries play upon only one of them. Subjectivism means, on the one hand, the freedom of the individual subject and, on the other, that man cannot pass beyond human subjectivity. It is the latter which is the deeper meaning of existentialism. When we say that man chooses himself, we do mean that every one of us must choose himself; but by that we also mean that in choosing for himself he chooses for all men. For in effect, of all the actions a man may take in order to create himself as he wills to be, there is not one which is not creative, at the same time, of an image of man such as he believes he ought to be. To choose between this or that is at the same time to affirm the value of that which is chosen; for we are unable ever to choose the worse. What we choose is always the better; and nothing can be better for us unless it is better for all. If, moreover, existence precedes essence and we will to exist at the same time as we fashion our image, that image is valid for all and for the entire epoch in which we find ourselves. Our responsibility is thus much greater than we had supposed, for it concerns mankind as a whole. If I am a worker, for instance, I may choose to join a Christian rather than a Communist trade union. And if, by that membership, I choose to signify that resignation is, after all, the attitude that best becomes a man, that man's kingdom is not upon this earth, I do not commit myself alone to that view. Resignation is my will for everyone, and my action is, in consequence, a commitment on behalf of all mankind. Or if, to take a more personal case, I decide to marry and to have children, even though this decision proceeds simply from my situation, from my passion or my desire, I am thereby committing not only myself, but humanity as a whole, to the practice of monogamy. I am thus responsible for myself and for all men, and I am creating a certain image of man as I would have him to be. In fashioning myself I fashion man.

## 2. Anguish, Abandonment, and Despair

This may enable us to understand what is meant by such terms—perhaps a little grandiloquent—as anguish, abandonment and despair. As you will soon see, it is very simple. First, what do we mean by "anguish"?—The existentialist frankly states that man is in anguish. His meaning is as follows—When a man commits himself to anything, fully realizing that he is not only choosing what he will be, but is thereby at the same time a legislator deciding for the whole of mankind—in such a moment a man cannot escape from the sense of complete and profound responsibility. There are many, indeed, who show no such anxiety. But we affirm that they are merely disguising their anguish or are in flight from it. Certainly, many people think that in what they are doing they commit no one but themselves to anything: and if you ask them, "What would happen if everyone did so?" they shrug their shoulders and reply, "Everyone does not do so." But in truth, one ought always to ask oneself what would happen if everyone did as one is doing; nor can one escape from that disturbing thought except by a kind of self-deception. The man who lies in self-excuse, by saying "Everyone will not do it" must be ill at ease in his conscience, for the act of lying implies the universal value which it denies. By its very disguise his anguish reveals itself. This is the anguish that **Kierkegaard** called "the anguish of Abraham." You know the story: An angel commanded Abraham to sacrifice his son; and obedience was obligatory, if it really was an angel who had appeared and said, "Thou, Abraham, shalt sacrifice thy son." But anyone in such a case would wonder, first, whether it was indeed an angel and secondly, whether I am really Abraham. Where are the proofs? [. . .] If an angel appears to me, what is the proof that it is an angel; or, if I hear voices, who can prove that they proceed from heaven and not from hell, or from my own subconsciousness or some pathological condition? Who can prove that they are really addressed to me?

Who, then, can prove that I am the proper person to impose, by my own choice, my conception of man upon mankind? I shall never find any proof whatever; there will be no sign to convince me of it. If a voice speaks to me, it is still I myself who must decide whether the voice is or is not that of an angel. If I regard a certain course of action as good, it is only I who choose to say that it is good and not bad. There is nothing to show that I am Abraham: nevertheless I also am obliged at every instant to perform actions which are examples. Everything happens to every man as though the whole human race had its eyes fixed upon what he is doing and regulated its conduct accordingly. So every man ought to say, "Am I really a man who has the right to act in such a manner that humanity regulates itself by what I do." If a man does not say that, he is dissembling his anguish. Clearly, the anguish with which we are concerned here is not one that could lead to quietism or inaction. It is anguish pure and simple, of the kind well known to all those who have borne responsibilities. When, for instance, a military leader takes upon himself the responsibility for an attack and sends a number of men to their death, he chooses to do it and at bottom he alone chooses. No doubt under a higher command, but its orders, which are more general, require interpretation by him and upon that interpretation depends the life of ten, fourteen or twenty men. In making the decision, he cannot but feel a certain anguish. All leaders know that anguish. It does not prevent their acting, on the contrary it is the very condition of their action, for the action presupposes that there is a plurality of possibilities, and in choosing one of these, they realize that it has value only because it is chosen. Now it is anguish of that kind which existentialism describes, and moreover, as we shall see, makes explicit through direct responsibility towards other men who are concerned. Far from being a screen which could separate us from action, it is a condition of action itself.

And when we speak of "abandonment"—a favourite word of Heidegger—we only mean to say that God does not exist, and that it is necessary to draw the consequences of his absence right to the end. The existentialist is strongly opposed to a certain type of secular moralism which seeks to suppress God at the least possible expense. Towards 1880, when the French professors endeavoured to formulate a secular morality, they said something like this: God is a useless and costly hypothesis, so we will do without it. However, if we are to have morality, a society, and a law-abiding world, it is essential that certain values

should be taken seriously; they must have an a priori existence ascribed to them. It must be considered obligatory a priori to be honest, not to lie, not to beat one's wife, to bring up children, and so forth; so we are going to do a little work on this subject, which will enable us to show that these values exist all the same, inscribed in an intelligible heaven although, of course, there is no God. In other words—and this is, I believe, the purport of all that we in France call radicalism—nothing will be changed if God does not exist; we shall rediscover the same norms of honesty, progress, and humanity, and we shall have disposed of God as an out-of-date hypothesis which will die away quietly of itself. The existentialist, on the contrary, finds it extremely embarrassing that God does not exist, for there disappears with Him all possibility of finding values in an intelligible heaven. There can no longer be any good a priori, since there is no infinite and perfect consciousness to think it. It is nowhere written that "the good" exists, that one must be honest or must not lie, since we are now upon the plane where there are only men. **Dostoevsky** once wrote: "If God did not exist, everything would be permitted"; and that, for existentialism, is the starting point. Everything is indeed permitted if God does not exist, and man is in consequence forlorn, for he cannot find anything to depend upon either within or outside himself. He discovers forthwith, that he is without excuse. For if indeed existence precedes essence, one will never be able to explain one's action by reference to a given and specific human nature; in other words, there is no determinism—man is free, man *is* freedom. Nor, on the other hand, if God does not exist, are we provided with any values or commands that could legitimize our behaviour. Thus we have neither behind us, nor before us in a luminous realm of values, any means of justification or excuse. We are left alone, without excuse. That is what I mean when I say that man is condemned to be free. Condemned, because he did not create himself, yet is nevertheless at liberty, and from the moment that he is thrown into this world he is responsible for everything he does. [. . .]

As an example by which you may the better understand this state of abandonment, I will refer to the case of a pupil of mine, who sought me out in the following circumstances. His father was quarrelling with his mother and was also inclined to be a "collaborator"; his elder brother had been killed in the German offensive of 1940 and this young man, with a sentiment somewhat primitive but generous, burned to avenge him. His mother was living alone with him, deeply afflicted by the semi-treason of his father and by the death of her eldest son, and her one consolation was in this young man. But he, at this moment, had the choice between going to England to join the Free French Forces or of staying near his mother and helping her to live. He fully realized that this woman lived only for him and that his disappearance—or perhaps his death—would plunge her into despair. He also realized that, concretely and in fact, every action he performed on his mother's behalf would be sure of effect in the sense of aiding her to live, whereas anything he did in order to go and fight would be an ambiguous action which might vanish like water into sand and serve no purpose. For instance, to set out for England he would have to wait indefinitely in a Spanish camp on the way through Spain; or, on arriving in England or in Algiers he might be put into an office to fill up forms. Consequently, he found himself confronted by two very different modes of action; the one concrete, immediate, but directed towards only one individual; and the other an action addressed to an end infinitely greater, a national collectivity, but for that very reason ambiguous—and it might be frustrated on the way. At the same time, he was hesitating between two kinds of morality; on the one side the morality of sympathy, of personal devotion and, on the other side, a morality of wider scope but of more debatable validity. He had to choose between those two. What could help him to choose? Could the Christian doctrine? No. Christian doctrine says: Act with charity, love your neighbour, deny yourself for others, choose the way which is hardest, and so forth. But which is the harder road? To whom does one owe the more brotherly love, the patriot or the mother? Which is the more useful aim, the general one of fighting in and for the whole community, or the precise aim of helping one particular person to live? Who can give an answer to that a priori? No

one. Nor is it given in any ethical scripture. The Kantian ethic says, Never regard another as a means, but always as an end. Very well; if I remain with my mother, I shall be regarding her as the end and not as a means: but by the same token I am in danger of treating as means those who are fighting on my behalf; and the converse is also true, that if I go to the aid of the combatants I shall be treating them as the end at the risk of treating my mother as a means. [. . .]

As for "despair," the meaning of this expression is extremely simple. It merely means that we limit ourselves to a reliance upon that which is within our wills, or within the sum of the probabilities which render our action feasible. Whenever one wills anything, there are always these elements of probability. If I am counting upon a visit from a friend, who may be coming by train or by tram, I presuppose that the train will arrive at the appointed time, or that the tram will not be derailed. I remain in the realm of possibilities; but one does not rely upon any possibilities beyond those that are strictly concerned in one's action. Beyond the point at which the possibilities under consideration cease to affect my action, I ought to disinterest myself. For there is no God and no prevenient design, which can adapt the world and all its possibilities to my will. When Descartes said, "Conquer yourself rather than the world," what he meant was, at bottom, the same—that we should act without hope.

**Marxists,** to whom I have said this, have answered: "Your action is limited, obviously, by your death; but you can rely upon the help of others. That is, you can count both upon what the others are doing to help you elsewhere, as in China and in Russia, and upon what they will do later, after your death, to take up your action and carry it forward to its final accomplishment which will be the revolution. Moreover you must rely upon this; not to do so is immoral." To this I rejoin, first, that I shall always count upon my comrades-in-arms in the struggle, insofar as they are committed, as I am, to a definite, common cause; and in the unity of a party or a group which I can more or less control—that is, in which I am enrolled as a militant and whose movements at every moment are known to me. In that respect, to rely upon the unity and the will of the party is exactly like my reckoning that the train will run on time or that the tram will not be derailed. But I cannot count upon men whom I do not know, I cannot base my confidence upon human goodness or upon man's interest in the good of society, seeing that man is free and that there is no human nature which I can take as foundational. I do not know where the Russian revolution will lead. I can admire it and take it as an example insofar as it is evident, today, that the proletariat plays a part in Russia which it has attained in no other nation. But I cannot affirm that this will necessarily lead to the triumph of the proletariat: I must confine myself to what I can see. Nor can I be sure that comrades-in-arms will take up my work after my death and carry it to the maximum perfection, seeing that those men are free agents and will freely decide, tomorrow, what man is then to be. Tomorrow, after my death, some men may decide to establish Fascism, and the others may be so cowardly or so slack as to let them do so. If so, Fascism will then be the truth of man, and so much the worse for us. In reality, things will be such as men have decided they shall be.

## 3. Objections

We have now, I think, dealt with a certain number of the reproaches against existentialism. You have seen that it cannot be regarded as a philosophy of quietism since it defines man by his action; nor as a pessimistic description of man, for no doctrine is more optimistic, the destiny of man is placed within himself. Nor is it an attempt to discourage man from action since it tells him that there is no hope except in his action, and that the one thing which permits him to have life is the deed. Upon this level therefore, what we are considering is an ethic of action and self-commitment. However, we are still reproached, upon these few data, for confining man within his individual subjectivity. There again people badly misunderstand us. [. . .]

This theory alone is compatible with the dignity of man, it is the only one which does not make man into an object. All kinds of materialism lead one to treat every man including oneself as an object— that is, as a set of pre-determined reactions, in no

way different from the patterns of qualities and phenomena which constitute a table, or a chair, or a stone. Our aim is precisely to establish the human kingdom as a pattern of values in distinction from the material world. But the subjectivity which we thus postulate as the standard of truth is no narrowly individual subjectivism, for as we have demonstrated, it is not only one's own self that one discovers in the *cogito*, but those of others too. Contrary to the philosophy of Descartes, contrary to that of Kant, when we say "I think" we are attaining to ourselves in the presence of the other, and we are just as certain of the other as we are of ourselves. Thus the man who discovers himself directly in the *cogito* also discovers all the others, and discovers them as the condition of his own existence. He recognizes that he cannot be anything (in the sense in which one says one is spiritual, or that one is wicked or jealous) unless others recognize him as such. I cannot obtain any truth whatsoever about myself, except through the mediation of another. The other is indispensable to my existence, and equally so to any knowledge I can have of myself. Under these conditions, the intimate discovery of myself is at the same time the revelation of the other as a freedom which confronts mine, and which cannot think or will without doing so either for or against me. Thus, at once, we find ourselves in a world which is, let us say, that of "inter-subjectivity." It is in this world that man has to decide what he is and what others are.

Furthermore, although it is impossible to find in each and every man a universal essence that can be called human nature, there is nevertheless a human universality of *condition*. It is not by chance that the thinkers of today are so much more ready to speak of the condition than of the nature of man. By his condition they understand, with more or less clarity, all the *limitations* which a priori define man's fundamental situation in the universe. His historical situations are variable: man may be born a slave in a pagan society or may be a feudal baron, or a proletarian. But what never vary are the necessities of being in the world, of having to labour and to die there. These limitations are neither subjective nor objective, or rather there is both a subjective and an objective aspect of them. Objective, because we meet with them everywhere and they are everywhere recognizable: and subjective because they are *lived* and are nothing if man does not live them—if, that is to say, he does not freely determine himself and his existence in relation to them. And, diverse though man's purpose may be, at least none of them is wholly foreign to me, since every human purpose presents itself as an attempt either to surpass these limitations, or to widen them, or else to deny or to accommodate oneself to them. Consequently every purpose, however individual it may be, is of universal value. Every purpose, even that of a Chinese, an Indian or a Negro, can be understood by a European. [. . .] In this sense we may say that there is a human universality, but it is not something given; it is being perpetually made. I make this universality in choosing myself; I also make it by understanding the purpose of any other man, of whatever epoch. This absoluteness of the act of choice does not alter the relativity of each epoch. [. . .]

This does not completely refute the charge of subjectivism. Indeed that objection appears in several other forms. [. . .]

People say to us, "You are unable to judge others." This is true in one sense and false in another. It is true in this sense, that whenever a man chooses his purpose and his commitment in all clearness and in all sincerity, whatever that purpose may be, it is impossible for him to prefer another. It is true in the sense that we do not believe in progress. Progress implies amelioration; but man is always the same, facing a situation which is always changing, and choice remains always a choice in the situation. The moral problem has not changed since the time when it was a choice between slavery and anti-slavery—from the time of the war of Secession [US Civil War], for example, until the present moment when one chooses between the M.R.P. [**Mouvement Républicain Populaire**] and the Communists.

We can judge, nevertheless, for, as I have said, one chooses in view of others, and in view of others one chooses himself. One can judge, first—and perhaps this is not a judgment of value, but it is a logical judgment—that in certain cases choice is founded upon an error, and in others upon the truth. One can judge a man by saying that he deceives himself.

Since we have defined the situation of man as one of free choice, without excuse and without help, any man who takes refuge behind the excuse of his passions, or by inventing some deterministic doctrine, is a self-deceiver. One may object: "But why should he not choose to deceive himself?" I reply that it is not for me to judge him morally, but I define his self-deception as an error. Here one cannot avoid pronouncing a judgment of truth. The self-deception is evidently a falsehood, because it is a dissimulation of man's complete liberty of commitment. Upon this same level, I say that it is also a self-deception if I choose to declare that certain values are incumbent upon me; I am in contradiction with myself if I will these values and at the same time say that they impose themselves upon me. [. . .] Furthermore, I can pronounce a moral judgment. For I declare that freedom, in respect of concrete circumstances, can have no other end and aim but itself; and when once a man has seen that values depend upon himself, in that state of forsakenness he can will only one thing, and that is freedom as the foundation of all values. [. . .] Kant declared that freedom is a will both to itself and to the freedom of others. Agreed: but he thinks that the formal and the universal suffice for the constitution of a morality. We think, on the contrary, that principles that are too abstract break down when we come to defining action. To take once again the case of that student; by what authority, in the name of what golden rule of morality, do you think he could have decided, in perfect peace of mind, either to abandon his mother or to remain with her? There are no means of judging. The content is always concrete, and therefore unpredictable; it has always to be invented. The one thing that counts, is to know whether the invention is made in the name of freedom.

Let us, for example, examine the two following cases, and you will see how far they are similar in spite of their difference. Let us take *The Mill on the Floss*. We find here a certain young woman, Maggie Tulliver, who is an incarnation of the value of passion and is aware of it. She is in love with a young man, Stephen, who is engaged to another, an insignificant young woman. This Maggie Tulliver, instead of heedlessly seeking her own happiness, chooses in the name of human solidarity to sacrifice herself and to give up the man she loves. On the other hand, La Sanseverina in Stendhal's *Chartreuse de Parme*, believing that it is passion which endows man with his real value, would have declared that a grand passion justifies its sacrifices, and must be preferred to the banality of such conjugal love as would unite Stephen to the little goose he was engaged to marry. It is the latter that she would have chosen to sacrifice in realizing her own happiness, and, as Stendhal shows, she would also sacrifice herself upon the plane of passion if life made that demand upon her. Here we are facing two clearly opposed moralities; but I claim that they are equivalent, seeing that in both cases the overruling aim is freedom. You can imagine two attitudes exactly similar in effect, in that one girl might prefer, in resignation, to give up her lover while the other preferred, in fulfilment of sexual desire, to ignore the prior engagement of the man she loved; and, externally, these two cases might appear the same as the two we have just cited, while being in fact entirely different. The attitude of La Sanseverina is much nearer to that of Maggie Tulliver than to one of careless greed. Thus, you see, the second objection is at once true and false. One can choose anything, but only if it is upon the plane of free commitment.

The [final] objection, stated by saying, "You take with one hand what you give with the other," means, at bottom, "your values are not serious, since you choose them yourselves." To that I can only say that I am very sorry that it should be so; but if I have excluded God the Father, there must be somebody to invent values. We have to take things as they are. And moreover, to say that we invent values means neither more nor less than this; that there is no sense in life a priori. Life is nothing until it is lived; but it is yours to make sense of, and the value of it is nothing else but the sense that you choose. Therefore, you can see that there is a possibility of creating a human community. I have been reproached for suggesting that existentialism is a form of humanism: people have said to me, "But you have written in your *Nausée* that the humanists are wrong, you have even ridiculed a certain type of humanism, why do you now go back upon that?" In reality, the word humanism has two very different meanings. One may understand

by humanism a theory which upholds man as the end-in-itself and as the supreme value. Humanism in this sense appears, for instance, in Cocteau's story *Round the World in 80 Hours*, in which one of the characters declares, because he is flying over mountains in an airplane, "Man is magnificent!" This signifies that although I personally have not built airplanes, I have the benefit of those particular inventions and that I personally, being a man, can consider myself responsible for, and honoured by, achievements that are peculiar to some men. It is to assume that we can ascribe value to man according to the most distinguished deeds of certain men. That kind of humanism is absurd, for only the dog or the horse would be in a position to pronounce a general judgment upon man and declare that he is magnificent, which they have never been such fools as to do—at least, not as far as I know. But neither is it admissible that a man should pronounce judgment upon Man. Existentialism dispenses with any judgment of this sort: an existentialist will never take man as the end, since man is still to be determined. [. . .]

But there is another sense of the word, of which the fundamental meaning is this: Man is all the time outside of himself: it is in projecting and losing himself beyond himself that he makes man to exist; and, on the other hand, it is by pursuing transcendent aims that he himself is able to exist. Since man is thus self-surpassing, and can grasp objects only in relation to his self-surpassing, he is himself the heart and centre of his transcendence. There is no other universe except the human universe, the universe of human subjectivity. This relation of transcendence as constitutive of man (not in the sense that God is transcendent, but in the sense of self-surpassing) with subjectivity (in such a sense that man is not shut up in himself but forever present in a human universe)—it is this that we call existential humanism. This is humanism, because we remind man that there is no legislator but himself; that he himself, thus abandoned, must decide for himself; also because we show that it is not by turning back upon himself, but always by seeking, beyond himself, an aim which is one of liberation or of some particular realization, that man can realize himself as truly human. [. . .]

## Study Questions

1. Sartre tells us that what existentialists have in common is "simply the fact that they believe that *existence* comes before *essence*." How does this belief challenge the theories of philosophers like Aristotle, Kant, and Mill, which find moral foundations in human nature?

2. Sartre identifies three states that follow from existentialism: anguish, abandonment, and despair. Explain the role each of these plays in Sartre's existentialist ethic.

3. That, when facing similar situations, the characters Maggie Tulliver in Eliot's novel *The Mill on the Floss* and La Sanseverina in Stendhal's novel *Chartreuse de Parme* choose so differently suggests opposing moralities are involved, but Sartre contends that an existentialist ethic accounts for both. Why is this? Does Sartre's response successfully address the "subjectivist" charge that existentialism makes it impossible to judge others?

4. Sartre says that existentialism is a humanism but only when we construe the meaning of "humanism" in one way and not another. Explain.

---

## Melville J. Herskovits

---

Melville Herskovits (1895–1963) was an American anthropologist of Jewish immigrant origins, who did his PhD with Franz Boas (1858–1942) at Columbia University, where he met his wife and collaborator Frances Shapiro Herskovits (1897–1972). The Herskovitses carried out fieldwork in Suriname, Dahomey (now the Republic of Benin), Haiti, Trinidad, and Brazil. As seen in this essay, their writings emphasized the richness and complexity of cultures in Africa and the African diaspora.

## Cultural Relativism and Cultural Values

### 1. Judging Cultures: Monogamy vs. Polygamy

All peoples form judgments about ways of life different from their own. When systematic study is undertaken, comparison gives rise to classification, and scholars have devised many schemes for classifying ways of life. Moral judgments have been drawn regarding the ethical principles that guide the behaviour and mould the value systems of different peoples. Their economic and political structures and their religious beliefs have been ranked in order of complexity, efficiency, desirability. Their art, music, and literary forms have been weighed.

It has become increasingly evident, however, that evaluations of this kind stand or fall with the acceptance of the premises from which they derive. In addition, many of the criteria on which judgment is based are in conflict, so that conclusions drawn from one definition of what is desirable will not agree with those based on another formulation.

A simple example will illustrate this. There are not many ways in which the primary family can be constituted. One man may live with one woman, one woman may have a number of husbands, one man may have a number of wives. But if we evaluate these forms according to their function of perpetuating the group, it is clear that they perform their essential tasks. Otherwise, the societies wherein they exist would not survive.

Such an answer will, however, not satisfy all those who have undertaken to study cultural evaluation. What of the moral questions inherent in the practice of monogamy as against polygamy, the adjustment of children raised in households where, for example, the mothers must compete on behalf of their offspring for the favours of a common husband? If monogamy is held to be the desired form of marriage, the responses to these questions are predetermined. But when we consider these questions from the point of view of those who live in polygamous societies, alternative answers, based on different conceptions of what is desirable, may be given.

Let us consider, for example, the life of a plural family in the West African culture of **Dahomey**. Here, within a compound, live a man and his wives. The man has his own house, as has each of the women and her children, after the basic African principle that two wives cannot successfully inhabit the same quarters. Each wife in turn spends a native week of four days with the common husband, cooking his food, washing his clothes, sleeping in his house, and then making way for the next. Her children, however, remain in their mother's hut. With pregnancy, she drops out of this routine, and ideally, in the interest of her child's health and her own, does not again visit her husband until the child has been born and weaned. This means a period of from three to four years, since infants are nursed two years and longer.

The compound, made up of these households, is a co-operative unit. The women who sell goods in the market, or make pottery, or have their gardens, contribute to its support. This aspect, though of great economic importance, is secondary to the prestige that attaches to the larger unit. This is why one often finds a wife not only urging her husband to acquire a second spouse but even aiding him by loans or gifts to make this possible.

Tensions do arise between the women who inhabit a large compound. Thirteen different ways of getting married have been recorded in this society, and in a large household those wives who are married in the same category tend to unite against all others. Competition for the regard of the husband is also a factor, when several wives try to influence the choice of an heir in favour of their own sons. Yet all the children of the compound play together, and the strength of the emotional ties between the children of the same mother more than compensates for whatever stresses may arise between brothers and sisters who share the same father but are of different mothers. Co-operation, moreover, is by no means a mere formality among the wives. Many common tasks are performed in friendly unison, and there is solidarity in the interest of women's prerogatives, or where the status of the common husband is threatened.

We may now return to the criteria to be applied in drawing judgments concerning polygamous as against monogamous families. The family structure of Dahomey is obviously a complex institution. If we but consider the possible lines of personal relations among the many individuals concerned, we see clearly how numerous are the ramifications of reciprocal right and obligation of the Dahomean family. The effectiveness of the Dahomean family is, however, patent. It has, for untold generations, performed its function of rearing the young; more than this, the very size of the group gives it economic resources and a resulting stability that might well be envied by those who live under different systems of family organization. Moral values are always difficult to establish, but at least in this society marriage is clearly distinguished from casual sex relations and from prostitution, in its supernatural sanctions and in the prestige it confers, to say nothing of the economic obligations toward spouse and prospective offspring explicitly accepted by one who enters into a marriage.

Numerous problems of adjustment do present themselves in an aggregate of this sort. It does not call for much speculation to understand the plaint of the head of one large compound when he said: "One must be something of a diplomat if one has many wives." Yet the sly digs in proverb and song, and the open quarrelling, involve no greater stress than is found in any small rural community where people are also thrown closely together for long periods of time. Quarrels between co-wives are not greatly different from disputes over the back fence between neighbours. And Dahomeans who know European culture, when they argue for their system, stress the fact that it permits the individual wife to space her children in a way that is in accord with the best precepts of modern gynaecology.

Thus polygamy, when looked at from the point of view of those who practise it, is seen to hold values that are not apparent from the outside. A similar case can be made for monogamy, however, when it is attacked by those who are enculturated to a different kind of family structure. And what is true of a particular phase of culture such as this, is also true of others. Evaluations are *relative* to the cultural background out of which they arise.

## 2. Cultural Relativism

*Cultural relativism* is in essence an approach to the question of the nature and role of values in culture. It represents a scientific, inductive attack on an age-old philosophical problem, using fresh, cross-cultural data, hitherto not available to scholars, gained from the study of the underlying value-systems of societies having the most diverse customs. The principle of cultural relativism, briefly stated, is as follows: *Judgments are based on experience, and experience is interpreted by each individual in terms of his own enculturation.* Those who hold for the existence of fixed values will find materials in other societies that necessitate a re-investigation of their assumptions. Are there absolute moral standards, or are moral standards effective only as far as they agree with the orientations of a given people at a given period of their history? We even approach the problem of the ultimate nature of reality itself. **Cassirer** holds that reality can only be experienced through the symbolism of language (25). Is reality, then, not defined and redefined by the ever-varied symbolisms of the innumerable languages of mankind?

Answers to questions such as these represent one of the most profound contributions of anthropology to the analysis of man's place in the world. When we reflect that such intangibles as right and wrong, normal and abnormal, beautiful and plain are absorbed as a person learns the ways of the group into which he is born, we see that we are dealing here with a process of first importance. Even the facts of the physical world are discerned through the enculturative screen, so that the perception of time, distance, weight, size, and other "realities" is mediated by the conventions of any given group.

No culture, however, is a closed system of rigid moulds to which the behaviour of all members of a society must conform. The psychological reality of culture tells us that a culture, as such, can *do* nothing. It is but the summation of the behaviour and habitual modes of thought of the persons who make up a particular society. Though by learning and habit these individuals conform to the ways of the group into which they have been born, they nonetheless vary in their reactions to the situations of living they commonly meet. They vary, too, in the degree to which they desire change, as whole cultures vary. This is but another way in which we see that culture is flexible and holds many possibilities of choice within its framework, and that to recognize the values held by a given people in no wise implies that these values are a constant factor in the lives of succeeding generations of the same group.

How the ideas of a people mediate their approach even to the physical world can be made plain by a few examples. Indians living in the southwestern part of the United States think in terms of *six* cardinal points rather than four. In addition to north, south, east and west, they include the directions "up" and "down." From the point of view that the universe is three dimensional, these Indians are entirely realistic. Among ourselves, even in airplane navigation, where three dimensions must be coped with as they need not by those who keep to the surface of the earth, we separate direction from height in instruments and in our thinking about position. We operate, conceptually, on two distinct planes. One is horizontal—"We are traveling ENE." One is vertical—"We are now cruising at 8,000 feet."

Or take a problem in the patterning of sound. We accept the concept of the wave length, tune pianos in accordance with a mechanically determined scale, and are thus conditioned to what we call true pitch. Some persons, we say, have absolute pitch; that is, a note struck or sung at random will immediately be given its place in the scale—"That's B flat." A composition learned in a given key, when transposed, will deeply trouble such a person, though those who are musically trained but do not have true pitch will enjoy such a transposed work, if the *relation* of each note to every other has not been disturbed. Let us assume that it is proposed to study whether this ability to identify a note is an inborn trait, found among varying but small percentages of individuals in various societies. The difficulty of probing such a question appears immediately once we discover that but few peoples have fixed scales, and none other than ourselves has the concept of true pitch! Those living in cultures without mechanically tuned and true instruments are free to enjoy notes that are as much as a quarter-tone "off," as we would say. As for the patterned progressions in which the typical scales and modal orientations of any musical convention are set, the number of such systems, each of which is consistent within its own limits, is infinite.

The principle that judgments are derived from experience has a sure psychological foundation. This has been best expressed by **Sherif** in his development of the hypothesis of "social norms." His experiments are fundamental, and his accessory concept of the "frame of reference," the background to which experience is referred, has become standard in social psychology. Because of its importance for an understanding of cultural differences, we shall briefly describe the work he did in testing his hypothesis that "experience appears to depend always on *relations*" (32).

The subjects were introduced into a dark room where a dim light appeared and disappeared when an electric key was pressed. Some subjects were brought into the room, first alone and later as members of groups, while others were exposed to the group situation before they were tested individually. Though the light was fixed, the autokinetic response to a situation like this is such that the subject perceives movement where there is none, since being in a room that is perfectly dark, he has no fixed point from which to judge motion. Judgments obtained from each subject *individually* conclusively demonstrated that individuals subjectively establish "a range of extent and a point (a standard or norm) within that range which is peculiar to the individual"

when no objective standard is available to them, and that in repetitions of the experiment the established range is retained. In the group situation, diversity of individual judgments concerning the extent of movement by the light became gradually less. But each group establishes a norm peculiar to itself, after which the individual member "perceives the situation in terms of the range and norm that he brings from the group situation" (105).

The general principle advanced on the basis of these results and those of many other relevant psychological experiments may be given in the words of Sherif: "The psychological basis of the established social norms, such as stereotypes, fashions, conventions, customs, and values, is the formation of common frames of reference as a product of the contact of individuals" (106). [. . .]

Numerous instances of how the norms posited by Sherif vary may be found in the anthropological literature. They are so powerful that they can flourish even in the face of what seems to the outsider an obvious, objectively verifiable fact. Thus, while recognizing the role of both father and mother in procreation, many peoples have conventions of relationship that count descent on but one side of the family. In such societies, it is common for incest lines to be so arbitrarily defined that "first cousins," as we would say, on the mother's side call each other brother and sister and regard marriage with one another with horror. Yet marriage within the same degree of biological relationship on the father's side may be held not only desirable, but sometimes mandatory. This is because two persons related in this way are by definition not considered blood relatives.

The very definition of what is normal or abnormal is relative to the cultural frame of reference. As an example of this, we may take the phenomenon of possession as found among African and New World Negroes. The supreme expression of their religious experience, possession, is a psychological state wherein a displacement of personality occurs when the god "comes to the head" of the worshipper. The individual thereupon is held to be the deity himself. This phenomenon has been described in pathological terms by many students whose approach is non-anthropological, because of its surface resemblance to cases in the records of medical practitioners, psychological clinicians, psychiatrists, and others. The hysteria-like trances, where persons, their eyes tightly closed, move about excitedly and presumably without purpose or design, or roll on the ground, muttering meaningless syllables, or go into a state where their bodies achieve complete rigidity, are not difficult to equate with the neurotic and even psychotic manifestations of abnormality found in Euro-American society.

Yet when we look beneath behaviour to meaning, and place such apparently random acts in their cultural frame of reference, such conclusions become untenable. For *relative to the setting in which these possession experiences occur, they are not to be regarded as abnormal at all*, much less psychopathological. They are *culturally* patterned, and often induced by learning and discipline. The dancing or other acts of the possessed persons are so stylized that one who knows this religion can identify the god possessing a devotee by the behaviour of the individual possessed. Furthermore, the possession experience does not seem to be confined to emotionally unstable persons. Those who "get the god" run the gamut of personality types found in the group. Observation of persons who frequent the cults, yet who, in the idiom of worship "have nothing in the head" and thus never experience possession, seems to show that they are far less adjusted than those who do get possessed. Finally, the nature of the possession experience in these cultures is so disciplined that it may only come to a given devotee under particular circumstances. In West Africa and Brazil the gods come only to those who have been designated in advance by the priest of their group, who lays his hands on their heads. In Haiti, for an initiate not a member of the family group giving a rite to become possessed at a ceremony is considered extremely "bad form" socially and a sign of spiritual weakness, evidence that the god is not under the control of his worshipper.

The terminology of psychopathology, employed solely for descriptive purposes, may be of some utility. But the connotation it carries of psychic instability, emotional imbalance, and departure from normality recommends the use of other words that do not invite such a distortion of cultural reality. For in these Negro societies, the meaning this experience holds for the people falls entirely in the realm of understandable, predictable, *normal* behaviour. This behaviour is known and recognized by all members as an experience that may come to any one of them, and is to be welcomed not only for the psychological security it affords, but also for the status, economic gain, aesthetic expression, and emotional release it vouchsafes the devotee.

## 3. Ethnocentrism

The primary mechanism that directs the evaluation of culture is *ethnocentrism*. Ethnocentrism is the point of view that one's own way of life is to be preferred to all others. Flowing logically from the process of early enculturation, it characterizes the way most individuals feel about their own culture, whether or not they verbalize their feeling. Outside the stream of Euro-American culture, particularly among non-literate peoples, this is taken for granted and is to be viewed as a factor making for individual adjustment and social integration. For the strengthening of the ego, identification with one's own group, whose ways are implicitly accepted as best, is all-important. It is when, as in Euro-American culture, ethnocentrism is rationalized and made the basis of programs of action detrimental to the well-being of other peoples that it gives rise to serious problems.

The ethnocentrism of non-literate peoples is best illustrated in their myths, folk tales, proverbs, and linguistic habits. It is manifest in many tribal names whose meaning in their respective languages signifies "human beings." The inference that those to whom the name does not apply are outside this category is, however, rarely, if ever, explicitly made. When the Suriname Bush Negro, shown a flashlight, admires it and then quotes the proverb: "White man's magic isn't black man's magic," he is merely reaffirming his faith in his own culture. He is pointing out that the stranger, for all his mechanical devices, would be lost in the Guiana jungle without the aid of his Bush Negro friends.

A myth of the origin of human races, told by the Cherokee Indians of the Great Smoky Mountains, gives another instance of this kind of ethnocentrism. The Creator fashioned man by first making and firing an oven and then, from dough he had prepared, shaping three figures in human form. He placed the figures in the oven and waited for them to get done. But his impatience to see the result of this, his crowning experiment in the work of creation, was so great that he removed the first figure too soon. It was sadly underdone—pale, an unlovely colour, and from it descended the white people. His second figure had fared well. The timing was accurate, the form, richly browned, that was to be the ancestor of the Indians, pleased him in every way. He so admired it, indeed, that he neglected to take out of the oven the third form, until he smelled it burning. He threw open the door, only to find this last one charred and black. It was regrettable, but there was nothing to be done; and this was the first Negro.

This is the more usual form that ethnocentrism takes among many peoples—a gentle insistence on the good qualities of one's own group, without any drive to extend this attitude into the field of action. With such a point of view, the objectives, sanctioned modes of behaviour, and value systems of peoples with whom one's own group comes into contact can be considered in terms of their desirability, then accepted or rejected without any reference to absolute standards. That differences in the manner of achieving commonly sought objectives may be permitted to exist without a judgment being entered on them involves a reorientation in thought for those in the Euro-American tradition, because in this tradition, a difference in belief or behaviour too often implies something is worse, or less desirable, and must be changed.

The assumption that the cultures of non-literate peoples are of inferior quality is the end product of a long series of developments in our intellectual history. It is not often recalled that the concept of progress, that strikes so deep into our thinking, is relatively recent. It is, in fact, a unique product of our culture. It is a part of the same historic stream that developed the scientific tradition and that developed the machine, thus giving Europe and America the final word in debates about cultural superiority. "He who makes the gun-powder wields the power," runs a Dahomean proverb. There is no rebuttal to an argument, backed by cannon, advanced to a people who can defend their position with no more than spears, or bows and arrows, or at best a flint-lock gun.

With the possible exception of technological aspects of life, however, the proposition that one way of thought or action is better than another is exceedingly difficult to establish on the grounds of any universally acceptable criteria. Let us take food as an instance. Cultures are equipped differently for the production of food, so that some peoples eat more than others. However, even on the subsistence level, there is no people who do not hold certain potential foodstuffs to be unfit for human consumption. Milk, which figures importantly in our diet, is rejected as food by the peoples of southeastern Asia. Beef, a valued element of the Euro-American cuisine, is regarded with disgust by Hindus. Nor need compulsions be this strong. The thousands of cattle that range the East African highlands are primarily wealth to be preserved, and not a source of food. Only the cow that dies is eaten—a practice that, though abhorrent to us, has apparently done no harm to those who have been following it for generations.

Totemic and religious taboos set up further restrictions on available foodstuffs, while the refusal to consume many other edible and nourishing substances is simply based on the enculturative conditioning. So strong is this conditioning that prohibited food consumed unwittingly may induce such a physiological reaction as vomiting. All young animals provide succulent meat, but the religious abhorrence of the young pig by the Mohammedan is no stronger than the secular rejection of puppy steaks or colt chops by ourselves. Ant larvae, insect grubs, locusts—all of which have caloric values and vitamin content—when roasted or otherwise cooked, or even when raw, are regarded by many peoples as delicacies. We never eat them, however, though they are equally available to us. On the other hand, some of the same peoples who feed on these with gusto regard substances that come out of tin cans as unfit for human consumption.

## 4. Morality: Cultural Universal Not Absolute

Before we terminate our discussion of cultural relativism, it is important that we consider certain questions that are raised when the cultural-relativistic position is advanced. "It may be true," it is argued, "that human beings live in accordance with the ways they have learned. These ways may be regarded by them as best. A people may be so devoted to these ways that they are ready to fight and die for them. In terms of survival value, their effectiveness may be admitted, since the group that lives in accordance with them continues to exist. But does this mean that all systems of moral values, all concepts of right and wrong, are founded on such shifting sands that there is no need for morality, for proper behaviour, for ethical codes? Does not a relativistic philosophy, indeed, imply a negation of these?"

To hold that values do not exist because they are relative to time and place is to fall prey to a fallacy that results from a failure to take into account the positive contribution of the relativistic position. For cultural relativism is a philosophy that recognizes the values set up by every society to guide its own life and that understands their worth to those who live by them, though they may differ from one's own. Instead of underscoring differences from absolute norms that, however objectively arrived at, are nonetheless the product of a given time or place, the relativistic point of view brings into relief the validity of every set of norms for the people who have them, and the values these represent.

It is essential, in considering cultural relativism, that we differentiate absolutes from universals. *Absolutes* are fixed, and, as far as convention is concerned, are not admitted to have variation, to differ from culture to culture, from epoch to epoch. *Universals*, on the other hand, are those least common denominators to be extracted from the range of variation that all phenomena of the natural or cultural world manifest. If we apply the distinction between these two concepts in drawing an answer to the points raised in our question, these criticisms are found to lose their force. To say that there is no absolute criterion of values or morals, or even, psychologically, of time or space, does not mean that such criteria, in differing *forms*, do not comprise universals in human culture. Morality is a universal, and so is enjoyment of beauty, and some standard for truth. The many forms these concepts take are but products of the particular historical experience of the societies that manifest them. In each, criteria are subject to continuous questioning, continuous change. But the basic conceptions remain, to channel thought and direct conduct, to give purpose to living.

In considering cultural relativism, also, we must recognize that it has three quite different aspects, which in most discussions of it tend to be disregarded. One of these is methodological, one philosophical, and one practical. As it has been put:

As method, relativism encompasses the principle of our science that, in studying a culture, one seeks to attain as great a degree of objectivity as possible; that one does not judge the modes of behaviour one is describing, or seek to change them. Rather, one seeks to understand the sanctions of behaviour in terms of the established relationships within the culture itself, and refrains from making interpretations that arise from a preconceived frame of reference. Relativism as philosophy concerns the nature of cultural values, and, beyond this, the implications of an epistemology that derives from a recognition of the force of enculturative conditioning in shaping thought and behaviour. Its practical aspects involve the application—the practice—of the philosophical principles derived from this method, to the wider, cross-cultural scene.

In these terms, the three aspects of cultural relativism can be regarded as representing a logical sequence which, in a broad sense, the historical development of the idea has also followed. That is, the methodological aspect, whereby the data from which the epistemological propositions flow are gathered, ordered and assessed, came first. For it is difficult to conceive of a systematic theory of cultural relativism—as against a generalized idea of live-and-let-live—without the pre-existence of the massive ethnographic documentation gathered by anthropologists concerning the similarities and differences between cultures the world over. Out of these data came the philosophical position, and with the philosophical position came speculation as to its implications for conduct. (Herskovits 24)

*Cultural* relativism, in all cases, must be sharply distinguished from concepts of the relativity of individual behaviour, which would negate all social controls over conduct. Conformity to the code of the group is a requirement for any regularity in life. Yet to say that we have a right to expect conformity to the code of our day for ourselves does not imply that we need expect, much less impose, conformity to our code on persons who live by other codes. The very core of cultural relativism is the social discipline that comes of respect for differences—of mutual respect. Emphasis on the worth of many ways of life, not one, is an affirmation of the values in each culture. Such emphasis seeks to understand and to harmonize goals, not to judge and destroy those that do not dovetail with our own. Cultural history teaches that, important as it is to discern and study the parallelisms in human civilizations, it is no less important to discern and study the different ways man has devised to fulfill his needs.

That it has been necessary to consider questions such as have been raised reflects an enculturative experience wherein the prevalent system of morals is not only consciously inculcated, but its exclusive claim to excellence emphasized. There are not many cultures, for example, where a rigid dichotomy between good and evil, such as we have set up, is insisted upon. Rather it is recognized that good and evil are but the extremes of a continuously varied scale between these poles that produces only different degrees of greyness. We thus return to the principle enunciated earlier, that "judgments are based on experience, and experience is interpreted by each individual in terms of his enculturation." In a culture where absolute values are stressed, the relativism of a world that encompasses many ways of living will be difficult to comprehend. Rather, it will offer a field day for value judgments based on the degree to which a given body of customs resembles or differs from those of Euro-American culture.

Once comprehended, however, and employing the field methods of the scientific student of man, together with an awareness of the satisfactions the most varied bodies of custom yield, this position gives us a leverage to lift us out of the ethnocentric morass in which our thinking about ultimate values has for so long bogged down. With a means of probing deeply into all manner of differing cultural orientations, of reaching into the significance of the ways of living of different peoples, we can turn again to our own culture with fresh perspective, and an objectivity that can be achieved in no other manner.

## Works Cited

Cassirer, E. *An Essay on Man: An Introduction to the Philosophy of Human Culture*. New Haven: Yale University Press, 1944.

Herskovits, M.J. "Tender- and Tough-Minded Anthropology and the Study of Values in Culture." *Southwestern Journal of Anthropology* 7 (1951): 22–31.

Sherif, M. *The Psychology of Social Norms*. New York: Harper & Row, 1936.

## Study Questions

1. Herskovits tells us that judgments about cultural practices are relative to the cultural backgrounds from which they arise. How does his example of monogamy versus polygamy illustrate this?

2. How does Herskovits define "cultural relativism," and how does Sherif's research on social norms provide an empirical basis for this definition? Use incest as an example.

3. How does Herskovits define "ethnocentrism"? Why does he believe that ethnocentrism has a different significance when engaged in by non-literate peoples versus Euro-Americans?

4. Herskovits suggests that differing cultural preferences in food provide a good analogy for relativism in other sorts of judgments, including moral and aesthetic ones. Does this imply that morality is subjective, no different from a like or dislike for anchovies on pizza? Your response should mention Herskovits's distinction between "absolutes" and "universals."

# ~ GENDER AND MORALITY ~

## Martha C. Nussbaum

Martha Nussbaum is Ernst Freund Distinguished Service Professor of Law and Ethics at the University of Chicago. She received a PhD in classical philology from Harvard University in 1975. Nussbaum's extensive collection of scholarly books and articles has won her numerous awards and honorary degrees, but also notable is her commitment to "public philosophy." Recent contributions to newspapers such as the *New York Times* and *Washington Post* and magazines such as *The Nation* and *New Republic* cover such topics as same-sex marriage, burqa bans, and the humanities' importance to democracy.

## Judging Other Cultures: The Case of Genital Mutilation

From *Sex and Social Justice*

### 1. The Case of Fauziya Kassindja

In June 1997, the Board of Immigration Appeals of the United States Immigration and Naturalization Service (INS) granted political asylum to a 19-year-old woman from Togo who had fled her home to escape the practice of genital mutilation (see Dugger, "U.S. Gives Asylum" and "A Refugee's Body"). Fauziya Kassindja is the daughter of Muhammed Kassindja, a successful owner of a small trucking business in Kpalimé. Her father opposed the ritual practice: He remembered his sister's screams during the rite and her suffering from a tetanus infection she developed afterwards. Hajia, his wife, recalled the death of her older sister from an infection associated with the rite; this tragedy led Hajia's family to exempt her from cutting, and she, too, opposed the practice for her children. During his lifetime, Muhammed, being wealthy, was able to defy the tribal customs of the Tchamba-Kunsuntu, to which he belonged. Both illiterate themselves, the Kassindjas sent Fauziya to a boarding school in Ghana, so that she could learn English and help her father in his business. Meanwhile, her four older sisters married men of their own choice, genitals intact.

Fauziya's family was thus an anomaly in the region. Rakia Idrissou, the local genital exciser, told a reporter that girls usually have the procedure between the ages of four and seven. If weak, they are held down by four women; if stronger, they require five women, one to sit on their chests and one for each arm and leg. They must be kept still, she said, because if they jerk suddenly the razor blade used for the surgery can cut too deep.

When Fauziya was fifteen, however, her father died. Her mother was summarily turned out of the house by hostile relatives, and an aunt took control of the household, ending Fauziya's education. "We don't want girls to go to school too much," this aunt told a reporter from *The New York Times*. The family patriarch then arranged for Fauziya to become the fourth wife of an electrician; her prospective husband insisted that she have the genital operation first. To avoid the marriage and the mutilation that would have preceded it, Fauziya decided to leave home; her mother gave her $3,000 of the $3,500 inheritance that was her only sustenance. On her wedding day, Fauziya left her aunt's house, flagged down a taxi, and, with nothing but the clothes on her back, asked the driver to take her across the border into Ghana, some 20 miles away. Once in Ghana, she got on a flight to Germany; with help from people who befriended her there, she got a flight to the United States.

On landing in Newark she confessed that her documents were false and asked for political asylum. After weeks of detention in an unsanitary and oppressive immigration prison, she got legal assistance—again with the help of her mother, who contacted a nephew who was working as a janitor in the Washington area. Scraping together $500, the nephew hired a law student at American University, Ms. Miller Bashir, to handle Fauziya's case. At first, Bashir was unsuccessful, and a Philadelphia immigration judge denied Fauziya's request for asylum. Through the determined efforts of activists, journalists, and law faculty at American University, she successfully appealed the denial. The appellate ruling stated that the practice of genital mutilation constitutes persecution and concluded: "It remains particularly true that women have little legal recourse and may face threats to their freedom, threats or acts of physical violence, or social ostracization for refusing to undergo this harmful traditional practice, or attempting to protect their female children."

## 2. Female Genital Mutilation

In recent years, the practice of female genital mutilation has been increasingly in the news, generating a complex debate about cultural norms and the worth of sexual functioning. This chapter attempts to describe and to sort out some aspects of this controversy. First, however, a word about nomenclature. Although discussions sometimes use the terms "female circumcision" and "clitoridectomy," "female genital mutilation" (FGM) is the standard generic term for all these procedures in the medical literature. "Clitoridectomy" standardly designates a subcategory, described shortly. The term "female circumcision" has been rejected by international medical practitioners because it suggests the fallacious analogy to male circumcision, which is generally believed to have either no effect or a positive effect on physical health and sexual functioning. Anatomically, the degree of cutting in the female operations described here is far more extensive. (The male equivalent of the clitoridectomy would be the amputation of most of the penis. The male equivalent of infibulation would be

"removal of the entire penis, its roots of soft tissue, and part of the scrotal skin" [Toubia, *FGM* 5].) This discussion is confined to cases that involve substantial removal of tissue and/or functional impairment; I make no comment on purely symbolic procedures that involve no removal of tissue, and these are not included under the rubric "female genital mutilation" by international agencies that study the prevalence of the procedure (Toubia, *FGM* 10).

Three types of genital cutting are commonly practised: (1) In *clitoridectomy*, a part or the whole of the clitoris is amputated and the bleeding is stopped by pressure or a stitch. (2) In *excision*, both the clitoris and the inner lips are amputated. Bleeding is usually stopped by stitching, but the vagina is not covered. (3) In *infibulation*, the clitoris is removed, some or all of the labia minora are cut off, and incisions are made in the labia majora to create raw surface. These surfaces are either stitched together or held in contact until they heal as a hood of skin that covers the urethra and most of the vagina (see Toubia, *FGM* 10–11, with anatomical drawings). Approximately 85 per cent of women who undergo FGM have type 1 or type 2; infibulation, which accounts for only 15 per cent of the total, nonetheless accounts for 80 to 90 per cent of all operations in certain countries, for example, the Sudan, Somalia, and Djibouti.

The practice of female genital mutilation remains extremely common in Africa, although it is illegal, and widely resisted, in most of the countries where it occurs. The World Health Organization estimates that overall, in today's world between 85 and 115 million women have had such operations. In terms of percentages, for example, 93 per cent of women in Mali have undergone genital cutting, 98 per cent in Somalia, 89 per cent of women in the Sudan, 43 per cent in the Central African Republic, 43 per cent in the Ivory Coast, and 12 per cent in Togo (see Toubia, *FGM* 25, reporting WHO data). Smaller numbers of operations are now reported from countries such as Australia, Belgium, France, the United Kingdom, and the United States.

Female genital mutilation is linked to extensive and in some cases lifelong health problems. These include infection, haemorrhage, and abscess at the time of the operation; later difficulties in urination and menstruation; stones in the urethra and bladder due to repeated infections; excessive growth of scar tissue at the site, which may become disfiguring; pain during intercourse; infertility (with devastating implications for a woman's other life chances); obstructed labour and damaging rips and tears during childbirth (Toubia). Complications from infibulations are more severe than those from clitoridectomy and incision; nonetheless, the false perception that clitoridectomy is "safe" frequently leads to the ignoring of complications.

Both in the implicated nations and outside, feminists have organized to demand the abolition of this practice, citing its health risks, its impact on sexual functioning, and the violations of dignity and choice associated with its compulsory and non-consensual nature. These opponents have been joined by many authorities in their respective nations, both religious and secular. In Egypt, for example, both the health minister, Ismail Sallem, and the new head of Al Azhar, the nation's leading Islamic institution, support a ban on the practice. The World Health Organization has advised health professionals not to participate in the practice since 1982 and repeated its strong opposition in 1994; the practice has also been condemned by the UN Commission on Human Rights, UNICEF, the World Medical Organization, Minority Rights Group International, and Amnesty International.

At the same time, however, other writers have begun to protest that the criticism of genital mutilation is inappropriate and "ethnocentric," a demonizing of another culture when we have many reasons to find fault with our own. They have also charged that the focus on this problem involves a Western glamorization of sexual pleasure that is inappropriate, especially when we judge other cultures with different moral norms. To encounter such positions we do not need to turn to scholarly debates. We find them in our undergraduate students, who are inclined to be ethical relativists on such matters, at least initially, hesitant to make any negative judgment of a culture other than their own. Because it seems important for anyone interested in political change in this area to understand these views in their popular and non-academic form, I shall illustrate them from student writings I have encountered both in my own teaching and in my research for a book on liberal education (see *Cultivating Humanity*).

## 3. Relativist Responses

Many students, like some participants in the academic debate, are general cultural relativists, holding that it is always inappropriate to criticize the practices of another culture, and that cultures can appropriately be judged only by their own internal norms. That general position would indeed imply that it is wrong for Westerners to criticize female genital mutilation, but not for any reasons interestingly specific to genital mutilation itself. For that reason, [. . .] I shall focus here on [three] criticisms that, while influenced by relativism, stop short of the general relativist thesis:

1  It is morally wrong to criticize the practices of another culture unless one is prepared to be similarly critical of comparable practices when they occur in one's own culture. (Thus, a typical student reaction is to criticize the "ethnocentrism" of a stance that holds that one's own culture is the benchmark for "the principles and practices that are appropriate for all people.")
2  It is morally wrong to criticize the practices of another culture unless one's own culture has eradicated all evils of a comparable kind. (Thus, a typical undergraduate paper comments that criticism of genital mutilation is unacceptable "when one considers the domestic problems we are faced with in our own cultures.")
3  Female genital mutilation is morally on a par with practices of dieting and body shaping in American culture. (I observed quite a few courses in which this comparison played a central role, and the comparison has often been suggested by my own students.) [. . .]

These are significant charges, which should be confronted. Feminist argument should not be condescending to women in developing countries who have their own views of what is good. Such condescension is all the more damaging when it comes from women who are reluctant to criticize the flaws in their own culture, for then it is reminiscent of the worst smugness of "white man's burden" colonialism. Our students are surely right to think that withholding one's own judgment until one has listened carefully to the experiences of members of the culture in question is a crucial part of intelligent deliberation. On the other hand, the prevalence of a practice, and the fact that even today many women endorse and perpetuate it, should not be taken as the final word, given that there also many women in African cultures who struggle against it, and given that those who do perpetuate it may do so in background conditions of intimidation and economic and political inequality. How, then, should we respond to these very common charges?

The first thesis is true, and it is useful to be reminded of it. Americans have all too often criticized other cultures without examining their own cultural shortcomings. It is less clear, however, that lack of self-criticism is a grave problem for Americans on such issues. We find no shortage of criticism of the ideal female body image, or of practices of dieting intended to produce it. Indeed, American feminists would appear to have devoted considerably more attention to these American problems than to genital mutilation, to judge from the success of books such as Naomi Wolf's *The Beauty Myth* and Susan Bordo's *Unbearable Weight*. Indeed, a review of the recent feminist literature suggests the problem may lie in exactly the opposite direction, in an excessive focusing on our own failings. We indulge in moral narcissism when we flagellate ourselves for our own errors while neglecting to attend to the needs of those who ask our help from a distance.

The second thesis is surely false. It is wrong to insist on cleaning up one's own house before responding to urgent calls from outside. Should we have said "Hands off Apartheid," on the grounds that racism persists in the United States? Or, during the Second World War, "Hands off the rescue of the Jews," on the grounds that in the 1930s and 1940s every nation that contained Jews

was implicated in anti-Semitic practices? It is and should be difficult to decide how to allocate one's moral effort between local and distant abuses. To work against both is urgently important, and individuals will legitimately make different decisions about their priorities. But the fact that a needy human being happens to live in Togo rather than Idaho does not make her less my fellow, less deserving of my moral commitment. And to fail to recognize the plight of a fellow human being because we are busy moving our own culture to greater moral heights seems the very height of moral obtuseness and parochialism.

We could add that FGM is not as such the practice of a single culture or group of cultures. As recently as in the 1940s, related operations were performed by US and British doctors to treat female "problems" such as masturbation and lesbianism (Toubia, *FGM* 21). Nor is there any cultural or religious group in which the practice is universal. As Nahid Toubia[1] puts it, "FGM is an issue that concerns women and men who believe in equality, dignity and fairness to all human beings, regardless of gender, race, religion or ethnic identity. . . . It represents a human tragedy and must not be used to set Africans against non-Africans, one religious group against another, or even women against men" (*FGM* 7).

If the third thesis were true, it might support a decision to give priority to the local in our political action (though not necessarily speech and writing): If two abuses are morally the same and we have better local information about one and are better placed politically to do something about it, that one seems to be a sensible choice to focus on in our actions here and now. But is the third thesis true? Surely not. Let us enumerate the differences.

1. Female genital mutilation is carried out by force, whereas dieting in response to culturally constructed images of beauty is a matter of choice, however seductive the persuasion. Few mothers restrict their children's dietary intake to unhealthy levels in order to make them slim; indeed most mothers of anorexic girls are horrified and deeply grieved by their daughters'

condition. By contrast, during FGM small girls, frequently as young as four or five, are held down by force, often, as in Togo, by a group of adult women, and have no chance to select an alternative. The choices involved in dieting are often not fully autonomous: They may be the product of misinformation and strong social forces that put pressure on women to make choices, sometimes dangerous ones, that they would not make otherwise. We should criticize these pressures and the absence of full autonomy created by them. And yet the distinction between social pressure and physical force should also remain salient, both morally and legally. [. . .]

2. Female genital mutilation is irreversible, whereas dieting is, famously, far from irreversible.

   Female genital mutilation is usually performed in conditions that in and of themselves are dangerous and unsanitary, conditions to which no child should be exposed; dieting is not.

3. Female genital mutilation is linked to extensive and in some cases lifelong health problems, even death. (In Kassindja's region, deaths are rationalized by the folk wisdom that profuse bleeding is a sign that a girl is not a virgin.) Dieting is linked to problems of this gravity only in the extreme cases of anorexia and bulimia, which, even, then, are reversible.

4. Female genital mutilation is usually performed on children far too young to consent even were consent solicited; dieting involves, above all, adolescents and young adults. Even when children are older, consent is not solicited. Typical is the statement of an Ivory Coast father of a 12-year old girl about to be cut. "She has no choice," he stated. "I decide. Her viewpoint is not important." His wife, who personally opposes the practice, concurs: "It is up to my husband," she states. "The man makes the decisions about the children" (Dugger, "African Ritual Pain").

5. In the United States, as many women as men complete primary education, and more women than men complete secondary education; adult literacy is 99 per cent for both females and males. In Togo, adult female literacy is 32.9 per cent (52 per cent that of men); in the Sudan, 30.6 per cent (56 per cent that of men); in the Ivory Coast, 26.1 per cent (56 per cent); in Burkina Faso, 8 per cent (29 per cent). Illiteracy is an impediment to independence; other impediments are supplied by economic dependency and lack of employment opportunities. These facts suggest limits to the notions of consent and choice, even as applied to the mothers or relatives who perform the operation, who may not be aware of the extent of resistance to the practice in their own and relevantly similar societies. To these limits we may add those imposed by political powerlessness, malnutrition, and intimidation. The wife of the patriarch in Fauziya Kassindja's clan told a reporter that she is opposed to the practice and would have run away like Fauziya had she been able—but nonetheless, she will allow the operation for her infant daughter. "I have to do what my husband says," she concludes. "It is not for women to give an order. I feel what happened to my body. I remember my suffering. But I cannot prevent it for my daughter."

6. Female genital mutilation means the irreversible loss of the capability for a type of sexual functioning that many women value highly, usually at an age when they are far too young to know what value it has or does not have in their own life. In the rare case in which a woman can make the comparison, she usually reports profound regret. Mariam Razak, a neighbour of the Kassindjas, was 15 when she was cut, with five adult women holding her down. She had had sex with the man who is now her husband prior to that time and found it satisfying. Now, they both say, things are difficult. Mariam compares the loss to having a terminal illness that lasts a lifetime. "Now," her husband says, "something was lost in that place. . . . I try to make her feel pleasure, but it doesn't work very well."

7. Female genital mutilation is unambiguously linked to customs of male domination. Even its official rationales, in terms of purity and propriety, point to aspects of sex hierarchy. Typical is the

statement of Egyptian farmer Said Ibrahim, upset about the government ban: "Am I supposed to stand around while my daughter chases men?" To which Mohammed Ali, age 17, added, "Banning it would make women wild like those in America." Sex relations constructed by the practice are relations in which intercourse becomes a vehicle for one-sided male pleasure rather than for mutuality of pleasure.

By contrast, the ideal female body image purveyed in the American media has multiple and complex resonances, including those of male domination, but also including those of physical fitness, independence, and boyish non-maternity.

These differences help explain why there is no serious campaign to make ads for diet programs, or the pictures of emaciated women in *Vogue*, illegal, whereas FGM is illegal in most of the countries in which it occurs. (In the Sudan, the practice is punishable by up to two years' imprisonment.) Such laws are not well enforced, but their existence is evidence of a widespread movement against the practice in the countries implicated. Women in local regions where the practice is traditional give evidence of acquiescing, insofar as they do, out of intimidation and lack of options; women in adjacent regions where the practice is not traditional typically deplore it, citing health risks, loss of pleasure, and unnecessary suffering.

These differences also explain why Fauziya Kassindja was able to win political asylum. We shall not see similar arguments for political asylum for American women who have been pressured by the culture to be thin—however much it remains appropriate to criticize the norms of female beauty displayed in *Vogue* (as some advertisers have begun to do), the practices of some mothers, and the many covert pressures that combine to produce eating disorders in our society. Similarly, whereas the prospect of footbinding of the traditional Chinese type (in which the bones of the feet were repeatedly broken and the flesh of the foot became rotten [for an especially vivid description of this practice, see Chang]) would, in my view, give grounds for political asylum;

the presence of advertisements for high-heeled shoes surely would not, however many problems may be associated with the fashion. Even the publication of articles urging women to undergo FGM should be seen as altogether different from forcing a woman to undergo the procedure.

## 4. Traditional Justifications of FGM

How, then, is FGM traditionally justified, when it is? In social terms, it is highly likely that FGM emerged as the functional equivalent to the seclusion of women. African women, unlike their counterparts in India, Pakistan, and elsewhere, are major agricultural producers. There is no barrier to women's work outside the home, and indeed the entire organization of agriculture in Africa traditionally rests on the centrality of female labour (Boserup). In India, women's purity is traditionally guaranteed by seclusion; in Africa, this guarantee was absent, and another form of control emerged. But this functional history clearly does not justify the practice. What arguments are currently available?

It is now generally agreed that there is no religious requirement to perform FGM. The prophet Mohammed's most cited statement about the practice (from a reply to a question during a speech) makes the process non-essential, and the force of his statement seems to have been to discourage extensive cutting in favour of a more symbolic type of operation.[2] The one reference to the operation in the *hadith* classifies it as a *makrama*, or non-essential practice. FGM is not practised at all in many Islamic countries, including Pakistan, Algeria, Tunisia, Saudi Arabia, Iran, and Iraq. Defences appealing to morality (FGM keeps women from extramarital sex) have resonance because they connect with the practice's likely original rationale, but they presuppose an unacceptable picture of women as whorish and childish. However sincerely such arguments are addressed, they should not be accepted by people with an interest in women's dignity. Defences in terms of physical beauty are trickier, because we know how much cultures differ in what they regard as beautiful, but even perceptions of beauty (also at issue in Chinese footbinding) should yield before evidence of impairment of health and sexual functioning. Arguments claiming that without the practice women will not be acceptable to men may state something true in local circumstances (as was also the case with footbinding) and may therefore provide a rationale for individual families to defer to custom as the best of a bad business (although this is less true now than formerly, given the widespread resistance to the practice in most areas where it occurs). Such arguments, however, clearly cannot justify the practice in moral or legal terms; similarly, arguments advising slaves to behave themselves if they do not want to be beaten may give good advice but cannot justify the institution of slavery.

The strongest argument in favour of the practice is an argument that appeals to cultural continuity. **Jomo Kenyatta** and others have stressed the constitutive role played by such initiation rites in the formation of a community and the disintegrative effect of interference. For this reason, Kenyatta opposed criminalization of the surgery and recommended a more gradual process of education and persuasion. Although one must have some sympathy with these concerns, it is still important to remember that a community is not a mysterious organic unity but a plurality of people standing in different relations of power to one another. It is not obvious that the type of cohesion that is effected by subordination and functional impairment is something we ought to perpetuate. Moreover, 60 years after Kenyatta's ambivalent defence, we see widespread evidence of resistance from within each culture, and there is reason to think that the practice is kept alive above all by the excisers themselves, paramedical workers who enjoy both high income and high prestige in the community from their occupation. These women frequently have the status of priestesses and have great influence over social perceptions (Toubia, *FGM* 29). Countries that move against the practice should certainly make provision for the economic security of these women, but this does not mean taking them as unbiased interpreters of cultural tradition. To the extent that an initiation ritual is still held to be a valuable source of cultural solidarity, such rituals can surely be practised (as they already are in some places) using a merely symbolic operation that does not remove any tissue.

## 5. Conclusion

Internal criticism is slowly changing the situation in the nations in which FGM has traditionally been practised. The 18-year-old son of the patriarch of the Kassindja family told reporters that he wanted to marry a woman who had not been cut, because teachers in his high school had influenced his thinking. The patriarch himself now favours making the practice optional, to discourage more runaways who give the family a bad name. The very fact that the age of cutting in Togo has been moving steadily down (from twelve to four), in order (the exciser says) to discourage runaways, gives evidence of mounting resistance to the practice. But many of the women and men in the relevant nations who are struggling against this practice are impoverished or unequal under the law or illiterate or powerless or in fear—and often all of these. There is no doubt that they wish outside aid. There is also no doubt that they encounter local opposition—as is always the case when one moves to change a deeply entrenched custom connected with the structures of power. (As I have suggested, some of the people involved have strong personal economic and status interests in the status quo.) Suzanne Aho, director of Togo's Office for the Protection and Promotion of the Family, explains that she tries to counsel men about women's rights of choice, but she encounters the dead weight of custom. Of the Kassindja patriarch she says: "'You cannot force her,' I told him. He understood, but he said it is a tradition."

These upholders of tradition are eager, often, to brand their internal opponents as Westernizers, colonialists, and any other bad thing that may carry public sentiment. Even so, Fauziya's father was accused of "trying to act like a white man." But this way of deflecting internal criticism should not intimidate outsiders who have reasoned the matter out, at the same time listening to the narratives of women who have been involved in the reality of FGM. The charge of "colonialism" presumably means that the norms of an oppressor group are being unthinkingly assimilated, usually to curry favour with that group. That is not at all what is happening in the case of FGM. In the United Nations, in Human Rights Watch, in many organizations throughout the world, and in countless local villages the issue has been debated. Even the not very progressive Immigration and Naturalization Service (INS) has been swayed by the data it collected. The vigour of internal resistance should give confidence to those outside who work to oppose the practice. Frequently external pressure can assist a relatively powerless internal group that is struggling to achieve change.

In short, international and national officials who have been culpably slow to recognize gender-specific abuses as human rights violations are beginning to get the idea that women's rights are human rights, and that freedom from FGM is among them. Without abandoning a broader concern for the whole list of abuses women suffer at the hands of unjust customs and individuals, we should continue to keep FGM on the list of unacceptable practices that violate women's human rights, and we should be ashamed of ourselves if we do not use whatever privilege and power has come our way to make it disappear forever.

## Notes

1. Toubia was the first woman surgeon in the Sudan. She is an advisor to the World Health Organization, vice chair of the Women's Rights Project of Human Rights Watch, and director of the Global Action against FGM Project at the Columbia University School of Public Health.
2. Mohammed told his listeners to "circumcise" but not to "mutilate," for not destroying the clitoris would be better for the man and would make the woman's face glow—a directive that many interpret as calling for "a male-type circumcision where the prepuce is removed, making the clitoris even more sensitive to touch" (Toubia, "*FGM*" 236).

## Works Cited

Boserup, E. *Women's Role in Economic Development.* 2nd ed. Aldershot, England: Gower Publishing, 1986.

Chang, J. *Wild Swans: Three Daughters of China.* London and New York: HarperCollins, 1992.

Dugger, C.W. "US Gives Asylum to Woman Who Fled Genital Mutilation." *New York Times* 20 June 1996.

Dugger, C.W. "A Refugee's Body Is Intact but Her Family Is Torn." *New York Times* 11 September 1996.

Dugger, C.W. "African Ritual Pain: Genital Cutting." *New York Times* 5 October 1996.

Kenyatta, J. *Facing Mount Kenya.* London: Secker and Warburg, 1938.

Nussbaum, M.C. *Cultivating Humanity: A Classical Defense of Reform in Higher Education.* Cambridge, MA: Harvard University Press, 1997.

Toubia, N. "Female Genital Mutilation." *Women's Rights, Human Rights.* Ed. J. Peters and A. Wolper. New York: Routledge, 1994. 224–37.

Toubia, N. *Female Genital Mutilation: A Call for Global Action.* New York: UNICEF, 1995.

## Study Questions

1. Nussbaum tells us that undergraduate students are likely to be moral relativists. As an undergraduate student, do you think that Nussbaum is correct about this?
2. What health risks are associated with FGM? Do you agree with international medical practitioners that "female genital mutilation" is a more appropriate term than "female circumcision"?
3. What three moral relativist theses does Nussbaum identify that lead undergraduate students to oppose criticisms of FGM by westerners? Which of Nussbaum's responses do you find most convincing, and which of Nussbaum's responses do you find least convincing?
4. What three traditional justifications of FGM does Nussbaum identify? Which of Nussbaum's responses do you find most convincing, and which of Nussbaum's responses do you find least convincing?

# Carol Gilligan

After majoring in English literature as an undergraduate, Carol Gilligan earned her PhD in social psychology at Harvard University. Gilligan was a long-time professor at the Harvard Graduate School of Education before moving to New York University in 2002. During her early years at Harvard, Gilligan collaborated with Lawrence Kohlberg (1927–87) in his influential research on moral development, but went on to criticize him for ignoring the experiences of girls and women. Gilligan's 1982 book, *In A Different Voice*, has sold more than 750,000 copies and been translated into 16 languages.

# Moral Orientation and Moral Development

## 1. Justice and Care

When one looks at an ambiguous figure like the drawing that can be seen as a young or old woman, or the image of the vase and the faces, one initially sees it in only one way. Yet even after seeing it in both ways, one way often seems more compelling. This phenomenon reflects the laws of perceptual organization that favour certain modes of visual grouping. But it also suggests a tendency to view reality as unequivocal and thus to argue that there is one right or better way of seeing.

The experiments of the **Gestalt psychologists** on perceptual organization provide a series of demonstrations that the same proximal pattern can be organized in different ways so that, for example, the same figure can be seen as a square or a diamond, depending on its orientation in relation to a surrounding frame. Subsequent studies show that the context influencing which of two possible organizations will be chosen may depend not only on the features of the array presented but also on the perceiver's past experience or expectation. Thus, a bird-watcher and a rabbit-keeper are likely to see the duck-rabbit figure in different ways; yet this difference does not imply that one way is better or a higher form of perceptual organization. It does, however, call attention to the fact that the rabbit-keeper, perceiving the rabbit, may not see the ambiguity of the figure until someone points out that it can also be seen as a duck.

This paper presents a similar phenomenon with respect to moral judgment, describing two moral perspectives that organize thinking in different ways.

The analogy to ambiguous figure perception arises from the observation that although people are aware of both perspectives, they tend to adopt one or the other in defining and resolving moral conflict. Since moral judgments organize thinking about choice in difficult situations, the adoption of a single perspective may facilitate clarity of decision. But the wish for clarity may also imply a compelling human need for resolution or closure, especially in the face of decisions that give rise to discomfort or unease. Thus, the search for clarity in seeing may blend with a search for justification, encouraging the position that there is one right or better way to think about moral problems. This question, which has been the subject of intense theological and philosophical debate, becomes of interest to the psychologist not only because of its psychological dimensions—the tendency to focus on one perspective and the wish for justification—but also because one moral perspective currently dominates psychological thinking and is embedded in the most widely used measure for assessing the maturity of moral reasoning.

In describing an alternative standpoint, I will reconstruct the account of moral development around two moral perspectives, grounded in different dimensions of relationship that give rise to moral concern. The justice perspective, often equated with moral reasoning, is recast as one way of seeing moral problems and a care perspective is brought forward as an alternate vision or frame. The distinction between justice and care as alternative perspectives or moral orientations is based empirically on the observation that a shift in the focus of attention from concerns about justice to concerns about care changes the definition of what constitutes a moral problem, and leads the same situation to be seen in different ways. Theoretically, the distinction between justice and care cuts across the familiar divisions between thinking and feeling, egoism and altruism, theoretical and practical reasoning. It calls attention to the fact that all human relationships, public and private, can be characterized *both* in terms of equality and in terms of attachment, and that both inequality and detachment constitute grounds for moral concern. Since everyone is vulnerable both to oppression and to abandonment, two moral visions—one of justice and one of care—recur in human experience. The moral injunctions, not to act unfairly toward others, and not to turn away from someone in need, capture these different concerns.

The conception of the moral domain as comprised of at least two moral orientations raises new questions about observed differences in moral judgment and the disagreements to which they give rise. Key to this revision is the distinction between differences in developmental stage (more or less adequate positions within a single orientation) and differences in orientation (alternative perspectives or frameworks). The findings reported in this paper of an association between moral orientation and gender speak directly to the continuing controversy over sex differences in moral reasoning. In doing so, however, they also offer an empirical explanation for why previous thinking about moral development has been organized largely within the justice framework.

## 2. Piaget and Kohlberg

My research on moral orientation derives from an observation made in the course of studying the relationship between moral judgment and action. Two studies, one of college students describing their experiences of moral conflict and choice, and one of pregnant women who were considering abortion, shifted the focus of attention from the ways people reason about hypothetical dilemmas to the ways people construct moral conflicts and choices in their lives. This change in approach made it possible to see what experiences people define in moral terms, and to explore the relationship between the understanding of moral problems and the reasoning strategies used and the actions taken in attempting to resolve them. In this context, I observed that women, especially when speaking about their own experiences of moral conflict and choice, often define moral problems in a way that eludes the categories of moral theory and is at odds with the assumptions that shape psychological thinking about morality and about the self. This discovery, that a different voice often guides the moral judgments and the actions of women, called attention to a major design problem in previous moral judgment research: namely, the use of all-male samples as the empirical basis for theory construction.

The selection of an all-male sample as the basis for generalizations that are applied to both males and females is logically inconsistent. As a research strategy, the decision to begin with a single-sex sample is inherently problematic, since the categories of analysis will tend to be defined on the basis of the initial data gathered and subsequent studies will tend to be restricted to these categories. **Piaget's** work on the moral judgment of the child illustrates these problems since he defined the evolution of children's consciousness and practice of rules on the basis of his study of boys playing marbles, and then undertook a study of girls to assess the generality of his findings. Observing a series of differences both in the structure of girls" games and "in the actual mentality of little girls," he deemed these differences not of interest because "it was not this contrast which we proposed to study." Girls, Piaget found, "rather complicated our interrogatory in relation to what we know about boys," since the changes in their conception of rules, although following the same sequence observed in boys, did not stand in the same relation to social experience. Nevertheless, he concluded that "in spite of these differences in the structure of the game and apparently in the players" mentality, we find the same process at work as in the evolution of the game of marbles" (76–84).

Thus, girls were of interest insofar as they were similar to boys and confirmed the generality of Piaget's findings. The differences noted, which included a greater tolerance, a greater tendency toward innovation in solving conflicts, a greater willingness to make exceptions to rules, and a lesser concern with legal elaboration, were not seen as germane to "the psychology of rules," and therefore were regarded as insignificant for the study of children's moral judgment. Given the confusion that currently surrounds the discussion of sex differences in moral judgment, it is important to emphasize that the differences observed by Piaget did not pertain to girls" understanding of rules *per se* or to the development of the idea of justice in their thinking, but rather to the way girls structured their games

and their approach to conflict resolution—that is, to their use rather than their understanding of the logic of rules and justice.

Kohlberg, in his research on moral development, did not encounter these problems since he equated moral development with the development of justice reasoning and initially used an all-male sample as the basis for theory and test construction. In response to his critics, Kohlberg has recently modified his claims, renaming his test a measure of "justice reasoning" rather than of "moral maturity" and acknowledging the presence of a care perspective in people's moral thinking. But the widespread use of Kohlberg's measure as a measure of moral development together with his own continuing tendency to equate justice reasoning with moral judgment leaves the problem of orientation differences unsolved. More specifically, Kohlberg's efforts to assimilate thinking about care to the six-stage developmental sequence he derived and refined by analyzing changes in justice reasoning (relying centrally on his all-male longitudinal sample), underscores the continuing importance of the points raised in this paper concerning (1) the distinction between differences in developmental stage within a single orientation and differences in orientation, and (2) the fact that the moral thinking of girls and women was not examined in establishing either the meaning or the measurement of moral judgment within contemporary psychology.

## 3. Cases

An analysis of the language and logic of men's and women's moral reasoning about a range of hypothetical and real dilemmas underlies the distinction elaborated in this paper between a justice and a care perspective. The empirical association of care reasoning with women suggests that discrepancies observed between moral theory and the moral judgments of girls and women may reflect a shift in perspective, a change in moral orientation. Like the figure-ground shift in ambiguous figure perception, justice and care as moral perspectives are not opposites or mirror-images of one another, with justice uncaring and care unjust. Instead, these perspectives denote different ways of organizing the basic elements of moral judgment: self, others, and the relationship between them. With the shift in perspective from justice to care, the organizing dimension of relationship changes from inequality/equality to attachment/detachment, reorganizing thoughts, feelings, and language so that words connoting relationship like "dependence" or "responsibility" or even moral terms such as "fairness" and "care" take on different meanings. To organize relationships in terms of attachment rather than in terms of equality changes the way human connection is imagined, so that the images or metaphors of relationship shift from hierarchy or balance to network or web. In addition, each organizing framework leads to a different way of imagining the self as a moral agent.

From a justice perspective, the self as moral agent stands as the figure against a ground of social relationships, judging the conflicting claims of self and others against a standard of equality or equal respect (the Categorical Imperative, the Golden Rule). From a care perspective, the relationship becomes the figure, defining self and others. Within the context of relationship, the self as a moral agent perceives and responds to the perception of need. The shift in moral perspective is manifest by a change in the moral question from "What is just?" to "How to respond?"

For example, adolescents asked to describe a moral dilemma often speak about peer or family pressure in which case the moral question becomes how to maintain moral principles or standards and resist the influence of one's parents or friends. "I have a right to my religious opinions," one teenager explains, referring to a religious difference with his parents. Yet, he adds, "I respect their views." The same dilemma, however, is also construed by adolescents as a problem of attachment, in which case the moral question becomes: how to respond both to oneself and to one's friends or one's parents, how to maintain or strengthen connection in the face of differences in belief. "I understand their fear of my new religious ideas," one teenager explains, referring to her religious disagreement with her parents, "but they really ought to listen to me and try to understand my beliefs."

One can see these two statements as two versions of essentially the same thing. Both teenagers present self-justifying arguments about religious disagreement; both address the claims of self and of others in a way that honours both. Yet each frames the problem in different terms, and the use of moral language points to different concerns. The first speaker casts the problem in terms of individual rights that must be respected within the relationship. In other words, the figure of the considering is the self looking on the disagreeing selves in relationship, and the aim is to get the other selves to acknowledge the right to disagree. In the case of the second speaker, figure and ground shift. The relationship becomes the figure of the considering, and relationships are seen to require listening and efforts at understanding differences in belief. Rather than the right to disagree, the speaker focuses on caring to hear and to be heard. Attention shifts from the grounds for agreement (rights and respect) to the grounds for understanding (listening and speaking, hearing and being heard). This shift is marked by a change in moral language from the stating of separate claims to rights and respect ("I have a right . . . I respect their views.") to the activities of relationship—the injunction to listen and try to understand ("I understand . . . they ought to listen . . . and try to understand."). The metaphor of moral voice itself carries the terms of the care perspective and reveals how the language chosen for moral theory is not orientation neutral.

The language of the public abortion debate, for example, reveals a justice perspective. Whether the abortion dilemma is cast as a conflict of rights or in terms of respect for human life, the claims of the fetus and of the pregnant woman are balanced or placed in opposition. The morality of abortion decisions thus construed hinges on the scholastic or metaphysical question as to whether the fetus is a life or a person, and whether its claims take precedence over those of the pregnant woman. Framed as a problem of care, the dilemma posed by abortion shifts. The connection between the fetus and the pregnant woman becomes the focus of attention and the question becomes whether it is responsible or irresponsible, caring or careless, to extend or to end this connection. In this construction, the abortion dilemma arises because there is no way not to act, and no way of acting that does not alter the connection between self and others. To ask what actions constitute care or are more caring directs attention to the parameters of connection and the costs of detachment, which become subjects of moral concern.

Finally, two medical students, each reporting a decision not to turn in someone who has violated the school rules against drinking, cast their decision in different terms. One student constructs the decision as an act of mercy, a decision to override justice in light of the fact that the violator has shown "the proper degrees of contrition." In addition, this student raises the question as to whether or not the alcohol policy is just, i.e., whether the school has the right to prohibit drinking. The other student explains the decision not to turn in a proctor who was drinking on the basis that turning him in is not a good way to respond to this problem, since it would dissolve the relationship between them and thus cut off an avenue for help. In addition, this student raises the question as to whether the proctor sees his drinking as a problem.

This example points to an important distinction, between care as understood or construed within a justice framework and care as a framework or a perspective on moral decision. Within a justice construction, care becomes the mercy that tempers justice; or connotes the special obligations or supererogatory duties that arise in personal relationships; or signifies altruism freely chosen—a decision to modulate the strict demands of justice by considering equity or showing forgiveness; or characterizes a choice to sacrifice the claims of the self. All of these interpretations of care leave the basic assumptions of a justice framework intact: the division between the self and others, the logic of reciprocity or equal respect.

As a moral perspective, care is less well elaborated, and there is no ready vocabulary in moral theory to describe its terms. As a framework for moral decision, care is grounded in the assumption that self and other are interdependent, an assumption reflected in a view of action as responsive and, therefore, as arising in relationship rather than the view of action as emanating from within the self and, therefore, "self governed." Seen as responsive, the self is by definition connected to others, responding

to perceptions, interpreting events, and governed by the organizing tendencies of human interaction and human language. Within this framework, detachment, whether from self or from others, is morally problematic, since it breeds moral blindness or indifference—a failure to discern or respond to need. The question of what responses constitute care and what responses lead to hurt draws attention to the fact that one's own terms may differ from those of others. Justice in this context becomes understood as respect for people in their own terms.

The medical student's decision not to turn in the proctor for drinking reflects a judgment that turning him in is not the best way to respond to the drinking problem, itself seen as a sign of detachment or lack of concern. Caring for the proctor thus raises the question of what actions are most likely to ameliorate this problem, a decision that leads to the question of what are the proctor's terms.

The shift in organizing perspective here is marked by the fact that the first student does not consider the terms of the other as potentially different but instead assumes one set of terms. Thus the student alone becomes the arbiter of what is *the* proper degree of contrition. The second student, in turn, does not attend to the question of whether the alcohol policy itself is just or fair. Thus each student discusses an aspect of the problem that the other does not mention.

## 4. In a Difference Voice

These examples are intended to illustrate two cross-cutting perspectives that do not negate one another but focus attention on different dimensions of the situation, creating a sense of ambiguity around the question of what is the problem to be solved. Systematic research on moral orientation as a dimension of moral judgment and action initially addressed three questions: (1) Do people articulate concerns about justice and concerns about care in discussing a moral dilemma? (2) Do people tend to focus their attention on one set of concerns and minimally represent the other? and (3) Is there an association between moral orientation and gender? Evidence from studies that included a common set of questions about actual experiences of moral conflict and matched samples of males and females provides affirmative answers to all three questions.

When asked to describe a moral conflict they had faced, 55 out of 80 (69 percent) educationally advantaged North American adolescents and adults raised considerations of both justice and care. Two-thirds (54 out of 80), however, focused their attention on one set of concerns, with focus defined as 75 percent or more of the considerations raised pertaining either to justice or to care. Thus the person who presented, say, two care considerations in discussing a moral conflict was more likely to give a third, fourth, and fifth than to balance care and justice concerns—a finding consonant with the assumption that justice and care constitute organizing frameworks for moral decision. The men and the women involved in this study (high school students, college students, medical students, and adult professionals) were equally likely to demonstrate the focus phenomenon (two-thirds of both sexes fell into the outlying focus categories). There were, however, sex differences in the direction of focus. With one exception, all of the men who focused, focused on justice. The women divided, with roughly one third focusing on justice and one third on care (Gilligan and Attanucci).

These findings clarify the different voice phenomenon and its implications for moral theory and for women. First, it is notable that if women were eliminated from the research sample, care focus in moral reasoning would virtually disappear. Although care focus was by no means characteristic of all women, it was almost exclusively a female phenomenon in this sample of educationally advantaged North Americans. Second, the fact that the women were advantaged means that the focus on care cannot readily be attributed to educational deficit or occupational disadvantage—the explanation Kohlberg and others have given for findings of lower levels of justice reasoning in women. Instead, the focus on care in women's moral reasoning draws attention to the limitations of a justice-focused moral theory and highlights the presence of care concerns in the moral thinking of both women and men. In this light, the Care/Justice group composed of one third of the women and one third of the men becomes of particular interest, pointing

to the need for further research that attends to the way people organize justice and care in relation to one another—whether, for example, people alternate perspectives, like seeing the rabbit and the duck in the rabbit-duck figure, or integrate the two perspectives in a way that resolves or sustains ambiguity.

Third, if the moral domain is comprised of at least two moral orientations, the focus phenomenon suggests that people have a tendency to lose sight of one moral perspective in arriving at moral decision—a liability equally shared by both sexes. The present findings further suggest that men and women tend to lose sight of different perspectives. The most striking result is the virtual absence of care-focus reasoning among the men. Since the men raised concerns about care in discussing moral conflicts and thus presented care concerns as morally relevant, a question is why they did not elaborate these concerns to a greater extent.

## Conclusion

In summary, it becomes clear why attention to women's moral thinking led to the identification of a different voice and raised questions about the place of justice and care within a comprehensive moral theory. It also is clear how the selection of an all-male sample for research on moral judgment fosters an equation of morality with justice, providing little data discrepant with this view. In the present study, data discrepant with a justice-focused moral theory comes from a third of the women. Previously, such women were seen as having a problem understanding "morality." Yet these women may also be seen as exposing the problem in a justice-focused moral theory. This may explain the decision of researchers to exclude girls and women at the initial stage of moral judgment research. If one begins with the premise that "all morality consists in respect for rules" (Piaget) or "virtue is one and its name is justice" (Kohlberg), then women are likely to appear problematic within moral theory. If one begins with women's moral judgments, the problem becomes how to construct a theory that encompasses care as a focus of moral attention rather than as a subsidiary moral concern. [. . .]

## Works Cited

Gilligan, C. *In a Different Voice: Psychological Theory and Women's Development*. Cambridge, MA: Harvard University Press, 1982.

Gilligan, C. and J. Attanucci. "Two Moral Orientations". Harvard University, unpublished manuscript, 1986.

Kohlberg, L. *The Psychology of Moral Development*. San Francisco, CA: Harper & Row, 1984.

Piaget, J. *The Moral Judgment of the Child*. New York: The Free Press Paperback Edition, 1965.

## Study Questions

1. What shortcomings does Gilligan identify in the empirical research upon which Piaget's and Kohlberg's influential theories of moral development are based?
2. Using an example, contrast the justice and care perspectives.
3. Of what importance is Gilligan's analogy of the duck-rabbit figure for understanding how the justice and care perspectives operate?
4. Is Gilligan claiming that *all* males and *all* females approach moral conflicts differently? If not, what *is* Gilligan claiming about the association between moral orientation and gender?

---

# Susan Sherwin

---

Susan Sherwin is an emeritus professor at Dalhousie University. She has a BA in mathematics and philosophy from York University. Sherwin's PhD dissertation, "Moral Foundations of Feminism," completed at Stanford University in 1974, was a pioneering work in feminist philosophy; her 1992 book, *No Longer Patient*, excerpted here, helped to establish feminist bioethics as a field. Sherwin's honours include election as a fellow of the Royal Society of Canada in 1999 and receiving the Killam Prize for outstanding career achievement in the humanities in 2006.

## Ethics, "Feminine" Ethics, and Feminist Ethics

From *No Longer Patient: Feminist Ethics and Health Care*

### 1. Traditional Ethics

Deontologists believe that ethics is a matter of determining which actions are required or prohibited as a matter of moral duty. These actions are right (or wrong) because they are required (or proscribed) by a moral law or set of rules that is binding on persons, independent of their specific interests. **Immanuel Kant** is the most influential of the deontologists, and although his most important work in ethics (*Groundwork of the Metaphysic of Morals*) was published more than two hundred years ago, his general approach is still widely followed today.

Kant proposed that the right-making characteristic of an action is defined by the logical nature of the principle it embodies. He believed that moral duties are identified by rational, free persons through the purely abstract process of reason. Kant argued that the moral law must be above personal considerations, that is, independent of the feelings of those involved in particular applications. The moral evaluation he called for explicitly disallows consideration of the specific circumstances of the agent or of other parties affected. Rather, moral conclusions must be reached through reasoning that has been abstracted from the circumstances of application, whereby agents decide if the maxims under which they would act could be willed to be universally binding. (For example, the maxim to tell the truth can be willed to be universal without contradiction, but the maxim to lie to take advantage of others' good faith cannot.) Kant was well aware that the specific consequences of performing an action prescribed by such a principle might be undesirable in a particular circumstance, but he believed that morality consists in following the moral law and not in pursuing the consequences we prefer. [. . .]

Deontological theories pay scant attention to the specific details of individuals' moral experiences and relationships. They admit that special obligations arise from specific relationships—for example, to friends and family—but little discussion is devoted to exploring the range or force of such duties. Almost all the theoretical work is concentrated on exploring the nature of general, rather than specific, obligations. [. . .]

Like many other moral theorists, Kant assumed that only men would fully qualify as moral agents. He believed that women—together with children and idiots—were unable (or unwilling) to engage in a process that requires them to ignore personal sentiments in their moral decision-making. Because of this "deficiency," he considered women inferior moral agents, unfit for public life. Rather than accept Kant's view of women as deficient moral agents, feminists generally judge his determination to discount the role of sentiment to be a mark of inadequacy in the theory itself. With many other critics, feminists reject the notion of a moral theory that is wholly detached from concern about consequences.

Consequentialists have an entirely different vision of morality from Kant's: they believe that the moral worth of an action is measured in terms of the worth of the consequences of the action. Consequentialists determine a measure against which states of affairs can be evaluated and hold that an action is right if it maximizes what is desirable in its outcome, in comparison with the results of all alternatives. The most familiar form of consequentialism is utilitarianism, in which consequences are evaluated in terms of the aggregate effects of an action on the welfare or happiness of persons (or sentient beings). Like other consequentialists, utilitarians deny that rules should be followed if they result in less desirable outcomes, even if those rules appear rational in the abstract.[1] Unlike Kantians, consequentialists believe that the particular feelings and attitudes both of agents and of those affected by the actions in question should be considered when determining the moral value of actions; in this sense, their analysis focuses on concrete experiences.

Those who promote consequentialism in its traditional formulations still operate on an abstract plane, however, because ultimately, rightness of an action is calculated by appeal to the total amount of happiness and suffering created by an act, without regard to whose happiness or suffering is at issue. For example, if a utilitarian can produce the greatest amount of happiness by performing an action that will benefit her enemies rather than her children, she is obligated to do that. Although the individual agent would find it preferable to benefit her loved ones rather than her enemies, and although her own pain at the outcome is an element to be considered in the calculation, the theory says that what is important is the total amount of happiness that will be produced by the act. There is no assurance that this requirement will allow her to act on behalf of those she loves, rather than on behalf of those she fears or loathes. [. . .] Moreover, utilitarianism is not directly concerned with merit or fairness in the provision of happiness. What is important about persons is their status as bearers of utility; an individual's relationship to the agent contemplating action and all other qualities that are specifically associated with the individual are of indirect relevance only.

Like Kantianism, then, consequentialism has usually been understood to demand a level of impartiality on the part of agents, which many people find psychologically unacceptable and morally repugnant. The details of the emotional lives and the relationships of the particular persons affected are rendered irrelevant from the moral point of view, except insofar as these details contribute to overall measures of happiness or suffering. All persons are essentially interchangeable for the purposes of both moral theories. Specifically, no special role is directly assigned to a person's status in dominance/subordination relationships. In both Kantian deontology and consequentialism moral agents are asked to distance themselves from their personal experience and concerns. Kant directs agents to think in terms of universal laws, without regard to the circumstances from which actions arise; consequentialists direct them to weigh their own interests equally with those of everyone else, and on most accounts there is no moral evaluation of the worth of the interests themselves. Both theories deny giving special weight to the details of individuals' actual positions in dominance hierarchies. This abstract neutrality is objectionable from the perspective of feminist ethics, which demands explicit focus on the social and political contexts of individuals in its moral deliberations. [. . .]

Among the many reasons women have identified for developing new approaches to ethics, perhaps the most obvious comes from the experience of being caught up short by the antiwoman bias that pervades so much of the existing theoretical work in ethics. Even the most cursory feminist review of the work of the leading moral theorists reveals that the existing proposals of philosophic ethics do not constitute the objective, impartial theories that they are claimed to be; rather, most theories reflect and support explicitly gender-biased and often blatantly misogynist values.

Perhaps this should come as no surprise, because the leading moral theorists have historically described their audience as being exclusively male. **Aristotle**'s theory of virtues, especially as it was developed in the *Nicomachean Ethics* and the *Politics*, made clear that there was a different set of virtues for (free) women from the one developed for (free) men; whereas men's virtues were those required for freedom and political life, women's virtues consisted in

obedience and silence.[2] Only the male virtues were treated as being of philosophic interest or genuine moral worth. This misogynist vision did not end with Aristotle, for his influence has continued for centuries: it was especially important in the development of the thought of the church fathers, who accepted his division of moral worth and made it a centrepiece of their theology, shaping Western values through the ages.

Most of the influential moral theorists in the history of Western thought, including not only Kant and Aristotle but also **Thomas Aquinas**, **Jean-Jacques Rousseau**, **G.W.F. Hegel**, **Friedrich Nietzsche**, and **Jean-Paul Sartre**, saw women as having a significantly different character from men, one they considered morally inferior because it was too focused on the particular and inattentive to the level of generality that moral thought was said to require. They took it as obvious that men were associated with reason (the essential feature of morality) and women were associated with inclination (a barrier to moral thought). Women's deficiency in this regard was taken as justification for excluding women from active roles in political life and for limiting their power and influence in the home. Moreover, many moral theorists believed that subordination was the natural condition of women and perceived in them a willingness to accept their status passively. Rousseau put it most bluntly: women were suited by nature "to please and to be subjected to man. . . . Woman is made to put up even with injustice from him. You will never reduce young boys to the same condition, their inner feelings rise in revolt against injustice; nature has not fitted them to put up with it" (quoted in Canovan, 86–7).

## 2. "Feminine" Ethics

Such views about the nature of moral agents in general and women in particular have not been restricted to the ivory-tower debates of philosophers; they are part of our cultural heritage and shape our daily lives. **Sigmund Freud**, for instance, also considered women incapable of justice because of their commitment to the personal and their unwillingness to evaluate ethical claims in abstraction. Lawrence Kohlberg, in seeking to develop cross-cultural data on the development of moral reasoning in human subjects, deliberately excluded women from his sample groups on the assumption that their inclusion would contaminate the data. In other words, he anticipated that women would follow different patterns in the development of their moral-reasoning skills and therefore excluded them from consideration when setting up a scale intended to measure the moral development of all agents. The evidence is that Kohlberg was right in this expectation; when the tests he developed on the basis of male norms for moral development are applied, men tend to score higher than women (Gilligan). In other words, according to Kohlberg's criteria of what constitutes moral reasoning, the statistical evidence shows women to be deficient in their moral development relative to men.

For years, feminists fought against men's claim that women pursue morality differently from men. They sought to establish an equality of moral ability between men and women; this equality was deemed necessary if women were to achieve equal political rights with men. Hence many important reformist thinkers and activists, including prominent figures of the Anglo-American feminist movement, argued that women have, at least in principle, the same moral capacities as men. Others, however, including leading feminists of the European community, accepted the claim that there is a gender difference in male and female moral thinking; they sought to have the feminine approach to moral thought recognized as a legitimate and important element, which needs to be added to discussions in the public sphere. These theorists argued that rather than disqualifying women from public life, women's distinctive moral perspective makes it urgent that they be included in public debates so that their voices can be heard. Recently, many feminists on both sides of the Atlantic have embraced this notion of women's different approach to moral reasoning.

Carol Gilligan has provided us with an important empirical study that seems to identify a gender difference in moral thinking. She found that when women are presented with moral conflicts, they tend to focus on details about the relationships that hold between the individuals concerned, and they seek out innovative solutions that protect the interests of all participants; that is, they strive to find options that avoid bringing harm to anyone. Men, in contrast, tend to try to identify the appropriate rules that govern the sort of situation described; they select the course of action most compatible with the dominant rule, even if someone's interests may be sacrificed to considerations of justice. Gilligan named the former an ethic of responsibility or care and the latter an ethic of justice. The empirical gender correlations are not perfect, because women sometimes opt for a justice solution and men sometimes choose in accordance with an ethic of care; but statistically, she found that girls and women are likely to choose responses that are sensitive to considerations of responsibility, whereas boys and men are likely to reflect considerations of justice in their analysis. On Gilligan's view, the ideal for all moral agents would be an ethics that includes elements of both approaches.

Thus it appears that Gilligan supports the assumption, common to Kant, Freud, and others, that women focus on the particular, expressing their concern for the feelings and special relationships of the persons involved in moral dilemmas, but unlike Kant and his followers (and also unlike her mentor, Kohlberg), she does not disallow such responses from the realm of the moral. Instead, she expands the definition of moral considerations, so that traditionally feminine thinking is recognized as morally relevant, rather than deficient. Gilligan thereby includes women's characteristic moral experiences and approach to moral decision-making in the field of legitimate moral thinking.

Not all women share Gilligan's analysis of how best to accommodate women's moral reasoning in the development of theoretical ethics. Jean Grimshaw and various other critics, both feminist and nonfeminist, have objected to Gilligan's insistence on two distinct ethics and have suggested that the considerations of care can be accommodated under the ethics of justice. As Chesire Calhoun argues, however, the point is not whether care can be subsumed under an ethic of justice; rather, what is significant is that the proponents of traditional ethics have chosen not to address issues of care. The cumulative effect of generations of male-defined theorizing amounts to gender bias and a denial of the ethical significance of women's perspective and concerns. [. . .]

Ethical models based on the image of ahistorical, self-sufficient, atom-like individuals are simply not credible to most women. Because women are usually charged with the responsibility of caring for children, the elderly, and the ill as well as the responsibility of physically and emotionally nurturing men both at work and at home, most women experience the world as a complex web of interdependent relationships, where responsible caring for others is implicit in their moral lives. The abstract reasoning of morality that centres on the rights of independent agents is inadequate for the moral reality in which they live. Most women find that a different model for ethics is necessary; the traditional ones are not persuasive.

Nel Noddings has taken Gilligan's move a step further; she, too, accepts that caring is morally significant, but she goes so far as to argue that it is the only legitimate moral consideration. In *Caring* she argues that everyone (men and women alike) ought to pursue a feminine ethic of caring and abandon the insensitive demands of the abstract moral rules of justice. She focuses on "how to meet the other morally" and defines the proper locus of ethical thought as the quality of relationships, rather than a quality of judgments or acts. An agent's moral obligation, in Noddings' view, is to meet others as "one-caring" and to maintain conditions that permit caring to flourish. These others, for their part, have a responsibility to exhibit reciprocity or, at least, to acknowledge the caring. Ethical behaviour, for Noddings, involves putting oneself at the service of others, seeing the world from their perspective, and acting "as though in my own behalf, but in behalf of the other" (33).

Other women engaged in moral theory have spoken of the ethics associated with the characteristically feminine activity of mothering. Most notably, Sara Ruddick has proposed that maternal thinking, the moral perspective appropriate to the demands of mothering, is a distinctive way of knowing and caring that has implications for such important social issues as pacifism and antimilitarism. She believes that women are particularly skilled at such thinking, whether or not they are mothers, because they have been raised to be mothers. [. . .]

Another important motivation for development of feminine ethics is recognition of the explicit maleness of the model pursued by those engaged in traditional ethics. As Annette Baier (1985b) has observed, the objective of most men who work in traditional ethics is the development of a comprehensive theory, but most female theorists do not seem interested in building an abstract, encompassing system. Baier challenges the suitability of a comprehensive, abstract model that rests on a few fundamental building blocks as a basis for theoretical ethics. Moreover, she calls into question the value of a moral theory that is defined in terms of abstract, universal principles, which are divorced from actual moral experience. In *Postures of the Mind* (Baier 1985a) she advises theorists to abandon the search for a rationalistic, universal system, chosen from purely theoretical concerns, and to concentrate instead on the search for a more accurate understanding of moral experience.

## 3. Feminist Ethics

Feminist ethics is different from feminine ethics. It derives from the explicitly political perspective of feminism, wherein the oppression of women is seen to be morally and politically unacceptable. Hence it involves more than recognition of women's actual experiences and moral practices; it incorporates a critique of the specific practices that constitute their oppression. Nevertheless, it is not altogether separate from what I have termed "feminine ethics."

In my view, feminist ethics must recognize the moral perspective of women; insofar as that includes the perspective described as an ethics of care, we should expand our moral agenda accordingly. Feminists have reason, however, to be cautious about the place of caring in their approach to ethics; it is necessary to be wary of the implications of gender traits within a sexist culture. Because gender differences are central to the structures that support dominance relations, it is likely that women's proficiency at caring is somehow related to women's subordinate status.

Within dominance relations, those who are assigned the subordinate position, that is, those with less power, have special reason to be sensitive to the emotional pulse of others, to see things in relational terms, and to be pleasing and compliant. Thus the nurturing and caring at which women excel are, among other things, the survival skills of an oppressed group that lives in close contact with its oppressors. [. . .]

Just as the gender associations that Gilligan identified have developed in a particular historical context, the attitudes that Ruddick (1984a) described as maternal thinking reflect the usual experience of mothering in Western, middle-class life, where a socially and economically defined nuclear family is assumed to be the norm. We should be wary of assuming gender-based dichotomies of moral thought too readily, whatever their empirical origin; such dualisms perpetuate assumptions of deep difference between men and women and limit our abilities to think creatively about genuinely gender-neutral ethical and power structures.

Another danger inherent in proposals for feminine ethics is that caring about the welfare of others often leads women to direct all their energies toward meeting the needs of others; it may even lead them to protect the men who oppress them. Hence feminists caution against valorizing the traits that help perpetuate women's subordinate status. Therefore, Barbara Houston warns that "women's distinctive morality is self-defeating, or highly dubious, when exercised in our relations with men, with those more powerful than ourselves, or when exercised in conditions in which the social constructions are likely to deform our caring or disguise it as a form of consent to the status quo" (252); or, as Catharine MacKinnon dryly phrased it, "Women value care because men have valued us according to the care we give them, and we could probably use some" (39).

Within the existing patterns of sexism, there is a clear danger that women will understand the prescriptions of feminine ethics to be directing them to pursue the virtues of caring, while men continue to focus on abstractions that protect their rights and autonomy. Although Gilligan sees the two perspectives of moral reasoning as complementary, not competitive, and believes that both elements must be incorporated into any adequate moral view, it is easy to read her evidence as entrenching the gender differences she uncovers. In a society where the feminine is devalued and equated with inferiority, it is not easy to perceive men embracing a moral approach described as feminine. Because the world is still filled with vulnerable, dependent persons who need care, if men do not assume the responsibilities of caring, then the burden for doing so remains on women.

Nonetheless, despite its politically suspect origins, caring is often a morally admirable way of relating to others. Feminists join with feminine ethicists in rejecting the picture that malestream[3] ethicists offer of a world organized around purely self-interested agents—a world many women judge to be an emotionally and morally barren place that we would all do well to avoid. Feminists perceive that the caring that women do is morally valuable, but most feminists believe that women need to distinguish between circumstances in which care is appropriately offered and those in which it is better withheld. Therefore, an important task of feminist ethics is to establish moral criteria by which we can determine when caring should be offered and when it should be withheld. Feminist analyses of power structures suggest that specific instances of moral caring should be evaluated in the context of the social and political relations that each instance supports or challenges (Houston and Diller). In feminist ethics, evaluating the moral worth of specific acts and patterns of caring involves making political judgments.

Feminist ethics also takes from feminine ethics its recognition that personal feelings, such as empathy, loyalty, or guilt, can play an ethically significant role in moral deliberations. I think, however, that the proponents of abstraction are right to insist that there are limits to the place of caring in ethics. We should guard against allowing preferences, especially those tied to feelings of personal animosity, from being granted full range in ethical matters. For example, it would not be appropriate to decide to withdraw life support from a patient because she has been aggressive, complaining, and unco-operative, and hence her caregivers do not like her. Although there is something morally abhorrent about the obligation to make moral decisions without regard for the effects on loved ones, there is also great danger in believing we are only responsible for the interests of those for whom we feel affection. Morality must include respect for sentiments, but it cannot give full authority to particular sentiments without considering both their source and their effects.[4] Because feminism arises from moral objections to oppression, it must maintain a commitment to the pursuit of social justice; that commitment is not always compatible with preferences derived from existing relationships and attitudes. Hence we must recognize that feminist ethics involves a commitment to considerations of justice, as well as to those of caring.

Feminist ethics takes its inspiration for other important features from what I have characterized as feminine ethics. It can agree with Gilligan that the morally relevant features of any decision-making situation include the agents' responsibilities to specific persons, including themselves. It also shares with feminine ethics a recognition of the significance of rooting ethical discussion in specific contexts and thus rejecting traditional ethical theory's commitment to purely abstract reasoning. Like feminine ethics, feminist ethics directs us to consider the details of experience when evaluating practices. For example, when one is asked to decide about a morally uncertain policy such as euthanasia, it is important to remember the terror and pain of any of our own friends and relatives who were denied that option and also the constraints we may have observed in specific individuals' ability to make such decisions once their illnesses took over their lives. We cannot adequately develop moral attitudes toward a controversial practice such as euthanasia if we restrict our reasoning to abstract rules about the duty to respect life or about the importance of autonomy.

In addition, feminist ethics shares with feminine ethics a rejection of the paradigm of moral subjects as autonomous, rational, independent, and virtually indistinguishable from one another; it seems clear that an ontology that considers only isolated, fully developed beings is not adequate for ethics (Whitbeck). We must reconceive the concept of the individual, which has been taken as the central concept of ethical theory in Western thought. People have historical roots; they develop within specific human contexts, and they are persons, to a significant degree, by virtue of their relations to others like themselves (Baier 1985a). We value persons as unique individuals whose lives are of concern to us, and in that respect, the individual person is still an important element of ethical thought. We cannot speak of the individual as the central unit of analysis, however, without considering that persons only exist in complex social relationships. Unless we recognize that a person's desires, needs, and beliefs are formed only within human society, we may mistakenly imagine ourselves and our interests to be independent from others and their interests. [. . .]

Most important, feminist ethics is characterized by its commitment to the feminist agenda of eliminating the subordination of women—and of other oppressed persons—in all of its manifestations. The principal insight of feminist ethics is that oppression, however it is practised, is morally wrong. Therefore, moral considerations demand that we uncover and examine the moral injustice of actual oppression in its many guises. When pressed, other sorts of moral theorists will acknowledge that oppressive practices are wrong, but such general declarations are morally inadequate in the face of insidious, systematic oppression. If we want moral change and not mere moral platitudes, then the particular practices that constitute oppression of one group by another must be identified and subjected to explicit moral condemnation; feminists demand the elimination of each oppressive practice.

Given the extent of sexism and other oppressive systems, such as racism, homophobia, and discrimination against the disabled, it is necessary to examine the particular effects of practices on the various oppressed groups. We cannot uncover and dismantle sexist (or racist) prejudices by proceeding with a gender-neutral (or race-neutral) account, because within a sexist (racist) society, such an account is more likely to mask bias than remove it. Marilyn Frye advises that if we want to understand the specific barriers that jointly constitute oppression, we must look at each barrier and ask certain questions about it: "Who constructs it and maintains it? Whose interests are served by its existence? Is it part of a structure which tends to confine, reduce and immobilize some group?" (14). In pursuing feminist ethics, we must continually raise the question, What does it mean for women? When, for example, feminists consider medical research, or the new reproductive technologies, they need to ask not only most of the standard moral questions but also the general questions of how the issue under consideration relates to the oppression of women and what the implications of a proposed policy would be for the political status of women. Unless such questions are explicitly asked, the role of practices in the oppression of women (or others) is unlikely to be apparent, and offensive practices may well be morally defended. According to feminist ethics, other moral questions and judgments come into play only if we can assure ourselves that the act or practice in question is not itself one of a set of interlocking practices that maintains oppressive structures.

In practice, the constraints imposed by feminist ethics mean that, for instance, we cannot discuss abortion purely in terms of the rights of fetuses, without noticing that fetuses are universally housed in women's bodies. We cannot discuss the acceptability of institutionalizing patients for mental illness without noting that women are far more likely to be diagnosed as mentally ill than are men. Any morally adequate discussion of such practices must come to terms with the fact that the resulting social policy will have profound implications on the lives of women. Feminist ethics demands that the effects of any decision on women's lives be a feature of moral discussion and decision-making. [. . .]

Feminist ethics is not an ethics whose conclusions are appropriate only to feminists. The subordination of one group of persons by another is morally wrong, as well as politically unjust, and all adequate moral theories ought to make that plain. Hence those engaged in ethical theorizing and policy formation should always ask about the connections between the subject at hand and patterns of oppression, especially, but not solely, those associated with sexism. Consideration of the feminist implications of any recommendation, whether on the level of moral theory, medical practice, or specific action, belongs in all ethical discussion. There are probably issues where the question will make no real difference to the outcome, because the effects of the practice on women are not distinct; for example, the ethical wrong of destroying the ozone layer for the sake of economic profit can probably be adequately explored without addressing the issues of women's subordination. There will be many surprising cases, however, where the issue is highly relevant, although hidden until raised, and this is true of far more cases than the work currently done by most non-feminist moral theorists indicates. To correct the gender bias that, until recently, has been central to ethical theorizing, it is necessary to make gender an explicit element of ethics (Calhoun).

I label this approach "feminist ethics" and not simply "ethics," because only feminists (male and female) have really concerned themselves with the details of oppression. The leading moral theorists in the mainstream tradition have not only failed to object to the oppression of women; they have often actively contributed to its perpetuation. They legitimized the subjection of women by insisting on women's moral, rational, and epistemological inferiority. Hence the ethical systems they proposed are not only inadequate but also morally wrong, because they promote behaviour and relationships that are morally reprehensible. In a world where women are systematically oppressed, an adequate ethics must address that oppression. Feminist ethics, in making explicit the moral offence of sexism and illuminating some of its many forms, is the only approach to ethics that lives up to this obligation. [. . .]

## Works Cited

Baier, A.C. *Postures of the Mind: Essays on Mind and Morals*. Minneapolis: University of Minnesota Press, 1985a.

Baier, A.C. "What Do Women Want in a Moral Theory?" *Nous* 19, 1 (1985b): 53–63.

Calhoun, C. "Justice, Care, and Gender Bias." *Journal of Philosophy* 85, 9 (1988): 451–63.

Canovan, M. "Rousseau's Two Concepts of Citizenship." *Women in Western Political Thought*. Ed. E. Kennedy and S. Mendus. Brighton: Wheatsheaf Books, 1984.

Freud, S. "Some Psychical Consequences of the Anatomical Distinction between the Sexes." *The Standard Edition of the Complete Psychological Works of Sigmund Freud*. Vol. 19. Trans. and ed. J. Strachey. London: Hogarth Press, 1925.

Frye, M. *The Politics of Reality: Essays in Feminist Theory*. Freedom, CA: Crossing Press, 1983.

Gilligan, C. *In a Different Voice: Psychological Theory and Women's Moral Development*. Cambridge, MA: Harvard University Press, 1982.

Grimshaw, J. *Philosophy and Feminist Thinking*. Minneapolis: University of Minnesota Press, 1986.

Houston, B. "Rescuing Womanly Virtues: Some Dangers of Moral Reclamation." *Science, Morality and Feminist Theory*. Ed. M. Hanen and K. Nielsen. *Canadian Journal of Philosophy* 13, suppl. (1987): 237–62.

Houston, B., and A. Diller. "Trusting Ourselves to Care." *RFR/DRF* 16, 3 (1987): 35–8.

MacKinnon, C. *Feminism Unmodified: Discourses on Life and Law*. Cambridge, MA: Harvard University Press, 1987.

Noddings, N. *Caring: A Feminine Approach to Ethics and Moral Education*. Berkeley: University of California Press, 1984.

O'Brien, M. *The Politics of Reproduction*. London: Routledge and Kegan Paul, 1981.

Ruddick, S. "Maternal Thinking." *Mothering: Essays in Feminist Theory*. Ed. J. Trebilcot. Totowa, NJ: Rowman & Allenheld, 1984a.

Ruddick, S. "Preservative Love and Military Destruction: Some Reflections on Mothering and Peace." *Mothering: Essays in Feminist Theory*. Ed. J. Trebilcot. Totowa, NJ: Rowman & Allenheld, 1984b.

Spelman, E.V. *Inessential Woman: Problems of Exclusion in Feminist Thought*. Boston: Beacon Press, 1988.

Whitbeck, C. "A Different Reality: Feminist Ontology." *Beyond Domination: New Perspectives on Women and Philosophy*. Ed. C.C. Gould. Totowa, NJ: Rowman & Allanheld, 1984.

## Notes

1. A modern form of utilitarianism, known as rule utilitarianism, does involve commitment to following moral rules. Its basic principle directs the agent to follow those rules that, if generally followed, would create the best consequences.

2. As Spelman has pointed out, yet another set of virtues was defined for slaves who are presumed to be male. What virtues were expected of slave women remains undefined.

3. Apparently, this handy feminist term originated with O'Brien in her influential book *The Politics of Reproduction*. It has been widely adopted by feminist critics in many disciplines, and it is hard to imagine how we ever got along without it.

4. I do not mean to imply that the proposals offered by Gilligan, Noddings, and others for an ethics of care are simply emotive theories directing us to "act according to our feelings." They are more sophisticated than that, specifying the nature of the relationships subsumed under the obligation to care; further, neither offers any basis for directing "negative" care or harm at others.

## Study Questions

1. Traditional deontological/Kantian and consequentialist/utilitarian approaches to moral demand impartiality. In what ways is such impartiality problematic?
2. Feminist historians of philosophy have pointed out that philosophers such as Aristotle, Kant, and Rousseau did not simply ignore women in their theorizing but attached specific assumptions to gender differences. What sorts of assumptions were these, and how were they implicated in the inferior status of women in society?
3. Compare "feminine" and "feminist" ethics. Be sure to consider both similarities and differences.
4. Why are feminist philosophers likely to consider it socially and politically risky for women to uncritically embrace a moral philosophy like Gilligan's that promotes a gender-based ideal of care?

---

# Catherine Wilson

---

Catherine Wilson is Regius Professor of Moral Philosophy at the University of Aberdeen; her previous positions were at the Graduate Center of the City University of New York, the University of British Columbia, the University of Alberta, and the University of Oregon. Wilson's writings focus on intersections of scientific knowledge with metaphysics, epistemology, and, as in this chapter from *Moral Animals*, ethics. She was elected a fellow of the Royal Society of Canada in 2003.

## Moral Equality and "Natural" Subordination

From *Moral Animals: Ideals and Constraints in Moral Theory*

### 1. Introduction

"When [a man] is in a co-operative and benevolent relation with a woman, his theme is the principle of abstract equality; the concrete inequality to which he can otherwise attest is not posited" (Beauvoir 27–8). **Simone de Beauvoir**'s remark has not lost its pertinence with regard to modern moral discourse. General moral theory discusses the obligations and entitlements of persons without regard to sex or gender. This discursive posture may express the presumption that between the ordinary run of philosophers and women there exists a co-operative and benevolent relationship. Or it can be interpreted as evasion.

**Aristotle**, **Rousseau**, and **Kant**, amongst others, took note of the division of labour and modes of life between the sexes. They considered the status of men and women relative to one another to pose interesting questions and believed themselves responsible for explaining the special obligations of women and the special privileges of men. Where the old philosophers explained women's subordination as best they could—and it would not have occurred to them to do so by reference to women's preferences or choices, as opposed to nature's plan for them—modern theorists of distributive justice are disinclined to take either an analytical or an evaluative position on the character of women's lives. Whether it is motivated by unease, uncertainty, or indifference, or entirely innocent, this is an oversight. The old philosophers were right to appreciate that men and women stood in a curious relationship to one another where the distribution of the components of well-being was concerned. We should aim to recover their interest in explaining and evaluating this noteworthy feature of our world and its relationship to our underlying natures. We need not reproduce their descriptive errors or their unacceptable prescriptions.

## 2. Are Women Objectively Deprived?

The belief that the division of the co-operative surplus between men and women of the same social class, if not between nations or classes, is more or less just, and that women's lives are overall exactly as good as men's, is held in large measure by both sexes. As Beauvoir notes, in face-to-face encounters, the impression that moral equality prevails may be irresistible (27). In modern families, questions such as the division of labour, the relative importance of one spouse's career compared with the other's, the investment of resources in further education, and other issues that have a bearing on individuals' social standing and their prospects are discussed openly and often reasonably, allowing for their emotional character, and agreement is ordinarily secured. Legal rights with respect to ownership, liability, and testimony are symmetrical between men and women in most developed countries.

At the same time, objective evidence for women's enjoyment of lower levels of well-being relative to men of their own reference group is not hard to come by. According to most anthropologists, women in nearly all existing and past cultures of record have lower status than men do in two respects: They are excluded by custom and tradition from prestigious occupations, employments, and activities; and they perform most basic maintenance activities such as feeding, nursing, and cleaning. Men, whether they are unemployed, employed in unskilled positions, or occupy lucrative and visible ones, tend to assume a partial or full exemption from maintenance. **E.O. Wilson** notes that "History records not a single culture in which women have controlled the political and economic lives of men. . . . Men have traditionally assumed the positions of chieftains, shamans, judges

and warriors. Their modern technocratic counterparts rule the industrial states and head the corporations and churches" (128). These conditions justify us in referring to women as existing in a condition of subordination.

Educational and employment prospects, legal protection, and access to credit have improved for women in many parts of the world, but women's lower standing is pronounced even in the wealthiest and most rights-conscious nations. The following observations pertain to Western liberal democracies *c.*2000 CE.

1. Executive positions such as judge, professor, general, director, president, minister, doctor, mayor, and board member are overwhelmingly held by men.
2. Men initiate and carry through most significant financial transactions involving the investment and expenditure of public and corporate funds. They own approximately 90 per cent of the world's wealth.
3. Men constitute the greater portion of the clientele in fine restaurants, first-class sections of airplanes, and luxury hotels.
4. Men win more prizes, are awarded more badges and medals, and have more buildings, bridges, and roads named after them than women.
5. Men appear more frequently in non-entertainment magazines, and as subjects of news programs. They are photographed more often performing tasks requiring specialized training and expertise.
6. Men come and go from the household with greater freedom than women. Recurrent or permanent defections from the household and the family by men are judged less severely than similar defections by women.
7. Men, with the exception of professional porters and caddies, carry fewer bags and sacks than women do, and push fewer prams, pushchairs, and shopping trolleys than women do.
8. Men come into contact with kitchen detritus, vomit, excrement, soiled clothing, and other taboo objects and substances less than women do.

Women are not numerous on the editorial boards of newspapers and magazines that collect and shape public opinion, or on the governing boards of research centres, universities, and regulatory agencies. Women, for the most part, do not decide where national boundaries are to be drawn, how cities are to be laid out, which drugs and surgical procedures to promote, how many airports or railways to build, what rights are to be enshrined in a constitution, and how many bombs and missiles of what kinds a country is to have and when it is to deploy them. [. . .]

Women experience deficits with respect to each of the known and necessary components of well-being—consumption, expression, affiliation, activity, participation, and respectful depiction. They are under-represented in the "active world" of the collective imagination. A careful tally of listings in the local entertainment guide should convince any reader that modern cinema is overwhelmingly concerned with men, their thoughts and ideas, their conflicts and struggles. Even television and the comics, with their more domestic focus, represent the world as approximately two-thirds male and one-third female. Women are more frequently photographed in a state of undress. They are rarely depicted as absorbed in a task, oblivious to the gaze. These representational trends are more evident in the modern world under liberal democratic regimes than they were at earlier times when the power and charisma of hereditary aristocracies elevated some women to positions of prestige and even influence in the absence of meritocratic competition and social mobility. Finally, women are more liable to depression than men and lack social resiliency. Their personal reputations are more vulnerable; their position and status always more precariously maintained. It is estimated that eight times as many women as men are abandoned by their spouses when they develop a serious illness, and widowers are far more likely to remarry than widows are; the ends of women's longer lives are often spent in a state of physical frailty and loneliness. The financial consequences of the death or defection of a partner are more serious for women than for men.

In short, women are less likely at any stage of life to be found amongst the beneficiaries of the ancient system of exemption and privilege, enjoying the kind of life Aristotle understood as a good life for members of the moral community.

## 3. Some Favoured Explanations for Female Subordination

Sociobiology—or, as it is now termed, "evolutionary psychology"—offers the latest and most credible approach to the question why women's status is lower than men's in most human societies. The general form of the answer is that women's and men's reproductive strategies not only are different but are especially conducive to social systems involving female subordination.

These strategies, it is alleged, have evolved through competition between members of the same sex to survive and reproduce. The winning strategies manifest themselves through emotions, aptitudes, and dispositions that are underpinned by differences in cerebral organization, in levels of circulating hormones, and in the presence or absence of receptors for these hormones throughout the body. While each individual is physiologically unique, differences whose workings are perceptible in ordinary life emerge at the statistical level. According to the hypothesis of evolutionary psychology, women typically possess certain attributes incompatible with high social status and/ or lack other attributes conducive to status. As a result, women have little motivation to strive to better their own status, and both men and women have little motivation to help them. The possession and lack of these attributes can be explained by conditions in the early adaptive environment and its pressure on the evolution of human physical and psychological traits. [. . .]

It will be useful to consider the three most prominent explanations for female subordination in the literature. The first focuses on male aggression and competition, the second on the physical encumbrances of maternity, and the third on female vulnerability and altruism.

## (a) Aggression and competition

Life is not easy for primate females. According to Wrangham and Peterson, writing in 1996:

> Among chimpanzees every adult male is dominant to every adult female, and he enjoys his dominance. She must move out of the way, acknowledge him with the appropriate call or gestures, bend to his whim—or risk punishment. The punishment by a bad tempered male can vary from a hit to a chase through trees and along the ground, until the female is caught and pulled and kicked and hit and dragged, screaming until her throat cramps, reminded to respect him the next time. (205)

Wrangham and Petersen infer that "Patriarchy is worldwide and history-wide, and its origins are detectable in the social lives of chimpanzees." The impression that male primates are hard on their own females is backed up by observation of other species. Barbara Smuts found that each female in a baboon troop was attacked by a male slightly more than once a week, and that, on average, each female could expect to receive a serious wound, one taking two or three months to heal, from a male once a year (88).

The human platform is different from that of *troglodytes* [chimpanzees] and baboons. Not only is sexual dimorphism reduced in humans, indicating selection pressures against large and threatening males, the human brain is further specialized for the inhibition of impulses and for moral ideation. Yet it is undeniable that men's differential ability to injure and kill women and women's awareness of their relative physical weakness facilitates control by men of women's behaviour and movements. It creates the expectation in men that women will do what they want them to do, and resigns women to the idea that they ought to behave as men want them to behave.

A related notion is that men's intrinsically higher levels of energy, sexual curiosity, and tolerance for pain translate into accomplishments women cannot expect to match. Competition between men for "access" to women who select them for their ability to provide "resources" is seen as a motivating force that spurs the male sex to ever more daring, worthwhile, and lucrative achievements in science, literature, the arts, politics, drama, and sports. Women, with their "larger gametes," are held to constitute a scarce resource, from which their non-competitive propensities follow.

## (b) Encumbrances of maternity

In nature, female primates are often accompanied by their young, sometimes an infant and a juvenile, sometimes two infants. Males in many species play with, protect, and take care of juveniles, but the mother–infant bond is intense and universal, and primate mothers may take an interest in their offspring and vice versa for their entire lives. The newly parturient female is hormonally a distinctive creature, and the inclination to respond to a baby's cries, to carry it around, keep track of it, and to feed it seems to depend on the conjunction of the mother's temperament and hard-wiring, social learning by observation of others, and on the behaviour of the child.

Much excited writing pro and con has focused on the question whether maternal care in humans is innate or "conditioned." "There is no such thing as the maternal instinct," Anne Oakley stated confidently in *Housewife* in 1974. "There is no biologically based drive which propels women into childbearing or forces them to become childrearers once the children are there" (199). But one might wonder exactly what is being disputed. Some women do not like children and are annoyed by their dependency; some are careless or vicious and manage to kill or hurt or malnourish them; some are overprotective and inadvertently harm their children, but most women desire and welcome the arrival of offspring and are capable parents. Involuntary childlessness is perhaps the greatest source of anguish in women's lives. [. . .]

Maternity seems to explain a good deal where women's subordination is concerned. Women can work, but maternity means that the work must be such that it is easily interrupted. Women's work must not be dangerous or too absorbing, since becoming motherless, or merely suffering maternal neglect, is a worse fate than becoming fatherless or suffering paternal neglect. It should not involve long journeys since young children have to be carried and cannot move at a comfortable adult speed on their own. All this results, according to the hypothesis, in specialization for detail work in or near the home on the part of women and in specialization for work involving travel, risk, and imagination to men.

Social inequality, on this view, follows from the fact that human males are not as interested in and committed to young children as human females are. While individual men may show high levels of interest and commitment and individual women low levels, the average differences between the sexes with respect to parental investment are thought to predict female social inferiority. By allocating more time to caring for and teaching children, women must invariably allocate less time to the production of other objects and states of affairs deemed valuable in a culture. Since childbearing is a salient feature of women, the disqualification of maternity attaches to the sex as a whole.

### (c) Vulnerability and altruism

The characteristics that specialize women for childbearing and childcare, even if they do not bear on intellectual, artistic, and practical competence, seem to put them at a disadvantage in modern competitive institutions. According to an argument that is rarely propounded aloud, quite apart from the physical encumbrances of maternity, women's greater sensitivity to physical and emotional pain, greater altruism, and overall lack of toughness lead them down different life pathways.

Women, it seems, do not attach the same importance to defeating and humiliating rivals as men do. It is known that drive levels tested in isolation are the same in males and females. Women have the same underlying desire to master tasks and to perform well as men do (Maccoby and Jacklin 134 ff). Yet when they are placed in competitive situations, the drive to defeat rivals appears to diminish. Boys appear to respond to competition with greater output, girls with less (149–50). In comparison

with men, women are observed to express more misgivings about their own abilities, to have lower expectations for themselves, and to be more tolerant of others" failures. They tend to refer their successes to extraneous factors (154 ff). To the frustration of their teachers, they often appear to be easily discouraged, and seem to require more coaching and personal attention to perform to a given level in professional life. According to Helen Fisher, females do not establish status ladders: "They form cliques instead—laterally connected subgroups of individuals who care for one another's infants and protect and nurture each other in times of social chaos. Females are less aggressive, less dominance oriented, and this network can remain stable—and relatively egalitarian for years" (222).

The explanation for this diffidence is thought to be as follows: Women depend on the help of other women to raise their children. This leads them to treat female friends and relatives in kind and conciliatory ways. At the same time, they compete with one another for male attention, but not by signalling their cognitive superiority, fierceness, or athleticism. Rather, a shapely figure, maidenly demeanour, and maternal inclinations are believed to impress men. It might be predicted by evolutionary psychologists that, while male–male competitions for prestige will be eagerly studied by males and females alike, female–female skill competitions (unlike beauty pageants) will be thought relatively uninteresting. Cross-sex competition will be avoided by humans or considered not to matter.

### 4. Historically Contingent Leveraging

Even if we accept the evolutionary psychologist's account of our underlying dispositions they do not predict and do not justify the current state of the world. A Martian ethologist given information concerning initial conditions in the early adaptive environment, and information about the competencies, drives, and tendencies of men and women would be unlikely to predict the present condition of the world, including male control of politics, economics, architecture, and culture, or the excess female risk of poverty and abandonment. The ethologist would assuredly not predict that men are more qualified as present-day politicians and artists. Nevertheless, *if* the Martian knew that one sex was going to gain supremacy in these areas, then, knowing *only* that men and women have the preferences and motivations just cited, it might well predict that the winning sex would be the male sex. If the Martian also knew that men are not more qualified than women to decide how things should go and that women do not prefer their condition of enhanced vulnerability, it could predict that Earth would become an unjust place.

The evolutionary psychologist may concede that our institutions have exaggerated the effects of our biology, but he is professionally unequipped to recognize the manner in which the history of our species has created a moral problem that was not present in the early adaptive environment of 75,000–300,000 years ago. Wilson refers to the accumulation of advantage in describing how "a small evolutionary change in the behaviour patterns of individuals can be amplified into a major social effect by the expanding upward distribution of the effect into multiple facets of social life" (11). This process of leveraging explains observed historical patterns in the relationship between men and women better than the supposition that they are a direct product of biological endowments that would have manifested themselves in any possible world.

Among the few remaining modern hunters and gatherers and nomadic herders whose lives are considered to resemble most closely those of our distant ancestors, female subordination is minimal, for the confinement and management of women is incompatible with survival. The emergence of permanent settlements and agriculture in the Neolithic altered the balance. Settlement created the need for intensive domestic work to keep dwelling places habitable, and women's larger caloric requirements in pregnancy and lactation and their lesser musculature encouraged sedentary habits that made them natural candidates for this job. Women became the chief tenders of gardens and fields, as they still are in small villages without draft animals or machinery, and the chief processors of grains and seeds. Arranged marriage and the ownership of women, perhaps suggested to the human mind by the ownership and controlled breeding of livestock, diverted men's energies from courtship and food-getting to cultural productions, displays, and politics.

With the advent of metalworking, the physically stronger males gained control of the manufacture and use of iron weapons and of plough agriculture, with its use of large draft animals, then cart transportation, then trade, and so money, writing, and administration (Harris). Women remained generalists; men specialized. The work they perform varies from culture to culture, but in all human societies, women perform a greater number of separate tasks than men do (Boulding 122). The urbanization movements of 2000 BCE marked the beginning of women's claustration, exaggerating, to the point of extreme distortion, the female features of modesty and the tendency to energy conservation.

With women's tasks increasingly sequestered and unseen by men, militaristic societies worried about the contagiousness and debilitating influence of femininity. Young men were removed as early as possible from the company of their mothers and sisters, reducing their mutual understanding and their companionship value for one another. The route to high political office proceeded through a military or, by the Middle Ages, a church career, and the development of large administrative structures and political organizations that operated in secrecy tended to women's exclusion (Boulding 122). Many unisexual institutions—boarding schools, monasteries, and formerly universities—replicate some features of military discipline and camaraderie. It is easy to state conditions under which a system of sex and gender hierarchy is well entrenched and self-perpetuating. The pathways for men leading to positions of power and influence must be clearly marked and well paved. The most prestigious educational institutions, with the best endowments and the finest facilities, and those requiring the highest parental investments, must be governed and staffed by males and restricted to them. Under such conditions, the actual competencies, dispositions, and preferences of women, though they cannot be entirely submerged, are thwarted.

Human institutions can be considered, like the nest of the bird, as entirely natural productions, springing from the needs and capacities of a species able, like nearly every species, to modify its own ambient environment. In this respect, we can agree that it is natural to create environments in which women occupy the crowded lower tiers of employment hierarchies and do not enjoy certain privileges. Nothing is added, in one sense, to the critique of institutions by insisting that exploitation and deprivation are merely cultural, for the admission that they are natural carries no implication as to the ease or difficulty of remedies. The cultural disability of lacking a high-school diploma is harder to compensate for than the natural disability of happening to lack a front tooth.

In another sense, however, the subordination of women is not natural, for it depends on contingencies that have nothing to do with sexual strategies of the early adaptive environment. If metal were not malleable at temperatures achievable with charcoal fires; if no wild animals had proved themselves amenable to domestication; if grain could not be stored for more than a week; and if no piles of stones over five feet high could stand, women would not be subordinated. This point is eloquently expressed by Sarah Hrdy:

> Incontestably, weaker individuals are often victimized by stronger ones. This can certainly be documented throughout the primates, but never on the scale in which it occurs among people, and never exclusively against a particular sex. . . . Only in human societies are females as a class subject to the sort of treatment that among other species would be rather randomly accorded the more defenseless members of the group—the very young, the disabled, or the very old—regardless of sex. . . . Human ingenuity, and with it the ability to build walls, to count, and tell tales, to transport food and store it, and particularly

to allocate labour (to control not just the reproductive but the productive capacities of other individuals), all of these eroded age-old female advantage. (185–7)

The same conditions, as observed earlier, that permit the most varied and spectacular expressions of human artistry and invention, permit at the same time the most varied and spectacular expressions of the will to dominate and control others.

## 5. The Argument from Heavy Costs

Women's past and present deprivations incriminate few identifiable individuals. History reveals for the most part a panorama of microethically unobjectionable choices and transactions, punctuated here and there by a noteworthy act of exceptional antifeminism. Nevertheless, the status of women presents us with a clear example of a moral dilemma. How much ought a well-off group to sacrifice in order to improve conditions for a less well-off group? To what extent does the vigorous and healthy self-interest of the former group, the fact that there is something that it is like to be a member of that group, and that the experiences of individuals within the group are profoundly influenced by membership in the group set limits on what can be asked of them? Moral concern mandates some transfer of advantage from better-off to worse-off, only the questions how much and how soon have no determinate answers. [. . .]

Greater social equality for women implies some costs for men. Even if we can anticipate benefits to the collective from a reversal of women's fortunes, some individuals will be worse off, for social status and financial reward are limited resources and their allocation is virtually a zero-sum game. The familiar multipliers of costs are likely to weigh in at this stage of reflection. The prospect of greater social equality in Western countries rouses sentiments of relative deprivation; our women seem to lack the biddable qualities they had only a generation or two ago and still have in many places. Affirmative action is seen as externally imposed and the sacrifices implied by greater equality will not be temporary.

In a world in which women are rarely judges or professors, and rarely receive incomes of over $100,000, my chances of enjoying these benefits are greatly increased if I am a man of the class that normally has access to these positions. In a society in which women are always domestic cleaners and preparers of food, my chances of having to take on these burdensome tasks are virtually nil if I am a man of any class whatsoever. Self-interested men, therefore, have overwhelming reasons to favour a division of labour along customary lines. Moral philosophers do not share these reasons, for they are technically precluded from theorizing as self-interested men. Though the propensity to treat statistical inequality between the sexes as though it does not matter or to deem it other than a proper subtopic of general moral and political theory need not imply a disregard for the professional role, it can betray a certain forgetfulness.

Conversely, moral theorists who are female are obliged to evaluate betterness relations from an impersonal perspective, not with respect to the outcome they happen to prefer for their own sex. They cannot ignore the fact that greater social equality may impose heavy costs on some groups and persons, reducing, prima facie, the prima facie obligation to strive for it. Suppose, for example, that by sacrificing one randomly chosen person by lethal injection, statistical equality between the sexes could be assured. Would it be right to do this? Clearly not. However, the utilitarian sacrificing action is not forbidden because it is always forbidden to worsen the condition of even one agent in ways he could not agree to, no matter what benefit follows. It is simply the case that I judge a world in which gender equality has been produced by an execution to be worse, all things considered, than our existing unfair world and I expect competent judges to support me in this claim.

It would take a brilliant imagination to work out a convincing scenario in which the sacrifice of a single human being would produce statistical equality between the sexes. Even an ordinary imagination, though, can work out convincing scenarios in which some sacrifices by human beings contribute to greater equality. What level of equality can we reasonably aim for? How much would it cost us?

A number of respected philosophers appear to be pessimistic on this score. They advance versions of the familiar argument from heavy costs. [. . .]

B.A.O. Williams, citing Nagel, presents the argument with unusual frankness. "It might just be," he ventures, "that [equality] is too hard and will not work":

> That is, there is a *Spielraum* for human beings, an area in which it is possible for human beings individually—or even for a time societally—to do things of a certain kind, but it is so against the grain that some things are just, to use the phrase used by Tom Nagel, too much to ask. Someone will come along and say, "Look it is possible to treat women just like men, at least almost just like men. But if we try to adopt this equality of treatment everywhere, there will be anxiety, disaster, collapse,—results which everybody knows are unacceptable to human society." This is certainly a respectable form of claim. (142)

Nagel agrees that it would be a mistake to try to extend juridical equality so far that it produces statistical equality (89–90). The state, he theorizes, exists in order to prevent serious and remediable harms to persons and can guarantee their juridical status—and it has done so, ending racial and sexual discrimination—but it is not responsible for supervising social outcomes. Further, "The impersonal desire for equality meets severe obstacles from individual motivation at every step; in regard to the basic institutions to which individuals are willing to give their allegiance, in the process of democratic politics, and in the operation of the economy" (95).

Williams' belief that it could be dangerous to throw open the doors for women by treating them equally everywhere reflects his conception of the social world as governed by *Sittlichkeit* even while the individual is ignobly fettered by ethical theory. His mood of gloomy foreboding might be supposed to arise from contemplation of the difficulties that would be involved in overcoming the disqualifications of maternity and in making women and institutions better adapted to each other than they currently are. Nevertheless, it seems to hint at something darker. Why does Williams think it is "certainly a respectable form of claim" that a world in which women were treated just like men would spell disaster for human society? We need to know what forms of anxiety, disaster, and collapse are more likely to occur, given women's actual propensities and dispositions, when they are treated more equally. Only then can we decide whether the costs associated with a more moral world are really much heavier than we are willing to bear.

One way to interpret this foreboding is as follows: Since Rousseau first expressed it, there has been a presumption in force that women's greater compassion and lesser interest in personal acquisition would enable men to operate as they pleased without the world becoming uninhabitable. Women's altruism, their willingness to "labour for love," would maintain the collective. Only half of mankind would be fuelled by *amour-propre* to engage in competitive displays and struggles, converting raw materials as fast as possible into artefacts and inventing new intellectual products. The other half would deal with the stresses and strains that are the inevitable by-product of such striving.

Imagine a world in which women are not only treated like men but behave like caricatures of men. A number of women become belligerent dictators, threatening other states. En masse, women adopt the specialist's mode of life, either displacing men or simply adding their labours and effort to double the amount of existing bridge-building, theorem-proving, and merging and acquiring. Further, women develop new predatory habits with respect to young men, and construct a commercial demi-monde parallel to the one we already have to relieve their newly manifest sexual boredom. They stop looking after men and attending to their needs. Social equality has been produced, but at the price of increased aggression and a faster rate of economic throughput, less devotion to the preservation of life. The world is now more dangerous, politically and psychologically, and less attractive than it used to be.

Another source of foreboding is the suspicion that a redistribution of social advantage from men to women might violate **Rawlsian principles of distributive justice** in worsening the position of the worst-off men. This might in turn have grave consequences for everyone. As a result of increased competition, men who were formerly able to find a social niche might be driven below the threshold of integration and esteem required to sustain productivity and goodwill. They might defect to a resentful and dangerous underclass. On this view, larger personal incomes, disproportionate respect, and social liberties are preferentially awarded to men in recognition of the fact that the worst-off men are an exceptionally disadvantaged class whose defection can also be dangerous to the collective. Preferential treatment for the gender helps to boost morale in this vulnerable subpopulation.

A third source of foreboding is this: The full participation of young mothers in the important institutions of the modern world seems to require state-funded, board-certified, round-the-clock daycare to enable them to meet the work, travel, and entertainment requirements of the modern corporation. This suggests that in any world in which women participate on an equal basis with men in all facets of culture and politics, the comforts of home will be diminished, the intimacies of marriage destroyed by exhaustion, and the acculturation of the young neglected. Overall good worlds, according to the argument from heavy costs, require socio-economic inequality between men and women. Greater equality is a moral luxury that is too expensive for us, not only in terms of money but in terms of our other values, including domestic comfort, responsibility to future generations, and freedom.

Should we be persuaded by these forecastings of doom? In considering this question, it is essential to keep in mind that it is unreasonable to reject all worse-for-someone states when some are morally better. It is often just, as well as relatively inexpensive, to worsen the condition of some people to improve that of others. The knowledge that humans are generally more averse to moving to lower levels of power and wealth than they are eager to advance to higher levels provides only one factual consideration relevant to the assessment of the overall costs of policy change.

The argument from heavy costs for a light, or hands-off, approach to sexual inequality cannot be dismissed out of hand. Its conclusion does not, however, approach the status of a confirmed theorem of the theory of distributive justice. The argument that the removal of the maternity disqualification and the adaptation of women to institutions and institutions to women will be so expensive and burdensome that it ought not be attempted is undermined by three considerations that are commonly recognized as defeaters of the argument from heavy costs. Male advantage reflects the enjoyment of ill-gotten gains; implies the violation of an implicit contract to co-operate for mutual benefit; and is the product of increasingly culpable ignorance.

Men and women face one another as competitors for the same scarce resources—material goods, autonomy, and respect. At the same time, they are co-operators, dedicated to tasks of interest to both sexes. Women's co-operative role cannot reduce their entitlement to the same level of well-being as men enjoy, nor has nature failed to endow them with the cognitive and emotional resources and dispositions they need to earn their half-share of the co-operative surplus. As competitors, women are nevertheless handicapped by their specialization for one of their co-operative roles—childbearing and the nurture of the young. As co-operators, women are easily exploited in virtue of their seemingly deficient performance as competitors.

The two sexes did not stand in morally precarious relations in the early adaptive environment before the accumulation of male advantage. The suggestion that, by getting in touch with their evolutionary roots, women will come to appreciate the appropriateness of their status is thought-provoking but ultimately unconvincing. The task of the prescriptive moralist is to envision distributive and redistributive protocols that compensate for handicaps and that limit the facility with which women can be exploited to perform the least desirable tasks of the community. [. . .]

## Works Cited

Beauvoir, S. de. *Le Deuxieme Sexe*. 2 vols. Paris: Gallimard, 1949.

Boulding, E. *The Underside of History*. Newbury Park: Sage, 1992.

Fisher, H. *The Anatomy of Love: The Natural History of Monogamy, Adultery and Divorce*. London and New York: Simon and Schuster, 1992.

Harris, M. "The Evolution of Gender Hierarchies: A Trial Formulation." *Sex and Gender Hierarchies*. Ed. B.D. Miller. Cambridge: Cambridge University Press, 1993. 57–80.

Hrdy, S.B. *The Woman that Never Evolved*. Cambridge, MA: Harvard University Press, 1981.

Maccoby, E., and C. Jacklin. *The Psychology of Sex Differences*. London: Oxford University Press, 1975.

Nagel. T. *Equality and Partiality*. New York: Oxford University Press, 1991.

Oakley, A. *Housewife*. London: Allen Lane, 1974.

Smuts, B. *Sex and Friendship in Baboons*. New York: Aldine, 1985.

Williams, B.A.O. "Conclusions." *Morality as a Biological Phenomenon*. Ed. G. Stent. Berkeley and Los Angeles: University of California Press, 1980.

Wilson, E.O. *On Human Nature*. Cambridge, MA: Harvard University Press, 1978.

Wrangham, R., and D. Peterson. *Demonic Males: Apes and the Origin of Human Violence*. London: Bloomsbury, 1996.

## Study Questions

1. Recall Gilligan's empirical findings that the perspective of justice is found more often in men and the perspective of care is found more often in women. What explanation might a sociobiologist or evolutionary psychologist provide?

2. Critically discuss the "objective evidence" that Wilson enlists to establish that the subordination of women persists, even in western liberal democracies.

3. What are three prominent explanations of how differences in male and female reproductive strategies promote the subordination of women in society? Wilson argues that women's subordination arose only contingently, not necessarily, from our biological natures. What contingent historical circumstances might be implicated in each of these explanations?

4. Critically assess the "argument from heavy costs."

# Film Notes

## Moral Foundations

*Atanarjuat: The Fast Runner* (Canada 2001, Zacharias Kunuk, 172 min; Inuktitut with subtitles): Based on an Inuit legend, love and betrayal lead to tragedy in a small community, where everyone depends on each other for survival.

*Atonement* (UK/France 2007, Joe Wright, 123 min): Promising young lives are devastated after a 13-year-old accuses her sister's lover of a rape he did not commit.

*Au revoir, les enfants* (France/West Germany/Italy 1987, Louis Malle, 104 min; French with subtitles): About a friendship between two 12-year-old students at a French boarding school in 1944; one boy is Jewish and being hidden by the priests.

*Dead Man Walking* (UK/USA 1995, Tim Robbins, 122 min): A Louisiana nun visits a death row inmate convicted of rape and murder.

*The Deer Hunter* (USA/UK 1978, Michael Cimino, 182 min): A story about three friends from a steel town in Pennsylvania whose lives are changed irrevocably by the Vietnam War.

*Divided We Fall* (Czech Republic 2000, Jan Hrebejk, 120 min; German and Czech with subtitles): A couple living in Prague agree to hide the son of their Jewish employers.

*The Fifth Horseman Is Fear* (Czechoslovakia 1965, Zbynek Brynych, 100 min; Czech with subtitles): A Jewish doctor in occupied Czechoslovakia, forbidden by the Nazis to practise medicine, agrees to treat a wounded partisan.

*The Hanging Garden* (UK/Canada 1997, Thom Fitzgerald, 91 min): Alternate realities coexist at a family wedding: one haunted by the memory of a 15-year-old boy hanging from a tree and the other attended by the bride's 25-year-old gay brother.

*High Noon* (USA 1952, Fred Zinnemann, 85 min): On the very day a sheriff is to retire and ride off into the sunset with his Quaker bride, duty compels him to defend the townspeople, who are too cowardly or corrupt to defend themselves, against a bad guy he sent away.

*Lifeboat* (USA 1944, Alfred Hitchcock, 97 min): During the Second World War, survivors of a torpedoed Navy ship and the sole survivor from the German U-boat find themselves together in a lifeboat.

*On the Waterfront* (USA 1954, Elia Kazan, 108 min): This film about a longshoreman who is compelled by his conscience to take on a corrupt union was Kazan's attempt to justify his co-operation with the House Un-American Activities Committee.

*Paradise Now* (Occupied Palestinian Territory/France/Germany/Netherlands/Israel 2005, Hany Abu-Assad, 90 min; Arabic with subtitles): Two Palestinians, best friends, both garage mechanics, are recruited as suicide bombers.

*Saving Private Ryan* (USA 1998, Steven Spielberg, 169 min): A Second World War squadron goes behind enemy lines to send Private Ryan home to his mother after his brothers die.

*Schindler's List* (USA 1993, Steven Spielberg, 195 min): Schindler manages to use his factories to save the lives of more than 1,000 Jewish workers while producing few goods for the war.

*The Sweet Hereafter* (Canada 1997, Atom Egoyan, 112 min): The fabric of a small British Columbia community is stretched after a tragic school bus accident kills 14 children and the families must decide whether to join a class-action lawsuit.

## Challenges to Moral Foundations

*Chinatown* (USA 1974, Roman Polanski, 130 min): A 1940s private eye who specializes in adultery cases is hired by a mysterious woman under false pretences and proceeds to uncover crime and corruption in a plan to steal water from LA.

*City of Hope* (USA 1991, John Sayles, 129 min): In a fictional New Jersey city, greed and corruption prevail, overwhelming goodness at every turn.

*Dogville* (Denmark/Sweden/Norway/Finland/UK/France/Germany/Netherlands 2003, Lars von Trier, 178 min): A vulnerable stranger enters a Depression-era Rocky Mountain town willing to work in return for assistance, but she encounters the worst of human nature.

*Eastern Promises* (UK/Canada/USA 2007, David Cronenberg, 100 min; some subtitles): When a midwife, using the diary of a young woman who died in childbirth, connects the baby to a London restaurant run by Russian mobsters, their code of loyalty is disrupted.

*Lord of War* (France/USA 2005, Andrew Niccol, 122 min; some subtitles): An arms dealer takes no responsibility for harms arising from the guns he sells.

*Yojimbo* (Japan 1961, Akira Kurosawa, 110 min; Japanese with subtitles): A samurai, unemployed with collapse of the feudal system, becomes a bodyguard (*yojimbo*) who plays two warring factions against each other.

## Moral Foundations/Challenges to Moral Foundations

*Casablanca* (USA 1942, Michael Curtiz, 102 min): The American owner of a nightclub in Morocco—populated by refugees, black-marketeers, Nazis, and the French Resistance alike—must decide where he stands.

*The Conversation* (USA 1974; Francis Ford Coppola; 113 min): A surveillance expert experiences a crisis of conscience.

*The Counterfeiters* (Austria/Germany 2007, Stefan Ruzowitzky, 98 min; German with subtitles): Inmates at the Sachsenhausen concentration camp carry out a counterfeiting operation that preserves their lives but at the same time supports the Nazi war effort.

*Crimes and Misdemeanors* (USA 1989, Woody Allen, 104 min): The crime is the arranged murder by a respected ophthamologist of his mistress. The doctor's egoism is countered by the moral relativism, religious morality, and existentialism of other characters.

*Do the Right Thing* (USA 1989, Spike Lee, 120 min): Palpable tensions among a Brooklyn neighbourhood's black, Italian, and Korean residents escalate over the course of one hot summer day that ends in tragedy.

*Fresh* (USA/France 1994, Boaz Yakin, 114 min): Fresh is an intelligent and perceptive 12-year-old boy who works as a runner for drug dealers in his Brooklyn neighbourhood.

*Hoop Dreams* (USA 1994, Steve James, 170 min): A documentary about two African-American boys from inner-city Chicago neighbourhoods who hope to play in the NBA and the values that nurture, sustain, and exploit them.

*LA Confidential* (USA 1997, Curtis Hanson, 138 min): About pervasive corruption in Los Angeles' overlapping worlds of tabloid journalism, organized crime, the movie industry, the sex trade, and crooked cops in the 1950s—with three cops at the centre of the drama.

*Michael Clayton* (USA 2007, Tony Gilroy, 119 min): Clayton is a fixer for a law firm that cleans up corporate messes—in this case, an agribusiness company facing a multibillion-dollar lawsuit for selling a cancer-causing herbicide.

*Quiz Show* (USA 1994, Robert Redford, 133 min): A congressional investigation follows when a disgruntled contestant blows the whistle on NBC's rigged 1950s quiz show, *Twenty-One*.

*A Simple Plan* (France/UK/Germany/USA/Japan 1998, Sam Raimi, 121 min): When three friends discover four million dollars in a crashed airplane, they proceed to compromise their values in ways that lead them along previously unimaginable paths.

## Gender and Morality

*A Brief Vacation* (Italy/Spain 1973, Vittorio De Sica, 112 min; Italian with subtitles): A woman who finds love in a TB sanatorium faces returning to the drudgery of her factory job, family responsibilities, and intolerable in-laws.

*Four Months, Three Weeks and Two Days* (Romania 2007, Cristian Mongiu, 113 min; Romanian with subtitles): A university student helps her roommate to secure an illegal abortion in 1980s Romania.

*In the Company of Men* (Canada/USA 1997, Neil LaBute, 97 min): Two men, in transit to spend six weeks at a regional office of their company, decide they will find a vulnerable woman, date her, and then dump her—as payback for a recent breakup.

*Kadosh* (Israel/France 1999, Amos Gitai, 110 min; Hebrew with subtitles): About two sisters forced like other women in their Hasidic Jewish community to live unhappy, restricted lives centred on childbearing.

*Moolaadé* (Senegal/France/Burkina Faso/Cameroon/Morocco/Tunisia 2004, Ousmane Sembene, 124 min; Bambara with subtitles): The title refers to the spirit-based protection a woman villager in Burkina Faso invokes when four girls resisting "circumcision" come to her.

*Thelma & Louise* (USA/France 1991, Ridley Scott, 130 min): Two working-class women from Arkansas take off on a weekend road trip, but after an attempted rape ends in a murder in a saloon parking lot, there is no going back.

*Vera Drake* (UK/France 2004, Mike Leigh, 125 min): In 1950s England, Vera's caring and compassionate character leads her to provide illegal abortions; her unaware family is devastated when she is caught.

*Water* (Canada/India 2005, Deepa Mehta, 117 min; Hindi with subtitles): Set in India in 1938, an eight-year-old widow, who barely understands she was married, experiences the oppressive practices associated with traditional Hindu law.

*You Can Count on Me* (USA 2000, Kenneth Lonergan, 111 min): The quite ordinary story of a divorced woman, with a young son, a brother she cannot count on, a boyfriend she is ambivalent about, and a boss she agrees to sleep with.

# PART IV

# The Just

## ▶ Introduction

Political philosophy's origins lie with Socrates, Plato, and Aristotle. The term "political" is derived from the Greek word *polis*, for "city-state." Philosophical questions about the *polis* that arose for these thinkers include: How did political institutions develop? What is the best form of government? How do politics and ethics differ? What is the nature of the relationship between citizen and state? How are political concepts such as justice and equality to be understood? Although we sometimes speak of the actions of an individual as just or unjust, the readings included in this section on "the just" focus on individuals as political beings and how societies are politically organized.

### Plato's *Crito*

In *Euthyphro*, we learn of the charges brought against Socrates: not believing in the city's gods, introducing new gods, and corrupting the young. In *Apology*, we follow the trial of Socrates, which culminates in his conviction and death sentence. In *Crito*, Socrates, who has been imprisoned for a month awaiting execution, is visited by his friend Crito. Crito tries to persuade Socrates to escape into exile, but Socrates chooses instead to accept the jury's penalty. In justifying his decision to Crito, Socrates invites philosophical reflection on several important questions about justice: the status of majority opinion and democratic government, the nature of the relationship between a state and its citizens, and the legitimacy of civil disobedience.

### Civil Disobedience

Citizens have a duty to obey the law, but what if the law conflicts with what a person's conscience says is right or what justice demands? In *Crito*, Socrates says that he is innocent of the charges brought against him, and yet that justice requires that he submit to the sentence rendered by the Athenian court. A citizen must obey the law, just as a servant obeys his master, or else persuade the state that the law is unjust. In acts of conscientious objection and civil disobedience, in contrast, citizens deliberately violate the law in order to fulfill their moral ideals or redress injustice in society.

Henry David Thoreau refused to pay his poll tax for six years because of his opposition to slavery and the US–Mexican War, and was arrested in July 1846. Thoreau's famous essay "Resistance to Civil Government" recounts his night in jail (he was released the next morning after his aunt paid the taxes) and justifies his act of civil disobedience. Thoreau argues that the individual is "a higher and independent power" than the state, and the source of the state's own power and authority. Individuals must act as their consciences dictate: they are moral agents primarily, and legal subjects and citizens of the state only secondarily. Thoreau inspired such well-known pacifists and civil disobedients as Leo Tolstoy, Mahatma Gandhi, and Martin Luther King, Jr.

King and other black civil rights leaders organized a campaign in Birmingham, Alabama, in April 1963 that included mass meetings, lunch counter and library sit-ins, church pray-ins, marches on city hall, a boycott of downtown merchants, and a voter registration drive. One week after the protests started, the city government obtained a state circuit court injunction. The campaign's leaders decided to disobey the injunction, and numerous protesters, including King, were arrested. King's famous "Letter from Birmingham Jail" responds to a statement written by eight "moderate" white Birmingham clergymen that condemned the protests as "unwise and untimely" and led by "outsiders," and urged local blacks to withdraw their support.

In "A Justification of Civil Disobedience," John Rawls defines civil disobedience as involving "a public, nonviolent, and conscientious act contrary to law usually done with the intent to bring about a change in the policies or laws of the government." Rawls's theory of justice as fairness, which identifies basic principles of justice that rational, free, and equal individuals would agree upon, underlies his account. Civil disobedience is justified, Rawls argues, when such fundamental rights (to vote, to religious freedom, to equality of opportunity) are violated and standard appeals to the sense of justice of the majority have failed.

By raising questions about justice and the relationship between citizen and state, the topic of civil disobedience provokes debate about the status of majority opinion and democratic government. King, for instance, defines an unjust law as one the majority inflicts on the minority, and notes that protesters in Birmingham sought to sway majority opinion by appealing to democratic ideals of freedom and equality.

## Democratic Government

Democracy first arose in ancient Greece. The term *demokratia* derives from *demos*, "people," and *kratia*, "power," and was used to describe Athens' direct form of government during the fifth and fourth centuries BCE, in which citizens attended and spoke at the *Ecclesia* (assembly) and were chosen by lot for the *Boule* (council) and popular courts like the one that tried Socrates. Democracy as reinvented in the modern era was less about the people directly governing themselves and more about the government's legitimacy as resting with the people.

For John Locke, the government's legitimacy depends on the terms of the "social contract" whereby individuals agree to leave the "state of nature" and enter society and form a government. Locke's *Second Treatise of Government* portrays humans in the state of nature as free and equal and governed by natural law. Reason forbids interfering with the life, liberty, health, or possessions of others: these are "natural rights," and their violation constitutes an injustice. Locke argues that private property arises in the state of nature when individuals mix their labour with what nature provides—by gathering apples, catching fish, farming land, etc. The social contract emerges from the shared desire to protect person and property, and the government's legitimate exercise of power is limited by this "common good."

England's parliamentary system was the outcome of battles, bloodshed, and beheadings that took place during Locke's lifetime: the monarch was stripped of the "divine right" to rule, and Parliament's supremacy was enshrined in the Bill of Rights of 1689. And yet, one century later, at the time of the French Revolution, only a tiny fraction of the population could vote and hold office. Pressure from middle-class merchants and working-class radicals led to passage of the Reform Acts of 1832, 1867, and 1884, which vastly extended male suffrage in England and Wales.

John Stuart Mill wrote *Considerations on Representative Government* during this period of parliamentary reform. Mill's support for extending male suffrage combines with proposals for systems of proportional representation and plural voting to protect against the "low grade of intelligence in the representative body" and "class legislation on the part of the numerical majority" that he fears will result. Mill also supports female suffrage, writing that sex is "as entirely irrelevant to political rights as difference in height or in the colour of the hair." Mill considers race entirely relevant, however: he argues that whereas Britain's colonies of the "European race" like Canada and Australia are ready for representative government, a "barbarous" colony like India requires the civilizing influence of a "good despot."

Despite Mill's support for female suffrage, women could not vote until 1918 in Britain and Canada (in Canada, though, the right to vote federally was limited to women also eligible to vote provincially—e.g., Quebec women could not vote at either level until 1939), and 1920 in the United States. Although women vote in similar numbers as men these days, they are under-represented in government. In "Quotas for Women," Anne Phillips evaluates four arguments that support efforts being made to raise the proportion of women elected: that successful women politicians provide role models, that it is unjust that rights and opportunities are available to men and not women, that democracy is undermined when women's interests are not represented, and that women bring different values and concerns to political life. Phillips examines a tension that emerges between the autonomy and accountability of representatives: if they have sufficient autonomy to be influenced by gender, are they sufficiently accountable to party platform?

In "Modernity, Persons, and Subpersons," Charles Mills writes: "Three decades of feminist scholarship have done much to demonstrate the political gender exclusions implicit in the ostensibly neutral 'men.' But the counter-narrative of *racial* subordination is not, at least within philosophy, as well developed, nor is the whiteness of 'men' inscribed on the concept's face in the same way as their masculinity is." According to mainstream narratives, egalitarianism emerged triumphant during the modern age, with Thomas Jefferson's opening words in the US Declaration of Independence emblematic: "We hold these truths to be self-evident, that all men are created equal." Uncomfortable truths about racism, e.g., that Jefferson owned slaves, are treated as "anomalies." Mills suggests replacing this "anomaly" view with the "symbiosis" view. The symbiosis view recognizes that modernity was about "racialized *white* equality," not "equality *simpliciter*," and that racism and egalitarianism coexist in the same theory.

## Multiculturalism

Cultural pluralism is nothing new: although ancient Athens might be supposed to be culturally homogeneous because citizens were Athenians by descent for several generations, slaves captured in foreign wars and resident aliens (*metics*) like Aristotle outnumbered citizens. However, the discourse of multiculturalism arose only in the last half of the twentieth century, with Canada, in 1971, becoming the first country in the world to adopt multiculturalism as an official government policy. Not surprisingly, Canadian political philosophers have been at the fore of debates about multiculturalism and the challenges it poses for the liberal democratic tradition.

In "The Politics of Recognition," Charles Taylor describes how the "demand for recognition" within multiculturalism draws on the identity-centred "politics of difference" to advocate differential treatment on the basis of cultural differences. This is at odds with the dignity-centred "politics of universalism" that underlies liberalism's assertion of the equality of individual rights and rejection of discrimination based on differences. Taylor recognizes that US-style "procedural liberalism" cannot accommodate the differential rights necessary to protect minority cultures. He defends an alternative form of liberalism that allows collective goals (e.g., the cultural survival of the Québécois), while protecting fundamental rights (e.g., religious freedom, not language of commercial signage).

In *Multicultural Citizenship*, Will Kymlicka defines two kinds of minority groups with different interests: "national minorities" are groups that were self-governing at the time of their incorporation into the larger political community and typically want to maintain themselves as distinct societies, and "ethnic groups" are immigrants who typically want to integrate into the wider society. Canada is a multination and polyethnic state because it includes minority groups of both kinds. Kymlicka's argument from equality draws on a liberal theory of justice to justify according minority groups three varieties of "group-differentiated rights": "self-government rights," "polyethnic rights," and "special representation rights."

In "Liberalism's Last Stand," Dale Turner distinguishes between two approaches Kymlicka takes to Aboriginal rights. The first approach, couched in the language of cultural protection, defines culture as a primary good and argues that Aboriginal peoples deserve special rights because as cultural minorities, they are susceptible to the dominant culture. The second approach, couched in the language of political sovereignty, argues that Aboriginal peoples deserve special rights because they are national minorities that were self-governing at the time of their incorporation. Turner criticizes Kymlicka for ignoring the historical basis of Aboriginal rights with his first approach and the specifics of the history surrounding "Aboriginal incorporation" with his second approach.

Himani Bannerji's "On the Dark Side of the Nation" is deeply skeptical about Canadian multiculturalism. Bannerji believes that multiculturalism creates new identities (e.g., "visible minority," "new Canadian") that increase the state's control over immigrants' lives. She also protests the opportunistic political use of people designated as "visible minorities" to downplay Quebec's demands by portraying Canada as multicultural, not English. And Bannerji criticizes Taylor for using First Nations and immigrant groups to solidify the status of the English and French as the "constitutive elements" of "the nation" and ignoring the history of racism and colonialism.

## ▶ Discussion Questions

1. What is "civil disobedience"? Provide a well-known example of an act of civil disobedience. Is there an existing law or government policy that you consider to be unjust? Would you consider opposing such a law or policy by participating in civil disobedience?
2. What does "democracy" mean to you? What is it to be "free" and "equal"? What "rights" do you have, and what guarantees these rights: nature or political convention?
3. Today, in Western countries, although women vote in equal numbers to men, they are under-represented in government. In Canada, how many members of Parliament are women, and what proportion of members is this? Do you think that this is a problem? Why or why not?
4. In 1971, Canada became the first country in the world to adopt multiculturalism as an official government policy. Four decades later, how well are we doing?

## ▶ Further Reading

Arblaster, Anthony. *Democracy*. 3rd edition. Buckingham and Philadelphia: Open University Press, 2002.

Benhabib, Seyla. *The Claims of Culture: Equality and Diversity in the Global Era*. Princeton and Oxford: Princeton University Press, 2002.

Gandhi, Mahatma. *The Essential Writings*. Ed. Judith M. Brown. Oxford and New York: Oxford University Press, 2008.

Young, Iris Marion. *Inclusion and Democracy*. Oxford and New York: Oxford University Press, 2000.

# Plato

Plato (429–347 BCE) was a citizen of the ancient Greek city-state of Athens, born into a wealthy family with anti-democratic inclinations. When Athens was defeated by Sparta in the Peloponnesian War (431–404 BCE), the oligarchy installed included Plato's mother's cousin Critias and brother Charmides. Pro-democratic forces regained control in 403, and it was at the hands of Athens' newly reconstituted democracy that Socrates was executed in 399. *Crito* covers Socrates' final days, as he refused his friends' help to escape and calmly accepted his death.

## *Crito* (or *On Duty*)

Characters: **Socrates**, Crito

SOCRATES. Why have you come at this time, Crito? Or isn't it still early?

CRITO. Yes, very early.

S. About what time?

C. Just before dawn.

S. I am surprised that the watchman of the prison was willing to let you in.

C. He is used to me by this time, Socrates, because I come here so often, and besides I have done something for him.

S. Have you just come, or some time ago?

C. Some little time ago.

S. Then why did you not wake me at once, instead of sitting by me in silence?

C. No, no, by Zeus, Socrates, I only wish I myself were not so sleepless and sorrowful. But I have been wondering at you for some time, seeing how sweetly you sleep; and I purposely refrained from waking you, that you might pass the time as pleasantly as possible. I have often thought throughout your life hitherto that you were of a happy disposition, and I think so more than ever in this present misfortune, since you bear it so easily and calmly.

S. Well, Crito, it would be absurd if at my age I were disturbed because I must die now.

C. Other men as old, Socrates, become involved in similar misfortunes, but their age does not in the least prevent them from being disturbed by their fate.

S. That is true. But why have you come so early?

C. To bring news, Socrates, sad news, though apparently not sad to you, but sad and grievous to me and all your friends, and to few of them, I think, so grievous as to me.

S. What is this news? Has the **ship come from Delos**, at the arrival of which I am to die?

C. It has not exactly come, but I think it will come today from the reports of some men who have come from Sunium and left it there. Now it is clear from what they say that it will come today, and so tomorrow, Socrates, your life must end.

S. Well, Crito, good luck be with us! If this is the will of the gods, so be it. However, I do not think it will come today.

C. What is your reason for not thinking so?

S. I will tell you. I must die on the day after the ship comes in, must I not?

C. So those say who have charge of these matters.

S. Well, I think it will not come in today, but tomorrow. And my reason for this is a dream which I had a little while ago in the course of this night. And perhaps you let me sleep just at the right time.

C. What was the dream?

S. I dreamed that a beautiful, fair woman, clothed in white raiment, came to me and called me and said, "Socrates, on the third day thou wouldst come to fertile Phthia" (Homer, *Iliad* ix, 363).

C. A strange dream, Socrates.

S. No, a clear one, at any rate, I think, Crito.

C. Too clear, apparently. But, my dear Socrates, even now listen to me and save yourself. Since, if you die, it will be no mere single misfortune to me, but I shall lose a friend such as I can never find again, and besides, many persons who do not know you and me well will think I could have saved you if I had been willing to spend money, but that I would not take the trouble. And yet what reputation could be more disgraceful than that of considering one's money of more importance than one's friends? For most people will not believe that we were eager to help you to go away from here, but you refused.

S. But, my dear Crito, why do we care so much for what most people think? For the most reasonable men, whose opinion is more worth considering, will think that things were done as they really will be done.

C. But you see it is necessary, Socrates, to care for the opinion of the public, for this very trouble we are in now shows that the public is able to accomplish not by any means the least, but almost the greatest of evils, if one has a bad reputation with it.

S. I only wish, Crito, the people could accomplish the greatest evils, that they might be able to accomplish also the greatest good things. Then all would be well. But now they can do neither of the two; for they are not able to make a man wise or foolish, but they do whatever occurs to them.

C. That may well be. But, Socrates, tell me this: you are not considering me and your other friends, are you, fearing that, if you escape, the informers will make trouble for us by saying that we stole you away, and we shall be forced to lose either all our property or a good deal of money, or be punished in some other way besides? For if you are afraid of anything of that kind, let it go; since it is right for us to run this risk, and even greater risk than this, if necessary, provided we save you. Now please do as I ask.

S. I am considering this, Crito, and many other things.

C. Well, do not fear this! for it is not even a large sum of money which we should pay to some men who are willing to save you and get you away from here. Besides, don't you see how cheap these informers are, and that not much money would be needed to silence them? And you have my money at your command, which is enough, I fancy; and moreover, if because you care for me you think you ought not to spend my money, there are foreigners here willing to spend theirs; and one of them, Simmias of Thebes, has brought for this especial purpose sufficient funds; and Cebes also and very many others are ready. So, as I say, do not give up saving yourself through fear of this. And do not be troubled by what you said in the court, that if you went away you would not know what to do with yourself. For in many other places, wherever you go, they will welcome you; and if you wish to go to Thessaly, I have friends there who will make much of you and will protect you, so that no one in Thessaly shall annoy you.

And besides, Socrates, it seems to me the thing you are undertaking to do is not even right—betraying yourself when you might save yourself. And you are eager to bring upon yourself just what your enemies would wish and just what those were eager for who wished to destroy you. And moreover, I think you are abandoning your children, too, for when you might bring them up and educate them, you are going to desert them and go away, and, so far as you are concerned, their fortunes in life will be whatever they happen to meet with, and they will probably meet with such treatment as generally comes to orphans in their destitution. No. Either one ought not to beget children, or one ought to stay by them and bring them up and educate them. But you seem to me to be choosing the laziest way; and you ought to choose as a good and brave man would choose, you who have been saying all your life that you cared for virtue. So I am shamed both for you and for us, your friends, and I am afraid people will think that this whole affair of yours has been conducted with a sort of cowardice on our part—both the fact that the case came before the court, when it might have been avoided, and the way in which the trial itself was carried on, and finally they will think, as the crowning absurdity of the whole affair, that this opportunity has escaped us through some base cowardice on our part, since we did not save you, and you did not save yourself, though it was quite possible if we had been of any use whatever. Take care, Socrates, that these things be not disgraceful, as well as evil, both to you and to us. Just consider, or rather it is time not to consider any longer, but to have finished considering. And there is just one possible plan; for all this must be done in the coming night. And if we delay it can no longer be done. But I beg you, Socrates, do as I say and don't refuse.

S. My dear Crito, your eagerness is worth a great deal, if it should prove to be rightly directed; but otherwise, the greater it is, the more hard to bear. So we must examine the question whether we ought to do this or not; for I am not only now but always a man who follows nothing but the reasoning which on consideration seems to me best. And I cannot, now that this has happened to us, discard the arguments I used to advance, but they seem to me much the same as ever, and I revere and honour the same ones as before. And unless we can bring forward better ones in our present situation, be assured that I shall not give way to you, not even if the power of the multitude frighten us with even more terrors than at present, as children are frightened with goblins, threatening us with imprisonments and deaths and confiscations of property. Now how could we examine the matter most reasonably? By taking up first what you say about opinions and asking whether we were right when we always used to say that we ought to pay attention to some opinions and not to others? Or were we right before I was condemned to death, whereas it has now been made clear that we were

talking merely for the sake of argument and it was really mere play and nonsense? And I wish to investigate, Crito, in common with you, and see whether our former argument seems different to me under our present conditions, or the same, and whether we shall give it up or be guided by it. But it used to be said, I think, by those who thought they were speaking sensibly, just as I was saying now, that of the opinions held by men some ought to be highly esteemed and others not. In God's name, Crito, do you not think this is correct? For you, humanly speaking, are not involved in the necessity of dying tomorrow, and therefore present conditions would not lead your judgment astray. Now say, do you not think we were correct in saying that we ought not to esteem all the opinions of men, but some and not others, and not those of all men, but only of some? What do you think? Is not this true?

C. It is.

S. Then we ought to esteem the good opinions and not the bad ones?

C. Yes.

S. And the good ones are those of the wise and the bad ones those of the foolish?

C. Of course.

S. Come then, what used we to say about this? If a man is an athlete and makes that his business, does he pay attention to every man's praise and blame and opinion or to those of one man only who is a physician or a trainer?

C. To those of one man only.

S. Then he ought to fear the blame and welcome the praise of that one man and not of the multitude.

C. Obviously.

S. And he must act and exercise and eat and drink as the one man who is his director and who knows the business thinks best rather than as all the others think.

C. That is true.

S. Well then; if he disobeys the one man and disregards his opinion and his praise, but regards words of the many who have no special knowledge, will he not come to harm?

C. Of course he will.

S. And what is this harm? In what direction and upon what part of the one who disobeys does it act?

C. Evidently upon his body; for that is what it ruins.

S. Right. Then in other matters, not to enumerate them all, in questions of right and wrong and disgraceful and noble and good and bad, which we are now considering, ought we to follow and fear the opinion of the many or that of the one, if there is anyone who knows about them, whom we ought to revere and fear more than all the others? And if we do not follow him, we shall injure and cripple that which we used to say is benefited by the right and is ruined by the wrong. Or is there nothing in this?

C. I think it is true, Socrates.

S. Well then, if through yielding to the opinion of the ignorant we ruin that which is benefited by health and injured by disease, is life worth living for us when that is ruined? And that is the body, is it not?

C. Yes.

S. Then is life worth living when the body is worthless and ruined?

C. Certainly not.

S. But is it worth living when that is ruined which is injured by the wrong and improved by the right? Or do we think that part of us, whatever it is, which is concerned with right and wrong, is less important than the body?

C. By no means.

S. But more important?

C. Much more.

S. Then, most excellent friend, we must not consider at all what the many will say of us, but what he who knows about right and wrong, the one man, and truth herself will say. And so you introduced the discussion wrongly in the first place, when you began by saying we ought to consider the opinion of the multitude about the right and the noble and the good and their opposites. But it might, of course, be said that the multitude can put us to death.

C. That is clear, too. It would be said, Socrates.

S. That is true. But, my friend, the argument we have just finished seems to me still much the same as before; and now see whether we still hold to this, or not, that it is not living, but living well which we ought to consider most important.

C. We do hold to it.

S. And that living well and living rightly are the same thing, do we hold to that, or not?

C. We do.

S. Then we agree that the question is whether it is right for me to try to escape from here without the permission of the Athenians, or not right. And if it appears to be right, let us try it, and if not, let us give it up. But the considerations you suggest, about spending money, and reputation, and bringing up my children, these are really, Crito, the reflections of those who lightly put men to death, and would bring them to life again, if they could, without any sense, I mean the multitude. But we, since our argument so constrains us, must consider only the question we just broached, whether we shall be doing right in giving money and thanks to these men who will help me to escape, and in escaping or aiding the escape ourselves, or shall in truth be doing wrong, if we do all these things. And if it appears that it is wrong for us to do them, it may be that we ought not to consider either whether we must die if we stay here and keep quiet or whether we must endure anything else whatsoever, but only the question of doing wrong.

C. I think what you say is right, Socrates; but think what we should do.

S. Let us, my good friend, investigate in common, and if you can contradict anything I say, do so, and I will yield to your arguments; but if you cannot, my dear friend, stop at once saying the same thing to me over and over, that I ought to go away from here without the consent of the Athenians; for I am anxious to act in this matter with your approval, and not contrary to your wishes. Now see if the beginning of the investigation satisfies you, and try to reply to my questions to the best of your belief.

C. I will try.

S. Ought we in no way to do wrong intentionally, or should we do wrong in some ways but not in others? Or, as we often agreed in former times, is it never right or honourable to do wrong? Or have all those former conclusions of ours been overturned in these few days, and have we old men, seriously conversing with each other, failed all along to see that we were no better than children? Or is not what we used to say most certainly true, whether the world agree or not? And whether we must endure still more grievous sufferings than these, or lighter ones, is not wrongdoing inevitably an evil and a disgrace to the wrongdoer? Do we believe this or not?

C. We do.

S. Then we ought not to do wrong at all.

C. Why, no.

S. And we ought not even to requite wrong with wrong, as the world thinks, since we must not do wrong at all.

C. Apparently not.

S. Well, Crito, ought one to do evil or not?

C. Certainly not, Socrates.

S. Well, then, is it right to requite evil with evil, as the world says it is, or not right?

C. Not right, certainly.

S. For doing evil to people is the same thing as wronging them.

C. That is true.

S. Then we ought neither to requite wrong with wrong nor to do evil to anyone, no matter what he may have done to us. And be careful, Crito, that you do not, in agreeing to this, agree to something you do not believe; for I know that there are few who believe or ever will believe this. Now those who believe this, and those who do not, have no common ground of discussion, but they must necessarily, in view of their opinions, despise one another. Do you therefore consider very carefully whether you agree and share in this opinion, and let us take as the starting point of our discussion the assumption that it is never right to do wrong or to requite wrong with wrong, or when we suffer evil to defend ourselves by doing evil in return. Or do you disagree and refuse your assent to this starting point? For I have long held this belief and I hold it yet, but if you have reached any other conclusion, speak and explain it to me. If you still hold to our former opinion, hear the next point.

C. I do hold to it and I agree with you; so go on.

S. Now the next thing I say, or rather ask, is this: "ought a man to do what he has agreed to do, provided it is right, or may he violate his agreements?"

C. He ought to do it.

S. Then consider whether, if we go away from here without the consent of the state, we are doing harm to the very ones to whom we least ought to do harm, or not, and whether we are abiding by what we agreed was right, or not.

C. I cannot answer your question, Socrates, for I do not understand.

S. Consider it in this way. If, as I was on the point of running away (or whatever it should be called), the laws and the commonwealth should come to me and ask, "Tell me, Socrates, what have you in mind to do? Are you not intending by this thing you are trying to do, to destroy us, the laws, and the entire state, so far as in you lies? Or do you think that state can exist and not be overturned, in which the decisions reached by the courts have no force but are made invalid and annulled by private persons?" What shall we say, Crito, in reply to this question and others of the same kind? For one might say many things, especially if one were an orator, about the destruction of that law which provides that the decisions reached by the courts shall be valid. Or shall we say to them, "The state wronged me and did not judge the case rightly"? Shall we say that, or what?

C. That is what we shall say, by Zeus, Socrates.

S. What then if the laws should say, "Socrates, is this the agreement you made with us, or did you agree to abide by the verdicts pronounced by the state?" Now if I were surprised by what they said, perhaps they would continue, "Don't be surprised at what we say, Socrates, but answer, since you are in the habit of employing the method of question and answer. Come, what fault do you find with us and the state, that you are trying to destroy us? In the first place, did we not bring you forth? Is it not through us that your father married your mother and begat you? Now tell us, have you any fault to find with those of us who are the laws of marriage?"

"I find no fault," I should say. "Or with those that have to do with the nurture of the child after he is born and with his education which you, like others, received? Did those of us who are assigned to these matters not give good directions when we told your father to educate you in music and gymnastics?" "You did," I should say. "Well then, when you were born and nurtured and educated, could you say to begin with that you were not our offspring and our slave, you yourself and your ancestors? And if this is so, do you think right as between you and us rests on a basis of equality, so that whatever we undertake to do to you it is right for you to retaliate? There was no such equality of right between you and your father or your master, if you had one, so that whatever treatment you received you might return it, answering them if you were reviled, or striking back if you were struck, and the like; and do you think that it will be proper for you to act so toward your country and the laws, so that if we undertake to destroy you, thinking it is right, you will undertake in return to destroy us laws and your country, so far as you are able, and will say that in doing this you are doing right, you who really care for virtue? Or is your wisdom such that you do not

see that your country is more precious and more to be revered and is holier and in higher esteem among the gods and among men of understanding than your mother and your father and all your ancestors, and that you ought to show to her more reverence and obedience and humility when she is angry than to your father, and ought either to convince her by persuasion or to do whatever she commands, and to suffer, if she commands you to suffer, in silence, and if she orders you to be scourged or imprisoned or if she leads you to war to be wounded or slain, her will is to be done, and this is right, and you must not give way or draw back or leave your post, but in war and in court and everywhere, you must do whatever the state, your country, commands, or must show her by persuasion what is really right, but that it is impious to use violence against either your father or your mother, and much more impious to use it against your country?" What shall we reply to this, Crito, that the laws speak the truth, or not?

C. I think they do.

S. "Observe then, Socrates," perhaps the laws would say, "that if what we say is true, what you are now undertaking to do to us is not right. For we brought you into the world, nurtured you, and gave a share of all the good things we could to you and all the citizens. Yet we proclaim, by having offered the opportunity to any of the Athenians who wishes to avail himself of it, that anyone who is not pleased with us when he has become a man and has seen the administration of the city and us, the laws, may take his goods and go away wherever he likes. And none of us stands in the way or forbids any of you to take his goods and go away wherever he pleases, if we and the state do not please him, whether it be to an Athenian colony or to a foreign country where he will live as an alien. But we say that whoever of you stays here, seeing how we administer justice and how we govern the state in other respects, has thereby entered into an agreement with us to do what we command; and we say that he who does not obey does threefold wrong, because he disobeys us who are his parents, because he disobeys us who nurtured him, and because after agreeing to obey us he neither obeys us nor convinces us that we are wrong, though we give him the opportunity and do not roughly order him to do what we command, but when we allow him a choice of two things, either to convince us of error or to do our bidding, he does neither of these things."

"We say that you, Socrates, will be exposed to these reproaches, if you do what you have in mind, and you not least of the Athenians but more than most others." If then I should say, "How so?" perhaps they might retort with justice that I had made this agreement with them more emphatically than most other Athenians. For they would say, "Socrates, we have strong evidence that we and the city pleased you; for you would never have stayed in it more than all other Athenians if you had not been better pleased with it than they; you never went out from the city to a festival, or anywhere else, except on military service, and you never made any other journey, as other people do, and you had no wish to know any other city or other laws, but you were contented with us and our city. So strongly did you prefer us and agree to live in accordance with us; and besides, you begat children in the city, showing that it pleased you. And moreover even at your trial you might have offered exile as your penalty, if you wished, and might have done with the state's consent what you are now undertaking to do without it. But you then put on airs and said you were not disturbed if you must die, and you preferred, as you said, death to exile. And now you are not ashamed to think of those words and you do not respect us, the laws, since you are trying to bring us to naught; and you are doing what the meanest slave would do, since you are trying to run away contrary to the compacts and agreements you made with us that you would live in accordance with us. First then, answer this question, whether we speak the truth or not when we say that you agreed, not in word, but by your acts, to live in accordance with us." What shall we say to this, Crito? Must we not agree that it is true?

C. We must, Socrates.

S. "Are you then," they would say, "not breaking your compacts and agreements with us, though you were not led into them by compulsion or fraud, and were not forced to make up your mind in a short time, but had seventy years, in which you could have gone away, if we did not please you and if you thought the agreements were unfair? But you preferred neither **Lacedaemon** nor **Crete**, which you are always saying are well governed, nor any other of the Greek states, or of the foreign ones, but you went away from this city less than the lame and the blind and the other cripples. So much more than the other Athenians were you satisfied with the city and evidently therefore with us, its laws; for who would be pleased with a city apart from its laws? And now will you not abide by your agreement? You will if you take our advice, Socrates; and you will not make yourself ridiculous by going away from the city.

"For consider. By transgressing in this way and committing these errors, what good will you do to yourself or any of your friends? For it is pretty clear that your friends also will be exposed to the risk of banishment and the loss of their homes in the city or of their property. And you yourself, if you go to one of the nearest cities, to Thebes or Megara—for both are well governed—will go as an enemy, Socrates, to their government, and all who care for their own cities will look askance at you, and will consider you a destroyer of the laws, and you will confirm the judges in their opinion, so that they will think their verdict was just. For he who is destroyer of the laws might certainly be regarded as a destroyer of young and thoughtless men. Will you then avoid the well-governed cities and the most civilized men? And if you do this will your life be worth living? Or will you go to them and have the face to carry on—what kind of conversation, Socrates? The same kind you carried on here, saying that virtue and justice and lawful things and the laws are the most precious things to men? And do you not think that the conduct of Socrates would seem most disgraceful? You cannot help thinking so. Or you will keep away from these places and go to Crito's friends in Thessaly; for there great disorder and lawlessness prevail, and perhaps they would be amused to hear of the ludicrous way in which you ran away from prison by putting on a disguise, a peasant's leathern cloak or some of the other things in which runaways dress themselves up, and changing your appearance. But will no one say that you, an old man, who had probably but a short time yet to live, clung to life with such shameless greed that you transgressed the highest laws? Perhaps not, if you do not offend anyone; but if you do, Socrates, you will have to listen to many things that would be a disgrace to you. So you will live as an inferior and a slave to everyone. And what will you do except feast in Thessaly, as if you had gone to Thessaly to attend a banquet? What will become of our conversations about justice and virtue? But perhaps you wish to live for the sake of your children, that you may bring them up and educate them? How so? Will you take them to Thessaly to be brought up and educated, making exiles of them, that you may give them that blessing also? Or perhaps you will not do that, but if they are brought up here while you are living, will they be better brought up and educated if you are not with them than if you were dead? Oh yes! your friends will care for them. Will they care for them if you go away to Thessaly and not if you go away to the dwellings of the dead? If those who say they are your friends are of any use, we must believe they will care for them in both cases alike.

"Ah, Socrates, be guided by us who tended your infancy. Care neither for your children nor for life nor for anything else more than for the right, that when you come to the home of the dead, you may have all these things to say in your own defence. For clearly if you do this thing it will not be better for you here, or more just or holier, no, nor for any of your friends, and neither will it be better when you reach that other abode. Now, however, you will go away wronged, if you do go away, not by us, the laws, but by men; but if you escape after so disgracefully requiting wrong with wrong and evil with evil, breaking your compacts and agreements with us, and injuring those whom you least ought to injure—yourself, your friends, your country and us—we shall be angry with you while you live, and there our brothers, the laws in Hades' realm, will not receive you graciously; for they will know that you tried, so far as in you lay, to destroy us. Do not let Crito persuade you to do what he says, but take our advice.

Be well assured, my dear friend, Crito, that this is what I seem to hear, as the **frenzied dervishes of Cybele** seem to hear the flutes, and this sound of these words re-echoes within me and prevents my hearing any other words. And be assured that, so far as I now believe, if you argue against these words you will speak in vain. Nevertheless, if you think you can accomplish anything, speak.

C. No, Socrates, I have nothing to say.

S. Then, Crito, let it be, and let us act in this way, since it is in this way that God leads us.

## Study Questions

1. Socrates refers to a "just agreement" that exists between citizens and the state (theorized by modern philosophers as the "social contract"). On what basis do individuals consent to this agreement, and what duties does it require of them as citizens?

2. In "Letter from Birmingham Jail," Martin Luther King, Jr., claims that Socrates was practising civil disobedience. Based on your reading of the *Crito*, do you agree or disagree?

3. When we think of democratic government, several slogans come to mind, such as "rule by the people for the people," "one person, one vote," and "majority rules." In what ways does Plato criticize the ideas associated with these slogans?

4. Given that Socrates' trial and execution followed the restoration of democratic government in Athens, what system of government might Plato have preferred instead? (Hint: he tells us we are to value the "good" opinions of "wise" people, i.e., those who understand "the just, beautiful, and good and their opposites.")

# ⌣ CIVIL DISOBEDIENCE ⌣

## Henry D. Thoreau

Henry David Thoreau (1817–62) was born in Concord, Massachusetts, and completed an undergraduate degree at Harvard College. Thoreau worked as a schoolteacher, as a land surveyor, and at his family's pencil factory while establishing himself as a poet, naturalist, and philosopher. *Walden*, Thoreau's best-known work, is about simple living in natural surroundings based on his experiences living alone for two years in a cabin on Walden Pond. Thoreau belonged to the New England transcendentalist movement founded by Ralph Waldo Emerson (1803–82), and the role of conscience, as immanence of spirit in the individual, is evident in this influential essay on civil disobedience, originally delivered as a lecture in 1847.

## Resistance to Civil Government

I heartily accept the motto,—"That government is best which governs least"; and I should like to see it acted up to more rapidly and systematically. Carried out, it finally amounts to this, which also I believe,— "That government is best which governs not at all"; and when men are prepared for it, that will be the kind of government which they will have. Government is at best an expedient; but most governments are usually, and all governments are sometimes, inexpedient. The objections which have been brought against a standing army, and they are many and weighty, and deserve to prevail, may also at last be brought against a standing government. The standing army is only an arm of the standing government. The government itself, which is only the mode which the people have chosen to execute their will, is equally liable to be abused and perverted before the people can act through it. Witness the present **Mexican war**, the work of comparatively a few individuals using the standing government as their tool; for, in the outset, the people would not have consented to this measure.

This American government,—what is it but a tradition, though a recent one, endeavouring to transmit itself unimpaired to posterity, but each instant losing some of its integrity? It has not the vitality and force of a single living man; for a single man can bend it to his will. It is a sort of wooden gun to the people themselves; and, if ever they should use it in earnest as a real one against each other, it will surely split. But it is not the less necessary for this; for the people must have some complicated machinery or other, and hear its din, to satisfy that idea of government which they have. Governments show thus how successfully men can be imposed on, even impose on themselves, for their own advantage. It is excellent, we must all allow; yet this government never of itself furthered any enterprise, but by the alacrity with which it got out of its way. *It* does not keep the country free. *It* does not settle the West. *It* does not educate. The character inherent in the American people has done all that has been accomplished; and it would have done somewhat more, if the government had not sometimes got in its way. For government is an expedient by which men would fain succeed in letting one another alone; and, as has been said, when it is most expedient, the governed are most let alone by it. [. . .]

But, to speak practically and as a citizen, unlike those who call themselves no-government men, I ask for, not at once no government, but *at once* a better government. Let every man make known what kind of a government would command his respect, and that will be one step toward obtaining it.

After all, the practical reason why, when the power is once in the hands of the people, a majority are permitted, and for a long period continue, to rule, is not because they are most likely to be in the right, nor because this seems fairest to the minority, but because they are physically the strongest. But a government in which the majority rule in all cases cannot be based on justice, even as far as men understand it. Can there not be a government in which majorities do not virtually decide right and wrong but conscience?—in which majorities decide only those questions to which the rule of expediency is applicable? Must the citizen ever for a moment, or in the least degree, resign his conscience to the legislator? Why has every man a conscience, then? I think that we should be men first, and subjects afterward. It is not desirable to cultivate a respect for the law, so much as for the right. The only obligation which I have a right to assume, is to do at any time what I think right. It is truly enough said, that a corporation has no conscience; but a corporation of conscientious men is a corporation *with* a conscience. Law never made men a whit more just; and, by means of their respect for it, even the well-disposed are daily made the agents of injustice. A common and natural result of an undue respect for law is, that you may see a file of soldiers, colonel, captain, corporal, privates, powder-monkeys and all, marching in admirable order over hill and dale to the wars, against their wills, aye, against their common sense and consciences, which makes it very steep marching indeed, and produces a palpitation of the heart. They have no doubt that it is a damnable business in which they are concerned; they are all peaceably inclined. Now, what are they? Men at all? or small moveable forts and magazines, at the service of some unscrupulous man in power? [. . .]

The mass of men serve the State thus, not as men mainly, but as machines, with their bodies. They are the standing army, and the militia, jailers, constables, *posse comitatus*, etc. In most cases there is no free exercise whatever of the judgment or of the moral sense; but they put themselves on a level with wood and earth and stones; and wooden men can perhaps be manufactured that will serve the purpose as well. Such command no more respect than men of straw, or a lump of dirt. They have the same sort of worth only as horses and dogs. Yet such as these even are commonly esteemed good citizens. Others, as most legislators, politicians, lawyers, ministers, and office-holders, serve the State chiefly with their heads; and, as they rarely make any moral distinctions, they are as likely to serve the devil, without intending it, as God. A very few, as heroes, patriots, martyrs, reformers in the great sense, and *men*, serve the State with their consciences also, and so necessarily resist it for the most part; and they are commonly treated by it as enemies. [. . .]

How does it become a man to behave toward this American government today? I answer that he cannot without disgrace be associated with it. I cannot for an instant recognize that political organization as *my* government which is the *slave's* government also.

All men recognize the right of revolution; that is, the right to refuse allegiance to and to resist the government, when its tyranny or its inefficiency are great and unendurable. But almost all say that such is not the case now. But such was the case, they think, in the Revolution of '75. If one were to tell me that this was a bad government because it taxed certain foreign commodities brought to its ports, it is most probable that I should not make an ado about it, for I can do without them: all machines have their friction; and possibly this does enough good to counterbalance the evil. At any rate, it is a great evil to make a stir about it. But when the friction comes to have its machine, and oppression and robbery are organized, I say, let us not have such a machine any longer. In other words, when a sixth of the population of a nation which has undertaken to be the refuge of liberty are slaves, and a whole country is unjustly overrun and conquered by a foreign army, and subjected to military law, I think that it is not too soon for honest men to rebel and revolutionize. What makes this duty the more urgent is the fact, that the country so overrun is not our own, but ours is the invading army. [. . .]

Does any one think that Massachusetts does exactly what is right at the present crisis? [. . .] Practically speaking, the opponents to a reform in Massachusetts are not a hundred thousand politicians at the South, but a hundred thousand merchants and farmers here, who are more interested in commerce and agriculture than they are in humanity, and are not prepared to do justice to the slave and to Mexico, *cost what it may*. I quarrel not with far-off foes, but with those who, near at home, cooperate with, and do the bidding of those far away, and without whom the latter would be harmless. We are accustomed to say, that the mass of men are unprepared; but improvement is slow, because the few are not materially wiser or better than the many. It is not so important that many should be as good as you, as that there be some absolute goodness somewhere; for that will leaven the whole lump. There are thousands who are *in opinion* opposed to slavery and to the war, who yet in effect do nothing to put an end to them; who, esteeming themselves children of **Washington** and **Franklin**, sit down with their hands in their pockets, and say that they know not what to do, and do nothing; who even postpone the question of freedom to the question of free-trade, and quietly read the prices-current along with the latest advices from Mexico, after dinner, and, it may be, fall asleep over them both. What is the price-current of an honest man and patriot today? They hesitate, and they regret, and sometimes they petition; but they do nothing in earnest and with effect. They will wait, well-disposed, for others to remedy the evil, that they may no longer have it to regret. At most, they give only a cheap vote, and a feeble countenance and God-speed, to the right, as it goes by them. [. . .]

All voting is a sort of gaming, like chequers or backgammon, with a slight moral tinge to it, a playing with right and wrong, with moral questions; and betting naturally accompanies it. The character of the voters is not staked. I cast my vote, perchance, as I think right; but I am not vitally concerned that that right should prevail. I am willing to leave it to the majority. Its obligation, therefore, never exceeds that of expediency. Even voting *for the right* is *doing* nothing for it. It is only expressing to men feebly your desire that it should prevail. A wise man will not leave the right to the mercy of chance, nor wish it to prevail through the power of the majority. There is but little virtue in the action of masses of men. When the majority shall at length vote for the abolition

of slavery, it will be because they are indifferent to slavery, or because there is but little slavery left to be abolished by their vote. [. . .]

It is not a man's duty, as a matter of course, to devote himself to the eradication of any, even the most enormous wrong; he may still properly have other concerns to engage him; but it is his duty, at least, to wash his hands of it, and, if he gives it no thought longer, not to give it practically his support. If I devote myself to other pursuits and contemplations, I must first see, at least, that I do not pursue them sitting upon another man's shoulders. I must get off him first, that he may pursue his contemplations too. See what gross inconsistency is tolerated. I have heard some of my townsmen say, "I should like to have them order me out to help put down an insurrection of the slaves, or to march to Mexico;—see if I would go"; and yet these very men have each, directly by their allegiance, and so indirectly, at least, by their money, furnished a substitute. [. . .]

How can a man be satisfied to entertain an opinion merely, and enjoy *it*? Is there any enjoyment in it, if his opinion is that he is aggrieved? If you are cheated out of a single dollar by your neighbour, you do not rest satisfied with knowing that you are cheated, or with saying that you are cheated, or even with petitioning him to pay you your due; but you take effectual steps at once to obtain the full amount, and see that you are never cheated again. Action from principle,—the perception and the performance of right,—changes things and relations; it is essentially revolutionary, and does not consist wholly with anything which was. It not only divides states and churches, it divides families; aye, it divides the *individual*, separating the diabolical in him from the divine.

Unjust laws exist: shall we be content to obey them, or shall we endeavour to amend them, and obey them until we have succeeded, or shall we transgress them at once? Men generally, under such a government as this, think that they ought to wait until they have persuaded the majority to alter them. They think that, if they should resist, the remedy would be worse than the evil. But it is the fault of the government itself that the remedy *is* worse than the evil. *It* makes it worse. Why is it not more apt to anticipate and provide for reform? Why does it not cherish its wise minority? Why does it cry and resist before it is hurt? Why does it not encourage its citizens to be on the alert to point out its faults, and *do* better than it would have them? Why does it always crucify Christ, and excommunicate **Copernicus** and **Luther**, and pronounce Washington and Franklin rebels? [. . .]

As for adopting the ways which the State has provided for remedying the evil, I know not of such ways. They take too much time, and a man's life will be gone. I have other affairs to attend to. I came into this world, not chiefly to make this a good place to live in, but to live in it, be it good or bad. A man has not everything to do, but something; and because he cannot do *everything*, it is not necessary that he should do *something* wrong. It is not my business to be petitioning the governor or the legislature any more than it is theirs to petition me; and, if they should not hear my petition, what should I do then? But in this case the State has provided no way: its very Constitution is the evil. [. . .]

I do not hesitate to say, that those who call themselves abolitionists should at once effectually withdraw their support, both in person and property, from the government of Massachusetts, and not wait till they constitute a majority of one, before they suffer the right to prevail through them. I think that it is enough if they have God on their side, without waiting for that other one. Moreover, any man more right than his neighbours, constitutes a majority of one already.

I meet this American government, or its representative the State government, directly, and face to face, once a year, no more, in the person of its tax-gatherer; this is the only mode in which a man situated as I am necessarily meets it; and it then says distinctly, Recognize me; and the simplest, the most effectual, and, in the present posture of affairs, the indispensablest mode of treating with it on this head, of expressing your little satisfaction with and love for it, is to deny it then. My civil neighbour, the tax-gatherer, is the very man I have to deal

with,—for it is, after all, with men and not with parchment that I quarrel,—and he has voluntarily chosen to be an agent of the government. How shall he ever know well what he is and does as an officer of the government, or as a man, until he is obliged to consider whether he shall treat me, his neighbour, for whom he has respect, as a neighbour and well-disposed man, or as a maniac and disturber of the peace, and see if he can get over this obstruction to his neighbourliness without a ruder and more impetuous thought or speech corresponding with his action? I know this well, that if one thousand, if one hundred, if ten men whom I could name,—if ten *honest* men only,—aye, if *one* HONEST man, in this State of Massachusetts, *ceasing to hold slaves*, were actually to withdraw from this copartnership, and be locked up in the county jail therefore, it would be the abolition of slavery in America. For it matters not how small the beginning may seem to be: what is once well done is done for ever. But we love better to talk about it: that we say is our mission. Reform keeps many scores of newspapers in its service, but not one man. [. . .]

Under a government which imprisons any unjustly, the true place for a just man is also a prison. The proper place today, the only place which Massachusetts has provided for her freer and less desponding spirits, is in her prisons, to be put out and locked out of the State by her own act, as they have already put themselves out by their principles. It is there that the fugitive slave, and the Mexican prisoner on parole, and the Indian come to plead the wrongs of his race, should find them; on that separate, but more free and honourable ground, where the State places those who are not *with* her but *against* her,—the only house in a slave-state in which a free man can abide with honour. If any think that their influence would be lost there, and their voices no longer afflict the ear of the State, that they would not be as an enemy within its walls, they do not know by how much truth is stronger than error, nor how much more eloquently and effectively he can combat injustice who has experienced a little in his own person. Cast your whole vote, not a strip of paper merely, but your whole influence. A minority is powerless while it conforms to the majority; it is not even a minority then; but it is irresistible when it clogs by its whole weight. If the alternative is to keep all just men in prison, or give up war and slavery, the State will not hesitate which to choose. If a thousand men were not to pay their tax-bills this year, that would not be a violent and bloody measure, as it would be to pay them, and enable the State to commit violence and shed innocent blood. This is, in fact, the definition of a peaceable revolution, if any such is possible. If the tax-gatherer, or any other public officer, asks me, as one has done, "But what shall I do?" my answer is, "If you really wish to do anything, resign your office." When the subject has refused allegiance, and the officer has resigned his office, then the revolution is accomplished. But even suppose blood should flow. Is there not a sort of bloodshed which the conscience is wounded? Through this wound a man's real manhood and immortality flow out, and he bleeds to an everlasting death. I see this blood flowing now. [. . .]

When I converse with the freest of my neighbours, I perceive that, whatever they may say about the magnitude and seriousness of the question, and their regard for the public tranquillity, the long and the short of the matter is, that they cannot spare the protection of the existing government, and they dread the consequences of disobedience to it to their property and families. For my own part, I should not like to think that I ever rely on the protection of the State. But, if I deny the authority of the State when it presents its tax-bill, it will soon take and waste all my property, and so harass me and my children without end. This is hard. This makes it impossible for a man to live honestly and at the same time comfortably in outward respects. It will not be worth the while to accumulate property; that would be sure to go again. You must hire or squat somewhere, and raise but a small crop, and eat that soon. You must live within yourself, and depend upon yourself, always tucked up and ready for a start, and not have many affairs. A man may grow rich in Turkey even, if he will be in all respects a good subject of the Turkish government. **Confucius** said,—"If a State is governed by the principles of reason, poverty and misery are subjects of shame; if a State is not governed by the principles of reason, riches and honours are the subjects of shame." No: until I want the protection of Massachusetts to be extended to me in some distant southern port, where my liberty is endangered, or until I am bent solely on building up an estate at home by peaceful enterprise, I can afford to refuse allegiance to Massachusetts, and her right to my property and life. It costs me less in every sense to incur the penalty of disobedience to the State, than it would to obey. I should feel as if I were worth less in that case. [. . .]

I have paid no poll-tax for six years. I was put into a jail once on this account, for one night; and, as I stood considering the walls of solid stone, two or three feet thick, the door of wood and iron, a foot thick, and the iron grating which strained the light, I could not help being struck with the foolishness of that institution which treated me as if I were mere flesh and blood and bones, to be locked up. I wondered that it should have concluded at length that this was the best use it could put me to, and had never thought to avail itself of my services in some way. I saw that, if there was a wall of stone between me and my townsmen, there was a still more difficult one to climb or break through, before they could get to be as free as I was. I did not for a moment feel confined, and the walls seemed a great waste of stone and mortar. I felt as if I alone of all my townsmen had paid my tax. They plainly did not know how to treat me, but behaved like persons who are underbred. In every threat and in every compliment there was a blunder; for they thought that my chief desire was to stand [on] the other side of that stone wall. I could not but smile to see how industriously they locked the door on my meditations, which followed them out again without let or hinderance, and *they* were really all that was dangerous. As they could not reach me, they had resolved to punish my body; just as boys, if they cannot come at some person against whom they have a spite, will abuse his dog. I saw that the State was half-witted, that it was timid as a lone woman with her silver spoons, and that it did not know its friends from its foes, and I lost all my remaining respect for it, and pitied it. [. . .]

I have never declined paying the highway tax, because I am as desirous of being a good neighbour as I am of being a bad subject; and, as for supporting schools, I am doing my part to educate my fellow-countrymen now. It is for no particular item in the tax-bill that I refuse to pay it. I simply wish to refuse allegiance to the State, to withdraw and stand aloof from it effectually. I do not care to trace the course of my dollar, if I could, till it buys a man, or a musket to shoot one with,—the dollar is innocent,—but I am concerned to trace the effects of my allegiance. In fact, I quietly declare war with the State, after my fashion, though I will still make what use and get what advantage of her I can, as is usual in such cases. [. . .]

The authority of government, even such as I am willing to submit to,—for I will cheerfully obey those who know and can do better than I, and in many things even those who neither know nor can do so well,—is still an impure one: to be strictly just, it must have the sanction and consent of the governed. It can have no pure right over my person and property but what I concede to it. The progress from an absolute to a limited monarchy, from a limited monarchy to a democracy, is a progress toward a true respect for the individual. Is a democracy, such as we know it, the last improvement possible in government? Is it not possible to take a step further towards recognizing and organizing the rights of man? There will never be a really free and enlightened State, until the State comes to recognize the individual as a higher and independent power, from which all its own power and authority are derived, and treats him accordingly. I please myself with imagining a State at last which can afford to be just to all men, and to treat the individual with respect as a neighbour; which even would not think it inconsistent with its own repose, if a few were to live aloof from it, not meddling with it, nor embraced by it, who fulfilled all the duties of neighbours and fellow-men. A State which bore this kind of fruit, and suffered it to drop off as fast as it ripened, would prepare the way for a still more perfect and glorious State, which also I have imagined, but not yet anywhere seen.

## Study Questions

1. What specific injustices are behind Thoreau's refusal to pay his poll tax and his accompanying plea "that it is not too soon for honest men to rebel and revolutionize"?

2. When we think of democratic government, several slogans come to mind, such as "rule by the people for the people," "one person, one vote," and "majority rules." What criticisms does Thoreau make of the ideas associated with these slogans? Why does he believe nonetheless that democracy counts as progress compared with absolute and limited monarchies?

3. As socially and politically aware citizens, we tend to react to unjust laws by voting, forming and expressing opinions, and petitioning for change. Why does Thoreau believe these steps are insufficient, and what does he demand of us instead?

4. According to Thoreau, what duties do individuals have to the state, and what authority does the state have over individuals? What is Thoreau's preferred system of government over the long term?

# Martin Luther King, Jr.

Martin Luther King, Jr. (1929–68) was born in Atlanta, Georgia. He had three degrees: a BA from Morehouse College, a BD from Crozer Theological Seminary, and a PhD from Boston University. King was pastor of a church in Montgomery, Alabama. He grew up during the time of segregation. After the Civil War, blacks were free but did not get equal rights. King very badly wanted to stop segregation. The Ku Klux Klan threatened his life, but the great Indian leader Mohandas Gandhi helped him understand not to use violence when fighting for civil rights. In "Letter from Birmingham Jail," King explains and defends this approach. King won the Nobel Peace Prize in 1964.—TG

## Letter from Birmingham Jail[1]

April 16, 1963
My Dear Fellow Clergymen:

While confined here in the Birmingham city jail, I came across your recent statement calling my present activities "unwise and untimely." Seldom do I pause to answer criticism of my work and ideas. If I sought to answer all the criticisms that cross my desk, my secretaries would have little time for anything other than such correspondence in the course of the day, and I would have no time for constructive work. But since I feel that you are men of genuine good will and that your criticisms are sincerely set forth, I want to try to answer your statement in what I hope will be patient and reasonable terms.

I think I should indicate why I am here in Birmingham, since you have been influenced by the view which argues against "outsiders coming in." I have the honour of serving as president of the Southern Christian Leadership Conference, an organization operating in every southern state, with headquarters in Atlanta, Georgia. We have some 85 affiliated organizations across the South, and one of them is the Alabama Christian Movement for Human Rights. Frequently we share staff, educational and financial resources with our affiliates. Several months ago the affiliate here in Birmingham asked us to be on call to engage in a non-violent direct-action program if such were deemed necessary. We readily consented, and when the hour came we lived up to our promise. So I, along with several members of my staff, am here because I was invited here. I am here because I have organizational ties here.

But more basically, I am in Birmingham because injustice is here. Just as the prophets of the eighth century BCE left their villages and carried their "thus saith the Lord" far beyond the boundaries of their home towns, and just as the Apostle Paul left his village of Tarsus and carried the gospel of Jesus Christ to the far corners of the Greco-Roman world, so am I compelled to carry the gospel of freedom beyond my own home town. Like Paul, I must constantly respond to the Macedonian call for aid.

Moreover, I am cognizant of the interrelatedness of all communities and states. I cannot sit idly by in Atlanta and not be concerned about what happens in Birmingham. Injustice anywhere is a threat to justice everywhere. We are caught in an inescapable network of mutuality, tied in a single garment of destiny. Whatever affects one directly, affects all indirectly. Never again can we afford to live with the narrow, provincial "outside agitator" idea. Anyone who lives inside the United States can never be considered an outsider anywhere within its bounds.

You deplore the demonstrations taking place in Birmingham. But your statement, I am sorry to say, fails to express a similar concern for the conditions that brought about the demonstrations. I am sure that none of you would want to rest content with the superficial kind of social analysis that deals merely with effects and does not grapple with underlying causes. It is unfortunate that demonstrations are taking place in Birmingham, but it is even more unfortunate that the city's white power structure left the Negro community with no alternative.

In any non-violent campaign there are four basic steps: collection of the facts to determine whether injustices exist; negotiation; self-purification; and direct action. We have gone through all these steps in Birmingham. There can be no gainsaying the fact that racial injustice engulfs this community. Birmingham is probably the most thoroughly segregated city in the United States. Its ugly record of brutality is widely known. Negroes have experienced grossly unjust treatment in the courts. There have been more unsolved bombings of Negro homes and churches in Birmingham than in any other city in the nation. These are the hard, brutal facts of the case. On the basis of these conditions, Negro leaders sought to negotiate with the city fathers. But the latter consistently refused to engage in good-faith negotiation.

Then, last September, came the opportunity to talk with leaders of Birmingham's economic community. In the course of the negotiations, certain promises were made by the merchants—for example, to remove the stores' humiliating racial signs. On the basis of these promises, the Reverend Fred Shuttlesworth and the leaders of the Alabama Christian Movement for Human Rights agreed to a moratorium on all demonstrations. As the weeks and months went by, we realized that we were the victims of a broken promise. A few signs, briefly removed, returned; the others remained.

As in so many past experiences, our hopes had been blasted, and the shadow of deep disappointment settled upon us. We had no alternative except to prepare for direct action, whereby we would present our very bodies as a means of laying our case before the conscience of the local and the national community. Mindful of the difficulties involved, we decided to undertake a process of self-purification. We began a series of workshops on non-violence, and we repeatedly asked ourselves: "Are you able to accept blows without retaliating?" "Are you able to endure the ordeal of jail?" We decided to schedule our direct-action program for the Easter season, realizing that except for Christmas, this is the main shopping period of the year. Knowing that a strong economic-withdrawal program would be the by-product of direct action, we felt that this would be the best time to bring pressure to bear on the merchants for the needed change.

Then it occurred to us that Birmingham's mayoral election was coming up in March, and we speedily decided to postpone action until after election day. When we discovered that the Commissioner of Public Safety, Eugene "Bull" Connor, had piled up enough votes to be in the run-off, we decided again to postpone action until the day after the run-off so that the demonstrations could not be used to cloud the issues. Like many others, we waited to see Mr Connor defeated, and to this end we endured postponement after postponement. Having aided in this community need, we felt that our direct-action program could be delayed no longer.

You may well ask: "Why direct action? Why sit-ins, marches and so forth? Isn't negotiation a better path?" You are quite right in calling for negotiation. Indeed, this is the very purpose of direct action. Non-violent direct action seeks to create such a crisis and foster such a tension that a community which has constantly refused to negotiate is forced to confront the issue. It seeks so to dramatize the issue that it can no longer be ignored. My citing the creation of tension as part of the work of the non-violent-resister may sound rather shocking. But I must confess that I am not afraid of the word "tension." I have earnestly opposed violent tension, but there is a type of constructive, non-violent tension which is necessary for growth. Just as Socrates felt that it was necessary to create a tension in the mind so that individuals could rise from the bondage of myths and half-truths to the unfettered realm of creative analysis and objective appraisal, so must we see the need for non-violent gadflies to create the kind of tension in society that will help men rise from the dark depths of prejudice and racism to the majestic heights of understanding and brotherhood.

The purpose of our direct-action program is to create a situation so crisis-packed that it will inevitably open the door to negotiation. I therefore concur with you in your call for negotiation. Too long has our beloved Southland been bogged down in a tragic effort to live in monologue rather than dialogue.

One of the basic points in your statement is that the action that I and my associates have taken in Birmingham is untimely. Some have asked: "Why didn't you give the new city administration time to act?" The only answer that I can give to this query is that the new Birmingham administration must be prodded about as much as the outgoing one, before it will act. We are sadly mistaken if we feel that the election of Albert Boutwell as mayor will bring the millennium to Birmingham. While Mr. Boutwell is a much more gentle person than Mr. Connor, they are both segregationists, dedicated to maintenance of the status quo. I have hope that Mr. Boutwell will be reasonable enough to see the futility of massive resistance to desegregation. But he will not see this without pressure from devotees of civil rights. My friends, I must say to you that we have not made a single gain in civil rights without determined legal and non-violent pressure. Lamentably, it is an historical fact that privileged groups seldom give up their privileges voluntarily. Individuals may see the moral light and voluntarily give up their unjust posture; but, as **Reinhold Niebuhr** has reminded us, groups tend to be more immoral than individuals.

We know through painful experience that freedom is never voluntarily given by the oppressor; it must be demanded by the oppressed. Frankly, I have yet to engage in a direct-action campaign that was "well timed" in the view of those who have not suffered unduly from the disease of segregation. For years now I have heard the word "Wait!" It rings in the ear of every Negro with piercing familiarity. This "Wait" has almost always meant "Never." We must come to see, with one of our distinguished jurists, that "justice too long delayed is justice denied."

We have waited for more than 340 years for our constitutional and God-given rights. The nations of Asia and Africa are moving with jet-like speed toward gaining political independence, but we still creep at horse-and-buggy pace toward gaining a cup of coffee at a lunch counter. Perhaps it is easy for those who have never felt the stinging darts of segregation to say, "Wait." But when you have seen vicious mobs lynch your mothers and fathers at will and drown your sisters and brothers at whim; when you have seen hate-filled policemen curse, kick and even kill your black brothers and sisters; when you see the vast majority of your twenty million Negro brothers smothering in an airtight cage of poverty in the midst of an affluent society; when you suddenly find your tongue twisted and your speech stammering as you seek to explain to your six-year-old daughter why she can't go to the public amusement park that has just been advertised on television, and see tears welling up in her eyes when she is told that Funtown is closed to coloured children, and see ominous clouds of inferiority beginning to form in her little mental sky, and see her beginning to distort her personality by developing an unconscious bitterness toward white people; when you have to concoct an answer for a five-year-old son who is asking: "Daddy, why do white people treat coloured people so mean?"; when you take a cross-county drive and find it necessary to sleep night after night in the uncomfortable corners of your automobile because no motel will accept you; when you are humiliated day in and day out by nagging signs reading "white" and "coloured"; when your first name becomes "nigger," your middle name becomes "boy" (however old you are) and your last name becomes "John," and your wife and mother are never given the respected title "Mrs"; when you are harried by day and haunted by night by the fact that you are a Negro, living constantly at tiptoe stance, never quite knowing what to expect next, and are plagued with inner fears and outer resentments; when you are forever fighting a degenerating sense of "nobodiness"—then you will understand why we find it difficult to wait. There comes a time when the cup of endurance runs over, and men are no longer willing to be plunged into the abyss of despair. I hope, sirs, you can understand our legitimate and unavoidable impatience.

You express a great deal of anxiety over our willingness to break laws. This is certainly a legitimate concern. Since we so diligently urge people to obey the Supreme Court's decision of 1954 outlawing segregation in the public schools, at first glance it may seem rather paradoxical for us consciously to break laws. One may well ask: "How can you advocate breaking some laws and obeying others?" The answer lies in the fact that there are two types of laws: just and unjust. I would be the first to advocate obeying just laws. One has not only a legal but a moral responsibility to obey just laws. Conversely, one has a moral responsibility to disobey unjust laws. I would agree with **St Augustine** that "an unjust law is no law at all."

Now, what is the difference between the two? How does one determine whether a law is just or unjust? A just law is a man-made code that squares with the moral law or the law of God. An unjust law is a code that is out of harmony with the moral law. To put it in the terms of **St Thomas Aquinas**: An unjust law is a human law that is not rooted in eternal law and natural law. Any law that uplifts human personality is just. Any law that degrades human personality is unjust. All segregation statutes are unjust because segregation distorts the soul and damages the personality. It gives the segregator a false sense of superiority and the segregated a false sense of inferiority. Segregation, to use the terminology of the Jewish philosopher **Martin Buber**, substitutes an "I–it" relationship for an "I–thou" relationship and ends up relegating persons to the status of things. Hence segregation is not only politically, economically and sociologically unsound, it is morally wrong and sinful. **Paul Tillich** has said that sin is separation. Is not segregation an existential expression of man's tragic separation, his awful estrangement, his terrible sinfulness? Thus it is that I can urge men to obey the 1954 decision of the Supreme Court, for it is morally right; and I can urge them to disobey segregation ordinances, for they are morally wrong.

Let us consider a more concrete example of just and unjust laws. An unjust law is a code that a numerical or power majority group compels a minority group to obey but does not make binding on itself. This is *difference* made legal. By the same token, a just law is a code that a majority compels a minority to follow and that it is willing to follow itself. This is *sameness* made legal.

Let me give another explanation. A law is unjust if it is inflicted on a minority that, as a result of being denied the right to vote, had no part in enacting or devising the law. Who can say that the legislature of Alabama which set up that state's segregation laws was democratically elected? Throughout Alabama all sorts of devious methods are used to prevent Negroes from becoming registered voters, and there are some counties in which, even though Negroes constitute a majority of the population, not a single Negro is registered. Can any law enacted under such circumstances be considered democratically structured?

Sometimes a law is just on its face and unjust in its application. For instance, I have been arrested on a charge of parading without a permit. Now, there is nothing wrong in having an ordinance which requires a permit for a parade. But such an ordinance becomes unjust when it is used to maintain segregation and to deny citizens the First-Amendment privilege of peaceful assembly and protest.

I hope you are able to see the distinction I am trying to point out. In no sense do I advocate evading or defying the law, as would the rabid segregationist. That would lead to anarchy. One who breaks an unjust law must do so openly, lovingly, and with a willingness to accept the penalty. I submit that an individual who breaks a law that conscience tells him is unjust, and who willingly accepts the penalty of imprisonment in order to arouse the conscience of the community over its injustice, is in reality expressing the highest respect for law.

Of course, there is nothing new about this kind of civil disobedience. It was evidenced sublimely in the **refusal of Shadrach, Meshach, and Abednego to obey the laws of Nebuchadnezzar**, on the ground that a higher moral law was at stake. It was practised superbly by the early Christians, who were willing to face hungry lions and the excruciating pain of chopping blocks rather than submit to certain unjust laws of the Roman Empire. To a degree, academic freedom is a reality today because Socrates practiced civil disobedience. In our own nation, the **Boston Tea Party** represented a massive act of civil disobedience.

We should never forget that everything Adolf Hitler did in Germany was "legal" and everything the **Hungarian freedom fighters** did in Hungary was "illegal." It was "illegal" to aid and comfort a Jew in Hitler's Germany. Even so, I am sure that, had I lived in Germany at the time, I would have aided and comforted my Jewish brothers. If today I lived in a Communist country where certain principles dear to the Christian faith are suppressed, I would openly advocate disobeying that country's anti-religious laws.

I must make two honest confessions to you, my Christian and Jewish brothers. First, I must confess that over the past few years I have been gravely disappointed with the white moderate. I have almost reached the regrettable conclusion that the Negro's great stumbling block in his stride toward freedom is not the **White Citizen's Counciler or the Ku Klux Klanner**, but the white moderate, who is more devoted to "order" than to justice; who prefers a negative peace which is the absence of tension to a positive peace which is the presence of justice; who constantly says: "I agree with you in the goal you seek, but I cannot agree with your methods of direct action"; who paternalistically believes he can set the timetable for another man's freedom; who lives by a mythical concept of time and who constantly advises the Negro to wait for a "more convenient season." Shallow understanding from people of good will is more frustrating than absolute misunderstanding from people of ill will. Lukewarm acceptance is much more bewildering than outright rejection.

I had hoped that the white moderate would understand that law and order exist for the purpose of establishing justice and that when they fail in this purpose they become the dangerously structured dams that block the flow of social progress. I had hoped that the white moderate would understand that the present tension in the South is a necessary phase of the transition from an obnoxious negative peace, in which the Negro passively accepted his unjust plight, to a substantive and positive peace, in which all men will respect the dignity and worth of human personality. Actually, we who engage in non-violent direct action are not the creators of tension. We merely bring to the surface the hidden tension that is already alive. We bring it out in the open, where it can be seen and dealt with. Like a boil that can never be cured so long as it is covered up but must be opened with all its ugliness to the natural medicines of air and light, injustice must be exposed, with all the tension its exposure creates, to the light of human conscience and the air of national opinion before it can be cured.

In your statement you assert that our actions, even though peaceful, must be condemned because they precipitate violence. But is this a logical assertion? Isn't this like condemning a robbed man because his possession of money precipitated the evil act of robbery? Isn't this like condemning Socrates because his unswerving commitment to truth and his philosophical inquiries precipitated the act by the misguided populace in which they made him drink hemlock? Isn't this like condemning Jesus because his unique God-consciousness and never-ceasing devotion to God's will precipitated the evil act of crucifixion? We must come to see that, as the federal courts have consistently affirmed, it is wrong to urge an individual to cease his efforts to gain his basic constitutional rights because the quest may precipitate violence. Society must protect the robbed and punish the robber.

I had also hoped that the white moderate would reject the myth concerning time in relation to the struggle for freedom. I have just received a letter from a white brother in Texas. He writes: "All Christians know that the coloured people will receive equal rights eventually, but it is possible that you are in too great a religious hurry. It has taken Christianity almost two thousand years to accomplish what it has. The teachings of Christ take time to come to earth." Such an attitude stems from a tragic misconception of time, from the strangely irrational notion that there is something in the very flow of time that will inevitably cure all ills. Actually, time itself is neutral; it can be used either destructively or constructively. More and more I feel that the people of ill will have used time much more effectively than have the people of good will. We will have to repent in this generation not merely for the hateful words and actions of the bad people but for the appalling silence of the good people. Human progress never rolls in on wheels of inevitability; it comes through the tireless efforts of men willing to be co-workers with God, and without this hard work, time itself becomes an ally of the forces of social stagnation. We must use time creatively, in the knowledge that the time is always ripe to do right. Now is the time to make real the promise of democracy and transform our pending national elegy into a creative psalm of brotherhood. Now is the time to lift our national policy from the quicksand of racial injustice to the solid rock of human dignity.

You speak of our activity in Birmingham as extreme. At first I was rather disappointed that fellow clergymen would see my non-violent efforts as those of an extremist. I began thinking about the fact that I stand in the middle of two opposing forces in the Negro community. One is a force of complacency, made up in part of Negroes who, as a result of long years of oppression, are so drained of self-respect and a sense of "somebodiness" that they have adjusted to segregation; and in part of a few middle-class Negroes who, because of a degree of academic and economic security and because in some ways they profit by segregation, have become insensitive to the problems of the masses. The other force is one of bitterness and hatred, and it comes perilously close to advocating violence. It is expressed in the various black nationalist groups that are springing up across the nation, the largest and best known being **Elijah Muhammad**'s Muslim movement. Nourished by the Negro's frustration over the continued existence of racial discrimination, this movement is made up of people who have lost faith in America, who have absolutely repudiated Christianity, and who have concluded that the white man is an incorrigible "devil."

I have tried to stand between these two forces, saying that we need emulate neither the "do nothingism" of the complacent nor the hatred and despair of the black nationalist. For there is the more excellent way of love and non-violent protest. I am grateful to God that, through the influence of the Negro church, the way of non-violence became an integral part of our struggle.

If this philosophy had not emerged, by now many streets of the South would, I am convinced, be flowing with blood. And I am further convinced that if our white brothers dismiss as "rabble rousers" and "outside agitators" those of us who employ non-violent direct action, and if they refuse to support our non-violent efforts, millions of Negroes will, out of frustration and despair, seek solace and security in black-nationalist ideologies—a development that would inevitably lead to a frightening racial nightmare.

Oppressed people cannot remain oppressed forever. The yearning for freedom eventually manifests itself, and that is what has happened to the American Negro. Something within has reminded him of his birthright of freedom, and something without has reminded him that it can be gained. Consciously or unconsciously, he has been caught up by the *Zeitgeist* [spirit of the time], and with his black brothers of Africa and his brown and yellow brothers of Asia, South America and the Caribbean, the United States Negro is moving with a sense of great urgency toward the promised land of racial justice. If one recognizes this vital urge that has engulfed the Negro community, one should readily understand why public demonstrations are taking place. The Negro has many pent-up resentments and latent frustrations, and he must release them. So let him march; let him make prayer pilgrimages to the city hall; let him go on freedom rides—and try to understand why he must do so. If his repressed emotions are not released in non-violent ways, they will seek expression through violence; this is not a threat but a fact of history. So I have not said to my people: "Get rid of your discontent." Rather, I have tried to say that this normal and healthy discontent can be channelled into the creative outlet of non-violent direct action. And now this approach is being termed extremist.

But though I was initially disappointed at being categorized as an extremist, as I continued to think about the matter I gradually gained a measure of satisfaction from the label. Was not Jesus an extremist for love: "Love your enemies, bless them that curse you, do good to them that hate you, and pray for them which despitefully use you, and persecute you." Was not Amos an extremist for justice: "Let justice roll down like waters and righteousness like an ever-flowing stream." Was not Paul an extremist for the Christian gospel: "I bear in my body the marks of the Lord Jesus." Was not **Martin Luther** an extremist: "Here I stand; I cannot do otherwise, so help me God." And **John Bunyan**: "I will stay in jail to the end of my days before I make a butchery of my conscience." And **Abraham Lincoln**: "This nation cannot survive half slave and half free." And **Thomas Jefferson**: "We hold these truths to be self-evident, that all men are created equal . . ." So the question is not whether we will be extremists, but what kind of extremists we will be. Will we be extremists for hate or for love? Will we be extremists for the preservation of injustice or for the extension of justice? In that dramatic scene on Calvary's hill three men were crucified. We must never forget that all three were crucified for the same crime— the crime of extremism. Two were extremists for immorality, and thus fell below their environment. The other, Jesus Christ, was an extremist for love, truth and goodness, and thereby rose above his environment. Perhaps the South, the nation and the world are in dire need of creative extremists.

I had hoped that the white moderate would see this need. Perhaps I was too optimistic; perhaps I expected too much. I suppose I should have realized that few members of the oppressor race can understand the deep groans and passionate yearnings of the oppressed race, and still fewer have the vision to see that injustice must be rooted out by strong, persistent and determined action. I am thankful, however, that some of our white brothers in the South have grasped the meaning of this social revolution and committed themselves to it. They are still all too few in quantity, but they are big in quality. Some—such as Ralph McGill, Lillian Smith, Harry Golden, James McBride Dabbs, Ann Braden and Sarah Patton Boyle—have written about our struggle in eloquent and prophetic terms. Others have marched with us down nameless streets of the South. They have languished in filthy, roach-infested jails, suffering the abuse and brutality of policemen who view them as "dirty nigger-lovers." Unlike so many of their moderate brothers and sisters, they have recognized the urgency of the moment and sensed the need for powerful "action" antidotes to combat the disease of segregation.

Let me take note of my other major disappointment. I have been so greatly disappointed with the white church and its leadership. Of course, there are some notable exceptions. I am not unmindful of the fact that each of you has taken some significant stands on this issue. I commend you, Reverend Stallings, for your Christian stand on this past Sunday, in welcoming Negroes to your worship service on a non-segregated basis. I commend the Catholic leaders of this state for integrating Spring Hill College several years ago.

But despite these notable exceptions, I must honestly reiterate that I have been disappointed with the church. I do not say this as one of those negative critics who can always find something wrong with the church. I say this as a minister of the gospel, who loves the church; who was nurtured in its bosom; who has been sustained by its spiritual blessings and who will remain true to it as long as the cord of life shall lengthen.

When I was suddenly catapulted into the leadership of the bus protest in Montgomery, Alabama, a few years ago, I felt we would be supported by the white church. I felt that the white ministers, priests and rabbis of the South would be among our strongest allies. Instead, some have been outright opponents, refusing to understand the freedom movement and misrepresenting its leaders; all too many others have been more cautious than courageous and have remained silent behind the anaesthetizing security of stained-glass windows.

In spite of my shattered dreams, I came to Birmingham with the hope that the white religious leadership of this community would see the justice of our cause and, with deep moral concern, would serve as the channel through which our just grievances could reach the power structure. I had hoped that each of you would understand. But again I have been disappointed.

I have heard numerous southern religious leaders admonish their worshipers to comply with a desegregation decision because it is the law, but I have longed to hear white ministers declare: "Follow this decree because integration is morally right and because the Negro is your brother." In the midst of blatant injustices inflicted upon the Negro, I have watched white churchmen stand on the sideline and mouth pious irrelevancies and sanctimonious trivialities. In the midst of a mighty struggle to rid our nation of racial and economic injustice, I have heard many ministers say: "Those are social issues, with which the gospel has no real concern." And I have watched many churches commit themselves to a completely otherworldly religion which makes a strange, un-Biblical distinction between body and soul, between the sacred and the secular.

I have travelled the length and breadth of Alabama, Mississippi and all the other southern states. On sweltering summer days and crisp autumn mornings I have looked at the South's beautiful churches with their lofty spires pointing heavenward. I have beheld the impressive outlines of her massive religious-education buildings. Over and over I have found myself asking: "What kind of people worship here? Who is their God? Where were their voices when the lips of Governor **Barnett** dripped with words of interposition and nullification? Where were they when Governor **Wallace** gave a clarion call for defiance and hatred? Where were their voices of support when bruised and weary Negro men and women decided to rise from the dark dungeons of complacency to the bright hills of creative protest?"

Yes, these questions are still in my mind. In deep disappointment I have wept over the laxity of the church. But be assured that my tears have been tears of love. There can be no deep disappointment where there is not deep love. Yes, I love the church. How could I do otherwise? I am in the rather unique position of being the son, the grandson and the great-grandson of preachers. Yes, I see the church as the body of Christ. But, oh! How we have blemished and scarred that body through social neglect and through fear of being non-conformists.

There was a time when the church was very powerful—in the time when the early Christians rejoiced at being deemed worthy to suffer for what they believed. In those days the church was not merely a thermometer that recorded the ideas and principles of popular opinion; it was a thermostat that transformed the mores of society. Whenever the early Christians entered a town, the people in power became disturbed and immediately sought to convict the Christians for being "disturbers of the peace" and "outside agitators." But the Christians pressed on, in the conviction that they were "a colony of heaven," called to obey God rather than man. Small in number, they were big in commitment. They were too God-intoxicated to be "astronomically intimidated." By their effort and example they brought an end to such ancient evils as infanticide and gladiatorial contests.

Things are different now. So often the contemporary church is a weak, ineffectual voice with an uncertain sound. So often it is an archdefender of the status quo. Far from being disturbed by the presence of the church, the power structure of the average community is consoled by the church's silent—and often even vocal—sanction of things as they are.

But the judgment of God is upon the church as never before. If today's church does not recapture the sacrificial spirit of the early church, it will lose its authenticity, forfeit the loyalty of millions, and be dismissed as an irrelevant social club with no meaning for the twentieth century. Every day I meet young people whose disappointment with the church has turned into outright disgust.

Perhaps I have once again been too optimistic. Is organized religion too inextricably bound to the status quo to save our nation and the world? Perhaps I must turn my faith to the inner spiritual church, the church within the church, as the true *ekklesia* and the hope of the world. But again I am thankful to God that some noble souls from the ranks of organized religion have broken loose from the paralyzing chains of conformity and joined us as active partners in the struggle for freedom. They have left their secure congregations and walked the streets of Albany, Georgia, with us. They have gone down the highways of the South on tortuous rides for freedom. Yes, they have gone to jail with us. Some have been dismissed from their churches, have lost the support of their bishops and fellow ministers. But they have acted in the faith that right defeated is stronger than evil triumphant. Their witness has been the spiritual salt that has preserved the true meaning of the gospel in these troubled times. They have carved a tunnel of hope through the dark mountain of disappointment.

I hope the church as a whole will meet the challenge of this decisive hour. But even if the church does not come to the aid of justice, I have no despair about the future. I have no fear about the outcome of our struggle in Birmingham, even if our motives are at present misunderstood. We will reach the goal of freedom in Birmingham and all over the nation, because the goal of America is freedom. Abused and scorned though we may be, our destiny is tied up with America's destiny. Before the pilgrims landed at Plymouth, we were here. Before the pen of Jefferson etched the majestic words of the Declaration of Independence across the pages of history, we were here. For more than two centuries our forebears laboured in this country without wages; they made cotton king; they built the homes of their masters while suffering gross injustice and shameful humiliation— and yet out of a bottomless vitality they continued to thrive and develop. If the inexpressible cruelties of slavery could not stop us, the opposition we now face will surely fail. We will win our freedom because the sacred heritage of our nation and the eternal will of God are embodied in our echoing demands.

Before closing I feel impelled to mention one other point in your statement that has troubled me profoundly. You warmly commended the Birmingham police force for keeping "order" and "preventing violence." I doubt that you would have so warmly commended the police force if you had seen its dogs sinking their teeth into unarmed, non-violent Negroes. I doubt that you would so quickly commend the policemen if you were to observe their ugly and inhumane treatment of Negroes here in the city jail; if you were to watch them push and curse old Negro women and young Negro girls; if you were to see them slap and kick old Negro men and young boys; if you were to observe them, as they did on two occasions, refuse to give us food because we wanted to sing our grace together. I cannot join you in your praise of the Birmingham police department.

It is true that the police have exercised a degree of discipline in handling the demonstrators. In this sense they have conducted themselves rather "non-violently" in public. But for what purpose? To preserve the evil system of segregation. Over the past few years I have consistently preached that non-violence demands that the means we use must be as pure as the ends we seek. I have tried to make clear that it is wrong to use immoral means to attain moral ends. But now I must affirm that it is just as wrong, or perhaps even more so, to use moral means to preserve immoral ends. Perhaps Mr. Connor and his policemen have been rather non-violent in public, as was Chief Pritchett in Albany, Georgia, but they have used the moral means of non-violence to maintain the immoral end of racial injustice. As **T.S. Eliot** has said: "The last temptation is the greatest treason: To do the right deed for the wrong reason."

I wish you had commended the Negro sit-inners and demonstrators of Birmingham for their sublime courage, their willingness to suffer and their amazing discipline in the midst of great provocation. One day the South will recognize its real heroes. They will be the **James Meredith**s, with the noble sense of purpose that enables them to face jeering and hostile mobs, and with the agonizing loneliness that characterizes the life of the pioneer. They will be old, oppressed, battered Negro women, symbolized in a 72-year-old woman in Montgomery, Alabama, who rose up with a sense of dignity and with her people decided not to ride segregated buses, and who responded with ungrammatical profundity to one who inquired about her weariness: "My feets is tired, but my soul is at rest." They will be the young high school and college students, the young ministers of the gospel and a host of their elders, courageously and non-violently sitting in at lunch counters and willingly going to jail for conscience" sake. One day the South will know that when these disinherited children of God sat down at lunch counters, they were in reality standing up for what is best in the American dream and for the most sacred values in our Judaeo-Christian heritage, thereby bringing our nation back to those great wells of democracy which were dug deep by the founding fathers in their formulation of the Constitution and the Declaration of Independence.

Never before have I written so long a letter. I'm afraid it is much too long to take your precious time. I can assure you that it would have been much shorter if I had been writing from a comfortable desk, but what else can one do when he is alone in a narrow jail cell, other than write long letters, think long thoughts, and pray long prayers?

If I have said anything in this letter that overstates the truth and indicates an unreasonable impatience, I beg you to forgive me. If I have said anything that understates the truth and indicates my having a patience that allows me to settle for anything less than brotherhood, I beg God to forgive me.

I hope this letter finds you strong in the faith. I also hope that circumstances will soon make it possible for me to meet each of you, not as an integrationist or a civil-rights leader but as a fellow clergyman and a Christian brother. Let us all hope that the dark clouds of racial prejudice will soon pass away and the deep fog of misunderstanding will be lifted from our fear-drenched communities, and in some not too distant tomorrow the radiant stars of love and brotherhood will shine over our great nation with all their scintillating beauty.

Yours for the cause of Peace and Brotherhood,
Martin Luther King, Jr.

## Note

1. Author's Note: This response to a published statement by eight fellow clergymen from Alabama [. . .] was composed under somewhat constricting circumstances. Begun on the margins of the newspaper in which the statement appeared while I was in jail, the letter was continued on scraps of writing paper supplied by a friendly Negro trusty, and concluded on a pad my attorneys were eventually permitted to leave me. Although the text remains in substance unaltered, I have indulged in the author's prerogative of polishing it for publication.

## Study Questions

1. What is King's response to the clergymen's portrayal of him as an "outsider" stirring up trouble in Birmingham? Do you agree or disagree?
2. Describe the four basic steps to be carried out in a non-violent campaign.
3. What is the Socratic method, and how is it used pedagogically? Why did King believe that the civil rights movement's use of non-violent civil disobedience played an analogous role in facilitating social and political change?
4. Provide an example of an act of non-violent civil disobedience that illustrates the apparent paradox that demonstrators consciously break some laws while urging people to uphold others. King resolves the paradox by saying that there are just and unjust laws. Critically evaluate the various ways in which King draws this distinction.

# John Rawls

John Rawls (1921–2002) is considered the most influential political philosopher of the twentieth century. Born in Baltimore, Rawls obtained his BA at Princeton in 1943, served in the Pacific during the Second World War, and returned to Princeton to earn his PhD in 1950. After a Fulbright year spent at Oxford in 1952–3, Rawls taught at Cornell, MIT, and, for more than 30 years, Harvard. Rawls' *A Theory of Justice* (1971) critiques utilitarianism and draws on the social contract tradition to defend a theory of justice as fairness that accommodates tension between democratic ideals of freedom and equality. These ideas are introduced in this 1969 essay on civil disobedience.

## The Justification of Civil Disobedience

### 1. Introduction

I should like to discuss briefly, and in an informal way, the grounds of civil disobedience in a constitutional democracy. Thus, I shall limit my remarks to the conditions under which we may, by civil disobedience, properly oppose legally established democratic authority; I am not concerned with the situation under other kinds of government nor, except incidentally, with other forms of resistance. My thought is that in a reasonably just (though of course not perfectly just) democratic regime, civil disobedience, when it is justified, is normally to be understood as a political action which addresses the sense of justice of the majority in order to urge reconsideration of the measures protested and to warn that in the firm opinion of the dissenters the conditions of social cooperation are not being honoured. This characterization of civil disobedience is intended to apply to dissent on fundamental questions of internal policy, a limitation which I shall follow to simplify our question.

### 2. The Social Contract Doctrine

[. . .] I believe that the appropriate conception [of justice], at least for an account of political obligation in a constitutional democracy, is that of the social contract theory from which so much of our political thought derives. If we are careful to interpret it in a suitably general way, I hold that this doctrine provides a satisfactory basis for political theory, indeed even for ethical theory itself, but this is beyond our present concern.[1] The interpretation I suggest is the following: that the principles to which social arrangements must conform, and in particular the principles of justice, are those which free and rational men would agree to in an original position of equal liberty; and similarly, the principles which govern men's relations to institutions and define their natural duties and obligations are the principles to which they would consent when so situated. It should be noted straightaway that in this interpretation of the contract theory the principles of justice are understood as the outcome of a hypothetical agreement. They are principles which would be agreed to if the situation of the original position were to arise. There is no mention of an actual agreement, nor need such an agreement ever be made. Social arrangements are just or unjust according to whether they accord with the principles for assigning and securing fundamental rights and liberties which would be chosen in the original position. This position is, to be sure, the analytic analogue of the traditional notion of the state of nature, but it must not be mistaken for a historical occasion. Rather it is a hypothetical situation which embodies the basic ideas of the contract doctrine; the description of this situation enables us to work out which principles would be adopted. I must now say something about these matters.

The contract doctrine has always supposed that the persons in the original position have equal powers and rights, that is, that they are symmetrically situated with respect to any arrangements for reaching agreement, and that coalitions and the like are excluded. But it is an essential element (which has not been sufficiently observed although it is implicit in **Kant**'s version of the theory) that there are very strong restrictions on what the contracting parties are presumed to know. In particular, I interpret the theory to hold that the parties do not know their position in society, past, present, or future; nor do they know which institutions exist. Again, they do not know their own place in the distribution of natural talents and abilities, whether they are intelligent or strong, man or woman, and so on. Finally, they do not know their own particular interests and preferences or the system of ends which they wish to advance: they do not know their conception of the good. In all these respects the parties are confronted with a veil of ignorance which prevents any one from being able to take advantage of his good fortune or particular interests or from being disadvantaged by them. What the parties do know (or assume) is that **Hume**'s circumstances of justice obtain: namely, that the bounty of nature is not so generous as to render cooperative schemes superfluous nor so harsh as to make them impossible. Moreover, they assume that the extent of their altruism is limited and that, in general, they do not take an interest in one another's interests. Thus, given the special features of the original position, each man tries to do the best he can for himself by insisting on principles calculated to protect and advance his system of ends whatever it turns out to be.

I believe that as a consequence of the peculiar nature of the original position there would be an agreement on the following two principles for assigning rights and duties and for regulating distributive shares as these are determined by the fundamental institutions of society: first, each person is to have an equal right to the most extensive liberty compatible with a like liberty for all; second, social and economic inequalities (as defined by the institutional structure or fostered by it) are to be arranged so that they are both to everyone's advantage and attached to positions and offices open to all. In view of the content of these two principles and their application to the main institutions of society, and therefore to the social system as a whole, we may regard them as the two principles of justice. Basic social arrangements are just insofar as they conform to these principles, and we can, if we like, discuss questions of justice directly by reference to them. But a deeper understanding of the justification of civil disobedience requires, I think, an account of the derivation of these principles provided by the doctrine of the social contract. Part of our task is to show why this is so.

## 3. The Grounds of Compliance with an Unjust Law

If we assume that in the original position men would agree both to the principle of doing their part when they have accepted and plan to continue to accept the benefits of just institutions (the principle of fairness), and also to the principle of not preventing the establishment of just institutions and of upholding and complying with them when they do exist, then the contract doctrine easily accounts for our having to conform to just institutions. But how does it account for the fact that we are normally required to comply with unjust laws as well? The injustice of a law is not a sufficient ground for not complying with it any more than the legal validity of legislation is always sufficient to require obedience to it. Sometimes one hears these extremes asserted, but I think that we need not take them seriously.

An answer to our question can be given by elaborating the social contract theory in the following way. I interpret it to hold that one is to envisage a series of agreements as follows: first, men are to agree upon the principles of justice in the original position. Then they are to move to a constitutional convention in which they choose a constitution that satisfies the principles of justice already chosen.

Finally they assume the role of a legislative body and, guided by the principles of justice, enact laws subject to the constraints and procedures of the just constitution. The decisions reached in any stage are binding in all subsequent stages. Now whereas in the original position the contracting parties have no knowledge of their society or of their own position in it, in both a constitutional convention and a legislature, they do know certain general facts about their institutions, for example, the statistics regarding employment and output required for fiscal and economic policy. But no one knows particular facts about his own social class or his place in the distribution of natural assets. On each occasion the contracting parties have the knowledge required to make their agreement rational from the appropriate point of view, but not so much as to make them prejudiced. They are unable to tailor principles and legislation to take advantage of their social or natural position; a veil of ignorance prevents their knowing what this position is. With this series of agreements in mind, we can characterize just laws and policies as those which would be enacted were this whole process correctly carried out.

In choosing a constitution the aim is to find among the just constitutions the one which is most likely, given the general facts about the society in question, to lead to just and effective legislation. The principles of justice provide a criterion for the laws desired; the problem is to find a set of political procedures that will give this outcome. I shall assume that, at least under the normal conditions of a modern state, the best constitution is some form of democratic regime affirming equal political liberty and using some sort of majority (or other plurality) rule. Thus it follows that on the contract theory a constitutional democracy of some sort is required by the principles of justice. At the same time it is essential to observe that the constitutional process is always a case of what we may call imperfect procedural justice: that is, there is no feasible political procedure which guarantees that the enacted legislation is just even though we have (let us suppose) a standard for just legislation. In simple cases, such as games of fair division,

there are procedures which always lead to the right outcome (assume that equal shares is fair and let the man who cuts the cake take the last piece). These situations are those of perfect procedural justice. In other cases it does not matter what the outcome is as long as the fair procedure is followed: fairness of the process is transferred to the result (fair gambling is an instance of this). These situations are those of pure procedural justice. The constitutional process, like a criminal trial, resembles neither of these; the result matters and we have a standard for it. The difficulty is that we cannot frame a procedure which guarantees that only just and effective legislation is enacted. Thus even under a just constitution unjust laws may be passed and unjust policies enforced. Some form of the majority principle is necessary but the majority may be mistaken, more or less wilfully, in what it legislates. In agreeing to a democratic constitution (as an instance of imperfect procedural justice) one accepts at the same time the principle of majority rule. Assuming that the constitution is just and that we have accepted and plan to continue to accept its benefits, we then have both an obligation and a natural duty (and in any case the duty) to comply with what the majority enacts even though it may be unjust. In this way we become bound to follow unjust laws, not always, of course, but provided the injustice does not exceed certain limits. We recognize that we must run the risk of suffering from the defects of one another's sense of justice; this burden we are prepared to carry as long as it is more or less evenly distributed or does not weigh too heavily. Justice binds us to a just constitution and to the unjust laws which may be enacted under it in precisely the same way that it binds us to any other social arrangement. Once we take the sequence of stages into account, there is nothing unusual in our being required to comply with unjust laws.

It should be observed that the majority principle has a secondary place as a rule of procedure which is perhaps the most efficient one under usual circumstances for working a democratic constitution. The basis for it rests essentially upon the principles of justice and therefore we may, when conditions allow, appeal to these principles against unjust legislation. The justice of the constitution does not ensure the justice of laws enacted under it; and while we often have both an obligation and a duty to comply with what the majority legislates (as long as it does not exceed certain limits), there is, of course, no corresponding obligation or duty to regard what the majority enacts as itself just. The right to make law does not guarantee that the decision is rightly made; and while the citizen submits in his conduct to the judgment of democratic authority, he does not submit his judgment to it. And if in his judgment the enactments of the majority exceed certain bounds of injustice, the citizen may consider civil disobedience. For we are not required to accept the majority's acts unconditionally and to acquiesce in the denial of our and others' liberties; rather we submit our conduct to democratic authority to the extent necessary to share the burden of working a constitutional regime, distorted as it must inevitably be by men's lack of wisdom and the defects of their sense of justice.

## 4. The Place of Civil Disobedience in a Constitutional Democracy

We are now in a position to say a few things about civil disobedience. I shall understand it to be a public, non-violent, and conscientious act contrary to law usually done with the intent to bring about a change in the policies or laws of the government (Bedau). Civil disobedience is a political act in the sense that it is an act justified by moral principles which define a conception of civil society and the public good. It rests, then, on political conviction as opposed to a search for self or group interest; and in the case of a constitutional democracy, we may assume that this conviction involves the conception of justice (say that expressed by the contract doctrine) which underlies the constitution itself. That is, in a viable democratic regime there is a common conception of justice by reference to which its citizens regulate their political affairs and interpret the constitution. Civil disobedience is a public act which the dissenter believes to be justified by this conception of justice, and for this reason it may be understood as addressing the sense of justice of the majority in order to urge reconsideration of the measures protested and to warn that, in the sincere opinion of the dissenters, the conditions of social cooperation are not being honoured. For the principles of justice express precisely such conditions, and their persistent and deliberate violation in regard to basic liberties over any extended period of time cuts the ties of community and invites either submission or forceful resistance. By engaging in civil disobedience a minority leads the majority to consider whether it wants to have its acts taken in this way, or whether, in view of the common sense of justice, it wishes to acknowledge the claims of the minority.

Civil disobedience is also civil in another sense. Not only is it the outcome of a sincere conviction based on principles which regulate civic life, but it is public and non-violent, that is, it is done in a situation where arrest and punishment are expected and accepted without resistance. In this way it manifests a respect for legal procedures. Civil disobedience expresses disobedience to law within the limits of fidelity to law, and this feature of it helps to establish in the eyes of the majority that it is indeed conscientious and sincere, that it really is meant to address their sense of justice (Fried). Being completely open about one's acts and being willing to accept the legal consequences of one's conduct is a bond given to make good one's sincerity, for that one's deeds are conscientious is not easy to demonstrate to another or even before oneself. No doubt it is possible to imagine a legal system in which conscientious belief that the law is unjust is accepted as a defence for noncompliance, and men of great honesty who are confident in one another might make such a system work. But as things are such a scheme would be unstable; we must pay a price in order to establish that we believe our actions have a moral basis in the convictions of the community.

The non-violent nature of civil disobedience refers to the fact that it is intended to address the sense of justice of the majority and as such it is a form of speech, an expression of conviction. To engage in violent acts likely to injure and to hurt is incompatible with civil disobedience as a mode of address. Indeed, an interference with the basic rights of others tends to obscure the civilly disobedient quality of one's act. Civil disobedience is non-violent in the further sense that the legal penalty for one's action is accepted and that resistance is not (at least for the moment) contemplated. Non-violence in this sense is to be distinguished from non-violence as a religious or pacifist principle. While those engaging in civil disobedience have often held some such principle, there is no necessary connection between it and civil disobedience. For on the interpretation suggested, civil disobedience in a democratic society is best understood as an appeal to the principles of justice, the fundamental conditions of willing social cooperation among free men, which in the view of the community as a whole are expressed in the constitution and guide its interpretation. Being an appeal to the moral basis of public life, civil disobedience is a political and not primarily a religious act. It addresses itself to the common principles of justice which men can require one another to follow and not to the aspirations of love which they cannot. Moreover, by taking part in civilly disobedient acts one does not foreswear indefinitely the idea of forceful resistance; for if the appeal against injustice is repeatedly denied, then the majority has declared its intention to invite submission or resistance and the latter may conceivably be justified even in a democratic regime. We are not required to acquiesce in the crushing of fundamental liberties by democratic majorities which have shown themselves blind to the principles of justice upon which justification of the constitution depends.

## 5. The Justification of Civil Disobedience

So far we have said nothing about the justification of civil disobedience, that is, the conditions under which civil disobedience may be engaged in consistent with the principles of justice that support a democratic regime. Our task is to see how the characterization of civil disobedience as addressed to the sense of justice of the majority (or to the citizens as a body) determines when such action is justified.

First of all, we may suppose that the normal political appeals to the majority have already been made in good faith and have been rejected, and that the standard means of redress have been tried. Thus, for example, existing political parties are indifferent to the claims of the minority, and attempts to repeal the laws protested have been met with further repression since legal institutions are in the control of the majority. While civil disobedience should be recognized, I think, as a form of political action within the limits of fidelity to the rule of law, at the same time it is a rather desperate act just within these limits, and therefore it should, in general, be undertaken as a last resort when standard democratic processes have failed. In this sense it is not a normal political action. When it is justified there has been a serious breakdown; not only is there grave injustice in the law but a refusal more or less deliberate to correct it.

Second, since civil disobedience is a political act addressed to the sense of justice of the majority, it should usually be limited to substantial and clear violations of justice and preferably to those which, if rectified, will establish a basis for doing away with remaining injustices. For this reason there is a presumption in favour of restricting civil disobedience to violations of the first principle of justice, the principle of equal liberty, and to barriers which contravene the second principle, the principle of open offices which protects equality of opportunity. It is not, of course, always easy to tell whether these principles are satisfied. But if we think of them as guaranteeing the fundamental equal political and civil liberties (including freedom of conscience and liberty of thought) and equality of opportunity, then it is often relatively clear whether their principles are being honoured. After all, the equal liberties are defined by the visible structure of social institutions; they are to be incorporated into the recognized practice, if not the letter, of social arrangements. When minorities are denied the right to vote or to hold certain political offices, when certain religious groups are repressed and others denied equality of opportunity in the economy, this is often obvious and there is no doubt that justice is not being given. However, the first part of the second principle which requires that inequalities be to everyone's advantage is a much more imprecise and controversial matter. Not only is there a problem of assigning it a determinate and precise sense, but even if we do so and agree on what it should be, there is often a wide variety of reasonable opinion as to whether the principle is satisfied. The reason for this is that the principle applies primarily to fundamental economic and social policies. The choice of these depends upon theoretical and speculative beliefs as well as upon a wealth of concrete information, and all of this mixed with judgment and plain hunch, not to mention in actual cases prejudice and self-interest. Thus unless the laws of taxation are clearly designed to attack a basic equal liberty, they should not be protested by civil disobedience; the appeal to justice is not sufficiently clear and its resolution is best left to the political process. But violations of the equal liberties that define the common status of citizenship are another matter. The deliberate denial of these more or less over any extended period of time in the face of normal political protest is, in general, an appropriate object of civil disobedience. We may think of the social system as divided roughly into two parts, one which incorporates the fundamental equal liberties (including equality of opportunity) and another which embodies social and economic policies properly aimed at promoting the advantage of everyone. As a rule civil disobedience is best limited to the former where the appeal to justice is not only more definite and precise, but where, if it is effective, it tends to correct the injustices in the latter.

Third, civil disobedience should be restricted to those cases where the dissenter is willing to affirm that everyone else similarly subjected to the same degree of injustice has the right to protest in a similar way. That is, we must be prepared to authorize others to dissent in similar situations and in the same way, and to accept the consequences of their doing so. Thus, we may hold, for example, that the widespread disposition to disobey civilly

clear violations of fundamental liberties more or less deliberate over an extended period of time would raise the degree of justice throughout society and would ensure men's self-esteem as well as their respect for one another. Indeed, I believe this to be true, though certainly it is partly a matter of conjecture. As the contract doctrine emphasizes, since the principles of justice are principles which we would agree to in an original position of equality when we do not know our social position and the like, the refusal to grant justice is either the denial of the other as an equal (as one in regard to whom we are prepared to constrain our actions by principles which we would consent to) or the manifestation of a willingness to take advantage of natural contingencies and social fortune at his expense. In either case, injustice invites submission or resistance; but submission arouses the contempt of the oppressor and confirms him in his intention. If straightaway, after a decent period of time to make reasonable political appeals in the normal way, men were in general to dissent by civil disobedience from infractions of the fundamental equal liberties, these liberties would, I believe, be more rather than less secure. Legitimate civil disobedience properly exercised is a stabilizing device in a constitutional regime, tending to make it more firmly just. [. . .]

The final condition, of a different nature, is the following. We have been considering when one has a right to engage in civil disobedience, and our conclusion is that one has this right should three conditions hold: when one is subject to injustice more or less deliberate over an extended period of time in the face of normal political protests; where the injustice is a clear violation of the liberties of equal citizenship; and provided that the general disposition to protest similarly in similar cases would have acceptable consequences. These conditions are not, I think, exhaustive, but they seem to cover the more obvious points; yet even when they are satisfied and one has the right to engage in civil disobedience, there is still the different question of whether one should exercise this right, that is, whether by doing so one is likely to further one's ends. Having established one's right to protest, one is then free to consider these tactical questions. We may be acting within our rights but still foolishly if our action only serves to provoke the harsh retaliation of the majority; and it is likely to do so if the majority lacks a sense of justice, or if the action is poorly timed or not well designed to make the appeal to the sense of justice effective. It is easy to think of instances of this sort, and in each case these practical questions have to be faced. From the standpoint of the theory of political obligation we can only say that the exercise of the right should be rational and reasonably designed to advance the protester's aims, and that weighing tactical questions presupposes that one has already established one's right, since tactical advantages in themselves do not support it.

## 6. Conclusion: Several Objections Considered

In a reasonably affluent democratic society justice becomes the first virtue of institutions. Social arrangements irrespective of their efficiency must be reformed if they are significantly unjust. No increase in efficiency in the form of greater advantages for many justifies the loss of liberty of a few. That we believe this is shown by the fact that in a democracy the fundamental liberties of citizenship are not understood as the outcome of political bargaining, nor are they subject to the calculus of social interests. Rather these liberties are fixed points which serve to limit political transactions and which determine the scope of calculations of social advantage. It is this fundamental place of the equal liberties which makes their systematic violation over any extended period of time a proper object of civil disobedience. For to deny men these rights is to infringe the conditions of social cooperation among free and rational persons, a fact which is evident to the citizens of a constitutional regime since it follows from the principles of justice which underlie their institutions. The justification of civil disobedience rests on the priority of justice and the equal liberties which it guarantees.

It is natural to object to this view of civil disobedience that it relies too heavily upon the existence of a sense of justice. Some may hold that the feeling for justice is not a vital political force, and that what moves men are various other interests, the desire for wealth, power, prestige, and so on. Now this is a large question the answer to which is highly conjectural, and each tends to have his own opinion. But there are two remarks which may clarify what I have said: first, I have assumed that there is in a constitutional regime a common sense of justice the principles of which are recognized to support the constitution and to guide its interpretation. In any given situation particular men may be tempted to violate these principles, but the collective force in their behalf is usually effective since they are seen as the necessary terms of cooperation among free men; and presumably the citizens of a democracy (or sufficiently many of them) want to see justice done. Where these assumptions fail, the justifying conditions for civil disobedience (the first three) are not affected, but the rationality of engaging in it certainly is. In this case, unless the costs of repressing civil dissent injures the economic self-interest (or whatever) of the majority, protest may simply make the position of the minority worse. No doubt as a tactical matter civil disobedience is more effective when its appeal coincides with other interests, but a constitutional regime is not viable in the long run without an attachment to the principles of justice of the sort which we have assumed.

Then, further, there may be a misapprehension about the manner in which a sense of justice manifests itself. There is a tendency to think that it is shown by professions of the relevant principles together with actions of an altruistic nature requiring a considerable degree of self-sacrifice. But these conditions are obviously too strong, for the majority's sense of justice may show itself simply in its being unable to undertake the measures required to suppress the minority and to punish as the law requires the various acts of civil disobedience. The sense of justice undermines the will to uphold unjust institutions, and so a majority despite its superior power may give way. It is unprepared to force the minority to be subject to injustice. Thus, although the majority's action is reluctant and grudging, the role of the sense of justice is nevertheless essential, for without it the majority would have been willing to enforce the law and to defend its position. Once we see the sense of justice as working in this negative way to make established injustices indefensible, then it is recognized as a central element of democratic politics.

Finally, it may be objected against this account that it does not settle the question of who is to say when the situation is such as to justify civil disobedience. And because it does not answer this question, it invites anarchy by encouraging every man to decide the matter for himself. Now the reply to this is that each man must indeed settle this question for himself, although he may, of course, decide wrongly. This is true on any theory of political duty and obligation, at least on any theory compatible with the principles of a democratic constitution. The citizen is responsible for what he does. If we usually think that we should comply with the law, this is because our political principles normally lead to this conclusion. There is a presumption in favour of compliance in the absence of good reasons to the contrary. But because each man is responsible and must decide for himself as best he can whether the circumstances justify civil disobedience, it does not follow that he may decide as he pleases. It is not by looking to our personal interests or to political allegiances narrowly construed, that we should make up our mind. The citizen must decide on the basis of the principles of justice that underlie and guide the interpretation of the constitution and in the light of his sincere conviction as to how these principles should be applied in the circumstances. If he concludes that conditions obtain which justify civil disobedience and conducts himself accordingly, he has acted conscientiously and perhaps mistakenly, but not in any case at his convenience.

In a democratic society each man must act as he thinks the principles of political right require him to. We are to follow our understanding of these principles, and we cannot do otherwise. There can be no morally binding legal interpretation of these principles, not even by a supreme court or legislature. Nor is there any infallible procedure for determining what or who is right. In our system the Supreme Court, Congress, and the President often put forward rival interpretations of the Constitution. Although the Court has the final say in settling any particular case, it is not immune from powerful political influence that may change its reading of the law of the land. The Court presents its point of view by reason and argument; its conception of the Constitution must, if it is to endure, persuade men of its soundness. The final court of appeal is not the Court, or Congress, or the President, but the electorate as a whole. The civilly disobedient appeal in effect to this body. There is no danger of anarchy as long as there is a sufficient working agreement in men's conceptions of political justice and what it requires. That men can achieve such an understanding when the essential political liberties are maintained is the assumption implicit in democratic institutions. There is no way to avoid entirely the risk of divisive strife. But if legitimate civil disobedience seems to threaten civil peace, the responsibility falls not so much on those who protest as upon those whose abuse of authority and power justifies such opposition.

## Note

1. By the social contract theory I have in mind the doctrine found in Locke, Rousseau, and Kant.

## Works Cited

Bedau, H.A. "On Civil Disobedience." *Journal of Philosophy* 58 (1961): 653–65.

Fried, C. "Moral Causation." *Harvard Law Review* (1964): 1258–70.

## Study Questions

1. Explain the roles played by Rawls' hypothetical devices of the "original position" and "veil of ignorance" in his theory of justice.

2. On what grounds does Rawls argue that we have a duty to comply with unjust laws?

3. What two senses of "civil" are implicated in civil disobedience, according to Rawls, and in what two ways is civil disobedience non-violent?

4. Rawls tells us that simply following constitutionally proper procedures in enacting a law does not make it just but also that simply finding a law to be unjust does not sanction disobeying it. Provide an example of an act of civil disobedience. Does it satisfy the four conditions Rawls identifies as providing justification for civil disobedience?

## ⌁ DEMOCRATIC GOVERNMENT ⌁

---

## John Locke

---

John Locke (1632–1704) received a classical education at Westminster School and Christ Church College, Oxford. After studying medicine at Oxford, Locke became personal physician, political advisor, and secretary to Anthony Ashley Cooper (later the first Earl of Shaftesbury). Shaftesbury's involvement in plots to prevent Charles II's succession by his Roman Catholic brother, James, forced Locke to flee to Holland; he returned after the Glorious Revolution of 1688. Shaped by England's seventeenth-century parliamentary struggles, civil wars, and revolutionary plots, Locke's *Second Treatise of Government*, published anonymously in 1689, inspired American revolutionaries less than a century later.

# From *Second Treatise of Government*

### Of the State of Nature [Ch. 2]

4. To understand political power right and derive it from its original, we must consider what state all men are naturally in, and that is a *state of perfect freedom* to order their actions and dispose of their possessions and persons as they think fit within the bounds of the law of nature, without asking leave or depending upon the will of any other man.

A *state* also *of equality*, wherein all the power and jurisdiction is reciprocal, no one having more than another; there being nothing more evident than that creatures of the same species and rank, promiscuously born to all the same advantages of nature and the use of the same faculties, should also be equal one amongst another without subordination or subjection, unless the lord and master of them all should, by any manifest declaration of his will, set one above another and confer on him, by an evident and clear appointment, an undoubted right to dominion and sovereignty. [. . .]

6. But though this be a *state of liberty*, yet *it is not a state of licence*: though man in that state has an uncontrollable liberty to dispose of his person or possessions, yet he has not liberty to destroy himself, or so much as any creature in his possession, but where some nobler use than its bare preservation calls for it. The *state of nature* has a law of nature to govern it, which obliges everyone: and reason, which is that law, teaches all mankind, who will but consult it, that being all *equal and independent*, no one ought to harm another in his life, health, liberty, or possessions: for men being all the workmanship of one omnipotent and infinitely wise maker; all the servants of one sovereign master, sent into the world by his order and about his business; they are his property whose workmanship they are, made to last during his, not one another's, pleasure: and being furnished with like faculties, sharing all in one community of nature, there cannot be supposed any such *subordination* among us that may authorize us to destroy one another, as if we were made for one another's uses as the inferior ranks of creatures are for ours. [. . .]

7. And that all men may be restrained from invading others' rights and from doing hurt to one another, and the law of nature be observed which willeth the peace and *preservation of all mankind*, the *execution* of the law of nature is, in that state, put into every man's hands, whereby everyone has a right to punish the transgressors of that law to such a degree as may hinder its violation: for the *law of nature* would, as all other laws that concern men in this world, be in vain if there were nobody that in the state of nature had a *power to execute* that law, and thereby preserve the innocent and restrain offenders. And if anyone in

the state of nature may punish another for any evil he has done, everyone may do so: for in that *state of perfect equality*, where naturally there is no superiority or jurisdiction of one over another, what any may do in prosecution of that law, everyone must needs have a right to do. [. . .]

9. I doubt not but this will seem a very strange doctrine to some men: but before they condemn it, I desire them to resolve me by what right any prince or state can put to death or *punish an alien* for any crime he commits in their country. It is certain their laws by virtue of any sanction they receive from the promulgated will of the legislative reach not a stranger: they speak not to him, nor, if they did, is he bound to hearken to them. The legislative authority by which they are in force over the subjects of that common-wealth hath no power over him. Those who have the supreme power of making laws in *England*, *France*, or *Holland* are to an *Indian*, but like the rest of the world, men without authority: and therefore, if by the law of nature every man hath not a power to punish offences against it as he soberly judges the case to require, I see not how the magistrates of any community can *punish an alien* of another country—since, in reference to him, they can have no more power than what every man naturally may have over another. [. . .]

14. It is often asked as a mighty objection, *where are* or ever were there any *men in such a state of nature?* To which it may suffice as an answer at present that since all princes and rulers of *independent* governments all through the world are in a state of nature, it is plain the world never was, nor ever will be, without numbers of men in that state. I have named all governors of *independent communities*, whether they are, or are not, in league with others: for it is not every compact that puts an end to the state of nature between men, but only this one of agreeing together mutually to enter into one community and make one body politic; other promises and compacts men may make one with another, and yet still be in the state of nature. The promises and bargains for truck, etc. between the two men in the desert island mentioned by *Garcilaso de la Vega* in his history of *Peru*, or between a *Swiss* and an *Indian* in the woods of *America*, are binding to them, though they are perfectly in a state of nature in reference to one another: for truth and keeping of faith belongs to men, as men, and not as members of society. [. . .]

## Of Property [Ch. 5]

25. Whether we consider natural *reason*, which tells us that men, being once born, have a right to their preservation, and consequently to meat and drink and such other things as nature affords for their subsistence: or *revelation*, which gives us an account of those grants God made of the world to *Adam* and to *Noah* and his sons, it is very clear that God, as king *David* says (*Psal.* cxv. 16), *has given the earth to the children of men*, given it to mankind in common. But this being supposed, it seems to some a very great difficulty how anyone should ever come to have a property in anything. [. . .] I shall endeavour to show how men might come to have a *property* in several parts of that which God gave to mankind in common, and that without any express compact of all the commoners.

26. God, who hath given the world to men in common, hath also given them reason to make use of it to the best advantage of life and convenience. The earth, and all that is therein, is given to men for the support and comfort of their being. And though all the fruits it naturally produces and beasts it feeds belong to mankind in common as they are produced by the spontaneous hand of nature, and nobody has originally a private dominion, exclusive of the rest of mankind, in any of them as they are thus in their natural state, yet being given for the use of men, there must of necessity be *a means to appropriate* them some way or other before they can be of any use or at all beneficial to any particular man. The fruit or venison which nourishes the wild *Indian* who knows no enclosure and is still a tenant in common must be his, and so his, i.e., a part of him, that another can no longer have any right to it, before it can do him any good for the support of his life.

27. Though the earth and all inferior creatures be common to all men, yet every man has a *property* in his own *person*: this nobody has any right to but

himself. The *labour* of his body and the *work* of his hands, we may say, are properly his. Whatsoever then he removes out of the state that nature hath provided and left it in, he hath mixed his *labour* with and joined to it something that is his own, and thereby makes it his *property*. It being by him removed from the common state nature hath placed it in, it hath by this *labour* something annexed to it that excludes the common right of other men: for this *labour* being the unquestionable property of the labourer, no man but he can have a right to what that is once joined to, at least where there is enough, and as good, left in common for others.

28. He that is nourished by the acorns he picked up under an oak, or the apples he gathered from the trees in the wood, has certainly appropriated them to himself. Nobody can deny but the nourishment is his. I ask then, when did they begin to be his? When he digested? Or when he ate? Or when he boiled? Or when he brought them home? Or when he picked them up? And it is plain, if the first gathering made them not his, nothing else could. That *labour* put a distinction between them and common: that added something to them more than nature, the common mother of all, had done; and so they became his private right. And will anyone say, he had no right to those acorns or apples he thus appropriated because he had not the consent of all mankind to make them his? Was it a robbery thus to assume to himself what belonged to all in common? If such a consent as that was necessary, man had starved, notwithstanding the plenty God had given him. [. . .]

31. It will perhaps be objected to this that if gathering the acorns or other fruits of the earth, etc. makes a right to them, then anyone may *engross* as much as he will. To which I answer, not so. The same law of nature that does by this means give us property does also *bound* that *property* too. God *has given us all things richly* (1 Tim. vi. 12) is the voice of reason confirmed by inspiration. But how far has he given it us? *To enjoy*. As much as anyone can make use of to any advantage of life before it spoils, so much he may by his labour fix a property in: whatever is beyond this is more than his share and belongs to others. Nothing was made by God for

man to spoil or destroy. And thus, considering the plenty of natural provisions there was a long time in the world and the few spenders, and to how small a part of that provision the industry of one man could extend itself and engross it to the prejudice of others, especially keeping within the *bounds* set by reason of what might serve for his *use*, there could be then little room for quarrels or contentions about property so established.

32. But the *chief matter of property* being now not the fruits of the earth and the beasts that subsist on it but *the earth itself*, as that which takes in and carries with it all the rest, I think it is plain that *property* in that too is acquired as the former. *As much land* as a man tills, plants, improves, cultivates, and can use the product of, so much is his *property*. He by his labour does, as it were, enclose it from the common. Nor will it invalidate his right to say everybody else has an equal title to it, and therefore he cannot appropriate, he cannot enclose, without the consent of all his fellow-commoners, all mankind. God, when he gave the world in common to all mankind, commanded man also to labour, and the penury of his condition required it of him. God and his reason commanded him to subdue the earth, i.e., improve it for the benefit of life, and therein lay out something upon it that was his own, his labour. He that in obedience to this command of God, subdued, tilled, and sowed any part of it thereby annexed to it something that was his *property*, which another had no title to, nor could without injury take from him.

33. Nor was this *appropriation* of any parcel of *land* by improving it any prejudice to any other man since there was still enough and as good left, and more than the yet unprovided could use. So that, in effect, there was never the less left for others because of his enclosure for himself: for he that leaves as much as another can make use of does as good as take nothing at all. Nobody could think himself injured by the drinking of another man, though he took a good draught, who had a whole river of the same water left him to quench his thirst: and the case of land and water, where there is enough of both, is perfectly the same.

37. This is certain, that in the beginning, before the desire of having more than man needed had

altered the intrinsic value of things, which depends only on their usefulness to the life of man; or had *agreed that a little piece of yellow metal*, which would keep without wasting or decay, should be worth a great piece of flesh or a whole heap of corn, though men had a right to appropriate by their labour, each one of himself, as much of the things of nature as he could use: yet this could not be much, nor to the prejudice of others, where the same plenty was still left to those who would use the same industry. To which let me add that he who appropriates land to himself by his labour does not lessen but increase the common stock of mankind: for the provisions serving to the support of human life produced by 1 acre of enclosed and cultivated land are (to speak much within compass) 10 times more than those which are yielded by an acre of land of an equal richness lying waste in common. And therefore he that encloses land and has a greater plenty of the conveniences of life from 10 acres than he could have from 100 left to nature may truly be said to give 90 acres to mankind: for his labour now supplies him with provisions out of 10 acres which were but the product of a hundred lying in common. I have here rated the improved land very low in making its product but as 10 to 1 when it is much nearer 100 to 1: for I ask, whether in the wild woods and uncultivated waste of *America*, left to nature, without any improvement, tillage, or husbandry, a thousand acres yield the needy and wretched inhabitants as many conveniences of life as ten acres of equally fertile land do in *Devonshire* where they are well cultivated? [. . .]

46. The greatest part of *things really useful* to the life of man, and such as the necessity of subsisting made the first commoners of the world look after as it doth the *Americans* now, *are* generally things of *short duration*—such as, if they are not consumed by use, will decay and perish of themselves: gold, silver, and diamonds are things that fancy or agreement hath put the value on, more than real use and the necessary support of life. Now of those good things which nature hath provided in common, everyone had a right (as hath been said) to as much as he could use, and *property* in all that he could effect

with his labour; all that his *industry* could extend to, to alter from the state nature had put it in, was his. He that *gathered* 100 bushels of acorns or apples had thereby a *property* in them; they were his goods as soon as gathered. He was only to look that he used them before they spoiled, else he took more than his share, and robbed others. And indeed it was a foolish thing, as well as dishonest, to hoard up more than he could make use of. If he gave away a part to anybody else so that it perished not uselessly in his possession, these he also made use of. And if he also bartered away plums that would have rotted in a week for nuts that would last good for his eating a whole year, he did no injury; he wasted not the common stock, destroyed no part of the portion of goods that belonged to others, so long as nothing perished uselessly in his hands. Again, if he would give his nuts for a piece of metal, pleased with its colour, or exchange his sheep for shells or wool for a sparkling pebble or a diamond, and keep those by him all his life, he invaded not the right of others. He might heap up as much of these durable things as he pleased, the *exceeding of the bounds of* his *just property* not lying in the largeness of his possession but the perishing of anything uselessly in it.

47. And thus *came in the use of money*, some lasting thing that men might keep without spoiling, and that by mutual consent men would take in exchange for the truly useful, but perishable supports of life.

48. And as different degrees of industry were apt to give men possessions in different proportions, so this *invention of money* gave them the opportunity to continue and enlarge them: for supposing an island, separate from all possible commerce with the rest of the world, wherein there were but a hundred families, but there were sheep, horses, and cows with other useful animals, wholesome fruits, and land enough for corn for a hundred thousand times as many, but nothing in the island, either because of its commonness or perishableness, fit to supply the place of *money*, what reason could anyone have there to enlarge his possessions beyond the use of his family and a plentiful supply to its *consumption*, either in what their own industry produced or they could barter for like perishable, useful commodities

with others? Where there is not something, both lasting and scarce, and so valuable to be hoarded up, there men will not be apt to enlarge their *possessions of land*, were it never so rich, never so free for them to take: for I ask, what would a man value 10,000 or 100,000 acres of excellent *land*, ready cultivated and well stocked too with cattle, in the middle of the inland parts of *America*, where he had no hopes of commerce with other parts of the world to draw money to him by the sale of the product? It would not be worth the enclosing, and we should see him give up again to the wild common of nature whatever was more than would supply the conveniences of life to be had there for him and his family.

49. Thus in the beginning all the world was *America*, and more so than that is now; for no such thing as *money* was anywhere known. Find out something that hath the *use and value of money* amongst his neighbours, you shall see the same man will begin presently to enlarge his possessions. [. . .]

## Of the Beginning of Political Societies [Ch. 8]

95. Men being, as has been said, by nature, all free, equal, and independent, no one can be put out of this estate and subjected to the political power of another without his own consent. The only way whereby anyone divests himself of his natural liberty and puts on the *bonds of civil society* is by agreeing with other men to join and unite into a community for their comfortable, safe, and peaceable living one amongst another, in a secure enjoyment of their properties and a greater security against any that are not of it. This any number of men may do because it injures not the freedom of the rest; they are left as they were in the liberty of the state of nature. When any number of men have so *consented to make one community or government*, they are thereby presently incorporated and make *one body politic*, wherein the *majority* have a right to act and conclude the rest.

96. For when any number of men have by the consent of every individual made a *community*, they have thereby made that *community* one body, with a power to act as one body, which is only by the will and determination of the *majority*: for that which acts any community, being only the consent of the individuals of it, and it being necessary to that which is one body to move one way, it is necessary the body should move that way whither the greater force carries it, which is the *consent of the majority*: or else it is impossible it should act or continue one body, *one community*, which the consent of every individual that united into it agreed that it should; and so everyone is bound by that consent to be concluded by the *majority*. And therefore we see that in assemblies empowered to act by positive laws, where no number is set by that positive law which empowers them, the *act of the majority* passes for the act of the whole.

97. And thus every man, by consenting with others to make one body politic under one government, puts himself under an obligation to everyone of that society to submit to the determination of the *majority* and to be concluded by it; or else this *original compact*, whereby he with others incorporates into *one society*, would signify nothing, and be no compact, if he be left free and under no other ties than he was in before in the state of nature. For what appearance would there be of any compact? What new engagement if he were no farther tied by any decrees of the society than he himself thought fit and did actually consent to? This would be still as great a liberty as he himself had before his compact, or anyone else in the state of nature hath who may submit himself and consent to any acts of it if he thinks fit.

98. For if *the consent of the majority* shall not, in reason, be received as *the act of the whole* and conclude every individual, nothing but the consent of every individual can make anything to be the act of the whole: but such a consent is next to impossible ever to be had if we consider the infirmities of health and avocations of business, which in a number, though much less than that of a commonwealth, will necessarily keep many away from the public assembly. To which if we add the variety of opinions and contrariety of interests, which unavoidably happen in all collections of men, the

coming into society upon such terms would be only like *Cato's* coming into the theatre, only to go out again. Such a constitution as this would make the mighty *Leviathan* of a shorter duration than the feeblest creatures, and not let it outlast the day it was born in: which cannot be supposed till we can think that rational creatures should desire and constitute societies only to be dissolved: for where the *majority* cannot conclude the rest, there they cannot act as one body, and consequently will be immediately dissolved again.

99. Whosoever therefore out of a state of nature unite into a *community* must be understood to give up all the power necessary to the ends for which they unite into society to the *majority* of the community, unless they expressly agreed in any number greater than the majority. And this is done by barely agreeing to *unite into one political society*, which is *all the compact* that is, or needs be, between the individuals that enter into or make up a *commonwealth*. And thus that which begins and actually *constitutes any political society* is nothing but the consent of any number of freemen capable of a majority to unite and incorporate into such a society. And this is that, and that only, which did or could give beginning to any *lawful government* in the world. [. . .]

## Of the Ends of Political Society and Government [Ch. 9]

123. If man in the state of nature be so free, as has been said; if he be absolute lord of his own person and possessions, equal to the greatest and subject to nobody, why will he part with his freedom? Why will he give up this empire and subject himself to the dominion and control of any other power? To which it is obvious to answer that though in the state of nature he hath such a right, yet the enjoyment of it is very uncertain and constantly exposed to the invasion of others: for all being kings as much as he, every man his equal, and the greater part no strict observers of equity and justice, the enjoyment of the property he has in this state is very unsafe, very unsecure. This makes him willing to quit a condition, which, however free, is full of fears and continual dangers: and it is not without reason that he seeks out and is willing to join in society with others who are already united, or have a mind to unite, for the mutual *preservation* of their lives, liberties, and estates, which I call by the general name, *property*.

124. The great and *chief end*, therefore, of men's uniting into commonwealths and putting themselves under government is *the preservation of their property*. To which in the state of nature there are many things wanting.

*First*, there wants an *established*, settled, known *law*, received and allowed by common consent to be the standard of right and wrong, and the common measure to decide all controversies between them: for though the law of nature be plain and intelligible to all rational creatures; yet men being biased by their interest, as well as ignorant for want of study of it, are not apt to allow of it as a law binding to them in the application of it to their particular cases.

125. *Secondly*, in the state of nature there wants *a known and indifferent judge* with authority to determine all differences according to the established law: for everyone in that state being both judge and executioner of the law of nature, men being partial to themselves, passion and revenge is very apt to carry them too far and with too much heat in their own cases, as well as negligence and unconcernedness to make them too remiss in other men's.

126. *Thirdly*, in the state of nature there often wants *power* to back and support the sentence when right and to *give* it due *execution*. They who by any injustice offended will seldom fail, where they are able, by force to make good their injustice; such resistance many times makes the punishment dangerous and frequently destructive to those who attempt it.

127. Thus mankind, notwithstanding all the privileges of the state of nature, being but in an ill condition while they remain in it, are quickly driven into society. Hence it comes to pass that we seldom find any number of men live any time together in this state. The inconveniences that they are therein exposed to by the irregular and uncertain exercise

of the power every man has of punishing the transgressions of others make them take sanctuary under the established laws of government, and therein seek *the preservation of their property*. It is this makes them so willingly give up every one his single power of punishing, to be exercised by such alone as shall be appointed to it among them, and by such rules as the community, or those authorized by them to that purpose, shall agree on. And in this we have the original right and rise of both the legislative and executive power, as well as of the governments and societies themselves. [. . .]

## Study Questions

1. Locke provides us with an account of how private property arises, without mutual consent, even though "the creator" gave "mankind" the earth in common. Outline Locke's account by making reference to both the land and the land's provisions. How does this account underwrite capitalist democracy?

2. Did Locke believe that Aboriginal peoples in the Americas were living in the state of nature or political societies? In what ways does Locke's account of property serve to justify the taking of Aboriginal lands by English (and other European) colonists?

3. According to Locke, when individuals leave the state of nature to unite into civil society, they give power up to the majority of the community. What reasons does he use to justify majority rule?

4. Locke tells us that the legislative and executive functions of government have their foundations in powers that, in the state of nature, belong to everyone. Explain what each of these powers is, and provide an example. What motivates people to accept limits on their enjoyment of these powers when they leave the state of nature to enter civil society?

---

# John Stuart Mill

---

John Stuart Mill (1806–73) had a career in public service, from 1823 to 1858, as an administrator at the East India Company, and from 1865 to 1868, as Liberal MP for Westminster. As an MP, Mill sought to extend suffrage to women as well as working-class men, advocated proportional representation, opposed voting by ballot, criticized the brutal military suppression of Jamaica's 1865 Morant Bay Rebellion, supported habeas corpus in Ireland, and favoured capital punishment. *On Liberty* (1859), Mill's most famous work in political philosophy, defends civil liberties, while *Considerations on Representative Government* (1861) defends that form of rule.

## From *Considerations on Representative Government*

### 1. That the Ideally Best Form of Government Is Representative Government [Ch. 3]

[. . .] [I]t is evident that the only government which can fully satisfy all the exigencies of the social state is one in which the whole people participate; that any participation, even in the smallest public function, is useful; that the participation should everywhere be as great as the general degree of improvement of the community will allow; and that nothing less can be ultimately desirable than the admission of all to a share in the sovereign power of the State. But since all cannot in a community exceeding a single small town participate personally in any but some very minor portions of the public business, it follows that the ideal type of a perfect government must be representative. [. . .]

## 2. Of True and False Democracy; Representation of All, and Representation of the Majority Only [Ch. 7]

It has been seen that the dangers incident to a representative democracy are of two kinds: danger of a low grade of intelligence in the representative body, and in the popular opinion which controls it; and danger of class legislation on the part of the numerical majority, these being all composed of the same class. We have next to consider how far it is possible so to organize the democracy as, without interfering materially with the characteristic benefits of democratic government, to do away with these two great evils, or at least to abate them in the utmost degree attainable by human contrivance.

The common mode of attempting this is by limiting the democratic character of the representation through a more or less restricted suffrage. But there is a previous consideration which, duly kept in view, considerably modifies the circumstances which are supposed to render such a restriction necessary. A completely equal democracy in a nation in which a single class composes the numerical majority cannot be divested of certain evils; but those evils are greatly aggravated by the fact that the democracies which at present exist are not equal but systematically unequal in favour of the predominant class. Two very different ideas are usually confounded under the name democracy. The pure idea of democracy, according to its definition, is the government of the whole people by the whole people, equally represented. Democracy as commonly conceived and hitherto practised is the government of the whole people by a mere majority of the people, exclusively represented. The former is synonymous with the equality of all citizens; the latter, strangely confounded with it, is a government of privilege, in favour of the numerical majority, who alone possess practically any voice in the State.

This is the inevitable consequence of the manner in which the votes are now taken, to the complete disfranchisement of minorities.

The confusion of ideas here is great, but it is so easily cleared up that one would suppose the slightest indication would be sufficient to place the matter in its true light before any mind of average intelligence. It would be so, but for the power of habit—owing to which the simplest idea, if unfamiliar, has as great difficulty in making its way to the mind as a far more complicated one. That the minority must yield to the majority, the smaller number to the greater, is a familiar idea; and accordingly men think there is no necessity for using their minds any further, and it does not occur to them that there is any medium between allowing the smaller number to be equally powerful with the greater and blotting out the smaller number altogether. In a representative body actually deliberating, the minority must of course be overruled; and in an equal democracy (since the opinions of the constituents, when they insist on them, determine those of the representative body) the majority of the people, through their representatives, will outvote and prevail over the minority and their representatives. But does it follow that the minority should have no representatives at all? Because the majority ought to prevail over the minority, must the majority have all the votes, the minority none? Is it necessary that the minority should not even be heard? Nothing but habit and old association can reconcile any reasonable being to the needless injustice. In a really equal democracy, every or any section would be represented, not disproportionately, but proportionately. A majority of the electors would always have a majority of the representatives; but a minority of the electors would always have a minority of the representatives. Man for man they would be as fully represented as the majority. Unless they are, there is not equal government, but a government of inequality and privilege: one part of the people rule over the rest; there is a part whose fair and equal share of influence in the representation is withheld from them—contrary to all just government, but, above all, contrary to the principle of democracy, which professes equality as its very root and foundation.

The injustice and violation of principle are not less flagrant because those who suffer by them are a minority; for there is not equal suffrage where every single individual does not count for as much as any other single individual in the community. But it is not only a minority who suffer. Democracy, thus constituted, does not even attain its ostensible object, that of giving the powers of government in all cases to the numerical majority. It does something very different: it gives them to a majority of the majority—who may be, and often are, but a minority of the whole. All principles are most effectually tested by extreme cases. Suppose then, that in a country governed by equal and universal suffrage, there is a contested election in every constituency, and every election is carried by a small majority. The Parliament thus brought together represents little more than a bare majority of the people. This Parliament proceeds to legislate, and adopts important measures by a bare majority of itself. What guarantee is there that these measures accord with the wishes of a majority of the people? Nearly half the electors, having been outvoted at the hustings, have had no influence at all in the decision; and the whole of these may be, a majority of them probably are, hostile to the measures, having voted against those by whom they have been carried. Of the remaining electors, nearly half have chosen representatives who, by supposition, have voted against the measures. It is possible, therefore, and not at all improbable, that the opinion which has prevailed was agreeable only to a minority of the nation, though a majority of that portion of it whom the institutions of the country have erected into a ruling class. If democracy means the certain ascendancy of the majority, there are no means of ensuring that but by allowing every individual figure to tell equally in the summing up. Any minority left out, either purposely or by the play of the machinery, gives the power not to the majority, but to a minority in some other part of the scale.

The only answer which can possibly be made to this reasoning is that as different opinions predominate in different localities, the opinion which is in a minority in some places has a majority in others, and on the whole every opinion which exists in the constituencies obtains its fair share of voices in the representation. And this is roughly true in the present state of the constituency; if it were not, the discordance of the House with the general sentiment of the country would soon become evident. But it would be no longer true if the present constituency were much enlarged; still less, if made co-extensive with the whole population; for in that case the majority in every locality would consist of manual labourers; and when there was any question pending, on which these classes were at issue with the rest of the community, no other class could succeed in getting represented anywhere. [. . .]

## 3. Of the Extension of the Suffrage [Ch. 8]

Democracy is not the ideally best form of government unless this weak side of it can be strengthened; unless it can be so organized that no class, not even the most numerous, shall be able to reduce all but itself to political insignificance, and direct the course of legislation and administration by its exclusive class interest. The problem is to find the means of preventing this abuse without sacrificing the characteristic advantages of popular government.

These twofold requisites are not fulfilled by the expedient of a limitation of the suffrage, involving the compulsory exclusion of any portion of the citizens from a voice in the representation. Among the foremost benefits of free government is that education of the intelligence and of the sentiments which is carried down to the very lowest ranks of the people when they are called to take a part in acts which directly affect the great interests of their country. [. . .] People think it fanciful to expect so much from what seems so slight a cause—to recognize a potent instrument of mental improvement in the exercise of political franchises by manual labourers. Yet, unless substantial mental cultivation in the mass of mankind is to be a mere vision, this is the road by which it must come. [. . .] It is by political discussion that the manual labourer, whose employment is a routine and whose way of life brings him in contact with no variety of impressions, circumstances, or ideas, is taught that remote causes and events which take place far off have a most sensible effect even on his personal interests; and it is from political discussion and collective political action that one whose daily occupations concentrate his interests in a small circle round himself learns to feel for and with his fellow-citizens, and becomes consciously a member of a great community. But political discussions fly over the heads of those who have no votes and are not endeavouring to acquire them. Their position, in comparison with the electors, is that of the audience in a court of justice, compared with the 12 men in the jury-box. [. . .]

Independently of all these considerations, it is a personal injustice to withhold from anyone, unless for the prevention of greater evils, the ordinary privilege of having his voice reckoned in the disposal of affairs in which he has the same interest as other people. If he is compelled to pay, if he may be compelled to fight, if he is required implicitly to obey, he should be legally entitled to be told what for; to have his consent asked and his opinion counted at its worth, though not at more than its worth. There ought to be no pariahs in a full-grown and civilized nation, no persons disqualified except through their own default. [. . .] No arrangement of the suffrage [. . .] can be permanently satisfactory in which any person or class is peremptorily excluded, in which the electoral privilege is not open to all persons of full age who desire to obtain it.

There are, however, certain exclusions, required by positive reasons, which do not conflict with this principle, and which, though an evil in themselves, are only to be got rid of by the cessation of the state of things which requires them. I regard it as wholly inadmissible that any person should participate in the suffrage without being able to read, write, and, I will add, perform the common operations of arithmetic. Justice demands, even when the suffrage does not depend on it, that the means of attaining these elementary acquirements should be within the reach of every person, either gratuitously or at an expense not exceeding what the poorest who earn their own living can afford. If this were really the case, people would no more think of giving the suffrage to a man who could not read than of giving it to a child who could not speak; and it would not be society that would exclude him, but his own laziness. When society has not performed its duty by rendering this amount of instruction accessible to all, there is some hardship in the case, but it is a hardship that ought to be borne. If society has neglected to discharge two solemn obligations, the more important and more fundamental of the two must be fulfilled first: universal teaching must precede universal enfranchisement. No one but those in whom an a priori theory has silenced common sense will maintain that power over others, over the whole community, should be imparted to people who have not acquired the commonest and most essential requisites for taking care of themselves, for pursuing intelligently their own interests and those of the persons most nearly allied to them. [. . .]

It is also important that the assembly which votes the taxes, either general or local, should be elected exclusively by those who pay something towards the taxes imposed. Those who pay no taxes, disposing by their votes of other people's money, have every motive to be lavish and none to economize. As far as money matters are concerned, any power of voting possessed by them is a violation of the fundamental principle of free government, a severance of the power of control from the interest in its beneficial exercise. It amounts to allowing them to put their hands into other people's pockets for any purpose which they think fit to call a public one [. . .]. That representation should be co-extensive with taxation, not stopping short of it but also not going beyond it, is in accordance with the theory of British institutions. But to reconcile this as a condition annexed to the representation with universality, it is essential, as it is on many other accounts desirable, that taxation in a visible shape should descend to the poorest class. In this country and in most others, there is probably no labouring family which does not contribute to the indirect taxes by the purchase of tea, coffee, sugar, not to mention narcotics or stimulants. But this mode of defraying a share of the public expenses is hardly felt [. . .]. It would be better that a direct tax in the simple form of a capitation should be levied on every grown person in the community; or that every such person should be admitted an elector on allowing himself to be rated *extra ordinem* to the assessed taxes; or that a small annual payment, rising and falling with the gross expenditure of the country, should be required from every registered elector—that so everyone might feel that the money which he assisted in voting was partly his own, and that he was interested in keeping down its amount.

However this may be, I regard it as required by first principles that the receipt of parish relief should be a peremptory disqualification for the franchise. He who cannot by his labour suffice for his own support has no claim to the privilege of helping himself to the money of others. By becoming dependent on the remaining members of the community for actual subsistence, he abdicates his claim to equal rights with them in other respects. Those to whom he is indebted for the continuance of his very existence may justly claim the exclusive management of those common concerns to which he now brings nothing, or less than he takes away. As a condition of the franchise, a term should be fixed, say five years previous to the registry, during which the applicant's name has not been on the parish books as a recipient of relief. To be an uncertified bankrupt or to have taken the benefit of the Insolvent Act should disqualify for the franchise until the person has paid his debts [. . .]. Non-payment of taxes, when so long persisted in that it cannot have arisen from inadvertence, should disqualify while it lasts. These exclusions are not in their nature permanent. They exact such conditions only as all are able, or ought to be able, to fulfil if they choose. [. . .]

In the long run, therefore (supposing no restrictions to exist but those of which we have now treated), we might expect that all except that (it is to be hoped) progressively diminishing class, the recipients of parish relief, would be in possession of votes, so that the suffrage would be, with that slight abatement, universal. That it should be thus widely expanded is, as we have seen, absolutely necessary to an enlarged and elevated conception of good government. Yet in this state of things, the great majority of voters in most countries, and emphatically in this, would be manual labourers; and the twofold danger, that of too low a standard of political intelligence and that of class legislation, would still exist in a very perilous degree. It remains to be seen whether any means exist by which these evils can be obviated.

They are capable of being obviated if men sincerely wish it, not by any artificial contrivance but by carrying out the natural order of human life which recommends itself to everyone in things in which he has no interest or traditional opinion running counter to it. In all human affairs, every person directly interested and not under positive tutelage has an admitted claim to a voice, and when his exercise of it is not inconsistent with the safety of the whole cannot justly be excluded from it. But though everyone ought to have a voice—that everyone should have an equal voice is a totally different proposition. When two persons who have a joint interest in any business differ in opinion, does justice require that both opinions should be held of exactly equal value? If, with equal virtue, one is superior to the other in knowledge and intelligence— or if, with equal intelligence, one excels the other in virtue—the opinion, the judgment, of the higher moral or intellectual being is worth more than that of the inferior: and if the institutions of the country virtually assert that they are of the same value, they assert a thing which is not. [. . .]

Now, national affairs are exactly such a joint concern, with the difference that no one needs ever be called upon for a complete sacrifice of his own opinion. It can always be taken into the calculation and counted at a certain figure, a higher figure being assigned to the suffrages of those whose opinion is entitled to greater weight. There is not, in this arrangement, anything necessarily invidious to those to whom it assigns the lower degrees of influence.

Entire exclusion from a voice in the common concerns is one thing: the concession to others of a more potential voice, on the ground of greater capacity for the management of the joint interests, is another. The two things are not merely different, they are incommensurable. Everyone has a right to feel insulted by being made a nobody and stamped as of no account at all. No one but a fool, and only a fool of a peculiar description, feels offended by the acknowledgment that there are others whose opinion, and even whose wish, is entitled to a greater amount of consideration than his. To have no voice in what are partly his own concerns is a thing which nobody willingly submits to; but when what is partly his concern is also partly another's, and he feels the other to understand the subject better than himself, that the other's opinion should be counted for more than his own accords with his expectations, and with the course of things which in all other affairs of life he is accustomed to acquiesce in. It is only necessary that his superior influence should be assigned on grounds which he can comprehend, and of which he is able to perceive the justice.

I hasten to say that I consider it entirely inadmissible, unless as a temporary makeshift, that the superiority of influence should be conferred in consideration of property. I do not deny that property is a kind of test; education in most countries, though anything but proportional to riches, is on the average better in the richer half of society than in the poorer. But the criterion is so imperfect; accident has so much more to do than merit with enabling men to rise in the world; and it is so impossible for anyone, by acquiring any amount of instruction, to make sure of the corresponding rise in station, that this foundation of electoral privilege is always, and will continue to be, supremely odious. To connect plurality of votes with any pecuniary qualification would be not only objectionable in itself but a sure mode of discrediting the principle and making its permanent maintenance impracticable. The Democracy, at least of this country, are not at present jealous of personal superiority, but they are naturally and most justly so of that which is grounded on mere pecuniary circumstances. The only thing

which can justify reckoning one person's opinion as equivalent to more than one is individual mental superiority; and what is wanted is some approximate means of ascertaining that. If there existed such a thing as a really national education or a trustworthy system of general examination, education might be tested directly. In the absence of these, the nature of a person's occupation is some test. An employer of labour is on the average more intelligent than a labourer, for he must labour with his head and not solely with his hands. A foreman is generally more intelligent than an ordinary labourer, and a labourer in the skilled trades than in the unskilled. A banker, merchant, or manufacturer is likely to be more intelligent than a tradesman because he has larger and more complicated interests to manage. In all these cases it is not the having merely undertaken the superior function but the successful performance of it that tests the qualifications, for which reason, as well as to prevent persons from engaging nominally in an occupation for the sake of the vote, it would be proper to require that the occupation should have been persevered in for some length of time (say three years). Subject to some such condition, two or more votes might be allowed to every person who exercises any of these superior functions. The liberal professions, when really and not nominally practised, imply, of course, a still higher degree of instruction; and wherever a sufficient examination or any serious conditions of education are required before entering on a profession, its members could be admitted at once to a plurality of votes. The same rule might be applied to graduates of universities, and even to those who bring satisfactory certificates of having passed through the course of study required by any school at which the higher branches of knowledge are taught, under proper securities that the teaching is real and not a mere pretence. The "local" or "middle class" examination for the degree of Associate, so laudably and public-spiritedly established by the Universities of Oxford and Cambridge, and any similar ones which may be instituted by other competent bodies (provided they are fairly open to all comers), afford a ground on which plurality of votes might with great advantage be accorded to those who have passed the test. All these suggestions are open to much discussion in the detail and to objections which it is of no use to anticipate. The time is not come for giving to such plans a practical shape, nor should I wish to be bound by the particular proposals which I have made. But it is to me evident that in this direction lies the true ideal of representative government and that to work towards it, by the best practical contrivances which can be found, is the path of real political improvement. [. . .]

In the preceding argument for universal, but graduated suffrage, I have taken no account of difference of sex. I consider it to be as entirely irrelevant to political rights as difference in height or in the colour of the hair. All human beings have the same interest in good government; the welfare of all is alike affected by it, and they have equal need of a voice in it to secure their share of its benefits. If there be any difference, women require it more than men, since, being physically weaker, they are more dependent on law and society for protection. Mankind have long since abandoned the only premises which will support the conclusion that women ought not to have votes. No one now holds that women should be in personal servitude; that they should have no thought, wish, or occupation but to be the domestic drudge of husbands, fathers, or brothers. It is allowed to unmarried, and wants but little of being conceded to married women, to hold property and have pecuniary and business interests in the same manner as men. It is considered suitable and proper that women should think, and write, and be teachers. As soon as these things are admitted, the political disqualification has no principle to rest on. The whole mode of thought of the modern world is with increasing emphasis pronouncing against the claim of society to decide for individuals what they are and are not fit for, and what they shall and shall not be allowed to attempt. [. . .]

But it is not even necessary to maintain so much in order to prove that women should have the suffrage. Were it as right, as it is wrong, that they should be a subordinate class, confined to domestic occupations and subject to domestic authority,

they would not the less require the protection of the suffrage to secure them from the abuse of that authority. Men, as well as women, do not need political rights in order that they may govern, but in order that they may not be misgoverned. The majority of the male sex are, and will be all their lives, nothing else than labourers in cornfields or manufactories; but this does not render the suffrage less desirable for them, nor their claim to it less irresistible, when not likely to make a bad use of it. Nobody pretends to think that woman would make a bad use of the suffrage. The worst that is said is that they would vote as mere dependents, at the bidding of their male relations. If it be so, so let it be. If they think for themselves, great good will be done, and if they do not, no harm. It is a benefit to human beings to take off their fetters even if they do not desire to walk. It would already be a great improvement in the moral position of women to be no longer declared by law incapable of an opinion, and not entitled to a preference, respecting the most important concerns of humanity.

## 4. Of the Government of Dependencies by a Free State [Ch. 18]

Free states, like all others, may possess dependencies, acquired either by conquest or by colonization, and our own is the greatest instance of the kind in modern history. It is a most important question how such dependencies ought to be governed.

It is unnecessary to discuss the case of small posts, like Gibraltar, Aden, or Heligoland, which are held only as naval or military positions. The military or naval object is in this case paramount, and the inhabitants cannot, consistently with it, be admitted to the government of the place, though they ought to be allowed all liberties and privileges compatible with that restriction, including the free management of municipal affairs, and, as a compensation for being locally sacrificed to the convenience of the governing state, should be admitted to equal rights with its native subjects in all other parts of the empire.

Outlying territories of some size and population, which are held as dependencies, that is, which are subject, more or less, to acts of sovereign power on the part of the paramount country, without being equally represented (if represented at all) in its legislature, may be divided into two classes. Some are composed of people of similar civilization to the ruling country, capable of, and ripe for, representative government, such as the British possessions in America and Australia. Others, like India, are still at a great distance from that state. [. . .]

It is now a fixed principle of the policy of Great Britain, professed in theory and faithfully adhered to in practice, that her colonies of European race, equally with the parent country, possess the fullest measure of internal self-government. They have been allowed to make their own free representative constitutions by altering in any manner they thought fit the already very popular constitutions which we had given them. Each is governed by its own legislature and executive, constituted on highly democratic principles. The veto of the Crown and of Parliament, though nominally reserved, is only exercised (and that very rarely) on questions which concern the empire, and not solely the particular colony. How liberal a construction has been given to the distinction between imperial and colonial questions is shown by the fact that the whole of the unappropriated lands in the regions behind our American and Australian colonies have been given up to the uncontrolled disposal of the colonial communities, though they might, without injustice, have been kept in the hands of the imperial government, to be administered for the greatest advantage of future emigrants from all parts of the empire. Every colony has thus as full power over its own affairs as it could have if it were a member of even the loosest federation, and much fuller than would belong to it under the Constitution of the United States, being free even to tax at its pleasure the commodities imported from the mother country. Their union with Great Britain is the slightest kind of federal union, but not a strictly equal federation, the mother country retaining to itself the powers of a federal government, though reduced in practice to their very narrowest limits. This inequality is, of course, as far as it goes, a disadvantage to the dependencies, which have no voice in foreign policy,

but are bound by the decisions of the superior country. They are compelled to join England in war without being in any way consulted previous to engaging in it. [. . .]

Thus far of the dependencies whose population is in a sufficiently advanced state to be fitted for representative government; but there are others which have not attained that state, and which, if held at all, must be governed by the dominant country, or by persons delegated for that purpose by it. This mode of government is as legitimate as any other, if it is the one which in the existing state of civilization of the subject people most facilitates their transition to a higher stage of improvement. There are [. . .] conditions of society in which a vigorous despotism is in itself the best mode of government for training the people in what is specifically wanting to render them capable of a higher civilization. There are others, in which the mere fact of despotism has indeed no beneficial effect, the lessons which it teaches having already been only too completely learned, but in which, there being no spring of spontaneous improvement in the people themselves, their almost only hope of making any steps in advance depends on the chances of a good despot. Under a native despotism, a good despot is a rare and transitory accident; but when the dominion they are under is that of a more civilized people, that people ought to be able to supply it constantly. The ruling country ought to be able to do for its subjects all that could be done by a succession of absolute monarchs, guaranteed by irresistible force against the precariousness of tenure attendant on barbarous despotisms, and qualified by their genius to anticipate all that experience has taught to the more advanced nation. Such is the ideal rule of a free people over a barbarous or semi-barbarous one. We need not expect to see that ideal realized; but, unless some approach to it is, the rulers are guilty of a dereliction of the highest moral trust which can devolve upon a nation; and if they do not even aim at it, they are selfish usurpers, on a par in criminality with any of those whose ambition and rapacity have sported from age to age with the destiny of masses of mankind.

## Study Questions

1. Why does Mill favour representative government over direct democracy? What criticisms does Mill make of "democracy as commonly conceived and hitherto practised," and what "pure idea of democracy" does he promote instead?
2. What "two great evils" does Mill associate with representative democracy? How does Mill's proposal of a system of proportional representation serve to mitigate these "evils"? How does Mill's proposal of a system of a "plurality of votes" serve to mitigate these "evils"?
3. Why, despite his fears, does Mill favour extending suffrage? Mill's position nonetheless falls short of universal suffrage. What classes of people does he contend should not be allowed to vote, and why? Do you agree or disagree?
4. Compare Mill's views on the political rights of British women and Britain's colonial subjects, e.g., in Canada and India.

---

## Anne Phillips

---

Anne Phillips is a professor of political and gender theory at the London School of Economics. Phillips has a BSc from the University of Bristol, an MSc from the University of London, and a PhD from the City University London. She was elected a fellow of the British Academy in 2003. Phillips is a feminist political theorist whose research broadens contemporary liberal theory by attending to such issues as democracy and representation, equality, multiculturalism, and difference. The 1995 book excerpted here concerns the challenge within liberal democracy that demands by underrepresented groups for inclusion ("politics of presence") pose to the traditional view that only a diversity of opinions matters ("politics of ideas").

## Quotas for Women

From *The Politics of Presence*

### 1. Introduction

[. . .] Arguments for raising the proportion of women elected have fallen broadly into four groups. There are those that dwell on the role model successful women politicians offer; those that appeal to principles of justice between the sexes; those that identify particular interests of women that would be otherwise overlooked; and those that stress women's different relationship to politics and the way their presence will enhance the quality of political life. The least interesting of these, from my point of view, is the role model. When more women candidates are elected, their example is said to raise women's self-esteem, encourage others to follow in their footsteps, and dislodge deep-rooted assumptions about what is appropriate to women and men. I leave this to one side, for I see it as an argument that has no particular purchase on politics per se. Positive role models are certainly beneficial, but I want to address those arguments that engage more directly with democracy.

### 2. Argument from Justice

The most immediately compelling of the remaining arguments is that which presents gender parity as a straightforward matter of justice: that it is patently and grotesquely unfair for men to monopolize representation. If there were no obstacles operating to keep certain groups of people out of political life, we would expect positions of political influence to be randomly distributed between the sexes. There might be some minor and innocent deviations, but any more distorted distribution is evidence of intentional or structural discrimination. In such contexts (that is, most contexts) women are being denied rights and opportunities that are currently available to men. There is a prima facie [at first sight] case for action.

There are two things to be said about this. One is that it relies on a strong position on the current sexual division of labour as inequitable and "unnatural." Consider the parallel under-representation of the very young and very old in politics. Most people will accept this as part of a normal and natural life-cycle, in which the young have no time for conventional politics, and the old have already contributed their share; and since each in principle has a chance in the middle years of life, this under-representation does not strike us as particularly unfair. The consequent "exclusion" of certain views or experiences may be said to pose a problem; but, however much people worry about this, they rarely argue for proportionate representation for the over-seventies and the under-twenty-fives.[1] The situation of women looks more obviously unfair in that women will be under-represented throughout their entire lives, but anyone wedded to the current division of labour can treat it as a parallel case. A woman's life-cycle typically includes a lengthy period of caring for children, and another lengthy period of caring for parents as they grow old. It is hardly surprising, then, that fewer women come forward as candidates, or that so few women are elected. Here, too, there may be an under-representation of particular experiences and concerns, but, since this arises quite "naturally" from particular life-cycles, it is not at odds with equality or justice.

I do not find the parallel convincing, but my reasons lie in a feminist analysis of the sexual division of labour as "unnatural" and unjust. The general argument from equal rights or opportunities translates into a specific case for gender parity in politics only when it is combined with some such analysis; failing this, it engages merely with the more overt forms of discrimination that exclude particular aspirants from political office. Justice requires us to eliminate discrimination (this is already implied in the notion of justice), but the argument for women's equal representation in politics depends on that further ingredient which establishes structural discrimination. Feminists will have no difficulty adding this, and the first point then reinforces the general argument. The case for the proportionate representation of women and men is not something we can deduce from an impossibly abstract equation of fair representation with proportional representation, as if each and every characteristic can be mapped out in the legislative assemblies. Nor is it automatically mandated by the discovery that there are fewer women in politics than men. Something else has to be added before we can move from a description of women's under-representation to an analysis of its injustice.

The second point is more intrinsically problematic, and relates to the status of representation as a political act. If we treat the under-representation of women in politics as akin to their under-representation in management or the professions, we seem to treat being a politician as on a continuum with all those other careers that should be opened up equally to women. In each case, there is disturbing evidence of sexual inequality; in each case, there should be positive action for change. The argument appeals to our sense of justice, but it does so at the expense of an equally strong feeling that being a politician is not just another kind of job. "Career politician" is still (and surely rightly) a term of abuse; however accurately it may describe people's activities in politics, it does not capture our political ideals. If political office *has* been reduced to yet another favourable and privileged position, then there is a clear argument from justice for making such office equally available to women. Most democrats, however, will want to resist pressures to regard political office in this way. So, while men have no "right" to monopolize political office, there is something rather unsatisfying in basing women's claim to political equality on an equal right to an interesting job.

Reformulating the equal right to political office as an equal right to participate in politics makes it sound much better, but does not otherwise help. A rough equality in political participation has entered firmly enough into the understanding (if not yet the practice) of political equality for us to see an imbalance between the sexes as a legitimate cause for concern. Extending this, however, to the sphere of representation simply asserts what has to be established: that representation is just another aspect of participation, to be judged by identical criteria. The under-representation of women in elected assemblies is not simply analogous to their under-representation in the membership of political parties or the attendance at political meetings; for, while we can quite legitimately talk of an equal "right" to political participation, we cannot so readily talk of an equal "right" to be elected to political office. As has already been noted, the deduction from one to the other lays itself open to irritated complaints of missing what is new about representation.

What we can more usefully do is turn the argument around, and ask by what "natural" superiority of talent or experience men could claim a right to dominate assemblies? The burden of proof then shifts to the men, who would have to establish either some genetic distinction which makes them better at understanding problems and taking decisions, or some more socially derived advantage which enhances their political skills. Neither of these looks particularly persuasive; the first has never been successfully established, and the second is no justification if it depends on structures of discrimination. There is no argument from justice that can defend the current state of affairs; and in this more negative sense, there *is* an argument from justice for parity between women and men. The case then approximates that more general argument about symbolic representation, stressing the social significance that attaches to the composition of political élites, and the way that exclusion from these reinforces wider assumptions about the inferiority of particular groups. But there is a troubling sense in which this still overlooks what is peculiar to representation as a political act. When democracy has been widely understood as a matter of representing particular policies or programs or ideas, this leaves a question mark over why the sex of the representative should matter.

## 3. Argument from Women's Interests

An alternative way of arguing for gender parity is in terms of the interests that would be otherwise discounted. This is an argument from political realism. In the heterogeneous societies contained by the modern nation-state, there is no transparently obvious "public interest," but rather a multiplicity of different and potentially conflicting interests which must be acknowledged and held in check. Our political representatives are only human, and as such they cannot pretend to any greater generosity of spirit than those who elected them to office. There may be altruists among them, but it would be unwise to rely on this in framing our constitutional arrangements. Failing Plato's solution to the intrusion of private interest (a class of Guardians with no property or family of their own), we must look to other ways of limiting tyrannical tendencies, and most of these will involve giving all interests their legitimate voice.

This, in essence, was **James Mill**'s case for representative government and an extended franchise, though he notoriously combined this with the argument that women could "be struck off without inconvenience" from the list of potential claimants, because they had no interests not already included in those of their fathers or husbands. (He also thought we could strike off "young" men under forty years of age.) Part of the argument for increasing women's political representation is a feminist rewrite and extension of this. Women occupy a distinct position within society: they are typically contracted, for example, in lower paid jobs; and they carry the primary responsibility for the unpaid work of caring for others. There are particular needs, interests, and concerns that arise from women's experience, and these will be inadequately addressed in a politics that is dominated by men. Equal rights to a vote have not proved strong enough to deal with this problem; there must also be equality among those elected to office.

One point made by Will Kymlicka is that this argument may not be enough to justify parity of presence. In a recent discussion of demands for group representation in Canada, he makes a useful distinction between arguments for equal or proportionate presence (where the number of women or Aboriginal peoples or francophone Canadians in any legislative assembly would correspond to their proportion in the citizenry as a whole), and the case for a threshold presence (where the numbers would reach the requisite level that ensured each group's concerns were adequately addressed). When the group in question is a numerically small minority, the threshold might prove larger than their proportion in the population as a whole; when the group composes half the population, the threshold might be considerably lower. On this basis, there could be an argument for greater than proportionate representation of Aboriginal peoples, for example, but less than proportionate representation of women—not that women would be formally restricted to 25 per cent or 30 per cent of the seats, but that they might not require any more than this in order to change the political agenda. It is the argument from justice that most readily translates into strict notions of equality; the argument from women's interests need not deliver such strong results.

The above is a qualification rather than a counter-argument, and in principle it still confirms the legitimacy of political presence. A potentially more damaging argument comes from those who query whether women do have a distinct and separate interest, and whether "women" is a sufficiently unified category to generate an interest of its own. If women's interests differed systematically from men's (or if women always

thought differently on political issues), then the disproportionate number of men in politics would seem self-evidently wrong. The concerns of one group would get minimal consideration; the concerns of another would have excessive weight. But where is the evidence for this claim? Does not the notion of a distinct "women's interest" just dissolve upon closer attention?

The idea that women have at least some interests distinct from and even in conflict with men's is, I think, relatively straightforward. Women have distinct interests in relation to child-bearing (for any foreseeable future, an exclusively female affair); and as society is currently constituted they also have particular interests arising from their exposure to sexual harassment and violence, their unequal position in the division of paid and unpaid labour, and their exclusion from most arenas of economic or political power. But all this may still be said to fall short of establishing a set of interests shared by all women. If interests are understood in terms of what women express as their priorities and goals, there is considerable disagreement among women; and, while attitude surveys frequently expose a "gender gap" between women and men, the more striking development over recent decades has been the convergence in the voting behaviour of women and men. There may be more mileage in notions of a distinct woman's interest if this is understood in terms of some underlying but as yet unnoticed "reality," but this edges uncomfortably close to notions of "false consciousness," which most feminists would prefer to avoid. Indeed, the presumption of a clearly demarcated woman's interest which holds true for all women in all classes and all countries has been one of the casualties of recent feminist critique, and the exposure of multiple differences between women has undermined more global understandings of women's interests and concerns. If there is no clearly agreed woman's interest, can this really figure as a basis for more women in politics?

There are two things to be said about this. The first is that the variety of women's interests does not refute the claim that interests are gendered. That some women do not bear children does not make pregnancy a gender-neutral event; that women disagree so profoundly on abortion does not make its legal availability a matter of equal concern to both women and men; that women occupy such different positions in the occupational hierarchy does not mean they have the same interests as men in their class. The argument from interest does not depend on establishing a unified interest of all women: it depends, rather, on establishing a difference between the interests of women and men.

Some of the interests of women will, of course, overlap with the interests of certain groups of men. The fact that women are more likely to depend on public transport, for example, forges a potential alliance with those men who have campaigned for better public transport on social or environmental grounds; and the fact that women are more likely to press the interests of children does not mean that no man would share their concerns. In these instances, it may be said that the election of more female representatives will introduce a new range of issues—but that many of these will be ones that some men will be happy to endorse. In other instances, the differences are more inherently conflictual. Women's claim to equal pay must, logically, imply a relative worsening of male earnings; and outside extraordinary growth conditions, women's claim to equal employment opportunities must reduce some of the openings currently available to men. Women have no monopoly on generosity of spirit, and even in these more conflictual situations they can expect to find a few powerful allies among the men. What they cannot really expect is the degree of vigorous advocacy that people bring to their own concerns.

The second point is more complex, and arises with particular pertinence when a history of political exclusion has made it hard even to articulate group concerns. When Hanna Pitkin explored **Edmund Burke**'s rather odd understanding of representation, she noted that he conceived of interests as a matter of "objective, impersonal, unattached reality" (168); this then became the basis on which he argued for "virtual"

representation, by people not even chosen by the interested group. Burke certainly thought that all major interests should be duly represented, but the very objectivity of the interests allowed for their representation by people who did not immediately share them. The more fixed the interests, the more definite and easily defined, the less significance seemed to attach to who does the work of representation. So if women's interests had a more objective quality (and were transparently obvious to any intelligent observer) there might be no particular case—beyond what I have already argued about vigorous advocacy—for insisting on representatives who also happen to be women. We might feel that men would be less diligent in pressing women's interests and concerns, that their declared "sympathy" would always be suspect. But if we all knew what these interests were, it would be correspondingly easy to tell whether or not they were being adequately pursued.

Interest would then more obviously parallel political ideas or beliefs. It would become something we could detach from particular experience, as we already detach the "interest" of pensioners, or children, or the long-term unemployed. Each of these (perhaps particularly the example of children) is problematic, but in each of them we can more legitimately claim to know what is in a group's interest. Attention then shifts to more traditional ways of strengthening the weight attached to the interests, perhaps through writing them into party programs or party commitments. The alternative emphasis on changing the composition of decision-making assemblies is particularly compelling where interests are not so precisely delineated, where the political agenda has been constructed without reference to certain areas of concern, and where much fresh thinking is necessary to work out what best to do. In such contexts there is little to turn to other than the people who carry the interests, and who does the representation then comes to be of equal significance with what political parties they represent. [. . .]

The more decisive problem with the argument from interests lies in the conditions for accountability to the interested group. Does the election of more women ensure their representation? At an intuitive level, an increase in the number of women elected seems likely to change both the practices and priorities of politics, increasing the attention given to matters of child care, for example, or ensuring that women's poor position in the labour market is more vigorously addressed. This intuition is already partially confirmed by the experience of those countries that have changed the gender composition of their elected assemblies. But what does this mean in terms of political representation? Elections are typically organized by geographical constituencies, which sometimes coincide with concentrations of particular ethnic or religious groups, or concentrations of certain social classes, but which never coincide with concentrations of women or men. Elections typically take place through the medium of political parties, each of which produces candidates who are said to represent that party's policies and programs and goals. In what sense can we say that the women elected through this process carry an additional responsibility to represent women? In the absence of mechanisms to establish accountability the equation of more women with more adequate representation of women's interests looks suspiciously undemocratic. If the interests of women are varied, or not yet fully formed, how do the women elected know what the women who elected them want? By what right do they claim their responsibility to represent women's concerns? The asymmetry between noting a problem of exclusion and identifying the difference that inclusion brings about is particularly pointed here. However plausible it is to say that male-dominated assemblies will not adequately address the needs and interests of women, it cannot be claimed with equal confidence that a more balanced legislature will fill this gap.

## 4. Argument from Women's Needs

The third way of formulating the case for gender parity approaches it from almost the opposite direction. It sees the inclusion of women as challenging the dominance of interest group politics, and expects women politicians to introduce a different set of values and concerns. This is something that has had a long history in feminist thinking; for, while women have repeatedly complained that their interests were being ignored by the men, the very same women have often presented their sex as the one that disdains interest and transcends the limits of faction. In the campaign for women's suffrage, for example, it was often suggested that women would bring a more generous morality to the political field; in the recent development of eco-feminism, it is often argued that women have a deeper, because trans-generational, relationship to the needs of the environment.

In some formulations of this, feminists have made a strong distinction between interest and need, arguing that the emphasis on interests treats politics as a matter of brokerage between different groups, and that the equation of politics with the rational calculation of interests is at odds with women's own understanding of their needs and goals. As Irene Diamond and Nancy Hartsock put it, "The reduction of all human emotions to interests, and interests to the rational search for gain reduces the human community to an instrumental, arbitrary, and deeply unstable alliance, one which rests on the private desires of isolated individuals" (719). Need, by contrast, is thought to appeal to a more basic and common humanity; instead of asserting a stake in political battle, it formulates claims in more obviously moral terms.

This distinction engages directly with that common objection to a politics of presence which views it as increasing the role of interest in politics. When the demand for more women in politics is formulated in terms of interest, this seems to accept a version of politics as a matter of competition between interest groups; it talks the language of defence or protection, and treats politics as a zero-sum game. But when the demand is formulated in terms of need, this potentially raises things to a higher plain. The substitution of needs talk for interests talk may then offer a more radical challenge to the practices of contemporary democracy, querying the very nature of the game as well as the composition of the players.

My own position on this is somewhat agnostic. Interest can sound rather grasping and competitive, but it does at least serve to remind us that there may be conflicts between different groups. Need has more obvious moral resonance, but it originates from a paternalist discourse which lends itself more readily to decisions by experts on behalf of the needy group (Jonasdottir). My own rather commonsensical solution is to use both terms together. Note, however, that the opposition between need and interest does not substantially alter what is at issue in demands for more women in politics, for need is as contested as interest, and either requires a female presence. As Nancy Fraser has argued, the interpretation of needs is itself a matter of political struggle, spanning three crucial moments: the struggle to establish (or deny) the political status of a given need; the struggle for the power to define and interpret the need; and the struggle to secure its satisfaction. At each moment it matters immensely who can claim the authoritative interpretation; and, while much of the battle for this rages across the full terrain of civil society, groups excluded from state agencies or legislative assemblies will have significantly less chance of establishing their own preferred version. Neither needs nor interests can be conceived as transparently obvious, and any fair interpretation of either then implies the presence of the relevant group.

The broader claim made by those who disdain the politics of interest is that increasing the proportion of women elected introduces new kinds of behaviour and values. It is often suggested, for example, that women will be less competitive, more co-operative, more prepared to listen to others; that women bring with them a different, and more generous, scale of values; that women raise the moral tenor of politics. These arguments are always associated with women's role as caring for others, and often more specifically with their role as mothers [e.g., Ruddick, 1980]. [. . .]

My problem with such arguments is not that they presume a difference between men and women. As

Catherine MacKinnon puts it in a nicely pointed question, "I mean, can you imagine elevating one half of a population and denigrating the other half and producing a population in which everyone is the same?" (37). We do not have to resort to either mysticism or socio-biology to explain social differences between women and men, and it would be most peculiar if the different responsibilities the sexes carry for caring for others did not translate into different approaches to politics and power. These initial differences may be far outweighed by the common experiences men and women will later share in making their way through political life. I incline to the view that politics is more formative than sex, and that the contrast between those who get involved in politics and those who do not is deeper than any gender difference between those who are elected. But this remains at a more speculative level. The real problem with basing the case for more women in politics on their supposed superiority over men is that this loads too much on women's role as mothers.

As Mary Dietz, in particular, has argued, the characteristics that make a good mother are not necessarily those that make a good citizen, and the generous care women may give to their dependent children is hardly a paradigm for a democratic politics that should be based on equality and mutual respect. Nor is it particularly useful to present women as better or more moral than men. "Such a premise would posit as a starting point precisely what a democratic attitude must deny—that one group of citizens' voices is generally better, more deserving of attention, more worthy of emulation, more moral, than another's. A feminist democrat cannot give way to this sort of temptation, lest democracy itself lose its meaning, and citizenship its special name" (17–18).

Which is not to say that women will not, or should not, make a difference. In a recent study of Norwegian MPs, Hege Skjeie uncovered a remarkable consensus across the parties and between the sexes that gender does and should make a difference, with a clear majority thinking that gender affects priorities and interests, and that women represent a new "politics of care." Translated into areas of policy initiative, this generated a rather predictable list: politicians of both sexes saw women as particularly concerned with policies on welfare, the environment, equality, education, and disarmament, and men as more interested in the economy, industry, energy, national security, and foreign affairs. (Transport was the only area regarded as equally "male" and "female"—not because transport is intrinsically more gender-neutral, but because it has become important, for different reasons, to both women and men.) Against the background of a strong Norwegian tradition of social representation, which has long assumed that political representatives should "mirror" differences between town and country and balance territorial concerns (Valen), it has been seen as perfectly legitimate and desirable that women politicians should represent different concerns. Indeed, "[a] mandate of "difference" is now attached to women politicians. . . .. Women have entered politics on a collective mandate, and their performance is judged collectively" (Skjeie 234).

The precise implications of this remain, however, ambiguous. The widely presumed association between women and a politics of care leaves it open whether women will concentrate on policies to enhance child care provision, thereby to increase women's participation in the labour market, or on policies that will raise the value and prestige of the care work that women do in the home. What resolves this in the Norwegian context is not so much gender as party. Women associated with parties on the left of the political spectrum are more likely to interpret a politics of care in terms of the first set of priorities, while women associated with parties on the right will tend to the second interpretation. In this as in other policy areas, party loyalties are usually decisive, and, though Skjeie notes a number of cases of women forming cross-party alliances on particular issues, she finds little evidence of women refusing the ultimate priorities of their parties. "The belief in women's difference could still turn into a mere litany on the importance of difference. Repeated often enough, the statement

that "gender matters" may in turn convince the participants that change can in fact be achieved by no other contribution than the mere presence of women" (258).

## 5. Representation as a Process

This leads directly into the key area of contention, already signalled in my discussion of interest. Either gender does make a difference, in which case it is in tension with accountability through political parties, or it does not make a difference, in which case it can look a rather opportunistic way of enhancing the career prospects of women politicians. Aside from the symbolic importance of political inclusion, and women's equal right to have their chance at a political career (a fair enough argument, but not intrinsically about democracy), we can only believe that the sex of the representatives matters if we think it will change what the representatives do. Yet in saying this, we seem to be undermining accountability through party programs. We are saying we expect our representatives to do more—or other—than they promised in the election campaign. If we are either surprised or disappointed, for example, by the limited capacity to act on a cross-party basis, this must be because we see an increase in the number of women politicians as challenging the dominance of the party system, or the tradition of voting along party lines. Those who have felt that tight controls of party discipline have worked to discourage serious discussion and debate may be happy enough with this conclusion. But in the absence of alternative mechanisms of consultation or accountability, it does read like a recipe for letting representatives do what *they* choose to do.

Though it is rarely stated in the literature, the argument from women's interests or needs or difference implies that representatives will have considerable autonomy; that they do have currently; and, by implication, that this ought to continue. Women's exclusion from politics is said to matter precisely because politicians do not abide by pre-agreed policies and goals—and feminists have much experience of this, gained through painful years of watching hard-won commitments to sexual equality drop off the final agenda. When there is a significant under-representation of women at the point of final decision, this can and does have serious consequences, and it is partly in reflection on this that many have shifted attention from the details of policy commitments to the composition of the decision-making group. Past experience tells us that all male or mostly male assemblies have limited capacity for articulating either the interests or needs of women, and that trying to tie them down to pre-agreed programs has had only limited effect. There is a strong dose of political realism here. Representatives *do* have autonomy, which is why it matters who those representatives are.

This is a fair enough comment on politics as currently practised, and shifting the gender balance of legislatures then seems a sensible enough strategy for the enfeebled democracies of the present day. But one might still ask whether representatives *should* have such autonomy, and whether it would change the importance attached to gender composition if the politicians were more carefully bound by their party's commitments and goals. [. . .]

This points to a significant area of divergence between current feminist preoccupations and what has long been the main thrust in radical democracy. Radical democrats distrust the wayward autonomy of politicians and the way they concentrate power around them, and they typically work to combat these tendencies by measures that will bind politicians more tightly to their promises, and disperse over-centralized power. Feminists have usually joined forces in support of the second objective: feminism is widely associated with bringing politics closer to home; and women are often intensely involved in local and community affairs. But when feminists insist that the sex of the representatives matters, they are expressing a deeper ambivalence towards the first objective. The politics of binding mandates turns the representatives into glorified messengers: it puts all the emphasis on to the content of the messages, and makes it irrelevant who the messengers are. In contesting the sex of the representatives, feminists are querying this version of democratic accountability. [. . .]

Much more can (and in my view should) be done to keep representatives accountable to the programs on which they were elected to office, and to bind them more closely to what they professed as their political beliefs. But there is no combination of reforms that can deliver express and prior commitments on every issue that will come to matter, and it is in those spaces where we have to rely on representatives exercising their own judgment that it can most matter who the representatives are. Behind the deceptive simplicity of the arguments for gender parity is this alternative—and more contested—understanding of representation. [. . .]

Representation [is] a process. Fair representation is not something that can be achieved in one moment, nor is it something that can be guaranteed in advance. Representation depends on the continuing relationship between representatives and the represented, and anyone concerned about the exclusion of women's voices or needs or interests would be ill-advised to shut up shop as soon as half those elected are women. This is already well understood in relation to the politics of ideas; for getting one's preferred party elected to government is usually seen as the beginning rather than the end of the process, and only the most sanguine of voters regards this as settling future policy direction. The warning is even more pointed in relation to the politics of presence, for the shared experience of women as women can only ever figure as a *promise* of shared concerns, and there is no obvious way of establishing strict accountability to women as a group. Changing the gender composition of elected assemblies is largely an enabling condition (a crucially important one, considering what is *disabled* at present) but it cannot present itself as a guarantee. It is, in some sense, a shot in the dark: far more likely to reach its target than when those shooting are predominantly male, but still open to all kinds of accident.

## Note

1. There *are* parties that operate quotas for youth (usually defined as under 30), but no one, to my knowledge, argues that voters aged between 18 and 25 should have a proportionate representation in parliament.

## Works Cited

Diamond, I., and N. Hartsock. "Beyond Interests in Politics: A Comment on Virginia Sapiro's "When are interests interesting?"" *American Political Science Review* 75, 3 (1981): 717–21.

Dietz, M. "Context Is All: Feminism and Theories of Citizenship." *Daedalus* 116, 4 (1987): 1–24.

Fraser, N. "Struggle Over Needs: Outline of a Socialist-Feminist Critical Theory of Late Capitalist Political Culture." *Unruly Practices: Power, Discourse and Gender in Contemporary Social Theory*. Cambridge: Polity Press, 1989.

Jonasdottir, A. "On the Concept of Interest, Women's Interests, and the Limitation of Interest Theory." *The Political Interests of Gender: Developing Theory and Research with a Feminist Face*. Eds. K.B. Jones and A. Jonasdottir. London: Sage, 1988.

Kymlicka, W. *Multicultural Citizenship: A Liberal Theory of Minority Rights*. Oxford: Oxford University Press, 1995.

MacKinnon, C.A. *Feminism Unmodified: Discourses on Life and Law*. Cambridge, MA: Harvard University Press, 1987.

Pitkin, H. *The Concept of Representation*. Berkeley: University of California Press, 1967.

Ruddick, S. "Maternal Thinking." *Feminist Studies* 6, 2 (1980): 342–67.

Skjeie, H. "The Rhetoric of Difference: On Women's Inclusion into Political Elites." *Politics and Society* 19, 2 (1991): 233–63.

Valen, H. "Norway: Decentralization and Group Representation." *Candidate Selection in Comparative Perspective*. Eds. M. Gallagher and M. Marsh. London: Sage, 1988.

## Study Questions

1. What is the "argument from justice" for raising the proportion of women elected? Which objection to this argument does Phillips find less convincing, and why? Which objection to this argument does Phillips find more convincing, and why?

2. What is the "argument from women's interests" for raising the proportion of women elected? On what basis does Phillips dismiss the objection indebted to recent feminist critique that "women" is not a sufficiently unified category for common interests? What "more decisive problem" does Phillips identify?

3. What is the "argument from women's needs" for raising the proportion of women elected? What concerns does Phillips express about this argument insofar as it rests on women's roles as caregivers, especially mothers?

4. In what ways does the feminist insistence that the sex of representatives matters serve to undermine accountability through political parties and the goals of radical democracy? What conclusions does Phillips draw about the nature of representation?

# Charles W. Mills

Charles W. Mills is John Evans Professor of Moral and Intellectual Philosophy at Northwestern University. He has a BSc in physics from the University of the West Indies and an MA and a PhD from the University of Toronto. Before joining Northwestern in 2007, Mills taught at the University of Oklahoma and the University of Illinois at Chicago. His first book, *The Racial Contract* (1997), won the Myers Outstanding Book Award. In this 2006 essay, Mills argues that the "moral egalitarianism" of liberal political theorists such as John Locke and John Stuart Mill did not escape the white supremacist and colonial relations of their time.

## Modernity, Persons, and Subpersons

### 1. Introduction

Mainstream narratives of modernity represent it as characterized by the triumph of moral egalitarianism. The Age of Revolution and the Age of Enlightenment are also supposed to be the Age of Equality. Thus the crucial texts of the period, whether political or scholarly, trumpet human equality—ostensibly unqualified—as a foundational principle. "We hold these truths to be self-evident," **Thomas Jefferson** ringingly asserts in the famous opening lines of the American Declaration of Independence, "that all men are created equal," and this is echoed 13 years later in the *liberté, égalité, fraternité* of the **French Revolution**. It is not, of course, that the ideal of human equality had never been put forward before—after all, **Stoicism** proclaimed it, and so, in a somewhat different fashion, did Christianity. But equality in the epoch of the Greco-Roman slave states could never become a general principle, while equality in the eyes of God, on the day of judgment, was never intended to contradict the justifiable social divisions of this world, as the Catholic Church's underwriting of the **feudal order** testifies. What marks the modern period is that egalitarianism, and the corresponding ideals of equal rights and freedoms, are taken to become the *dominant* norm, and to do so within the *secular* sphere. Thus the orthodox narrative of modernity provides a periodization in which the ascriptive hierarchies of the ancient and medieval epochs—patrician and plebeian, lord and serf—are contrasted with the unqualified "men," the "persons," of the modern period. Moral egalitarianism—equality of moral status—is then taken as the norm and as constituting the basis for juridical and political egalitarianism, equality before the law and equality of citizenship.

In this narrative, the leading moral and political Western philosophers of the period—**Thomas Hobbes, John Locke, David Hume, Jean-Jacques Rousseau, Immanuel Kant, G.W. F. Hegel, John Stuart Mill, Karl Marx**—are represented as the theoretical spokesmen for equality and advocates for competing moral/political visions ramifying from it. The original egalitarian formulations are historically most closely linked to contractarian liberalism and the natural rights tradition. As one author writes about contractarianism in general: "The emergence of the notion of the social contract is hence linked intimately with the emergence of the idea of the equality of human beings" (Forsyth 37). But the specificity of this connection is contingent. Equality is supposed to be a general axiom, independent of these commitments, and thus to be found also in the proto-utilitarianism of Hume, and the later developed utilitarianism of Mill, where the felicific calculus is founded on the principle that each one counts for one. So while deontological/rights-based and consequentialist/welfare-based liberalisms may disagree on other issues, they are united on liberal equality. [. . .] [Normative equality is also the starting point of] other Western political theories more ambiguously related, or outright hostile, to the liberal tradition: Rousseau's radical republicanism, Hegel's communitarianism, Marx's communism. So though these writers will go on to fight about numerous other issues [. . .] the *fact* of this equality is itself an unquestioned truism. It serves as the framework, the overarching conceptual picture, within which other debates can take place, since *this* debate has been settled. Thus it tacitly imposes a certain conceptual and normative logic, pointing us away from certain areas of inquiry, indeed almost foreclosing the question of their legitimacy. As Will Kymlicka writes, in the opening of his introduction to political philosophy, "the idea that each person matters equally is at the heart of all plausible [modern] political theories" (5).

This narrative, this framing paradigm, is a very powerful and influential one; indeed, it is hegemonic. What I want to argue in this chapter is that it is profoundly misleading, deeply wrong, that it radically mystifies the recent past, and that it needs to be confronted and discredited if our sociopolitical categories are to be true to the world they are supposed to be mapping. Three decades of feminist scholarship have done much to demonstrate the political gender exclusions implicit in the ostensibly neutral "men." But the counternarrative of *racial* subordination is not, at least within philosophy, as well developed, nor is the whiteness of "men" inscribed on the concept's face in the same way as their masculinity is. So even when racism is conceded, and discussed, it tends to be within the official framework of egalitarian assumptions, generating a language of "deviations," "anomalies," "contradictions," and "ironies." It is (reluctantly) admitted that these theorists may have been racist, but this concession is not taken to challenge the logic of the basic framework itself. Since equality is the globally dominant norm, the normative default mode, racism has to be a deviation. Thus one speaks of the "irony" of Jefferson's having been a slaveholder, or the

"contradiction" of the need for **black Jacobins** to carry out a separate **Haitian Revolution** (James). We would find it absurd, clearly counterfactual, to describe the ancient or medieval periods as characterized by egalitarianism, since the whole point about the social systems of these periods is that inequality is the rule. Yet we do not find it equally absurd to conceptualize the modern period as basically one of equality.

What I am arguing for, then, is a reconceptualization of our narrative of modernity, a fundamental paradigm shift in how we think about liberalism, personhood, and egalitarianism. I am suggesting that racism is most illuminatingly seen as *a normative system in its own right*, to be thought of in the same terms and in the same conceptual space as the familiar normative systems of ancient and medieval class hierarchy. I will argue that there was a category in European thought for people of colour as less-than-full persons, as what I have called elsewhere "subpersons," and that this inferior metaphysical standing justifies their differential normative treatment (*Blackness Visible* and *Racial Contract*). So it is not that Hobbes, Locke, Hume, Kant, Hegel, Mill, Marx, and others meant their theories of moral and political egalitarianism to apply in the same way and with full force to all humans, to which application their racist statements were lamentable deviations. (Rousseau's environmentalism makes him a trickier case, and so I will exclude him.) Rather, I am suggesting, we need to see their racist statements as part of the *same* theory as their egalitarian statements and to recognize that their moral, juridical, and political prescriptions, and their philosophies of history, follow different rules for whites than for nonwhites. So instead of seeing these theorists as spokesmen for equality *simpliciter*, we need to start seeing them as spokesmen for a racialized *white* equality. And instead of seeing the Age of Modernity as the Age of Equality, we need to start seeing it as the Age of Global White Supremacy, the age in which whites, being metaphysically and morally superior to all other races, are teleologically destined to rule over them.

## 2. Persons, Subpersons, and Racism as "Symbiosis"

The insight that racism should itself be conceptualized as a theory of personhood, with implications for the normative, is not new. **Sojourner Truth** is supposed to have asked, "An ain't I a woman?" (see Painter). **W.E.B. Du Bois** pointed out that for white racist thought, blacks were a "*tertium quid*" [third thing], "somewhere between men and cattle" (122), and **Frantz Fanon** stated that "the black is not a man" (8). In one of the classic texts of anti-imperialism, **Jean-Paul Sartre** explicitly argued that "there is nothing more consistent than a racist humanism. . . . On the other side of the ocean there was a race of less-than-humans" (26). But, at least until recently, there has been little systematic exploration in philosophy of the ramifications of this idea, and such work as has been done [. . .] has mostly been from the perspective and with the vocabulary of Continental philosophy, the discourse of First World Self in relation to Third World Other. In the analytic mainstream, which is obviously the crucial location for the goal of influencing debate in the profession, far less has been written [. . .].

This neglect is all the more striking since, with the decline of utilitarianism's stature in recent decades, and the resurgence of Kantian "deontological liberalism," it is precisely the language of personhood that is now all-pervasive. The concept of *persons*—entities who, by virtue of their characteristics, are protected by a certain normative armour of rights and freedoms, entitled to be treated in a certain way—has become the central pillar of contemporary moral discourse. Thus debates about abortion are often fought over the actual or potential personhood of the fetus; animal rights theorists charge that restricting full moral concern to human persons is speciesist; and issues of metaphysical and political autonomy, of freedom of the will and citizenship rights, are discussed in terms of what personhood demands.

But what characterizes these discussions is a Eurocentrically ahistorical view of personhood and its prerequisites. Humanness is not necessary for personhood, because of the possibility of intelligent aliens. But (adult) humanness *is* generally taken as sufficient, or at least strongly presumptively sufficient, for personhood, apart from possible exceptions like the brain-dead. So white moral and political philosophers tend to write as if, apart from these kinds of exceptions, moral equality can be presupposed for humans (not merely normatively, as an ideal, but factually, as an accepted norm). And I want to challenge and disrupt this framework of assumptions by formally introducing the concept of a "subperson" (*Untermensch*)—referring to those humans who, though adult, are, because of their race, deservedly *not* treated as full persons—and arguing that this expanded conceptual apparatus better tracks the actual recent global history, and the actual views of the canonical Western moral/political philosophers, than the conventional account and its standard terms.

In approaching this issue, I am going to draw on a contemporary debate in American political theory, since I think that, with appropriate adjustments and modifications, the terms of the debate can be mapped onto, and illuminate, the corresponding positions in political philosophy. In a landmark 1993 article, later expanded into a prizewinning book, *Civic Ideals*, Rogers Smith argues that the dominant conceptualizations of the American polity in the literature have been fundamentally misleading. Citing the work of **Alexis de Tocqueville**, **Gunnar Myrdal**, and **Louis Hartz** as emblematic, Smith points out that the dominant framing of the United States has been as an egalitarian liberal democracy, for which racism and racial exclusion have been an "anomaly." In large measure because of the centrality to their analysis of European class categories, commentators have been blinded to the fact that "the relative egalitarianism that prevailed among white men (at first, moderately propertied white men) was surrounded by an array of fixed, ascriptive hierarchies, all largely unchallenged by the leading American revolutionaries" (*Civic Ideals* 17).

Smith emphasizes that it is not that these theorists have altogether ignored the history of racial oppression (Native American expropriation,

African slavery, **Jim Crow**, etc.), but that they have conceptualized it in a misleading way, one that leaves intact the mainstream picture of the polity. Tocqueville, for example, "treated racism as mere prejudice, ignoring the burgeoning scientific racism in Jacksonian America," and even though "he correctly saw racism as prevalent throughout the nation," he still wrote in "unqualified terms about America's supposedly egalitarian conditions" and relegated "blacks and Native Americans to the status of tangents in a final chapter" (21–2). Myrdal's famous book, *An American Dilemma*, was focused precisely on racism, and—with the help of a research team that included many leading black social scientists—provided massive documentation of the systemic subordination of blacks across the country in all spheres of social, political, and economic life. And he conceded that "far from being an exceptional or marginal phenomenon, moreover, the nation's racial ordering . . . affected virtually all aspects of American life." But again, when it came to the question of how this subordination should be *conceived* (for example, in his introduction to the book), he framed it in terms of a violation of the liberal egalitarian American ideals that white citizens were, nonetheless, still thought of as endorsing, giving rise to the tragic dilemma of the title (23).

So racism and white supremacy are not thought of as rising to the level of the ideological and political; rather, they are "prejudices," hangovers from the pre-modern. As Smith comments, it then becomes possible, remarkably, to represent as an egalitarian liberal democracy a country in which for most of its existence people of colour were subordinated, whether enslaved, expropriated, segregated, disenfranchised, or deprived of equal socioeconomic opportunities. And what makes this feat of evasion possible is, in part, the ignoring of the facts, but in addition, and more important, the *mapping* of the conceptual terrain in such a way that the facts are deprived of their proper significance. This history of domination is not framed, as it should be, as an account of a white-supremacist political system, in which some citizens are superior to others. And the beliefs justifying this rule are not seen, as they should

be, as the ideology of white supremacy but demoted to the status of "prejudice," the "non-rational," "interest-driven deviations." Smith points out that these racist traditions "provide elaborate, principled arguments for giving legal expression to people's ascribed place in various hereditary, inegalitarian cultural and biological orders, valorized as natural, divinely approved, and just." But later writers in the Tocquevillian mode read "egalitarian principles as America's true principles, while treating the massive inequalities in American life as products of prejudice, not rival principles" (18, 27). Smith's move is therefore to contrapose to the mainstream "anomaly" view what he calls the "multiple traditions" view, which recognizes racism and white supremacy as alternative political and ideological traditions in their own right within the political culture. So it is not that there is one liberal egalitarian tradition, with racism as an anomaly. Rather, there are multiple traditions. Another position, in the spirit of Smith's, but more radical, is the "symbiosis" view, which would claim that actually racism *is* the dominant tradition, and that liberal egalitarianism has been racially inflected from the start.

Now what I want to suggest is that, writ large—that is, transferred to the global stage—and writ high—that is, elevated to the level of abstraction appropriate to philosophy—these terms can assist and elucidate the present debate. For modernity in philosophy is standardly presented in analogous terms (though obviously, since philosophy is a non-empirical discipline, with even less attention to the history of racism): as introducing personhood and liberal equality as the global norm, for which racism is the anomaly. And what I want to argue for is a reconceptualization of the philosophy of modernity along "multiple traditions" or "symbiosis" lines. My own preference is for the "symbiosis" view, but the important thing to recognize is that, whichever of these is chosen, the anomaly view is utterly inaccurate as a characterization both of the United States and of recent global history.[1] As Matthew Frye Jacobson comments about the United States, but I would claim with more general validity: "Exclusions based upon race and gender did not represent mere lacunae in an otherwise liberal philosophy of political standing; nor were the nation's exclusions simply contradictions of the democratic creed. Rather . . . these inclusions and exclusions formed an inseparable, interdependent figure and ground in the same ideological tapestry" (22–3). And this, I am claiming, is the story of modernity itself. The idea of a person is linked with that of a subperson as figure and ground, symbiotically related. [. . .]

Putting this simply, the contrast between the orthodox "anomaly" view of racism and the "symbiosis" view I am advocating can be represented as follows. Let T be the (egalitarian) moral/political theory of the philosopher in question; *p* stand for person; and *sp* for subperson. Mainstream commentary is basically saying that

For philosopher P:

T asserts egalitarianism for all *p*, where *p* is race-neutral.

Racist statements are then an exception, and not part of T.

And what, by contrast, I am recommending as an interpretive framework is

For philosopher P:

T asserts egalitarianism for all *p*, where whiteness is (generally) a necessary condition for being a *p*.[2]

T asserts nonegalitarianism for *sp*, where nonwhiteness is (generally) a sufficient condition for being an *sp*.

Racist statements are then part of T, not an exception.

On both views, racism can be admitted—the charge is not that mainstream views cannot concede racism. The crucial question is *how* they frame it, whether as anomaly/contradiction, et cetera, or as an integral/symbiotic part of the theory.

It will be appreciated, then, that this semantic innovation, so simple to describe, would, if adopted, quite radically transform our view of modern Western moral/political philosophy. We would have to start thinking of these theorists, and their theories, quite differently from how they are presented in the standard textbook. This does not rule out, of course, a sanitized reappropriation and retrieval of their theories. But it would have to be explicitly acknowledged that that *is* what we are doing, that we are not reading them as they intended. So it is not that liberalism and egalitarianism, abstract L and E, were historically meant to extend to everybody. Rather, we would need to talk about racialized liberalism and racialized egalitarianism, RL and RE. Racism would then emerge, as it should, as a normative system in its own right—indeed, as the *actual* normative system obtaining for most of the modern period. And just as the hierarchical ideologies of the ancient and medieval world were multiply tiered, with different standings (of class) for different sets of human beings, we would be forced to acknowledge that (actual, historical) liberalism also is a two-tiered ideology, with a different status assigned to, and correspondingly differentiated norms prescribed for, whites and nonwhites. The orthodox narrative of modernity would have to be rewritten; the orthodox cartography of the political would have to be redrawn.

Apart from being—unlike the present narrative—true to the actual historical record, and so demanding implementation on those grounds alone, this transformation would have the great virtue of uniting the conceptual spaces and periodization times of the white political and the nonwhite political. As emphasized at the start, the mainstream narrative orients us toward certain players, certain dates, in keeping with a macro-picture of global history in which an egalitarian modernity triumphantly succeeds the hierarchical ancient and medieval epochs. So there is a segregation of events, an apartheid of the historical calendar, a colour coding of concepts. Textbooks provide an account of the history of Western political philosophy that moves smoothly from Plato to **John Rawls** without dealing with race, as if, in the modern period, Western theorists were proclaiming their egalitarian views as applicable to everybody. The views of known racist theorists—**Joseph de Gobineau**, **Houston Stuart Chamberlain**, Adolf Hitler—are usually excluded from these accounts, and the racism of Enlightenment theorists is not highlighted or even mentioned. The West is constructed in such a way that racism and white racial domination have been no part of the history of the West, and the normative superiority of whites to nonwhites, justified by these theorists, has been no part of that history. We have a history of the official political proscenium [theatre stage in front of curtain] with a certain cast of actors (**Whigs and Tories**; liberals and conservatives; socialists, anarchists, and fascists), and these other players (abolitionists, anti-imperialists, **Pan-Africanists** . . .) seem to be on a different stage, a stage so oddly related to the familiar one that it hardly seems political at all. Similarly, we are all familiar with 1776 and 1789 as crucial dates for human liberation: the American and French Revolutions. But how many of us would be able to come up unassisted with the date of the Haitian Revolution or the end of New World slavery? [. . .]

## 3. The Symbiosis of Racism and Egalitarianism in Locke and Mill

I now want to turn to the concrete illustration of what I am contending is this symbiotic relationship in the work of [. . .] Locke [. . .] and Mill. [. . .] What we need to examine is how the traditional account of their views needs to be modified once we recognize that a dichotomized logic, whether explicit or implicit, can be argued to be at work in their texts, and that the same egalitarian rules which specify one set of norms and a certain history and prognosis for persons specify a different set of rules and a different history and prognosis for subpersons. Moreover, since moral equality is at the normative heart of the liberal-democratic polity [. . .], and the normative theorization of it, ramifying through the

legislative branch and the functioning of the state, a moral *in*equality will be similarly all-encompassing in its practical and theoretical ramifications. [. . .]

### 3.1. Locke

[. . .] Locke is central to the liberal-democratic mainstream: the celebrated Whig champion of property rights, limited government, parliamentarianism, and the right to revolt against despotic rule. [. . .] Locke's [(putative) moral egalitarianism] is foundational. As he states in the "Second Treatise": "To understand Political Power right, and derive it from its Original, we must consider what State all Men are naturally in, and that is, a *State of perfect Freedom* to order their Actions. . . . A *State* also *of Equality*, wherein all the Power and Jurisdiction is reciprocal, no one having more than another" (269). Thus he is the spokesman for a principled opposition to the ascriptive hierarchy of **Sir Robert Filmer**'s Tory patriarchalism (*Patriarcha*). Property is the normative concept most central to Locke's universe, being used to denote both legitimate possessions and rights. We own ourselves; we own our bodies and our labour; we appropriate the world by mixing our labour with nature; and others are duty-bound to respect our property rights and our rights as our private "property."

But if Locke is the theoretical champion of proprietarian liberalism, he is also, as James Tully reminds us, a *colonial* theorist, though in political philosophy this connection is usually ignored. He "was one of the six or eight men who closely invigilated and helped to shape the old colonial system during the **Restoration**," played a policy-making role in the Carolina government (including taking a hand in writing their 1669 *Fundamental Constitution*), and had investments in the slave-trading Royal Africa Company (168). Thus Locke's theoretical and practical writings directly concerned two groups of nonwhites, Native Americans and Africans. And in both cases, it can be argued—though admittedly more controversially in the second case—it is clear that they could not have counted as equal "persons" for him.

The Native American case is clear-cut [. . .], and, as Tully points out, is the subject of a huge body of literature outside philosophy. Like Hobbes, Locke characterizes Native Americans as still being in the state of nature, though a late stage. Since Locke's state of nature, unlike Hobbes', is not intrinsically warlike, this is less of an indictment for Locke than it is for the earlier theorist. But it does, nonetheless, inevitably say something about their development: These are not people who have reached the stage of instituting the commonwealth, civil society. As Tully comments, "Amerindian political organization is disregarded . . . thereby dispossessing Amerindian governments of their authority and nationhood and permitting Europeans to deal with them and punish them on an individual basis" (178).

Moreover, their activities *in* the state of nature also leave much to be desired. God may have given the world to "mankind in common," but in the light of the divine imperative to earn a living by the sweat of your brow, he gave it pre-eminently to "the Industrious and Rational." Indeed, these are virtually "co-implicative," since reason is demonstrated by the recognition of natural law, and natural law mandates that we appropriate the world through mixing our labour with it. The "freedom" in the state of nature, then, is not *licence*, but constrained by obligations of various kinds, among which is economic productivity.

Now Locke believes not merely in the labour theory of property, but, as with most of the British political economists, the labour theory of value. He says that 90 per cent, or perhaps even 99 per cent, of the value of manufactured goods comes from labour; their natural base is worth only a tiny fraction of the final total. So refusal to mix one's labour with nature, or doing so in a desultory way, leaves the world far less valuable than, counterfactually, it *could* be if such mixing were taking place. Insofar as Native Americans are negligent on this score, then, they are falling short of their natural-law duty to improve the world and add value to it. Moreover, since they are singled out as a *group*—it is not a matter of *some* Native Americans being stigmatized, but the group as a whole—this is a general characteristic of them.

Locke's proviso forbids an appropriation of the world that results in "enough and as good" not being left for others, and "waste and spoilage" resulting. The usual examples cited are attempts to monopolize some natural good, for example, the only water source for miles around, and the wasteful non-consumption of actually appropriated goods, for example rotting deer carcasses, baskets of putrid apples, and the like. But equally important, arguably, are examples of incompetent or inefficient appropriation that do not add enough value to leave "enough and as good" for others, while—through the blocking of the superior methods of the more "industrious and rational"—generating "waste and spoilage" of *counterfactual*, *potential* goods: the virtual goods that could have been produced, but cannot now be. In other words, if a given plot of land could generate 100V of value if efficiently utilized, and because of Native Americans" (putative) inferior techniques, only 1V has been generated, then 99V of potential value has been wasted.

The Lockean injunction to appropriate the world thus leads naturally to the expropriation of those in occupation of certain sectors of the world who are not making proper use of it. What seems like a theory of general application to *all* peoples, with uniform colourless norms and prescriptions, turns out to have sharply differentiated consequences for *some* people. But mainstream philosophy does not highlight this distinction. Tully comments, "The fact that the chapter (ch. 5: 'On Property') is organized around a contrast between Europe, where appropriation without consent is not permitted because political societies exist, and America, where appropriation without consent is permitted because it is a state of nature, is rarely mentioned. That the argument justifies European settlement in America without the consent of the native people, one of the most contentious and important events of the seventeenth century and one of the formative events of the modern world, is normally passed over in silence" (173). In effect, then, Native Americans, by virtue of their deficient appropriation, lose the moral status of equality that the opening chapters announce all people to have. And again, I would claim, this should not be seen as an inconsistency, but a corollary of their subpersonhood. Locke provides us with a normative theory of what is required of persons as self-owning proprietors, and the efficient, value-adding appropriation of the world is one of the key prerequisites. Insofar as Native Americans fall short of these requirements, they can legitimately be treated as less than full persons. And in fact the Lockean argument, directly, or somewhat modified, would become the central justification for displacing native peoples in North America, Australia, and parts of Africa. The land was deemed "vacant," *terra nullius* [no one's land], *vacuum domicilium* [empty domicile], consistent with a moral/juridical doctrine that denies personhood to certain kinds of humans.

The more controversial case is African slavery, because here one has not a developed textual rationale whose implications have been ignored by philosophers, but a textual silence, or a seeming inconsistency with the actual text. In *Two Treatises of Government,* Locke opposes slavery except under tightly specified conditions: that it must come about through a just war, for example, the enslavement of the defeated prosecutors of a war of aggression, and it must not extend to the hereditary enslavement of wives and children (*Second Treatise*, ch. 16, "On Conquest"). Clearly, the Atlantic slave trade massively violated both these stipulations. Yet, as noted, Locke himself had earlier had investments in the slave trade, and either wrote, or had a large hand in writing, the Carolina Constitution, which enshrined hereditary slavery.

How is this apparent inconsistency to be explained? There is a large literature on the subject, which Wayne Glausser, in a survey article from fifteen years ago, divided into three main categories: (1) Locke's participation in slavery as "a deviation from his theory," "an unfortunate but minor lapse"; (2) Locke's participation as justified by a "tortured logic"; (3) Locke's participation as "part of the fabric of Lockean philosophy, however embarrassing that might be for modern admirers of one of the founding liberals" (199).

As one would expect, I am most sympathetic to the third alternative. A "deviation" so great is hardly plausible (and would, of course, not remotely be "minor"), especially since, as Jennifer Welchman points out in an article, Locke was intimately familiar with the details of American slavery, since "most of the correspondence conducted by the Council [of Trade and Plantations] passed over Locke's desk" (72). The logic of the second set of theories is indeed tortured, requiring, for example, that Locke seriously believe the captured Africans were themselves the aggressors; moreover, it would not explain his countenancing of hereditary slavery. The third set includes different variants, one being the representation of Locke as a "bourgeois theorist" for whom "protections against enslavement are less fundamental . . . than provisions for capitalist growth" (Glausser 211). But this seems to me to underestimate the role of morality, even in the degraded role of moral rationalization. Bourgeois theorists no less than other theorists need to feel morally in the right about what they are doing, and it is difficult to believe that such inconsistency with Locke's own liberal principles (if conceived of as universalist and race-neutral) could simply have been ignored by Locke. [. . .]

So the explanation in terms of racism (the other variant of the third group), which, for one reason or another, would exclude blacks as inferior humans from the *Second Treatise* prohibitions, seems most convincing to me, though admittedly there is no smoking gun. [. . .]

## 3.2. Mill

The standard critique of consequentialist liberalism for decades has been, in Rawls' famous words, that "Utilitarianism does not take seriously the distinction between persons," so that, unlike deontological, rights-based liberalism, individuals" rights are subject to the calculus of welfare maximization (27). So personhood, it is claimed, is not as securely and foundationally lodged in the normative apparatus of the theory as with the contractarians. But utilitarians would, of course, challenge this characterization, and in any case Mill's *On Liberty* is unquestionably a great paean to individual self-realization.

Yet there are those lines in chapter 1 right after the statement of the harm principle where, after insisting on the individual's "absolute" independence and "sovereignty" over matters concerning himself, Mill casually and offhandedly asserts that "this doctrine is meant to apply only to human beings in the maturity of their faculties," not children, those "still in a state to require being taken care of by others," nor, for the same reason, "those backward states of society in which the race itself may be considered as in its nonage": "Despotism is a legitimate mode of government in dealing with barbarians, provided the end be their improvement, and the means justified by actually effecting that end. Liberty, as a principle, has no application to any state of things anterior to the time when mankind have become capable of being improved by free and equal discussion" (13–14).

So easy to read through and miss the significance of—as generations of liberal-arts students throughout the Western world studying this universally assigned text have doubtless done—unless, as noted, you have a background theory contextualizing Mill's remarks and showing that they are *not* casual and offhand after all. No less than with his contractarian fellow-liberals, Mill's "individuals" are not "humans" *simpliciter*, but racially divided, with different rules applying to different subsets. As several recent commentators have reminded us [. . .], Mill the famous liberal and champion of individual liberty was also Mill the employee of the East India Company. He was a colonial official and a theorist of colonial rule, who never intended his domestic pronouncements to be extended without qualification to the colonies. But [. . .] Western commentators who have noticed these remarks have generally framed them in the language of "inconsistencies" and "anomalies." In a recent book, Souffrant characterizes such accounts as "aberration theories," since they claim that "Mill's work on intervention and his tacit support of the colonization of one group by another are inconsistent with his overall philosophy" (5). By contrast, Souffrant insists

> Mill's Utilitarianism does not contradict his interventionist posture in international affairs. . . . [H]e would permit the qualified intervention of a more civilized group in the affairs of uncivilized others. . . . Advocates of the second aberration theory [Souffrant identifies several varieties] assume that Mill's ban against encroachment is universal and that it applies to the international environment as well as the domestic. But in Mill's eyes, the immature [such as barbarians] are exempt from the protection of the principle of liberty and open to intervention . . . . [W]hen Mill speaks of individuality, he is referring to an attribute of mature individuals, human beings who have been brought up within the confines of particular societies. Mature individuals enjoy having had a formative period contributing to their maturity. . . . He believes furthermore that in his time individuality is an attribute exclusive to the European nations. (5–6, 8, 54–5)

As we have seen before, then, there is an anthropology underlying seemingly transparent and straightforward claims about "humans" or "individuals," which either overtly or in effect racializes the criteria for full enjoyment of personhood. Mehta comments that the obvious contrasts between Lockean and utilitarian liberalism should not blind us to the common "anthropological basis of [their] universalistic claims" (48, n. 2). Mill's theory makes it possible to reconcile liberalism at home and in the white settler states with despotism abroad in the nonwhite colonies, because of the different levels of maturity of the respective populations. India as a civilization is "infantilized," seen as analogous to a child that is not ready to direct its own affairs. So the justifiable lack of freedom is both individual and national, micro and macro; as with the other theorists, normative inegalitarianism for individuals has ramifications on the political level. As Mehta points out, Mill's comments in *On Liberty* have their larger echo in a chapter in *Considerations on Representative Government*, "a revealing document on the increasing relevance of cultural, civilizational, linguistic, and racial categories in defining the constituency of Mill's liberalism":

Mill . . . divides colonized countries into two classes. The first of these classes is composed of countries "of similar civilization to the ruling country; capable of and ripe for representative government: such as the British possessions in America and Australia" [in other words, white settler states]. The other class includes "others, like India, [that] are still at a great distance from that state." Mill goes on to celebrate England's realization that countries in the first class must be the beneficiaries of "the true principle of government," namely representative government. . . . Regarding the second class of countries—countries with a population whose civilization, culture, language, and race were different from the British—Mill's attitude is strikingly different and his recommendations correspondingly so. Not only is Mill opposed to dismembering colonialism, he is equally opposed to these countries being internally democratic. . . . He goes on: "Such is the ideal rule of a free people over a barbarous or semi-barbarous one." (70–1)

Thus Mehta concludes, with Souffrant, that there is no "inconsistency" or "aberration" here: Rather, "it is by reference to utility that Mill comes to the view that representative institutions are appropriate for Europe and its predominantly white colonies and not for the rest of the world. *The bracketing of India, among others, is not therefore the mark of an embarrassing theoretical inconsistency*, precisely because at the theoretical level, the commitment to representative institutions is subsequent, and not prevenient, to considerations of utility" (73, my emphasis). In effect, "under conditions of backwardness or for children, the principle of liberty would sanction behaviour that would be contrary to utility maximization. Under such conditions alternative norms are required to remain consistent with the progress associated with utility" (99). What I have characterized, following the political science literature on race, as "anomaly" theories of racism are thus as mistaken at the more abstract level of political philosophy as they are in political science; rather, a "symbiosis" analysis is the appropriate one.

So we get Mill wrong if we treat his "individuals" as colourless, and his consequentialist principles as applying in the same way to all adult humans. Mill's praiseworthy progressiveness on gender did not extend to race. His defence of freedom in the white world becomes a defence of despotism for people of colour in the colonies, not because—the deontological versus utilitarian debate—"person" is subject to welfare maximization but, more fundamentally (in the sense of a premise common to *both* sides of the liberal debate), because he did not see people of colour as full persons in the first place. He shared with his theoretical adversaries a vision of nonwhites as humans not fully human, not fully mature and capable of directing themselves. Both on the individual and on the political level, nonwhites were in effect subpersons for him.

## 4. Conclusion

By looking at these [two] theorists, then, I believe I have shown—admittedly more controversially in some cases than in others—how radically misleading orthodox philosophical narratives of modernity are. The vaunted egalitarianism of the modern world is really colour coded, reserved for whites. Humanness is not presumptively sufficient for personhood but requires additional achievements. Whether because of [. . .] inferior and inefficient appropriative skills [. . .] or mental immaturity, nonwhites are denied the status of full persons. Thus the wide differences between these theorists' versions of egalitarianism and liberalism mask a common commitment to European superiority and European domination. Insofar as our textbooks, encyclopedia summaries, journal articles, and classroom presentations continue to depict them as if they were arguing in a racially inclusive fashion, insofar as we continue to utilize the framework of "anomaly," "contradiction," and "inconsistency" in talking about their racism, we are fundamentally misrepresenting their thought and blinding ourselves both to the real architecture of their theories and the corresponding real architecture of the world their theories helped to bring about and rationalize. We are also endorsing a fictive moral/political topography. For taking the presumptive normative personhood of all humans, independent of race, as *already* accomplished—part of the moral/political territory—profoundly distorts the actual moral economy of the past few hundred years. The political struggles around race, conquest, slavery, imperialism, colonization, segregation; the battles for abolition, independence, self-government, equal rights, first-class citizenship; the movements of aboriginal peoples, slaves, colonial populations, black Americans, and other subordinated people of colour; and the texts of all these movements, vanish into a conceptual abyss papered over by the seemingly minor, but actually tremendously question-begging, assumption that all humans are and have been acknowledged as equal persons. The formal recognition of the category of the subperson not only brings these embarrassing realities into the same discursive universe as mainstream Western political theory, but it overturns the sanitized and amnesiac assumptions of that universe by forcing the admission that—at its foundational origins, its modern genesis—*this category was its own*, that Western political theory's liberalism, humanism, and egalitarianism were all racialized: all white.

## Notes

1. The problem with the "multiple traditions" view is that it carries the connotation that these two "traditions" are, if not equally influential, at least roughly on a par with one another. One may also get the image of two traditions fighting it out and alternating in power. But both these pictures are quite misleading as characterizations of the American polity.

2. The qualification is necessary because of a point of disanalogy between gender and race—that while there is only one subordinate gender, there are several subordinate non-white races, and their respective statuses may differ over time and from one theorist's writings to another's. So while blacks and Native Americans are fairly consistently seen as subpersons in racist theory, some Asians (Indians, Chinese) have on occasion been judged to be almost equal to whites.

## Works Cited

Du Bois, W.E.B. *The Souls of Black Folk*. New York: Signet Classic, 1969.

Fanon, F. *Black Skin, White Masks*. Trans. C.L. Markmann. New York: Grove Press, 1967.

Filmer, R. *Patriarcha and Other Writings*. Ed. J.P. Sommerville. New York: Cambridge University Press, 1991.

Forsyth, M. "Hobbes's Contractarianism: A Comparative Analysis." *The Social Contract from Hobbes to Rawls*. Eds. D. Boucher and P. Kelly. New York: Routledge, 1994. 35–50.

Glausser, W. "Three Approaches to Locke and the Slave Trade." *Journal of the History of Ideas* 51 (1990): 199–216.

Jacobson, M.F. *Whiteness of a Different Color: European Immigrants and the Alchemy of Race*. Cambridge, MA: Harvard University Press, 1998.

James, C.L.R. *The Black Jacobins: Toussaint L'Ouverture and the San Domingo Revolution*. 2nd ed. New York: Vintage, 1963.

Kymlicka, W. *Contemporary Political Philosophy: An Introduction*. Oxford: Clarendon Press, 1990.

Locke, J. *Two Treatises of Government*. Ed. P. Laslett. New York: Cambridge University Press, 1988.

Mehta, U.S. *Liberalism and Empire: A Study in Nineteenth-Century British Liberal Thought*. Chicago: University of Chicago Press, 1999.

Mill, J.S. *Considerations on Representative Government*. Ed. C. V. Shields. New York: Liberal Arts Press, 1958.

Mill, J.S. *On Liberty with The Subjection of Women and Chapters on Socialism*. Ed. S. Collini. New York: Cambridge University Press, 1989.

Mills, C.W. *Blackness Visible: Essays on Philosophy and Race*. Ithaca, NY: Cornell University Press, 1998.

Mills, C.W. *The Racial Contract*. Ithaca, NY: Cornell University Press, 1997.

Myrdal, G. *An American Dilemma: The Negro Problem and Modern Democracy*. 2 vols. New Brunswick, NJ: Transaction, 1996.

Painter, N.I. *Sojourner Truth: A Life, a Symbol*. New York: W. W. Norton, 1996.

Rawls, J. *A Theory of Justice*. Cambridge, MA: Harvard University Press, 1971.

Sartre, J.-P. Preface to *The Wretched of the Earth*. Trans. C. Farrington. New York: Grove Weidenfeld, 1968. 7–31.

Smith, R.M. "Beyond Tocqueville, Myrdal, and Hartz: The Multiple Traditions in America." *American Political Science Review* 87 (1993): 549–66.

Smith, R.M. *Civic Ideals: Conflicting Visions of Citizenship in U.S. History*. New Haven, CT: Yale University Press, 1997.

Souffrant, E.M. *Formal Transgression: John Stuart Mill's Philosophy of International Affairs*. Lanham, MD: Rowman & Littlefield, 2000.

Tully, J. "Rediscovering America: The *Two Treatises* and Aboriginal Rights." *Locke's Philosophy: Content and Context*. Ed. G. A. J. Rogers. Oxford: Clarendon Press, 1994. 165–96.

Welchman, J. "Locke on Slavery and Inalienable Rights." *Canadian Journal of Philosophy* 25 (1995): 67–81.

## Study Questions

1. Why does Mills contend that moral and political philosophers of the modern period should be seen as "spokesmen for a racialized *white* equality" not "equality *simpliciter*," and that the "Age of Modernity" should be seen as the "Age of Global White Supremacy" not the "Age of Equality"?

2. Compare the mainstream "anomaly" view of egalitarianism and racism with the "multiple traditions" view (of Smith) and the "symbiosis" view (of Mills). How does the view we adopt change our understanding of the history of political philosophy in the West?

3. How do Locke's labour theories of property and value illustrate the "symbiotic relationship" between egalitarianism and racism and "dichotomized logic" of persons and subpersons, according to Mills? Explain why Locke's political philosophy served to justify the European expropriation of Native American land.

4. How do Mill's works on individual liberty and representative government and their underlying utilitarianism illustrate the "symbiotic relationship" between egalitarianism and racism and "dichotomized logic" of persons and subpersons, according to Mills? Explain why Mill's political philosophy served to justify British imperial rule of India.

# ∿ MULTICULTURALISM ∿

## Charles Taylor

Charles Taylor is an emeritus professor at McGill University. A bilingual Quebecer, Taylor has a BA in history from McGill and a BA in politics, philosophy, and economics, an MA, and a DPhil from Oxford. He is a Companion of the Order of Canada and won the Social Sciences and Humanities Research Council Gold Medal in 2003 and the Templeton Prize in 2007. Taylor is also a public intellectual: his books find audiences beyond philosophy, he recently co-chaired Quebec's Consultation Committee on Accommodation Practices Related to Cultural Differences, and he was a candidate in several federal elections. The title of this 1992 essay refers to competing demands concerning recognition in the public sphere: liberalism's same treatment for everyone versus multiculturalism's respect for difference.

## The Politics of Recognition

### 1. Politics of Universalism vs. Politics of Difference

[. . .] [T]he discourse of recognition has become familiar to us, on two levels: First, in the intimate sphere, where we understand the formation of identity and the self as taking place in a continuing dialogue and struggle with significant others. And then in the public sphere, where a politics of equal recognition has come to play a bigger and bigger role. [. . .]

I want to concentrate here on the public sphere, and try to work out what a politics of equal recognition has meant and could mean.

In fact, it has come to mean two rather different things. [. . .] With [the modern notion of] dignity has come a politics of universalism, emphasizing the equal dignity of all citizens, and the content of this politics has been the equalization of rights and entitlements. What is to be avoided at all costs is the existence of "first-class" and "second-class" citizens. Naturally, the actual detailed measures justified by this principle have varied greatly, and have often been controversial. For some, equalization has affected only civil rights and voting rights; for others, it has extended into the socio-economic sphere. People who are systematically handicapped by poverty from making the most of their citizenship rights are deemed on this view to have been relegated to second-class status, necessitating remedial action through equalization. But through all the differences of interpretation, the principle of equal citizenship has come to be universally accepted. Every position, no matter how reactionary, is now defended under the colours of this principle. Its greatest, most recent victory was won by the civil rights movement of the 1960s in the United States. It is worth noting that even the adversaries of extending voting rights to blacks in the southern states found some pretext consistent with universalism, such as "tests" to be administered to would-be voters at the time of registration.

By contrast, [. . .] the modern notion of identity has given rise to a politics of difference. There is, of course, a universalist basis to this as well, making for the overlap and confusion between the two. *Everyone* should be recognized for his or her unique identity. But recognition here means something else. With the politics of equal dignity, what is established is meant to be universally the same, an identical basket of rights and immunities; with the politics of difference, what we are asked to recognize is the unique identity of this individual or group, their distinctness from everyone else. The idea is that it is precisely this distinctness that has been ignored, glossed over, assimilated to a dominant or majority identity. And this assimilation is the cardinal sin against the ideal of authenticity.

Now underlying the demand is a principle of universal equality. The politics of difference is full of denunciations of discrimination and refusals of second-class citizenship. This gives the principle of universal equality a point of entry within the politics of dignity. But once inside, as it were, its demands are hard to assimilate to that politics. For it asks that we give acknowledgement and status to something that is not universally shared. Or, otherwise put, we give due acknowledgement only to what is universally present—everyone has an identity—through recognizing what is peculiar to each. The universal demand powers an acknowledgment of specificity.

The politics of difference grows organically out of the politics of universal dignity through one of those shifts with which we are long familiar, where a new understanding of the human social condition imparts a radically new meaning to an old principle. Just as a view of human beings as conditioned by their socioeconomic plight changed the understanding of second-class citizenship, so that this category came to include, for example, people in inherited poverty traps, so here the understanding of identity as formed in interchange, and as possibly so malformed, introduces a new form of second-class status into our purview. As in the present case, the socioeconomic redefinition justified social programs that were highly controversial. For those who had not gone along with this changed definition of equal status, the various redistributive programs and special opportunities offered to certain populations seemed a form of undue favouritism.

Similar conflicts arise, today around the politics of difference. Where the politics of universal dignity fought for forms of non-discrimination that were quite "blind" to the ways in which citizens differ, the politics of difference often redefines non-discrimination as requiring that we make these distinctions the basis of differential treatment. So members of aboriginal bands will get certain rights and powers not enjoyed by other Canadians, if the demands for native self-government are finally agreed on, and certain minorities will get the right to exclude others in order to preserve their cultural integrity, and so on.

To proponents of the original politics of dignity, this can seem like a reversal, a betrayal, a simple negation of their cherished principle. Attempts are therefore made to mediate, to show how some of these measures meant to accommodate minorities can after all be justified on the original basis of dignity. These arguments can be successful up to a point. For instance, some of the (apparently) most flagrant departures from "difference-blindness" are reverse discrimination measures, affording people from previously unfavoured groups a competitive advantage for jobs or places in universities. This practice has been justified on the grounds that historical discrimination has created a pattern within which the unfavoured struggle at a disadvantage. Reverse discrimination is defended as a temporary measure that will eventually level the playing field and allow the old "blind" rules to come back into force in a way that doesn't disadvantage anyone. This argument seems cogent enough—wherever its factual basis is sound. But it won't justify some of the measures now urged on the grounds of difference, the goal of which is not to bring us back to an eventual "difference-blind" social space but, on the contrary, to maintain and cherish distinctness, not just now but forever. After all, if we're concerned with identity, then what is more legitimate than one's aspiration that it never be lost?[1]

So even though one politics springs from the other, by one of those shifts in the definition of key terms with which we're familiar, the two diverge quite seriously from each other. One basis for the divergence comes out even more clearly when we go beyond what each requires that we acknowledge—certain universal rights in one case, a particular identity on the other—and look at the underlying intuitions of value.

The politics of equal dignity is based on the idea that all humans are equally worthy of respect. It is underpinned by a notion of what in human beings commands respect, however we may try to shy away from this "metaphysical" background. For **Kant**, whose use of the term *dignity* was one of the earliest influential evocations of this idea, what commanded respect in us was our status as rational agents, capable of directing our lives through principles (434). Something like this has been the basis for our intuitions of equal dignity ever since, though the detailed definition of it may have changed.

Thus, what is picked out as of worth here is a *universal human potential*, a capacity that all humans share. This potential, rather than anything a person may have made of it, is what ensures that each person deserves respect. Indeed, our sense of the importance of potentiality reaches so far that we extend this protection even to people who through some circumstance that has befallen them are incapable of realizing their potential in the normal way—handicapped people, or those in a coma, for instance.

In the case of the politics of difference, we might also say that a universal potential is at its basis, namely, the potential for forming and defining one's own identity, as an individual, and also as a culture. This potentiality must be respected equally in everyone. [. . .]

These two modes of politics, then, both based on the notion of equal respect, come into conflict. For one, the principle of equal respect requires that we treat people in a difference-blind fashion. The fundamental intuition that humans command this respect focuses on what is the same in all. For the other, we have to recognize and even foster particularity. The reproach the first makes to the second is just that it violates the principle of non-discrimination. The reproach the second makes to the first is that it negates identity by forcing people into a homogeneous mould that is untrue to them. This would be bad enough if the mould were itself neutral—nobody's mould in particular. But the complaint generally goes further. The claim is that the supposedly neutral set of difference-blind principles of the politics of equal dignity is in fact a reflection of one hegemonic culture. As it turns out, then, only the minority or suppressed cultures are being forced to take alien form. Consequently, the supposedly fair and difference-blind society is not only inhuman (because suppressing identities) but also, in a subtle and unconscious way, itself highly discriminatory.

This last attack is the cruellest and most upsetting of all. The liberalism of equal dignity seems to have to assume that there are some universal, difference-blind principles. Even though we may not have defined them yet, the project of defining them remains alive and essential. Different theories may be put forward and contested—and a number (**Rawls**, Dworkin, Habermas) have been proposed in our day—but the shared assumption of the different theories is that one such theory is right.

The charge levelled by the most radical forms of the politics of difference is that "blind" liberalisms are themselves the reflection of particular cultures. And the worrying thought is that this bias might not just be a contingent weakness of all hitherto proposed theories, that the very idea of such a liberalism may be a kind of pragmatic contradiction, a particularism masquerading as the universal. [. . .]

## 2. Quebec in Canada: Two Conceptions of Rights-Liberalism

Are the critics correct?

The fact is that there are forms of this liberalism of equal rights that in the minds of their own proponents can give only a very restricted acknowledgment of distinct cultural identities. The notion that any of the standard schedules of rights might apply differently in one cultural context than they do in another, that their application might have to take account of different collective goals, is considered quite unacceptable. The issue, then, is whether this restrictive view of equal rights is the only possible interpretation. If it is, then it would seem that the accusation of homogenization is well founded. But perhaps it is not. I think it is not, and perhaps the best way to lay out the issue is to see it in the context of the Canadian case, where this question has played a role in the impending breakup of the country. In fact, two conceptions of rights-liberalism have confronted each other, albeit in confused fashion, throughout the long and inconclusive constitutional debates of recent years.

The issue came to the fore because of the adoption in 1982 of the Canadian Charter of Rights, which aligned our political system in this regard with the American one in having a schedule of rights offering a basis for judicial review of legislation at all levels of government. The question had to arise how to relate this schedule to the claims for distinctness put forward by French Canadians, and particularly Quebecers, on the one hand, and Aboriginal peoples on the other. Here what was at stake was the desire of these peoples for survival, and their consequent demand for certain forms of autonomy in their self-government, as well as the ability to adopt certain kinds of legislation deemed necessary for survival.

For instance, Quebec has passed a number of laws in the field of language. One regulates who can send their children to English-language schools (not francophones or immigrants); another requires that businesses with more than 50 employees be run in French; a third outlaws commercial signage in any language other than French. In other words, restrictions have been placed on Quebecers by their government, in the name of their collective goal of survival, which in other Canadian communities might easily be disallowed by virtue of the Charter. The fundamental question was: Is this variation acceptable or not?

The issue was finally raised by a proposed constitutional amendment, named after the site of the conference where it was first drafted, Meech Lake. The Meech amendment proposed to recognize Quebec as a "distinct society," and wanted to make this recognition one of the bases for judicial interpretation of the rest of the constitution, including the Charter. This seemed to open up the possibility for variation in its interpretation in different parts of the country. For many, such variation was fundamentally unacceptable. Examining why brings us to the heart of the question of how rights-liberalism is related to diversity.

The Canadian Charter follows the trend of the last half of the twentieth century, and gives a basis for judicial review on two basic scores. First, it defines a set of individual rights that are very similar to those protected in other charters and bills of rights in Western democracies, for example, in the United States and Europe. Second, it guarantees equal treatment of citizens in a variety of respects, or, alternatively put, it protects against discriminatory treatment on a number of irrelevant grounds, such as race or sex. There is a lot more in our Charter, including provisions for linguistic rights and aboriginal rights, that could be understood as according powers to collectivities, but the two themes I singled out dominate in the public consciousness.

This is no accident. These two kinds of provisions are now quite common in entrenched schedules of rights that provide the basis for judicial review. In this sense, the Western world, perhaps the world as a whole, is following American precedent. The Americans were the first to write out and entrench a bill of rights, which they did during the ratification of their Constitution and as a condition of its successful outcome. One might argue that they weren't entirely clear on judicial review as a method of securing those rights, but this rapidly became the practice. The first amendments protected individuals, and sometimes state governments, against encroachment by the new federal government. It was after the Civil War, in the period of triumphant Reconstruction, and particularly with the Fourteenth Amendment, which called for "equal protection" for all citizens under the laws, that the theme of non-discrimination became central to judicial review. But this theme is now on a par with the older norm of the defence of individual rights, and in public consciousness perhaps even ahead.

For a number of people in "English Canada," a political society's espousing certain collective goals threatens to run against both of these basic provisions of our Charter, or indeed any acceptable bill of rights. First, the collective goals may require restrictions on the behaviour of individuals that may violate their rights. For many non-francophone Canadians, both inside and outside Quebec, this feared outcome had already materialized with

Quebec's language legislation. For instance, Quebec legislation prescribes, as already mentioned, the type of school to which parents can send their children; and in the most famous instance, it forbids certain kinds of commercial signage. This latter provision was actually struck down by the Supreme Court as contrary to the Quebec Bill of Rights, as well as the Charter, and only re-enacted through the invocation of a clause in the Charter that permits legislatures in certain cases to override decisions of the courts relative to the Charter for a limited period of time (the so-called notwithstanding clause).

But second, even if overriding individual rights were not possible, espousing collective goals on behalf of a national group can be thought to be inherently discriminatory. In the modern world it will always be the case that not all those living as citizens under a certain jurisdiction will belong to the national group thus favoured. This in itself could be thought to provoke discrimination. But beyond this, the pursuit of the collective end will probably involve treating insiders and outsiders differently. Thus the schooling provisions of Law 101 forbid (roughly speaking) francophones and immigrants to send their children to English-language schools, but allow Canadian anglophones to do so.

This sense that the Charter clashes with basic Quebec policy was one of the grounds of opposition in the rest of Canada to the **Meech Lake Accord**. The cause for concern was the distinct society clause, and the common demand for amendment was that the Charter be "protected" against this clause, or take precedence over it. There was undoubtedly in this opposition a certain amount of old-style anti-Quebec prejudice, but there was also a serious philosophical point, which we need to articulate here.

Those who take the view that individual rights must always come first, and, along with non-discrimination provisions, must take precedence over collective goals, are often speaking from a liberal perspective that has become more and more widespread in the Anglo-American world. Its source is, of course, the United States, and it has recently been elaborated and defended by some of the best philosophical and legal minds in that society,

including John Rawls, Ronald Dworkin, [. . .] and others. There are various formulations of the main idea, but perhaps the one that encapsulates most clearly the point that is relevant to us is the one expressed by Dworkin in his short paper entitled "Liberalism."

Dworkin makes a distinction between two kinds of moral commitment. We all have views about the ends of life, about what constitutes a good life, which we and others ought to strive for. But we also acknowledge a commitment to deal fairly and equally with each other, regardless of how we conceive our ends. We might call this latter commitment "procedural," while commitments concerning the ends of life are "substantive." Dworkin claims that a liberal society is one that as a society adopts no particular substantive view about the ends of life. The society is, rather, united around a strong procedural commitment to treat people with equal respect. The reason that the polity as such can espouse no substantive view, cannot, for instance, allow that one of the goals of legislation should be to make people virtuous in one or another meaning of that term, is that this would involve a violation of its procedural norm. For, given the diversity of modern societies, it would unfailingly be the case that some people and not others would be committed to the favoured conception of virtue. They might be in a majority; indeed, it is very likely that they would be, for otherwise a democratic society probably would not espouse their view. Nevertheless, this view would not be everyone's view, and in espousing this substantive outlook the society would not be treating the dissident minority with equal respect. It would be saying to them, in effect, "your view is not as valuable, in the eyes of this polity, as that of your more numerous compatriots."

There are very profound philosophical assumptions underlying this view of liberalism, which is rooted in the thought of Immanuel Kant. Among other features, this view understands human dignity to consist largely in autonomy, that is, in the ability of each person to determine for himself or herself a view of the good life. Dignity is associated less with any particular understanding of the good life, such that someone's departure from this would detract from his or her own dignity, than with the power to consider and espouse for oneself some view or other. We are not respecting this power equally in all subjects, it is claimed, if we raise the outcome of some people's deliberations officially over that of others. A liberal society must remain neutral on the good life, and restrict itself to ensuring that however they see things, citizens deal fairly with each other and the state deals equally with all.

The popularity of this view of the human agent as primarily a subject of self-determining or self-expressive choice helps to explain why this model of liberalism is so strong. But we must also consider that it has been urged with great force and intelligence by liberal thinkers in the United States, and precisely in the context of constitutional doctrines of judicial review. Thus it is not surprising that the idea has become widespread, well beyond those who might subscribe to a specific Kantian philosophy, that a liberal society cannot accommodate publicly espoused notions of the good. This is the conception, as Michael Sandel has noted, of the "procedural republic," which has a very strong hold on the political agenda in the United States, and which has helped to place increasing emphasis on judicial review on the basis of constitutional texts at the expense of the ordinary political process of building majorities with a view to legislative action.

But a society with collective goals like Quebec's violates this model. It is axiomatic for Quebec governments that the survival and flourishing of French culture in Quebec is a good. Political society is not neutral between those who value remaining true to the culture of our ancestors and those who might want to cut loose in the name of some individual goal of self-development. It might be argued that one could after all capture a goal like *survivance* for a proceduralist liberal society. One could consider the French language, for instance, as a collective resource that individuals might want to make use of, and act for its preservation, just as one does for clean air or green spaces. But this can't capture the full thrust of policies designed for cultural survival. It is not just a matter of having

the French language available for those who might choose it. This might be seen to be the goal of some of the measures of federal bilingualism over the last twenty years. But it also involves making sure that there is a community of people here in the future that will want to avail itself of the opportunity to use the French language. Policies aimed at survival actively seek to *create* members of the community, for instance, in their assuring that future generations continue to identify as French-speakers. There is no way that these policies could be seen as just providing a facility to already existing people.

Quebecers, therefore, and those who give similar importance to this kind of collective goal, tend to opt for a rather different model of a liberal society. On their view, a society can be organized around a definition of the good life, without this being seen as a depreciation of those who do not personally share this definition. Where the nature of the good requires that it be sought in common, this is the reason for its being a matter of public policy. According to this conception, a liberal society singles itself out as such by the way in which it treats minorities, including those who do not share public definitions of the good, and above all by the rights it accords to all of its members. But now the rights in question are conceived to be the fundamental and crucial ones that have been recognized as such from the very beginning of the liberal tradition: rights to life, liberty, due process, free speech, free practice of religion, and so on. On this model, there is a dangerous overlooking of an essential boundary in speaking of fundamental rights to things like commercial signage in the language of one's choice. One has to distinguish the fundamental liberties, those that should never be infringed and therefore ought to be unassailably entrenched, on one hand, from privileges and immunities that are important, but that can be revoked or restricted for reasons of public policy—although one would need a strong reason to do this—on the other.

A society with strong collective goals can be liberal, on this view, provided it is also capable of respecting diversity, especially when dealing with those who do not share its common goals;

and provided it can offer adequate safeguards for fundamental rights. There will undoubtedly be tensions and difficulties in pursuing these objectives together, but such a pursuit is not impossible, and the problems are not in principle greater than those encountered by any liberal society that has to combine, for example, liberty and equality, or prosperity and justice.

Here are two incompatible views of liberal society. One of the great sources of our present disharmony is that the two views have squared off against each other in the last decade. The resistance to the "distinct society" that called for precedence to be given to the Charter came in part from a spreading procedural outlook in English Canada. From this point of view, attributing the goal of promoting Quebec's distinct society to a government is to acknowledge a collective goal, and this move had to be neutralized by being subordinated to the existing Charter. From the standpoint of Quebec, this attempt to impose a procedural model of liberalism not only would deprive the distinct society clause of some of its force as a rule of interpretation, but bespoke a rejection of the model of liberalism on which this society was founded. Each society misperceived the other throughout the Meech Lake debate. But here both perceived each other accurately—and didn't like what they saw. The rest of Canada saw that the distinct society clause legitimated collective goals. And Quebec saw that the move to give the Charter precedence imposed a form of liberal society that was alien to it, and to which Quebec could never accommodate itself without surrendering its identity (see Laforest).

I have delved deeply into this case because it seems to me to illustrate the fundamental questions. There is a form of the politics of equal respect, as enshrined in a liberalism of rights, that is inhospitable to difference, because (a) it insists on uniform application of the rules defining these rights, without exception, and (b) it is suspicious of collective goals. Of course, this doesn't mean that this model seeks to abolish cultural differences. This would be an absurd accusation. But I call it inhospitable to difference because it can't accommodate what the members of distinct societies really aspire to, which is survival. This is (b) a collective goal, which (a) almost inevitably will call for some variations in the kinds of law we deem permissible from one cultural context to another, as the Quebec case clearly shows.

I think this form of liberalism is guilty as charged by the proponents of a politics of difference. Fortunately, however, there are other models of liberal society that take a different line on (a) and (b). These forms do call for the invariant defence of *certain* rights, of course. There would be no question of cultural differences determining the application of *habeas corpus*, for example. But they distinguish these fundamental rights from the broad range of immunities and presumptions of uniform treatment that have sprung up in modern cultures of judicial review. They are willing to weigh the importance of certain forms of uniform treatment against the importance of cultural survival, and opt sometimes in favour of the latter. They are thus in the end not procedural models of liberalism, but are grounded very much on judgments about what makes a good life—judgments in which the integrity of cultures has an important place.

Although I cannot argue it here, obviously I would endorse this kind of model. Indisputably, though, more and more societies today are turning out to be multicultural, in the sense of including more than one cultural community that wants to survive. The rigidities of procedural liberalism may rapidly become impractical in tomorrow's world. [. . .]

## Note

1. Will Kymlicka [. . .] tries to argue for a kind of politics of difference, notably in relation to Aboriginal rights in Canada, but from a basis that is firmly within a theory of liberal neutrality. He wants to argue on the basis of certain cultural needs—minimally, the need for an integral and undamaged cultural language with which one can define and pursue his or

her own conception of the good life. In certain circumstances, with disadvantaged populations, the integrity of the culture may require that we accord them more resources or rights than others. The argument is quite parallel to that made in relation to socio-economic inequalities that I mentioned above.

But where Kymlicka's interesting argument fails to recapture the actual demands made by the groups concerned—say Indian bands in Canada, or French-speaking Canadians—is with respect to their goal of survival. Kymlicka's reasoning is valid (perhaps) for existing people who find themselves trapped within a culture under pressure, and can flourish within it or not at all. But it doesn't justify measures designed to ensure survival through indefinite future generations. For the populations concerned, however, that is what is at stake. We need only think of the historical resonance of "la survivance" among French Canadians.

## Works Cited

Dworkin, R. *Taking Rights Seriously*. London: Duckworth, 1977.

Dworkin, R. "Liberalism." *Public and Private Morality*. Ed. S. Hampshire. Cambridge: Cambridge University Press, 1978.

Dworkin, R. *A Matter of Principle*. Cambridge, MA: Harvard University Press, 1985.

Habermas, J. *Theorie des kommunikativen Handelns*. Frankfurt: Suhrkarmp, 1981.

Kant, I. *Grundlegung der Metaphysik der Sitten*. Berlin: Gruyter, 1968.

Laforest, G. "L'esprit de 1982." *Le Québec et la restructuration du Canada, 1980-1992*. Eds. L. Balthasar, G. Laforest, and V. Lemieux. Quebec: Septentrion, 1991.

Rawls, J. *A Theory of Justice*. Cambridge, MA: Harvard University Press, 1971.

Rawls, J. "Justice as Fairness: Political Not Metaphysical." *Philosophy & Public Affairs* 14 (1985): 223–51.

Sandel, M. "The Procedural Republic and the Unencumbered Self." *Political Theory* 12 (1984): 81–96.

## Study Questions

1. Compare the two different meanings of the "politics of recognition" Taylor identifies in the public sphere: the "politics of universalism" based on dignity and the "politics of difference" based on identity. Provide an example that illustrates the tension between these.

2. In an endnote, Taylor notes that Kymlicka has sought to defend "a kind of politics of difference . . . within a theory of liberal neutrality." What is Kymlicka's approach, and why does Taylor believe it fails?

3. Describe the theoretical commitments of US-style procedural liberalism. Explain why Taylor believes that this version of liberalism underlies the views of many in English Canada concerning the Canadian Charter of Rights and Freedoms and language laws in Quebec.

4. Taylor believes that multiculturalism requires an alternative, non-procedural, form of liberalism that is conducive to the aspirations of cultural groups. Describe Taylor's preferred version of liberalism, and explain how it supports "distinct society" status for Quebec.

# Will Kymlicka

Will Kymlicka is a professor and Canada Research Chair in political philosophy at Queen's University. Kymlicka has a BA from Queen's and a BPhil and DPhil from Oxford. He taught previously at the University of Toronto, the University of Ottawa, and Carleton University. Kymlicka was named a fellow of the Royal Society of Canada in 2003 and received the Killam Prize in 2004. Kymlicka's *Multicultural Citizenship*, excerpted here, won awards from the Canadian and American Political Science Associations for its groundbreaking defence of group-based minority rights within a liberal political framework. Since its publication in 1995, the book has been translated into at least 18 languages.

# From *Multicultural Citizenship: A Liberal Theory of Minority Rights*

## 1. The Politics of Multiculturalism [Ch. 2]

Modern societies are increasingly confronted with minority groups demanding recognition of their identity, and accommodation of their cultural differences. This is often phrased as the challenge of "multiculturalism." But the term "multicultural" covers many different forms of cultural pluralism, each of which raises its own challenges. There are a variety of ways in which minorities become incorporated into political communities, from the conquest and colonization of previously self-governing societies to the voluntary immigration of individuals and families. These differences in the mode of incorporation affect the nature of minority groups, and the sort of relationship they desire with the larger society. [. . .]

In this chapter, I focus on two broad patterns of cultural diversity. In the first case, cultural diversity arises from the incorporation of previously self-governing, territorially concentrated cultures into a larger state. These incorporated cultures, which I call "national minorities," typically wish to maintain themselves as distinct societies alongside the majority culture, and demand various forms of autonomy or self-government to ensure their survival as distinct societies.

In the second case, cultural diversity arises from individual and familial immigration. Such immigrants often coalesce into loose associations which I call "ethnic groups." They typically wish to integrate into the larger society, and to be accepted as full members of it. While they often seek greater recognition of their ethnic identity, their aim is not to become a separate and self-governing nation alongside the larger society, but to modify the institutions and laws of the mainstream society to make them more accommodating of cultural differences.

These are just general patterns, of course, not laws of nature. [. . .] But we cannot begin to understand and evaluate the politics of multiculturalism unless we see how the historical incorporation of minority groups shapes their collective institutions, identities, and aspirations. I will begin by describing the nature of these two broad categories, and then consider the specific demands associated with each.

## 1.1. Multination States and Polyethnic States

One source of cultural diversity is the coexistence within a given state of more than one nation, where "nation" means a historical community, more or less institutionally complete, occupying a given territory or homeland, sharing a distinct language and culture. A "nation" in this sociological sense is closely related to the idea of a "people" or a "culture"—indeed, these concepts are often defined in terms of each other. A country which contains more than one nation is, therefore, not a nation-state but a multination state, and the smaller cultures form "national minorities." The incorporation of different nations into a single state may be involuntary, as occurs when one cultural community is invaded and conquered by another, or is ceded from one imperial power to another, or when its homeland is overrun by colonizing settlers. But the formation of a multi-nation state may also arise voluntarily, when different cultures agree to form a federation for their mutual benefit. [. . .]

Canada's historical development has involved the federation of three distinct national groups (English, French, and Aboriginals).[1] The original incorpora-tion of the Québécois and Aboriginal communities into the Canadian political community was invol-untary. Indian homelands were overrun by French settlers, who were then conquered by the English. While the possibility of secession is very real for the Québécois, the historical preference of these groups [. . .] has not been to leave the federation, but to renegotiate the terms of federation, so as to increase their autonomy within it. [. . .]

Many other Western democracies are also multi-national, either because they have forcibly incorpo-rated indigenous populations (e.g., Finland and New Zealand), or because they were formed by the more or less voluntary federation of two or more European cultures (e.g., Belgium and Switzerland). In fact, many countries throughout the world are multina-tional, in the sense that their boundaries were drawn to include the territory occupied by pre-existing, and often previously self-governing, cultures. This is true of most countries throughout the former Communist bloc and the Third World.

To say that these countries are "multination" states is not to deny that the citizens view them-selves for some purposes as a single people. For example, the Swiss have a strong sense of common loyalty, despite their cultural and linguistic divisions. Indeed, multination states cannot survive unless the various national groups have an allegiance to the larger political community they cohabit.

Some commentators describe this common loy-alty as a form of national identity, and so consider Switzerland a nation-state. I think this is misleading. We should distinguish "patriotism," the feeling of allegiance to a state, from national identity, the sense of membership in a national group. In Switzerland as in most multination states, national groups feel allegiance to the larger state only because the larger state recognizes and respects their distinct national existence. The Swiss are patriotic, but the Switzerland they are loyal to is defined as a federation of distinct peoples. For that reason, it is best seen as a multi-nation state, and the feelings of common loyalty it engenders reflect a shared patriotism, not a common national identity.

The second source of cultural pluralism is immi-gration. A country will exhibit cultural pluralism if it accepts large numbers of individuals and fami-lies from other cultures as immigrants, and allows them to maintain some of their ethnic particularity. This has always been a vital part of life in Australia, Canada, and the United States, which have the three highest per capita rates of immigration in the world. Indeed, well over half of all legal immi-gration in the world goes into one of these three countries.

Prior to the 1960s, immigrants to these coun-tries were expected to shed their distinctive heritage and assimilate entirely to existing cultural norms. This is known as the "Anglo-conformity" model of immigration. Indeed, some groups were denied entry if they were seen as unassimilable (e.g. restric-tions on Chinese immigration in Canada and the United States, the "white-only" immigration policy in Australia). Assimilation was seen as essential for political stability, and was further rationalized through ethnocentric denigration of other cultures.

This shared commitment to Anglo-conformity is obscured by the popular but misleading con-trast between the American "melting-pot" and the Canadian "ethnic mosaic." While "ethnic mosaic" carries the connotation of respect for the integrity of immigrant cultures, in practice it simply meant that immigrants to Canada had a choice of two dominant cultures to assimilate to. [. . .]

However, beginning in the 1970s, under pressure from immigrant groups, all three countries rejected the assimilationist model, and adopted a more toler-ant and pluralistic policy which allows and indeed encourages immigrants to maintain various aspects of their ethnic heritage. It is now widely (though far from unanimously) accepted that immigrants should be free to maintain some of their old customs regarding food, dress, religion, and to associate with each other to maintain these practices. This is no longer seen as unpatriotic or "unamerican."

But it is important to distinguish this sort of cultural diversity from that of national minorities. Immigrant groups are not "nations," and do not occupy homelands. Their distinctiveness is manifested primarily in their family lives and in voluntary associations, and is not inconsistent with their institutional integration. They still participate within the public institutions of the dominant culture(s) and speak the dominant language(s). For example, immigrants (except for the elderly) must learn English to acquire citizenship in Australia and the United States, and learning English is a mandatory part of children's education. In Canada, they must learn either of the two official languages (French or English). [. . .]

Immigration is not only a "New World" phenomenon. Many other countries also accept immigrants, although not in the same magnitude as the United States, Canada, and Australia. Since World War II, Britain and France have accepted immigrants from their former colonies. Other countries which accept few immigrants nonetheless accept refugees from throughout the world (e.g., Sweden). In yet other countries, "guest-workers" who were originally seen as only temporary residents have become *de facto* immigrants. For example, Turkish guest-workers in Germany have become permanent residents, with their families, and Germany is often the only home known to their children (and now grandchildren). All these countries are exhibiting increasing "polyethnicity."

Obviously, a single country may be both multinational (as a result of the colonizing, conquest, or confederation of national communities) and polyethnic (as a result of individual and familial immigration). Indeed, all of these patterns are present in Canada— the Indians were overrun by French settlers, the French were conquered by the English, although the current relationship between the two can be seen as a voluntary federation, and both the English and French have accepted immigrants who are allowed

to maintain their ethnic identity. So Canada is both multinational and polyethnic. [. . .]

## 1.2. Three Forms of Group-Differentiated Rights

Virtually all liberal democracies are either multinational or polyethnic, or both. The "challenge of multiculturalism" is to accommodate these national and ethnic differences in a stable and morally defensible way (Gutmann 1993). In this section, I will discuss some of the most important ways in which democracies have responded to the demands of national minorities and ethnic groups.

In all liberal democracies, one of the major mechanisms for accommodating cultural differences is the protection of the civil and political rights of individuals. It is impossible to overstate the importance of freedom of association, religion, speech, mobility, and political organization for protecting group difference. These rights enable individuals to form and maintain the various groups and associations which constitute civil society, to adapt these groups to changing circumstances, and to promote their views and interests to the wider population. The protection afforded by these common rights of citizenship is sufficient for many of the legitimate forms of diversity in society. [. . .]

However, it is increasingly accepted in many countries that some forms of cultural difference can only be accommodated through special legal or constitutional measures, above and beyond the common rights of citizenship. Some forms of group difference can only be accommodated if their members have certain group-specific rights—what Iris Young calls "differentiated citizenship" (258). [. . .]

It is these special group-specific measures for accommodating national and ethnic differences that I will focus on. There are at least three forms of group-specific rights: (1) self-government rights; (2) polyethnic rights; and (3) special representation rights. [. . .]

1. *Self-government rights.* In most multination states, the component nations are inclined to demand some form of political autonomy or

territorial jurisdiction, so as to ensure the full and free development of their cultures and the best interests of their people. At the extreme, nations may wish to secede, if they think their self-determination is impossible within the larger state.

The right of national groups to self-determination is given (limited) recognition in international law. According to the United Nations' Charter, "all peoples have the right to self-determination." However, the UN has not defined "peoples," and it has generally applied the principle of self-determination only to overseas colonies, not internal national minorities, even when the latter were subject to the same sort of colonization and conquest as the former. This limitation on self-determination to overseas colonies (known as the "salt-water thesis") is widely seen as arbitrary, and many national minorities insist that they too are "peoples" or "nations," and, as such, have the right of self-determination. They demand certain powers of self-government which they say were not relinquished by their (often involuntary) incorporation into a larger state.

One mechanism for recognizing claims to self-government is federalism, which divides powers between the central government and regional subunits (provinces/states/cantons). Where national minorities are regionally concentrated, the boundaries of federal subunits can be drawn so that the national minority forms a majority in one of the subunits. Under these circumstances, federalism can provide extensive self-government for a national minority, guaranteeing its ability to make decisions in certain areas without being outvoted by the larger society.

For example, under the federal division of powers in Canada, the province of Quebec (which is 80 per cent francophone) has extensive jurisdiction over issues that are crucial to the survival of the French culture, including control over education, language, culture, as well as significant input into immigration policy. The other nine provinces also have these powers, but the major impetus behind the existing division of powers, and indeed behind the entire federal system, is the need to accommodate the Québécois. At the time of Confederation, most English Canadian leaders were in favour of a unitary state, like Britain, and agreed to a federal system primarily to accommodate French Canadians. [. . .]

Federalism can only serve as a mechanism for self-government if the national minority forms a majority in one of the federal subunits, as the Québécois do in Quebec. This is not true of most indigenous peoples in North America, who are fewer in number and whose communities are often dispersed across state/provincial lines. Moreover, with few exceptions (such as the Navaho), no redrawing of the boundaries of these federal subunits would create a state, province, or territory with an indigenous majority. It would have been possible to create a state or province dominated by an Indian tribe in the nineteenth century, but, given the massive influx of settlers since then, it is now virtually inconceivable.

One exception concerns the Inuit in the north of Canada, who wish to divide the Northwest Territories into two, so that they will form the majority in the eastern half (to be called "Nunavut"). This redrawing of federal boundaries is seen as essential to the implementation of the Inuit's right of self-government, and has recently been approved by the federal government.[2]

For the other indigenous peoples in North America, however, self-government has been primarily tied to the system of reserved lands (known as tribal "reservations" in the United States, and band "reserves" in Canada). Substantial powers have been devolved from the federal government to the tribal/band councils which govern each reserve. Indian tribes/bands have been acquiring increasing control over health, education, family law, policing, criminal justice, and resource development. They are becoming, in effect, a third order of government, with a collection of powers that is carved out of both federal and state/provincial jurisdictions. However, the administrative difficulties are daunting. Indian tribes/bands differ enormously in the sorts of powers they desire. Moreover, they are territorially located within existing states/provinces, and must co-ordinate their self-government with state/provincial agencies. The exact scope and mechanisms of indigenous self-government in Canada and the United States therefore remain unclear. [. . .]

Self-government claims, then, typically take the form of devolving political power to a political unit substantially controlled by the members of the national minority, and substantially corresponding to their historical homeland or territory. It is important to note that these claims are not seen as a temporary measure, nor as a remedy for a form of oppression that we might (and ought) someday to eliminate. On the contrary, these rights are often described as "inherent," and so permanent (which is one reason why national minorities seek to have them entrenched in the constitution).

2. *Polyethnic rights.* As I noted earlier, immigrant groups in the last thirty years have successfully challenged the "Anglo-conformity" model which assumed that they should abandon all aspects of their ethnic heritage and assimilate to existing cultural norms and customs. At first, this challenge simply took the form of demanding the right freely to express their particularity without fear of prejudice or discrimination in the mainstream society. It was the demand, as Walzer put it, that "politics be separated from nationality—as it was already separated from religion" (6–11).

But the demands of ethnic groups have expanded in important directions. It became clear that positive steps were required to root out discrimination and prejudice, particularly against visible minorities. For this reason, anti-racism policies are considered part of the "multiculturalism" policy in Canada and Australia, as are changes to the education curriculum to recognize the history and contribution of minorities. However, these policies are primarily directed at ensuring the effective exercise of the common rights of citizenship, and so do not really qualify as group-differentiated citizenship rights.

Some ethnic groups and religious minorities have also demanded various forms of public funding of their cultural practices. This includes the funding of ethnic associations, magazines, and festivals. Given that most liberal states provide funding to the arts and museums, so as to preserve the richness and diversity of our cultural resources, funding for ethnic studies and ethnic associations can be seen as falling under this heading. Indeed, some people defend this funding simply as a way of ensuring that ethnic groups are not discriminated against in state funding of art and culture. Some people believe that public funding agencies have traditionally been biased in favour of European-derived forms of cultural expression, and programmes targeted at ethnic groups remedy this bias. A related demand [. . .] is for the provision of immigrant language education in schools.

Perhaps the most controversial demand of ethnic groups is for exemptions from laws and regulations that disadvantage them, given their religious practices. For example, Jews and Muslims in Britain have sought exemption from Sunday closing or animal slaughtering legislation; Sikh men in Canada have sought exemption from motorcycle helmet laws and from the official dress-codes of police forces, so that they can wear their turban; Orthodox Jews in the United States have sought the right to wear the yarmulka during military service; and Muslim girls in France have sought exemption from school dress-codes so that they can wear the *chador*.

These group-specific measures—which I call "polyethnic rights"—are intended to help ethnic groups and religious minorities express their cultural particularity and pride without it hampering their success in the economic and political institutions of the dominant society. Like self-government rights, these polyethnic rights are not seen as temporary, because the cultural differences they protect are not something we seek to eliminate. But, [. . .] unlike self-government rights, polyethnic rights are usually intended to promote integration into the larger society, not self-government.

3. *Special representation rights.* While the traditional concern of national minorities and ethnic groups has been with either self-government or polyethnic rights, there has been increasing interest by these groups, as well as other non-ethnic social groups, in the idea of special representation rights.

Throughout the Western democracies, there is increasing concern that the political process is "unrepresentative," in the sense that it fails to reflect the diversity of the population. Legislatures in most of these countries are dominated by middle-class, able-bodied, white men. A more representative process, it is said, would include members of ethnic and racial minorities, women, the poor, the disabled, etc. The under-representation of historically disadvantaged groups is a general phenomenon. In the United States and Canada, women, racial minorities, and indigenous peoples all have under one-third of the seats they would have based on their demographic weight. People with disabilities and the economically disadvantaged are also significantly under-represented.

One way to reform the process is to make political parties more inclusive, by reducing the barriers which inhibit women, ethnic minorities, or the poor from becoming party candidates or party leaders; another way is to adopt some form of proportional representation, which has historically been associated with greater inclusiveness of candidates.

However, there is increasing interest in the idea that a certain number of seats in the legislature should be reserved for the members of disadvantaged or marginalized groups. During the debate in Canada over the Charlottetown Accord, for example, a number of recommendations were made for the guaranteed representation of women, ethnic minorities, official language minorities, and Aboriginals.

Group representation rights are often defended as a response to some systemic disadvantage or barrier in the political process which makes it impossible for the group's views and interests to be effectively represented. Insofar as these rights are seen as a response to oppression or systemic disadvantage, they are most plausibly seen as a temporary measure on the way to a society where the need for special representation no longer exists—a form of political "affirmative action." Society should seek to remove the oppression and disadvantage, thereby eliminating the need for these rights.

However, the issue of special representation rights for groups is complicated, because special representation is sometimes defended, not on grounds of oppression, but as a corollary of self-government.

A minority's right to self-government would be severely weakened if some external body could unilaterally revise or revoke its powers, without consulting the minority or securing its consent. Hence it would seem to be a corollary of self-government that the national minority be guaranteed representation on any body which can interpret or modify its powers of self-government (e.g., the Supreme Court). Since the claims of self-government are seen as inherent and permanent, so too are the guarantees of representation which flow from it (unlike guarantees grounded on oppression). [. . .]

## 2. Justice and Minority Rights [Ch. 6]

[. . .] [M]any liberals believe that people's interest in cultural membership is adequately protected by the common rights of citizenship, and that any further measures to protect this interest are illegitimate. They argue that a system of universal individual rights already accommodates cultural differences, by allowing each person the freedom to associate with others in the pursuit of shared religious or ethnic practices. Freedom of association enables people from different backgrounds to pursue their distinctive ways of life without interference. Every individual is free to create or join various associations, and to seek new adherents for them, in the "cultural marketplace." Every way of life is free to attract adherents, and if some ways of life are unable to maintain or gain the voluntary adherence of people that may be unfortunate, but it is not unfair. On this view, giving political recognition or support to particular cultural practices or associations is unnecessary and unfair. It is unnecessary, because a valuable way of life will have no difficulty attracting adherents. And it is unfair, because it subsidizes some people's choices at the expense of others.

Proponents of this "strict separation of state and ethnicity" view need not deny that people have a deep bond to their own culture (although some do). They may just argue that cultures do not need state assistance to survive. If a societal culture is worth saving, one could argue, the members of the culture will sustain it through their own choices. If the culture is decaying, it must be because some people no longer find it worthy of their allegiance. The state, on this view, should not interfere with the cultural market-place—it should neither promote nor inhibit the maintenance of any particular culture. Rather, it should respond with "benign neglect" to ethnic and national differences.

I think this common view is not only mistaken, but actually incoherent. The idea of responding to cultural differences with "benign neglect" makes no sense. Government decisions on languages, internal boundaries, public holidays, and state symbols unavoidably involve recognizing, accommodating, and supporting the needs and identities of particular ethnic and national groups. The state unavoidably promotes certain cultural identities, and thereby disadvantages others. Once we recognize this, we need to rethink the justice of minority rights claims. In this chapter, I will argue that some self-government rights and polyethnic rights are consistent with, and indeed required by, liberal justice. [. . .]

## 2.1. The Equality Argument

Many defenders of group-specific rights for ethnic and national minorities insist that they are needed to ensure that all citizens are treated with genuine equality. On this view, "the accommodation of differences is the essence of true equality,"[3] and group-specific rights are needed to accommodate our differences. I think this argument is correct, within certain limits.

Proponents of "benign neglect" will respond that individual rights already allow for the accommodation of differences, and that true equality requires equal rights for each individual regardless of race or ethnicity. [. . .] This assumption that liberal equality precludes group-specific rights is relatively recent, and arose in part as an (over-)generalization of the racial desegregation movement in the United States. It has some superficial plausibility. In many cases, claims for group-specific rights are simply an attempt by one group to dominate and oppress another.

But some minority rights eliminate, rather than create, inequalities. Some groups are unfairly disadvantaged in the cultural market-place, and political recognition and support rectify this disadvantage. I will start with the case of national minorities. The viability of their societal cultures may be undermined by economic and political decisions made by the majority. They could be outbid or outvoted on resources and policies that are crucial to the survival of their societal cultures. The members of majority cultures do not face this problem. Given the importance of cultural membership, this is a significant inequality which, if not addressed, becomes a serious injustice.

Group-differentiated rights—such as territorial autonomy, veto powers, guaranteed representation in central institutions, land claims, and language rights—can help rectify this disadvantage, by alleviating the vulnerability of minority cultures to majority decisions. These external protections ensure that members of the minority have the same opportunity to live and work in their own culture as members of the majority. [. . .]

These rights may impose restrictions on the members of the larger society, by making it more costly for them to move into the territory of the minority (e.g., longer residency requirements, fewer government services in their language), or by giving minority members priority in the use of certain land and resources (e.g., indigenous hunting and fishing rights). But the sacrifice required of non-members by the existence of these rights is far less than the sacrifice members would face in the absence of such rights.

Where these rights are recognized, members of the majority who choose to enter the minority's homeland may have to forgo certain benefits they are accustomed to. This is a burden. But without such rights, the members of many minority cultures face the loss of their culture, a loss which we cannot reasonably ask people to accept.

Any plausible theory of justice should recognize the fairness of these external protections for national minorities. They are clearly justified, I believe, within a liberal egalitarian theory, such as Rawls's and Dworkin's, which emphasizes the importance of rectifying unchosen inequalities. Indeed inequalities in cultural membership are just the sort which Rawls says we should be concerned about, since their effects are "profound and pervasive and present from birth" (96).

This equality-based argument will only endorse special rights for national minorities if there actually is a disadvantage with respect to cultural membership, and if the rights actually serve to rectify the disadvantage. Hence the legitimate scope of these rights will vary with the circumstances. In North America, indigenous groups are more vulnerable to majority decisions than the Québécois or Puerto Ricans, and so their external protections will be more extensive. For example, restrictions on the sale of land which are necessary in the context of indigenous peoples are not necessary, and hence not justified, in the case of Quebec or Puerto Rico.

At some point, demands for increased powers or resources will not be necessary to ensure the same opportunity to live and work in one's culture. Instead, they will simply be attempts to gain benefits denied to others, to have more resources to pursue one's way of life than others have. This was clearly the case with apartheid, where whites constituting under 20 per cent of the population controlled 87 per cent of the land mass of the country, and monopolized all the important levers of state power.

One could imagine a point where the amount of land reserved for indigenous peoples would not be necessary to provide reasonable external protections, but rather would simply provide unequal opportunities to them. Justice would then require that the holdings of indigenous peoples be subject to the same redistributive taxation as the wealth of other advantaged groups, so as to assist the less well off in society. In the real world, of course, most indigenous peoples are struggling to maintain the bare minimum of land needed to sustain the viability of their communities. But it is possible that their land holdings could exceed what justice allows.

The legitimacy of certain measures may also depend on their timing. For example, many people have suggested that a new South African constitution should grant a veto power over certain important decisions to some or all of the major national groups. This sort of veto power is a familiar feature of various "consociational democracies" in Europe, and [. . .] under certain circumstances it can promote justice. But it would probably be unjust to give privileged groups a veto power before there has been a dramatic redistribution of wealth and opportunities (Adam 295). A veto power can promote justice if it helps protect a minority from unjust policies that favour the majority; but it is an obstacle to justice if it allows a privileged group the leverage to maintain its unjust advantages.

So the ideal of "benign neglect" is not in fact benign. It ignores the fact that the members of a national minority face a disadvantage which the members of the majority do not face. In any event, the idea that the government could be neutral with respect to ethnic and national groups is patently false. [. . .] One of the most important determinants of whether a culture survives is whether its language is the language of government—i.e., the language of public schooling, courts, legislatures, welfare agencies, health services, etc. When the government decides the language of public schooling, it is providing what is probably the most important form of support needed by societal cultures, since it guarantees the passing on of the language and its associated traditions and conventions to the next generation. Refusing to provide public schooling in a minority language, by contrast, is almost inevitably condemning that language to ever-increasing marginalization.

The government therefore cannot avoid deciding which societal cultures will be supported. And if it supports the majority culture, by using the majority's language in schools and public agencies, it cannot refuse official recognition to minority languages on the ground that this violates "the separation of state and ethnicity." This shows that the analogy between religion and culture is mistaken. [. . .] Many liberals say that just as the state should not recognize, endorse, or support any particular church, so it should not recognize, endorse, or support any particular cultural group or identity. But the analogy does not work. It is quite possible for a state not to have an established church. But the state cannot help but give at least partial establishment to a culture when it decides which language is to be used in public schooling, or in the provision of state services. The state can (and should) replace religious oaths in courts with secular oaths, but it cannot replace the use of English in courts with no language. [. . .]

One could argue that decisions about the language of schooling and public services should be determined, not by officially recognizing the existence of various groups, but simply by allowing each political subunit to make its own language policy on a democratic basis. If a national minority forms a majority in the relevant unit, they can decide to have their mother tongue adopted as an official language in that unit. But this is because they are a local majority, not because the state has officially recognized them as a "nation."

This is sometimes said to be the American approach to language rights, since there is no constitutional definition of language rights in the United States. But in fact the American government has historically tried to make sure that such "local" decisions are always made by political units that have an anglophone majority. [. . .] Decisions about state borders, or about when to admit territories as states, have been explicitly made with the aim of ensuring that there will be an anglophone majority. States in the American south-west and Hawaii were only offered statehood when the national minorities residing in those areas were outnumbered by settlers and immigrants. And some people oppose offering statehood to Puerto Rico precisely on the grounds that it will never have an anglophone majority (Rubinstein; Glazer).

This illustrates a more general point. Leaving decisions about language to political subunits just pushes back the problem. What are the relevant political units—what level of government should make these decisions? Should each neighbourhood be able to decide on the language of public schooling and public services in that neighbourhood? Or should this decision be left to larger units, such as cities or provinces? And how do we decide on the boundaries of these subunits? If we draw municipal or provincial boundaries in one way, then a national minority will not form even a local majority. But if we draw the boundaries another way, then the national minority will form a local majority. In a multination state, decisions on boundaries and the division of

powers are inevitably decisions about which national group will have the ability to use which state powers to sustain its culture. [. . .]

The whole idea of "benign neglect" is incoherent, and reflects a shallow understanding of the relationship between states and nations. In the areas of official languages, political boundaries, and the division of powers, there is no way to avoid supporting this or that societal culture, or deciding which groups will form a majority in political units that control culture-affecting decisions regarding language, education, and immigration.

So the real question is, what is a fair way to recognize languages, draw boundaries, and distribute powers? And the answer, I think, is that we should aim at ensuring that all national groups have the opportunity to maintain themselves as a distinct culture, if they so choose. This ensures that the good of cultural membership is equally protected for the members of all national groups. In a democratic society, the majority nation will always have its language and societal culture supported, and will have the legislative power to protect its interests in culture-affecting decisions. The question is whether fairness requires that the same benefits and opportunities should be given to national minorities. The answer, I think, is clearly yes.

Hence group-differentiated self-government rights compensate for unequal circumstances which put the members of minority cultures at a systemic disadvantage in the cultural market-place, regardless of their personal choices in life. This is one of many areas in which true equality requires not identical treatment, but rather differential treatment in order to accommodate differential needs. [. . .]

Let me now turn to polyethnic rights for ethnic groups. I believe there is an equality-based argument for these rights as well, which also invokes the impossibility of separating state from ethnicity, but in a different way. [. . .] The context of choice for immigrants, unlike national minorities, primarily involves equal access to the mainstream culture(s). Having uprooted themselves from their old culture, they are expected to become members of the national societies which already exist in their new country.

Hence promoting the good of cultural membership for immigrants is primarily a matter of enabling integration, by providing language training and fighting patterns of discrimination and prejudice. Generally speaking, this is more a matter of rigorously enforcing the common rights of citizenship than providing group-differentiated rights. Insofar as common rights of citizenship in fact create equal access to mainstream culture, then equality with respect to cultural membership is achieved.

But even here equality does justify some group-specific rights. Consider the case of public holidays. Some people object to legislation that exempts Jews and Muslims from Sunday closing legislation, on the ground that this violates the separation of state and ethnicity. But almost any decision on public holidays will do so. In the major immigration countries, public holidays currently reflect the needs of Christians. Hence government offices are closed on Sunday, and on the major religious holidays (Easter, Christmas). This need not be seen as a deliberate decision to promote Christianity and discriminate against other faiths (although this was undoubtedly part of the original motivation). Decisions about government holidays were made when there was far less religious diversity, and people just took it for granted that the government work-week should accommodate Christian beliefs about days of rest and religious celebration.

But these decisions can be a significant disadvantage to the members of other religious faiths. And having established a work-week that favours Christians, one can hardly object to exemptions for Muslims or Jews on the ground that they violate the separation of state and ethnicity. These groups are simply asking that their religious needs be taken into consideration in the same way that the needs of Christians have always been taken into account. Public holidays are another significant embarrassment for the "benign neglect" view, and it is interesting to note how rarely they are discussed in contemporary liberal theory.

Similar issues arise regarding government uniforms. Some people object to the idea that Sikhs or Orthodox Jews should be exempted from requirements regarding headgear in the police or military.

But here again it is important to recognize how the existing rules about government uniforms have been adopted to suit Christians. For example, existing dress-codes do not prohibit the wearing of wedding rings, which are an important religious symbol for many Christians (and Jews). And it is virtually inconceivable that designers of government dress-codes would have ever considered designing a uniform that prevented people from wearing wedding rings, unless this was strictly necessary for the job. Again, this should not be seen as a deliberate attempt to promote Christianity. It simply would have been taken for granted that uniforms should not unnecessarily conflict with Christian religious beliefs. Having adopted dress-codes that meet Christian needs, one can hardly object to exemptions for Sikhs and Orthodox Jews on the ground that they violate "benign neglect."

One can multiply the examples. For example, many state symbols such as flags, anthems, and mottoes reflect a particular ethnic or religious background ("In God We Trust"). The demand by ethnic groups for some symbolic affirmation of the value of polyethnicity (e.g., in government declarations and documents) is simply a demand that their identity be given the same recognition as the original Anglo-Saxon settlers.

It may be possible to avoid some of these issues by redesigning public holidays, uniforms, and state symbols. It is relatively easy to replace religious oaths with secular ones, and so we should. It would be more difficult, but perhaps not impossible, to replace existing public holidays and work-weeks with more "neutral" schedules for schools and government offices.

But there is no way to have a complete "separation of state and ethnicity." In various ways, the ideal of "benign neglect" is a myth. Government decisions on languages, internal boundaries, public holidays, and state symbols unavoidably involve recognizing, accommodating, and supporting the needs and identities of particular ethnic and national groups. Nor is there any reason to regret this fact. There is no reason to regret the existence of official languages and public holidays, and no one gains by creating unnecessary conflicts between government regulations and religious beliefs. The only question is how to ensure that these unavoidable forms of support for particular ethnic and national groups are provided fairly—that is, how to ensure that they do not privilege some groups and disadvantage others. In so far as existing policies support the language, culture, and identity of dominant nations and ethnic groups, there is an argument of equality for ensuring that some attempts are made to provide similar support for minority groups, through self-government and polyethnic rights.

## Notes

1. It is important to note that Aboriginal peoples are not a single nation. The term "Aboriginal" covers three categories of Aboriginals (Indian, Inuit, and Métis), and the term Indian itself is a legal fiction, behind which there are numerous distinct Aboriginal nations with their own histories and separate community identities.

2. The new territory of Nunavut came into existence on 1 April 1999.—LG

3. This phrase is from the judgment of the Canadian Supreme Court in explaining its interpretation of the equality guarantees under the Canadian Charter of Rights (*Andrews v. Law Society of British Columbia* 1 SCR 143; 56 DLR (4th) 1).

## Works Cited

Adam, H. "The Failure of Political Liberalism." *Ethnic Power Mobilized: Can South Africa Change?* Eds. H. Adam and H. Giliomee. New Haven, CT: Yale University Press, 1979. 258–85.

Dworkin, R. "What is Equality? Part II: Equality of Resources." *Philosophy and Public Affairs* 10, 4 (1981): 283–345.

Glazer, N. *Ethnic Dilemmas: 1964–1982.* Cambridge, MA: Harvard University Press, 1983.

Gutmann, A. "The Challenge of Multiculturalism to Political Ethics." *Philosophy and Public Affairs* 22, 3 (1993): 171–206.

Rawls, J. *A Theory of Justice*. London: Oxford University Press, 1971.

Rubinstein, A. "Is Statehood for Puerto Rico in the National Interest?" *In Depth: A Journal for Values and Public Policy* (Spring 1993): 87–99.

Walzer, M. "Pluralism in Political Perspective." *The Politics of Ethnicity*. Ed. M. Walzer. Cambridge, MA: Harvard University Press, 1982. 1–28.

Young, I. M. "Polity and Group Difference: A Critique of the Ideal of Universal Citizenship." *Ethics* 99, 2 (1989): 250–74.

## Study Questions

1. Kymlicka tells us that Canada is both a multination and polyethnic state, but not a nation. What does he mean by this? Do you agree or disagree?

2. On Kymlicka's account, what is an example of a minority group in Canada that is exercising the right of self-government, and what purpose does this right serve? On Kymlicka's account, what is an example of a minority group in Canada that is exercising a polyethnic right, and what purpose does this right serve?

3. What is the "benign neglect" view of cultural differences? Making reference to an example, explain why Kymlicka believes that this view is "not only mistaken, but actually incoherent."

4. In 1999, the Supreme Court of Canada issued a decision in the Donald Marshall case that recognized the right of the Mi'kmaq and Maliseet bands to earn a moderate livelihood from year-round fishing, hunting, and gathering. The decision was based on the existence of signed treaties dating to the 1760s. How might Kymlicka's argument from equality be used both to support and undermine these treaty rights?

# Dale Turner

Dale Turner is an associate professor of government and Native American studies at Dartmouth College. A Teme-Augama Anishnabai from northern Ontario, Turner has a BA from Concordia University and a PhD from McGill University. Turner specializes in political theory, with particular interest in theoretical and practical meanings of "sovereignty," especially "tribal" sovereignty. In this chapter from his 2006 book, *This Is Not a Peace Pipe*, Turner challenges Will Kymlicka's influential liberal theory of minority rights.

## Liberalism's Last Stand: Minority Rights and the (Mis)recognition of Aboriginal Sovereignty

From *This Is Not a Peace Pipe: Towards a Critical Indigenous Philosophy*

### 1. Introduction

Aboriginal rights, as they are entrenched in Canada's Constitution Act, 1982, [sections 15 and 35], can be interpreted as rights that are accorded to Aboriginal peoples by virtue of their membership in minority cultures. This characterization of Aboriginal rights, derived from various styles of liberalism, does not recognize the legitimacy of indigenous forms of political sovereignty. Sovereignty does not play an important role in determining the content of Aboriginal special rights because within the framework of liberal thought, it simply does not exist.[1] [. . .] Aboriginal rights, [. . .] if they exist at all, are subsumed within the superior forms of sovereignty held by the provincial and federal governments.

In this chapter I examine what many consider a generous account of Aboriginal rights and raise several serious concerns about this liberal characterization of Aboriginal rights. Since most Aboriginal communities claim that their "special" rights flow from their legitimate political sovereignty, I take issue with liberal claims that Aboriginal rights imply a type of "minority right." I then suggest why most Aboriginal peoples do not subscribe to liberalism's descriptions of their rights as minority rights. In view of Aboriginal understandings of their political sovereignty, justice demands that contemporary and future policy makers include Aboriginal voices when drafting legislation and policies that affect the welfare of Aboriginal peoples. In other words, a robust account of Aboriginal rights must include greater Aboriginal participation.

From an Aboriginal perspective, it is unfortunate that an investigation into the meaning of Aboriginal sovereignty must begin with an examination of liberalism. This is necessary because Aboriginal conceptions of sovereignty are not fully recognized as legitimate by Canada's federal and provincial governments. As Will Kymlicka states in *Liberalism, Community, and Culture*:

> For better or worse, it is predominantly non-Aboriginal judges and politicians who have the ultimate power to protect and enforce Aboriginal rights, and so it is important to find a justification of them that such people can recognize and understand. Aboriginal people have their own understanding of self-government drawn from their own experience, and that is important. But it is also important, politically, to know how non-Aboriginal Canadians—Supreme Court Justices, for example—will understand Aboriginal rights and relate them to their own experiences and traditions. . . . On the standard interpretation of liberalism, Aboriginal rights are viewed as matters of discrimination and/or privilege, not of equality. They will always, therefore, be viewed with the kind of suspicion that

led liberals like Trudeau to advocate their abolition. Aboriginal rights, at least in their robust form, will only be secure when they are viewed, not as competing with liberalism, but as an essential component of liberal political practice. (154)

This imperative, which I refer to as "Kymlicka's constraint," represents a profound reality check for Aboriginal peoples. I agree with Kymlicka that Aboriginal rights "in their robust form" ought not to compete with liberalism. But it is not simply a matter of waking liberals from their colonial slumbers in order to show them that Aboriginal forms of sovereignty make sense in the language of political liberalism. Indigenous peoples have tried for more than five hundred years to make colonial governments recognize the legitimacy of indigenous forms of political sovereignty.

I will use Kymlicka's classification of Aboriginal rights of governance as a special class of minority rights in order to show that his theory of minority rights requires us to include, and recognize, Aboriginal explanations of political sovereignty. So in one sense, I am contributing to the rich tradition of Aboriginal voices that have argued in favour of Aboriginal sovereignty. I differ from my predecessors in that I am not justifying or generating a theory of Aboriginal sovereignty at all; rather, I am going to engage Kymlicka's version of liberalism and show that it is not tenable *unless* it recognizes Aboriginal understandings of political sovereignty.

But my goals are not solely philosophical. I believe that Aboriginal conceptions of political sovereignty must be included in political liberalism's justification of Aboriginal rights so that the racist and oppressive public policies that have held Aboriginal peoples captive for more than one hundred thirty years can be changed. One way of renewing a just relationship—and more importantly, renewing hope among Aboriginal peoples—is to help non-Aboriginal peoples understand better the meaning and significance of Aboriginal forms of political sovereignty. The precise content of a theory of Aboriginal sovereignty will remain open, as indeed it should; the meaning of Aboriginal sovereignty in all its diversity is best understood by listening to the myriad voices of Aboriginal peoples themselves.

My discussion will fall into two sections. In the first, I briefly discuss Kymlicka's liberal theory of minority rights. For Kymlicka, Aboriginal rights are a special class of rights within a general theory of minority rights. He argues that Aboriginal rights do not pose a problem for liberalism, since they can be subsumed within a more general liberal theory of rights. Arguably, his liberalism offers the most generous accommodation of Aboriginal rights in contemporary liberalism; in fact, he is a strong advocate of Aboriginal self-government.

In the second section, I examine more closely Kymlicka's characterization of Aboriginal communities as "national minorities" that somehow became "incorporated" into the Canadian state. Kymlicka himself points out that this notion of incorporation is problematic and fraught with historical injustice. I will emphasize that a thorough understanding of "Aboriginal incorporation" (my own term) goes to the heart of our understandings of Aboriginal sovereignty and especially of how we ought to understand the historical relationship between Aboriginal peoples and the European newcomers.

In the limited space of this chapter, [. . .] I cannot provide a fully developed "theory" of Aboriginal forms of political sovereignty. I do, however, have room to suggest what I consider a more fruitful way of approaching this complex issue without necessarily discarding Kymlicka's liberalism. Essentially, in this chapter, I take up Kymlicka's idea of Aboriginal incorporation to show that a thorough investigation of the meaning of this concept requires a radical shift in our understandings of historical interpretation, political sovereignty, and most importantly, Aboriginal peoples" place in the Canadian state.

## 2. Kymlicka on the Liberal Theory of Minority Rights

Kymlicka begins *Liberalism, Community, and Culture* by stating that he will be examining the "broader account of the relationship between the individual and society" (1). In other words, he is interested in the individual's sense of belonging to a community and, therefore, to a culture. He proposes to defend an interpretation of liberalism—one influenced by **Rawls** and Dworkin—against communitarian objections that it possesses only a "thin" theory of culture. Communitarians mean by this objection that contemporary liberal theorists attach little value to the role culture plays in shaping an individual's moral and political identity. Supposedly, contemporary liberalism is unable to generate a rich or "thick" theory of culture, given the diversity of cultures prevalent in most constitutional democracies. There are two facets to the liberal-communitarian debate that Kymlicka wants to examine: the communitarian critiques demanding thick theories of culture, and the failure of both liberals and communitarians to deal with cultural diversity.

Kymlicka focuses on liberalism as a normative political philosophy, and examines what he takes to be the fundamental moral commitments made by a liberal political theory. The philosophical issue at hand is this: How is an individual to determine what her essential interest is when she deliberates about her moral status in the world? For Kymlicka, our essential interest is the fact that we attempt to live a good life; that is, we value most those things a good life contains. However, the current set of beliefs we hold to be of greatest value may be the wrong ones. So it is imperative that we be able to deliberate so that we can change our minds (when we come to consider certain beliefs that we have held to be inimical to the good life). Thus for Kymlicka our essential interest is living *the* good life—as opposed to the life we currently believe to be good (12). Next, according to Kymlicka, we must revise these beliefs from "the inside." An individual can lead a good life only if she makes choices according to the values she holds to be true. Kymlicka has two preconditions for what he takes to be the necessary conditions for the fulfilment of our essential interest in leading a good life. First, we must lead our life from the inside—that is, from the set of beliefs we value as the best for our pursuit of

the good life. Second, we must be free to question these beliefs (13).

Kymlicka introduces culture into his theory because we must evaluate our beliefs in a cultural context. In his earlier book *Liberalism, Community, and Culture*, he does not offer a substantive understanding of culture, because he is not interested in exploring culture per se, but rather in establishing a set of rationally devised cultural conditions: "Individuals must have the cultural *conditions* conducive to acquiring an awareness of different views of the good life, and to acquiring the ability to intelligently examine and re-examine these views" (13; emphasis added). These cultural conditions must allow individuals to live their lives from the inside; furthermore, these individuals must have the freedom to question their beliefs in "the light of whatever information and examples and arguments our culture can provide." The culture Kymlicka is referring to as "ours" has shown great concern for the rights of individuals. The liberal's explicit interest in the individual has forged the traditional liberal concerns for (Kymlicka's list) "education, freedom of expression, freedom of press, artistic freedom, etc." (13).

Kymlicka offers a more substantive discussion of culture in *Multicultural Citizenship: A Liberal Theory of Minority Rights*: "The sort of culture that I will focus on is a *societal culture*—that is, a culture which provides its members with meaningful ways of life across the full range of human activities, including social, educational, religious, recreational, and economic life, encompassing both public and private spheres. These cultures tend to be territorially concentrated, and based on a shared language" (76; emphasis added).

Moreover, a societal culture is "institutionally" embodied. Clearly, Kymlicka has the same type of community in mind here as he offered in *Liberalism, Community, and Culture*; specifically, a legitimate societal culture is "modern" and shares a common identity with an underlying commitment to individual equality and opportunity (76–7). The public policies of this type of societal culture are guided by three imperatives: first, the government must treat people as equals; second, the government must treat all individuals with equal concern and respect; and third, the government must provide all individuals with the appropriate liberties and resources they need to examine and act on their beliefs. These criteria constitute a liberal conception of justice. So for Kymlicka, it is vital for an individual to choose what is best for the good life and to be free to act on these choices: "For meaningful individual choice to be possible, individuals need not only access to information, the capacity to reflectively evaluate it, and freedom of expression and association. They also need access to a societal culture. Group-differentiated measures that secure and promote this access may, therefore, have a legitimate role to play in a liberal theory of justice" (84).

Cultural membership, then, is a primary good in Kymlicka's liberalism. Because culture is a primary good for all individuals, governments ought to preserve the integrity of the plurality of cultures from which individuals make their choices. Kymlicka identifies "two broad patterns of cultural diversity." In the first instance, "cultural diversity arises from the *incorporation* of *previously* self-governing, territorially concentrated cultures into a larger state. These incorporated cultures, which I call "national minorities," typically wish to maintain themselves as distinct societies alongside the majority culture, and demand various forms of autonomy or self-government to ensure their survival as distinct societies" (10; emphasis added).

The second pattern of cultural diversity arises out of "individual and familial immigration." Essentially, immigrants came to Canada under the assumption that they were going to become part of the existing societal culture; in a sense, they left behind their own societal cultures in order to join another. One of the main arguments of *Multicultural Citizenship* is that national minorities have stronger claims to group-differentiated rights than cultures that have immigrated to Canada from other parts of the world. In the Canadian context, the national minorities consist of the English and Scottish newcomers, the French newcomers, and the Aboriginal peoples.

Kymlicka claims that national minorities, as *previously* self-governing cultures, *incorporated* to form the Canadian state. He adds: "The incorporation of different nations into a single state may be involuntary, as occurs when one cultural community is invaded and conquered by another, or is ceded from one imperial power to another, or when its homeland is overrun by colonizing settlers" (11).

From an Aboriginal perspective, the Canadian state came into existence through all three practices: some Aboriginal communities were conquered,[2] some communities ceded powers to the British Crown and later to the Canadian governments, and many communities were simply overrun by colonial newcomers. Of course, these three practices were not exclusive to one another; most Aboriginal communities experienced all three forms of incorporation. I will return to the issue of Aboriginal incorporation later; first I will take a closer look at Kymlicka's justification for the special rights held by national minorities.

In Chapter 6 of *Multicultural Citizenship*, "Justice and Minority Rights," Kymlicka provides several overlapping arguments to justify minority rights, or group-differentiated rights, within a liberal democratic state. He discusses three arguments in favour of recognizing minority rights: the equality argument, the argument from historical agreement, and the diversity argument. As we will see shortly, his theory is driven by the equality argument; the historical agreement and diversity arguments, although meritorious on their own, ultimately depend on the equality argument for normative support.

Kymlicka's main motive in providing three overlapping justifications for minority rights is to show that the concept of "benign neglect" is untenable for political liberalism. Advocates of the benign neglect view argue that recognition of universal individual rights resolves any problems associated with demands for special cultural recognition—according to this view, substantive differences between cultures are unproblematic because the state grants the same package of rights to all individuals. For their part, advocates of group-differentiated rights contend that there are substantive differences between the diverse cultures and that legitimate recognition of this diversity requires the state to allocate different packages of rights accordingly. Kymlicka argues that "the state unavoidably promotes certain cultural identities, and thereby disadvantages others. Once we recognize this, we need to rethink the justice of minority rights claims" (108). The equality argument is intended to resolve the conflict between the benign neglect view of rights and the group-differentiated rights view.

The normative role of equality, in Kymlicka's equality argument, now functions at the level of the national minorities. Since cultural membership is a primary good *and* Aboriginal peoples constitute a national minority, those peoples are accorded special rights by the state—where the state is implicitly understood as *the* ultimate legitimate expression of political sovereignty. Aboriginal rights are a legitimate class of rights since liberals give credence to the intuition that prior occupancy has at least some normative weight in a theory of justice; indeed, in Kymlicka's theory this intuition is what generates the legitimacy of national minorities.[3] The special rights that Aboriginal peoples possess are rights of governance, one of three forms of group-differentiated rights in Kymlicka's theory of minority rights. These rights—the inherent rights that are legitimate from the initial formation of the Canadian state—are the strongest form of group rights in Kymlicka's classification of minority rights. The other forms of group-differentiated rights—ethnic rights and special representation rights—are allocated to certain groups that arrived after the Canadian state was formed and do not entail rights of governance.

Kymlicka's equality argument can be summarized as follows. The national minorities (Aboriginal peoples, the English, and the French) are the fundamentally privileged sovereign groups in Kymlicka's characterization of the Canadian multinational state. National minorities have rights of governance because they were the initial legitimate entities that formed the multinational state of Canada. However, for various reasons, the national minorities relinquished or transferred certain powers to the larger political union. Kymlicka notes that the creation of the multinational state may not have arisen from a just

context; however, this poses no significant problem for his theory because his view of the political relationship *today* is premised on the fundamental political recognition of equality between the incorporating national minorities. I believe this assumption goes to the core of the meaning of Canadian sovereignty, especially Aboriginal sovereignty.

I want to point out, though, that there are two normative dimensions to Kymlicka's theory of minority rights and that it is important to keep them separate. First, there is the cultural dimension. Aboriginal cultures are unfairly vulnerable to influence by the dominant culture; for this reason, they are afforded special rights in order to protect their integrity. Aboriginal peoples constitute a kind of collective, and because of this their special rights are premised on two facts: that cultural membership is a primary good *and* that Aboriginal cultures are vulnerable to the unfair influences of the dominant culture. This is the broad context from which liberals have discussed the legitimacy of collective rights for groups.

The second normative dimension to Kymlicka's theory of minority rights involves the language of political sovereignty. Kymlicka does not use the word "sovereignty"; even so, he brings the language of political sovereignty into his theory when he introduces the concept of national minorities. National minorities are defined as communities that were self-governing at the time of incorporation. Aboriginal communities constitute national minorities because normative weight is given to the fact that Aboriginal peoples occupied Canada first and therefore were self-governing societies. Thus the status of Aboriginal peoples as a national minority is based on the assumption that in the past they were self-governing, or sovereign.

Both these normative dimensions—cultural minority and national minority—are at work in Kymlicka's justification for Aboriginal rights of governance. However, liberals have discussed Aboriginal rights mostly in the language of cultural protection, rather than in the language of Aboriginal sovereignty. Kymlicka is right to raise the fact that Aboriginal peoples constitute a national minority, but there is no good reason for Aboriginal sovereignty—which is implicit in their status as a national minority—to disappear from the discussion of Aboriginal rights of governance in a contemporary context. If we take seriously the claim that Aboriginal peoples were self-governing nations before contact, we must re-examine our understandings of Aboriginal incorporation. This is because Aboriginal incorporation calls into question the nature of the formation of the Canadian state. Kymlicka is sensitive to the fact that Aboriginal peoples have suffered greatly throughout the history of the relationship; nonetheless, he sidesteps the issue of Aboriginal incorporation. Interestingly, the cultural and sovereignty dimensions of Kymlicka's theory both yield interpretations that advocate Aboriginal rights of governance, though I will claim that the second interpretation offers a more fruitful approach to capturing Aboriginal understandings of their sovereignty.

The cultural dimension of Kymlicka's theory does support Aboriginal sovereignty. Aboriginal peoples constitute a national minority; it follows that if our theory of justice deems it necessary, rights of governance can be accorded to them. Since culture is a primary good for all individuals, including Aboriginal individuals, the state ought to ensure policies that protect the integrity of all cultures. Since Aboriginal cultures are unfairly vulnerable to decimation by the overpowering dominant culture in Canada, justice demands that they be accorded special rights. Within a distributive theory of justice, these special rights *may* be rights of governance.

But it is important to note that the rights accorded to Aboriginal groups are justified only "if there actually is a disadvantage with respect to cultural membership, and if the rights actually serve to rectify the disadvantage." Kymlicka adds:

> One could imagine a point where the amount of land reserved for indigenous peoples would not be necessary to provide reasonable external protections, but rather would simply provide unequal opportunities to them. Justice would then require that the holdings of indigenous peoples be subject to the same

redistributive taxation as the wealth of other advantaged groups, so as to assist the less well off in society. In the real world, of course, most indigenous peoples are struggling to maintain the bare minimum of land needed to sustain the viability of their communities. But it is possible that their land holdings could exceed what justice allows. (*MC* 110)

The point behind this passage, as Kymlicka explains in the accompanying footnote, is that he places Aboriginal rights squarely in a theory of distributive justice. Aboriginal cultures, as national minorities, can exercise their rights of governance only to the extent that they do not offset the balance of fairness in relation to the remaining cultures in Canada. This proviso leads to a weaker form of Aboriginal sovereignty because the rights of Aboriginal governance are recognized only to the extent that they do not trump the sovereignty of the Canadian state. Aboriginal peoples argue that limiting their rights in this ahistorical way misrecognizes the source of their right of governance.

## 3. Aboriginal Incorporation and Aboriginal Sovereignty

Aboriginal perspectives must be included in the discourse that determines the meaning and content of their rights. We can retain the idea that Aboriginal communities are national minorities; but then we ought to focus on the problem of Aboriginal incorporation in order to determine the *current* political status of *particular* Aboriginal communities. This is because many Aboriginal communities maintain that they are *still* self-governing nations and that they have not in fact relinquished or ceded all of their powers to the state. Aboriginal incorporation calls into question our understandings of Aboriginal peoples' political relationships with the Canadian state. From this perspective, Aboriginal rights of governance can be recognized in a much deeper sense than in the first interpretation. This is because Aboriginal sovereignty does not have to dissipate after the formation of the Canadian state; more importantly, it lies in the forefront of any current discussion about Aboriginal rights.

This indigenous approach differs from the first in that it facilitates a stronger conception of Aboriginal sovereignty, something like the one provided by **the Gitxsan people**, who believe that "the ownership of territory is a marriage of the Chief and the land. Each Chief has an ancestor who encountered and acknowledged the life of the land. From such encounters come power. The land, the plants, the animals and the people all have spirit—they all must be shown respect. That is the basis of our law" (Wa and Uukw 7). The "voice" that arises within a strong conception of Aboriginal sovereignty arises directly from the community itself—that is, from the people who hold the traditional knowledge of their community and who are recognized by their citizens as legitimately expressing the meaning of their political sovereignty. However, for Canadian governments, recognition of a strong conception of Aboriginal sovereignty entails acceptance of the possibility that there are Aboriginal communities in Canada that remain sovereign political entities. Canadian governments have refused to recognize Aboriginal sovereignty in any form; until Aboriginal peoples participate as equals in the discourse that determines the meaning of their political sovereignty—and the rights of governance that follow from that sovereignty—legislative instruments and the meanings of rights as found in section 35(1) of the *Canadian Constitution* will remain undefined and elusive for policy-makers.

Of course, this does not bring us any closer to the meaning of Aboriginal sovereignty. The first step we must take to better understand what Aboriginal peoples themselves mean by sovereignty is to listen to their understandings of the historical relationship itself. But it matters very much *how we* have this dialogue. For example, Kymlicka uses the word "incorporation" to capture the historical significance of the early period of the relationship. This commits us to a particular interpretation of history. Such interpretations play pivotal roles in determining the meaning of Aboriginal sovereignty. The frustrating problem

for Aboriginal peoples is that their interpretations of history have not been recognized as legitimate. [. . .] A liberal theory of rights, in the context of Aboriginal peoples, functions ahistorically: it begins from a rationally constructed theory of distributive justice that bestows a set of fundamental rights on all individuals and, as a consequence, a set of special rights on individuals who belong to minority cultures. As I have tried to show by examining Kymlicka's theory of minority rights, it is possible for a version of liberalism to recognize that some Aboriginal communities are self-governing nations; what remains unresolved is a rich understanding of the meaning of Aboriginal sovereignty. This difference may not mean much to liberals and to Aboriginal policy-makers, as a liberal theory of justice has in some sense distributed fairly special rights to Aboriginal peoples. However, sovereignty lies at the very core of Aboriginal existence, and history is the main source for understanding the complex nature of Aboriginal forms of political sovereignty.

Kymlicka does allow historical interpretations to find their way into a liberal theory of justice when he invokes his second argument in favour of group-differentiated rights. The argument from historical agreement is meant to provide further normative support to the more fundamental equality argument, while addressing the issues surrounding the dissolution of Aboriginal sovereignty. Kymlicka points out that proponents of group-differentiated rights have had difficulty convincing opponents with historical arguments: "Those people who think that group-differentiated rights are unfair have not been appeased by pointing to agreements that were made by previous generations in different circumstances, often undemocratically and in conditions of substantial inequality in bargaining power." He goes on to ask: "Why should not governments do what principles of equality require now, rather than what outdated and often unprincipled agreements require?" (116).

His answer is to question a fundamental assumption underlying the equality argument: "The equality argument assumes that the state must treat its citizens with equal respect. But there is a prior question of determining which citizens should be governed by which states" (116). For Aboriginal people like Harold Cardinal, this raises an extremely serious problem for liberalism. If we invoke the equality argument without looking at history, we gloss over the fact that Aboriginal peoples became citizens in many different ways, most of them unjust. More importantly, Aboriginal peoples in some communities simply are not citizens of the Canadian state. Canadian political leaders, policy-makers, and especially judges have unilaterally assumed that for better or worse, Canada's Aboriginal peoples have become citizens of Canada in the fullest sense. Essentially, this is how Kymlicka uses the term incorporation; his theory implicitly subsumes the fact that Aboriginal peoples have become citizens of the Canadian state and, more importantly, that they *may* have relinquished their original sovereignty in this process of incorporation.[4]

This is where Kymlicka's concept of incorporation becomes most useful for my investigation of Aboriginal sovereignty. If the incorporation process was unjust—as Kymlicka suggests was the case for many Aboriginal communities—we have to reassess the validity of Aboriginal incorporation in a much fuller investigation. It is not enough to leave the investigation with the claim that the incorporation was unjust and that therefore the Canadian state should accord Aboriginal peoples special rights to rectify past wrongs. [. . .]

The relevant issue for Aboriginal peoples is not whether we ought to rectify past injustices in order to balance the scales of a liberal distributive justice system, but rather how governments can come to recognize the legitimacy of Aboriginal forms of sovereignty in order to renew the political relationship on more just foundations.[5] Kymlicka's theory can be interpreted in a way that at least makes room for Aboriginal peoples to speak for themselves. This is an important first step for liberalism, but it is only a first step. [. . .] History and Western philosophy have not been kind to Aboriginal ways of understanding the world, so it is vital that Aboriginal voices be listened to and respected as philosophically legitimate participants in the discourse on Aboriginal sovereignty.

How this ought to happen is a serious practical and philosophical problem. European philosophers developed a discourse *about* Aboriginal peoples, and therefore their philosophical "theories" did not require Aboriginal participation. This lack of philosophical participation is significant because it demonstrates that some Europeans in early colonial America [e.g., Locke] cared little about Aboriginal ways of thinking. I hope that by engaging in this investigation we may start on a path that examines the concept of Aboriginal sovereignty in a richer and more inclusive discourse.

To put it simply, if we want to understand better the meaning of what is commonly termed "indigenous," "tribal," or "Aboriginal" sovereignty, we must *listen* to what Aboriginal peoples have to say about its meaning. This inclusion process, which itself requires explanation, does not mean that anything will actually get done in practice, or that enlightenment will automatically follow merely by including Aboriginal voices in legal and philosophical discourses. Aboriginal sovereignty is a normative political concept for several overlapping reasons: Aboriginal peoples assert it, constitutions recognize it, comprehensive and specific land claims are negotiated because of it, and public policies have been designed and implemented to undermine it. Yet Aboriginal peoples and the various Canadian governments cannot agree on the meaning of the political relationship itself. Defining or characterizing the relationship would go far towards situating Aboriginal understandings of political sovereignty.

I have attempted to argue in this chapter that Kymlicka's liberalism does not require the participation of Aboriginal peoples in order to determine the content of their "special" rights. This is because Aboriginal rights are justified within a theory of distributive justice that does not fully recognize the legitimacy of Aboriginal sovereignty. Many Aboriginal people contend that their rights of governance flow from their political sovereignty and that these rights ought to be recognized by the Canadian governments (perhaps this is the significance of section 35(1)). It is precisely this fact of Aboriginal experience that Canadian governments have refused to recognize in any serious fashion. I am suggesting that Kymlicka's theory of minority rights can be reformulated in a way that allows Aboriginal voices into the dominant, non-Aboriginal discourse on Aboriginal rights. However, to do so in a just way requires a re-examination of Aboriginal incorporation between Aboriginal peoples and the Canadian state. The meaning of Aboriginal incorporation is problematic because Aboriginal interpretations have not been recognized by the dominant colonial governments; therefore, it matters how we go about understanding its meaning. [. . .] The minority rights view does not require the participation of Aboriginal voices when the meaning and content of their rights are being deliberated. The problem of Aboriginal participation remains unresolved. [. . .]

## Notes

1. I am using the concept of indigenous, or Aboriginal, sovereignty in this chapter to capture (albeit crudely) the special relationship that Aboriginal peoples have to their territories.
2. Strictly speaking, at least in the Canadian legal and political context, Aboriginal peoples were never "conquered." I take *conquered* to be the most destructive form of the "overrun" practice of colonization. For example, the Beothuck of Newfoundland can be said to have been conquered, but only to the extent that they no longer exist. From an Aboriginal perspective, as long as an Aboriginal community is occupying a homeland it remains unconquered.
3. Kymlicka includes the English and the French as holding prior occupancy because they were self-governing entities at the time the Canadian state was formed; however, Aboriginal peoples think of prior occupancy in the context of the time *before* arrival of the Europeans. The difference between the two interpretations is that in Kymlicka's view we don't question the legitimacy of French and English sovereignty before the time of Confederation.
4. I say that Aboriginal peoples *may* have relinquished their sovereignty because Kymlicka leaves it as an open issue whether the possibility exists that some communities remain sovereign—for example, the Cree of northern Quebec, the Mohawk of Kahnawake, and the Gitxsan and Wet'suwet'en people of British Columbia.
5. Of course, this is not to say that compensation ought not to play a role in renewing the relationship.

## Works Cited

Cardinal, H. *The Unjust Society: The Tragedy of Canada's Indians*. Edmonton, AB: Hurtig, 1969.

Kymlicka, W. *Liberalism, Community, and Culture*. Oxford: Oxford University Press, 1989.

Kymlicka, W. *Multicultural Citizenship: A Liberal Theory of Minority Rights*. Oxford: Oxford University Press, 1995.

Wa, G., and D. Uukw. *The Spirit in the Land: Statements of the Gitksam and Wet'suwet'en Hereditary Chiefs in the Supreme Court of British Columbia 1987–1990*. Gabriola, BC: Reflections, 1992.

## Study Questions

1. What does Turner mean by "Kymlicka's constraint"?

2. Why does Kymlicka view culture as a primary good? How does this view of culture support multiculturalism as official government policy and, more specifically, governance and other special rights for Aboriginal cultures?

3. Explain why Turner charges that Kymlicka's support for Aboriginal self-government does not go far enough by making reference to his

distinctions between "weak" versus "strong" forms of Aboriginal sovereignty and "ahistorical" versus "historical" approaches to assigning rights.

4. Turner argues that Kymlicka "sidesteps" the question of "Aboriginal incorporation" by paying insufficient attention to Canada's formation as a "multination" state. What "radical shift in our understandings" follows, according to Turner, once we focus on this question?

---

## Himani Bannerji

---

Himani Bannerji is a professor of sociology at York University. She has a BA from Visva Bharati University, an MA from Jadavpur University, and an MA and a PhD from the University of Toronto. Bannerji is well known as a Marxist, feminist, anti-racist, and post-colonial theorist; she is also a poet and author of children's stories. Bannerji's *Inventing Subjects: Studies in Hegemony, Patriarchy and Colonialism* (2002) won the 2005 Rabindra Memorial Prize. In this 1996 essay, Bannerji challenges the complacency of Canadians surrounding the success of multiculturalism.

## On the Dark Side of the Nation: Politics of Multiculturalism and the State of "Canada"

### 1. The Personal and the Political: A Chorus and a Problematic

When the women's movement came along and we were coming to our political consciousness, one of its slogans took us by surprise and thrilled and activated us: "the personal is political!" Since then years have gone by, and in the meanwhile I have found myself in Canada, swearing an oath of allegiance to the Queen of England, giving up the passport of a long-fought-for independence, and being assigned into the category of "visible minority." These years have produced their own consciousness in me, and I have learnt that also the reverse is true: the political is personal.

The way this consciousness was engendered was not ideological, but daily, practical, and personal. It came from having to live within an all-pervasive presence of the state in our everyday life. It began with the Canadian High Commission's rejection of my two-year-old daughter's visa and continued with my airport appearance in Montreal, where I was interrogated at length. What shook me was not the fact that they interviewed me, but rather their tone of suspicion about my somehow having stolen my way "in."

As the years progressed, I realized that in my life, and in the lives of other non-white people around me, this pervasive presence of the state meant everything—allowing my daughter and husband to come into the country; permitting me to continue my studies or to work, to cross the border into the USA and back; allowing me the custody of my daughter, although I had a low income; "landing" me so I could put some sort of life together with some predictability. Fear, anxiety, humiliation, anger, and frustration became the wire-mesh that knit bits of my life into a pattern. The quality of this life may be symbolized by an incident with which my final immigration interview culminated after many queries about a missing "wife" and the "head of the family." I was facing an elderly, bald, white man, moustached and blue-eyed—who said he had been to India. I made some polite rejoinder and he asked me—"Do you speak Hindi?" I replied that I understood it very well and spoke it with mistakes. "Can you translate this sentence for me?" he asked, and proceeded to say in Hindi what in English amounts to "Do you want to fuck with me?" A wave of heat rose from my toes to my hair roots. I gripped the edge of my chair and stared at him—silently. His hand was on my passport, the pink slip of my "landing" document lay next to it. Steadying my voice I said, "I don't know Hindi that well." "So you're a PhD student?" My interview continued. I sat rigid and concluded it with a schizophrenic intensity. On Bloor Street in Toronto, sitting on the steps of a church—I vomited. I was a landed immigrant.

Throughout these 25 years I have met many non-white and Third World legal and illegal "immigrants" and "new Canadians" who feel that the machinery of the state has us impaled against its spikes. In beds, in workplaces, in suicides committed over deportations, the state silently, steadily rules our lives with "regulations." How much more intimate could we be—this state and we? It has almost become a person—this machinery—growing with and into our lives, fattened with our miseries and needs, and the curbing of our resistance and anger.

But simultaneously with the growth of the state we grew too, both in numbers and protest, and became a substantial voting population in Canada. We demanded some genuine reforms, some changes—some among us even demanded the end of racist capitalism—and instead we got "multiculturalism." "Communities" and their leaders or representatives were created by and through the state, and they called for funding and promised "essential services" for their "communities," such as the preservation of their identities. There were advisory bodies, positions, and even arts funding created on the basis of ethnicity and community. A problem of naming arose, and hyphenated cultural and political identities proliferated. Officially constructed identities came into being and we had new names—immigrant, visible minority, new Canadian, and ethnic. In the mansion of the state small back rooms were accorded to these new political players on the scene. Manoeuvring for more began. As the state came deeper into our lives—extending its political, economic, and moral regulation, its police violence and surveillance—we simultaneously officialized ourselves. It is as though we asked for bread and were given stones, and could not tell the difference between the two.

## 2. In or Of the Nation? The Problem of Belonging

The state and the "visible minorities" (the non-white people living in Canada) have a complex relationship with each other. There is a fundamental unease with how our difference is construed and constructed by the state, how our otherness in relation to Canada is projected and objectified. We cannot be successfully ingested, or assimilated, or made to vanish from where we are not wanted. We remain an ambiguous presence, our existence a question mark in the side of the nation, with the potential to disclose much about the political unconscious and consciousness of Canada as an "imagined community" (Anderson). Disclosures accumulate slowly, while we continue to live here as outsider—insiders of the nation which offers a proudly multicultural profile to the international community. We have the awareness that we have arrived into somebody's state, but what kind of state; whose imagined community or community of imagination does it embody? And what are the terms and conditions of our "belonging" to this state of a nation? Answers to these questions are often indirect and not found in the news highway of Canadian media. But travelling through the side-roads of political discursivities and practices we come across markers for social terrains and political establishments that allow us to map the political geography of this nation-land where we have "landed."

We locate our explorations of Canada mainly in that part where compulsorily English-speaking visible minorities reside, a part renamed by Charles Taylor (1993) and others as "Canada outside of Quebec" (COQ). But we will call it "English Canada" as in common parlance. This reflects the binary cultural identity of the country to whose discourse, through the notions of the two solitudes, survival, and bilingualism, "new comers" are subjected.[1] Conceptualizing Canada within this discourse is a bleak and grim task: since "solitude" and "survival" (with their **Hobbes**ian and **Darwin**ist aura) are hardly the language of communitarian joy in nation making.

What, I asked when I first heard of these solitudes, are they? And why survival, when Canada's self-advertisement is one of a wealthy industrial nation? Upon my immigrant inquiries these two solitudes turned out to be two invading European nations—the French and the English—which might have produced two colonial-nation states in this part of North America. But history did not quite work out that way. Instead of producing two settler colonial countries like Zimbabwe (Rhodesia) and South Africa, they held a relationship of conquest and domination with each other. After the **battle at the Plains of Abraham**, one conquered nation/nationality, the French, continued in an uneasy and subjected relation to a state of "Canada," which they saw as "English," a perception ratified by this state's rootedness in the English Crown. The colonial French then came to a hyphenated identity of "franco-something," or declared themselves (at least within one province) as plain "Québécois." They have been existing ever since in an unhappy state, their promised status as a "distinct society" notwithstanding. Periodically, and at times critically, Quebec

challenges "Canadian" politics of "unity" and gives this politics its own "distinct" character. These then are the two solitudes, the protagonists who, to a great extent, shape the ideological parameters of Canadian constitutional debates, and whose "survival" and relations are continually deliberated. And this preoccupation is such a "natural" of Canadian politics that all other inhabitants are only a minor part of the problematic of "national" identity. This is particularly evident in the role, or lack thereof, accorded to the First Nations of Canada in the nation-forming project. Even after **Elijah Harper**'s intervention in the **Meech Lake Accord**, the deployment of the Canadian Army against the Mohawk peoples and the long stand-off that followed, constant land claims and demands for self-government/self-determination, there is a remarkable and a determined political marginalization of the First Nations. And yet their presence as the absent signifiers within Canadian national politics works at all times as a bedrock of its national definitional project, giving it a very particular contour through the same absences, silences, exclusions, and marginalizations. In this there is no distinction between "COQ" or English Canada and Quebec. One needs only to look at the **siege at Oka** to realize that as far as these "others" are concerned, Europeans continue the same solidarity of ruling and repression, blended with competitive manipulations, that they practised from the dawn of their conquests and state formations.

The Anglo–French rivalry therefore needs to be read through the lens of colonialism. If we want to understand the relationship between visible minorities and the state of Canada/English Canada/COQ, colonialism is the context or entry point that allows us to begin exploring the social relations and cultural forms which characterize these relations. The construction of visible minorities as a social imaginary and the architecture of the "nation" built with a "multicultural mosaic" can only be read together with the engravings of conquests, wars, and exclusions. It is the nationhood of this Canada, with its two solitudes and their survival anxieties and aggressions against "native others," that provides the epic painting in whose dark corners we must look for the later "others." We have to get past and through these dual monoculturalist assumptions or paradigms in order to speak about "visible minorities," a category produced by the multiculturalist policy of the state. This paper repeats, in its conceptual and deconstructive movements, the motions of the people themselves who, "appellated" as refugees, immigrants, or visible minorities, have to file past immigration officers, refugee boards, sundry ministries, and posters of multi-featured/coloured faces that blandly proclaim "Together we are Ontario"—lest we or they forget!

We will examine the assumptions of "Canada" from the conventional problematic and thematic of Canadian nationhood, that of "Fragmentation or Integration?" currently resounding in post-referendum times. I look for my place within this conceptual topography and find myself in a designated space for "visible minorities in the multicultural society and state of Canada." This is existence in a zone somewhere between economy and culture. It strikes me then that this discursive mode in which Canada is topicalized does not anywhere feature the concept of class. Class does not function as a potential source for the theorization of Canada, any more than does race as an expression for basic social relations of contradiction. Instead the discursivities rely on hegemonic cultural categories such as English or French Canada, or on notions such as national institutions, and conceive of differences and transcendences, fragmentation and integration, with regard to an ideological notion of unity that is perpetually in crisis. This influential problematic is displayed in a *Globe and Mail* editorial of 29 March 1994. It is typically preoccupied with themes of unity and integration or fragmentation, and delivers a lecture on these to Lucien Bouchard of the Bloc Québécois.

> It has been an educational field trip for Lucien Bouchard. On his first venture into "English Canada" (as he insists on calling it) since becoming leader of Her Majesty's Loyal Opposition, Mr. Bouchard learned, among other things, there is such a thing as Canadian Nationalism: not just patriotism,

nor yet that self-serving little prejudice that parades around as Canadian Nationalism— mix equal parts elitism, statism, and Anti-Americanism—but a genuine fellow-feeling that binds Canadians to one another across this country—and includes Quebec.

Lest this statement appear to the people of Quebec as passing off "English Canada" disguised as "the nation" and locking Quebec in a vice grip of "unity" without consent or consultation, the editor repeats multiculturalist platitudes meant to mitigate the old antagonisms leading to "separatism." The demand for a French Canada is equated with "self-serving little prejudice" and "patriotism," and promptly absorbed into the notion of a culturally and socially transcendent Canada, which is supposedly not only non-French, but non-English as well. How can this nonpartisan, transcendent Canada be articulated except in the discourse of multiculturalism? Multiculturalism, then, can save the day for English Canada, conferring upon it a transcendence, even though the same transcendent state is signalled through the figure of Her Majesty the Queen of England and the English language. The unassimilable "others" who, in their distance from English Canada, need to be boxed into this catch-all phrase now become the moral cudgel with which to beat Quebec's separatist aspirations. The same editorial continues:

> Canada is dedicated to the ideal that people of different languages and cultures may, without surrendering their identity, yet embrace the human values they have in common: the "two solitudes" of which the poet wrote, that "protect and touch and greet each other," were a definition of love, not division.

But this poetic interpretation of solitudes, like the moral carrot of multicultural love, is quickly followed by a stick. Should Quebec not recognize this obligation to love, but rather see it as a barrier to self-determination, Canada will not tolerate this. We are then confronted with other competing self-determinations in one breath, some of which ordinarily would not find their advocate in *Globe and Mail* editorials. What of the self-determination of the Cree, of the anglophones, of federalists of every stripe? What of the self-determination of the Canadian nation? Should Mr. Bouchard and his kind not recognize this national interest, it is argued, then the province's uncertainties are only beginning. In the context of the editorial's discourse, these uncertainties amount to the threat of a federalist anglophone war. The "self-determination of the Cree" is no more than an opportunistic legitimation of Canada in the name of all others who are routinely left out of its construction and governance. These "different (from the French) others," through the device of a state-sponsored multiculturalism, create the basis for transcendence necessary for the creation of a universalist liberal democratic statehood. They are interpellated or bound into the ideological state apparatus through their employment of tongues which must be compulsorily, officially unilingual—namely, under the sign of English.[2]

"Canada," with its primary inscriptions of "French" or "English," its colonialist and essentialist identity markers, cannot escape a fragmentary framework. Its imagined political geography simplifies into two primary and confrontational possessions, cultural typologies, and dominant ideologies. Under the circumstances, all appeal to multiculturalism on the part of "Canada Outside Quebec" becomes no more than an extra weight on the "English" side. Its "difference-studded unity," its "multicultural mosaic," becomes an ideological sleight of hand pitted against Quebec's presumably greater cultural homogeneity. The two solitudes glare at each other from the barricades in an ongoing colonial war. But what do either of these solitudes and their reigning essences have to do with those whom the state has named "visible minorities" and who are meant to provide the ideological basis for the Canadian state's liberal/universal status? How does their very "difference," inscribed with inferiority and negativity—their otherwise troublesome particularity—offer the very particularist state of "English Canada" the legitimating device of transcendence through

multiculturalism? Are we not still being used in the war between the English and the French?

It may seem strange to "Canadians" that the presence of the First Nations, the "visible minorities" and the ideology of multiculturalism are being suggested as the core of the state's claim to universality or transcendence. Not only in multiplying pawns in the old Anglo–French rivalry but in other ways as well, multiculturalism may be seen less as a gift of the state of "Canada" to the "others" of this society, than as a central pillar in its own ideological state apparatus. This is because the very discourse of nationhood in the context of "Canada," given its evolution as a capitalist state derived from a white settler colony with aspirations to liberal democracy, needs an ideology that can mediate fissures and ruptures more deep and profound than those of the usual capitalist nation state. That is why usually undesirable others, consisting of non-white peoples with their ethnic or traditional or underdeveloped cultures, are discursively inserted in the middle of a dialogue on hegemonic rivalry. The discourse of multiculturalism, as distinct from its administrative, practical relations, and forms of ruling, serves as a culmination for the ideological construction of "Canada." This places us, on whose actual lives the ideology is evoked, in a peculiar situation. On the one hand, by our sheer presence we provide a central part of the distinct pluralist unity of Canadian nationhood; on the other hand, this centrality is dependent on our "difference," which denotes the power of definition that "Canadians" have over "others." In the ideology of multicultural nationhood, however, this difference is read in a power-neutral manner rather than as organized through class, gender, and race. Thus at the same moment that difference is ideologically evoked it is also neutralized, as though the issue of difference were the same as that of diversity of cultures and identities, rather than those of racism and colonial ethnocentrism—as though our different cultures were on a par or could negotiate with the two dominant ones! The hollowness of such a pluralist stance is exposed in the shrill indignation of anglophones when rendered a "minority" in Quebec, or the angry desperation of francophones in Ontario. The issue of the First Nations—their land claims, languages, and cultures—provides another dimension entirely, so violent and deep that the state of Canada dare not even name it in the placid language of multiculturalism.

The importance of the discourse of multiculturalism to that of nation making becomes clearer if we remember that "nation" needs an ideology of unification and legitimation.[3] As Benedict Anderson points out, nations need to imagine a principle of "com-unity" or community even where there is little there to postulate any.[4] A nation, ideologically, cannot posit itself on the principle of hate, according to Anderson, and must therefore speak to the sacrificing of individual, particularist interests for the sake of "the common good." This task of "imagining community" becomes especially difficult in Canada—not only because of class, gender, and capital, which ubiquitously provide contentious grounds in the most culturally homogeneous of societies—but because its socio-political space is saturated by elements of surplus domination due to its Eurocentric/racist/colonial context. Ours is not a situation of coexistence of cultural nationalities or tribes within a given geographical space. Speaking here of culture without addressing power relations displaces and trivializes deep contradictions. It is a reductionism that hides the social relations of domination that continually create "difference" as inferior and thus signifies continuing relations of antagonism. The legacy of a white settler colonial economy and state and the current aspirations to imperialist capitalism mark Canada's struggle to become a liberal democratic state. Here a cultural pluralist interpretive discourse hides more than it reveals. It serves as a fantastic evocation of "unity," which in any case becomes a reminder of the divisions. Thus to imagine "com-unity" means to imagine a common-project of valuing difference that would hold good for both Canadians and others, while also claiming that the sources of these otherizing differences are merely cultural. As that is impossible, we consequently have a situation where no escape is possible from divisive social relations. The nation state's need for an ideology that can avert a complete rupture becomes desperate, and gives rise to a multicultural ideology which both needs and creates "others" while subverting demands for anti-racism and political equality.

## 3. Charles Taylor on "Reconciling Solitudes": "First Level" vs. "Deep" Diversity

Let me illustrate my argument by means of Charles Taylor's thoughts on the Canadian project of nation making. Taylor is comparable to Benedict Anderson insofar as he sees "nation" primarily as an expression of civil society, as a collective form of self-determination and definition. He therefore sees that culture, community, tradition, and imagination are crucial for this process. His somewhat romantic organicist approach is pitted against neo-liberal projects of market ideologies misnamed as "reform." Taylor draws his inspiration, among many sources, from an earlier European romantic tradition that cherishes cultural specificities, local traditions, and imaginations. This presents Taylor with the difficult task of "reconciling solitudes" with some form of a state while retaining traditional cultural identities in an overall ideological circle of "Canadian" nationhood. This is a difficult task at all times, but especially in the Canadian context of Anglo–French rivalry and the threat of separatism. Thus Taylor, in spite of his philosophical refinement, is like others also forced into the recourse of "multiculturalism as a discourse," characterized by its reliance on diversity. The constitution then becomes a federal Mosaic tablet for encoding and enshrining this very moral/political mandate. But Taylor is caught in a further bind, because Canada is more than a dual monocultural entity. Underneath the "two solitudes," as he knows well, Canada has "different differences," a whole range of cultural identities which cannot (and he feels should not) be given equal status with the "constituent elements" of "the nation," namely, the English and the French. At this point Taylor has to juggle with the contending claims of these dominant or "constituent" communities and their traditions, with the formal equality of citizenship in liberal democracy, and with other "others" with their contentious political claims and "different cultures." This juggling, of course, happens best in a multicultural language, qualifying the claim of the socio-economic equality of "others" with the language of culture and tolerance, converting difference into diversity in order to mitigate the power relations underlying it. Thus Taylor, in spite of his organicist, communitarian-moral view of the nation and the state, depends on a modified liberal pluralist discourse which he otherwise finds "American," abstract, empty, and unpalatable.

*Reconciling the Solitudes* and *Multiculturalism and the Politics of Recognition* are important texts for understanding the need for the construction of the category of visible minorities to manage contentions in the nationhood of Canada. Even though Taylor spends little time actually discussing either the visible minorities or the First Nations, their importance for the creation of a national ideology is brought out by his discussion of Anglo–French contestation. Their visceral anxieties about loss of culture are offset by "other" cultural presences that are minoritized with respect to both, while the commonality of Anglo-French culture emerges in contrast. Taylor discovers that the cultural essences of COQ have something in common with Quebec—their Europeanness—in spite of the surface of diversity. This surface diversity, he feels, is not insurmountable within the European-Anglo framework, whose members" political imagination holds enough ground for some sort of commonality.

> What is enshrined here is what one might call *first level diversity*. There are great differences in culture and outlook and background in a population that nevertheless shares the same idea of what it is to belong to Canada. Their patriotism and manner of belonging is uniform, whatever their differences, and this is felt to be necessary if the country is to hold together. (*Reconciling* 182)

Taylor must be speaking of those who are "Canadians" and not "others": the difference of

visible minorities and First Nations peoples is obviously not containable in this "first level diversity" category. As far as these "others" are concerned the Anglo-European (COQ) and French elements have much in common in both "othering" and partially "tolerating" them. Time and time again, especially around the so-called Oka crisis, it became clear that liberal pluralism rapidly yields to a fascist "sons of the soil" approach as expressed by both the Quebec state and its populace, oblivious to the irony of such a claim. It is inconsistent of Taylor to use this notion of "first level diversity" while also emphasizing the irreducible cultural ontology of Quebec as signalled by the concept of a "deep diversity" (183). But more importantly, this inconsistency accords an ownership of nationhood to the Anglo-French elements. He wrestles, therefore, to accommodate an Anglo-French nationality, while the "deep diversities" of "others," though nominally cited, are erased from the political map just as easily as the similarity of the "two nations" vis-à-vis those "others." Of course, these manipulations are essential for Taylor and others if the European (colonial) character of "Canada" is to be held status quo. This is a **Trudeau**-like stance of dual unification in which non-European "others" are made to lend support to the enterprise by their existence as a tolerated, managed difference.

This multicultural take on liberal democracy, called the "politics of recognition" by Taylor, is informed by his awareness that an across-the-board use of the notion of equality would reduce the French element from the status of "nation" to that of just another minority. This of course must not be allowed to happen, since the French are, by virtue of being European co-conquerors, one of the "founding nations." At this point Taylor adopts the further qualified notion of visible minorities as integral to his two-in-one nation-state schema. For him as for other majority ideologues they constitute a minority of minorities. They are, in the scheme of things, peripheral to the essence of Canada, which is captured by "Trudeau's remarkable achievement in extending bilingualism" to reflect the "Canadian" character of "duality" (164). This duality Taylor considers as currently under a threat of irrelevancy, not from anglo monoculturism, but from the ever-growing presence of "other" cultures. "Already one hears Westerners saying . . . that their experience of Canada is of a multicultural mosaic" (182). This challenge of the presence of "others" is, for Taylor, the main problem for French Canadians in retaining their equality with English Canadians. But it is also a problem for Taylor himself, who sees in this an unsettling possibility for the paradigm of "two solitudes" or "two nations" to which he ultimately concedes. In order to project the irreducible claims of the two dominant and similar cultures, he refers fleetingly and analogically, though frequently, to aboriginal communities: "visible minorities" also enter his discourse, but both are terms serving to install a "national" conversation between French and English, embroidering the dialogue of the main speakers. His placement of these "other" social groups is evident when he says: "something analogous [to the French situation] holds for aboriginal communities in this country; their way of being Canadian is not accommodated by first level diversity" (182). Anyone outside of the national framework adopted by Taylor would feel puzzled by the analogical status of the First Nations brought in to negotiate power sharing between the two European nations. Taylor's approach is in keeping with texts on nationalism, culture, and identity that relegate the issues of colonialism, racism, and continued oppression of the Aboriginal peoples and the oppression visited upon "visible minorities" to the status of footnotes in Canadian politics.

Yet multiculturalism as an ideological device both enhances and erodes Taylor's project. Multiculturalism, he recognizes at one level, is plain realism—an effect of the realization that many (perhaps too many) "others" have been allowed in, stretching the skin of tolerance and "first level diversity" tightly across the body of the nation. Their "deep diversity" cannot be accommodated simply within the Anglo-French duality. The situation is so murky that, "more fundamentally, we face a challenge to our very conception of diversity" (182). "Difference," he feels, has to be more "fundamentally" read into the "nation":

In a way, accommodating difference is what Canada is all about. Many Canadians would concur in this. (181)

Many of the people who rallied around the Charter and multiculturalism to reject the distinct society are proud of their acceptance of diversity—and in some respects rightly so. (182)

But this necessary situational multiculturalism acknowledged by Taylor not only creates the transcendence of a nation built on difference, it also introduces the claims of "deep diversities" on all sides. Unable to formulate a way out of this impasse Taylor proposes an ideological utopia of "difference" (devoid of the issue of power) embodied in a constitutional state, a kind of cultural federalism:

To build a country for everyone, Canada would have to allow for second-level or "deep" diversity in which a plurality of ways of belonging would also be acknowledged and accepted. Someone of, say, Italian extraction in Toronto or Ukrainian extraction in Edmonton might indeed feel Canadian as a bearer of individual rights in a multicultural mosaic. His or her belonging would not "pass through" some other community, although the ethnic identity might be important to him or her in various ways. But this person might nevertheless accept that a Québécois or a Cree or a Dene might belong in a very different way, that these persons were Canadian through being members of their national communities. Reciprocally, the Québécois, Cree, or Dene would accept the perfect legitimacy of the "mosaic" identity. (183)

This utopian state formation of Taylor founders, as do those of others, on the rocky shores of the reality of how different "differences" are produced, or are not just forms of diversity. For all of Taylor's pleas for recognizing two kinds of diversity, he does not ever probe into the social relations of power that create the different differences. It is perhaps significant from this point of view that he speaks of the "deep diversities" of Italians or Ukrainians but does not mention those of the blacks, South Asians, or the Chinese. In other words, he cannot raise the spectre of real politics, of real social, cultural, and economic relations of white supremacy and racism. Thus he leaves out of sight the relations and ideologies of ruling that are intrinsic to the creation of a racist civil society and a racializing colonial-liberal state. It is this foundational evasion that makes Taylor's proposal so problematic for those whose "differences" in the Canadian context are not culturally intrinsic but constructed through "race," class, gender, and other relations of power. This is what makes us skeptical about Taylor's retooling of multicultural liberal democracy by introducing the concept of "deep diversity" as a differentiated citizenship into the bone marrow of the polity, while leaving the Anglo-French European "national" (colonial and racist) core intact. He disagrees with those for whom

> [the] model of citizenship has to be uniform, or [they think] people would have no sense of belonging to the same polity. Those who say so tend to take the United States as their paradigm, which has indeed been hostile to deep diversity and has sometimes tried to stamp it out as "un-American." (183)

This, for Taylor, amounts to the creation of a truly Canadian polity that needs a "united federal Canada" and is able to deliver "law and order, collective provision, regional equality and mutual self-help" (183). None of these categories—for example, that of "law and order"—is characteristically problematized by Taylor. His model "Canada" is not to be built on the idea of a melting pot or of a uniform citizenship based on a rationalist and functional view of polity. That would, according to him, "straight-jacket" deep diversity. Instead,

> The world needs other models to be legitimated in order to allow for more humane and less constraining modes of political cohabitation. Instead of pushing ourselves to the point of break up in the name of a uniform model, we would do our own and some other peoples a favour by exploring the space of deep diversity. (184)

What would this differentiated citizenship look like in concrete example, we ask? Taylor throws in a few lines about **Basques, Catalans, and Bretons**. But those few lines are not answer enough for us. Though this seems to be an open invitation to join the project of state and nation making, the realities of a colonial capitalist history—indentures, reserves, First Nations without a state, immigrants and citizens, illegals, refugees, and "Canadians"—make it impossible. They throw us against the inscription of power-based "differences" that construct the self-definition of the Canadian state and its citizenship. We realize that class, "race," gender, sexual orientation, colonialism, and capital cannot be made to vanish by the magic of Taylor's multiculturalism, managed and graduated around a core of dualism. His inability to address current and historical organizations of power, his inability to see that this sort of abstract and empty invitation to "difference" has always enhanced the existing "difference" unless real social equality and historical redress can be possible—these erasures make his proposal a touch frightening for us. This is why I shudder to "take the deep road of diversity together" with Charles Taylor (184). Concentration and labour camps, Japanese internment, the Indian Act and reserves, apartheid and ethnic "homelands" extend their long shadows over the project of my triumphal march into the federal utopia of a multiculturally differentiated citizenship. But what becomes clear from Taylor's writings is the importance of a discourse of difference and multiculturalism for the creation of a legitimate nation space for Canada. Multiculturalism becomes a mandate of moral regulation as an antidote to any, and especially Quebec's, separatism. [. . .]

## Notes

1. For an exposition of the notions of "solitude" and "survival" see Atwood.
2. For an elaboration of these concepts see Althusser.
3. For a clarification of my use of this concept see Habermas, *Legitimation Crisis*. This use of "legitimacy" is different from Taylor's Weberian use of it in *Reconciling the Solitudes*.
4. Anderson says, "I . . . propose the following definition of the nation: it is an imagined political community—and imagined as both inherently limited and sovereign. It is *imagined* because the members of even the smallest nation will never know most of their fellow members, meet them, or even hear of them, yet in the minds of each lives the image of their communion" (6).

## Works Cited

Althusser, L. "Ideology and Ideological State Apparatuses (Notes towards an Investigation)." *Lenin and Philosophy and Other Essays*. London: New Left Books, 1977.

Anderson, B. *Imagined Community*. London: Verso, 1991.

Atwood, M. *Survival: A Thematic Guide to Canadian Literature*. Toronto: House of Anansi Press, 1972.

Habermas, J. *Legitimation Crisis*. Boston: Beacon Press, 1975.

Taylor, C. *Multiculturalism and "The Politics of Recognition."* Princeton: Princeton University Press, 1992.

Taylor, C. *Reconciling the Solitudes: Essays on Canadian Federalism and Nationalism*. Ed. G. Laforest. Montreal and Kingston: McGill-Queen's University Press, 1993.

## Study Questions

1. What point is Bannerji making when she reverses the slogan of the women's movement "The personal is political" to say "The political is personal"? Why does Bannerji hold that the arrival of multiculturalism as official government policy made the problem even worse?
2. Bannerji is skeptical that multiculturalism is as positive for "minorities" as it is generally portrayed. What role does Bannerji believe instead is played by multiculturalism—and Aboriginal peoples and "visible minorities," in particular—in Canadian society?
3. How does Benedict Anderson define "nation"? What use does Bannerji make of Anderson's definition in her critique of Canadian multiculturalism?
4. Bannerji characterizes Taylor's distinction between "first level diversity" and "second level diversity" as "a kind of cultural federalism." Providing examples, explain the nature of Taylor's distinction. What sorts of events from Canadian and European colonial history make Bannerji skeptical of Taylor's account of multiculturalism, and why?

# Film Notes

### Civil Disobedience

*Gandhi* (UK/India 1982, Richard Attenborough, 191 min): Biography of the man who led campaigns of non-violent civil disobedience to win rights for Indians in South Africa and free India from British rule.

*Police, Adjective* (Romania 2009, Corneliu Porumboiu, 115 min): Conscience and the law are at odds for a Bucharest police officer hesitant to arrest a teenager suspected of selling drugs.

### Democratic Government

*Antz* (USA 1998, Eric Darnell and Tim Johnson, 83 min): An animated political parable about a worker ant named Z who asserts his individuality in his colony's conformist society.

*Good Night, and Good Luck* (USA/France/UK/Japan 2005, George Clooney, 93 min): Despite corporate and sponsorship pressures, broadcast journalist Edward R. Murrow and the CBS newsroom challenge Senator Joseph McCarthy's anti-Communist attack on civil liberties.

*Seven Days in May* (USA 1964, John Frankenheimer, 118 min): After the US signs a nuclear disarmament treaty with the Soviet Union, a popular general plans a coup to oust the unpopular president.

*Silver City* (USA 2004, John Sayles, 128 min): A murder mystery accompanies a political satire about a Colorado gubernatorial candidate backed by industrial polluters.

*Wag the Dog* (USA 1997, Barry Levinson, 97 min): Just weeks from an election, the US president is caught in a sex scandal, and to distract the media, a war with Albania is invented.

### Civil Disobedience/Democratic Government

*Born on the Fourth of July* (USA 1989, Oliver Stone, 145 min): Adapted from the autobiography of Ron Kovic who joined the Marines out of high school, was paralyzed by a bullet to the spine in Vietnam, and emerged from embittered anger to become an anti-war activist.

*The Great Debaters* (USA 2007, Denzel Washington, 126 min): Based on the remarkable story of a debate team from Wiley College, a Black institution in the segregated US South of the 1930s, that won the national championship.

*Iron Jawed Angels* (USA 2004, Katja von Garnier, 125 min): About US suffragists Alice Paul and Lucy Burns who broke from the mainstream women's movement to form a more radical wing in the fight for passage of the 19th Amendment.

*Once Upon a Time . . . When We Were Colored* (USA 1995, Tim Reid, 115 min): Four generations of life as experienced in a Black community in segregated rural Mississippi, from 1946 to arrival of the civil rights movement in 1962.

*Sophie Scholl: The Final Days* (Germany 2005, Marc Rothemund, 120 min; German with subtitles): Sophie belonged to the White Rose, a student protest group in Munich, and was tried and executed in 1943 for distributing leaflets against Hitler and the war.

*This Is What Democracy Looks Like* (USA 2000, Jill Friedberg and Rick Rowley, 72 min): Documentary about the protests at the World Trade Organization summit meeting in Seattle in 1999. *Battle in Seattle* (Canada/USA/Germany 2007, Stuart Townsend, 99 min) provides a fictionalized account.

*The Untold Story of the Suffragists of Newfoundland* (Canada 1999, Greg Malone, 54 min): Docudrama about the struggle waged by Newfoundland women on their way to winning the right to vote in 1925.

*Water* (Canada/India 2005, Deepa Mehta, 117 min; Hindi with subtitles): Set in India in 1938, an eight-year-old widow, who barely understands she was married, experiences the oppressive practices associated with traditional Hindu law.

*Z* (France/Algeria, Costas Gavras, 127 min; French, Russian, and English with subtitles): A judicial investigation implicates high-ranking military and police officials in the assassination of the leader of the political opposition in Greece in 1963.

## Multiculturalism

*Crash* (USA/Germany 2004, Paul Haggis, 112 min): The film begins with discovery of a body beside a free-way and, by retracing the 24 hours prior, portrays the bigotry and distrust that characterize the intersecting lives of LA's racially and ethnically diverse residents.

*Gran Torino* (USA/Germany 2008, Clint Eastwood, 116 min): Walt is a retired Detroit autoworker, full of racist vitriol, who gets to know, and like, his Hmong neighbours after the teenage son, threatened by gang members, tries to steal his prized 1972 Gran Torino.

*Lone Star* (USA 1996, John Sayles, 134 min): In a Texas border town with longstanding racial tensions, secrets from the past come to be unearthed along with the skeleton of a much-hated sheriff murdered 25 years previously.

## Civil Disobedience/Multiculturalism

*Do the Right Thing* (USA 1989, Spike Lee, 120 min): Palpable tensions among a Brooklyn neighbour-hood's Black, Italian, and Korean residents escalate over the course of one hot summer day that ends in tragedy.

## Civil Disobedience/Democratic Government/ Multiculturalism

*The Battle of Algiers* (Italy/Algeria 1966, Gillo Pontecorvo, 121 min; Italian, French, English, and Arabic with subtitles): An unflinching look at Algeria's War of Independence, 1954–62, in which guerrilla warfare by the Front de Libération Nationale was met with targeted killing and torture by the French.

*Kanehsatake: 270 Years of Resistance* (Canada 1993, Alanis Obomsawin, 119 min): Documentary about the "Oka Crisis"—the armed standoff at Kanehsatake between the Mohawks, Quebec police, and Canadian army during the summer of 1990.

*Persepolis* (France/USA 2007, Vincent Paronnaud and Marjane Satrapi, 96 min; French, English, Persian, and German with subtitles): Animated film based on Satrapi's autobiographical graphic novel about coming of age during the Iranian Revolution.

*Thunderheart* (USA 1992, Michael Apted, 119 min): An FBI agent is assigned to investigate a murder on a Sioux reservation in South Dakota because he has Native American ancestry, and ends up becoming sen-sitized to political issues and uncovering a conspiracy.

# PART V

# The Beautiful

## ▶ Introduction

Since the eighteenth century, the area of philosophy that studies "the beautiful" has been called aesthetics, a label derived from the idea of philosophers of that century (e.g., Hume, Kant) that humans are equipped with a sense of "taste," by means of which we experience pleasure in what is beautiful. Aesthetic experiences are consequently diverse: a glimpse of a bald eagle, a walk on a beach, a spoken word performance, a drumming ceremony, a Van Gogh exhibit, or a Hitchcock film. Philosophers of aesthetics ask what art is, and how to evaluate it. Philosophy's traditional question about the meaning of life can be rephrased as a question about what makes a beautiful life. Our lives become unfinished canvasses in a painter's studio or stories that in their telling and retelling create meaning for us, with authenticity valued no less than in artworks.

Although these questions about art and aesthetics and what makes a beautiful life go back to Plato, interestingly, he distinguishes between art and beauty, and treats them in opposite ways.

### Plato, "Art as Imitation"

In Book 10 of *The Republic*, Socrates, conversing with Glaucon, criticizes artists for being "imitators" whose works convey knowledge only of appearances, not reality. The "mimetic" or "imitative" theory of art assumes different levels of reality, reminiscent of the cave analogy. The couch in an artist's painting "imitates" a particular couch in terms of appearance. The particular couch "resembles" the idea or form of Couch, the "real couch" or "couch in itself," that guided its production by the carpenter. Similarly, Homer's poems, like the artist's couch, are "three removes from nature," whereas the legislator or general, like the carpenter, has knowledge.

### Plato, "Diotima on Beauty: Socrates' Speech in *Symposium*"

For Plato, "the beautiful" is the form most closely related to that of "the good." Diotima tells Socrates that "Love" wants goodness to be made one's own forever, and amorous behaviour "begets" on what is beautiful to bring immortality forth. For women and less gifted men, this is by having children. For statesmen like Solon or poets like Homer, it is through laws or poems left to posterity. For philosophers like Socrates, it involves knowledge of eternal essences. Diotima's stepwise guide to achieving knowledge of "the beautiful" begins with the sexual initiation and moral education of youth by their elders and culminates in the pursuit of practical and theoretical knowledge within a philosophical community.

## Art and Aesthetics

In "On the Metaphysics of the Beautiful and Aesthetics," Arthur Schopenhauer is inspired by Plato, and yet he rejects Plato's imitative theory of art. Schopenhauer holds that the conception for any "genuine" work of art comes from the artist's "apprehension" of "Platonic Ideas" in a process of "pure knowing" in which the will ceases activity and "genius" takes hold. The "essence" of the work of art is to show form without matter: in contrast to Socrates' painted couch at "three removes from nature," for Schopenhauer, "the picture stands nearer to the Idea than does reality." "Will-free knowing" is also the basis of aesthetic pleasure: all suffering ceases as the intellect intuits the idea in the work in the absence of the will.

Arthur Danto's "The Artworld" critiques Plato's theory of art. Not only is imitation neither a necessary nor a sufficient condition for defining art, but the Socratic approach to conceptual definition wrongly suggests that artworks can readily be identified as such. Danto contends that the "Imitation Theory" (IT) was replaced by the "Reality Theory" (RT) because IT could not accept post-impressionist paintings as art. RT claims that inasmuch as an artwork is not an imitation of a real object (e.g., Socrates' artist's painted couch), it is, like the real object imitated (e.g., Socrates' carpenter's couch), itself a real object. Similarly, for modern art. By allowing different senses of "is," we recognize that **Rauschenberg**'s bed both is and is not a bed.

Alfred Lessing's "What Is Wrong with a Forgery?" addresses the title's question using the case of **van Meegeren**'s *Christ and the Disciples of Emmaus*, which was discovered to be a forgery after being authenticated as a Vermeer, displayed in a Rotterdam museum, and highly praised by critics. Lessing argues that forgeries are not necessarily aesthetically inferior, as the case of *The Disciples* shows. Canvassing non-aesthetic—historical, biographical, economic, and sociological—criteria instead, Lessing concludes that it is the lack of originality expected of the creative arts that makes the forgery wrong: the use of colour and lighting in the *The Disciples* was original with Vermeer in the seventeenth century, not with van Meegeren in the twentieth century.

In "The Aesthetics of Cultural Appropriation," James O. Young argues that culturally appropriated artworks are not necessarily aesthetically inferior. Young rejects the "cultural experience argument" that an artist has to be a member of a specific culture (e.g., African-American) to create an aesthetically successful work (e.g., blues music). Although, unlike Lessing, Young holds that aesthetic properties belong not just to the artwork but to contextual features of its production that determine how it is to be interpreted and evaluated—so that the aesthetic merit of a work can be affected by knowledge that it was done by an outsider—he concludes that works by outsiders need not be inauthentic and therefore aesthetically inferior.

## A Beautiful Life

In *A Confession*, Leo Tolstoy, the famous Russian novelist, despairs at his inability to answer what he had come to regard as "the most important and profound of life's questions": what is the meaning of his life and life in general. Science was telling him that life is meaningless, the result of "a transitory, casual cohesion of particles" that eventually disintegrates into nothingness. The prospect left him unable to find purpose in his activities and without a will to live. Eventually, faith provides Tolstoy with the answer to his questions. Just as Plato's Diotima tells Socrates that mortal beings seek immortality, Tolstoy finds meaning in finite human lives through the infinitude of God and heaven.

In "The Meanings of Lives," Susan Wolf argues that secular philosophy cannot provide a positive answer to Tolstoy's question about the meaning of life in general, but this does not mean that there is no positive answer to Tolstoy's question about the meaning of his life, or anyone else's. Beginning with three paradigms of meaningless lives, Wolf arrives at a definition of a meaningful life as "one that is actively and at least somewhat successfully engaged in a project (or projects) of positive value." Wolf contends that there is objective value in the world and that what makes a project of positive value, therefore, is an objective, not subjective, matter. To assume otherwise, she says, egocentrically ignores that "we are tiny specks in a vast universe."

Bernard Williams challenges Lucretius's contention that death is never an evil since we are not around to experience the loss. Williams argues that it is better to live a longer life than a shorter one because we are provided with a greater opportunity to satisfy our desires—in particular, what he calls "categorical desires." But this does not imply that we should want to live forever. Williams' title, "The Makropulos Case," refers to the story of a woman who is 342 years old and, being bored, decides to stop taking the elixir that keeps her alive. Williams agrees that immortality would be tedious. Thus, he dismisses Plato's conception of a beautiful life as striving for immortality; in particular, eternal bliss for the philosopher who succeeds in contemplating the Forms is an illusion.

## ▶ Discussion Questions

1. Is art (e.g., painting, sculpture, music, film, literature, etc.) a source of knowledge?
2. Imagine your life as a creative endeavour, and suppose you are nearing its end and reflecting on what you have done and experienced along the way. On what grounds would you say that yours has been a beautiful life? Would you judge the lives of others on such grounds, or is this a judgment that can be made only by the person whose life it is?
3. Do you want to live forever?

## ▶ Further Reading

Heidegger, Martin. "The Origin of the Work of Art." *Poetry, Language, Thought*. Trans. Albert Hofstadter. New York: Harper & Row, 1971.

Heyes, Cressida J. *Self-Transformations: Foucault, Ethics, and Normalized Bodies*. Oxford and New York: Oxford University Press, 2007.

Kernohan, Andrew. *A Guide for the Godless: The Secular Path to Meaning*. Halifax: self-published, 2008; http://myweb.dal.ca/kernohan/godless.

Lopes, Dominic McIver. *Sight and Sensibility: Evaluating Pictures*. Oxford: Oxford University Press, 2005.

---

# Plato

---

Plato (429–347 BCE) composed his works as dialogues, not treatises, thus drawing on the literary tradition of poets and playwrights. Nevertheless, in *The Republic*, Plato deems the arts a threat to the ideal city because they inflame people's passions and promote illusion instead of truth.

## Art as Imitation

From *The Republic*

Characters: **Socrates, Glaucon**

1. "And truly," I [Socrates] said, "many other considerations assure me that we were entirely right [in Book 3] in our organization of the state, and especially, I think, in the matter of poetry." "What about it?" he [Glaucon] said. "In refusing to admit at all so much of it as is imitative; for that it is certainly not to be received is, I think, still more plainly apparent now that we have distinguished the several parts of the soul." "What do you mean?" "Why, between ourselves—for you will not betray me to the tragic poets and all other imitators—that kind of art seems to be a corruption of the mind of all listeners who do not possess as an antidote a knowledge of its real nature." "What is your idea in saying this?" he said. "I must speak out," I said, "though a certain love and reverence for **Homer** that has possessed me from a boy would stay me from speaking. For he appears to have been the first teacher and beginner of all these beauties of tragedy. Yet all the same we must not honour a man above truth, but, as I say, speak our minds."

"By all means," he said. "Listen, then, or rather, answer my question." "Ask it," he said. "Could you tell me in general what imitation is? For neither do I myself quite apprehend what it would be at." "It is likely, then," he said, "that *I* should apprehend!" "It would be nothing strange," said I, "since it often happens that the dimmer vision sees things in advance of the keener." "That is so," he said; "but in your presence I could not even be eager to try to state anything that appears to me, but do you yourself consider it." "Shall we, then, start the inquiry at this point by our customary procedure? We are in the habit, I take it, of positing a single idea or form in the case of the various multiplicities to which we give the same name. Do you not understand?" "I do." "In the present case, then, let us take any multiplicity you please; for example, there are many couches and tables." "Of course." "But these utensils imply, I suppose, only two ideas or forms, one of a couch and one of a table." "Yes." "And are we not also in the habit of saying that the craftsman who produces either of them fixes his eyes on the idea or form, and so makes in the one case the couches and in the other the tables that we use, and similarly of other things? For surely no craftsman makes the idea itself. How could he?" "By no means." "But now consider what name you would give to this craftsman." "What one?" "Him who makes all the things that all handicrafts-men severally produce." "A truly clever and wondrous man you tell of." "Ah, but wait, and you will say so indeed, for this same handicraftsman is not only able to make all implements, but he produces all plants and animals, including himself,[1] and thereto earth and heaven and the gods and all things in heaven and in Hades under the earth." "A most marvellous sophist," he said. "Are you incredulous?" said I. "Tell me, do you deny altogether the possibility of such a craftsman, or do you admit that in a sense there could be such a creator of all these things, and in another sense not? Or do you not perceive that you yourself would be able to make all these things in a way?" "And in what way, I ask you," he said. "There is no difficulty," said I, "but it is something that the craftsman can make everywhere and quickly. You could do it most quickly if you should choose to take a mirror and carry it about everywhere. You will speedily produce the sun and all the things in the sky, and speedily the earth and your-self and the other animals and implements and plants and all the objects of which we just now spoke." "Yes," he said, "the appearance of them, but not the reality and the truth." "Excellent," said I, "and you come to the aid of the argument opportunely. For I take it that the painter too belongs to this class of producers, does he not?" "Of course." "But you will say, I suppose, that his creations are not real and true. And yet, after a fashion, the painter too makes a couch, does he not?" "Yes," he said, "the appearance of one, he too."

2. "What of the cabinet-maker? Were you not just now saying that he does not make the idea or form which we say is the real couch, the couch in itself, but only some particular couch?" "Yes, I was." "Then if he does not make that which really is, he could not be said to make real being but something that resembles real being but is not that. But if anyone should say that being in the complete sense belongs to the work of the cabinet-maker or to that of any other handicraftsman,

it seems that he would say what is not true." "That would be the view," he said, "of those who are versed in this kind of reasoning."[2] "We must not be surprised, then, if this too is only a dim adumbration in com-parison with reality." "No, we must not." "Shall we, then, use these very examples in our quest for the true nature of this imitator?" "If you please," he said. "We get, then, these three couches, one, that in nature which, I take it, we would say that God produces, or who else?" "No one, I think." "And then there was one which the carpenter made." "Yes," he said. "And one which the painter. Is not that so?" "So be it." "The painter, then, the cabinet-maker, and God, there are these three presiding over three kinds of couches." "Yes, three." "Now God, whether because he so willed or because some compulsion was laid upon him not to make more than one couch in nature, so wrought and created one only, the couch which really and in itself is. But two or more such were never created by God and never will come into being." "How so?" he said. "Because," said I, "if he should make only two, there would again appear one of which they both would possess the form or idea, and that would be the couch that really is in and of itself, and not the other two."[3] "Right," he said. "God, then, I take it, knowing this and wishing to be the real author of the couch that has real being and not of some particular couch, nor yet a particular cabinet-maker, produced it in nature unique." "So it seems." "Shall we, then, call him its true and natural begetter, or something of the kind?" "That would certainly be right," he said, "Since it is by and in nature that he has made this and all other things." "And what of the carpenter? Shall we not call him the creator of a couch?" "Yes." "Shall we also say that the painter is the creator and maker of that sort of thing?" "By no means." "What will you say he is in relation to the couch?" "This," said he, "Seems to me the most reasonable designation for him, that he is the imitator of the thing which those others pro-duce." "Very good," said I; "the producer of the prod-uct three removes from nature you call the imitator?" "By all means," he said. "This, then, will apply to the maker of tragedies also, if he is an imitator and is in his nature three removes from the king and the truth, as are all other imitators." "It would seem so." "We are in agreement, then, about the imitator. But tell me now this about the painter. Do you think that what he tries to imitate is in each case that thing itself in nature or the works of the craftsmen?" "The works of the craftsmen," he said. "Is it the reality of them or the appearance? Define that further point." "What do you mean?" he said. "This: Does a couch differ from itself according as you view it from the side or the front or in any other way? Or does it differ not at all in fact though it appears different, and so of other things?" "That is the way of it," he said: "it appears other but differs not at all." "Consider, then, this very point. To which is painting directed in every case, to the imitation of reality as it is or of appearance as it appears? Is it an imitation of a phantasm or of the truth?" "Of a phantasm," he said. "Then the mimetic art is far removed from truth, and this, it seems, is the reason why it can produce everything, because it touches or lays hold of only a small part of the object and that a phantom; as, for example, a painter, we say, will paint us a cobbler, a carpenter, and other craftsmen, though he himself has no expertness in any of these arts, but nevertheless if he were a good painter, by exhibiting at a distance his picture of a carpenter he would deceive children and foolish men, and make them believe it to be a real carpenter." "Why not?" "But for all that, my friend, this, I take it, is what we ought to bear in mind in all such cases: When anyone reports to us of someone, that he has met a man who knows all the crafts and everything else that men severally know, and that there is nothing that he does not know more exactly than anybody else, our tacit rejoinder must be that he is a simple fellow, who apparently has met some magician or sleight-of-hand man and imitator and has been deceived by him into the belief that he is all-wise, because of his own inability to put to the proof and distinguish knowledge, ignorance, and imitation." "Most true," he said.

3. "Then," said I, "have we not next to scrutinize tragedy and its leader Homer, since some people tell us that these poets know all the arts and all things human pertaining to virtue and vice, and all things divine? For the good poet, if he is to poetize things rightly, must, they argue, create with knowledge or else be unable to create. So we must consider whether these critics have not fallen in with such imitators and been deceived by them, so that looking upon their works they cannot perceive that these are three removes from reality, and easy to produce without knowledge of the truth. For it is phantoms, not realities, that they produce. Or is there something in their claim, and do good poets really know the things about which the multitude fancy they speak well?" "We certainly must examine the matter," he said. "Do you suppose, then, that if a man were able to produce both the exemplar and the semblance, he would be eager to abandon himself to the fashioning of phantoms and set this in the forefront of his life as the best thing he had?" "I do not." "But, I take it, if he had genuine knowledge of the things he imitates he would far rather devote himself to real things than to the imitation of them, and would endeavour to leave after him many noble deeds and works as memorials of himself, and would be more eager to be the theme of praise than the praiser." "I think so," he said; "for there is no parity in the honour and the gain." "Let us not, then, demand a reckoning from Homer or any other of the poets on other matters by asking them, if any one of them was a physician and not merely an imitator of a physician's talk, what men any poet, old or new, is reported to have restored to health as **Asclepius** did, or what disciples of the medical art he left after him as Asclepius did his descendants; and let us dismiss the other arts and not question them about them; but concerning the greatest and finest things of which Homer undertakes to speak, wars and generalship and the administration of cities and the education of men, it surely is fair to question him and ask, "Friend Homer, if you are not at the third remove from truth and reality in human excellence, being merely that creator of phantoms whom we defined as the imitator, but if you are even in the second place and were capable of knowing what pursuits make men better or worse in private or public life, tell us what city was better governed owing to you, even as Lacedaemon [Sparta] was because of **Lycurgus**, and many other cities great and small because of other legislators. But what city credits you with having been a good legislator and having benefited them? Italy and Sicily say this of **Charondas** and we of **Solon**. But who says it of you?" Will he be able to name any?" "I think

not," said Glaucon; "at any rate none is mentioned even by the Homerids themselves." "Well, then, is there any tradition of a war in Homer's time that was well conducted by his command or counsel?" "None." "Well, then, as might be expected of a man wise in practical affairs, are many and ingenious inventions for the arts and business of life reported of Homer as they are of **Thales the Milesian** and **Anacharsis the Scythian**?" "Nothing whatever of the sort." "Well, then, if no public service is credited to him, is Homer reported while he lived to have been a guide in education to men who took pleasure in associating with him and transmitted to posterity a certain Homeric way of life just as **Pythagoras** was himself especially honoured for this, and his successors, even to this day, denominating a certain way of life the Pythagorean, are distinguished among their contemporaries?" "No, nothing of this sort either is reported; for Creophylos[4], Socrates, the friend of Homer, would perhaps be even more ridiculous than his name as a representative of Homeric culture and education, if what is said about Homer is true. For the tradition is that Homer was completely neglected in his own lifetime by that friend of the flesh."

4. "Why, yes, that is the tradition," said I; "but do you suppose, Glaucon, that, if Homer had really been able to educate men and make them better and had possessed not the art of imitation but real knowledge, he would not have acquired many companions and been honoured and loved by them? But are we to believe that while **Protagoras of Abdera** and **Prodicus of Ceos** and many others are able by private teaching to impress upon their contemporaries the conviction that they will not be capable of governing their homes or the city unless they put them in charge of their education, and make themselves so beloved for this wisdom that their companions all but carry them about on their shoulders, yet, forsooth, that Homer's contemporaries, if he had been able to help men to achieve excellence, would have suffered him or **Hesiod** to roam about rhapsodizing and would not have clung to them far rather than to their gold, and constrained them to dwell with them in their homes, or failing to persuade them, would themselves have escorted them wheresoever they went until they should have sufficiently imbibed their culture?" "What you say seems to me to be altogether true, Socrates," he said. "Shall we, then, lay it down that all the poetic tribe, beginning with Homer, are imitators of images of excellence and of the other things that they "create," and do not lay hold on truth? But, as we were just now saying, the painter will fashion, himself knowing nothing of the cobbler's art, what appears to be a cobbler to him and likewise to those who know nothing but judge only by forms and colours?" "Certainly." "And similarly, I suppose, we shall say that the poet himself, knowing nothing but how to imitate, lays on with words and phrases the colours of the several arts in such fashion that others equally ignorant, who see things only through words, will deem his words most excellent, whether he speak in rhythm, metre and harmony about cobbling or generalship or anything whatever. So mighty is the spell that these adornments naturally exercise; though when they are stripped bare of their musical colouring and taken by themselves, I think you know what sort of a showing these sayings of the poets make. For you, I believe, have observed them." "I have," he said. "Do they not," said I, "resemble the faces of adolescents, young but not really beautiful, when the bloom of youth abandons them?" "By all means," he said. "Come, then," said I, "consider this point: The creator of the phantom, the imitator, we say, knows nothing of the reality but only the appearance. Is not that so?" "Yes."

## Notes

1. Tr.: It is a tempting error to refer this to God, as I once did. [. . .] But the producer of everything, including himself, is the imitator generalized and then exemplified by the painter and the poet.

2. Tr.: An indirect reference to Plato and his school.

3. Tr.: The famous argument of the third man.

4. Tr.: "Of the beef-clan." The scholiast says he was a Chian and an epic poet.

## Study Questions

1. Socrates tells us that the god, the carpenter, and the painter make three different kinds of couches (or beds in other translations). What are these? Why does Socrates characterize the painter's couch as "three removes from nature"?

2. Evaluate Socrates' argument that great works of literature cannot provide us with knowledge.

---

# Plato

---

In Plato's (429–347 BCE) *Symposium*, beauty provides a "ladder of love" that ascends to knowledge of truth and goodness. The expression "Platonic love" comes from this intellectual striving for "the beautiful."

## Diotima on Beauty: Socrates' Speech in *Symposium*

"And now I shall let you alone, and proceed with the discourse upon Love which I heard one day from a Mantinean woman named Diotima[1]: in this subject she was skilled, and in many others too; for once, by bidding the Athenians offer sacrifices ten years before the plague, she procured them so much delay in the advent of the sickness. Well, I also had my lesson from her in love-matters; so now I will try and follow up the points on which Agathon and I have just agreed by narrating to you all on my own account, as well as I am able, the speech she delivered to me. [. . .]

"I observed: [. . .] 'of what use is he [Love] to mankind?'

"'That is the question, Socrates,' she replied, 'on which I will try to enlighten you. [. . .] Now, suppose someone were to ask us: In what respect is he Love of beautiful things, Socrates and Diotima? But let me put the question more clearly thus: What is the love of the lover of beautiful things?'

"'That they may be his,' I replied.

"'But your answer craves a further query,' she said, "Such as this: What will he have who gets beautiful things?'

"This question I declared I was quite unable now to answer offhand.

"'Well,' she proceeded, 'imagine that the object is changed, and the inquiry is made about the good instead of the beautiful. Come, Socrates (I shall say), what is the love of the lover of good things?'

"'That they may be his,' I replied.

"'And what will he have who gets good things?'

"'I can make more shift to answer this,' I said; 'he will be happy.'

"'Yes,' she said, 'the happy are happy by acquisition of good things, and we have no more need to ask for what end a man wishes to be happy, when such is his wish: the answer seems to be ultimate.'

"'Quite true,' I said.

"'Now do you suppose this wish or this love to be common to all mankind, and that everyone always wishes to have good things? Or what do you say?'

"'Even so,' I said; 'it is common to all.'

"'Well then, Socrates,' she said, 'we do not mean that all men love, when we say that all men love the same things always; we mean that some people love and others do not?'

"'I am wondering myself,' I replied.

"'But you should not wonder,' she said; 'for we have singled out a certain form of love, and applying thereto the name of the whole, we call it love; and there are other names that we commonly abuse.'

"'As, for example—?' I asked.

"'Take the following: you know that *poetry* is more than a single thing. For of anything whatever that passes from not being into being the whole cause is composing or poetry; so that the productions of all arts are kinds of poetry, and their craftsmen are all poets.'

"'That is true.'

"'But still, as you are aware,' said she, 'they are not called poets: they have other names, while a single section disparted from the whole of poetry—merely the business of music and metres—is entitled with the name of the whole. This and no more is called poetry; those only who possess this branch of the art are poets.'

"'Quite true,' I said.

"'Well, it is just the same with love. Generically, indeed, it is all that desire of good things and of being happy—Love most mighty and all-beguiling. Yet, whereas those who resort to him in various other ways—in money-making, an inclination to sports, or philosophy—are not described either as loving or as lovers, all those who pursue him seriously in one of his several forms obtain, as loving and as lovers, the name of the whole.'

"'I fancy you are right,' I said. [. . .]

"'Then we may state unreservedly that men love the good?'

"'Yes,' I said.

"'Well now, must we not extend it to this, that they love the good to be theirs?'

"'We must.'

"'And do they love it to be not merely theirs but theirs always?'

"'Include that also.'

"'Briefly then,' said she, 'love loves the good to be one's own forever.'

"'That is the very truth,' I said.

"'Now if love is always for this,' she proceeded, 'what is the method of those who pursue it, and what is the behaviour whose eagerness and straining are to be termed love? What actually is this effort? Can you tell me?'

"'Ah, Diotima,' I said; 'in that case I should hardly be admiring you and your wisdom, and sitting at your feet to be enlightened on just these questions.'

"'Well, I will tell you,' said she; 'it is begetting on a beautiful thing by means of both the body and the soul.'

"'It wants some divination to make out what you mean,' I said; 'I do not understand.'

"'Let me put it more clearly,' she said. 'All men are pregnant, Socrates, both in body and in soul: on reaching a certain age our nature yearns to beget. This it cannot do upon an ugly person, but only on the beautiful: the conjunction of man and woman is a begetting for both. It is a divine affair, this engendering and bringing to birth, an immortal element in the creature that is mortal; and it cannot occur in the discordant. The ugly is discordant with whatever is divine, whereas the beautiful is accordant. Thus Beauty presides over birth as Fate and Lady of Travail; and hence it is that when the pregnant approaches the beautiful it becomes not only gracious but so exhilarate, that it flows over with begetting and bringing forth; though when it meets the ugly it coils itself close in a sullen dismay: rebuffed and repressed, it brings not forth, but goes in labour with the burden of its young. Therefore when a person is big and teeming-ripe he feels himself in a sore flutter for the beautiful, because its possessor can relieve him of his heavy pangs. For you are wrong, Socrates, in supposing that love is of the beautiful.'

"'What then is it?'

"'It is of engendering and begetting upon the beautiful.'

"'Be it so,' I said.

"'To be sure it is,' she went on; 'and how of engendering? Because this is something ever-existent and immortal in our mortal life. From what has been admitted, we needs must yearn for immortality no less than for good, since love loves good to be one's own forever. And hence it necessarily follows that love is of immortality.'

"All this instruction did I get from her at various times when she discoursed of love-matters; and one time she asked me, 'What do you suppose, Socrates, to be the cause of this love and desire? For you must have observed the strange state into which all the animals are thrown, whether going on earth or winging the air, when they desire to beget: they are all sick and amorously disposed, first to have union one with another, and next to find food for the newborn; in whose behalf they are ready to fight hard battles, even the weakest against the strongest, and to sacrifice their lives; to be racked with starvation themselves if they can but nurture their young, and be put to any sort of shift. As for men,' said she, 'one might suppose they do these things on the promptings of reason; but what is the cause of this amorous condition in the animals? Can you tell me?'

"Once more I replied that I did not know; so she proceeded: 'How do you design ever to become a master of love-matters, if you can form no notion of this?'

"'Why, it is just for this, I tell you, Diotima—as I stated a moment ago—that I have come to see you, because I noted my need of an instructor. Come, tell me the cause of these effects as well as of the others that have relation to love-matters.'

"'Well then,' she said, 'if you believe that love is by nature bent on what we have repeatedly admitted, you may cease to wonder. For here, too, on the same principle as before, the mortal nature ever seeks, as best it can, to be immortal. In one way only can it succeed, and that is by generation; since so it can always leave behind it a new creature in place of the old. It is only for a while that each live thing can be described as alive and the same, as a man is said to be the same person from childhood until he is advanced in years: yet though he is called the same he does not at any time possess the same properties; he is continually becoming a new person, and there are things also which he loses, as appears by his hair, his flesh, his bones, and his blood and body altogether. And observe that not only in his body but in his soul besides we find none of his manners or habits, his opinions, desires, pleasures, pains or fears, ever abiding the same in his particular self; some things grow in him, while others perish. And here is a yet stranger fact: with regard to the possessions of knowledge, not merely do some of them grow and others perish in us, so that neither in what we know are we ever the same persons; but a like fate attends each single sort of knowledge. What we call *conning* implies that our knowledge is departing; since forgetfulness is an egress of knowledge, while conning substitutes a fresh one in place of that which departs, and so

preserves our knowledge enough to make it seem the same. Every mortal thing is preserved in this way; not by keeping it exactly the same forever, like the divine, but by replacing what goes off or is antiquated with something fresh, in the semblance of the original. Through this device, Socrates, a mortal thing partakes of immortality, both in its body and in all other respects; by no other means can it be done. So do not wonder if everything naturally values its own offshoot; since all are beset by this eagerness and this love with a view to immortality.'

"On hearing this argument I wondered, and said: 'Really, can this in truth be so, most wise Diotima?'

"Whereat she, like our perfect professors, said: 'Be certain of it, Socrates; only glance at the ambition of the men around you, and you will have to wonder at the unreasonableness of what I have told you, unless you are careful to consider how singularly they are affected with the love of winning a name, 'and laying up fame immortal for all time to come.'[2] For this, even more than for their children, they are ready to run all risks, to expend money, perform any kind of task, and sacrifice their lives. 'Do you suppose,' she asked, 'that **Alcestis would have died for Admetus, or Achilles have sought death on the corpse of Patroclus**, or your own **Codrus** have welcomed it to save the kingdom of his children, if they had not expected to win 'a deathless memory for valour,' which now we keep? Of course not. I hold it is for immortal distinction and for such illustrious renown as this that they all do all they can, and so much the more in proportion to their excellence. They are in love with what is immortal. Now those who are teeming in body betake them rather to women, and are amorous in this way: by getting children they acquire an immortality, a memorial, and a state of bliss, which in their imagining they 'for all succeeding time procure.' But pregnancy of soul—for there are persons,' she declared, 'who in their souls still more than in their bodies conceive those things which are proper for soul to conceive and bring forth; and what are those things? Prudence, and virtue in general; and of these the begetters are all the poets and those craftsmen who are styled *inventors*. Now by far the highest and fairest part of prudence is that which concerns the regulation of cities and habitations; it is called sobriety and justice. So when a man's soul is so far divine that it is made pregnant with these from his youth, and on attaining manhood immediately desires to bring forth and beget, he too, I imagine, goes about seeking the beautiful object whereon he may do his begetting, since he will never beget upon the ugly. Hence it is the beautiful rather than the ugly bodies that he welcomes in his pregnancy, and if he chances also on a soul that is fair and noble and well-endowed, he gladly cherishes the two combined in one; and straightway in addressing such a person he is resourceful in discoursing of virtue and of what should be the good man's character and what his pursuits; and so he takes in hand the other's education. For I hold that by contact with the fair one and by consorting with him he bears and brings forth his long-felt conception, because in presence or absence he remembers his fair. Equally too with him he shares the nurturing of what is begotten, so that men in this condition enjoy a far fuller community with each other than that which comes with children, and a far surer friendship, since the children of their union are fairer and more deathless. Everyone would choose to have got children such as these rather than the human sort—merely from turning a glance upon **Homer** and **Hesiod** and all the other good poets, and envying the fine offspring they leave behind to procure them a glory immortally renewed in the memory of men. Or only look,' she said, 'at the fine children whom **Lycurgus** left behind him in Lacedaemon [Sparta] to deliver his country and—I may almost say—the whole of Greece; while **Solon** is highly esteemed among you for begetting his laws; and so are diverse men in diverse other regions, whether among the Greeks or among foreign peoples, for the number of goodly deeds shown forth in them, the manifold virtues they begot. In their name has many a shrine been reared because of their fine children; whereas for the human sort never any man obtained this honour.

"'Into these love-matters even you, Socrates, might haply be initiated; but I doubt if you could approach the rites and revelations to which these, for the properly instructed, are merely the avenue.

However I will speak of them,' she said, 'and will not stint my best endeavours; only you on your part must try your best to follow. He who would proceed rightly in this business must not merely begin from his youth to encounter beautiful bodies. In the first place, indeed, if his conductor guides him aright, he must be in love with one particular body, and engender beautiful converse therein; but next he must remark how the beauty attached to this or that body is cognate to that which is attached to any other, and that if he means to ensue beauty in form, it is gross folly not to regard as one and the same the beauty belonging to all; and so, having grasped this truth, he must make himself a lover of all beautiful bodies, and slacken the stress of his feeling for one by regarding it with contempt and counting it a trifle. But his next advance will be to set a higher value on the beauty of souls than on that of the body, so that however little the grace that may bloom in any likely soul it shall suffice him for loving and caring, and for bringing forth and soliciting such converse as will tend to the betterment of the young; and that finally he may be constrained to contemplate the beautiful as appearing in our observances and our laws, and to behold it all bound together in kinship and so estimate the body's beauty as a slight affair. From observances he should be led on to the branches of knowledge, that there also he may behold a province of beauty, and by looking thus on beauty in the mass may escape from the mean, meticulous slavery of a single instance, where he must centre all his care, like a lackey, upon the beauty of a particular child or man or single observance; and turning rather towards the main ocean of the beautiful may by contemplation of this bring forth in all their splendour many fair fruits of discourse and meditation in a plenteous crop of philosophy; until with the strength and increase there acquired he descries a certain single knowledge connected with a beauty which has yet to be told. And here, I pray you,' said she, 'give me the very best of your attention.

"'When a man has been thus far tutored in the lore of love, passing from view to view of beautiful things, in the right and regular ascent, suddenly he will have revealed to him, as he draws to the close of his dealings in love, a wondrous vision, beautiful in its nature; and this, Socrates, is the final object of all those previous toils. First of all, it is ever-existent and neither comes to be nor perishes, neither waxes nor wanes; next, it is not beautiful in part and in part ugly, nor is it such at such a time and other at another, nor in one respect beautiful and in another ugly, nor so affected by position as to seem beautiful to some and ugly to others. Nor again will our initiate find the beautiful presented to him in the guise of a face or of hands or any other portion of the body, nor as a particular description or piece of knowledge, nor as existing somewhere in another substance, such as an animal or the earth or sky or any other thing; but existing ever in singularity of form independent by itself, while all the multitude of beautiful things partake of it in such a way that, though all of them are coming to be and perishing, it grows neither greater nor less, and is affected by nothing. So when a man by the right method of boy-loving ascends from these particulars and begins to catch sight of that beauty, he is almost able to lay hold of the final secret. Such is the right approach or induction to love-matters. Beginning from obvious beauties he must for the sake of that highest beauty be ever climbing aloft, as on the rungs of a ladder, from one to two, and from two to all beautiful bodies; from personal beauty he proceeds to beautiful observances, from observance to beautiful learning, and from learning at last to that particular study which is concerned with the beautiful itself and that alone; so that in the end he comes to know the very essence of beauty. In that state of life above all others, my dear Socrates,' said the Mantinean woman, 'a man finds it truly worthwhile to live, as he contemplates essential beauty. This, when once beheld, will outshine your gold and your vesture, your beautiful boys and striplings, whose aspect now so astounds you and makes you and many another, at the sight and constant society of your darlings, ready to do without either food or drink if that were any way possible, and only gaze upon them and have their company. But tell me, what would happen if one of you had the fortune to look upon essential beauty entire, pure and unalloyed; not infected with the flesh and colour of humanity, and ever so much more of mortal trash? What if he could behold the divine beauty itself, in its unique form? Do you call it a pitiful life for a man to lead—looking that way, observing that vision by the proper means, and having it ever with him? Do but consider,' she said, 'that there only will it befall him, as he sees the beautiful through that which makes it visible, to breed not illusions but true examples of virtue, since his contact is not with illusion but with truth. So when he has begotten a true virtue and has reared it up he is destined to win the friendship of Heaven; he, above all men, is immortal.'

"This, Phaedrus and you others, is what Diotima told me, and I am persuaded of it; in which persuasion I pursue my neighbours, to persuade them in turn that towards this acquisition the best helper that our human nature can hope to find is Love." [. . .]

## Notes

1. Tr.: These names suggest a connection respectively with prophecy and with the favour of Heaven.

2. Tr.: Diotima breaks into verse of her own composing.

## Study Questions

1. Diotima tells Socrates that because love desires good things to be ours not just now but forever, love also desires immortality. How do humans as mortal beings "partake" in immortality during our lives?

2. Socrates' speech outlines the contribution of love and beauty to philosophical training. What are the steps by which it is possible to "ascend" to knowledge of "the very essence of beauty"? How are gender and sexuality implicated in this account?

## ∾ ART AND AESTHETICS ∾

### Arthur Schopenhauer

Arthur Schopenhauer (1788–1860) was a German philosopher inspired by Plato and Kant. Although expected to pursue a career in business, Schopenhauer instead chose philosophy, studying at the Universities of Göttingen and Berlin and receiving a doctorate from Jena. Schopenhauer believed that the will, free and self-determining but without rationality or purpose, is the fundamental metaphysical principle, and that life's constant suffering is caused by the frustration of desires. This 1851 essay argues that genuine art involves the expression of Platonic forms.

## On the Metaphysics of the Beautiful and Aesthetics

205. [. . .] The real problem of the metaphysics of the beautiful may be very simply expressed by our asking how satisfaction with and pleasure in an object are possible without any reference thereof to our willing.

Thus everyone feels that pleasure and satisfaction in a thing can really spring only from its relation to our will or, as we are fond of expressing it, to our aims, so that pleasure without a stirring of the will seems to be a contradiction. Yet the beautiful, as such, quite obviously gives rise to our delight and pleasure, without its having any reference to our personal aims and so to our will.

My solution has been that in the beautiful we always perceive the essential and original forms of animate and inanimate nature and thus **Plato**'s Ideas thereof, and that this perception has as its condition their essential correlative, the *will-free subject of knowing*, in other words a pure intelligence without aims and intentions. On the occurrence of an aesthetic apprehension, the will thereby vanishes entirely from consciousness. But it alone is the source of all our sorrows and sufferings. This is the origin of that satisfaction and pleasure which accompany the apprehension of the beautiful. It therefore rests on the removal of the entire possibility of suffering. If it should be objected that the possibility of pleasure would then also be abolished, it should be remembered that, as I have often explained, happiness or satisfaction is of a *negative* nature, that is, simply

the end of a suffering, whereas pain is that which is positive. And so with the disappearance of all willing from consciousness, there yet remains the state of pleasure, in other words absence of all pain and here even absence of the possibility thereof. For the individual is transformed into a subject that merely knows and no longer wills; and yet he remains conscious of himself and of his activity precisely as such. As we know, the world as *will* is the first world (*ordine prior*), and the world as *representation*, the second (*ordine posterior*). The former is the world of craving and therefore of pain and a thousand different woes. The latter, however, is in itself essentially painless; moreover, it contains a spectacle worth seeing, altogether significant, and at least entertaining. Aesthetic pleasure consists in the enjoyment thereof. To become a pure subject of knowing means to be quit of oneself;[1] but since in most cases people cannot do this, they are, as a rule, incapable of that purely objective apprehension of things, which constitutes the gift of the artist.

206. However, let the individual will leave free for a while the power of representation which is assigned to it, and let it exempt this entirely from the service for which it has arisen and exists so that, for the time being, such power relinquishes concern for the will or for one's own person, this being its only natural theme and thus its regular business, but yet it does not cease to be energetically active and

to apprehend clearly and with rapt attention what is intuitively perceptible. That power of representation then becomes at once perfectly *objective*, that is to say, the true mirror of objects or, more precisely, the medium of the objectification of the will that manifests itself in the objects in question. The inner nature of the will now stands out in the power of representation the more completely, the longer intuitive perception is kept up, until it has entirely exhausted that inner nature. Only thus does there arise with the pure subject the pure object, that is, the perfect manifestation of the will that appears in the intuitively perceived object, this manifestation being just the (Platonic) *Idea* thereof. But the apprehension of such an Idea requires that, while contemplating an object, I disregard its position in time and space and thus its individuality. For it is this *position* which is always determined by the law of causality and puts that object in some relation to me as an individual. Therefore only when that position is set aside does the object become the *Idea* and do I at the same time become the pure subject of knowing. Thus through the fact that every painting for ever fixes the fleeting moment and tears it from time, it already gives us not the individual thing, but the *Idea*, that which endures and is permanent in all change. Now for that required change in the subject and object, the condition is not only that the power of knowledge is withdrawn from its original servitude and left entirely to itself, but also that it nevertheless remains active with the whole of its energy, in spite of the fact that the natural spur of its activity, the impulse of the will, is now absent. Here lies the difficulty and in this the rarity of the thing; for all our thoughts and aspirations, all our seeing and hearing, are naturally always in the direct or indirect service of our countless greater and smaller personal aims. Accordingly it is the *will* that urges the power of knowledge to carry out its function and, without such impulse, that power at once grows weary. Moreover, the knowledge thereby awakened is perfectly adequate for practical life, even for the special branches of science which are directed always only to the *relations* of things, not to the real and true inner nature thereof; and so all their knowledge proceeds on the

guiding line of the **principle of sufficient reason** [or ground], this element of relations. Thus wherever it is a question of knowledge of cause and effect, or of other grounds and consequents, and hence in all branches of natural science and mathematics, as also of history, inventions, and so forth, the knowledge sought must be a *purpose of the will*, and the more eagerly this aspires to it, the sooner will it be attained. Similarly, in the affairs of state, war, matters of finance or trade, intrigues of every kind, and so on, the *will* through the vehemence of its craving must first compel the intellect to exert all its strength in order to discover the exact clue to all the grounds and consequents in the case in question. In fact, it is astonishing how far the spur of the will can here drive a given intellect beyond the usual degree of its powers. And so for all outstanding achievements in such things, not merely a fine or brilliant mind is required, but also an energetic will which must first urge the intellect to laborious effort and restless activity, without which such achievements cannot be effected.

Now it is quite different as regards the apprehension of the objective original essence of things which constitutes their (Platonic) Idea and must be the basis of every achievement in the fine arts. Thus the will, which was there so necessary and indeed indispensable, must here be left wholly out of the question; for here only that is of any use which the intellect achieves entirely of itself and from its own resources and produces as a free-will offering. Here everything must go automatically; knowledge must be active without intention and so must be will-less. For only in the state of *pure knowing*, where a man's will and its aims together with his individuality are entirely removed from him, can that purely objective intuitive perception arise wherein the (Platonic) Ideas of things are apprehended. But it must always be such an apprehension which precedes the conception, i.e., the first and always intuitive knowledge. This subsequently constitutes the real material and kernel, as it were the soul, of a genuine work of art, a poem, and even a real philosophical argument. The unpremeditated, unintentional, and indeed partly unconscious and instinctive element that has at all times been observed in the works of *genius*, is just a consequence of the fact that the original artistic knowledge is one that is entirely separate from, and independent of, the will, a will-free, will-less knowledge. And just because the will is the man himself, we attribute such knowledge to a being different from him, to genius. A knowledge of this kind has not, as I have often explained, the principle of sufficient reason [or ground] for its guiding line and is thus the antithesis of a knowledge of the first kind. By virtue of his objectivity, the genius with *reflectiveness* perceives all that others do not see. This gives him as a poet the ability to describe nature so clearly, palpably, and vividly, or as a painter, to portray it.

On the other hand, with the *execution* of the work, where the purpose is to communicate and present what is known, the *will* can, and indeed must, again be active, just because there exists a *purpose*. Accordingly, the principle of sufficient reason [or ground] here rules once more, whereby the means of art are suitably directed to the ends thereof. Thus the painter is concerned with the correctness of his drawing and the treatment of his colours; the poet with the arrangement of his plan and then with expression and metre.

But since the intellect has sprung from the will, it therefore presents itself objectively as brain and thus as a part of the body which is the objectification of the will. Accordingly, as the intellect is originally destined to serve the will, the activity natural to it is of the kind previously described, where it remains true to that natural form of its knowledge which is expressed by the principle of sufficient reason [or ground], and where it is brought into activity and maintained therein by the will, the primary and original element in man. Knowledge of the second kind, on the other hand, is an abnormal activity, unnatural to the intellect; accordingly, it is conditioned by a decidedly abnormal and thus very rare excess of intellect and of its objective phenomenon, the brain, over the rest of the organism and beyond the measure required by the aims of the will. Just because this excess of intellect is abnormal, the phenomena springing therefrom sometimes remind one of madness.

Here knowledge then breaks with and deserts its origin, the will. The intellect which has arisen merely to serve the will and, in the case of almost all men, remains in such service, their lives being absorbed in such use and in the results thereof, is used abnormally, as it were abused, in all the *free* arts and sciences; and in this use are set the progress and honour of the human race. In another way, it can even turn itself against the will, in that it abolishes this in the phenomena of holiness.

However, that purely objective apprehension of the world and of things which, as primary and original knowledge, underlies every artistic, poetical, and purely philosophical conception, is only a fleeting one, on subjective as well as objective grounds. For this is due in part to the fact that the requisite exertion and attention cannot be maintained, and also to the fact that the course of the world does not allow us at all to remain in it as passive and indifferent spectators, like the philosopher according to the definition of **Pythagoras**. On the contrary, everyone must act in life's great puppet-play and almost always feels the wire which also connects him thereto and sets him in motion.

207. Now as regards the *objective* element of such aesthetic intuitive perception, the (Platonic) *Idea*, this may be described as that which we should have before us if time, this formal and subjective condition of our knowledge, were withdrawn, like the glass from the kaleidoscope. For example, we see the development of the bud, blossom, and fruit and are astonished at the driving force that never wearies of again going through this cycle. Such astonishment would vanish if we could know that, in spite of all that change, we have before us the one and unalterable Idea of the plant. However, we are unable intuitively to perceive this Idea as a unity of bud, blossom, and fruit, but are obliged to know it by means of the form of *time*, whereby it is laid out for our intellect in those successive states.

208. If we consider that both poetry and the plastic arts take as their particular theme an *individual* in order to present this with the greatest care and

accuracy in all the peculiarities of its individual nature down to the most insignificant; and if we then review the sciences that work by means of *concepts*, each of which represents countless individuals by determining and describing, once for all, the characteristic of their whole species; then on such a consideration the pursuit of art might seem to us insignificant, trifling, and almost childish. But the essence of art is that its one case applies to thousands, since what it implies through that careful and detailed presentation of the individual is the revelation of the (Platonic) *Idea* of that individual's species. For example, an event, a scene from human life, accurately and fully described and thus with an exact presentation of the individuals concerned therein, gives us a clear and profound knowledge of the Idea of humanity itself, looked at from some point of view. For just as the botanist plucks a single flower from the infinite wealth of the plant world and then dissects it in order to demonstrate the nature of the plant generally, so does the poet take from the endless maze and confusion of human life, incessantly hurrying everywhere, a single scene and often only a mood or feeling, in order then to show us what are the life and true nature of man. We therefore see that the greatest minds, **Shakespeare** and **Goethe**, **Raphael** and **Rembrandt**, do not regard it as beneath their dignity to present with the greatest accuracy, earnestness, and care an individual who is not even outstanding, and to give down to the smallest detail a graphic description of all his peculiarities. For only through intuitive perception is the particular and individual thing grasped; I have, therefore, defined poetry as the art of bringing the imagination into play by means of words.

If we want to feel directly and thus become conscious of the advantage which knowledge through intuitive perception, as that which is primary and fundamental, has over abstract knowledge and thus see how art reveals more to us than any science can, let us contemplate, either in nature or through the medium of art, a beautiful and mobile human countenance full of expression. What a much deeper insight into the essence of man, indeed of nature generally, is given by this than by all the words and abstractions they express! Incidentally, it may be observed here that what, for a beautiful landscape is the sudden glimpse of the sun breaking through the clouds, is for a beautiful countenance the appearance of its laughter. Therefore, *ridete, puellae, ridete!* ["Laugh, girls, laugh!"][2]

209. However, what enables a *picture* to bring us more easily than does something actual and real to the apprehension of a (Platonic) Idea and so that whereby the picture stands nearer to the Idea than does reality, is generally the fact that the work of art is the object which has already passed through a subject. Thus it is for the mind what animal nourishment, namely the vegetable already assimilated, is for the body. More closely considered, however, the case rests on the fact that the work of plastic art does not, like reality, show us that which exists only once and never again, thus the combination of *this* matter with *this* form, such combination constituting just the concrete and really particular thing, but that it shows us *the form alone*, which would be the Idea itself if only it were given completely and from every point of view. Consequently, the picture at once leads us away from the individual to the mere form. This separation of the form from matter already brings it so much nearer to the Idea. But every picture is such a separation, whether it be a painting or a statue. This severance, this separation, of the form from matter belongs, therefore, to the character of the aesthetic work of art, just because the purpose thereof is to bring us to the knowledge of a (Platonic) *Idea*. It is, therefore, *essential* to the work of art to give the form alone without matter, and indeed to do this openly and avowedly. Here is to be found the real reason why wax figures make no aesthetic impression and are, therefore, not works of art (in the aesthetic sense); although, if they are well made, they produce a hundred times more illusion than can the best picture or statue. If, therefore, deceptive imitation of the actual thing were the purpose of art, wax figures would necessarily occupy the front rank. Thus they appear to give not merely the form, but also the matter as well; and so they produce the illusion of our having before us the thing itself.

Therefore, instead of having the true work of art that leads us away from what exists only once and never again, i.e. the individual, to what always exists an infinite number of times, in an infinite number of individuals, i.e. the mere form or Idea, we have the wax figure giving us apparently the individual himself and hence that which exists only once and never again, yet without that which lends value to such a fleeting existence, that is, without life. Therefore the wax figure causes us to shudder since its effect is like that of a stiff corpse.

It might be imagined that it was only the statue that gave form without matter, whereas the painting gave matter as well, insofar as it imitated, by means of colour, matter, and its properties. This, however, would be equivalent to understanding form in the purely geometrical sense, which is not what was meant here. For in the philosophical sense, form is the opposite of matter and thus embraces also colour, smoothness, texture, in short every quality. The statue is certainly the only thing that gives the purely geometrical form alone, presenting it in marble, thus in a material that is clearly foreign to it; and so in this way, the statue plainly and obviously isolates the form. The painting, on the other hand, gives us no matter at all, but the mere appearance of the form, not in the geometrical but in the philosophical sense just stated. The painting does not even give this form, but the mere appearance thereof, namely its effect on only one sense, that of sight, and even this only from one point of view. Thus even the painting does not really produce the illusion of our having before us the thing itself, that is, form and matter; but even the deceptive truth of the picture is still always under certain admitted conditions of this method of presentation. For example, through the inevitable falling away of the parallax of our two eyes, the picture always shows us things only as a one-eyed person would see them. Therefore even the painting gives only *the form* since it presents merely the effect thereof and indeed quite one-sidedly, namely on the eye alone. [. . .]

Akin to the foregoing consideration is the following where, however, the form must again be understood in the geometrical sense. Black and white copper engravings and etchings correspond to a nobler and more elevated taste than do coloured engravings and water colours, although the latter make a greater appeal to those of less cultivated taste. This is obviously due to the fact that black and white drawings give the *form* alone, *in abstracto* so to speak, whose apprehension is (as we know) intellectual, that is, the business of the intuitively perceiving understanding. Colour, on the other hand, is merely a matter of the sense-organ and in fact of quite a special adaptation therein (qualitative divisibility of the retina's activity). In this respect, we can also compare the coloured copper engravings to rhymed verses and black and white ones to the merely metrical.

215. The origin of the fundamental idea for a work of art has been very appropriately called its *conception*; for it is the most essential thing just as is procreation to the origin of man; and like this it requires not exactly time, but rather mood and opportunity. Thus the object in general, as that which is the male, practises a constant act of procreation on the subject, as that which is the female. Yet this act becomes fruitful only at odd happy moments and with favoured subjects; but then there arises from it some new and original idea which, therefore, lives on. And as with physical procreation, fruitfulness depends much more on the female than on the male; if the former (the subject) is in the mood suitable for conceiving, almost every object now falling within its apperception will begin to speak to it, in other words, to create in it a vivid, penetrating, and original idea. Thus the sight of a trifling object or event has sometimes become the seed of a great and beautiful work; for instance, by suddenly looking at a tin vessel, **Jacob Boehme** was put into a state of illumination and introduced into the innermost depths of nature. Yet ultimately everything turns on our own strength; and just as no food or medicine can impart or replace vital force, so no book or study can furnish an individual and original mind. [. . .]

## Notes

1. The pure subject of knowing occurs in our forgetting ourselves in order to be absorbed entirely in the intuitively perceived objects, so that they alone are left in consciousness.

2. Tr.: Presumably taken from Martial's *Epigrammata*, II. 41.

## Study Questions

1. Schopenhauer begins with the premise that the "real problem of the metaphysics of the beautiful" arises from an apparent contradiction: our personal desires (thus will) determine whether we find something pleasurable, and yet we take pleasure in the beautiful independently of our personal desires (thus will). Do you agree or disagree?

2. In contrast to Plato, Schopenhauer places the "picture" (e.g., painting or statue) nearer to the "Platonic Idea" than reality. Using a specific artwork as an example, explain the process by which viewers are supposed to arrive at knowledge of a Platonic Idea. What accounts for the source of pleasure that accompanies this "apprehension" of the beautiful?

3. Why does Schopenhauer contend that "art reveals more to us than any science can"? Do you agree or disagree?

4. Schopenhauer holds that the conception of a work of art is preceded by the artist's apprehension of the Platonic Ideas of things, a process of "genius" associated with "abnormal" and "excess" intellect. How is gender implicated in this portrayal of artistic creativity?

---

# Arthur Danto

---

Arthur C. Danto is Johnsonian Professor Emeritus of Philosophy at Columbia University. Danto received a BA from Wayne State University, where he studied art and history, and an MA and PhD from Columbia. Danto's research interests include philosophy of art and philosophical psychology. Art critic at *The Nation* since 1984, Danto's *Encounters and Reflections: Art in the Historical Present* won the National Book Critics Circle Award in 1990. This influential 1964 essay critiques Plato's theory of art as imitation and lays the groundwork for subsequent institutional theories of art.

## The Artworld

*Hamlet: Do you see nothing there?*
*The Queen: Nothing at all; yet all that is I see.*
                    —Shakespeare: *Hamlet*, Act III, Scene IV

### 1. Introduction

Hamlet and **Socrates**, though in praise and deprecation respectively, spoke of art as a mirror held up to nature. As with many disagreements in attitude, this one has a factual basis. Socrates saw mirrors as but reflecting what we can already see; so art, insofar as mirrorlike, yields idle accurate duplications of the appearances of things, and is of no cognitive benefit whatever. Hamlet, more acutely, recognized a remarkable feature of reflecting surfaces, namely that they show us what we could not otherwise perceive—our own face and form—and so art, insofar as it is mirrorlike, reveals us to ourselves, and is, even by Socratic criteria, of some cognitive utility after all. As a philosopher, however, I find Socrates' discussion defective on other, perhaps less profound grounds than these. If a mirror-image of *o* is indeed an imitation of *o*, then, if art is imitation, mirror-images are art. But in fact mirroring objects no more is art than returning weapons to a madman is justice; and reference to mirrorings would be just the sly sort of counterinstance we would expect Socrates to bring forward in rebuttal of the theory he instead uses them to illustrate. If that theory requires us to class *these* as art, it thereby shows its inadequacy: "is an imitation" will not do as a sufficient condition for "is art." Yet, perhaps because artists *were* engaged in imitation, in Socrates' time and after, the insufficiency of the theory was not noticed until the invention of photography. Once rejected as a sufficient condition, mimesis was quickly discarded as even a necessary one; and since the achievement of **Kandinsky**, mimetic features have been relegated to the periphery of critical concern, so much so that some works survive in spite of possessing those virtues, excellence in which was once celebrated as the essence of art, narrowly escaping demotion to mere illustrations.

It is, of course, indispensable in Socratic discussion that all participants be masters of the concept up for analysis, since the aim is to match a real defining expression to a term in active use, and the test for adequacy presumably consists in showing that the former analyzes and applies to all and only those things of which the latter is true. The popular disclaimer notwithstanding, then, Socrates' auditors purportedly knew what art was as well as what they liked; and a theory of art, regarded here as a real definition of "Art," is accordingly not to be of great use in helping men to recognize instances of its application. Their antecedent ability to do this is precisely what the adequacy of the theory is to be tested against, the problem being only to make explicit what they already know. It is *our* use of the term that the theory allegedly means to capture, but we are supposed able, in the words of a recent writer, "to separate those objects which are works of art from those which are not, because . . . we know how correctly to use the word 'art' and to apply the phrase 'work of art.'" Theories, on this account, are somewhat like mirror-images on Socrates' account, showing forth what we already know, wordy reflections of the actual linguistic practice we are masters in.

But telling artworks from other things is not so simple a matter, even for native speakers, and these days one might not be aware he was on artistic terrain without an artistic theory to tell him so. And part of the reason for this lies in the fact that terrain is constituted artistic in virtue of artistic theories, so that one use of theories, in addition to helping us discriminate art from the rest, consists in making art possible. Glaucon and the others could hardly have known what was art and what not: otherwise they would never have been taken in by mirror-images.

## 2. Reality Theory vs. Imitation Theory of Art

Suppose one thinks of the discovery of a whole new class of artworks as something analogous to the discovery of a whole new class of facts anywhere, viz., as something for theoreticians to explain. In science, as elsewhere, we often accommodate new facts to old theories via auxiliary hypotheses, a pardonable enough conservatism when the theory in question is deemed too valuable to be jettisoned all at once. Now the Imitation Theory of Art (IT) is, if one but thinks it through, an exceedingly powerful theory, explaining a great many phenomena connected with the causation and evaluation of artworks, bringing a surprising unity into a complex domain. Moreover, it is a simple matter to shore it up against many purported counterinstances by such auxiliary hypotheses as that the artist who deviates from mimeticity is perverse, inept, or mad. Ineptitude, chicanery, or folly are, in fact, testable predications. Suppose, then, tests reveal that these hypotheses fail to hold, that the theory, now beyond repair, must be replaced. And a new theory is worked out, capturing what it can of the old theory's competence, together with the heretofore recalcitrant facts. One might, thinking along these lines, represent certain episodes in the history of art as not dissimilar to certain episodes in the history of science, where a conceptual revolution is being effected and where refusal to countenance certain facts, while in part due to prejudice, inertia, and self-interest, is due also to the fact that a well-established, or at least widely credited, theory is being threatened in such a way that all coherence goes.

Some such episode transpired with the advent of post-impressionist paintings. In terms of the prevailing artistic theory (IT), it was impossible to accept these as art unless inept art: otherwise they could be discounted as hoaxes, self-advertisements, or the visual counterparts of madmen's ravings. So to get them accepted *as* art, on a footing with the **Transfiguration** (not to speak of a **Landseer stag**), required not so much a revolution in taste as a theoretical revision of rather considerable proportions, involving not only the artistic enfranchisement of these objects, but an emphasis upon newly significant features of accepted artworks, so that quite different accounts of their status as artworks would now have to be given. As a result of the new theory's acceptance, not only were post-impressionist paintings taken up as art, but numbers of objects (masks, weapons, etc.) were transferred from anthropological museums (and heterogeneous other places) to *musées des beaux arts*, though, as we would expect from the fact that a criterion for the acceptance of a new theory is that it account for whatever the older one did, nothing had to be transferred out of the *musée des beaux arts*—even if there were internal rearrangements as between storage rooms and exhibition space. Countless native speakers hung upon suburban mantelpieces innumerable replicas of paradigm cases for teaching the expression "work of art" that would have sent their **Edwardian** forebears into linguistic apoplexy.

To be sure, I distort by speaking of a theory: historically, there were several, all, interestingly enough, more or less defined in terms of the IT. Art-historical complexities must yield before the exigencies of logical exposition, and I shall speak as though there were one replacing theory, partially compensating

for historical falsity by choosing one which was actually enunciated. According to it, the artists in question were to be understood not as unsuccessfully imitating real forms but as successfully creating new ones, quite as real as the forms which the older art had been thought, in its best examples, to be creditably imitating. Art, after all, had long since been thought of as creative (**Vasari** says that God was the first artist), and the **post-impressionists** were to be explained as genuinely creative, aiming, in **Roger Fry**'s words, "not at illusion but reality." This theory (RT) furnished a whole new mode of looking at painting, old and new. Indeed, one might almost interpret the crude drawing in **Van Gogh** and **Cézanne**, the dislocation of form from contour in **Rouault** and **Dufy**, the arbitrary use of colour planes in **Gauguin** and the **Fauves**, as so many ways of drawing attention to the fact that these were *non-imitations*, specifically intended not to deceive. Logically, this would be roughly like printing "Not Legal Tender" across a brilliantly counterfeited dollar bill, the resulting object (counterfeit *cum* inscription) rendered incapable of deceiving anyone. It is not an illusory dollar bill, but then, just because it is non-illusory it does not automatically become a real dollar bill either. It rather occupies a freshly opened area between real objects and real facsimiles of real objects: it is a non-facsimile, if one requires a word, and a new contribution to the world. Thus, Van Gogh's *Potato Eaters*, as a consequence of certain unmistakable distortions, turns out to be a non-facsimile of real-life potato eaters; and inasmuch as these are not facsimiles of potato eaters, Van Gogh's picture, as a non-imitation, had as much right to be called a real object as did its putative subjects. By means of this theory (RT), artworks re-entered the thick of things from which Socratic theory (IT) had sought to evict them: if no *more* real than what carpenters wrought, they were at least no *less* real. The Post-Impressionist won a victory in ontology.

It is in terms of RT that we must understand the artworks around us today. Thus **Roy Lichtenstein** paints comic-strip panels, though ten or twelve feet high. These are reasonably faithful projections onto a gigantesque scale of the homely frames from the daily tabloid, but it is precisely the scale that counts. A skilled engraver might incise **The Virgin and the Chancellor Rollin** on a pinhead, and it would be recognizable as such to the keen of sight, but an engraving of a **Barnett Newman** on a similar scale would be a blob, disappearing in the reduction. A *photograph* of a Lichtenstein is indiscernible from a photograph of a counterpart panel from **Steve Canyon**; but the photograph fails to capture the scale, and hence is as inaccurate a reproduction as a black-and-white engraving of **Botticelli**, scale being essential here as colour there. Lichtensteins, then, are not imitations but *new entities*, as giant whelks [marine snails] would be. **Jasper Johns**, by contrast, paints objects with respect to which questions of scale are irrelevant. Yet his objects cannot be imitations, for they have the remarkable property that any intended copy of a member of this class of objects is automatically a member of the class itself, so that these objects are logically inimitable. Thus, a copy of a numeral just *is* that numeral: a painting of 3 is a 3 made of paint. Johns, in addition, paints targets, flags, and maps. Finally, in what I hope are not unwitting footnotes to Plato, two of our pioneers—Robert Rauschenberg and **Claes Oldenburg**—have made genuine beds.

Rauschenberg's bed hangs on a wall, and is streaked with some desultory housepaint. Oldenburg's bed is a rhomboid, narrower at one end than the other, with what one might speak of as a built-in perspective: ideal for small bedrooms. As beds, these sell at singularly inflated prices, but one *could* sleep in either of them: Rauschenberg has expressed the fear that someone might just climb into his bed and fall asleep. Imagine, now, a certain Testadura ["hard head"]—a plain speaker and noted philistine—who is not aware that these are art, and who takes them to be reality simple and pure. He attributes the paintstreaks on Rauschenberg's bed to the slovenliness of the owner, and the bias in the Oldenburg bed to the ineptitude of the builder or the whimsy, perhaps, of whoever had it "custom-made." These would be mistakes, but mistakes of rather an odd kind, and not terribly different from that made by the stunned birds who pecked the sham grapes of **Zeuxis**. They mistook art for reality, and so has Testadura. But it was meant to

*be* reality, according to RT. Can one have mistaken reality for reality? How shall we describe Testadura's error? What, after all, prevents Oldenburg's creation from being a misshapen bed? This is equivalent to asking what makes it art, and with this query we enter a domain of conceptual inquiry where native speakers are poor guides: *they* are lost themselves.

## 3. The *Is* of Artistic Identification

To mistake an artwork for a real object is no great feat when an artwork is the real object one mistakes it for. The problem is how to avoid such errors, or to remove them once they are made. The artwork is a bed, and not a bed-illusion; so there is nothing like the traumatic encounter against a flat surface that brought it home to the birds of Zeuxis that they had been duped. Except for the guard cautioning Testadura not to sleep on the artworks, he might never have discovered that this was an artwork and not a bed; and since, after all, one cannot discover that a bed is not a bed, how is Testadura to realize that he has made an error? A certain sort of explanation is required, for the error here is a curiously philosophical one, rather like, if we may assume as correct some well-known views of P.F. Strawson, mistaking a person for a material body when the truth is that a person *is* a material body in the sense that a whole class of predicates, sensibly applicable to material bodies, are sensibly, and by appeal to no different criteria, applicable to persons. So you cannot *discover* that a person is not a material body.

We begin by explaining, perhaps, that the paintstreaks are not to be explained away, that they are *part* of the object, so the object is not a mere bed with—as it happens—streaks of paint spilled over it, but a complex object fabricated out of a bed and some paintstreaks: a paint-bed. Similarly, a person is not a material body with—as it happens—some thoughts superadded, but is a complex entity made up of a body and some conscious states: a conscious-body. Persons, like artworks, must then be taken as irreducible to *parts* of themselves, and are in that sense primitive. Or, more accurately, the paintstreaks are not part of the real object—the bed—which happens to be part of the artwork, but are, *like* the bed, part of the artwork as such. And this might be generalized into a rough characterization of artworks that happen to contain real objects as parts of themselves: not every part of an artwork *A* is part of a real object *R* when *R* is part of *A* and can, moreover, be detached from *A* and seen *merely* as *R*. The mistake thus far will have been to mistake *A* for *part* of itself, namely *R*, even though it would not be incorrect to say that *A* is *R*, that the artwork is a bed. It is the "is" which requires clarification here.

There is an *is* that figures prominently in statements concerning artworks which is not the *is* of either identity or predication; nor is it the *is* of existence, of identification, or some special *is* made up to serve a philosophic end. Nevertheless, it is in common usage, and is readily mastered by children. It is the sense of *is* in accordance with which a child, shown a circle and a triangle and asked which is him and which his sister, will point to the triangle saying "That is me"; or, in response to my question, the person next to me points to the man in purple and says "That one is Lear"; or in the gallery I point, for my companion's benefit, to a spot in the painting before us and say "That white dab is Icarus." We do not mean, in these instances, that whatever is pointed to stands for, or represents, what it is said to be, for the *word* "Icarus" stands for or represents Icarus: yet I would not in the same sense of *is* point to the word and say "That is Icarus." The sentence "That *a* is *b*" is perfectly compatible with "That *a* is not *b*" when the first employs this sense of *is* and the second employs some other, though *a* and *b* are used nonambiguously throughout. Often, indeed, the truth of the first *requires* the truth of the second. The first, in fact, is incompatible with "That *a* is not *b*" only when the *is* is used nonambiguously throughout. For want of a word I shall designate this the *is* of *artistic identification*; in each case in which it is used, the *a* stands for some specific physical property of, or physical part of, an object; and, finally, it is a necessary condition for something to be an artwork that some part or property of it be designable by the subject of a sentence that employs this special *is*. It is an *is*, incidentally, which has near-relatives in

marginal and mythical pronouncements. (Thus, one is **Quetzalcoatl**; those *are* the **Pillars of Hercules**.)

Let me illustrate. Two painters are asked to decorate the east and west walls of a science library with frescoes to be respectively called *Newton's First Law* and *Newton's Third Law*. These paintings, when finally unveiled, look, scale apart, as follows:

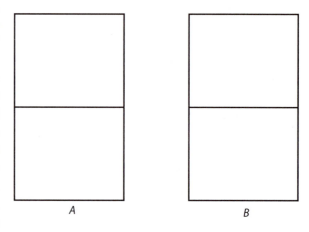

As objects I shall suppose the works to be indiscernible: a black, horizontal line on a white ground, equally large in each dimension and element. *B* explains his work as follows: a mass, pressing downward, is met by a mass pressing upward: the lower mass reacts equally and oppositely to the upper one. *A* explains his work as follows: the line through the space is the path of an isolated particle. The path goes from edge to edge, to give the sense of its *going beyond*. If it ended or began within the space, the line would be curved: and it is parallel to the top and bottom edges, for if it were closer to one than to another, there would have to be a force accounting for it, and this is inconsistent with its being the path of an *isolated* particle.

Much follows from these artistic identifications. To regard the middle line as an edge (mass meeting mass) imposes the need to identify the top and bottom half of the picture as rectangles, and as two distinct parts (not necessarily as two masses, for the line could be the edge of *one* mass jutting up—or down—into empty space). If it is an edge, we cannot thus take the entire area of the painting as a single space: it is rather composed of two forms, or one form and a non-form. We could take the entire area as a single space only by taking the middle horizontal as a *line* which is not an edge. But this almost requires a three-dimensional identification of the whole picture: the area can be a flat surface which the line is *above* (*Jet-flight*), or *below* (*Submarine-path*), or *on* (*Line*), or *in* (*Fissure*), or *through* (*Newton's First Law*)—though in this last case the area is not a flat surface but a transparent cross section of absolute space. We could make all these prepositional qualifications clear by imagining perpendicular cross sections to the picture plane. Then, depending upon the applicable prepositional clause, the area is (artistically) interrupted or not by the horizontal element. If we take the line as *through* space, the edges of the picture are not really the edges of the space: the space goes beyond the picture if the line itself does; and we are in the same space as the line is. As *B*, the edges of the picture can be *part* of the picture in case the masses go right to the edges, so that the edges of the picture are *their* edges. In that case, the vertices of the picture would be the vertices of the masses, except that the masses have four vertices more than the picture itself does: here four vertices would be part of the art work which were not part of the real object. Again, the faces of the masses could be the face of the picture, and in looking at the picture, we are looking at these faces: but *space* has no face, and on the reading of *A* the work has to be read as faceless, and the face of the physical object would not be part of the artwork. Notice here how one artistic identification engenders another artistic identification, and how, consistently with a given identification, we are *required* to give others and *precluded* from still others: indeed, a given identification determines how many elements the work is to contain. These different identifications are incompatible with one another, or generally so, and each might be said to make a different artwork, even though each artwork contains the identical real object as part of itself—or at least parts of the identical real object as parts of itself. There are, of course, senseless identifications: no one could, I think, sensibly

read the middle horizontal as **Love's Labour's Lost** or **The Ascendency of St Erasmus**. Finally, notice how acceptance of one identification rather than another is in effect to exchange one *world* for another. We could, indeed, enter a quiet poetic world by identifying the upper area with a clear and cloudless sky, reflected in the still surface of the water below, whiteness kept from whiteness only by the unreal boundary of the horizon.

And now Testadura, having hovered in the wings throughout this discussion, protests that *all he sees is paint*: a white painted oblong with a black line painted across it. And how right he really is: that is all he sees or that anybody can, we aesthetes included. So, if he asks us to show him what there is further to see, to demonstrate through pointing that this is an artwork (*Sea and Sky*), we cannot comply, for he has overlooked nothing (and it would be absurd to suppose he had, that there was something tiny we could point to and he, peering closely, say "So it is! A work of art after all!"). We cannot help him until he has mastered the *is of artistic identification* and so *constitutes* it a work of art. If he cannot achieve this, he will never look upon artworks: he will be like a child who sees sticks as sticks.

But what about pure abstractions, say something that looks just like *A* but is entitled No. 7? The 10th Street abstractionist blankly insists that there is nothing here but white paint and black, and none of our literary identifications need apply. What then distinguishes him from Testadura, whose philistine utterances are indiscernible from his? And how can it be an artwork for him and not for Testadura, when they agree that there is nothing that does not meet the eye? The answer, unpopular as it is likely to be to purists of every variety, lies in the fact that this artist has returned to the physicality of paint through an atmosphere compounded of artistic theories and the history of recent and remote painting, elements of which he is trying to refine out of his own work; and as a consequence of this his work belongs in this atmosphere and is part of this history. He has achieved abstraction through rejection of artistic identifications, returning to the real world from which such identifications remove us (he thinks), somewhat in the mode of Ch'ing Yuan, who wrote:

> Before I had studied Zen for thirty years, I saw mountains as mountains and waters as waters. When I arrived at a more intimate knowledge, I came to the point where I saw that mountains are not mountains, and waters are not waters. But now that I have got the very substance I am at rest. For it is just that I see mountains once again as mountains, and waters once again as waters.

His identification of what he has made is logically dependent upon the theories and history he rejects. The difference between his utterance and Testadura's "This is black paint and white paint and nothing more" lies in the fact that he is still using the *is* of artistic identification, so that his use of "That black paint is black paint" is not a tautology. Testadura is not at that stage. To see something as art requires something the eye cannot decry—an atmosphere of artistic theory, a knowledge of the history of art: an artworld.

## 4. Brillo Cartons as Artwork

Mr **Andy Warhol**, the Pop artist, displays facsimiles of Brillo cartons, piled high, in neat stacks, as in the stockroom of the supermarket. They happen to be of wood, painted to look like cardboard, and why not? To paraphrase the critic of the *Times*, if one may make the facsimile of a human being out of bronze, why not the facsimile of a Brillo carton out of plywood? The cost of these boxes happens to be 2 x 10³ that of their homely counterparts in real life—a differential hardly ascribable to their advantage in durability. In fact the Brillo people might, at some slight increase in cost, make their boxes out of plywood without these becoming artworks, and Warhol might make *his* out of cardboard without their ceasing to be art. So we may forget questions of intrinsic value, and ask why the Brillo people cannot manufacture art and why Warhol cannot *but* make artworks. Well, his are made by hand, to be sure. Which is like an insane reversal of **Picasso's** strategy in pasting the label from a bottle of Suze [French brand of bitters] onto a drawing, saying as it were that the academic artist, concerned with exact imitation, must always fall short of the real thing: so why not just *use* the real thing? The Pop artist laboriously reproduces machine-made objects by hand, e.g., painting the labels on coffee cans (one can hear the familiar commendation "Entirely made by hand" falling painfully out of the guide's vocabulary when confronted by these objects). But the difference cannot consist in craft: a man who carved pebbles out of stones and carefully constructed a work called *Gravel Pile* might invoke the labour theory of value to account for the price he demands; but the question is, What makes it art? And why need Warhol *make* these things anyway? Why not just scrawl his signature across one? Or crush one up and display it as *Crushed Brillo Box* ("A protest against mechanization . . .") or simply display a Brillo carton as *Uncrushed Brillo Box* ("A bold affirmation of the plastic authenticity of industrial . . .")? Is this man a kind of **Midas**, turning whatever he touches into the gold of pure art? And the whole world consisting of latent artworks waiting, like the bread and wine of reality, to be transfigured, through some dark mystery, into the indiscernible flesh and blood of the sacrament? Never mind that the Brillo box may not be good, much less great art. The impressive thing is that it is art at all. But if it is, why are not the indiscernible Brillo boxes that are in the stockroom? Or *has* the whole distinction between art and reality broken down?

Suppose a man collects objects (ready-mades), including a Brillo carton; we praise the exhibit for variety, ingenuity, what you will. Next he exhibits nothing but Brillo cartons, and we criticize it as dull, repetitive, self-plagiarizing—or (more profoundly) claim that he is obsessed by regularity and repetition, as in **Marienbad**. Or he piles them high, leaving a narrow path; we tread our way through the smooth opaque stacks and find it an unsettling experience, and write it up as the closing in of consumer products, confining us as prisoners: or we say he is a modern pyramid builder. True, we don't say these things about the stockboy. But then a stockroom is not an art gallery, and we cannot readily separate the Brillo cartons from the gallery they are in, any more than we can separate the Rauschenberg bed from the paint upon it. Outside the gallery, they are pasteboard cartons. But then, scoured clean of paint, Rauschenberg's bed is a bed, just what it was before it was transformed into art. But then if we think this matter through, we discover that the artist has failed, really and of necessity, to produce a mere real object. He has produced an artwork, his use of real Brillo cartons being but an expansion of the resources available to artists, a contribution to *artists' materials*, as oil paint was, or *tuche*.

What in the end makes the difference between a Brillo box and a work of art consisting of a Brillo Box is a certain theory of art. It is the theory that takes it up into the world of art, and keeps it from collapsing into the real object which it is (in a sense of *is* other than that of artistic identification). Of course, without the theory, one is unlikely to see it as art, and in order to see it as part of the artworld, one must have mastered a good deal of artistic theory as well as a considerable amount of the history of recent New York painting. It could not have been art fifty years ago. But then there could not have been, everything being equal, flight insurance in the Middle Ages, or **Etruscan** typewriter erasers. The world has to be ready for certain things, the artworld no less than the real one. It is the role of artistic theories, these days as always, to make the artworld, and art, possible. It would, I should think, never have occurred to the **painters of Lascaux** that they were producing *art* on those walls. Not unless there were neolithic aestheticians.

## Study Questions

1. What is the "Imitation Theory of Art" or "IT"? Why, according to Danto, does it provide neither necessary nor sufficient conditions for defining art?

2. What is the "Real Theory of Art" or "RT"? Recalling Plato's distinction between the carpenter's and painter's couches, explain how the artworks of Rauschenberg and Oldenburg support RT over IT.

3. How does Danto use the distinction between "person" and "material body" to explain the "*is* of artistic identification" that constitutes Rauschenberg's bed as an artwork? How does Danto use the Newton frescoes to illustrate how the *is* of artistic identification constitutes identical paintings as different artworks?

4. Describe how Danto uses the concept "the artworld" to explain why a pure abstraction is an artwork even though it represents nothing and a Brillo box is an artwork in an art gallery but not a stock room.

# Alfred Lessing

Alfred (Fred) Lessing was born in 1936, into a Jewish family in The Hague, Netherlands. Lessing survived the Holocaust as a "hidden child," spending most of the war separated from his family and forced to conceal his identity. After the war, the Lessings immigrated to the United States. Lessing has a BA from Carleton College, in Minnesota, a PhD from Yale University, and was a philosophy professor at Oakland University in Rochester, Michigan, when he published this influential article in 1965. Lessing's response to the question he poses in the article's title is that forgeries lack the originality that is expected for artistic works. Today, Lessing is a clinical psychologist in private practice in Birmingham, Michigan, and active as a lecturer about the Holocaust.

## What Is Wrong with a Forgery?

### 1. *The Disciples* and van Meegeren's Dilemma

This paper attempts to answer the simple question: What is wrong with a forgery? It assumes, then, that something *is* wrong with a forgery. This is not an unreasonable assumption when one considers that the term *forgery* can be defined only in reference to a contrasting phenomenon which must somehow *include* the notion of genuineness or authenticity. When thus defined there can be little doubt that the concept of forgery is a normative one. It is clear, moreover, that it is a negative concept implying the absence or negation of value. The problem arises when we ask what kind of value we are speaking of. It appears to be generally assumed that in the case of artistic forgeries we are dealing with the absence or negation of aesthetic value. If this were so, a forgery would be an aesthetically inferior work of art. This, as I will try to show, is not the case. Pure aesthetics cannot explain forgery. [. . .]

Somehow critics have never understood this and have again and again allowed themselves to be forced into an embarrassing position upon the discovery of some forgery or other. Perhaps the classic, certainly the most celebrated, case in point was that of **Han van Meegeren** who in 1945 disturbed the complacent tranquility of the world of art and art critics by confessing that he was the artist responsible for eight paintings of which six had been sold as legitimate **Vermeer**s and two as **de Hoogh**s. It is not hard to imagine the discomfort felt by critics at that time, especially when we recall how thoroughly successful van Meegeren was in perpetrating his fraud. Here, for example, are some of the words with which the discovery of van Meegeren's *Christ and the Disciples at Emmaus* was announced to the world by Abraham Bredius, at that time probably the world's expert on Vermeer:

> . . . we have here a—I am inclined to say—*the* masterpiece of Johannes Vermeer of Delft . . . quite different from all his other paintings and yet every inch a Vermeer. The subject is *Christ and the Disciples at Emmaus* and the colors are magnificent—and characteristic. . . .
>
> In no other picture by the great Master of Delft do we find such sentiment, such a profound understanding of the Bible story—a sentiment so nobly human expressed through the medium of the highest art. . . .
>
> The reproduction [accompanying Bredius's article] can only give a very inadequate idea of the splendid luminous effect of the rare combination of colors of this magnificent painting by one of the greatest artists of the Dutch School.

The picture referred to hung in the Boymans Museum in Rotterdam for seven years. During that time thousands upon thousands admired and praised the painting. There was no doubt in anyone's mind that this was one of the greatest of Vermeer's paintings and, indeed, one of the most beautiful works of art in the world. It was undoubtedly this universal judgment of aesthetic excellence which accounts largely for the sensational effects of van Meegeren's confession in 1945.

It is of course embarrassing and irritating for an expert to make a mistake in his field. And it *was*, as it turned out, a mistake to identify the painting as a Vermeer. But it should be obvious from the words of Bredius just quoted that there is more involved here than a mere matter of misidentification. "The colors are magnificent," he writes. "The highest art . . . this magnificent painting . . . *the* masterpiece of Vermeer": this is more than identification. This clearly is aesthetic praise. And it is just the fact that the critics heaped such lavish praise on a picture which turned out to have been painted by a second-rate contemporary artist that made the van Meegeren case such a painful affair for them. To their way of thinking, which I am trying to show was not very logical, they were now apparently faced with the dilemma of either admitting that they had praised a worthless picture or continuing to do so.

This was of course precisely the trap that van Meegeren had laid for the critics. It was, in fact, the whole *raison d'être* of his perpetrating the fraud. He deliberately chose this extreme, perhaps pathological, way of exposing what he considered to be false aesthetic standards of art critics. In this respect his thinking was no more logical than that of the critics. His reasoning, at least about his first forgery *The Disciples*, was in effect as follows: Once my painting has been accepted and admired as a genuine Vermeer, I will confess publicly to the forgery and thus force the critics either to retract their earlier judgments of praise, thereby acknowledging their fallibility, or to recognize that I am as great an artist as Vermeer. The dilemma as stated contains a difficulty to which we shall come back later. What is important historically is that the critics accepted van Meegeren's dilemma as a genuine one (thereby becoming the dupes of a logical forgery as well as an artistic one).

## 2. Forgeries Need Not Lack Aesthetic Value

The plain fact is that aesthetically it makes no difference whether a work of art is authentic or a forgery, and instead of being embarrassed at having praised a forgery, critics should have the courage of their convictions and take pride in having praised a work of beauty. Perhaps if critics did respond in this way we should be less inclined to think that so often their judgments are historical, biographical, economical, or sociological instead of aesthetic. For in a sense, of course, van Meegeren proved his point. Perhaps it is a point for which such radical proof was not even necessary. We all know very well that it is just the preponderance in the art world of non-aesthetic criteria such as fame of the artist and the age or cost of the canvas which is largely responsible for the existence of artistic forgeries in the first place. We all know that a few authentic pen and ink scratches by **Picasso** are far more valuable than a fine landscape by an unknown artist. If we were offered a choice between an inferior (but genuine) **Degas** sketch and a beautiful Jones or Smith or X, how many of us would choose the latter? In a museum that did not label its paintings, how many of us would not feel uneasy lest we condemn one of the greats or praise an unknown? But, it may be argued, all this we know. It is simply a fact and, moreover, probably an unavoidable, understandable—even a necessary—fact. Is this so serious or regrettable? The answer of course is that it is indeed serious and regrettable that the realm of art should be so infested with non-aesthetic standards of judgment that it is often impossible to distinguish artistic from economic value, taste or fashion from true artistic excellence, and good artists from clever businessmen.

This brings us to the point of our discussion so far. The matter of genuineness versus forgery is but yet another non-aesthetic standard of judgment. The fact that a work of art is a forgery is an item of information about it on a level with such information as how old the artist was when he created it, the political situation in the time and place of its creation, the price it originally fetched, the kind of materials used in it, the stylistic influences discernible in it, the psychological state of the artist, his purpose in painting it, and so on. All such information belongs to areas of interest peripheral at best to the work of art as aesthetic object, areas such as biography, history of art, sociology, and psychology. It is not denied here that such areas of interest may be important and that their study may even help us to become better art appreciators. But it is denied that the information with which they deal is of the essence of the work of art or of the aesthetic experience which it engenders.

It would be merely foolish to assert that it is of no interest whatsoever to know that *The Disciples* is a forgery. But to the man who has never heard of either Vermeer or van Meegeren and who stands in front of *The Disciples* admiring it, it can make no difference whether he is told that it is a seventeenth century Vermeer or a twentieth century van Meegeren in the style of Vermeer. And when some deny this and argue vehemently that indeed it does make a great deal of difference, they are only admitting that *they* do know something about Vermeer and van Meegeren and the history of art and the value and reputation of certain masters. They are only admitting that *they* do not judge a work of art on purely aesthetic grounds, but also take into account when it was created, by whom, and how great a reputation it or its creator has. And instead of seeking justification in the fact that in truth it is difficult to make a pure, aesthetic judgment, unbiased by all our knowledge of the history and criticism of art, they generally confuse matters of aesthetics even more by rationalizing that it is the complexity of the aesthetic experience which accounts for the difference made by the knowledge that a work of art is a forgery. That the aesthetic experience is complex I do not deny. But it is not so complex that such items of information as the place and date of creation or the name of the creator of a work of art have to be considered. The fact that *The Disciples* is a forgery is

just that, a fact. It is a fact *about* the painting which stands entirely apart from it as an object for aesthetic contemplation. The knowledge of this fact can neither add anything to nor subtract anything from the aesthetic experience (as aesthetic), except insofar as preoccupation with it or disappointment on its account may in some degree prevent us from having an aesthetic experience at all. Whatever the reasons for the removal of *The Disciples* from the walls of the Boymans Museum in Rotterdam, they were assuredly not aesthetic.

## 3. Forgeries Need Not Be Morally or Legally Wrong

And yet, we can all sympathize, or at least understand, why *The Disciples* was removed. It was, after all, a forgery and even if we grant that it is not a matter of aesthetics, it still seems self-evident that forgery remains a normative term implying a defect or absence in its object. In short, we still need to answer our question: What is wrong with a forgery?

The most obvious answer to this question, after the aesthetic one, is that forgery is a moral or legal normative concept, and that thus it refers to an object which, if not necessarily aesthetically inferior, is always morally offensive. Specifically, the reason forgery is a moral offence, according to this view, is of course that it involves *deception*. Reasonable and commonsensical as this view seems at first, it does not, as I will try to show, answer our question adequately.

Now it cannot be denied, I think, that we do in fact often intend little more than this moral connotation when we speak of forgery. Just because forgery is a normative concept we implicitly condemn any instance of it because we generally assume that it involves the breaking of a legal or moral code. This assumption is, however, only sometimes correct. It is important to note this because historically by far the majority of artistic fakes or forgeries have not been legal forgeries. Most often they have been the result of simple mistakes, misunderstandings, and lack of information about given works of art. We can, as a point of terminology, exclude all such instances from the category of forgery and restrict the term to only those cases involving deliberate deception. There is, after all, a whole class of forgeries, including simple copies, misattributions, composites, and works "in the manner of" some reputable artist, which represent deliberate frauds. In these cases of forgery, which are undoubtedly the most notorious and disconcerting, someone, e.g., artist or art dealer, has passed off a work of art as being something which it is not. The motive for doing so is almost always economic, but occasionally, as with van Meegeren, there is involved also a psychological motive of personal prestige or revenge. In any case, it seems clear that—if we leave out of consideration the factor of financial loss, which can of course be considerable, as again the van Meegeren case proved—such deliberate forgeries are condemned by us on moral grounds, that is, because they involve conscious deception.

Yet, as a final answer to our question as to what is wrong with a forgery, this definition fails. The reason is the following: Although to some extent it is true that passing *anything* off as *anything* that it is not constitutes deception and is thus an undesirable or morally repugnant act, the case of deception we have in mind when we define forgery in terms of it is that of passing off the inferior as the superior. Although, strictly speaking, passing off a genuine de Hoogh as a Vermeer is also an immoral act of deception, it is hard to think of it as a forgery at all, let alone a forgery in the same sense as passing off a van Meegeren as a Vermeer is. The reason is obviously that in the case of the de Hoogh a superior work is being passed off as a superior work (by another artist), while in the van Meegeren case an inferior work is passed off as a superior work.

What is needed, then, to make our moral definition of forgery more accurate is the specification "passing off the inferior as the superior." But it is just at this point that this common-sense definition of artistic forgery in moral terms breaks down. For we are now faced with the question of what is meant by superior and inferior in art. The moral definition

of forgery says in effect that a forgery is an inferior work passed off as a superior one. But what is meant here by inferior? We have already seen that the forgery is not necessarily *aesthetically* inferior. What, then, does it mean? Once again, what is wrong with a forgery?

The attempt to define forgery in moral terms fails because it inevitably already assumes that there exists a difference between genuine works of art and forgeries which makes passing off the latter as the former an offence against a moral or legal law. For only if such a difference does in fact exist can there be any rationale for the law. It is of course precisely this assumed real difference which we are trying to discover in this paper.

## 4. Forgeries Lack the Originality Characteristic of the Creative Arts

It seems to me that the offence felt to be involved in forgery is not so much against the spirit of beauty (aesthetics) or the spirit of the law (morality) as against the spirit of art. Somehow, a work such as *The Disciples* lacks artistic integrity. Even if it is beautiful and even if van Meegeren had not forged Vermeer's signature, there would still be something wrong with *The Disciples*. What? is still our question.

We may approach this problem by considering the following interesting point. The concept of forgery seems to be peculiarly inapplicable to the performing arts. It would be quite nonsensical to say, for example, that the man who played the **Bach suites** for unaccompanied cello and whom at the time we took to be **Pablo Casals** was in fact a forger. Similarly, we should want to argue that the term *forgery* was misused if we should read in the newspaper that **Margot Fonteyn**'s performance in *Swan Lake* last night was a forgery because as a matter of fact it was not Margot Fonteyn who danced last night but rather some unknown person whom everyone mistook for Margot Fonteyn. Again, it is difficult to see in what sense a performance of, say, *Oedipus Rex* or *Hamlet* could be termed a forgery.

Here, however, we must immediately clarify our point, for it is easily misunderstood. There is, of course, a sense in which a performance of *Hamlet* or *Swan Lake* or the Bach suites could be called a forgery. If, for example, someone gave a performance of *Hamlet* in which every gesture, every movement, every vocal interpretation had been copied or imitated from the performance of *Hamlet* by **Laurence Olivier**, we could, I suppose, call the former a forgery of the latter. But notice that in that case we are interpreting the art of acting not as a performing art but as a creative art. For what is meant is that Olivier's interpretation and performance of *Hamlet* is itself an original and creative work of art which can be forged. Similar comments would apply to Margot Fonteyn's *Swan Lake* and Casal's Bach suites and, in fact, to every performance.

My point is then that the concept of forgery applies only to the creative and not to the performing arts. It can be denied of course that there is any such ultimate distinction between creative and performing arts. But we shall still have to admit, I think, that the duality on which it is based—the duality of creativity or originality, on the one hand, and reproduction or technique, on the other—is real. We shall have to admit that originality and technique are two elements of all art; for not only can it be argued that a performance requires more than technique, namely originality, but also that the creation of a work of art requires more than originality, namely technique.

The truth of the matter is probably that both performances and works of art vary greatly and significantly in the degree to which they possess these elements. Their relative presence in works of art and performances makes, in fact, an interesting way of categorizing the latter. But it would be wrong to assert that these two elements are inseparable. I can assure the reader that a portrait painted by myself would be technically almost totally incompetent, and yet even I would not deny that it might be original. On the other hand, a really skilful copy of, for example, a **Rembrandt** drawing may be technically perfect and yet lack all originality. These two examples establish the two extreme cases of a kind

of continuum. The copy of Rembrandt is of course the forgery *par excellence*. My incompetent portrait is as far removed from being a forgery as any work can be. Somewhere in between lies the whole body of legitimate performances and works of art.

The implications of this long and devious argument are as follows. Forgery is a concept that can be made meaningful only by reference to the concept of originality, and hence only to art viewed as a *creative*, not as a reproductive or technical activity. The element of performance or technique in art cannot be an object for forgery because technique is not the kind of thing that can be forged. Technique is, as it were, public. One does or does not possess it or one acquires it or learns it. One may even pretend to have it. But one cannot forge it because in order to forge it one must already possess it, in which case there is no need to forge it. It is not Vermeer's technique in painting light which van Meegeren forged. That technique is public and may be had by anyone who is able and willing to learn it. It is rather Vermeer's discovery of this technique and his use of it, that is, Vermeer's originality, which is forged. The light, as well as the composition, the colour, and many other features, of course, were original with Vermeer. They are not original with van Meegeren. They are forged.

## 5. Concepts of Originality in Art

At this point our argument could conclude were it not for the fact that the case which we have used throughout as our chief example, *Christ and the Disciples at Emmaus*, is not in fact a skilful copy of a Vermeer but a novel painting in the style of Vermeer. This threatens our definition of forgery since this particular forgery (always assuming it *is* a forgery) obviously possesses originality in some sense of the word.

The problem of forgery, in other words, is a good deal more complex than might at first be supposed, and before we can rest content with our definition of forgery as works of art lacking originality, it must be shown that the concept of originality can indeed account for the meaning of forgery as an untrue or objectionable thing in all instances, including even such a bizarre case as that of van Meegeren's *Disciples at Emmaus*. It thus becomes important to examine the various possible meanings that the term *originality* may have in the context of art in order to determine in what sense *The Disciples* does and does not possess it, and hence in what sense it can meaningfully and justifiably be termed a forgery.

1) A work of art may be said to be original in the sense of being a particular object not identical with any other object. But this originality is trivial since it is a quality possessed by all things. *Particularity* or *self-identity* would be better names for it.

2) By originality in a work of art we may mean that it possesses a certain superficial individuality which serves to distinguish it from other works of art. Thus, for example, a certain subject matter in a particular arrangement painted in certain colours may serve to identify a painting and mark it as an original work of art in the sense that its subject matter is unique. Probably the term *individuality* specifies this quality more adequately than *originality*.

It seems safe to assert that this quality of individuality is a necessary condition for any work of art to be called original in any significant sense. It is, however, not a necessary condition for a work to be called beautiful or to be the object of an aesthetic experience. A good reproduction or copy of a painting may be the object of aesthetic contemplation and yet it lacks all originality in the sense which we are here considering. Historically many forgeries are of this kind, i.e., more or less skilful copies of existing works of art. They may be described as being forgeries just because they lack this kind of originality and hence any other kind of originality as well. It is to be noticed that the quality which makes such a copy a forgery, i.e., its lack of individuality, is not a quality which exists in the work of art as such. It is a fact about the work of art which can be known only by placing the latter in the context of the history of art and observing whether any identical work predates it.

As we said above, it is not this kind of originality which is lacking in *The Disciples*.

3) By originality in art we may mean the kind of imaginative novelty or spontaneity which is a mark of every good work of art. It is the kind of originality which attaches to individual works of art and which can be specified in formal or technical terms such as composition, balance, colour intensity, perspective, harmony, rhythm, tempo, texture, rhyme, alliteration, suspense, character, plot, structure, choice of subject matter, and so on. Here again, however, in order for this quality to be meaningfully called originality, a reference must be made to a historical context in terms of which we are considering the particular work of art in question, e.g., this work of art is original because the artist has done something with the subject and its treatment which has never been done before, or this work is not original because many others just like it predate it.

In any case, *The Disciples* does, by common consent, possess this kind of originality and is therefore in this sense at least not a forgery.

4) The term *originality* is sometimes used to refer to the great artistic achievement of a specific work of art. Thus we might say that whereas nearly all of **Milton**'s works are good and original in the sense of (c) above, **Paradise Lost** has a particularly profound originality possessed only by really superlative works of art. It is hard to state precisely what is meant by this use of the term *originality*. In justifying it we should probably point to the scope, profundity, daring, and novelty of the conception of the work of art in question as well as to the excellence of its execution. No doubt this kind of originality differs from that discussed under (c) above only in degree.

It is to be noted that it cannot be the lack of this kind of originality which defines a forgery since, almost by definition, it is a quality lacking in many—maybe the majority of—legitimate works of art. Moreover, judging from the critical commentary with which *The Disciples* was received at the time of its discovery—commentary unbiased by the knowledge that it was a forgery—it seems reasonable to infer that the kind of originality meant here is in fact one which *The Disciples* very likely possesses.

5) Finally, it would seem that by originality in art we can and often do mean the artistic novelty and achievement not of one particular work of art but of the totality of artistic productions of one man or even one school. Thus we may speak of the originality

of Vermeer or **El Greco** or **Mozart** or **Dante** or **Impressionism** or the **Metaphysical Poets** or even the Greeks or the **Renaissance**, always referring, I presume, to the artistic accomplishments achieved and embodied in the works of art belonging to the particular man, movement, or period. In the case of Vermeer we may speak of the originality of the artist's sense of design in the genre picture, the originality of his use of bright and pure colours, and of the originality of his treatment and execution of light.

It is to be noticed first of all that this meaning of originality, too, depends entirely on a historical context in which we are placing and considering the accomplishment of one man or one period. It would be meaningless to call Impressionism original, in the sense here considered, except in reference to the history of art which preceded it. Again, it is just because Vermeer's sense of pictorial design, his use of bright colours, and his mastery of the technique of painting light are not found in the history of art before him that we call these things original in Vermeer's work. Originality, even in this more profound sense, or rather especially in this more profound sense, is a quality definable only in terms of the history of art.

A second point of importance is that while originality as here considered is a quality which attaches to a whole corpus or style of works of art, it can be considered to exist in one particular work of art in the sense that that work of art is a typical example of the style or movement to which it belongs and therefore embodies the originality of that style or movement. Thus we may say that Vermeer's *A Painter in His Studio* is original because in this painting (as well as in several others, of course) we recognize those characteristics mentioned earlier (light, design, colour, etc.) which are so typical of Vermeer's work as a whole and which, when we consider the whole of Vermeer's work in the context of the history of art, allow us to ascribe originality to it.

Turning our attention once more to *The Disciples*, we are at last in a position to provide an adequate answer to our question as to the meaning of the term forgery when applied to a work of art such as *The Disciples*. We shall find, I think, that the fraudulent character of this painting is adequately defined by stating that it lacks originality in the fifth and final sense which we have here considered. Whatever kinds of originality it can claim—and we have seen that it possesses all the kinds previously discussed—it is *not* original in the sense of being the product of a style, period, or technique which, when considered in its appropriate historical context, can be said to represent a significant achievement. It is just this fact which differentiates this painting from a genuine Vermeer! The latter, when considered in its historical context, i.e., the seventeenth century, possesses the qualities of artistic or creative novelty which justify us in calling it original. *The Disciples*, on the other hand, in *its* historical context, i.e., the twentieth century, is not original, since it presents nothing new or creative to the history of art even though, as we have emphasized earlier, it may well be as beautiful as the genuine Vermeer pictures.

It is to be noted that in this definition of forgery the phrase "appropriate historical context" refers to the date of production of the particular work of art in question, not the date which in the history of art is appropriate to its style or subject matter. In other words, what makes *The Disciples* a forgery is precisely the disparity or gap between its stylistically appropriate and its actual date of production. It is simply this disparity which we have in mind when we say that forgeries such as *The Disciples* lack integrity.

It is interesting at this point to recall van Meegeren's reasoning in perpetrating the Vermeer forgeries. "Either," he reasoned, "the critics must admit their fallibility or else acknowledge that I am as great an artist as Vermeer." We can see now that this reasoning is not sound. For the notion of greatness involved in it depends on the same concept of historical originality which we have been considering. The only difference is that we are now thinking of it as an attribute of the artist rather than of the works of art. Van Meegeren's mistake was in thinking that Vermeer's reputation as a great artist depended on his ability to paint beautiful pictures. If this were so, the dilemma which van Meegeren posed to the critics would have been a real one, for his picture is undeniably beautiful. But, in fact, Vermeer is *not* a great artist only because he could paint beautiful pictures. He is great for that reason plus something else. And that something else is precisely the fact of his originality, i.e., the fact that he painted certain pictures in a certain manner *at a certain time in the history and development of art.* Vermeer's art represents a genuine creative achievement in the history of art. It is the work not merely of a master craftsman or technician, but of a creative genius as well. And it is for the latter rather than for the former reason that we call Vermeer great. [. . .]

## Work Cited

Bredius, A. "A New Vermeer." *The Burlington Magazine* Nov 1937: 210–1.

## Study Questions

1. Describe the dilemma van Meegeren assumed he was creating for the critics when he painted *Christ and the Disciples at Emmaus* in order to pass it off as a work by the seventeenth-century Dutch master Vermeer.
2. What makes a forgery wrong, according to Lessing, and why does this analysis show that van Meegeren did not present the critics with a dilemma after all?
3. What are the five senses of originality in art identified by Lessing? In which sense(s) is *The Disciples* original and in which sense(s) is it not?
4. Lessing emphasizes that aesthetic judgment is autonomous: what makes a painting beautiful is independent of non-aesthetic—e.g., biographical, historical, sociological, or psychological—considerations. What qualities do you think are implicated in aesthetic judgments of beauty?

---

# James O. Young

---

James O. Young is a professor and chair of philosophy at the University of Victoria. He has a BA from Simon Fraser University, an MA from the University of Waterloo, and a PhD from Boston University. Young specializes in philosophy of language and philosophy of art. He has written three books: *Global Anti-Realism* (1995), *Art and Knowledge* (2001), and, excerpted here, *Cultural Appropriation and the Arts* (2008).

## The Aesthetics of Cultural Appropriation

From *Cultural Appropriation and the Arts*

### 1. The Aesthetic Handicap Thesis

In this chapter [. . .] I will ask whether an artwork that employs appropriated content [. . .] will necessarily have (qua product of cultural appropriation) aesthetic flaws. Potentially both interpretive and creative artists suffer from a handicap. For example, both a Westerner who performs Beijing opera and a Chinese who paints landscapes in the style of Monet could suffer from an aesthetic handicap. I will reach the conclusion that the works of artists who appropriate content [. . .] do not necessarily suffer from aesthetic flaws. On the contrary, artists who engage in cultural appropriation may produce works of considerable aesthetic merit. [. . .]

This chapter is divided into [five] sections. After this introductory section, I will consider the claim that works by outsiders have flaws that can be detected without any information about who produced them. In the third section I will consider and accept the proposal that at least some of the aesthetic properties of an artwork depend, in part, on the cultural context in which it was produced. This is to admit that the fact that artists have engaged in content appropriation can affect the aesthetic properties of their works. An argument can be given for the conclusion that the effect is negative. In the fourth section I present arguments for the claim that works by outsiders who engage in content appropriation are flawed because they are inauthentic. In the fifth section these arguments are refuted. [. . .]

In assessing the aesthetic handicap thesis, we need to bear in mind that aesthetic properties come in two varieties. **Nelson Goodman** famously wrote that "the aesthetic properties of a picture include not only those found by looking at it but also those that determine how it is to be looked at" (111–12). Goodman limited his remarks to pictures, but presumably the same point applies to other sorts of artworks. Once we extend Goodman's point to other classes of artworks, we would say that the first class of properties includes those that can be heard as well as those that can be seen. Presumably it also includes properties of literary works that are apprehended by intellectual experience. So the triteness or didacticism of a novel that readers can experience, without knowing anything about the circumstances of the work's production, belongs to the first category. The second sort of property will include the categories to which artworks belong, and which influence the interpretation and evaluation of a work. In order to discover these properties of an artwork, audiences must do more than inspect the work. Audiences need to learn about the circumstances of the work's production and, in particular, the context in which the work was produced.

Given Goodman's distinction, the aesthetic handicap thesis can be interpreted in two ways. The first possibility is that, try as they may, when artists appropriate from another culture, they will produce works that have immediately observable aesthetic flaws. On this first interpretation of the thesis, one does not need to know who produced the work for its flaws to be apparent. That is, the thesis is that when outsiders appropriate content, they will always employ it ineffectively. We will be able to tell, for example, just by listening to a blues performance by a non-African American that it has certain flaws. [. . .]

The alternative interpretation of the aesthetic handicap thesis states that the aesthetic flaws of works by cultural appropriators are properties of Goodman's second sort. On this interpretation of the thesis, the fact that a work employs content from a culture other than the artist's own, or represents a culture other than the artist's, is an aesthetic property. Specifically, it is a negative aesthetic property that detracts from a work's aesthetic value. Perhaps, for example, once a work is known to be by an outsider it will be experienced as (and actually be) insincere or unoriginal.

## 2. The Cultural Experience Argument

A common sort of argument tries to establish that works by outsiders will have observable aesthetic flaws. This argument starts from the premise that the ability to use a style successfully is linked to participation in a culture. On this view, artists cannot successfully employ a style unless they have had experiences available only to members of a culture. In other words, the experience of living as a member of a given culture is a necessary condition of being able to create successful works of the types developed by the culture. We may call this the *cultural experience argument* for the aesthetic handicap thesis.

This sort of argument is made about the appropriation of African-American music. A well-known advocate of this view is Amiri Baraka (the blues musician formerly known as LeRoi Jones). He has maintained that a musician cannot learn to produce the blues (or to produce the blues well) except via "the peculiar social, cultural, economic, and emotional experience of a black man in America. The idea of a white blues singer seems an even more violent contradiction of terms than the idea of a middle-class blues singer. The materials of blues were not available to the white American" (148). (The debate about the appropriation of the blues is often formulated with reference to race or ethnicity. References to race can be replaced by references to culture.) Crucial to this experience was the discrimination to which African Americans were subject. Baraka writes that "The blues was conceived by freedmen and ex-slaves . . . as an emotional confirmation of, and reaction to, the way in which most Negroes were still forced to exist in the United States" (142). Many non-African Americans do not simply lack the experience of being a member of African-American culture and experiencing discrimination. Given their skin pigmentation, they cannot have this experience. [. . .]

The conclusion of the cultural experience argument is that artists who lack the requisite cultural background are bound to produce works or performances of a poor aesthetic quality. According to Baraka, the result of the appropriation of the blues was commercialized and diluted music. [. . .] Since the blues originated in a specific cultural context, the cultural experience argument has an initial plausibility. Many performances of blues by musicians whose cultural background is non-African-American undeniably are aesthetically poor. They do not measure up to the standards established by pioneering African-American blues artists such as Ma Rainey, John Lee Hooker, Muddy Waters, and so on.

Despite its initial plausibility, the cultural experience argument faces telling objections. The first point to make is that even if artists cannot successfully master a style or genre developed in another culture, it does not follow that they are condemned to aesthetic failure when they engage in cultural appropriation. We need to distinguish between two ways in which artists can engage in content appropriation. The first may be called *non-innovative content appropriation*. We would have an example of such appropriation if an American performer were to attempt to enter into the tradition of Japanese epic ballad recitation by chanting (in Japanese) the **Tale of the Heike** while accompanying himself on a *biwa*. Artists engaged in non-innovative content appropriation are not creating a new category of artwork, but adding to a category that already exists. They attempt to succeed by the standards already established within the

culture from which they are appropriating. In this case, a non-Japanese performer is trying to master the techniques of an existing Japanese tradition.

Alternatively an artist might engage in *innovative content appropriation*. Artists who engage in this sort of appropriation appropriate a style or a motif from a culture but use it in a way that would not be found in the culture in which it originated. **Picasso** was engaged in innovative content appropriation (specifically: motif appropriation) when he borrowed ideas from African carvers in such paintings as *Les Demoiselles d'Avignon*. Although African carving influenced Picasso, he did not produce a work that belongs to any tradition of African carving. Similarly, **Ravel** borrowed from African-American culture in such jazz-influenced works as the Sonata for Violin and Cello (1922), the Sonata for Violin and Piano (1927), and the two piano concerti (the Piano Concerto for the Left Hand in D Major, composed for Paul Wittgenstein, and the Concerto in G Major) he composed between 1929 and 1931. Although these are not jazz compositions, we find in them innovative content appropriation. [. . .]

Equipped with the distinction between innovative and non-innovative content appropriation we are in a position to see the first problem with the cultural experience argument. At best it shows that artists who engage in non-innovative content appropriation are doomed to aesthetic failure. Perhaps the middle-class white college student who sings the blues, imitating the singers he has heard in recordings, will inevitably produce derivative and uninspired music. Perhaps my imaginary American performer will never be able to recite epic Japanese poetry as well as a Japanese. Even if this is so, the cultural experience argument provides us with no reason to believe that outsiders will not be able to make aesthetically successful innovative re-use of styles and motifs developed by other cultures. I take it that the examples of motif appropriation by Picasso and Ravel are sufficient to establish this point.

Even Baraka, who endorses the aesthetic handicap thesis, acknowledges this point. Middle-class whites are, on his view, unable to produce good music in an African-American style. Still, he admits that they are able to appropriate from African-American culture and produce something valuable. Baraka concedes this in the contexts of a discussion of the trumpet playing of **Bix Beiderbecke**. According to Baraka, Beiderbecke's playing was "certainly an appropriation of black New Orleans brass style, most notably King Oliver's" (151). At the same time, Baraka recognizes that Beiderbecke was a successful musician. He "played "white jazz" . . . music that is the product of attitudes expressive of a peculiar culture." Still, "the serious white musician" such as Beiderbecke was in a position to make creative re-use of what he had appropriated and he produced good music (154). [. . .]

The response just given to the cultural experience argument does not completely undermine the argument. It may still be successful against non-innovative appropriation. If so, this would be worrying since much cultural appropriation is likely to be non-innovative. Picasso, Ravel, and Beiderbecke were great artists and less talented and innovative artists will perform much cultural appropriation. A little reflection is sufficient to show that the cultural experience argument is unable even to show that non-innovative content appropriation will necessarily suffer from observable aesthetic flaws.

Very little evidence exists for the claim that mastery of an artistic style is linked to membership in a culture but vast amounts of evidence can be marshalled in support of the opposite claim. Many examples can be given of artists from diverse cultures who are successful practitioners of the same style. (At least, they are apparently successful. Consideration of the second sort of aesthetic property is still pending.) Consider **bel canto** singing, originally produced in the context of Italian culture. Singers with diverse cultural backgrounds have fully mastered the style: Kathleen Battle (an African-American) and Kiri Te Kanawa (half Maori) no less than Cecelia Bartoli. The greatest composer in the French baroque style was Jean-Baptiste Lully (born Giovanni Battista Lulli in Florence). Arguably the most proficient master of the Italian baroque style was *Il caro Sassone* ["the dear Saxon"], George Frederic Handel.

What is true of Italian musical styles is as true of those that originated in the context of African-American culture. Ray Eldridge, the distinguished African-American jazz trumpeter, was an adherent of the cultural experience argument. He once bet Leonard Feather, the music critic, that he could reliably tell the difference between jazz performances by African Americans and non-African Americans. If anyone could tell the difference, Eldridge could. Widely regarded as the greatest trumpet soloist of his time, Eldridge's credentials were impeccable. Put to the test, he failed miserably. In blind listening situations, he misidentified the cultural origins of the performer more than half of the time. (Feather conducted a series of "blindfold tests" for *Down Beat* during his long tenure at that magazine.)

Let us return to our starting point: the blues. It is possible to name any number of outsiders who are good blues musicians by the standards established by insiders. Marcia Ball, John Hammond, James Harman, Charlie Musslewhite, Stevie Ray Vaughan, and Johnny Winter are all examples of outsiders (relative to African-American culture) who are successful blues musicians by the standards of insiders. Many of them are multiple winners of W. C. Handy Blues Awards. Presumably such a distinguished bluesman as Buddy Guy would notice the flaws in the blues of Eric Clapton, a born and bred Englishman. Yet Guy has said with reference to Clapton that "all I want to do is hear him play. Race, size, color, nothing matters when a guy's got it, and Eric's got it" (in Taylor 313). Guy was perfectly aware that Clapton is an outsider relative to African-American culture. [. . .]

The fact that there is no hard and fast link between culture and artistic success should not surprise us. The cultural experience argument only alleged that experience of living in a culture was a necessary condition of being able to create successful works in certain categories. It never said that such experience was a sufficient condition of being able to do so. Nor should it have. After all, many people belong to a given culture and yet are unable to produce successful works of art in the categories typical of their culture. (I, for example, am unable to produce a successful work of art in any of the genres characteristic of my culture.) Given that membership in a culture is not a sufficient condition of being able to produce good works of a certain sort, we might well ask what else is necessary.

It is probably impossible to specify sufficient conditions for the successful production of works in any genre but it is fairly easy to identify a few necessary conditions. Aspiring artists must undergo a process of training. (Sometimes, an artist can be self-trained.) Artists must study successful works of the sort that they aspire to produce. They must become familiar with techniques and materials. Often they need to learn the significance of certain symbols, conventions, and so on. [. . .] Perhaps, most importantly, artists must repeatedly practise their craft. These are the really important preconditions of being a successful artist in any style. Notice that no mention is made of the cultural background of the aspiring artist. The required training can be undertaken by anyone. Being able to work in a given style is like learning a language and there is no reason why outsiders cannot learn this language every bit as well as insiders.

## 3. Aesthetic Properties and Cultural Context

In the previous section I assumed that if outsiders who engage in cultural appropriation labour under an aesthetic handicap, they will produce works with observable aesthetic flaws. I have argued that when outsiders engage in non-innovative appropriation they are successful when experience cannot reliably distinguish their works from those produced by good insider artists. Even if we cannot immediately determine which works are by outsiders, we cannot rule out the possibility that their works inevitably have aesthetic flaws. Perhaps they have flaws because of the second sort of aesthetic property Goodman identified. Perhaps facts about the origin of works by outsiders will enable us to see or interpret works by outsiders in new ways. Perhaps when we reinterpret works by outsiders, flaws will become apparent.

A long and distinguished tradition in aesthetics would have us reject Goodman's distinction. According to this empiricist tradition, nothing

is relevant to the aesthetic value of a work of art besides its observable properties. Facts about the intentions, beliefs, provenance, or (most importantly given present concerns) the cultural background of an artist have no relevance to the aesthetic properties of a work of art. Anyone who subscribes to this tradition will believe that much of what follows in this section is not only unnecessary but misguided. I am inclined, however, to think that Goodman's distinction cannot be disregarded.

The way in which information about the origin of an artwork can affect its aesthetic properties can be illustrated by a well-known literary thought experiment. **Jorge Luis Borges** famously compared the *Don Quixote* (1605) of Cervantes and the (imaginary) *Don Quixote* of Pierre Menard. In Part I, Chapter 9, of Cervantes' *Quixote* we find the following passage: "Truth, whose mother is history, who is the rival of time, depositor of deeds, witness of the past, example and lesson to the present, and warning to the future . . ." Menard in the early twentieth century, Borges imagines, writes instead: "Truth, whose mother is history, who is the rival of time, depositor of deeds, witness of the past, example and lesson to the present, and warning to the future. . ." Written in the seventeenth century, Cervantes' "enumeration is a mere rhetorical eulogy of history." For Menard, the contemporary of **William James**, the same passage is a statement of pragmatism: "Historical truth, for him, is not what took place; it is what we think took place" (102). This illustrates how information about the origin of a literary work can influence how it is interpreted and what properties it has.

The same point can be made in less fanciful terms. In the early eighteenth century, King George I described the work of the architect Sir Christopher Wren as "amusing, awful and artificial." He meant that it was amazing, awe-inspiring, and artistic. Obviously, the King's words do not have the same meaning today. The meanings of words depend on the contexts in which they are originally used. The meaning of words in a work of literature contributes to its aesthetic properties. Consequently, the aesthetic properties of a literary work depend on the work's original context. A similar point can be made about the properties of musical and visual artworks. Certain harmonies will be dissonant if produced in the eighteenth century. The same harmonies will not be dissonant in a twentieth-century composition.

An even more general argument shows that the aesthetic properties of an artwork can depend on facts about its production. I have in mind the argument in Kendall Walton's classic paper, "Categories of Art." Walton argued that we can only determine what aesthetic properties an artwork has once we have determined the category to which it belongs. Indeed, a work only has aesthetic properties in the context of a category. One cannot, for example, say that a painting is gaudy *tout court*. First we must determine the category to which it belongs. Imagine that we are presented with a brightly coloured landscape. If it belongs to the category of **Wu School** landscape painting (exemplified by the works of Shen Zhou), it may very well be gaudy. If the painting belongs to the category of post-impressionist landscapes (say it is in the style of **Van Gogh** or **Matisse**), then probably it is not gaudy. In determining the category to which a work of art belongs we take into account a wide variety of factors. Among these factors will be knowledge about artists and their historical contexts. The culture of an artist is a large part of the historical context.

A few examples will illustrate how the cultural background of an artist can have an impact on the aesthetic properties of a work. Imagine that we have a certain number of artworks which are thought to have been produced by insiders. One is apparently a typical Mississippi Delta blues. Another is a novel about the *ante bellum* [pre–Civil War] American south, reputedly written by a freed slave. Imagine now that it turns out that the blues piece was not performed by an African-American insider, but is rather by a university student from Beijing. Or imagine that it turns out that a slave owner wrote the novel in question. [. . .] The cultural milieu of an artist is an important part of a work's original context. So it could well be that critics are justified in revising their assessment of the works in question. They may have been wrong when they judged the novel to be a sensitive and poignant indictment of slavery. Perhaps it is a sly parody of African-American manners.

Similarly, the blues performance will not have been a heartfelt expression of the plight of poor African-American sharecroppers. The judgment that it was is mistaken, even though no observable features of the performance would justify the conclusion that the judgment is mistaken.

## 4. Authenticity and Appropriation

Even if the aesthetic properties of an artwork depend on the cultural context in which it was produced, we still do not have an argument that shows that works produced by outsiders are necessarily subject to aesthetic flaws. No developed philosophical literature directly supports the aesthetic handicap thesis. There is, however, a literature that can be adapted to argue for the thesis. In introducing his distinction between the two types of aesthetic properties, Goodman was concerned about forgeries. Goodman, and many writers who have followed his lead, have held that forgeries and originals have different aesthetic properties. This could be the case even when a forgery and an original cannot be distinguished simply by experience of the works. A number of writers have suggested that forgeries and originals originate in different contexts and that this has an impact on the aesthetic properties of the works. In the case of forgeries, the impact is thought to be negative. One might similarly maintain that the cultural backgrounds of artists affect the aesthetic properties of artworks and affect them negatively.

Several philosophers have advanced arguments that open up this possibility. Colin Radford put the question in the following terms. He asked whether a critic could "be justified in feeling differently about a painting after he has learned . . . that it was not what he thought" (67). He has in mind the discovery that a painting is not, say, by **Vermeer** but by **van Meegeren**. (Famously, Han van Meegeren produced several paintings that he attributed to the great seventeenth-century Dutch master.) The same issue can arise in the context of cultural appropriation. Radford is only one example of a philosopher who has presented variations on what we may call the *authenticity argument*.

In Radford's version of the argument, we are asked to imagine that the discovery that some painting is a forgery is not accompanied by any discovery of observable aesthetic flaws. Imagine, for example, that some work is now known to be by van Meegeren, and not by Vermeer, but that everyone still agrees that the painting is very fine. Unlike other van Meegerens, it displays a profound knowledge of anatomy, the modelling is excellent, it contains no flaws in the perspective, the composition is balanced, and so on. The best critics agree that it is emotionally charged. There may still be grounds for revising the assessment of the painting given when it was thought to be by Vermeer. For example, when thought to be by Vermeer the work could be judged to be original. When known to be by van Meegeren, Radford suggests, the painting now looks derivative. It is not an expression of an original perspective, and in this sense, the work is not authentic.

Radford is not the only philosopher to argue along these lines. W.E. Kennick presents a related argument and explicitly extends it to cover the case of cultural appropriation. He writes that "I cannot, for example, even if I had the appropriate technical skills, paint a picture in the style of the thirteenth-century Chinese master Mu Ch'i (or Fa Ch'ang). The best I can do is *imitate* (ape, mimic) his style" (7). Kennick was primarily concerned about forgery. His point is, however, one that can be applied to acts of cultural appropriation. Kennick went on to observe that "The *Caravaggisti*, because they were in the suitable historical and geographical position to do so, adapted, *in parte*, the style of **Caravaggio**" (7). He might have added that the *Caravaggisti* were in the right cultural position to paint in the style of Caravaggio. [. . .] Since cultures have changed, no one today, Kennick leads us to believe, can authentically paint in the style of Mu Chi or Caravaggio. Anyone who tried would produce an inauthentic imitation instead of a bold, original work. [. . .]

Martin A. Bestman reaches a similar conclusion. He states that no one today can authentically paint in the style of—he varies the example—**Masaccio**. His reason for stating this is that any present-day artist "stands in a different relationship to his craft than those painters of a half millennium ago whose style he captures. He, after all, has to 'act to forget' the technical progress of his craft. Further, the content of his painting—its symbols, allusion, and interests—speak to a social world long gone" (116). Anyone who attempts to appropriate the style of painters from long ago is condemned, on this view, to produce works that are inauthentic.

Bestman is concerned in this passage with artists who employ styles from the past. He goes on to suggest that a similar inauthenticity will exist when an artist appropriates something from foreign contemporary cultures. He does not develop this point, but one can easily imagine how the argument would go. Suppose I were to sculpt a house pole in the style of the Songish or Salish cultures of Vancouver Island and suppose that I am a technically gifted sculptor. I could include the Thunderbird (eagle) and other totems without having the smallest idea about their mythological significance. As used by an insider, an image may have rich symbolic significance. It may be the insigne of a clan or of a deity. As used by an outsider, the same image is simply a strong graphic design. Since the outsider's work lacks the symbolic or cultural significance of works by insiders, there is a sense in which it is inauthentic. Moreover, Bestman would say that outsiders are also not employing the full range of skills they have as (let us suppose) academy-trained sculptors. This suggests that their work would be inauthentic in another way: they are not fully expressing themselves.

## 5. Authentic Appropriation

Each of the versions of the authenticity argument just presented leads to the conclusion that outsiders who appropriate content will produce works that are inauthentic. Before these arguments can be assessed we need to say a little more about the concept of authenticity. We need to be clearer about what authenticity is and why it is an aesthetic virtue. I will consider [three] sorts of authenticity. Not all of these sorts of authenticity are aesthetic virtues.

The first point to make is that we are not here concerned with authenticity in the sense of being produced by insiders. In this sense, the authenticity of an artwork depends on its provenance. We may say that a work is authentic when it is in a style and genre of a given culture and insiders (relative to that culture) have produced it. Otherwise, it is inauthentic. Works that are authentic in this sense I will call *provenance authentic*.

Many people are concerned with provenance authenticity. Insider artists are justifiably upset when works by outsiders are represented as works by insiders. Apart from anything else, such fraud can harm the economic interests of insiders. Outsiders are also harmed. Collectors of, for example, Australian aboriginal art and the art of North American First Nations, often want to know that an artwork has been produced by an insider. Misrepresentation of the origins of arts and crafts is common. According to one estimate, aboriginal Australians paint only about half of the didgeridoos sold (www.didjshop.com/authenticity.html). Many fewer are cut by aboriginal craftsmen. Nevertheless, almost all of the instruments are sold as "authentic aboriginal didgeridoos." [. . .]

Here provenance authenticity is not at stake. For a start, we are concerned with works that are, by hypothesis, known to be by outsiders. More importantly, provenance authenticity is not, in itself, an aesthetic merit. A work could be provenance authentic but have a low aesthetic value. After all, every culture is home to poor artists. More importantly still, the suggestion that provenance inauthenticity is an aesthetic demerit begs the question. At issue is the question of whether works by outsiders necessarily have an aesthetic flaw qua works by outsiders. One cannot argue for the conclusion that they do by reiterating that such works are produced by outsiders.

We can identify a second sort of authenticity that plausibly is an aesthetic property. Authenticity, in this second sense of the word, is the property of being the product of an artist's individual genius. An inauthentic work is derivative or even imitative. Kennick and Radford seem to be concerned with this sort of authenticity. It is also akin to a sort of authenticity discussed by Peter Kivy. I will borrow Kivy's term and say that works that are an expression of an artist's individual genius are characterized by *personal authenticity*. Those that are not are characterized by personal inauthenticity. Personal authenticity is an aesthetic merit. All things being equal, a work of art that is an original expression of an artist's genius is more valuable than a derivative one. The original artwork opens up new perspectives. It excites the imagination in new ways.

Now we need to ask the question of whether works by outsiders are necessarily characterized by personal inauthenticity. I do not see why this should be so. In order to see that appropriation can result in authentic works, we can begin by recalling the distinction between innovative and non-innovative content appropriation. There may be a reason to think that non-innovative content appropriation will not be personally authentic. It is in the nature of such works to be heavily indebted to other works. We have no similar reason to think that innovative content appropriation will be personally inauthentic. On the contrary, innovative content appropriation seems likely to result in personally authentic works.

Still, perhaps the artist who engages in non-innovative content appropriation necessarily produces personally inauthentic works. Certainly, anyone who engages in non-innovative content appropriation produces a work that is, to some extent, derivative. That said, every work of art, or at least every work of art that audiences can appreciate, is derivative to some extent. Unless a work fits into some category of artwork, audiences have no idea about how to appreciate it (Carroll 211ff). It does not follow from this that a work is not personally authentic. A debt to an existing tradition does not remove the possibility of personal authenticity. Any tradition provides scope for artists to innovate. Artworks can owe a great deal to previously existing works and still be personally authentic.

Certainly artists who borrowed liberally from others have produced some of the greatest art of all time. **Johann Sebastian Bach** was a conservative composer whose style closely approximates the style of his immediate predecessors. Or consider the music of **George Frederic Handel**. As long ago as the eighteenth century, Uvedale Price remarked that

"If ever there was a truly great and original genius in any art, Handel was that genius in music; and yet, what may seem no slight paradox, there never was a greater plagiary. He seized [that is, appropriated], without scruple or concealment, whatever suited his purpose" (573). And yet, in borrowing from others, Handel created great masterpieces. **William Boyce** remarked of Handel's borrowings that "He takes other men's pebbles and polishes them into diamonds." Handel was quite unashamed of his appropriation of material from other composers. When asked about a theme he had appropriated from **Bononcini**, Handel is said to have replied, "It's much too good for him; he did not know what to do with it." Artists such as Bach and Handel could, though they were greatly indebted to their predecessors, produce personally authentic compositions. Though they borrowed from others they also contributed a spark of individual genius. [. . .]

The examples of borrowing I have just given are not examples of cultural appropriation. (Though perhaps, in borrowing from Bononcini, Handel was engaged in cultural appropriation. [. . .]) One might grant that works that draw on other works can be personally authentic, but still think that outsiders are more likely to produce derivative work than insiders. I see no reason to believe that this is so. All artists working within a tradition depend on earlier artists, and in this sense, their work is derivative. This is as true of insiders as it is of outsiders. Indeed, in many artistic traditions, innovation is not valued. Consider, for example, the sculptures for the housing of spirits produced by the Kalabari of southern Nigeria. Close resemblance to previously existing sculptures is stated as a desideratum of new ones (Layton 7–8). Consequently, if anything, one might expect that the outsider, who may have the benefit of exposure to a wider range of artistic styles, may have an advantage over the insider. Broader artistic experience will make it easier to produce works characterized by personal authenticity.

Turn now to a consideration of a third sort of authenticity, one suggested by Bestman's remarks. [. . .] A work of art can be authentic in the sense that it is something to which the producing artist is fully committed. To say that artists are committed to their work is to say that they understand the full significance of all of the elements of their work and that they embrace their work's perspectives on the world. Artists could be ignorant of the significance of symbols and other elements of their works. Alternatively, they could be aware of the significance of the elements of their works, but not embrace them. For example, I might not believe a myth I retell. In either case, the work would be inauthentic. This sort of inauthenticity is akin to the authenticity discussed by existentialists such as **Heidegger** and **Sartre**. Existentialists expect individuals to be fully committed to everything that they do. Inspired by the existentialists, I will identify another sort of authenticity, *existential authenticity*.

Before proceeding any further, we need to ask whether existential authenticity is an aesthetic merit. One can make a case on either side of this question. As we have already seen, a well-established aesthetic school instructs us to pay attention only to the perceptible qualities of artworks. According to this school, artists' grasp of the significance of the elements of their artworks is irrelevant to the interpretation and appreciation of their works. If this sort of approach to interpretation and appreciation is right, we still need to be concerned about existential authenticity. It may be the case that artists who are unfamiliar with the significance of symbols and imagery that they employ will not use them skilfully. If so, this will be apparent from an examination of the work.

Many people believe that artists' commitment to their work is more important than the previous paragraph suggests. A work of art (at least very often) presents a perspective on the world. It matters to audiences that artists are committed to the perspectives presented in their works. Consider for example two artists, one a Christian and the other an atheist, who both paint a Crucifixion. Imagine also that the paintings are visually indistinguishable. Audiences, particularly audiences of Christians, might very well care about whether an artist is committed to the Christian perspective on Christ's Passion. In all probability, if a church is going to commission an altarpiece, it will commission the painting from the artist who is committed to the perspective presented in the painting. They may do so on the grounds that the Christian's altarpiece is existentially authentic while the atheist's painting is not. This may indicate that existential authenticity is an aesthetic virtue.

An example that is more explicitly a case of cultural appropriation seems to lead to the same conclusion. A musician who is a member of mainstream American culture could sing the blues without a full awareness of the significance of this style and its elements. This musician may use the words "mojo" and "hep" without any idea of their meanings within African-American culture. More generally, the musician might perform blues numbers without any idea of the cultural significance that the blues has for African-American culture. Such a singer would produce existentially inauthentic performances. An audience from African-American culture may well perceive this as an aesthetic flaw. [. . .]

This strikes me as a plausible position, but a contrary position also seems plausible. Consider, for example, performances of Bach's church cantatas. These cantatas had a very specific cultural significance. They were written for Lutheran church services and Bach was deeply committed to the idea that they presented a Christian perspective. (He marked each of them S.D.G.—*Sola Dei Gloria.*) Presumably only a Lutheran or, at any rate, a Christian can give an existentially authentic performance of these works. If existential authenticity is an aesthetic virtue, it follows that a performance not by a Christian has an aesthetic flaw. Nevertheless it seems credible that a performance by Chinese atheists or Israeli Jews could be an aesthetic triumph. The same point can be made about the works of outsiders who engage in cultural appropriation. An outsider may not be able to produce an existentially authentic work in the style of insiders, but perhaps it could be (like some atheists' performance of, say, Bach's "Ich habe genug") an aesthetic success.

The claim that (at least some) artworks and performances by outsiders must be existentially inauthentic (and deeply aesthetically flawed) and the claim that they can be aesthetically successful both seem plausible. Perhaps the contradiction is only apparent. One could say that the aesthetic value of an artwork or a performance is relative to an audience. Perhaps relative to secular music lovers the atheists' performance of "Ich habe genug" is an aesthetic triumph. Perhaps, on the other hand, relative to the devout Lutheran audience the performance is an aesthetic failure because it is existentially inauthentic. One might posit a similar relativity in the context of cultural appropriation. The African-American audience might find a blues performance existentially inauthentic, and so badly aesthetically flawed. The audience of outsiders might be unconcerned by the same existential inauthenticity. Relative to them, the same blues performance [. . .] has high aesthetic value.

It would be better to resolve this issue without recourse to relativism. I am skeptical about the claim that existential authenticity is an aesthetic virtue. (At a certain point I want to say that the audiences of Christians and African-Americans that I have just imagined are unreasonably prejudiced against certain works.) In any case, even if we grant that existential authenticity is an aesthetic virtue, it does not follow that artists who engage in cultural appropriation cannot produce existentially authentic works and performances. Certainly, some outsiders will produce existentially inauthentic works. The middle-class college student who parrots blues lyrics without understanding their significance is just such an outsider but not all outsiders produce such inauthentic works. One way for outsiders to produce existentially authentic works is to engage in innovative content appropriation. Consider again Picasso's appropriation of motifs from West African carvers. Very likely Picasso was unaware of the significance these motifs had within their original cultural context. It does not follow from this that *Les Demoiselles d'Avignon* is not existentially authentic. Good artists can endow the elements of their artworks with a fresh significance. This is precisely what Picasso and other artists have done. These artists will not produce existentially authentic instances of works in the categories that insiders possess. But they will produce instances of works in new categories and there is no reason why these cannot be existentially authentic and works of high aesthetic value. The insiders may judge that the work has a low aesthetic value because artists cannot produce an existentially authentic example of a work in the style of insiders. This judgment would be mistaken since it miscategorizes the work.

Still, even if this argument is accepted, it may seem that non-innovative content appropriation will be existentially inauthentic. To a large extent this conclusion can be avoided. An atheist who sings a Bach cantata can be fully committed to the work as an expression of themes of repentance, forgiveness, or longing, even if these themes are removed from their original theological contexts. Similarly, artists can use content appropriated from another culture to express perspectives to which they are fully committed. In both of these cases, we can say that artists have produced works or performances characterized by existential authenticity. Insiders may still regard the works as existentially inauthentic since

the outsider does not accept certain beliefs current in their culture. The response to this should be that this is irrelevant. The artist is fully committed to his work and this is sufficient to make it existentially authentic. Still, it must be admitted that outsiders cannot produce existentially authentic works or performances if they simply ape the artistic practices of members of another culture. Sometimes artists will ape others, and to the extent that existential inauthenticity is an aesthetic flaw, these artists will produce unsuccessful works of art. [. . .]

I conclude that in many senses of the word "authentic," outsiders can produce authentic works in styles appropriated from other cultures. Even if we accept, as I do, that the aesthetic properties of artworks depend on the cultural context in which they were produced, outsiders who engage in cultural appropriation do not labour under an aesthetic handicap that condemns them to produce seriously flawed works of art.

## Works Cited

Bestman, M.A. "Anachronistic Inauthenticity in Art." *Journal of Aesthetic Education* 18, 3 (1984): 115–18.

Borges, J.L. "Pierre Menard, Author of the Quixote." *Borges: A Reader*. Eds. E. Rodriguez Monegal and A. Reid. New York: E.P. Dutton, 1981. 96–103.

Carroll, N. "Art, Creativity and Tradition." *The Creation of Art: New Essays in Philosophical Aesthetics*. Cambridge: Cambridge University Press, 2003.

Goodman, N. *Languages of Art*. Indianapolis, IN: Bobbs-Merrill, 1968.

Jones, L. *Blues People*. New York: William Morrow, 1963.

Kennick, W.E. "Art and Inauthenticity." *Journal of Aesthetics and Art Criticism* 44 (1985): 3–12.

Kivy, P. *Authenticities: Philosophical Reflection on Musical Performance*. Ithaca, NY: Cornell University Press, 1995.

Layton, R. *The Anthropology of Art*. 2nd ed. Cambridge: Cambridge University Press, 1991.

Price, U. *On the Picturesque: With an Essay on the Origin of Taste*. Edinburgh: Caldwell, Lloyd, 1842.

Radford, C. "Fakes." *Mind* 87 (1978): 66–76.

Taylor, P.C. "So Black and Blue: Response to Rudinow." *Journal of Aesthetics and Art Criticism* 53 (1995): 313–17.

Walton, K. "Categories of Art." *Philosophical Review* 79 (1970): 334–67.

## Study Questions

1. How does Goodman's distinction between two kinds of aesthetic properties provide Young with two alternative interpretations of the "aesthetic handicap thesis"?

2. What is the "cultural experience argument"? For what reasons does Young dismiss this argument when it comes to both "non-innovative" and "innovative cultural appropriation"?

3. What are Young's reasons for arguing that the empiricist tradition in aesthetics wrongly restricts judgments about an artwork's aesthetic value to its observable properties? Provide an example that shows how cultural appropriation might diminish a work's aesthetic value because it lacks authenticity.

4. Of the three kinds of authenticity Young identifies, which two does he consider relevant to an artwork's aesthetic value? Do you agree or disagree with Young's position that cultural appropriation need not produce works that are inauthentic in either of these two senses?

# ꕥ A BEAUTIFUL LIFE ꕥ

## Leo Tolstoy

Lev (Leo) Nikolayevich Tolstoy (1828–1910) was of Russian nobility. Tolstoy studied at Kazan University (1844–7), but did not complete a degree. Tolstoy began to write fiction while in the army (1851–5), with immediate success. Drinking, gambling, and brothels also occupied Tolstoy's time, but after marrying in 1862, he settled at the family estate and wrote the novels for which he is famous, *War and Peace* (1865–9) and *Anna Karenina* (1878). Yet, Tolstoy was in personal crisis, the topic of *A Confession*. Tolstoy's subsequent essays and novels embraced pacifism and asceticism and attacked the church, leading to his excommunication in 1901. Having decided to leave his family and live out his days at a monastery, Tolstoy died of pneumonia en route.

# From *A Confession*

### 1. Meaning of Life [Sec. 3]

[. . .] Returning from there I married. The new conditions of happy family life completely diverted me from all search for the general meaning of life. My whole life was centred at that time in my family, wife and children, and therefore in care to increase our means of livelihood. My striving after self-perfection, for which I had already substituted a striving for perfection in general, i.e., progress, was now again replaced by the effort simply to secure the best possible conditions for myself and my family.

So another 15 years passed.

In spite of the fact that I now regarded authorship as of no importance, I still continued to write during those 15 years. I had already tasted the temptation of authorship—the temptation of immense monetary rewards and applause for my insignificant work—and I devoted myself to it as a means of improving my material position and of stifling in my soul all questions as to the meaning of my own life or life in general.

I wrote: teaching what was for me the only truth, namely, that one should live so as to have the best for oneself and one's family.

So I lived; but five years ago something very strange began to happen to me. At first I experienced moments of perplexity and arrest of life, as though I did not know what to do or how to live; and I felt lost and became dejected. But this passed, and I went on living as before. Then these moments of perplexity began to recur oftener and oftener, and always in the same form. They were always expressed by the questions: What is it for? What does it lead to?

At first it seemed to me that these were aimless and irrelevant questions. I thought that it was all well known, and that if I should ever wish to deal with the solution it would not cost me much effort; just at present I had no time for it, but when I wanted to I should be able to find the answer. The questions however began to repeat themselves frequently, and to demand replies more and more insistently; and like drops of ink always falling on one place they ran together into one black blot.

Then occurred what happens to everyone sickening with a mortal internal disease. At first trivial signs of indisposition appear to which the sick man pays no attention; then these signs reappear more and more often and merge into one uninterrupted period of suffering. The suffering increases, and before the sick man can look round, what he took for a mere indisposition has already become more important to him than anything else in the world—it is death!

That was what happened to me. I understood that it was no casual indisposition but something very important, and that if these questions constantly repeated themselves they would have to be answered. And I tried to answer them. The questions seemed such stupid, simple, childish ones; but as soon as I touched them and tried to solve them I at once became convinced, first, that they are not childish and stupid but the most important and profound of life's questions; and secondly that, occupying myself with my Samára estate, the education of my son, or the writing of a book, I had to know *why* I was doing it. As long as I did not know why, I could do nothing and could not live. Amid the thoughts of estate management which greatly occupied me at that time, the question would suddenly occur: "Well, you will have 6,000 *desyatínas* [unit equivalent to about 1.09 hectares] of land in Samára Government and 300 horses, and what then?" . . . And I was quite disconcerted and did not know what to think. Or when considering plans for the education of my children, I would say to myself: "What for?" Or when considering how the peasants might become prosperous, I would suddenly say to myself: "But what does it matter to me?" Or when thinking of the fame my works would bring me, I would say to myself, "Very well; you will be more famous than Gógol or Púshkin or Shakespeare or Molière, or than all the writers in the world—and what of it?" And I could find no reply at all. The questions would not wait, they had to be answered at once, and if I did not answer them it was impossible to live. But there was no answer.

I felt that what I had been standing on had collapsed and that I had nothing left under my feet. What I had lived on no longer existed, and there was nothing left.

## 2. An Eastern Fable [Sec. 4]

And all this befell me at a time when all around me I had what is considered complete good fortune. I was not yet fifty; I had a good wife who loved me and whom I loved, good children, and a large estate which without much effort on my part improved and increased. I was respected by my relations and acquaintances more than at any previous time. I was praised by others and without much self-deception

could consider that my name was famous. And far from being insane or mentally diseased, I enjoyed on the contrary a strength of mind and body such as I have seldom met with among men of my kind; physically I could keep up with the peasants at mowing, and mentally I could work for eight and ten hours at a stretch without experiencing any ill results from such exertion. And in this situation I came to this—that I could not live, and, fearing death, had to employ cunning with myself to avoid taking my own life.

My mental condition presented itself to me in this way: my life is a stupid and spiteful joke someone has played on me. Though I did not acknowledge a "someone" who created me, yet such a presentation— that someone had played an evil and stupid joke on me by placing me in the world—was the form of expression that suggested itself most naturally to me.

Involuntarily it appeared to me that there, somewhere, was someone who amused himself by watching how I lived for thirty or forty years: learning, developing, maturing in body and mind, and how, having with matured mental powers reached the summit of life from which it all lay before me, I stood on that summit—like an arch-fool—seeing clearly that there is nothing in life, and that there has been and will be nothing. And *he* was amused. [. . .]

But whether that "someone" laughing at me existed or not, I was none the better off. I could give no reasonable meaning to any single action or to my whole life. I was only surprised that I could have avoided understanding this from the very beginning—it has been so long known to all. Today or tomorrow sickness and death will come (they had come already) to those I love or to me; nothing will remain but stench and worms. Sooner or later my affairs, whatever they may be, will be forgotten, and I shall not exist. Then why go on making any effort? . . . How can man fail to see this? And how go on living? That is what is surprising! One can only live while one is intoxicated with life; as soon as one is sober it is impossible not to see that it is all a mere fraud and a stupid fraud! That is precisely what it is: there is nothing either amusing or witty about it, it is simply cruel and stupid.

There is an Eastern fable, told long ago, of a traveller overtaken on a plain by an enraged beast.

Escaping from the beast he gets into a dry well, but sees at the bottom of the well a dragon that has opened its jaws to swallow him. And the unfortunate man, not daring to climb out lest he should be destroyed by the enraged beast, and not daring to leap to the bottom of the well lest he should be eaten by the dragon, seizes a twig growing in a crack in the well and clings to it. His hands are growing weaker and he feels he will soon have to resign himself to the destruction that awaits him above or below, but still he clings on. Then he sees that two mice, a black one and a white one, go regularly round and round the stem of the twig to which he is clinging and gnaw at it. And soon the twig itself will snap and he will fall into the dragon's jaws. The traveller sees this and knows that he will inevitably perish; but while still hanging he looks around, sees some drops of honey on the leaves of the twig, reaches them with his tongue and licks them. So I too clung to the twig of life, knowing that the dragon of death was inevitably awaiting me, ready to tear me to pieces; and I could not understand why I had fallen into such torment. I tried to lick the honey which formerly consoled me, but the honey no longer gave me pleasure, and the white and black mice of day and night gnawed at the branch by which I hung. I saw the dragon clearly and the honey no longer tasted sweet. I only saw the unescapable dragon and the mice, and I could not tear my gaze from them. And this is not a fable but the real unanswerable truth intelligible to all.

The deception of the joys of life which formerly allayed my terror of the dragon now no longer deceived me. No matter how often I may be told, "You cannot understand the meaning of life so do not think about it, but live," I can no longer do it: I have already done it too long. I cannot now help seeing day and night going round and bringing me to death. That is all I see, for that alone is true. All else is false.

The two drops of honey which diverted my eyes from the cruel truth longer than the rest: my love of family, and of writing—art as I called it—were no longer sweet to me.

"Family" . . . said I to myself. But my family—wife and children—are also human. They are placed just as I am: they must either live in a lie or see the terrible truth. Why should they live? Why should I love them, guard them, bring them up, or watch them? That they may come to the despair that I feel, or else be stupid? Loving them, I cannot hide the truth from them: each step in knowledge leads them to the truth. And the truth is death.

"Art, poetry?" . . . Under the influence of success and the praise of men, I had long assured myself that this was a thing one could do though death was drawing near—death which destroys all things, including my work and its remembrance; but soon I saw that that too was a fraud. It was plain to me that art is an adornment of life, an allurement to life. But life had lost its attraction for me, so how could I attract others? As long as I was not living my own life but was borne on the waves of some other life—as long as I believed that life had a meaning, though one I could not express—the reflection of life in poetry and art of all kinds afforded me pleasure: it was pleasant to look at life in the mirror of art. But when I began to seek the meaning of life and felt the necessity of living my own life, that mirror became for me unnecessary, superfluous, ridiculous, or painful. I could no longer soothe myself with what I now saw in the mirror, namely, that my position was stupid and desperate. It was all very well to enjoy the sight when in the depth of my soul I believed that my life had a meaning. Then the play of lights—comic, tragic, touching, beautiful, and terrible—in life amused me. But when I knew life to be meaningless and terrible, the play in the mirror could no longer amuse me. No sweetness of honey could be sweet to me when I saw the dragon and saw the mice gnawing away my support. [. . .]

## 3. Exact vs. Abstract Science [Sec. 6]

In my search for answers to life's questions I experienced just what is felt by a man lost in a forest.

He reaches a glade, climbs a tree, and clearly sees the limitless distance, but sees that his home is not and cannot be there; then he goes into the dark wood and sees the darkness, but there also his home is not.

So I wandered in that wood of human knowledge, amid the gleams of mathematical and experimental science which showed me clear horizons but in a direction where there could be no home, and also amid the darkness of the abstract sciences where I was immersed in deeper gloom the further I went, and where I finally convinced myself that there was, and could be, no exit.

Yielding myself to the bright side of knowledge, I understood that I was only diverting my gaze from the question. However alluringly clear those horizons which opened out before me might be, however alluring it might be to immerse oneself in the limitless expanse of those sciences, I already understood that the clearer they were the less they met my need and the less they applied to my question.

"I know," said I to myself, "what science so persistently tries to discover, and along that road there is no reply to the question as to the meaning of my life." In the abstract sphere I understood that notwithstanding the fact, or just because of the fact, that the direct aim of science is to reply to my question, there is no reply but that which I have myself already given: "What is the meaning of my life?" "There is none." Or: "What will come of my life?" "Nothing." Or: "Why does everything exist that exists, and why do I exist?" "Because it exists."

Inquiring for one region of human knowledge, I received an innumerable quantity of exact replies concerning matters about which I had not asked: about the chemical constituents of the stars, about the movement of the sun towards the constellation Hercules, about the origin of species and of man, about the forms of infinitely minute imponderable particles of ether; but in this sphere of knowledge the only answer to my question, "What is the meaning of my life?" was: "You are what you call your "life"; you are a transitory, casual cohesion of particles. The mutual interactions and changes of these particles produce in you what you call your "life." That cohesion will last some time; afterwards the interaction of these particles will cease and what you call "life" will cease, and so will all your questions. You are an accidentally united little lump of something. That little lump ferments. The little lump calls that fermenting its "life." The lump will disintegrate

and there will be an end of the fermenting and of all the questions." So answers the clear side of science and cannot answer otherwise if it strictly follows its principles.

From such a reply one sees that the reply does not answer the question. I want to know the meaning of my life, but that it is a fragment of the infinite, far from giving it a meaning destroys its every possible meaning. The obscure compromises which that side of experimental exact science makes with abstract science when it says that the meaning of life consists in development and in cooperation with development, owing to their inexactness and obscurity cannot be considered as replies.

The other side of science—the abstract side—when it holds strictly to its principles, replying directly to the question, always replies, and in all ages has replied, in one and the same way: "The world is something infinite and incomprehensible. Human life is an incomprehensible part of that incomprehensible 'all.'" [. . .]

## 4. Faith vs. Reason [Sec. 8]

[. . .] I long lived in this state of lunacy, which, in fact if not in words, is particularly characteristic of us very liberal and learned people. But thanks either to the strange physical affection I have for the real labouring people, which compelled me to understand them and to see that they are not so stupid as we suppose, or thanks to the sincerity of my conviction that I could know nothing beyond the fact that the best I could do was to hang myself, at any rate I instinctively felt that if I wished to live and understand the meaning of life, I must seek this meaning not among those who have lost it and wish to kill themselves, but among those billions of the past and the present who make life and who support the burden of their own lives and of ours also. And I considered the enormous masses of those simple, unlearned, and poor people who have lived and are living and I saw something quite different. I saw that, with rare exceptions, all those billions who have lived and are living do not fit into my divisions, and that I could not class them as not understanding the question, for they themselves state it and reply to it with extraordinary clearness. Nor could I consider them **epicureans**, for their life consists more of privations and sufferings than of enjoyments. Still less could I consider them as irrationally dragging on a meaningless existence, for every act of their life, as well as death itself, is explained by them. To kill themselves they consider the greatest evil. It appeared that all mankind had a knowledge, unacknowledged and despised by me, of the meaning of life. It appeared that reasonable knowledge does not give the meaning of life, but excludes life: while the meaning attributed to life by billions of people, by all humanity, rests on some despised pseudo-knowledge.

Rational knowledge, presented by the learned and wise, denies the meaning of life, but the enormous masses of men, the whole of mankind, receive that meaning in irrational knowledge. And that irrational knowledge is faith, that very thing which I could not but reject. It is God, One in Three; the creation in six days; the devils and angels, and all the rest that I cannot accept as long as I retain my reason.

My position was terrible. I knew I could find nothing along the path of reasonable knowledge except a denial of life; and there—in faith—was nothing but a denial of reason, which was yet more impossible for me than a denial of life. From rational knowledge it appeared that life is an evil, people know this and it is in their power to end life; yet they lived and still live, and I myself live, though I have long known that life is senseless and an evil. By faith it appears that in order to understand the meaning of life I must renounce my reason, the very thing for which alone a meaning is required.

## 5. Finite and Infinite [Sec. 9]

A contradiction arose from which there were two exits. Either that which I called reason was not so rational as I supposed, or that which seemed to me irrational was not so irrational as I supposed. And I began to verify the line of argument of my rational knowledge.

Verifying the line of argument of rational knowledge I found it quite correct. The conclusion that life is nothing was inevitable; but I noticed a mistake.

The mistake lay in this, that my reasoning was not in accord with the question I had put. The question was: "Why should I live, that is to say, what real, permanent result will come out of my illusory transitory life—what meaning has my finite existence in this infinite world?" And to reply to that question I had studied life.

The solution of all the possible questions of life could evidently not satisfy me, for my question, simple as it at first appeared, included a demand for an explanation of the finite in terms of the infinite, and vice versa.

I asked: "What is the meaning of my life, beyond time, cause, and space?" And I replied to quite another question: "What is the meaning of my life within time, cause, and space?" With the result that, after long efforts of thought, the answer I reached was: "None."

In my reasonings I constantly compared (nor could I do otherwise) the finite with the finite, and the infinite with the infinite; but for that reason I reached the inevitable result: force is force, matter is matter, will is will, the infinite is the infinite, nothing is nothing—and that was all that could result.

It was something like what happens in mathematics, when thinking to solve an equation, we find we are working on an identity. The line of reasoning is correct, but results in the answer that a equals a, or x equals x, or o equals o. The same thing happened with my reasoning in relation to the question of the meaning of my life. The replies given by all science to that question only result in—identity.

And really, strictly scientific knowledge—that knowledge which begins, as Descartes' did, with complete doubt about everything—rejects all knowledge admitted on faith and builds everything afresh on the laws of reason and experience, and cannot give any other reply to the question of life than that which I obtained: an indefinite reply. Only at first had it seemed to me that knowledge had given a positive reply—the reply of **Schopenhauer**: that life has no meaning and is an evil. But on examining the matter I understood that the reply is not positive, it was only my feeling that so expressed it. Strictly expressed, as it is by the **Brahmins** and by **Solomon** and Schopenhauer, the reply is merely indefinite, or an identity: o equals o, life is nothing. So that philosophic knowledge denies nothing, but only replies that the question cannot be solved by it—that for it the solution remains indefinite.

Having understood this, I understood that it was not possible to seek in rational knowledge for a reply to my question, and that the reply given by rational knowledge is a mere indication that a reply can only be obtained by a different statement of the question and only when the relation of the finite to the infinite is included in the question. And I understood that, however irrational and distorted might be the replies given by faith, they have this advantage, that they introduce into every answer a relation between the finite and the infinite, without which there can be no solution.

In whatever way I stated the question, that relation appeared in the answer. How am I to live?—According to the law of God. What real result will come of my life?—Eternal torment or eternal bliss. What meaning has life that death does not destroy?—Union with the eternal God: heaven.

So that besides rational knowledge, which had seemed to me the only knowledge, I was inevitably brought to acknowledge that all live humanity has another irrational knowledge—faith which makes it possible to live. Faith still remained to me as irrational as it was before, but I could not but admit that it alone gives mankind a reply to the questions of life, and that consequently it makes life possible. Reasonable knowledge had brought me to acknowledge that life is senseless—my life had come to a halt and I wished to destroy myself. Looking around on the whole of mankind I saw that people live and declare that they know the meaning of life. I looked at myself—I had lived as long as I knew a meaning of life and had made life possible.

Looking again at people of other lands, at my contemporaries and at their predecessors, I saw the same thing. Where there is life, there since man began faith has made life possible for him, and the chief outline of that faith is everywhere and always identical.

Whatever the faith may be, and whatever answers it may give, and to whomsoever it gives them, every such answer gives to the finite existence of man an infinite meaning, a meaning not destroyed by sufferings, deprivations, or death. This means that only in faith can we find for life a meaning and a possibility. What, then, is this faith? And I understood that faith is not merely "the evidence of things not seen," etc., and is not a revelation (that defines only one of the indications of faith), is not the relation of man to God (one has first to define faith and then God, and not define faith through God); it not only agreement with what has been told one (as faith is most usually supposed to be), but faith is a knowledge of the meaning of human life in consequence of which man does not destroy himself but lives. Faith is the strength of life. If a man lives he believes in something. If he did not believe that one must live for something, he would not live. If he does not see and recognize the illusory nature of the finite, he believes in the finite; if he understands the illusory nature of the finite, he must believe in the infinite. Without faith he cannot live. [. . .]

## 6. Meaning of Life in Faith [Sec. 10]

[. . .] For all humanity to be able to live, and continue to live attributing a meaning to life, they, those billions, must have a different, a real, knowledge of faith. Indeed, it was not the fact that we, with Solomon and Schopenhauer, did not kill ourselves that convinced me of the existence of faith, but the fact that those billions of people have lived and are living, and have borne Solomon and us on the current of their lives.

And I began to draw near to the believers among the poor, simple, unlettered folk: pilgrims, monks, sectarians, and peasants. The faith of these common people was the same Christian faith as was professed by the pseudo-believers of our circle. Among them, too, I found a great deal of superstition mixed with the Christian truths; but the difference was that the superstitions of the believers of our circle were quite unnecessary to them and were not in conformity with their lives, being merely a kind of epicurean diversion; but the superstitions of the believers among the labouring masses conformed so with their lives that it was impossible to imagine them to oneself without those superstitions, which were a necessary condition of their life. The whole life of believers in our circle was a contradiction of their faith, but the whole life of the working-folk believers was a confirmation of the meaning of life which their faith gave them. And I began to look well into the life and faith of these people, and the more I considered it the more I became convinced that they have a real faith which is a necessity to them and alone gives their life a meaning and makes it possible for them to live. In contrast with what I had seen in our circle—where life without faith is possible and where hardly one in a thousand acknowledges himself to be a believer— among them there is hardly one unbeliever in a thousand. In contrast with what I had seen in our circle, where the whole of life is passed in idleness, amusement, and dissatisfaction, I saw that the whole life of these people was passed in heavy labour, and that they were content with life. In contradistinction to the way in which people of our circle oppose fate and complain of it on account of deprivations and sufferings, these people accepted illness and sorrow without any perplexity or opposition, and with a quiet and firm conviction that all is good. In contradistinction to us, who the wiser we are the less we understand the meaning of life, and see some evil irony in the fact that we suffer and die, these folk live and suffer, and they approach death and suffering with tranquillity and in most cases gladly. In contrast to the fact that a tranquil death, a death without horror and despair, is a very rare exception in our circle, a troubled, rebellious, and unhappy death is the rarest exception among the people. And such

people, lacking all that for us and for Solomon is the only good of life and yet experiencing the greatest happiness, are a great multitude. I looked more widely around me. I considered the life of the enormous mass of the people in the past and the present. And of such people, understanding the meaning of life and able to live and to die, I saw not two or three, or tens, but hundreds, thousands, and millions. And they all—endlessly different in their manners, minds, education, and position, as they were—all alike, in complete contrast to my ignorance, knew the meaning of life and death, laboured quietly, endured deprivations and sufferings, and lived and died seeing therein not vanity but good.

And I learnt to love these people. The more I came to know their life, the life of those who are living and of others who are dead of whom I read and heard, the more I loved them and the easier it became for me to live. So I went on for about two years, and a change took place in me which had long been preparing and the promise of which had always been in me. It came about that the life of our circle, the rich and learned, not merely became distasteful to me, but lost all meaning in my eyes. All our actions, discussions, science and art, presented itself to me in a new light. I understood that it is all merely self-indulgence, and that to find a meaning in it is impossible; while the life of the whole labouring people, the whole of mankind who produce life, appeared to me in its true significance. I understood that *that* is life itself, and that the meaning given to that life is true: and I accepted it. [. . .]

## Study Questions

1. Describe Tolstoy's state of mind, and its effects on his family and work, that resulted from his inability to answer the questions, "What is it for?" "What does it lead to?" Do you think he was having a mid-life crisis? Should he have sought treatment for depression?
2. Explain the metaphorical significance of the Eastern fable recounted by Tolstoy.
3. What answer does "exact science" provide to Tolstoy's question, "What is the meaning of my

life?" What answer does "abstract science" provide? What does Tolstoy finally realize about the structure of his question that makes it unanswerable by science/rational knowledge but answerable by faith/irrational knowledge?
4. What is your response to Tolstoy's claim that "working-folk believers" have meaningful lives whereas affluent, educated, nonbelievers have meaningless lives? What is your response to Tolstoy's claim that "without faith we cannot live"?

# Susan Wolf

Susan Wolf is Edna J. Koury Distinguished Professor at University of North Carolina at Chapel Hill. She has a BA from Yale and an MA and a PhD from Princeton. Before joining UNC in 2002, Wolf held positions at Harvard, Maryland, and Johns Hopkins. Wolf's research is in ethics and its links with philosophy of mind, philosophy of action, political philosophy, and aesthetics. Wolf was recently president of the eastern division of the American Philosophical Association. In this article, she offers what she considers to be an objective definition of what makes a life meaningful.

## The Meanings of Lives

### 1. Introduction

This question, "What is the meaning of life?" was once taken to be a paradigm of philosophical inquiry. Perhaps, outside of the academy, it still is. In philosophy classrooms and academic journals, however, the question has nearly disappeared, and when the question is brought up, by a naive student, for example, or a prospective donor to the cause of a liberal arts education, it is apt to be greeted with uncomfortable embarrassment.

What is so wrong with the question? One answer is that it is extremely obscure, if not downright unintelligible. It is unclear what exactly the question is supposed to be asking. Talk of meaning in other contexts does not offer ready analogies for understanding the phrase "the meaning of life." When we ask the meaning of a word, for example, we want to know what the word stands for, what it represents. But life is not part of a language, or of any other sort of symbolic system. It is not clear how it could "stand for" anything, nor to whom. We sometimes use "meaning" in non-linguistic contexts: "Those dots mean measles." "Those footprints mean that someone was here since it rained." In these cases, talk of meaning seems to be equivalent to talk of evidence, but the contexts in which such claims are made tend to specify what hypotheses are in question within relatively fixed bounds. To ask what life means, without a similarly specified context, leaves us at sea.

Still, when people do ask about the meaning of life, they are evidently expressing some concern or other, and it would be disingenuous to insist that the rest of us haven't the faintest idea what that is. The question at least gestures toward a certain set of concerns with which most of us are at least somewhat familiar. Rather than dismiss a question with which many people have been passionately occupied as pure and simple nonsense, it seems more appropriate to try to interpret it and reformulate it in a way that can be more clearly and unambiguously understood. Though there may well be many things going on when people ask, "What is the meaning of life?" the most central among them seems to be a search to find a purpose or a point to human existence. It is a request to find out why we are here (that is, why we exist at all), with the hope that an answer to this question will also tell us something about what we should be doing with our lives.

If understanding the question in this way, however, makes the question intelligible, it might not give reason to reopen it as a live philosophical problem. Indeed, if some of professional philosophy's discomfort with discussion of the meaning of life comes from a desire to banish ambiguity and obscurity from the field, as much comes, I think, from the thought that the question, when made clearer, has already been answered, and that the answer is depressing. Specifically, if the question of the Meaning of Life is to be identified with the question of the purpose of life, then the standard view, at least among professional philosophers, would seem to be that it all depends on the existence of God. In other words, the going opinion seems to be that if there is a God, then there is at least a chance that there is a purpose, and so a meaning to life. God may have created us for a reason, with a plan in mind. But to go any further along this branch of thinking is not in the purview of secular philosophers. If, on the other hand, there is no God, then there can be no meaning, in the sense of a point or a purpose to our existence. We are simply a product of physical processes—there are no reasons for our existence, just causes.

At the same time that talk of Life having a Meaning is banished from philosophy, however, the talk of lives being more or less *meaningful* seems to be on the rise. Newspapers, magazines, self-help manuals are filled with essays on how to find meaning in your life; sermons and therapies are built on the truism that happiness is not just a matter of material comfort, or sensual pleasure, but also of a deeper kind of fulfillment. Though philosophers to date have had relatively little to say about what gives meaning to individual lives, passing references can be found throughout the literature; it is generally acknowledged as an intelligible and appropriate thing to want in one's life. Indeed, it would be crass to think otherwise.

But how can individual lives have meaning if life as a whole has none? Are those of us who suspect there is no meaning *to* life deluding ourselves in continuing to talk about the possibility of finding meaning *in* life? (Are we being short-sighted, failing to see the implications of one part of our thought on another?) Alternatively, are these expressions mere homonyms, with no conceptual or logical connections between them? Are there simply two wholly unconnected topics here?

Many of you will be relieved to hear that I do not wish to revive the question of whether there is a meaning to life. I am inclined to accept the standard view that there is no plausible interpretation of that question that offers a positive answer in the absence of a fairly specific religious metaphysics. An understanding of meaningfulness in life, however, does seem to me to merit more philosophical attention than it has so far received, and I will have some things to say about it here. Here, too, I am inclined to accept the standard view—or a part of the standard view—viz., that meaningfulness is an intelligible feature to be sought in a life, and that it is, at least sometimes, attainable but not everywhere assured. But what that feature is—what we are looking for—is controversial and unclear, and so the task of analyzing or interpreting that feature will take up a large portion of my remarks today. With an analysis proposed, I shall return to the question of how a positive view about the possibility of meaning in lives can fit with a negative or agnostic view about the meaning of life. The topics are not, I think, as unconnected as might at first seem necessary for their respectively optimistic and pessimistic answers to coexist. Though my discussion will offer nothing new in the way of an answer to the question of the meaning of life, therefore, it may offer a somewhat different perspective on that question's significance.

## 2. What Makes a Meaningful Life?

Let us begin, however, with the other question, that of understanding what it is to seek meaning in life. What do we want when we want a meaningful life? What is it that makes some lives meaningful, others less so?

If we focus on the agent's, or the subject's, perspective—on a person wanting meaning in her life, her feeling the need for more meaning—we might incline toward a subjective interpretation of the feature being sought. When a person self-consciously looks for something to give her life meaning, it signals a kind of unhappiness. One imagines, for example, the alienated housewife, whose life seems to her to be a series of endless chores. What she wants, it might appear, is something that she can find more subjectively rewarding.

This impression is reinforced if we consider references to "meaningful experiences." (The phrase might be applied, for example, to a certain kind of wedding or funeral.) The most salient feature of an event that is described as meaningful seems to be its "meaning a lot" *to* the participants. To say that a ceremony, or, for that matter, a job, is meaningful seems at the very least to include the idea that it is emotionally satisfying. An absence of meaning is usually marked by a feeling of emptiness and dissatisfaction; in contrast, a meaningful life, or meaningful part of life, is necessarily at least somewhat rewarding or fulfilling. It is noteworthy, however, that meaningful experiences are not necessarily particularly happy. A trip to one's birthplace may well be meaningful; a visit to an amusement park is unlikely to be so.

If we step back, however, and ask ourselves, as observers, what lives strike us as especially meaningful, if we ask what sorts of lives exemplify meaningfulness, subjective criteria do not seem to be in the forefront. Who comes to mind? Perhaps, **Gandhi**, or **Albert Schweitzer**, or **Mother Teresa**; perhaps **Einstein** or **Jonas Salk**. **Cézanne**, or **Manet**, **Beethoven**, **Charlie Parker**. **Tolstoy** is an interesting case to which I shall return. Alternatively, we can look to our neighbours, our colleagues, our relatives—some of whom, it seems to me, live more meaningful lives than others. Some, indeed, of my acquaintance seem to me to live lives that are paradigms of meaning—right up there with the famous names on the earlier lists; while others (perhaps despite their modicum of fame) would score quite low on the meaningfulness scale. If those in the latter category feel a lack of meaning in their lives—well, they are right to feel it, and it is a step in the right direction that they notice that there is something about their lives that they should try to change.

What is it to live a meaningful life, then? What does meaningfulness in life amount to? It may be easier to make progress by focusing on what we want to avoid. In that spirit, let me offer some paradigms, not of meaning*ful*, but of meaning*less* lives.

For me, the idea of a meaningless life is most clearly and effectively embodied in the image of a person who spends day after day, or night after night, in front of a television set, drinking beer and watching situation comedies. Not that I have anything against television or beer. Still the image, understood as an image of a person whose life is lived in hazy passivity, a life lived at a not unpleasant level of consciousness, but unconnected to anyone or anything, going nowhere, achieving nothing—is,

I submit, as strong an image of a meaningless life as there can be. Call this case The Blob.

If any life, any human life, is meaningless, the Blob's life is. But this doesn't mean that any meaningless life must be, in all important respects, like the Blob's. There are other paradigms that highlight by their absences other elements of meaningfulness.

In contrast to the Blob's passivity, for example, we may imagine a life full of activity, but silly or decadent or useless activity. (And again, I have nothing against silly activity, but only against a life that is wholly occupied with it.) We may imagine, for example, one of the idle rich who flits about, fighting off boredom, moving from one amusement to another. She shops, she travels, she eats at expensive restaurants, she works out with her personal trainer.

Curiously, one might also take a very un-idle rich person to epitomize a meaningless life in a slightly different way. Consider, for example, the corporate executive who works twelve-hour, seven-day weeks, suffering great stress, for the sole purpose of the accumulation of personal wealth. Related to this perhaps is David Wiggins' example of the pig farmer who buys more land to grow more corn to feed more pigs to buy more land to grow more corn to feed more pigs.

These last three cases of the idle rich, the corporate executive and the pig farmer are in some ways very different, but they all share at least this feature: they can all be characterized as lives whose dominant activities seem pointless, useless, or empty. Classify these cases under the heading Useless.

A somewhat different and I think more controversial sort of case to consider involves someone who is engaged, even dedicated, to a project that is ultimately revealed as bankrupt, not because the person's values are shallow or misguided, but because the project fails. The person may go literally bankrupt: for example, a man may devote his life to creating and building up a company to hand over to his children, but the item his company manufactures is rendered obsolete by technology shortly before his planned retirement. Or consider a scientist whose life's work is rendered useless by the announcement of a medical breakthrough just weeks before his own research would have yielded the same results. Perhaps more poignantly, imagine a woman whose life is centred around a relationship that turns out to be a fraud. Cases that fit this mould we may categorize under the heading Bankrupt. [. . .]

If the cases I have sketched capture our images of meaninglessness more or less accurately, they provide clues to what a positive case of a meaningful life must contain. In contrast to the Blob's passivity, a person who lives a meaningful life must be actively engaged. But, as the Useless cases teach us, it will not do to be engaged in just anything, for any reason or with any goal—one must be engaged in a project or projects that have some positive value, and in some way that is non-accidentally related to what gives them value. Finally, in order to avoid Bankruptcy, it seems necessary that one's activities be at least to some degree successful (though it may not be easy to determine what counts as the right kind or degree of success). Putting these criteria together, we get a proposal for what it is to live a meaningful life: viz., a meaningful life is one that is actively and at least somewhat successfully engaged in a project (or projects) of positive value.

Several remarks are needed to qualify and refine this proposal. First, the use of the word "project" is not ideal: it is too suggestive of a finite, determinate task, something one takes on, and, if all goes well, completes. Among the things that come to mind as projects are certain kinds of hobbies or careers, or rather, specific tasks that fall within the sphere of such hobbies or careers: things that can be seen as accomplishments, like the producing of a proof or a poem or a pudding, the organizing of a union or a high school band. Although such activities are among the things that seem intuitively to contribute to the meaningfulness of people's lives, there are other forms of meaningfulness that are less directed, and less oriented to demonstrable achievement, and we should not let the use of the word "project" distort or deny the potential of these things to give meaningfulness to life. Relationships, in particular, seem at best awkwardly described as projects. Rarely does one deliberately take them on and, in some cases, one doesn't even have to work at them—one

may just have them and live, as it were, within them. Moreover, many of the activities that are naturally described as projects—coaching a school soccer team, planning a surprise party, reviewing an article for a journal—have the meaning they do for us only because of their place in the non-projectlike relationships in which we are enmeshed and with which we identify. In proposing that a meaningful life is a life actively engaged in projects, then, I mean to use "projects" in an unusually broad sense, to encompass not only goal-directed tasks but other sorts of ongoing activities and involvements as well.

Second, the suggestion that a meaningful life should be "actively engaged" in projects should be understood in a way that recognizes and embraces the connotations of "engagement." Although the idea that a meaningful life requires activity was introduced by contrast to the life of the ultra-passive Blob, we should note that meaning involves more than mere, literal activity. The alienated housewife, presumably, is active all the time—she buys groceries and fixes meals, cleans the house, does the laundry, chauffeurs the children from school to soccer to ballet, arranges doctors' appointment and babysitters. What makes her life insufficiently meaningful is that her heart, so to speak, isn't in these activities. She does not identify with what she is doing—she does not embrace her roles as wife, mother, and homemaker as expressive of who she is and wants to be. We may capture her alienated condition by saying that though she is active, she is not actively engaged. (She is, one might say, just going through the motions.) In characterizing a meaningful life, then, it is worth stressing that living such a life is not just a matter of having projects (broadly construed) and actively and somewhat successfully getting through them. The projects must engage the person whose life it is. Ideally, she would proudly and happily embrace them, as constituting at least part of what her life is about.

Finally, we must say more about the proposal's most blatantly problematic condition—viz, that the project's engagement with which can contribute to a meaningful life must be projects "of positive value." The claim is that meaningful lives must be engaged in projects of positive value—but who is to decide which projects have positive value, or even to guarantee that there is such a thing?

I would urge that we leave the phrase as unspecific as possible in all but one respect. We do not want to build a theory of positive value into our conception of meaningfulness. As a proposal that aims to capture what most people mean by a meaningful life, what we want is a concept that "tracks" whatever we think of as having positive value. This allows us to explain at least some divergent intuitions about meaningfulness in terms of divergent intuitions or beliefs about what has positive value, with the implication that if one is wrong about what has positive value, one will also be wrong about what contributes to a meaningful life. (Thus, a person who finds little to admire in sports—who finds ridiculous, for example, the sight of grown men trying to knock a little ball into a hole with a club, will find relatively little potential for meaning in the life of an avid golfer; a person who places little stock in esoteric intellectual pursuits will be puzzled by someone who strains to write, much less read, a lot of books on **supervenience**.)

The exception I would make to this otherwise maximally tolerant interpretation of the idea of positive value is that we exclude merely subjective value as a suitable interpretation of the phrase.

It will not do to allow that a meaningful life is a life involved in projects that seem to have positive value from the perspective of the one who lives it. Allowing this would have the effect of erasing the distinctiveness of our interest in meaningfulness; it would blur or remove the difference between an interest in living a meaningful life and an interest in living a life that feels or seems meaningful. That these interests are distinct, and that the former is not merely instrumental to the latter can be seen by reflecting on a certain way the wish or the need for meaning in one's life may make itself felt. What I have in mind is the possibility of a kind of epiphany, in which one wakes up—literally or figuratively—to the recognition that one's life to date has been meaningless. Such an experience would be nearly unintelligible if a lack of meaning were to be understood as a lack of a certain kind of subjective impression. One can hardly understand the idea of

waking up to the thought that one's life to date has seemed meaningless. To the contrary, it may be precisely because one did not realize the emptiness of one's projects or the shallowness of one's values until that moment that the experience I am imagining has the poignancy it does. It is the sort of experience that one might describe in terms of scales falling from one's eyes. And the yearning for meaningfulness, the impulse to do something about it, will not be satisfied (though it may be eliminated) by putting the scales back on, so to speak. If one suspects that the life one has been living is meaningless, one will not bring meaning to it by getting therapy or taking a pill that, without changing one's life in any other way, makes one believe that one's life has meaning.

To care that one's life is meaningful, then, is, according to my proposal, to care that one's life is actively and at least somewhat successfully engaged in projects (understanding this term broadly) that not just seem to have positive value, but that really do have it. To care that one's life be meaningful, in other words, is in part to care that what one does with one's life is, to pardon the expression, at least somewhat objectively good. We should be careful, however, not to equate objective goodness with moral goodness, at least not if we understand moral value as essentially involving benefitting or honouring humanity. The concern for meaning in one's life does not seem to be the same as the concern for moral worth, nor do our judgments about what sorts of lives are meaningful seem to track judgments of moral character or accomplishment.

To be sure, some of the paradigms of meaningful lives are lives of great moral virtue or accomplishment—I mentioned Gandhi and Mother Teresa, for example. Others, however, are not. Consider **Gauguin**, **Wittgenstein**, **Tchaikovsky**—morally unsavoury figures all, whose lives nonetheless seem chock full of meaning. If one thinks that even they deserve moral credit, for their achievements made the world a better place, consider instead Olympic athletes and world chess champions, whose accomplishments leave nothing behind but their world records. Even more important, consider the artists, scholars, musicians, athletes of our more ordinary sort. For us, too, the activities of artistic creation and research, the development of our skills and our understanding of the world give meaning to our lives—but they do not give moral value to them.

It seems then that meaning in life may not be especially moral, and that indeed lives can be richly meaningful even if they are, on the whole, judged to be immoral. Conversely, that one's life is at least moderately moral, that it is lived, as it were, above reproach, is no assurance of its being moderately meaningful. The alienated housewife, for example, may be in no way subject to moral criticism. (And it is debatable whether even the Blob deserves specifically moral censure.)

That people do want meaning in their lives, I take it, is an observable, empirical fact. We have already noted the evidence of self-help manuals, and therapy groups. What I have offered so far is an analysis of what that desire or concern amounts to. I want now to turn to the question of whether the desire is one that it is good that people have, whether, that is, there is some positive reason why they *should* want this.

## 3. Why Seek a Meaningful Life?

At a minimum, we may acknowledge that it is at least not bad to want meaning in one's life. There is, after all, no harm in it. Since people do want this, and since there are no moral objections to it, we should recognize the concern for meaning as a legitimate concern, at least in the weak sense that people should be allowed to pursue it. Indeed, insofar as meaningfulness in one's life is a significant factor in a life's overall well-being, we should do more than merely allow its pursuit: we should positively try to increase opportunities for people to live lives of meaning.

Most of us, however, seem to have a stronger positive attitude toward the value of meaningfulness than this minimum concession admits. We do not think it is merely all right for people to want meaning in their lives—as it is all right for people to like country music, or to take an interest in figure skating. We think people positively ought to care that their lives be meaningful. It is disturbing, or at least regrettable, to find someone who doesn't care about this. Yet this positive assessment ought to strike us, at least initially, as somewhat mysterious. What is the good, after all, of living a meaningful life, and to whom?

Since a meaningful life is not necessarily a *morally* better life than a meaningless one (the Olympic athlete may do no more good nor harm than the idly rich socialite), it is not necessarily better *for the world* that people try to live or even succeed in living meaningful lives. Neither is a meaningful life assured of being an especially happy one, however. Many of the things that give meaning to our lives (relationships to loved ones, aspirations to achieve) make us vulnerable to pain, disappointment and stress. From the inside, the Blob's hazy passivity may be preferable to the experience of the tortured artist or political crusader. By conventional standards, therefore, it is not clear that caring about or even succeeding in living a meaningful life is better *for the person herself*.

Yet, as I have already mentioned, those of us who do care that our lives be meaningful tend to think that it is a positively good thing that we do. We not only want to live meaningful lives, we want to want this—we approve of this desire, and think it is better for others if they have this desire, too. If, for example, you see a person you care about conducting her life in a way that you find devoid of worth—she is addicted to drugs, perhaps, or just to television, or she is overly enthusiastic in her career as a corporate lawyer—you are apt to encourage her to change, or at least hope that she will find a new direction on her own. Your most prominent worry may well be that she is heading for a fall. You fear that at some point she will wake up to the fact that she has been wasting or misdirecting her life, a point that may come too late for easy remedy and will, in any case, involve a lot of pain and self-criticism. But the fear that she will wake up to the fact that she has been wasting her life (and have difficulty turning her life around) may not be as terrible as the fear that she won't wake up to it. If you came to feel secure that no painful moment of awakening would ever come because your friend (or sister or daughter) simply does not care whether her life is meaningful, you might well think that this situation is not better but worse. We seem to think there is something regrettable about a person living a meaningless life, even if the person herself does not mind that she is. We seem to think she *should* want meaning in her life, even if she doesn't realize it.

What, though, is the status of this "should," the nature or source of the regret? The mystery that I earlier suggested we should feel about our value in meaningfulness is reflected in the uneasy location of this judgment. If my own reaction to the woman who doesn't care whether her life is meaningful is typical, the thought that she should, or ought to care is closer to a prudential judgment than it is to a moral one. (If there is a moral objection to a person who lives a meaningless life and is content with that, it is not, in my opinion, a very strong one. The Blob, after all, is not hurting anyone, nor is the idle rich jet-setter. She may, for example, give money to environmental causes to offset the damage she is doing in her SUV, and write generous cheques to Oxfam and UNICEF on a regular basis.) The thought that it is too bad if a person does not live a meaningful life (even if she doesn't mind) seems rather to be the thought that it is too bad *for her*.

The closest analogue to this thought in the history of ethics of which I am aware is **Aristotle**'s conception of *eudaimonia*. His conception of the virtuous life as the happiest life is offered as a conclusion of an enlightened self-interest. According to standard conceptions of self-interest, however (either **hedonistic** or preference-based), it is not obvious why this should be so, and, unfortunately, Aristotle himself does not address the question explicitly. Rather, he seems to think that if you do not just see that the virtuous life, in which one aims for and achieves what is "fine," is a better, more desirable life for yourself, that just shows that you were not well brought up, and in that case, there is no point trying to educate you.

Our question, the question of whether and what kind of reason there is for a person to strive for a meaningful life, is not quite the same as the question of whether and what kind of reason there is to aspire to virtue,—though, when one is careful to interpret "virtue" in the broad and not specifically moral way that Aristotle uses the term, it is closer than it might seem. Still, as I say, Aristotle does not really address the question, and so, though I take my line of thought to be Aristotelian in spirit, a scholarly study of Aristotle's texts is not likely to be an efficient way of finding an answer to the question ourselves.

What reason is there, then, if any, for a person to want to live a meaningful life? I have said that we seem to think it would be better for her, that it is, at least roughly, in her self-interest. At the same time, the thought that she should care about meaning seems to depend on claims from outside herself. Even if there are no desires latent in her psychology which meaningfulness would satisfy, we seem to think, there is reason why she should have such desires. She seems to be making some kind of mistake.

If my analysis of what is involved in living a meaningful life is right, then the question of why one should care about living a meaningful life is equivalent to the question of why one should care that one's life be actively and somewhat successfully engaged in projects of positive value. The source of perplexity seems, in particular, to be about the reason to care that one's projects be positively valuable. As long as you are engaged by your activities, and they make you happy, why should one care that one's activities be objectively worthwhile?

The answer, I believe, is that to devote one's life entirely to activities whose value is merely subjective, to devote oneself to activities whose sole justification is that it is good for you, is, in a sense I shall try to explain, practically **solipsistic**. It flies in the face of one's status as, if you will, a tiny speck in a vast universe, a universe with countless perspectives of equal status with one's own, from which one's life might be assessed. Living a life that is engaged with and so at least partially focused on projects whose value has a non-subjective source is a way of acknowledging one's non-privileged position. It harmonizes, in a way that a purely egocentric life does not, with the fact that one is not the centre of the universe.

The basic idea is this: The recognition of one's place in the universe, of one's smallness, one might say, or one's insignificance, and of the independent existence of the universe in which one is a part involves, among other things, the recognition of "the mereness" of one's subjective point of view. To think of one's place in the universe is to recognize the possibility of a perspective, of infinitely many perspectives, really, from which one's life is merely gratuitous; it is to recognize the possibility of a perspective, or rather of infinitely many perspectives, that are indifferent to whether one exists at all, and so to whether one is happy or sad, satisfied or unsatisfied, fulfilled or unfulfilled.

In the face of this recognition, a life that is directed solely to its subject's own fulfillment, or, to its mere survival or towards the pursuit of goals that are grounded in nothing but the subject's own psychology, appears either solipsistic or silly.

A person who lives a largely egocentric life—who devotes, in other words, lots of energy and attention and care toward himself, who occupies himself more specifically with satisfying and gratifying himself, expresses and reveals a belief that his happiness matters. Even if it doesn't express the view that his happiness matters objectively, it at least expresses the idea that it matters to him. To be solely devoted to his own gratification, then, would express and reveal the fact that his happiness is *all* that matters, at least all that matters to him. If, however, one accepts a framework that recognizes distinctions in non-subjective value, (and if one believes, as seems only reasonable, that what has non-subjective value has no special concentration in or connection to oneself) this attitude seems hard to justify.

To accept that framework is, after all, to accept the view that some things are better than others. To me, it makes sense partially to understand this literally: Some *things*, it seems to me, are better than others: people, for example, are better than rocks or mosquitoes, and a **Vermeer** painting is better than the scraps on my compost heap. What is essential, though, is that accepting a framework that recognizes distinctions in non-subjective value involves seeing the world as value-filled, as containing with it distinctions of better and worse, of more and less worthwhile, if not of better and worse objects per se, then of better and worse features of the world, or activities, or

opportunities to be realized. Against this background, a life solely devoted to one's own gratification or to the satisfaction of one's whims seems gratuitous and hard to defend. For, as I have said, to live such a life expresses the view that one's happiness is all that matters, at least to oneself. But why should this be the only thing that matters, when there is so much else worth caring about? [. . .]

I am suggesting that we can have a reason to do something or to care about something that is grounded not in our own psychologies, nor specifically in our own desires, but in a fact about the world. The fact in question in this case is the fact that we are, each of us, specks in a vast and value-filled universe, and that as such we have no privileged position as a source of or possessor of objective value. To devote oneself wholly to one's own satisfaction seems to me to fly in the face of this truth, to act "as if" one is the only thing that matters, or perhaps, more, that one's own psychology is the only source of (determining) what matters. By focusing one's attention and one's energies at least in part on things, activities, aspects of the world that have value independent of you, you implicitly acknowledge your place and your status in the world. Your behaviour, and your practical stance, is thus more in accord with the facts.

Admittedly, this is not the sort of reason that one must accept on pain of inconsistency or any other failure of logic. Just as a person may simply not care whether her life is meaningful, so she may also simply not care whether her life is in accord with, or harmonizes with the facts. (It is one thing to say we should live in accord with the facts of physics, geography, and the other sciences. Living in accordance with these facts has evident instrumental value—it helps us get around in the world. But living in a way that practically acknowledges, or harmonizes with the fact that we are tiny specks in a value-filled world will not make our lives go better that way.) Such a person cannot be accused in any strict sense of irrationality. Like non-instrumental reasons to be moral, the reason to care about living a worthwhile life is not one that narrow rationality requires one to accept. At the same time, it seems appropriate to characterize my suggestion [. . .] as one that appeals to reason in a broader sense. For my suggestion is that an interest in living a meaningful life is an appropriate response to a fundamental truth, and that failure to have such a concern constitutes a failure to acknowledge that truth.

## 4. Meaning of Life

As we have already seen, the truth to which I am proposing a meaningful life provides a response is the truth that we are, each of us, tiny specks in a vast and value-filled universe. [. . .] It opposes what children and many adults may have a tendency to assume—namely, that they are the centre of the universe, either the possessor or the source of all value. [. . .] My proposal is that an appropriate response to our status as specks in a vast universe is a concern and aspiration to have one's life wrapped up with projects of positive value.

Perhaps, however, I have not made it clear why this is an appropriate response. The question may seem especially pressing because the thought that we are tiny specks in a vast universe, and the sense that it calls for or demands a response has, in the past, tended to move philosophers in a different direction. Specifically, the thought that we are tiny specks in a vast universe was in the past closely associated with that murky and ponderous question to which I referred at the beginning of my [paper]—the question of The Meaning of Life. The thought that we are tiny specks in a vast universe has indeed often evoked that question, and, to those who either do not believe in or do not want to rest their answers in the existence of a benevolent God, it has more or less immediately seemed also to indicate an answer. Considering their answer to the question of the Meaning of Life and contrasting it with my response to the fact of our smallness, may clarify the substance of my proposal.

The train of thought I have in mind is one that has, with variations, been expressed by many distinguished philosophers, including **Camus** [and] Tolstoy [. . .]. For them, the recognition of our place in the universe—our smallness, or our speckness, if

you will—seems to warrant the conclusion not only that there is no meaning to life as such but also that each individual life is necessarily absurd.

On the view of these philosophers, a life can be meaningful only if it can mean something *to* someone, and not just to *someone*, but to someone other than oneself and indeed someone of more intrinsic or ultimate value than oneself. Of course, anyone can live in such a way as to make her life meaningful to *someone* other than herself. She can maintain her relationship with parents and siblings, establish friendships with neighbours and colleagues. She can fall in love. If all else fails, she can have a child who will love her, or two children, or six. She can open up an entire clinic for God's sake. But if a life that is devoted solely to yourself, a life that is good to no one other than yourself lacks meaning, these philosophers not implausibly think, so will a life that is devoted to any other poor creature, for he or she will have no more objective importance than you have, and so will be no more fit a stopping place by which to ground the claim of meaningfulness than you. Nor, according to this train of thought, will it help to expand your circle, to be of use or to have an effect on a larger segment of humankind. If each life is individually lacking in meaning, then the collective is meaningless as well. If each life has but an infinitesimal amount of value, then although one's meaning will increase in proportion to one's effect, the total quantity of meaning relative to the cosmos will remain so small as to make the effort pathetic.

From the perspective of these philosophers, if there is no God, then human life, each human life, must be objectively meaningless, because if there is no God, there is no appropriate being *for whom* we could have meaning.

From this perspective, my suggestion that the living of a worthwhile life constitutes a response to a recognition of our place in the universe might seem ridiculously nearsighted, as if, having acknowledged the mereness of my own subjectivity, I then failed to acknowledge the equal mereness of the subjectivity of others. But I think this misunderstands the point in my proposal of living a life that realizes non-subjective value, a misunderstanding that derives from too narrow a view about what an appropriate and satisfactory response to the fact of our place in the universe must be.

The philosophers I have been speaking about—we can call them the pessimists—take the fundamental lesson to be learned from the contemplation of our place in the universe to be that we are cosmically insignificant, a fact that clashes with our desire to be very significant indeed. If God existed, such philosophers might note, we would have a chance at being significant. For God himself, is presumably very significant and so we could be significant by being or by making ourselves significant to Him. In the absence of a God, however, it appears that we can only be significant to each other, to beings, that is, as pathetically small as ourselves. We want to be important, but we cannot be important, and so our lives are absurd.

The pessimists are right about the futility of trying to make ourselves important. Insofar as contemplation of the cosmos makes us aware of our smallness, whether as individuals or as a species, we simply must accept it and come to terms with it. Some people do undoubtedly get very upset, even despondent when they start to think about their cosmic insignificance. They want to be important, to have an impact on the world, to make a mark that will last forever. When they realize that they cannot achieve this, they are very disappointed. The only advice one can give to such people is: Get Over It.

Rather than fight the fact of our insignificance, however, and of the mereness of our subjectivity, my proposal is that we live in a way that acknowledges the fact, or, at any rate, that harmonizes with it. Living in a way that is significantly focused on, engaged with, and concerned to promote or realize value whose source comes from outside of oneself, does seem to harmonize with this, whereas living purely egocentrically does not. Living lives that attain or realize some non-subjective value may not make us meaningful, much less important, to anyone other than ourselves, but it will give us something to say, to think, in response to the recognition of perspectives that we ourselves imaginatively adopt that are indifferent to our existence and to our well-being.

At the beginning of this paper, I raised the question of how the meaning of life—or the absence of such meaning—was related to the meaningfulness of particular lives. As I might have put it, does it really make sense to think that there can be meaningful lives in a meaningless world? In light of this discussion, we can see how the answer to that question might be "yes" while still holding on to the idea that the similar wording of the two phrases is not merely coincidental.

If I am right about what is involved in living a meaningful life—if, that is, living a meaningful life is a matter of at least partly successful engagement in projects of positive value—then the possibility of living meaningful lives despite the absence of an overall meaning *to* life can be seen to depend on the fact that distinctions of value (that is, of objective value) do not rely on the existence of God or of any overarching purpose to the human race as a whole. Whether or not God exists, the fact remains that some objects, activities and ideas are better than others. Whether or not God exists, some ways of living are more worthwhile than others. Some activities are a waste of time.

People are sometimes tempted to think that if God doesn't exist, then nothing matters. They are tempted to think that if we will all die, and eventually all traces of our existence will fade from all consciousness, there is no point to doing anything; nothing makes any difference. Tolstoy evidently thought this sometimes, and gave eloquent voice to that view. But the reasoning is ridiculous. If one activity is worthwhile and another is a waste, then one has reason to prefer the former, even if there is no God to look down on us and approve. More generally, we seem to have reason to engage ourselves with projects of value whether God exists and gives life a purpose or not.

Putting things this way, however, fails to explain why we use the language of meaning to describe lives engaged in activities of worth. Putting things this way there seems to be no connection at all between the question of whether there is a meaning to life and the question of whether individual lives can be meaningful. I believe, however, that there is a connection, that shows itself, or perhaps that consists in the fact that the wish for both kinds of meaning are evoked by the same thought, and that, perhaps, either kind of meaning would be an appropriate and satisfying response to that thought. The thought in question is the thought (the true thought) that we are tiny specks in a vast universe. It is a thought that is apt to be upsetting when it first hits you—at least in part because, looking back from that position, it may seem that one had until then lived "as if" something opposite were true. One had lived perhaps until then as if one were the centre of the universe, the sole possessor or source of all value. One had all along assumed one had a special and very important place in the world, and now one's assumption is undermined. One can see how, in this context, one might wish for a meaning to life. For if there were a meaning—a purpose, that is, to human existence that can be presumed to be of great importance, then, by playing a role, by contributing to that purpose, one can recover some of the significance one thought one's life had. Like the pessimistic philosophers I talked about a few minutes ago, I doubt that that path is open to us. But there seems another way one can respond to the thought, or to the recognition of our relatively insignificant place in the universe, that is more promising, and that can, and sometimes does, provide a different kind of comfort. If one lived one's life, prior to the recognition of our smallness, as if one was the centre of the universe, the appropriate response to that recognition is simply *to stop living that way*. If one turns one's attention to other parts of the universe—even to other specks like oneself—in a way that appreciates and engages with the values or valuable objects that come from outside oneself, then one corrects one's practical stance. If, in addition, one is partly successful in producing, preserving, or promoting value—if one does some good, or realizes value, then one has something to say, or to think in response to the worry that one's life has no point.

Only if some suggestion like mine is right can we make sense of the intuitions about meaningfulness to which I called attention in the earlier part of this paper. According to those intuitions the difference between a meaningful and a meaningless life is not a difference between a life that does a lot of good, and a life that does a little. (Nor is it a difference between a life that makes a big splash and one that, so to speak, sprays only a few drops.) It is rather a difference between a life that does good or is good or realizes value and a life that is essentially a waste. According to these intuitions, there is as sharp a contrast between the Blob and a life devoted to the care of a single needy individual as there is between the Blob and someone who manages to change the world for the better on a grand scale. Indeed, there may be an equally sharp contrast between the Blob and the monk of a contemplative order whose existence confers no benefit or change on anyone else's life at all. Ironically, along this dimension, Tolstoy fares exceptionally well.

Thus it seems to me that even if there is no meaning to life, even if, that is, life as a whole has no purpose, no direction, no point, that is no reason to doubt the possibility of finding and making meaning in life—that is no reason, in other words, to doubt the possibility of people living meaningful lives. In coming to terms with our place and our status in the universe, it is natural and appropriate that people should want to explore the possibility of both types of meaning. Even if philosophers have nothing new or encouraging to say about the possibility of meaning of the first sort, there may be some point to elaborating the different meanings of the idea of finding meaning in life, and in pointing out the different forms that coming to terms with the human condition can take.

## Work Cited

Wiggins, D. "Truth, Invention, and the Meaning of Life." *Proceedings of the British Academy* 62 (1976): 331–78.

## Study Questions

1. Describe how Wolf begins with three paradigms of meaningless lives as a method of arriving at her definition of what constitutes a meaningful life. Based on Wolf's definition, assess the meaningfulness of your own life.

2. Provide an example of a life that is meaningful in a subjective sense. Provide an example of a life that is meaningful in an objective sense. Evaluate Wolf's argument for claiming that we should prefer lives that are objectively, not merely subjectively, meaningful.

3. Wolf cautions us not to equate meaningful lives with moral or happy lives. Provide examples of someone living a meaningful but not moral life, a meaningful but not happy life, a moral but not meaningful life, and a happy but not meaningful life.

4. Why do the philosophers Wolf calls "pessimists" believe that the question "What is the meaning of life?" *and* the question "What makes a meaningful life?" depend on god's existence? Wolf finds these questions not as closely connected as other philosophers assume, but not unconnected either. Explain why.

---

# Bernard Williams

---

Bernard Williams (1929–2003) is considered one of the most influential British philosophers of the twentieth century. Williams studied classics at Balliol College, Oxford, and spent his National Service flying Spitfires in Canada. Williams' career was divided between Oxford, University College London, Bedford College, Cambridge, and Berkeley. Williams is especially well known for his critiques of utilitarian and Kantian moral theories; he focused instead on the Aristotelian question of what makes a good life. In this famous 1972 essay, Williams argues that while it is better to live a longer than a shorter life, we should not want to live forever.

## The Makropulos Case: Reflections on the Tedium of Immortality

### 1. Introduction

[. . .] Immortality, or a state without death, would be meaningless, I shall suggest; so, in a sense, death gives the meaning to life. That does not mean that we should not fear death (whatever force that injunction might be taken to have, anyway). Indeed, there are several very different ways in which it could be true at once that death gave the meaning to life and that death was, other things being equal, something to be feared. Some existentialists, for instance, seem to have said that death was what gave meaning to life, if anything did, just because it was the fear of death that gave meaning to life; I shall not follow them.

I shall rather pursue the idea that from facts about human desire and happiness and what a human life is, it follows both that immortality would be, where conceivable at all, intolerable, and that (other things being equal) death is reasonably regarded as an evil. Considering whether death can reasonably be regarded as an evil is in fact as near as I shall get to considering whether it should be feared: they are not quite the same question.

My title is that, as it is usually translated into English, of a play by Karel Capek which was made into an opera by Janacek and which tells of a woman called Elina Makropulos, *alias* Emilia Marty, *alias* Ellian Macgregor, alias a number of other things with the initials "EM," on whom her father, the Court physician to a sixteenth-century Emperor, tried out an elixir of life. At the time of the action she is aged 342. Her unending life has come to a state of boredom, indifference, and coldness. Everything is joyless: "in the end it is the same," she says, "singing and silence." She refuses to take the elixir again; she dies; and the formula is deliberately destroyed by a young woman among the protests of some older men.

EM's state suggests at least this, that death is not necessarily an evil, and not just in the sense in which almost everybody would agree to that, where death provides an end to great suffering, but in the more intimate sense that it can be a good thing not to live too long. It suggests more than that, for it suggests that it was not a peculiarity of EM's that an endless life was meaningless. That is something I shall follow out later. First, though, we should put together the suggestion of EM's case, that death is not necessarily an evil, with the claim of some philosophies and religions that death is necessarily not an evil. Notoriously, there have been found two contrary bases on which that claim can be mounted: death is said by some not to be an evil because it is not the end, and by others, because it is. [. . .]

## 2. Is Death an Evil, and Is It Better to Die Later than Earlier?

### 2.1. Two Arguments from Lucretius

Most famous, perhaps, among those who have found comfort in the second option, the prospect of annihilation, was **Lucretius**, who, in the steps of **Epicurus**, and probably from a personal fear of death which in some of his pages seems almost tangible, addresses himself to proving that death is never an evil. Lucretius has two basic arguments for this conclusion [in *de Rerum Natura* or *On the Nature of Things*], and it is an important feature of them both that the conclusion they offer has the very strong consequence—and seems clearly intended to have the consequence— that, for oneself at least, it is all the same whenever one dies, that a long life is no better than a short one. That is to say, death is never an evil in the sense not

merely that there is no one for whom dying is an evil, but that there is no time at which dying is an evil—sooner or later, it is all the same.

The first argument (Ch. III, lines 870ff, 898ff.) seeks to interpret the fear of death as a confusion, based on the idea that we shall be there after death to repine our loss of the *praemia vitae*, the rewards and delights of life, and to be upset at the spectacle of our bodies burned, and so forth. The fear of death, it is suggested, must necessarily be the fear of some experiences had when one is dead. But if death is annihilation, then there are no such experiences: in the Epicurean phrase, when death is there, we are not, and when we are there, death is not. So, death being annihilation, there is nothing to fear. The second argument (line 1091) addresses itself directly to the question of whether one dies earlier or later, and says that one will be the same time dead however early or late one dies, and therefore one might as well die earlier as later. And from both arguments we can conclude *nil igitur mors est ad nos, neque pertinet hilum*—death is nothing to us, and does not matter at all (line 830).

The second of these arguments seems even on the face of things to contradict the first. For it must imply that if there *were* a finite period of death, such that if you died later you would be dead for less time, then there *would* be some point in wanting to die later rather than earlier. But that implication makes sense, surely, only on the supposition that what is wrong with dying consists in something undesirable about the condition of being dead. And that is what is denied by the first argument.

More important than this, the oddness of the second argument can help to focus a difficulty already implicit in the first. The first argument, in locating the objection to dying in a confused objection to being dead, and exposing that in terms of a confusion with being alive, takes it as genuinely true of life that the satisfaction of desire, and possession of the *praemia vitae*, are good things. It is not irrational to be upset by the loss of home, children, possessions—what is irrational is to think of death as, in the relevant sense, *losing* anything. But now if we consider two lives, one very short and cut off before the *praemia* have been acquired, the other fully provided with the *praemia* and containing their enjoyment to a ripe age, it is very difficult to see why the second life, by these standards alone, is not to be thought better than the first. But if it is, then there must be something wrong with the argument which tries to show that there is nothing worse about a short life than a long one. The argument locates the mistake about dying in a mistake about consciousness, it being assumed that what commonsense thinks about the worth of the *praemia vitae* and the sadness of their (conscious) loss is sound enough. But if the *praemia vitae* are valuable; even if we include as necessary to that value consciousness that one possesses them; then surely getting to the point of possessing them is better than not getting to that point, longer enjoyment of them is better than shorter, and more of them, other things being equal, is better than less of them. But if so, then it just will not be true that to die earlier is all the same as to die later, nor that death is never an evil—and the thought that to die later is better than to die earlier will not be dependent on some muddle about thinking that the dead person will be alive to lament his loss. It will depend only on the idea, apparently sound, that if the *praemia vitae* and consciousness of them are good things, then longer consciousness of more *praemia* is better than shorter consciousness of fewer *praemia*.

## 2.2. Argument from Categorical Desire

Is the idea sound? A decent argument, surely, can be marshalled to support it. If I desire something, then, other things being equal, I prefer a state of affairs in which I get it from one in which I do not get it, and (again, other things being equal) plan for a future in which I get it rather than not. But one future, for sure, in which I would not get it would be one in which I was dead. To want something, we may also say, is to that extent to have reason for resisting what excludes having that thing: and death certainly does that, for a very large range of things that one wants.[1] If that is right, then for any of those things, wanting something itself gives one a reason for avoiding death. Even though if I do not succeed, I will not know that, nor what I am missing, from the perspective of the wanting agent it is rational to aim for

states of affairs in which his want is satisfied, and hence to regard death as something to be avoided; that is, to regard it as an evil.

It is admittedly true that many of the things I want, I want only on the assumption that I am going to be alive; and some people, for instance some of the old, desperately want certain things when nevertheless they would much rather that they and their wants were dead. It might be suggested that not just these special cases, but really all wants, were conditional on being alive; a situation in which one has ceased to exist is not to be compared with others with respect to desire-satisfaction—rather, if one dies, all bets are off. But surely the claim that all desires are in this sense conditional must be wrong. For consider the idea of a rational forward-looking calculation of suicide: there can be such a thing, even if many suicides are not rational, and even though with some that are, it may be unclear to what extent they are forward-looking (the obscurity of this with regard to suicides of honour is an obscurity in the notion of shame). In such a calculation, a man might consider what lay before him, and decide whether he did or did not want to undergo it. If he does decide to undergo it, then some desire propels him on into the future, and *that* desire at least is not one that operates conditionally on his being alive, since it itself resolves the question of whether he is going to be alive. He has an unconditional, or (as I shall say) a *categorical* desire.

The man who seriously calculates about suicide and rejects it, only just has such a desire, perhaps. But if one is in a state in which the question of suicide does not occur, or occurs only as total fantasy—if, to take just one example, one is happy—one has many such desires, which do not hang from the assumption of one's existence. If they did hang from that assumption, then they would be quite powerless to rule out that assumption's being questioned, or to answer the question if it is raised; but clearly they are not powerless in those directions—on the contrary they are some of the few things, perhaps the only things, that have power in that direction. Some ascetics have supposed that happiness required reducing one's desires to those necessary for one's existence, that is, to those that one has to have granted that one exists at all; rather, it requires that some of one's desires should be fully categorical, and one's existence itself wanted as something necessary to them.

To suppose that one can in this way categorically want things implies a number of things about the nature of desire. It implies, for one thing, that the reason I have for bringing it about that I get what I want is not merely that of avoiding the unpleasantness of not getting what I want. But that must in any case be right—otherwise we should have to represent every desire as the desire to avoid its own frustration, which is absurd.

About what those categorical desires must be, there is not much of great generality to be said, if one is looking at the happy state of things: except, once more against the ascetic, that there should be not just enough, but more than enough. But the question might be raised, at the impoverished end of things, as to what the minimum categorical desire might be. Could it be *just* the desire to remain alive? The answer is perhaps "no." In saying that, I do not want to deny the existence, the value, or the basic necessity of a sheer reactive drive to self-preservation: humanity would certainly wither if the drive to keep alive were not stronger than any perceived reasons for keeping alive. But if the question is asked, and it is going to be answered calculatively, then the bare categorical desire to stay alive will not sustain the calculation—that desire itself, when things have got that far, has to be sustained or filled out by some desire for something else, even if it is only, at the margin, the desire that future desires of mine will be born and satisfied. But the best insight into the effect of categorical desire is not gained at the impoverished end of things, and hence in situations where the question has actually come up. The question of life being desirable is certainly transcendental in the most modest sense, in that it gets by far its best answer in never being asked at all. [. . .]

## 3. Immortality

But now—if death, other things being equal, is a misfortune; and a longer life is better than a shorter

life; and we reject the Lucretian argument that it does not matter when one dies; then it looks as though—other things always being equal—death is at any time an evil, and it is always better to live than die. [. . .] But wider consequences follow. For if all that is true, then it looks as though it would be not only always better to live, but better to live always, that is, never to die. If Lucretius is wrong, we seem committed to wanting to be immortal.

### 3.1. EM and the Indefinite Extension of Embodied Life

That would be, as has been repeatedly said, with other things equal. No one need deny that since, for instance, we grow old and our powers decline, much may happen to increase the reasons for thinking death a good thing. But these are contingencies. We might not age; perhaps, one day, it will be possible for some of us not to age. If that were so, would it not follow then that, more life being *per se* better than less life, we should have reason so far as that went (but not necessarily in terms of other inhabitants) to live for ever? EM indeed bears strong, if fictional, witness against the desirability of that; but perhaps she still laboured under some contingent limitations, social or psychological, which might once more be eliminated to bring it about that really other things were equal. Against this, I am going to suggest that the supposed contingencies are not really contingencies; that an endless life would be a meaningless one; and that we could have no reason for living eternally a human life. There is no desirable or significant property which life would have more of, or have more unqualifiedly, if we lasted for ever. In some part, we can apply to life **Aristotle's** marvellous remark about Plato's Form of the Good: "nor will it be any the more good for being eternal: that which lasts long is no whiter than that which perishes in a day" (*Ethica Nicomachea* [Nicomachean Ethics] 1096b4[2]). But only in part; for, rejecting Lucretius, we have already admitted that more days may give us more than one day can.

If one pictures living for ever as living as an embodied person in the world rather as it is, it will be a question, and not so trivial as may seem, of what age one eternally is. EM was 342; because for 300 years she had been 42. This choice (if it was a choice) I am personally, and at present, well disposed to salute—if one had to spend eternity at any age, that seems an admirable age to spend it at. Nor would it necessarily be a less good age for a woman: that at least was not EM's problem, that she was too old at the age she continued to be at. Her problem lay in having been at it for too long. Her trouble was it seems, boredom: a boredom connected with the fact that everything that could happen and make sense to one particular human being of 42 had already happened to her. Or, rather, all the sorts of things that could make sense to one woman of a certain character; for EM has a certain character, and indeed, except for her accumulating memories of earlier times, and no doubt some changes of style to suit the passing centuries, seems always to have been much the same sort of person.

There are difficult questions, if one presses the issue, about this constancy of character. How is this accumulation of memories related to this character which she eternally has, and to the character of her existence? Are they much the same kind of events repeated? Then it is itself strange that she allows them to be repeated, accepting the same repetitions, the same limitations—indeed, *accepting* is what it later becomes, when earlier it would not, or even could not, have been that. The repeated patterns of personal relations, for instance, must take on a character of being inescapable. Or is the pattern of her experiences not repetitious in this way, but varied? Then the problem shifts, to the relation between these varied experiences, and the fixed character: how can it remain fixed, through an endless series of very various experiences? The experiences must surely happen to her without really affecting her; she must be, as EM is, detached and withdrawn.

EM, of course, is in a world of people who do not share her condition, and that determines certain features of the life she has to lead, as that any personal relationship requires peculiar kinds of concealment. That, at least, is a form of isolation which would disappear if her condition were generalized. But to suppose more generally that boredom and inner death would be eliminated if everyone were similarly becalmed, is an empty hope: it would be a world of **Bourbons**, learning nothing and forgetting nothing, and it is unclear how much could even happen.

The more one reflects to any realistic degree on the conditions of EM's unending life, the less it seems a mere contingency that it froze up as it did. That it is not a contingency, is suggested also by the fact that the reflections can sustain themselves independently of any question of the particular character that EM had; it is enough, almost, that she has a human character at all. Perhaps not quite. One sort of character for which the difficulties of unending life would have less significance than they proved to have for EM might be one who at the beginning was more like what she is at the end: cold, withdrawn, already frozen. For him, the prospect of unending cold is presumably less bleak in that he is used to it. But with him, the question can shift to a different place, as to why he wants the unending life at all; for, the more he is at the beginning like EM is at the end, the less place there is for categorical desire to keep him going, and to resist the desire for death. In EM's case, her boredom and distance from life both kill desire and consist in the death of it; one who is already enough like that to sustain life in those conditions may well be one who had nothing to make him want to do so. But even if he has, and we conceive of a person who is stonily resolved to sustain for ever an already stony existence, his possibility will be of no comfort to those, one hopes a larger party, who want to live longer because they want to live more.

To meet the basic anti-Lucretian hope for continuing life which is grounded in categorical desire, EM's unending life in this world is inadequate, and necessarily so relative to just those desires and conceptions of character which go into the hope. That is very important, since it is the most direct response, that which should have been adequate if the hope is both coherent and what it initially seemed to be. It also satisfied one of two important conditions which must be satisfied by anything which is to be adequate as a fulfillment of my anti-Lucretian hope, namely that it should clearly be *me* who lives for ever. The second important condition is that the state in which I survive should be one which, to me looking forward, will be adequately related, in the life it presents, to those aims which I now have in wanting to survive at all. That is a vague formula, and necessarily so, for what exactly that relation will be must depend to some extent on what kind of aims and (as one might say) prospects for myself I now have. What we can say is that since I am propelled forward into longer life by categorical desires, what is promised must hold out some hopes for those desires. The limiting case of this might be that the promised life held out some hope just to that desire mentioned before, that future desires of mine will be born and satisfied; but if that were the only categorical desire that carried me forward into it, at least this seems demanded, that any image I have of those future desires should make it comprehensible to me how in terms of my character they could be my desires. [. . .]

### 3.3. Life after Death

Nothing of this, and nothing much like this, was in the minds of many who have hoped for immortality; for it was not in this world that they hoped to live for ever. As one might say, their hope was not so much that they would never die as that they would live after their death, and while that in its turn can be represented as the hope that one would not really die, or, again, that it was not really oneself that would die, the change of formulation could point to an after-life sufficiently unlike this life, perhaps, to earth the current of doubt that flows from EM's frozen boredom.

But in fact this hope has been and could only be modelled on some image of a more familiar untiring or unresting or unflagging activity or satisfaction; and what is essentially EM's problem, one way or another, remains. In general we can ask, what it is about the imaged activities of an eternal life which would stave off the principle hazard to which EM succumbed, boredom. The Don Juan in Hell joke, that heaven's prospects are tedious and the devil has the best tunes, though a tired fancy in itself, at least serves to show up a real and (I suspect) a profound difficulty, of providing any model of an unending, supposedly satisfying, state or activity which would

not rightly prove boring to anyone who remained conscious of himself and who had acquired a character, interests, tastes and impatiences in the course of living, already, a finite life. The point is not that for such a man boredom would be a tiresome consequence of the supposed states or activities, and that they would be objectionable just on the **utilitarian** or **hedonistic** ground that they had this disagreeable feature. If that were all there was to it, we could imagine the feature away, along no doubt with other disagreeable features of human life in its present imperfection. The point is rather that boredom, as sometimes in more ordinary circumstances, would be not just a tiresome effect, but a reaction almost perceptual in character to the poverty of one's relation to the environment. Nothing less will do for eternity than something that makes boredom *unthinkable*. What could that be? Something that could be guaranteed to be at every moment utterly absorbing? But if a man has and retains a character, there is no reason to suppose that there is anything that could be that. If, lacking a conception of the guaranteedly absorbing activity, one tries merely to think away the reaction of boredom, one is no longer supposing an improvement in the circumstances, but merely an impoverishment in his consciousness of them. Just as being bored can be a sign of not noticing, understanding, or appreciating enough, so equally not being bored can be a sign of not noticing, or not reflecting, enough. One might make the immortal man content at every moment, by just stripping off from him consciousness which would have brought discontent by reminding him of other times, other interests, other possibilities. Perhaps, indeed, that is what we have already done, in a more tempting way, by picturing him just now as at every moment totally absorbed—but that is something we shall come back to.

Of course there is in actual life such a thing as justified but necessary boredom. Thus—to take a not entirely typical example—someone who was, or who thought himself, devoted to the radical cause might eventually admit to himself that he found a lot of its rhetoric excruciatingly boring. He might think that he ought not to feel that, that the reaction was wrong, and merely represented an unworthiness of his, an unregenerate remnant of intellectual superiority. However, he might rather feel that it would not necessarily be a better world in which no one was bored by such rhetoric and that boredom was, indeed, a perfectly worthy reaction to this rhetoric after all this time; but for all that, the rhetoric might be necessary. A man at arms can get cramp from standing too long at his post, but sentry-duty can after all be necessary. But the threat of monotony in eternal activities could not be dealt with in that way, by regarding immortal boredom as an unavoidable ache derived from standing ceaselessly at one's post. (This is one reason why I said that boredom in eternity would have to be *unthinkable*.) For the question would be unavoidable, in what campaign one was supposed to be serving, what one's ceaseless sentry-watch was for.

Some philosophers have pictured an eternal existence as occupied in something like intense intellectual enquiry. Why that might seem to solve the problem, at least for them, is obvious. The activity is engrossing, self-justifying, affords, as it may appear, endless new perspectives, and by being engrossing enables one to lose oneself. It is that last feature that supposedly makes boredom unthinkable, by providing something that is, in that earlier phrase, at every moment totally absorbing. But if one is totally and perpetually absorbed in such an activity, and loses oneself in it, then as those words suggest, we come back to the problem of satisfying the conditions that it should be me who lives for ever, and that the eternal life should be in prospect of some interest. Let us leave aside the question of people whose characteristic and most personal interests are remote from such pursuits, and for whom, correspondingly, an immortality promised in terms of intellectual activity is going to make heavy demands on some theory of a "real self" which will have to emerge at death. More interesting is the content and value of the promise for a person who *is*, in this life, disposed to those activities. For looking at such a person as he now is, it seems quite unreasonable to suppose that those activities would have the fulfilling or liberating character that they do have for him, if they were in fact all he could do or conceive of doing. If they are genuinely fulfilling, and do not operate (as they can) merely as a compulsive diversion, then the ground and shape of the satisfactions that the intellectual inquiry offers him, will relate to *him*, and not just to the inquiry. The *Platonic introjection*, seeing the satisfactions of studying what is timeless and impersonal as being themselves timeless and impersonal, may be a deep illusion, but it is certainly an illusion. [. . .]

## 4. Conclusion

Suppose, then, that categorical desire does sustain the desire to live. So long as it remains so, I shall want not to die. Yet I also know, if what has gone before is right, that an eternal life would be unliveable. In part, as EM's case originally suggested, that is because categorical desire will go away from it: in those versions, such as hers, in which I am recognizably myself, I would eventually have had altogether too much of myself. There are good reasons, surely, for dying before that happens. But equally, at times earlier than that moment, there is reason for not dying. Necessarily, it tends to be either too early or too late. EM reminds us that it can be too late, and many, as against Lucretius, need no reminding that it can be too early. If that is any sort of dilemma, it can, as things still are and if one is exceptionally lucky, be resolved, not by doing anything, but just by dying shortly before the horrors of not doing so become evident. Technical progress may, in more than one direction, make that piece of luck rarer. But as things are, it is possible to be, in contrast to EM, *felix opportunitate mortis*—as it can be appropriately mistranslated, lucky in having the chance to die.

## Notes

1. Obviously the principle is not exceptionless. For one thing, one can want to be dead: the content of that desire may be obscure, but whatever it is, a man presumably cannot be *prevented* from getting it by dying. More generally, the principle does not apply to what I elsewhere ("Egoism and Altruism") call *non-I desire*.

2. Bekker numbers (e.g., "1096b4"), the usual way scholars cite Aristotle, correspond with the Prussian Academy of Sciences' nineteenth-century publication of Aristotle's complete works, edited by August Immanuel Bekker (1785–1781): "1096" refers to the page number, "b" refers to the column, and "4" refers to the line number.

## Work Cited

Williams, B. "Egoism and Atruism." *Problems of the Self*. Cambridge: Cambridge University Press, 1973. 250–265.

## Study Questions

1. What are Lucretius's two arguments for the conclusion that death is never an evil? What is Williams's objection?
2. Explain what a categorical desire is by making reference to one of yours. Why does Williams consider categorical desires to be significant in determining the meaningfulness of our lives?
3. Describe the story line and philosophical implications of *The Makropulos Case*, the play written by Capek and composed as an opera by Janácek in the 1920s. What would *you* do, were you to find yourself in Elina's situation? Do you agree or disagree with Williams' assessment of what her (and your) life would be like?
4. On what basis does Williams dismiss the objection that indefinite life *after* death escapes the problems associated with Elina's situation of indefinite extension of embodied life? Do you agree or disagree with Williams' assessment of this alternative version of immortality?

# Film Notes

## Art and Aesthetics/A Beautiful Life

*Amadeus* (USA 1984, Milos Forman, 160 min): After attempting suicide, composer Antonio Salieri is placed in an insane asylum, where he confesses to a priest his jealousy of Mozart and his role in Mozart's death.

*Camille Claudel* (France 1988, Bruno Nuytten, 175 min; French with subtitles): A biography of the late-nineteenth-century French sculptor, who was determined to succeed as a woman artist but as student then model, mistress, and collaborator of Rodin, gradually goes mad.

*Everlasting Moments* (Sweden/Denmark/Norway/Finland/Germany 2008, Jan Troell, 131 min; Swedish and Finnish with subtitles): Maria Larsson has seven children and an alcoholic husband who works on the docks, but the photos she takes bring a measure of independence.

*Ghost World* (USA/UK/Germany 2001, Terry Zwigoff, 111min): Social outcasts Enid and Rebecca graduate from high school without plans for the future, except the art class Enid must make up.

*The Hours* (USA/UK 2002, Stephen Daldry, 114 min): The novel *Mrs. Galloway* links author Virginia Woolf to two women living in different times and places: LA housewife Laura Brown in 1951 and New York editor Clarissa Vaughan in 2001.

*La Vie en Rose* (France/UK/Czech Republic 2007, Olivier Dahan, 140 min; French with subtitles): About the life of French singer Édith Piaf who went from the streets to stardom, living hard, and dying early.

*Mephisto* (West Germany/Hungary/Austria 1981, István Szabó, 144 min): An actor of modest talent trades integrity and morality for ambition when the Nazis come to power in Germany.

*Mona Lisa Smile* (USA 2003, Mike Newell, 117 min): Set in the 1950s, Katherine Watson relocates from Berkeley to teach art at Wellesley College, where students are educated to become wives and mothers.

*Pleasantville* (USA 1998, Gary Ross, 124 min): David and Jennifer are magically transported into the perfect-seeming world of white picket fences in the 1950s sitcom *Pleasantville*, where, as Bud and Mary Sue, they become the stimulus for change.

*Pollock* (USA 2000, Ed Harris 122 min): About the life and work of painter Jackson Pollock and the postwar New York art world in which his abstract expressionism took hold. *Who the #$&% Is Jackson Pollock?* (USA 2006, Harry Moses, 74 min) is a documentary about Teri Horton, a retired semi-truck driver, who sets out to prove to the art world that the painting she bought at a thrift store for $5 was painted by Pollock.

*Round Midnight* (USA/France 1986, Bertrand Tavernier, 133 min): Dale Turner (played by jazz legend Dexter Gordon) is an American tenor saxophonist who, nearing the end of a life shortened by alcohol and drugs, headlines a Paris club in 1959.

*Séraphine* (France/Belgium 2008, Martin Provost, 125 min; French, German, and Latin with subtitles): About Séraphine de Senlis, impoverished cleaning lady by day and divinely-inspired painter by night.

*Vincent* (Australia/Belgium 1987, Paul Cox, 105 min): With a soundtrack based entirely on Vincent Van Gogh's letters to his brother Theo, the film is about the places, landscapes, and sequences that inspired the painter and the techniques he used. *Vincent and Theo* (Netherlands/UK/France/Italy/Germany 1990, Robert Altman, 138 min) and *Lust for Life* (USA 1956, Vincente Minnelli, 122 min) are biographies of Van Gogh.

## A Beautiful Life

*Amélie* (France/Germany 2001, Jean-Pierre Jeunet, 122 min; French with subtitles): Amélie is a shy and lonely, but unusually imaginative, waitress in a Paris café who decides that her life's purpose is to bring other people happiness.

*American Beauty* (USA 1999, Sam Mendes, 122 min): A 42-year-old magazine writer who hates his job and is unloved by his family, Lester's midlife crisis includes a crush on his teenage daughter's cheerleader friend, a sports car, and a fast-food job.

*Chariots of Fire* (UK 1981, Hugh Hudson, 124 min): About two British sprinters who won gold medals at the 1924 Olympics but competed for very different reasons: Harold Abrahams, a Jewish student at Cambridge, and Eric Liddell, from a Scottish missionary family.

*Cries and Whispers* (Sweden 1972, Ingmar Bergman, 91 min; Swedish with subtitles): Agnes is dying of cancer in the company of her two sisters, Maria and Karin, who cannot love, and her servant, Anna, who can.

*Departures* (Japan 2008, Yōjirō Takita, 130 min; Japanese with subtitles): A cellist in a Tokyo orchestra that goes under moves back to his hometown and takes the low-caste job of undertaker's assistant.

*Down and Out in Beverley Hills* (USA 1986, Paul Mazursky, 103 min): The lives of members of a Beverly Hills family are changed when a homeless man who tried to drown himself in their pool comes to live with them.

*Gattaca* (USA 1997, Andrew Niccol, 112 min): About a society not far into the future. Naturally born "In-Valid" Vincent dreams of becoming an astronaut, but the job is restricted to genetically engineered "Valids."

*Ikiru* (Japan 1952, Akira Kurosawa, 143 min; Japanese with subtitles): Mr. Watanabe's life consists of a bureaucratic job shuffling papers and a strained relationship with his son. When he learns that he is dying of cancer, he decides to try to figure out how to live.

*Into the Wild* (USA 2007, Sean Penn, 148 min): Twenty-year-old Christopher McCandless graduates from Emory University and decides to live in the Alaskan wilderness instead of going to law school.

Based on Jon Krakauer's book, which relied on McCandless's journals.

*Leaving Las Vegas* (France/USA/UK 1995, Mike Figgis, 111 min): Having lost his job and wife and kid, alcoholic screenwriter Ben Sanderson arrives in Las Vegas to drink himself to death and enters a relationship with a prostitute, Sera.

*Man Push Cart* (USA 2005, Ramin Bahrani, 87 min): Camus' *Myth of Sisyphus* inspired this story of Ahmad, a Pakistani immigrant, once a rock star, who struggles each night to manoeuvre his pushcart to a Manhattan corner to sell coffee and bagels in the morning.

*Orlando* (UK/Italy/France/Netherlands 1992, Sally Potter, 93 min): Orlando is an attractive youth, a favourite of the aging Queen Elizabeth I who bequeaths him an estate on condition that he not grow old. Partway across the ensuing centuries, Orlando becomes a woman.

*The Sea Inside* (Spain/France/Italy 2004, Alejandro Amenábar, 125 min; Spanish, Catalan, and Galician with subtitles): Ramón Sampedro, a Galician fisherman who became a quadriplegic in a diving accident as a young man, campaigns for the right to die.

*The Straight Story* (France/UK/USA 1999, David Lynch, 112 min): The true story of 73-year-old Alvin Straight who drove his tractor-style lawn mower from Iowa to Wisconsin to reconcile with his brother.

*Taste of Cherry* (Iran/France 1997, Abbas Kiarostami, 95 min; Persian with subtitles): Mr. Badii wants to commit suicide and, driving around Tehran's outskirts, asks a soldier, seminarian, and taxidermist for help.

*Vagabond* (France 1985, Agnès Varda, 105 min; French with subtitles): A pseudo-documentary about a young woman found frozen to death in a field, based on interviews with people she encountered during her preceding months as a vagabond.

# Glossary

**"Achilles [would] have sought death on the corpse of Patroclus"**: in Homeric tradition, Patroclus was killed in the Trojan war after convincing his friend Achilles, who had withdrawn, to lend him men, horses, and armour.

**Agricola, Georgius (1494–1555)**: Latinized name for German-born Georg Bauer, who combined his work as a physician with the study of geology and mining.

**"Alcestis would have died for Admetus"**: in Greek mythology, Alcestis died for her husband Admetus, king of Pherae in Thessaly, and was restored to life.

**Anacharsis, the Scythian**: travelled to Athens early in sixth century BCE, where he became friends with **Solon** and valued for his outsider's perspective on Athenian institutions.

**analytic**: a statement's truth depends on its logical form or meanings of its constituent terms; for **Kant**, the predicate concept is contained within the subject concept.

**a posteriori**: known on the basis of experience.

**a priori**: known independent of experience.

**Aquinas, St Thomas (1225–74)**: Dominican philosopher and theologian, canonized in 1323 and well known for his commentaries on **Aristotle** and reconciliation of faith and reason.

**Archimedes (c. 287–c. 212 BCE)**: Greek mathematician, natural philosopher, and engineer who lived in Syracuse, Sicily.

**Aristophanes (c. 450–388 BCE)**: comedic playwright who lived in Athens.

**Aristotle (384–322 BCE)**: see p. 314.

**Asclepius**: son of Apollo and god of medicine in Greek mythology.

**Augustine, St (354–430)**: philosopher and theologian who lived in present-day Algeria.

**"authors of *Port-Royal Grammar*" (1660) and *Port-Royal Logic* (1662)**: Antoine Arnauld (1612–94), Claude Lancelot (1615–75), and Pierre Nicole (1625–95), who were Jansenist scholars associated with the Port Royal abbey in Paris.

**Bach, Johann Sebastian (1685–1750)**: German composer of the Baroque period, responsible for a prodigious output of vocal and instrumental works in his church and court employments as organist and musical director.

**Bacon, Francis (1561–1626)**: see p. 256.

**Barnett, Ross R. (1898–1987)**: elected governor of Mississippi on a segregationist platform, during his 1960-4 term, he jailed Freedom Riders and denied **James Meredith** admission to University of Mississippi calling Meredith's attempt "our greatest crisis" since the Civil War.

**"Basques, Catalans, and Bretons"**: examples of national and linguistic minorities accorded some political autonomy by the state—the Basques live in a region of the Pyrenees that straddles France and Spain, the Catalans live in a region of northeastern Spain that borders France and includes Barcelona, and the Bretons live in the Brittany region of France.

**"battle at the Plains of Abraham"**: on 13 September 1759, British forces under James Wolfe defeated French forces under Louis-Joseph de Montcalm just upstream from Quebec, leading to the city's surrender a few days later.

**Beauvoir, Simone de (1908–86)**: see p. 45.

**Beauzée, Nicolas (1717–89)**: French grammarian whose *Grammaire generale* was published in 1767.

**Bebel, August (1840–1913)**: cabinetmaker who cofounded the German Social-Democratic Party and whose 1879 book *Woman and Socialism* argued that the promise of socialism could not be fulfilled without freedom and equality of women.

**Beethoven, Ludwig van (1770–1827):** German pianist and composer whose piano, chamber, and orchestral works, despite his progressive hearing loss, elevated the status of instrumental over vocal music.

**Beiderbecke, Leon Bix (1903–31):** US jazz musician (cornet and piano) and composer from Iowa, famous for improvisation and being, with Louis Armstrong, one of jazz's first soloists.

*bel canto* ("beautiful singing"): a vocal style in Italian opera that dates to the Baroque period.

**Bergson, Henri (1859–1941):** French philosopher whose ideas that intuition (not the intellect) apprehends reality and evolution is a creative process guided by an *élan vital* (life force) were widely influential during the early decades of the twentieth century.

**Berkeley, George (1685–1753):** see p. 179.

*biwa:* a short-necked, fretted lute.

**Black Death:** bubonic plague that arose in China in the early 1330s and spread along trade routes, killing one-third of Europe's population between 1347 and 1350.

**"black Jacobins":** the Jacobins were radical revolutionaries during the **French Revolution**; C.L.R. James' *The Black Jacobins* is about the **Haitian Revolution** and influence of France.

**Boehme, Jacob (1575–1624):** German shoemaker who after an epiphany caused by sunlight reflected from a pewter dish began to write mystical religious works that influenced seventeenth-century Protestantism and nineteenth-century Romanticism.

**Bononcini, Giovanni Battista (1670–1747):** Italian composer and cellist of the Baroque period whose operas competed with **Handel**'s in London during the 1720s.

**Borges, Jorge Luis (1899–1986):** writer born in Buenos Aires, Argentina, well known for his short stories, essays, and poems.

**Borgia, Cesare (1475/76–1507):** Italian military leader and ruler under the patronage of his father, Pope Alexander VI.

**Bossuet, Jacques-Bénigne (1627–1704):** French bishop, theologian, and orator who served as tutor to the Dauphin in the court of Louis XIV and defended the divine right of kings.

**Boston Tea Party:** in December 1773, Massachusetts patriots, some dressed as Mohawk Indians, dumped 342 crates of Darjeeling tea from ships in Boston Harbor to protest British tax policies.

**Botticelli, Sandro (1444/5–1510):** Italian **Renaissance** painter of the Florentine school, known for his vibrant use of colour.

**Bourbons:** important ruling house of Europe; descendants of Louis I, duc de Bourbon 1327–42, included monarchs of France, Spain, Naples, and Sicily from the seventeenth to nineteenth century.

**Boyce, William (1711–79):** English composer and organist of the Baroque period.

**Boyle, Robert (1627–91):** English natural philosopher and founding member of the Royal Society, famous for his air pump experiments and contributions to experimental method.

**Brahmins:** highest caste, of priests, in traditional Hindu societies in India and Nepal; *Brahman* is Sanskrit for a transcendent power that supports and upholds everything in the universe.

**Brahms, Johannes (1833–97):** German composer and pianist who combined nineteenth-century Romantic and eighteenth-century Classical styles.

*Brown v Board of Education*: in 1954, the US Supreme Court ruled that the doctrine of "separate but equal" has no place in public education and violates the Fourteenth Amendment's guarantee of equal protection of the laws.

**Buber, Martin (1878–1965):** Jewish philosopher, theologian, and editor whose best-known work, *Ich und Du* (1923), defends dialogical philosophy and the distinction between "I–It" and "I–Thou'" as two fundamentally different kinds of relations.

**Buffon (1707–88):** Georges-Louis Leclerc, Comte de Buffon, was a French zoologist who criticized Linnaean taxonomy and speculated about evolution.

**Buñuel, Luis (1900–83):** Spanish-born surrealist who made documentary films in Spain, France, the United States, and Mexico.

**Bunyan, John (1628–88):** author of *The Pilgrim's Progress*, he was a tinker who became a Puritan preacher imprisoned for dissent from the Church of England.

**Burke, Edmund (1729–97):** Anglo-Irish political philosopher and longstanding parliamentarian; a founder of British conservatism who supported the independence of elected representatives and criticized the dangers of mob rule with the **French Revolution**.

**Butler, Joseph (1692–1752):** English philosopher and bishop in the Church of England who defended traditional views on morality and religion.

**Camus, Albert (1913–60):** French journalist, playwright, novelist, and essayist whose "philosophy of the absurd" concerns the impossibility of answering the ultimate question whether life has meaning in face of inevitable death.

**Canal, Giovanni Antonio, or Canaletto (1697–1768):** artist known especially for paintings of his birthplace, Venice.

**Cantillon, Richard (1680–1734):** an important early theorist in economics due to his treatise *Essai sur la nature du commerce en général*.

**Cantor, Georg (1845–1918):** German mathematician who founded set theory.

**Caravaggio, Michelangelo Merisi di (1571–1610):** Italian painter who broke with convention by using posed models and dramatic lighting to create realistic works.

**Carnap, Rudolf (1891–1970):** born in Germany, a leading member of the **Vienna Circle** before emigrating from Prague to the United States in 1935.

**"Cartesian fashion":** a reference to **Descartes**' dualist belief that the universe comprises two distinct substances: immaterial mind and material body.

**Casals, Pablo (1876–1973):** Spanish cellist, conductor, and composer who went into exile in France, then Puerto Rico, when Franco took power in 1939; as a 13-year-old, stumbled on sheet music for **Bach**'s suites for cello at a Barcelona second-hand shop, eventually making these compositions famous with his performances and recordings.

**Cassirer, Ernst (1874–1945):** trained in the neo-Kantian tradition; as a Jew, forced to leave Germany in 1933, ultimately ending up in the United States; sought to provide a unified account of knowledge in the natural and human sciences with his philosophy of symbolic forms.

**Cézanne, Paul (1839–1906):** French **Post-Impressionist** painter considered a great influence on the development of modern art.

**Chamberlain, Houston Stewart (1855–1927):** British-born Germanophile whose anti-Semitic, conservative, and nationalistic writings were popular among Germans, including Hitler, during the early decades of the twentieth century.

**Charondas:** lawgiver from the Sicilian city of Catana, a colony of ancient Greece.

**Codrus:** legendary Athenian king who engineered his death at the hands of Dorian invaders once he learned that an oracle had said they would succeed by sparing the king.

**conceptualism:** medieval position on the problem of universals that holds that general terms such as "human" refer to abstract concepts of the mind.

**Condillac (1714–80):** French empiricist philosopher Étienne Bonnot, Abbé de Condillac, in his 1776 *Commerce and Government*, advanced the theory that value depends on the utility of a commodity in relation to subjective needs.

**Confucius (551–479 BCE):** thinker, politician, and educator whose influence on the history of Chinese thought has been compared to **Socrates**' influence on Western thought.

**Constable, John (1776–1837):** English artist known for his landscape paintings.

**Copernicus, Nicolaus (1473–1543):** Polish astronomer whose heliocentric theory of the universe challenged the prevailing geocentrism of the Ptolemaic system.

**Cuvier, Georges (1769–1832):** French zoologist whose "comparative anatomy" explained structural differences in terms of functional differences and formed the basis of his classification system.

**Dahomey:** a kingdom that profited from the slave trade in the eighteenth century, was made a French colony in the 1890s, and, after gaining independence in 1960, was renamed Benin in 1975.

**Dante Alighieri (1265–1321):** Italian poet and philosopher, and political exile from Florence; his epic poem *The Divine Comedy* is about his journey through the afterlife.

**Darwin, Charles (1809–82):** British naturalist whose 1831–6 voyage on *HMS Beagle* promoted the development of a theory of evolution finally published in 1859 as *The Origin of Species*.

**Daumier, Honoré-Victorin (1808–79):** French caricaturist, lithographer, painter, and sculptor.

**Degas, Edgar (1834–1917):** French painter, printmaker, sculptor, and photographer who called himself a Realist, not an **Impressionist**, and for whom ballerinas, race horses, and Paris cafés were frequent subjects.

**de Hooch (de Hoogh), Pieter de (1629–84):** Dutch painter especially known for his use of light and portrayal of interior scenes viewed through windows and corridors.

**deme:** smallest political unit to which citizens of Athens belonged.

**Democritus (c. 460-370 BCE):** Greek philosopher who developed the atomic theory proposed by his teacher, **Leucippus**, that the universe is composed of an infinite number of solid, indivisible, and indestructible bodies of various sizes and shapes moving about in an infinite void.

**Descartes, René (1596–1650):** see p. 171.

**Diderot, Denis (1713–84):** as general editor of the *Encyclopédie*, toiled for 25 years to fulfill the French Enlightenment's goal of providing a systematization of knowledge that could serve as a rational basis for the common good.

**Dostoevsky, Fyodor (1821–81):** Russian novelist and journalist; after four years spent at hard labour in Siberia once his death sentence for socialist politics was commuted, the theme of redemption through suffering and faith came to predominate in his writings.

**Du Bois, W.E.B. (1868–1963):** scholar, editor, and activist who was the first African American to earn a PhD from Harvard University, a founding member of the NAACP, and fought racial injustice throughout his life.

**Dufy, Raoul (1877–1953):** French painter who worked in a variety of media including oils, watercolours, textiles, and woodcuts.

**Duhem, Pierre (1861–1916):** French physicist who also published important works in history and philosophy of science.

**Edwardian:** era that includes the reign of King Edward VII in Great Britain, 1901–10.

**Einstein, Albert (1879–1955):** besides his famous contributions to physics (special and general theories of relativity, explanation of Brownian motion of molecules, photon theory of light), also made important contributions to philosophy of science.

**El Greco, Domenikos Theotokopoulos (1541–1614):** born in Crete and trained as an icon painter, he studied Renaissance painting in Venice and Rome before settling in Toledo, Spain, where he perfected his distinctive style of elongated figures and contrasts of light and colour.

**Eliot, T.S. (1888–1965):** influential poet and playwright who worked as a teacher, bank clerk, and literary editor; born in St Louis and educated at Harvard but eventually became a British citizen; won the 1948 Nobel Prize in Literature.

**Empedocles of Acragas (in Sicily) (c. 495–35 BCE):** philosopher, poet, politician, and physician, who held that effluences emitted by sensory organs and objects make perception possible.

**Epicureans:** followers of **Epicurus**.

**Epicurus (341–270 BCE):** Greek philosopher who held that happiness (pursuit of pleasure, peace of mind) is the goal of human life and that sensations of pleasure and pain are the best guides to what is right and wrong.

**Etruscan:** literate culture inhabiting the Italian peninsula (Etruria) during the first millennium BCE.

**"famous clock at Strasburg":** Strasbourg Cathedral's astronomical clock, completed in 1574, measured time, served as a calendar, and displayed the motions of the planets, while various automata entertained passersby.

**Fanon, Frantz (1925–61):** his influential works on racism and decolonization are rooted in experiences growing up in Martinique, studying medicine and psychiatry in France, treating patients affected by torture during the Algerian War of Independence, and joining that cause.

**Fauves:** French artists led by **Matisse** who, by presenting nature with vivid colours and broad brushstrokes, brought about the first of the early twentieth-century avant-garde movements.

**FDR or Franklin Delano Roosevelt (1882–1945):** as thirty-second president of the United States, held office from the height of the Great Depression through World War II.

**Feigl, Herbert (1902–88):** member of the **Vienna Circle** who immigrated to the United States in 1931 and defended the identity theory of mind and brain.

**feudal order:** decentralized political and economic order of medieval Europe wherein lords exchanged land for vassals' military service, or, in a broader social sense, peasants' labour.

**Filmer, Robert (1588–1653):** Royalist during the English Civil Wars, his *Patriarcha; or the Natural Power* *of Kings* (1680), which **Locke** sought to refute, asserts the biblical basis of the king's absolute power as Adam's direct descendant by one of Noah's sons.

**Fonteyn, Margot (1919–91):** renowned English ballerina who spent her entire long career, from age 14 to 60, with the Royal Ballet (previously Vic-Wells and Sadler's Wells Ballets).

**Fortbonnais, François Véron de (1722–1800):** French economist who advocated protectionist policies such as import duties.

**Franklin, Benjamin (1706–90):** son of a poor candle and soap maker who became a civic-minded scientist, inventor, writer, diplomat, and, as signatory to the Declaration of Independence, Treaty of Paris, and Constitution, a founding father of the United States.

**Frege, Gottlob (1848–1925):** German mathematician, logician, and philosopher who invented predicate calculus, (unsuccessfully) sought to reduce mathematics to logic, and made a lasting contribution to philosophy of language by distinguishing sense and reference.

**"French existentialists":** likely a reference by Sartre to his contemporaries Simone de **Beauvoir** (1908–86), Albert **Camus** (1913–60), and Maurice **Merleau-Ponty** (1908–61).

**French Revolution (1789–1799):** in 1789, commoners of the Third Estate declared themselves the National Assembly and proceeded to abolish the feudal system, adopt a declaration of individual rights, seize church property, and force King Louis XVI to accept a constitutional monarchy; in 1792, the monarchy was abolished and a republic declared; the Reign of Terror took place 1793–4 after the Jacobins took control of parliament; Napoleon Bonaparte's coup d'état brought the revolution to a close in 1799.

**"frenzied dervishes of Cybele":** a fertility goddess with ecstatic followers, worship of Cybele spread from the Anatolian kingdom of Phrygia to Greece in the sixth or fifth century BCE.

**Freud, Sigmund (1856–1939):** Viennese neurologist who founded psychoanalysis, known in his day as the "talking cure," and whose theories of the mind gave us concepts such as repression, the unconscious, Oedipus complex, and id–ego–superego.

**Fry, Roger (1866–1934):** English critic and artist, member of the Bloomsbury group, and champion of modern art.

**Galileo Galilei (1564–1642):** Italian mathematician who was a central figure in the scientific revolution and famously condemned by the Catholic Inquisition for his defence of **Copernicus**'s theory.

**Gandhi, Mohandas (1869–1948):** called *Mahatma* (great soul), led movements to achieve basic rights for Indians in South Africa and free India from British rule using a method of non-violent resistance, which he named *satyagraha* (devotion to truth).

**Gauguin, Paul (1848–1903):** French **Post-Impressionist** painter and printmaker who in travels to Brittany, Martinique, and Tahiti sought to capture the "pure' and "primitive" in his art; he abandoned not just his Danish wife and their five children but children arising from his many sexual liaisons, often involving girls only 13 or 14 years old.

**Gestalt psychology:** an approach based on the perception of patterned wholes as not simply aggregations of parts that originated in Germany and Austria in the 1910s and provided foundations for modern theories of perception; *Gestalt* translates as "shape' or "form."

**Giacometti, Alberto (1901–66):** Swiss sculptor, painter, and draftsman.

**GI Bill of Rights (officially, the Servicemen's Readjustment Act of 1944):** provided US World War II veterans with education and training subsidies, unemployment benefits, and loan guaranties for homes, farms, and businesses in order to ease their transition to civilian life.

**Gilbert, William (1544–1603):** English physician and scientist known especially for his research on electricity and magnetism.

**Giotto di Bondone (1267–1337):** Italian painter during the late Middle Ages/early **Renaissance**, famous for the frescos adorning the inside of Padua's Scrovegni (Arena) Chapel.

**"the Gitxsan people":** First Nation that asserts its right to self-government and ownership of its traditional territory in the Skeena River watershed region of northwestern British Columbia.

**Glaucon:** name of **Plato**'s younger brother.

**Gobineau, Joseph Arthur (1816–82):** French writer and diplomat best known for the four-volume *Essay on the Inequality of Human Races*, published in 1853–5, which defends a racialist account of the rise and fall of civilizations, deeming "whites," in particular "Aryans," to be superior.

**Goethe, Johann Wolfgang von (1749–1832):** celebrated German writer whose poems, novels, plays, essays, and scientific treatises influenced nineteenth-century literature and philosophy.

**Goodman, Nelson (1906–98):** see p. 205.

**Haydn, Joseph (1732–1809):** Austrian composer who contributed to the development of the symphony and string quartet.

**Haitian Revolution:** began with the slave uprising of 1791, included the abolition of slavery in 1793 and defeat of Napoleon's forces in 1803, and ended with the declaration of Saint Domingue's (renamed Haiti) independence from France on 1 January 1804.

*Hamlet*: tragedy by **William Shakespeare** about a Danish prince's desire to avenge the murder of his father by his uncle.

**Handel, George Frederic (1685–1759):** German-born composer of the Baroque period who produced many operas and oratios (e.g., *Messiah*) over a career spent mostly in England.

**Hare, R.M. (1919–2002):** British moral philosopher known for his defence of "prescriptivism," i.e., that while moral judgments are not matters of fact, they are not expressions of feelings (emotivism) either, but commands that universalize preferences.

**Harper, Elijah (1949–):** Cree from Red Sucker Lake, Manitoba who served as Band Chief, provincial MLA (Rupertsland) and cabinet minister, and federal MP (Churchill); as MLA, delayed passage of the **Meech Lake Accord** to protest lack of attention to Aboriginal issues.

**Hartz, Louis (1919–86):** US political scientist, son of Russian Jewish immigrants, whose classic 1955 book *The Liberal Tradition in America* explains the dominance of **Locke**an liberalism by the absence of a **feudal order** to overcome.

**hedonistic:** motivated by the desire to seek pleasure and avoid pain.

**Hegel, Georg Wilhelm Friedrich (1770–1831):** German philosopher in the post-Kantian idealist tradition who argued in *Phenomenology of Spirit* that experience of the objective world requires mutual recognition of self-consciousness.

**Heidegger, Martin (1889–1976):** German philosopher whose 1927 *Being and Time* provides a phenomenological analysis of human existence.

**Heliogabalus (or Elagabalus):** a reference to the Syrian-born teenaged Roman emperor Marcus Aurelius Antoninus (204–22), famed for decadence and debauchery during his four-year rule, after the sun-god he sought to elevate.

**Helmholtz, Hermann von (1821–94):** German physiologist and physicist who invented the ophthalmoscope and contributed theories of vision, the geometry of space, conservation of energy, and fluid dynamics.

**Hesiod:** Greek poet who is supposed to have lived a century after **Homer** and composed works of theological and philosophical authority in ancient Greece.

**Hobbes, Thomas (1588–1679):** English philosopher whose 1651 book *Leviathan* justifies the absolute rule of sovereigns as what would be agreed to by free and equal individuals acting in their own self-interest in a state of nature.

**"Hobbesian contractualism":** a reference to Hobbes's theory that the prescriptive force of moral norms derives from the mutual consent of rational agents attempting to maximize their self-interest.

**Homer:** Greek poet who is supposed to have composed the *Iliad* and *Odyssey*, which emerged from oral tradition to become the most influential works of literature in the ancient world.

**Humboldt, Wilhelm von (1767–1835):** contributed to linguistics, anthropology, aesthetics, and political philosophy; established the University of Berlin in 1810 (now Humboldt University), inaugurating today's familiar model of universities that combine teaching and research.

**Hume, David (1711–76):** see p. 71 and p. 188.

**"Hungarian freedom fighters":** the Hungarian Revolution of 1956 was a spontaneous but widespread uprising that almost succeeded in establishing the nation's independence before being crushed by Soviet troops.

**Huxley, Thomas Henry (1825–95):** English zoologist characterized as "**Darwin**'s bulldog" because of his outspoken defence of Darwin's theory before scientific and public audiences.

**Impressionism/ists:** a movement by an independent group of artists who held eight exhibitions in Paris 1874–86 outside the official Salon; their short brushstrokes and bright colours broke with tradition, providing a spontaneous appearance to depictions of rural landscapes and urban scenes alike.

**Ingres, Jean-Auguste-Dominique (1780–1867):** French painter who contributed portraits and works inspired by literary and historical themes.

**Ishmael:** according to *Genesis*, Abraham's eldest son, born to Sarah's handmaiden Hagar.

**James, William (1842–1910):** US physiologist, philosopher, and psychologist who is credited as a founder of psychology as a scientific discipline and pragmatism in philosophy.

**Jaspers, Karl (1883–1969):** psychologist and philosopher who is considered, with **Heidegger**, to have founded existentialism in Germany.

**Jefferson, Thomas (1743–1826):** US founding father who authored the Declaration of Independence, insisted that the constitution be amended by a bill of rights, and served as the third president.

**"Jim Crow laws":** a reference to the white supremacist system of racial segregation maintained in the US South from the end of Reconstruction in 1877 until passage of the Civil Rights Act of 1964 and Voting Rights Act of 1965.

**Johns, Jasper (1930–):** US painter, print-maker, and sculptor whose representations of maps, flags, and targets in the 1950s encouraged artists to move away from Abstract Expressionism.

**Joyce, James (1882–1941):** Irish novelist and poet who, in self-imposed exile on the continent, used innovative techniques to capture the Dublin of his youth.

**Kandinsky, Wassily (1866–1944):** considered the founder of abstract art, the Russian-born artist and art theorist's paintings found inspiration in spirituality, music, and geometry.

**Kant, Immanuel (1724–1804):** see p. 78 and p. 197.

**Kenyatta, Jomo (1889–1978):** Kenya's first prime minister and president after independence from Britain in 1963; studied with anthropologist Bronislaw Malinowski (1884–1942) at London School of Economics and defended "female circumcision" in *Facing Mount Kenya: The Tribal Life of the Gikuyu*, published in 1938.

**Kepler, Johannes (1571–1630):** German astronomer and mathematician who proposed three laws of planetary motion: the orbits of the planets are ellipses with the sun at one of the foci; the line connecting a planet to the sun sweeps out equal areas in equal times; and the square of the period of a planet's orbit around the sun is proportional to the cube of its mean distance from the sun.

**Keynes, John Maynard (1883–1946):** British economist who revolutionized economics with his 1936 depression-era *General Theory of Employment, Interest and Money*, which advised government spending to maintain full employment during economic downturns.

**Kierkegaard, Søren (1813–55):** Danish philosopher known as the "father of existentialism."

**"king archon":** government official who presided over cases of alleged religious offences during **Plato**'s time.

**Kuhn, Thomas (1922–96):** physicist and historian and philosopher of science whose 1962 book, *The Structure of Scientific Revolutions*, sold more than 1 million copies in 16 languages.

**Landseer stag:** English artist Edwin Henry Landseer (1802–73) is known for his paintings of animals, especially dogs, horses, and stags.

**Laplace, Pierre-Simon (1749–1827):** mathematician dubbed "**Newton** of France" for his contributions to calculus, astronomy, physics, and probability theory.

**Larissa:** capital of Thessaly, a region of ancient Greece ruled by the Aleuadai, an aristocratic family; orator, rhetorician, and philosopher Gorgias of Leontini (in Sicily) died there in 375 BCE.

**Law, John (1671–1729):** his 1705 *Money and Trade Considered, with a Proposal for Supplying the Nation with Money* urged the adoption of paper currency; in France, the experiment resulted in an economic crisis when the note-issuing Bank Générale collapsed.

**Leibniz, Gottfried Wilhelm (1646–1716):** born and educated in Leipzig, Germany; made important contributions to metaphysics, epistemology, logic, natural philosophy, and theology.

**Leucippus (fifth century BCE):** considered the founder of atomism in ancient Greek philosophy.

**Lincoln, Abraham (1809–65):** as sixteenth US president, his office was defined by the Civil War—in

1861, when southern states seceded in response to his anti-slavery platform, his resolve to preserve the union provoked war; in 1865, he was assassinated by an actor sympathetic to the Confederate cause just days after the war ended.

**Lichtenstein, Roy (1923–97):** US artist who influenced the development of Pop Art with paintings inspired by comic strips and advertisements.

**Linnaeus, Carl (1707–78):** Swedish botanist and physician called the "father of taxonomy" for his creation of a hierarchical system (of species, genera, orders, classes, and kingdoms) and binomial names (genus and species, e.g., *Homo sapiens*).

**Locke, John (1632–1704):** see p. 13, p. 105, and p. 453.

***Love's Labour's Lost:*** an early play by **William Shakespeare** written around 1593–4, in which a king and three lords forswear the company of women for three years of study.

**Lucretius:** **Epicurean** poet who wrote the philosophical poem *De Rerum Natura* ("On the Nature of Things") in the middle of the first century BCE.

**Luther, Martin (1483–1546):** German monk who took on the Catholic Church and Pope Leo X in 1517 by publishing "95 Theses" opposing the sale of indulgences; the newly invented printing press spread these ideas across Europe, with the resulting Protestant Reformation bringing about the end of medieval feudalism and birth of the modern age.

**Lyceum:** a gymnasium in Athens' eastern suburbs used for military training, physical exercise, and philosophical discussion; **Aristotle** established his school there in 335 BCE.

**Lycurgus:** legendary creator of Sparta's constitution about whom little historically is known.

**Manet, Édouard (1832–83):** French painter whose work was often rejected by the Paris Salon and on occasion provoked scandal; associated with **Impressionists** such as **Monet** and Renoir.

**Marcel, Gabriel (1889–1973):** French philosopher, playwright, and drama critic.

***Marienbad:*** *Last Year in Marienbad* is a 1961 surrealist film directed by Alain Resnais and written by Alain Robbe-Grillet.

**Marx, Karl (1818–83):** German émigré writer whose philosophical, economic, and political ideas were central to the socialist-democratic and communist movements of the nineteenth and twentieth centuries—e.g., that modes of production that arise to satisfy material needs are basic to forms of society and consciousness ("dialectical" and "historical materialism"), that inevitable class struggle between workers alienated from their labour ("proletariat") and owners who profit from that labour ("bourgeois") will result in the revolutionary overthrow of capitalism and institution of a classless society, and that social and economic equality and freedom arising from the recognition of interdependence within a community are more basic than liberalism's equality before the law and freedom from interference.

**Masaccio, or Thommaso di Giovanni di Mone Casai (1401–28):** Italian **Renaissance** painter who pioneered use of light and perspective to create naturalistic three-dimensional figures.

**Matisse, Henri (1869–1954):** innovative French artist who used diverse media (painting, drawing, sculpture, paper cutouts, graphic arts) and styles (**Impressionism**, **Fauvism**, Cubism).

**Mead, George Herbert (1863–1931):** American pragmatist philosopher whose theory of the self's development through communication has been influential in sociology and social psychology.

**Meech Lake Accord (1987):** an attempt to bring Quebec into the constitutional family by recognizing its status as a distinct society and increasing provincial powers; the agreement failed when all the provinces did not ratify it within the three-year deadline.

**Meredith, James (1933–):** in October 1962, by Supreme Court order, he became the first African-American student to enrol at the University of Mississippi; his arrival on campus was met with a riot that resulted in two deaths and the mobilization of federal troops by President Kennedy.

**Merleau-Ponty, Maurice (1908–61):** see p. 222.

**Metaphysical Poets:** seventeenth-century poets, such as John Donne (1572–1631), George Herbert (1593–1633), and Andrew Marvell (1621–78), who challenged Elizabethan stylistic conventions by approaching topics such as love and spirituality with reason, wit, and hyperbole.

**"Mexican war":** the US–Mexican War (1846–8) followed the 1845 US annexation of Texas and resulting dispute with Mexico over the new state's borders; for supporters, the war was an opportunity to fulfil the "manifest destiny" of the United States to expand to the Pacific, while northern abolitionist opponents saw the war as an attempt of southern states to expand slavery.

**Michelangelo (1475–1564):** Italian painter, sculptor, architect, poet, anatomist, and military engineer—a true "**Renaissance** man."

**microbes:** organisms such as bacteria, fungi, and protozoa that are visible under the microscope but not with the naked eye.

**Midas:** in Greek mythology, a king of Phrygia who is granted the favour that all he touches be turned to gold by the god Dionysus.

**Mill, James (1773–1836):** Scottish political philosopher, historian, and social reformer best known today as **John Stuart Mill**'s father and Jeremy Bentham's utilitarian ally.

**Mill, John Stuart (1806–73):** see p. 329 and 459.

**Milton, John (1608–74):** English poet and essayist who defended Puritan, parliamentarian, libertarian, and republican causes and was a civil servant in Cromwell's government.

**Mondrian, Piet (1872–1944):** Dutch painter who developed a nonrepresentational art form he called "Neo-Plasticism."

**Monet, Claude (1840–1926):** French painter who worked outdoors to produce naturalistic landscapes and seascapes in the bright colours characteristic of **Impressionism**.

**Montaigne, Michel de (1533–92):** French philosopher who emphasized the importance of freely exercising one's own judgment rather than providing rational justification for prevailing beliefs.

**Morgan, John Pierpont (1837–1913):** US banker and financier who provided photographer Edward Sheriff Curtis with support for *The North American Indian*.

**Mother Teresa (1910–97):** awarded the Nobel Peace Prize in 1979 and beatified by Pope John Paul II in 2003 for decades of tending to the destitute, sick, and dying of Calcutta; conservative Catholic who opposed contraception and abortion.

**Mouvement Républicain Populaire:** Christian-Democratic party that existed in France between 1944 and 1967.

**Mozart, Wolfgang Amadeus (1756–91):** Austrian composer and pianist of the Classical period; a child prodigy who wrote minuets at age five and performed before royalty at age six.

**Muhammad, Elijah (1897–1975):** born Elijah Poole, he joined the newly formed Nation of Islam after moving to Detroit from Georgia; as leader, he promoted economic self-sufficiency for blacks and sought to establish "a nation within a nation."

**Myrdal, Gunnar (1898–1987):** Swedish economist, sociologist, and politician awarded the Nobel Prize for Economics in 1974; spent 1938–40 in the United States, invited by the Carnegie Corporation of New York to study race relations (a foreigner, it was thought, would be more objective), and published *An American Dilemma* in 1944.

**"Negroes of Haiti":** A reference to the **Haitian Revolution**.

**"neo-Platonic or Hermetic view":** Plotinus (204–70) is regarded as the founder of neo-Platonism, a synthesis of Christian, Gnostic, and traditional Platonic thought; neo-Platonism's resurgence during the early **Renaissance** coincided with the translation of works (wrongly) attributed to the ancient Egyptian Hermes Trismegistus.

**"Nestor or Thersites at the siege of Troy":** As recounted by **Homer** in the *Iliad* and *Odyssey*, both Nestor and Thersites fought on the side of the Achaeans who laid siege to Troy; Nestor is characterized as a brave, honourable elder statesman, while Thersites is characterized as an ugly, malicious, bad-tempered rank-and-file soldier.

**Newman, Barnett (1905–70):** US painter who sought to express feelings and ideas through abstract shapes; the National Gallery of Canada's purchase of *Voice of Fire* in 1989 was controversial.

**Newton, Isaac (1642–1727):** English natural philosopher who is best known for the theory of universal gravitation but also invented calculus and made important discoveries in optics.

**Niebuhr, Reinhold (1892–1971):** preacher and professor considered the most influential US theologian of the twentieth century; held that individuals can overcome the sinfulness of human nature in their personal relationships but the egoism of groups is unavoidable.

**Nietzsche, Friedrich (1844–1900):** see p. 346.

**nominalism:** medieval position on the problem of universals that holds that only particulars (e.g., individual humans) exist and that universals (e.g., humanity) exist in name only.

**"Occam's razor":** reference to the view attributed to medieval philosopher William of Ockham (c. 1287–1347) that entities should not be posited in the absence of compelling reasons.

*Oedipus Rex:* tragedy by Athenian playwright Sophocles (c. 495–406 BCE) about King Oedipus's exile from Thebes after discovering he had killed his father and married his mother.

**Oldenburg, Claes (1929–):** Swedish-born US artist who combines sculpture with performance art and architecture and is considered a founder of Pop Art for his depictions of everyday objects; *Bedroom Ensemble*, 1963 is displayed at the National Gallery of Canada.

**Olivier, Laurence (1907–89):** acclaimed English actor, director, and producer whose adaptation of *Hamlet* for film in 1948 won Oscars for Best Actor and Best Picture.

**"painters of Lascaux":** a reference to Paleolithic paintings, mostly of animals, on walls of an interconnected series of caves in Lascaux in southwestern France that date to 17,000 BCE.

**Palladio, Andrea (1508–80):** chief architect of the Venetian Republic during the Italian **Renaissance** who designed palaces, villas, and churches with Roman influences ("Palladian style").

**Pan-Africanists:** theorists who promote the unity and solidarity of African peoples on that continent and worldwide; the movement arose in the decolonization and national liberation struggles of the twentieth century.

**(great) Panathenaea:** a festival held every four years to honour the goddess Athena, which included a procession to the Acropolis to place a sacred cloth (*peplos*) on a wooden statue of her.

*Paradise Lost:* **Milton**'s influential epic poem about Adam and Eve's expulsion from paradise, published in 1667, after being dictated over the preceding decade by the blind author.

**Parker, Charlie (1920–55):** US jazz saxophonist and composer who pioneered the movement from swing to bebop in the 1940s.

**Parker, Dorothy (1893–1967):** US writer and critic, who worked at *Vogue*, *Vanity Fair*, and *The New Yorker* and was known for her wit.

**Pascal, Blaise (1623–62):** contributed to the scientific and theological debates of mid-seventeenth-century France and is especially known for his argument (in *Pensées*) that religious belief is not an unreasonable wager; spent his entire life in poor health.

**Peirce, Charles Sanders (1839–1914):** founder of American pragmatism who worked as a scientist for the US Coast and Geodetic Survey and made important contributions to logic and philosophy of science.

**Piaget, Jean (1896–80):** Swiss psychologist, biologist, and philosopher whose research in developmental psychology and genetic epistemology reflected his broader interest in the growth of knowledge.

**Picasso, Pablo (1881–1973):** founder of "Cubism"; born in Spain, but spent most of his career in France producing paintings, sculptures, drawings, prints, and ceramics.

**Piero della Francesca (c. 1425/20–1492):** Italian **Renaissance** painter who also contributed mathematical treatises.

**Pilate, Pontius:** as Roman prefect of Judea between 26 and 36 CE, ordered Jesus' execution.

**Pillars of Hercules:** two promontories at eastern end of Strait of Gibraltar (Rock of Gibraltar and either Jebel Musa or Monte Hacho), by legend said to have been formed by Hercules.

**Pindar (518–438 BCE):** one of the most famous poets of ancient Greece.

**Place, U.T. (1924–2000):** British philosopher and psychologist who convinced Smart to adopt the identity theory of mind and brain while both were at University of Adelaide in the early 1950s; today, his brain is on display there, bearing the question, "Did this Brain Contain the Consciousness of U.T. Place?"

**Plato (429–347 BCE):** see pp. 8, 161, 305, 420, 532, and 536.

**"Pope's three crowns":** although the significance of the papal tiara's three crowns is debated, according to the Vatican website (www.vatican.va), they symbolize "the triple power of the Pope: father of kings, governor of the world, and Vicar of Christ."

**Popper, Karl Raimund (1902–94):** see p. 262.

**Post-Impressionists:** term coined by **Fry** in 1910 to refer to a group of artists (**Cézanne**, **Gauguin**, Seurat, **Van Gogh**) whose more expressive and abstract works of the late 1880s moved beyond the naturalism of **Impressionism**.

**principle of sufficient reason:** principle stipulating that everything must have a reason or cause.

**Prodicus of Ceos (an Athenian colony off the coast of Attica):** fifth-century BCE rhetorician who drew fine distinctions between meanings of similar words.

**Protagoras of Abdera (a city on the Aegean coast of Thrace):** fifth-century BCE **Sophist** who advanced the relativist claim that "man is the measure of all things."

**Pythagoras (c. 570–490 BCE):** influenced ancient Greek philosophers like **Plato** with his views on a cosmos structured by numerical ratios, reincarnation, and immortality of the soul.

**quarks:** elementary particles in physics that make up neutrons and protons and account for the "strong force" that holds the nucleus together.

**Quetzalcoatl:** mythical figure of a feathered serpent in Mesoamerican cultures.

**Quine, Willard van Orman (1908–2000):** US philosopher who challenged key tenets of logical empiricism and championed naturalism, the position that empirical science provides the only path to knowledge.

**Raphael, or Raffaello Sanzio (1483–1520):** Italian **Renaissance** painter, printmaker, and architect whose *School of Athens*, a representation of **Plato's** Academy, hangs in the Vatican palace.

**Ravel, Maurice (1875–1937):** French composer known for precision, innovation, and openness to influences as diverse as flamenco and jazz.

**Rauschenberg, Robert (1925–2008):** US artist who influenced the movement from Abstract Expressionism to modern art with his experimental approach that combined not just objects and images but forms of artistic expression in works.

**Rawls, John (1921–2002):** see p. 444.

**"Rawlsian principles of distributive justice":** **Rawls'** theory of "justice as fairness" proposes that social and economic inequalities be attached to positions and offices open to all (principle of equality of opportunity), in a way that benefits the least advantaged members of society (difference principle).

**"refusal of Shadrach, Meshach and Abednego to obey the laws of Nebuchadnezzar":** a biblical story wherein Nebuchadnezzar, Babylon's king, casts three Hebrews into a burning furnace for refusing to worship him over their god, and they emerge unscathed.

**Reichenbach, Hans (1891–1953):** important logical empiricist who lost his position at University of Berlin in 1933 and relocated to Istanbul then UCLA; especially known today for the "context of discovery"–"context of justification" distinction.

**Reid, Thomas (1710–96):** Scottish philosopher who defended common-sense solutions to philosophical problems.

**Rembrandt van Rijn (1606–69):** Dutch artist whose paintings, drawings, and etchings include portraits and depictions of historical and religious themes.

**Renaissance:** post–Middle Ages period in European culture, 1350–1600, characterized as a "rebirth" insofar as inspiration provided by the civilizations of ancient Greece and Rome promoted the flourishing of art, literature, philosophy, and science.

**Restoration:** in 1660, the monarchy in Britain was restored with the coronation of Charles II whose father was removed during the English Civil Wars and subsequently beheaded by the Puritan-controlled Parliament.

**Rouault, Georges (1871–1958):** French artist whose paintings and prints capture spirituality and sympathy for the poor.

**Rousseau, Jean-Jacques (1712–78):** Swiss philosopher recognized for his contributions to political philosophy and moral psychology and his influence on **Kant**.

**Roussel, Raymond (1877–1933):** eccentric, self-published French writer who developed an avant-garde following; Foucault wrote about Roussel in *Death and the Labyrinth*, trans. Charles Ruas (Garden City, NY: Doubleday, 1986).

**Salk, Jonas (1914–95):** US physician and medical researcher who developed the first polio vaccine in the early 1950s.

**Sartre, Jean-Paul (1905–80):** see p. 360.

**Schlick, Moritz (1882–1936):** see p. 84.

**Schopenhauer, Arthur (1788–1860):** see p. 541.

**Schweitzer, Albert (1875–1965):** philosopher, theologian, concert organist, pastor, physician, and winner of the 1952 Nobel Peace Prize for his work as a medical missionary in Africa.

**Seth:** according to *Genesis*, Adam and Eve's son, born after Cain slew Abel.

**Shakespeare, William (1564–1616):** preeminent English actor, playwright, and poet from Stratford-upon-Avon whose works continue to inspire audiences around the world.

**Shaw, George Bernard (1856–1950):** moved from Dublin to London as a young adult to become a successful playwright and active in socialist politics; won the Nobel Prize in Literature in 1925.

**Sherif, Muzafer (1906–88):** one of the founders of social psychology.

**"ship come from Delos":** on the day before **Socrates**' trial, a ship dedicated to Apollo that commemorated Theseus's legendary victory over the Minotaur left for Delos; no executions could take place until the ship returned to Athens.

**"siege at Oka":** opposition by the Mohawks of Kanesatake to the town of Oka's plan to expand a golf course and build condominiums at the site of a burial ground resulted in a 78-day standoff between Mohawk warriors and the Sûreté du Québec and Canadian Armed Forces during the summer of 1990.

**Socrates (469–399 BCE):** Athenian philosopher, made famous by **Plato**'s dialogues for his question-and-answer mode of engaging others in the search for knowledge.

**solipsism:** the position that only the reality of one's own mind can be known with certainty—not material things, the body, or other minds.

**Solomon:** according to biblical sources, powerful and wise king of Israel during tenth century BCE, who decided which of two women was the mother of a baby by judging their reactions to the prospect of cutting it in half.

**Solon (c. 638–558 BCE):** celebrated Athenian lawgiver and one of the Seven Sages of ancient Greece.

**Sophists:** from fifth century BCE, intellectuals who travelled to different Greek cities and lectured and taught for a fee.

*Steve Canyon:* adventure comic strip by Milton Caniff (1907–88) that ran from 1947 to 1988.

**Stevenson, Charles Leslie (1908–79):** US philosopher who specialized in meta-ethics and is known for his rigorous defence of ethical emotivism.

**Stoics/Stoicism:** philosophical rivals to the **Epicureans** in Hellenistic Greece; believed that though only virtues are good, other things that accord with nature (e.g., health, wealth) also have value and are to be rationally preferred—in this, the passions are not to be trusted.

**supervenience:** a set of properties *A* supervenes on another set of properties *B* just in case two things cannot differ in their *A*-properties without also differing in their *B*-properties.

*Swan Lake:* ballet by Russian composer Pyotr Ilyich **Tchaikovsky** (1840–93), inspired by a folk tale, about a prince, Siegfried, who falls in love with a white swan, Odette.

**synthetic:** a statement's truth depends on the way the world is; for **Kant**, the predicate concept goes beyond or amplifies the subject concept.

*Tale of the Heike:* tells the story of two warring clans in twelfth-century Japan.

**tautology:** logical truth.

**Tchaikovsky, Pyotr Ilyich (1840–93):** Russian composer of emotive musical works of great public appeal; anxiety over his homosexuality provoked him into a short-lived marriage.

**Thales the Milesian (c. 620–546 BCE):** first of the Seven Sages of ancient Greece and founder of natural philosophy; theorized that water is the origin of all things, predicted the solar eclipse of 585 BCE, and introduced geometry to Greece from Egypt.

*The Ascendancy of St Erasmus:* likely a reference to *The Martyrdom of St Erasmus*, created in 1628 by French painter Nicolas Poussin (1594–1665) as an altarpiece for St. Peter's Basilica.

*The Virgin and the Chancellor Rollin:* painting by Flemish artist Jan van Eyck (c. 1390–1441), one of the first to use oils, now displayed at the Musée du Louvre in Paris.

**Tillich, Paul (1886–1965):** German philosopher and theologian influenced by existentialism who sought to reconcile reason and revelation; immigrated to the United States when the Nazis took power.

**Tocqueville, Alexis de (1805–59):** French political scientist, historian, and politician whose two-volume *Democracy in America*, based on his nine-month visit in 1831–2 as a civil servant charged with studying prison reforms, reflected on the significance of the American experience for the democratization underway in his own society.

**Tolstoy (1828–1910):** see p. 573.

**Tournefort, Joseph Pitton de (1656–1708):** French botanist and physician who is credited with contributing to the modern genus concept.

*Transfiguration:* **Raphael**'s last painting, left unfinished when he died in 1520, is exhibited in the Vatican Museum; St. Peter's Basilica in Rome contains a mosaic copy.

**transfinite numbers:** cardinal numbers that describe the sizes of equivalent infinite sets.

**Trudeau, Pierre Elliott (1919–2000):** first elected as an MP in 1965, he gained attention for liberalizing laws on divorce, homosexuality, and abortion as justice minister and was elected Liberal leader in 1968; as prime minister in 1968–79 and 1980–4, his commitment to federalism lay behind such lasting contributions of his governments as the institution of official bilingualism in 1969 and multiculturalism in 1971 and passage of the Constitution Act and its accompanying Charter of Rights and Freedoms in 1982.

**Truman, Harry S. (1884–1972):** became thirty-third president of the United States when **FDR** died in April 1945; responsible for the decision to drop atomic bombs on Hiroshima and Nagasaki.

**Truth, Sojourner (1797–1883):** after escaping from slavery in New York, she became a travelling preacher who was active in the abolitionist, suffrage, and temperance movements.

**Turing Machine:** idea introduced in 1936 by mathematician Alan Turing (1912–54) as a thought experiment to address the question whether a method exists that could decide for any mathematical statement whether or not it is provable; the machine was modelled on a teleprinter, with a paper tape that could move in both directions and a "head" that could read symbols and erase and print new ones—see http://plato.stanford.edu/entries/turing.

**Turgot, Anne-Robert-Jacques (1727–81):** French economist who promoted competition and free markets and influenced Adam Smith's *Wealth of Nations*.

**utilitarian:** maximization of the good, which is often equated with pleasure or happiness.

**Van Gogh, Vincent (1853–90):** Dutch painter whose 10-year career as an artist was cut tragically short by a self-inflicted gunshot wound.

**van Meegeren, Han (1889–1947):** Dutch artist who rejected the cubism and surrealism of his contemporaries to paint in the tradition of the Dutch Golden Age; angered by critics who found his work unoriginal, began to forge paintings by Dutch masters; in 1945, confessed to forgery after being charged with treason for having sold a Vermeer to Nazi leader Hermann Göring during the war.

**Vasari, Giorgio (1511–74):** Italian painter, architect, and biographer who shaped subsequent views of the **Renaissance**'s importance.

**Velásquez, Diego (1599–1660):** Spanish master who created his most famous work, *Las Meninas*, in his capacity as court painter for King Philip IV.

**verifiability theory of meaning:** holds that the meaning of a sentence is the method of its verification; if a sentence cannot be verified by logic or sense experience, it is meaningless.

**Vermeer, Johannes (1632–75):** painter from the Dutch city of Delft whose small body of work focuses on domestic subjects and makes exceptional use of light and colours.

**Vienna Circle:** group of scientists and philosophers who, during the 1920s–30s, advocated a scientific—logical, empirical, and anti-metaphysical—approach to philosophy known as logical positivism.

**Voltaire, or François-Marie d'Arouet (1694–1778):** author of plays, stories, and poems with philosophical themes (e.g., *Candide* satirized **Leibniz**'s belief that God created the best of all possible worlds) who, as a philosopher, introduced the empiricism of **Locke** and **Newton** to France and contributed to the *Encyclopédie*.

**Waismann, Friedrich (1896–1959):** member of the **Vienna Circle** who immigrated to England in 1937, teaching at Cambridge then Oxford.

**Wallace, George C. (1919–98):** four-time governor of Alabama and four-time US presidential candidate who vowed in his first inaugural address as governor in January 1963, "segregation now, segregation tomorrow, and segregation forever!" and later that year fulfilled his campaign pledge to stand "in the schoolhouse door" by blocking James A. Hood and Vivian J. Malone from registering at University of Alabama.

**Warhol, Andy (1928–87):** US Pop artist; already a successful commercial artist and illustrator when he became a celebrity in the early 1960s for his paintings of comic-strip characters, advertising images, and celebrities and his sculptures of household products.

**Washington, George (1732–99):** Virginia planter, commander in chief of the Continental Army during the American Revolution, presided over the Constitutional Conference in Philadelphia in 1787, and became the first US president in 1789.

**Whewell, William (1794–1866):** central figure in Victorian science who wrote on architecture, mineralogy, geology, physics, astronomy, political economy, theology, moral philosophy, and philosophy of science.

**"Whigs and Tories":** during the Exclusion Crisis of 1679–85, Whigs opposed the succession of Charles II by his Catholic brother James, while Tories supported the monarchy.

**"White Citizen's Counciler or the Ku Klux Klanner":** White Citizens' Councils originated in Mississippi in 1954 in opposition to *Brown v Board of Education* and were composed of prominent community members who could retaliate socially and economically against integrationists; the more clandestine Ku Klux Klan, founded by Confederate Army veterans after the Civil War and revived in the 1920s and again in the 1950s, relied on violent means such as lynching to maintain white supremacy.

**Whitehead, Alfred North (1861–1947):** British mathematician and philosopher who made important contributions to logic, philosophy of science, and metaphysics.

**Wilson, E.O. (1929–):** Harvard biologist who founded the discipline of sociobiology as the systematic study of the biological basis of social behaviour when he published *Sociobiology: The New Synthesis* in 1975.

**Wittgenstein, Ludwig (1889–1951):** see p. 227.

**Wu School:** during the Ming dynasty in China (1368–1644), a group of scholar-amateur painters from the Wu region around the city of Suzhou, led by Shen Zhou (1427–1509).

**Zeuxis (fifth c. BCE):** ancient Greek painter who in a contest with his rival Parrhasius painted a bowl of fruit so realistic that a bird tried to steal a grape; however, Parrhasius won when it was realized that the curtain "concealing" his painting was itself the painting.

# Credits

**ARISTOTLE** From *Nicomachean Ethics*, trans. H. Rackham (Cambridge, MA: Harvard University Press and London: William Heinemann, 1947), 5, 11–7, 27–33, 71–5, 83–95, 111–3, 613–23 (odd pages).

**A.J. AYER** "Critique of Ethics" from *Language, Truth, and Logic* by A.J. Ayer (New York: Dover, 1952), 104–14.

**FRANCIS BACON** "Aphorisms Concerning the Interpretation of Nature and the Kingdom of Man" from *The Works of Francis Bacon*, eds. James Spedding, Robert Leslie Ellis, and Douglas Denon Heath, vol. 4 (London: Longman, 1860), 47–66, 113–5.

**HIMANI BANNERJI** "On the Dark Side of Nation: Politics of Multiculturalism and the State of 'Canada'", *Journal of Canadian Studies* 31, 3, 1996. Used with permission.

**MARCIA BARON** "Crime, Genes, and Responsibility" by Marcia Baron, in *Genetics and Criminal Behavior*, ed. David Wasserman and Robert Wachbroit, © Cambridge University Press, 2001, 201–6, 213–20. Reprinted with the permission of Cambridge University Press.

**JOHN BEATTY** "Teleology and the Relationship Between Biology and the Physical Sciences in the Nineteenth Century" from *Some Truer Method: Reflections on the Heritage of Newton*, ed. Frank Durham and Robert D. Purrington (New York: Columbia University Press, 1990), 113–44. Reprinted with permission of the publisher.

**GEORGE BERKELEY** From "Three Dialogues between Hylas and Philonous, in Opposition to Sceptics and Atheists" in *The Principles of Human Knowledge, Three Dialogues between Hylas and Philonous*, ed. G.J. Warnock (Glasgow: Fontana Press, 1962), 149–54, 158–66, 169–73, 193, 195, 197–8.

**ANJAN CHAKRAVARTTY** "Realism and Anti-Realism; Metaphysics and Empiricism" from *A Metaphysics for Scientific Realism: Knowing the Unobservable* by Anjan Chakravartty (Cambridge: Cambridge University Press, 2007), 3–16, 26. Reprinted with the permission of Cambridge University Press.

**LORRAINE CODE** "Public Knowledge, Public Trust: Toward Democratic Epistemic Practices" from *Ecological Thinking: The Politics of Epistemic Location* by Lorraine Code (2006), pp. 237–9, 241–7, 250–2, 268–75. By permission of Oxford University Press, USA.

**ARTHUR DANTO** "The Artworld" by Arthur Danto from *The Journal of Philosophy* 61, 19 (1964): 571–81. Used by permission.

**SIMONE DE BEAUVOIR** Introduction to *The Second Sex*, trans. and ed. H.M. Parshley (New York: Random House, 1952), xv–xxix, xxxi–xxxiv.

**RENÉ DESCARTES** Meditations I and II from *The Method, Meditations and Philosophy of Descartes*, trans. John Veitch (New York: Tudor Publishing, Co., 1901), 219–33.

**BARON D'HOLBACH** "Of the System of Man's Free Agency" from *The System of Nature or Laws of the Moral and Physical World*, vol. 1, trans. H.D. Robinson (New York: Burt Franklin, 1868), 88–90, 92–3, 95–103.

**JOHN DUPRÉ** "Natural Kinds and Biological Taxa" in *The Philosophical Review*, Volume 90, no. 1, pp. 66–90. Copyright, 1981, Cornell University. All rights reserved. Reprinted by permission of the publisher, Duke University Press, www.dukeupress.edu.

**MICHEL FOUCAULT** From *The Order of Things: An Archaeology of the Human Sciences*, Michel Foucault, copyright © 1970 Tavistock Publications. Reproduced by permission of Taylor & Francis Books UK.

**HARRY FRANKFURT** "Alternate Possibilities and Moral Responsibility" by Harry Frankfurt, from *The Journal of Philosophy* 66, 23 (1969): 829–39.

**CAROL GILLIGAN** "Moral Orientation and Moral Development" by Carol Gilligan, in *Women and Moral*

**J.J.C. SMART** "Sensations and Brian Processes", *The Philosophical Review* 68, 2 (1959): 141–56.

**CHARLES TAYLOR** "The Politics of Recognition" from *Multiculturalism and the Politics of Recognition* by Charles Taylor. Copyright © 1992 Princeton University Press, 1994 expanded paperback edition (Multiculturalism: Examining the Politics of Recognition). Reprinted by permission of Princeton University Press.

**HENRY D. THOREAU** "Resistance to Civil Government" from *Aesthetic Papers*, ed. Elizabeth P. Peabody (New York: G.P. Putnam, 1849).

**LEO TOLSTOY** From *A Confession, The Gospel in Brief, and What I Believe*, trans. Aylmer Maude (London: Oxford University Press, 1921), 14–22, 30–2, 46–51, 55–8; *My Confession* was first circulated in Russia in 1882.

**DALE TURNER** "Liberalism's Last Stand: Minority Rights and the (Mis)recognition of Aboriginal Sovereignty" from *This Is Not a Peace Pipe: Towards a Critical Indigenous Philosophy* by Dale Turner (Toronto: University of Toronto Press, 2006), 57–70. Used with permission of University of Toronto Press and McGill-Queens University Press.

**BERNARD WILLIAMS** "The Makropulos Case: Reflections on the Tedium of Immortality" from *Problems of the Self* by Bernard Williams (Cambridge: Cambridge University Press, 1973), 82–7, 89–100. Reprinted by permission of Cambridge University Press.

**CATHERINE WILSON** "Moral Equality and 'Natural' Subordination" from *Moral Animals: Ideals and Constraints in Moral Theory* by Catherine Wilson (2004) pp. 254–5, 257–61, 266–7, 270–83. By permission of Oxford University Press.

**LUDWIG WITTGENSTEIN** From *Philosophical Investigations*, 1st ed., trans. G.E.M. Anscombe (Basil Blackwell, 1953), 91–102.

**SUSAN WOLF** "The Meanings of Lives" by Susan Wolf in *Introduction to Philosophy: Classical and Contemporary Readings*, ed. John Perry, Michael Bratman, and John Martin Fischer (New York and Oxford: Oxford University Press, 2007), 62–73. By permission of the author.

**JAMES O. YOUNG** "The Aesthetics of Cultural Appropriation" from *Cultural Appropriation and the Arts* by James O. Young (Malden, MA: Blackwell, 2008), 32–52, 55.

# Index